Index to Poetry for Children and Young People

1964-1969

Index to Poetry for Children and Young People

1964-1969

A TITLE, SUBJECT, AUTHOR, AND FIRST LINE INDEX TO POETRY IN COLLECTIONS FOR CHILDREN AND YOUNG PEOPLE

Compiled by
John E. and Sara W. Brewton
and
G. Meredith Blackburn III

THE H. W. WILSON COMPANY NEW YORK 1972

INDEX TO POETRY FOR CHILDREN AND YOUNG PEOPLE
COPYRIGHT © 1972
By John E. Brewton, Sara W. Brewton, and G. Meredith Blackburn III

International Standard Book Number 0-8242-0435-2
Library of Congress Catalog Card Number 71-161574

PRINTED IN THE UNITED STATES OF AMERICA

INTRODUCTION

The INDEX TO POETRY FOR CHILDREN AND YOUNG PEOPLE: 1964-1969 is a dictionary index to 117 collections of poems for children and young people published from 1964 through 1969, with title, subject, author, and first line entries. A few publications of earlier date are included. More than 11,000 poems by approximately 2,000 authors and translators are classified under more than 2,000 subjects.

The INDEX TO POETRY FOR CHILDREN AND YOUNG PEOPLE: 1964-1969 is in effect a supplement to INDEX TO CHILDREN'S POETRY but because of the larger number of books at the 7-12 grade level, it seemed appropriate to give the present volume a new, more inclusive title.

Scope. The carefully selected list of books of poetry for children and young people which are indexed includes collections for the very young child (e.g., books such as those classed in "Easy Books" in the *Children's Catalog*, Mother Goose, etc.); collections for the elementary school grades (e.g., the range of collections in class 821.08 in the *Children's Catalog*); and collections suitable for junior and senior high-school age (e.g., such collections as those found in class 821.08 in the *Junior High School Library Catalog* and in the *Senior High School Library Catalog*). In addition to anthologies or collections of poetry by more than one poet, volumes by individual poets (e.g., books by David McCord, Phyllis McGinley), and collections of selected poems by a single author (e.g., *Poems of Robert Burns*, selected by L. Frankenberg and *Poems of Emily Dickinson*, selected by Helen Plotz) are also included. Books partly in prose and partly in verse (e.g., *Flowers of Delight*, an agreeable garland of prose and poetry, 1765-1830) are indexed; as well as collections of poems on a single subject (e.g., *America Forever New*, compiled by Sara and John E. Brewton, and *A Book of Love Poems*, compiled by William Cole). The inclusion of comprehensive collections (e.g., *The Cherry Tree*, edited by Gregory Grigson) gives the index a wide range.

Selection of Collections Included. Selection of the 117 collections included is based on a list of titles voted on by consulting librarians and teachers in various parts of the United States. A comprehensive list of anthologies and volumes of poetry by individual authors was sent to the selected consultants, their advice secured, and the final selection made. A list of consultants follows this Introduction.

Entries. Entries are of four types: title, subject, author, and reference from first line to title. The addition of collection symbols to title, subject, and author entries makes these complete within themselves, thus obviating the necessity for cross references.

1. TITLE ENTRY. The fullest information is given in this entry. Although the symbols designating the books in which the poems are to be found are given in author and subject entries as well as in the title entries, the title entry is the only one

which gives full name of author, when known, and full name of translator. References to the title entry have been made (a) from variant titles (e.g., One old ox. See "One old Oxford ox opening oysters"); (b) from titles of selections to the source title (e.g., Mercy. See The merchant of Venice); and (c) from first lines (e.g., "I know a funny little man." See Mr Nobody).

The title entry includes:

(a) Title, followed by first line in parentheses when needed to distinguish between poems with the same title.

(b) Variant titles, indented under the main title. When the same poem apears in different books with different titles, one title, generally the one appearing in the most collections, has been chosen as the title entry and all variations have been indented and listed under this title.

(c) Full name of author, when known.

(d) Full name of translator.

(e) Symbols for collections in which the poem is to be found.

In order to bring together selections from a single source, selections are listed under source titles. An example follows:

Alice's adventures in wonderland, sels. Lewis Carroll
"Beautiful soup, so rich and green."—BlO
Beautiful soup.—SmM
Turtle soup.—ClF

All entries subordinated under source titles are entered in their alphabetical position and referred to the source entry. Examples follow:

Beautiful soup. See Alice's adventures in wonderland—"Beautiful soup, so rich and green"
"**Beautiful** soup, so rich and green." See Alice's adventures in wonderland
Turtle soup. See Alice's adventures in wonderland—"Beautiful soup, so rich and green"

A group title (e.g., Limericks, Nonsense verses, Rhyming riddles) under which several poems appear has been subordinated as a variant to a title under which the poem appears in another book. Otherwise it has been subordinated to its own first line. Examples follow:

"**There** was an old man who said, How." Edward Lear.—BlO—BrLl
Limericks.—HoB
Nonsense verses.—HuS-3
"**I** never speak a word." Mary Austin
Rhyming riddles.—ArT-3

2. Subject Entry. Entries are grouped by specific subjects. For example, under **Animals** are listed the poems about animals in general, while poems about specific animals are grouped under names of animals, as **Dogs**. A single poem is often classified under a number of subject headings (e.g., "The **mountain** and the squirrel," is listed under the subject headings **Fables**, **Mountains**, **Squirrels**, and **Talents**).

Both *See* and *See also* references have been made freely to and from related subjects. These are filed at the beginning of the entries for the subject. Examples follow:

Agriculture. See Farm life; Harvests and harvesting

Animals. See also Circus; Fables; also names of classes of the animal kingdom, as Birds; also names of animals, as Cats

In order that individual poems or selections from longer poems which have been subordinated to source titles in the title entries may be classified according to subject and may also be readily identified as to sources, they have been entered under subject headings as follows:

Spring
A lover and his lass. From As you like it. W. Shakespeare.—ShS

Variant titles and titles of selections subordinate to source titles are treated in the same way as under the title and author entries.

The subject entry gives:

(a) Title, followed by first line in parentheses when needed to distinguish between poems with the same title.

(b) Name, including initials, of author.

(c) Symbols for collections in which the poem is to be found.

3. Author Entry. All titles are listed alphabetically under the name of the author. Variant titles and titles of selections subordinated under source titles are entered in their proper alphabetical place and referred to the main title or source title.

The author entry gives, under the full name of the author:

(a) Title, followed by first line in parentheses when needed to distinguish between poems with the same title.

(b) Symbols for collections in which the poem is to be found.

(c) Cross references from variant titles to main titles.

(d) Cross references from titles of selections to source titles.

4. First Line References. The first line is always given in quotation marks, even when it is also the title. When the title differs from first line, reference is made from first line to title.

Arrangement. The arrangement is alphabetical. Articles are always retained at the beginning of title and first line, but the articles (except articles in dialect and foreign articles) are disregarded in the alphabeting. Such entries are alphabeted by the word following the article and this word is printed in boldface (e.g., The **cat,** is filed under C). Articles in dialect and foreign articles are filed under the dialect or foreign article (e.g., **Da** boy from Rome, is filed under D and **La** belle dame sans merci, is filed under L). Abbreviations are filed as if spelled in full (e.g., **St** is filed as Saint). Contractions are filed as one word (e.g., **I'd** is filed as Id). Hyphenated words are filed as separate words. An exception is made if the hyphen is part of the word (e.g., **A-hunting**). To facilitate quick use the entries beginning **O** and **Oh** have been filed together, under O. Likewise, names beginning **Mac** and **Mc** have been filed together as Mac. Punctuation has been disregarded in filing.

Grades. The books have been graded and the grades are given in parentheses in the Analysis of Books Indexed and in the Key to Symbols. The grading is only approximate and is given to indicate in general the grades for which each book is suitable. A book that is comprehensive in nature and is suitable for a wide range of grades up to and beyond the twelfth grade is designated (r), reference.

Uses. The INDEX TO POETRY FOR CHILDREN AND YOUNG PEOPLE should serve as a practical reference book for all who desire to locate poems for children and young people by subject, author, title, or first line. It should prove especially useful to librarians, teachers in elementary and secondary schools, teachers and students of literature for children and young people, radio and television artists, parents, young people, and children. The variety of subject classifications should be particularly useful to anyone preparing programs for special occasions, to teachers planning activities around interests of children and young people, to parents who desire to share poetry, and to anyone searching for poems on a given topic. The Analysis of Books Indexed, which gives in detail the contents of each book, number of poems included, number of authors represented, and number of poems in each group or classification, should prove valuable in the selection of collections for purchase or use. The comprehensiveness of the books indexed insures the usefulness of the INDEX to those interested in poetry from the nursery through the secondary school and beyond.

Acknowledgments. The compilers thank the consultants who cooperated in checking lists of titles to be included. Evelyn Stephenson gave invaluable assistance. Thanks are also due the publishers who generously supplied copies of the books which are included in the INDEX.

JOHN EDMUND BREWTON
SARA WESTBROOK BREWTON
G. MEREDITH BLACKBURN III

CONSULTANTS

Mrs. Muriel F. Boardman
1406 Euclid Avenue 2
Berkeley, California 94708

Miss Anne Jo Carter
Library Supervisor
Metropolitan Public Schools
Nashville, Tennessee 37204

Miss Laurie Dudley
Coordinator of Children's Services
Dallas Public Library
1954 Commerce Street
Dallas, Texas 75201

Miss Anne T. Eaton
118 East 31st Street
New York, New York 10016

Miss Edith Edmonds
Elementary School Librarian
Hubbard Woods School
Chatfield Road
Winnetka, Illinois 60093

Miss Shirley Ellison
Children's Librarian
New Westminster Public Library
716 - 6th Avenue
New Westminster, B.C., Canada

Miss Helen Fuller
Supervisor, Work with Boys and Girls
Public Library
Long Beach, California 90802

Mrs. Peggy Gadbow
Director of Library Services
Missoula Public Schools
Missoula, Montana 59801

Miss Elvajean Hall
Supervisor of Library Services
c/o Division of Instruction
Newton Public Schools
88 Chestnut Street
West Newton, Massachusetts 02165

Mrs. Dorothy W. Heald, Consultant
Educational Media
State Department of Education
Tallahassee, Florida 32304

Miss Mildred L. Krohn
Coordinator of Libraries
Shaker Heights City School District
15600 Parkland Drive
Shaker Heights, Ohio 44120

Miss Lucille R. Menihan, Librarian
Baker School
Great Neck, New York 11020

Miss Jean A. Merrill
Children's Department
Kansas City, Missouri Public Library
Kansas City, Missouri 64106

Miss Beryl Robinson
Readers' Adviser
Children's Department
Boston Public Library
Boston, Massachusetts 02117

CONSULTANTS

Miss Marian Schroether
Children's Librarian
Waukegan Public Library
Waukegan, Illinois 60085

Mrs. Helen Tyler
Library Consultant
Elementary School Libraries
Eugene Public Schools
275 Seventh Avenue, East
Eugene, Oregon 97401

Miss Frances Sullivan
Children's Librarian
Wichita City Library
Wichita, Kansas 67202

Mrs. Madelyn C. Wankmiller
Supervisor, Work with Children
Free Public Library
Worcester, Massachusetts 01608

Miss Jane B. Wilson
Specialist in Children's Work
State Library
Raleigh, North Carolina 27602

CONTENTS

ANALYSIS OF BOOKS OF POETRY INDEXED

Grades are given in parentheses at the end of each entry: (k), kindergarten or preschool grade; (1), first grade; (2), second grade, etc. Comprehensive general collections are designated (r), reference.

Adoff, Arnold, ed. I am the darker brother; an anthology of modern poems by Negro Americans; il. by Benny Andrews. Macmillan 1968 (5-12)

Contents: 64 poems by 29 authors grouped as follows: Like I am, 13; Genealogy, 9; Shall be remembered, 9; If we must die, 7; I am the darker brother, 18; and The hope of your unborn, 8. Also Foreword by Charlemae Rollins; Preface by Arnold Adoff; Notes; Biographies. Indexed by authors and first lines.

Agree, Rose H., comp. How to eat a poem and other morsels; food poems for children; il. by Peggy Wilson. Pantheon bks. 1967 (3-6)

Contents: 64 poems by 31 authors grouped as follows: From soup to nuts, 31; Snacks, 9; Tutti-frutti, 8; and Mind your manners, 16. Indexed by authors and first lines.

Aiken, Conrad. Cats and bats and things with wings; il. by Milton Glaser. Atheneum 1965 (k-4)

Contents: 16 poems ungrouped.

Aldan, Daisy, comp. Poems from India; il. by Joseph Low. Crowell 1969 (7-12)

Contents: 102 poems by 78 authors and 39 translators grouped as follows: Poems of ancient India, 16; Sanskrit court poetry, 11; Other poems of the middle period, 9; Old Tamil poetry, 10; and Poems of modern India, 56. Also Introduction. Indexed by authors, titles, and translators.

Arbuthnot, May Hill and Root, Jr., Shelton L., comps. Time for poetry; il. by Arthur Paul. Third general edition. Scott, Foresman 1967 (r)

Contents: The book is divided into two parts: Part one: Poetry time and Part two: Keeping poetry and children together. Part one: Poetry time contains 760 poems by 251 authors grouped as follows: All sorts of people, 98; The animal fair, 135; Traveling we go, 51; Let's play, 89; How ridiculous, 91; Magic and make-belive, 38; Wind and water, 56; Round the clock, 36; Round the calendar, 113; and Wisdom and beauty, 53. Thirteen additional poems are included in the Introduction and prose discussions in Part two. Also Bibliography. Indexed by authors, first lines, and titles.

Baron, Virginia Olsen, ed. Here I am; an anthology of poems written by young people in some of America's minority groups; il. by Emily Arnold McCully. Dutton 1969 (5-12)

Contents: 115 poems by 86 authors grouped as follows: Who am I, 13; How do I feel, 11; About the world, 8; About seasons and nature, 31; About life and people, 15; About places, 14; Sometimes I wonder, 9; And I dream, 7; and But there is still much mystery, 7. Also Foreword. Indexed by authors and first lines.

Baron, Virginia Olsen, ed. Seasons of time, Tanka poetry of ancient Japan; il. by Yasuhide Kobashi. Dial 1968 (4-up)

Contents: 79 poems by 44 authors grouped as follows: Introductory poem, 1; Spring, 22; Summer, 12; Autumn, 24; Winter, 10; and This world, 10. Also Introduction. Indexed by authors.

Behn, Harry, tr. Cricket songs; Japanese haiku translated by Harry Behn, with pictures selected from Sesshu and other Japanese masters. Harcourt 1964 (4-up)

Contents: 85 haikus by 35 authors ungrouped. Also brief comment on Haiku and The pictures.

Behn, Harry. Golden hive; il. by the author. Harcourt 1966 (3-5)

Contents: 42 poems ungrouped.

Belting, Natalia. Calendar moon; il. by Bernarda Bryson. Holt 1964 (5-up)

Contents: 27 poems ungrouped.

Blake, William. Poems of William Blake; selected by Amelia H. Munson; il. by William Blake. Crowell 1964 (7-12)

Contents: 95 poems grouped as follows: From poetical sketches, 14; Songs of innocence and of experience, 45; Verses and fragments, 30; and From the prophetic books, 6. Also introduction, William Blake. Indexed by first lines and titles.

Blishen, Edward, comp. Oxford book of poetry for children; il. by Brian Wildsmith. Watts 1963 (r)

Contents: 171 poems by 62 authors grouped as follows: The moon's in a fit, 23; Children, you are very little, 8; There I met a pretty miss, 10; The world of waters is our home, 12; What bird so sings, 11; A story I'll to you unfold, 7; O'er ditches and mires, 5; Sweet sprites, 7; Come wind, come weather, 11; He is of the tribe of tiger, 10; Other creatures, 19; We'll let each other alone, 5; O'er vales and hills, 17; A chip hat had she on, 11; Sigh as you sing, 7; With sweet-briar and bon-fire, 5; and Rock them, rock them, lullaby, 3. Also Introduction. Indexed by authors and first lines.

Bogan, Louise and Smith, William Jay, comps. Golden journey; poems for young people; woodcuts by Fritz Kredel. Reilly 1965 (2-6)

Contents: 206 poems by 107 authors grouped as follows: Introductory poem, 1; What is pink, 17; Slight things, 13; The wind and the rain, 6; A pea-green gamut, 18; Birds, beasts, and flowers, 34; Spring and summer, 7; In between are the people, 11; Go, lovely rose, 9; Many love music, 15; They went to sea in a sieve, 10; Ballads, 4; The sea, 6; The dark hills, 6; All that's past, 11; Here and now, 7; Lyrebird country, 10; When you are old, 6; The moon and the sun, 5; and Year's end, 10. Also Introduction. Indexed by authors and titles.

ANALYSIS OF BOOKS OF POETRY INDEXED

Bontemps, Arna, ed. American Negro poetry. Hill and Wang 1963 (r)

Contents: 171 poems by 55 authors grouped by authors. Also Introduction; Biographical notes. Indexed by titles.

Bontemps, Arna, comp. Hold fast to dreams; poems old and new. Follett 1969 (5-up)

Contents: 122 poems by 68 authors grouped as follows: Dream variations, 12; I hear America singing, 9; Spring thunder, 11; The sound of trees, 7; Bats, loons, and other creatures, 8; Sea fever, 7; Winners and losers, 17; How do I love thee, 10; After August, 12; Strong men, 10; The poet and his song, 12; and Nothing happens only once, 7. Also introduction, On integrating the old with the new. Indexed by authors, first lines, and titles.

Bramblett, Ella, comp. Shoots of green; poems for young gardeners; il. by Ingrid Fetz. Crowell 1968 (k-3)

Contents: 107 poems by 55 authors grouped as follows: Spring is coming, 8; To dig and delve, 8; How does your garden grow, 22; To pop into the pot, 10; Fly away home, 23; Come buy, come buy, 8; I found a four-leaf clover, 6; Fires in the fall, 8; and A song of seasons, 14. Indexed by authors, first lines, and titles.

Brewton, Sara and Brewton, John E., comps. America forever new; il. by Ann Grifalconi. Crowell 1968 (5-up)

Contents: 211 poems by 131 authors grouped as follows: This is our land, 18; You, whoever you are, 22; Conceived in liberty, 33; Lonesome water, 19; The American dimension: *Change and diversity,* 42; Rolling waters, 19; Sidewalks of America, 35; Americans are always moving on, 15; and We have tomorrow, 8. Indexed by authors, first lines, and titles.

Brewton, Sara and Brewton, John E., comps. Laughable limericks; il. by Ingrid Fetz. Crowell 1965 (3-up)

Contents: 251 poems by 49 authors grouped as follows: Introductory, 1; Bugs, bees, and birds, 15; Crawlers, croakers, and creepers, 6; Animals—friendly and tame, 18; Animals—not so friendly and tame, 25; Laughs anatomical, 30; Behavior—scroobious and strange, 39; Accidents—more or less fatal, 16; Food and eating, 19; Clothing and dress, 14; School and college, 8; Music and musicians, 9; Science and mathematics, 10; Courtship, 16; Writing limericks, 17; and Try singing these, 8. Also Foreword. Indexed by authors and first lines.

Brewton, Sara and Brewton, John E., comps. Shrieks at midnight; macabre poems, eerie and humorous; il. by Ellen Raskin. Crowell 1969 (4-up)

Contents: 157 poems by 73 authors grouped as follows: Shrieks at midnight, 12; A whiff of murder, 20; Gather up the fragments, 21; He just goes fffff-ut, 8; Mix you into stuffin', 13; Shiverous beasts, 22; Such a pleasant familee, 23; Go doucement doucement to the cemetery, 12; Angels, sing-a ling-a ling, 7; and Grave humor, 19. Also Foreword. Indexed by authors, first lines, and titles.

Briggs, Raymond, il. Fee fi fo fum; a picture book of nursery rhymes. Coward 1964 (k-3)
Contents: 20 nursery rhymes ungrouped.

Briggs, Raymond, comp. and il. Mother Goose treasury. Coward 1966 (k-3)
Contents: 408 nursery rhymes and 897 illustrations. Indexed by first lines and familiar titles.

Browning, Robert. Poems of Robert Browning; selected by Rosemary Sprague; il. by Robert Galster. Crowell 1964 (7-12)
Contents: 57 poems grouped as follows: Men and women speak, 14; Two hearts beating each to each, 19; Boot, saddle, to horse and away, 13; and Oh, the wild joys of living, 11. Also introduction, I have made my life my own. Indexed by first lines and titles.

Burns, Robert. Hand in hand we'll go; ten poems by Robert Burns; il. by Nonny Hogrogian. Crowell 1965 (3-up)
Contents: 10 poems ungrouped.

Burns, Robert. Poems of Robert Burns; selected by Lloyd Frankenberg; il. by Joseph Low. Crowell 1967 (7-12)
Contents: 53 poems grouped as follows: Aye rowth o' rhymes, 19; Tam o' Shanter, 1; The jolly beggars, 1; and Gin a body kiss a body, 32. Also Scotch, Scottish, and Scots, an introduction to Robert Burns; and a Glossary. Indexed by first lines and titles.

Byron, George Gordon, Lord. Poems of George Gordon, Lord Byron; selected by Horace Gregory; il. by Virgil Burnett. Crowell 1969 (7-12)
Contents: 20 poems grouped as follows: Occasional pieces, 13; From Childe Harold's pilgrimage, 2; From Don Juan, 4; and Beppo, 1. Also Introduction and Letters. Indexed by first lines and titles.

Causley, Charles, comp. Dawn and dusk; poems of our time chosen and introduced to boys and girls by Charles Causley; with designs by Gerald Wilkinson. Watts First American publication 1963 (5-up)
Contents: 91 poems by 50 authors grouped as follows: Songs and ballads, 25; The other world, 12; Carnival of animals, 16; People and places, 18; and Occasions, seasons and festivals, 20. Also Introduction and brief biographical sketches of the contributors. Indexed by authors and first lines.

Causley, Charles, comp. Modern ballads and story poems; il. by Anne Netherwood. Watts 1965 (5-up)
Contents: 44 poems by 42 authors ungrouped. Also Introduction and notes. Indexed by authors and first lines.

Chaucer, Geoffrey. Taste of Chaucer; selections from The Canterbury tales chosen and edited by Anne Malcolmson; il. by Enrico Arno. Harcourt 1964 (7-12)
Contents: 10 selections from The Canterbury tales: The prologue and 9 of the tales. Also An introduction to Geoffrey Chaucer, glossary, and notes.

Ciardi, John. You know who; il. by Edward Gorey. Lippincott 1964 (1-5)
Contents: 27 poems ungrouped.

Clark, Leonard, comp. Flutes and cymbals; il. by Shirley Hughes. Crowell 1969 (3-7)

Contents: 82 poems by 63 authors grouped as follows: Words and music, 9; Town and country, 10; Around the year, 14; Wind and water, 10; Home and away, 8; Man and beast, 11; Long ago, 10; and Christmas and other feasts, 10. Also Introduction. Indexed by authors and first lines.

Coatsworth, Elizabeth Jane. Down half the world; il. by Zena Bernstein. Macmillan 1968 (4-up)

Contents: 74 poems ungrouped. Also Note.

Coatsworth, Elizabeth Jane. Sparrow bush; rhymes by Elizabeth Coatsworth; wood engravings by Stefan Martin. Norton 1966 (4-up)

Contents: 53 poems ungrouped. Also Author's preface.

Coffey, Dairine, comp. Dark tower; nineteenth century narrative poems. Atheneum 1967 (5-up)

Contents: 14 poems by 11 authors ungrouped. Also An author's notes.

Cole, William, ed. Birds and the beasts were there; animal poems selected by William Cole; woodcuts by Helen Siegl. World 1963 (5-up)

Contents: 293 poems by 163 authors grouped as follows: Small animals of the woods and fields, 53; Under the water and on the shore, 17; Slitherers, creepers, and hardshells, 15; Dogs, 22; Cats, 20; Horses and donkeys, 17; The farmyard, 25; Big beasts, wild beasts, 31; Buzzers, leapers, and flyers, 17; Birds, 54; Animals all together, 10; and Impossible animals, 12. Also Introduction. Indexed by authors and titles.

Cole, William, ed. Beastly boys and ghastly girls; il. by Tomi Ungerer. World 1964 (4-6)

Contents: 70 poems by 38 authors grouped as follows: Introductory poem, 1; Put some mustard in your shoe, 13; Wriggling, giggling, noise, and tattling, 11; They spill their broth on the tablecloth, 11; The naughtiest children I know, 11; Never stew your sister, 13; and And beat him when he sneezes, 10. Indexed by authors and titles.

Cole, William, ed. Book of love poems; il. by Lars Bo. Viking 1965 (6-up)

Contents: 170 poems by 114 authors grouped as follows: Love awakening and first love, 17; Longing and loneliness, 16; What is this thing, 26; He writes about her, 27; She writes about him, 18; Together, 24; Love lost and love dead, 26; and Love stories, 16. Also Introduction. Indexed by authors and titles.

Cole, William, ed. Book of nature poems; il. by Robert Andrew Parker. Viking 1969 (6-up)

Contents: 246 poems by 143 authors grouped as follows: Introductory verse, 1; O feel the gentle air, 31; Green thoughts in a green shade, 22; Of Neptune's empire let us sing, 29; A blaze of noons, 21; Wait for the moon to rise, 23; Season of mists and mellow fruitfulness, 19; About the woodlands I will go, 21; The wind stood up and gave a shout, 18; When icicles hang by the wall, 28; and To stand and stare, 33. Also Introduction. Indexed by authors and titles.

Cole, William, ed. Oh, what nonsense; il. by Tomi Ungerer. Viking 1966 (3-5)
Contents: 50 poems by 22 authors ungrouped. Also Introduction. Indexed by authors and titles.

Cole, William, comp. Sea, ships and sailors; poems, songs and shanties selected by William Cole; il. by Robin Jacques. Viking 1967 (5-up)
Contents: 85 poems by 54 authors grouped as follows: Buccaneers, battles and bad men, 10; The moods of the sea, 9; Of ships and men, 13; The sillies, 7; Songs and shanties, 12; Storms, wrecks and disasters, 11; Under the sea, 11; and Sea stories, 12. Also Introduction. Indexed by authors and titles.

Colum, Padraic, ed. Roofs of gold; poems to read aloud. Macmillan 1964 (5-up)
Contents: 82 poems by 54 authors ungrouped. Also Introduction; Notes. Indexed by authors and first lines.

DeForest, Charlotte B., comp. Prancing pony; nursery rhymes from Japan adapted into English by Charlotte B. DeForest; with kusa-e illustrations by Keiko Hida. Walker 1968 (k-3)
Contents: 53 Japanese nursery rhymes ungrouped.

De La Mare, Walter. Bells and grass; il. by Dorothy P. Lathrop. Viking reissue 1963 (4-8)
Contents: 90 poems ungrouped. Also Introduction. Indexed by first lines and titles.

Dickinson, Emily. Letter to the world; poems for young readers chosen and introduced by Rumer Godden; decorated by Prudence Seward. Macmillan 1968 (7-12)
Contents: 44 poems ungrouped. Also Introduction by Rumer Godden. Indexed by first lines.

Dickinson, Emily. Poems of Emily Dickinson; selected by Helen Plotz; il. by Robert Kipniss. Crowell 1964 (7-12)
Contents: 211 poems grouped as follows: Introduction, 1; Portraits and daily faces, 35; Experiment of green, 57; Divine majority, 28; The soul unto itself, 46; and Bulletins from immortality, 44. Also introduction, Emily Dickinson herself; and Answers to riddle poems. Indexed by first lines.

Doob, Leonard W., ed. Crocodile has me by the leg; African poems; il. by Solomon Irein Wangboje. Walker 1967 (5-up)
Contents: 50 traditional poems grouped as follows: Mother and child, 8; Good advice, 12; Hunger, 6; Two good insults, 2; Songs to sing and dance to, 20; and The sorrows of death, 2. Also Preface.

Downie, Mary Alice and Robertson, Barbara, comps. Wind has wings; poems from Canada; il. by Elizabeth Cleaver. Walck 1968 (4-up)
Contents: 77 poems by 48 authors and translators ungrouped. Indexed by authors.

Dunning, Stephen; Lueders, Edward; and Smith, Hugh, comps. Reflections on a gift of watermelon pickle . . . and other modern verse. Lothrop 1967 (7-12)
Contents: 114 poems by 97 authors grouped in fifteen sections without titles. Also Note; Interpretation. Indexed by authors and titles.

Dunning, Stephen; Leuders, Edward; and Smith, Hugh, comps. Some haystacks don't even have any needle, and other complete modern poems. Lothrop 1969 (7-12)

Contents: 135 poems by 93 authors grouped in seventeen sections without titles. Also Foreword. Indexed by authors and titles.

Farjeon, Eleanor. Around the seasons; il. by Jane Paton. Walck 1969 (2-5)

Contents: 20 poems ungrouped.

Farjeon, Eleanor. Then there were three, being Cherrystones, The mulberry bush, and The starry floor; il. by Isobel and John Morton-Sale. Lippincott 1965 (4-8)

Contents: 76 poems grouped as follows: Introductory poem, 1; Cherrystones, 26; The mulberry bush, 24; and The starry floor, 25.

Fisher, Aileen. Cricket in a thicket; il. by Feodor Rojankovsky. Scribner 1963 (k-3)

Contents: 39 poems grouped as follows: Six legs and eight, 9; Four legs and two, 8; Sunflowers high and pumpkins low, 10; and Warm days and cold, 12. Indexed by titles.

Fisher, Aileen. In one door and out the other; a book of poems; il. by Lillian Hoban. Crowell 1969 (k-3)

Contents: 64 poems ungrouped.

Fisher, Aileen. In the woods, in the meadow, in the sky; il. by Margot Tomes. Scribner 1965 (k-3)

Contents: 48 poems grouped as follows: In the woods, 16; In the meadow, 16; and In the sky, 16. Indexed by titles.

Fraser, Kathleen. Stilts, somersaults, and headstands; game poems based on a painting by Peter Breughel. Atheneum 1968 (2-6)

Contents: 20 poems ungrouped. Also Introduction.

Gasztold, Carmen Bernos de. Creatures' choir, tr. fr. the French and with a foreword by Rumer Godden; il. by Jean Primrose. Viking 1965 (3-up)

Contents: 26 poems ungrouped. Also Foreword by Rumer Godden.

Greenaway, Kate. Kate Greenaway treasury; an anthology of the illustrations and writings of Kate Greenaway, edited and selected by Edward Ernest, assisted by Patricia Tracy Lowe. World 1967 (r)

Contents: 105 poems by 12 authors grouped as follows: Under the window, verses written and illustrated by Kate Greenaway, 18; Birthday book, verses by Mrs Sale Barker, 39; Mother Goose, traditional rhymes, 16; A day in a child's life, poems set to music by Myles B. Foster, 9; Little Ann, story poems by Jane and Ann Taylor, 8; Marigold garden, verses written and illustrated by Kate Greenaway, 13; A apple pie, traditional text, 1; and The Pied Piper of Hamelin by Robert Browning, 1. Also Introduction by Ruth Hill Viguers; Kate Greenaway, a biographical sketch by M. H. Spielman and G. S. Layard; Artist and critic, a selection from Kate Greenaway's letters to and from John Ruskin; A century of Kate Greenaway by Anne Carroll Moore (excerpts); Kate Greenaway's book of games, and Bibliography.

Gregory, Horace and Zaturenska, Marya, comps. Silver swan; poems of romance and mystery; wood engravings by Diana Bloomfield. Holt 1966 (6-12)

Contents: 98 poems by 87 authors grouped as follows: Introductory poem, 1; Flowers in the valley, 14; What terra lemnia gave thee birth, 12; Do you not hear the aziola cry, 9; Flowers: For Heliodora, 14; The dancer lone and white, 14; Fair-haired angel of the evening, 8; Three formes of Heccate, 7; Under a juniper tree, 5; The trumpet blowing, 5; and Mermen keep the tone and time, 9. Also Foreword and Notes. Indexed by authors, first lines, and titles.

Grigson, Geoffrey, comp. Cherry tree. Vanguard 1962 (r)

Contents: 604 poems by 185 authors grouped as follows: Idle fyno, 42; Never stew your sister, 29; April and May, 31; Amo amas, 19; The grief of love, 17; A bunch of songs, 15; Creatures of the air, 28; Creatures of the field, 22; Tales and ballads, 14; Charms and spells, 36; Enchantments, 16; Shore and sea, 31; Ships on the sea, 15; A thousand fearful wrecks, 7; The summer, 16; The flowers, 12; The garden, 9; Journeys, 12; London poems, 18; Autumn poems, 12; The cherry fair, 17; The cries of war, 23; O mortal man, 17; Life and death, 25; Winter, 15; Moon and stars, 24; The days of Christmas, 19; The poet's voice, 33; and I think you stink, 30. Also introduction, To the reader; and brief introductions to each section. Indexed by authors, first lines, and titles.

Hannum, Sara and Reed, Gwendolyn E., comps. Lean out of the window; an anthology of modern poetry; il. by Ragna Tischler. Atheneum 1965 (4-7)

Contents: 89 poems by 41 authors ungrouped. Also Introduction by Siddie Joe Johnson. Indexed by authors and titles.

Hayden, Robert, ed. Kaleidoscope; poems by American Negro poets. Harcourt 1967 (7-12)

Contents: 142 poems by 42 authors grouped by authors. Also introduction and sketches of authors.

Hine, Al, ed. This land is mine; an anthology of American verse; il. by Leonard Vosburgh. Lippincott 1965 (5-up)

Contents: 109 poems by 71 authors grouped as follows: The colonies, 15; A new nation, 19; A nation divided, 15; A nation grows, 30; The United States and a world at war, 6; Between wars, 6; World war II and after, 16; and History is, 2. Also Introduction; and introductions to each section. Indexed by authors and first lines.

Hollowell, Lillian, ed. Book of children's literature. Third edition. Holt 1966 (r)

Contents: 265 poems by 86 authors arranged in two general sections: Traditional poetry and Modern poetry. In the section on Traditional poetry are Mother Goose rhymes, 62; and Ballads, 4. In the section on Modern poetry are the following groupings: Humor and nonsense, 36; Ballads and other narratives, 6; Everyday life—play, home, people, 46; Beasts, birds, flowers, and insects, 35; Water, weather, and other natural phenomena, 26; Lullabies and other songs, 15; Months, special days, seasons, 21; and Supernatural, 14. Also general introduction, What is poetry; and introductions to Traditional poetry and to Modern poetry. Indexed by authors and titles.

Howard, Coralie, comp. Lyric poems; il. by Mel Fowler. Watts 1968 (7-12)
Contents: 111 poems by 78 authors and 22 translators ungrouped. Also Foreword. Indexed by authors, first lines, and titles.

Huber, Miriam Blanton, ed. Story and verse for children. Third edition. Macmillan 1965 (r)
Contents: Two sections of this book are devoted to poetry. The first section, Verse, contains 246 poems by 104 authors grouped as follows: Boys and girls, 34; In feathers and fur and such, 45; The world and all, 52; Fairies and make-believe, 28; For fun, 19; The day's work, 19; Guideposts, 18; Our country, 15; and Stories in verse, 16. Also Verse for children; References: Verse for children; Collections of verse; Books of verse. The second section, Mother Goose rhymes, contains 65 rhymes; also Mother Goose rhymes: Origin and significance; Mother Goose rhymes: Suggested grades; Books of Mother Goose rhymes; and A B C books. Indexed by authors and titles.

Issa. Few flies and I, Haiku by Issa, selected by Jean Merrill and Ronni Solbert from translations by R. H. Blyth and Nobuyuki Yuasa; il. by Ronni Solbert. Pantheon bks. 1969 (4-up)
Contents: 95 poems by Issa ungrouped. Also Introduction to Issa.

Larrick, Nancy, comp. On city streets; an anthology of poetry; il. with photographs by David Sagarin. M. Evans 1968 (3-5)
Contents: 88 poems by 51 authors grouped as follows: Roaring, clanking, sirens screaming, 17; Tall people, short people, 24; A little boy stood on the corner, 12; Like bees in a tunnelled hive, 11; The park is green and quiet, 6; Night song, 11; and Let me pry loose old walls, 7. Also introduction, On city streets. Indexed by authors, first lines, and titles.

Larrick, Nancy, comp. Piper, pipe that song again; poems for boys and girls; il. by Kelly Oechsli. Random 1965 (2-5)
Contents: 78 poems by 47 authors ungrouped. Also an introduction, Piper, pipe that song again. Indexed by authors and titles.

Larrick, Nancy, ed. Piping down the valleys wild; poetry for the young of all ages; il. by Ellen Raskin. Delacorte 1968 (2-8)
Contents: 247 poems by 99 authors grouped as follows: Introductory poem, 1; I'm shouting, I'm singing, I'm swinging through trees, 17; Sing a song of laughter, 23; I like it when it's mizzly and just a little drizzly, 18; I saw a star slide down the sky, 12; I saw a spooky witch out riding on her broom, 16; I wonder what the spring will shout, 17; I chanced to meet, 13; I'd take the hound with the drooping ears, 22; I heard a bird sing, 16; I found new-born foxes, 27; I know a place that's oh, so green, 17; Yet there isn't a train I wouldn't take, 6; I must go down to the seas again, 7; The city spreads its wings, 11; I was one of the children told, 17; and A dozen dreams to dance to you, 7. Also introduction, Piping down the valley wild. Indexed by authors, first lines, and titles.

Larrick, Nancy, comp. Poetry for holidays; drawings by Kelly Oechsli. Garrard 1966 (3-6)
Contents: 57 poems by 33 authors ungrouped. Indexed by authors.

Lewis, Claudia. Poems of earth and space; il. by Symeon Shimin. Dutton 1967 (3-7)
Contents: 24 poems ungrouped.

Lewis, Richard, ed. In a spring garden; il. by Ezra Jack Keats. Dial 1965 (4-up)
Contents: 23 haiku by 10 authors ungrouped.

Lewis, Richard, comp. Miracles; poems by children of the English-speaking world. Simon 1966 (2-6)
Contents: 177 poems by children between the ages of 5 and 13 from the United States, New Zealand, Ireland, Kenya, Uganda, Canada, England, Australia, India, and the Philippines grouped as follows: Poetry, 3; Morning, 5; Spring, 12; The wind and the rain, 17; Playing, 13; Summer, 8; Creatures, 16; The sea, 15; Autumn, 12; People, 17; Feelings, 31; Winter, 10; and Night, 18. Also Introductory note.

Lewis, Richard, ed. Moment of wonder; a collection of Chinese and Japanese poetry; il. with paintings by Chinese and Japanese masters. Dial 1964 (5-up)
Contents: 130 poems by 80 authors grouped as follows: Preface, 6; The family of nature, 31; Landscapes of the sky and earth, 27; The passage of seasons, 32; and The ages of man, 34. Also Preface and brief introductions to each section. Indexed by authors.

Lewis, Richard, ed. Moon, for what do you wait; poems by Tagore; il. by Ashley Bryan. Atheneum 1967 (2-up)
Contents: 17 poems by Rabindranath Tagore ungrouped.

Lewis, Richard, ed. Of this world, a poet's life in poetry; photographs by Helen Buttfield. Dial 1968 (5-up)
Contents: 78 poems by Issa grouped in four parts after brief background passages on Issa's life as follows: Part 1, 18; Part 2, 20; Part 3, 19; and Part 4, 21.

Lewis, Richard, ed. Out of the earth I sing; poetry and songs of primitive peoples of the world; il. with halftone reproductions of primitive paintings, carving, sculpture, and weaving. Norton 1968 (r)
Contents: 124 traditional poems and songs grouped as follows: The white light of morning, 20; We pray for children, 11; Every living creature, 22; Something I've killed, 8; The voice of the thunders, 11; A whispered word, 13; The night comes down, 19; and A long journey, 20. Also Introduction; Appendix. Indexed by first lines.

Lindsay, Vachel. Selected poems of Vachel Lindsay edited by Mark Harris. Macmillan 1967 (7-12)
Contents: 87 poems grouped as follows: United States rhythms, 16; Home town, 17; Runes of the road, 11; Politics, 27; and Songs, prayers, and supplications to the muse, 16. Also Introduction.

Livingston, Myra Cohn. Crazy flight, and other poems; il. by James J. Spanfeller. Harcourt 1969 (1-4)
Contents: 42 poems ungrouped.

Livingston, Myra Cohn, ed. Tune beyond us; il. by James J. Spanfeller. Harcourt 1968 (5-up)

Contents: 143 poems by 67 authors grouped as follows: Introductory poem, 1; "Home is where one starts from . . .," 12; ". . . every atom belonging to me . . .," 12; ". . . the land where the bong-tree grows," 12; "Come away, O human child," 8; ". . . imaginary gardens with real toads . . .," 10; "Oh! Why was I born with a different face?" 16; "I learn by going where I have to go," 17; "What was the name of that cat?" 8; "Green, how much I want you green," 15; ". . . music heard so deeply That it is not heard at all, but you are the music While the music lasts," 11; "I hear an army charging upon the land," 8; and ". . . a newer, mightier world, varied world," 13. Also Editor's note. Indexed by authors, first lines, titles, and translators.

Longfellow, Henry Wadsworth. Poems by Henry Wadsworth Longfellow selected by Edmund Fuller; etchings by John Ross and Clare Romano Ross. Crowell 1967 (5-9)

Contents: 52 poems grouped as follows: Songs of memory and other lyrics, 21; Story in song, 14; Poems of principle, 7; Sonnets, 9; and Excerpts from Michael Angelo: A fragment, 1. Also Introduction. Indexed by first lines and titles.

McCord, David. All day long; fifty rhymes of the never was and always is; il. by Henry B. Kane. Little 1966 (5-9)

Contents: 51 poems ungrouped including an introductory poem.

McCord, David. Every time I climb a tree; il. by Marc Simont. Little 1967 (1-3)

Contents: 25 poems selected from the author's "All day long," "Far and few," and "Take sky," ungrouped.

McGinley, Phyllis, comp. Wonders and surprises. Lippincott 1968 (5-up)

Contents: 107 poems by 66 authors grouped as follows: Strangenesses, 12; The animal kingdom, 10; Love and kisses, 11; Gentlemen and ladies, 9; The poison pen, 10; Trumpet sounds, 9; Far-off places, 8; The changing year, 9; Relatively speaking, 10; A bouquet of ballads, 7; and Simple nonsense, 12. Also Foreword. Indexed by authors and titles.

McGinley, Phyllis. Wreath of Christmas legends; il. by Leonard Weisgard. Macmillan 1967 (4-up)

Contents: 15 poems ungrouped.

Merriam, Eve. Catch a little rhyme; il. by Imero Gobbato. Atheneum 1966 (1-4)

Contents: 27 poems ungrouped.

Merriam, Eve. Independent voices; il. by Arvis Stewart. Atheneum 1968 (5-12)

Contents: 7 poems ungrouped. Also A note to the reader.

Merriam, Eve. It doesn't always have to rhyme; il. by Malcolm Spooner. Atheneum 1964 (4-up)

Contents: 59 poems ungrouped.

Milne, A. A. Christopher Robin book of verse; with decorations and illustrations in full color by E. H. Shepard. Dutton 1967 (1-4)

Contents: 24 poems ungrouped.

Mizumura, Kazue. I see the wind; il. by the author. Crowell 1966 (k-3)
Contents: 17 poems ungrouped.

Montgomerie, Norah and Montgomerie, William, eds. Book of Scottish nursery rhymes; il. by T. Ritchie and N. Montgomerie. Oxford 1965 (k-3)
Contents: 200 Scottish nursery rhymes ungrouped. Also Introduction; and Some words you may not know. Indexed by first lines.

Morrison, Lillian, comp. Sprints and distances; sports in poetry and poetry in sport; il. by Clare and John Ross. Crowell 1965 (6-12)
Contents: 160 poems by 131 authors grouped as follows: The games, 40; Races and contests, 28; Pleasures of the country, 36; The joys of locomotion, 24; Instruction in the art, 10; The road all runners come, 12; and Into lucid air, 10. Also Foreword; Prefatory note. Indexed by authors, first lines, titles, and sports.

O'Neill, Mary. Fingers are always bringing me news; il. by Don Bolognese. Doubleday 1969 (k-4)
Contents: 14 poems ungrouped.

O'Neill, Mary. Hailstones and halibut bones; adventures in color; il. by Leonard Weisgard. Doubleday 1961 (k-4)
Contents: 14 poems ungrouped.

Opie, Iona and Opie, Peter, comps. Family book of nursery rhymes; il. by Pauline Baynes. Oxford 1964 (k-3) (Originally published by Penguin books as The Puffin book of nursery rhymes.)
Contents: 358 nursery rhymes ungrouped. Also Preface; and Incidentally —Some notes on particular rhymes. Indexed by first lines and principal subjects of the rhymes.

Parker, Elinor, comp. Here and there; 100 poems about places; il. by Peter Spier. Crowell 1967 (5-up)
Contents: 100 poems by 73 authors grouped as follows: America, 40; Around the world, 52; and Off the map, 8. Indexed by authors, first lines, and titles.

Plotz, Helen, comp. Earth is the Lord's; poems of the spirit; il. with wood engravings by Clare Leighton. Crowell 1965 (7-12)
Contents: 181 poems by 108 authors grouped as follows: The vision splendid, 53; Praise doubt, 28; God's familiars, 18; All creatures here below, 36; and Our daily bread, 46. Also Introduction. Indexed by authors, first lines, and titles.

Poe, Edgar Allan. Poems of Edgar Allan Poe selected by Dwight Macdonald; il. by Ellen Raskin. Crowell 1965 (7-12)
Contents: 34 poems grouped as follows: The music of things, 9; Out of space and out of time, 10; and I have not been as others were, 15. Also Introduction and A note on selection and arrangement. Indexed by first lines and titles.

Reed, Gwendolyn, comp. Bird songs; il. by Gabriele Margules. Atheneum 1969 (2-5)
Contents: 81 poems by 62 authors and translators grouped as follows: Cock Robin, 5; And Jenny Wren, 4; Love's horn doth blow, 5; Within the bush, 4; In the dark of December, 6; Summer is coming, 5; Cages and nets, 6; Children of the wind, 20; Listening . . . watching, 7; Te whit, te whoo, 4; Hark, hark, the lark, 3; Caw, caw, caw, 4; and Silence and songs, 8. Indexed by authors and titles.

Reed, Gwendolyn, comp. Out of the ark; an anthology of animal verse; il. by Gabriele Margules. Atheneum 1968 (5-up)
Contents: 135 poems by 92 authors ungrouped. Also Notes. Indexed by authors and titles.

Reed, Gwendolyn, comp. Songs the Sandman sings; il. by Peggy Owens Skillen. Atheneum 1969 (k-2)
Contents: 55 poems by 39 authors grouped as follows: Time for bed, 13; Tucked in, 9; Lullabies, 14; Moonlight and starlight, 8; While you're asleep, 7; and Now I lay me down to sleep, 4.

Reed, Philip, comp. and il. Mother Goose and nursery rhymes. Atheneum 1963 (k-3)
Contents: 67 nursery rhymes ungrouped. Indexed by first lines.

Reeves, James, comp. One's none; old rhymes for new tongues; il. by Bernadette Watts. Watts 1969 (k-3)
Contents: 95 nursery rhymes ungrouped.

Shakespeare, William. Seeds of time; selections from Shakespeare compiled by Bernice Grohskopf; il. by Kelly Oechsli. Atheneum 1963 (5-up)
Contents: 48 selections from Shakespeare ungrouped. Indexed by titles and sources.

Smith, John, comp. My kind of verse; il. by Uri Shulevitz. Macmillan 1968 (5-9)
Contents: 206 poems by 113 authors grouped as follows: Songs and simples, 35; Magic and mystery, 25; Tall tales, 14; Odd bods, 25; Places, weathers, creatures, things, 56; Stuff and nonsense, 20; and Wisdoms, praise, prayers and graces, 31. Also Introduction, and Notes on the poems. Indexed by authors and first lines.

Stephens, James. A singing wind; selected poems by James Stephens; edited by Quail Hawkins; il. by Harold Goodwin. Macmillan 1968 (7-12)
Contents: 82 poems grouped as follows: In green ways, 14; A honeycomb, 15; In the two lights, 6; Heels and head, 17; Less than daintily, 7; The golden bird, 15; and Miscellany, 8. Also Introduction. Indexed by first lines.

Stephenson, Marjorie, comp. Fives sixes and sevens; il. by Denis Wrigley. Warne 1968 (k-3)
Contents: 106 poems by 49 authors grouped as follows: Fives, 39; Sixes, 32; and Sevens, 35.

Tennyson, Alfred, Lord. Poems of Alfred, Lord Tennyson; selected by Ruth Greiner Rausen; il. by Virgil Burnett. Crowell 1964 (7-12)
Contents: 74 poems ungrouped. Also introduction, About Alfred, Lord Tennyson. Indexed by first lines and titles.

Thomas, Edward. Green roads; poems by Edward Thomas chosen and with an introduction by Eleanor Farjeon; il. by Diana Bloomfield. Holt 1965 (6-12)

Contents: 55 poems grouped as follows: One, 35; Two, 6; Three, 7; Four, 6; and Five, 1. Also Foreword, Walking with Edward Thomas by Eleanor Farjeon. Indexed by first lines and titles.

Thompson, Blanche Jennings, ed. All the silver pennies, combining Silver pennies and More silver pennies; il. by Ursula Arndt. Macmillan 1967 (3-8)

Contents: 176 poems by 111 authors arranged in two parts: Part one for younger children, 90 poems; and Part two for older children, 86 poems. Also an Introduction. Brief introductory comments precede each poem. Indexed by authors, first lines, and titles.

Tudor, Tasha, comp. and il. Wings from the wind, an anthology of poetry. Lippincott 1964 (4-up)

Contents: 65 poems by 39 authors grouped as follows: Thoughts, 27; As the earth turns, 19; Birds of the air, beasts of the field, 15; and Nonsense, 4.

Vries, Leonard de, ed. Flowers of delight, culled from the Osborne collection of early children's books; embellished with some 700 woodcuts and engravings on wood and copper of which upwards of 125 are colored. Pantheon bks. 1965 (r)

Contents: 167 poems by 12 known authors. Also prose selections. Also The Osborne collection by H. C. Campbell, chief librarian of the Toronto Public Library; The anthologist's apology; Notes on the original books; Some writers, illustrators and publishers; and Bibliography.

Weiss, Renée Karol, comp. Paper zoo; a collection of animal poems by modern American poets; il. by Ellen Raskin. Macmillan 1968 (4-up)

Contents: 16 poems by 16 authors ungrouped. Also Afterwords.

Whitman, Walt. Walt Whitman's America; selections and drawings by James Daugherty. World 1964 (5-up)

Contents: 11 poems grouped as follows: I hear America singing, 10; and The American dream, 1. Also prose selections.

Wildsmith, Brian, comp. and il. Brian Wildsmith's Mother Goose; a collection of nursery rhymes. Watts 1965 (k-3)

Contents: 86 nursery rhymes ungrouped. Indexed by first lines.

Wordsworth, William. Poems of William Wordsworth; selected by Elinor Parker; wood engravings by Diana Bloomfield. Crowell 1964 (7-12)

Contents: 66 poems grouped as follows: Still glides the stream, 7; The still, sad music of humanity, 15; Sing, ye birds, sing, 21; The visionary gleam, 11; and The glory and the dream, 12. Also introduction, The poet—his life and his art. Indexed by first lines and titles.

Wyndham, Robert, ed. Chinese Mother Goose rhymes; il. by Ed Young. World 1968 (k-2)

Contents: 41 traditional rhymes ungrouped. Also Author's note.

Yeats, William Butler. Running to paradise; poems by W. B. Yeats; an introductory selection by Kevin Crossley-Holland; il. by Judith Valpy. Macmillan 1968 (7-12)

Contents: 47 poems ungrouped. Also Introduction. Indexed by first lines.

KEY TO SYMBOLS FOR BOOKS INDEXED

Grades are given in parentheses at the end of each entry: (k), kindergarten or preschool grade; (1), first grade; (2), second grade, etc. Comprehensive general collections are designated (r), reference.

Space is left under each symbol where the library call number may be inserted.

AdIa Adoff, A. ed. I am the darker brother. Macmillan 1968 (5-12)

AgH Agree, R. H. comp. How to eat a poem and other morsels. Pantheon bks. 1967 (3-6)

AiC Aiken, C. Cats and bats and things with wings. Atheneum 1965 (k-4)

AlPi Aldan, D. comp. Poems from India. Crowell 1969 (7-12)

ArT-3 Arbuthnot, M. H. and Root, Jr., S. L. comps. Time for poetry. Third general edition. Scott, Foresman 1967 (r)

BaH Baron, V. O. ed. Here I am. Dutton 1969 (5-12)

BaS Baron, V. O. ed. Seasons of time. Dial 1968 (4-up)

BeCm Belting, N. Calendar moon. Holt 1964 (5-up)

BeCs Behn, H. tr. Cricket songs. Harcourt 1964 (4-up)

BeG Behn, H. Golden hive. Harcourt 1966 (3-5)

BlO Blishen, E. comp. Oxford book of poetry for children. Watts 1963 (r)

BlP Blake, W. Poems of William Blake. Crowell 1964 (7-12)

BoA Bontemps, A. ed. American Negro poetry. Hill and Wang 1963 (r)

BoGj Bogan, L. and Smith W. J. comps. Golden journey. Reilly 1965 (2-6)

BoH Bontemps, A. comp. Hold fast to dreams. Follett 1969 (5-up)

BrA Brewton, S. and J. E. comps. America forever new. Crowell 1968 (5-up)

BrF Briggs, R. comp. and il. Fee fi fo fum. Coward 1964 (k-3)

BrLl Brewton, S. and J. E. comps. Laughable limericks. Crowell 1965 (3-up)

BrMg Briggs, R. comp. and il. Mother Goose treasury. Coward 1966 (k-3)

BrP Browning, R. Poems of Robert Browning. Crowell 1964 (7-12)

BrSg Bramblett, E. comp. Shoots of green. Crowell 1968 (k-3)

BrSm Brewton, S. and J. E. comps. Shrieks at midnight. Crowell 1969 (4-up)

BuH Burns, R. Hand in hand we'll go. Crowell 1965 (3-up)

BuPr Burns, R. Poems of Robert Burns. Crowell 1967 (7-12)

ByP Byron, G. G. Poems of George Gordon, Lord Byron. Crowell 1969 (7-12)

CaD Causley, C. comp. Dawn and dusk. Watts 1963 (5-up)

CaMb Causley, C. comp. Modern ballads and story poems. Watts 1965 (5-up)

ChT Chaucer, G. Taste of Chaucer. Harcourt 1964 (7-12)

CiYk Ciardi, J. You know who. Lippincott 1964 (1-5)

ClF Clark, L. comp. Flutes and cymbals. Crowell 1969 (3-7)

CoB Cole, W. ed. Birds and the beasts were there. World 1963 (5-up)

CoBb Cole, W. ed. Beastly boys and ghastly girls. World 1964 (4-6)

CoBl Cole, W. ed. Book of love poems. Viking 1965 (6-up)

CoBn Cole, W. ed. Book of nature poems. Viking 1969 (6-up)

CoD Coffey, D. comp. Dark tower. Atheneum 1967 (5-up)

CoDh Coatsworth, E. J. Down half the world. Macmillan 1968 (4-up)

CoO Cole, W. ed. Oh, what nonsense. Viking 1966 (3-5)

CoR Colum, P. ed. Roofs of gold. Macmillan 1964 (5-up)

CoSb Coatsworth, E. J. Sparrow bush. Norton 1966 (4-up)

CoSs Cole, W. ed. Sea, ships and sailors. Viking 1967 (5-up)

DeBg De La Mare, W. Bells and grass. Viking reissue 1963 (4-8)

DePp DeForest, C. B. comp. Prancing pony. Walker 1968 (k-3)

DiL Dickinson, E. Letter to the world. Macmillan 1968 (7-12)

DiPe Dickinson, E. Poems of Emily Dickinson. Crowell 1964 (7-12)

DoC Doob, L. W. ed. Crocodile has me by the leg. Walker 1967 (5-up)

DoW Downie, M. A. and Robertson, B. comps. Wind has wings. Walck 1968 (4-up)

DuR Dunning, S.; Lueders, E., and Smith, H. comps. Reflections on a gift of watermelon pickle. Lothrop 1967 (7-12)

DuS Dunning, S.; Lueders, E., and Smith, H. comps. Some haystacks don't even have any needle. Lothrop 1969 (7-12)

FaA Farjeon, E. Around the seasons. Walck 1969 (2-5)

FaT Farjeon, E. Then there were three. Lippincott 1965 (4-8)

FiC Fisher, A. Cricket in the thicket. Scribner 1963 (k-3)

FiI Fisher, A. In the woods, in the meadow, in the sky. Scribner 1965 (k-3)

FiIo Fisher, A. In one door and out the other. Crowell 1969 (k-3)

FrS Fraser, K. Stilts, somersaults and headstands. Atheneum 1968 (2-6)

GaC Gasztold, C. B. de. Creature's choir. Viking 1965 (3-up)

GrCt Grigson, G. comp. Cherry tree. Vanguard 1962 (r)

GrS Gregory, H. and Zaturenska, M. comps. Silver swan. Holt 1966 (6-12)

GrT Greenaway, K. Kate Greenaway treasury. World 1967 (r)

HaK Hayden, R. ed. Kaleidoscope. Harcourt 1967 (7-12)

HaL Hannum, S. and Reed, G. E. comps. Lean out of the window. Atheneum 1965 (4-7)

HiL Hine, A. ed. This land is mine. Lippincott 1965 (5-up)

HoB Hollowell, L. ed. Book of children's literature. Third edition. Holt 1966 (r)

HoL Howard, C. comp. Lyric poems. Watts 1968 (7-12)

HuS-3 Huber, M. B. ed. Story and verse for children. Third edition. Macmillan 1965 (r)

KEY TO SYMBOLS FOR BOOKS INDEXED

IsF Issa. Few flies and I. Pantheon bks. 1969 (4-up)

LaC Larrick, N. comp. On city streets. M. Evans 1968 (3-5)

LaP Larrick, N. comp. Piper, pipe that song again. Random 1965 (2-5)

LaPd Larrick, N. ed. Piping down the valleys wild. Delacorte 1968 (2-8)

LaPh Larrick, N. comp. Poetry for holidays. Garrard 1966 (3-6)

LeI Lewis, R. ed. In a spring garden. Dial 1965 (4-up)

LeM Lewis, R. comp. Miracles. Simon 1966 (2-6)

LeMf Lewis, R. ed. Moon, for what do you wait. Atheneum 1967 (2-up)

LeMw Lewis, R. ed. Moment of wonder. Dial 1964 (5-up)

LeO Lewis, R. ed. Out of the earth I sing. Norton 1968 (r)

LeOw Lewis, R. ed. Of this world. Dial 1968 (5-up)

LeP Lewis, C. Poems of earth and space. Dutton 1967 (3-7)

LiC Livingston, M. C. Crazy flight, and other poems. Harcourt 1969 (1-4)

LiP Lindsay, V. Selected poems of Vachel Lindsay. Macmillan 1963 (7-12)

LiT Livingston, M. C. ed. Tune beyond us. Harcourt 1968 (5-up)

LoPl Longfellow, H. W. Poems of Henry Wadsworth Longfellow. Crowell 1967 (5-9)

McAd McCord, D. All day long. Little 1966 (5-9)

McE McCord, D. Every time I climb a tree. Little 1967 (1-3)

McWc McGinley, P. Wreath of Christmas legends. Macmillan 1967 (4-up)

McWs McGinley, P. comp. Wonders and surprises. Lippincott 1968 (5-up)

MeC Merriam, E. Catch a little rhyme. Atheneum 1966 (1-4)

MeI Merriam, E. It doesn't always have to rhyme. Atheneum 1964 (4-up)

MeIv Merriam, E. Independent voices. Atheneum 1968 (5-12)

MiC Milne, A. A. Christopher Robin book of verse. Dutton 1967 (1-4)

MiI Mizumura, K. I see the wind. Crowell 1966 (k-3)

MoB Montgomerie, N. and W. eds. Book of Scottish nursery rhymes. Oxford 1965 (k-3)

MoS Morrison, L. comp. Sprints and distances. Crowell 1965 (6-12)

OnF O'Neill, M. Fingers are always bringing me news. Doubleday 1969 (k-4)

OnH O'Neill, M. Hailstones and halibut bones. Doubleday 1961 (k-4)

OpF Opie, I. and P. comps. Family book of nursery rhymes. Oxford 1964 (k-3)

PaH Parker, E. comp. Here and there. Crowell 1967 (5-up)

PlE Plotz, H. comp. Earth is the Lord's. Crowell 1965 (7-12)

PoP Poe, E. A. Poems of Edgar Allan Poe. Crowell 1965 (7-12)

ReBs Reed, G. comp. Bird songs. Atheneum 1969 (2-5)

ReMg Reed, P. comp. and il. Mother Goose and nursery rhymes. Atheneum 1963 (k-3)

ReO Reed, G. comp. Out of the ark. Atheneum 1968 (5-up)

ReOn Reeves, J. comp. One's none. Watts 1969 (k-3)

ReS Reed, G. comp. Songs the Sandman sings. Atheneum 1969 (k-2)

ShS Shakespeare, W. Seeds of time. Atheneum 1963 (5-up)

SmM Smith, J. comp. My kind of verse. Macmillan 1968 (5-9)

StF Stephenson, M. comp. Fives sixes and sevens. Warne 1968 (k-3)

StS Stephens, J. Singing wind. Macmillan 1968 (7-12)

TeP Tennyson, A. Poems of Alfred, Lord Tennyson. Crowell 1964 (7-12)

ThA Thompson, B. J. ed. All the silver pennies. Macmillan 1967 (3-8)

ThG Thomas, E. Green roads. Holt 1965 (6-12)

TuW Tudor, T. comp. and il. Wings from the wind. Lippincott 1964 (4-up)

VrF Vries, L. de. ed. Flowers of delight. Pantheon bks. 1965 (r)

WeP Weiss, R. K. comp. Paper zoo. Macmillan 1968 (4-up)

WhA Whitman, W. Walt Whitman's America. World 1964 (5-up)

WiMg Wildsmith, B. comp. and il. Brian Wildsmith's Mother Goose. Watts 1965 (k-3)

WoP Wordsworth, W. Poems of William Wordsworth. Crowell 1964 (7-12)

WyC Wyndham, R. ed. Chinese Mother Goose rhymes. World 1968 (k-2)

YeR Yeats, W. B. Running to paradise. Macmillan 1968 (7-12)

KEY TO ABBREVIATIONS

ad. adapted
at. attributed
bk. book
comp. compiler, compiled
comps. compilers
ed. edition, editor
eds. editors
il. illustrated, illustrator
ils. illustrators
k kindergarten or preschool grade
pseud. pseudonym
pseuds. pseudonyms
r reference
rev. revised
rev ed revised edition
sel. selection
sels. selections
tr. translator
tr. fr. translated from
trs. translators
wr. at. wrongly attributed

DIRECTIONS FOR USE

SEE KEY TO SYMBOLS, p. XXV

The TITLE ENTRY is the main entry and gives the fullest information, including title (with the first line in parentheses when needed to distinguish between poems with the same title); variant titles; full name of author; translator; and symbols for collections in which the poem is to be found. VARIANT TITLES and titles with variant first lines are also listed in their alphabetical order, with *See* references to the main title.

"**Above** the mountain." Shiki, tr. fr. the Japanese by Harry Behn.—BeCs
A **Christmas** carol ("In the bleak mid-winter") Christina Georgina Rossetti.—GrCt
My gift.—LaPh (sel.)
My gift. See A Christmas carol ("In the bleak mid-winter")

Titles of poems are grouped according to subject, in alphabetical order under a subject heading. The SUBJECT ENTRY gives the title of poem; name of author with initials only; first line where needed for identification; variant titles; source title for subordinate selections; and the symbols for the collections in which the poem is to be found.

Cats
The cat ("The black cat yawns") M. B. Miller.—ArT-3—CoB—HoB—HuS-3—StF
The cursing of the cat. From Philip (or Phylip) Sparrow. J. Skelton.—ReO
O cat of carlish kind.—GrCt
"Dame Trot and her cat." Mother Goose.—StF
Dame Trot.—BrMg

The AUTHOR ENTRY gives the full name of the author; title of poem with its variants (first line in parentheses when needed for identification); and the symbols for the collections in which the poem is to be found. Included under the author entry are references from variant titles, and from titles of selections to the source title.

Carryl, Charles Edward
Davy and the goblin, sels.
Robinson Crusoe's story.—CoSs—HoB
Robinson Crusoe's island.—ArT-3
Robinson Crusoe's story. See Davy and the goblin
Robinson Crusoe's island. See Davy and the goblin —Robinson Crusoe's story

FIRST LINES of poems, enclosed in quotation marks, are listed in their alphabetical order with references to the title entry where all the information may be found. First lines are enclosed in quotation marks even when used as titles.

"**I** have fallen in love with American names." See American names
"**Taffy** is a Welshman." See "Taffy was a Welshman"

When the source of a poem is more familiar than the title of the poem, or when only selections from a longer work are given, such titles are grouped under the source title. All titles subordinated to SOURCE TITLES are also entered in their alphabetical order with references to the source title.

As you like it, sels. William Shakespeare
A lover and his lass.—ShS
"Under the greenwood tree."—ArT-3—CoBn—ShS—TuW
A **lover** and his lass. See As you like it
"**Under** the greenwood tree." See As you like it

INDEX TO POETRY FOR CHILDREN AND YOUNG PEOPLE

Accidents—*Continued*
Epitaph. R. Armour.—BrSm
Falling in the creek. I. Heke.—LeM
Hallelujah. A. E. Housman.—BrSm
"He shot at Lee Wing." Unknown.—BrSm
Hell's bells. M. Fishback.—BrSm
"Here's little Jim Nast of Pawtucket." H. Lofting.—BrLl
Highway: Michigan. T. Roethke.—DuS
"Humpty Dumpty ligs in t' beck." Mother Goose.—OpF
"Humpty Dumpty sat on a wall . . . (four score men)." Mother Goose.—HuS-3—OpF
"Jack and Jill went up the hill." Mother Goose. —HuS-3—OpF—WiMg
"Jack and Jill."—GrT
Jack and Jill and old Dame Dob.—BrMg
"A new servant maid named Maria." Unknown.—BrLl
Primer of consequences. V. Brasier.—BrSm
"Ruth and Johnnie." Unknown.—BrSm
The scarred girl. J. Dickey.—DuS
Sir Smashum Uppe. E. V. Rieu.—CoO
The swift bullets. C. Wells.—BrSm
The termite. O. Nash.—BrSm
"There was a young fellow named Hall." Unknown.—BrLl—SmM
"There once was a young man named Hall."—BrSm
"There was a young fellow named Weir." Unknown.—BrLl
"There was a young man of Herne bay." Unknown.—BrLl
"There was an old lady named Crockett." W. J. Smith.—BrLl—BrSm
"Wirgele-Wargele, auf der bank." Mother Goose.—OpF
"An **accomplished** acrobat." Issa, tr. fr. the Japanese by Nobuyuki Yuasa.—IsF
Achilles
"There was a young man named Achilles." E. M. Robinson.—BrLl
Achilles Deatheridge. Edgar Lee Masters.—BrA
Acker, William
Long I have loved to stroll. tr.—GrCt
Acorn, Milton
Poem in June.—DoW
Acorn Bill. Ruth Ainsworth.—StF
Acorns. See also Oak trees
Acorn Bill. R. Ainsworth.—StF
Acquainted with the night. Robert Frost.—GrCt —LaC—LaPd
Acrobat. See A circus garland
"**Across** a sage-grown upland." See The path of the padres
"**Across** the dim frozen fields of night." See Night train
"**Across** the narrow beach we flit." See The sandpiper
"**Across** the seas of Wonderland to Mogadore we plodded." See Forty singing seamen
"**Across** the silent stream." See From the hills of dream
"**Across** the sparkling snowfields and the dark pines." See Day moon
Acrostics
An enigma. E. A. Poe.—PoP
Acton, Harold and Ch'en Shih-hsiang
The country in spring, trs.—LeMw
Several people. trs.—LeMw
The song of the wind bell. trs.—LeMw
Summer rain. trs.—LeMw
Actors and acting
Hazardous occupations. C. Sandburg.—HoL
The puppet play. P. Colum.—CoR
Adam and Eve. See also Eden, Garden of
Adam lay a-bowndyn. Unknown.—GrCt
Adam's curse. W. B. Yeats.—YeR
All the way. W. De La Mare.—DeBg
The animals mourn with Eve. From Eve. C. G. Rossetti.—ReO
Eve. R. Hodgson.—SmM
Eve speaks to Adam. From Paradise lost. J. Milton.—GrCt
Expulsion from Paradise. From Paradise lost. J. Milton.—GrCt
Genesis. E. J. Coatsworth.—CoDh
"**Adam** and Eve gaed up my sleeve." See Tickling game
"**Adam** Birkett took his gun." See Birkett's eagle
Adam lay i-bowndyn. Unknown.—GrCt
"**Adam** lay i-bowndyn, bowndyn in a bond." See Adam lay i-bowndyn
Adams, Franklin P. (F. P. A., pseud.)
A ballade of lawn tennis.—MoS
Baseball note.—MoS
Baseball's sad lexicon.—MoS
Adams, James Barton
The cowboy's life. at.—ArT-3—BrA
Adams, Léonie
Country summer.—BoGj
Song from a country fair. BoGj
Adams, Lucy
Barrow.—BaH
Adam's curse. William Butler Yeats.—YeR
Addison, Joseph
"The spacious firmament on high."—PlE
Addition. See Arithmetic
Address from the printer to his little readers. Unknown, at. to William Darton.—VrF
Address to a child during a boisterous winter evening. Dorothy Wordsworth.—BlO
Address to a haggis. Robert Burns.—BuPr
Address to a lark, sel. John Clare
Address to a lark singing in winter.—ReBs
Address to a lark singing in winter. See Address to a lark.
Address to a mummy. Horace Smith.—CoR
Address to the deil. Robert Burns.—BuPr
Address to the toothache. Robert Burns.—BuPr
Address to the unco guid. Robert Burns.—BuPr
Adeler, Max
Willie.—CoBb
Adieu. Paul Lewenstein.—SmM
"**Adieu,** farewell earth's bliss." See Lord, have mercy on us

Adigal, Ilango
The lover's song. See Shilappadakaram
Shilappadakaram, sels.
The lover's song.—AlPi
Song of the playing ball.—AlPi
Song of the playing ball. See Shilappadakaram
Adjuration. Charles Enoch Wheeler.—BoA
Adlestrop. Edward Thomas.—BlO—BoGj—PaH—ThG
The **admiral's** ghost. Alfred Noyes.—ArT-3
Adolphus Elfinstone. Gelett Burgess.—CoBb
"**Adolphus** Elfinstone of Nachez." See Adolphus Elfinstone
Adon 'Olam. Unknown, tr. fr. the Hebrew by F. De Sola Mendes.—PlE
Adonais, sel. Percy Bysshe Shelley
Go thou to Rome.—GrCt
Adulescentia. Robert Fitzgerald.—MoS (sel.)
Adults
Grown-up fingers. M. O'Neill.—OnF
Grownups. M. Duskin.—LeM
Adventure ("It's not very far to the edge of town") Harry Behn.—ArT-3
Adventure ("The little men of meadow land") Nancy Byrd Turner.—HuS-3
Adventure ("There's a place I've dreamed about far away") Harry Behn.—BeG
Adventure and adventurers. See also Explorers and exploration; Frontier and pioneer life; Gipsies; Heroes and heroines; Hunters and hunting; Indians of the Americas; Roads and trails; Seamen; Wayfaring life
Adventure ("It's not very far to the edge of town") H. Behn.—ArT-3
Adventure ("The little men of meadow land") N. B. Turner.—HuS-3
Adventure ("There's a place I've dreamed about far away") H. Behn.—BeG
"Adventure most unto itself." E. Dickinson.—DiPe
Aventures of Isabel. O. Nash.—BrSm (sel.)—LaP (sel.)—LaPd (sel.)
The adventures of Oberon, king of the fairies, while searching for Queen Mab. From Nymphidia, the court of fairy. M. Drayton.—ReO
The adventures of Tom Bombadil, sels. J. R. R. Tolkien.—LiT (Complete)
Oliphaunt.—ClF
Perry-the-winkle.—ArT-3
The ballad of Kon-Tiki. I. Serraillier.—CoSs
Childe Roland to the dark tower came. R. Browning.—BrP—CoD
Eldorado. E. A. Poe.—PaH—PoP
Momotara. Unknown.—ArT-3
Ulysses. A. Tennyson.—TeP
The voyage of Maeldune. A. Tennyson.—TeP
"**Adventure** most unto itself." Emily Dickinson.—DiPe
Adventures of Isabel. Ogden Nash.—BrSm (sel.)—LaP (sel.)—LaPd (sel.)
The **adventures** of Oberon, king of the fairies, while searching for Queen Mab. See Nymphidia, the court of fairy
The **adventures** of Tom Bombadil, sels. J. R. R. Tolkien.—LiT (Complete)
Oliphaunt.—ClF
Perry-the-winkle.—ArT-3
The **adversary.** Phyllis McGinley.—McWs
Advertisement for a divertissement. Eve Merriam.—MeI
Advertising
Advertisement for a divertissement. E. Merriam.—MeI
Memorial to the great big beautiful self-sacrificing advertisers. F. Ebright.—HiL
A paradox. Unknown.—BrSm
A rhyme about an electrical advertising sign. V. Lindsay.—LiP
Advice. See also Conduct of life
Advice to children. C. Wells.—CoO
Advice to travelers. W. Gibson.—DuR
Apples and water. R. Graves.—CaD
Ballad of the soldier. B. Brecht.—LiT
Good advice. Unknown.—ArT-3
"If a jackal bothers you, show him a hyena." Unknown.—DoC
"Never get up till the sun gets up." Unknown.—DoC
Staying alive. D. Wagoner.—CoBn—DuS
Warning. J. Ciardi.—LaPd
Advice. See "He that would thrive"
Advice to children. Carolyn Wells.—CoO
Advice to travelers. Walker Gibson.—DuR
"**Ae** fond kiss, and then we sever." Robert Burns.—BuPr
Aeiou, Jonathan Swift.—BlO
Aeneid, sels. Virgil
The boat race; tr. fr. the Latin by Rolfe Humphries.—MoS
The boxing match; tr. fr. the Latin by Rolfe Humphries.—MoS
Aeroplane. Mary McB. Green.—ArT-3
Aeroplanes. See Airplanes
Aesop
The ass in the lion's skin.—ReO
Afar in the desert. Thomas Pringle.—ReO (sel.)
"**Afar** in the desert I love to ride." See Afar in the desert
Affection. See Friendship; Kindness; Love
Affliction. See Blind; Cripples
Afforestation. E. A. Wodehouse.—MoS
"**Afoot** and light-hearted, I take to the open road." See Song of the open road
"**Afraid?** Of whom am I afraid." Emily Dickinson.—DiPe
Africa
The African affair. B. McM. Wright.—BoA
African China. M. B. Tolson.—HaK
African Christmas. J. Press.—CaD
African dance. L. Hughes.—ThA
African sunrise. G. M. Lutz.—DuR
April. N. Belting.—BeCm
December. N. Belting.—BeCm
Far from Africa: Four poems. M. Danner.—BoA
Heritage. C. Cullen.—BoA
January. N. Belting.—BeCm

Africa—*Continued*
May-June. N. Belting.—BeCm
Morning light the dew-drier. M. E. L. Newsome.—BoA
O Daedalus, fly away home. R. E. Hayden.—AdIa—BoH
Stanley meets Mutesa. J. D. Rubadiri.—BoH
Ula Masonda's dream. W. Plomer.—CaMb
The **African** affair. Bruce McM. Wright.—BoA
African China. Melvin B. Tolson.—HaK
African Christmas. John Press.—CaD
African dance. Langston Hughes.—ThA
African sunrise. Gertrude May Lutz.—DuR
After a bath. Aileen Fisher.—StF
"**After** a flock of flies." Issa, tr. fr. the Japanese.—LeOw
"**After** a wedding or baby shower." See What are the most unusual things you find in garbage cans
After all and after all. Mary Carolyn Davies.—ArT-3—ThA
After apple-picking. Robert Frost.—CoR
". . . **after** dinner." See Conversations about Christmas
After ever happily; or, The princess and the woodcutter. Ian Serraillier.—CoBl
"**After** great pain, a formal feeling comes." Emily Dickinson.—DiL
"**After** my bath." See After a bath
After rain ("In the autumn sky the clouds are thinned") Tu Fu, tr. fr. the Chinese by Chi Hwang Chu and Edna Worthley Underwood.—HoL
After rain ("The rain is clinging to the round rose-cheek") Eleanor Farjeon.—HoB
After rain ("The rain of a night and a day and a night") Edward Thomas.—ThG
After reading certain books. Mary Coleridge.—PlE
After reading the sad story of the fall of Babylon. Vachel Lindsay.—LiP
After reading translations of ancient texts on stone and clay. Charles Reznikoff.—GrS
"**After** such years of dissension and strife." See Dust to dust
"**After** tea, while others knit." See Grandad's pipe
"**After** the beautiful rain." See Pearls on the grass
"**After** the bells hummed." Bashō, tr. fr. the Japanese by Harry Behn.—BeCs
"**After** the bronzed, heroic traveller." See The mapmaker on his art
"**After** the businesses had moved, before." See The produce district
"**After** the cloud embankments." See Reconnaissance
"**After** the dark of night." See Daybreak
"**After** the first powerful plain manifesto." See The express
After the rain is over. Aileen Fisher.—FiI
After the salvo. Herbert Asquith.—LiT
After the sea ship. Walt Whitman.—CoSs
"**After** the sea ship, after the whistling winds." See After the sea ship
"**After** the sky." See After the rain is over
"**After** the storm." Nōin, tr. fr. the Japanese by Kenneth Rexroth.—BaS
After the winter. Claude McKay.—AdIa
"**After** those first days." See Death of a bird
After-thought. William Wordsworth.—WoP
After winter. Sterling Brown.—BoH
Aftermath. Henry Wadsworth Longfellow.—LoPl
Afternoon
Abracadabra. D. Livesay.—DoW
Afternoon. M. Stearns.—ArT-3
Afternoon: Amagansett beach. J. H. Wheelock.—CoBn
Afternoon on a hill. E. St V. Millay.—ArT-3—ClF—Hus-3—LaPd
City afternoon. B. Howes.—BrA
Summer afternoon. R. Souster.—CoBn
Village before sunset. F. Cornford.—CoBn
Afternoon. Monroe Stearns.—ArT-3
Afternoon: Amagansett beach. John Hall Wheelock.—CoBn
Afternoon on a hill. Edna St Vincent Millay.—ArT-3—ClF—HuS-3—LaPd
Afterwards ("I like to have a home life in the house") Gertrude Stein.—HaL (sel.)
Afterwards ("When the present has latched its postern behind my tremulous stay") Thomas Hardy.—CoBn—GrCt
Afton water. See Sweet Afton
"**Again** and again through the day." See Cat
"**Again** rejoicing Nature sees." See Song
"**Again** the day." See If the stars should fall
"**Again** the sacred parable." See An elegy for a dead child in the street
"**Against** a white wall I stand." See In camera
"**Against** the day of sorrow." See Trifle
"**Against** the evening sky the trees are black." See The winter trees
"**Against** the moon the icicles hang black." See Winter thaw
"**Agatha** Morley." See Dust
Age. See also Birthdays; Old age; Youth; Youth and age
Characteristics of a child three years old. W. Wordsworth.—WoP
"Crawl, laugh." Issa.—LeOw
"I asked him how old he was." Issa.—IsF
Of all the barbarous middle ages. From Don Juan. G. G. Byron.—ByP
"The **aged** dog." Issa, tr. fr. the Japanese by R. H. Blyth.—IsF
The **aged** stranger. Bret Harte.—BrA
The **ageing** athlete. Neil Weiss.—MoS
Aghadoe. John Todhunter.—CoBl
Agincourt, Battle of, 1415
Before Agincourt. From King Henry V. W. Shakespeare.—GrCt
Before battle.—ShS
Aglaura, sel. John Suckling
Why so pale and wan.—CoBl

Agnew, Edith
Ambition.—ArT-3
Progress.—BrA
Agrawal, Kedar Nath
Spring wind.—AlPi
Agriculture. See Farm life; Harvests and harvesting
"**Ah,** broken is the golden bowl, — the spirit flown forever." See Lenore
"**Ah,** did you once see Shelley plain." See Memorabilia
Ah fading joy. John Dryden.—GrCt
"**Ah** fading joy, how quickly art thou past." See Ah fading joy
"**Ah,** Faustus." See The tragical history of Dr Faustus
"**Ah,** God, to see the branches stir." See The old vicarage, Grantchester
"**Ah,** how poets sing and die." See Dunbar
"**Ah,** I remember well—and how can I." See First flame
"**Ah** little road all whirry in the breeze." See The road
Ah, sun-flower. William Blake.—BlP
The sun-flower.—GrCt
"**Ah,** sun-flower, weary of time." See Ah, sun-flower
"**Ah,** the peasant who." Hosokawa Yusai, tr. fr. the Japanese by Shoson Yasuda.—LeMw
"**Ah,** then the grassy-meäded Mäy." See Zummer stream
"**Ah,** through the open door." See Spring morning
"**Ah,** to be." Issa, tr. fr. the Japanese by R. H. Blyth.—IsF—LeOw
"**Ah** what avails the sceptered race." See Rose Aylmer
"**Ah,** would I were a pastrycook." See For Mopsa
"**Ah,** you should see Cynddylan on a tractor." See Cynddylan on a tractor
"**Ahoy** and ahoy, birds." See Wings and wheels
Ahsoak, Lula
Myself.—BaH
Ahvakana, Martha
My rough sketch.—BaH
Aiken, Conrad
The argument, sel.
"Do not believe your Shakespeare's grief." —ReO
Atlantis. See Priapus and the pool
The bat.—AiC
The birdcage.—ReBs
The cassowary.—AiC
The cat.—AiC
The coming forth by day of Osiris Jones, sel.
The nursery.—HaL
The crab. AiC
The crocodile.—AiC
Discordants.—CoBl
"Do not believe your Shakespeare's grief." See The argument
The elephant.—AiC
"The fallow deer."—AiC
The frog.—AiC
The goats.—AiC
The grasshopper.—AiC
Hatteras calling.—CoBn
Improvisations: Light and snow.—CoBl (sel.) —CoBn (sel.)
John Deth, sel.
"With myriad voices grass was filled."—ReO
The lion.—AiC
The mandrill.—AiC
The nursery. See The coming forth by day of Osiris Jones
The octopus.—AiC
The owl.—AiC
Portrait of a girl. See Priapus and the pool
Preludes for Memnon.—CoBl (sel.)
Priapus and the pool, sels.
Atlantis.—GrS
Portrait of a girl.—BoGj
"When trout swim down Great Ormond street."—HoL—McWs
The rhinoceros.—AiC
The seal.—AiC
Senlin. See Senlin: A biography
Senlin: A biography, sel.
Senlin.—HaL
Stone too can pray.—PlE—SmM
"Watch long enough, and you will see the leaf."—HoL
"When trout swim down Great Ormond street." See Priapus and the pool
"With myriad voices grass was filled." See John Deth
Aiken Drum. Unknown.—BlO
"There came a man to our town."—MoB (sel.)
Ainsworth, Ruth
Acorn Bill.—StF
Black monkeys.—StF
"One, two (what shall I do)."—StF
Riddles.—StF
The snowman.—StF
Air
Dinosaur air. C. Lewis.—LeP
John Coil. Unknown.—BrSm
"The **air** breathes frost. A thin wind beats." See City autumn
"The **air** is filled with faces of the torchmouth ghouls." See The cremation ground
"The **air** is like a butterfly." See Easter
Air pilots. See Aviators
Airlift. Aileen Fisher.—FiI
"The **airplane** taxis down the field." See Taking off
Airplanes. See also Aviators
Aeroplane. M. M. Green.—ArT-3
At the airport. H. Nemerov.—DuS—McWs
Chairoplane chant. N. B. Turner.—StF
Cockpit in the clouds. D. Dorrance.—ArT-3
Death of an aircraft. C. Causley.—CaMb
Ego. P. Booth.—DuS
Flying. K. Starbird.—LaPd
From an airplane. H. Behn.—BeG
Malfunction. R. E. Albert.—DuS
The man in the dead machine. D. Hall.—DuS

Aldridge, Richard
The pine bough.—HoL
Alexander, Cecil Frances
"All things bright and beautiful."—HoB
Alexander, John T.
The winning of the TV West.—BoH—BrA
Alexander and Campaspe, sel. John Lyly
"Who is't now we hear."—ReBs
Alexander Campbell, sels. Vachel Lindsay
I. My fathers came from Kentucky.—BrA—LiP
II. Written in a year when many of my people died.—LiP
III. A rhymed address to all renegade Campbellites, exhorting them to return.—LiP
"**Alexander** Graham Bell." See Alexander Graham Bell did not invent the telephone
Alexander Graham Bell did not invent the telephone. Robert P. Tristram Coffin.—ArT-3
Alexandria, Egypt
Mine argosy from Alexandria. From The jew of Malta. C. Marlowe.—GrCt
Algonquin Indians. See Indians of the Americas—Algonquin
Algy. Unknown.—BrSm
"**Algy** saw a bear." See Algy
Alhashmi, Rahm Ali
Ghazal. tr.—AlPi
"**Alice,** dear, what ails you." See A frosty night
Alice's adventures in wonderland, sels. Lewis Carroll
"Beautiful soup, so rich and green."—BlO
Beautiful soup.—SmM
Turtle soup.—ClF
Father William.—BoGj—LaP (sel.)—LaPd (sel.)
You are old, Father William.—HoB
"You are old, Father William, the young man said."—ArT-3
"How doth the little crocodile."—ArT-3—BlO—BrSm—HoB—LaP
The lobster quadrille.—HoB
The mock turtle's song.—GrCt
"Speak roughly to your little boy."—BlO
The dutchess' lullaby.—CoBb
Alien. Donald Jeffrey Hayes.—BoA
All, all a-lonely. Unknown.—GrCt
"**All,** all of a piece throughout." See The secular masque
"**All** along the backwater." See The wind in the willows—Ducks' ditty
"**All** animals like me." Raymond Souster.—DoW
All around the town, sels. Phyllis McGinley
"B's the bus."—ArT-3
"C is for the circus."—ArT-3
"E is the escalator."—ArT-3
"F is the fighting firetruck."—ArT-3—LaP
"J's the jumping jay-walker."—ArT-3
"P's the proud policeman."—ArT-3
"Q is for the quietness."—LaC
"R is for the restaurant."—ArT-3
"U is for umbrellas."—ArT-3
"V is for the vendor."—BrSg
"W is for windows."—ArT-3
"**All** busy punching tickets." See Crickets
"**All** but blind." Walter De La Mare.—LaPd
"**All** day a strong wind blew." See A strong wind
"**All** day and night, save winter, every weather." See Aspens
All day I hear. See Chamber music—The noise of waters
"**All** day I hear the noise of waters." See Chamber music—The noise of waters
"**All** day in gray rain." Bashō, tr. fr. the Japanese by Harry Behn.—BeCs
All day long. David McCord.—McAd
"**All** day long, day after day." See The Nile
"**All** day long the clouds go by." See Flight
All-day sucker. Aileen Fisher.—FiIo
"**All** day, the burning furnace of the plain." See The road to Granada
"**All** day the great guns barked and roared." See Molly Pitcher
"**All** day the plane had searched for them, the wild." See The ballad of Kon-Tiki
"**All** day—when early morning shone." See The swallows
"**All** dripping in tangles green." See The tuft of kelp
"**All** flesh is grass and so are feathers too." See Epitaph on Lady Ossory's bullfinch
"**All** hail, once pleasing, once inspiring shade." See Lines written in Windsor forest
"**All** I could see from where I stood." See Renascence
"**All** in green went my love riding." E. E. Cummings.—BoGj—MoS
"**All** in the Downs the fleet was moored." See Black-eyed Susan
"**All** in the golden weather, forth let us ride today." See The King's highway
All in the path of a power mower. Richard Gillman.—DuS
"**All** kinds of cicadas singing." Issa, tr. fr. the Japanese by R. H. Blyth.—IsF
"**All** look and likeness caught from earth." See Phantom
"**All** my life." See Death song of a song maker
"**All** my life, I guess, I've loved the clouds." See The clouds
"**All** my life long." See Circus hand
"**All** nature seems at work. Slugs leave their lair." See Work without hope
"**All** night and all day the wind roared in the trees." See Mid-country blow
"**All** night the wind swept over the house." See Winter morning
"**All** night they marched, the infantrymen under pack." See 1936
All of a sudden. Elizabeth Jane Coatsworth.—CoSb
"**All** of a sudden, bicycles are toys." See A certain age
"**All** of a sudden the big nasturtiums." See The big nasturtiums
All on a Christmas morning. Elizabeth Jane Coatsworth.—CoSb
All one people. See The people, yes

"**All** over America railroads ride through roses." See Landscape as metal and flowers
"**All** peacefully gliding." See The rapid
"**All** right, armorer." See Directions to the armorer
"**All** service ranks the same with God." See Pippa passes
"**All** that I know." See My star
"**All** that is left." See The little trumpet
All that's past. Walter De La Mare.—BoGj
"**All** the bells were ringing." Christina Georgina Rossetti.—ArT-3
"**All** the breath and the bloom of the year in the bag of one bee." See Summum bonum
All the fishes far below. Elizabeth Jane Coatsworth.—CoSb
"**All** the flowers are sleeping." See Blue jay
"**All** the gods do I perceive in thy body." See Bhagavad Gita—Arjuna's paean to Krishna
"**All** the long night." See The happy farmer
"**All** the night in woe." See The little girl found
"**All** the night o'er and o'er." Unknown.—MoB
All the way. Walter De La Mare.—DeBg
"**All** the way from Adam." See All the way
"**All** the while." Issa, tr. fr. the Japanese by Nobuyuki Yuasa.—IsF
"**All** these hurt." Vainateya, tr. fr. the Sanskrit by P. Lal.—AlPi
"**All** things bright and beautiful." Cecil Frances Alexander.—HoB
"**All** things of earth have an end, and in the midst." Unknown, tr. fr. the Aztec.—LeO
"**All** things uncomely and broken, all things worn out and old." See The lover tells of the rose in his heart
All things will die. Alfred Tennyson.—TeP
All thoughts, all creeds. Alfred Tennyson.—TeP
"**All** thoughts, all creeds, all dreams are true." See All thoughts, all creeds
"**All** through the garden I went and went." See The butterbean tent
"**All** under the leaves, the leaves of life." See The seven virgins
"**All** visible, visibly." See Runner
All winter. Aileen Fisher.—FiC
All wool. Abbie Farwell Brown.—ArT-3
All work and no play. Mother Goose.—BrMg
"**All** work and no play makes Jack a dull boy." See All work and no play
All your fortunes we can tell ye. See Masque of gipsies
"**All** your young beauty is to me." Unknown, tr. fr. the Somali.—LeO
Allen, Hervey
  The tower of Genghis Khan.—PaH
Allen, Hillary
  Wild horse.—LeM
Allen, Marie Louise
  First snow.—ArT-3
  The mitten song.—ArT-3
  My zipper suit.—ArT-3
Allen, Samuel
  American Gothic. See To Satch
  If the stars should fall.—AdIa
  A moment please.—AdIa—BoA—HaK
  To Satch.—BoA—HaK
    American Gothic.—AdIa
    To Satch; or, American Gothic.—MoS
  To Satch; or, American Gothic. See To Satch
Allen, Steve
  Flight.—DuS
Alley, Rewi
  Under the frontier post. tr.—GrCt
  War. tr.—GrCt
  The white horse. tr.—GrCt
Allie. Robert Graves.—BoGj—CaD—HaL
"**Allie,** call the birds in." See Allie
Alligator on the escalator. Eve Merriam.—LaC—MeC
Alligators
  Alligator on the escalator. E. Merriam.—LaC—MeC
Alligoshee. Mother Goose.—BrMg
Alling, Kenneth Slade
  Moth.—HoL
Allingham, William
  The elf singing.—HuS-3
  The fairies.—BlO—CoR—GrCt—HoB—LaPd
    "Up the airy mountain."—HuS-3
  "Four ducks on a pond."—BlO—DuR
  The mill.—GrCt
  Robin Redbreast.—HoB—ReBs
  "Up the airy mountain." See The fairies
Allison, Young Ewing
  Derelict.—CoSs
Alliteration; or, The siege of Belgrade. Unknown.—GrCt
"**Allow** me; I'm the wind." See Spring wind
Almanacs
  Marjorie's almanac. T. B. Aldrich.—BrSg
Alone ("The abode of the nightingale is bare") Walter De La Mare—GrCt
Alone ("From childhood's hour I have not been") Edgar Allan Poe.—PoP
Alone ("How sad it is to be alone") Kathie Mann.—BaH
Alone ("I never had walked quite so far") Joseph Paget-Fredericks.—HuS-3
"**Alone** in the greenwood must I roam." Unknown.—MoB
"**Alone** in the night." See Stars
"**Alone** on the shore in the pause of the nighttime." See The full heart
"**Along** about then, the middle of May." See Elm seed blizzard
"**Along** the black." See Night ride
"**Along** the cold post road." Issa, tr. fr. the Japanese by Nobuyuki Yuasa.—IsF
"**Along** the line of smoky hills." See Indian summer
"**Along** the long, dark hallway." See The memory-filled house
"**Along** the thousand roads of France." See The good Joan

Alphabet
The A B C bunny. W. Gág.—ArT-3
"A was an apple-pie." Mother Goose.—OpF
A, apple pie.—BrMg—GrT
Mother Goose rhymes, 38.—HoB
The tragical death of A apple-pye.—VrF
Aeiou, J. Swift.—BlO
The alphabet of Goody Two Shoes. Unknown. —VrF
An alphabetical arrangement of animals for little naturalists. S. Sketch.—VrF
Backwards. E. Merriam.—MeC
Confusions of the alphabet. J. Wain.—CaD
A curious discourse that passed between the twenty-five letters at dinner-time. Unknown. —VrF
Great A. Mother Goose.—BrMg
A jamboree for j. E. Merriam.—MeI
The lesson. Unknown.—GrT
A riddle. C. M. Fanshawe.—GrCt
Tom Thumb's picture alphabet. Mother Goose. —BrMg
"**Alphabet** noodles." See Baby Toodles
An **alphabet** of famous Goops. Gelett Burgess. —CoBb (sel.)
The **alphabet** of Goody Two Shoes. Unknown. —VrF
An **alphabetical** arrangement of animals for little naturalists. Sally Sketch.—VrF
Alpine. R. S. Thomas.—CoBn
Alps mountains
"In lands I never saw, they say." E. Dickinson.—DiPe
"Our lives are Swiss." E. Dickinson.—DiL—DiPe
"**Also** Ulysses once—that other war." See Kilroy
"**Alter?** When the hills do." Emily Dickinson.—DiPe
"An **altered** look about the hills." Emily Dickinson.—DiL—DiPe
Altgeld, John Peter (about)
The eagle that is forgotten. V. Lindsay.—LiP
"**Although** both grasses and trees." Funya no Yasuhide.—BaS
"**Although** I can see him still." See The fisherman
"**Although** I'd lie lapped in linen." See Under the round tower
"**Although** I've been to Kankakee." See Schenectady
"**Although** my father's only child." See Cecilia
"**Although** she feeds me bread of bitterness." See America
Alton Locke, sel. Charles Kingsley
The sands of Dee.—BlO—ClF—CoSs
Altshuler, Nathan
"Hungry tree."—LeM
Alumasa, Joseph
My old grandfather.—LeM
Aluskak, John
Hunting.—BaH
Alvarez, Victor
The Cuban emigrant.—BaH
Always with us—the black preacher. Herman Melville.—ReBs
"**Amazing** monster, that, for aught I know." See The fish, the man, and the spirit
The **amber** bead. See A trapped fly
The **ambiguous** dog. Arthur Guiterman.—CoB
Ambition. See also Conduct of life; Success
Ambition ("I got pocketed behind 7X-3824") M. Bishop.—BrA
Ambition ("When I am grown an hombre") E. Agnew.—ArT-3
Andrea del Sarto. R. Browning.—BrP
The boy. R. M. Rilke.—LiT—SmM
"But can see better there, and laughing there." G. Brooks.—HaK
Drug store. J. V. A. Weaver.—HiL
Merlin and the gleam. A. Tennyson.—TeP
"When I am a man, then I shall be a hunter, O father." Unknown.—LeO
Your world. G. D. Johnson.—BoA—BoH
Ambition ("I got pocketed behind 7X-3824") Morris Bishop.—BrA
Ambition ("When I am grown an hombre") Edith Agnew.—ArT-3
"The **ambulance** flies at a furious gait." See Hell's bells
Ambulances
Hell's bells. M. Fishback.—BrSm
"**Amelia** mixed the mustard." Alfred Edward Housman.—LiT
America. See also names of countries, as Mexico; United States
America ("Although she feeds me bread of bitterness") C. McKay.—BoH
America ("The Guardian Prince of Albion burns in his nightly tent") W. Blake.—BlP (sel.)
America for me. H. Van Dyke.—ThA
America was promises. A. MacLeish.—BrA (sel.)
America the beautiful. K. L. Bates.—PlE
American child. P. Engle.—BrA
American laughter. K. A. Robinson.—BrA
American letter. A. MacLeish.—BrA (sel.)
American names. S. V. Benét.—BrA—PaH
The birds of America. J. Broughton.—BrA
Brown river, smile. J. Toomer.—BoA
Eagle plain. R. Francis.—BrA
Europe and America. D. Ignatow.—BrA
I hear America singing. W. Whitman.—ArT-3 —BrA—HoB—HuS-3—WhA
"I hear America singing, the varied carols I hear."—LaPd
I hear America griping. M. Bishop.—BrA
I sing America now. J. Stuart.—BrA
"I, too, sing America." L. Hughes.—AdIa
I, too.—BoA—HaK
Invocation. From John Brown's body. S. V. Benét.—BrA
Les isles d'Amerique. E. J. Coatsworth.—CoDh
Localities. C. Sandburg.—BrA
Midwest town. R. D. Peterson.—BrA

America—*Continued*
The new world ("There was a strange and unknown race") P. Engle.—BrA
The new world ("This America is an ancient land") E. L. Masters.—BrA (sel.)
"Next to of course God America I." E. E. Cummings.—BrA—HiL
Our heritage. J. Stuart.—BrA
Shine, Republic. R. Jeffers.—BrA
Traveling America. J. Struther.—BrA
"What is America." J. F. Velez.—BaH
America—Discovery and exploration. See also names of explorers, as Columbus, Christopher
The Pinta, the Nina and the Santa Maria; and many other cargoes of light. J. Tagliabue. —BrA
The story of Vinland. S. Lanier.—HiL
"**America.**" See The Pinta, the Nina and the Santa Maria; and many other cargoes of light
America ("Although she feeds me bread of bitterness") Claude McKay.—BoH
America ("The Guardian Prince of Albion burns in his nightly tent") William Blake.—BlP (sel.)
America for me. Henry Van Dyke.—ThA
"**America** is West and the wind blowing." See American letter
America the beautiful. Katherine Lee Bates.—PlE
"**America** was always promises." See America was promises
America was promises. Archibald MacLeish.—BrA (sel.)
American ballads. See Cowboys—Songs
American child. Paul Engle.—BrA
American Colonial history. See United States—History—Colonial period
"The **American** eagle is not aware he is." See Eagle plain
American Gothic. See To Satch
An **American** in England. Elinor Wylie.—PaH
American Indians. See Indians of the Americas
American laughter. Kenneth Allan Robinson.—BrA
American letter. Archibald MacLeish.—BrA (sel.)
"**American** muse, whose strong and diverse heart." See John Brown's body—Invocation
American names. Stephen Vincent Benét.—BrA —PaH
American revolution. See United States—History —Revolution
American yarns. See The people, yes—"They have yarns"
Americans
American child. P. Engle.—BrA
An American in England. E. Wylie.—PaH
American laughter. K. A. Robinson.—BrA
American letter. A. MacLeish.—BrA
Americans are afraid of lizards. K. Shapiro.—BrA
"Americans are always moving on." From Western star. S. V. Benét.—BrA
The coming American. S. W. Foss.—BrA (sel.)
Immigrants. N. B. Turner.—BrA
Men. A. MacLeish.—BrA
Trail breakers. J. Daugherty.—BrA
Americans are afraid of lizards. Karl Shapiro.—BrA
"**Americans** are always moving on." See Western star
Amey, David
My uncle Jack.—LeM
"**Amid** curled leaves and green." See Peach tree with fruit
"**Amid** pale green milkweed." See Dead doe
Amis, Kingsley
Autobiographical fragment.—CaD
Amittai, Levi Ben
Kibbutz Sabbath.—PlE
Amma, Balamani
The housewife.—AlPi
Amo amas. John O'Keefe.—CoBl—GrCt
"**Amo,** amas, I love a lass." See Amo amas
Amoebas
Ode to the amoeba. A. Guiterman.—DuS
"**Among** the fox-red fallen leaves I surprised him. Snap." See The squirrel
"**Among** the hills of St Jerome." See At St Jerome
Among the leaves. Elizabeth Jane Coatsworth.—CoSb
"**Among** the leaves of grass." Issa, tr. fr. the Japanese by R. H. Blyth.—LeOw
Among the millet. Archibald Lampman.—DoW
"**Among** the orchard weeds, from every search." See Hen's nest
"**Among** the stripped and sooty twigs of the wild-cherry tree." See The white blackbirds
"**Among** the taller wood with ivy hung." See The vixen
"**Ample** make this bed." Emily Dickinson.—DiPe
An **amulet.** Samuel Menashe.—SmM
"**Amy** Elizabeth Ermyntrude Annie." Queenie Scott Hopper.—ArT-3
Anacreontics. Alfred Tennyson.—TeP
Anashuya and Vijaya. William Butler Yeats.—LiT
Anatomy. See Body, Human; also names of parts of the body, as Hands
Anatomy of the world: The first anniversary, sel. John Donne
"Doth not a Tenarif, or higher hill."—GrCt
"The **ancestral** house talks to me. Wherever I move." See The house
Ancestry. See also Heritage
"Each morning." From Hymn for Lanie Poo. L. Jones.—AdIa
Graveyard. R. P. T. Coffin.—BrA
The house. R. Debee.—AlPi
"Lady Clara Vere de Vere." A. Tennyson.—TeP
Let us now praise famous men. From Ecclesiasticus, Bible, Apocrypha.—GrCt
Lineage. M. Walker.—HaK
My fathers came from Kentucky. From Alexander Campbell. V. Lindsay.—BrA—LiP

A pastoral. R. Hillyer.—CoBn
"The pedigree of honey." E. Dickinson.—DiPe
Square-toed princes. R. P. T. Coffin.—BrA
The **anchorage.** Pat Wilson.—CoSs
The **ancient** elf. James Stephens.—StS
Ancient history. Arthur Guiterman.—DuR—McWs
The **ancient** mansion, sel. George Crabbe
Spring to winter.—GrCt
"An **ancient** saga tells us how." See Dead cow farm
And a big black crow is cawing. Elizabeth Jane Coatsworth.—CoSb
And angling, too. See Don Juan
"**And** angling, too, that solitary vice." See Don Juan—And angling, too
"**And** can the physician make sick men well." Unknown.—BlO
"**And** David lamented with this lamentation over Saul and over Jonathan his son." See The second book of Samuel—David's lament
"**And** death shall have no dominion." Dylan Thomas.—PlE
"**And** Dick said, Look what I have found." See Crescent moon
"**And** every sky was blue and rain." See To deck a woman
"**And** every time I pass." See Construction
"**And** God stepped out on space." See The creation
"**And** here is dear old Boston." See The new order
"**And** here where all is waste and wild." See Syracuse
"**And** I." See The lost world
"**And** I have come upon this place." See L'an trentiesme de mon eage
"**And** I step on the bus." See The one I always get
"**And** in September, O what keen delight." See September
And it was windy weather. James Stephens.—ClF—StS
"**And** it's baking, Bessy Bell." See Singing game
And laughter sounded. Elizabeth Jane Coatsworth.—CoDh
"**And** nigh this toppling reed, still as the dead." See The pike
"**And** not one word for Biddy, the placid one." See Biddy
"**And** now at last." See John Brown's body—Robert E. Lee
"**And** now both bands in close embraces met." See A match at football—Heaps on heaps
"**And** now, said the governor, gazing abroad on the piled-up store." See The first Thanksgiving day
"**And** now the dark comes on, all full of chitter noise." See The sound of night
"**And** now the storm blast came, and he." See The rime of the ancient mariner
"**And** now they nigh approachèd to the stead." See The faerie queene—The mermaids
"**And** now you live dispersed on ribbon roads." See The rock
"**And** o'er the first bumbarrel's next." See Birds' nests
And off he went just as proud as you please. John Ciardi.—CiYk
And on this shore. M. Carl Holman.—BoA
And once. Myra Cohn Livingston.—LiC
"**And** once, a stranger smiled at me." See And once
"**And** one morning while in the woods I stumbled suddenly upon the thing." See Between the world and me
"**And** sedge-warblers, clinging so light." See Sedge-warblers
"**And** she looked at me." See Someone
"**And** she was there. The little boat." See Orpheus' dream
And she washed his feet with her tears, and wiped them with the hairs of her head. Edward Sherburne.—GrCt
"**And** silence." See The end of man is his beauty
"**And** tell how Oberon doth fare." See Nymphidia, the court of fairy—The adventures of Oberon, king of the fairies, while searching for Queen Mab
"**And** the first gray of morning filled the east." See Sohrab and Rustum
"**And** the Lord was not in the whirlwind." See Visitations: VII
"**And** the old women gathered." Mari Evans.—HaK
"**And** the subway gives such refinement." See The subway
"**And** then." See Stars
"**And** then I pressed the shell." See The shell
And then it rained. Mark Van Doren.—CoBn
"**And** then it rained, oh, then it rained." See And then it rained
"**And** then she saw me creeping." See Fossils
And there was a great calm. Thomas Hardy.—GrCt
"**And** they both lived happily ever after." See After ever happily; or, The princess and the woodcutter
"**And** this is good old Boston." See Boston
"**And** thou hast walked about—how strange a story." See Address to a mummy
"**And** timid, funny, brisk little bunny." Christina Georgina Rossetti.—ArT-3
"**And** we marched against them there in the next spring." See Conquistador
And were a little changed. Elizabeth Jane Coatsworth.—CoDh
"**And** what is so rare as a day in June." See The vision of Sir Launfal—A day in June
"**And** when night comes they will sing serenades." See Evening
"**And** when you come home." See Coming home
"**And** while they talked and talked, and while they sat." See The breath of life
"**And** who shall separate the dust." See Common dust
And yet fools says. George S. Holmes.—ArT-3

And you, Helen. Edward Thomas.—ThG
"**And** you, Helen, what should I give you." See And you, Helen
Anderson, Karen
"I feel relaxed and still."—LeM
Anderson, Patrick
Canoe.—MoS
Andes mountains
Condors. P. Colum.—BoGj
André. Gwendolyn Brooks.—ArT-3—HoB
Andrea del Sarto. Robert Browning.—BrP
Andresen, Sally
Fall.—DuR
"**Andrew** Airpump ask'd his aunt her ailment." See Peter Piper's practical principles of plain and perfect pronunciation
Andrew Jackson. Martha Keller.—BrA
"**Andrew** Jackson was eight feet tall." See The statue of old Andrew Jackson
Andrewes, Francis
"I bear, in sign of love." See Shepherdess' valentine
Shepherdess' valentine, sel.
"I bear, in sign of love."—ReBs
Andrews, Brian
The doors.—LeM
"**Andy** Pandy, fine and dandy." Mother Goose. —OpF
Ane sang of the birth of Christ, with the tune of baw lula low. Martin Luther, tr. fr. the German by John Wedderburn.—GrCt
"**Ane,** twa, three." Unknown.—MoB
Anecdote of the jar. Wallace Stevens.—HoL
The **angel.** William Blake.—BlP
The **angel** in the apple tree. Winifred Welles.—HuS-3
"An **angel,** robed in spotless white." See Dawn
"The **angel** that presided o'er my birth." William Blake.—BlP
"An **angel** told Mary." See A Christmas carol
Angelo, Michael (about)
Michael Angelo, A fragment. H. W. Longfellow.—LoP (sel.)
Angels
The angel. W. Blake.—BlP
The angel in the apple tree. W. Welles.—HuS-3
"The angels came a-mustering." Unknown.—PlE
"At the round earth's imagin'd corners, blow." J. Donne.—PlE
Blow your trumpets, angels.—GrCt
Azrael. From Tales of a wayside inn. H. W. Longfellow.—LoPl
"I heard an angel singing." W. Blake.—BlP
Israfel. E. A. Poe.—PoP
"My joy, my jockey, my Gabriel." G. Barker. —CaD
Night. W. Blake.—BlP—BrSg (sel.)—CoBn—ReS (sel.)
Stone angel. A. Ridler.—PlE
To the evening star. W. Blake.—BlP—CoBn—GrCt—GrS
The visitation. E. Jennings.—CaMb
"The **angels** came a-mustering." Unknown, tr. by Israel Zangwill.—PlE
Anger
Mad as the mist and snow. W. B. Yeats.—GrCt
"Mine enemy is growing old." E. Dickinson.—DiPe
One, two, three. N. K. Sethi.—AlPi
A poison tree. W. Blake.—BlP—GrS
Angler's choice. H. J. Gottlieb.—DuR
The **angler's** reveille. Henry Van Dyke.—HuS-3
The **angler's** song. Izaak Walton.—MoS (sel.)
Angling. See Fishermen and fishing
Angling. Ann and Jane Taylor.—VrF
Angus, Marion
Alas, poor queen.—GrS
Anil (A. R. Deshpandi)
The trail.—AlPi
Animal crackers. Christopher Morley.—HoB—ThA
"**Animal** crackers, and cocoa to drink." See Animal crackers
The **animal** fair. Unknown.—LaP
The **animal** store. Rachel Field.—ArT-3—HuS-3—LaP—LaPd
Animal tracks
Tracks in the snow ("Out of the dark") E. J. Coatsworth.—HoB
Tracks in the snow ("Wherever fox or cat or crow") E. J. Coatsworth.—CoSb
Animals. See also Circus; Fables; also names of classes of the animal kingdom, as Birds; also names of animals, as Elephants
About the bloath. S. Silverstein.—CoB
Afar in the desert. T. Pringle.—ReO (sel.)
"All animals like me." R. Souster.—DoW
"All but blind." W. De La Mare.—LaPd
All in the path of a power mower. R. Gillman. —DuS
All winter. A. Fisher.—FiC
Allie. R. Graves.—BoGj—CaD—HaL
An alphabetical arrangement of animals for little naturalists. S. Sketch.—VrF
Animal crackers. C. Morley.—HoB—ThA
The animal fair. Unknown.—LaP
The animal store. R. Field.—ArT-3—Hus-3—LaP—LaPd
Animals. From Song of myself. W. Whitman. —CoB
"I think I could turn and live with animals."—LaPd
Song of myself.—Lit—SmM
Animals' houses. J. Reeves.—StF
The animals in the ark. Unknown.—GrCt
The animals mourn with Eve. From Eve. C. G. Rossetti.—ReO
Another riddle. From Love's labour's lost. W. Shakespeare.—ShS
Are you a marsupial. J. Becker.—CoB
At night. A. Fisher.—FiC
At the zoo. A. A. Milne.—MiC
Ballad of the robin. P. McGinley.—McWc
Ballade of a zoo buff. M. Bracker.—CoB
The barnyard. M. Burnham.—ArT-3

Beautiful Sunday. J. Falstaff.—CoBn
The bestiary. W. R. Benét.—ReO (sel.)
"Beware, my child." S. Silverstein.—CoO—LaPd
Big little boy. E. Merriam.—MeC
The boar and the dromedar. H. Beissel.—DoW
Boo moo. D. McCord.—McAd
Bow-wow. Mother Goose.—BrMg
Boy in a pond. From The runaway. J. Whaler.—ReO
Busy summer. A. Fisher.—FiI
The butterfly's ball and the grasshopper's feast. W. Roscoe.—VrF
"Calico pie." E. Lear.—CoB—TuW
The catipoce. J. Reeves.—CoB
Christmas eve legend. F. M. Frost.—HoB
Christmas in the woods. F. M. Frost.—ArT-3 (sel.)
The Christmas present. P. Hubbell.—LaPd
"Cold winter now is in the wood." E. J. Coatsworth.—ArT-3—TuW
The contrary waiter. E. Parker.—CoO
Dance of the animals. Unknown.—DoC—LeO
Daybreak. D. McCord.—McAd
"Dear Father." M. W. Brown.—LaPd
A dirge. From The white devil. J. Webster.—BlO
Call for the robin-redbreast.—GrCt
"Do not believe your Shakespeare's grief." From The argument. C. Aiken.—ReO
"The dog will come when he is called." A. O'Keefe.—BlO
"Don't ever cross a crocodile." K. Starbird.—ArT-3—LaPd
The doze. J. Reeves.—CoB
The egg. L. E. Richards.—ArT-3
Eyes are lit up. R. P. T. Coffin.—SmM
"F was a fussy flamingo." C. Wells.—BrLl
Familiar friends. J. S. Tippett.—HoB—StF
Farm yard at evening. J. Clare.—CoB (sel.)
Feather or fur. J. Becker.—ArT-3
Feet. A. Fisher.—FiC
Finder, please return to Henry Thoreau. E. J. Coatsworth.—CoDh
First and last. D. McCord.—McAd
Fooba wooba John. Unknown.—CoO
Foot, fin or feather. From Psalm CXLVII. C. Smart.—ReO
The friendly beasts. Unknown.—LaPh
The gallows. E. Thomas.—CoB—ThG
A garden path. M. Justus.—BrSg
Genesis. E. J. Coatsworth.—CoDh
The gifts of the animals to man. From Shepherd song. P. Sidney.—ReO
Good morning. M. Sipe.—ArT-3
Grace. W. De La Mare.—DeBg
Green hill neighbors. F. M. Frost.—ArT-3
"Hey, diddle, diddle, the cat and the fiddle." Mother Goose.—ArT-3
The cat and the fiddle.—BrMg—OpF
"Hey diddle diddle."—HuS-3—WiMg
Mother Goose rhymes, 17.—HoB
"Higgledy, piggledy, see how they run." K. Greenaway.—ArT-3
Higgledy, piggledy.—GrT
"Higglety, pigglety, pop." Mother Goose.—StF
Higglety, pigglety.—BrMg
"His father died." Unknown.—MoB
His grange; or, Private wealth. R. Herrick.—BoGj
The history of the flood. J. Heath-Stubbs.—CaMb
Hoddley, poddley. Mother Goose.—BrMg
How to tell the wild animals. C. Wells.—ArT-3
"I had a wee cock and I loved it well." Unknown.—MoB
I love animals and dogs. H. A. Farley.—LeM
I sing for the animals. Unknown.—LeO
"If a jackal bothers you, show him a hyena." Unknown.—DoC
In a million years. C. Lewis.—LeP
In the fashion. A. A. Milne.—LaP
Inside the zoo. E. Merriam.—MeC
The intruder. J. Reeves.—LaPd
Jump or jiggle. E. Beyer.—ArT-3
"Katie Beardie had a cow." Unknown.—MoB
Knowing. A. Fisher.—FiIo
Laughing time. W. J. Smith.—HoB
The legend of the cat. P. McGinley.—McWc
"Let no one suppose." J. Reeves.—CoB
Lion. W. J. Smith.—CoB—WeP
The little black dog. Mother Goose.—BrMg
Little Blue Ben. Mother Goose.—BrMg
The little coward. A. and J. Taylor.—VrF
Little donkey close your eyes. M. W. Brown.—LaP—LaPd
The little girl lost. W. Blake.—BlP
The long black grave. E. J. Coatsworth.—CoDh
A long time ago. Unknown.—CoSs
Lost. D. McCord.—McE
The lost son. T. Roethke.—LiT (sel.)
The lost world. R. Jarrell.—LiT (sel.)
The marsh. W. D. Snodgrass.—CoBn
Midnight. T. Middleton.—BlO
Minstrel's song. Unknown.—DoC
Mr Zoo. E. Merriam.—MeI
Mixed beasts, sels. K. Cox
The bumblebeaver.—ArT-3
The kangarooster.—ArT-3
The octopussycat.—ArT-3
Momotara. Unknown.—ArT-3
My brother Bert. T. Hughes.—CoBb
Not me. S. Silverstein.—CoB
Oddity land. E. Anthony.—HoB
Old friends. A. Muir.—CoB
Old Jake Sutter. K. Starbird.—ArT-3
The old lady who swallowed a fly. Unknown.—BrSm
Old Noah's ark. Unknown.—CoB
On our way. E. Merriam.—MeC
Open House. A. Fisher.—FiI
Open the door. M. Edey.—ArT-3
"Out of the ark's grim hold." From The flaming terrapin. R. Campbell.—CoB (sel.)—ReO
Pad and pencil. D. McCord.—McAd—McE

Storm at night. E. J. Coatsworth.—CoSb
Stupidity street. R. Hodgson.—CoB—HaL—LaPd—ThA
Tit for tat. W. De La Mare.—CoB
To a linnet in a cage. F. Ledwidge.—CoR
To a starved hare in the garden in winter. C. T. Turner.—SmM
Tom's sleeping song. From Jonathan Gentry. M. Van Doren.—HaL
Animals—Mythical. See also names of mythical animals, as Griffins
"That bright chimeric beast." C. Cullen.—BoA
Animals—Prehistoric. See also Dinosaurs
Conversation by Loch Ness. E. J. Coatsworth. —CoDh
Animals. See Song of myself
"**Animals** are restless." See Winter
Animals' houses. James Reeves.—StF
The **animals** in the ark. Unknown.—GrCt
The **animals** mourn with Eve. See Eve
"**Ann.**" See Ann's fan
"**Ann,** Ann." See Alas, alack
"**Anna** Mariar she sat on the fire." Mother Goose. —BrMg—OpF
Annabel Lee. Edgar Allan Poe.—CoR—HuS-3—PoP
Anne. Mother Goose.—ReOn
Anne Rutledge. See The Spoon River anthology
"**Annie** Bolanny." Unknown.—GrCt
"**Annie** has run to the mill dam." See Dreamland
"**Announced** by all the trumpets of the sky." See The snowstorm
Ann's fan. Eve Merriam.—MeC
Annus mirabilis, sels. John Dryden
The fire of London.—GrCt
"So have I seen some fearful hare maintain"
Annus mirabilis.—CoB
Another little boy. Ann and Jane Taylor.—VrF
Another riddle. See Love's labour's lost
Another song of a fool. William Butler Yeats.—ReO
Answer to a child's question. Samuel Taylor Coleridge.—BlO—CoB—ReBs
An **answer** to the parson. William Blake.—BlP
Answering your question. David McCord.—McAd
"An **ant** on the tablecloth." See Departmental; or, The end of my ant Jerry
The **ant** village. Marion Edey.—ArT-3
"An **antelope** eating a cantaloupe." See From the sublime to the ridiculous to the ridiculously sublime
Antelopes
The gazelle. C. B. de Gasztold.—GaC
Gazelles and unicorns. From The long road. J. Gray.—GrCt
"One day I went out to the zoo." G. T. Johnson.—BrLl
"Please don't kill my antelope." Unknown.—LeO
Prayer to the moon. Unknown.—LeO
Anthem for doomed youth. Wilfred Owen.—BoH—GrCt
Anthony, Edward
Oddity land.—HoB
Anthony, Saint (about)
And laughter sounded. E. J. Coatsworth.—CoDh
Anthony, Tina
"A little egg."—LeM
Antichrist. Edwin Muir.—PlE
Antin, David
"Regarding a door."—DuS
Antin, Esther
Corn.—BrSg
Antique shop. Carl Carmer.—ThA
Antiquity. See Time
"**Anton** Leeuwenhoek was Dutch." See The microscope
Antonio. Laura E. Richards.—ArT-3—LaPd
"**Antonio,** Antonio." See Antonio
Antony and Cleopatra, sel. William Shakespeare
Clouds.—ShS
Ants
The ant village. Marion Edey.—ArT-3
Ants and sailboats. D. McCord.—McAd
"As I was walking slowly." A. E. Housman.—LiT
Departmental; or, The end of my ant Jerry. R. Frost.—DuS—McWs
Jungles of grass. A. Fisher.—FiC
The people. E. M. Roberts.—ArT-3—BoGj
Ants and sailboats. David McCord.—McAd
"The **ants** are walking under the ground." See The people
The **anxious** farmer. Burges Johnson.—CoBn
Any bird. Ilo Orleans.—BrSg
Any day now. David McCord.—BrSm
"**Any** star is enough." See Some short poems—Star guides
"**Anybody.**" See Desert
Anyte of Tegea
The dolphin's tomb.—ReO
"The **aoudads** are horned creatures." See Truth will out
Apache Indians. See Indians of the Americas—Apache
Apartment house. Gerald Raftery.—BrA—DuR—LaC
Apathy
Insouciance. J. W. Dickson.—DuS
Pooh. W. De La Mare.—DeBg
Ape. See Creatures in the zoo
"**Apis,** the men you boxed with, grateful that you." See The world's worst boxer
Apollo
Callicles' song. From Empedocles on Etna. M. Arnold.—GrCt
An **apology** for the bottle volcanic. Vachel Lindsay.—LiP
Apostrophe to man. Edna St Vincent Millay.—DuS
Appalachia. See also Dialect—American—Appalachian; also states in the region, as Kentucky
Appalachian front. R. L. Weeks.—BrA
Appalachian front. Robert Lewis Weeks.—BrA

Appearances. See The taming of the shrew
"**Applause** flutters onto the open air." See A snapshot for Miss Bricka who lost in the semi-final round of the Pennsylvania lawn tennis tournament at Haverford, July, 1960
The **apple-barrel** of Johnny Appleseed. Vachel Lindsay.—BrA
"An **apple** for the king." Mother Goose.—ReOn
An **apple** gathering. Christina Georgina Rossetti. —CoBl
"**Apple** pie, pudding, and pancakes." Mother Goose.—OpF
The **apple** tree. See "As I went up the apple tree"
The **apple** tree ("I am hiding in the crooked apple tree") James Stephens.—LiT
Apple trees
The angel in the apple tree. W. Welles.—HuS-3
The apple tree. J. Stephens.—LiT
"As I went up the apple tree." Mother Goose. —OpF
The apple tree.—BrMg
The fairy from the apple-seed. V. Lindsay.—LiP
"Here's to thee, good apple tree." Mother Goose.—OpF
Apples.—BrMg
"Here's to thee."—BlO
Twelfth night.—TuW
The merry policeman. J. Stephens.—StS
Oh dear. Mother Goose.—BrMg
The old ones. F. Bellerby.—CaD
"Old Roger is dead and laid in his grave." Mother Goose.—OpF
Old Roger.—BrMg
A pastoral. R. Hillyer.—CoBn
The planting of the apple tree. W. C. Bryant. —HuS-3
Unharvested. R. Frost.—CoBn
"Up in the green orchard there is a green tree." Mother Goose.—OpF
"**Applecumjockaby,** blindfold eye." See Blindman's in
Apples
Adam lay i-bowndyn. Unknown.—GrCt
After apple-picking. R. Frost.—CoR
The apple-barrel of Johnny Appleseed. V. Lindsay.—BrA
An apple gathering. C. G. Rossetti.—CoBl
Apples and water. R. Graves.—CaD
Apples in New Hampshire. M. Gilchrist.—CoBn
Autumn. P. Hubbell.—LaPd
Blackbirds. W. De La Mare.—DeBg
The boys and the apple-tree. A. and J. Taylor.—GrT
Cider song. M. Weston.—CoBn
The cow in apple time. R. Frost.—ReO
Dividing. D. McCord.—AgH
Lemons and apples. M. Neville.—ArT-3
Moonlit apples. J. Drinkwater.—CoBn
The orchard. W. De La Mare.—DeBg
Sweet apple. J. Stephens.—StS
"There was a young lady of Ryde." Unknown. —BrSm—LaPd
Verdancy. Unknown.—BrSm
Apples. See "Here's to thee, good apple tree"
Apples and water. Robert Graves.—CaD
"The **apples** falling from the tree." See Night magic
Apples in New Hampshire. Marie Gilchrist.—CoBn
Appleseed, Johnny (about). See Chapman, John
Appoggiatura. Donald Jeffrey Hayes.—BoA
An **appointment.** William Butler Yeats.—YeR
April
"An altered look about the hills." E. Dickinson.—DiL—DiPe
April ("The creeks and the streams and the Great River are full") N. Belting.—BeCm
April ("It's lemonade, it's lemonade, it's daisy") M. Masters.—DuR
April ("The little goat") Y. Winters.—CoB—DuR
April ("The roofs are shining from the rain") S. Teasdale.—ArT-3—HuS-3—LaPd
April ("The season of planting is finished") N. Belting.—BeCm
An April child. Unknown.—DePp
April day: Binsey. M. Hamburger.—CaD
April fool. H. Summers.—CaD
April rain song. L. Hughes.—ArT-3—LaP—LaPd
April's amazing meaning. G. Dillon.—CoBl
Heigh-ho, April. E. Farjeon.—FaA
April ("The creeks and the streams and the Great River are full") Natalia Belting.—BeCm
April ("It's lemonade, it's lemonade, it's daisy") Marcia Masters.—DuR
April ("The little goat") Y. Winters.—CoB—DuR
April ("The roofs are shining from the rain") Sara Teasdale.—ArT-3—Hus-3—LaPd
April ("The season of planting is finished") Natalia Belting.—BeCm
An **April** child. Unknown, ad. fr. the Japanese by Charlotte B. DeForest.—DePp
April day: Binsey. Michael Hamburger.—CaD
April fool. Hal Summers.—CaD
April 4, 1968. Michael Goode.—BaH
April rain song. Langston Hughes.—ArT-3—LaP —LaPd
April's amazing meaning. George Dillon.—CoBl
"**April's** amazing meaning doubtless lies." See April's amazing meaning
Arabian nights
Aladdin. J. R. Lowell.—CoR
Aladdin and the jinn. V. Lindsay.—LiP
Dates. From Thousand and one nights. Unknown.—HoL
The sorceress. V. Lindsay.—LaPd
The time of the Barmacides. J. C. Mangan.—CoR
Arapaho Indians. See Indians of the Americas—Arapaho

Arbor day. See also Chapman, John; Forests and forestry; Trees; also names of trees, as Apple trees
Arbor day. D. B. Thompson.—BrSg
Arbor day. Dorothy Brown Thompson.—BrSg
Arbutus
"Pink, small, and punctual." E. Dickinson.—DiPe
Archbishop Tait. Unknown.—GrCt
"The **archer** is awake." See Peace on earth
Archery. See also Bows and arrows; Robin Hood
The Zen archer. J. Kirkup.—PlE
Archy and Mehitabel, sels. Don Marquis
The flattered lightning bug.—CoB
Freddy the rat perishes.—CoB
Pete at the seashore.—CoB
Short course in natural history.—CoB
Arctic regions. See also Eskimos
A man is buried where the cold winds blow. D. G. Matumeak.—BaH
"**Are** not the joys of morning sweeter." William Blake.—BlP
"**Are** not the mountains, waves, and skies, a part." See Childe Harold's pilgrimage
"**Are** the reindeer in the rain, dear." See Conversation between Mr and Mrs Santa Claus
Are we their equals. Helen Geltman.—LeM
Are you a marsupial. John Becker.—CoB
"**Are** you awake, Gemelli." See Star-talk
"**Are** You looking for us? We are here." See The 151st psalm
"**Are** you too proud to kiss me." Rabindranath Tagore.—LeMf
"**Aren't** you cold up there in the windy sky." See To a day moon
Arethusa
Arethusa. P. B. Shelley.—CoD
Arethusa. Percy Bysshe Shelley.—CoD
"**Arethusa** arose." See Arethusa
The **argument**, sel. Conrad Aiken
"Do not believe your Shakespeare's grief."—ReO
An **argument.** Vachel Lindsay.—LiP
An **argument** against the empirical method. See Some short poems
Argumentation
The blind men and the elephant. J. G. Saxe.—BoH
Ariel's dirge. See The tempest—Full fathom five
Ariel's song. See The tempest—"Come unto these yellow sands"
Ariel's song. See The tempest—Full fathom five
Ariel's song. See The tempest—Where the bee sucks
"**Arise** and arm, ye spectral forms." See Atharva Veda—To secure victory in battle
Arithmetic. See also Mathematics
Arithmetic. C. Sandburg.—BoH—DuR
"Multiplication is vexation." Mother Goose.—ReMg
A number of numbers. E. Merriam.—MeC
You know who. J. Ciardi.—CiYk
Arithmetic. Carl Sandburg.—BoH—DuR
"**Arithmetic** is where numbers fly like pigeons in and out of your head." See Arithmetic
Arizona
Arizona nature myth. J. Michie.—SmM
Arizona village. R. S. Davieau.—BrA
At Boot Hill in Tombstone, Arizona. Unknown.—BrSm
John Coil. Unknown.—BrSm
The painted hills of Arizona. E. Curran.—PaH
Arizona nature myth. James Michie.—SmM
Arizona village. Robert Stiles Davieau.—BrA
Arjuna's paean to Krishna. See Bhagavad Gita
Arkansas
Variations for two pianos. D. Justice.—DuS
Arkell, Reginald
A public nuisance.—MoS
Armadillos
"There once was an arch armadillo." C. Wells.—BrLl
The **armful.** Robert Frost.—LiT
Armistice day. See Veteran's day
Armor. See Arms and armor
Armour, Richard
Epitaph.—BrSm
Fish story.—DuR
One down.—MoS
Arms and armor
The arsenal at Springfield. H. W. Longfellow.—LoPl
Directions to the armorer. E. Olson.—DuS
This excellent machine. J. Lehmann.—DuS
When the assault was intended to the city. From Arms and the Muse. J. Milton.—CoR
Arms and the Muse, sel. John Milton
When the assault was intended to the city.—CoR
Armstrong, Martin
A bird's epitaph.—ReBs
The **army** of the Sidhe. Lady Gregory.—ThA
Arnold, Matthew
Callicles' song. See Empedocles on Etna
Dover beach.—ClF (sel.)—CoBl—PlE
Empedocles on Etna, sel.
Callicles' song.—GrCt
The forsaken merman.—BlO—CoSs—SmM
The scholar gipsy.—GrCt
Sohrab and Rustum.—CoD
"**Around** the church." See Poems
"**Around** the house the flakes fly faster." See Birds at winter nightfall
"**Around** the rick, around the rick." Mother Goose.—BrMg
Arran. Unknown, tr. fr. the Old Irish by Kenneth Jackson.—GrCt
"**Arran** of the many stags." See Arran
"**Arrived** in heaven, when his sands were run." See The crusader
The **arrow** and the song. Henry Wadsworth Longfellow.—LoPl
Arrows. See Archery; Bows and arrows
Ars poetica. Archibald MacLeish.—BoH
The **arsenal** at Springfield. Henry Wadsworth Longfellow.—LoPl

Arsenals. See Arms and armor
Art and artists. See also names of artists, as Toulouse-Lautrec, Henri Marie Raymond de
Art review. K. Fearing.—DuS
From a 19th century Kansas painter's notebook. D. Ettter.—DuS
How to paint the portrait of a bird. J. Prevert. —SmM
The mapmaker on his art. H. Nemerov.—DuS
Pad and pencil. D. McCord.—McAd—McE
Pictor ignotus. R. Browning.—BrP
Sadie's playhouse. M. Danner.—HaK
"The spider as an artist." E. Dickinson.—DiPe
Tom Agnew, Bill Agnew. C. G. Rossetti.—GrCt
Ungainly things. R. Wallace.—DuS
Art review. Kenneth Fearing.—DuS
"**Art** thou gone in haste." See Pursuit of love
"**Art** thou pale for weariness." See To the moon
Arthur, King (about). See also Galahad, Sir; Lancelot, Sir
Idylls of the king, sels. A. Tennyson
Blow trumpet.—TeP
If love be love.—TeP
Morte d' Arthur.—CoD—TeP
Rain, rain, and sun.—TeP
"When good King Arthur ruled this land." Mother Goose.—OpF
Good King Arthur.—BrF
King Arthur.—BrMg
"**Arthur** O'Bower has broken his band." Mother Goose.—OpF
The high wind.—GrCt
Wind.—MoB
"**Arthur** of Bower has broken his bands." See "Arthur O'Bower has broken his band"
Arthur Ridgewood, M.D. Frank Marshall Davis. —HaK
"**Arthur** with a lighted taper." See Science for the young
"The **artichoke.**" See Artichoke
Artichoke. Pabol Neruda, tr. by Ben Belitt.—LiT
Artichokes
Artichoke. P. Neruda.—LiT
"**As** a black child I was a dreamer." See Four sheets to the wind and a one-way ticket to France, 1933
"**As** a child." See Four sheets to the wind and a one-way ticket to France, 1933
"**As** a diversion." Issa, tr. fr. the Japanese by R. H. Blyth.—IsF
"**As** a fletcher makes straight his arrow." See Dhamma-pada—Thought
As a flower I come. Sundaram, tr. fr. the Gujarati by the author.—AlPi
"**As** a fond mother, when the day is o'er." See Nature
"**As** a friend to the children commend me the yak." See The yak
"**As** a naked man I go." See In waste places
As a plane tree by the water. Robert Lowell.—GrS
As a possible lover. LeRoi Jones.—BoA
"**As** ah walked oot, yah Sunday morn." See Bleeberrying
"**As** bird to nest, when, moodily." See Sarasvati
"**As** birds are fitted to the boughs." Louis Simpson.—CoBl—HoL
As black as ink. Mother Goose.—ReOn
"**As** black as ink and isn't ink." See As black as ink
"**As** down the road she wambled slow." See Bessie Bobtail
"**As** evening falls." Shunzei.—BaS
"**As** evening fell the day's oppression lifted." See Embassy
"**As** for this world." Semimaru.—BaS
"**As** Frances was playing, and turning around." See The dizzy girl
"**As** glass may yet be whole." See The scarred girl
"**As** he trudg'd along to school." See The story of Johnny Head-in-air
"**As** high as a castle." Mother Goose.—OpF
"**As** I." See A memory
"**As** I am now so you will be." See A curt addendum
"**As** I came down from Lebanon." Clinton Scollard.—PaH
"**As** I came over the humpbacked hill." See The green fiddler
"**As** I came over Windy Gap." See Running to paradise
"**As** I came past by Garrick." See The robin's last will
"**As** I came to the edge of the woods." See Come in
"**As** I curl up to go to sleep." See The night
"**As** I lay awake in the white moonlight." See Sleepyhead
"**As** I lie here wondering." See Wondering
"**As** I listened from a beach-chair in the shade." See Their lonely betters
"**As** I look into each different face." See Through the varied patterned lace
"**As** I look into the mirror I see my face." See Mirror, mirror
As I looked out. Unknown.—StF
"**As** I looked out on Sunday last." See As I looked out
"**As** I looked, the poplar rose in the shining year." See The deceptive present, the phoenix year
"**As** I row over the plain." Fujiwara no Tadamichi, tr. fr. the Japanese by Kenneth Rexroth.—BaS
"**As** I rowed out to the light-house." See The light-house-keeper's white-mouse
"**As** I sat in the gloaming." See The voice
"**As** I sat on a sunny bank." Unknown.—GrCt
"**As** I sat under a sycamore tree." Unknown.—SmM
As I sit. Calvin Begay.—BaH
"**As** I stood at the door." See In the college of surgeons

"As I walk'd by myself." Mother Goose.—GrCt—ReOn
By myself.—BrMg
"As I walk'd thinking through a little grove." See On a wet day
"As I walked out in the streets of Laredo." See The cowboy's lament
"As I walked out one morning for pleasure." See Whoopee ti yi yo, git along little dogies
"As I walked through my garden." See Butterfly
"As I wander'd the forest." See The wild flower's song
"As I was a-hoeing, a-hoeing my lands." See The six badgers
"As I was a-walking." Unknown.—ReBs
The lark in the morning.—GrCt
"As I was a-walking the streets of Laredo." See The cowboy's lament
"As I was going by Charing cross." Mother Goose.—BlO—OpF
"As I was going o'er London bridge." Mother Goose.—BrMg
"As I was going o'er misty moor." See Misty moor
"As I was going o'er Tipple Tine." Mother Goose.—OpF
"As I went over Tipple Tyne."—GrCt
"As I was going out one day." Unknown.—CoO
"As I was going to Banbury." Mother Goose.—OpF
Banbury fair.—BrMg
"As I was going to Derby." See The Derby ram
"As I was going to St Ives." Mother Goose.—HuS-3—OpF—ReMg—WiMg
Going to St Ives.—BrMg
Mother Goose rhymes, 26.—HoB
"As I was going to sell my butter." Mother Goose.—OpF
"As I was going to sell my eggs." Mother Goose.—OpF
Bandy legs.—BrMg
"As I was going up Pippen hill." See "As I went up Pippin hill"
"As I was going up the hill." Mother Goose.—OpF
Jack the piper.—GrCt
"As I was laying on the green." Unknown.—McWs
"As I was sticking handbills on Prince Albert's prim anatomy." See A reunion in Kensington
As I was walking. Kate Greenaway.—GrT
"As I was walking all alane." See The wee, wee man
"As I was walking down our lane." See Ice storm
"As I was walking in a field of wheat." Mother Goose.—BrMg—OpF
"As I was walking slowly." Alfred Edward Housman.—LiT
"As I was walking up the street." See As I was walking
"As I watch over." See Seagull
"As I went by a dyer's door." See The dyer
"As I went by by Humbydrum." Unknown.—MoB
"As I went by my little pig-sty." Unknown.—OpF
"As I went by the Luckenbooths." Unknown.—MoB
"As I went down by Havre de Grace." Elinor Wylie.—PaH
"As I went down to Dymchurch wall." See In Romney marsh
"As I went out a crow." See The last word of a bluebird
"As I went over Lincoln bridge." Mother Goose.—OpF
Mister Rusticap.—BrMg
"As I went over London bridge." Unknown.—GrCt
"As I went over the water." Mother Goose.—SmM
Two little blackbirds.—BrMg
"As I went over Tipple Tyne." See "As I was going o'er Tipple Tine"
"As I went through the garden gap." Mother Goose
Mother Goose rhymes, 31.—HoB
"As I went to Bonner." Mother Goose.—ReMg
A strange pig.—BrMg
"As I went up a slippery gap." Mother Goose.—OpF
Uncle Davy.—BrMg
"As I went up Brandy hill." See Brandy hill
"As I went up by yonder hill." Unknown.—MoB
"As I went up Pippin hill." Mother Goose.—BlO
"As I was going up Pippen hill."—OpF
Pippen hill.—BrMg
"As I went up the apple tree." Mother Goose.—OpF
The apple tree.—BrMg
"As I went up the garden." Unknown.—MoB—StF
"As I went up the humber jumber." Unknown.—OpF
"As I went up to Craigbilly fair." See Craigbilly fair
"As if a voice had called, I woke." See The border bird
"As imperceptibly as grief." Emily Dickinson.—DiPe
"As inward love breeds outward talk." See The angler's song
"As it befell on a bright holiday" See The bitter withy
"As Joseph was a-walking." See The cherry-tree carol
As kingfishers catch fire. Gerard Manley Hopkins.—PlE
"As kingfishers catch fire, dragonflies draw flame." See As kingfishers catch fire
"As light as a feather." Mother Goose.—OpF
"As lily grows up easily." See Peggy Mitchell
"As long as I live." See Me

Asses. See Donkeys
Asses. Padraic Colum.—HaL (sel.)
The **assignation,** sel. Edgar Allan Poe
To one in paradise.—PoP
Assyria—History
The destruction of Sennacherib.—G. G. Byron. —ByP
"The **Assyrian** came down like the wolf on the fold." See The destruction of Sennacherib
Astronauts
Blue. C. Lewis.—LeP
No man on any moon. C. Lewis.—LeP
Outward. L. Simpson.—LiT
Astronomy. See also Moon; Planets; Stars; Sun; Tides; World
Star-swirls. R. Jeffers.—DuS
"When I heard the learn'd astronomer." W. Whitman.—HoL
At a child's baptism. Vassar Miller.—BoGj
"**At** a little grass hut in the valley of the river." See From my study at the mouth of the valley
At a vacation exercise, sel. John Milton
Rivers arise: A fragment.—GrCt
At Amberley Wild Brooks. Andrew Young.—ReO
"**At** Atri in Abruzzo, a small town." See Tales of a wayside inn—The bell of Atri
At Boot Hill in Tombstone, Arizona. Unknown. —BrSm
At Brill. See "At Brill on the hill"
"**At** Brill on the hill." Mother Goose.—OpF
At Brill.—BrMg
Brill.—ReOn
At Carmel. Mary Austin.—BrA
At Christmas. Unknown.—ClF
At Christmas time. Aileen Fisher.—FiIo
At church. Elizabeth Turner.—VrF
"**At** church last Sunday afternoon." See At church
At dawn. Rose Fyleman.—HoB
At Dunwich. Anthony Thwaite.—CaMb
"**At** dusk." See If the owl calls again.
"**At** dusk I met you first where the dirt road bends." See The opossum
At Easter time. Laura E. Richards.—HoB
"**At** evening when the lamp is lit." See The land of story-books
"**At** every stroke his brazen fins do take." See The progress of the soul—The whale
At Feng Ting temple. Li T'ai-po, tr. fr. the Chinese by Henry H. Hart.—LeMw
"**At** fifteen I joined the army." See The return
"**At** first there was neither Being nor non-Being." See Rig Veda—The song of creation
"**At** Flores in the Azores Sir Richard Grenville lay." See The Revenge
"**At** four o'clock in the morning." See Waking time
At Galway races. William Butler Yeats.—MoS
At grass. Philip Larkin.—CaD—MoS
At Great Torrington, Devon. Unknown.—BrSm
"**At** half past four, mornings in June." See The fisher
"**At** half-past three a single bird." Emily Dickinson.—DiPe
At Heron lodge. Wang Chih-huan, tr. fr. the Chinese by Witter Bynner and Kiang Kang-hu.—LeMw
At home. See Pancakes
At last. Walter De La Mare.—DeBg
"**At** last, in sunshine." Onitsura, tr. fr. the Japanese by Harry Behn.—BeCs
"**At** least to pray is left, is left." Emily Dickinson.—DiPe
"**At** mid-day then along the lane." See Old Jack Noman
"**At** midnight, in the month of June." See The sleeper
"**At** midnight's stroke." See The legend of the cat
At Mrs Appleby's. Elizabeth Upham McWebb. —ArT-3—HuS-3
At Mount Vernon. Aileen Fisher.—HoB
At night. Aileen Fisher.—FiC
"**At** night may I roam." Unknown, tr. fr. the Teton Sioux.—LeO
"**At** poet's tears." See Song
At St Jerome. Frances Harrison.—DoW
At school. Kate Greenaway.—GrT
"**At** seven sharp the morning rings." See Getting up
"**At** six o'clock." See The sound of morning in New Mexico
"**At** sunset, when the night-dews fall." See The snail
At the airport. Howard Nemerov.—DuS—McWs
"**At** the altar." Issa, tr. fr. the Japanese by R. H. Blyth.—IsF
"**At** the boarding house where I live." See Folk song
At the bottom of the well. Louis Untermeyer.—BoGj
At the carnival. Anne Spencer.—HaK
"**At** the corner of Wood street, when daylight appears." See The reverie of poor Susan
"**At** the end of my yard there is a vat." Unknown.—GrCt
"**At** the end of the bough." See Sweet apple
At the end of the field. Aileen Fisher.—FiC
"**At** the end of the garden." See Pumpkins
"**At** the flower-vase." Issa, tr. fr. the Japanese by R. H. Blyth.—IsF
At the grave of Henry Vaughan. Siegfried Sassoon.—PlE
At the keyhole. Walter De La Mare.—BlO
At the lion's cage. Peter Kane Dufault.—CoB
"**At** the meadow's edge." See On an autumn night
"**At** the midnight in the silence of the sleep-time." See Asolando—Epilogue
"**At** the midnight of the year." See Revelation
"**At** the morning exhibition." Issa, tr. fr. the Japanese by R. H. Blyth.—IsF
"**At** the next vacancy for God, if I am elected." See In place of a curse

"**At** the round earth's imagin'd corners, blow." John Donne.—PlE
Blow your trumpets, angels.—GrCt
At the sea-side. Robert Louis Stevenson.—ArT-3
"**At** the siege of Belle isle." See Belle isle
At the tennis clinic. I. L. Martin.—MoS
"**At** the time that turned the heat of the earth." Unknown, tr. fr. the Maori.—LeO
"**At** the time when blossoms." Unknown, tr. fr. the Chinese by Arthur Waley.—LeMw
"**At** the time when the earth became hot." Unknown, tr. fr. the Hawaiian.—LeO
"**At** the top of the house the apples are laid in rows." See Moonlit apples
At the windowed horizon. Elizabeth Jane Coatsworth.—CoDh
At the zoo. A. A. Milne.—MiC
"**At** the zoo I remarked to an emu." Unknown.—BrLl
"**At** twilight." Elizabeth Jane Coatsworth.—CoDh
At war. Russell Atkins.—BoA
Atalanta
Atalanta's race. W. Morris.—CoD
Atalanta's race. William Morris.—CoD
Atharva Veda, sels. Unknown, tr. fr. the Sanskrit by A. A. MacDonnell
A charm against cough.—AlPi
An imprecation against foes and sorcerers.—AlPi
To secure victory in battle.—AlPi
Athens, Greece
"Maid of Athens, ere we part." G. G. Byron.—ByP
"**Athirst** in spirit, through the gloom." See The prophet
Atkins, Russell
At war.—BoA
Irritable song.—BoA
It's here in the.—BoA
Athletes and athletics. See also names of sports, as Baseball
The ageing athlete. N. Weiss.—MoS
Athletes. W. Gibson.—MoS
Athletic employment. Unknown.—MoS
The breed of athletes. Euripides.—MoS
To an athlete dying young. From A Shropshire lad. A. E. Housman.—MoS
Athletes. Walker Gibson.—MoS
Athletic employment. Unknown.—MoS
Atlantic Charter, A. D. 1620-1942. See The island
Atlantis
Atlantis. From Priapus and the pool. C. Aiken.—GrS
Atlantis. See Priapus and the pool
Atomic age
"And the Lord was not in the whirlwind." From Visitations: VII. L. MacNeice.—PlE
Any day now. D. McCord.—BrSm
Atomic courtesy. E. Jacobson.—BrSm
Back again from Yucca Flats. R. S. Kelley.—BrA
Mother Goose, circa 2054. I. Sekula.—BrSm
Primer of consequences. V. Brasier.—BrSm
Rhymes for a modern nursery, sels. P. Dehn
"Hey diddle diddle (the physicists)."—DuR
"In a cavern, in a canyon."—BrSm
"Little Miss Muffet (crouched)."—BrSm—DuR
Song, on reading that the cyclotron has produced cosmic rays, blasted the atom in to twenty-two particles, solved the mystery of the transmutation of elements and devil knows what. S. Hoffenstein.—BrSm
Atomic courtesy. Ethel Jacobson.—BrSm
Atsumi, Prince
"Mirrored in the waters of the Kamunabi river."—BaS
Attar, Farid-uddin
Then from a ruin.—ReBs
"An **attorney** was taking a turn." See The briefless barrister
Atwell, Roy
Some little bug.—BrS (sel.)
Aubade: Dick the donkey boy. Osbert Sitwell.—CaD
An **auctioneer** ("A going! a going! for nothing 'tis going") Unknown, at. to William Darton.—VrF
Auctioneer ("Now I go down here and bring up a moon") Carl Sandburg.—LaPd
Auctioneers
An auctioneer ("A going! a going! for nothing 'tis going") Unknown.—VrF
Auctioneer ("Now I go down here and bring up a moon") C. Sandburg.—LaPd
Horse and hammer. P. K. Dufault.—CoB
Auden, W. H.
Embassy.—DuS
Epitaph on a tyrant.—HoL
For the time being: A Christmas oratorio, sel.
"He is the way."—PlE
"He is the way." See For the time being: A Christmas oratorio
In memory of W. B. Yeats.—GrCt (sel.)
In Schrafft's.—McWs
James Honeyman.—CaMb—SmM
The night mail.—GrCt
Nursery rhyme.—GrS
"O what is that sound which so thrills the ear."—CaD—GrS
"Over the heather the wet wind blows." See Roman wall blues
Roman wall blues.—SmM
"Over the heather the wet wind blows."—CaD
Runner.—MoS
Sext.—LiT (sel.)
Their lonely betters.—BoGj—HaL
The unknown citizen.—DuS
Who's who.—McWs
— and Sjöberg, Leif
"Lord—Thine the day." trs.—PlE
Audubon, John James (about)
John James Audubon. R. C. and S. V. Benét.—HiL
Audubon, drafted. LeRoi Jones.—HaK

Autumn—*Continued*
Autumn ("I love the fitful gust that shakes") J. Clare.—ClF
Autumn ("Now are the autumn days hospitable to wild geese") Manovinoda.—AlPi
Autumn ("Summer's flurry") H. Behn.—BeG
Autumn ("The thistledown's flying, though the winds are all still") J. Clare.—CoBn
Autumn ("A touch of cold in the autumn night") T. E. Hulme.—HaL—SmM
Autumn birds. J. Clare.—ReO
Autumn bluebirds. A. Fisher.—FiC
"The autumn breeze." Issa.—LeOw
"The autumn breeze is blowing." Buson.—LeMw
"An autumn evening (a man)." Issa.—LeOw
Autumn fancies. Unknown.—HuS-3
Autumn fires. R. L. Stevenson.—ArT-3—BrSg
Autumn flight. A. Karanikas.—BoH
Autumn in Carmel. G. Sterling.—PaH
Autumn leaves. A. Fisher.—FiI
Autumn scene. B. Dowling.—CoBn
Autumn squall: Lake Erie. L. I. Russo.—BrA
The autumn wind. J. Clare.—CoBn
Autumn woods. J. S. Tippett.—ArT-3—HoB—StF
Autumn's passing. H. I. Rostron.—StF
"Because the mist." Kiyowara Fukayabu.—BaS
"A chestnut falls." Bashō.—LeMw
City autumn. J. M. March.—LaC
The city of falling leaves. A. Lowell.—ArT-3
A day in autumn. R. S. Thomas.—CoBn
"The deer which (or that) lives." Onakatomi Yoshinobu.—BaS—LeMw
"Down, down." E. Farjeon.—ArT-3
"Even for the space of a flash." Unknown.—BaS
Fall ("The geese flying south") S. Andresen.—DuR
Fall ("The last of October") A. Fisher.—ArT-3—BrSg
Fall of the year. A. Fisher.—FiC
Fall surprises. A. Fisher.—FiIo
For autumn. E. Farjeon.—FaA
The golden tickseed. G. Davidson.—BoH
Horse-chestnut time. K. Starbird.—LaPd
"How will you manage." Princess Daihaku.—BaS
"I like fall." A. Fisher.—LaPh
Immortal autumn. A. MacLeish.—GrS
"In a gust of wind the white dew." Bunya (*or* Funya) no Asayasu.—BaS—LeMw
"In my loneliness." Ryōzen.—BaS
"In the empty mountains." Hitomaro.—BaS
"In the evening." Minamoto no Tsunenobu.—BaS
"In the mountain village." Minamoto no Morotada.—BaS
Indian summer ("Along the line of smoky hills") W. Campbell.—DoW
Indian summer ("These are the days when early") H. Behn.—BeG
An Indian summer day on the prairie. V. Lindsay.—HuS-3
"A leaf crashes gently to the ground." J. Hodgman.—LeM
"A leaf looks prickly and sharp." Peter Johnson.—LeM
The leaves are green. Unknown.—ReOn
"The morns are meeker than they were." E. Dickinson.—ArT-3—DiL—DiPe
Autumn.—BoH—CoBn—TuW
"Nobody gives it to you." M. C. Livingston.—LiC
October. R. Frost.—BoGj
On an autumn night. A. Fisher.—FiI
"The pampas grass." Issa.—LeMw
"A passing shower." Unknown.—BaS
Pastoral X. R. Hillyer.—HaL
Pencil and paint. E. Farjeon.—LaPd
Rain of leaves. A. Fisher.—FiI
Red in autumn. E. Gould.—StF
Reflection. Tomonori.—LeMw
The reunion. O. Dodson.—BoH
Rich days. W. H. Davies.—CoBn
The ripe and bearded barley. Unknown.—CoBn—GrCt
Robin Redbreast. W. Allingham.—HoB—ReBs
"Rushes in a watery place." C. G. Rossetti.—GrCt—LaPd
"Solitude." E. Merriam.—MeI
Song ("The feathers of the willow") R. W. Dixon.—BlO—CoBn
Song ("Why fadest thou in death") R. W. Dixon.—GrCt
"There are two ripenings, one of sight." E. Dickinson.—DiPe
"There is a fading time." Unknown.—BaS
"These are the days when birds come back." E. Dickinson.—DiPe
"Thou shalt see the field-mouse peep." From Fancy. J. Keats.—ReO
To autumn ("O autumn, laden with fruit, and stained") W. Blake.—BlP—CoBn
To autumn ("Season of mists and mellow fruitfulness") J. Keats.—ClF (sel.)—CoBn—CoR
Tree. J. Hunter.—LeM
The trees and the wind. E. Farjeon.—FaA
Two lives and others. W. T. Scott.—DuR
Warning. A. Fisher.—FiC
"When I count." Minamoto no Shitagō.—BaS
When the frost is on the punkin. J. W. Riley.—CoBn
"Where are you going." Issa.—LeOw
"While I stay alone." Unknown.—BaS
Autumn. See "The morns are meeker than they were"
Autumn ("The clock is striking autumn at the apple vendor's fair") Patricia Hubbell.—LaPd
Autumn ("I love the fitful gust that shakes") John Clare.—ClF
Autumn ("Now are the autumn days hospitable to wild geese") Manovinoda, tr. fr. the Sanskrit by Daniel H. H. Ingalls.—AlPi
Autumn ("Summer's flurry") Harry Behn.—BeG
Autumn ("The thistledown's flying, though the winds are all still") John Clare.—CoBn

Autumn ("A touch of cold in the autumn night") T. E. Hulme.—HaL—SmM
Autumn birds. John Clare.—ReO
Autumn bluebirds. Aileen Fisher.—FiC
"The **autumn** breeze." Issa, tr. fr. the Japanese by R. H. Blyth.—LeOw
"The **autumn** breeze is blowing." Buson, tr. fr. the Japanese by R. H. Blyth.—LeMw
"An **autumn** evening (a man)." Issa, tr. fr. the Japanese by R. H. Blyth.—LeOw
"An **autumn** evening (it is)." Issa. tr. fr. the Japanese by R. H. Blyth.—LeOw
Autumn fancies. Unknown.—HuS-3
Autumn fires. Robert Louis Stevenson.—ArT-3—BrSg
Autumn flight. Alexander Karanikas.—BoH
"**Autumn** has come and things begin." See Tree
Autumn in Carmel. George Sterling.—PaH
Autumn leaves. Aileen Fisher.—FiI
"The **autumn** moon." Issa, tr. fr. the Japanese by R. H. Blyth.—IsF
Autumn scene. Basil Dowling.—CoBn
Autumn squall: Lake Erie. Lola Ingres Russo.—BrA
"The **autumn** wind (the shadow)." Issa, tr. fr. the Japanese.—LeOw
"The **autumn** wind (there are)." Issa, tr. fr. the Japanese by R. H. Blyth.—LeOw
The **autumn** wind ("The autumn's wind on suthering wings") John Clare.—CoBn
Autumn woods. James S. Tippett.—ArT-3—HoB—StF
Autumn's passing. Hilda I. Rostron.—StF
"The **autumn's** wind on suthering wings." See The autumn wind
Aux Tuileries 1790. Elizabeth Jane Coatsworth.—CoDh
Averitt, Eleanor
November day.—DuR
Aversion to physic overcome. Mary Elliott.—VrF
Aviators
Ego. P. Booth.—DuS
An Irish airman foresees his death. W. B. Yeats.—BoGj—HoL—YeR
The man in the dead machine. D. Hall.—DuS
To an aviator. D. W. Hicky.—ThA
To Beachey, 1912. C. Sandburg.—ArT-3
Vapor trails. G. Snyder.—DuS
"**Avoid** and pass us by, O curse." See Atharva Veda—An imprecation against foes and sorcerers
"**Avoid** the reeking herd." See The eagle and the mole
The **Avondale** mine disaster. Unknown.—HiL
"**Awa'** wi' your witchcraft o' beauty's alarms." See A lass wi' a tocher
Awake. See The song of Solomon
"**Awake** to the cold light." See March
Awaken. Sally Bingham.—LeM
Award. Ray Durem.—AdIa
Aware. D. H. Lawrence.—CoBn
"**Away** beyond the Jarboe tree." See Strange tree
"**Away** floats the butterfly." Unknown.—WyC
"**Away** in a manger." See Cradle hymn
Away with bloodshed. Alfred Edward Housman.—BrSm
"Away with bloodshed, I love not such."—LiT
"**Away** with bloodshed, I love not such." See Away with bloodshed
"The **axe** has cut the forest down." See Conquest
"**Ay,** little larky, what's the reason." See Address to a lark—Address to a lark singing in winter
"**Ay** me, ay me, I sigh to see the scythe afield." See How time consumeth all earthly things
"**Ay,** tear her tattered ensign down." See Old Ironsides
"**Ay,** waukin, O." Robert Burns.—BuPr
Ayres, Philip
On Lydia distracted.—GrS
Ayscough, Florence. See also Lowell, Amy and Ayscough, Florence
The city of stones. tr.—LeMw
Aytoun, William Edmonstone
The massacre of the Macpherson.—GrCt
The **aziola.** Percy Bysshe Shelley.—GrS
Azrael. See Tales of a wayside inn
The **Aztec** city. Eugene Fitch Ware.—PaH
Aztec Indians. See Indians of the Americas—Aztec
Aztecs
The Aztec city. E. F. Ware.—PaH
"The **azur'd** vault, the crystal circles bright." See Heaven and earth

B

B., R. L.
Silly Willy.—BrSm
B is for beanseed. Eleanor Farjeon.—BrSg
B stands for bear. See A moral alphabet
"**Ba-a,** ba-a, black sheep, have you any wool." See "Baa, baa, black sheep"
"**Baa,** baa, black sheep." Mother Goose.—ArT-3—BrMg—HuS-3—OpF—WiMg
Mother Goose rhymes, 21.—HoB
Bab-Lock-Hythe. Laurence Binyon.—MoS
"The **babe** was in the cradle laid." See Going to bed
The **babes** in the wood. Unknown.—BlO
Babies. See also Childhood recollections; Children and childhood; Finger-play poems; Lullabies; Mother Goose; Nursery play
An April child. Unknown.—DePp
"Babies are crying." P. John.—BaH
"Baby and I." Mother Goose.—BrMg
Baby mine. K. Greenaway.—GrT
Baby Toodles. J. S. Newman.—CoBb
Babylon, Babylon, Babylon the great. V. Lindsay.—LiP
Bartholomew. N. Gale.—ThA
"Be quiet, my baby." Unknown.—DoC
Blessings upon an infant. Unknown.—DoC
Breakfast and puss. A. and J. Taylor.—VrF

Babies—*Continued*
"Bump, bump, please go away." Unknown.—WyC
A bunch of roses. J. B. Tabb.—ThA
Burial. M. Van Doren.—CaMb
By the firelight. L. A. G. Strong.—CaD
"Dear little baby." Unknown.—WyC
Giant Bonaparte. Mother Goose.—BrMg
"A girl in the army." Mother Goose.—BrMg
"Hap and row, hap and row." Unknown.—MoB
"The heaven is bright." Unknown.—WyC
"How many days has my baby to play." Mother Goose.—ArT-3
"Hush, my child." Unknown.—DoC
"I have a wee bit Highlandman." Unknown.—MoB
"If your mother has set out to fish." Unknown.—DoC
Infant joy. W. Blake.—BlP—BoGj—TuW
Infant sorrow. W. Blake.—BlP
"Johnnie Crack and Flossie Snail." From Under Milk Wood. D. Thomas.—BoGj—CaD—HaL—LaPd
Kevin's fingers. M. O'Neill.—OnF
Learning to go alone. A. and J. Taylor.—VrF
Little. D. Aldis.—ArT-3
"Little Blue Shoes." K. Greenaway.—ArT-3
"Mother dear." Unknown.—DoC
"Mother moon, bless baby." Unknown.—LeO
Newborn fingers. M. O'Neill.—OnF
A pavane for the nursery. W. J. Smith.—BoGj—CoBl
Short history of man. J. Holmes.—McWs
The tender nurse. M. Elliott.—VrF
To baby. K. Greenaway.—GrT
Upon a child. R. Herrick.—SmM
"Why do you cry." Unknown.—DoC
"The **babies** are born." Mary Bryant.—BaH
"**Babies** are crying." Pricilla John.—BaH
Baboons. See Monkeys
"**Babushka,** the grandmother, snug in her room." See A legend from Russia
"**Baby** and I." Mother Goose.—BrMg
"**Baby,** baby, naughty baby." See Giant Bonaparte
"A **baby** born in April." See An April child
Baby camel. Vadim Korostylev, tr. fr. the Russian by Babette Deutsch.—CoB
Baby mine. Kate Greenaway.—GrT
"**Baby** mine, over the trees." See Baby mine.
Baby playing. Roderick Crilly Clarke.—LeM
Baby seed song. Edith Nesbit.—HoB—ThA
Baby seeds. Unknown.—BrSg
"**Baby** swimming down the river." See Lullaby
Baby Toodles. Joseph S. Newman.—CoBb
"A **baby** warbler." Kikaku, tr. fr. the Japanese by Harry Behn.—BeCs
Babylon
After reading the sad story of the fall of Babylon. V. Lindsay.—LiP
Babylon, Babylon, Babylon the great. V. Lindsay.—LiP
The destruction of Jerusalem by the Babylonian hordes. I. Rosenberg.—GrS
"How many miles to Babylon." Mother Goose.—OpF—ReMg—TuW
Babylon.—BrMg—GrCt
Babylon. See "How many miles to Babylon"
Babylon, Babylon, Babylon, the great. Vachel Lindsay.—LiP
Bachelors
The two old bachelors. E. Lear.—BrSm
Bachman, Ingeborg
To the sun.—CoBn
Back again from Yucca Flats. Reeve Spencer Kelley.—BrA
"**Back** from the kill." See Contest
Back yard, July night. William Cole.—CoBn
Backwards. Eve Merriam.—MeC
Bacmeister, Rhoda W.
Galoshes.—ArT-3
Bacon, Josephine Dodge Daskam
The sleepy song.—HuS-3—ThA
Bacon, Martha
Wanderer's night song.—ReS
Bacon, Peggy
Cobbler.—LaC
Fatigue.—LaC
The **bad** kittens. Elizabeth Jane Coatsworth.—ThA
The **bad** rider. See "I had a little pony"
Badger. John Clare.—ClF (sel.)—CoB
Badgers
Badger. J. Clare.—ClF (sel.)—CoB
The six badgers. R. Graves.—BoGj—CoB
The **bagel.** David Ignatow.—DuS
The **bagpipe** man. Nancy Byrd Turner.—ArT-3
"The **bagpipe** man came over our hill." See The bagpipe man
Bagpipers
The bagpipe man. N. B. Turner.—ArT-3
Bagpipes. See "Puss came dancing out of the barn"
Bahe, Stanley
"Walking (in the forest)."—BaH
Bailey, Philip James
The great black crow.—CoB
Bairstow, John
"A moth flies round the window."—LeM
The **bait.** John Donne.—MoS
Baker, Barbara
A spike of green.—BrSg
Baker, Karle Wilson
Days.—ArT-3—ThA
Bakers
"Baby and I." Mother Goose.—BrMg
The baker's boy. M. E. L. Newsome.—AgH
The butcher's boy." K. Greenaway.—GrT
"Charley, Charley." Mother Goose.—WiMg
Charley.—BrF
"Ginger, Ginger, broke the winder." Mother Goose.—OpF
Ginger.—BrMg
"I wouldna have a baker, ava, va, va." Unknown.—MoB

I'll be a baker. A. Fisher.—FiIo
"Pat-a-cake, pat-a-cake, baker's man."—HuS-3—OpF—ReMg—WiMg
Pat-a-cake.—BrMg
The **baker's** boy. Mary Effie Lee Newsome.—AgH
"The **baker's** boy delivers loaves." See The baker's boy
Balaclava, Battle of, 1854
The charge of the Light Brigade. A. Tennyson.—TeP
Balade. Geoffrey Chaucer.—GrCt
Balcony. Federico García Lorca, tr. fr. the Spanish by W. S. Merwin.—LiT
"**Bald** heads forgetful of their sins." See The scholars
Baldwin, A. W. I.
Ten little dicky-birds.—StF
Baldwin, Michael
Death on a live wire.—CaMb
Bale, John
Wassail, wassail.—GrCt
The **ball** and the club. Forbes Lindsay.—MoS
The **ball** poem. John Berryman.—LaC (sel.)
Ballad. Henry Treece.—CaD
A **ballad** of a mine. Robin Skelton.—CaMb
Ballad of another Ophelia. D. H. Lawrence.—GrCt
The **ballad** of banners. John Lehmann.—CaMb
The **ballad** of Billy Rose. Leslie Norris.—CaMb
The **ballad** of east and west. Rudyard Kipling.—ArT-3
The **ballad** of Father Gilligan. William Butler Yeats.—McWs—PlE—YeR
A **ballad** of John Silver. John Masefield.—CoSs
Ballad of Johnny Appleseed. Helmer O. Oleson.—ArT-3
The **ballad** of Kon-Tiki. Ian Serraillier.—CoSs
The **ballad** of Reading gaol. Oscar Wilde.—CoD
The **ballad** of red fox. Melvin Walker La Follette.—HaL
A **ballad** of remembrance. Robert E. Hayden.—AdIa—BoA
The **ballad** of Semmerwater. William Watson.—BlO
The **ballad** of Sir Patrick Spens. See Sir Patrick Spens
The **ballad** of Sir Thopas. See The Canterbury tales
The **ballad** of Sue Ellen Westerfield. Robert E. Hayden.—Hak
The **ballad** of the Billycock. Anthony C. Deane.—CoSs
The **ballad** of the boll weevil. Unknown.—HiL
A **ballad** of the Boston tea-party. Oliver Wendell Holmes.—HiL
Ballad of the flood. Edwin Muir.—CaMb
Ballad of the Goodly Fere. Ezra Pound.—CaMb
The **ballad** of the harp-weaver. Edna St Vincent Millay.—ArT-3
The **ballad** of the light-eyed little girl. Gwendolyn Brooks.—LiT
Ballad of the little square. Federico García Lorca, tr. fr. the Spanish by Stephen Spender and J. L. Gili.—LiT
A **ballad** of the mulberry road. Ezra Pound.—HaL
Ballad of the nightingale. Phyllis McGinley.—McWc
The **ballad** of the oysterman. Oliver Wendell Holmes.—SmM
Ballad of the robin. Phyllis McGinley.—McWc
Ballad of the rosemary. Phyllis McGinley.—McWc
Ballad of the soldier. Bertolt Brecht, tr. fr. the German by H. R. Hays.—LiT
Ballad of the two tapsters. Vernon Watkins.—CaMb
Ballad of the Western Island in the North country. Unknown, tr. by Arthur Waley.—GrS
Ballade by the fire. Edwin Arlington Robinson.—BoH
Ballade of a zoo buff. Milton Bracker.—CoB
A **ballade** of lawn tennis. Franklin P. Adams.—MoS
Ballads—American. See Cowboys—Songs
Ballads—Old English and Scottish
The bitter withy. Unknown.—GrCt
The bonnie earl of Moray. Unknown.—BlO
The coasts of high Barbary. Unknown.—BlO
The crafty farmer. Unknown.—ArT-3
The drowned lady. Unknown.—GrCt
Flowers in the valley. Unknown.—BlO—GrS
Get up and bar the door. Unknown.—ArT-3—BlO—HoB—LaPd
The gipsy laddie. Unknown.—BlO
The Golden Vanity. Unknown.—BlO—CoSs
The great Silkie of Sule Skerry. Unknown.—GrCt
Green broom. Unknown.—BlO
Jackie Faa. Unknown.—GrCt
"A knight came riding from the East." Unknown.—BlO
The laily worm and the machrel of the sea. Unknown.—GrCt—ReO
Lord Randal. Unknown.—ClF
Lord Ullin's daughter. T. Campbell.—CoR
"O, where are you going." Unknown.—MoB
The outlandish knight. Unknown.—BrSm
The raggle, taggle gypsies. Unknown.—ArT-3—HuS-3
The wraggle taggle gypsies.—McWs
Robin Hood and Allin-a-Dale. Unknown.—HoB
Robin Hood and Little John. Unknown.—HuS-3
Robin Hood and the Bishop of Hereford. Unknown.—BlO
Robin Hood and the ranger. Unknown.—HuS-3
Robin Hood rescuing the widow's three sons. Unknown.—ArT-3
The royal fisherman. Unknown.—GrCt
Sir Patrick Spens. Unknown.—BlO—BoGj—HoB
The ballad of Sir Patrick Spens.—CoR
Sir Patrick Spence.—ArT-3—CoSs

Ballads—Old English and Scottish—*Continued*
The strange visitor. Unknown.—GrCt—MoB
Thomas Rymer and the queen of Elfland. Unknown.—GrCt
The wee croodin doo. Unknown.—MoB
The wife of Usher's well. Unknown.—ArT-3—GrCt
Ballet school. Babette Deutsch.—HoL
The **balloon** ("As when a man, that sails in a balloon") Alfred Tennyson.—CoR
Balloon ("Dear little balloon") Kathleen Fraser. —FrS
The **balloon** ("I went to the park") Karla Kuskin.—LaPd
The **balloon** man. Dorothy Aldis.—ArT-3
Balloons
The balloon ("As when a man, that sails in a balloon") A. Tennyson.—CoR
Balloon ("Dear little balloon") K. Fraser.—FrS
The balloon ("I went to the park") K. Kuskin. —LaPd
The balloon man. D. Aldis.—ArT-3
"What's the news of the day." Mother Goose. —OpF
What's the news.—BrMg
"Who knows if the moon's." E. E. Cummings. —HaL
Baltic, Battle of the, 1801
The battle of the Baltic. T. Campbell.—CoR
Baltimore, Maryland
Incident. C. Cullen.—AdIA—HoB—HoL—ThA
Bam, bam, bam. Eve Merriam.—LaPd—MeC
Bana
Summer.—AlPi
Bananas
"Bananas and cream." D. McCord.—McE
In memory of Anna Hopewell. Unknown.—BrSm
When monkeys eat bananas. D. McCord.—McAd
"**Bananas** and cream." David McCord.—McE
"**Bananas** ripe and green, and ginger-root." See The tropics in New York
Banbury fair. See "As I was going to Banbury"
Bandit. A. M. Klein.—DoW
Bandits. See Crime and criminals
The **bandog.** Walter De La Mare.—ArT-3
Bandy legs. See "As I was going to sell my eggs"
"**Bang,** bang, bang." See The history of the flood
Bangs, John Kendrick
As to the restless brook.—CoO
I met a little elf man. See The little elf-man
The little elf. See The little elf-man
The little elf-man.—ArT-3—HoB
I met a little elf man.—HuS-3
The little elf.—LaPd—ThA
My dog.—HuS-3
The **banjo** player. Fenton Johnson.—HaK
Banking coal. Jean Toomer.—BoH
The **banks** o' Doon. Robert Burns.—BuPr—CoBl
Bannockburn, Battle of, 1314
Scots, wha hae. R. Burns.—BuPr
Bapat, Vasant
Then go at once.—AlPi
Baptism
At a child's baptism. V. Miller.—BoGj
Baptism. C. G. Bell.—BrA
Baptist. S. Menashe.—SmM
"I'm ceded, I've stopped being theirs." E. Dickinson.—DiPe
Baptism. Charles G. Bell.—BrA
Baptist. Samuel Menashe.—SmM
Bar-room matins. Louis MacNeice.—PlE
Barbara Frietchie. John Greenleaf Whittier.—HiL
The **barber.** Unknown, at. to William Darton.—VrF
Barber, barber. See "Barber, barber, shave a pig"
"**Barber,** barber, shave a pig." Mother Goose.—OpF—ReMg
Barber, barber.—BrMg
Mother Goose rhymes, 20.—HoB
"A **barber** who lived in Batavia." Unknown.—BrLl
The **barber's.** Walter De La Mare.—BoGj
Barbers and barbershops
The barber. Unknown.—VrF
"Barber, barber, shave a pig." Mother Goose. —OpF—ReMg
Barber, barber.—BrMg
Mother Goose rhymes, 20.—HoB
"A barber who lived in Batavia." Unknown.—BrLl
The barber's. W. De La Mare.—BoGj
"Hippety hop to the barber shop." Mother Goose.—ArT-3
"A lion emerged from his lair." J. G. Francis. —BrLl
"There once was a barber of Kew." C. Monkhouse.—BrLl
Barbershops. See Barbers and barbershops
"**Bare-handed** reach." See End of winter
"**Barefooted** bat." See The barefoot bat
The **barefoot** bat. Unknown, ad. fr. the Japanese by Charlotte B. DeForest.—DePp
"**Barefoot** I went and made no sound." See The viper
Baring-Gould, Sabine
Child's evening hymn.—ReS
Barker, George
"My joy, my jockey, my Gabriel."—CaD
Barker, Sale
Birthday book.—GrCt (sels.)
Barker, Shirley
March weather.—HoL
"A **barking** sound the shepherd hears." See Fidelity
Barley
"Bent down by a storm." Jōsō.—BeCs
"The ears of barley, too." Issa.—IsF
The ripe and bearded barley. Unknown.—CoBn—GrCt
The **barn** owl. Samuel Butler.—SmM
Barnes, Kate
Hector the dog.—CoB

Barnes, William
The dove.—ReBs
An englyn on a yellow greyhound.—ReO
The hearth of Urien.—GrCt
"In wintry midnight, o'er a stormy main." tr. —GrCt
The leaves.—CoBn—GrCt
Lullaby.—ReS
May.—GrCt
The spring.—CoBn
Times o' year.—CoBn
A winter night.—GrCt
The woodlands.—CoBn
Zummer stream.—CoBn
Barney, William D.
The panther possible.—DuS
Barney Bodkin. Mother Goose.—ReOn
"**Barney** Bodkin broke his nose." See Barney Bodkin
Barns
The barnyard. M. Burnham.—ArT-3
The boy in the barn. H. Read.—CaD
Human things. H. Nemerov.—CoBn
Lamplighter barn. M. C. Livingston.—ArT-3
Three lovely holes. W. Welles.—HuS-3
The wagon in the barn. J. Drinkwater.—ThA
"**Barnum** and Bayley." Unknown.—MoB
The **barnyard.** Maude Burnham.—ArT-3
Baro, Gene
The ferns.—SmM
Under the boughs.—CoBn
The **baron's** war, sel. Michael Drayton
The Severn.—GrCt
Barrax, Gerald William
Black Narcissus.—HaK
Christmas 1959 et cetera.—HaK
The death of a squirrel in McKinley park.—HaK
Patroness.—HaK
The sacrifice.—HaK
"**Barrels** are very rare." See Shouting into a barrel
Barrington, Patrick
I had a hippopotamus.—CoB
Barrow. Lucy Adams.—BaH
"**Barrow** was a quiet town." See Barrow
Barry, Shirley
Skeleton.—LeM
Barter. Sara Teasdale.—ThA
The **Bartholdi** statue. John Greenleaf Whittier. —HiL
Bartholomew. Norman Gale.—ThA
"**Bartholomew** is very sweet." See Bartholomew
Barua, Hem
A snapshot.—AlPi
Baruch, Dorothy W.
Automobile mechanics.—ArT-3
Different bicycles.—ArT-3
Merry-go-round.—Art-3—HuS-3
Stop—go.—ArT-3
The **base** stealer. Robert Francis.—ArT-3—BoGj —DuR—MoS
Baseball
The base stealer. R. Francis.—ArT-3—BoGj—DuR—MoS
Baseball note. F. P. Adams.—MoS
Baseball's sad lexicon. F. P. Adams.—MoS
Casey at the bat. E. L. Thayer.—BoH—MoS
Cobb would have caught it. R. Fitzgerald.—DuS—LiT—MoS
Decline and fall of a Roman umpire. O. Nash. —MoS
The double-play. R. Wallace.—DuS—MoS
Dream of a baseball star. G. Corso.—LaC
Hits and runs. C. Sandburg.—MoS
Line-up for yesterday. O. Nash.—MoS
Pitcher. R. Francis.—DuS—MoS
Polo grounds. R. Humphries.—MoS
To Lou Gehrig. J. Kieran.—MoS
To Satch. S. Allen.—BoA—HaK
American Gothic.—AdIa
To Satch; or, American Gothic.—MoS
The umpire ("Everyone knows he's blind as a bat") W. Gibson.—MoS
The umpire ("The umpire is a lonely man") M. Bracker.—MoS
Villanelle. M. D. Feld.—MoS
Where, O where. M. Bracker.—MoS
Baseball note. Franklin P. Adams.—MoS
Baseball's sad lexicon. Franklin P. Adams.—MoS
Basham, A. L.
The cloud messenger. tr.—AlPi (sel.)
A description of famine. tr.—AlPi
Gita Govinda, sel.
Krishna's longing. tr.—AlPi
Hammira-mahakavya, sel.
Radhadevi's dance. tr.—AlPi
In praise of celibacy. See Sutra-krtanga
Krishna's longing. See Gita Govinda
Naladiyar, sel.
Observations. tr.—AlPi
Observations. See Naladiyar
Old age. See Thera-gatha and Theri-gatha
Radhadevi's dance. See Hammira-mahakavya
Sutra-krtanga, sel.
In praise of celibacy. tr.—AlPi
Thera-gatha and Theri-gatha, sel.
Old age. tr.—AlPi
Bashford, Henry Howarth
Parliament hill.—ThA
Bashkin, Vasily
Eagles.—CoB
Bashō
"Above the ruins."—BeCs
"After the bells hummed."—BeCs
"All day in gray rain."—BeCs
"A cautious crow clings."—BeCs
"A chestnut falls."—LeMw
"Farewell, like a bee."—BeCs
"High on a mountain."—BeCs
"I've just come from a place."—LeI
"Lightning flickering."—BeCs
"Listen, what stillness."—BeCs
"Little bird flitting."—BeCs
"Little gray cuckoo."—LeMw
"My horse clip-clopping."—BeCs

Bashō—*Continued*
"An old silent pond."—BeCs
On the road to Nara.—ArT-3
"One dream all heroes."—BeCs
"The sea in the dusk."—BeCs
"The seed of all song."—BeCs
"A small hungry child."—BeCs
"Spring departing."—LeMw
"Summer in the world."—LeMw
"Wake up, old sleepy."—BeCs
"You light the fire."—LeMw
Basketball
Ex-basketball player. J. Updike.—DuS
Foul shot. E. A. Hoey.—DuR
"The **bat**." Buson, tr. fr. the Japanese by R. H. Blyth.—LeI
The **bat** ("Airy-mouse, hairy-mouse") Arthur Guiterman.—CoB
The **bat** ("Being a mammal, I have less care than birds") Ruth Herschberger.—DuR
The **bat** ("By day the bat is cousin to the mouse") Theodore Roethke.—BoGj—CoB—DuR—LaPd—SmM
The **bat** ("Lightless, unholy, eldritch thing") Ruth Pitter.—CaD—CoB
Bat ("On summer eves with wild delight") See Childhood. John Clare
The **bat** ("What's that") Conrad Aiken.—AiC
The **bat** baby. See Bats ("A bat is born")
"**Bat,** bat, come under my hat." See To the bat
"A **bat** is born." See Bats
"The **bat** is dun with wrinkled wings." Emily Dickinson.—DiPe
Bates, Clara Doty
Who likes the rain.—ArT-3—StF
Bates, Katherine Lee
America the beautiful.—PlE
The **bath.** Harry Graham.—BrSm
Bathing
After a bath. A. Fisher.—StF
The bath. H. Graham.—BrSm
For a little girl that did not like to be washed. A. and J. Taylor.—VrF
"He who bathes among crocodiles." Unknown.—LeO
It is time, you know. J. Ciardi.—CiYk
Ivory. D. McCord.—McAd
The tub. G. S. Chappell.—StF
The voyage of Jimmy Poo. J. A. Emanuel.—BoA
Washing. J. Drinkwater.—HuS-3
"Waves, coming up against the rocks." Unknown.—LeO
Bathsheba (about)
In the late afternoon. E. J. Coatsworth.—CoDh
Bats
The barefoot bat. Unknown.—DePp
"The bat." Buson.—LeI
The bat ("Airy-mouse, hairy-mouse") A. Guiterman.—CoB
The bat ("Being a mammal, I have less care than birds") R. Herschberger.—DuR
The bat ("By day the bat is cousin to the mouse") T. Roethke.—BoGj—CoB—DuR—LaPd—SmM
The bat ("Lightless, unholy, eldritch thing") R. Pitter.—CaD—CoB
Bat ("On summer eves with wild delight") From Childhood. J. Clare.—ReO
The bat ("What's that") C. Aiken.—AiC
"The bat is dun with wrinkled wings." E. Dickinson.—DiPe
Bats ("A bat is born") R. Jarrell.—DuS—ReO—WeP
The bat baby.—McWs (sel.)
The bats ("In the June twilight, we looked without knowing why") W. Bynner.—BoH
"Cheese and bread." Unknown.—MoB
A round trip. Unknown.—DePp
To the bat. Mother Goose.—BrMg
Bats ("A bat is born") Randall Jarrell.—DuS—ReO—WeP
The bat baby.—McWs (sel.)
The **bats** ("In the June twilight, we looked without knowing why") Witter Bynner.—BoH
"**Batter** my heart, three person'd God." John Donne.—PlE
The **battle.** Louis Simpson.—DuS
Battle hymn of the republic. Julia Ward Howe.—HiL—PlE
The **battle** of Clothesline bay. Wallace Irwin.—CoSs
The **battle** of New Orleans. Thomas Dunn English.—HiL
The **battle** of the Baltic. Thomas Campbell.—CoR
Battles. See also Naval battles; names of battles, as Balaclava, Battle of, 1854; Warships
The battle. L. Simpson.—DuS
The battle of Clothesline bay. W. Irwin.—CoSs
To secure victory in battle. From Atharva Veda. Unknown.—AlPi
Under the frontier post. Wang Chan-Ling.—GrCt
Battleships. See Naval battles; Warships
Bavarian gentians. D. H. Lawrence.—BoGj
"The **bawl** of a steer." See The cowboy's life
Baxter, James K.
A rope for Harry Fat.—CaMb
"The **bay** was anchor, sky." See Offshore
Baybars, Taner
Waves against a dog.—SmM
"**Be** a good boy." Issa, tr. fr. the Japanese by R. H. Blyth.—LeOw
"**Be** brave." Issa, tr. fr. the Japanese by Nobuyuki Yuasa.—IsF
"**Be** careful what." See Zoo manners
"**Be** gay, be merry, and don't be wary of milking the modest minute." See Song, on reading that the cyclotron has produced cosmic rays, blasted the atom into twenty-two particles, solved the mystery of the transmutation of elements and devil knows what

"**Be** kind." Unknown, tr. fr. the aboriginal (Australia).—LeO
"**Be** kind and tender to the frog." See The frog
Be like the bird. Victor Hugo.—ArT-3
"**Be** like the bird, who." See Be like the bird
"**Be** my circle." Myra Cohn Livingston.—LiC
Be my non-valentine. Eve Merriam.—MeI
"**Be** near me when my light is low." See In memoriam—When my light is low
"**Be** not afraid of every danger." See The old wives' tale—A spell
"**Be** not frighted with our fashion." See Masque of gipsies—All your fortunes we can tell ye
"**Be** quiet, my baby." Unknown.—DoC
"**Be** still, my child." Unknown, tr. fr. the Basari. —DoC—LeO
Beach fire. Frances M. Frost.—ArT-3
Beaches. See Seashore
The **bead** mat. Walter De La Mare.—DeBg
Beads
  Overheard on a saltmarsh. H. Monro.—ArT-3 —BoGj—DuR—McWs—ThA
  A trapped fly.—HoL
    The amber bead.—GrCt
The **beagles.** W. R. Rodgers.—MoS
"The **beams** of heaven have been eaten." See Darkness
The **bean** eaters. Gwendolyn Brooks.—HaK
Beans
  B is for beanseed. E. Farjeon.—BrSg
  The bean eaters. G. Brooks.—HaK
  How to sow beans. Unknown.—BrSg
  Jack and the beanstalk. P. Goedicke.—DuS
"A **beanseed,** a beanseed." See B is for beanseed
The **bear.** Carmen Bernos de Gasztold, tr. fr. the French by Rumer Godden.—GaC
"**Bear** down lightly." See To destiny
"A **bear,** however hard he tries." See Teddy bear
"A **bear** went over the mountain." Mother Goose. —HuS-3
Beards
  Old Mr Bows. E. Horsbrugh.—CoO
  "There was an old man in a tree (whose whiskers)." E. Lear.—BrLl
  "There was an old man named Michael Finnegan." Unknown.—ArT-3
  "There was an old man with a beard." E. Lear.—ArT-3—BrLl—GrCt—LaPd
    Limericks.—HoB
    Nonsense verses.—HuS-3
  Whiskers. J. Brown.—LeM
Bears
  Adventures of Isabel. O. Nash.—BrSm (sel.)—LaP (sel.)—LaPd (sel.)
  Algy. Unknown.—BrSm
  B stands for bear. From A moral alphabet. H. Belloc.—BrSm
  The bear. C. B. de Gasztold.—GaC
  "A bear went over the mountain." Mother Goose.—HuS-3
  Big Bear and Little Bear. E. Farjeon.—FaT
  "A cheerful old bear at the zoo." Unknown.—BrLl
  Far away. E. J. Coatsworth.—CoSb
  Fragment of a bylina. A. S. Pushkin.—LiT
  The friend. A. A. Milne.—MiC
  Furry bear. A. A. Milne.—HuS-3—MiC
  Grizzly. B. Harte.—CoB—ReO
  Grizzly bear. M. Austin.—ArT-3—BoGj—LaP—LaPd
  Infant innocence. A. E. Housman.—GrCt
  The lady and the bear. T. Roethke.—BoGj
  Lines and squares. A. A. Milne.—MiC
  Little Katy. Unknown.—BrSm
  The monotony song. T. Roethke.—LiT
  Night watchmen. W. Garthwaite.—ReS
  Teddy bear. A. A. Milne.—MiC
  "There was an old person of Ware." E. Lear
    Limericks.—HoB
  Us two. A. A. Milne.—ArT-3—MiC
  Waiting. H. Behn.—ArT-3—BrSg
  "When a cub, unaware being bare." E. Merriam.—BrLl
  "Who are you, asked the cat of the bear." E. J. Coatsworth.—ArT-3
  Willy. Richard Moore.—DuS
Beasts. See Animals
"**Beat** the drum. Rum-pum-pum." Unknown.—WyC
Beaumont, Francis
  Fit only for Apollo.—GrCt
  Pining for love.—CoBl
—and Fletcher, John
  Jolly red nose. See "Nose, nose, jolly red nose"
  The knight of the burning pestle, sel.
    The month of May.—GrCt
  The month of May. See The knight of the burning pestle
  "Nose, nose, jolly red nose." at.—ClF
    Jolly red nose.—BrMg
Beau's reply. William Cowper.—ReO
"**Beauteous,** yea beauteous more than these." See A song to David
The **beautiful.** Unknown, tr. fr. the Hawaiian.—LeO
"A **beautiful** kite." Issa, tr. fr. the Japanese by R. H. Blyth.—IsF—LeOw
"**Beautiful** must be the mountains whence ye come." See Nightingales
Beautiful soup. See Alice's adventures in wonderland—"Beautiful soup, so rich and green"
"**Beautiful** soup, so rich and green." See Alice's adventures in wonderland
Beautiful Sunday. Jake Falstaff.—CoBn
Beauty
  Barter. S. Teasdale.—ThA
  The beautiful. Unknown.—LeO
  Beauty ("Beauty is seen") E-Yeh-Shure.—ArT-3
  Beauty ("What does it mean? Tired, angry, and ill at ease") E. Thomas.—ThG
  Beauty extolled. H. Noel.—GrCt
  The black finger. A. W. Grimké.—BoA
  Black is a soul. J. White.—AdIa

Beauty—*Continued*
Blue girls. J. C. Ransom.—GrCt—McWs
The coin. S. Teasdale.—ArT-3—ThA
Composed upon Westminster bridge, September 3, 1802. W. Wordsworth.—ArT-3—GrCt—PaH—WoP
"The day will bring some lovely thing." G. N. Crowell.—ArT-3
Ella. G. Brooks.—AgH
"Estranged from beauty none can be." E. Dickinson.—DiPe
Gay Head. N. Abeel.—PaH
The glory. E. Thomas.—ThG
A gospel of beauty. V. Lindsay.—LiP (Complete)
I. The proud farmer
II. The Illinois village
III. On the building of Springfield
He remembers forgotten beauty. W. B. Yeats.—YeR
"I died for beauty, but was scarce." E. Dickinson.—DiPe
In the fields. C. Mew.—CoBn—SmM
Leisure. W. H. Davies.—ArT-3—CoBn—SmM—TuW
Loveliness. H. Conkling.—ArT-3
Lovel's song. B. Jonson.—HoL
Manhole covers. K. Shapiro.—BoGj—BoH—BrA
Night. S. Teasdale.—ArT-3—ThA
It is not far.—HuS-3
No jewel. W. De La Mare.—DeBg
On a lonely spray. J. Stephens.—StS
Pied beauty. G. M. Hopkins.—BoGj—HoL—PlE—SmM
Reflection. L. Sarett.—ThA
"Spring rain." Chiyo-ni.—LeMw
"Swift things are beautiful." E. J. Coatsworth.—ArT-3—DuR—HuS-3
Taught me purple. E. T. Hunt.—LaC
Theme. From Theme and variations. J. Stephens.—StS
"There is a trinity of loveliest things." Rippo.—LeMw
A thing of beauty. From Endymion. J. Keats.—HuS-3
The three cherry trees. W. De La Mare.—GrS
"The voice that beautifies the land." Unknown.—LeO
The washerman. U. Joshi.—AlPi
Waves of thought. Panikkar.—AlPi
The weaving. H. L. Cook.—ThA
Who pilots ships. D. W. Hicky.—ThA
Beauty, Personal
Alas! poor queen. M. Angus.—GrS
Deirdre. J. Stephens.—StS
Karintha. J. Toomer.—HaK (sel.)
Lovely dames. W. H. Davies.—GrS
The lover praises his lady's bright beauty. S. O'Sheel.—CoBl
Mary. W. Blake.—BlP
Me, Alexander Soames. K. Kuskin.—ArT-3
No images. W. Cuney.—BoA—BoH
Petrarch for Laura. C. McAllistair.—GrS
A pretty wench. Mother Goose.—BrMg
Rose-cheeked Laura. T. Campion.—GrS
Sestina. Dante.—GrS
She walked unaware. P. MacDonogh.—CoBl
She walks in beauty. G. G. Byron.—ByP—CoR
To Helen. E. A. Poe.—CoBl—GrCt—PoP
"A young lady sings in our choir." Unknown.—BrLl
Beauty ("Beauty is seen") E-Yeh-Shure.—ArT-3
Beauty ("What does it mean? Tired, angry, and ill at ease") Edward Thomas.—ThG
Beauty extolled. Henry Noel.—GrCt
"**Beauty** has a coldness." See Ella
"**Beauty** is a lily." See Reflection
"**Beauty** is seen." See Beauty
"The **beauty** of manhole covers—what of that." See Manhole covers
The **beaver.** Carmen Bernos de Gasztold, tr. fr. the French by Rumer Godden.—GaC
Beavers
The beaver. C. B. de Gasztold.—GaC
"**Because** I am poor." Unknown, tr. fr. the Kiowa.—LeO
"**Because** I believe in the community of little children." See The massacre of the innocents
"**Because** I could not stop for death." Emily Dickinson.—DiL—DiPe
"**Because** I feel that, in the heavens above." See To my mother
"**Because** I had loved so deeply." See Compensation
"**Because** the mist." Kiyowara Fukayabu.—BaS
"**Because** the treetops of the peak." Hitomaro, tr. fr. the Japanese by Arthur Waley.—LeMw
"**Because** the warden is a cousin, my." See Deer hunt
Bechtel, Louise Seaman
Grandfather frog.—ArT-3
Becker, John
Are you a marsupial.—CoB
Feather or fur.—ArT-3
The hoopee.—CoB
Becket, sel. Alfred Tennyson
Duet.—GrS
Beclouded. See "The sky is low, the clouds are mean"
Bed. See Go to bed
Bed in summer. Robert Louis Stevenson.—BoGj—HuS-3
Bed-time. See also Good-night poems; Lullabies
Bed in summer. R. L. Stevenson.—BoGj—HuS-3
Bedtime ("Come, let's to bed") Mother Goose.—BrMg
Bedtime ("Down with the lambs") Mother Goose.—BrMg
Bedtime ("Father") A. Fisher.—FiIo
Bedtime ("Five minutes, five minutes more, please") E. Farjeon.—ArT-3—ReS
Bedtime ("Ladybugs haven't a house to sweep") A. Fisher.—FiC
The bellman's song. Unknown.—ReS
Calling all cowboys. J. Ciardi.—CiYk

"Diddle, diddle, dumpling, my son John." Mother Goose.—HuS-3—OpF—WiMg
Diddle, diddle, dumpling.—BrMg
Mother Goose rhymes, 14.—HoB
Drummer and sot. Unknown.—VrF
Early supper. B. Howes—BoGj
Escape at bedtime. R. L. Stevenson.—ArT-3—ReS
Fragment of an English opera. A. E. Housman.—LiT
Go to bed. Mother Goose.—GrCt—ReOn—ReS
Bed.—BrMg
"Go to bed, Tom." Mother Goose.—OpF
Going to bed ("The babe was in the cradle laid") E. Turner.—ReS—VrF
Going to bed ("Down upon my pillow warm") A. and J. Taylor.—VrF
Going to bed ("Go to bed late") Mother Goose.—BrMg
Going to bed ("I'm always told to hurry up") M. Chute.—HoB—LaP—LaPd
Goodnight. Mother Goose.—BrMg
The great news. J. Ciardi.—CiYk
The happy family. J. Ciardi.—CoO
Hark. W. De La Mare.—DeBg
Hippity hop to bed. L. F. Jackson.—ArT-3—ReS
The house of dream. W. De La Mare.—DeBg
The huntsmen. W. De La Mare.—ArT-3—HuS-3
In the dark. A. A. Milne.—MiC
"In the evening glow." K. Mizumura.—MiI
June's tune. E. Merriam.—MeC
"Keep a poem in your pocket." B. S. De Regniers.—LaPd
A lantern. W. De La Mare.—DeBg
"Lazy Zany Addlepate." Unknown.—OpF
Lully. W. De La Mare.—DeBg
"The man in the moon (looked out)." Mother Goose.—BrMg—ReS
"A moth flies round the window." J. Bairstow. LeM
The night. A. Goodman.—LeM
Night watchmen. W. Garthwaite.—ReS
No bed. W. De La Mare.—DeBg
Nurse's song. W. Blake.—BlP—ClF—HoB—ReS
The old man in the moon. Unknown.—ReS
The plumpuppets. C. Morley.—ArT-3—ReS
Putting on a nightgown. Mother Goose.—BrMg
Prayer before sleeping. Unknown.—ReS
Seven gifts. Unknown.—DePp
Sleepy Harry. A. and J. Taylor.—GrT—VrF
"Sluggardy-guise, sluggardy-guise." Unknown. —OpF
Someone at my house said. J. Ciardi.—CiYk
Someone lost his head at bedtime but he got it back. J. Ciardi.—CiYk
Storm at night. E. J. Coatsworth.—CoSb
Ten o'clock. P. Hubbell.—LaC
Three a-bed. Mother Goose.—BrMg
Tired Tim. W. De La Mare.—ArT-3—ReS
"To bed, to bed." Mother Goose.—OpF
Bedtime.—BrMg
Let's go to bed.—GrCt—ReS
To the young locust tree outside the window. C. Lewis.—LeP
The unwritten song. F. M. Ford.—ReS
"Wee Willie Winkie runs through the town." Mother Goose.—HuS-3—WiMg
Mother Goose rhymes, 6.—HoB
Wee Willie Winkie.—MoB—ReS
Willie Winkie.—BrMg
Where. W. De La Mare.—DeBg
"Wild young birds that sweetly sing." M. W. Brown.—LaPd
Beddoes, Thomas Lovell
The bride's tragedy, sel.
Song.—ReBs
A crocodile.—CoB
"The mighty thoughts of an old world."—BoGj
Song.—GrS
Song. See "The mighty thoughts of an old world"
Song ("A ho. A ho") See The bride's tragedy
Song ("Old Adam, the carrion crow")—CoB
Bedouin song. Bayard Taylor.—CoBl
Beds
Fred's bed. E. Merriam.—MeC
Inscription for an old bed. W. Morris.—ReS
The land of counterpane. R. L. Stevenson.—HoB—HuS-3
My bed is a boat. R. L. Stevenson.—HuS-3
"There once was an arch armadillo." C. Wells. —BrLl
Two in bed. A. B. Ross.—ArT-3
Bedtime. See Bed-time
Bedtime. See "To bed, to bed"
Bedtime ("Come, let's to bed") Mother Goose.—BrMg
Bedtime ("Down with the lambs") Mother Goose. —BrMg
Bedtime ("Father") Aileen Fisher.—FiIo
Bedtime ("Five minutes, five minutes more, please") Eleanor Farjeon.—ArT-3—ReS
Bedtime ("Ladybugs haven't a house to sweep") Aileen Fisher.—FiC
"**Bedtime's** come fu' little boys." See Lullaby
"**Bee-balm** for humming-birds." See Garden song
"The **bee**, he has white honey." See Dulce ridentem
The **bee-orchis.** Andrew Young.—GrCt
Bee song. Carl Sandburg.—LaPd
Beech ("I like the circling proud old family beech") David McCord.—McAd
The **beech** ("Strength leaves the hand I lay on this beech bole") Andrew Young.—CoBn
Beech trees
Beech ("I like the circling proud old family beech") D. McCord.—McAd
The beech ("Strength leaves the hand I lay on this beech bole") A. Young.—CoBn
Beecher, Henry Ward (about)
Henry Ward Beecher. See "The Reverend Henry Ward Beecher"
"The Reverend Henry Ward Beecher." O. W. Holmes.—BrLl
Henry Ward Beecher.—GrCt

Beeching, Henry Charles
Prayer.—MoS
Beehive. Jean Toomer.—AdIa
Beer, Morris Abel
Manhattan.—BrA
Beer, Patricia
The fifth sense.—CaMb
Beerbohm, Max
Brave Rover.—ReO
Bees. See also Honey
Airlift. A. Fisher.—FiI
"As I was going o'er Tipple Tine." Mother Goose.—OpF
"As I went over Tipple Tyne."—GrCt
The bee-orchis. A. Young.—GrCt
Bee song. C. Sandburg.—LaPd
Beehive. J. Toomer.—AdIa
Bees. M. Chute.—HoB
Bees in lavender. E. Farjeon.—FaA
The bees' song. W. De La Mare.—McWs
"Bless you, bless you, burnie-bee." Mother Goose.—OpF
Bumble bee ("Black and yellow") M. W. Brown.—LaPd
Bumblebee ("The bumblebee is bumbly") D. McCord.—McAd
Buzzy old bees. A. Fisher.—FiI
The canticle of the bees. P. McGinley.—McWc
"Farewell, like a bee." Bashō.—BeCs
"God made the bees." Unknown.—BlO
The golden hive. H. Behn.—ArT-3—BeG
Hammock. D. McCord.—McAd
Honey-bees. From King Henry V. W. Shakespeare.—CoB
The humble-bee. From Troilus and Cressida. W. Shakespeare.—ShS
Julius Caesar and the honey-bee. C. T. Turner. —ReO
The lilac spires. E. J. Coatsworth.—CoSb
Little busy bee. I. Watts.—HuS-3
"The nearest dream recedes, unrealized." E. Dickinson.—DiPe
"Partake as doth bee." E. Dickinson.—DiPe
"The pedigree of honey." E. Dickinson.—DiPe
"The poor little bee." Unknown.—LeO
"Red-currant jelly." M. M. Stephenson.—StF
Spelling bee. E. Farjeon.—FaT
"There once was a boy of Bagdad." Unknown. —BrLl
"There was a bee sat on a wall." Mother Goose.—ReMg
"There was an old man in a tree (who was horribly)." E. Lear.—ArT-3—BrLl
Limericks.—HoB
Two old crows. V. Lindsay.—HaL
Waiting. H. Behn.—ArT-3—BrSg
"What does the bee do." C. G. Rossetti.—ArT-3
Where the bee sucks. From The tempest. W. Shakespeare.—BlO—SmM
Ariel's song.—LaPd
Merrily, merrily.—ShS
"Where the bee sucks, there suck I."—ArT-3
"**Bees.**" See Busy summer
Bees. Marchette Chute.—HoB
Bees in lavender. Eleanor Farjeon.—FaA
"**Bees** in the late summer sun." See Bee song
"**Bees** in winter." See The canticle of the bees
The **bees'** song. Walter De La Mare.—McWs
Beethoven, Ludwig van (about)
Beethoven's death mask. S. Spender.—LiT
Beethoven's death mask. Stephen Spender.—LiT
"**Beetle.**" See Cracker time
Beetle. Hugh Finn.—CoB
"A **beetle** caught my eye, one day." See Beetle
Beetles
Beetle. H. Finn.—CoB
Clock-a-clay. J. Clare.—BlO
Cracker time. A. Fisher.—FiC
Fly away. E. J. Coatsworth.—CoSb
The harnet and the bittle. J. Y. Akerman.—GrCt
I want you to meet. D. McCord.—McE
Jungles of grass. A. Fisher.—FiC
The ladybird ("Dear God") C. B. de Gasztold. —GaC
Ladybird ("Lady, Lady Landers") Unknown. —MoB
"Ladybird, ladybird (fly away home)." Mother Goose.—BrMg—SmM
Mother Goose rhymes, 57.—HoB
"Ladybird, ladybird (where do you hide)." I. O. Eastwick.—BrSg
"Lady bug, lady bug (fly away, do)." Unknown.—WyC
Lullaby. Unknown.—LeO
Seen by moonlight. E. J. Coatsworth.—CoSb
"Wee man o' leather." Unknown.—GrCt
Before Agincourt. See King Henry V
Before battle. See King Henry V—Before Agincourt
Before breakfast ("I went out in the early morning") Elizabeth Jane Coatsworth.—CoSb
Before breakfast ("Mother has to comb her hair") Aileen Fisher.—FiIo
"**Before** I got my eye put out." Emily Dickinson. —DiPe
"**Before** I knew how cruel." See Gossip
"**Before** I melt." See The snowflake
"**Before** she has her floor swept." See Portrait by a neighbor
Before tea. A. A. Milne.—MiC
"**Before** the children say goodnight." See The happy family
"**Before** you love." See A proverb
Beg parding. Unknown.—CoO—GrCt
"'**Beg** parding, Mrs Harding." See Beg parding
Begay, Calvin
As I sit.—BaH
Daddy.—BaH
"The **beggar** at the door for fame." Emily Dickinson.—DiPe
"The **beggar** on the bridge." Issa, tr. fr. the Japanese by R. H. Blyth.—IsF—LeOw
The **beggar** speaks. Vachel Lindsay.—LiP
The **beggar** wind. Mary Austin.—CoBn
Beggarman. Eleanor Farjeon.—FaT

Beggars
The ballad of Semmerwater. W. Watson.—BlO
"A beautiful kite." Issa.—IsF—LeOw
"The beggar on the bridge." Issa.—IsF—LeOw
The beggar speaks. V. Lindsay.—LiP
Beggarman. E. Farjeon.—FaT
The beggar's valentine. V. Lindsay.—LiP
Charity. E. Turner.—VrF
Christmas. Mother Goose.—ArT-3—BrMg
Beggar's rhyme.—LaPh
Craigbilly fair. Unknown.—GrCt
"Hark, hark, the dogs do bark." Mother Goose. —ArT-3—OpF—ReMg—WiMg
The beggars.—BrMg
"Hark, hark."—BrF
Mother Goose rhymes, 23.—HoB
The jolly beggars. R. Burns.—BuPr
The little beggar girl. A. and J. Taylor.—VrF
The old beggar man. A. and J. Taylor.—VrF
St Martin and the beggar. T. Gunn.—CaMb
Soft wings. J. Stephens.—StS
Under the round tower. W. B. Yeats.—GrS
"What a pretty kite." Issa.—BeCs
The **beggars.** See "Hark, hark, the dogs do bark"
Beggar's rhyme. See Christmas ("Christmas is coming, the geese are getting fat")
The **beggar's** valentine. Vachel Lindsay.—LiP
"**Beginning** to dangle beneath." See In the marble quarry
"**Begone,** calm." See A spell of weather
Behavior. See also Conduct of life; Etiquette
Adolphus Elfinstone. G. Burgess.—CoBb
An alphabet of famous Goops. G. Burgess.—CoBb (sel.)
"Amelia mixed the mustard." A. E. Housman. —LiT
Any day now. D. McCord.—BrSm
At church. E. Turner.—VrF
Aunt Eliza. Unknown.—BrSm
Aunt Maud. Unknown.—BrSm
Autobiographical fragment. K. Amis.—CaD
Aversion to physic overcome. M. Elliott.—VrF
B stands for bear. From A moral alphabet. H. Belloc.—BrSm
Belsnickel. A. Guiterman.—CoBb
Beware, or be yourself. E. Merriam.—MeI
A boy. B. Graves.—LeM
"The boy stood in the supper-room." Unknown.—CoO
The boy who laughed at Santa Claus. O. Nash. —CoBb
The boys and the apple-tree. A. and J. Taylor. —GrT
Bringing him up. Lord Dunsany.—CoBb
Bronzeville man with a belt in the back. G. Brooks.—AdIa
Brother and sister. L. Carroll.—BrSm—CoBb—GrCt
Can someone tell me why. J. Ciardi—CiYk
Careless Maria. E. Turner.—VrF
The careless niece. C. Wells.—BrSm
Careless Willie. Unknown.—CoBb
"Children when they're very sweet." J. Ciardi. —CoBb
A children's don't. H. Graham.—CoBb (sel.)
Come and play in the garden. J. Taylor.—GrT
The contrary boy. G. V. Drake.—CoBb
Corner. R. Pomeroy.—DuS
"Country bumpkin." Issa.—LeOw
The cruel boy. E. Turner.—VrF
Dan Dunder. J. Ciardi.—CoBb
"Ding, dong, bell, pussy's in the well." Mother Goose.—OpF
"Ding, dong, bell."—ArT-3—BrMg—ReMg —WiMg
Mother Goose rhymes, 8.—HoB
Dirge for a bad boy. E. V. Rieu.—CoBb
Dirty Jim. J. Taylor.—GrT
Disappointment. E. Turner.—VrF
The dizzy girl. E. Turner.—VrF
"Don't-care didn't care." Unknown.—BlO
A double limerick or twiner. W. De La Mare. —BrLl
Drawing teeth. E. Turner.—VrF
Dressed or undressed. E. Turner.—VrF
The dunce. E. Turner.—VrF
"Excuse me." E. L. Dailey.—BaH
Extremely naughty children. E. Godley.—CoBb
Fairies. M. Chute.—ThA
Four children. Mother Goose.—BrMg
Get up or you'll be late for school, silly. J. Ciardi.—CiYk
Gifts for a good boy. Unknown.—DePp
"Ginger, Ginger, broke the winder." Mother Goose.—OpF
Ginger.—BrMg
"Godfrey Gordon Gustavus Gore." W. B. Rands.—ArT-3—CoBb—HoB
Going to school. E. Turner.—VrF
Good and bad. Unknown.—DePp
Good and bad children. R. L. Stevenson.—BlO —CoBb
The good girl. E. Turner.—VrF
The good little girl. A. A. Milne.—CoBb
The good scholar. E. Turner.—VrF
Henry King, who chewed bits of string, and was early cut off in dreadful agonies. H. Belloc.—BrSm—CoBb
"Here in this book, collected for you." W. Cole.—CoBb
"Here's Sulky Sue." Mother Goose.—OpF
Sulky Sue.—BrMg
"Here's the tailor with his sheers." Unknown. —VrF
The hoyden. E. Turner.—VrF
"I am a nice nice boy." M. O'Connor.—LeM
I want to know. J. Drinkwater.—HoB
"An important young man of Quebec." J. H. Pitman.—BrLl
Inhuman Henry; or, Cruelty to fabulous animals. A. E. Housman.—CoBb
Jane, do be careful. I. Page.—CoBb
"Jeremiah Obadiah, puff, puff, puff." Mother Goose.—OpF
Jeremiah Obadiah.—BrMg
Jim, who ran away from his nurse, and was eaten by a lion. H. Belloc.—BrSm—CoBb—GrCt

Behavior—*Continued*
Jittery Jim. W. J. Smith.—CoBb
Johnny. E. Rounds.—BrSm
"Johnny went to church one day." Unknown. —CoBb
Lemons and apples. M. Neville.—ArT-3
The little girl that beat her sister. A. and J. Taylor.—VrF
"Little Jack Horner." Mother Goose.—HuS-3 —OpF—WiMg
Jack Horner.—BrMg
Mother Goose rhymes, 7.—HoB
Little Katy. Unknown.—BrSm
"Little Polly Flinders." Mother Goose.—OpF —WiMg
Polly Flinders.—BrMg
Little Willie. Unknown.—BrSm
Lucy and Dicky. E. Turner.—VrF
Lullaby. P. L. Dunbar.—HoB
Maria Jane. A. Scott-Gatty.—CoBb
Matilda ("Matilda got her stockings wet") F. G. Evans.—CoBb
Matilda ("Matilda told such dreadful lies") H. Belloc.—BlO
Meddlesome Matty. A. and J. Taylor.—GrT
Miss Peggy. E. Turner.—VrF
Miss Sophia. E. Turner.—VrF
Mr Nobody. Unknown.—HuS-3
Mrs Elsinore. M. C. Livingston.—LiC
Modifications. R. Koertge.—DuS
The mouth and the body. P. Mwanikih.—LeM
"My mother said, I never should." Mother Goose.—BlO—BrMg
"My mother said that I never should."—OpF
"My parents kept me from children who were rough." S. Spender.—CaD
Naughty Sam. E. Turner.—VrF
"Nothing to do." S. Silverstein.—CoBb
"Now to be good if you'll begin." Unknown. —VrF
A nursery song. L. E. Richards.—HoB
"Oh, no." M. M. Dodge.—CoBb
"On little Harry's christ'ning day." M. Elliott. —VrF
The opportune overthrow of Humpty Dumpty. G. W. Carryl.—CoBb
The orphans. H. S. Horsley.—VrF
Our polite parents. C. Wells.—CoBb
Peeking in. A. Fisher.—FiIo
Please. J. Ciardi.—CiYk
"Polly, Dolly, Kate and Molly." Unknown.—CoBb
Polly Picklenose. L. F. Jackson.—CoBb
Psychological prediction. V. Brasier.—CoBb
The quiet child. R. Field.—ReS
Rebecca. H. Belloc.—DuR—TuW
"Said a sheep to her child, My dear Ruth." J. G. Francis.—BrLl
"Sarah Cynthia Sylvia Stout." S. Silverstein.—CoBb
The sash. E. Turner.—VrF
Science for the young. W. Irwin.—BrSm (sel.) —CoBb
Seven gifts. Unknown.—DePp
Sh. J. S. Tippett.—ArT-3
"Simple Simon met a pieman." Mother Goose. —HuS-3—OpF—ReMg—WiMg
The history of Simple Simon.—VrF
Mother Goose rhymes, 49.—HoB
Simple Simon.—BrMg
Sister Nell. Unknown.—CoBb
Sleepy Harry. A. and J. Taylor.—GrT—VrF
So still. A. Fisher.—FiIo
Someone was up in that tree. J. Ciardi.—CiYk
Sometimes. E. Merriam.—MeC
A song about myself. J. Keats.—SmM
Song against children. A. Kilmer.—ThA
"Speak roughly to your little boy." From Alice's adventures in wonderland. L. Carroll.—BlO
The dutchess' lullaby.—CoBb
The story of Augustus who would not have any soup. H. Hoffmann.—AgH—BoGj—BrSm —CoBb
The story of Augustus.—ArT-3
The story of Johnny Head-in-air. H. Hoffmann.—ArT-3—CoBb
Such a pleasant familee. W. Irwin.—BrSm
Sulking. A. and J. Taylor.—VrF
Susan and Patty. E. Turner.—VrF
Tardiness. G. Burgess.—CoBb
"There was a little girl, and she had a little curl." Mother Goose.—OpF—WiMg
Jemima.—BlO—CoBb
Mother Goose rhymes, 15.—HoB
"There was a young fellow of Ealing." Unknown.—BrLl
"There was a young girl of Asturias." Unknown
Two limericks.—CoBb
"There was a young lady from Woosester." Unknown.—BrLl
"There was a young lady of Oakham." Unknown
Two limericks.—CoBb
"There was a young lady of Russia." E. Lear. —BrLl
"There was an old man of Thermopylae." E. Lear.—BrLl
"There was an old person of Burton." E. Lear. —BrLl
"There was an old person of Grange." E. Lear—BrLl
"There was an old person of Ischia." E. Lear. —BrLl
"There was an old person of Shoreham." E. Lear.—BrLl
Think of eight numbers. S. Silverstein.—CoBb
"This little fellow." Unknown.—WyC
Three bad children. K. Greenaway.—GrT
Three bad ones. Mother Goose.—CoBb
To mystery land. K. Greenaway.—GrT
"Tommy was a silly boy." K. Greenaway.—ArT-3
Two people. E. V. Rieu.—CoBb
A visit to Newgate. H. S. Horsley.—VrF
Warning to children. R. Graves.—BlO

The watchman. H. S. Horsley.—VrF
What she did in the morning, I wouldn't know, she was seated there in the midst of her resilient symptoms, always. Merrill Moore.—DuS
What the Lord High Chamberlain said. V. W. Cloud.—CoBb
"When Jacky's a good boy." Mother Goose.—OpF
Cakes and custard.—BrMg
Reward.—AgH
"When we went out with grandmamma." K. Greenaway.—GrT
Where's Mary. I. O. Eastwick.—ArT-3
Whittington and his cat. Unknown.—VrF
Who's here. E. Merriam.—MeI
"Wilhelmina Mergenthaler." H. P. Taber.—CoBb
Willie. M. Adeler.—CoBb
Won't. W. De La Mare.—DeBg
Young Sammy Watkins. Unknown.—CoBb
"**Behind** him lay the gray Azores." See Columbus
"**Behind** me the moon." Kikaku, tr. fr. the Japanese by Harry Behn.—BeCs
"**Behind** our house there is a mere." See The white drake
Behind the waterfall. Winifred Welles.—ArT-3—HuS-3
Behn, Harry
"Above the mountain." tr.—BeCs
"Above the ruins." tr.—BeCs
"Above tides of leaves." tr.—BeCs
Adventure ("It's not very far to the edge of town")—ArT-3
Adventure ("There's a place I've dreamed about far away")—BeG
"After the bells hummed." tr.—BeCs
"All day in gray rain." tr.—BeCs
"Asleep in the sun." tr.—BeCs
"At last, in sunshine." tr.—BeCs
Autumn.—BeG
"A baby warbler." tr.—BeCs
"Behind me the moon." tr.—BeCs
"Bent down by a storm." tr.—BeCs
"Beyond the dark trees." tr.—BeCs
"Beyond the temple." tr.—BeCs
The Blackfoot chieftains.—BeG
"Brightly the sun shines." tr.—BeCs
Brightness. tr.—BeG
"Broken and broken." tr.—BeCs
"Butterfly, these words." tr.—BeCs
Canticle of spring.—BeG
"A cautious crow clings." tr.—BeCs
Ceremony.—BeG
A Christmas carol.—HoB
"A cloud shimmering." tr.—BeCs
Crickets.—BeG
"Day darken, frogs say." tr.—BeCs
Deer.—CoB—LiT
Discovery.—BeG
Dragonfly.—LiT
The dream.—LiT
The errand.—BeH
"Even stones under." tr.—BeCs
"Evening shadows touch." tr.—BeCs
"Farewell, like a bee." tr.—BeCs
The first Christmas eve.—BeG
Flowers.—BrSg
Follow the leader.—ArT-3
Fourth of July.—BeG
A friendly mouse.—BeG
"Frog-school competing." tr.—BeCs
From an airplane.—BeG
Gardeners.—BeG
Ghosts.—BeG
Gila monster.—LiT
The gnome.—ArT-3—LaPd
The golden hive.—ArT-3—BeG
Growing up.—LaPd—LaPh
Hallowe'en.—ArT-3—HuS-3—LaPd—LaPh
Hansi.—BeG
"High on a mountain." tr.—BeCs
"Ho, for the May rains." tr.—BeCs
"Hop out of my way." tr.—BeCs
"How cool cut hay smells." tr.—BeCs
"A hungry owl hoots." tr.—BeCs
"I must go begging." tr.—BeCs
"Idly my ship glides." tr.—BeCs
"If the white herons." tr.—BeCs
"If things were better." tr. BeCs
"In spring the chirping." tr.—BeCs
Indian summer.—BeG
"It is nice to read." tr.—BeCs
Killdees.—BeG
The kite.—ArT-3
The lake.—BeG
"Leaf falling on leaf." tr.—BeCs
"The least of breezes." tr.—BeCs
Lesson.—BrSg
"Lightly a new moon." tr.—BeCs
"Lightning flickering." tr.—BeCs
"Listen, what stillness." tr.—BeCs
"Little bird flitting." tr.—BeCs
Lost.—BeG
March wind.—BeG
Miss Jones.—BeG
Mr Potts.—BeG
Mr Pyme.—ArT-3—LaPd
"A mountain village." tr.—BeCs
"My horse clip-clopping." tr.—BeCs
Northern summer.—BeG
"Now the moon goes down." tr.—BeCs
"O foolish ducklings." tr.—BeCs
"O moon, why must you." tr.—BeCs
"Of what use are twigs." tr.—BeCs
"An old silent pond." tr.—BeCs
"One dream all heroes." tr.—BeCs
"One man and one fly." tr.—BeCs
Our country.—BeG
"Out of one wintry." tr.—BeCs
"Out of the sky, geese." tr.—BeCs
"Over the deepest." tr.—BeCs
"Over the wintry." tr.—BeCs—LaPd
The Painted desert.—BeG
Perrin's walk.—BeG
"Poor crying cricket." tr.—BeCs
"Puffed by a wind, sails." tr.—BeCs

Behn, Harry—*Continued*
Purification. tr.—BeG
"Rain went sweeping on." tr.—BeCs
"The red sun sinks low." tr.—BeCs
"A river leaping." tr.—BeCs
River's song.—BeG
Roosters and hens.—BeG
Santa Fe west.—BeG
"The sea hawk hunting." tr.—BeCs
"The sea in the dusk." tr.—BeCs
"The seed of all song." tr.—BeCs
September.—BeG
"Since my house burned down." tr.—BeCs
"A small hungry child." tr.—BeCs
A small migration.—BeG
"Snow fell until dawn." tr.—BeCs
Song to cloud.—BeG
"A spark in the sun."—BeCs—BrSg
Spring.—ArT-3—LaP
"Spring is almost gone." tr.—BeCs
Spring rain.—ArT-3
The storm.—BeG
Summer.—BeG
"Sun low in the west." tr.—BeCs
Sunrise and sun.—BeG
"Swift cloud shadows." tr.—BeCs
Swing song.—ArT-3
Teddy bear.—ArT-3
"That duck, bobbing up." tr.—BeCs
"This fall of new snow." tr.—BeCs
This happy day.—ArT-3
Thunder dragon.—BeG
"The tight string broke and." tr.—BeCs
"Tonight in this town." tr.—BeCs
Traveling song. tr.—BeG
"A tree frog trilling." tr.—BeCs
Trees.—ArT-3—HoB
"Turning from watching." tr.—BeCs
Two views of the planet earth.—BeG
Waiting.—ArT-3—BrSg
"Waiting in darkness." tr.—BeCs
"Wake up, old sleepy." tr.—BeCs
"Washing my rice hoe." tr.—BeCs
"We rowed into fog." tr.—BeCs
"Well, hello down there." tr.—BeCs
"What a pretty kite." tr.—BeCs
"What a wonderful." tr.—BeCs
"When my canary." tr.—ArT-3—BeCs
"When spring is gone, none." tr.—BeCs
"Where does he wander." tr.—BeCs
"Whose scarf could this be." tr.—BeCs
"Wild ducks have eaten." tr.—BeCs
Windy morning.—ArT-3
Winter night.—BeG
"**Behold**, four kings in majesty rever'd." See The rape of the lock—The playing cards
"**Behold** her, single in the field." See The solitary reaper
"**Behold** the scraggly cassowary." See The cassowary
Beier, Ulli
Erin (Elephant). tr.—ReO
"**Being** a mammal, I have less care than birds." See The bat
"**Being** fat. Myra Cohn Livingston.—LiC
Being gypsy. Barbara Young.—ArT-3
Being nobody. Karen Crawford.—LeM
"**Being** out of heart with government." See An appointment
"**Being** your slave, what should I do but tend." See Sonnets. William Shakespeare
Beissel, Henry
The boar and the dromedar.—DoW
Beleaguered cities. F. L. Lucas.—ClF (sel.)
The **belfry** of Bruges. Henry Wadsworth Longfellow.—PaH
Belgrade, Siege of, 1789
Alliteration; or, The siege of Belgrade. Unknown.—GrCt
Belief. See Faith
"**Believe** in Orion. Believe." See The lights in the sky are stars
Belisarius (about)
Belisarius. H. W. Longfellow.—LoPl
Belisarius. Henry Wadsworth Longfellow.—LoPl
Belitt, Ben
Artichoke. tr.—LiT
Diver. tr.—LiT
A few things explained. tr.—LiT (sel.)
Belkin, Fyodor
Rooster.—CoB
Bell, Alexander Graham (about)
Alexander Graham Bell did not invent the telephone. R. P. T. Coffin.—ArT-3
Bell, Charles G.
Baptism.—BrA
The gar.—BrA
"A **bell** and a rattle." See The cradle trap
"**Bell** horses, bell horses, what time of day." Mother Goose.—ArT-3
Race starting.—BrMg
The **bell** of Atri. See Tales of a wayside inn
Bellamy, William
"There's a lady in Kalamazoo."—BrLl
Belle isle. Mother Goose.—ReOn
Bellerby, Frances
The old ones.—CaD
The **belles** of Mauchline. Robert Burns.—BuH
"The **belles** of the eighties were soft." See Reflections outside of a gymnasium
The **bellman's** song. Unknown.—ReS
Belloc, Hilaire
B stands for bear. See A moral alphabet
The dodo.—GrCt
The early morning.—CoBn
The elephant.—ArT-3
The frog.—BoGj—HoB
Henry King, who chewed bits of string, and was early cut off in dreadful agonies.—BrSm—CoBb
Jim, who ran away from his nurse, and was eaten by a lion.—BrSm—CoBb—GrCt
Juliet.—CoBl
Matilda.—BlO
The moon's funeral.—ThA
A moral alphabet, sel.
B stands for bear.—BrSm
On a hand.—CoBl

On a politician.—BrSm—McWs
The python.—BrSm
Rebecca.—DuR—TuW
The rhinoceros.—GrCt
Sarah Byng.—BoGj
The South Country.—PaH
Tarantella.—PaH—ThA
The vulture.—AgH
The yak.—BlO

Bellows, Isabel Frances
"M is for mournful Miss Molly."—BrLl

Bells
"After the bells hummed." Bashō.—BeCs
The belfry of Bruges. H. W. Longfellow.—PaH
The bell of Atri. From Tales of a wayside inn. H. W. Longfellow.—LoPl
The bells. E. A. Poe.—BoH—PoP
The bells of heaven. R. Hodgson.—BoGj—CoB—PlE—ThA
The bells of Shandon. Father Prout.—CoR—GrCt—PaH
Chimes. F. Meynell.—TuW
Christmas bells. H. W. Longfellow.—LaPh (sel.)
Donne redone. J. P. Tierney.—BrSm
Doorbells. R. Field.—ArT-3—HuS-3
"How still the bells in steeples stand." E. Dickinson.—DiL—DiPe
Jingle bells. Mother Goose.—BrMg
"Merry are the bells, and merry would they ring." Mother Goose.—OpF
Merry are bells.—ArT-3
"The nightingales sing." Ukō.—LeI
"A nut and a kernel." Mother Goose.—OpF
On bell-ringers. Voltaire.—BrSm
"Oranges and lemons." Mother Goose.—BrMg—OpF—SmM—WiMg
London bells.—GrCt
Ring out, wild bells. From In memoriam. A. Tennyson.—ArT-3—LaPh—TeP
"Roast beef and marshmallows." Mother Goose.—OpF
"Roon, roon, rosie." Unknown.—MoB
The song of the wind bell. Ch'en Meng-chia.—LeMw
The temple bells of Yun Sui. Yang Wan-li.—LeMw

"There was an old man, who said, Well." E. Lear.—BrLl

The **bells.** Edgar Allan Poe.—BoH—PoP

The **bells** of heaven. Ralph Hodgson.—BoGj—CoB—PlE—ThA

The **bells** of Shandon. Father Prout.—CoR—GrCt—PaH

"**Below** the thunders of the upper deep." See The kraken

Belshazzar
"Belshazzar had a letter." E. Dickinson.—DiPe
Vision of Belshazzar. G. G. Byron.—ByP—CoR

"**Belshazzar** had a letter." Emily Dickinson.—DiPe

Belsnickel. Arthur Guiterman.—CoBb

Belting, Natalia (M.)
April ("The creeks and the streams and the Great River are full")—BeCm
April ("The season of planting is finished")—BeCm
August ("The hot sun has ripened the corn")—BeCm
August ("When the earth was not as old as it is now")—BeCm
"The dark gray clouds."—LaPd
December ("Furry grandfather sleeps")—BeCm
December ("The rice-cutting moons have gone")—BeCm
February ("Put the pine tree in its pot by the doorway")—BeCm
February ("The sun is coming")—BeCm
January ("The mountain passes are deep in snow")—BeCm
January ("The summer corn ripens")—BeCm
July ("The giant cactus is ripe in the desert")—BeCm
July ("The grandfathers were instructed")—BeCm
June ("The gentle winds blow")—BeCm
June ("There is no night")—BeCm
March ("It is time. The geese fly overhead, returning")—BeCm
March ("Winter has packed her brown garments")—BeCm
May ("Night is almost gone")—BeCm
May ("The Seven Stars are shining again")—BeCm
May-June ("The food pits are empty")—BeCm
May-June ("In the beginning man did not have cattle")—BeCm
November ("Cold flings itself out of the north")—BeCm
November ("The crops are in from the fields")—BeCm
October ("The harvest is finished. Winter stays its coming")—BeCm
October ("The villages stand on the lake-edge")—BeCm
"The seasons were appointed, and the times."—BeCm
September ("Beyond the Shining mountains")—BeCm
September ("The dry fingers of the sun have wiped up the dampness around the grass roots")—BeCm
"Some say the sun is a golden earring."—LaPd

"**Ben-Arabie** was the camel." See Exile

"**Ben** Battle was a soldier bold." See Faithless Nelly Gray

"**Ben** Franklin munched a loaf of bread while walking down the street." See Benjamin Franklin

Benally, Raymond
Crucifixion.—BaH

Benbow, John (about)
The death of Admiral Benbow. Unknown.—BlO

"**Bend** low again, night of summer stars." See Summer stars

Bender, Jill
"Walking into the woods I see."—LeM
Bendig, Margaret
"Inviting, rippling waters."—LeM
"**Bending** over." Issa, tr. fr. the Japanese by Nobuyuki Yuasa.—IsF
"**Beneath** its morning caul, this ravaged land." See Dakota badlands
"**Beneath** the high solemn dusk of Westminster." See Birthday party
"**Beneath** the pine tree where I sat." See All day long
Beneath the snowy trees. Aileen Fisher.—FiI
"**Beneath** the waters." See Undersea
"**Beneath** these fruit-tree boughs that shed." See The green linnet
"**Beneath** these stones repose the bones." See On an old toper buried in Durham churchyard, England
"**Beneath** this plain pine board is lying." See Joshua Hight
"**Beneath** time's roaring cannon." See Three poems about Mark Twain—When the Mississippi flowed in Indiana
Benedict, Saint (about)
"Saint Francis and Saint Benedight." W. Cartwright.—PlE
A house blessing.—GrCt
Benediction. Donald Jeffrey Hayes.—BoA
Benét, Rosemary Carr and Stephen Vincent
Abraham Lincoln.—ArT-3
Benjamin Franklin.—ArT-3
Captain Kidd.—HiL—TuW
Clipper ships and captains.—HuS-3
Cotton Mather.—HiL
Daniel Boone.—BrA—HoL
John James Audubon.—HiL
Johnny Appleseed.—HoB
"Lewis and Clark."—HuS-3
Nancy Hanks.—ArT-3—HuS-3
Negro spirituals.—BrA
Southern ships and settlers.—BrA
"Thomas Jefferson."—ArT-3
Benét, Stephen Vincent
American names.—BrA—PaH
"Americans are always moving on." See Western star
Dulce ridentem.—HaL
Invocation. See John Brown's body
"It was noon when the company marched to the railroad station." See John Brown's body
John Brown's body, sels.
Invocation.—BrA
"It was noon when the company marched to the railroad station"
From John Brown's body.—HiL
Robert E. Lee.—BrA
"There was a girl I used to go with."—HaL
"Three elements."—PlE
Nightmare number three.—McWs
1936.—McWs
A nonsense song.—TuW
Robert E. Lee. See John Brown's body
"There was a girl I used to go with." See John Brown's body
"Three elements." See John Brown's body
Western star, sel.
"Americans are always moving on."—BrA
—See also Benét, Rosemary Carr, jt. auth.
Benét, William Rose
The bestiary.—ReO (sel.)
The fancy.—MoS
The fawn in the snow.—ReO
Jesse James.—HiL
Benjamin Franklin ("Ben Franklin munched a loaf of bread while walking down the street") Rosemary Carr and Stephen Vincent Benét.—ArT-3
Benjamin Franklin ("Every day, every day") Eve Merriam.—MeIv
Bennett, Gwendolyn B.
Hatred.—BoA
Heritage.—BoA
Sonnet I.—BoA
Sonnett II.—BoA
Bennett, Henry Holcomb
The flag goes by.—ArT-3
Bennett, John
"There's a tune, said a sly Bengalese."—BrLl
Bennett, Peggy
Bird thou never wert.—CoB
Greed.—CoB
Lord of jesters, prince of fellows.—CoB
Over the green sands.—CoB
Pearls among swine.—CoB
Plain talk for a pachyderm.—CoB
Rose's calf.—CoB
A snap judgment of the llama.—CoB
Tatterdemalion.—CoB
Truth will out.—CoB
Bennett, Rowena Bastin
Boats.—ArT-3
Conversation between Mr and Mrs Santa Claus.—ArT-3
The freight train.—LaP—LaPd
Meeting the Easter bunny.—ArT-3
A modern dragon.—ArT-3—LaPd
Motor cars.—ArT-3—LaP
Smoke animals.—LaPd
Benson, Michael
Scrapyard.—LeM
"**Bent** down by a storm." Jōsō, tr. fr. the Japanese by Harry Behn.—BeCs
Bentley, Beth
A waltz in the afternoon.—CoBl
Bentley, E. (Edmund) C. (Clerihew)
George III.—McWs
Beppo. George Gordon Byron.—ByP
Berchan
The Fort of Rathangan.—GrCt
The old Fort of Rathangan.—HoL
The old Fort of Rathangan. See The Fort of Rathangan
Bergengren, Ralph
The worm.—BrSg
Bermuda
Bermudas. A. Marvell.—GrCt—HiL

Bermudas. Andrew Marvell.—GrCt—HiL
Berries. See also names of berries, as Blackberries
Berries. I. O. Eastwick.—BrSg
Elfin berries. R. Field.—AgH
A way of looking. C. Lewis.—LeP
Berries ("Red berry") Ivy O. Eastwick.—BrSg
Berries ("There was an old woman") Walter De La Mare.—HoB
Berryman, John
The ball poem.—LaC (sel.)
"**Berryman** and Baxter." See The little black hen
"**Beside** that tent and under guard." See Geronimo
"**Beside** the bay of Okura." See Weeping cherry trees
"**Beside** the old earth-colored." See Vacant house
Besides that. James Stephens.—StS
Bessie Bobtail. James Stephens.—StS
"The **best** game the fairies play." Rose Fyleman. —ArT-3
Best of all. Aileen Fisher.—FiC
The **bestiary.** William Rose Benét.—ReO (sel.)
Betai, Sunderji G.
Roses and thorns.—AlPi
"**Betimes** a wise guest." See Always with us—the black preacher
Betjeman, John
East Anglian bathe.—MoS
Harrow-on-the-hill.—CaD
Hunter trials.—CaD
The Olympic girl.—MoS
Seaside golf.—MoS
A Shropshire lad.—CaMb
A subaltern's love-song.—McWs
Sunday morning, King's Cambridge.—PlE
"**Better** hatred than the friendship of fools." See Naladiyar—Observations
"**Better** to be the rock above the river." See La Crosse at ninety miles an hour
"**Better** to see your cheek grown hollow." See Madman's song
"**Betty** Botter bought some butter." Mother Goose.—OpF
Betty Botter's batter.—BrMg
Betty Botter's batter. See "Betty Botter bought some butter"
"**Between** Botallack and the light." See A ballad of a mine
"**Between** our house and Jack's next door." See The cellar hole
"**Between** the dark and the daylight." See The children's hour
"**Between** the full moon and the hoarfrost." See The three deer
"**Between** the grey pastures and the dark wood." See The valley of white poppies
"**Between** the green of summer." See Going south so soon
Between the walls of the valley. Elisabeth Peck. —BrA
Between the world and me. Richard Wright.—AdIa—BoA
"**Between** two hawks, which flies the higher pitch." See King Henry VI—Comparisons
Bevington, Helen
Italian excursion.—McWs
Report from the Carolinas.—BrA (sel.)
Beware. See The tempest
"**Beware** lest you should get a toss." See The rhinoceros
"**Beware,** my child." Shelley Silverstein.—CoO—LaPd
Beware of the doggerel. Eve Merriam.—MeI
Beware, or be yourself. Eve Merriam.—MeI
"**Beware.** The Israelite of old, who tore." See The warning
Beyer, Evelyn
Jump or jiggle.—ArT-3
Beyer, William
The trap.—DuR
"**Beyond** the dark trees." Shiki, tr. fr. the Japanese by Harry Behn.—BeCs
"**Beyond** the east the sunrise, beyond the west the sea." See Wander-thirst
"**Beyond** the fence she hesitates." See Midwife cat
"**Beyond** the field where crows cawed at a hawk." See Two lives and others
"**Beyond** the great valley an odd instinctive rising." See Ascent to the Sierras
"**Beyond** the Shining mountains." See September
"**Beyond** the temple." Shiki, tr. fr. the Japanese by Harry Behn.—BeCs
"**Beyond** the turning sea's far foam." See At war
Bhagavad Gita, sels. Unknown, tr. fr. the Sanskrit by P. Lal
Arjuna's paean to Krishna.—AlPi
Who is the man of poise.—AlPi
Bharati, Dharmavir
Evening clouds.—AlPi
Bhartrahari
Good men.—AlPi
Bhavabhuti
The cremation ground.—AlPi
Bialik, H. N.
For Hanukkah.—ArT-3
Bible—Apocrypha
Let us now praise famous men. See Ecclesiasticus
Bible—New Testament
Charity. See First epistle of Paul to the Corinthians
"For God hath not given us the spirit of fear." See Second Timothy
The Lord's prayer. See Gospel according to Matthew
"Whatsoever things are true." See Philippians
Bible—Old Testament
Awake. See The song of Solomon
"But they that wait upon the Lord shall renew their strength." See Isaiah
"Cast thy bread upon the waters." See Ecclesiastes
"Comfort ye, comfort ye my people." See Isaiah

Bible—Old Testament—*Continued*
David's lament. See The second book of Samuel
The earth is the Lord's. See Psalms—Psalm 24
"For, lo, the winter is past." See The song of Solomon—The song of songs
"Hast thou given the horse strength." See Job
"He that is slow to anger is better than the mighty." See Proverbs
The heavens. See Psalms—Psalm 19
"How is the gold become dim." See The lamentations of Jeremiah
"I am the rose of Sharon." See The song of Solomon
Laudate dominum. See Psalms—Psalm 150
The Lord is my shepherd. See Psalms—Psalm 23
"Lord thou hast been our dwelling place." See Psalms—Psalm 90
"Man that is born of a woman." See Job
A merry heart. See Proverbs—"A soft answer turneth away wrath"
"My soul is weary of my life." See Job
"O sing unto the Lord a new song." See Psalms—Psalm 98
Psalm 19. See Psalms
Psalm 23. See Psalms
Psalm 24. See Psalms
Psalm 37. See Psalms
Psalm 90. See Psalms
Psalm 95. See Psalms
Psalm 98. See Psalms
Psalm 100. See Psalms
Psalm 103. See Psalms
Psalm 107. See Psalms
Psalm 136. See Psalms
Psalm 147. See Psalms
Psalm 150. See Psalms
Remember now thy Creator. See Ecclesiastes
"A soft answer turneth away wrath." See Proverbs
The song of songs. See The song of Solomon
They that go down to the sea. See Psalms—Psalm 107
The war horse. See Job—"Hast thou given the horse strength"
"The wolf also shall dwell with the lamb." See Isaiah
Bible characters. See also names of Bible characters, as Adam and Eve
After reading translations of ancient texts on stone and clay. C. Reznikoff.—GrS
Bible stories. L. W. Reese.—ThA
By chapel as I came. Unknown.—GrCt
The confession stone. O. Dodson.—HaK (sel.)
Daniel. V. Lindsay.—GrCt—LiP
The Daniel jazz.—SmM
Peter and John. E. Wylie.—CaMb
Three helpers in battle. M. Coleridge.—PlE
Bible stories. Lizette Woodworth Reese.—ThA
Bickerstaffe, Isaac
An expostulation.—CoBl
Jolly miller. See Love in a village
Love in a village, sel.
Jolly miller.—BrMg
"There was a jolly miller once."—OpF—WiMg
"There was a jolly miller once." See Love in a village—Jolly miller
Bicycalamity. Edmund W. Peters.—MoS
The **bicycle.** Jerzy Harasymowicz, tr. fr. the Polish by Edmund Ordon.—DuS
Bicycles and bicycling
Bicycalamity. E. W. Peters.—MoS
The bicycle. J. Harasymowicz.—DuS
Bicycles. A. Voznesensky.—LiT
A certain age. P. McGinley.—DuS
Different bicycles. D. W. Baruch.—ArT-3
On a bicycle. Y. Yevtushenko.—LiT (sel.)
Bicycles. Andrei Voznesensky, tr. fr. the Russian by Anselm Hollo.—LiT
"The **bicycles** lie." See Bicycles
Biddy. Fred Lape.—CoB
Big Bear and Little Bear. Eleanor Farjeon.—FaT
"The **big** blue-jean, the summer-bored boy next door." See Carry me back
The **big** boy. See "When I was a little boy (my mammy)"
The **big** clock. Unknown.—ArT-3
Big dam. W. R. Moses.—BrA
Big Goliath, little David. Eve Merriam.—MeC
"A **big** Jack, cutting outward toward blue." See Growing up
Big little boy. Eve Merriam.—MeC
The **big** nasturtiums. Robert Beverly Hale.—CoBn
"The **big** rat said to the little rats." See Pioneer rat
The **big** Rock Candy mountains. Unknown.—GrCt
"**Big** trucks with apples." See Country trucks
Big wind. Theodore Roethke.—BoGj
"A **big** young bareheaded woman." See Proletarian portrait
Bilhana
"Even now." See Fifty stanzas for a thief
Fifty stanzas for a thief, sel.
"Even now."—AlPi
"**Billy** boy Blue, come blow me your horn." See "Little Boy Blue, come blow your horn"
Billy Taylor. Unknown.—ReOn
"**Billy** Taylor's a jolly sailor." See Billy Taylor
Billy the Kid.—Unknown.—HiL
Bingham, Sally
Awaken.—LeM
Binker. A. A. Milne.—MiC
"**Binker**—what I call him—is a secret of my own." See Binker
Binsey poplars felled 1879. Gerard Manley Hopkins.—CoBn
Binyon, Laurence
Bab-Lock-Hythe.—MoS
"The **birch** begins to crack its outer sheath." See A young birch
Birch trees
The spirit of the birch. A. Ketchum.—ThA

A young birch. R. Frost.—CoBn
A **bird.** See "A bird came down the walk"
"A **bird.**" See A living
The **bird** ("As poor old Goode") Walter De La Mare.—DeBg
The **bird** ("O clear and musical") Elinor Wylie. —McWs
Bird cage, sel. Theodore Roethke
The heron.—CoB—HoL—LaPd—ReBs
"A **bird** came down the walk." Emily Dickinson.—ArT-3—BoGj—CoB—DiL—DiPe—LaP —LaPd—TuW
A bird.—BrSg—HuS-3
"**Bird** cries, bird-threshings." See Squirrel with jays
"A **bird** flies and has wings." See Birds
"A **bird** in the air, a fish in the sea." Mother Goose.—OpF
"The **bird** is lost." See Yardbird's skull
The **bird-man.** William Henry Davies.—SmM
The **bird** of night. Randall Jarrell.—ReBs
"**Bird** of the wilderness." See The skylark
A **bird** song in the ravine. Wang Wei, tr. fr. the Chinese by Arthur Christy.—LeMw
"The **bird-song** is the echo of the morning light." Rabindranath Tagore.—LeMf
Bird talk. Aileen Fisher.—HoB
Bird thou never wert. Peggy Bennett.—CoB
"The **bird** wishes it were a cloud." Rabindranath Tagore.—LeMf
The **birdcage.** Conrad Aiken.—ReBs
"A **birdie** with a yellow bill." See Time to rise
Birds. See also names of birds, as Robins
Albert. D. Abse.—SmM
The angler's reveille. H. Van Dyke.—HuS-3
Any bird. I. Orleans.—BrSg
As when emotion too far exceeds its cause. G. C. Oden.—BoA—HaK
"At half-past three a single bird." E. Dickinson.—DiPe
Augury. S. George.—GrS
Autumn birds. J. Clare.—ReO
Be like the bird. V. Hugo.—ArT-3
"Be still, my child." Unknown.—DoC—LeO
Beau's reply. W. Cowper.—ReO
The bird ("As poor old Goodie") W. De La Mare.—DeBg
The bird ("O clear and musical") E. Wylie.—McWs
"A bird came down the walk." E Dickinson.—ArT-3—BoGj—CoB—DiL—DiPe—LaP—LaPd—TuW
A bird.—BrSg—HuS-3
The bird-man. W. H. Davies.—SmM
A bird song in the ravine. Wang Wei.—LeMw
"The bird-song is the echo of the morning light." R. Tagore.—LeMf
Bird talk. A. Fisher.—HoB
"The bird wishes it were a cloud." R. Tagore. —LeMf
The birdcage. C. Aiken.—ReBs
"Birds." L. Kitagaki.—BaH
Birds ("A bird flies and has wings.") R. Fabrizio.—SmM
The birds ("One day I saw some birds") R. Vasquez.—BaH
Birds asleep. M. C. Livingston.—LiC
Birds at winter nightfall. T. Hardy.—ReBs
A bird's epitaph. M. Armstrong.—ReBs
Birds in the fens. From Polyolbion. M. Drayton.—GrCt
Birds in the garden. Unknown.—StF
The birds know. E. Farjeon.—FaA
Birds must sing. A. Rye.—SmM
The birds of America. J. Broughton.—BrA
The birds of the air. Mother Goose..—ReOn
Birds on a stone. Mother Goose.—ReOn
Two birds.—BrMg
The blind man. A. Young.—ReBs
The blinded bird. T. Hardy.—CoB—PlE
The blossom. W. Blake.—BlP—BoGj
The border bird. W. De La Mare.—DeBg
The bugle-billed bazoo. J. Ciardi.—HoB
Cape Ann. From Landscapes. T. S. Eliot.—BoGj—CaD—HoL
Ceremony. H. Behn.—BeG
Come, come away. From The merry beggars. R. Brome.—ReBs
"The common cormorant or shag." Unknown. —BlO—GrCt
The common cormorant.—SmM
Dawn. G. Bottomley.—ReBs
Dead and gone. A. Thwaite.—CaD
A dead bird. From A summer wish. A. Young. —CoB
Death of a bird. J. Silkin.—CaD
December bird. A. Fisher.—LaPh
The dodo. H. Belloc.—GrCt
The echoing cliff. A. Young.—ReBs
The falcon. E. Wylie.—HaL
The feather. W. De La Mare.—DeBg
The flight of birds. J. Clare.—CoB
The flying fish. J. Gray.—GrCt
"Follow, follow, follow." J. Stephens.—StS
Forgive my guilt. R. P. T. Coffin.—DuR
Four birds. Unknown.—GrCt
Hail, Bishop Valentine. From An epithalamium on the Lady Elizabeth and Count Palatine being married on St Valentine's day. J. Donne.—GrCt
The hoopee. J. Becker.—CoB
"The hototogisu is singing." Issa.—IsF
How many birds. Unknown.—ReOn
How to paint the portrait of a bird. J. Prévert.—SmM
"I bear, in sign of love." From Shepherdess' valentine. F. Andrewes.—ReBs
"I cleaned." Issa.—IsF
" I heard a bird sing." O. Herford.—ArT-3—CoB—LaP—LaPd—ThA
"I know the trusty almanac." From May-day. R. W. Emerson.—ReBs
"I like the birds because." Z. White.—BaH
In Glencullen. J. M. Synge.—ReBs
In praise of May. Unknown.—ReBs

Birds—*Continued*
"In the evening glow." K. Mizumura.—MiI
Joe. D. McCord.—ArT-3—HoB—McE
John James Audubon. R. C. and S. V. Benét. —HiL
King David. W. De La Mare.—LiT
Lady lost. J. C. Ransom.—ReO
"Let us go, then, exploring." V. Woolf.—CoBn
The liberator. Wu-ti.—ReBs
"Little bird flitting." Bashō.—BeCs
"A little green bird sat on a fence rail." Mother Goose
Mother Goose rhymes, 22.—HoB
A little morning music. D. Schwartz.—CoBn
Little Trotty Wagtail. J. Clare.—BlO
A living. D. H. Lawrence.—CoB
Looking for a sunset bird in winter. R. Frost. —ReBs
The making of birds. K. Tynan.—ReBs
Midsummer. S. H. Calverley.—ReBs
A minor bird. R. Frost.—HaL
Misconceptions. R. Browning.—BrP
"Mossy clear water." Issa.—LeOw
"Most she touched me by her muteness." E. Dickinson.—ReBs
The nonny. J. Reeves.—CoB
"Now—more near ourselves than we." E. E. Cummings.—WeP
On a spaniel, called Beau, killing a young bird. W. Cowper.—ReO
"Once I saw a little bird." Mother Goose.—HuS-3
The ousel cock. From A midsummer-night's dream. W. Shakespeare.—SmM
"Out in the marsh reeds." Tsurayuki.—BaS
Overtones. W. A. Percy.—BoH
"People buy a lot of things." A. Wynne.—LaPd
Playing with a pet bird. K. Fraser.—FrS
"Poor bird." W. De La Mare.—DeBg
"Quickly fly away." Issa.—IsF
The rivals. J. Stephens.—ReBs—StS—ThA
"The saddest noise, the sweetest noise." E. Dickinson.—ClF (sel.)
The sermon of St Francis. H. W. Longfellow. —LoPl
The serpent. T. Roethke.—LiT
"Sing in the silent sky." C. G. Rossetti.—ReBs
"Sitting." T. N. Tsosie.—BaH
Small birds. P. Quennell.—ReBs
The snow lies light. W. W. Christman.—ReBs (sel.)
"So by chance it may be you've not heard." D. McCord.—BrLl
Song. From The bride's tragedy. T. L. Beddoes.—ReBs
The soul of birds. P. Mitra.—AlPi
"Startled." Saigyo Hōshi.—BaS
Stay-at-homes. A. Fisher.—FiI
The storm. W. De La Mare.—DeBg
Stupidity street. R. Hodgson.—CoB—HaL—LaPd—ThA
Sympathy. P. L. Dunbar.—AdIa—BoA
Telegraph poles. P. Dehn.—SmM
Ten little dicky-birds. A. W. I. Baldwin.—StF
"There once was an old man who said, Hush." E. Lear.—BrLl
"There was a fat man of Bombay." Mother Goose
Mother Goose rhymes, 46.—HoB
"There was an old man in a tree (whose whiskers)." E. Lear.—BrLl
"There was an old man on whose nose." E. Lear
Limericks.—HoB
"There was an old man who said, Hush." E. Lear.—BrLl
Limericks.—BoGj
Nonsense verses.—HuS-3
The three singing birds. J. Reeves.—LaPd
Time to rise. R. L. Stevenson.—HoB—HuS-3
Tiny Eenanennika. W. De La Mare.—DeBg
Tom's sleeping song. From Jonathan Gentry. M. Van Doren.—HaL
The tree of life. Unknown.—ReBs
Two birds flying. Unknown.—DePp
Two guests from Alabama. From Out of the cradle endlessly rocking. W. Whitman.—ReO
"Two little dicky birds." Mother Goose.—WiMg
"Walking." T. N. Tsosie.—BaH
"Washing my rice hoe." Buson.—BeCs
"The waterfowl." Ginkō.—LeMw
"A wee bird sat upon a tree." Unknown.—MoB
What bird so sings. J. Lyly.—BlO
"When I was a little girl (about seven years old)." Mother Goose.—SmM
A little girl.—BrMg
"When I was a wee thing." Unknown.—MoB
The white bird. H. Chattopadhyaya.—AlPi
"Why chidest thou the tardy spring." From May-day. R. W. Emerson.—ReBs
Why the owl wakes at night. P. McGinley.—McWc
"A widow bird sate mourning for her love." From Charles IV. P. B. Shelley.—BlO
Song from Charles IV.—SmM
"Will it go crying." Furubito.—BaS
"The wind was once a man." Unknown.—LeO
Winter feast. F. M. Frost.—BrSg
Winter song. J. R. Jiménez.—LiT
Yardbird's skull. O. Dodson.—AdIa—BoA
The yellow bird. Unknown.—ReBs
The zobo bird. F. A. Collymore.—BoGj

Birds—Eggs and nests
The bird's nest. J. Drinkwater.—HuS-3—LaPd
Birds' nests. J. Clare.—ReBs
The brown thrush. L. Larcom.—HoB
"The common cormorant or shag." Unknown. —BlO—GrCt
The common cormorant.—SmM
The dove's song. Unknown.—StF
The emperor's bird's-nest. H. W. Longfellow. —ReBs
Fifty faggots. E. Thomas.—ThG
"I have found out a gift for my fair." From A pastoral ballad. W. Shenstone.—ReBs

"In this fleeting world." Issa.—LeOw
"November bares the robin's nest." D. McCord.—McAd
The robin and the wren. Unknown.—BlO
The secret. Unknown.—ArT-3—HoB
"The swallows are homing." E. Farjeon.—FaA
Talents differ. L. E. Richards.—ArT-3
"Tammy, Tammy Titmouse." Unknown.—MoB
"There was an old man with a beard." E. Lear.—ArT-3—BrLl—GrCt—LaPd
Limericks.—HoB
Nonsense verses.—HuS-3
The two nests. From Childhood. F. Carlin.—ReBs
"Wee chookie birdie." Unknown.—MoB
What robin told. G. Cooper.—ArT-3
Who stole the nest. L. M. Child.—StF
Within the bush. From A rose-bud, by my early walk. R. Burns.—ReBs
Birds—Migration
August 28. D. McCord.—McE
Children of the wind. From The people, yes. C. Sandburg.—HuS-3
These children of the wind.—ReBs
Fall. S. Andresen.—DuR
Going south so soon. A. Fisher.—FiC
The last word of a bluebird. R. Frost.—ArT-3—BoGj—HuS-3—TuW
On the wing. A. Fisher.—FiI
"Something told the wild geese." R. Field.—ArT-3—CoB—HoL—HuS-3—LaPd—SmM—TuW
When snow will come. E. J. Coatsworth.—CoSb
Wild geese. E. Chipp.—ArT-3
"The wild geese returning." Tsumori Kunimoto.—BaS—LaPd—LeMw
Wild goose. C. Heath.—DuR
"**Birds**." Lynn Kitagaki.—BaH
Birds ("A bird flies and has wings") Ray Fabrizio.—SmM
The **birds** ("One day I saw some birds") Rosalia Vasquez.—BaH
"**Birds** are flying past me." Debra Fong.—BaH
"The **birds** are gone to bed, the cows are still." See Hares at play
"The **birds** are singing music." Desmond Garton.—LeM
Birds asleep. Myra Cohn Livingston.—LiC
Birds at winter nightfall. Thomas Hardy.—ReBs
A **bird's** epitaph. Martin Armstrong.—ReBs
"The **birds** go fluttering in the air." See The silent snake
"The **birds** have all flown." See November
"The **birds** have hid, the winds are low." See Evening
Birds in the fens. See Polyolbion
"The **birds** in the first light twitter and whistle." See A little morning music
Birds in the garden. Unknown.—StF
The **birds** know. Eleanor Farjeon.—FaA
"The **birds** know.—You can hear they know." See The birds know
Birds must sing. Anthony Rye.—SmM
The **bird's** nest. John Drinkwater.—HuS-3—LaPd
Birds' nests. John Clare.—ReBs
"**Birds** of a feather flock together." Mother Goose.—ReMg
The **birds** of America. James Broughton.—BrA
Birds of paradise
The birds of paradise. J. P. Bishop.—BoGj
The captive bird of paradise. R. Pitter.—GrS
The **birds** of paradise. John Peale Bishop.—BoGj
Birds of passage, sel. Henry Wadsworth Longfellow
The leap of Roushan Beg.—HuS-3
The **birds** of the air. Mother Goose.—ReOn
Birds on a stone. Mother Goose.—ReOn
Two birds.—BrMg
Birkett's eagle. Dorothy S. Howard.—CaMb
Birney, Earle
David.—DuS
Québec May.—DoW
Birth. See also Birthdays
"The angel that presided o'er my birth." W. Blake.—BlP
"An autumn evening (it is)." Issa.—LeOw
"The babies are born." M. Bryant.—BaH
Birth of Henri Quatre. E. J. Coatsworth.—CoDh
Birthplace revisited. G. Corso.—LaC
The cabin. E. J. Coatsworth.—CoDh
The evil eye. J. Ciardi.—CaMb
"Highlandman, Highlandman." Unknown.—MoB
An Irish legend. P. McGinley.—McWc
"Little lad, little lad." Mother Goose.—GrT—TuW
Look, Edwin. E. St V. Millay.—BoGj
The phoenix self-born. From Metamorphoses. Ovid.—GrCt
Sea born. H. Vinal.—BoH
Birth of Henri Quatre. Elizabeth Jane Coatsworth.—CoDh
A **birthday** ("My heart is like a singing bird") Christina Georgina Rossetti.—BlO—CoBl
Birthday ("The next best thing to Christmas") Aileen Fisher.—FiIo
The **birthday** ("On Christmas eve, some say") Phyllis McGinley.—McWc
Birthday book. Sale Barker.—GrCt (sels.)
The **birthday** bus. Mary Ann Hoberman.—ArT-3
Birthday cake. Aileen Fisher.—LaPd
The **birthday** child. Rose Fyleman.—LaPh
Birthday party. Elizabeth Jane Coatsworth.—CoDh
Birthday present. Aileen Fisher.—FiC
Birthdays
An April child. Unknown.—DePp
A birthday ("My heart is like a singing bird") C. G. Rossetti.—BlO—CoBl
Birthday ("The next best thing to Christmas") A. Fisher.—FiIo
Birthday book. S. Barker.—GrCt (sels.)
The birthday bus. M. A. Hoberman.—ArT-3
Birthday cake. A. Fisher.—LaPd
The birthday child. R. Fyleman.—LaPh
Birthday party. E. J. Coatsworth.—CoDh

The **blackbird** ("In the far corner") Humbert Wolfe.—ArT-3—BoGj—HuS-3
The **blackbird** ("O blackbird, sing me something well") Alfred Tennyson.—TeP
The **blackbird** by Belfast lough. Unknown, tr. fr. the Irish by Frank O'Connor.—ReBs
A **blackbird** singing. R. S. Thomas.—CoB
A **blackbird** suddenly. Joseph Auslander.—ArT-3—TuW
Blackbirds
"A I went over the water." Mother Goose.—SmM
Two little blackbirds.—BrMg
The blackbird ("In the far corner") H. Wolfe.—ArT-3—BoGj—HuS-3
The blackbird ("O blackbird, sing me something well") A. Tennyson.—TeP
The blackbird by Belfast lough. Unknown.—ReBs
A blackbird singing. R. S. Thomas.—CoB
A blackbird suddenly. J. Auslander.—ArT-3—TuW
Blackbirds. W. De La Mare.—DeBg
Dead and gone. A. Thwaite.—CaD
O what if the fowler. C. Dalmon.—CoB—ReBs
"Sing a song of sixpence." Mother Goose.—BrF—BrMg—HuS-3—OpF—SmM—WiMg
Mother Goose rhymes, 61.—HoB
Vespers. T. E. Brown.—CoB
The white blackbirds. E. Farjeon.—FaA
Blackbirds. Walter De La Mare.—DeBg
Blackburn, Paul
The stone.—DuS
Blackburn, Thomas
Ganga.—CaMb
Jonah.—CaD
"**Blackened** and bleeding, helpless, panting, prone." See Chicago
Blackfeet Indians. See Indians of the Americas—Blackfeet
The **Blackfoot** chieftains. Harry Behn.—BeG
"**Blackman.**" See Why prejudice
Blackout. Arthur Gregor.—GrS
The **blacksmith.** Mother Goose.—ReOn
Blacksmiths and blacksmithing
The blacksmith. Mother Goose.—ReOn
Felix Randal. G. M. Hopkins.—CoR
"An old dame to the blacksmith went." Unknown.—VrF
"Pitty Patty Polt." Mother Goose.—StF
The unemployed blacksmith. J. Woods.—McWs
The village blacksmith. H. W. Longfellow.—HuS-3—LoPl—TuW
Blacktail deer. Lew Sarett.—CoB
"The **blacktail** held his tawny marble pose." See Blacktail deer
Blackthorn. Mother Goose.—ReOn
"**Blackthorn,** blackthorn." See Blackthorn
Blackwell, Arlene
"What if this world was full of happiness."—BaH
Blackwell, Elizabeth (about)
Elizabeth Blackwell. E. Merriam.—MeIv
Blackwell, Harriet Gray
Hill people.—BrA
Blades, Leslie B.
Out of blindness.—DuS
Blake, Teddy
"Life."—BaH
Blake, William
Ah, sun-flower.—BlP
The sun-flower.—GrCt
America.—BlP (sel.)
"And did those feet in ancient time." See Milton
The angel.—BlP
"The angel that presided o'er my birth."—BlP
An answer to the parson.—BlP
"Are not the joys of morning sweeter."—BlP
Auguries of innocence.—BlP—CoB (sel.)—SmM (sel.)
"Awake, awake, my little boy." See The land of dreams
The blossom.—BlP—BoGj
The book of Thel.—BlP (sel.)
Thel's motto.—GrCt (sel.)
"The caverns of the grave I've seen."—BlP
The chimney sweeper ("A little black thing among the snow")—BlP
The chimney sweeper ("When my mother died I was very young")—BlP
The clod and the pebble.—BlP
A cradle song ("Sleep, sleep, beauty bright")—BlP
A cradle song ("Sweet dreams, form a shade")—BlP
Cromek speaks.—BlP
The crystal cabinet.—BlP
Dedication of the illustrations to Blair's grave.—BlP—GrCt
A divine image ("Cruelty has a human heart")—BlP—GrCt
The divine image ("To mercy, pity, peace, and love" —BlP
A dream.—BlP—ReO
Earth's answer.—BlP
The ecchoing green.—BlP
Enitharmon's song. See Vala
Eternity.—BlP
Ethinthus, queen of waters. See Europe
Europe, sel.
Ethinthus, queen of waters.—GrCt
The everlasting gospel.—BlP (sel.)
The fly.—BlO—BlP
The four Zoas.—BlP (sel.)
The garden of love.—BlP
The golden net.—GrS
"Great things are done when men and mountains meet."—BlP
The grey monk.—BlP
Holy Thursday ("Is this a holy thing to see")—BlP
Holy Thursday ("'Twas on a Holy Thursday, their innocent faces clean")—BlP
The human abstract.—BlP

"Why was Cupid a boy."—BlP
The wild flower's song.—BlP
William Bond.—BlP
"You say their pictures well painted be."—BlP
"**Blazing** in gold and quenching in purple." Emily Dickinson.—DiL—DiPe
"**Blazoned** upon the shadows in her stiff gorgeousness." See The infanta
Bleeberrying. Jonathan Denwood.—CaMb
Blennerhassett's island. See The new pastoral
"**Bless** the four corners of this house." See House blessing
"**Bless** the Lord, O my soul." See Psalms—Psalm 103
"**Bless** you, bless you, burnie-bee." Mother Goose. —OpF
"**Blessed** art Thou." See Blessing for light
"**Blessed** art Thou, O God our Lord." See Blessings for Chanukah
A **blessing.** James Wright.—DuS
Blessing for light. Unknown.—ThA
Blessings
Benediction. D. J. Hayes.—BoA
A blessing. J. Wright.—DuS
Blessing for light. Unknown.—ThA
Blessings for Chanukah. J. E. Sampter.—ArT-3
Blessings upon an infant. Unknown.—DoC
"Every morning when I wake." From Under Milk Wood. D. Thomas.—HaL
"God bless the master of this house." Mother Goose.—HuS-3
Christmas carol.—ArT-3
"Saint Francis and Saint Benedight." W. Cartwright.—PlE
A house blessing.—GrCt
"You who cultivate fields." Unknown.—DoC
Blessings for Chanukah. Jessie E. Sampter.—ArT-3
Blessings upon an infant. Unknown.—DoC
Blind
"All but blind." W. De La Mare.—LaPd
The ballad of Billy Rose. L. Norris—CaMb
The blind boy. C. Cibber.—CoR
The blind man. A. Young.—ReBs
The blind men and the elephant. J. G. Saxe. —BoH
"The blind sparrow." Gyôdai.—LeI
The blinded bird. T. Hardy.—CoB—PlE
Mimi's fingers. M. O'Neill.—OnF
On his blindness. J. Milton.—GrCt
Out of blindness. L. B. Blades.—DuS
A solitude. D. Levertov.—DuS
A visit to the blind asylum. H. S. Horsley.—VrF
The **blind** boy. Colley Cibber.—CoR
The **blind** man. Andrew Young.—ReBs
"**Blind** man, blind man." See Blind man's buff
"A **blind** man. I can stare at him." See A solitude
Blind man's buff ("Blind man, blind man") Mother Goose.—BrMg
Blind man's buff ("Blindman! Blindman! Blundering about") Eleanor Farjeon.—FaT
The **blind** men and the elephant. John Godfrey Saxe.—BoH
"The **blind** sparrow." Gyôdai, tr. fr. the Japanese by R. H. Blyth.—LeI
"**Blind** to all reasoned aim, this furtive folk." See The termites
"**Blind** with love, my daughter." See Pain for a daughter
The **blinded** bird. Thomas Hardy.—CoB—PlE
"**Blindman,** blindman, blundering about." See Blind man's buff
Blindman's buff. Kathleen Fraser.—FrS
Blindman's in. Walter De La Mare.—DeBg
Blok, Alexander
Little catkins.—PlE
"**Block** the cannon; let no trumpet sound." See Sunset horn
The **blood** horse. Barry Cornwall.—CoB
"A **blood-red** bird with one green eye." See Roundelay
The **bloody** conquests of mighty Tamburlaine. See Tamburlaine the Great
The **blossom.** William Blake.—BlP—BoGj
The **blossoming** of love. Dharmakirti, tr. fr. the Sanskrit by Daniel H. H. Ingalls.—AlPi
"The **blossoms** fall like snowflakes." See Butterflies
"**Blow,** blow. The winds are so hoarse they cannot blow." See Storm at sea
"**Blow,** blow, thou winter wind." See As you like it
"**Blow,** blow, what shall I do now." See Afternoon
Blow, bugle, blow. See The princess—The bugle song
Blow me eyes. Wallace Irwin.—CoBl
Blow the stars home. Eleanor Farjeon.—LaPd
"**Blow** the stars home, wind, blow the stars home." See Blow the stars home
Blow trumpet. See Idylls of the king
"**Blow** trumpet, for the world is white with May." See Idylls of the king—Blow trumpet
"**Blow,** wind, blow." See "Blow wind, blow, and go mill, go"
"**Blow,** wind, blow." See Winter night
"**Blow** wind, blow, and go mill, go." Mother Goose.—ArT-3—HuS-3—OpF
"Blow, wind, blow."—BrMg
The windmill.—VrF
"**Blow,** winds, and crack your cheeks, rage, blow." See King Lear—The storm
Blow, ye winds. Unknown.—CoSs
Blow your trumpets, angels. See "At the round earth's imagin'd corners, blow"
Blowing bubbles. See Soap bubbles
Blowing bubbles. Kathleen Fraser.—FrS
Blue (Color)
Blue. C. Lewis.—LeP
Blue flowers. R. Field.—BrSg
The Blue Ridge. H. Monroe.—BoH
Blue winter. R. Francis.—HoL
Little Blue Ben. Mother Goose.—BrMg
What is blue. M. O'Neill.—OnH

Blue. Claudia Lewis.—LeP
The **blue** and the gray. Francis Miles Finch.—HiL
Blue-butterfly day. Robert Frost.—BrSg
"A **blue** day." See March
"**Blue** evening falls." Unknown, tr. fr. the Papago.—LeO
Blue flowers. Rachel Field.—BrSg
Blue girls. John Crowe Ransom.—GrCt—McWs
"**Blue** is the color of the sky." See What is blue
Blue jay. Hilda Conkling.—CoB—ReBs
Blue jays. See Jays
Blue moon butterfly. Paul Williams.—LeM
"**Blue** mountains to the north of the walls." See Taking leave of a friend
The **Blue** Ridge. Harriet Monroe.—BoH
Blue stars and gold. James Stephens.—StS
"**Blue** water . . . a clear moon." Li T'ai-po, tr. fr. the Chinese by Shigeyoshi Obata.—LeMw
Blue winter. Robert Francis.—HoL
Blueberries
Bleeberrying. J. Denwood.—CaMb
In the blueberry bushes. E. J. Coatsworth.—CoSb
The pioneer woman—in the North country. E. Tietjens.—BrA
Bluebird. Aileen Fisher.—FiI
Bluebirds
Autumn bluebirds. A. Fisher.—FiC
Bluebird. A. Fisher.—FiI
The last word of a bluebird. R. Frost.—ArT-3—BoGj—HuS-3—TuW
"**Blues.**" See Get up, blues
Blunden, Edmund
The dog from Malta. See A Maltese dog
The hurrying brook.—CoBn
A Maltese dog. tr.—ArT-3
The dog from Malta. tr.—CoB
The midnight skaters.—BoGj
The pike.—ReO (sel.)
Blunt, Wilfrid Scawen
The old squire.—MoS
Bly, Robert
Driving to town late to mail a letter.—CoBn
Love poem.—CoBl
Blyth, R. H.
"The aged dog." tr.—IsF
"Ah, to be." tr.—IsF—LeOw
"All kinds of cicadas singing." tr.—IsF
"Among the leaves of grass." tr.—LeOw
"As a diversion." tr.—IsF
"As one of us." tr.—LeOw
"As we grow old." tr.—LeOw
"At the altar." tr.—IsF
"At the flower-vase." tr.—IsF
"At the morning exhibition." tr.—IsF
"The autumn breeze." tr.—LeOw
"The autumn breeze is blowing." tr.—LeMw
"An autumn evening (it is)." tr.—LeOw
"An autumn evening (a man)." tr.—LeOw
"The autumn moon." tr.—IsF
"The autumn wind (there are)." tr.—LeOw
"The bat." tr.—LeI
"Be a good boy." tr.—LeOw
"A beautiful kite." tr.—IsF—LeOw
"The beggar on the bridge also." tr.—IsF
"The blind sparrow." tr.—LeI
"A butterfly came." tr.—LeOw
"By the light of the next room." tr.—LeOw
"The cherry-blossoms (they have)." tr.—IsF
"A chestnut falls." tr.—LeMw
"The chicken." tr.—LeI
"The child sobs." tr.—IsF—LeOw
"The child sways on the swing." tr.—LeMw
"Children are the children of the wind." tr.—LeMw
"Click, clack." tr.—LeOw
"Come and play with me." tr.—LeOw
"Coming along the mountain path." tr.—LeMw
"The cool breeze." tr.—IsF—LeOw
"The coolness." tr.—LeOw
"The crow." tr.—IsF
"A day of spring." tr.—LeI
"The dogs." tr.—IsF
"The dragon-fly." tr.—IsF
"Each time a wave breaks." tr.—LeMw
"The ears of barley, too." tr.—IsF
"Even among insects, in this world." tr.—IsF
"Even on a small island." tr.—IsF
"An exhausted sparrow," tr.—IsF—LeOw
"The face of the dragonfly." tr.—LeMw
"The feeble plant." tr.—LeOw
"The fireflies flit." tr.—IsF
"The first firefly (it was off)." tr.—LeOw
"The first firefly (why do you)." tr.—IsF
"A flash of lightning." tr.—LeI
"The flying butterfly." tr.—IsF
"For you fleas too." tr.—IsF
"The frog." tr.—LeI
"Frogs squatting this way." tr.—IsF
"The full moon." tr.—LeOw
"Getting colder." tr.—LeOw
"Grasshopper (be the keeper)." tr.—IsF
"Grasshopper (do not trample)." tr.—LeI
"Hail." tr.—LeMw
"Helter-skelter." tr.—IsF
"The hototogisu is singing." tr.—IsF
"How happy, how affectionate they are." tr.—LeOw
"How lovely." tr.—LeI—LeMw
"How much." tr.—LeOw
"I borrowed my cottage." tr.—IsF
"I could eat it." tr.—LeMw
"If only she were here." tr.—LeOw
"If you are tender to them." tr.—IsF
"I'm going to turn over." tr.—IsF
"In my old age." tr.—LeOw
"In our house." tr.—IsF—LeOw
"In the dawn of day." tr.—IsF
"In the wintry grove." tr.—LeOw
"Insects on a bough." tr.—IsF
"I've just come from a place." tr.—LeI
"Just being here." tr.—IsF—LeOw
"Just simply alive." tr.—LeI
"The kingfisher." tr.—LeMw
"Little garden at the gate." tr.—IsF—LeOw
"Little-Plum-Tree village." tr.—IsF
"Little sparrow." tr.—LeOw

"The long night." tr.—LeMw
"Look snail." tr.—IsF—LeOw
"Making his way through the crowd." tr.—IsF —LeOw
"The moon in the water." tr.—LeI
"The moon over the mountains." tr.—IsF
"The mosquitoes." tr.—IsF
"My hut is so small." tr.—IsF
"No doubt the boss." tr.—IsF
"Now I am going out." tr.—LeOw
"O butterfly." tr.—LeMw
"O owl." tr.—IsF
"Off with you." tr.—IsF
"The pampas grass." tr.—LeMw
"The peony." tr.—LeMw
"People are few." tr.—IsF—LeMw
"The puppy asleep." tr.—LeI
"Rain is leaking in." tr.—IsF
"A red morning sky." tr.—LeI
"Round my hut." tr.—LeOw
"The school servant." tr.—LeMw
"Searching for the visitor's shoes." tr.—LeMw
"She has put the child to sleep." tr.—LeOw
"The smoke." tr.—LeOw
"The snail." tr.—IsF
"Spring departing." tr.—LeMw
"Spring rain (everything)." tr.—LeMw
"Steal this one." tr.—IsF
"Stillness." tr.—LeI
"Summer in the world." tr.—LeMw
"The swallow." tr.—LeMw
"Swatted out." tr.—IsF
"That stone." tr.—IsF
"These flowers of the plum." tr.—LeMw
"Throwing them up to the moon." tr.—LeMw
"To wake alive, in this world." tr.—LeMw
"The toad. It looks as if." tr.—LeI
"Under the cherry-blossoms." tr.—IsF
"Visiting the graves." tr.—IsF—LeOw
"Voices." tr.—LeI
"The waterfowl." tr.—LeMw
"We human beings." tr.—IsF
"Well, now, let's be off." tr.—IsF
"What happiness." tr.—LeMw
"Where can he be going." tr.—LeMw
"Whose is it then." tr.—IsF
"Why." tr.—LeMw
"Wild goose, O wild goose." tr.—LeOw
"With that voice." tr.—LeMw
"With the evening breeze." tr.—LeI
"The woodpecker." tr.—LeOw
"The wren." tr.—IsF—LeOw
"You light the fire." tr.—LeMw
Boa constrictor. Shelley Silverstein.—CoO
The **boar.** See Venus and Adonis
The **boar** and the dromedar. Henry Beissel.—DoW
Boars
The boar. From Venus and Adonis. W. Shakespeare.—CoB
The **boat** race. See Aeneid
Boat races. See Races and racing—Boat
"The **boat** sails away, like a bird on the wing." See Sailor's dance
"The **boatman** he can dance and sing." See Dance the boatman
Boats and boating. See also Canoes and canoeing; Ferries; Races and racing—Boat; Ships
Ants and sailboats. D. McCord.—McAd
Bab-Lock-Hythe. L. Binyon.—MoS
Boats. R. B. Bennett.—ArT-3
The boats are afloat. Chu Hsi.—LeMw
A boatwoman. Chao Yeh.—LeMw
Carrying their coracles. From Upon Appleton house. A. Marvell.—GrCt
The coracle. From Pharsalia. Lucan.—GrCt
Crew cut. D. McCord.—MoS
Dance the boatman. Unknown.—HiL
Down the Mississippi. J. G. Fletcher.—BrA (sel.)—PaH
Drifting. T. B. Read.—PaH
East river. R. Thomas.—BrA
Eight oars and a coxswain. A. Guiterman.—MoS
Ezra Shank. Unknown.—BrSm
Ferry-boats. J. S. Tippett.—ArT-3
"Ferry me across the water." C. G. Rossetti. —BoGj—GrCt—LaPd
Fleeing to safety. R. Chettur.—LeM
"A flock of little boats." S. Menashe.—SmM
Freight boats. J. S. Tippett.—HuS-3
I had a boat. M. Coleridge.—SmM
"I may be a boy." K. Mizumura.—MiI
"Idly my ship glides." Otsuji.—BeCs
If only. R. Fyleman.—HuS-3
The Jumblies. E. Lear.—ArT-3—BlO—BoGj—GrCt—HuS-3—SmM
Lost. C. Sandburg.—DuR—LaPd
Morning on the Lièvre. A. Lampman.—MoS
My bed is a boat. R. L. Stevenson.—HuS-3
Offshore. P. Booth.—MoS
Paper boats. R. Tagore.—BoH—ThA
"Puffed by a wind, sails." Kyorai.—BeCs
The rapid. C. Sangster.—DoW
The river boats. D. W. Hicky.—BrA
River night.—F. M. Frost.—LaC
River travel. Ts'ui Hao.—LeMw
"Row, row, row your boat." Unknown.—MoS
Sailboat, your secret. R. Francis.—MoS
Tee-wee's boat. Mother Goose.—BrMg
"There was an old man in a boat." E. Lear.—BrLl
Limericks.—HoB
Vacationer. W. Gibson.—MoS
Where go the boats. R. L. Stevenson.—ArT-3 —BoGj—HoB
Whistles. R. Field.—ArT-3—HuS-3
Young Argonauts. S. Wingfield.—MoS
Boats. Rowena Bastin Bennett.—ArT-3
The **boats** are afloat. Chu Hsi, tr. fr. the Chinese by Kenneth Rexroth.—LeMw
"The **boats** as Van Gogh painted them." See Les Saintes-Maries-de-la-Mer
"**Boats** sail on the rivers." Christina Georgina Rossetti.—ArT-3—HoB—HuS-3
"**Boats** that carry sugar." See Freight boats
A **boatwoman.** Chao Yeh, tr. fr. the Chinese by Teresa Li.—LeMw

"**Bobbie** Shaftoe's gone to sea." See "Bobby Shaftoe's gone to sea"
Bobby Shaftoe. See "Bobby Shaftoe's gone to sea"
"**Bobby** Shaftoe's gone to sea." Mother Goose.—MoB—WiMg
Bobby Shaftoe.—BrMg
Mother Goose rhymes, 1.—HoB
Bobolinks
Robert of Lincoln. W. C. Bryant.—CoB—HoB
Bobwhite. Robert Hillyer.—CoB
Bodenheim, Maxwell
Poet to his love.—CoBl
Body, Human. See also names of parts of body, as Hands
"Being fat." M. C. Livingston.—LiC
Body and spirit. E. J. Coatsworth.—CoDh
"I'd rather have fingers than toes." G. Burgess.—BrLl
Johnny. E. Rounds.—BrSm
The mouth and the body. P. Mwanikih.—LeM
"There once was a girl of New York." C. Monkhouse.—BrLl
"Two deep clear eyes." W. De La Mare.—DeBg
"Your little hands." S. Hoffenstein.—CoBl
Body and spirit. Elizabeth Jane Coatsworth.—CoDh
"The **body** keeps an accurate count of years." See Body and spirit
Bogan, Louise
M., singing.—BoGj
Musician.—BoGj
Question in a field.—HoL
Variation on a sentence.—HoL
"**Bohunkus** would take off his hat, and bow and smile, and things like that." See An Alphabet of famous Goops
Boilleau, Joan
I saw a ghost.—ArT-3
Boker, George Henry
The cruise of the Monitor.—HiL
"**Bold** Lanty was in love, you see, with lively Rosie Carey." See Lanty Leary
Boleyn, Anne
"O death, rock me on sleep." at.—GrCt
Boleyn, Anne (about)
"O death, rock me on sleep." A. Boleyn. at.—GrCt
Boll weevils
The ballad of the boll weevil. Unknown.—HiL
"**Bolt** and bar the front door." See Hallowe'en
"**Bolt** and bar the shutter." See Mad as the mist and snow
Bonac. John Hall Wheelock.—PaH
Bonaparte, Napoleon. See Napoleon Bonaparte I, Emperor of France (about)
Boncho
"How cool cut hay smells."—BeCs
"The red sun sinks low."—BeCs
Bond, Caroline
Cornwall.—LeM
Bond, Horace Julian
The bishop of Atlanta: Ray Charles.—BoA
Bones
At the keyhole. W. De La Mare.—BlO
Bones. W. De La Mare.—BrSm—DuL
Jerry Jones. Unknown.—BrSm
The stone troll. From The hobbit. J. R. R. Tolkien.—LiT
Bones. Walter De La Mare.—BrSm—DuL
"**Bonfire** smoke swirls upward." See Autumn's passing
Bonneville dam
The fish counter at Bonneville. W. Stafford.—BrA
The **bonnie** blue flag. Annie Chambers Ketchum.—HiL
The **bonnie** cravat. Mother Goose.—ArT-3
"**Bonnie** lady." Unknown.—MoB
"**Bonnie** Maggie, braw Maggie." Unknown.—MoB
"The **bonnie** moor-hen." Unknown.—MoB
The **bonny,** bonny owl. See Kenilworth
The **bonny** earl of Moray. Unknown.—BlO
"**Bonny** lass, canny lass." Mother Goose.—OpF
Bonny Saint John. Unknown.—MoB
Bontemps, Arna
A black man talks of reaping.—AdIa—BoA—BoH—HaK
Close your eyes.—BoA—HaK
The daybreakers.—AdIa—BoA
Golgotha is a mountain.—BoA
Idolatry.—BoA
Nocturne at Bethesda.—BoA
Reconnaissance.—BoA—BoH—HaK
Southern mansion.—AdIa—BoA—BrA—HaK
To a young girl leaving the hill country.—HaK
A tree design.—BoH
Bonum omen. Walter De La Mare.—DeBg
Boo moo. David McCord.—McAd
The **book** of Kells. Howard Nemerov.—PlE
Book of the dead, sel. Unknown, tr. fr. the Egyptian by Robert Hillyer
He is like the lotus.—PlE
The **book** of Thel. William Blake.—BlP (sel.)
Thel's motto.—GrCt (sel.)
Book-moth. Unknown, tr. fr. the old English by Charles W. Kennedy.—ReO
The **book-worms.** Robert Burns.—GrCt
Booker T. and W. E. B. Dudley Randall.—HaK
Books. See The prelude. William Wordsworth
Books and reading
Address from the printer to his little readers. Unknown.—VrF
After reading certain books. M. Coleridge.—PlE
Book-moth. Unknown.—ReO
The book-worms. R. Burns.—GrCt
Books. From The prelude. W. Wordsworth.—WoP
"Books fall open." D. McCord.—McAd
The daisy. E. Turner.—VrF
The day is done. H. W. Longfellow.—LoPl
Development. R. Browning.—BrP
The dunce of a kitten. A. and J. Taylor.—VrF
Fairy tale. A. Fisher.—FiIo

"First come was Cherrystones." E. Farjeon.—FaT
Forget it. D. McCord.—McAd
"He ate and drank the precious words." E. Dickinson.—DiPe
"Here in this book, collected for you." W. Cole.—CoBb
I, says the poem. E. Merriam.—ArT-3—MeI
In a spring still not written of. R. Wallace.—CoBn
The land of story-books. R. L. Stevenson.—ArT-3
The new book. E. Turner.—VrF
O leave novéls. R. Burns.—BuPr
On first looking into Chapman's Homer. J. Keats.—CoR—GrCt
Oz. D. McCord.—McAd
Rapid reading. D. McCord.—McAd
Sarah Byng. H. Belloc.—BoGj
"There is an old fellow named Mark." J. M. Flagg.—BrLl
"There is no frigate like a book." E. Dickinson.—BoGj—DiL—DiPe
"This land was white." Mother Goose.—BrMg
"The way I read a letter's—this." E. Dickinson.—DiL
"When the wind and the rain." E. J. Coatsworth.—CoSb
"Who hath a book." W. D. Nesbit.—ArT-3
A world to do. T. Weiss.—GrS
"**Books** fall open." David McCord.—McAd
"**Bookshelves** empty, tables lampless, walls." See Moving
Booman. Mother Goose.—ReOn
"**Booming** thundering sound." See Dancing
Boone, Daniel (about)
Cumberland gap. Unknown.—BrA
Daniel Boone ("Daniel Boone at twenty-one") A. Guiterman.—HuS-3
Daniel Boone ("When Daniel Boone goes by, at night") R. C. and S. V. Benét.—BrA—HoL
Boot and saddle. See Cavalier tunes
"**Boot,** saddle, to horse, and away." See Cavalier tunes—Boot and saddle
Booth, Philip
Crossing.—BrA—DuR
Ego.—DuS
First lesson.—MoS
Green song.—CoBn
Instruction in the art.—MoS
Maine.—BrA
The misery of mechanics.—DuS
Offshore.—MoS
Propeller.—DuS
The round.—CoBn
Booth, William (about)
General William Booth enters into heaven." V. Lindsay.—LiP
"**Booth** led boldly with his big bass drum." See General William Booth enters into heaven
Boots and shoes. See also Shoemakers
The barefoot bat. Unknown.—DePp
Bump. Bang. Bump. J. Ciardi.—CiYk
Choosing shoes. F. Wolfe.—ArT-3—StF
"Cock a doodle doo (my dame)." Mother Goose.—BrMg
"Cock-a-doodle-do."—ReMg
Cock and hen. Unknown.—MoB
"Diddle, diddle, dumpling, my son John." Mother Goose.—HuS-3—OpF—WiMg
Diddle, diddle, dumpling.—BrMg
Mother Goose rhymes, 14.—HoB
Galoshes. R. W. Bacmeister.—ArT-3
Happiness. A. A. Milne.—ArT-3—MiC
"Little Betty Blue." Mother Goose.—GrT—HuS-3—OpF
Moon. Mother Goose.—BrMg
New shoes. A. Wilkins.—ArT-3
Please tell this someone to take care. J. Ciardi.—CiYk
Sale. J. Miles.—DuS
"Searching for the visitor's shoes." Koka.—LeMw
Shoes. T. Robinson.—ArT-3
Skylark. Unknown.—MoB
"There was a young woman of Ayr." Unknown.—BrLl
"There was an old man from Peru." Unknown.—LaPd
"There was an old man of Toulouse." E. Lear.—BrLl
"There was an old woman who lived in a shoe." Mother Goose.—HuS-3—OpF—ReMg—WiMg
Mother Goose rhymes, 52.—HoB
"Two brothers we are." Mother Goose.—BrMg
Velvet shoes. E. Wylie.—ArT-3—BoGj—HuS-3—ThA
"A wandering tribe called the Sioux." Unknown.—BrLl
Borden, Lizzie (about)
Lizzie Borden. Unknown.—BrSm
The **border** bird. Walter De La Mare.—DeBg
Border songs. Lu Lun, tr. fr. the Chinese by Witter Bynner and Kiang Kang-hu.—LeMw
Boredom
Afternoon. M. Stearns.—ArT-3
On Dean Inge. H. Wolfe.—GrCt
Borland, Hal
Caravans.—ThA
"**Born** I was to meet with age." See On himself
"**Born** in a fence-corner." See Tumbling Mustard
"**Born,** nurtured, wedded, prized, within the pale." See La Fayette
"**Born** of the sorrowful of heart." See For Paul Laurence Dunbar
Bose, Buddhadeva
Frogs.—AlPi
Bossidy, John Collins
Boston.—BrA
Boston, Massachusetts
As a plane tree by the water. R. Lowell.—GrS
A ballad of the Boston tea-party. O. W. Holmes.—HiL
Boston. J. C. Bossidy.—BrA

Boston, Massachusetts—*Continued*
A foreigner comes to earth on Boston Common. H. Gregory.—PlE
The new order. P. McGinley.—BrA
So much the worse for Boston. V. Lindsay.—LiP (sel.)
Boston. John Collins Bossidy.—BrA
"A **Boston** boy went out to Yuma." D. D.—BrSm
Boston Charlie. Walt Kelly.—BoGj
The **Bothie** of Tober-na-Vuolich. Arthur Hugh Clough.—CoBn (sel.)
"The **bottle** of perfume that Willie sent." Unknown.—BrLl
Bottles
"Around the rick, around the rick." Mother Goose.—BrMg
Song of the pop-bottlers. M. Bishop.—McWs
Bottomley, Gordon
Dawn.—ReBs
"A louse crept out of my lady's shift."—GrCt
"The **boughs** do shake and the bells do ring." See Harvest
Boughton, Thea
"Fluttering helplessly."—LeM
Bounce ball rhymes. See Play
Bound no'th blues. Langston Hughes.—BoA
"**Bound** to a boy's swift feet, hard blades of steel." See River skater
"**Bound** to my heart as Ixion to the wheel." See Dirge for the new sunrise
The **Bourbons** at Naples. Elizabeth Jane Coatsworth.—CoDh
Bourinot, Arthur S.
A legend of Paul Bunyan.—BrA
"**Bourtree,** bourtree, crookit rung." See The elder tree
Borie, Smith Palmer
The chariot race. See The Georgics
The Georgics, sel.
The chariot race. tr.—MoS
"**Bow** down my soul in worship very low." See St Isaac's church, Petrograd
Bow-wow. Mother Goose.—BrMg
"**Bow-wow,** says the dog." See Bow-wow
"**Bow** wow, wow." Mother Goose.—ArT-3—HuS-3—OpF
Tom Tinker's dog.—BrMg
"**Bowed** by the weight of centuries he leans." See The man with the hoe
Bowl away. Kate Greenaway.—GrT
"**Bowl** away. Bowl away." See Bowl away
Bowles, W. L.
The greenwood.—ClF (sel.)
Bowling
"O, I say, you Joe." From Songs from an island in the moon. W. Blake.—LiT
Bowra, C. M.
Earth and sky. tr.—PlE
Bows and arrows
The arrow and the song. H. W. Longfellow.—LoPl
Crooked-heart. J. Stephens.—StS
"I have no wings, but yet I fly." M. Austin
Rhyming riddles.—ArT-3
"Jack, Jack Joe." Mother Goose.—OpF
"My bow, its lower part, I drew back." Unknown.—LeO
Prayer to the moon. Unknown.—LeO
"Robin-a-Bobbin." Mother Goose.—BrMg
"Robin-a-Bobin bent his bow."—ReMg
The **box.** Myra Cohn Livingston.—LiC
Boxer. Joseph P. Clancy.—MoS
The **boxer's** face. Lucilius, tr. fr. the Latin by Humbert Wolfe.—MoS
Boxing
The ballad of Billy Rose. L. Norris.—CaMb
Boxer. J. P. Clancy.—MoS
The boxer's face. Lucilius.—MoS
The boxing match. From Aeneid. Virgil.—MoS
The fancy. W. R. Benét.—MoS
First fight. V. Scannell.—SmM
Gallantly within the ring. J. H. Reynolds.—MoS
The nonpareil's grave.—M. J. McMahon.—MoS
On Hurricane Jackson. A. Dugan.—MoS
The world's worst boxer. Lucilius.—MoS
The **boxing** match. See Aeneid
"A **boy.**" See In praise of Johnny Appleseed
A **boy** ("A boy tried to get killed") Benny Graves.—LeM
The **boy** ("I want to become like one of those") Rainer Maria Rilke, tr. fr. the German by M. D. Herter Norton; and by J. B. Leishman.—LiT—SmM
The **boy** and the frogs. Richard Scrafton Sharpe.—VrF
"A **boy** at Sault Ste Marie." Unknown.—BrLl
Boy Blue. See "Little Boy Blue, come blow your horn"
"The **boy** climbed up into the tree." See The rescue
The **boy** fishing. E. J. Scovell.—ClF—SmM
Boy in a pond. See The runaway
The **boy** in the barn. Herbert Read.—CaD
Boy into heron. Celia Randall.—SmM
A **boy** looking at big David. May Swenson.—LiT
"The **boy** stood in the supper-room." Unknown.—CoO
"**Boy,** the giant beauty." See Instruction in the art
"A **boy** tried to get killed." See A boy
A **boy** went walking. Unknown.—StF
The **boy** who laughed at Santa Claus. Ogden Nash.—CoBb
"A **boy** who played tunes on a comb." Unknown.—BrLl
Boy with frogs. Sy Kahn.—DuR
Boy with his hair cut short. Muriel Rukeyser.—CoR
The **boy** with the little bare toes. Frederick William Harvey.—StF
Boyd, Thomas
Love on the mountain.—CoBl
Boyden, Polly Chase
Mud.—ArT-3
New Mexico.—ArT-3
Boyhood. See Boys and boyhood

Boylan, Robert
Wild West.—DuS
Boys and boyhood. See also Babies; Childhood recollections; Children and childhood
Aubade: Dick the donkey boy. O. Sitwell.—CaD
Boy in a pond. From The runaway. J. Whaler.—ReO
The boy in the barn. H. Read.—CaD
The boy with the little bare toes. F. W. Harvey.—StF
Boys' names. E. Farjeon.—ArT-3
A boy's place. R. Burgunder.—LaPd
A boy's song. J. Hogg.—BlO
Come to think of it. J. Ciardi.—CiYk
Farm child. R. S. Thomas.—CaD—CoBn
"I am a nice nice boy." M. O'Connor.—LeM
"I may be a boy." K. Mizumura.—MiI
Kansas boy. R. Lechlitner.—BrA—DuR
The little boy found. W. Blake.—BlP
The little boy lost ("Father, father where are you going") W. Blake.—BlP
A little boy lost ("Nought loves another as itself") W. Blake.—BlP
Little boys of Texas. R. P. T. Coffin.—BrSm
Me, Alexander Soames. K. Kuskin.—ArT-3
Someone was up in that tree. J. Ciardi.—CiYk
Son. J. A. Emanuel.—BoH
Timothy Winters. C. Causley.—SmM
Two Indian boys. J. L. Concha.—BaH
"What are little boys made of." Mother Goose.—OpF—ReMg—WiMg
Boys and girls.—BrMg
Mother Goose rhymes, 10—HoB
"When I was a little boy (my mammy)." Mother Goose.—OpF—TuW
The big boy.—BrMg
Wishes. K. Greenaway.—GrT—HoB
Boys and girls. See "What are little boys made of"
"**Boys** and girls come out to play." See "Girls and boys, come out to play"
The **boys** and the apple-tree. Ann and Jane Taylor.—GrT
"**Boys** like puppets dangling." See Spring is a looping-free time
Boys' names. Eleanor Farjeon.—ArT-3
A **boy**'s place. Rose Burgunder.—LaPd
A **boy**'s song. James Hogg.—BlO
"**Braced** against the rise and fall of ocean." See Korea bound, 1952
Bracker, Milton
Ballade of a zoo buff.—CoB
The umpire.—MoS
Where, O where.—MoS
"A **brackish** reach of shoal off Madaket." See The Quaker graveyard in Nantucket
Braddock, Edward (about)
Braddock's fate, with an incitement to revenge. S. Tilden.—HiL
Braddock's fate, with an incitement to revenge Stephen Tilden.—HiL
Brahma. Ralph Waldo Emerson.—PlE
Brahms, Johannes (about)
"A modern composer named Brahms." Unknown.—BrLl
Brain
"The brain is wider than the sky." E. Dickinson.—DiL—DiPe
"The brain within its groove." E. Dickinson.—DiPe
My brain. A. Laurance.—LeM
"There was a young man at the War Office." J. W. Churton.—BrLl
"The **brain** is wider than the sky." Emily Dickinson.—DiL—DiPe
"The **brain** within its groove." Emily Dickinson.—DiPe
Braithwaite, William Stanley
Rhapsody.—BoA—BoH
Scintilla.—BoA
Braley, Berton
"Young Frankenstein's robot invention."—BrLl
Branch, Anna Hempstead
Connecticut road song.—PaH
Song for my mother.—ArT-3
"A **branch** of willow." Issa, tr. fr. the Japanese by Nobuyuki Yuasa.—IsF
"The **brandish't** sword of God before them blazed." See Paradise lost—Expulsion from Paradise
Brandy hill. Mother Goose.—ReOn
Brasier, Virginia
Generosity.—HuS-3
Heartbeat of democracy.—HuS-3
Primer of consequences.—BrSm
Psychological prediction.—CoBb
Wind weather.—HuS-3
"The **brass** band blares." See Circus
Brass spittoons. Langston Hughes.—BoA
"**Brave** flowers, that I could gallant it like you." See A contemplation upon flowers
The **brave** man. Wallace Stevens.—LiT
"**Brave** news is come to town." Mother Goose.—OpF
"Braw news is come to town."—MoB
Jemmy Dawson.—BrMg
The **brave** old duke of York. See "Oh, the brave old duke of York"
The **brave** priest. Mother Goose.—BrMg
Brave Rover. Max Beerbohm.—ReO
Brave Wolfe. Unknown.—HiL
Bravery. See Courage
"**Braw** news is come to town." See "Brave news is come to town"
The **braw** wooer. Robert Burns.—BuPr
Brazil
Brazilian happenings. R. O'Connell.—DuS
A private letter to Brazil. G. C. Oden.—BoA—HaK
Rolling down to Rio. R. Kipling.—PaH
Brazilian happenings. Richard O'Connell.—DuS
Bread
Bread and cherries. W. De La Mare.—BrSg
A charm. R. Herrick.—GrCt
"Hot cross buns." Mother Goose.—WiMg
Good Friday.—BrMg

Bread—*Continued*
The loaves. R. Everson.—DoW
Sing-song. C. G. Rossetti.—StF
The toaster. W. J. Smith.—AgH—ArT-3—DuR
Bread and cherries. Walter De La Mare.—BrSg
"**Bread** and milk for breakfast." See Sing-song
"**Break**, break, break." Alfred Tennyson.—BlO—BoGj—TeP
Breakfast
Before breakfast ("I went out in the early morning") E. J. Coatsworth.—CoSb
Before breakfast ("Mother has to comb her hair") A. Fisher.—FiIo
Breakfast. E. Farjeon.—AgH
Breakfast and puss. A. and J. Taylor.—VrF
Clover for breakfast. F. M. Frost.—HuS-3
The king's breakfast. A. A. Milne.—MiC
Mummy slept late and daddy fixed breakfast. J. Ciardi.—ArT-3—LaPd
No breakfast for Growler. A. and J. Taylor.—VrF
Sing-song. C. G. Rossetti.—StF
Sit up when you sit down. J. Ciardi.—CiYk
"There was a young man of Calcutta." Unknown.—BrLl
Breakfast. Eleanor Farjeon.—AgH
Breakfast and puss. Ann and Jane Taylor.—VrF
"The **breaking** waves dashed high." See The landing of the Pilgrim Fathers
The **breath** of life. James Stephens.—StS
"**Breathes** there the man with soul so dead." See The lay of the last minstrel
"**Breathless,** we flung us on the windy hill." See The hill
Brecht, Bertolt
Ballad of the soldier.—LiT
Changing the wheel.—HoL
Children's crusade 1939.—CaMb
Coal for Mike.—LiT
Iron.—HoL
The mask of evil.—LiT
Of swimming in lakes and rivers.—MoS
Questions of a studious working man.—SmM
The **breed** of athletes. Euripides, tr. fr. the Greek by Moses Hadas.—MoS
Breeze. Marie Hourigan.—LeM
"A **breeze** wipes creases off my forehead." See Poem in June
Brennan, Eileen
One kingfisher and one yellow rose.—ReBs
Brennan, Joseph Payne
The cat.—BrSm
Breton, Nicholas
The merry country lad. See The passionate shepherd
The passionate shepherd, sel.
The merry country lad.—ReO
The **bricklayer.** Unknown, at. to William Darton.—VrF
Bridal ballad. Edgar Allan Poe.—PoP
Brides and bridegrooms
"As the sun rose over the mountain." Unknown.—WyC
"Beat the drum. Rum-pum-pum." Unknown.—WyC
Bridal ballad. E. A. Poe.—PoP
A faery song. W. B. Yeats.—YeR
The frogs' wedding. E. J. Coatsworth.—CoSb
The griesly wife. J. Manifold.—CaMb
The host of the air. W. B. Yeats.—LiT—YeR
Light for a bride. Unknown.—DePp
Lochinvar. From Marmion. W. Scott.—CoR—HuS-3
Love and a question. R. Frost.—CaMb
Prothalamion. E. Spenser.—GrCt
The purist. O. Nash.—BoGj—BrSm
Song. From The bride's tragedy. T. L. Beddoes.—ReBs
The wedding bells. K. Greenaway.—GrT
Wedding procession from a window. J. A. Emanuel.—HaK
The **bride's** tragedy, sel. Thomas Lovell Beddoes
Song.—ReBs
"The **bridge** of dreams." Teika.—BaS
Bridges, Robert
The cliff-top.—CoBn
The first spring morning.—CoBn—SmM
I have loved flowers.—BoGj
"I heard a linnet courting."—ReO
The idle flowers.—CoBn—GrCt
London snow.—CoBn—GrCt
Nightingales.—GrS—ReO
"Spring goeth all in white."—CoBn—GrCt
Bridges. See also names of bridges, as Brooklyn bridge
Bridges. D. McCord.—McAd
"Bryan O'Lynn and his wife and his wife's mother." Mother Goose.—OpF
The burnt bridge. L. MacNeice.—GrS
Covered bridge. R. P. T. Coffin.—BrA
"If you chance to be crossing." Unknown.—WyC
The old bridge. H. Conkling.—ThA
The old bridge at Florence. H. W. Longfellow.—LoPl—PaH
On London bridge, and the stupendous sight, and structure thereof. J. Howell.—GrCt
On the bridge. K. Greenaway.—GrT
Trip: San Francisco. L. Hughes.—BrA
"With its fog-shroud the." From Poems. J. Lester.—HaK
Bridges. David McCord.—McAd
"**Bridges** are essential in a place." See Covered bridge
"**Brief,** on a flying night." See Chimes
The **briefless** barrister. John G. Saxe.—BrSm
The **brigade** must not know, sir. Unknown.—HiL
"A **bright** red flower he wears on his head." Unknown.—WyC
"**Bright** sun, hot sun, oh, to be." See Gone
"**Brightly** the sun shines." Ontei, tr. fr. the Japanese by Harry Behn.—BeCs
Brightness. Unknown, tr. fr. the Eskimo by Harry Behn.—BeG
Brill. See "At Brill on the hill"
"**Bring** daddy home." See Daddy

"**Bring** me men to match my mountains." See The coming American
"**Bring** me soft song, said Aladdin." See Aladdin and the jinn
"**Bring** me those needles, Martha." See The confession stone
"**Bring** out your dust, the dustman cries." See The dustman
"**Bring** the comb and play upon it." See Marching song
Bring us in good ale. Unknown.—ClF
"**Bring** us in no brown bread for that is made of bran." See Bring us in good ale
Bringing him up. Lord Dunsany.—CoBb
Britannia's pastorals, sels. William Browne
  The frolic mariners of Devon.—GrCt
  So shuts the marigold her leaves.—GrCt
"A **Briton** who shot at his king." David Ross.—BrSm
Brittany
  The rocks of Brittany. From The Canterbury tales. G. Chaucer.—ChT
"**Brittle** the snow on the gables." See Brittle world
Brittle world. Lew Sarett.—ThA
"The **broad** beach." See Afternoon: Amagansett beach
"**Broad** is the gate and wide the path." See The bath
The **broad** water. Mother Goose.—ReOn
Broadway: Twilight. Tom Prideaux.—LaC
Brody, Alter
  A city park.—LaC
"**Broken** and broken." Chosu, tr. fr. the Japanese by Harry Behn.—BeCs
The **broken-hearted** gardener. Unknown.—GrCt
The **broken** oar. Henry Wadsworth Longfellow.—LoPl
"The **broken** pillar of the wing jags from the clotted shoulder." See Hurt hawks
Brome, Richard
  Come, come away. See The merry beggars
  The merry beggars, sel.
    Come, come away.—ReBs
The **broncho** that would not be broken. Vachel Lindsay.—ArT-3—CoB—CoR—LiP
Brontë, Emily
  "I gazed upon the cloudless moon."—GrCt
  The morning star.—GrCt
  "The night is darkening round me."—HoL
  The night wind.—CoR—GrCt
  "No coward soul is mine."—PlE
The **brook**. Alfred Tennyson.—BlO—BoGj—ClF—CoBn
  Song of the brook.—TeP
"**Brook** and road." See The Simplon pass
The **brook** in February. Charles G. D. Roberts.—CoBn—DoW
The **brook** of the heart. See "Have you got a brook in your little heart"
"The **brook** wound through the woods behind." See The crayfish
Brooke, Rupert
  Doubts.—GrS
  The fish.—ReO (sel.)
  The hill.—CoBl
  The old vicarage, Grantchester.—PaH (sel.)
  There's wisdom in women.—CoBl
  The young man in April.—CoBl
Brooklyn bridge
  Brooklyn bridge. V. Mayakovsky.—LiT
  Brooklyn bridge at dawn. R. Le Gallienne.—ArT-3
  To Brooklyn bridge. H. Crane.—HiL—PaH
Brooklyn bridge. Vladimir Mayakovsky, tr. fr. the Russian by Max Hayward and George Reavey.—LiT
Brooklyn bridge at dawn. Richard Le Gallienne.—ArT-3
Brooklyn, New York
  Fortune. L. Ferlinghetti.—DuR—LaC
Brooks, Gwendolyn
  André.—ArT-3—HoB
  The ballad of the light-eyed little girl.—LiT
  The bean eaters.—HaK
  Bronzeville man with a belt in the back.—AdIa
  "But can see there, and laughing there."—HaK
  The Chicago Defender sends a man to Little Rock, Fall, 1967.—BoA
  The crazy woman.—BoH—LiT
  Cynthia in the snow.—ArT-3
  Ella.—AgH
  Flags.—BoA
  Hunchback girl: She thinks of heaven.—HaK
  Mentors.—HaK
  Negro hero.—HaK
  The old-marrieds.—BoA
  Old tennis player.—MoS
  Otto.—LaPd—LaPh
  Pete at the zoo.—HaL—LaPd
  Piano after war.—BoA—HaK
  The preacher: Ruminates behind the sermon.—LiT
  Rudolph is tired of the city.—LaPd
  A song in the front yard.—AdIa—BoH
  Strong men, riding horses.—HaK
  To a winter squirrel.—BoH
  Tommy.—BrSg
  Vern.—ArT-3—LaC
  We real cool.—AdIa—BoH—LaC
Brooks, Jonathan
  The resurrection.—BoA
Brooks
  As to the restless brook. J. K. Bangs.—CoO
  The brook. A. Tennyson.—BlO—BoGj—ClF—CoBn
    Song of the brook.—TeP
  The brook in February. C. G. D. Roberts.—CoBn—DoW
  The gleaming stream. C. Minor.—BaH
  The hurrying brook. E. Blunden.—CoBn
  Hyla brook. R. Frost.—CoBn

Brooks—*Continued*
"I sits with my toes in the brook." Unknown. —OpF
Zummer stream. W. Barnes.—CoBn
Broom balancing. Kathleen Fraser.—FrS
Brooms
Broom balancing. K. Fraser.—FrS
The witch.—McE
"**Broomsticks** and witches." See Hallowe'en
Brother and sister. Lewis Carroll.—BrSm—CoBb —GrCt
Brother Jonathan's lament for Sister Caroline. Oliver Wendell Holmes.—HiL
"**Brother** little fly flies around and looks at the sun." See The little fly
"**Brother** to the firefly." See Morning light the dew-drier
Brotherhood
The ballad of east and west. R. Kipling.—ArT-3
Bar-room matins. L. MacNeice.—PlE
The cable hymn. J. G. Whittier.—HiL
Dark testament. P. Murray.—BoA
The jingo and the minstrel. V. Lindsay.—LiP
A man's a man for a' that. R. Burns.—BoH—BuPr
"Ring around the world." A. Wynne.—ArT-3 —HuS-3
Sew the flags together. V. Lindsay.—LiP
Tableau. C. Cullen.—BrA—HaK
Through the varied patterned lace. M. Danner.—HaK
The wedding of the rose and the lotus. V. Lindsay.—LiP
"You, whoever you are." W. Whitman.—BrA
Brothers and sisters
"As I went up the garden." Unknown.—MoB —StF
Boy with his hair cut short. M. Rukeyser.—CoR
Brother and sister. L. Carroll.—BrSm—CoBb—GrCt
"Brothers and sisters have I none." Unknown. —OpF
The brothers: Two Saltimbanques. J. Logan. —DuS
Careless Willie. Unknown.—CoBb
Cradle song for a boy. Unknown.—LeO
A double limerick or twiner. W. De La Mare. —BrLl
The eel.—BrSm
Five little sisters. K. Greenaway.—GrT
Little. D. Aldis.—ArT-3
Little brother's secret. K. Mansfield.—ArT-3—ThA
The little girl that beat her sister. A. and J. Taylor.—VrF
Little Willie ("Little Willie, mad as hell") Unknown.—BrSm
Little Willie ("Little Willie, once in ire") Unknown.—BrSm
My brother ("My brother is inside the sheet") D. Aldis.—ArT-3
My brother ("Today I went to market with my mother") D. Aldis.—HoB
My brother Bert. T. Hughes.—CoBb
"My little golden sister." Unknown.—WyC
The new book. E. Turner.—VrF
The penny whistle. E. Thomas.—ThG
Poems for my brother. O. Dodson.—AdIa
Quarrelsome children. E. Turner.—VrF
"Sing me a song." C. G. Rossetti.—HoB
Sister Nell. Unknown.—CoBb
The sisters. A. Tennyson.—TeP
Sometimes. E. Merriam.—MeC
To my sister. W. Wordsworth.—WoP
Trip upon trenchers. Mother Goose.—ReOn
A sad song.—BrMg
The twins ("In form and feature, face and limb") H. S. Leigh.—ArT-3—BrSm
The twins ("The two-ones is the name for it") E. M. Roberts.—ArT-3
"Two brothers there were of Sioux City." Unknown.—BrLl
Two in bed. A. B. Ross.—ArT-3
"Two little sisters went walking one day." Unknown.—WyC
War. J. Langland.—DuS
Waterwings. K. Fraser.—FrS
Young Sammy Watkins. Unknown.—CoBb
"**Brothers** and sisters have I none." Unknown.—OpF
The **brothers**: Two Saltimbanques. John Logan. —DuS
Broughton, James
The birds of America.—BrA
"**Brow**, brow, brenty." Unknown.—MoB
Brower, Alfred
"Luther Leavitt is a whale hunter."—BaH
Brown, Abbie Farwell
All wool.—ArT-3
Brown, Audrey Alexandra
The strangers.—DoW
Brown, Barry
"Drums, drumming."—BaH
"What will become."—BaH
Brown, Beatrice Curtis
Jonathan Bing.—ArT-3—LaP—LaPd
A new song to sing about Jonathan Bing.—CoO
Brown, Jane
Whiskers.—LeM
Brown, John (about)
Brown of Ossawatomie. J. G. Whittier.—HiL
Glory hallelujah; or, John Brown's body. Unknown.—HiL
John Brown's body, sels. S. V. Benét
Invocation.—BrA
"It was noon when the company marched to the railroad station"
From John Brown's body.—HiL
Robert E. Lee.—BrA
"There was a girl I used to go with.—HaL
"Three elements."—PlE
Brown, Margaret Wise
Bumble bee.—LaPd

"Dear Father."—LaPd
The fish with the deep sea smile.—LaPd
"How do you know it's spring."—BrSg
Little donkey close your eyes.—LaP—LaPd
The secret song.—LaP—LaPd
"Wild young birds that sweetly sing."—LaPd
Brown, Palmer
"The spangled pandemonium."—ArT-3
Brown, Sheri
A real dream.—BaH
Brown, Spencer
Bits of glass.—HoL
Brown, Sterling A.
After winter.—BoH
Mose.—HaK
Old Lem.—AdIa
Revelations.—HaK
Sister Lou.—BoA
Sporting Beasley.—HaK
Strange legacies.—HaK
Strong men.—BoH
When de saints go ma'chin' home.—BoA
Brown, T. E.
Vespers.—CoB
Brown, Thomas (or **Tom**)
Doctor Fell. tr.—BrMg—GrCt
"I do not like thee, Dr Fell."—ReMg
"I do not like thee, Dr Fell." See Doctor Fell
Brown (Color)
What is brown. M. O'Neill.—OnH
"**Brown** and furry." Christina Georgina Rossetti. —BrSg
Caterpillar.—BoGj—CoB—HoB—HuS-3—LaP
"**Brown** bunny sits inside his burrow." See The rabbit
The **brown** cow. Unknown.—VrF
"The **brown-dappled** fawn." See The fawn in the snow
A **brown** girl dead. Countee Cullen.—HaK
"**Brown** is the color of a country road." See What is brown
"**Brown** lived at such a lofty farm." See Brown's descent; or, The willy-nilly slide
Brown of Ossawatomie. John Greenleaf Whittier.—HiL
Brown penny. William Butler Yeats.—CoBl—YeR
Brown river, smile. Jean Toomer.—BoA
The **brown** thrush. Lucy Larcom.—HoB
Browne, William
Britannia's pastorals, sels.
The frolic mariners of Devon.—GrCt
So shuts the marigold her leaves.—GrCt
The frolic mariners of Devon. See Britannia's pastorals
Harlem sounds: Hallelujah corner.—BoA
So shuts the marigold her leaves. See Britannia's pastorals
Song of the syrens.—GrCt
"**Brownie,** it isn't my fault." See September
Brownies. See Fairies
Browning, Elizabeth Barrett
The cry of the children.—ClF (sel.)
How do I love thee. See Sonnets from the Portuguese
"How do I love thee? Let me count the ways." See Sonnets from the Portuguese
"If thou must love me, let it be for naught." See Sonnets from the Portuguese
Lady Geraldine's courtship.—CoD
Sonnets from the Portuguese, sels.
"How do I love thee? Let me count the ways."—CoBl
How do I love thee.—BoH
"If thou must love me, let it be for naught."—CoBl
Browning, Robert
Abt Vogler.—BrP
"All service ranks the same with God." See Pippa passes
Andrea del Sarto.—BrP
Asolando, sel.
Epilogue.—BrP
Bishop Blougram's apology, sel.
If once we choose belief.—BrP
The bishop orders his tomb at Saint Praxed's church.—BrP
Boot and saddle. See Cavalier tunes
Caliban on Setebos; or, Natural theology in the island.—BrP
Cavalier tunes, sels.
I. Marching along.—BrP
II. Give a rouse.—BrP
III. Boot and saddle.—BrP
Childe Roland to the dark tower came.—BrP
"Day." See Pippa passes
Deaf and dumb.—BrP
De gustibus.—BrP
Development.—BrP
Epilogue. See Asolando
Fra Lippo Lippi.—BrP
Give a rouse. See Cavalier tunes
"Here's to Nelson's memory."—BrP
Hervé Riel.—CoSs
Home-thoughts, from abroad.—BrP—CoBn—PaH
Home-thoughts, from the sea.—BrP
House.—BrP
How they brought the good news from Ghent to Aix.—ArT-3—BrP—CoR—HuS-3
If once we choose belief. See Bishop Blougram's apology
In a gondola, sel.
"The moth's kiss, first."—BrP
In three days.—BrP
Incident of the French camp.—BrP—CoR
La Saisiaz, sel.
Prologue.—BrP
The laboratory.—BrP
The last ride together.—BrP
Life in a love.—BrP
A likeness.—BrP
The lost leader.—BrP
Love in a life.—BrP
Marching along. See Cavalier tunes
Meeting at night.—BrP—CoBl—HoL—TuW
Memorabilia.—BrP
Misconceptions.—BrP
"The moth's kiss, first." See In a gondola

Browning, Robert—*Continued*
My last duchess.—BrP
My star.—BrP
Now.—BrP
"Oh day, if I squander a wavelet of thee." See Pippa passes
Oh, our manhood's prime vigor. See Saul
One word more, sel.
Phases of the moon.—GrCt
"Overhead the tree-tops meet." See Pippa passes
Parting at morning.—BrP
The patriot.—BrP
Phases of the moon. See One word more
Pictor ignotus.—BrP
The Pied Piper of Hamelin.—ArT-3—BrP—GrT—HoB—HuS-3
"Rats."—CoB (sel.)
Pippa passes, sels.
"All service ranks the same with God."—BrP
"Day."—BrP
"Oh day, if I squander a wavelet of thee."—BrP
"Overhead the tree-tops meet."—BrP
"The year's at the spring."—BrP—HoB
Pippa's song.—BoGj—LaPd
Song.—TuW
You'll love me yet.—BrP
Pippa's song. See Pippa passes—"The year's at the spring"
Popularity.—BrP
Porphyria's lover.—BrP
Prologue. See La Saisiaz
Prospice.—BrP
Rabbi Ben Ezra.—BrP
"Rats." See The Pied Piper of Hamelin
Saul, sel.
Oh, our manhood's prime vigor.—BrP
Soliloquy of the Spanish cloister.—BrP—CoD
Song ("Nay but you, who do not love her")—BrP—CoBl
Song ("The year's at the spring") See Pippa passes—"The year's at the spring"
Summum bonum.—CoBl
A toccata of Galuppi's.—BrP
Two in the Campagna.—BrP—CoBl (sel.)
Up at a villa—down in the city.—BrP
Why I am a liberal.—BrP
A woman's last word.—BrP
"The year's at the spring." See Pippa passes
You'll love me yet. See Pippa passes
Browning, Robert (about)
Development. R. Browning.—BrP
House. R. Browning.—BrP
Why I am a liberal. R. Browning.—BrP
Brown's descent; or, The willy-nilly slide. Robert Frost.—ArT-3
Bronzeville man with a belt in the back. Gwendolyn Brooks.—AdIa
"**Bruadar** and Smith and Glinn." Douglas Hyde.—McWs
Bruce, John
The pike.—MoS
Bruce, Robert, King of Scotland (about)
Scots, wha hae. R. Burns.—BuPr
Bruges, Belgium
The belfry of Bruges. H. W. Longfellow.—PaH
"The **bruisers** of England, the men of tremendous renown." See The fancy
Brumana. James Elroy Flecker.—PaH
Bryan, William Jennings (about)
Bryan, Bryan, Bryan, Bryan. V. Lindsay.—LiP
Bryan, Bryan, Bryan, Bryan. Vachel Lindsay.—LiP
"**Bryan** O'Lynn and his wife and his wife's mother." Mother Goose.—OpF
Bryant, Juanita
The city.—BaH
"The world's coming to an end."—BaH
Bryant, Mary
"The babies are born."—BaH
Bryant, Veronica
"The world was meant to be peaceful."—BaH
Bryant, William Cullen
The death of the flowers.—CoBn
The planting of the apple tree.—HuS-3
Robert of Lincoln.—CoB—HoB
Song of Marion's men.—HiL
Thanatopsis.—CoBn
"**B's** the bus." See All around the town
The **bubble.** Kenneth Hopkins.—CaD
"**Bubbles** are big enough." See Blowing bubbles
The **buccaneer.** Nancy Byrd Turner.—ArT-3
Buchan, Tom
Dolphins at Cochin.—CoSs
Buckingham palace. A. A. Milne.—LaPd—MiC
Buddha
"All kinds of cicadas singing." Issa.—IsF
"At the morning exhibition." Issa.—IsF
"The Buddha." Issa.—IsF
"The **Buddha.**" Issa, tr. fr. the Japanese by Nobuyuki Yuasa.—IsF
The **buds.** James Stephens.—StS
Buff. Mother Goose.—BrMg
The **buffalo.** Laura E. Richards.—CoO
Buffalo Bill. See Cody, William Frederick (about)
"**Buffalo** Bill's." E. E. Cummings.—LiT
Buffalo Bill's defunct.—BrA
Portrait.—HoL
Buffalo Bill's defunct. See "Buffalo Bill's"
Buffalo dusk. Carl Sandburg.—ArT-3—LaPd—ReO
"The **buffalo** goes with his head on high." Unknown, tr. fr. the Lango.—LeO
The **buffalo** skinners. Unknown.—HiL
"The **buffalo,** the buffalo." See The buffalo
Buffaloes
The buffalo. L. E. Richards.—CoO
Buffalo dusk. C. Sandburg.—ArT-3—LaPd—ReO
"The buffalo goes with his head on high." Unknown.—LeO
The buffalo skinners. Unknown.—HiL
The flower-fed buffaloes. V. Lindsay.—ArT-3—BoGj—BrA—CoB—GrCt—LiP
The ghost of the buffaloes. V. Lindsay.—LiP

Hunting song. Unknown.—LeO
The passing of the buffalo. H. Garland.—HuS-3
"The **buffaloes** are gone." See Buffalo dusk
The **bugle-billed** bazoo. John Ciardi.—HoB
The **bugle** song. See The princess
"The **bugle** sounds the measured call to prayers." See Sunday: New Guinea
"A **bugler** named Dougal MacDougal." Ogden Nash.—BrLl
Edouard.—McWs
Bugles
The bugle song. From The princess. A. Tennyson.—HoB—HuS-3
Blow, bugle, blow.—GrCt
Song.—BlO
"The splendor falls on castle walls."—ArT-3—BoGj
The splendour falls.—CoR
"A bugler named Dougal MacDougal." O. Nash.—BrLl
Edouard.—McWs
"No one cares less than I." E. Thomas.—ThG
The trumpet. E. Thomas.—GrS—ThG
Bugs. See Insects
"**Build** me straight, O worthy master." See The building of the ship
Build-on rhymes
"Anna Mariar she sat on the fire." Mother Goose.—BrMg—OpF
Craigbilly fair. Unknown.—GrCt
"For want of a nail." Mother Goose.—ReMg
A nail.—BrMg
"I went down the garden." Unknown.—OpF
The mad man. Mother Goose.—BrMg
There was a man.—SmM
A man of double deed. Mother Goose.—BrMg
There was a man.—SmM
Not ragged-and-tough. Unknown.—GrCt
The old lady who swallowed a fly. Unknown.—BrSm
The story of the old woman and her pig. Mother Goose.—BrMg
Swinging. Mother Goose.—BrMg
"This is the house that Jack built." Mother Goose.—HuS-3—OpF
The house that Jack built.—BrMg
This is the key. Mother Goose.—BlO
The key of the kingdom.—BrMg
The twelve days of Christmas. Mother Goose.—BrMg—LaPh
"The first day of Christmas my true love sent to me."—OpF
The thirteen days.—ReOn
Thirteen Yule days.—MoB
The Yule days.—GrCt
"What's in there." Mother Goose.—BrMg—MoB—ReOn
"When I was a lad as big as my dad." Mother Goose.—OpF
When I was a lad.—BrF
"**Build** your houses, build your houses, build your slums." See Beleaguered cities
The **builders.** Sara Henderson Hay.—DuR
Builders and building. See also Work; also types of builders, as Carpenters
Bam, bam, bam. E. Merriam.—LaPd—MeC
The building of the ship. H. W. Longfellow.—LoPl
The concrete mixer. T. Langley.—LeM
Concrete mixers. P. Hubbell.—LaPd
Construction. M. C. Livingston.—LiC
The hammers. R. Hodgson.—BoGj
Song of the builders. J. W. Murton.—BrA
The **building** of the ship. Henry Wadsworth Longfellow.—LoPl
The **bull.** Ralph Hodgson.—ReO (sel.)
The **bull** calf. Irving Layton.—CoB
Buller, A. H. Reginald
"There was a young lady of Bright."—ArT-3—BrLl
Bulls
The bull. R. Hodgson.—ReO (sel.)
Sarah Byng. H. Belloc.—BoGj
Bumble bee. Margaret Wise Brown.—LaPd
The **bumblebeaver.** See Mixed beasts
Bumblebee. David McCord.—McAd
"The **bumblebee** is bumbly." See Bumblebee
Bump. Bang. Bump. John Ciardi.—CiYk
"**Bump,** bump, please go away." Unknown.—WyC
A **bunch** of roses. John Banister Tabb.—ThA
"A **bunch** of the boys were whooping it up in the Malamute saloon." See The shooting of Dan McGrew
Bunches of grapes. Walter De La Mare.—ArT-3—BoGj
"**Bunches** of grapes, says Timothy." See Bunches of grapes
"A **bundle** of grass on her head." See A village girl
"A **bundle** is a funny thing." See Bundles
Bundles
The armful. R. Frost.—LiT
Bundles. J. Farrar.—ArT-3
Bundles. John Farrar.—ArT-3
Bunner, Henry Cuyler
Grandfather Watts's private Fourth.—ArT-3
Bunya (or **Funya**) **no Asayasu**
"In a gust of wind the white dew."—BaS—LeMw
Bunyan, John
Neither hook nor line.—MoS
The pilgrim. See The pilgrim's progress
The pilgrim's progress, sels.
The pilgrim.—ArT-3—ClF
The shepherd boy sings in the valley of humiliation.—PlE
The shepherd boy sings in the valley of humiliation. See The pilgrim's progress
Upon the lark and the fowler.—CoB
Upon the snail.—CoB—GrCt
Bunyan, Paul (about)
A legend of Paul Bunyan. A. S. Bourinot.—BrA
The **bunyip.** Douglas Stewart.—ReO
Bunyips
The bunyip. D. Stewart.—ReO

Burford, William
Space.—HoL
Burgess, Clinton Brooks
"Said Mrs Isosceles Tri."—BrLl
Burgess, Gelett
Adolphus Elfinstone.—CoBb
An alphabet of famous Goops.—CoBb (sel.)
Felicia Ropps.—CoBb
"I never saw a purple cow."—BlO
The purple cow.—ArT-3—LaPd
"I wish that my room had a floor."—LaP
Relativity and levitation.—BrLl
"I'd rather have fingers than toes."—BrLl
The jilted funeral.—BrSm
The purple cow. See "I never saw a purple cow"
Relativity and levitation. See "I wish that my room had a floor"
Table manners.—CoBb
Tardiness.—CoBb
"There's nothing in afternoon tea."—BrLl
Burgunder, Rose
A boy's place.—LaPd
Getting up.—ArT-3
Trains.—ArT-3
Upside down.—ArT-3
Burial. Mark Van Doren.—CaMb
The **burial** of Sir John Moore. Charles Wolfe.—CoR
The burial of Sir John Moore after Corunna.—GrCt
The **burial** of Sir John Moore after Corunna. See The burial of Sir John Moore
Burnham, Maude
The barnyard.—ArT-3
Burials. See Funerals
The **burning** bush. Norman Nicholson.—PlE
Burning in the night. Thomas Wolfe.—BrA
Burns, Alvin
Black is beautiful.—BaH
Burns, Robert
Address to a haggis.—BuPr
Address to the deil.—BuPr
Address to the toothache.—BuPr
Address to the unco guid.—BuPr
"Ae fond kiss, and then we sever."—BuPr
Afton water. See Sweet Afton
Auld lang syne.—BuPr
"Ay, waukin, O."—BuPr
The banks o' Doon.—BuPr—CoBl
The belles of Mauchline.—BuH
The book-worms.—GrCt
The braw wooer.—BuPr
Comin' thro' the rye.—BuPr
The daisy. See To a mountain daisy
The death and dying words of poor Mailie.—BuPr
The deil's awa wi' th' exciseman.—BuPr
Duncan Davison.—BuPr
Duncan Gray.—BuPr
The dusty miller.—BuH
Elegy on Willie Nicol's mare.—BuPr
Epistle to James Smith.—BuPr
Epitaph on Holy Willie.—BuPr
Epitaph on John Dove, innkeeper.—BuPr
The gallant weaver.—BuH
"Green grow the rashes, O."—BuPr
Highland Mary.—BuPr
The holy fair.—BuPr
Holy Willie's prayer.—BuPr
I'm o'er young to marry yet.—BuPr
"It was a' for our rightfu' king."—BuPr
John Anderson my jo.—BuH—BuPr
John Barleycorn: A ballad.—BuPr
The jolly beggars.—BuPr
A lass wi' a tocher.—BuPr
A man's a man for a' that.—BoH—BuPr
Mary Morison.—BuPr
My heart's in the Highlands.—BuH (sel.)—BuPr—ClF—MoS
"My heart's in the Highlands, my heart is not here."—BlO—PaH
"My heart's in the Highlands, my heart is not here." See My heart's in the Highlands
O leave novéls.—BuPr
"O were my love yon lilac fair."—GrCt
"O wert thou in the cauld blast."—BuPr
"O whistle an' I'll come to ye, my lad."—BuPr—CoBl
"Of a' the airts the wind can blaw."—BuPr
On Dr Babington's looks.—BuPr
On the Duchess of Gordon's reel dancing.—BuPr
"One night as I did wander."—BuH
Poor Mailie's elegy.—BuPr
A red, red rose.—ArT-3—BoH—BuH—BuPr—CoBl—GrCt
The rigs o' barley.—BuPr
A rose-bud, by my early walk, sel.
Within the bush.—ReBs
Scots, wha hae.—BuPr
Song.—CoBn
Sweet Afton.—BuPr
Afton water.—CoBn
Sweet Tibbie Dunbar.—BuH
Tam o' Shanter.—BuPr
The Tarbolton lasses.—BuPr
There's a youth in this city.—BuPr
To a louse, on seeing one on a lady's bonnet at church.—BuH—BuPr—CoB
To a mountain daisy.—BuPr
The daisy.—CoBn
To a mouse.—BuH—BuPr—CoB—ReO
The toad-eater.—BuPr
Up in the morning early.—BuPr
"Up in the morning's no' for me."—BlO (sel.)
"Up in the morning's no' for me." See Up in the morning early
"Wha is that at my bower-door."—BuPr
Whistle o'er the lave o't.—BuPr
Willie brew'd a peck o' maut.—BuPr
Within the bush. See A rose-bud, by my early walk
Burns, Robert (about)
Epistle to James Smith. R. Burns.—BuPr
Burnshaw, Stanley
House in St Petersburg.—GrS

The **burnt** bridge. Louis MacNeice.—GrS
"**Burnt** lawns and iron bound pastures." See Midsummer
Burr, Amelia Josephine
Night magic.—ThA
Rain in the night.—ArT-3—ThA
Burr conspiracy. See United States—History—Burr conspiracy
"A **burro** once, sent by express." See Advice to travelers
Burrows, Abe
Sea chanty.—CoSs
"**Bury** her at even." Michael Field.—SmM
"**Bury** her deep, down deep." See Cat's funeral
"**Bury** me, the bishop said." See St Swithin
"**Bury** the great duke." See Ode on the death of the Duke of Wellington
The **buses** headed for Scranton. Ogden Nash.—McWs
"The **buses** headed for Scranton travel in pairs." See The buses headed for Scranton
Bush, Jocelyn
The little red sled.—ArT-3
Buson
"Above tides of leaves."—BeCs
"Asleep in the sun."—BeCs
"The autumn breeze is blowing."—LeMw
"The bat."—LeI
"Day darken, frogs say."—BeCs
"Evening shadows touch."—BeCs
"A flash of lightning."—LeI
"Now the moon goes down."—BeCs
"O foolish ducklings."—BeCs
"Of what use are twigs."—BeCs
"The peony."—LeMw
"Spring is almost gone."—BeCs
"Sun low in the west."—BeCs
"Washing my rice hoe."—BeCs
"What happiness."—LeMw
"Whose scarf could this be."—BeCs
"With the evening breeze."LeI
Busses
The birthday bus. M. A. Hoberman.—ArT-3
"B's the bus." From All around the town. P. McGinley.—ArT-3
The buses headed for Scranton. O. Nash.—McWs
Jittery Jim. W. J. Smith.—CoBb
The one I always get. M. C. Livingston.—LiC
Busy carpenters. James S. Tippett.—HuS-3
"**Busy**, curious, thirsty fly." Unknown.—ClF
Busy summer. Aileen Fisher.—FiI
"**But** as they left the dark'ning heath." See Marmion—Flodden
"**But** can see there, and laughing there." Gwendolyn Brooks.—HaK
"**But** do not let us quarrel any more." See Andrea del Sarto
"**But** give me holly, bold and jolly." Christina Georgina Rossetti.—ArT-3
"**But** God's own descent." See Kitty Hawk
"**But** in the crowding darkness not a word did they say." See The old-marrieds
But no. Elizabeth Jane Coatsworth.—CoDh
"**But** now the salmon-fishers moist." See Upon Appleton house—Carrying their coracles
"**But** outer space." Robert Frost.—LiT
But these things also. Edward Thomas.—ThG
"**But** these things also are spring's." See But these things also
"**But** they that wait upon the Lord shall renew their strength." See Isaiah
Butchers
The butcher's boy. K. Greenaway.—GrT
Shopping for meat in winter. O. Williams.—HoL
The **butcher's** boy. Kate Greenaway.—GrT
"A **butcher's** boy met a baker's boy." See The butcher's boy
Butler, Samuel
The barn owl.—SmM
A martial mouse.—ReO
Butter
"Come, butter, come." Mother Goose.—HuS-3
Churning.—BrMg
The **butterbean** tent. Elizabeth Madox Roberts.—BoGj—BrSg—HuS-3
Buttercup cow. Elizabeth Rendall.—ArT-3
"**Buttercup** cow has milk for me." See Buttercup cow
Buttercup days. A. A. Milne.—MiC
"**Buttercup,** the cow, had a new baby calf." See The new baby calf
Buttercups
"Are you too proud to kiss me." R. Tagore.—LeMf
Buttercup days. A. A. Milne.—MiC
"Buttercups and daisies." M. Howitt.—OpF
"**Buttercups** and daisies." Mary Howitt.—OpF
Buttered pippin-pies. John Davies of Hereford.—GrCt
Butterflies
Another song of a fool. W. B. Yeats.—ReO
"Asleep in the sun." Buson.—BeCs
"At the flower-vase." Issa.—IsF
"Away floats the butterfly." Unknown.—WyC
Blue-butterfly day. R. Frost.—BrSg
Blue moon butterfly. P. Williams.—LeM
"Brown and furry." C. G. Rossetti.—BrSg
Caterpillar.—BoGj—CoB—HoB—HuS-3—LaP
Butterflies. Chu Miao Tuan.—LeMw
Butterfly ("As I walked through my garden") H. Conkling.—ArT-3
Butterfly ("Of living creatures most I prize") W. J. Smith.—ArT-3—BoGj
"A butterfly came." Issa.—LeOw
Butterfly tongues. A. Fisher.—FiI
Butterfly wings. A. Fisher.—FiI
The butterfly's ball and the grasshopper's feast. W. Roscoe.—VrF
Envoi. A. C. Swinburne.—BoGj
White butterflies.—LaPd
The example. W. H. Davies.—ReO
"The flying butterfly." Issa.—IsF
Flying crooked. R. Graves.—HoL—ReO
"Fuzzy wuzzy, creepy crawly." L. A. Vanada.—ArT-3

Butterflies—*Continued*
"Ha, the butterfly." Unknown.—LeI
Hammock. D. McCord.—McAd
"Helter-skelter." Issa.—IsF
"How happy, how affectionate they are." Issa. —LeOw
"The king of yellow butterflies." V. Lindsay. —CoB
The lilac spires. E. J. Coatsworth.—CoSb
A magic carpet. T. Weiss.—WeP
"O butterfly." Chiyo-ni.—LeMw
Patroness. G. W. Barrax.—HaK
The prayer of the butterfly. C. B. de Gasztold.—LiT
"Softly." Issa.—LeMw
Song of the butterfly. Unknown.—LeO
Sparrows or butterflies. Unknown.—DePp
To a butterfly. W. Wordsworth.—BrSg (sel.) —CoB (sel.)—WoP
"Two butterflies went out at noon." E. Dickinson.—DiPe
"Wake up, old sleepy." Bashō.—BeCs
When snow will come. E. J. Coatsworth.—CoSb
Butterflies. Chu Miao Tuan, tr. fr. the Chinese by Henry H. Hart.—LeMw
"**Butterflies** flit to and fro." See The child in school
"A **butterfly**." See Summer
Butterfly ("As I walked through my garden") Hilda Conkling.—ArT-3
Butterfly ("Of living creatures most I prize") W. J. Smith.—ArT-3—BoGj
"The **butterfly**, a cabbage-white." See Flying crooked
"A **butterfly** came." Issa, tr. fr. the Japanese by R. H. Blyth.—LeOw
"The **butterfly** is O flutter by." See A magic carpet
"**Butterfly**, these words." Soseki, tr. fr. the Japanese by Harry Behn.—BeCs
Butterfly tongues. Aileen Fisher.—FiI
Butterfly wings. Aileen Fisher—FiI
The **butterfly's** ball and the grasshopper's feast. William Roscoe.—VrF
Butterworth, Hezekiah
The death of Jefferson.—HiL
Buttons
About buttons. D. Aldis.—ThA
Butts, Mary Frances
Night.—ReS
Winter night.—ArT-3
Buxton, John
Harebell.—SmM
"**Buy** me a milking pail." Unknown.—MoB
Buzzy old bees. Aileen Fisher.—FiI
By a chapel as I came. Unknown.—GrCt
"**By** a flat rock on the shore of the sea." See The rock
By a lake in Minnesota. James Wright.—BrA
"**By** a route obscure and lonely." See Dreamland
"**By** day it's a very good girl am I." See The quiet child
"**By** day the bat is cousin to the mouse." See The bat
"**By** far." See Extremely naughty children
"**By** June our brook's run out of song and speed." See Hyla brook
By myself. See "As I walk'd by myself"
"**By** numbers here from shame or censure free." See London—Poverty in London
"**By** reason of despair we set forth behind you." See The murder of Moses
By Sandy waters. Jesse Stuart.—BrA
"**By** shoal, by stream." See Wanderer's night song
"**By** sloth on sorrow fathered." See Lollocks
By the deep nine. W. Pearce.—GrCt
By the Exeter river. Donald Hall.—CaMb
By the firelight. L. A. G. Strong.—CaD
"**By** the flow of the inland river." See The blue and the gray
"**By** the garden fence chrysanthemums grow." See Chrysanthemum colors
"**By** the glim of a midwinterish early morning." See Son and father
"**By** the Isar, in the twilight." See River roses
"**By** the light of the next room." Issa, tr. fr. the Japanese by R. H. Blyth.—LeOw
"**By** the long flow of green and silver water." See Water and shadow
By the river. Judith Gautier, tr. fr. the French by Stuart Merrill.—GrS
"**By** the rude bridge that arched the flood." See Concord hymn
"**By** the sandy water I breathe the odor of the sea." Unknown, tr. fr. the Papago.—LeO
By the sea. Christina Georgina Rossetti.—CoBn
"**By** the shores of Gitche Gumee." See The song of Hiawatha—Hiawatha's childhood
By the spring at sunset. Vachel Lindsay.—LiP
By the statue of King Charles at Charing cross. Lionel Johnson.—CoR
"**By** the swimming." Robert Sward.—DuS
"**By** the wave rising, by the wave breaking." See The crow
"**By** those soft tods of wooll." See A conjuration, to Electra
"**By** thys fyre I warme my handys." See The months
"**By** word laid low." Unknown.—GrCt
"**Bye** baby bunting." Mother Goose.—ArT-3—HuS-3—OpF—WiMg
Mother Goose rhymes, 40.—HoB
Rabbit skin.—BrMg
Bynner, Witter
The bats.—BoH
A dance for rain.—PaH
I need no sky.—PlE
Pittsburgh.—BrA
Prayer.—PlE
—and Kiang Kang-hu
At Heron lodge, trs.—LeMw
Border songs, trs.—LeMw
"The days and months do not last long." trs. —LeMw

From my study at the mouth of the valley. trs.—LeMw
A green stream. trs.—MoS
"How can a deep love seem deep love." trs.—LeMw
A moonlight night. trs.—LeMw
Byron, George Gordon (Noël), Lord
And angling, too. See Don Juan
"Are not the mountains, waves, and skies, a part." See Childe Harold's pilgrimage
Beppo.—ByP
Childe Harold's pilgrimage, sels.
"Are not the mountains, waves, and skies, a part."—CoBn
The ocean.—CoSs
Deep and dark blue ocean.—GrCt
On Rome.—ByP
Waterloo.—ByP
Deep and dark blue ocean. See Childe Harold's pilgrimage—The ocean
The destruction of Sennacherib.—ByP
Don Juan, sels.
And angling, too.—MoS
Fragment.—ByP
Haidée.—ByP
The isles of Greece.—ByP—CoR—GrCt—PaH (sel.)
Of all the barbarous middle ages.—ByP
Fragment. See Don Juan
Haidée. See Don Juan
The isles of Greece. See Don Juan
"Maid of Athens, ere we part."—ByP
The ocean. See Childe Harold's pilgrimage
Of all the barbarous middle ages. See Don Juan
On Rome. See Childe Harold's pilgrimage
The prisoner of Chillon.—CoD
She walks in beauty.—ByP—CoR
"So we'll go no more a roving."—ByP
Song.—CoBl
We'll go no more a-roving.—BoH
Song. See "So we'll go no more a roving"
Stanzas ("Could love for ever")—ByP
Stanzas ("When a man hath no freedom to fight for at home")—ByP
Stanzas for music.—ByP
Stanzas to Augusta.—ByP
Stanzas written in passing the Ambracian gulf.—ByP
Stanzas written on the road between Florence and Pisa.—ByP
To Thomas Moore.—ByP
Vision of Belshazzar.—ByP—CoR
Waterloo. See Childe Harold's pilgrimage
We'll go no more a-roving. See "So we'll go no more a roving"
Written after swimming from Sestos to Abydos.—ByP
Byron, George Gordon (Noël), Lord (about)
Fragment. From Don Juan. G. G. Byron.—ByP

C

"**C** is for the circus." See All around the town
Cabbages
"Careful Katie cooked a crisp and crinkly cabbage." Mother Goose.—OpF
"Patches and patches." Mother Goose.—OpF
The **cabin.** Elizabeth Jane Coatsworth.—CoDh
The **cable** hymn. John Greenleaf Whittier.—HiL
Cables
The cable hymn. J. G. Whittier.—HiL
"**Cackle,** cackle." See Goose feathers
Cactuses
July. N. Belting.—BeCm
Caesar, Gaius Julius (about)
Julius Caesar and the honey-bee. C. T. Turner.—ReO
"**Caged** lightly by two-by-fours, rigged flat." See Propeller
Cairns, Diane
The flower.—LeM
"A **cake** of soap, a toothpick mask." See Ivory
Cakes and cookies
The bagel. D. Ignatow.—DuS
Birthday cake. A. Fisher.—LaPd
Catherine. K. Kuskin.—LaPd
Christmas cookies. A. Fisher.—AgH
Hot cake. Shu Hsi.—ClF (sel.)
"The moon's the north wind's cooky." V. Lindsay.—HoB—HuS-3—LaP—LaPd—ThA
"Oh dear, oh. My cake's all dough." Mother Goose.—OpF
Spice cake. A. Fisher.—AgH
Cakes and custard. See "When Jacky's a good boy"
Calcutta, India
Calcutta. A. Chakravarty.—AlPi
Calcutta. Amiya Chakravarty, tr. fr. the Bengali by Martin Kirkman.—AlPi
Caliban in the coal mines. Louis Untermeyer.—LaPd
Caliban on Setebos; or, Natural theology in the island. Robert Browning.—BrP
"**Calico** pie." Edward Lear.—BlO—TuW
California
California winter. K. Shapiro.—BrA (sel.)
In California there are two hundred and fifty-six religions. R. E. Albert.—DuS
Song of the redwood-tree. W. Whitman.—PaH (sel.)
The star in the hills. W. Stafford.—DuS
California winter. Karl Shapiro.—BrA (sel.)
Call for the robin-redbreast. See The white devil—A dirge
"**Call** for the robin red-breast and the wren." See The white devil—A dirge
"**Call** it neither love nor spring madness." See Without name
"**Call** the cows home." See Thunder
Callanan, Jeremiah John
The convict of Clonmel. tr.—MoS
Callicles' song. See Empedocles on Etna
Calling all cowboys. John Ciardi.—CiYk

Calling in the cat. Elizabeth Jane Coatsworth.—ReO
Calliopes
The kallyope yell. V. Lindsay.—LiP
Calm after storm. Frank Yerby.—BoA
"**Calm** is all nature as a resting wheel." See Written in very early youth
Calm is the morn. See In memoriam
"**Calm** is the morn without a sound." See In memoriam—Calm is the morn
Calm of evening. Hsieh T'iao, tr. fr. the Chinese by Henry H. Hart.—LeMw
"**Calm** was the day, and through the trembling air." See Prothalamion
"**Calmly** I step on the brakes." See The flat
Calverley, Charles Stuart
The cat. See Sad memories
Sad memories, sel.
The cat.—GrCt
Calverley, Sybil Horatia
Midsummer.—ReBs
Calves
The bull calf. I. Layton.—CoB
Johnny Armstrong. Mother Goose.—ReOn
The new baby calf. E. H. Newlin.—ArT-3
The pasture. R. Frost.—ArT-3—BoGj—CoB—LaP—LaPd—ThA
"There was an old man (and he had a calf)." Mother Goose.—BrMg
The young calves. R. P. T. Coffin.—ArT-3—HuS-3
"**Cam** you by the salmon fishers." See Singing game
Cambridge, England
Cambridge. F. Cornford.—ClF
Residence at Cambridge. From The prelude. W. Wordsworth.—WoP
Cambridge, Massachusetts
In the churchyard at Cambridge. H. W. Longfellow.—LoPl
Cambridge. Frances Cornford.—ClF
Camden, William
On a puritanicall lock-smith.—BrSm
"**Came** the relief. What, sentry, ho." See Relieving guard
The **camel.** Carmen Bernos de Gasztold, tr. fr. the French by Rumer Godden.—GaC—ReO
Camels
Baby camel. V. Korostylev.—CoB
The camel. C. B. de Gasztold.—GaC—ReO
Exile. V. Sheard.—CoB
The plaint of the camel. From Davy and the goblin. C. E. Carryl.—HuS-3—ThA
Twelfth night: Song of the camels. E. J. Coatsworth.—BoH
Cameron, Norman
Green, green is El Aghir.—CaMb
Campbell, Alexander (about)
Alexander Campbell, sels. V. Lindsay
I. My fathers came from Kentucky.—BrA—LiP
II. Written in a year when many of my people died.—LiP
III. A rhymed address to all renegade Campbellites, exhorting them to return.—LiP
Campbell, Alice B.
Sally and Manda.—LaP
Campbell, David
"The magpie singing his delight."—ReBs
Campbell, Joseph (Seosamh MacCathmhaoil, pseud.)
"I will go with my father a-ploughing."—ArT-3
Campbell, Roy
The flaming terrapin, sel.
"Out of the ark's grim hold."—CoB (sel.)—ReO
Horses on the Camargue.—CaD—ReO
Mithraic emblems, sel.
To the sun.—PlE
"Out of the ark's grim hold." See The flaming terrapin
To the sun. See Mithraic emblems
Tristan da Cunha.—CoR
The zebras.—CoB
Campbell, Thomas
The battle of the Baltic.—CoR
Hohenlinden.—CoR—GrCt
The jilted nymph.—CoBl
Lord Ullin's daughter.—CoR
Sleep upon the world. See Vesper
Vesper.—ReO
Sleep upon the world. tr.—GrCt
Campbell, Wilfred
Indian summer.—DoW
The winter lakes.—CoBn
Campion, Thomas
XVIII. See The third book of ayres
In praise of Neptune.—CoBn
Never weather-beaten sail.—GrCt
Rose-cheeked Laura.—GrS
The soldier's dream.—CoR
"There is a garden in her face."—BoGj
The third book of ayres, sel.
XVIII.—GrS
To shades of underground.—GrCt
Camptown. John Ciardi.—HiL
"**Can** I forget." See Childhood
"**Can** I forget that winter night." See A leap-year episode
"**Can** I see another's woe." See On another's sorrow
"**Can** it be that there is no moon." Narihira.—BaS
Can someone tell me why. John Ciardi.—CiYk
"**Can** you hear the spelling bee." See Spelling bee
"**Can** you wash your father's shirt." Mother Goose.—OpF
The **canal** bank. James Stephens.—StS
Canals. See names of canals, as Panama canal
Canaries
The canary. E. Turner.—VrF
"When my canary." Shiki.—ArT-3—BeCs
The **canary.** Elizabeth Turner.—VrF

"**Canary** birds feed on sugar and seed." See Davy and the goblin—The plaint of the camel
"**Candle,** candle." See Christmas chant
"**Candle,** candle, burning clear." See The house of dream
"The **candle** is out." See The lady
"The **candle** screamed with fury." See Candles
Candles
  Candles ("The candle screamed with fury") S. Heitler.—LeM
  Candles ("The days of our future stand before us") C. P. Cavafy.—SmM
  Green candles. H. Wolfe.—SmM
  "He climbed up the candlestick." Unknown. —WyC
  "A little girl (dressed)." Mother Goose.—OpF
  "Little Nancy Etticoat." Mother Goose.—BrMg —GrCt—HuS-3
    "Little Nanny Etticoat."—ArT-3
    Mother Goose rhymes, 30.—HoB
  The tallow chandler. Unknown.—VrF
Candles ("The candle screamed with fury") Susan Heitler.—LeM
Candles ("The days of our future stand before us") C. P. Cavafy, tr. by Rae Dalven.—SmM
Candy
  All-day sucker. A. Fisher.—FiIo
  "Andy Pandy, fine and dandy." Mother Goose. —OpF
  Colter's candy. Unknown.—MoB
  Jelly beans. A. Fisher.—FiIo
  "Nauty pauty." Mother Goose.—AgH
    Jack-a-Dandy.—BrMg
Candy house. Elizabeth Jane Coatsworth.—CoSb
Cane, Melville
  Fog, the magician.—ThA
  Rural dumpheap.—BrA
  Snow toward evening.—ArT-3—LaPd
Cane
  Carma. J. Toomer.—HaK (sel.)
A **cane.** Aileen Fisher.—FiIo
"A **canner,** exceedingly canny." Carolyn Wells. —BrLl
Cannes, Frances
  Eclogue. E. Lear.—LiT
Cannibals
  "A certain young man of great gumption." Unknown.—BrLl—BrSm
  A paradox. Unknown.—BrSm
Canning, George
  The cat and the bird.—GrCt—ReBs
  Ipecacuanha.—GrCt
"**Canny** moment, lucky fit." See The nativity chant
Canoe. Patrick Anderson.—MoS
The **canoe** speaks. Robert Louis Stevenson.—MoS (sel.)
Canoes and canoeing
  Canoe. P. Anderson.—MoS
  The canoe speaks. R. L. Stevenson.—MoS (sel.)
  Hiawatha's sailing. From The song of Hiawatha. H. W. Longfellow.—LoPl
  Lullaby. R. Hillyer.—DuR—HaL—ReS
  Paddling song. Unknown.—LeO
  The rousing canoe song. H. Fraser.—DoW
The **Canterbury** tales, sels. Geoffrey Chaucer
  The ballad of Sir Thopas.—ChT
  Chanticleer and the fox.—ChT
  The fortunes of the great.—ChT
  Patient Griselda.—ChT
  Phoebus and the crow.—ChT
    Lat take a cat.—GrCt (sel.)
    Take any bird.—ReO (sel.)
  The prologue.—ChT
    "Whan that Aprille with his shoures sote." —GrCt
  The rocks of Brittany.—ChT
  The story of Constance.—ChT
  Three men in search of death.—ChT
  The wily chemist.—ChT
Canticle of spring. Harry Behn.—BeG
The **canticle** of the bees. Phyllis McGinley.—McWc
Canyons
  Between the walls of the valley. E. Peck.—BrA
  Clouds across the canyon. J. G. Fletcher.—PaH
The **cap** and bells. William Butler Yeats.—GrCt —YeR
Cape Ann, Massachusetts
  Cape Ann. From Landscapes. T. S. Eliot.—BoGj—CaD
Cape Ann. See Landscapes
Cape Hatteras
  Hatteras calling. C. Aiken.—CoBn
Cape Horn
  Cape Horn gospel. J. Masefield.—CoSs
Cape Horn gospel. John Masefield.—CoSs
Cape Race
  The way of Cape Race. E. J. Pratt.—DoW
Capes, Molly
  Hallowe'en.—ThA
"**Capital** I gave a party." See Confusions of the alphabet
Capital punishment. See Punishment.
"A **capital** ship for an ocean trip." See Davy and the goblin—A nautical ballad
Caps. See Hats
Captain Kidd. Rosemary Carr and Stephen Vincent Benét.—HiL—TuW
"**Captain** or colonel, or knight in arms." See Arms and the Muse—When the assault was intended to the city
Captain Pink of the Peppermint. Wallace Irwin. —CoSs
"The **captain** stood on the carronade: First Lieutenant, says he." See The old navy
Captain Stratton's fancy. John Masefield.—CoSs
The **captive** bird of paradise. Ruth Pitter.—GrS
The **captive** lion. William Henry Davies.—CoB
"The **car** stands still." See Time

"**Caravals** on the unmapped river." See Evening clouds
"A **caravan** from China comes." Richard Le Gallienne.—ThA
Caravans
"A caravan from China comes. R. Le Gallienne.—ThA
Caravans ("Great, grey caravans moving in the night") H. Borland.—ThA
Caravans ("I've seen caravans") I. Thompson. —StF
The pedlar's caravan. W. B. Rands.—BlO
Caravans ("Great, grey caravans moving in the night") Hal Borland.—ThA
Caravans ("I've seen caravans") Irene Thompson.—StF
Carcassonne, France
Carcassonne. G. Nadaud.—PaH
Carcassonne. Gustave Nadaud.—PaH
The **cardinal.** Robert Penn Warren.—ReBs
Cardinal birds. See Red birds
"**Cardinal,** lover of shade." See The cardinal
Cardwell, Warren
The grass.—LeM
The **careful** angler. Robert Louis Stevenson.—MoS
"The **careful** angler chose his nook." See The careful angler
"A **careful** hen had hatch'd her brood." See The jewel on the dunghill
"**Careful** Katie cooked a crisp and crinkly cabbage." Mother Goose.—OpF
Carefulness
The careful angler. R. L. Stevenson.—MoS
"Careful Katie cooked a crisp and crinkly cabbage." Mother Goose.—OpF
The careless fairy. N. B. Turner.—HoB
Careless Maria. E. Turner.—VrF
The careless niece. C. Wells.—BrSm
Careless Willie. Unknown.—CoBb
Jane, do be careful. I. Page.—CoBb
Please tell this someone to take care. J. Ciardi.—CiYk
Vain and careless. R. Graves.—CaD—HaL
The **careless** fairy. Nancy Byrd Turner.—HoB
Careless Maria. Elizabeth Turner.—VrF
The **careless** niece. Carolyn Wells.—BrSm
Careless Willie. Unknown.—CoBb
Carelessness. See Carefulness
Carentan, France
Carentan O Carentan. L. Simpson.—CaMb
Carentan O Carentan. Louis Simpson.—CaMb
Cares and joys. See King Henry VI
The **cares** of a caretaker. Wallace Irwin.—CoO
Carew, Thomas
The youthful spring.—ClF
Cargoes
Cargoes. J. Masefield.—ArT-3—CoR—CoSs—ThA
Country trucks. M. Shannon.—ArT-3
Freight boats. J. S. Tippett.—HuS-3
The freight train. R. B. Bennett.—LaP—LaPd
"I saw a ship a-sailing." Mother Goose.—ArT-3 —HuS-3—ReMg—WiMg
I saw a ship.—CoSs—SmM
Mother Goose rhymes, 60.—HoB
A ship a-sailing.—BrMg
Mine argosy from Alexandria. From The Jew of Malta. C. Marlowe.—GrCt
Red iron ore. Unknown.—ArT-3
The ships of Yule. B. Carman.—DoW
Song of the truck. D. Frankel.—BrA
The train dogs. Pauline Johnson.—DoW
Cargoes. John Masefield.—ArT-3—CoR—CoSs—ThA
Carlin, Francis (James Francis Carlin MacDonnell)
Childhood, sel.
The two nests.—ReBs
The two nests. See Childhood
Carma. Jean Toomer.—HaK (sel.)
Carman, Bliss
The daisies.—CoBn
The gravedigger.—CoBn
The ships of Yule.—DoW
Carmel, California
At Carmel. M. Austin.—BrA
Autumn in Carmel. G. Sterling.—PaH
Carmel Point. M. P. MacSweeney.—DuR
Carmel Point. Margaret Phyllis MacSweeney.—DuR
Carmer, Carl
Antique shop.—ThA
The cathedral of St Louis.—ThA
Slave quarter.—ThA
Carnevali, Emanuel
In this hotel.—GrS
Carnivals
At the carnival. A. Spencer.—HaK
"**Carol,** brothers, carol." William Muhlenberg.—ArT-3
A **carol** for children. Ogden Nash.—PlE
A **carol** for Christmas eve. Eleanor Farjeon.—HoB
Carol of the brown king. Langston Hughes.—LaPh
The **carol** of the poor children. Richard Middleton.—SmM
"A **carol** round the ruddy hearth." See For Christmas day
The **carousel** ("An empty carousel in a deserted park") G. C. Oden.—BoA—HaK
The **carousel** ("With a roof and its shadow it rotates") Rainer Maria Rilke, tr. fr. the German by M. D. Herter Norton.—LiT
Carousels. See Merry-go-rounds
Carpenter. Edward Verrall Lucas.—HuS-3
Carpenters and carpentry
Busy carpenters. J. S. Tippett.—HuS-3
Carpenter. E. V. Lucas.—HuS-3
Industrious Carpenter Dan. W. Irwin.—CoSs
The man of the house. D. Wagoner.—DuS
The walrus and the carpenter. From Through the looking-glass. L. Carroll.—BlO—HoB—HuS-3
"The time has come, the walrus said."—ArT-3 (sel.)

Carr, Mary Jane
When a ring's around the moon.—ArT-3
Carr, Teddy
Whoops a daisy.—LeM
Carrera Andrade, Jorge
"It rained in the night."—HoL
Carriage. Eleanor Farjeon.—FaT
Carriages and carts. See also Wagons
Carriage. E. Farjeon.—FaT
Coach. E. Farjeon.—FaT
The deacon's masterpiece; or, The wonderful one-horse shay. O. W. Holmes.—HuS-3
Farm cart. E. Farjeon.—FaT
Pushcart row. R. Field.—BrSg
"Up at Piccadilly, oh." Mother Goose.—ClF—ReOn
The coachman.—BrMg
The wagon in the barn. J. Drinkwater.—ThA
Carrier, Constance
Black water and bright air.—MoS
The **carrion** crow. See "A carrion crow sat on an oak"
"A **carrion** crow sat on an oak." Mother Goose. —BlO—ReMg—SmM
The carrion crow.—BrMg
Carroll, Lewis, pseud. (Charles Lutwidge Dodgson)
Alice's adventures in wonderland, sels.
"Beautiful soup, so rich and green."—BlO
Beautiful soup.—SmM
Turtle soup.—ClF
Father William.—BoGj—Lap (sel.)—LaPd (sel.)
You are old, Father William.—HoB
"You are old, Father William, the young man said."—ArT-3
"How doth the little crocodile."—ArT-3—BlO—BrSm—HoB—LaP
The lobster quadrille.—HoB
The mock turtle's song.—GrCt
"Speak roughly to your little boy."—BlO
The dutchess' lullaby.—CoBb
Beautiful soup. See Alice's adventures in wonderland—"Beautiful soup, so rich and green"
"Beautiful soup, so rich and green." See Alice's adventures in wonderland
Brother and sister.—BrSm—CoBb—GrCt
The dutchess' lullaby. See Alice's adventures in wonderland—"Speak roughly to your little boy"
Father William. See Alice's adventures in wonderland
"His sister named Lucy O'Finner."—BrLl
"How doth the little crocodile." See Alice's adventures in wonderland
Humpty Dumpty's poem. See Through the looking-glass
Humpty Dumpty's recitation. See Through the looking-glass—Humpty Dumpty's poem
"I'll tell thee everything I can." See Through the looking-glass
Jabberwocky. See Through the looking-glass
The king-fisher song. See Sylvie and Bruno concluded
The lobster quadrille. See Alice's adventures in wonderland
The mock turtle's song. See Alice's adventures in wonderland—The lobster quadrille
The pig-tale. See Sylvie and Bruno
"Speak roughly to your little boy." See Alice's adventures in wonderland
A strange wild song. See Sylvie and Bruno
Sylvie and Bruno, sels.
The pig-tale.—ReO
A strange wild song.—HuS-3
Sylvie and Bruno concluded, sel.
The king-fisher song.—BlO
"There was a young lady of station."—BrLl
"There was once a young man of Oporta."—BrLl
Through the looking-glass, sels.
Humpty Dumpty's poem.—BlO
Humpty Dumpty's recitation.—GrCt
"I'll tell thee everything I can."—AgH
Jabberwocky.—ArT-3—BoGj—HoB
The walrus and the carpenter.—BlO—HoB—HuS-3
"The time has come, the walrus said." —ArT-3 (sel.)
"The time has come, the walrus said." See Through the looking-glass—The walrus and the carpenter
Turtle soup. See Alice's adventures in wonderland—"Beautiful soup, so rich and green"
The walrus and the carpenter. See Through the looking-glass
You are old, Father William. See Alice's adventures in wonderland—Father William
"You are old, Father William, the young man said." See Alice's adventures in wonderland —Father William
"A **carrot** has a green fringed top." See Vegetables
Carruth, Hayden
New Orleans.—BrA
On a certain engagement south of Seoul.—BrA
Salt Lake City.—BrA
Carry me back. John Holmes.—BrA
Carrying their coracles. See Upon Appleton house
Carryl, Charles Edward
Davy and the goblin, sels.
A nautical ballad.—HuS-3—ThA
The plaint of the camel.—HuS-3
Robinson Crusoe's story.—CoSs—HoB
Robinson Crusoe's island.—ArT-3
A nautical ballad. See Davy and the goblin
The plaint of the camel. See Davy and the goblin
The post captain.—CoSs
Robinson Crusoe's island. See Davy and the goblin—Robinson Crusoe's story
Robinson Crusoe's story. See Davy and the goblin
Carryl, Guy Wetmore
The opportune overthrow of Humpty Dumpty.—CoBb

"**Cars.**" See Central park tourney
"The **cart** that carries hay." See Farm cart
Cartwright, William
A house blessing. See "Saint Francis and Saint Benedight"
"Saint Francis and Saint Benedight."—PlE
A house blessing.—GrCt
"**Carved** by a mighty race whose vanished hands." See The sphinx speaks
Carving away in the mist. Mangesh Padgaonkar, tr. fr. the Marathi by R. P. Sirkar.—AlPi
Casabianca. Elizabeth Bishop.—GrS
Casey at the bat. Ernest Lawrence Thayer.—BoH—MoS
Casey Jones. Unknown.—BlO—HiL—McWs
Cassie O'Lang. Unknown.—BrSm
Cassiopeia
"Queen Cassiopeia." E. Farjeon.—FaT
Cassowaries
The cassowary. C. Aiken.—AiC
The **cassowary.** Conrad Aiken.—AiC
"**Cast** our caps and cares away." John Fletcher.—SmM
"**Cast** thy bread upon the waters." See Ecclesiastes
Castle. Eleanor Farjeon.—FaT
The **castle** yonder. John Dudley.—LeM
Castles
Castle. E. Farjeon.—FaT
The castle yonder. J. Dudley.—LeM
Elegiac stanzas, suggested by a picture of Peele castle, in a storm, painted by Sir George Beaumont. W. Wordsworth.—WoP
Grongar hill. J. Dyer.—ClF (sel.)—GrCt
Knocking over castles made with marbles. K. Fraser.—FrS
"Midways of a walled garden." From Golden wings. W. Morris.—GrCt
The ogre entertains. E. J. Coatsworth.—CoDh
Castro, Victor
Color.—BaH
Casual lines. Su Shih, tr. fr. the Chinese by Teresa Li.—LeMw
"**Cat.**" Eleanor Farjeon.—BlO—CoB
Cat ("Again and again through the day") Jibanananda Das, tr. fr. the Bengali by Lila Ray.—AlPi
The **cat** ("The black cat yawns") Mary Britton Miller.—ArT-3—CoB—HoB—HuS-3—StF
A **cat** ("She had a name among the children") Edward Thomas.—BlO—ThG
A **cat** ("Silently licking his gold-white paw") John Gittings.—LeM
The **cat** ("They call me cruel. Do I know if mouse or songbird feels") See Sad memories
The **cat** ("Who pads through the wood") Joseph Payne Brennan.—BrSm
The **cat** ("Who would not love") Conrad Aiken.—AiC
The **cat** ("Within that porch, across the way") William Henry Davies.—BlO
Cat and mouse. Ted Hughes.—PlE
The **cat** and the bird. George Canning.—GrCt—ReBs
The **cat** and the fiddle. See "Hey, diddle, diddle, the cat and the fiddle"
The **cat** and the moon. William Butler Yeats.—BoGj—CoB—CoR—HaL—LiT—YeR
Cat & the weather. Mary Swenson.—CoB
Cat asks mouse out. Stevie Smith.—CaD
A **cat** called Little Bell. Unknown, ad. fr. the Japanese by Charlotte B. DeForest.—DePp
"A **cat** came fiddling out of a barn." Mother Goose.—HuS-3—WiMg
Mother Goose rhymes, 45.—HoB
"**Cat,** if you go outdoors you must walk in the snow." See On a night of snow
"A **cat** in despondency sighed." Unknown.—BrLl
Cat on couch. Barbara Howes.—CoB
"The **cat** runs races with her tail. The dog." See Signs of winter
"The **cat** sat asleep by the side of the fire." Mother Goose.—OpF
"**Cat** takes a look at the weather." See Cat & the weather
"The **cat** that comes to my window sill." See That cat
"The **cat** was once a weaver." See What the gray cat sings
"The **cat** went here and there." See The cat and the moon
Catalogue. Rosalie Moore.—DuR
"The **cataract,** whirling to the precipice." See Fragment
A **catch.** Mary Ann Hoberman.—AgH
Catch a little rhyme. Eve Merriam.—LaPd—MeC
"**Catch** and shake the cobra garden hose." See Puppy
Catch him, crow. Mother Goose.—BrF—BrMg
"**Catch** him, crow. Carry him, kite." See Catch him, crow
"**Catch** the wooden fish." Kathleen Fraser.—FrS
Catching a whale. Mary Elliott.—VrF
Catching dragonflies. Unknown, ad. fr. the Japanese by Charlotte B. DeForest.—DePp
Cater, Catherine
Here and now.—BoA
Caterpillar. See "Brown and furry"
Caterpillars
About caterpillars. A. Fisher.—FiI
"Brown and furry." C. G. Rossetti.—BrSg
Caterpillar.—BoGj—CoB—HoB—HuS-3—LaP
Caterpillars. A. Fisher.—FiC
Cocoons. D. McCord.—McE
"Fuzzy wuzzy, creepy crawly." L. S. Vanada.—ArT-3
"How soft a caterpillar steps." E. Dickinson.—DiL
Only my opinion. M. Shannon.—ArT-3—HuS-3
The tickle rhyme. I. Serraillier.—CoO—LaP
Caterpillars. Aileen Fisher.—FiC
The **cathedral** of St Louis. Carl Carmer.—ThA
Cather, Willa Sibert
Spanish Johnny.—McWs

The **cats'** tea-party. Frederick E. Weatherly.—ArT-3
"Cat's whiskers." Kazue Mizumura.—MiI
"The **cattie** rade to Paisley, to Paisley, to Paisley." Unknown.—MoB
"The **cattie** sat in the kiln-ring." Unknown.—MoB
Cattle. See also Bulls; Calves; Cowboys—Songs; Cows
A drover. P. Colum.—PaH
The herd boy. Lu Yu.—GrCt—LeMw
I have twelve oxen. Unknown.—GrCt
May-June. N. Belting.—BeCm
Mulholland's contract. R. Kipling.—CoSs
Old Blue. R. P. T. Coffin.—ReO
The ox-tamer. W. Whitman.—CoB
The prayer of the ox. C. B. de Gasztold.—LiT—McWs
Catton, Bruce
Names from the war.—BrA
Catullus, Gaius Valerius (about)
Frater ave atque vale. A. Tennyson.—GrCt—TeP
The **cauld** lad's song. See The ghost's song
Causley, Charles
Death of an aircraft.—CaMb
Innocent's song.—CaD
Nursery rhyme of innocence and experience.—BoGj—CaD
Timothy Winters.—SmM
Caution. See "Mother, may I go out to swim"
"The **cautious** collapsible cow." Arthur Guiterman.—BrLl
"A **cautious** crow clings." Bashō, tr. fr. the Japanese by Harry Behn.—BeCs
Cavafy, C. P.
Candles.—SmM
Cavalier tunes, sels. Robert Browning
I. Marching along.—BrP
II. Give a rouse.—BrP
III. Boot and saddle.—BrP
Cavaliers
Cavalier tunes, sels. R. Browning
I. Marching along.—BrP
II. Give a rouse.—BrP
III. Boot and saddle.—BrP
His cavalier. R. Herrick.—BoGj
Cavalry crossing a ford. Walt Whitman.—GrCt—WhA
Cavendish, M.
Song by Lady Happy, as a sea-goddess.—GrS
"The **caverns** of the grave I've seen." William Blake.—BlP
Caves
Mnemonic for spelunking. E. Merriam.—MeI
Staffa. J. Keats.—GrS
Ula Masondo's dream. W. Plomer.—CaMb
Caw. Walter De La Mare.—DeBg
"**Caw** Hawkie, drive Hawkie." Unknown.—MoB
Cawein, Madison (Julius)
Ku-Klux.—HiL
Proem.—CoBn
"**Cease** to lament for that thou canst not help." See Two gentlemen of Verona—Time
"**Ceaseless** are the waters, ceaselessly flowing, ceaselessly cleaning, never sleeping." See Rig Veda—To the waters
Cecilia. Unknown, tr. fr. the French by William McLennan.—DoW
Celandines
To the small celandine. W. Wordsworth.—WoP
Celebrated return. Clarence Major.—BoA
Celery
Celery. O. Nash.—HoB
Celery. Ogden Nash.—HoB
"**Celery** raw." See Celery
"**Celestial** choir, enthron'd in realms of light." See His Excellency, General Washington
The **cellar** hole. David McCord.—McAd
Cellars
The cellar hole. D. McCord.—McAd
Root cellar. T. Roethke.—CoBn—HoL
Cemeteries. See also Epitaphs; Tombs
The dead at Clonmacnois. T. W. Rolleston.—PaH
Elegy in a country churchyard. G. K. Chesterton.—McWs
God's-acre. H. W. Longfellow.—LoPl
"Grasshopper (be the keeper)." Issa.—IsF
Graveyard. R. P. T. Coffin.—BrA
In the churchyard at Cambridge. H. W. Longfellow.—LoPl
The Indian burying ground. P. Freneau.—HiL
The Jewish cemetery at Newport. H. W. Longfellow.—LoPl—PaH
Lost graveyards. E. J. Coatsworth.—CoDh
On a politician. H. Belloc.—BrSm—McWs
The Quaker graveyard in Nantucket. R. Lowell.—PaH
Quiet fun. H. Graham.—BrSm
Spooks. N. Crane.—BrSm
Vacation. W. Stafford.—BrA
"**Censers** are swinging." See The soul of the city receives the gift of the Holy Spirit
The **centaur.** May Swenson.—DuS—LiT
Centaurs
The centaur. M. Swenson.—DuS—LiT
The centaurs. J. Stephens.—CoB—StS
The **centaurs.** James Stephens.—CoB—StS
A **centipede.** See "A centipede was happy quite"
The **centipede** ("The centipede is not quite nice") A. P. Herbert.—CoB
The **centipede** ("With innumerable little footsteps") Carmen Bernos de Gasztold, tr. fr. the French by Rumer Godden.—GaC
"The **centipede** is not quite nice." See The centipede
"A **centipede** was happy quite." Unknown.—BlO
A centipede.—ArT-3
Centipedes
The centipede ("The centipede is not quite nice") A. P. Herbert.—CoB
The centipede ("With innumerable little footsteps") C. B. de Gasztold.—GaC
"A centipede was happy quite." Unknown.—BlO
A centipede.—ArT-3

Centipedes—*Continued*
The horny-goloch. Unknown.—CoB
Earwig.—MoB
Central park tourney. Mildred Weston.—BrA—DuR—LaC
Ceremonies for Christmas. Robert Herrick.—ArT-3
Ceremony. Harry Behn.—BeG
A **certain** age. Phyllis McGinley.—DuS
"A **certain** young fellow named Beebee." Unknown.—BrLl
"A **certain** young gallant named Robbie." Unknown.—BrLl
"A **certain** young man of great gumption." Unknown.—BrLl—BrSm
"**Chaff** is in my eye." See Song for an unlucky man
Chaffee, Eleanor Alletta
The cobbler.—ArT-3
Chain. Paul Petrie.—CoB
The **chair** house. Elizabeth Jane Coatsworth.—CoSb
Chairoplane chant. Nancy Byrd Turner.—StF
Chairs
Chairoplane chant. N. B. Turner.—StF
Old chairs. Mother Goose.—BrMg
Riddles. R. Ainsworth.—StF
The table and the chair. E. Lear.—HoB—HuS-3
Chakravarty, Amiya
Calcutta.—AlPi
Challenge. Samuel Hazo.—MoS
Chamber music, sels. James Joyce
"Lean out of the window."—CoBl—HaL
Goldenhair.—GrCt—ThA
"My love is in a light attire."—HaL
The noise of waters.—ArT-3
All day I hear.—HoL
"All day I hear the noise of waters."—LiT
"Strings in the earth and air."—HaL
The **chamber** over the gate. Henry Wadsworth Longfellow.—LoPl
The **chameleon** ("The chameleon changes his color") A. P. Herbert.—CoB
The **chameleon** ("Two travellers of such a cast") James Merrick.—ClF (sel.)
"The **chameleon** changes his color." See The chameleon
"A **chameleon,** when he's feeling blue." Eve Merriam.—BrLl
Chameleons. See Lizards
Chamisso, Adelbert von
A tragic story.—HoB
Chan, Fang-shēng
Sailing homeward.—ArT-3—LeM—ThA
Chang Liang-ch'en
"Whose are this pond and house."—LeMw
Chang Yin-nan and Walmsley, Lewis C.
Egret dyke, trs.—LeMw
Two songs of spring wandering. trs.—LeMw
White Stone Bank. trs.—LeMw
Change
"Alter? When the hills do." E. Dickinson.—DiPe
Courthouse square. H. Merrill.—BrA
"The days and months do not last long." Pai Ta-shun.—LeMw
For my people. M. Walker.—AdIa—BoA—HaK
House in Denver. T. H. Ferril.—BrA
"I could not prove the years had feet." E. Dickinson.—DiPe
Modifications. R. Koertge.—DuS
Mutability. W. Wordsworth.—WoP
The old men admiring themselves in the water. W. B. Yeats.—BoGj—LiT—YeR
Progress. E. Agnew.—BrA
Texas. A. Lowell.—BrA
Trail breakers. J. Daugherty.—BrA
"The world turns and the world changes." From The rock. T. S. Eliot.—ArT-3
Changeling. Barbara Young.—ThA
Changelings
Changeling. B. Young.—ThA
Solitude. W. De La Mare.—DeBg
Changing the wheel. Bertolt Brecht, tr. fr. the German by Michael Hamburger.—HoL
Channel U. S. A.—live. Adrien Stoutenburg.—BrA—HiL
Chanson innocente, sels. E. E. Cummings
"In just."—DuR
"Little tree."—CoR—HaL
Chanson innocente II.—LaPd
A **chant** out of doors. Marguerite Wilkinson.—ThA
Chanteys. See Work songs
Chanticleer ("High and proud on the barnyard fence") John Farrar.—ArT-3
Chanticleer ("Of all the birds from east to west") Katherine Tynan.—ArT-3—TuW
Chanticleer and the fox. See The Canterbury tales
Chanukah. See Jews
Chao Yeh
A boatwoman.—LeMw
"**Chap** at the door." See Face game
Chapman, George
The masque of the twelve months, sel. at.
"Shine out, fair sun, with all your heat."—GrCt
"Shine out, fair sun, with all your heat." See The masque of the twelve months
Chapman, John (about)
The apple-barrel of Johnny Appleseed. V. Lindsay.—BrA
Ballad of Johnny Appleseed. H. O. Oleson.—ArT-3
In praise of Johnny Appleseed. V. Lindsay.—HuS-3—LiP
Johnny Appleseed. R. C. and S. V. Benét.—HoB
Johnny Appleseed speaks of the apple-blossom amaranth that will come to this city. V. Lindsay.—LiP
Johnny Appleseed's hymn to the sun. V. Lindsay.—LiP

Johnny Appleseed's ship comes in. V. Lindsay. —LiP
Johnny Appleseed's wife from the palace of Eve. V. Lindsay.—LiP
Chappell, George S.
The tub.—StF
Character. See Conduct of life
The **character** of Holland. Andrew Marvell.—GrCt (sel.)
Character of the happy warrior. William Wordsworth.—WoP
Characteristics of a child three years old. William Wordsworth.—WoP
Characterization. Yogesvara, tr. fr. the Sanskrit by Daniel H. H. Ingalls.—AlPi
Charcoal burner. Unknown, at. to William Darton.—VrF
Charcoal burners
Charcoal burner. Unknown.—VrF
The **charge** of the Light Brigade. Alfred Tennyson.—TeP
Charity
The blinded bird. T. Hardy.—CoB—PlE
Charity ("Do you see that old beggar who stands at the door") E. Turner.—VrF
Charity ("Though I speak with the tongues of men and of angels") From First epistle of Paul to the Corinthians, Bible, New Testament.—HuS-3
The fan. E. Turner.—VrF
The new penny. E. Turner.—VrF
The poor cripple girl. H. S. Horsley.—VrF
Substantiations. Vallana.—AlPi
Charity ("Do you see that old beggar who stands at the door") Elizabeth Turner.—VrF
Charity ("Though I speak with the tongues of men and of angels") See First epistle of Paul to the Corinthians
Charles, Ray (about)
The bishop of Atlanta: Ray Charles. H. J. Bond.—BoA
Charles d'Orléans (Comte d'Angoulême)
Confession.—GrCt
Charles I, of England (about)
"As I was going by Charing cross." Mother Goose.—BlO—OpF
By the statue of King Charles at Charing cross.—CoR
Give a rouse. From Cavalier tunes. R. Browning.—BrP
King Charles upon the scaffold. From An Horatian ode upon Cromwell's return from Ireland. A. Marvell.—GrCt
Charles II, of England (about)
Impromptu on Charles II. J. Wilmot, Earl of Rochester.—GrCt
On Charles II.—McWs
Charles IV, sel. Percy Bysshe Shelley
"A widow bird sate mourning for her love."—BlO
Song from Charles IV.—SmM
Charleston, South Carolina
Dusk. D. Heyward.—PaH
Charley. See "Charley, Charley"
Charley Barley. Mother Goose.—BrMg
"**Charley** Barley, butter and eggs." See Charley Barley
"**Charley,** Charley." Mother Goose.—WiMg
Charley.—BrF
"**Charley** Wag, Charley Wag." Mother Goose.—AgH—OpF
"Charlie Wag."—BrMg
"**Charlie** Wag." See "Charley Wag, Charley Wag"
Charlie Warlie. Mother Goose.—BrMg
"**Charlie** Warlie had a cow." See Charlie Warlie
A **charm** ("If ye fear to be affrighted") Robert Herrick.—GrCt
A **charm** ("Thou moon, that aidest us with thy magic might") John Dryden.—GrCt
A **charm** against a magpie. Unknown.—GrCt
A **charm** against cough. See Atharva Veda
A **charm** against the toothache. John Heath-Stubbs.—CaD—SmM
A **charm** for spring flowers. Rachel Field.—ArT-3 —TuW
"**Charm** me asleep, and melt me so." See To musique, to becalme his fever
"A **charming** old lady of Settle." Edward Lear. BrLl
Charms
An amulet. S. Menashe.—SmM
"Bump, bump, please go away." Unknown.—WyC
A charm ("If ye fear to be affrighted") R. Herrick.—GrCt
A charm ("Thou moon, that aidest us with thy magic might") J. Dryden.—GrCt
A charm against a magpie. Unknown.—GrCt
A charm against cough. From Atharva Veda. Unknown.—AlPi
A charm against the toothache. J. Heath-Stubbs.—CaD—SmM
A charm for spring flowers. R. Field.—ArT-3 —TuW
"Come, butter, come." Mother Goose.—HuS-3
Churning.—BrMg
"Eastward I stand, mercies I beg." Unknown. —PlE
XVIII. From The third book of ayres. T. Campion.—GrS
"The fair maid who, the first of May." Mother Goose.—OpF
The fair maid.—ReOn
The first of May.—BrMg
Mother Goose rhymes, 34.—HoB
Hempseed. Mother Goose.—ReOn
"Hiccup, hiccup." Unknown.—MoB
Ladybird. Unknown.—MoB
"Magpie, magpie, chatter and flee." Mother Goose.—OpF
To the magpie.—BrMg
The peddler of spells. Lu Yu.—LeMw
"Rain, rain, go away (come again)." Mother Goose.—ArT-3
To the rain.—BrMg
A spell of invisibility. From The tragical history of Dr Faustus. C. Marlowe.—GrCt

Charms—*Continued*
Struthill well. Unknown.—MoB
A talisman. Marianne Moore.—BoGj—HoL
Witches' charm. B. Jonson.—BlO
The witch's song. Mother Goose.—BrMg
Chase, Betty
Why prejudice.—BaH
"**Chasing** the fireflies." K. Mizumura.—MiI
Chattahoochee river
Song of the Chattahoochee. S. Lanier.—BrA—CoBn
Chattopadhyaya, Harindranath
The white bird.—AlPi
Chaucer, Geoffrey
Balade.—GrCt
The ballad of Sir Thopas. See The Canterbury tales
The Canterbury tales, sels.
The ballad of Sir Thopas.—ChT
Chanticleer and the fox.—ChT
The fortunes of the great.—ChT
Patient Griselda.—ChT
Phoebus and the crow.—ChT
Lat take a cat.—GrCt (sel.)
Take any bird.—ReO (sel.)
The prologue.—ChT
"Whan that Aprille with his shoures sote."—GrCt
The rocks of Brittany.—ChT
The story of Constance.—ChT
Three men in search of death.—ChT
The wily alchemist.—ChT
Chanticleer and the fox. See The Canterbury tales
The fortunes of the great. See The Canterbury tales
Lat take a cat. See The Canterbury tales—Phoebus and the crow
Patient Griselda. See The Canterbury tales
Phoebus and the crow. See The Canterbury tales
The prologue. See The Canterbury tales
The rocks of Brittany. See The Canterbury tales
The story of Constance. See The Canterbury tales
Take any bird. See The Canterbury tales—Phoebus and the crow
Three men in search of death. See The Canterbury tales
"Whan that Aprille with his shoures sote." See The Canterbury tales—The prologue
The wily alchemist. See The Canterbury tales
Chaucer, Geoffrey (about)
Chaucer. H. W. Longfellow.—LoPl
Chaucer's Thames. W. Morris.—ClF (sel.)
Chaucer. Henry Wadsworth Longfellow.—LoPl
Chaucer's Thames. William Morris.—ClF (sel.)
Check. James Stephens.—ArT-3—HaL—ReS—StS—ThA
"**Cheer** up, ye young men all, let nothing fright you." See Brave Wolfe
"A **cheerful** and industrious beast." See Mixed beasts—The Bumblebeaver
"A **cheerful** old bear at the zoo." Unknown.—BrLl
Cheerfulness. See Happiness; Laughter; Optimism
Cheers. Eve Merriam.—DuR—MeI
"**Cheese** and bread." Unknown.—MoB
"**Cheese** and bread for gentlemen." Mother Goose.—OpF
"A **cheese** that was aged and gray." Unknown.—BrLl
Ch'en Fu
Returning.—LeMw
Ch'en Meng-chia
The song of the wind bell.—LeMw
Ch'en Shih-hsiang. See Acton, Harold and Ch'en Shih-hsiang
Cheney, John Vance
Evening.—ReS (sel.)
Cheney, W.
Tragedy.—CoO
Cherokee Indians. See Indians of the Americas—Cherokee
Cherries
"As I went through the garden gap." Mother Goose
Mother Goose rhymes, 31.—HoB
Bread and cherries. W. De La Mare.—BrSg
A cherry fair. Unknown.—GrCt
"Cherry pie black." E. Farjeon.—FaT
Cherry-stones ("How many cherries") E. Farjeon.—AgH
"How many cherries."—FaT
Cherry stones ("Tinker, tailor") Mother Goose.—BrMg
The child and the sparrow. T. Westwood.—ReBs
"Come a riddle, come a riddle." Unknown.—MoB
Miss Cherry. W. De La Mare.—DeBg
"Mother shake the cherry-tree." C. G. Rossetti.—ArT-3
Next year. E. Farjeon.—FaT
"Riddle me, riddle me ree (a little man)." Mother Goose.—BrMg
Song for a hot day. E. J. Coatsworth.—HuS-3
This year. E. Farjeon.—FaT
Under the boughs. G. Baro.—CoBn
"**Cherries,** ripe cherries." See Bread and cherries
"The **cherry** blossoms (of the)." Yekei Hoshi.—BaS
"The **cherry** blossoms (they have)." Issa, tr. fr. the Japanese by R. H. Blyth.—IsF
A **cherry** fair. Unknown.—GrCt
"**Cherry** pie black." Eleanor Farjeon.—FaT
Cherry-stones ("How many cherries") Eleanor Farjeon.—AgH
"How many cherries."—FaT
Cherry stones ("Tinker, tailor, soldier, sailor") Mother Goose.—BrMg
"The **cherry** tree blossomed. Black was my hair." Tomonori, tr. fr. the Japanese by Chi' Hwang Chu and Edna Worthley Underwood.—LeMw

The **cherry-tree** carol. Unknown.—GrCt
"As Joseph was a-walking."—HuS-3
Cherry trees
The cherry blossoms (of the)." Yekei Hoshi.—BaS
"The cherry-blossoms (they have)." Issa.—IsF
"The cherry tree blossomed. Black was my hair." Tomonori.—LeMw
The cherry-tree carol. Unknown.—GrCt
"As Joseph was a-walking."—HuS-3
The cherry trees. E. Thomas.—ThG
Cuckoo, cherry tree. Mother Goose.—BrMg
Loveliest of trees. From A Shropshire lad. A. E. Housman.—BlO—CoBn—HuS-3—SmM—TuW
"Loveliest of trees, the cherry now."—GrCt
"A mosquito bit me." Issa.—IsF
"Oh, fair to see." C. G. Rossetti.—ArT-3
The prancing pony. Unknown.—DePp
Under the boughs. G. Baro.—CoBn
"Under the cherry-blossoms." Issa.—IsF
Weeping cherry trees. Unknown.—DePp
The **cherry** trees. Edward Thomas.—ThG
"The **cherry** trees bend over and are shedding." See The cherry trees
Chess
The game of chess. E. Pound.—LiT
Chesterman, Hugh
Noah and the rabbit.—ReO
Chesterton, Gilbert Keith
A Christmas carol.—ArT-3
Elegy in a country churchyard.—McWs
In the evening.—LiT
The song of Quoodle.—BoGj
"A **chestnut** falls." Bashō, tr. fr. the Japanese by R. H. Blyth.—LeMw
Chestnut trees
"Above the ruins." Bashō.—BeCs
Chestnuts
"First I am frosted." M. Austin
Rhyming riddles.—ArT-3
Horse-chestnut time. K. Starbird.—LaPd
"How fits his umber coat." E. Dickinson.—DiPe
Chettur, Rajiv
Fleeing to safety.—LeM
Cheyenne Indians. See Indians of the Americas—Cheyenne
Chi' Hwang Chu and Underwood, Edna Worthley
After rain. trs.—HoL
"The cherry tree blossomed. Black was my hair." trs.—LeMw
"How the great moon crushes the cloud." trs.—LeMw
Neighbors. trs.—LeMw
Chicago
Chicago. C. Sandburg.—PaH
Night. From The windy city. C. Sandburg.—LaC
Tonight in Chicago. Unknown.—BrA
Chicago fire, 1870
Chicago. B. Harte.—HiL
Chicago ("Blackened and bleeding, helpless, panting, prone") Bret Harte.—HiL
Chicago ("Hog butcher for the world") Carl Sandburg.—PaH
The **Chicago** Defender sends a man to Little Rock, Fall, 1967. Gwendolyn Brooks.—BoA
Chickadee. Hilda Conkling.—ArT-3
"The **chickadee** in the appletree." See Chickadee
Chicakdees
Chickadee. H. Conkling.—ArT-3
"Tammy, Tammy Titmouse." Unknown.—MoB
"The **chicken.**" Unknown, tr. fr. the Japanese by R. H. Blyth.—LeI
Chicken. Walter De La Mare.—ArT-3
Chicken come clock. Mother Goose.—ReOn
"**Chicken** come clock around the rock." See Chicken come clock
Chickens
Biddy. F. Lape.—CoB
"A bright red flower he wears on his head." Unknown.—WyC
Chanticleer ("High and proud on the barnyard fence") J. Farrar.—ArT-3
Chanticleer ("Of all the birds from east to west") K. Tynan.—ArT-3—TuW
Chanticleer and the fox. From The Canterbury tales. G. Chaucer.—ChT
"The chicken." Unknown.—LeI
Chicken. W. De La Mare.—ArT-3
The chickens ("Said the first little chicken") Unknown.—StF
Five little chickens.—LaPd
The chickens ("What a fearful battle") R. Fyleman.—ArT-3
Chicks and ducks. Unknown.—StF
The cock. Unknown.—VrF
"Cock a doodle doo (my dame)." Mother Goose.—BrMg
"Cock-a-doodle-do."—ReMg
Cock and hen ("Ilka day") Unknown.—MoB
Cock and hen ("Lock the dairy door") Mother Goose.—BrMg
What the cock and hen say.—ReOn
Cock-crow. E. Thomas.—ThG
"The cock doth crow." Mother Goose.—ArT-3
"Cocks crow in the morn." Mother Goose.—ArT-3—ReMg
"Come and see." Unknown.—WyC
Fingers in the nesting box. R. Graves.—CoB
The fox and the rooster. E. Rees.—ArT-3
The hen and the carp. I. Serraillier.—CoB
The hens. E. M. Roberts.—ArT-3—BoGj—CoB—HuS-3—LaPd—ThA—TuW
The hen's nest. J. Clare.—ReO
"Hickety, pickety, my black hen." Mother Goose.—OpF—ReMg—WiMg
"Higgledy, piggledy, my black hen."—ArT-3—HuS-3
Mother Goose rhymes, 18.—HoB
My black hen.—BrMg
"I had a wee cock and I loved it well." Unknown.—MoB
The jewel on the dunghill. R. S. Sharpe.—VrF
The little black hen. A. A. Milne.—MiC

Chickens—*Continued*
The mother hen. C. B. de Gasztold.—GaC
"An old lady living in Worcester." Unknown. —BrLl
"Old Mother Minchin." J. Kenward.—SmM
The prayer of the cock. C. B. de Gasztold.—ArT-3
"A pullet in the pen." Mother Goose.—AgH
"The Reverend Henry Ward Beecher." O. W. Holmes.—BrLl
Henry Ward Beecher.—GrCt
Rooster. F. Belkin.—CoB
Roosters and hens. H. Behn.—BeG
"The silly bit chicken." Unknown.—MoB
"There was an old man who lived in Middle Row." Mother Goose.—OpF
Five hens.—BrMg
Wild spurs. Owen.—LeM
The **chickens** ("Said the first little chicken") Unknown.—StF
Five little chickens.—LaPd
The **chickens** ("What a fearful battle") Rose Fyleman.—ArT-3
Chicks and ducks. Unknown.—StF
"The **chief** defect of Henry King." See Henry King, who chewed bits of string, and was early cut off in dreadful agonies
"A **chieftain,** to the Highlands bound." See Lord Ullin's daughter
Ch'ien Ch'i
From my study at the mouth of the valley.—LeMw
Chien Hsu
"A piece of colored cloud shines on the stone wall."—LeMw
Child, Lydia Maria
Thanksgiving day.—HuS-3—LaPh
Who stole the nest.—StF
The **child.** Ivor Popham.—PlE
The **child** and the sparrow. Thomas Westwood. —ReBs
The **child** in school. Unknown, tr. fr. the Chinese by Alan S. Lee.—LeMw
The **child** in the orchard. Edward Thomas.—ThG
"The **child** is holy and most wise." See The child
Child labor
The cry of the children. E. B. Browning.—ClF (sel.)
The **child** next door. Rose Fyleman.—ThA
"The **child** next door has a wreath on her hat." See The child next door
Child on top of a greenhouse. Theodore Roethke.—DuR—HaL
The **child** on the cliffs. Edward Thomas.—ThG
The **child** on the curbstone. Elinor Wylie.—LaC
"A **child** should have pockets." See Pockets
"The **child** sobs." Issa, tr. fr. the Japanese by R. H. Blyth.—IsF—LeOw
"A **child** stretched forth." Torai, tr. by Nobuyuki Yuasa.—LeMw
"The **child** sways on the swing." Issa, tr. fr. the Japanese by R. H. Blyth.—LeMw
A **child** that has a cold. Thomas Dibdin.—GrCt
"A **child** that has a cold we may suppose." See A child that has a cold
Child with malaria. Clark Mills.—DuS
Childe Harold's pilgrimage, sels. George Gordon Byron
"Are not the mountains, waves, and skies, a part."—CoBn
The ocean.—CoSs
Deep and dark blue ocean.—GrCt
On Rome.—ByP
Waterloo.—ByP
Childe Roland to the dark tower came. Robert Browning.—BrP—CoD
Childhood. See Children and childhood
Childhood, sel. Francis Carlin
The two nests.—ReBs
Childhood, sel. John Clare
Bat.—ReO
Childhood ("Can I forget") Henri Percikow.—LaC
Childhood ("Oh there is blessing in this gentle breeze") See The prelude. William Wordsworth
Childhood ("When I was a child I knew red miners") Margaret Walker.—HaK
Childhood recollections
August from my desk. R. Flint.—BrA—DuR
The bells of Shandon. Father Prout.—CoR—GrCt—PaH
A boy's song. J. Hogg.—BlO
Childhood. H. Percikow.—LaC
The chums. T. Roethke.—DuS
The ecchoing green. W. Blake.—BlP
Fern hill. D. Thomas.—BoGj—CoR
Flame-heart. C. McKay.—BoA
Fortune. L. Ferlinghetti.—DuR—LaC
From a childhood. R. M. Rilke.—GrS
A memory. L. A. G. Strong.—CaD
My lost youth. H. W. Longfellow.—BoGj—CoR—LoPl
Nurses' song. W. Blake.—BlP
Poem in October. D. Thomas.—CaD
Yardbird's skull. O. Dodson.—AdIa—BoA
"Children." Issa, tr. fr. the Japanese by Nobuyuki Yuasa.—IsF
Children and childhood. See also Babies; Boys and boyhood; Childhood recollections; Girls and girlhood
A—apple pie. W. De La Mare.—DeBg
"Ah, to be." Issa.—IsF—LeOw
Alone. E. A. Poe.—PoP
American child. P. Engle.—BrA
At a child's baptism. V. Miller.—BoGj
The babes in the wood. Unknown.—BlO
Ballad of the little square. F. G. Lorca.—LiT
"Be still, my child." Unknown.—DoC—LeO
The birthday. P. McGinley.—McWc
A black man talks of reaping.—AdIa—BoA—BoH—HaK
A carol for children. O. Nash.—PlE
Characteristics of a child three years old. W. Wordsworth.—WoP
The child. I. Popham.—PlE
The child in the orchard. E. Thomas.—ThG

Child on top of a greenhouse. T. Roethke.—DuR—HaL
The child on the cliffs. E. Thomas.—ThG
Child with malaria. C. Mills.—DuS
Childhood ("Oh there is blessing in this gentle breeze") From The prelude. W. Wordsworth.—WoP
Childhood ("When I was a child I knew red miners") M. Walker.—HaK
"Children." Issa.—IsF
"Children are the children of the wind." Santaro.—LeMw
Children's crusade 1939. B. Brecht.—CaMb
A children's don't. H. Graham.—CoBb (sel.)
The children's hour. H. W. Longfellow.—TuW
The child's morning. W. T. Scott.—DuR
Clinton south of Polk. C. Sandburg.—BrA
The collier. V. Watkins.—CaD
"Come away, away children." Unknown.—BlO
Cornwall. C. Bond.—LeM
The cry of the children. E. B. Browning.—ClF (sel.)
Ditty for a child losing his first tooth. Unknown.—DoC
The dreamer. W. Childress.—DuS
Early supper. B. Howes.—BoGj
The ecchoing green. W. Blake.—BlP
"An exhausted sparrow." Issa.—IsF—LeOw
Extremely naughty children. E. Godley.—CoBb
Foreign children. R. L. Stevenson.—BoGj—HoB
The forsaken merman. M. Arnold.—BlO—CoSs—SmM
Four children. Mother Goose.—BrMg
Good and bad children. R. L. Stevenson.—BlO—CoBb
Hiawatha's childhood. From The song of Hiawatha. H. W. Longfellow.—ArT-3—HuS-3
Holy Thursday ("Is this a holy thing to see") W. Blake.—BlP
Holy Thursday ("'Twas on a Holy Thursday, their innocent faces clean") W. Blake.—BlP
Indian children. A. Wynne.—ArT-3—HuS-3
Kids. From Some short poems. W. Stafford.—GrCt
Little children. T. N. Tsosie.—BaH
The massacre of the innocents. W. J. Smith.—PlE
Mutterings over the crib of a deaf child. James Wright.—DuS
"My children, my children." Unknown.—LeO
"My parents kept me from children who were rough." S. Spender.—CaD
Rough.—HoL
Nurse's song ("When the voices of children are heard on the green and laughing") W. Blake.—BlP—ClF—HoB—ReS
Nurse's song ("When the voices of children are heard on the green and whisp'rings") W. Blake.—BlP
On the seashore. R. Tagore.—AlPi
"Overhead the tree-tops meet." From Pippa passes. R. Browning.—BrP
The Pied Piper of Hamelin. R. Browning.—ArT-3—BrP—GrT—HoB—HuS-3
"Rats."—CoB (sel.)
"Ring around the world." A. Wynne.—ArT-3—HuS-3
Saturday's child. C. Cullen.—BoH—HaK
A small migration. H. Behn.—BeG
Song against children. A. Kilmer.—ThA
The stern parent. H. Graham.—CoBb—GrCt
The stolen child. W. B. Yeats—YeR
"There was an old woman who lived in a shoe." Mother Goose.—HuS-3—OpF—ReMg—WiMg
Mother Goose rhymes, 52.—HoB
Three years she grew. W. Wordsworth.—WoP
"Throughout the world." Unknown.—LeO
We are seven. W. Wordsworth.—WoP
"We pray that the beetles appear." Unknown.—LeO
"Why dost thou weep, my child." Unknown.—LeO
Won't. W. De La Mare.—DeBg
A world to do. T. Weiss.—GrS

"The **children** are singing." See Singing
"**Children** are the children of the wind." Santaro, tr. fr. the Japanese by R. H. Blyth.—LeMw
"**Children** born of fairy stock." See I'd love to be a fairy's child
"The **children** celebrate a failure and a treason." See Fifth of November
"**Children,** for this small book some thanks are due." See Address from the printer to his little readers
"Children, if you dare to think." See Warning to children
"The **children** of Israel prayed for bread." See Old Sam's wife
"The **children** of Israel wanted bread." See Old Sam's wife
"**Children** of the future age." See A little girl lost
Children of the wind. See The people, yes
"The **children** sing." See Ballad of the little square
"**Children** when they're very sweet." John Ciardi.—CoBb
"**Children,** you are very little." See Good and bad children
Children's crusade 1939. Bertolt Brecht, tr. fr. the German by Michael Hamburger.—CaMb
A **children's** don't. Harry Graham.—CoBb (sel.)
The **children's** hour. Henry Wadsworth Longfellow.—TuW
"**Children's** voices in the orchard." See Landscapes—New Hampshire

Childress, William
The dreamer.—DuS
Korea bound, 1952.—BrA

A **child's** day, sels. Walter De La Mare
"Softly, drowsily"
A child's day, Part II.—ArT-3
A child's day begins.—HuS-3
"This little morsel of morsels here."—AgH

A **child's** day, Part II. See A child's day—"Softly, drowsily"
A **child's** day begins. See A child's day—"Softly, drowsily"
Child's evening hymn. Sabine Baring-Gould.—ReS
A **child's** grace. Robert Herrick.—PlE
  Another grace for a child.—BoGj
  Grace before meals.—GrT
  Grace before meat.—GrCt
  Grace for a child.—SmM
The **child's** morning. Winfield Townley Scott.—DuR
A **child's** pet. William Henry Davies.—CoB
Child's prayer. Mary Lundie Duncan.—GrT
A **child's** prayer at evening. Charles G. D. Roberts.—ReS
Child's song. See A garden song
Chiliasm. Richard Eberhart.—PlE
Chill of the eve. James Stephens.—StS
Chillicothe, Ohio
  A siding near Chillicothe. R. Lattimore.—BrA
Chimes. Francis Meynell.—TuW
The **chimney** sweeper ("A little black thing among the snow") William Blake.—BlP
The **chimney** sweeper ("Sweep, sweep, sweep, sweep, cries little Jack") Elizabeth Turner.—VrF
The **chimney** sweeper ("When my mother died I was very young") William Blake.—BlP
Chimney sweeps
  The chimney sweeper ("A little black thing among the snow") W. Blake.—BlP
  The chimney sweeper ("Sweep, sweep, sweep, sweep, cries little Jack") E. Turner.—VrF
  The chimney sweeper ("When my mother died I was very young") W. Blake.—BlP
  "Eaper Weaper, chimney sweeper." Mother Goose.—ReMg
  Wmffre the sweep. R. Humphries.—PlE
Chimneys
  "Black within, and red without." Mother Goose.—BrMg
    Mother Goose rhymes, 27.—HoB
"**Chimpanzee,** you have kindly eyes." See Lord of jesters, prince of fellows
China
  But no. E. J. Coatsworth.—CoDh
  "A caravan from China comes." R. Le Gallienne.—ThA
  The Ching-Ting mountain. Li T'ai-po.—LiT
  Digging for China. R. Wilbur.—BoGj
  March. N. Belting.—BeCm
  The most-sacred mountain. E. Tietjens.—PaH
  The road to China. O. B. Miller.—StF
  Shantung; or, The empire of China is crumbling down. V. Lindsay.—LiP
  To his friend, Wei. Li T'ai-po.—LiT (sel.)
  The tower of Genghis Khan. H. Allen.—PaH
  The wall of China. P. Colum.—CoR
China—History
  The nefarious war. Li T'ai-po.—LiT
  Under the frontier post. Wang Chang-Ling.—GrCt
  War. Li T'ai-po.—GrCt
Chinaware. See Pottery
Chinese
  African China. M. B. Tolson.—HaK
  The Chinese bumboatman. Unknown.—CoSs
  The Chinese nightingale. V. Lindsay.—LiP
  From Cadillac mountain. E. J. Coatsworth.—CoDh
  "He shot at Lee Wing." Unknown.—BrSm
  The people of Tao-chow. Po Chü-i.—GrCt
  The river-merchant's wife: A letter. Li T'ai-po.—BoH—CoBl—LiT
  The women of Yueh. Li T'ai-po.—HoL
The **Chinese** bumboatman. Unknown.—CoSs
The **Chinese** nightingale. Vachel Lindsay.—LiP
"**Ching-a-ring-a-ring-ching,** Feast of Lanterns." Mother Goose.—OpF
The **Ching-Ting** mountain. Li T'ai-po, tr. fr. the Chinese by Shigeyoshi Obata.—LiT
"**Chip** the glasses and crack the plates." See The hobbit—Dwarves 'song
Chipmunk. James S. Tippett.—HuS-3
Chipmunk, chipmunk. Mark Van Doren.—ReS
"**Chipmunk,** chipmunk, little and small." See Chipmunk, chipmunk
Chipmunks
  Chipmunk. J. S. Tippett.—HuS-3
  Chipmunks. M. Pomeroy.—CoB
  The chipmunk's song. R. Jarrell.—LaPd
Chipmunks. Marnie Pomeroy.—CoB
"**Chipmunks** jump, and." See Valentine
The **chipmunk's** song. Randall Jarrell.—LaPd
Chipp, Elinor
  Wild geese.—ArT-3
Chippewa Indians. See Indians of the Americas—Chippewa
Chisoku
  "The face of the dragonfly."—LeMw
Chitre, Dilip
  Poem. tr.—AlPi
Chivalry. See also Knights and knighthood; Romance; also names of knights, as Arthur, King
  The rhyme of the chivalrous shark. W. Irwin.—BrSm
Chiyo
  "I must go begging."—BeCs
  "If the white herons."—BeCs
  "Where does he wander."—BeCs
Chiyo-ni
  "O butterfly (everything)."—LeMw
  "Spring rain."—LeMw
"**Chlora,** come view my soul, and tell." See The gallery
Ch'n Ta-kao
  Her birthday. tr.—LeMw
The **choice.** Dorothy Parker.—CoBl
"**Choose** the darkest part o' the grove." See Oedipus—Incantation to Oedipus
Choosing
  The choice. D. Parker.—CoBl
  Choosing. E. Farjeon.—ArT-3
  Choosing a kitten. Unknown.—HuS-3
  Choosing shoes. F. Wolfe.—ArT-3—StF

Christmas eve under Hooker's statue. Robert Lowell.—HiL
A **Christmas** folk-song. Lizette Woodworth Reese.—ArT-3—ThA
Christmas in the woods. Frances M. Frost.—ArT-3 (sel.)
"**Christmas** is coming, the geese are getting fat." See Christmas
Christmas lullaby for a new-born child. Yvonne Gregory.—BoA
Christmas morning. Elizabeth Madox Roberts.—HuS-3
Christmas mouse. Aileen Fisher.—LaPh
Christmas 1959 et cetera. Gerald William Barrax.—HaK
Christmas 1945. Al Hine.—HiL
The **Christmas** present. Patricia Hubbell.—LaPd
The **Christmas** pudding. Unknown.—ArT-3—LaPh
A **Christmas** sonnet. Edwin Arlington Robinson.—PlE
Christmas stocking. Eleanor Farjeon.—LaPh
Christmas time. See Marmion
Christmas tree ("I'll find me a spruce") Aileen Fisher.—LaPh
Christmas tree ("My kitten thinks") Aileen Fisher.—FiIo—LaPd
Christmas trees
Best of all. A. Fisher.—FiC
Christmas tree ("I'll find me a spruce") A. Fisher.—LaPh
Christmas tree ("My kitten thinks") A. Fisher.—FiIo—LaPd
Come Christmas. D. McCord.—McAd—McE
"Little tree." From Chanson innocente. E. E. Cummings.—CoR—HaL
Chanson innocente II.—LaPd
Roundelay. I. Gardner.—HoL
Christopher Marlowe. See Henry Reynolds, of poets and poesy
"**Christopher** Robin." See Sneezles
"**Christopher** Robin goes." See Hoppity
Christy, Arthur
A bird song in the ravine. tr.—LeMw
Midnight in the garden. tr.—LeMw
On visiting a clear spring. tr.—LeMw
River travel. tr.—LeMw
Chrysanthemum colors. Unknown, ad. fr. the Japanese by Charlotte B. DeForest.—DePp
Chrysanthemums
Chrysanthemum colors. Unknown.—DePp
Reflection. Tomonori.—LeMw
"The white chrysanthemum." Mitsune.—BaS
Chu Hsi
The boats are afloat.—LeMw
Chu Miao Tuan
Butterflies.—LeMw
Ch'u Ta-kao
Longing for the south country. tr.—LeMw
Walking by the stream. tr.—LeMw
Chucklehead. Patricia Robbins.—ArT-3
"**Chuff,** chuff, chuff. An' a mountainbluff." See A song of Panama
The **chums.** Theodore Roethke.—DuS
Church, Richard
Mirage.—SmM
Churches
"Around the church." From Poems. J. Lester.—HaK
At church. E. Turner.—VrF
At Dunwich. A. Thwaite.—CaMb
The birds of the air. Mother Goose.—ReOn
By a chapel as I came. Unknown.—GrCt
The cathedral of St Louis. C. Carmer.—ThA
Divina commedia. H. W. Longfellow.—LoPl
The forsaken merman. M. Arnold.—BlO—CoSs—SmM
"Johnny went to church one day." Unknown.—CoBb
Les Saintes-Maries-de-la-Mer. A. Ross.—CaD
The little vagabond. W. Blake.—BlP
Poet to his love. M. Bodenheim.—CoBl
St Isaac's church, Petrograd. C. McKay.—BoA—HaK
Santa Maria Maggiore, Rome. E. Jennings.—CaD
A song of always. E. Rosenzweig.—ArT-3—ThA
Sunday morning, King's Cambridge. J. Betjeman.—PlE
"When I was a little girl (about seven years old)." Mother Goose.—SmM
A little girl.—BrMg
"When I was a wee thing." Unknown.—MoB
When Mahalia sings. Q. Prettyman.—AdIa
"The **churches,** Lord, all the dark churches." See Crag Jack's apostasy
Churchyards. See Cemeteries
Churning. See "Come, butter, come"
Churns and churning
"Come, butter, come." Mother Goose.—HuS-3
Churning.—BrMg
Churton, J. W.
"There was a young man at the War Office."—BrLl
Chute, Marchette (Gaylord)
Bees.—HoB
Early spring.—BrSg
Easter parade.—LaPh
Fairies.—ThA
Food.—AgH—LaC
Going to bed.—HoB—LaP—LaPd
Hallowe'en.—LaPh
My dog.—ArT-3—LaPd—ThA
Picnics.—AgH
Presents.—LaP—LaPh
Skiing.—LaP
Snowflakes.—LaP—LaPd
Spring.—BrSg
Spring planting.—BrSg
Spring rain.—ArT-3—LaP
Undersea.—LaP
Ciardi, John
About the teeth of sharks.—CoB
And off he went just as proud as you please.—CiYk
The bugle-billed bazoo.—HoB
Bump. Bang. Bump.—CiYk

Ciardi, John—*Continued*
Calling all cowboys.—CiYk
Camptown.—HiL
Can someone tell me why.—CiYk
"Children when they're very sweet."—CoBb
Come to think of it.—CiYk
The cow.—DuS
Dan Dunder.—CoBb
Elegy for Jog.—DuR
The evil eye.—CaMb
Get up or you'll be late for school, silly.—CiYk
The great news.—CiYk
Halloween.—ArT-3
The happy family.—CoO
"I said to a bug in the sink."—BrLl
If you should fall, don't forget this.—CiYk
In place of a curse.—DuS
Is this someone you know.—CiYk
It is time, you know.—CiYk
The light-house-keeper's white-mouse.—LaPd
A loud proud someone.—CiYk
The man in the onion bed.—CoO
Mummy slept late and daddy fixed breakfast. —ArT-3—LaPd
The pinwheel's song.—LaPd
Please.—CiYk
Please don't tell him.—CiYk
Please tell this someone to take care.—CiYk
Poor little fish.—CiYk
Rain sizes.—HuS-3
"The reason for the pelican."—HoB—LaP—LaPd
The river is a piece of sky.—ArT-3—HuS-3—LaPd
"Said a crow in the top of a tree."—BrLl
Sit up when you sit down.—CiYk
Some cook.—AgH—LaP—LaPd
Someone asked me.—CiYk
Someone at my house said.—CiYk
Someone had a helping hand.—CiYk
Someone lost his head at bedtime but he got it back.—CiYk
Someone made me proud of you.—CiYk
Someone showed me the right way to run away.—CiYk
Someone slow.—CiYk
Someone was up in that tree.—CiYk
Warning.—LaPd
What night would it be.—LaPd—LaPh
What someone said when he was spanked on the day before his birthday.—CiYk
What someone told me about Bobby Link.—AgH—CiYk
Why no one pets the lion at the zoo.—DuR
You know who.—CiYk
Cibber, Colley
The blind boy.—CoR
Cider song. Mildred Weston.—CoBn
"**Cinda** came." See Whistling
Cinderella
After all and after all. M. C. Davies.—ArT-3—ThA
Parvenu. V. Lindsay.—LiP
"**Cinderella.**" Unknown.—CoO
Circle one. Owen Dodson.—BoH—HaK
Circles
"Be my circle." M. C. Livingston.—LiC
Circles. From The people, yes. C. Sandburg. —BrA
Circles. See The people, yes
Circuit through the hills. Thakur Prasad Singh, tr. fr. the Hindi by J. Mauch.—AlPi
Circus. See also Animals; Clowns; also names of circus animals, as Lions
"C is for the circus." From All around the town. P. McGinley.—ArT-3
Circus. E. Farjeon.—HoB
A circus garland, sels. R. Field.—HuS-3 (Complete)
Acrobat
The elephant
The girl on the milk-white horse
The performing seal
Circus hand. P. Dehn.—SmM
The circus parade. O. B. Miller.—ArT-3
The circus ship Euzkera. W. Gibson.—CoSs
Hazardous occupations. C. Sandburg.—HoL
Holding hands. L. M. Link.—ArT-3—LaP
Horses. L. MacNeice.—CaD
Our circus. L. L. Randall.—ArT-3
A windy circus. L. Ray.—AlPi
Circus. Eleanor Farjeon.—HoB
A **circus** garland, sels. Rachel Field.—HuS-3 (Complete)
Acrobat
The elephant
The girl on the milk-white horse
The performing seal
Circus hand. Paul Dehn.—SmM
"A **circus** of battleships carrying heavy laughter passes." See Celebrated return
The **circus** parade. Olive Beaupré Miller.—ArT-3
The **circus** ship Euzkera. Walker Gibson.—CoSs
Cities and city life. See also names of cities, as San Francisco
Beleaguered cities. F. L. Lucas.—ClF (sel.)
Birthplace revisited. G. Corso.—LaC
Burning in the night. T. Wolfe.—BrA
Cities and science. From Poet always next but one. D. McCord.—BrA
The city. J. Bryant.—BaH
City afternoon. B. Howes.—BrA
City autumn. J. M. March.—LaC
City fingers. M. O'Neill.—OnF
City in summer. M. C. Livingston.—LiC
The city in the sea. E. A. Poe.—GrS—PoP
City lights. R. Field.—LaP—LaPd
City number. C. Sandburg.—LaC
The city of golf. R. F. Murray.—MoS
The city of stones. Liu Yü-hsi.—LeMw
A city park. A. Brody.—LaC
City: San Francisco. L. Hughes.—BrA
City.—LaP—LaPd
City sparrow. A. Kreymborg.—LaC
City streets and country roads.—E. Farjeon.—ArT-3
City traffic. E. Merriam.—LaC—LaPd—MeI
City trees. E. St V. Millay.—BoH—LaC

Cockpit in the clouds. D. Dorrance.—ArT-3
Commuter. E. B. White.—LaC
Concrete mixers. P. Hubbell.—LaPd
December. S. Vanderbilt.—LaC
"Drums, drumming." B. Brown.—BaH
Ellis park. H. Hoyt.—ThA
Exiled. E. St V. Millay.—PaH
Faces. S. Teasdale.—LaC
Flight. J. Tate.—LaC
Fools gaze at painted courts. From Polyolbion. M. Drayton.—GrCt
The greatest city. W. Whitman.—LaC
The ice-cream man. R. Field.—HoB
"In the streets I have just left." C. Reznikoff.—LaC
Kid in the park. L. Hughes.—LaC
A kingdom of clouds. M. Copeland.—LeM
Manhole covers. K. Shapiro.—BoGj—BoH—BrA
On the expressway. R. Dana.—LaC
Our largest and smallest cities. N. Rhodes.—LaC
People who must. C. Sandburg.—LaC—LaPd
Prelude I. T. S. Eliot.—ArT-3
Prelude.—CaD—LaC
The produce district. T. Gunn.—DuS
Rudolph is tired of the city. G. Brooks.—LaPd
A sad song about Greenwich village. F. Park.—LaC
Snow in the city. R. Field.—ArT-3—LaP
Song of the builders. J. W. Murton.—BrA
The street. O. Paz.—LaC
Subway rush hour. L. Hughes.—LaC
Summer. C. G. Rossetti.—CoBn
A sweet country life. Unknown.—ReOn
Tall city. S. N. Pulsifer.—LaC
To the city in the snow. A. O'Gara Ruggeri.—ThA
Trinity place. P. McGinley.—LaC
Until we built a cabin. A. Fisher.—ArT-3
Up at a villa—down in the city. R. Browning.—BrP
Winter. J. M. Synge.—SmM
Cities and science. See Poet always next but one
"**Cities** and science serve each other well." See Poet always next but one—Cities and science
"**Cities** and thrones and powers." Rudyard Kipling.—BoGj
City ("In the morning the city") See City: San Francisco
The **city** ("The city is full of people") Juanita Bryant.—BaH
City afternoon. Barbara Howes.—BrA
City autumn. Joseph Moncure March.—LaC
City fingers. Mary O'Neill.—OnF
"The **city** fingers work in city ways." See City fingers
"The **city** has streets." See City streets and country roads
City in summer. Myra Cohn Livingston.—LiC
The **city** in the sea. Edgar Allan Poe.—GrS—PoP
"The **city** is full of people." See The city
City life. See Cities and city life; Ghettoes, also names of cities, as San Francisco
City lights. Rachel Field.—LaP—LaPd
The **city** of falling leaves. Amy Lowell.—ArT-3
The **city** of golf. Robert Fuller Murray.—MoS
"**City** of mist and rain and blown grey spaces." See Edinburgh
The **city** mouse and the garden mouse. Christina Georgina Rossetti.—ArT-3—HoB—HuS-3
"The city mouse lives in a house."—BrSg
"The **city** mouse lives in a house." See The city mouse and the garden mouse
City number. Carl Sandburg.—LaC
The **city** of stones. Liu Yu-hsi, tr. fr. the Chinese by Florence Asycough.—LeMw
A **city** park. Alter Brody.—LaC
"The **city** rolls." See On the expressway
City: San Francisco. Langston Hughes.—BrA
City.—LaP—LaPd
City sparrow. Alfred Kreymborg.—LaC
City streets and country roads. Eleanor Farjeon.—ArT-3
City traffic. Eve Merriam.—LaC—LaPd—MeI
City trees. Edna St Vincent Millay.—BoH—LaC
Civil war. See United States—History—Civil war
"**Civile,** res ago." See See, Will, 'ere's a go
Civilities. Thomas Whitbread.—MoS
The **clam.** Shelley Silverstein.—CoB
Clams
The clam. S. Silverstein.—CoB
Clancy, Joseph P.
Boxer.—MoS
"**Clapping** her platter stood plump Bess." See Chicken
Clare, John
Address to a lark, sel.
Address to a lark singing in winter.—ReBs
Address to a lark singing in winter. See Address to a lark
Autumn ("I love the fitful gust that shakes")—ClF
Autumn ("The thistledown's flying, though the winds are all still")—CoBn
Autumn birds.—ReO
The autumn wind.—CoBn
Badger.—ClF (sel.)—CoB
Bat. See Childhood
Birds' nests.—ReBs
Childhood, sel.
Bat.—ReO
Clock-a-clay.—BlO
Come hither, my dear one.—CoBl
Deluge.—CoBn
The evening star.—GrCt
Farm yard at evening.—CoB (sel.)
First love.—GrCt
The flight of birds.—CoB
Fragment.—CoBn
Gipsies.—GrCt
The gipsy camp.—GrCt
Grasshoppers.—CoB
Hares at play.—ReO
The hedgehog. See The shepherd's calendar
Hen's nest.—ReO
I pass in silence.—CoBl

Clare, John—*Continued*
Let me then my birds alone. See Summer evening
Little Trotty Wagtail.—BlO
Love.—GrCt
March.—ReO
Mouses's nest.—CoB—GrCt
The ragwort.—GrCt
The red robin.—ReBs
The shepherd's calendar, sel.
The hedgehog.—ReO
Signs of winter.—CoBn—HoL
Snowstorm.—CoBn
Summer.—CoBn
Summer evening, sel.
Let ye then my birds alone.—ReBs
Summer images.—GrCt
The thrush's nest.—BlO—BoGj—SmM
To Mary: It is the evening hour.—GrCt
A vision.—GrCt
The vixen.—CoB
Winter in the fens.—CoBn
Clark, Ann Nolan
In my mother's house, sels.
Irrigation.—HuS-3
Mountains.—HuS-3
Irrigation. See In my mother's house
Mountains. See In my mother's house
Clark, Badger
Cottonwood leaves.—ArT-3
Clark, Leonard
The Goole captain.—CaD
Revelation.—SmM
Clarke, Austin
A strong wind.—CoBn
Clarke, Etain Mary
The field of the mice and the marigold.—LeM
Clarke, F. W.
The rhyme of the rain machine.—CoBn
Clarke, Molly
Runaway engine.—StF
Clarke, Roderick Crilly
Baby playing.—LeM
Classé, Margaret
Hate.—BaH
"I believe one day when."—BaH
"When I pray."—BaH
"**Clean** birds by sevens." See A charm against a magpie
"**Clean** the spittoons, boy." See Brass spittoons
Cleanliness. See also Bathing
The battle of Clothesline bay. W. Irwin.—CoSs
Before tea. A. A. Milne.—MiC
Dirty Jim. J. Taylor.—GrT
For a little girl that did not like to be washed. A. and J. Taylor.—VrF
Going too far. M. Howells.—ArT-3
The obedient child. M. Elliott.—VrF
Slovenly Peter. H. Hoffmann.—CoBb
Cleanthes
God leads the way.—PlE
"**Clear** and cool, clear and cool." See The tide river
"**Clear** and high, a mountain." See The hike
"**Clear,** cold water." Issa, tr. fr. the Japanese.—LeOw
"**Clear** is the bottom of the lake." Yakamochi.—BaS
"The **clear** note." Issa, tr. fr. the Japanese by Nobuyuki Yuasa.—IsF
"**Clearly** the blue river chimes in its flowing." See All things will die
Clerk, John
The miller.—GrCt
A **cliché.** Eve Merriam.—MeI
"A **cliché** is what we all say." See A cliché
"**Click,** clack." Issa, tr. fr. the Japanese by R. H. Blyth.—LeOw
The **cliff-top.** Robert Bridges.—CoBn
"The **cliff-top** has a carpet." See The cliff-top
"**Cliffs** that rise a thousand feet." See Sailing homeward
Climbing
Climbing. A. Fisher.—ArT-3—FiI
Climbing in Glencoe. A. Young.—MoS
David. E. Birney.—DuS
"Every time I climb a tree." D. McCord.—ArT-3—LaP—LaPd—McE
Having climbed to the topmost peak of the Incense-burner Mountain. Po Chü-i.—MoS
High brow. R. Fitch.—MoS
The mountains. W. Gibson.—MoS
On Middleton Edge. A. Young.—MoS
Tree climbing. K. Fraser.—FrS
Climbing. Aileen Fisher.—ArT-3—FiI
Climbing in Glencoe. Andrew Young.—MoS
Clinton south of Polk. Carl Sandburg.—BrA
Clipper ships and captains. Rosemary Carr and Stephen Vincent Benét.—HuS-3
Clock-a-clay. John Clare.—BlO
"The **clock** is striking autumn at the apple vendor's fair." See Autumn
Clock time by the geyser. John White.—BrSm
The **clock** tower. Colleen Thibaudeau.—DoW
Clocks and watches
"As round as a biscuit." Mother Goose.—OpF
The big clock. Unknown.—ArT-3
The clock tower. C. Thibaudeau.—DoW
Clocks and watches. Unknown.—StF
"Oh, no." M. M. Dodge.—CoBb
Someone slow. J. Ciardi.—CiYk
Town and country. Unknown.—DePp
Clocks and watches. Unknown.—StF
The **clod** and the pebble. William Blake.—BlP
"**Close** by the margin of the brook." See Dame Duck's lecture
"**Close** now thine eyes, and rest secure." See A good-night
"**Close** your eyes." See Pussy willows
Close your eyes. Arna Bontemps.—BoA—HaK
The **closing** of the rodeo. William Jay Smith.—HoL—McWs—MoS
"**Clothed** in yellow, red, and green." Mother Goose.—BrMg
"**Clothes** make no sound when I tread ground." See A riddle from the Old English

Clothing and dress. See also names of clothing, as Boots and shoes
About buttons. D. Aldis.—ThA
Aiken Drum. Unknown.—BlO
"There came a man to our town."—MoB (sel.)
"As I was going up the hill." Mother Goose.—OpF
Jack and the piper.—GrCt
"As I went by my little pig-sty." Unknown.—OpF
As soon as it's fall. A. Fisher.—FiC
The ballad of the harp-weaver. E. St V. Millay.—ArT-3
The bonnie cravat. Mother Goose.—ArT-3
"Bonnie Maggie, braw Maggie." Unknown.—MoB
Bronzeville man with a belt in the back. G. Brooks.—AdIa
Company clothes. A. Fisher.—FiIo
Cotton. E. Farjeon.—FaT
Crinolines and bloomers; or, The battle between Monsieur Worth and Mrs Bloomer. Unknown.—HiL
"Dancy-diddlety-poppety-pin." Mother Goose. OpF
Dressed or undressed. E. Turner.—VrF
Dressing. A. Fisher.—FiIo
A dressmaker. J. Kenward.—SmM
The dyer. Unknown.—GrCt
Easter parade. M. Chute.—LaPh
Five little sisters. K. Greenaway.—GrT
A furrier. Unknown.—VrF
Furry bear. A. A. Milne.—HuS-3—MiC
"Hark, hark, the dogs do bark." Mother Goose. —ArT-3—OpF—ReMg—WiMg
The beggars.—BrMg
"Hark, hark."—BrF
Mother Goose rhymes, 23.—HoB
Hector Protector. Mother Goose.—BrMg
"Hey, Cocky doo." Unknown.—MoB
"Hey diddle dinkety poppety pet." Mother Goose.—OpF
"I'm going in a train." Unknown.—MoB
"Johnny shall have a new bonnet." Mother Goose.—GrT
"Johnny, come lend me your fiddle."—MoB
Jonathan Bing. B. C. Brown.—ArT-3—LaP—LaPd
King Stephen. From Othello. W. Shakespeare. —ShS
Little Fanny. Unknown.—VrF
Little Freddy. Unknown.—VrF
The little kittens. E. L. Follen.—ArT-3
"A louse crept out of my lady's shift." G. Bottomley.—GrCt
McDonogh day in New Orleans. M. B. Christian.—BoA
My zipper suit. M. L. Allen.—ArT-3
"Nobody's nicer." A. Fisher.—FiIo
Nurse outwitted. M. Elliott.—VrF
Old Abram Brown. Mother Goose.—ReOn
On the gift of a cloak. Hugo of Orleans, known as Primas.—LiT
Patterns. A. Lowell.—BoH—CoBl
"The poor benighted Hindoo." C. Monkhouse. —BrLl
Pretty Polly. B. H. Reece.—CoBl
Rags. E. Farjeon.—FaT
Red stockings. Mother Goose.—BrMg
"Said an envious, erudite ermine." O. Herford.—BrLl
The sash. E. Turner.—VrF
Satin. E. Farjeon.—FaT
Silk. E. Farjeon.—FaT
Sleepy John. C. Tringress.—StF
The soldier and the maid. Mother Goose.—BrMg
"Soldier, soldier, won't you marry me." Unknown.—BlO
Sporting Beasley. S. A. Brown.—HaK
Tailor. E. Farjeon.—FaT
"A tapir who lived in Malay." O. Herford.—BrLl
"There was a young lady of Durban." Unknown.—BrLl
"There was a young man of Bengal." Unknown.—BrLl
"There was a young person of Crete." E. Lear.—BrLl
"There was an old lady whose folly." E. Lear. —BrLl
"There was an old man of the cape." R. L. Stevenson.—BrLl
There's a youth in this city. R. Burns.—BuPr
The three foxes. A. A. Milne.—BoGj—HuS-3—MiC
Tommy O'Linn. Mother Goose.—BrMg
Troubles. D. Aldis.—HuS-3
Turvey. Mother Goose.—ReOn
Upon Julia's clothes. R. Herrick.—GrCt—HoL
Wake. L. Hughes.—BrSm
"When a cub, unaware being bare." E. Merriam.—BrLl
"When I was a little girl (about seven years old)." Mother Goose.—SmM
A little girl.—BrMg
"Wilhelmina Merganthaler." H. P. Taber.—CoBb
The young ones, flip side. J. A. Emanuel.—HaK
Cloud, Virginia Woodward
What the Lord High Chamberlain said.—CoBb
The **cloud** messenger. Kalidasa, tr. fr. the Sanskrit by A. L. Basham.—AlPi (sel.)
"A **cloud** on top of Evergreen mountain is singing." Unknown, tr. fr. the Papago.—LeO
"A **cloud** shimmering." Shurin, tr. fr. the Japanese by Harry Behn.—BeCs
Clouds. See also Weather
Among the millet. A. Lampman.—DoW
"As high as a castle." Mother Goose.—OpF
"The bird wishes it were a cloud." R. Tagore. —LeMf
The cloud messenger. Kalidasa.—AlPi (sel.)

Clouds—*Continued*
"A cloud on top of Evergreen mountain is singing." Unknown.—LeO
"A cloud shimmering." Shurin.—BeCs
The clouds ("All my life, I guess, I've loved the clouds") D. McCord.—McAd
Clouds ("Clouds are like waves") P. Kuramoto.—LeM
Clouds ("Sometimes we see a cloud that's dragonish") From Antony and Cleopatra. W. Shakespeare.—ShS
Clouds ("These clouds are soft fat horses") J. Reaney.—DoW
Clouds ("White sheep, white sheep") C. G.. Rossetti.—HuS-3—LaP
"White sheep, white sheep."—ArT-3
Clouds ("Wonder where they come from") A. Fisher.—FiI
Clouds across the canyon. J. G. Fletcher.—PaH
Clouds in a wild storm. Darcy May.—LeM
The clouds that are so light. E. Thomas.—ThG
"The dark gray clouds." N. Belting.—LaPd
Ella. G. Brooks.—AgH
Ensnare the clouds. E. J. Coatsworth.—CoDh
Evening clouds. D. Bharati.—AlPi
How strange it is. C. Lewis.—LeP
"Let's ride." Issa.—LeOw
The loaves. R. Everson.—DoW
"The moorhens are chirping." Issa.—LeOw
Night clouds. A. Lowell.—ThA
"A piece of colored cloud shines on the stone well." Chien Hsu.—LeMw
Pony clouds. P. Hubbell.—ArT-3
The rhyme of the rain machine. F. W. Clarke. —CoBn
The scared clouds. H. Hodgins.—LeM
Song to cloud. H. Behn.—BeG
Substantiations. Vallana.—AlPi
"There was a wee wifie rowed (or row't) up in a blanket." Mother Goose.—MoB—OpF
"This little cloud, and this." Unknown.—DoC
Watching clouds. J. Farrar.—HuS-3
The **clouds** ("All my life, I guess, I've loved the clouds") David McCord.—McAd
Clouds ("Clouds are like waves") Paul Kuramoto.—LeM
Clouds ("Sometimes we see a cloud that's dragonish") See Antony and Cleopatra
Clouds ("These clouds are soft fat horses") James Reaney.—DoW
Clouds ("White sheep, white sheep") Christina Georgina Rossetti.—HuS-3—LaP
"White sheep, white sheep."—ArT-3
Clouds ("Wonder where they come from") Aileen Fisher.—FiI
Clouds across the canyon. John Gould Fletcher. —PaH
"**Clouds** are like waves." See Clouds
"The **clouds** are stuck and scared to move." See The scared clouds
"**Clouds** are torn." See The Painted desert
"The **clouds** float by." Jackson O'Donnell.—LeM
Clouds in a wild storm. Darcy May.—LeM
The **clouds** that are so light. Edward Thomas.—ThG
"The **clouds** were all brushed up and back." See Snow advent
Clough, Arthur Hugh
The Bothie of Tober-na-Vuolich.—CoBn (sel.)
Columbus.—BrA
The latest decalogue.—GrCt
Say not. See "Say not the struggle naught availeth"
"Say not the struggle naught availeth."—PlE
Say not.—TuW
Where lies the land.—CoSs—GrCt
Clover
After the rain is over. A. Fisher.—FiI
Clover for breakfast. F. M. Frost.—HuS-3
I found. M. C. Livingston.—BrSg
Clover for breakfast. Frances M. Frost.—HuS-3
The **clown.** Dorothy Aldis.—LaPd
Clowns. See also Circus
The clown. D. Aldis.—LaPd
Clowns. L. MacNeice.—CaD
Clowns. Louis MacNeice.—CaD
"**Clowns,** clowns and." See Clowns
Coach. Eleanor Farjeon.—FaT
"The **coach** is at the door at last." See Farewell to the farm
Coaches. See Carriages and carts
The **coachman.** See "Up at Piccadilly, oh"
Coal
Banking coal. J. Toomer.—BoH
"Black I am and much admired." Mother Goose.—BrMg
Coal for Mike. B. Brecht.—LiT
Coal for Mike. Bertolt Brecht, tr. fr. the German by H. R. Hays.—LiT
Coals. Walter De La Mare.—DeBg
Coaster wagon. Aileen Fisher.—FiIo
The **coasts** of high Barbary. Unknown.—BlO
A **coat.** William Butler Yeats.—YeR
Coatsworth, Elizabeth Jane
All of a sudden.—CoSb
All on a Christmas morning.—CoSb
All the fishes far below.—CoSb
Among the leaves.—CoSb
And a big black crow is cawing.—CoSb
And laughter sounded.—CoDh
And were a little changed.—CoDh
Asleep.—CoSb
At the windowed horizon.—CoDh
"At twilight."—CoDh
Aux Tuileries 1790.—CoDh
The bad kittens.—ThA
Before breakfast.—CoSb
Birth of Henri Quatre.—CoDh
Birthday party.—CoDh
Body and spirit.—CoDh
The Bourbons at Naples.—CoDh
But no.—CoDh
The cabin.—CoDh
Calling in the cat.—ReO
Candy house.—CoSb
The chair house.—CoSb

"Cold winter now is in the wood."—ArT-3—TuW
Columbus and the mermaids.—CoDh
Concrete trap.—CoB
Conquest.—BrA
The wilderness is tamed.—HuS-3
Conversation by Loch Ness.—CoDh
Crow in springtime.—CoSb
Danger.—CoSb
Daniel Webster's horses.—BrA—CoDh
Dark kingdom.—CoB
Day moon.—CoDh
Dedicated to her highness.—CoDh
Deer at dusk.—CoSb
Dialogue.—CoDh
Ducks at twilight.—CoSb
Early dark.—CoSb
Earth and the kisses of men.—CoDh
The empresses.—CoDh
Ensnare the clouds.—CoDh
Far away.—CoSb
"The Fates."—CoDh
Finder, please return to Henry Thoreau.—CoDh
The fish.—CoSb
Fly.—CoDh
Fly away.—CoSb
Fog.—CoDh
The frogs' wedding.—CoSb
From Cadillac mountain.—CoDh
The furrows of the unicorn.—CoDh
Genesis.—CoDh
Hang Fu.—CoDh
"Hard from the southeast blows the wind."—ArT-3
Harmony.—CoDh
"He who has never known hunger."—ArT-3
Heavy is the heat.—CoDh
"Heigh-ho."—CoSb
The horns.—CoDh
"A horse would tire."—ArT-3
The horses.—CoSb
The house plants.—CoSb
"How gray the rain."—ArT-3
I took a little stick.—CoSb
Ice storm.—CoSb
In the blueberry bushes.—CoSb
In the late afternoon.—CoDh
The infanta.—CoDh
January.—HoB
Johnsonia.—CoDh
July storm.—CoDh
The kangaroo.—ArT-3—HuS-3
Keep away.—CoDh
The lady.—CoDh
A lady comes to an inn.—ArT-3—CoDh
Late October.—CoSb
Les isles d'Amerique.—CoDh
The lights.—CoSb
Like arrows.—CoSb
The lilac spires.—CoSb
The long black grave.—CoDh
Lost graveyards.—CoDh
The maple.—CoSb
March.—LaPd
March in New Mexico.—CoDh
Mary Tudor.—CoDh
May morning.—CoSb
Meditation at Elsinore.—CoDh
Montezuma's song.—CoDh
Moses.—CoDh
The mouse.—ArT-3—CoB—ReS—ThA
The Navajo.—BrA
Night in early spring.—CoSb
Night piece.—CoDh
Night wind in spring.—CoDh
The Nile.—PaH
Now fall asleep.—ReS
Now in the stillness.—CoDh
Oak leaves.—HuS-3
The ogre entertains.—CoDh
On a night of snow.—CoB—DuR
On an overgrown hill.—CoDh
On the hills.—CoDh
Or hounds to follow on a track.—CoSb
Patterns of life.—CoDh
Pioneer rat.—CoSb
Poem to hunger.—CoDh
"Pretty Futility."—AgH
The rabbits' song outside the tavern.—ArT-3
Return.—CoDh
Rhyme.—CoSb
Riddle.—CoSb
Romanesque frieze.—CoDh
Running moon.—CoSb
Saint John.—CoDh
Samson.—CoDh
"The sea gull curves his wings."—ArT-3
Sea gull.—CoB
Seen by moonlight.—CoSb
"Shoe the horse."—CoSb
"Sing a song of kittens."—CoSb
Sketch for an island.—CoDh
Some day.—CoSb
Song for a hot day.—HuS-3
Song for snow.—McWs
Song of the earth.—CoDh
Song of the parrot.—HuS-3
Song to green.—CoDh
The sparrow bush.—CoSb
Split the stones.—CoDh
The starry nevers.—CoSb
Storm at night.—CoSb
Straws.—BrA
Sudden storm.—CoSb
The sun is first to rise.—HuS-3
Sunday.—BrA—LaC
"Swift things are beautiful."—ArT-3—DuR—HuS-3
Syracuse.—PaH
The telephone brought you back.—CoDh
This is a night.—CoDh
Three.—CoSb
The three deer.—CoDh
To a day moon.—CoSb
Tracks in the snow ("Out of the dark")—HoB

This is my country.—PaH
Thunder pools.—HaL
Tree-sleeping.—HaL
The young calves.—ArT-3—HuS-3
Coffins
"It isn't the cough." Unknown.—BrSm
Cohen, Leonard
For Anne.—CoBl
A kite is a victim.—MoS
Cohen, S. J.
A reunion in Kensington.—SmM
The **coin.** Sara Teasdale.—ArT-3—ThA
Cokeham, V.
"There is an umbrella."—LeM
"**Cold** and raw the north wind doth blow." See Winter
"A **cold** and starry darkness moans." See Ghosts
Cold are the crabs. Edward Lear.—BoGj
"**Cold** are the crabs that crawl on yonder hills." See Cold are the crabs
Cold blows the wind. John Hamilton.—ClF (sel.)
"**Cold,** clear, and blue, the morning heaven." See The morning star
"A **cold** coming we had of it." See Journey of the Magi
"**Cold** flings itself out of the north." See November
Cold logic. Barney Hutchinson.—MoS
"**Cold** Mountain is full of weird sights." Hanshan, tr. fr. the Chinese by Burton Watson. —LeMw
"**Cold** snuggle." See Spider
"**Cold** was the night—the clock struck ten." See The watchman
"**Cold** winter now is in the wood." Elizabeth Jane Coatsworth.—ArT-3—TuW
Cole, Charlotte Druitt
Three mice.—StF
Cole, William
Back yard, July night.—CoBn
"Here in this book, collected for you."—CoBb
Just dropped in.—BoGj
Undersea fever.—CoSs
Coleridge, Mary
After reading certain books.—PlE
I had a boat.—SmM
Three helpers in battle.—PlE
Coleridge, Samuel Taylor
Answer to a child's question.—BlO—CoB—ReBs
Hunting song.—BlO
In dispraise of the moon.—CoBn
The knight's tomb.—ClF
Kubla Khan.—BoGj—CoR—GrCt—McWs (sel.) —PaH
Nightingales.—GrCt
Phantom.—GrS
The rime of the ancient mariner.—CoR—CoSs (sel.)
Work without hope.—CoBn
Coleridge, Sara
The garden year. See "January brings the snow"
"January brings the snow."—ArT-3
The garden year.—HuS-3
Colin Clout's come home again, sel. Edmund Spenser
Her heards be thousand fishes.—GrCt
Coliseum (Rome)
The coliseum. E. A. Poe.—PoP
The **coliseum.** Edgar Allan Poe.—PoP
The **collar.** George Herbert.—PlE
"A **collegiate** damsel named Breeze." Unknown. —BrLl
"**Collie** puppies in a dooryard." See Wonder
The **collier.** Vernon Watkins.—CaD
Collins, Leslie M.
Stevedore.—BoA
"**Collop** Monday." Unknown.—MoB
Colly my cow. Mother Goose.—ReOn
Collymore, Frank A.
The zobo bird.—BoGj
Colm, Saint (about)
The pets. R. Farren.—ReO
"**Colm** had a cat." See The pets
"**Colonel** B." See Afforestation
Colonial period. See United States—History—Colonial period
Color ("They say that") Victor Castro.—BaH
Color ("What is the difference") Eve Merriam.—MeI
"**Color**—caste—denomination." Emily Dickinson. —PlE
"The **color** is dark blue." See Night time
Colorado
The Colorado trail. Unknown.—McWs
The **Colorado** trail. Unknown.—McWs
Colors. See also names of colors, as Yellow
Black and gold. N. B. Turner.—ArT-3—LaPh
Chrysanthemum colors. Unknown.—DePp
Color. E. Merriam.—MeI
"The colors live." M. O'Neill.—OnH
"Like acrobats on a high trapeze." M. O'Neill. —OnH
Song to bring fair weather. Unknown.—LeO
"What is pink? a rose is pink." C. G. Rossetti. —ArT-3
What is pink.—BoGj—BrSg—HuS-3
"The **colors** live." Mary O'Neill.—OnH
"The **colour'd** sampler's work displays." See The school-girl in 1820
"**Colouring** the tissued air." See A windy circus
Colter's candy. Unknown.—MoB
"**Coltrane** must understand how." See Soul
Colum, Padraic
Asses.—HaL (sel.)
Condors.—BoGj
Dahlias.—BoGj
A drover.—PaH
"I saw the wind today."—BoGj
Reminiscence II.—HaL
The wind.—CoR—LaPd
Irises.—CoBn
Monkeys.—CoB
The old woman of the roads.—HuS-3—ThA
Otters.—ReO
River-mates.—CoB

Come loose every sail to the breeze. Unknown. —CoSs
"**Come** loose ev'ry sail to the breeze." See Come loose every sail to the breeze
"**Come,** my darling, come away." See Learning to go alone
Come night, come Romeo. See Romeo and Juliet
"**Come** night; come, Romeo; come, thou day in night." See Romeo and Juliet—Come night, come Romeo
"**Come** on in." Unknown.—MoS
"**Come** on, owl." Issa, tr. fr. the Japanese by Lewis Mackenzie.—LeI
"**Come** out, fireflies." Issa, tr. fr. the Japanese.—LeOw
"**Come** out for a while and look from the outside in." See Christmas eve
"**Come** out, 'tis now September." See The ripe and bearded barley
Come out with me. A. A. Milne.—MiC
"**Come** out with me, cried the little red sled." See The little red sled
"**Come,** peep at London's famous town." See Introduction
"**Come** play with me." See To a squirrel at Kyle-Na-No
"**Come,** pussy, will you learn to read." See The dunce of a kitten
"**Come,** roses, with your colour and fragrance." See Roses and thorns
"**Come,** rouse up, ye bold-hearted Whigs of Kentucky." See Old Tippecanoe
"**Come,** take up your hats, and away let us haste." See The butterfly's ball and the grasshopper's feast
"**Come** the little clouds out of the ice-caves." See Indian songs—Rain chant
"**Come** to me broken dreams and all." See The still voice of Harlem
Come to think of it. John Ciardi.—CiYk
"**Come** trotting up." See Foal
"**Come** unto these yellow sands." See The tempest
"**Come** with me, under my coat." See The coolin
"**Come** with rain, O loud southwester." See To the thawing wind
"**Comes** a cry from Cuban water." See Cuba libre
"**Comes** the deer to my singing." See Hunting song
"**Comes** the time of leaves breaking." See Birds must sing
Comets
Halley's comet. E. Farjeon.—FaT
"I am like a slip of comet." G. M. Hopkins.—LiT
Comfort. See Some short poems
"**Comfort** ye, comfort ye, my people." See Isaiah
Comin' thro' the rye. Robert Burns.—BuPr
"**Coming** along the mountain path." Taigi, tr. fr. the Japanese by R. H. Blyth.—LeMw
The **coming** American. Sam Walter Foss.—BrA (sel.)
"**Coming** down the mountain in the twilight." See Where the hayfields were
The **coming** forth by day of Osiris Jones, sel. Conrad Aiken
The nursery.—HaL
"**Coming** from nowhere." Bonita Jones.—BaH
Coming home. Myra Cohn Livingston.—LiC
"**Coming** home in the cold wind." See March in New Mexico
The **coming** of the plague. Weldon Kees.—DuS
The **coming** star. Juan Ramón Jiménez, tr. fr. the Spanish by H. R. Hays.—LiT
"**Coming** upon it unawares." See Pittsburgh
"A **comma** hung above the park." See Comma in the sky
Comma in the sky. Aileen Fisher.—FiI
A **commercial** for spring. Eve Merriam.—MeI
Commercials
A commercial for spring. E. Merriam.—MeI
Commissary report. Stoddard King.—BrSm
The **common** cormorant. See "The common cormorant or shag"
"The **common** cormorant or shag." Unknown.—BlO—GrCt
The common cormorant.—SmM
Common dust. Georgia Douglas Johnson.—BoA
Communication. See also Mail service; Radio; Railroads; Rides and riding; Roads and trails; Telegraph; Telephones; Television
And yet fools say. G. S. Holmes.—ArT-3
How they brought the good news from Ghent to Aix. R. Browning.—ArT-3—BrP—CoR—HuS-3
Commuter. E. B. White.—LaC
"**Commuter**—one who spends his life." See Commuter
Company. Aileen Fisher.—FiIo
Company clothes. Aileen Fisher.—FiIo
Companions. See King Henry VI
Compensation. Paul Laurence Dunbar.—BoA
The **complaint** of Henrie, Duke of Buckinghame, sel. Thomas Sackville
Midnight was come.—ReO
Complaints
Caliban in the coal mines. L. Untermeyer.—LaPd
Eclogue. E. Lear.—LiT
The invisible man. C. K. Rivers.—HaK
The mouse. E. J. Coatsworth.—ArT-3—CoB—ReS—ThA
The plaint of the camel. From Davy and the goblin. C. E. Carryl.—HuS-3—ThA
Rain. J. W. Riley.—CoBn
Composed on a May morning, 1838. William Wordsworth.—WoP
Composed upon Westminster bridge, September 3, 1802. William Wordsworth.—ArT-3—GrCt—PaH—WoP
Computers
Univac to univac. L. B. Salomon.—DuS
Concanen, Matthew
Heaps on heaps. See A match at football
A match at football, sel.
Heaps on heaps. —MoS

Conceit
Cowboy. Unknown.—GrCt
"Duck, you are merely boasting." Unknown. —LeO
Ego. P. Booth.—DuS
The egotistical orchestra. E. Merriam.—MeI
In the fashion. A. A. Milne.—LaP
"Noah an' Jonah an' Cap'n John Smith." D. Marquis.—CoSs
The song of Mr Toad. From The wind in the willows. K. Grahame.—BoGj
There's a youth in this city. R. Burns.—BuPr
The wolf and the lioness. E. Rees.—ArT-3
Concha, Joseph Leonard
Two Indian boys.—BaH
Concord, Massachusetts
Concord hymn. R. W. Emerson.—BrA—HiL—HuS-3—PaH—TuW
Concord hymn. Ralph Waldo Emerson.—BrA—HiL—HuS-3—PaH—TuW
The **concrete** mixer. Timothy Langley.—LeM
Concrete mixers. Patricia Hubbell.—LaPd
Concrete trap. Elizabeth Jane Coatsworth.—CoB
Conder, Alan
Prayer to go to Paradise with the donkeys. tr. —CoB
Condors
Condors. P. Colum.—BoGj
"Said the condor, in tones of despair." O. Herford.—BrLl
Condors. Padraic Colum.—BoGj
Conduct of life. See also Behavior; Etiquette; Proverbs; also names of traits of character, as Perseverance
Address to the unco guid. R. Burns.—BuPr
After reading certain books. M. Coleridge.—PlE
The ancient elf. J. Stephens.—StS
Another song of a fool. W. B. Yeats.—ReO
Appearances. From The taming of the shrew. W. Shakespeare.—ShS
The armful. R. Frost.—LiT
As I sit. C. Begay.—BaH
"As I walk'd by myself." Mother Goose.—GrCt—ReOn
By myself.—BrMg
Athletic employment. Unknown.—MoS
Barter. S. Teasdale.—ThA
"Be kind." Unknown.—LeO
Be like the bird. V. Hugo.—ArT-3
"Belshazzar had a letter." E. Dickinson.—DiPe
Black is beautiful. A. Burns.—BaH
The blind boy. C. Cibber.—CoR
Blue girls. J. C. Ransom.—GrCt—McWs
The building of the ship. H. W. Longfellow. —LoPl
Character of the happy warrior. W. Wordsworth.—WoP
Close your eyes. A. Bontemps.—BoA—HaK
"Cocks crow in the morn." Mother Goose.—ArT-3—ReMg
The coming American. S. W. Foss.—BrA (sel.)
A contemplation upon flowers. H. King.—CoBn
The cradle trap. L. Simpson.—LiT
Do you fear the wind. H. Garland.—ArT-3—ThA
The eagle and the mole. E. Wylie.—ReO
Epigram. Viryamitra.—AlPi
Eternity. W. Blake.—BlP
The example. W. H. Davies.—ReO
Fergus and the druid. W. B. Yeats.—LiT
"Forbidden fruit a flavor has." E. Dickinson. —DiPe
The four Zoas. W. Blake.—BlP (sel.)
Generosity. V. Brasier.—HuS-3
Get up, blues. J. A. Emanuel.—BoA—LiT
"Go to the shine that's on a tree." R. Eberhart.—HoL—LiT
The goat paths. J. Stephens.—BoGj—ReO—StS
Good men. Bhartrihari.—AlPi
"Great things are done when men and mountains meet." W. Blake.—BlP
"Had I not seen the sun." E. Dickinson.—DiPe
Hey, ho, the wind and the rain. From Twelfth night. W. Shakespeare.—ShS
His cavalier. R. Herrick.—BoGj
The human abstract. W. Blake.—BlP
I bid you keep some few small dreams. H. Frazee-Bower.—ThA
I dream a world. L. Hughes.—BoA—BoH
"I never hear the word escape." E. Dickinson.—DiL—DiPe
"I rose up at the dawn of day." W. Blake.—BlP
I strove with none. W. S. Landor.—GrCt
"I thought that nature was enough." E. Dickinson.—DiPe
"I took my power in my hand." E. Dickinson. —DiPe
The duel.—LiT
I wish. J. Stephens.—StS
Idle fyno. Unknown.—GrCt
"If humility and purity be not in the heart." From The rock. T. S. Eliot.—ArT-3
"If I can stop one heart from breaking." E. Dickinson
Not in vain.—BoH
If we must die. C. McKay.—AdIa—BoA—HaK
"If you trap the moment before it's ripe." W. Blake.—BlP
I'll walk the tightrope. M. Danner.—HaK
"It is not growing like a tree." From To the immortal memory of that noble pair, Sir Lucius Cary and Sir H. Morison. B. Jonson.—GrCt
"It's such a little thing to weep." E. Dickinson.—DiPe
James Honeyman. W. H. Auden.—CaMb—SmM
Kid stuff. F. Horne.—BoA—BoH—HaK—LiT
The latest decalogue. A. H. Clough.—GrCt
The leaden-eyed. V. Lindsay.—LiP
Leaf and sun. N. Farber.—HoL
Letter to my sister. A. Spencer.—BoA
Lies. Y. Yevtushenko.—DuS
"The life that tied too tight escapes." E. Dickinson.—DiPe
A little song of life. L. W. Reese.—ThA

Madman's song. E. Wylie.—HaL—ThA
"A man of words and not of deeds." Mother Goose.—BlO—ReMg
A man of words.—ReOn
Mrs Gilfillan. J. Reeves.—LiT
Mother to son. L. Hughes.—BoA—BoH—HoB—HuS-3—LaC
The motion of the earth. N. Nicholson.—LiT
Motto. Unknown.—ArT-3
My kind o' man. P. L. Dunbar.—BoA
Name or person. Li T'ai-po.—SmM
A nation's strength. R. W. Emerson.—BrA (sel.)
Night practice. M. Swenson.—LiT
"No man exists." Unknown.—DoC
"Not with a club the heart is broken." E. Dickinson.—DiPe
"Oh day, if I squander a wavelet of thee." From Pippa passes. R. Browning.—BrP
The oak. A. Tennyson.—TeP
On looking up by chance at the constellations. R. Frost.—LiT
One good turn deserves another. Unknown.—BrSm
Outward show. From The merchant of Venice. W. Shakespeare.—ShS
"Partake as doth the bee." E. Dickinson.—DiPe
Perhaps. B. Kaufman.—HaK
The petal of a rose. J. Stephens.—StS
Precepts. From Mahabharata. Unknown.—AlPi
A question of weather. K. C. Katrak.—AlPi
Revelation. L. Clark.—SmM
Revelations. S. A. Brown.—HaK
"The riddle we can guess." E. Dickinson.—DiPe
School. H. S. Horsley.—VrF
Short sermon. Unknown.—ArT-3
The smile. W. Blake.—BlP
"A soft answer turneth away wrath." From Proverbs, Bible, Old Testament.—ArT-3
A merry heart.—HuS-3
Song of a Hebrew. D. Abse.—SmM
Sorrows of Werther. W. M. Thackeray.—BrSm
"A spider danced a cosy jig." I. Layton.—DoW
Steps. R. Heckman.—BaH
Strange legacies. S. A. Brown.—HaK
Ten commandments, seven deadly sins, and five wits. Unknown.—GrCt
Thanatopsis. W. C. Bryant.—CoBn
"That distance was between us." E. Dickinson.—DiPe
Thought. From Dhamma-pada. Unknown.—AlPi
Time. From Two gentlemen of Verona. W. Shakespeare.—ShS
To a skylark. P. B. Shelley.—CoR
"To fight aloud is very brave." E. Dickinson.—DiPe
"To hear an oriole sing." E. Dickinson.—DiPe
To James. From Notes found near a suicide. F. Horne.—BoA—BoH—HaK
To Miss Rápida. J. R. Jiménez.—LiT
To my son. S. Sassoon.—McWs
To the virgins, to make much of time. R. Herrick.—GrCt
The twins. J. Stephens.—StS
Villanelle. M. D. Feld.—MoS
A vision. J. Clare.—GrCt
The way. E. Muir.—GrS—HaL
"We never know how high we are." E. Dickinson.—DiPe
"We play at paste." E. Dickinson.—DiPe
What are years. Marianne Moore.—PlE
"What if this world was full of happiness." A. Blackwell.—BaH
When you walk. J. Stephens.—LaPd—StS
White primit falls. Unknown.—GrCt
"Who goes to dine must take his feast." E. Dickinson.—DiPe
"Who has not found the heaven—below." E. Dickinson.—DiPe
Who is the man of poise. From Bhagavad Gita. Unknown.—AlPi
"Who loves the rain." F. Shaw.—ThA
Who misses or who wins. W. M. Thackeray.—MoS
"Who never lost, are unprepared." E. Dickinson.—DiPe
Why. V. C. Howard.—BaH
Coney Island, New York
A Coney Island life. J. L. Weil.—BrA—CoSs—DuR
A **Coney** Island life. J. L. Weil.—BrA—CoSs—DuR
Confederate States of America. See also United States—History—Civil War
Brother Jonathan's lament for Sister Caroline. O. W. Holmes.—HiL
The rebel. I. Randolph.—HiL
The **confession** ("It's no joke at all, I'm not that sort of poet") Wen Yi-tuo.—GrCt
Confession ("My ghostly fadir, I me confess") Charles d'Orléans.—GrCt
The **confession** stone. Owen Dodson.—HaK (sel.)
Confidence. Miriam Lasanta.—BaH
Confusions of the alphabet. John Wain.—CaD
Confucius (about)
The most-sacred mountain. E. Tietjens.—PaH
The **Congo.** Vachel Lindsay.—LiP
Congreve, William
False, or inconstancy.—CoBl
Conjecture. Asokbijay Raha, tr. fr. the Bengali by Lila Ray.—AlPi
A **conjuration,** to Electra. Robert Herrick.—GrS
The **conjuror.** Edward Verrall Lucas.—HoB
Conkling, Grace Hazard
The goatherd.—ArT-3
The snail.—BrSg
Conkling, Hilda
Blue jay.—CoB—ReBs
Butterfly.—ArT-3
Chickadee.—ArT-3
Dandelion.—ArT-3—BrSg—HoB—LaPd
Easter.—ArT-3
Fairies.—ArT-3—ThA
Hills.—HuS-3
I am. ArT-3

Conkling, Hilda—*Continued*
Little snail.—ArT-3
Loveliness.—ArT-3
Moon song.—ThA
Mouse.—ArT-3—HuS-3
The old bridge.—ThA
Water.—ArT-3—LaPd
Weather.—ArT-3
Connecticut
Connecticut road song. A. H. Branch.—PaH
Connecticut road song. Anna Hempstead Branch. —PaH
"A **connoisseur** of pearl." See African China
The **conquered** one. Debbie Jackson.—BaH
The **conqueror** worm. See Ligeia
Conquest ("The axe has cut the forest down") Elizabeth Jane Coatsworth.—BrA
The wilderness is tamed.—HuS-3
Conquest ("My pathway lies through worse than death") Georgia Douglas Johnson.—BoA—BoH
Conquistador. Archibald MacLeish.—HiL (sel.)
Consequences. Eleanor Farjeon.—FaT
Conservation
"Black spruce and Norway pine." From The river. P. Lorentz.—BrA
"**Consider** this odd little snail." David McCord. —BrLl
A **considerable** speck. Robert Frost.—CoB
Consolation. Aileen Fisher.—FiIo
Constant, John
Winter.—LeM
The **constant** lover. John Suckling.—HoL
"Out upon it, I have loved"—CoBl
Constellations. See Stars; also names of constellations, as Pleiades
Construction. See also Builders and building
The bricklayer. Unknown.—VrF
Construction ("And every time I pass") M. C. Livingston.—LiC
Construction ("The house frames hang like spider webs") P. Hubbell.—LaC
On watching the construction of a skyscraper. B. Raffel.—DuR—LaC
Prayers of steel. C. Sandburg.—LaC—LaPd
A time for building. M. C. Livingston.—LaPd
Construction ("And every time I pass") Myra Cohn Livingston.—LiC
Construction ("The house frames hang like spider webs") Patricia Hubbell.—LaC
"**Consulting** summer's clock." Emily Dickinson. —DiPe
"**Contemplate** Pliny's crocodile." See The bestiary
A **contemplation** upon flowers. Henry King.—CoBn
Contentment
After the winter. C. McKay.—AdIa
The ass and the lap-dog. R. S. Sharpe.—VrF
The blind boy. C. Cibber.—CoR
Comfort. From Some short poems. W. Stafford.—DuS
The frogs who wanted a king. J. Lauren.—BoH
"Gladly I'll live in a poor mountain hut." Unknown.—LeMw
Here lies my wife. J. Dryden.—BrSm
I hear America griping. M. Bishop.—BrA
"Into my heart an air that kills." From A Shropshire lad. A. E. Housman.—GrCt
Into my heart.—BoGj
Johnny Fife and Johnny's wife. M. P. Meigs. —ArT-3
The lake isle of Innisfree. W. B. Yeats.—ArT-3 —CoR—PaH—ThA—YeR
Meditations of a tortoise dozing under a rosetree near a beehive at noon while a dog scampers about and a cuckoo calls from a distant wood. E. V. Rieu.—ArT-3—CoB
Montana wives. G. Haste.—BrA
Old Jake Sutter. K. Starbird.—ArT-3
The pioneer woman—in the North country. E. Tietjens.—BrA
Raccoon. W. J. Smith.—ArT-3
Unsatisfied yearning. R. K. Munkittrick.—DuR
When the drive goes down. D. Malloch.—BrA —HuS-3
Contest. Florence Victor.—MoS
Continental crossing. Dorothy Brown Thompson. —BrA
The **contrary** boy. Gaston V. Drake.—CoBb
Contrary Mary. See "Mary, Mary, quite contrary"
The **contrary** waiter. Edgar Parker.—CoO
Conversation
Conversation about Christmas. D. Thomas.—LiT (sels.)
Conversation between Mr and Mrs Santa Claus. R. B. Bennett.—ArT-3
Conversation by Loch Ness. E. J. Coatsworth. —CoDh
Conversation in Avila. P. McGinley.—PlE
Conversation on V. O. Dodson.—HaK
Conversation with myself. E. Merriam.—MeI
Conversational. Unknown.—CoBl
Talk. D. H. Lawrence.—ClF
"Whispers." M. C. Livingston.—LaPd
You'd say it was a funeral. J. Reeves.—BrSm
Conversation about Christmas. Dylan Thomas. —LiT (sels.)
Conversation between Mr and Mrs Santa Claus. Rowena Bastin Bennett.—ArT-3
Conversation by Loch Ness. Elizabeth Jane Coatsworth.—CoDh
Conversation in Avila. Phyllis McGinley.—PlE
Conversation on V. Owen Dodson.—HaK
Conversation with myself. Eve Merriam.—MeI
Conversational. Unknown.—CoBl
Conversion. J. T. Lillie.—CoB
The **convict** of Clonmel. Unknown, tr. fr. the Irish by Jeremiah John Callanan.—MoS
"**Coo-coo-roo** of the girls." Unknown.—DoC
"**Coo-pe-coo,** coo-pe-coo." See The dove's song
Cook, Harold Lewis
The weaving.—ThA
Cookies. See Cakes and cookies
Cooks and cooking. See also Food and eating; also names of foods, as Cakes and cookies

"Betty Botter bought some butter." Mother Goose.—OpF
Betty Botter's batter.—BrMg
Catherine. K. Kuskin.—LaPd
The Christmas pudding. Unknown.—ArT-3—LaPh
"Hokey pokey winkey wum." Mother Goose.—OpF
"If I were my mother." A. Fisher.—FiIo
"Mary Ann, Mary Ann." Mother Goose.—OpF
"Oh dear, oh. My cake's all dough." Mother Goose.—OpF
Pancakes. C. G. Rossetti.—ClF
At home.—AgH
The prologue. From The Canterbury tales. G. Chaucer.—ChT
"Whan that Aprille with his shoures sote."—GrCt
Some cook. J. Ciardi.—AgH—LaP—LaPd
"There is an old cook in N. Y." Unknown.—BrLl
"There was an old lady of Brooking." Unknown.—BrLl
"There were three cooks of Colebrook." Mother Goose.—OpF
Three cooks.—BrMg
"**Cool** as a cucumber." See Lilly McQueen
"The **cool** breeze." Issa, tr. fr. the Japanese by R. H. Blyth.—IsF—LeOw
The **coolin.** James Stephens.—StS
"The **coolness.**" Issa. tr. fr. the Japanese by R. H. Blyth.—LeOw
Coons. See Raccoons
Cooper, George
Frogs at school.—HoB
October's party.—HoB
What robin told.—ArT-3
The wonderful weaver.—HoB
Cooper, Julian
A warm winter day.—CoBn
"The **cop** slumps alertly on his motorcycle." See Corner
Copeland, Maura
A kingdom of clouds.—LeM
The setting of the sun.—LeM
Coppard, Alfred Edgar
Winter field.—ReBs
The **coracle.** See Pharsalia
"The **corbie** with his roupie throat." See The raven and the crow
Corinna. David McCord.—McAd
Corinna's going a-Maying. Robert Herrick.—CoBn
Corinthians, I. See First epistle of Paul to the Corinthians
Coriolanus, sel. William Shakespeare.
Coriolanus's farewell to his fellow-citizens as he goes into banishment.—McWs
Coriolanus's farewell to his fellow-citizens as he goes into banishment. See Coriolanus
Corn. Esther Antin.—BrSg
Corn and cornfields
August. N. Belting.—BeCm
Corn. E. Antin.—BrSg
"The corn grows up." Unknown.—LeO
The cornfield. E. M. Roberts.—BoGj
The cornfields. V. Lindsay.—LiP
John Barleycorn: A ballad. R. Burns.—BuPr
The song of the cornpopper. L. E. Richards.—HoB
The standing corn. E. Farjeon.—FaA
"The **corn** grows up." Unknown, tr. fr. the Navajo.—LeO
Corner ("The cop slumps alertly on his motorcycle") Ralph Pomeroy.—DuS
The **corner** ("Good news to tell") Walter De La Mare.—DeBg
The **corner** of the field. Frances Cornford.—CoBl
The **cornfield.** Elizabeth Madox Roberts.—BoGj
Cornfields. See Corn and cornfields
The **cornfields.** Vachel Lindsay.—LiP
"The **cornfields** rise above mankind." See The cornfields
Cornford, Frances
Cambridge. ClF
The corner of the field.—CoBl
The country bedroom.—BlO
Country idyll.—CoB
Dogs. StF
Night song.—CoB
To a fat lady seen from the train.—BoGj—SmM
Village before sunset.—CoBn
Weekend stroll.—CoBn
Cornish, William
Spring.—CoBn—GrCt
Cornwall, Barry, pseud. (Bryan Waller Procter)
The blood horse.—CoB
The owl.—CoB
Cornwall, England
A ballad of a mine. R. Skelton.—CaMb
Cornwall. C. Bond.—LeM
Cornwall. Caroline Bond.—LeM
Corporal Bull. See "Here's Corporal Bull"
Corpus Christi carol. Unknown.—GrCt
The falcon.—SmM
Corso, Gregory
Birthplace revisited.—LaC
Dream of a baseball star.—MoS
Italian extravaganza.—LaC
Poets hitchhiking on the highway.—DuR
Cortez, Hernando (about)
Cortez. W. K. Seymour.—SmM
Cortez. William Kean Seymour.—SmM
"**Cortez** one night trod." See Cortez
The **cosmic** fabric. Yakov Polonsky.—PlE
Costello, Pauline
Playing.—LeM
Cottage. Eleanor Farjeon.—FaT—StF
Cottage boy. Mary Elliott.—VrF
A **cottage** in Fife. See "In a cottage in Fife"
Cotton, Charles
Evening quatrains.—GrCt
Winter, sel.
Winter's troops.—GrCt
Winter's troops. See Winter
Cotton, John
Pumpkins.—CoBn

Cotton
The ballad of the boll weevil. Unknown.—HiL
Cotton. E. Farjeon.—FaT
Cotton. Eleanor Farjeon.—FaT
"The **cotton** blouse you wear, your mother said." See McDonogh day in New Orleans
Cotton Mather. Rosemary Carr and Stephen Vincent Benét.—HiL
Cottonwood leaves. Badger Clark.—ArT-3
Coué, Émile (about)
On Monsieur Coué. C. C. Inge.—BrLl
"**Coughing** in a shady grove." See Ipecacuanha
Coughs
A charm against cough. From Atharva Veda. Unknown.—AlPi
Ipecacuanha. G. Canning.—GrCt
It isn't the cough. Unknown.—BrSm
"**Could** any mortal lip divine." Emily Dickinson. —DiPe
Could be. Langston Hughes.—LaC
"**Could** be Hastings street." Langston Hughes.—LaC
Could it have been a shadow. Monica Shannon. —ArT-3—HuS-3
"**Could** love for ever." See Stanzas
"**Could** you tell me the way to somewhere." See Somewhere
"**Count** the white horses you meet on the way." See White horses
"**Count** this among my heartfelt wishes." See Fish story
Counting
"Ane, twa, three." Unknown.—MoB
Black monkeys. R. Ainsworth.—StF
Counting. F. Johnson.—BoA
Counting petals. A. Fisher.—FiC
A counting rhyme. M. M. Stephenson.—StF
Five. C. Tringress.—StF
A number of numbers. E. Merriam.—MeC
"One old Oxford ox opening oysters." Mother Goose.—OpF
One old ox.—GrCt
"One, two (what shall I do)." R. Ainsworth.—StF
"One's none." Mother Goose.—OpF—ReOn
The sheepherder. L. Sarett.—BrA
Ten little dicky-birds. A. W. I. Baldwin.—StF
"Ten little Injuns." Mother Goose.—OpF
Ten little squirrels. Mother Goose.—StF
"There was an old woman and she went one." Unknown.—OpF
"With a hop, and a skip, and a jump." W. O'Neill.—StF
Counting. Fenton Johnson.—BoA
Counting out. Unknown.—MoB
A **counting-out** rhyme. See "Intery, mintery, cutery-corn"
Counting-out rhyme ("Silver bark of beech, and sallow") Edna St Vincent Millay.—BoGj—DuR
Counting out rhyme ("Zeenty, peenty, heathery, mithery") Unknown.—GrCt
Counting-out rhymes
Brandy hill. Mother Goose.—ReOn
"Cinderella." Unknown.—CoO
Counting out. Unknown.—MoB
Counting-out rhyme ("Silver bark of beech, and sallow") E. St Vincent Millay.—BoGj—DuR
Counting out rhyme ("Zeenty, peenty, heathery, mithery") Unknown.—GrCt
Elder belder. Mother Goose.—ReOn
Ex and squarey. Unknown.—GrCt
"Hinx, minx." Mother Goose.—BrMg—ReOn
Hurly burly. Mother Goose.—ReOn
"Intery, mintery, cutery-corn." Mother Goose. —ArT-3—TuW
A counting-out rhyme.—ClF
"Intry, mintry, cutry, corn."—HuS-3
"One, two, buckle my shoe." Mother Goose.—HuS-3—WiMg
Mother Goose rhymes, 37.—HoB
"One, two."—ArT-3—BrMg—OpF
"One two three (father caught a flea)." Unknown.—CoO
"One, two, three, four (Mary at the cottage door)." Mother Goose.—OpF
"1, 2, 3, 4, 5 (I caught a hare alive)." Mother Goose.—ArT-3
"One-ery, two-ery, tickery, seven." Mother Goose.—BrMg
A pretty maid. Mother Goose.—BrMg
Counting petals. Aileen Fisher.—FiC
A **counting** rhyme. M. M. Stephenson.—StF
"The **countless** gold of a merry heart." See Riches
Countries. See names of countries, as Mexico
Country. See Country life
The **country** bedroom. Frances Cornford.—BlO
"**Country** bumpkin." Issa, tr. fr. the Japanese.—LeOw
Country fingers. Mary O'Neill.—OnF
Country idyll. Frances Cornford.—CoB
The **country** in spring. Lin Keng, tr. fr. the Chinese by Harold Acton and Ch'en Shih-hsiang.—LeMw
Country life. See also Farm life; Village life
"Amy Elizabeth Ermyntrude Annie." Q. S. Hopper.—ArT-3
A boys' song. J. Hogg.—BlO
City streets and country roads. E. Farjeon.—ArT-3
"Come, little children, wake from sleep. A. and J. Taylor.—VrF
The country bedroom. F. Cornford.—BlO
Country fingers. M. O'Neill.—OnF
Country summer. L. Adams.—BoGj
Daybreak. W. De La Mare.—DeBg
Fingers in the nesting box. R. Graves.—CoB
Fools gaze at painted courts. From Polyolbion. M. Drayton.—GrCt
Former barn lot. M. Van Doren.—HaL—LaPd
The green roads. E. Thomas.—ThG
The hens. E. M. Roberts.—ArT-3—BoGj—CoB—HuS-3—LaPd—ThA—TuW
"Hie away, hie away." From Waverley. W. Scott.—ArT-3
Hie away.—SmM
I dream of a place. W. De La Mare.—DeBg

"I went up the high hill." Mother Goose.—OpF
Where I went.—BrMg
If I were to own. E. Thomas.—ThG
Immalee. C. G. Rossetti.—BlO—CoBn
"It rained in the night." J. Carrera Andrade.—HoL
Laughing song. W. Blake.—ArT-3—BlP—BoGj
The merry country lad. From The passionate shepherd. N. Breton.—ReO
"Minnie and Mattie." C. G. Rossetti.—ArT-3—BoGj
"My father he died, but I can't tell you how." Unknown.—BlO
Of the mean and sure estate. T. Wyatt.—ReO (sel.)
Ploughing on Sunday. W. Stevens.—BoGj—SmM—WeP
Psalm of the fruitful field. A. M. Klein.—DoW
Reynard the fox. J. Masefield.—ReO (sel.)
Rudolph is tired of the city. G. Brooks.—LaPd
A small migration. H. Behn.—BeG
Summer. C. G. Rossetti.—CoBn
A sweet country life. Unknown.—ReOn
Town and country ("In town you have expensive clocks") Unknown.—DePp
Town and country ("My child, the town's a fine place") T. Moult.—ClF
Until we built a cabin. A. Fisher.—ArT-3
Up at a villa—down in the city. R. Browning.—BrP
"Walking into the woods I see." J. Bender.—LeM
"We'll to the woods no more." A. E. Housman.—HaL
Where the hayfields were. A. MacLeish.—HaL
Country summer. Léonie Adams.—BoGj
Country trucks. Monica Shannon.—ArT-3
"The **country** vegetables scorn." See V is for vegetables
Couplet countdown. Eve Merriam.—MeI
Courage. See also Conduct of life; Heroes and heroines; Perseverance
"Be brave." Issa.—IsF
Courage ("Courage is the price that life exacts for granting peace") A. Earhart.—ThA
Courage ("Cowards die many times before their deaths") From Julius Caesar. W. Shakespeare.—ShS
"Courage has a crimson coat." N. B. Turner.—ThA
El hombre. W. C. Williams.—HoL
For my people. M. Walker.—AdIa—BoA—HaK
The forsaken. D. C. Scott.—DoW (sel.)
"I took my power in my hand." E. Dickinson.—DiPe
The duel.—LiT
If we must die. C. McKay.—AdIa—BoA—HaK
In time of crisis. R. R. Patterson.—AdIa
The pilgrim ("The sword sang on the barren heath") W. Blake.—ArT-3
"The sword sung on the barren heath."—BlP
The pilgrim ("Who would true valour see") From The pilgrim's progress. J. Bunyan.—ArT-3—ClF
Prospice. R. Browning.—BrP
Strong men, riding horses. G. Brooks.—HaK
Courage ("Courage is the price that life exacts for granting peace") Amelia Earhart.—ThA
Courage ("Cowards die many times before their deaths") See Julius Caesar
"**Courage** has a crimson coat." Nancy Byrd Turner.—ThA
"**Courage,** he said, and pointed toward the land." See The lotos-eaters
"**Courage** is the price that life exacts for granting peace." See Courage
"A **course** in rabbit reading." See Rapid reading
Court jesters
The cap and bells. W. B. Yeats.—GrCt—YeR
Court trials
A rope for Harry Fat. J. K. Baxter.—CaMb
Courtesy. See Etiquette
Courthouse square. Herbert Merrill.—BrA
Courtship. See also Love
Anne. Mother Goose.—ReOn
Antonio. L. E. Richards.—ArT-3—LaPd
"As I went up Pippin hill." Mother Goose.—BlO
"As I was going up Pippen hill."—OpF
Pippen hill.—BrMg
Blow me eyes. W. Irwin.—CoBl
"Bonny lass, canny lass." Mother Goose.—OpF
"The bottle of perfume that Willie sent." Unknown.—BrLl
The braw wooer. R. Burns.—BuPr
The canal bank. J. Stephens.—StS
The choice. D. Parker.—CoBl
Cobbler, cobbler, mend my shoe. E. Farjeon.—FaT
Cock Robin. Mother Goose.—ReOn
Comin' thro' the rye. R. Burns.—BuPr
Conversational. Unknown.—CoBl
The coolin. J. Stephens.—StS
The corner of the field. F. Cornford.—CoBl
The courtship and marriage of Jerry and Kitty. Unknown.—VrF
"Curly Locks, Curly Locks, wilt thou be mine." Mother Goose.—WiMg
"Curly Locks, Curly Locks."—BrMg
The daisies. J. Stephens.—StS
"Down by the river." Mother Goose.—BrMg
Duncan Davison. R. Burns.—BuPr
Duncan Gray. R. Burns.—BuPr
Dusty miller. Mother Goose.—BrMg
"O the dusty miller."—MoB
Flowers in the valley. Unknown.—BlO—GrS
Fossils. J. Stephens.—StS
"Green grow the rashes, O." R. Burns.—BuPr
I call and I call. R. Herrick.—GrCt
"I heard a linnet courting." R. Bridges.—ReO
"I'll gie you a pennyworth o' preens." Unknown.—MoB
"It was on a merry time." Mother Goose.—OpF
"I've found something." Unknown.—MoB

Cowboys—Songs
The buffalo skinners. Unknown.—HiL
Cowboy's lament. Unknown.—GrCt—HiL
"As I walked out in the streets of Laredo."—McWs
The cowboy's life. Unknown.—BrA
Whoopee ti yi yo, git along little dogies. Unknown.—ArT-3
Git along, little dogies.—HuS-3
Cowboy's lament. Unknown.—GrCt—HiL
"As I walked out in the streets of Laredo."—McWs
The **cowboy's** life. Unknown, at. to James Barton Adams.—ArT-3—BrA
Cowie, Reg
Time.—LeM
Cowley, Abraham
Great Diocletian.—GrCt (sel.)
Sleep.—GrCt (sel.)
Cowley, Malcolm
Tumbling Mustard.—BrA
Cowper, William
Beau's reply.—ReO
The diverting history of John Gilpin.—CoR
Epitaph on a hare.—BlO—CoB
Light shining out of darkness.—PlE
Loss of the Royal George.—CoSs
On the loss of the Royal George.—CoR
On a spaniel, called Beau, killing a young bird.—ReO
On the loss of the Royal George. See Loss of the Royal George
The poplar field.—CoR—GrCt
The snail.—CoB
The solitude of Alexander Selkirk.—CoR
Squirrel in sunshine.—CoB
Truth.—CoB (sel.)
The woodman's dog.—CoB
Cows
"Bonnie lady." Unknown.—MoB
The brown cow. Unknown.—VrF
Buttercup cow. E. Rendall.—ArT-3
"The cautious collapsible cow." A. Guiterman.—BrLl
"Caw Hawkie, drive Hawkie." Unknown.—MoB
Charlie Warlie. Mother Goose.—BrMg
Colly my cow. Mother Goose.—ReOn
Country idyll. F. Cornford.—CoB
The cow ("The cow is of the bovine ilk") O. Nash.—CoB
Cow ("Cows are not supposed to fly") W. J. Smith.—CoO
The cow ("The friendly cow all red and white") R. L. Stevenson.—ArT-3—BlO—HoB—HuS-3—SmM
The cow ("A greensweet breathing") J. Ciardi.—DuS
The cow in apple time. R. Frost.—ReO
Cows. J. Reeves.—BlO—CoB—StF
"Cushy cow, bonny, let down thy milk." Mother Goose.—HuS-3—OpF—ReMg
Milking.—BrMg
"Four stiff-standers." Mother Goose.—BrMg—GrCt—OpF
Riddle.—BrF
Frighted by a cow. E. Turner.—VrF
The gracious and the gentle thing. R. P. T. Coffin.—ReO
Green afternoon. F. M. Frost.—ArT-3
Hexameter and pentameter. Unknown.—GrCt
"I had a little cow (hey-diddle)." Mother Goose.—OpF
"I had a little cow and to save her." Mother Goose.—OpF
"I heard a cow low, a bonnie cow low." Unknown.—MoB
"I never saw a purple cow." G. Burgess.—BlO
The purple cow.—ArT-3—LaPd
Jonathan. Unknown.—ArT-3
Man and cows. A. Young.—CaD
"Milk-white moon, put the cows to sleep." C. Sandburg.—HuS-3
Milking time. E. M. Roberts.—BoGj—HoB
Moo. R. Hillyer.—CoB
Night and noises. G. Foster.—LeM
No. M. C. Livingston.—LiC
The old woman's three cows. Mother Goose.—BrMg
Pretty cow. A. Taylor.—HuS-3
The cow.—VrF
"There was a little man and he had a little cow." Mother Goose.—OpF
"There was an old lady who said, How." E. Lear
Limericks.—HoB
"There was an old man who said, How." E. Lear.—BlO—BrLl
Limericks.—HoB
Nonsense verses.—HuS-3
"There was an old soldier of Bister." Unknown.—BrLl
"There's a cow on the mountain." Unknown.—WyC
"This little cow eats grass." Unknown.—WyC
Cows. James Reeves.—BlO—CoB—StF
"The **cows** are dressed in suede." See Late October
"**Cows** are not supposed to fly." See Cow
Cox, Kenyon
The bumblebeaver. See Mixed beasts
The kangarooster. See Mixed beasts
Mixed beasts, sels.
The bumblebeaver.—ArT-3
The kangarooster.—ArT-3
The octopussycat.—ArT-3
The octopussycat. See Mixed beasts
Coxe, Louis O.
Watching bird.—CoB
"The **coyote** sat." Mae Verna Tso.—BaH
Coyotes
"The coyote sat." M. V. Tso.—BaH
February. N. Belting.—BeCm
"The grey quails were bunched together." Unknown.—LeO

Cozens, F. H.
"There was a young curate named Stone."—BrLl
The **crab.** Conrad Aiken.—AiC
Crab-apple. Ethel Talbot.—ArT-3
Crabbe, George
The ancient mansion, sel.
Spring to winter.—GrCt
Spring to winter. See The ancient mansion
Crabs
The crab. C. Aiken.—AiC
The crabs. R. Lattimore.—DuS
The dead crab. A. Young.—ReO
"Old Mr Chang, I've heard it said." Unknown.—WyC
"Sitting on the stone, O crab." Unknown.—LeO
Song of the four little shell-animals. Unknown.—LeO
A thousand stones. C. Lewis.—LeP
The **crabs.** Richmond Lattimore.—DuS
"**Crack** of jibing canvas, dazzle-white in the sun." See Wind, waves, and sails
Cracker time. Aileen Fisher.—FiC
Crackers. See Cakes and cookies
The **crackling** twig. James Stephens.—StS
Cradle hymn. Martin Luther.—ArT-3—HoB—LaPh
Cradle song ("From groves of spice") Sarojini Naidu.—ThA
A **cradle** song ("Golden slumbers kiss your eyes") See Pleasant comedy of patient Grissell
Cradle song ("Hush, honey, hush") Herbert Read.—CaD
A **cradle** song ("Hush, my dear, lie still and slumber") Isaac Watts.—HoB
Cradle song ("O my deir hert, young Jesus sweit") Unknown.—PlE
Cradle song ("Out in the dark something complains") F. R. Higgins.—ReS
A **cradle** song ("Sleep, sleep, beauty bright") William Blake.—BlP
A **cradle** song ("Sweet and low, sweet and low") See The princess—Sweet and low
A **cradle** song ("Sweet dreams, form a shade") William Blake.—BlP
Cradle song for a boy. Unknown, tr. fr. the Tlingit.—LeO
Cradle songs. See Lullabies
The **cradle** trap. Louis Simpson.—LiT
The **crafty** farmer. Unknown.—ArT-3
Crag Jack's apostasy. Ted Hughes.—PlE
Craigbilly fair. Unknown.—GrCt
Craik, Jill
Fire.—LeM
Cranberry road. Rachel Field.—ThA
Crane, Hart
March.—CoBn
To Brooklyn bridge.—HiL—PaH
Crane, Nathalia, pseud. (Clara Ruth Abarbanel)
Spooks.—BrSm
Crane, Stephen
"Fast rode the knight."—LiT
"There was one I met upon the road."—PlE
War is kind.—HiL
Crane, Walter
The crocus.—BrSg
Cranes (Birds)
The dying crane. M. Drayton.—ReO
I hear the crane. From Du Bartas his divine weeks. J. Sylvester.—ReO
"In the evening calm the cranes search for prey." Unknown.—BaS
The sandhill crane. M. Austin.—ArT-3—CoB
"Startled." Saigyo Hōshi.—BaS
"When the frost lies white." Unknown.—BaS
The wolf and the crane. E. Rees.—ArT-3
Crapsey, Adelaide
November night.—HoL
"The **craving** of Samuel Rouse for clearance to create." See The slave and the iron lace
Crawford, Deborah
I cannot tell.—BaH
Crawford, Isabella V.
Love me, love my dog.—DoW
Crawford, Karen
Being nobody.—LeM
"**Crawl,** laugh." Issa, tr. fr. the Japanese.—LeOw
The **crayfish.** Robert Wallace.—CoB
A **crazy** flight. Myra Cohn Livingston.—LiC
"**Crazy** jay blue." E. E. Cummings.—CoB
"The **crazy** old vinegar man is dead. He never had missed a day before." See The vinegar man
"The **crazy** tugs." See East river
The **crazy** woman. Gwendolyn Brooks.—BoH—LiT
"A **cream** of phosphorescent light." See Jonah
"The **cream,** the bay." See Carriage
Creation
"All things bright and beautiful." C. F. Alexander.—HoB
"At the time when the earth became hot." Unknown.—LeO
The creation ("And God stepped out on space"). J. W. Johnson.—ArT-3
"Up from the bed of the river."—PlE (sel.)
The creation ("There was no sun") From Metamorphoses. Ovid.—ClF
Ducks. F. W. Harvey.—CoB (sel.)
Genesis. E. J. Coatsworth.—CoDh
"I wonder why." E. V. Lee.—BaH
The making of birds. K. Tynan.—ReBs
"The seasons were appointed, and the times." N. Belting.—BeCm
The song of creation. From Rig Veda. Unknown.—AlPi
Stars. F. S. Edsall.—ThA
The **creation** ("And God stepped out on space") James Weldon Johnson.—ArT-3
"Up from the bed of the river."—PlE (sel.)
The **creation** ("There was no sun") See Metamorphoses
Creatures in the zoo, sel. Babette Deutsch
Ape.—DuS
Crécy, Battle of, 1346
The eve of Crécy. W. Morris.—GrS

The **creditor.** Louis MacNeice.—PlE
"The **creeks** and the streams and the Great River are full." See April
Creeley, Robert
The invoice.—DuS
"Love comes quietly."—CoBl
Creep. Linda Kershaw.—LeM
Cremation
The cremation ground. Bhavabhuti.—AlPi
The cremation of Sam McGee. R. W. Service.—ArT-3—BrSm
The **cremation** ground. Bhavabhuti, tr. fr. the Sanskrit by Daniel H. H. Ingalls.—AlPi
The **cremation** of Sam McGee. Robert W. Service.—ArT-3—BrSm
"**Crescendo.**" See Starry night I
Crescent moon. Elizabeth Madox Roberts.—ArT-3
Crew cut. David McCord.—MoS
A **cricket.** Aileen Fisher.—FiC
"**Cricket** come back. You've left your drum behind." Unknown, tr. fr. the Lamba.—LeO
Crickets
"At the altar." Issa.—IsF
"Be a good boy." Issa.—LeOw
A cricket. A. Fisher.—FiC
"Cricket come back. You've left your drum behind." Unknown.—LeO
Crickets ("All busy punching tickets") D. McCord.—LaPd
Crickets ("We cannot say that crickets sing") H. Behn.—BeG
"Farther in summer than the birds." E. Dickinson.—DiPe
The grasshopper and the cricket. L. Hunt.—CoB
"I'm going to turn over." Issa.—IsF
"Now I am going out." Issa.—LeOw
On the grasshopper and cricket. J. Keats.—CoB
On the grasshopper and the cricket.—ReO
"On the top of a mountain." Unknown.—WyC
"Poor crying cricket." Kikaku.—BeCs
Splinter. C. Sandburg.—ArT-3
"Tonight in this town." Unknown.—BeCs
Crickets ("All busy punching tickets") David McCord.—LaPd
Crickets ("We cannot say that crickets sing") Harry Behn.—BeG
"The **crickets** call through the long, long night." See Johnny Appleseed's wife from the palace of Eve
"The **cries** of hate are as loud as drums." See Hate
Crime and criminals. See also Murder
Bandit. A. M. Klein.—DoW
Billy the Kid. Unknown.—HiL
The gallant highwayman. J. De Mille.—DoW
Hangman's tree. L. Z. White.—BrA
The highwayman. A. Noyes.—ArT-3—CoBl
Jesse James. W. R. Benét.—HiL
The leap of Roushan Beg. From Birds of passage. H. W. Longfellow.—HuS-3
Macavity: The mystery cat.—ArT-3—CoB—LiT—SmM
Psychological prediction. V. Brasier.—CoBb
A visit to Newgate. H. S. Horsley.—VrF
Crimean war, 1854-1856
The Crimean war heroes. W. S. Landor.—McWs
The **Crimean** war heroes. Walter Savage Landor.—McWs
Crinolines and bloomers; or, The battle between Monsieur Worth and Mrs Bloomer. Unknown.—HiL
The **cripple.** Robert P. Tristram Coffin.—HuS-3
Cripples
The lame boy and the fairy. V. Lindsay.—LiP
The cripple. R. P. T. Coffin.—HuS-3
A **critic.** Walter Savage Landor.—GrCt
Criticism. See Critics and criticism
Critics and criticism
A critic. W. S. Landor.—GrCt
The curse. J. M. Synge.—GrCt
A little learning. From An essay on criticism. A. Pope.—GrCt
Poets and critics. A. Tennyson.—TeP
Sonnet. W. Wordsworth.—WoP
To a captious critic. P. L. Dunbar.—HaK
To Christopher North. A. Tennyson.—TeP
A **crocodile** ("Hard by the lilied Nile I saw") Thomas Lovell Beddoes.—CoB
The **crocodile** ("O crocodile") Conrad Aiken.—AiC
Crocodiles
A crocodile ("Hard by the lilied Nile I saw") T. L. Beddoes.—CoB
The crocodile ("O crocodile") C. Aiken.—AiC
The cruel naughty boy. Unknown.—CoBb
"Don't ever cross a crocodile." K. Starbird.—ArT-3—LaPd
"He who bathes among crocodiles." Unknown.—LeO
"How doth the little crocodile." From Alice's adventures in wonderland. L. Carroll.—ArT-3—BlO—BrSm—HoB—LaP
"If you should meet a crocodile." Unknown.—LaPd
The monkeys and the crocodile. L. E. Richards.—ArT-3—BrSm—HoB—LaP
"Silent logs floating." M. Goodson.—LeM
"There was an old man of Boulak." E. Lear.—BrLl
The **crocus.** Walter Crane.—BrSg
"The **crocus,** while the days are dark." See The year's round
Crocuses
The crocus. W. Crane.—BrSg
Crocuses. Jōsa.—ArT-3
Crocuses. Jōsa.—ArT-3
Croesus, King of Lydia (about)
The fortunes of the great. From The Canterbury tales. G. Chaucer.—ChT
Cromek speaks. William Blake.—BlP
Cromwell, Oliver (about)
Cromwell dead. From A poem upon the death of Oliver Cromwell. A. Marvell.—GrCt
Cromwell dead. See A poem upon the death of Oliver Cromwell

Crooked-heart. James Stephens.—StS
"**Crooked** heels." See The cobbler
The **crooked** man. See "There was a crooked man, and he went a crooked mile"
"The **crooked** paths." See The goat paths
"The **crops** are in from the fields." See November
Cross. Langston Hughes.—AdIa—BoA
"**Cross-legged** on his bed." See Son
The **cross** of snow. Henry Wadsworth Longfellow.—LoPl
"**Cross-patch.**" Mother Goose.—BrMg—GrCt—WiMg
"**Cross-patch,** draw the latch." See "Cross-patch"
Crossing. Philip Booth.—BrA—DuR
Crossing Kansas by train. Donald Justice.—DuR
Crossing the bar. Alfred Tennyson.—TeP
Crouch, Pearl Riggs
A story in the snow.—ArT-3
"The **crow.**" Issa, tr. fr. the Japanese by R. H. Blyth.—IsF
The **crow** ("By the wave rising, by the wave breaking") P. K. Page.—DoW
Crow ("A hundred autumns he has wheeled") Mark Van Doren.—ReO
The **crow** ("Thou dusky spirit of the wood") Henry David Thoreau.—ReBs
The **crow** and the lark. See The merchant of Venice
"The **crow** doth sing as sweetly as the lark." See The merchant of Venice—The crow and the lark
"The **crow** flew so fast." Richard Wright
Hokku poems.—BoA
"The **crow** goes flopping on from wood to wood." See The flight of birds
Crow in springtime. Elizabeth Jane Coatsworth.—CoSb
"The **crow** killed the pussy, O." Unknown.—MoB
"The **crow**—the crow, the great black crow." See The great black crow
"**Crow,** with shiny clothes." Bonita Jones.—BaH
Crowell, Grace Noll
"The day will bring some lovely thing."—ArT-3
Shooting stars.—HoB
Crows
Absolutes. G. Keyser.—DuR
Always with us—the black preacher. H. Melville.—ReBs
"A carrion crow sat on an oak." Mother Goose.—BlO—ReMg—SmM
The carrion crow.—BrMg
"A cautious crow flies." Bashō.—BeCs
Caw. W. De La Mare.—DeBg
"The crow." Issa.—IsF
The crow ("By the wave rising, by the wave breaking") P. K. Page.—DoW
Crow ("A hundred autumns he has wheeled") M. Van Doren.—ReO
The crow ("Thou dusky spirit of the wood") H. D. Thoreau.—ReBs
The crow and the lark. From The merchant of Venice. W. Shakespeare.—ShS
"The crow flew so fast." R. Wright
Hokku poems.—BoA
Crow in springtime. E. J. Coatsworth.—CoSb
"The crow killed the pussy, O." Unknown.—MoB
Crows ("I like to walk") D. McCord.—ArT-3—DuR—LaPd—TuW
The crows ("I shortcut home between Wade's tipsy shocks") L. B. Drake.—DuR
Dust of snow. R. Frost.—ArT-3—LaPd—ReBs—ThA—TuW
The farmer's gun. A. Young.—ReO
Flight. G. Johnston.—DoW
The gnome. H. Behn.—ArT-3—LaPd
The great black crow. P. J. Bailey.—CoB
"It's silly for the day to be so long." Issa.—LeOw
Night crow. T. Roethke.—HoL—ReBs
"On the first of March." Mother Goose.—MoB—OpF
The crows.—BrMg
Phoebus and the crow. From The Canterbury tales. G. Chaucer.—ChT
Lat take a cat.—GrCt (sel.)
Take any bird.—ReO (sel.)
"Pick, crow, pick, and have no fear." Mother Goose.—OpF
The raven and the crow. Unknown.—MoB
"Said a crow in the top of a tree." J. Ciardi.—BrLl
Short song. Mother Goose.—BrMg
Song. T. L. Beddoes.—CoB
"There was a crow sat on a stone." Mother Goose.—ReMg
"There was a jolly frog in the river did swim, O." Unknown.—OpF
"There were two crows sat on a stone." Mother Goose.—MoB—OpF
Two old crows. V. Lindsay.—HaL
A warning to crows. Unknown.—DePp
The **crows.** See "On the first of March"
Crows ("I like to walk") David McCord.—ArT-3—DuR—LaPd—TuW
The **crows** ("I shortcut home between Wade's tipsy shocks") Leah Bodine Drake.—DuR
Crucifixion. See Easter; Jesus Christ
Crucifixion. Raymond Benally.—BaH
Cruciform. Winifred Welles.—HoL
The **cruel** boy. Elizabeth Turner.—VrF
Cruel clever cat. Geoffrey Taylor.—GrCt
The **cruel** naughty boy. Unknown.—CoBb
Cruel Tom. Mother Goose.—ReOn
"**Cruel** winter wind." Johnson James.—BaH
"**Cruelty** has a human heart." See A divine image
The **cruise** of the Monitor. George Henry Boker.—HiL
The **crusader.** Dorothy Parker.—BrSm
Crusades
Children's crusade 1939. B. Brecht.—CaMb
The crusader. D. Parker.—BrSm
"King Arthur's men have come again." V. Lindsay.—LiP

Romanesque frieze. E. J. Coatsworth.—CoDh
"A **crust** of bread and a corner to sleep in." See Life
The **cry** of the children. Elizabeth Barrett Browning.—ClF (sel.)
Crying
"Be still, my child." Unknown.—DoC—LeO
The crying child. E. Turner.—VrF
Giant Bonaparte. Mother Goose.—BrMg
"It's such a little thing to weep." E. Dickinson.—DiPe
The lizard is crying. F. G. Lorca.—LiT—SmM
The man in the onion bed. J. Ciardi.—CoO
Rice pudding. A. A. Milne.—CoBb—MiC
The sad story of a little boy that cried. Unknown.—CoBb
Why. W. De La Mare.—DeBg
"Why do you cry." Unknown.—DoC
"Why dost thou weep, my child." Unknown. —LeO
The **crying** child. Elizabeth Turner.—VrF
The **crystal** cabinet. William Blake.—BlP
Cuba
Cuba libre. J. Miller.—HiL
Cuba libre. Joaquin Miller.—HiL
The **Cuban** emigrant. Victor Alvarez.—BaH
Cubans
The Cuban emigrant. V. Alvarez.—BaH
"The **cubs** of bears a living lump appear." See The phoenix self-born
Cuchulain (about)
The death of Cuchulain. W. B. Yeats.—GrCt
The **cuckoo.** See "The cuckoo is a merry bird"
Cuckoo ("Cuckoo, cuckoo") Andrew Young.—GrCt
The **cuckoo** ("If the cuckoo were") Kodo, tr. fr. the Japanese by Kenneth Yasuda.—LeMw
The **cuckoo** ("Repeat that, repeat") Gerard Manley Hopkins.—CoB
"The **cuckoo** and the gowk." See How many birds
"**Cuckoo,** bubbling your green words across half Berkshire." See Hearing the cuckoo
Cuckoo, cherry tree. Mother Goose.—BrMg
"The **cuckoo** comes in April." Mother Goose.—OpF
"**Cuckoo,** cuckoo." See Cuckoo
"**Cuckoo,** cuckoo, cherry tree." See Cuckoo, cherry tree
"**Cuckoo,** cuckoo, what do you do." See To the cuckoo
Cuckoo in the pear-tree. William Brighty Rands. —ReBs
"The **cuckoo** is a merry bird." Mother Goose.—OpF
The cuckoo.—CoB—GrCt
"The **cuckoo** is a pretty bird." See "The cuckoo is a merry bird"
"The **cuckoo** sat in the old pear-tree." See Cuckoo in the pear-tree
The **cuckoo** song. Unknown.—GrCt
Cuckoos
Cuckoo ("Cuckoo, cuckoo") A. Young.—GrCt
The cuckoo ("If the cuckoo were") Kodo.—LeMw
The cuckoo ("Repeat that, repeat") G. M. Hopkins.—CoB
Cuckoo, cherry tree. Mother Goose.—BrMg
"The cuckoo comes in April." Mother Goose. —OpF
Cuckoo in the pear-tree. W. B. Rands.—ReBs
"The cuckoo is a merry bird." Mother Goose. —OpF
The cuckoo.—CoB—GrCt
The cuckoo song. Unknown.—GrCt
Cuckoos. A. Young.—GrCt
"The cuckoo's a bonnie bird." Unknown.—MoB
Cuckoo's palace. W. B. Rands.—ReBs
Hearing the cuckoo. J. Heath-Stubbs.—CaD
"In the leafy treetops." Yakamochi.—BaS
"Little gray cuckoo." Bashō.—LeMw
"On summer nights." Tsurayuki.—BaS
"Sunshine and rain." Mother Goose.—OpF
To the cuckoo ("Cuckoo, cuckoo, what do you do") Mother Goose.—BrMg
To the cuckoo ("Not the whole warbling grove in concert heard") W. Wordsworth.—WoP
To the cuckoo ("O blithe new-comer. I have heard") W. Wordsworth.—WoP
To the cuckoo ("O cuckoo, shall I call thee bird") F. H. Townsend.—GrCt
"Turned towards the moon." Yakamochi.—BaS
Cuckoos. Andrew Young.—GrCt
"The **cuckoo's** a bonnie bird." Unknown.—MoB
"The **cuckoo's** a bonny bird." See "The cuckoo is a merry bird"
Cuckoo's palace. William Brighty Rands.—ReBs
Cullen, Countee
A brown girl dead.—HaK
Epitaphs: For Paul Laurence Dunbar. See For Paul Laurence Dunbar
For a mouthy woman.—BrSm
For a pessimist.—BrSm
For John Keats.—HaK
Four epitaphs.—BoA
For my grandmother
Four epitaphs.—BoA
For Paul Laurence Dunbar.—HaK
Epitaphs: For Paul Laurence Dunbar.—BoH
Four epitaphs.—BoA
From the dark tower.—AdIa—HaK
Heritage.—BoA
"I have wrapped my dreams in a silken cloth."—ThA
If you should go.—BoH
Incident.—AdIa—HoB—HoL—ThA
Leaves.—BoH
The litany of the dark people.—PlE
Saturday's child.—BoH—HaK
Simon the Cyrenian speaks.—BoA
Spring reminiscence.—BoH
Tableau.—BrA—HaK
"That bright chimeric beast."—BoA
The unknown color.—BoH

Cynddylan on a tractor. R. S. Thomas.—CaD
Cynthia in the snow. Gwendolyn Brooks.—ArT-3
Cynthia's revels, sel. Ben Jonson
Hymn to Diana.—GrCt
Cypress trees
The black finger. A. W. Grimké.—BoA

D

D., D.
"A Boston boy went out to Yuma."—BrSm
D., H., pseud. (Hilda Doolittle; Mrs. Richard Aldington)
"Never more will the wind."—GrS
Oread.—BoGj
Storm.—ArT-3
"**Dab** a pin in my lottery book." Unknown.—MoB
"**Dad** went somewhere." See Daddy
Daddy ("Bring daddy home") Mother Goose.—BrMg
Daddy ("Dad went somewhere") Calvin Begay.—BaH
Daddy fell into the pond. Alfred Noyes.—LaP—LaPd
"**Daddy** fixed the breakfast." See Mummy slept late and daddy fixed breakfast
Daddy longlegs. Aileen Fisher.—FiI
Daedalus
O Daedalus, fly away home. R. E. Hayden.—AdIa—BoH
"**Daffadowndilly.**" See "Daffy-down-dilly has now come to town"
Daffodils
"Daffodils." From The winter's tale. W. Shakespeare.—ArT-3—BrSg—TuW
The daffodils ("The daffodils, the daffodils") A. Fisher.—FiC
The daffodils. ("I wandered lonely as a cloud") W. Wordsworth.—BoGj—HoB—HuS-3—TuW
I wandered lonely.—CoR
"I wandered lonely as a cloud."—BlO—BoH—CoBn—SmM—WoP
Daffodils ("In spite of cold and chills") Kikuriō.—ArT-3
"Daffy-down-dilly has now come to town." Mother Goose.—OpF—ReMg
Daffadowndilly.—ArT-3
Daffy-down-dilly.—BrMg—BrSg
Mother Goose rhymes, 5.—HoB
"Growing in the vale." C. G. Rossetti.—ArT-3
Sweet Daffadowndilly.—HoB
"I saw green banks of daffodils." From Home thoughts in Laventi. E. W. Tennant.—ArT-3
To daffodils. R. Herrick.—CoBn—HoL
To daffadills.—BoGj
"**Daffodils.**" See The winter's tale
The **daffodils** ("The daffodils, the daffodils") Aileen Fisher.—FiC
The **daffodils** ("I wandered lonely as a cloud") William Wordsworth.—BoGj—HoB—HuS-3—TuW
I wandered lonely.—CoR
"I wandered lonely as a cloud."—BlO—BoH—CoBn—SmM—WoP
Daffodils ("In spite of cold and chills") Kikuriō.—ArT-3
"The **daffodils**, the daffodils." See The daffodils
Daffy-down-dilly. See "Daffy-down-dilly has now come to town"
"**Daffy-down-dilly** has come up to town." See "Daffy-down-dilly has now come to town"
"**Daffy-down-dilly** has new come to town." See "Daffy-down-dilly has now come to town"
"**Daffy-down-dilly** has now come to town." Mother Goose.—OpF—ReMg
Daffadowndilly.—ArT-3
Daffy-down-dilly.—BrMg—BrSg
Mother Goose rhymes, 5.—HoB
Dagonet's canzonet. Ernest Rhys.—GrS
Dahl, Roald
James and the giant peach.—CoB (sel.)
Dahlias
Dahlias. P. Colum.—BoGj
Dahlias. Padraic Colum.—BoGj
Daiches, David
To Kate, skating better than her date.—MoS
Daihaku, Princess
"How will you manage."—BaS
Dailey, Esther L.
"Excuse me."—BaH
The **daily** grind. Fenton Johnson.—BoA
"**Daintily** the women of Syracuse." See Women of Syracuse
"**Dainty** Miss Apathy." See Pooh
Daisies
"Buttercups and daisies." M. Howitt.—OpF
The daisies ("In the scented bud of the morning-O") J. Stephens.—StS
The daisies ("Over the shoulders and slopes of the dune") B. Carman.—CoBn
Daisies ("The stars are everywhere to-night") A. Young.—BoGj
The daisy. E. Turner.—VrF
Daisy's song. J. Keats.—CoBn
The field daisy. A. and J. Taylor.—VrF
Mary. W. De La Mare.—DeBg
To a mountain daisy. R. Burns.—BuPr
The daisy.—CoBn
To the daisy. W. Wordsworth.—WoP
To the same flower. W. Wordsworth.—WoP
The **daisies** ("In the scented bud of the morning-O") James Stephens.—StS
The **daisies** ("Over the shoulders and slopes of the dune") Bliss Carman.—CoBn
Daisies ("The stars are everywhere to-night") Andrew Young.—BoGj
The **daisy** ("Papa, said Eugene, is a daisy a book") Elizabeth Turner.—VrF
The **daisy** ("Wee, modest, crimson-tipped flow'r") See To a mountain daisy
Daisy's song. John Keats.—CoBn

Dakota badlands. Elizabeth Landeweer.—BrA
Dakota Indians. See Indians of the Americas—Dakota
Daley's dorg Wattie. W. T. Goodge.—CoB
The **dalliance** of the leopards. Unknown, tr. fr. the Sanskrit by E. Powys Mathers.—HoL
Dalmon, Charles
O what if the fowler.—CoB—ReBs
Dalven, Rae
Candles. tr.—SmM
Dame Duck's lecture. Anne Hawkshawe.—StF
"**Dame,** get up and bake your pies." Mother Goose.—WiMg
Dame Trot. See "Dame Trot and her cat"
"**Dame** Trot and her cat." Mother Goose.—StF
Dame Trot.—BrMg
Dams. See also names of dams, as Bonneville dam
Big dam. W. R. Moses.—BrA
Dan Dunder. John Ciardi.—CoBb
"**Dan** Dunder is a blunder." See Dan Dunder
Dana, Robert
On the expressway.—LaC
The **dance** ("In Breughel's great picture, The Kermess") William Carlos Williams.—BoGj
Dance ("Left and right and swing around") James Stephens.—StS
A **dance** for rain. Witter Bynner.—PaH
Dance of burros. Dilys Laing.—CoB
Dance of the animals. Unknown, tr. fr. the Pygmie.—DoC—LeO
Dance the boatman. Unknown.—HiL
"**Dance** there upon the shore." See To a child dancing in the wind
"**Dance** to your daddie." See "Dance to your daddy"
"**Dance** to your daddy." Mother Goose.—BrMg—MoB
"Dance to your daddie."—ArT-3
Dancers. See Dances and dancing
Dances and dancing
African dance. L. Hughes.—ThA
Ballet school. B. Deutsch.—HoL
The cat and the moon. W. B. Yeats.—BoGj—CoB—CoR—HaL—LiT—YeR
"Cock a doodle doo (my dame)." Mother Goose.—BrMg
"Cock-a-doodle-do."—ReMg
The dance ("In Breughel's great picture, The Kermess") W. C. Williams.—BoGj
Dance ("Left and right and swing around") J. Stephens.—StS
A dance for rain. W. Bynner.—PaH
Dance of the animals. Unknown.—DoC—LeO
Dancing ("Booming thundering sound") Alex M.—LeM
Dancing ("A hop, a skip, and off you go") E. Farjeon.—HuS-3
Dancing ("Oh dear, I must wear my red slippers to-day") E. Turner.—VrF
The dancing sea. From Orchestra. J. Davies.—GrCt
The dutiful mariner. W. Irwin.—CoSs
"First the heel." Unknown.—MoB
Fairy dance. From A midsummer-night's dream. W. Shakespeare.—ShS
A fishy square dance. E. Merriam.—MeI
Jazzonia. L. Hughes.—BoA—HaK
"Jock plays them rants so lively." Unknown.—MoB
"Katie Beardie had a cow." Unknown.—MoB
Kids. From Some short poems. W. Stafford.—GrCt
Lily McQueen. S. Jackson.—CoBl
The lobster quadrille. From Alice's adventures in wonderland. L. Carroll.—HoB
The mock turtle's song.—GrCt
Midsummer magic. I. O. Eastwick.—ArT-3
"My arms, they wave high in the air." Unknown.—LeO
"O, the mill, mill, O." Unknown.—MoB
On the Duchess of Gordon's reel dancing. R. Burns.—BuPr
Peruvian dance song. Unknown.—LeO
A piper. S. O'Sullivan.—ArT-3—LaPd
The potatoes' dance. V. Lindsay.—HoB—ThA
Radhadevi's dance. From Hammira-mahakavya. N. Suri.—AlPi
Shadow dance. I. O. Eastwick.—ArT-3—LaP
Tam o'Shanter. R. Burns.—BuPr
Tarantella. H. Belloc.—PaH—ThA
"There was an old lady of France." E. Lear.—BrLl
"There'd be an orchestra." From Thousand-and-first ship. F. S. Fitzgerald.—BoGj
"Throwing them up to the moon." Unknown.—LeMw
To a child dancing in the wind. W. B. Yeats.—YeR
Undersea. M. Chute.—LaP
Upon his mistress dancing. J. Shirley.—McWs
A waltz in the afternoon. B. Bentley.—CoBl
When a ring's around the moon. M. J. Carr.—ArT-3
Where the hayfields were. A. MacLeish.—HaL
"Who learned you to dance." Unknown.—MoB
You were shattered. G. Ungaretti.—LiT (sel.)
The zobo bird. F. A. Collymore.—BoGj
Dancing. See Dances and dancing
Dancing ("Booming thundering sound") Alex M.—LeM
Dancing ("A hop, a skip, and off you go") Eleanor Farjeon.—HuS-3
Dancing ("Oh dear, I must wear my red slippers to-day") Elizabeth Turner.—VrF
"**Dancing** dancing down the street." See Rain
"**Dancing** in dust, dancing in sun, to you." See Song to cloud
The **dancing** sea. See Orchestra
"**Dancy-diddlety-poppety-pin.**" Mother Goose.—OpF
Dandelion. Hilda Conkling.—ArT-3—BrSg—HoB—LaPd
Dandelions
Dandelion. H. Conkling.—ArT-3—BrSg—HoB—LaPd
Dandelions. F. M. Frost.—ArT-3
Dandelions everywhere. A. Fisher.—FiC

"The dandelion's pallid tube." E. Dickinson.—DiPe
"Gently, gently, the wind blows." K. Mizumura.—MiI
Dandelions. Frances M. Frost.—ArT-3
Dandelions everywhere. Aileen Fisher.—FiC
"The **dandelion's** pallid tube." Emily Dickinson. —DiPe
Danger. Elizabeth Jane Coatsworth.—CoSb
Dangerous sport. Elizabeth Turner.—VrF
The **dangers** of foot-ball. See Trivia
Daniel
Daniel. V. Lindsay.—GrCt—LiP
The Daniel jazz.—SmM
Daniel, Samuel
First flame.—CoBl
Daniel. Vachel Lindsay.—GrCt—LiP
The Daniel jazz.—SmM
Daniel Boone ("Daniel Boone at twenty-one") Arthur Guiterman.—HuS-3
Daniel Boone ("When Daniel Boone goes by, at night") Rosemary Carr and Stephen Vincent Benét.—BrA—HoL
"**Daniel** Boone at twenty-one." See Daniel Boone
The **Daniel** jazz. See Daniel
Daniel Webster's horses. Elizabeth Jane Coatsworth.—BrA—CoDh
Daniells, Roy
The mole.—DoW
Noah.—DoW
Daniélou, Alain
The lover's song. See Shilappadakaram
Shilappadakaram, sels.
The lover's song. tr.—AlPi
Song of the playing ball. tr.—AlPi
Song of the playing ball. See Shilappadakaram
"**Dank,** limber verses, stuft with lakeside sedges." See Some of Wordsworth
Danner, Margaret
Far from Africa: Four poems.—BoA
I'll walk the tightrope.—HaK
Sadie's playhouse.—HaK
The slave and the iron lace.—BoA
These beasts and the Benin bronze.—HaK
Through the varied patterned lace.—HaK
"**Danny** dawdles." See Spring fever
Danny Murphy. James Stephens.—CoR—StS
"**Danny** was a rascal." See The buccaneer
Dante (Durante Alighieri)
Sestina.—GrS
Dante (Durante Alighieri) (about)
Dante. H. W. Longfellow.—LoPl
Divina commedia. H. W. Longfellow.—LoPl
Dante. Henry Wadsworth Longfellow.—LoPl
"**Darby** and Joan were dressed in black." See Alligoshee
"A **daring** young lady of Guam." Unknown.—BrLl
Darius, King of Persia (about)
Daniel. V. Lindsay.—GrCt—LiP
The Daniel jazz.—SmM
"**Darius** the Mede was a king and a wonder." See Daniel
Dark affections. See The merchant of Venice
"**Dark** brown is the river." See Where go the boats
Dark Danny. Ivy O. Eastwick.—ArT-3
"**Dark** Danny has eyes." See Dark Danny
"**Dark,** dark night." Lynette Joass.—LeM
"A **dark,** elusive shadow." See Shadows
Dark eyes at Forest Hills. I. L. Martin.—MoS
"**Dark** fills the sky with his big black cloak." Beverley Dinsdale.—LeM
The **dark** forest. Edward Thomas.—ThG
"The **dark** gray clouds." Natalia Belting.—LaPd
The **dark** hills. Edwin Arlington Robinson.—BoGj —BoH
"**Dark** hills at evening in the west." See The dark hills
"**Dark** is the forest and deep, and overhead." See The dark forest
Dark kingdom. Elizabeth Jane Coatsworth.—CoB
Dark symphony. Melvin B. Tolson.—BoA
Dark testament. Paul Murray.—BoA
Darley, George
The enchanted spring.—CoBn
Nepenthe, sels.
The phoenix.—GrCt
The unicorn.—GrCt
"O'er the wild gannet's bath."—CoSs—GrCt
The phoenix. See Nepenthe
The sea ritual.—GrS
Song of the mermaids.—GrCt
The unicorn. See Nepenthe
The **darkling** thrush. Thomas Hardy.—CoR
Darkness. Murari, tr. fr. the Sanskrit by Daniel H. H. Ingalls.—AlPi
"The **darkness** darts, the moon curls up." Janine. —LeM
"**Darkness** has called to darkness, and disgrace." See As a plane tree by the water
Darkness song. Unknown, tr. fr. the Iroquois.—LeO
"The **darkness** was a richness in the room." See From a childhood
Darton, William
Address from the printer to his little readers. at.—VrF
An auctioneer. at.—VrF
The barber. at.—VrF
The bricklayer. at.—VrF
Charcoal burner. at.—VrF
The dust man.—VrF
The flower-pot man.—VrF
A furrier. at.—VrF
The gardener. at.—VrF
The grocer. at.—VrF
The hatter. at.—VrF
Introduction.—VrF
"A sweet chubby fellow."—VrF
The tallow-chandler. at.—VrF
The tambour worker. at.—VrF
The tinman. at.—VrF
Darwin, Erasmus
The loves of the plants, sel.
Stay thy soft murmuring.—ReO
Stay thy soft murmuring. See The loves of the plants

Das, Jibanananda
Cat.—AlPi
Dates (Fruit)
Dates. From Thousand and one nights. Unknown.—HoL
Datta, Jyotirmoy
Follow sleep, fall asleep. tr.—AlPi
A little girl, Rumi's fancy. tr.—AlPi
Monologue of a dying man.—AlPi
Daugherty, James
Trail breakers.—BrA
"**Daughter** of the woman with a low brow, my companion." See On the death of a wife
"**Dave** Garroway's Mr J. Fred Muggs often thumps." See These beasts and the Benin bronze
Davenant, Sir William
Jealousy.—CoBl
"The lark now leaves his wat'ry nest."—GrCt
Storm at sea.—CoR
David, King of Israel (about)
Big Goliath, little David. E. Merriam.—MeC
A boy looking at big David. M. Swenson.—LiT
David's lament. From The second book of Samuel, Bible, Old Testament.—GrCt
King David. W. De La Mare.—LiT
"King David and King Solomon." J. B. Naylor.—SmM
A song to David. C. Smart.—GrCt
"Beauteous, yea beauteous more than these."—PlE (sel.)
David. Earle Birney.—DuS
"**David** and I that summer cut trails on the Survey." See David
David's lament. See The second book of Samuel
Davidson, Gustav
The golden tickseed.—BoH
Davidson, John
In Romney marsh.—PaH
A runnable stag.—CoB—MoS—ReO
Summer.—CoBn
Davieau, Robert Stiles
Arizona village.—BrA
Davies, Sir John
The dancing sea. See Orchestra
I know myself a man. See Nosce teipsum
Much knowledge, little reason. See Nosce teipsum
Nosce teipsum, sels.
I know myself a man.—GrCt
Much knowledge, little reason.—GrCt
Orchestra, sel.
The dancing sea.—GrCt
Davies, John, of Hereford
Buttered pippin-pies.—GrCt
Davies, Mary Carolyn
After all and after all.—ArT-3—ThA
"The day before April."—ThA
I'll wear a shamrock.—ArT-3
Davies, William Henry
The bird-man.—SmM
The captive lion.—CoB
The cat.—BlO
A child's pet.—CoB
The example.—ReO
The fog.—ArT-3—LaC
Frost.—CoBn
Happy wind.—SmM
Jenny Wren.—CoB—ReBs
Leisure.—ArT-3—CoBn—SmM—TuW
Lovely dames.—GrS
The mirror.—ThA
My garden.—CoBn
The rain.—ArT-3—BrSg
Rich days.—CoBn
Sheep.—ClF—ReO
Sport.—CoB
A strange meeting.—BlO
To sparrows fighting.—ReBs
Davis, Fannie Stearns (Fanny Stearns Gifford)
Evening song.—ThA
Moon folly.—ThA
Souls.—ThA
Davis, Frank Marshall
Arthur Ridgewood, M.D.—HaK
Flowers of darkness.—AdIa—BoA
Four glimpses of night.—BoA
Giles Johnson, Ph.D.—HaK
Hands of a brown woman.—BoH
Robert Whitmore.—HaK
Davis, Glenn
The jellyfish.—LeM
Davis, Robert A.
Dust bowl.—AdIa
Dawson, Stephen
A madman.—LeM
Davy and the goblin, sels. Charles Edward Carryl
A nautical ballad.—HuS-3—ThA
The plaint of the camel.—HuS-3
Robinson Crusoe's story.—CoSs—HoB
Robinson Crusoe's island.—ArT-3
"**Davy** Crockett in his woodman dress." See Lament for the Alamo
"**Davy** Davy Dumpling." See Davy Dumpling
Davy Dumpling. Mother Goose.—BrMg
Dawn ("An angel, robed in spotless white") Paul Laurence Dunbar.—BoA
Dawn ("A thrush is tapping a stone") Gordon Bottomley.—ReBs
"**Dawn?** blinks fawn." See Daybreak
"**Dawn** breaking as I woke." See Alba
"**Dawn** breaks." See Awaken
"**Dawn** came slowly." See War
"**Dawn** turned on her purple pillow." See Winter solstice
"A **dawn** wind blows." Susan Morrison.—LeM
Day, Crystal
Wife and husband.—LeM
Day. See also Afternoon; Bed-time; Evening; Morning; Night
"At night may I roam." Unknown.—LeO
"Day." From Pippa passes. R. Browning.—BrP
"A day! Help! Help! Another day." E. Dickinson.—DiPe
Day moon. E. J. Coatsworth.—CoDh
Day of these days. L. Lee.—CoBn

Daylight and moonlight. H. W. Longfellow.—LoPl
"I gazed upon the cloudless moon." E. Brontë.—GrCt
"It's silly for the day to be so long." Issa.—LeOw
"Oh day, if I squander a wavelet of thee." From Pippa passes. R. Browning.—BrP
Song to bring fair weather. Unknown, tr. fr. the Nootka.—LeO
This happy day. H. Behn.—ArT-3
"What a wonderful." Shiki.—BeCs
"What is this." Unknown.—LeO
"The woodpecker." Issa.—LeOw
"**Day.**" See Pippa passes
"The **day** before April." Mary Carolyn Davies.—ThA
"**Day** by day I float my paper boats one by one down the running stream." See Paper boats
"**Day** darken, frogs say." Buson, tr. fr. the Japanese by Harry Behn.—BeCs
Day-dreamer. Unknown, tr. fr. the German by Louis Untermeyer.—ArT-3
"A **day!** Help! Help! Another day." Emily Dickinson.—DiPe
A **day** in autumn. R. S. Thomas.—CoBn
A **day** in June. See The vision of Sir Launfal
"The **day** is cold, and dark, and dreary." See The rainy day
"The **day** is done." See Evening hymn
"The **day** is done." See Returning
The **day** is done. Henry Wadsworth Longfellow.—LoPl
"The **day** is done, and the darkness." See The day is done
"The **day** is warm." See Going barefoot—June
Day-Lewis, C. (Cecil)
Christmas eve.—PlE
The great magicians.—PlE
A parting shot.—CaD
Son and father.—PlE
"The sun came out in April."—CaMb
Third enemy speaks.—PlE
Day moon. Elizabeth Jane Coatsworth.—CoDh
"A **day** of spring." Issa, tr. fr. the Japanese.—LeOw
"A **day** of spring." Onitsura, tr. fr. the Japanese by R. H. Blyth.—LeI
Day of these days. Laurie Lee.—CoBn
"The **day** we die." Unknown, tr. fr. the Bushman.—LeO
"The **day** when Charmus ran with five." See A mighty runner, variation of a Greek theme
"The **day** will bring some lovely thing." Grace Noll Crowell.—ArT-3
"A **day** with sky so wide." See The motion of the earth
Daybreak ("After the dark of night") Walter De La Mare.—DeBg
Daybreak ("Dawn? blinks fawn") David McCord.—McAd
Daybreak ("Daybreak comes first") Carl Sandburg.—LaPd
Daybreak ("A wind came up out of the sea") Henry Wadsworth Longfellow.—LoPl
"**Daybreak** comes first." See Daybreak
Daybreak in Alabama. Langston Hughes.—BrA
The **daybreakers.** Arna Bontemps.—AdIa—BoA
Daylight and moonlight. Henry Wadsworth Longfellow.—LoPl
Days. See Days of the week
Days ("Some days my thoughts are just cocoons —all cold, and dull and blind") Karle Wilson Baker.—ArT-3—ThA
Days ("What are days for") Philip Larkin.—SmM
"The **days** and months do not last long." Pai Ta-shun, tr. by Witter Bynner.—LeMw
"The **days** are clear." Christina Georgina Rossetti.—ArT-3
"The **days** are short." See January
"The **days** grow long, the mountains." See South wind
"The **day's** grown old, the fainting sun." See Evening quatrains
Days in the month. See "Thirty days hath September"
"The **days** of our future stand before us." See Candles
Days of the week
"As Tommy Snooks and Bessie Brooks." Mother Goose.—WiMg
Tommy and Bessy.—BrMg
"Collop Monday." Unknown.—MoB
Days. P. Larkin.—SmM
"How many days has my baby to play." Mother Goose.—ArT-3
Monday. Unknown.—StF
"Monday's child is fair of face." Mother Goose.—HuS-3—WiMg
A week of birthdays.—BrMg
Mother Goose rhymes, 35.—HoB
"The morn's silver Saturday." Unknown.—MoB
Open the door. M. Edey.—ArT-3
"Solomon Grundy." Mother Goose.—BrMg—WiMg
"They that wash on Monday." Mother Goose.—BlO—OpF
Days of the week—Sunday
Beautiful Sunday. J. Falstaff.—CoBn
Mourning poem for the queen of Sunday. R. E. Hayden.—DuS
Ploughing on Sunday. W. Stevens.—BoGj—SmM—WeP
"Q is for the quietness." From All around the town. P. McGinley.—LaC
Sunday ("This is the day when all through the town") E. J. Coatsworth.—BrA—LaC
Sunday ("Up early while everyone sleeps") V. Rutsala.—DuS
Sunday at the end of summer. H. Nemerov.—CoBn
Sunday: New Guinea. K. Shapiro.—BrA
Those winter Sundays. R. E. Hayden.—AdIa—DuS
Days of the week—Monday
"Monday's the fast." Unknown.—MoB

Days of the week—Saturday
Saturday in the county seat. E. L. Jacobs.—BrA
Saturday's child. C. Cullen.—BoH—HaK
"The **days** shorten, the south blows wide for showers now." See Salmon-fishing
The **deacon's** masterpiece; or, The wonderful one-hoss shay. Oliver Wendell Holmes.—HuS-3
Dead and gone. Anthony Thwaite.—CaD
The **dead** at Clonmacnois. Thomas William Rolleston.—PaH
A **dead** bird. See A summer wish
Dead cow farm. Robert Graves.—LiT
The **dead** crab. Andrew Young.—ReO
Dead doe. Jim Harrison.—HoL
"**Dead.** Is it possible? He, the bold rider." See Custer's last charge
A **dead** mole. Andrew Young.—CoB
The **dead** ones. Myra Cohn Livingston.—LiC
Deaf and dumb. Robert Browning.—BrP
Deafness
Deaf and dumb. R. Browning.—BrP
Mutterings over the crib of a deaf child. James Wright.—DuS
The old wife and the ghost. J. Reeves.—BrSm—HoB—LaPd
"Old wife, old wife." Unknown.—MoB
Deane, Anthony C.
The ballad of the Billycock.—CoSs
"**Dear** Ann, wherever you are." See To Ann Scott-Moncrieff
"**Dear** babe, that sleepest cradled by my side." See Frost at midnight
"**Dear** children, they asked in every town." See The kings from the east
"**Dear** critic, who my lightness so deplores." See To a captious critic
Dear dark head. Samuel Ferguson.—CoBl
"**Dear,** dear, what can the matter be." See Oh dear
"**Dear** Father." Margaret Wise Brown.—LaPd
"**Dear** God." See The ladybird
"**Dear** God (give us a flood)." See The prayer of the little ducks
"**Dear** God, give me time." See The prayer of the ox
"**Dear** little baby." Unknown.—WyC
"**Dear** little balloon." See Balloon
"**Dear** mother, dear mother, the church is cold." See The little vagabond
"**Dear** mother, said a little fish." See The little fish that would not do as it was bid
"**Dear** my friend and fellow-student, I would lean my spirit o'er you." See Lady Geraldine's courtship
"**Dear** Smith, the slee'st, pawkie thief." See Epistle to James Smith
"**Dear** Uncle, whisper'd William Brown." See The sensitive figure
Dearmer, Geoffrey
The giraffe.—CoB
The Turkish trench dog.—CoB

Death. See also Death and immortality; Laments; Life—Life and death; Love—Love and death
"Ah, Faustus." From The tragical history of Dr Faustus. C. Marlowe
From Dr Faustus.—GrCt
"All things of earth have an end, and in the midst." Unknown.—LeO
All things will die. A. Tennyson.—TeP
"Ample make this bed." E. Dickinson.—DiPe
"And death shall have no dominion." D. Thomas.—PlE
Annabel Lee. E. A. Poe.—CoR—HuS-3—PoP
Arthur Ridgewood, M.D. F. M. Davis.—HaK
At last. W. De La Mare.—DeBg
"At the round earth's imagin'd corners, blow." J. Donne.—PlE
Blow your trumpets, angels.—GrCt
Athletes. W. Gibson.—MoS
Aunt Helen. T. S. Eliot.—McWs
Aunt Jane Allen. F. Johnson.—AdIa
Azrael. From Tales of a wayside inn. H. W. Longfellow.—LoPl
The babes in the wood. Unknown.—BlO
Beethoven's death mask. S. Spender.—LiT
The bicycle. J. Harasymowicz.—DuS
The bird. W. De La Mare.—DeBg
The bonny earl of Moray. Unknown.—BlO
Booman. Mother Goose.—ReOn
A boy. B. Graves.—LeM
"Break, break, break." A. Tennyson.—BlO—BoGj—TeP
A brown girl dead. C. Cullen.—HaK
"Buffalo Bill's." E. E. Cummings.—LiT
Buffalo Bill's defunct.—BrA
Portrait.—HoW
Burial. M. Van Doren.—CaMb
The city in the sea. E. A. Poe.—GrS—PoP
"Color—caste—denomination." E. Dickinson.—PlE
The convict of Clonmel. Unknown.—MoS
Courage. From Julius Caesar. W. Shakespeare.—ShS
Cromwell dead. From A poem upon the death of Oliver Cromwell. A. Marvell.—GrCt
Cross. L. Hughes.—AdIa—BoA
The cross of snow. H. W. Longfellow.—LoPl
Crossing the bar. A. Tennyson.—TeP
The dark hills. E. A. Robinson.—BoGj—BoH
David. E. Birney.—DuS
"The day we die." Unknown.—LeO
Dead and gone. A. Thwaite.—CaD
A dead bird. From A summer wish. A. Young.—CoB
Dead doe. J. Harrison.—HoL
Death ("Slow creatures, slow") J. Stephens.—StS
Death ("Who set that endless silence") J. Erwin.—LeM
The death and dying words of poor Mailie. R. Burns.—BuPr
Death be not proud. From Holy sonnets. J. Donne.—GrCt
Sonnet.—HoL

Death by water. From The waste land. T. S. Eliot.—CaD
Death of a bird. J. Silkin.—CaD
Death of a dog. B. Deutsch.—DuS
The death of a father. H. S. Horsley.—VrF
The death of a mother. H. S. Horsley.—VrF
The death of a squirrel in McKinley park. G. W. Barrax.—HaK
The death of Admiral Benbow. Unknown.—BlO
Death of an airplane. C. Causley.—CaMb
The death of Cuchulain. W. B. Yeats.—GrCt
Death of Samson. From Samson Agonistes. J. Milton.—GrCt
The death of the flowers. W. C. Bryant.—CoBn
Death on a live wire. M. Baldwin.—CaMb
Death song of a song maker. Unknown.—LeO
Derelict. Y. E. Allison.—CoSs
Dido my dear, alas, is dead. From Shepheardes calendar. E. Spenser.—GrCt
Didymus. L. MacNeice.—PlE
Donne redone. J. P. Tierney.—BrSm
Doubts. R. Brooke.—GrS
The dree night. Unknown.—GrCt
Dust. S. K. Russell.—BrSm—DuR
The dying crane. M. Drayton.—ReO
The dying swan. Unknown.—GrCt
"Each that we lose takes part of us." E. Dickinson.—DiPe
Ecstasy. R. A. Taylor.—GrS
Epilogue. From Asolando. R. Browning.—BrP
Erin (Elephant). Unknown.—ReO
Fable. Merrill Moore.—DuS
False gods. W. De La Mare.—PlE
Farewell to the warriors. Unknown.—LeO
"Fear no more the heat o' the sun." From Cymbeline. W. Shakespeare.—GrCt
Fear no more.—BoH—CoR
Felix Randal. G. M. Hopkins.—CoR
Fidelity. W. Wordsworth.—ClF
"Finite to fail, but infinite to venture." E. Dickinson.—DiPe
Flannan isle. W. W. Gibson.—BlO—CoSs
For a dead kitten. S. H. Hay.—DuR
For E. McG. E. Pound.—MoS
Freddy the rat perishes. From Archy and Mehitabel. D. Marquis.—LaC
Futility. W. Owen.—HoL
General Monk. Mother Goose.—BrMg
Giles Johnson, Ph.D. F. M. Davis.—HaK
"The glories of our blood and state." J. Shirley.—GrCt
"Go and tell Aunt Nancy." Unknown.—BlO
Go down death. J. W. Johnson.—BoA
God's-acre. H. W. Longfellow.—LoPl
Golden gates. Unknown.—BrSm
Golgotha is a mountain. A. Bontemps.—BoA
Grieve not for me. Unknown.—BrSm
"He found my being, set it up." E. Dickinson.—DiPe
Henry King, who chewed bits of string, and was early cut off in dreadful agonies. H. Belloc.—BrSm—CoBb
"Hey nonny no." Unknown.—GrCt
"How many times these low feet staggered." E. Dickinson.—DiPe
"I am a wanderer, I shall die stretched out." Unknown.—LeO
"I believe one day when." M. Classé.—BaH
I bless this man. From Nemea II. Pindar.—MoS
"I died for beauty, but was scarce." E. Dickinson.—DiPe
"I have a rendezvous with death." A. Seeger.—HiL
"I heard a fly buzz when I died." E. Dickinson.—DiPe
"I saw no doctor, but, feeling queer inside." From The Greek anthology. Unknown.—BrSm
If we must die. C. McKay.—AdIa—BoA—HaK
In memory of Jane Fraser. G. Hill.—CaD
In the churchyard at Cambridge. H. W. Longfellow.—LoPl
Incident of the French camp. R. Browning.—BrP—CoR
An Irish airman foresees his death. W. B. Yeats.—BoGj—HoL—YeR
An Irish legend. P. McGinley.—McWc
"Is God dead." M. Radcliffe.—LaC
"It isn't the cough." Unknown.—BrSm
"It was not death, for I stood up." E. Dickinson.—DiPe
Italian extravaganza. G. Corso.—LaC
January. R. S. Thomas.—CoB
Joshua Hight. Unknown.—BrSm
Keep away. E. J. Coatsworth.—CoDh
A king is dead. From King Henry VI. W. Shakespeare.—GrCt
The knifesmith. D. Howard.—SmM
Last song of Sitting Bull. Unknown.—LeO
The legend of Rabbi Ben Levi. From Tales of a wayside inn. H. W. Longfellow.—LoPl
Life after death. Pindar.—PlE
Little elegy. X. J. Kennedy.—BoGj
The little peach. E. Field.—AgH—BrSm
Little Willie. Unknown.—BrSm—McWs
Willie's epitaph.—SmM
The long black grave. E. J. Coatsworth.—CoDh
Long sleep. D. Short.—LeM
Lord, have mercy on us. T. Nashe.—GrCt
Lord Waterford. Unknown.—GrCt
Lowery cot. L. A. G. Strong.—CaD
Lucy Gray; or, Solitude. W. Wordsworth.—WoP
Madrigal macabre. S. Hoffenstein.—BrSm
Malfunction. R. E. Albert.—DuS
A man is buried where the cold winds blow. D. G. Matumeak.—BaH
Mentors. G. Brooks.—HaK
The midnight skaters. E. Blunden.—BoGj
Monologue of a dying man. J. Datta.—AlPi
The moon's funeral. H. Belloc.—ThA
Morte d'Arthur. From Idylls of the king. A. Tennyson.—CoD—TeP
Murder. P. Milosevic.—LeM
My city. J. W. Johnson.—BoH
My grasshopper. M. C. Livingston.—BrSg

"We only came to sleep." Unknown.—LeO
The wee croodin doo. Unknown.—MoB
We'll go to sea no more. Unknown.—CoSs—GrCt
The fishermen's song.—MoB (sel.)
"What inn is this." E. Dickinson.—DiPe
"What will you do, God, when I die." R. M. Rilke.—PlE
When de saints go ma'chin' home. S. A. Brown.—BoA
When I am dead. O. Dodson.—HaK
"When I was small, a woman died." E. Dickinson.—DiPe
When in the darkness. A. Tennyson.—TeP
"When you have gone." Unknown.—LeO
"Where is Paris and Heleyne." Thomas of Hales.—GrCt
"Whether my bark went down at sea." E. Dickinson.—DiPe
White rose. S. Sitwell.—GrS
"Who killed Cock Robin." Mother Goose.—OpF
The death and burial of Cock Robin.—BrMg—VrF
Willie. M. Adeler.—CoBb
Without benefit of declaration. L. Hughes.—BoA
Women of Syracuse. E. J. Coatsworth.—CoDh
Yardbird's skull. O. Dodson.—AdIa—BoA
The yew-tree. V. Watkins.—PlE
Young Sammy Watkins. Unknown.—CoBb
Death and immortality. See also Immortality
"Afraid? Of whom am I afraid." E. Dickinson.—DiPe
"Because I could not stop for death." E. Dickinson.—DiL—DiPe
Even such is time. W. Raleigh.—GrCt
"Exultation is the going." E. Dickinson.—DiPe
The hatch. N. Farber.—HoL
He is like the lotus. From Book of the dead. Unknown.—PlE
"I came from under the earth." Unknown.—LeO
"I never lost as much but twice." E. Dickinson.—DiL—DiPe
"If I die tomorrow." G. Mahapatra.—AlPi
In memoriam, sels. A. Tennyson
Calm is the morn.—GrCt—TeP
"Dip down upon the northern shore."—TeP
A happy lover.—TeP
"I envy not in any moods."—TeP
"I sometimes hold it half a sin."—TeP
"I trust I have not wasted breath."—TeP
I wage not any feud.—TeP
My Lord and King.—GrCt—TeP
Now fades the east.—TeP
"Oh yet we trust that somehow good."—PlE
Oh yet we trust.—TeP
Ring out, wild bells.—ArT-3—LaPh—TeP
Strong Son of God.—PlE
Prologue.—TeP
There rolls the deep.—TeP
What hope is here.—TeP
When my light is low.—TeP
"My flowers shall not perish." Unknown.—LeO
"My life closed twice before its close." E. Dickinson.—DiPe
Nothing will die. A. Tennyson.—TeP
"Our journey had advanced." E. Dickinson.—DiL—DiPe
"Safe in their alabaster chambers." E. Dickinson.—DiL—DiPe
"That such have died enables us." E. Dickinson.—DiPe
"There came a day at summer's full." E. Dickinson.—DiPe
"This world is not conclusion." E. Dickinson.—DiPe
" 'Twas just this time last year I died." E. Dickinson.—DiPe
Vastness. A. Tennyson.—TeP
"We only came to sleep." Unknown.—LeO
What are years. Marianne Moore.—PlE
The white island. R. Herrick.—GrCt
"Who abdicated ambush." E. Dickinson.—DiPe
Death ("Slow creatures, slow") James Stephens.—StS
Death ("Who set that endless silence") John Erwin.—LeM
The **death** and burial of Cock Robin. See "Who killed Cock Robin"
The **death** and dying words of poor Mailie. Robert Burns.—BuPr
"**Death** at the headlands, Hesiod, long ago." See Hesiod, 1908
Death be not proud. See Holy sonnets
"**Death** be not proud, though some have callèd thee." See Holy sonnets—Death be not proud
Death by water. See The waste land
Death of a bird. John Silkin.—CaD
Death of a dog. Babette Deutsch.—DuS
The **death** of a father. Henry Sharpe Horsley.—VrF
The **death** of a mother. Henry Sharpe Horsley.—VrF
The **death** of a squirrel in McKinley park. Gerald William Barrax.—HaK
The **death** of Admiral Benbow. Unknown.—BlO
Death of an aircraft. Charles Causley.—CaMb
The **death** of Cuchulain. William Butler Yeats.—GrCt
The **death** of Jefferson. Hezekiah Butterworth.—HiL
Death of Samson. See Samson Agonistes
Death of the cat. Ian Serraillier.—CoB
The **death** of the flowers. William Cullen Bryant.—CoBn
Death on a live wire. Michael Baldwin.—CaMb
Death song of a song maker. Unknown, tr. fr. the Yokut.—LeO

De Banville, Theodore
The goddess.—GrS
Debee, Rajlukshmee
The house.—AlPi
The **debt.** Paul Laurence Dunbar.—BoA—BoH—HaK
A **decade.** Amy Lowell.—CoBl
Deceit
Appearances. From The taming of the shrew. W. Shakespeare.—ShS
"Love to faults is always blind." W. Blake.—BlP
Outward show. From The merchant of Venice. W. Shakespeare.—ShS
Sigh no more. From Much ado about nothing. W. Shakespeare.—CoBl
The wily alchemist. From The Canterbury tales. G. Chaucer.—ChT
December
December ("Frost is the quietest thing that grows") T. W. Ramsey.—SmM
December ("Furry grandfather sleeps") N. Belting.—BeCm
December ("I like days") A. Fisher.—LaPh
December ("A little boy stood on the corner") S. Vanderbilt.—LaC
December ("The rice-cutting moons have gone") N. Belting.—BeCm
"When cold December." E. Sitwell.—McWs
December ("Frost is the quietest thing that grows") T. W. Ramsey.—SmM
December ("Furry grandfather sleeps") Natalia Belting.—BeCm
December ("I like days") Aileen Fisher.—LaPh
December ("A little boy stood on the corner") Sanderson Vanderbilt.—LaC
December ("The rice-cutting moons have gone") Natalia Belting.—BeCm
December bird. Aileen Fisher.—LaPh
The **deceptive** present, the phoenix year. Delmore Schwartz.—CoBn
"**Deck** us all with Boston Charlie." See Boston Charlie
Decline and fall of a Roman umpire. Ogden Nash.—MoS
De Coccola, Raymond and King, Paul
Manerathiak's song. trs.—DoW
The wind has wings. trs.—DoW
Decoration day. See Memorial day
"A **decrepit** old gas man named Peter." Unknown.—BrLl
Dedicated to her highness. Elizabeth Jane Coatsworth.—CoDh
Dedication of the illustrations to Blair's grave. William Blake.—BlP—GrCt
"**Deedle** deedle dumpling, my son John." Mother Goose.—OpF
The pasty.—BrMg
Deep and dark blue ocean. See Childe Harold's pilgrimage—The ocean
"**Deep** asleep, deep asleep." See The ballad of Semmerwater
"**Deep** in Alabama earth." See Alabama earth
"**Deep** in my soul there roared the crashing thunder." See Calm after storm
"**Deep** in the Georgia night when all." See Georgia towns
"**Deep** in the marsh and dappled woods." See Watching bird
"**Deep** in the stable tied with rope." See Country idyll
Deer
Blacktail deer. L. Sarett.—CoB
"The clear note." Issa.—IsF
The cripple. R. P. T. Coffin.—HuS-3
Dead doe. J. Harrison.—HoL
"The deer." Issa.—IsF
Deer. H. Behn.—CoB—LiT
Deer at dusk. E. J. Coatsworth.—CoSb
Deer hunt. J. Jerome.—DuR
"The deer which (or that) lives." Onakatomi Yoshinobu.—BaS—LeMw
Earthy anecdote. W. Stevens.—BoGj
"The fallow deer." C. Aiken.—AiC
The fallow deer at the lonely house. T. Hardy—BlO
The fawn. E. St V. Millay.—CoB
The fawn in the snow. W. R. Benét.—ReO
Green afternoon. F. M. Frost.—ArT-3
A hunted deer. Unknown.—DePp
Hunting song. Unknown.—LeO
I have a fawn. T. Moore.—ClF
"In summer the rains come and the grass grows up." Unknown.—LeO
Landscape, deer season. B. Howes.—BoGj
"Leaping the torrent." Issa.—IsF
Like arrows. E. J. Coatsworth.—CoSb
Moose hunting. T. Willis.—BaH
The nymph complaining for the death of her fawn. A. Marvell.—ReO (sel.)
"On the porch." Issa.—IsF
A runnable stag. J. Davidson.—CoB—MoS—ReO
The three deer. E. J. Coatsworth.—CoDh
Traveling through the dark. W. Stafford.—DuS
The white stag. E. Pound.—HaL
"The **deer.**" Issa, tr. fr. the Japanese by Nobuyuki Yuasa.—IsF
Deer. Harry Behn.—CoB—LiT
Deer at dusk. Elizabeth Jane Coatsworth.—CoSb
Deer hunt. Judson Jerome.—DuR
Deer mouse. Aileen Fisher.—FiC
"The **deer** which (or that) lives." Onakatomi Yoshinobu, tr. fr. the Japanese by Arthur Waley.—BaS—LeMw
DeForest, Charlotte B.
An April child. ad.—DePp
The barefoot bat. ad.—DePp
A cat called Little Bell. ad.—DePp
Catching dragonflies. ad.—DePp
Chrysanthemum colors. ad.—DePp
A dream party. ad.—DePp
Falling snow. ad.—DePp
Firefly party. ad.—DePp
The fisherman. ad.—DePp
A flower lullaby. ad.—DePp

Flower song. ad.—DePp
The frogs' call. ad.—DePp
Getting-up time. ad.—DePp
A ghost story. ad.—DePp
Gifts for a good boy. ad.—DePp
Good and bad. ad.—DePp
A hunted deer. ad.—DePp
In the spring. ad.—DePp
Light for a bride. ad.—DePp
"Little Miss Moon." ad.—DePp
The lonely boy. ad.—DePp
Long-posed elf. ad.—DePp
A lost snowflake. ad.—DePp
The millstream. ad.—DePp
Morning-glories. ad.—DePp
Mountains on mountains. ad.—DePp
The penniless hawk. ad.—DePp
Pigeon playmates. ad.—DePp
The prancing pony. ad.—DePp
A question. ad.—DePp
Rain riddle. ad.—DePp
A round trip. ad.—DePp
Seven gifts. ad.—DePp
Sleepy sparrows. ad.—DePp
Snowman. ad.—DePp
The song of the frog. ad.—DePp
Sparrows or butterflies. ad.—DePp
The spinners. ad.—DePp
The tea roaster. ad.—DePp
Thorn song. ad.—DePp
Three seagulls. ad.—DePp
To see a nightingale. ad.—DePp
Town and country. ad.—DePp
Twins. ad.—DePp
Two birds flying. ad.—DePp
Two puppies. ad.—DePp
A warning to crows. ad.—DePp
Weeping cherry trees. ad.—DePp
Where do rivers go. ad.—DePp
Why rabbits jump. ad.—DePp
Wild geese flying. ad.—DePp
Wind message. ad.—DePp
A winter's dream. ad.—DePp

De Gasztold, Carmen Bernos. See Gasztold, Carmen Bernos de

De gustibus. Robert Browning.—BrP

Dehn, Paul
Circus hand.—SmM
"Hey diddle diddle (the physicists)." See Rhymes for a modern nursery
How to paint the portrait of a bird. tr.—SmM
"In a cavern, in a canyon." See Rhymes for a modern nursery
"Little Miss Muffet (crouched)." See Rhymes for a modern nursery
Rhymes for a modern nursery, sels.
"Hey diddle diddle (the physicists)."—DuR
"In a cavern, in a canyon."—BrSm
"Little Miss Muffet (crouched)."—BrSm—DuR
Tailor's song.—SmM
Telegraph poles.—SmM

"The **deil** cam fiddlin thro' the town." See The deil's awa wi' th' exciseman
The **deil's** awa wi' th' exciseman. Robert Burns.—BuPr
Deirdre. James Stephens.—StS
Dekker, Thomas
A cradle song. See Pleasant comedy of patient Grissell
Golden slumbers. See Pleasant comedy of patient Grissell—A cradle song
Pleasant comedy of patient Grissell, sel.
A cradle song.—BlO
Golden slumbers.—SmM
Troynovant.—GrCt
De La Mare, Walter (Walter Ramal; Walter Rand, pseuds.)
A-apple pie.—DeBg
Alas, alack.—ArT-3
"All but blind."—LaPd
All that's past.—BoGj
All the way.—DeBg
Alone.—GrCt
As Lucy went a-walking.—SmM
At last.—DeBg
At the keyhole.—BlO
The bandog.—ArT-3
The barber's.—BoGj
The bead mat.—DeBg
The bees' song.—McWs
Berries.—HoB
The bird.—DeBg
Blackbirds.—DeBg
Blindman's in.—DeBg
Bones.—BrSm—DuL
Bonum omen.—DeBg
The border bird.—DeBg
Bread and cherries.—BrSg
Bunches of grapes.—ArT-3—BoGj
Caw.—DeBg
Chicken.—ArT-3
A child's day, sels.
"Softly, drowsily"
A child's day, Part II.—ArT-3
A child's day begins.—HuS-3
"This little morsel of morsels here."—AgH
A child's day begins. See A child's day—"Softly, drowsily"
A child's day, Part II. See A child's day—"Softly, drowsily"
Coals.—DeBg
Come—gone.—DeBg
The corner.—DeBg
The cupboard.—ArT-3—StF
Daybreak.—DeBg
Done for.—BlO—DeBg
Double Dutch.—ClF
A double limerick or twiner ("There was an old man with a gun")—BrLl
A double limerick or twiner ("There was an old person of Dover")—BrLl
The eel.—BrSm
Dreamland.—DeBg
Echo ("Seven sweet notes")—DeBg

The wind.—DeBg
Winter.—GrCt
Won't.—DeBg
Delany, Clarissa Scott
Solace.—BoA
Delaware Indians. See Indians of the Americas —Delaware
DeL. Bonnette, Jeanne
Vacant house.—DuS
"The **delicate** corner shot." See Civilities
"A **delicate** fabric of bird song." See May day
"**Delighter** of men's hearts is the wind." See Rig Veda—To the wind
Deluge. John Clare.—CoBn
De Madariaga, S.
Spanish folk song. tr.—ClF
Demille, A. B.
The ice king.—DoW
De Mille, James
The gallant highwayman.—DoW
"Sweet maiden of Passamaquoddy."—DoW
Dempsey, Jack (about)
The nonpareil's grave. M. J. McMahon.—MoS
Denby, Edwin
A girl.—CoBl
De Nerval, Gerard
Fantasy.—GrS
Denise. Robert Beverly Hale.—CoB
Denney, Revel
Fixer of midnight.—DuS
Tennis in San Juan.—MoS
The **dentist.** Rose Fyleman.—ArT-3
Dentists
The dentist. R. Fyleman.—ArT-3
Denver, Colorado
House in Denver. T. H. Ferril.—BrA
Denwood, Jonathan
Bleeberrying.—CaMb
De Onis, Harriet
Silly song. tr.—LiT
Departmental; or, The end of my ant Jerry. Robert Frost.—DuS—McWs
Depot in a river town. Miller Williams.—DuS
"**Deprived** of other banquet." Emily Dickinson. —DiPe
The **Derby** ram. Mother Goose.—BrMg
De Regnier, Beatrice Schenk
"I looked in the mirror."—LaPd
"Keep a poem in your pocket."—LaPd
Derelict. Young Ewing Allison.—CoSs
A **description** of famine. Unknown, tr. fr. the Tamil by A. L. Basham.—AlPi
Desert ("Anybody") Langston Hughes.—HaK
The **desert** ("Sand drums of the desert") Ronald King.—BaH
The **deserted** house ("I am afraid") Julie Fairbun.—LeM
The **deserted** house ("Life and thought have gone away") Alfred Tennyson.—TeP
Deserts
Afar in the desert. T. Pringle.—ReO (sel.)
Desert ("Anybody") L. Hughes.—HaK
The desert ("Sand drums of the desert") R. King.—BaH
"I went down into the desert." V. Lindsay.—LiP
"In the desert sand." N. Leonard.—BaH
Sand of the desert in an hour-glass. H. W. Longfellow.—LoPl
Deshpandi, A. R. See Anil
Design. Robert Frost.—HoL
"**Desolate** and lone." See Lost
The **despairing** lover. William Walsh.—CoBl
The **destruction** of Jerusalem by the Babylonian hordes. Isaac Rosenberg.—GrS
The **destruction** of Sennacherib. George Gordon Byron.—ByP
"**Detestable** race, continue to expunge yourself, die out." See Apostrophe to man
Detroit, Michigan
Detroit. D. Hall.—BrA
Detroit. Donald Hall.—BrA
Deutsch, Babette
Ape. See Creatures in the zoo
Baby camel. tr.—CoB
Ballet school.—HoL
Creatures in the zoo, sel.
Ape.—DuS
Death of a dog.—DuS
Eagles. tr.—CoB
Fireworks.—DuR
Little catkins. tr.—PlE
Morning workout.—MoS
The prophet. tr.—PlE
Put out my eyes. tr.—HoL
Rooster. tr.—CoB
We are all workmen. tr.—PlE
"What will you do, God, when I die." tr.—PlE
—and Yarmolinsky, Avrahm
Grapes. trs.—HoL
A **deux.** William Wood.—CoBl
Development. Robert Browning.—BrP
Devil
Address to the deil. R. Burns.—BuPr
After reading certain books. M. Coleridge.—PlE
Birkett's eagle. D. S. Howard.—CaMb
Chiliasm. R. Eberhart.—PlE
The deil's awa wi' th' exciseman. R. Burns.—BuPr
The devil. Mother Goose.—BrMg
The devil's bag. J. Stephens.—LiT
Lucifer in the train. A. C. Rich.—PlE
Morning star. E. Farjeon.—FaT
Satan journeys to the Garden of Eden. From Paradise lost. J. Milton.—GrCt
Tam o'Shanter. R. Burns.—BuPr
"What though the field be lost." From Paradise lost. J. Milton.—PlE
The **devil.** Mother Goose.—BrMg
The **devil's** bag. James Stephens.—LiT
"**Devouring** time, blunt thou the lion's paw." See Sonnets. William Shakespeare
Dew
The broad water. Mother Goose.—ReOn
The dew. A. Epstein.—LeM
Dew on a spider web. M. Stone.—LeM
The dewdrop. E. Farjeon.—FaA

"Hush-a-ba, babby, lie still, lie still." Unknown.—MoB
"Hush-a-ba, birdie, croon, croon." Mother Goose.—MoB
Hush-a-ba, birdie.—ReS
Scottish lullaby.—BrMg
"Hush you, hush you." Unknown.—MoB
"I had a little manikin, I set him on my thumbikin." Unknown.—MoB
"I had a wee cock and I loved it well." Unknown.—MoB
"I have a wee bit Highlandman." Unknown. —MoB
"I heard a cow low, a bonnie cow low." Unknown.—MoB
"I wouldna have a baker, ava, va, va." Unknown.—MoB
"I'll gie you a pennyworth o' preens." Unknown.—MoB
"I'll give you a pin to stick in your thumb." Unknown.—MoB
The innumerable Christ. H. MacDiarmid.—PlE
"I've found something." Unknown.—MoB
Jackie Faa. Unknown.—GrCt
"Jean, Jean, Jean." Unknown.—MoB
"Jock plays them rants so lively." Unknown. —MoB
"Katie Beardie had a cow." Unknown.—MoB
Kissin'. Unknown.—CoBl
The laily worm and the machrel of the sea. Unknown.—GrCt—ReO
Lament for the Makaris. W. Dunbar.—GrCt
"Lingle, lingle, land tang." Unknown.—MoB
Lord Randal. Unknown.—ClF
"Madam Pussie's coming hame." Unknown.—MoB
The massacre of the Macpherson. W. E. Aytoun.—GrCt
"Me and my grannie." Unknown.—MoB
"The midges dance aboon the burn." R. Tannahill.—CoBn
The miller. J. Clerk.—GrCt
Molecatcher. A. D. Mackie.—CoB
"Monday's the fast." Unknown.—MoB
"The morn's silver Saturday." Unknown.—MoB
"Mousie, mousie, come to me." Unknown.—MoB
"My mother said that I must go." Unknown. —MoB
"My wheelie goes round." Unknown.—MoB
"O can you sew cushions." Unknown.—MoB
"O Sandy is a Highland lad." Unknown.—MoB
"O such a hurry-burry." Unknown.—MoB
"O what's the rhyme to porringer." Unknown. —MoB
"O, when I was a wee thing." Unknown.—MoB
"O, where are you going?" Unknown.—MoB
"Old wife, old wife." Unknown.—MoB
"On the first of March." Mother Goose.—MoB —OpF
The crows.—BrMg
"Paddy on the railway." Unknown.—MoB
Parley of beasts. H. MacDiarmid.—ReO
"Pussy, pussy baudrons." Unknown.—MoB
"The Quaker's wife sat down to bake." Unknown.—MoB
"Queen Mary, Queen Mary, my age is sixteen." Unknown.—MoB
Queen Mary's men. Unknown.—MoB
"Rain, rain, rattle stanes." Unknown.—MoB
The raven and the crow. Unknown.—MoB
"Rise up, goodwife, and shake your feathers." Unknown.—MoB
"The robin came to the wren's nest." Unknown.—MoB
Robin Redbreast's testament. Unknown.—MoB
"Robin, Robin Redbreast (cutty, cutty wran)." Unknown.—MoB
"Roon, roon, rosie." Unknown.—MoB
"Round about the porridge pot." Unknown.—MoB
"Sandy, quo he, lend me your mill." Unknown.—MoB
"The silly bit chicken." Unknown.—MoB
Singing game ("And it's baking, Bessy Bell") Unknown.—MoB
Singing game ("Cam you by the salmon fishers") Unknown.—MoB
Singing game ("Johnnie Johnson's ta'en a notion") Unknown.—MoB
Singing game ("Roses up and roses down") Unknown.—MoB
Skylark. Unknown.—MoB
Snow. Unknown.—MoB
Struthill well. Unknown.—MoB
"Tam o the linn came up the gate." Unknown.—MoB
"Tammy, Tammy Titmouse." Unknown.—MoB
"There dwelt a puddy in a well." Unknown.—MoB
"There was a wee bit mousikie (or moosikie)." Unknown.—BlO—MoB—OpF
"There was a wee wifie rowed (or row't) up in a blanket." Mother Goose.—MoB—OpF
"This is the way the ladies ride (jimp and small)." Unknown.—MoB
Thomas Rymer and the queen of Elfland. Unknown.—GrCt
Thumb and finger game. Unknown.—MoB
Tickling game ("Adam and Eve gaed up my sleeve") Unknown.—MoB
Tickling game ("There was a man") Unknown.—MoB
Tickling game ("There was a wee mouse") Unknown.—MoB
Times o' year. W. Barnes.—CoBn
To the city of London. W. Dunbar.—GrCt
"Trot, trot, horsie." Unknown.—MoB
The two rivers. Unknown.—GrCt
Tweed and Till.—CoBn
"Wash well the fresh fish, wash well the fresh fish." Unknown.—MoB
"Weaverie, weaverie wabster." Unknown.—MoB
"A wee bird sat upon a tree." Unknown.—MoB
"Wee chookie birdie." Unknown.—MoB

Dialect—Scottish—*Continued*
The wee croodin doo. Unknown.—MoB
The wee, wee man. Unknown.—MoB
We'll go to sea no more. Unknown.—CoSs—GrCt
The fishermen's song.—MoB (sel.)
"West wind to the bairn." Unknown.—MoB
"When I was a wee thing." Unknown.—MoB
"When I was one, I was in my skin." Unknown.—MoB
"Who learned you to dance." Unknown.—MoB
"Who saw the Forty-second." Unknown.—MoB
The wife of Usher's well. Unknown.—ArT-3—GrCt
"A wife was sitting at her reel ae night." Unknown.—BlO
The strange visitor.—GrCt—MoB
"Will you buy syboes." Unknown.—MoB
"Willie, Willie Waddy." Unknown.—MoB
The woodlands. W. Barnes.—CoBn
Wren and dove. Unknown.—MoB
"Yokie pokie." Unknown.—MoB
"Your plack and my plack." Unknown.—MoB
Zummer stream. W. Barnes.—CoBn
Dialect quatrain. Marcus B. Christian.—BoA
Dialogue ("In the monotonous heat") Elizabeth Jane Coatsworth.—CoDh
Dialogue ("Rosalind is your love's name") See As you like it
Diamond cut diamond. Ewart Milne.—ArT-3—CoB
Diana
Hymn to Diana. From Cynthia's revels. B. Jonson.—GrCt
"**Diana** Fitzpatrick Mauleverer James." A. A. Milne.—ArT-3
Dibdin, Charles
A child that has a cold.—GrCt
The sailor's consolation.—CoSs—HuS-3
Tom Bowling.—CoSs
"**Dick.**" See Dick's trick
Dickens, Charles
The ivy green. See The Pickwick papers
The Pickwick papers, sel.
The ivy green.—CoBn
"**Dickery**, dickery, dare." Mother Goose.—OpF—WiMg
The flying pig.—BrMg
Dickey, James
The aura.—DuS
In the marble quarry.—BrA
The scarred girl.—DuS
Dickey, William
Memoranda.—DuS
"**Dickie** found a broken spade." See The worm
Dickinson, Emily
"Adventure most unto itself."—DiPe
"Afraid? Of whom am I afraid."—DiPe
"Alter? When the hills do."—DiPe
"An altered look about the hills."—DiL—DiPe
"Ample make this bed."—DiPe
"As imperceptibly as grief."—DiPe
"Ashes denote that fire was."—DiPe
"At half-past three a single bird."—DiPe
"At least to pray is left, is left."—DiPe
Autumn. See "The morns are meeker than they were"
"The bat is dun with wrinkled wings."—DiPe
"Because I could not stop for death."—DiL—DiPe
Beclouded. See "The sky is low, the clouds are mean"
"Before I got my eye put out."—DiPe
"The beggar at the door for fame."—DiPe
"Belshazzar had a letter."—DiPe
A bird. See "A bird came down the walk"
"A bird came down the walk."—ArT-3—BoGj—CoB—DiL—DiPe—LaP—LaPd—TuW
A bird.—BrSg—HuS-3
"Blazing in gold and quenching in purple."—DiL—DiPe
"The brain is wider than the sky."—DiL—DiPe
"The brain within its groove."—DiPe
The brook of the heart. See "Have you got a brook in your little heart"
"Color—caste—denomination."—PlE
"Consulting summer's clock."—DiPe
"Could any mortal lip divine."—DiPe
"The dandelion's pallid tube."—DiPe
"A day! Help! Help! Another day."—DiPe
"Deprived of other banquet."—DiPe
"Did we abolish frost."—DiPe
Divinest sense. See "Much madness is divinest sense"
"Drab habitation of whom."—DiPe
"A drop fell on the apple tree"
Summer shower.—CoBn
"A drunkard cannot meet a cork."—DiPe
The duel. See "I took my power in my hand"
"Each that we lose takes part of us."—DiPe
"Elysium is as far as to."—DiPe
"Essential oils are wrung."—DiPe
"Estranged from beauty none can be."—DiPe
"An everywhere of silver."—DiPe
"Experiment to me."—DiPe
"Exultation is the going."—DiPe
"A face devoid of love or grace."—DiPe
"Faith is a fine invention."—DiPe
"Falsehood of thee could I suppose."—DiPe
"Fame is a bee."—DiPe
"Fame is the tint that scholars leave."—DiPe
"Farther in summer than the birds."—DiPe
"A feather from the whippowil"
Pine bough.—DiL
"Finite to fail, but infinite to venture."—DiPe
"Forbidden fruit a flavor has."—DiPe
"From all the jails the boys and girls."—DiPe
"Garlands for queens may be."—DiPe
"God gave a loaf to every bird."—DiPe
"The grass so little has to do."—DiPe
"Had I not seen the sun."—DiPe
"Have you got a brook in your little heart"
The brook of the heart.—CoBl
"He ate and drank the precious words."—DiPe
"He found my being, set it up."—DiPe
"He put the belt around my life."—DiPe
"Her losses make our gains ashamed."—DiPe
"His bill an auger is."—DiPe

"Hope is a subtle glutton."—DiPe
"Hope is the thing with feathers."—ArT-3—DiL
"How fits his umber coat."—DiPe
"How happy is the little stone."—DiPe
"How many times these low feet staggered."—DiPe
"How much the present moment means."—DiPe
"How soft a caterpillar steps."—DiL
"How still the bells in steeples stand."—DiL—DiPe
How the sun rose. See "I'll tell you how the sun rose"
Humming bird. See "A route of evanescence"
"I asked no other thing."—DiPe
"I bet with every wind that blew."—DiPe
"I can wade grief."—DiPe
"I could not prove the years had feet."—DiPe
"I died for beauty, but was scarce."—DiPe
"I dwell in possibility."—DiPe
"I envy seas whereon he rides."—DiPe
"I felt a cleavage (or cleaving) in my mind."—DiL—DiPe
"I found the phrase to every thought."—DiPe
"I gave myself to him."—DiPe
"I had been hungry all the years."—DiPe
"I had no time to hate, because."—DiPe
"I have no life but this."—DiPe
"I heard a fly buzz when I died."—DiPe
"I held a jewel in my fingers."—DiL—DiPe
"I know some lonely houses off the road."—DiL
"I like to see it lap the miles."—DiL—DiPe—LaPd
"I never hear the word escape."—DiL—DiPe
"I never lost as much but twice."—DiL—DiPe
"I never saw a moor."—ArT-3—DiL—DiPe—ThA
"I started early, took my dog."—DiL—DiPe
"I stepped from plank to plank."—DiPe
"I taste a liquor never brewed."—DiL—DiPe
"I think that the root of the wind is water."—DiPe
"I thought that nature was enough."—DiPe
"I took my power in my hand."—DiPe
  The duel.—LiT
I was a phoebe.—ReBs
"I years had been from home."—DiPe
"If I can stop one heart from breaking"
  Not in vain.—BoH
"If you were coming in the fall."—DiPe
"I'll tell you how the sun rose."—DiL—DiPe—LaPd
  How the sun rose.—HuS-3
"I'm ceded, I've stopped being theirs."—DiPe
"I'm nobody. Who are you."—ArT-3—DiL—DiPe—LaPd
"Immured the whole of life."—DiPe
"In lands I never saw, they say."—DiPe
"In snow thou comest."—DiPe
"In this short life."—DiPe
"The infinite a sudden guest."—DiPe
"It dropped so low in my regard."—DiPe
"It is a lonesome glee."—DiPe
"It makes no difference abroad."—DiPe
"It sifts from leaden sieves."—DiPe
"It troubled me as once I was."—DiPe
"It was not death, for I stood up."—DiPe
"It's all I have to bring to-day."—DiPe
"It's such a little thing to weep."—DiPe
"I've nothing else to bring, you know"
  With flowers.—SmM
"A lady red upon the hill"
  The waking year.—CoBn
"The life that tied too tight escapes."—DiPe
"The life we have is very great."—DiPe
"A light exists in spring."—DiPe
"Like mighty footlights burned the red."—DiPe
"Like rain it sounded till it curved."—DiPe
"The lilac is an ancient shrub."—DiPe
"A little madness in the spring."—DiPe
"Love is anterior to life."—DiPe
"Love is done when love's begun."—DiPe
"Mine enemy is growing old."—DiPe
The moon. See "The moon was but a chin of gold"
"The moon is distant from the sea."—DiPe
"The moon was but a chin of gold"
  The moon.—HoB
Morning. See "Will there really be a morning"
"The morns are meeker than they were."—ArT-3—DiL—DiPe
  Autumn.—BoH—CoBn—TuW
"Most she touched me by her muteness."—ReBs
"Much madness is divinest sense."—DiPe
  Divinest sense.—HoL
"The mushroom is the elf of plants."—DiPe
"Musicians wrestle everywhere."—DiPe
"My country need not change her gown."—BrA—DiPe
"My life closed twice before its close."—DiPe
"My life had stood a loaded gun."—DiPe
"My period had come for prayer."—PlE
"A narrow fellow in the grass."—BoGj—CoB—DiL—DiPe—LiT—ReO
  The snake.—WeP
"The nearest dream recedes, unrealized."—DiPe
"No matter where the saints abide."—DiPe
"No passenger was known to flee."—DiPe—HoL
"No rack can torture me."—DiPe
"None can experience stint."—DiPe
Not in vain. See "If I can stop one heart from breaking"
"Not with a club the heart is broken."—DiPe
"Of all the souls that stand create."—DiPe
"Of all the sounds despatched abroad."—DiPe
"Of Brussels it was not."—DiPe
"Of God we ask one favor."—PlE
"One blessing had I, than the rest."—DiPe
"One dignity delays for all."—DiPe
"One need not be a chamber to be haunted."—DiPe
"The only news I know."—DiPe

"Who has not found the heaven—below."—DiPe
"Who never lost, are unprepared."—DiPe
"Who never wanted,—maddest joy."—DiL—DiPe
"Wild nights. Wild nights."—DiPe
"Will there really be a morning."—DiPe
Morning.—HoB
"The wind begun (or began) to rock the grass."—DiL—DiPe
A thunder-storm.—CoBn
With flowers. See "I've nothing else to bring you know"
A word. See "A word is dead"
"A word is dead"
A word.—ArT-3
"The world is not conclusion."—PlE
"You cannot put a fire out."—DiPe
Dickinson, Ken
Raindrops.—LeM
Dick's trick. Eve Merriam.—MeC
Dickson, John W.
Insouciance.—DuS
Dicky Dilver. Mother Goose.—BrMg
"**Did** ever you hear." See Grasshoppers
"**Did** we abolish frost." Emily Dickinson.—DiPe
"**Did** you ever go early." See Meadow morning
"**Did** you ever look." See Raccoons
"**Did** you ever take umbrage." See Having words
"**Did** you know, did you know." See The earth
"**Did** you say something." See The parrot
Diddle, diddle, dumpling. See "Diddle, diddle, dumpling, my son John"
"**Diddle,** diddle, dumpling, my son John." Mother Goose.—HuS-3—OpF—WiMg
Diddle, diddle, dumpling.—BrMg
Mother Goose rhymes, 14.—HoB
"**Diddle-me-diddle-me-dandy-O.**" Mother Goose.—OpF
Dido
Dido my dear, alas, is dead. From Shepheardes calendar. E. Spenser.—GrCt
Dido my dear, alas, is dead. See Shepheardes calendar
Didymus. Louis MacNeice.—PlE
Diekmann, Conrad
Winter trees.—MoS
Different bicycles. Dorothy W. Baruch.—ArT-3
"The **difficulty** to think at the end of the day." See A rabbit as king of the ghosts
Digging. Edward Thomas.—ThG
Digging for China. Richard Wilbur.—BoGj
"**Dill** double for Booman." See Booman
"A **dillar,** a dollar." See "A diller, a dollar, a ten o'clock scholar"
"A **diller,** a dollar, a ten o'clock scholar." Mother Goose.—ArT-3
"A dillar, a dollar."—WiMg
"A diller, a dollar."—OpF—ReMg
Mother Goose rhymes, 12.—HoB
Ten o'clock scholar.—BrMg
Dillon, George
April's amazing meaning.—CoBl
Dilly dilly. Unknown.—AgH
"**Dim** vales—and shadowy floods." See Fairy-land
"A **diner** while dining at Crewe." Unknown.—BrLl
"I raised a great hullabaloo."—LaPd
Dinesen, Isak
Zebra.—BoGj
Ding, ding. Eve Merriam.—MeC
"**Ding,** dong, bell." See "Ding, dong, bell, pussy's in the well"
"**Ding,** dong, bell, pussy's in the well." Mother Goose.—OpF
"Ding, dong, bell."—ArT-3—BrMg—ReMg—WiMg
Mother Goose rhymes, 8.—HoB
"**Dingty** diddlety." See My mammy's maid
Dinky. Theodore Roethke.—CoO—LiT
Dinner
Corinna. D. McCord.—McAd
Thanksgiving dinner. A. Fisher.—FiIo
"**Dinner.**" See Corinna
Dinosaur air. Claudia Lewis.—LeP
The **dinosaur** bones. Carl Sandburg.—DuS
"The **dinosaur** bones are dusted every day." See The dinosaur bones
Dinosaurs
Dinosaur air. C. Lewis.—LeP
The dinosaur bones. C. Sandburg.—DuS
"There once was a plesiosaurus." Unknown.—BrLl
"The **dinosaurs** are not all dead." See Steam shovel
Dinsdale, Beverley
"Dark fills the sky with his big black cloak."—LeM
Diocletian, Gaius Aurelius Valerius (about)
Great Diocletian. A. Cowley.—GrCt (sel.)
Diop, Birago
Omen.—HoL
"**Dip** and swing." See The rose on the wind
"**Dip** down upon the northern shore." See In memoriam
Directions to the armorer. Elder Olson.—DuS
A **dirge** ("Call for the robin red-breast and the wren") See The white devil
Dirge ("1-2-3 was the number he played but today the number came 3-2-1") Kenneth Fearing.—HiL
A **dirge** ("Rough wind, that moanest loud") Percy Bysshe Shelley.—GrCt
A **dirge** ("Why were you born when the snow was falling") Christina Georgina Rossetti.—GrCt
Dirge for a bad boy. E. V. Rieu.—CoBb
Dirge for the new sunrise. Edith Sitwell.—PlE
Dirges. See Laments
"**Dirt** and." See The streetcleaner's lament
Dirty Jim. Jane Taylor.—GrT
Disappointment
Disappointment. E. Turner.—VrF
Hugh Selwyn Mauberley. E. Pound.—HiL
Old gray squirrel. A. Noyes.—CoSs
Tangerines. A. Karanikas.—BoH
"**Disasters** will strike. Despite the infinite." See Warning

Discontent. See Content
Discordants. Conrad Aiken.—CoBl
"**Discovering** God is waking one morning." John L'Heureux.—CoBn
Discovery ("I walked by chance") Yuan Mei, tr. fr. the Chinese by Henry H. Hart.—LeMw
Discovery ("In a puddle left from last week's rain") Harry Behn.—BeG
The **discovery** ("There was an Indian, who had known no change") See There was an Indian
Disease. See Sickness
"A **dish** full of all kinds of flowers." Unknown.—OpF
Dishes. See Pottery
Dishonesty. See Truthfulness and falsehood
Dishman, Nelda
Trees.—LeM
Disillusionment of ten o'clock. Wallace Stevens.—HaL
Dislikes. See Likes and dislikes
The **dismantled** ship. Walt Whitman.—ClF—HoL
Disobedience. See Obedience
Disobedience. A. A. Milne.—MiC
"**Distracted** with care." See The despairing lover
Ditto marks; or, How do you amuse a muse. Eve Merriam.—MeI
Ditty for a child losing his first tooth. Unknown.—DoC
"**Dive** into grass." See First day of summer
The **diver** ("I would like to dive") W. W. E. Ross.—DoW
Diver ("The rubber man") Pablo Neruda, tr. by Ben Belitt.—LiT
The **diver** ("Sank through easeful") Robert E. Hayden.—DuS—HaK
The **diverting** history of John Gilpin. William Cowper.—CoR
Dividing. David McCord.—AgH
Divina commedia. Henry Wadsworth Longfellow.—LoPl
A **divine** image ("Cruelty has a human heart") William Blake.—BlP—GrCt
The **divine** image ("To mercy, pity, peace, and love") William Blake.—BlP
Divinest sense. See "Much madness is divinest sense"
Diving. See Swimming and diving
Dixon, Richard Watson
Song ("The feathers of the willow")—BlO—CoBn
Song ("Why fadest thou in death")—GrCt
The **dizzy** girl. Elizabeth Turner.—VrF
"**Do** diddle di do." See Jim Jay
"**Do** not believe your Shakespeare's grief." See The argument
"**Do** not forget, Lord." See The prayer of the cock
"**Do** not let any woman read this verse." See Deirdre
"**Do** not stifle me with the strange scent." See Alien
"**Do** not weep, maiden, for war is kind." See War is kind
"**Do** skyscrapers ever grow tired." See Skyscrapers
"**Do** those girls set out." Tsurayuki.—BaS
"**Do** ye remember . . . Surelye I remember." See The old shepherds
"**Do** you ask what the birds say? The sparrow, the dove." See Answer to a child's question
"**Do** you ever wonder." See Grasses
"**Do** you ever wonder." See Like a bug
"**Do** you fear the force of the wind." See Do you fear the wind
Do you fear the wind. Hamlin Garland.—ArT-3—ThA
"**Do** you hear the cry as the pack goes by." See Wind-wolves
"**Do** you know the hour when all opposites meet." See The time is
"**Do** you know the muffin man." Eleanor Farjeon.—FaT
"**Do** you know what I could wish." See Song for a hot day
"**Do** you not hear the aziola cry." See The aziola
"**Do** you remember." See Notes found near a suicide—To James
"**Do** you remember an inn." See Tarantella
"**Do** you remember that night." George Petrie, tr. fr. the Gaelic by Eugene O'Curry.—CoBl—GrS
Do you remember the night. See "Do you remember that night"
"**Do** you see that old beggar who stands at the door." See Charity
"**Do** you suppose it's really really true." See Run, kitty, run
"**Do** you suppose the babbling brook." See As to the restless brook
"**Do** you think we skip." See The zobo bird
Dobell, Sydney
Fragment of a sleepy song.—ReS
Dobson, (Henry) Austin
A garden song.—CoBn
The **doctor.** David McCord.—McAd
"**Doctor** Faustus was a good man." Mother Goose.—ReMg
Doctor Fell. Martial, tr. fr. the Latin by Thomas Brown.—BrMg—GrCt
"I do not like thee, Dr Fell."—ReMg
"A **doctor** fell in a deep well." Unknown.—BrSm
Doctor Foster. See "Doctor Foster went to Gloucester (in a shower)"
Doctor Foster ("Old Doctor Foster") Mother Goose.—BrMg
"**Doctor** Foster went to Gloster." See "Doctor Foster went to Gloucester (in a shower)"
"**Doctor** Foster went to Gloucester (in a shower)." Mother Goose.—OpF
Doctor Foster.—BrMg—CoO
"Doctor Foster went to Gloster."—WiMg
Doctor Mohawk. Vachel Lindsay.—LiP
Doctors
"And can the physician make sick men well." Unknown.—BlO
Arthur Ridgewood, M.D. F.M. Davis.—HaK
Bones. W. De La Mare.—BrSm—DuL

The doctor. D. McCord.—McAd
"A doctor fell in a deep well." Unknown.—BrSm
"I saw no doctor, but, feeling queer inside." From The Greek anthology. Unknown.—BrSm
Matilda. F. G. Evans.—CoBb
Seagulls. F. H. Savage.—DuS
Similia similibus. J. H. Morgan.—BrSm
Songs accompanying healing magic. Unknown.—DeC
"I sweep this hut"
"This is a root"
"Surgeons must be very careful." E. Dickinson.—DiPe
Witch doctor. R. E. Hayden.—BoA
Dodge, Mary Mapes
Lazy Lou.—CoBb
"Oh, no."—CoBb
"There once was a knowing raccoon."—BrLl
"There once was a man with a sneeze."—BrLl
Trouble in the greenhouse.—BrSg
The **dodo**. Hilaire Belloc.—GrCt
"The **dodo** used to walk around." See The dodo
Dodson, Owen
Circle one.—BoH—HaK
The confession stone.—HaK (sel.)
Conversation on V.—HaK
Drunken lover.—BoA
Hymn written after Jeremiah preached to me in a dream.—BoA—HaK
Poems for my brother Kenneth, VII.—AdIa
The reunion.—BoH
Sailors on leave.—BoA
Sickle pears.—BoA
"Sorrow is the only faithful one."—AdIa—BoA
When I am dead.—HaK
Yardbird's skull.—AdIa—BoA
"**Does** everyone have to die? Yes, everyone." See Fable
"**Does** the eagle know what is in the pit." See The book of Thel
Doffing the bonnet. James Stephens.—StS
Dog. William Jay Smith.—BoGj
The **dog** and the shadow. Richard Scrafton Sharpe.—VrF
Dog around the block. E. B. White.—LaC—McWs
"**Dog** around the block, sniff." See Dog around the block
"The **dog** beneath the cherry tree." See The ambiguous dog
"A **dog** emerges from the flies." See Nino, the wonder dog
"The **dog** fox rolls on his lolling tongue." See The hunt
The **dog** from Malta. See A Maltese dog
Dog, midwinter. Raymond Souster.—CoB
Dog-star. Eleanor Farjeon.—FaT
The **dog** Trim. Unknown.—VrF
"The **dog** will come when he is called." Adelaide O'Keefe.—BlO
"The **doggies** gaed to the mill." Unknown.—MoB
Dogs
"The aged dog." Issa.—IsF
Albert. D. Abse.—SmM
The ambiguous dog. A. Guiterman.—CoB
The animal store. R. Field.—ArT-3—HuS-3—LaP—LaPd
The ass and the lap-dog. R. S. Sharpe.—VrF
The bandog. W. De La Mare.—ArT-3
Beagles. W. R. Rodgers.—MoS
Beau's reply. W. Cowper.—ReO
Beware of the doggerel. E. Merriam.—MeI
Birthday present. A. Fisher.—FiC
"Bow, wow, wow." Mother Goose.—ArT-3—HuS-3—OpF
Tom Tinker's dog.—BrMg
Brave Rover. M. Beerbohm.—ReO
The buccaneer. N. B. Turner.—ArT-3
Buff. Mother Goose.—BrMg
Daley's dorg Wattie. W. T. Goodge.—CoB
Death of a dog. B. Deutsch.—DuS
Denise. R. B. Hale.—CoB
Dog. W. J. Smith.—BoGj
The dog and the shadow. R. S. Sharpe.—VrF
Dog around the block. E. B. White.—LaC—McWs
Dog, midwinter. R. Souster.—CoB
Dog-star. E. Farjeon.—FaT
The dog Trim. Unknown.—VrF
"The doggies gaed to the mill." Unknown.—MoB
"The dogs." Issa.—IsF
Dogs. F. Cornford.—StF
Dogs and weather. W. Welles.—ArT-3—HuS-3
The dog's cold nose. A. Guiterman.—CoB
"Dogs have as much right as people in Nevada." H. Witt.—DuS
The duel. E. Field.—ArT-3—HoB—HuS-3—ReS
Elegy for Jog. J. Ciardi.—DuR
An elegy on the death of a mad dog. O. Goldsmith.—BrSm—CoR
An englyn on a yellow greyhound. W. Barnes.—ReO
Engraved on the collar of a dog, which I gave to his royal highness. A. Pope.—GrCt
The extraordinary dog. N. B. Turner.—ArT-3
"A farmer's dog leaped over the stile." Unknown.—BlO
Fidelity. W. Wordsworth.—ClF
Full of the moon. K. Kuskin.—LaP—LaPd
"A girl in the army." Mother Goose.—BrMg
Gluskap's hound. T. G. Roberts.—DoW
The hairy dog. H. Asquith.—ArT-3—HoB—HuS-3—LaP—LaPd
Hansi. H. Behn.—BeG
"Hark, hark, the dogs do bark." Mother Goose.—ArT-3—OpF—ReMg—WiMg
The beggars.—BrMg
"Hark, hark."—BrF
Mother Goose rhymes, 23.—HoB
Hector the dog. K. Barnes.—CoB
The house dog's grave. R. Jeffers.—CoB
"The hydrogen dog and the cobalt cat." F. Winsor.—BrSm

"**Domelike** top, speckled comets converging." See The jellyfish
The **dome** of night. Claudia Lewis.—LeP
Don Juan, sels. George Gordon Byron
And angling, too.—MoS
Fragment.—ByP
Haidée.—ByP
The isles of Greece.—ByP—CoR—GrCt—PaH (sel.)
Of all the barbarous middle ages.—ByP
Don Quixote (about)
The windmill addresses Don Quixote. E. J. Coatsworth.—CoDh
Donall Oge: Grief of a girl's heart. Unknown, tr. fr. the Irish by Lady Gregory.—CoBl
The grief of a girl's heart.—GrCt
Done for. Walter De La Mare.—BlO—DeBg
The **dong** with a luminous nose. Edward Lear. —GrCt
The **donkey.** See "Donkey, donkey, old and grey"
The **donkey.** See "If I had a donkey"
The **donkey** ("I saw a donkey") Gertrude Hind. —CoB
Donkey ("Whose little beast") Mark Van Doren. —PlE
The **donkey** and the fluke. Eve Merriam.—MeC
"A **donkey** caught a fluke swimming round in the sea." See The donkey and the fluke
"**Donkey,** donkey, do not bray." Mother Goose. —OpF
"**Donkey,** donkey, old and grey." Mother Goose. —OpF
The donkey.—BrMg
Donkey riding. Unknown.—DoW—StF
Donkeys
Advice to travelers. W. Gibson.—DuR
The ass and the lap-dog. R. S. Sharpe.—VrF
The ass in the lion's skin. Aesop.—ReO
Asses. P. Colum.—HaL (sel.)
Aubade: Dick the donkey boy. O. Sitwell.—CaD
Dance of burros. D. Laing.—CoB
The donkey ("I saw a donkey") G. Hind.—CoB
Donkey ("Whose little beast") M. Van Doren. —PlE
The donkey and the fluke. E. Merriam.—MeC
"Donkey, donkey, do not bray." Mother Goose. —OpF
"Donkey, donkey, old and grey." Mother Goose.—OpF
The donkey.—BrMg
"If I had a donkey." Mother Goose.—OpF
The donkey.—BrMg
"If I had a donkey that wouldn't go."—WiMg
The little donkey. Unknown.—VrF
The monotony song. T. Roethke.—LiT
My donkey. Unknown.—ArT-3
Nicholas Nye. W. De La Mare.—BlO—CoB—HoB—ReO
The prayer of the donkey. C. B. de Gasztold. —ArT-3
Prayer to go to Paradise with the donkeys. F. Jammès.—CoB—ReO
Francis Jammès: A prayer to go to Paradise with the donkeys.—ArT-3—PlE
"This being's most despised by man." Unknown.—OpF
"This rustic maid enjoys her ride." M. Elliott. —VrF
"Up in the north, a long way off." Unknown. —OpF
"A **donkey's** tail is very nice." See The monotony song
Donne, John
Anatomy of the world: The first anniversary, sel.
"Doth not a Tenarif, or higher hill."—GrCt
"At the round earth's imagin'd corners, blow." —PlE
"Blow your trumpets, angels."—GrCt
The bait.—MoS
"Batter my heart, three person'd God."—PlE
"Blow your trumpets, angels." See "At the round earth's imagin'd corners, blow"
Death be not proud. See Holy sonnets
"Doth not a Tenarif, or higher hill." See Anatomy of the world: The first anniversary
An epithalamium on the Lady Elizabeth and Count Palatine being married on St Valentine's day, sel.
Hail, Bishop Valentine.—GrCt
Hail, Bishop Valentine. See An epithalamium on the Lady Elizabeth and Count Palatine being married on St Valentine's day
Holy sonnets, sel.
Death be not proud.—GrCt
Sonnet.—HoL
Hymn to God my God, in my sickness.—GrCt
A hymne to God the Father.—PlE
The progress of the soul, sel.
The whale.—GrCt
The whale. See The progress of the soul
Donne, John (about)
Donne redone. J. P. Tierney.—BrSm
Donne redone. Joseph Paul Tierney.—BrSm
"**Don't** ask me how he managed." See The worm
"**Don't** be polite." See How to eat a poem
"**Don't** begrudge." See Beware, or be yourself
Don't bomb human nature out of existence. John Tagliabue.—DuS
"**Don't** care didn't care." Unknown.—BlO
"**Don't** ever cross a crocodile." Kaye Starbird.—ArT-3—LaPd
"**Don't** ever grab." See The crab
Don't ever seize a weasel by the tail. Jack Prelutsky.—CoO
"**Don't** kill." Issa, tr. fr. the Japanese by Nobuyuki Yuasa.—IsF
"**Don't** look in the engagement calendar for memories." See And were a little changed
"**Don't** make any noise." See Creep
"**Don't** pull me up. I got to live." See The weed
"**Don't** shirk." See Good advice
"**Don't** step on the primrose." See Three don'ts

"**Don't** tell papa his nose is red." See A children's don't

"**Don't** you feel sorry." See All winter

"**Don't** you feel sorry." See Moles

"**Don't** you think a daddy longlegs." See Daddy longlegs

"**Don't** you think it's probable." See Little talk

Doolittle, Hilda. See D., H., pseud.

Doom

Conjecture. A. Raha.—AlPi

"The **door** is shut fast." See Who's in

"The **door** of death is made of gold." See Dedication of the illustrations to Blair's grave

Doorbells. See Bells

Doorbells. Rachel Field.—ArT-3—HuS-3

Doors

Doorbells. R. Field.—ArT-3—HuS-3

The doors ("The doors in my house") B. Andrews.—LeM

Doors ("An open door says, Come in") C. Sandburg.—HaL

"Godfrey Gordon Gustavus Gore." W. B. Rands.—ArT-3—CoBb—HoB

Green candles. H. Wolfe.—SmM

"In one door." A. Fisher.—FiIo

The man who hid his own front door. E. MacKinstry.—ArT-3

My uncle Jack. D. Amey.—LeM

Open the door. M. Edey.—ArT-3

Rebecca. H. Belloc.—DuR—TuW

"Regarding a door." D. Antin.—DuS

The revolving door. Newman Levy.—BrSm

"There was a young lady of Norway." E. Lear.—ArT-3—BrLl

Nonsense verses.—HuS-3

The **doors** ("The doors in my house") Brian Andrews.—LeM

Doors ("An open door says, Come in") Carl Sandburg.—HaL

"The **doors** in my house." See The doors

d'Orléans, Charles. See Charles d'Orléans

Dormice

The dormouse ("The dormouse chews a hole") P. Hill.—CoB

The dormouse ("A raindrop fell down on a dormouse's nose") M. M. Stephenson.—StF

The elf and the dormouse. O. Herford.—ArT-3—HoB—ThA

The **dormouse** ("The dormouse chews a hole") Pati Hill.—CoB

The **dormouse** ("A raindrop fell down on a dormouse's nose") M. M. Stephenson.—StF

"The **dormouse** chews a hole." See The dormouse

Dorrance, Dick

Cockpit in the clouds.—ArT-3

"**Dot** a dot dot dot a dot dot." See Weather

"**Doth** not a Tenarif, or higher hill." See Anatomy of the world: The first anniversary

"**Doth** some one say that there be gods above." See There are no gods

"A **doting** father once there was." See Piano practice

Double Dutch. Walter De La Mare.—ClF

"A **double** flower we were." See A waltz in the afternoon

A **double** limerick or twiner ("There was an old man with a gun") Walter De La Mare.—BrLl

A **double** limerick or twiner ("There was an old person of Dover") Walter De La Mare.—BrLl

The eel.—BrSm

The **double-play.** Robert Wallace.—DuS—MoS

Double trouble. Eve Merriam.—MeI

Doubt

Adjuration. C. E. Wheeler.—BoA

Antichrist. E. Muir.—PlE

A Christmas sonnet. E. A. Robinson.—PlE

Crag Jack's apostasy. T. Hughes.—PlE

Didymus. L. MacNeice.—PlE

The flight. S. Teasdale.—CoBl

If once we choose belief. From Bishop Blougram's apology. R. Browning.—BrP

Letter across doubt and distance. M. C. Holman.—BoA

Praise doubt. M. Van Doren.—PlE

There are no gods. Euripides.—PlE

"Thou art indeed just, Lord, if I contend." G. M. Hopkins.—PlE

The triumph of doubt. J. P. Bishop.—PlE

Why art thou silent. W. Wordsworth.—WoP

Doubts. Rupert Brooke.—GrS

Douglass, Frederick (about)

Frederick Douglass ("Susan B. Anthony led him onto the platform") E. Merriam.—MeIv

Frederick Douglass ("When it is finally ours, this freedom, this liberty, this beautiful") R. E. Hayden.—AdIa—BoA—HaK

The **dove.** William Barnes.—ReBs

The **dove** says. Mother Goose.—BrMg

"The **dove** says, Coo, coo." See The dove says

Dover, England

Dover beach. M. Arnold.—ClF (sel.)—CoBl—PlE

Dover beach. Matthew Arnold.—ClF (sel.)—CoB —PlE

Doves. See Pigeons

The **doves** of my eyes. G. P. Mohanty, tr. fr the Oriya by J. M. Mohanty.—AlPi

"The **doves** of my eyes rise to the sky's steel body." See The doves of my eyes

The **dove's** song. Unknown.—StF

Dowd, Emma C.

Fun in a garret.—ArT-3

Dowling, Basil

Autumn scene.—CoBn

"**Down.**" See Black is a soul

"**Down.**" See The grasshopper

Down. Aileen Fisher.—FiIo

"**Down** by the river." Mother Goose.—BrMg

Down by the salley gardens. William Butler Yeats.—CoBl

"**Down** by the salley gardens my love and I did meet." See Down by the salley gardens

"**Down** cellar, said the cricket." See The potatoes' dance

"**Down** dip the branches." Mark Van Doren.—ReS
"**Down,** down." Eleanor Farjeon.—ArT-3
"**Down** in a deep dark ditch sat an old crow munching a beanstalk." See Hexameter and pentameter
"**Down** in a green and shady bed." See The violet
"**Down** in the silent hallway." See Unsatisfied yearning
"**Down** in the valley." See Skipping
Down on Roberts' farm. Claude Reeves.—HiL
"**Down** on the rooftops." See Down
"**Down** the dripping pathway dancing through the rain." See Rainy song
"**Down** the hill in our wagon we go." See Coaster wagon
"**Down** the meadow." See On a windy day
Down the Mississippi. John Gould Fletcher.—BrA (sel.)—PaH
"**Down** the stream the swans all glide." Spike Milligan.—StF
"**Down** the Yellowstone, the Milk, the White and Cheyenne." See The river
"**Down** through the wintry air." See Late snowflakes
"**Down** upon my pillow warm." See Going to bed
"**Down** with the lambs." See Bedtime
"**Downhill** I came, hungry, and yet not starved." See The owl
"**Downstream** they have killed the river and built a dam." See The fish counter at Bonneville
Dowson, Ernest
Non sum qualis eram bonae sub regno Cynarae.—CoBl
To his mistress.—CoBl
Vitae summa brevis spem nos vetat incohare longam.—GrCt
The **doze.** James Reeves.—CoB
"**Dozens** of girls would storm up." See Girl crazy—Embraceable you
"A **dozen** machines." See A time for building
"**Drab** habitation of whom." Emily Dickinson.—DiPe
Dragon flies. See Dragonflies
Dragonflies
Catching dragonflies. Unknown.—DePp
"The dragon-fly." Issa.—IsF
The dragon-fly. From The two voices. A. Tennyson.—ReO
Dragonfly ("His small feet") H. Behn.—LiT
A dragonfly ("When the heat of the summer") E. Farjeon.—FaA—LaPd
"The face of the dragonfly." Chisoku.—LeMw
Flying. K. Starbird.—LaPd
"I wonder in what fields today." Kaga no Chiyo.—LeMw
"I would I were." Unknown.—LeO
"Where does he wander." Chiyo.—BeCs
"**Dragonflies,** hey." See Catching dragonflies
The **dragon-fly.** See The two voices
"The **dragon-fly.**" Issa, tr. fr. the Japanese by R. H. Blyth.—IsF
Dragonfly ("His small feet") Harry Behn.—LiT
A **dragonfly** ("When the heat of the summer") Eleanor Farjeon.—FaA—LaPd
Dragons
"As the sun came up, a ball of red." Unknown.—WyC
A modern dragon. R. B. Bennett.—ArT-3—LaPd
"Sir Eglamour that worthy knight." Unknown.—BlO
Thunder dragon. H. Behn.—BeG
The toaster. W. J. Smith.—AgH—ArT-3—DuR
Us two. A. A. Milne.—ArT-3—MiC
Drake, Gaston V.
The contrary boy.—CoBb
Drake, Leah Bodine
The crows.—DuR
"**Drake** he's in his hammock an' a thousand mile away." See Drake's drum
Drake's drum. Henry Newbolt.—CoSs
"**Drank** lonesome water." See Lonesome water
Drawing teeth. Elizabeth Turner.—VrF
Drayton, Michael
The adventures of Oberon, king of the fairies, while searching for Queen Mab. See Nymphidia, the court of fairy
The baron's war, sel.
The Severn.—GrCt
Birds in the fens. See Polyolbion
Christopher Marlowe. See To Henry Reynolds, of poets and poesy
The dying crane.—ReO
Fools gaze at painted courts. See Polyolbion
Hawking. See Polyolbion
Idea, sel.
"Since there's no help, come, let us kiss and part."—CoBl
Nymphidia, the court of fairy, sel.
The adventures of Oberon, king of the fairies, while searching for Queen Mab.—ReO
Polyolbion, sels.
Birds in the fens.—GrCt
Fools gaze at painted courts.—GrCt
Hawking.—MoS
Wrestlers.—MoS
The Severn. See The baron's war
"Since there's no help, come, let us kiss and part." See Idea
To Henry Reynolds, of poets and poesy, sel.
Christopher Marlowe.—GrCt
To the Virginian voyage.—HiL
Wrestlers. See Polyolbion
Drake, Sir Francis (about)
The admiral's ghost. A. Noyes.—ArT-3
Drake's drum. H. Newbolt.—CoSs
A **dream** ("Life is a dream") Irene Ellen Nez.—BaH
A **dream** ("Once a dream did weave a shade") William Blake.—BlP—ReO
The **dream** ("One night I dreamed") Harry Behn.—LiT

Dream deferred. See Lenox avenue mural
Dream-land. Edgar Allan Poe.—PoP
Dream of a baseball star. Gregory Corso.—MoS
The **dream** of all the Springfield writers. Vachel Lindsay.—LiP
A **dream** of wrecks. See King Richard III
A **dream** party. Unknown, ad. fr. the Japanese by Charlotte B. DeForest.—DePp
Dream variation. Langston Hughes.—AdIa—BoA
A **dream** within a dream. Edgar Allan Poe.—GrCt (sel.)—PoP
The **dream** woman. Patricia Hubbell.—ArT-3
The **dreamer.** William Childress.—DuS
"**Dreaming** of a prince." See After all and after all
"**Dreaming** of honeycombs to share." See Waiting
Dreamland. Walter De La Mare.—DeBg
Dreams. See also Visions
André. G. Brooks.—ArT-3—HoB
The angel. W. Blake.—BlP
The Blue Ridge. H. Monroe.—BoH
"The bridge of dreams." Teika.—BaS
Chanticleer and the fox. From The Canterbury tales. G. Chaucer.—ChT
Cornwall. C. Bond.—LeM
A dream ("Life is a dream") I. E. Nez.—BaH
A dream ("Once a dream did weave a shade") W. Blake.—BlP—ReO
The dream ("One night I dreamed") H. Behn.—LiT
Dream-land. E. A. Poe.—PoP
Dream of a baseball star. G. Corso.—MoS
A dream of wrecks. From King Richard III. W. Shakespeare.—GrCt
Dream variation. L. Hughes.—AdIa—BoA
A dream within a dream. E. A. Poe.—GrCt (sel.)—PoP
The dream woman. P. Hubbell.—ArT-3
The dreamer. W. Childress.—DuS
Dreamland. W. De La Mare.—DeBg
Dreams ("Dreams are funny") A. Fisher.—FiIo
Dreams ("Hold fast to dreams") L. Hughes.—BoH—DuR—HoB—McWs
Dreams ("Oh, that my young life were a lasting dream") E. A. Poe.—PoP
"Drums, drumming." B. Brown.—BaH
Evening star. E. Farjeon.—FaT
Fantasy. G. D. Nerval.—GrS
"The first of all my dreams was of." E. E. Cummings.—GrS
"A Friday night's dream on a Saturday told." Mother Goose.—OpF
From a childhood. R. M. Rilke.—GrS
From the hills of dream. W. Sharp.—ThA
Get this garbage out of my life. P. Goggins.—BaH
Green park dream. M. C. Livingston.—LiC
He wishes for the cloths of heaven. W. B. Yeats.—HoL—ThA—YeR
Hold fast your dreams. L. Driscoll.—ArT-3
The host of the air. W. B. Yeats.—LiT—YeR
The house of dream. W. De La Mare.—DeBg
I bid you keep some few small dreams. H. Frazee-Bower.—ThA
I dream a world. L. Hughes.—BoA—BoH
I dream of a place. W. De La Mare.—DeBg
I had a boat. M. Coleridge.—SmM
"I have wrapped my dreams in a silken cloth." C. Cullen.—ThA
If you should go. C. Cullen.—BoH
"In the dream." Issa.—LeOw
Known of old. W. De La Mare.—DeBg
The land of dreams. W. Blake.—BlP
Lenox avenue mural. L. Hughes.—BoA
Dream deferred.—LaC
"Longing pleases me like sweet fragrance." Unknown.—DoC
"The nearest dream recedes, unrealized." E. Dickinson.—DiPe
"The mighty thoughts of an old world." T. L. Beddoes.—BoGj—GrS
"One stormy night." V. L. Jones.—BaH
Orpheus' dream. E. Muir.—GrS
Paper boats. R. Tagore.—BoH—ThA
Peter and John. E. Wylie.—CaMb
Promise me a rose. B. Merrill.—CoBl
A real dream. S. Brown.—BaH
The rose on the wind. J. Stephens.—StS
The shepherd. W. De La Mare.—DeBg
"Since I am convinced." Saigyo Hōshi.—BaS
Sleep and dreams. P. Kelso.—LeM
The sluggard. Lucilius.—MoS
The soldier's dream. T. Campbell.—CoR
The still voice of Harlem. C. K. Rivers.—AdIa—HaK
The subway. C. K. Rivers.—HaK
"There was a young lady named Wemyss." Unknown.—BrLl
"There was an old man from Peru." Unknown.—LaPd
This old countryside. M. J. Fuller.—BaH
Trifle. G. D. Johnson.—BoA—BoH
Trinity: A dream sequence. N. L. Madgett.—HaK (sel.)
Ula Masondo's dream. W. Plomer.—CaMb
Under the moon. W. B. Yeats.—PaH
The valley of white poppies. W. Sharp.—ThA
"What will become." B. Brown.—BaH
Why. W. De La Mare.—DeBg
A winter's dream. Unknown.—DePp
Dreams ("Dreams are funny") Aileen Fisher.—FiIo
Dreams ("Hold fast to dreams") Langston Hughes.—BoH—DuR—HoB—McWs
Dreams ("Oh, that my young life were a lasting dream") Edgar Allan Poe.—PoP
"**Dreams** are funny." See Dreams
The **dree** night. Unknown.—GrCt
Dreidel song. Efraim Rosenzweig.—ArT-3
Dress. See Clothing and dress
Dressed or undressed. Elizabeth Turner.—VrF
"**Dressed** up in my melancholy." See Song
Dressing. Aileen Fisher.—FiIo
Dressing a doll. Mary Elliott.—VrF
A **dressmaker.** Jean Kenward.—SmM
Drifting. Thomas Buchanan Read.—PaH

"**Drifting** night in the Georgia pines." See O Daedalus, fly away home

Drillich, Richard
Rain.—LeM

A **drink**. Aileen Fisher.—FiIo

"**Drink** to me only with thine eyes." See Song to Celia

Drinking. See Drinks and drinking

Drinks and drinking
The Abbot Adam of Angers. Unknown.—LiT
Ballad of the two tapsters. V. Watkins.—CaMb
Bring us in good ale. Unknown.—ClF
"Busy, curious, thirsty fly." Unknown.—ClF
Butterfly tongues. A. Fisher.—FiI
Captain Stratton's fancy. J. Masefield.—CoSs
Cider song. M. Weston.—CoBn
"Come gather round me, Parnellites." W. B. Yeats.—YeR
A drink. A. Fisher.—FiIo
Drummer and sot. Unknown.—VrF
"A drunkard cannot meet a cork." E. Dickinson.—DiPe
"Eat at pleasure." Mother Goose.—AgH
Epitaph on John Dove, innkeeper. R. Burns.—BuPr
Gin by pailfuls. W. Scott.—GrCt
A glass of beer. J. Stephens.—McWs—StS
A health unto his majesty. J. Savile.—GrCt
John Barleycorn: A ballad. R. Burns.—BuPr
"Johnnie Crack and Flossie Snail." From Under Milk Wood. D. Thomas.—BoGj—CaD—HaL—LaPd
"King Arthur's men have come again." V. Lindsay.—LiP
Lemonade. D. McCord.—McAd
"The man in the moon drinks claret." Mother Goose.—BrMg
Mazilla and Mazura. Unknown.—GrCt
Mrs Swartz. D. Marquis.—HiL
Old Boniface. Mother Goose.—BrMg
On an old toper buried in Durham churchyard, England. Unknown.—BrSm
Sally Birkett's ale. Unknown.—GrCt
Song to Celia. B. Jonson.—BoH
A strange meeting. W. H. Davies.—BlO
Tam o'Shanter. R. Burns.—BuPr
"There was a young lady from Lynn." Unknown.—BrLl
The young lady of Lynn.—GrCt
"There was once a giraffe who said, What." O. Herford.—BrLl
Wassail, wassail. J. Bale.—GrCt
"We be soldiers three." Unknown.—GrCt
What someone told me about Bobby Link. J. Ciardi.—AgH—CiYk
Willie brew'd a peck o' maut. R. Burns.—BuPr
"Wine and cakes for gentlemen." Mother Goose.—ReMg
Wine and cakes.—BrMg—VrF

Drinkwater, John
The bird's nest.—HuS-3—LaPd
I want to know.—HoB
Moonlit apples.—CoBn
Snail.—BoGj
The sun.—ArT-3—HuS-3
The wagon in the barn.—ThA
Washing.—HuS-3

Driscoll, Louise
Hold fast your dreams.—ArT-3
Thanksgiving.—LaPh (sel.)

"The **driver** rubbed at his nettly chin." See To the four courts, please

"The **drivers** are washing the concrete mixers." See Concrete mixers

Driving to town late to mail a letter. Robert Bly.—CoBn

"A **drop** drew out of the ocean, toward the moon's height." See Since I left the ocean

"A **drop** fell on the apple tree." Emily Dickinson
Summer shower.—CoBn

"A **drop** of rain." Issa, tr. fr. the Japanese by Nobuyuki Yuasa.—ArT-3—LeI

"**Dropping** back with the ball ripe in my palm." See The passer

"A **drove** of rams and ewes and woolly lambs." See Two poems

A **drover**. Padraic Colum.—PaH

The **drowned** lady. Unknown.—GrCt

Drowning
A ballad of a mine. R. Skelton.—CaMb
The bitter withy. Unknown.—GrCt
By the Exeter river. D. Hall.—CaMb
Death by water. From The waste land. T. S. Eliot.—CaD
A dream of wrecks. From King Richard III. W. Shakespeare.—GrCt
The drowned lady. Unknown.—GrCt
Ezra Shank. Unknown.—BrSm
The giddy girl. E. Turner.—VrF
Isabel. Unknown.—DoW
Lord Ullin's daughter. T. Campbell.—CoR
Lowlands. Unknown.—GrCt
Lycidas. J. Milton.—GrCt
Ophelia's death. From Hamlet. W. Shakespeare.—GrCt
The outlandish knight. Unknown.—BrSm
Peg. Mother Goose.—BrMg
Piano practice. I. Serraillier.—CoBb
Rousecastle. D. Wright.—CaMb—CoSs
The sands of Dee. From Alton Locke. C. Kingsley.—BlO—ClF—CoSs
A Shropshire lad. J. Betjeman.—CaMb
Silly Willy. R. L. B.—BrSm
The stern parent. H. Graham.—CoBb—GrCt
The three fishers. C. Kingsley.—CoSs
The two rivers. Unknown.—GrCt
Tweed and Till.—CoBn

"**Drowsily** come the sheep." See Slumber song

"The **drowsy** wind." See The fickle wind

Drug store. John V. A. Weaver.—HiL

Druids
Fergus and the druid. W. B. Yeats.—LiT

"The **drum** drums health." See Praise song for a drummer

"**Drum** on your drums, batter on your banjos." See Jazz fantasia

Drummer and sot. Unknown.—VrF

Drummers and drums
"Cricket come back. You've left your drum behind." Unknown.—LeO
"Drums, drumming." B. Brown.—BaH
Praise song for a drummer. Unknown.—DoC
"The rat-a-tat-tat." Issa.—IsF
Drummond, William, of Hawthornden
Saint John the Baptist.—PlE
Thrice happy he.—CoBn
Drums. See Drummers and drums
"**Drums,** drumming." Barry Brown.—BaH
"**Drunk** or sober, go to bed, Tom." See Drummer and sot
"A **drunkard** cannot meet a cork." Emily Dickinson.—DiPe
Drunken lover. Owen Dodson.—BoA
"The **dry** fingers of the sun have wiped up the dampness around the grass roots." See September
The **dry** salvages, sel. T. S. Eliot
"I do not know much about gods; but I think that the river."—ArT-3
Dryads. See Fairies
Dryden, John
Absalom and Achitopel, sel.
Thomas Shadwell the poet.—GrCt
Ah fading joy.—GrCt
"All, all of a piece throughout." See The secular masque
Annus mirabilis, sels.
The fire of London.—GrCt
"So have I seen some fearful hare maintain"
Annus mirabilis.—CoB
A charm.—GrCt
The fire of London. See Annus mirabilis
The flood. See Metamorphoses
Here lies my wife.—BrSm
Incantation to Oedipus. See Oedipus
Jacob Tonson, his publisher.—GrCt
Metamorphoses, sels.
The flood. tr.—GrCt
The phoenix self-born. tr.—GrCt
Oedipus, sel.
Incantation to Oedipus.—GrS
The phoenix self-born. See Metamorphoses
The secular masque, sel.
"All, all of a piece throughout."—GrCt
"So have I seen some fearful hare maintain." See Annus mirabilis
Thomas Shadwell the poet. See Absalom and Achitopel
Du Bartas his divine weeks, sel. Joshua Sylvester
I hear the crane.—ReO
Dublin, Ireland
The gals o' Dublin town. Unknown.—CoSs
DuBois, William Edward Burghardt (about)
Booker T. and W. E. B. D. Randall.—HaK
Dubuque, Iowa
Old Dubuque. D. Etter.—BrA
The **duchess** of Malfi. John Webster.—GrCt (sel.)
The **duck.** Edith King.—HuS-3
"The **duck,** and mallard first, the falconer's only sport." See Polyolbion—Birds in the fens
The **duck** and the kangaroo. Edward Lear.—HoB
"**Duck** hunting is my favorite sport." See Hunting
"The **duck** is whiter than whey is." See Quack
"**Duck,** you are merely boasting." Unknown, tr. fr. the Yoruba.—LeO
Duckett, Alfred A.
Sonnet.—BoA
The **ducklings.** Aileen Fisher.—FiC
Ducks
Chicks and ducks. Unknown.—StF
Dame Duck's lecture. A. Hawkshawe.—StF
The duck. E. King.—HuS-3
The duck and the kangaroo. E. Lear.—HoB
"Duck, you are merely boasting." Unknown.—LeO
The ducklings. A. Fisher.—FiC
Ducks ("When God had finished the stars and whirl of colored suns") F. W. Harvey.—CoB (sel.)
The ducks ("When our ducks waddle to the pond") A. Wilkins.—ArT-3
Ducks at dawn. J. S. Tippett.—ArT-3
Ducks at twilight. E. J. Coatsworth.—CoSb
Duck's ditty. From The wind in the willows. K. Grahame.—ArT-3—BoGj—CoB—LaP—LaPd—TuW
Charley Barley. Mother Goose.—BrMg
"Four ducks on a pond." W. Allingham.—BlO—DuR
Four little ducks. D. McCord.—McAd
The hunter. O. Nash.—CoB—MoS
Hunting. J. Aluskak.—BaH
"I saw a ship a-sailing." Mother Goose.—ArT-3—HuS-3—ReMg—WiMg
I saw a ship.—CoSs—SmM
Mother Goose rhymes, 60.—HoB
A ship a-sailing.—BrMg
In the park. R. Fyleman.—HuS-3
"I've just come from a place." Bashō.—LeI
Mallard. R. Warner.—CoB
"My boat is turned up at both ends." Unknown.—WyC
Nell Flaherty's drake. Unknown.—ReO
"O foolish ducklings." Buson.—BeCs
The prayer of the little ducks. C. B. de Gasztold.—ArT-3—LaPd
Quack. W. De La Mare.—ArT-3—CoB—DeBg
"Spring rain." Issa.—LeOw
"That duck, bobbing up." Jōsō.—BeCs
"There was a little man, and he had a little gun." Mother Goose.—ReMg
The little man.—BrMg
"There was a little man."—OpF
'There was an old lady of France." E. Lear.—BrLl
A true blue gentleman. K. Patchen.—ReO
"Two ducks swim to the shore." Hiroshige.—LeMw
The white drake. Unknown.—DoW
Who likes the rain. C. D. Bates.—ArT-3—StF
"Wild ducks have eaten." Yasui.—BeCs

Ducks ("When God had finished the stars and whirl of colored suns") Frederick William Harvey.—CoB (sel.)
The **ducks** ("When our ducks waddle to the pond") Alice Wilkins.—ArT-3
Ducks at dawn. James S. Tippett.—ArT-3
Ducks at twilight. Elizabeth Jane Coatsworth.—CoSb
Ducks' ditty. See The wind in the willows
Dudley, John
The castle yonder.—LeM
The **duel.** See "I took my power in my hand"
The **duel** ("The gingham dog and the calico cat") Eugene Field.—ArT-3—HoB—HuS-3—ReS
The **duel** ("Schott and Willing did engage") Unknown.—BrSm
Duels
The duel ("The gingham dog and the calico cat") E. Field.—ArT-3—HoB—HuS-3—ReS
The duel ("Schott and Willing did engage") Unknown.—BrSm
"I took my power in my hand." E. Dickinson.—DiPe
The duel.—LiT
Duet. See Becket
Dufault, Peter Kane
At the lion's cage.—CoB
Horse and hammer.—CoB
Dugan, Alan
On Hurricane Jackson.—MoS
The **duke** of Grafton. Unknown.—GrCt
Dulce ridentem. Stephen Vincent Benét.—HaL
"**Dull** masses of dense green." See Down the Mississippi
Dunbar, Paul Laurence
Compensation.—BoA
Dawn.—BoA
The debt.—BoA—BoH—HaK
Harriet Beecher Stowe.—HaK
The haunted oak.—HaK
Life.—BoA
Lullaby.—HoB
My sort o' man.—BoA
The paradox.—HaK
The party.—BoA
The poet.—HaK
The poet and his song.—BoH
Robert Gould Shaw.—HaK
A song.—BoA—BoH
Sympathy.—AdIa—BoA
To a captious critic.—HaK
We wear the mask.—AdIa—BoA—BoH
Dunbar, Paul Laurence (about)
Dunbar. A. Spencer.—HaK
For Paul Laurence Dunbar. C. Cullen.—HaK
Epitaphs: For Paul Laurence Dunbar.—BoH
Four epitaphs.—BoA
The poet and his song. P. L. Dunbar.—BoH
Dunbar, William
Lament for the makaris.—GrCt
To the city of London.—GrCt
To the Princess Margaret Tudor.—GrS
Dunbar. Anne Spencer.—HaK
Duncan, Mary Lundie
Child's prayer.—GrT
Duncan, Thomas W.
Village portrait.—ThA
Duncan Davison. Robert Burns.—BuPr
Duncan Gray. Robert Burns.—BuPr
"**Duncan** Gray cam' here to woo." See Duncan Gray
The **dunce** ("Miss Bell was almost six years old") Elizabeth Turner.—VrF
The **dunce** ("Ring the bells, ring") Mother Goose.—BrMg
The **dunce** ("This is a sight to give us pain") Mary Elliott.—VrF
The **dunce** of a kitten. Ann and Jane Taylor.—VrF
Dunsany, Lord (Edward John Moreton Drax Plunkett)
Bringing him up.—CoBb
Dunstan, Saint (about)
The devil. Mother Goose.—BrMg
"**Durable** bird pulls interminable worm." See To a tidelands oil pump
Durem, Ray
Award.—AdIa
"**During** that summer." See Reflections on a gift of watermelon pickle received from a friend called Felicity
"**During** the strike, the ponies were brought up." See The ponies
Durston, Georgia Roberts
The hippopotamus.—ArT-3
The wolf.—ArT-3
Dusk ("The sunset bloomed") Eve Recht.—LeM
Dusk ("They tell me she is beautiful, my city") DuBose Heyward.—PaH
Duskin, Marc
Grownups.—LeM
Dust
Common dust. G. D. Johnson.—BoA
Dust. S. K. Russell.—BrSm—DuR
Dust bowl. R. A. Davis.—AdIa
Dust to dust. T. Hood.—BrSm
A peck of gold. R. Frost.—BoH—LaPd
"This quiet dust was gentlemen and ladies." E. Dickinson.—DiL
This quiet dust.—McWs
Two somewhat different epigrams. L. Hughes.—HaK
Dust. Sydney King Russell.—BrSm—DuR
"**Dust** always blowing about the town." See A peck of gold
Dust bowl. Robert A. Davis.—AdIa
"**Dust** in a cloud, blinding weather." See Apples and water
Dust of snow. Robert Frost.—ArT-3—LaPd—ReBs—ThA—TuW
Dust to dust. Thomas Hood.—BrSm
The **dustman** ("Bring out your dust! the dustman cries") William Darton, rev. by Ann and Jane Taylor.—VrF
The **dustman** ("Every Thursday morning") Clive Sansom.—StF

The **dusty** miller ("Hey the dusty miller") Robert Burns.—BuH
Dusty miller ("Oh the little rusty dusty miller") Mother Goose.—BrMg
"O the dusty miller."—MoB
A **Dutch** picture. Henry Wadsworth Longfellow. —LoPl
The **dutchess'** lullaby. See Alice's adventures in wonderland—"Speak roughly to your little boy"
The **dutiful** mariner. Wallace Irwin.—CoSs
Duty. See also Conduct of life
The dutiful mariner. W. Irwin.—CoSs
The legend beautiful. From Tales of a wayside inn. H. W. Longfellow.—LoPl
Ode to duty. W. Wordsworth.—WoP
Song of the Chattahoochee. S. Lanier.—BrA—CoBn
Dwarfs
Dwarves' song. From The hobbit. J. R. R. Tolkien.—LiT
The people of Tao-chow. Po Chü-i.—GrCt
The stone troll. From The hobbit. J. R. R. Tolkien.—LiT
Dwarves' song. See The hobbit
"**D'ye** ken John Peel with his coat so gray." See John Peel
Dyer, Edward
The lowest trees have tops.—HoL
A modest love.—CoBl
A modest love. See The lowest trees have tops
Dyer, John
Grongar hill.—ClF (sel.)—GrCt
The **dyer.** Unknown.—GrCt
The **dying** crane. Michael Drayton.—ReO
The **dying** swan. Unknown.—GrCt
Dyment, Clifford
Meeting.—CoB (sel.)
The snow.—SmM
The winter trees.—ClF

E

"**E** is the egotist dread." Oliver Herford.—BrLl
"**E** is the escalator." See All around the town
E-Yeh-Shuré (Louise Abeita)
Beauty.—ArT-3
"**Each** birthday wish." See The wish
"**Each** known mile comes late." See The train runs late to Harlem
"**Each** morning." See Hymn for Lanie Poo
"**Each** season, more lovely." Yakamochi.—BaS
"**Each** that we lose takes part of us." Emily Dickinson.—DiPe
"**Each** time a wave breaks." Nissha, tr. fr. the Japanese by R. H. Blyth.—LeMw
"**Each** time that I look at a fine landscape." Po Chü-i, tr. fr. the Chinese by Arthur Waley. —LeMw
"**Eagerly.**" See Four glimpses of night
The **eagle** ("He clasps the crag with crooked hands") Alfred Tennyson.—BlO—BoGj—CoB —LaPd—TeP—TuW
The **eagle** ("The sun's rays") Unknown, tr. fr. the Papago.—LeO
The **eagle** and the mole. Elinor Wylie.—ReO
Eagle plain. Robert Francis.—BrA
The **eagle** that is forgotten. Vachel Lindsay.—LiP
Eagles
Birkett's eagle. D. S. Howard.—CaMb
"The clouds float by." J. O'Donnell.—LeM
The eagle ("He clasps the crag with crooked hands") A. Tennyson.—BlO—BoGj—CoB—LaPd—TeP—TuW
The eagle ("The sun's rays") Unknown.—LeO
The eagle and the mole. E. Wylie.—ReO
Eagle plain. R. Francis.—BrA
Eagles. V. Bashkin.—CoB
"The red sun sinks low." Boncho.—BeCs
"See how the doves flutter and huddle." Unknown.—DoC
Sunset. V. Lindsay.—ReS
"There are the eagles crying, swooping from side to side." Unknown.—LeO
Eagles. Vasily Bashkin, tr. fr. the Russian by Babette Deutsch.—CoB
"The **eagle's** shadow runs across the plain." See Zebra
"**Eaper** Weaper, chimney sweeper." Mother Goose.—ReMg
Earhart, Amelia
Courage.—ThA
Early astir. Herbert Read.—CaD
Early dark. Elizabeth Jane Coatsworth.—CoSb
"**Early,** early I walked in the city." See Early astir
"**Early** I rose." See Papago love song
"**Early** in the morning." See The dream woman
"**Early** in the morning, before the day began." See The angel in the apple tree
The **early** morning. Hilaire Belloc.—CoBn
Early one morning ("Early one morning in May I set out") Edward Thomas.—ThG
Early one morning ("Early one morning, just as the sun was rising") Unknown.—GrCt
"**Early** one morning in May I set out." See Early one morning
"**Early** one morning, just as the sun was rising." See Early one morning
Early spring ("I've looked in all the places") Marchette Chute.—BrSg
Early spring ("Once more the heavenly power") Alfred Tennyson.—TeP
Early supper. Barbara Howes.—BoGj
"**Early** this morning." See The strangers
Ears
"The ears of barley, too." Issa, tr. fr. the Japanese by R. H. Blyth.—IsF
Someone at my house said. J. Ciardi.—CiYk
Earth. See World
Earth. See "If this little world to-night"

The **earth** ("Did you know, did you know") Eleanor Farjeon.—FaT
Earth ("A planet doesn't explode of itself, said drily") John Hall Wheelock.—DuR
Earth and sky ("O potent earth, and heaven God-built") Euripides, tr. fr. the Greek by C. M. Bowra.—PlE
Earth and sky ("Oh sky, you look so drear") Eleanor Farjeon.—BrSg
Earth and the kisses of men. Elizabeth Jane Coatsworth.—CoDh
"The **earth** has drunk the snow." See The fisherman
"**Earth** has not anything to show more fair." See Composed upon Westminster bridge, September 3, 1802
"The **earth** is lighter." See Song for snow
"The **earth** is not an old woman." Devendra Satyarthi, tr. fr. the Panjabi by P. Machwe. —AlPi
The **earth** is the Lord's. See Psalms—Psalm 24
"The **earth** is the Lord's, and the fulness thereof." See Psalms—Psalm 24
"The **earth** is what gives us life." See The good earth
"The **earth** lies here in giant folds and creases." See High wheat country
Earth, moon, and sun. Claudia Lewis.—LeP
"**Earth** out of earth is worldly wrought." See Earth upon earth
"**Earth** rais'd up her head." See Earth's answer
"**Earth,** receive an honored guest." See In memory of W. B. Yeats
Earth upon earth. Unknown.—GrCt
Earth's answer. William Blake.—BlP
Earthy anecdote. Wallace Stevens.—BoGj
"An **eartly** nourris sits and sings." See The Great Silkie of Sule Skerry
Earwig. See The horny-goloch
East Anglian bathe. John Betjeman.—MoS
East river, New York
East river. R. Thomas.—BrA
East river. Rosemary Thomas.—BrA
Easter
At Easter time. L. E. Richards.—HoB
Easter ("The air is like a butterfly") J. Kilmer. —ArT-3—LaPd—LaPh
Easter ("On Easter morn") H. Conkling.—ArT-3
Easter hymn. A. E. Housman.—PlE
Easter lily. M. B. Miller.—LaPh
Easter morning. A. Fisher.—LaPh
Easter parade. M. Chute.—LaPh
Easter Sunday. S. Scottus.—LiT
For Jim, Easter eve. A. Spencer.—BoA
In memoriam, Easter, 1915. E. Thomas.—ThG
The little black hen. A. A. Milne.—MiC
Loveliest of trees. From A Shropshire lad. A. E. Housman.—BlO—CoBn—HuS-3—SmM —TuW
"Loveliest of trees, the cherry now."—GrCt
Meeting the Easter bunny. R. B. Bennett.—ArT-3
Seven stanzas at Easter. J. Updike.—PlE
Time for rabbits. A. Fisher.—FiC—LaPh
What if. M. C. Livingston.—LiC
Easter ("The air is like a butterfly") Joyce Kilmer.—ArT-3—LaPd—LaPh
Easter ("On Easter morn") Hilda Conkling.—ArT-3
Easter hymn. Alfred Edward Housman.—PlE
Easter lily. Mary Britton Miller.—LaPh
Easter morning. Aileen Fisher.—LaPh
Easter parade. Marchette Chute.—LaPh
Easter Sunday. Sedulius Scottus, tr. fr. the Latin by Helen Waddell.—LiT
The **eastern** gate. Unknown, tr. fr. the Chinese by Arthur Waley.—LeMw
Eastman, Max
Rainy song.—BoH
"**Eastward** I stand, mercies I beg." Unknown, tr. fr. the Anglo-Saxon by Sarah Plotz.—PlE
Eastwick, Ivy O.
Berries.—BrSg
Dark Danny.—ArT-3
First snow.—ArT-3
Halloween.—HoB—LaPh
"Ladybird, ladybird (where do you hide)."—BrSg
Midsummer magic.—ArT-3
Shadow dance.—ArT-3—LaP
Snow in spring.—LaPd
Thanksgiving.—BrSg
Three don'ts.—BrSg
The three horses.—HoB
Waking time.—ArT-3
Where's Mary.—ArT-3
An **easy** decision. Kenneth Patchen.—DuS—HaL
"**Eat** at pleasure." Mother Goose.—AgH
Eat-it-all Elaine. Kaye Starbird.—LaPd
Eating. See Food and eating
"**Eating** a meal." Issa, tr. fr. the Japanese.—LeOw
Eating fish. George Johnston.—DoW
"**Eating** the songbird, does it eat." See The snowy owl
Eberhart, Richard
Chiliasm.—PlE
"Fishing for snakes."—LiT
"Go to the shine that's on a tree."—HoL—LiT
La Crosse at ninety miles an hour.—BrA
Man is God's nature.—PlE
Rumination.—HoL—SmM
Ebright, Fredrick
Memorial to the great beautiful self-sacrificing advertisers.—HiL
The **ecchoing** green. William Blake.—BlP
Ecclesiastes, sels. Bible, Old Testament
"Cast thy bread upon the waters."—ArT-3
Remember now thy Creator.—GrCt
Ecclesiasticus, sel. Bible, Apocrypha
Let us now praise famous men.—GrCt
Echo ("Seven sweet notes") Walter De La Mare. —DeBg
Echo ("Who called? I said, and the words") Walter De La Mare.—McWs
Echo ("You") Mildred Weston.—CoBn

Echoes
The bugle song. From The princess. A. Tennyson.—HoB—HuS-3
Blow, bugle, blow.—GrCt
Song.—BlO
"The splendor falls on castle walls."—ArT-3—BoGj
The splendour falls.—CoR
The ecchoing green. W. Blake.—BlP
Echo ("Seven sweet notes") W. De La Mare.—DeBg
Echo ("Who called? I said, and the words") W. De La Mare.—McWs
Echo ("You") M. Weston.—CoBn
The echoing cliff. A. Young.—ReBs
"In the wintry grove." Issa.—LeOw
"The nightingales sing." Ukō.—LeI
The **echoing** cliff. Andrew Young.—ReBs
Eclipse. Claudia Lewis.—LeP
Eclogue. Edward Lear.—LiT
Ecstasy. Rachel Annand Taylor.—GrS
The **Eddystone** light. Unknown.—CoSs
Edelman, Katherine
Irish grandmother.—BrA
Eden, Patience
Epitaph for a grim woman.—McWs
Eden, Garden of
Expulsion from Paradise. From Paradise lost. J. Milton.—GrCt
Satan journeys to the Garden of Eden. From Paradise lost. J. Milton.—GrCt
Edey, Marion
The ant village.—ArT-3
Christmas eve.—LaPh
The jolly woodchuck.—ArT-3—LaPd
The little fox.—ArT-3
Open the door.—ArT-3
So many monkeys.—ArT-3
"Trot along, pony."—ArT-3
Edinburgh, Scotland
Edinburgh. A. Noyes.—PaH
Edinburgh. Alfred Noyes.—PaH
Edison, Thomas A. (about)
And yet fools say. G. S. Holmes.—ArT-3
Edouard. See "A bugler named Dougal MacDougal"
Edsall, Florence Small
Stars.—ThA
"**Edward** the third had seven sons." See Ballad of the banners
Eeka, neeka. Walter De La Mare.—DeBg
"**Eeka,** neeka, leeka, lee." See Eeka, neeka
The **eel.** See A double limerick or twiner
Eels
A double limerick or twiner. W. De La Mare.—BrLl
The eel.—BrSm
Song of hate for eels. A. Guiterman.—CoB
"**Eftsoons** they saw an hideous host array'd." See The faerie queene—Sea monsters
The **egg.** Laura E. Richards.—ArT-3
Eggs. See also Birds—Eggs and nests
"As I was walking in a field of wheat." Mother Goose.—BrMg—OpF
"As white as milk (as soft as silk)." Mother Goose.—OpF
The egg. L. E. Richards.—ArT-3
The hen and the carp. I. Serraillier.—CoB
"Humpty Dumpty and his brother." Mother Goose.—OpF
"Humpty Dumpty ligs in t' beck." Mother Goose.—OpF
"Humpty Dumpty sat on a spoon." Mother Goose.—OpF
"Humpty Dumpty sat on a wall . . . (all the king's horses)." Mother Goose.—GrT—OpF—WiMg
Humpty Dumpty.—BrMg
Mother Goose rhymes, 25.—HoB
"Humpty Dumpty sat on a wall . . . (four score men)." Mother Goose.—HuS-3—OpF
"Humpty Dumpty went to town." Mother Goose.—OpF
"In marble halls as white as milk." Mother Goose.—BrMg—GrCt—HuS-3—OpF
In marble halls.—ReOn—SmM
"A little egg." T. Anthony.—LeM
"A long white barn." Unknown.—GrCt
"Old Mother Goose, when." Mother Goose.—WiMg
Old Mother Goose and the golden egg.—BrMg
"There's a wee wee house." Unknown.—MoB
"Wirgele-Wargele, auf der bank." Mother Goose.—OpF
Ego. Philip Booth.—DuS
The **egotistical** orchestra. Eve Merriam.—MeI
Egotists. See Pride and vanity
Egret dyke. Wang Wei, tr. fr. the Chinese by Chang Yin-nan and Lewis C. Walmsley.—LeMw
Egrets. See Herons
Egrets. Judith Wright.—BoGj
Egypt
The sphinx speaks. F. Saltus.—PaH
Egyptians
Love lyric. Unknown.—HoL
"**Eight** are the lights." Ilo Orleans.—ThA
Eight oars and a coxswain. Arthur Guiterman.—MoS
"**Eight** oars compel." See Eight oars and a coxswain
"**Eight** o'clock." Christina Georgina Rossetti.—ArT-3
"**Eight** o'clock bells are ringing." Unknown.—MoB
XVIII. See The third book of ayres
"**Eily,** Eily." See Hushing song
El capitan-general. Charles Godfrey Leland.—CoSs
El hombre. William Carlos Williams.—HoL
Elder belder. Mother Goose.—ReOn
"**Elder** belder, limber lock." See Elder belder
The **elder** tree. Unknown.—GrCt
Elder trees
The elder tree. Unknown.—GrCt
Eldorado. Edgar Allan Poe.—PaH—PoP

Eldridge, Paul
Wang Peng's recommendation for improving the people.—BrSm
Electra
A conjuration, to Electra. R. Herrick.—GrS
Electricity
And yet fools say. G. S. Holmes.—ArT-3
Death on a live wire. M. Baldwin.—CaMb
Elegiac stanzas, suggested by a picture of Peele castle, in a storm, painted by Sir George Beaumont. William Wordsworth.—WoP
Elegies. See Laments
Elegies, sel. Ovid
To verse let kings give place, tr. fr. the Latin by Christopher Marlowe.—GrCt
Elegy. Chidiock Tichborne.—GrCt
An **elegy** for a dead child in the street. Raghavendra Rao.—AlPi
Elegy for a dead soldier. Karl Shapiro.—HiL
Elegy for a jazz musician. Ernest Kroll.—DuS
Elegy for a nature poet. Howard Nemerov.—CoBn
Elegy for Jog. John Ciardi.—DuR
Elegy in a country churchyard. Gilbert Keith Chesterton.—McWs
An **elegy** on the death of a mad dog. Oliver Goldsmith.—BrSm—CoR
Elegy on Willie Nicol's mare. Robert Burns.—BuPr
The **elephant** ("The elephant grows very old") Conrad Aiken.—AiC
The **elephant** ("Here comes the elephant") Herbert Asquith.—ArT-3—StF
Elephant ("In his travels, the elephant") David McFadden.—DoW
The **elephant** ("When people called this beast to mind") Hilaire Belloc.—ArT-3
The **elephant** ("With wrinkled hide and great frayed ears") See A circus garland
"The **elephant** always carries his trunk." See The elephant's trunk
"The **elephant** grows very old." See The elephant
The **elephant** knocked the ground. Adrian Mitchell.—SmM
"The **elephant** knocked the ground with a stick." See The elephant knocked the ground
The **elephant**; or, The force of habit. Alfred Edward Housman.—LiT
"**Elephant** who brings death." See Erin (Elephant)
Elephants
The blind men and the elephant. J. G. Saxe.—BoH
"The dark gray clouds." N. Belting.—LaPd
The elephant ("The elephant grows very old") C. Aiken.—AiC
The elephant ("Here comes the elephant") H. Asquith.—ArT-3—StF
Elephant ("In his travels, the elephant") D. McFadden.—DoW
The elephant ("When people call this beast to mind") H. Belloc.—ArT-3
The elephant ("With wrinkled hide and great frayed ears") From A circus garland. R. Field.—HuS-3
The elephant knocked the ground. A. Mitchell.—SmM
The elephant; or, The force of habit. A. E. Housman.—LiT
The elephant's trunk. A. Wilkins.—ArT-3
Eletelephony. L. E. Richards.—ArT-3—BoGj—HoB—LaPd
Erin (Elephant). Unknown.—ReO
The handiest nose. A. Fisher.—FiC
Holding hands. L. M. Link.—ArT-3—LaP
"I asked my mother for fifteen cents." Unknown.—ArT-3
"In this jungle." M. C. Livingston.—LiC
Oliphaunt. From The adventures of Tom Bombadil. J. R. R. Tolkien.—ClF
Pete at the zoo. G. Brooks.—HaL—LaPd
Plain talk for a pachyderm. P. Bennett.—CoB
Tehachapi mountains. M. C. Livingston.—LiC
"An **elephant's** nose." See The handiest nose
The **elephant's** trunk. Alice Wilkins.—ArT-3
"**Elephants** walking." See Holding hands
Eletelephony. Laura E. Richards.—ArT-3—BoGj—HoB—LaPd
Eleusis, Greece
The greater mystery. J. M. O'Hara.—PaH
The **elf** and the dormouse. Oliver Herford.—ArT-3—HoB—ThA
"**Elf,** elf, long-nosed elf." See Long-nosed elf
"An **elf** sat on a twig." See The elf singing
The **elf** singing. William Allingham.—HuS-3
"**Elf,** will you sell me your berries bright." See Elfin berries
Elfin berries. Rachel Field.—AgH
Eliot, T. (Thomas) S. (Stearns)
"And now you live dispersed on ribbon roads." See The rock
Ash Wednesday, sel.
Lady, three white leopards.—GrS
Aunt Helen.—McWs
Cape Ann. See Landscapes
Death by water. See The waste land
The dry salvages, sel.
"I do not know much about gods; but I think that the river."—ArT-3
Forgive us, O Lord. See Murder in the cathedral
Growltiger's last stand.—CoR
"I do not know much about gods; but I think that the river." See The dry salvages
"If humility and purity be not in the heart." See The rock
Journey of the Magi.—PlE
Lady, three white leopards. See Ash Wednesday
Landscapes, sels.
Cape Ann.—BoGj—CaD—HoL
New Hampshire.—HaL
The love song of J. Alfred Prufrock, sel.
"The yellow fog that rubs its back upon the window-panes."—ArT-3
Yellow fog.—HaL

The **enchanted** spring. George Darley.—CoBn
Enchantment
All, all a-lonely. Unknown.—GrCt
The enchanted knight. E. Muir.—CaD
The griesly wife. J. Manifold.—CaMb
The laily worm and the machrel of the sea. Unknown.—GrCt—ReO
Lonesome water. R. Helton.—BrA
The milk-white dove. Unknown.—GrCt
My hat. S. Smith.—SmM
The reverie of poor Susan. W. Wordsworth.—WoP
Tom. O. Sitwell.—CaD
The two witches. R. Graves.—CaD
What the gray cat sings. A. Guiterman.—LiT—ReS
Encountering. Mary Jo Fuller.—BaH
Encounters with a Doppelganger, sel. George D. Painter
A meeting.—SmM
The **end** of man is his beauty. LeRoi Jones.—BoA
The **end** of summer. Edna St Vincent Millay.—CoBn
The **end** of the world. Archibald MacLeish.—McWs
End of winter. Eve Merriam.—MeI
The **ending** of the year. Eleanor Farjeon.—FaA
"An **endless** line of splendor." See Foreign missions in battle array
Endurance. See Perseverance
Endymion, sel. John Keats
A thing of beauty.—HuS-3
Enemies
"Mine enemy is growing old." E. Dickinson.—DiPe
Eng, Betty
Rain.—BaH
Engine. James S. Tippett.—HoB
The **engineer.** A. A. Milne.—MiC
Engineers. See also Railroads
Casey Jones. Unknown.—BlO—HiL—McWs
The engineer. A. A. Milne.—MiC
England
Adlestrop. E. Thomas.—BlO—BoGj—PaH—ThG
An American in England. E. Wylie.—PaH
Brumana. J. E. Flecker.—PaH
The crystal cabinet. W. Blake.—BlP
Elegy in a country churchyard. G. K. Chesterton.—McWs
England ("No lovelier hills than thine have laid") W. De La Mare.—PaH
England ("This royal throne of kings, this scepter'd isle") From King Richard II. W. Shakespeare.—ShS
This England.—PaH
"The fields from Islington to Marybone." From Jerusalem I. W. Blake.—GrCt
The frolic mariners of Devon. From Britannia's pastorals. W. Browne.—GrCt
The Georges. W. S. Landor.—GrCt
The ghost of Roger Casement. W. B. Yeats.—YeR
"Hey ding a ding, and ho ding a ding." Mother Goose.—OpF
Home-thoughts, from abroad. R. Browning.—BrP—CoBn—PaH
Home-thoughts, from the sea. R. Browning.—BrP
"I travelled among unknown men." W. Wordsworth.—WoP
The island. C. Morley.—PaH
Jerusalem. W. Blake.—BlP (sel.)
London, 1802. W. Wordsworth.—WoP
Milton. W. Blake.—BlP (sel.)
Jerusalem.—PlE (sel.)
The month of May. From The knight of the burning pestle. F. Beaumont and J. Fletcher.—GrCt
The path to Shottery. C. O. Skinner.—ThA
Traveling America. J. Struther.—BrA
Victoria. E. Farjeon.—BlO
A visit to Chelsea college. H. S. Horsley.—VrF
When I have borne in memory. W. Wordsworth.—WoP
England—History. See also European war, 1914-1918; French and Indian war, 1754-1763; Naval battles; Warships; World war, 1939-1945; also names of battles, as Agincourt, Battle of, 1415
America. W. Blake.—BlP
The ballad of banners. J. Lehmann.—CaMb
"Barnum and Bayley." Unknown.—MoB
The burial of Sir John Moore. C. Wolfe.—CoR
The burial of Sir John Moore after Corunna.—GrCt
Flodden. From Marmion. W. Scott.—ClF
Hervé Riel. R. Browning.—CoSs
Louisburg. Unknown.—HiL
"O what's the rhyme to porringer." Unknown.—MoB
Ode to Hengist and Horsa. R. Jeffers.—GrS
The song of the western men. R. S. Hawker.—CoR
England ("No lovelier hills than thine have laid") Walter De La Mare.—PaH
England ("This royal throne of kings, this scepter'd isle") See King Richard II
Engle, Paul
American child.—BrA
In a bar near Shibuya Station, Tokyo.—BrA
The new world.—BrA (sel.)
English, Thomas Dunn
The battle of New Orleans.—HiL
The **English** in Virginia. Charles Reznikoff.—GrS
Englishmen
"A Briton who shot at his king." D. Ross.—BrSm
"Fee, fi, fo, fum." Mother Goose.—BrF
"Fe, fi, fo, fum."—BrSm
The giant.—BrMg
An **englyn** on a yellow greyhound. William Barnes.—ReO
Engraved on the collar of a dog, which I gave to his royal highness. Alexander Pope.—GrCt

An **enigma**. Edgar Allan Poe.—PoP
"The **enigmatic** moon has at long last died." See Stevedore
Enitharmon's song. See Vala
"**Enjoy** the pleasure." See Mahabharata—Precepts
An **enjoyable** evening in the village near the lake. Lin Ho-ching, tr. by Max Perleberg.—LeMw
Ensign, Deborah
Mirror, mirror.—LeM
Ensnare the clouds. Elizabeth Jane Coatsworth.—CoDh
Enter November. Eleanor Farjeon.—FaA
Envoi. Algernon Charles Swinburne.—BoGj
White butterflies.—LaPd
Envy. See also Jealousy
"I envy seas whereon he rides." E. Dickinson.—DiPe
Mary. W. Blake.—BlP
Oh lucky Jim. Unknown.—GrCt
An **epicurean** ode. John Hall.—GrS
Epigram ("Hail, young lion, I would say a word") Viryamitra, tr. fr. the Sanskrit by Daniel H. H. Ingalls.—AlPi
Epigram ("Isn't it") Alfred Kreymborg.—CoBl
Epilogue. See Asolando
Epilogue to the adventures while preaching the gospel of beauty. Vachel Lindsay.—LiP
Epistle to Dr Arbuthnot, sels. Alexander Pope
Sporus.—GrCt
Why did I write?—GrCt
Epistle to James Smith. Robert Burns.—BuPr
Epistrophe. LeRoi Jones.—HaK
Epitaph ("Here he lies moulding") Leslie Mellichamp.—BrSm
Epitaph ("Insured for every accident") Richard Armour.—BrSm
Epitaph for a godly man's tomb. Robert Wild.—GrCt
Epitaph for a grim woman. Patience Eden.—McWs
Epitaph for a postal clerk. X. J. Kennedy.—BrSm
Epitaph for any New Yorker. Christopher Morley.—BrSm
Epitaph of Graunde Amoure. See The palace of pleasure
Epitaph on a hare. William Cowper.—BlO—CoB
Epitaph on a tyrant. W. H. Auden.—HoL
Epitaph on Elizabeth, L. H. Ben Jonson.—HoL
Epitaph on Holy Willie. Robert Burns.—BuPr
Epitaph on John Dove, innkeeper. Robert Burns.—BuPr
Epitaph on John Knott. Unknown.—BrSm—GrCt
Epitaph on Lady Ossory's bullfinch. Horace Walpole.—GrCt—ReO
Epitaph on Martha Snell. Unknown.—BlO
Epitaph on the proofreader of the Encyclopedia Britannica. Christopher Morley.—BrSm
Epitaphs
At Boot Hill in Tombstone, Arizona. Unknown.—BrSm
At Great Torrington, Devon. Unknown.—BrSm
A bird's epitaph. M. Armstrong.—ReBs
Cassie O'Lang. Unknown.—BrSm
Epitaph ("Here he lies moulding") L. Mellichamp.—BrSm
Epitaph ("Insured for every accident") R. Armour.—BrSm
Epitaph for a godly man's tomb. R. Wild.—GrCt
Epitaph for a grim woman. P. Eden.—McWs
Epitaph for a postal clerk. X. J. Kennedy.—BrSm
Epitaph for any New Yorker. C. Morley.—BrSm
Epitaph of Graunde Amoure. From The palace of pleasure. S. Hawes.—GrCt
Epitaph on a hare. W. Cowper.—BlO—CoB
Epitaph on a tyrant. W. H. Auden.—HoL
Epitaph on Elizabeth, L. H. B. Jonson.—HoL
Epitaph on Holy Willie. R. Burns.—BuPr
Epitaph on John Dove, innkeeper. R. Burns.—BuPr
Epitaph on John Knott. Unknown.—BrSm—GrCt
Epitaph on Lady Ossory's bullfinch. H. Walpole.—ReO
Epitaph on Martha Snell. Unknown.—BlO
Epitaph on the proofreader of the Encyclopedia Britannica. C. Morley.—BrSm
For my grandmother. C. Cullen
Four epitaphs.—BoA
For Paul Laurence Dunbar. C. Cullen.—HaK
Epitaphs: For Paul Laurence Dunbar.—BoH
Four epitaphs.—BoA
Here lies my wife. J. Dryden.—BrSm
In memory of Anna Hopewell. Unknown.—BrSm
John Bun. Unknown.—BrSm
John Coil. Unknown.—BrSm
Lester Young. T. Joans.—BoA
Manhattan epitaphs: Lawyer. A. Kreymborg.—LaC
On a monument in France which marks the last resting place of an army mule. Unknown.—BrSm
On a tired housewife. Unknown.—SmM
On an old toper buried in Durham churchyard, England. Unknown.—BrSm
On Samuel Pease. Unknown.—BrSm
On the Reverend Jonathan Doe. Unknown.—GrCt
Outside the chancel door. Unknown.—BrSm
The Spoon River anthology, sels. E. L. Masters
Anne Rutledge.—BrA—HiL
Knowlt Hoheimer.—HoL
The village atheist.—PlE
Tombstone. L. M. and J. L. Hymes, Jr.—ArT-3
Upon a child. R. Herrick.—SmM
Upon a maid. R. Herrick.—GrCt
Wang Peng's recommendation for improving the people. P. Eldridge.—BrSm
"Within this grave do lie." Unknown.—BrSm
An **epithalamium** on the Lady Elizabeth and Count Palatine being married on St Valentine's day, sel. John Donne

Hail, Bishop Valentine.—GrCt
Epstein, Amy
The dew.—LeM
"**Ere** yet the sun is high." See The iris
Erie canal
The Erie canal. Unknown.—BrA
The **Erie** canal. Unknown.—BrA
Erin (Elephant). Unknown, tr. fr. the Yoruba by Ulli Beier.—ReO
Ermine
"Said an envious, erudite ermine." O. Herford.—BrLl
The **errand.** Harry Behn.—BeH
Erulkar, Mary
The third continent.—AlPi
Erwin, John
Death.—LeM
Esbensen, Barbara Juster
Prediction.—ArT-3
Seascape.—ArT-3
Escalators
Alligator on the escalator. E. Merriam.—LaC—MeC
"E is the escalator." From All around the town. P. McGinley.—ArT-3
Escape at bedtime. Robert Louis Stevenson.—ArT-3—ReS
"**Escape** me." See Life in a love
Escapes
I, too, I, too. J. H. Wheelock.—SmM
The owl. E. Thomas.—GrCt—ReBs—ThG
Eskimo chant. Unknown, tr. fr. the Eskimo by Knud Rasmussen.—DoW
"There is joy in."—LeO
Eskimos
Eskimo chant. Unknown.—DoW
"There is joy in."—LeO
"I arise from rest with movements swift." Unknown.—LeO
Manerathiak's song. Unknown.—DoW
May. N. Belting.—BeCm
"My arms, they wave high in the air." Unknown.—LeO
The rousing canoe song. H. Fraser.—DoW
The train dogs. Pauline Johnson.—DoW
The wind has wings. Unknown.—DoW
An **essay** on criticism, sel. Alexander Pope
A little learning.—GrCt
"**Essential** oils are wrung." Emily Dickinson.—DiPe
"**Estella,** Estella, they're cooking up paella." See Song in praise of paella
Esthonia
October. N. Belting.—BeCm
"**Estranged** from beauty none can be." Emily Dickinson.—DiPe
"**Eternities**—now numbering six or seven." See Saint Peter relates an incident of Resurrection day
Eternity. See Time
Eternity. William Blake.—BlP
"**Eternity's** low voice." Mark Van Doren.—PlE
Ethinthus, queen of waters. See Europe
"**Ethinthus,** queen of water, how thou shinest in the sky." See Europe—Ethinthus, queen of waters
Etiquette
An alphabet of famous Goops. G. Burgess.—CoBb (sel.)
Atomic courtesy. E. Jacobson.—BrSm
The bath. H. Graham.—BrSm
The gallant highwayman. J. De Mille.—DoW
The good girl. E. Turner.—VrF
"A lady there was of Antigua." C. Monkhouse.—BrLl
Manners. K. Greenaway.—GrT
"Manners in the dining room." Mother Goose.—AgH
Of courtesy. A. Guiterman.—ArT-3
On politeness. H. S. Horsley.—VrF
Our polite parents. C. Wells.—CoBb
Politeness. E. Turner.—VrF
"A rather polite man of Hawarden." Unknown.—BrLl
Sit up when you sit down. J. Ciardi.—CiYk
Table manners. G. Burgess.—CoBb
"There was a young man so benighted." Unknown.—BrLl
"There was an old lady of Chertsey." E. Lear.—BlO—BrLl
"There's a dowager near Sneden Landing." Unknown.—BrLl
Under-the-table manners. Unknown.—StF
The visitor. K. Pyle.—CoBb
Zoo manners. E. Mathias.—StF
Etter, Dave
From a 19th century Kansas painter's notebook.—DuS
Old Dubuque.—BrA
Snow country.—BrA
Étude géographique. Stoddard King.—BrA
Euclid
Euclid. V. Lindsay.—HoL—LiT
Euclid. Vachel Lindsay.—HoL—LiT
Eulalie—A song. Edgar Allan Poe.—PoP
Euripides
The breed of athletes.—MoS
Earth and sky.—PlE
There are no gods.—PlE
Europa
Europa. W. Plomer.—CaMb
Europa. William Plomer.—CaMb
Europe. See also names of European countries, as France
America for me. H. Van Dyke.—ThA
Europe and America. D. Ignatow.—BrA
Europe, sel. William Blake
Ethinthus, queen of waters.—GrCt
Europe and America. David Ignatow.—BrA
European war, 1914-1918. See also Veteran's day
Abraham Lincoln walks at midnight. V. Lindsay.—BoH—BrA—HiL—LiP
And there was a great calm. T. Hardy.—GrCt
Blackout. A. Gregor.—GrS
Early one morning. E. Thomas.—ThG
Everyone sang. S. Sassoon.—HaL—SmM

European war, 1914-1918—*Continued*
Hugh Selwyn Mauberley. E. Pound.—HiL
"I have a rendezvous with death." A. Seeger. —HiL
In Flanders fields. J. McCrae.—ThA
In memoriam, Easter, 1915. E. Thomas.—ThG
Lights out. E. Thomas.—ThG
The merciful hand. V. Lindsay.—LiP
1936. S. V. Benét.—McWs
"No one cares less than I." E. Thomas.—ThG
The statue of old Andrew Jackson. V. Lindsay.—LiP
"This is no case of petty right or wrong." E. Thomas.—ThG
Euwer, Anthony
"For beauty I am not a star."—BrLl
"The hands they were made to assist."—BrLl
"No matter how grouchy you're feeling."—BrLl
Evangeline, sel. Henry Wadsworth Longfellow
Prologue.—LoPl
Evans, F. Gwynne
Little Thomas.—CoBb
Matilda.—CoBb
Evans, Mari
"And the old women gathered."—HaK
The emancipation of George-Hector (a colored turtle).—BoA
"If there be sorrow."—HaK
The rebel.—AdIa—BoA
Status symbol.—AdIa
When in Rome.—BoA
The world I see.—HaK
Eve. See Adam and Eve
Eve, sel. Christina Georgina Rossetti
The animals mourn with Eve.—ReO
Eve. Ralph Hodgson.—SmM
The **eve** of Christmas. James Kirkup.—CaD
The **eve** of Crécy. William Morris.—GrS
The **eve** of St Agnes. John Keats.—CoD
Eve speaks to Adam. See Paradise lost
"**Eve,** with her basket was." See Eve
"**Even** among insects, in this world." Issa, tr. fr. the Japanese by R. H. Blyth.—IsF
"**Even** as the snow fell." Issa, tr. fr. the Japanese by Lewis Mackensie.—LeMw
"**Even** for the space of a flash." Unknown.—BaS
"**Even** now." See Fifty stanzas for a thief
Even numbers. Carl Sandburg.—LaC
"**Even** on a small island." Issa, tr. fr. the Japanese by R. H. Blyth.—IsF
"**Even** stones under." Onitsura, tr. fr. the Japanese by Harry Behn.—BeCs
Even such is time. Walter Raleigh.—GrCt
"**Even** such is time, which takes in trust." See Even such is time
"**Even** the shrewd and bitter." See Rhymes to be traded for bread—Prologue
"**Even** though." See Scat scitten
Evening. See also Night
"At twilight." E. J. Coatsworth.—CoDh
"Blue evening falls." Unknown.—LeO
Calm of evening. Hsieh T'iao.—LeMw
Child's evening hymn. S. Baring-Gould.—ReS
Chill of the eve. J. Stephens.—StS
An enjoyable evening in the village near the lake. Lin Ho-ching.—LeMw
Evening ("And when night comes they will sing serenades") W. J. Turner.—PaH
Evening ("The birds have hid, the winds are low") J. V. Cheney.—ReS (sel.)
Evening ("Prince Absalom and Sir Rotherham Redde") E. Sitwell.—CaMb
An evening air. S. Sen.—AlPi
Evening at the seashore. N. V. Sharma.—AlPi
Evening hymn. E. M. Roberts.—ArT-3
Evening in the Great Smokies. D. Heyward.—PaH
Evening over the forest. B. Mayor.—ClF
Evening: Ponte al Mare, Pisa. P. B. Shelley.—ClF (sel.)
Evening quatrains. C. Cotton.—GrCt
"Evening shadows touch." Buson.—BeCs
Farm yard at evening. J. Clare.—CoB (sel.)
Georgia dusk. J. Toomer.—BoA—HaK
"Hard from the southeast blows the wind." E. J. Coatsworth.—ArT-3
Hesperus. J. Stephens.—StS
In the evening. G. K. Chesterton.—LiT
Prelude I. T. S. Eliot.—ArT-3
Prelude.—CaD—LaC
Returning. Ch'en Fu.—LeMw
Senlin. From Senlin: A biography. C. Aiken. —HaL
Snow toward evening. M. Cane.—ArT-3—LaPd
Stopping by woods on a snowy evening. R. Frost.—ArT-3—BoGj—CoBn—HuS-3—LaPd
The sun is first to rise. E. J. Coatsworth.—HuS-3
"This is my rock." D. McCord.—HuS-3—LaPd —McE
To the evening star. W. Blake.—BlP—CoBn—GrCt—GrS
Twilight calm. C. G. Rossetti.—CoBn
Twilight song. J. Hunter-Duvar.—DoW
Whale at twilight. E. J. Coatsworth.—CoDh
What she said. M. Kantan.—AlPi
Evening ("And when night comes they will sing serenades") W. J. Turner.—PaH
Evening ("The birds have hid, the winds are low") John Vance Cheney.—ReS (sel.)
Evening ("Prince Absalom and Sir Rotherham Redde") Edith Sitwell.—CaMb
An **evening** air. Samar Sen, tr. fr. the Bengali by the author.—AlPi
Evening at the seashore. Nalin Vilochan Sharma, tr. fr. the Hindi by J. Mauch.—AlPi
"The **evening,** blue, voluptuous, of June." See The walk on the beach
"**Evening** brings the sparrows home." See The nightingale
Evening clouds. Dharmavir Bharati, tr. fr. the Hindi by Vidya Niwas Misra and L. E. Nathan.—AlPi
Evening hymn. Elizabeth Madox Roberts.—ArT-3
Evening in the Great Smokies. DuBose Heyward.—PaH
Evening over the forest. Beatrice Mayor.—ClF

Evening: Ponte al Mare, Pisa. Percy Bysshe Shelley.—ClF (sel.)
Evening quatrains. Charles Cotton.—GrCt
"**Evening** shadows touch." Buson, tr. fr. the Japanese by Harry Behn.—BeCs
Evening song. Fannie Stearns Davis.—ThA
The **evening** star ("Hesperus, the day is gone") John Clare.—GrCt
Evening star ("Quiet mist, the milk of dreams") Eleanor Farjeon.—FaT
"**Evenings.**" See Setting the table
"**Ever,** ever." See Why
The **everlasting** gospel. William Blake.—BlP (sel.)
Everson, Ronald
The loaves.—DoW
"**Every** branch big with it." See Snow in the suburbs
"**Every** button has a door." See About buttons
"**Every** day coming." See The sun
"**Every** day, every day." See Benjamin Franklin
"**Every** Monday." See Monday
"**Every** morning when I wake." See Under Milk Wood
"**Every** morning when the sun." See This happy day
"**Every** rose on the little tree." See The little rose tree
"**Every** spring my mother sows." See Gardeners
"**Every** spring the pussy willows." See Pussy willows
"**Every** step we walk." See Steps
"**Every** Thursday morning." See The dustman
"**Every** time I climb a tree." David McCord.—ArT-3—LaP—LaPd—McE
"**Every** time the bucks went clattering." See Earthy anecdote
"**Every** valley drinks." See Winter rain
"**Everybody** laugh." Leonard Hale.—BaH
"**Everybody** says." Dorothy Aldis.—ThA
Everyday. Linda Curry.—BaH
"**Everyday** someone dies." See Everyday
"**Everyone** grumbled. The sky was grey." See Daddy fell into the pond
"**Everyone** knows he's blind as a bat." See The umpire
Everyone sang. Siegfried Sassoon.—HaL—SmM
"**Everyone** suddenly burst out singing." See Everyone sang
"**Everything** is black and gold." See Black and gold
"**Everything** that I can spy." James Stephens.—StS
"**Everything** was white as white." See White morning
"**Everything's** been different." See The birthday child
"An **everywhere** of silver." Emily Dickinson.—DiPe
"**Evie-ovie.**" See Skipping
Evil
The mask of evil. B. Brecht.—LiT
The **evil** eye. John Ciardi.—CaMb
Ewing, Juliana Horatia
A friend in the garden.—BrSg—HuS-3
Ex and squarey. Unknown.—GrCt
"**Ex** and squarey, Virgin Mary." See Ex and squarey
The **example.** William Henry Davies.—ReO
Ex-basketball player. John Updike.—DuS
Excelsior. Henry Wadsworth Longfellow.—LoPl
"**Excepting** the diner." See Poem to be read at 3 A.M.
The **excursion.** Tu Fu, tr. fr. the Chinese by Amy Lowell and Florence Ayscough.—MoS
"**Excuse** me." Esther Lee Dailey.—BaH
"**Excuse** me." Issa, tr. fr. the Japanese by Nobuyuki Yuasa.—IsF
"**Excuse** us, animals in the zoo." Annette Wynne. —ArT-3
Exeunt. Richard Wilbur.—CoBn—HoL
"An **exhausted** sparrow." Issa, tr. fr. the Japanese by R. H. Blyth.—IsF—LeOw
Exile. Virna Sheard.—CoB
Exiled. Edna St Vincent Millay.—PaH
"Th' **expanded** waters gather on the plain." See Metamorphoses—The flood
Experience. Dorothy Parker.—CoBl
"**Experiment** to me." Emily Dickinson.—DiPe
An **explanation** of the grasshopper. Vachel Lindsay.—HuS-3
Exploration. See Explorers and exploration
Explorers and exploration. See also names of explorers, as Columbus, Christopher
Earth and the kisses of men. E. J. Coatsworth. —CoDh
Morning light the dew-drier. M. E. L. Newsome.—BoA
The new world. P. Engle.—BrA
The path of the padres. E. D. Osborne.—BrA
The unexplorer. E. St V. Millay.—HaL
Explosions
"A decrepit old gas man named Peter." Unknown.—BrLl
"A little boy down in Natchez." Unknown.—BrLl
"Said a foolish young lady of Wales." L. Reed. —BrLl
An **expostulation.** Isaac Bickerstaffe.—CoBl
The **express.** Stephen Spender.—BoGj—CoR
Expulsion from Paradise. See Paradise lost
The **extraordinary** dog. Nancy Byrd Turner.—ArT-3
Extremely naughty children. Elizabeth Godley. —CoBb
"**Exultation** is the going." Emily Dickinson.—DiPe
"The **eye** can hardly pick them out." See At grass
"The **eye** penetrates into the thoughts of others." Steven Terry.—LeM
"**Eye** winker." See The features
Eyes
"The eye penetrates into the thoughts of others." S. Terry.—LeM
Eyes are lit up. R. P. T. Coffin.—SmM
Little donkey close your eyes. M. W. Brown. —LaP—LaPd
The look. S. Teasdale.—BoH—CoBl

Eyes—*Continued*
Man of Thessaly. Mother Goose.—BrMg
The powerful eyes o' Jeremy Tait. W. Irwin.—CoSs
"There was a man in our town." Mother Goose.—OpF
"There was a young lady whose eyes." E. Lear
Limericks.—BoGj
To Helen. E. A. Poe.—PoP
Eyes are lit up. Robert P. Tristram Coffin.—SmM
"**Eyes** like the morning star." See The Colorado trail
"The **eyes** of the pioneer woman are blue, blue as the." See The pioneer woman—in the North country
"The **eyes** of time flash." See Time
Ezekiel, Nissim
Night of the scorpion.—AlPi
Ezra Shank. Unknown.—BrSm

F

FBI
Award. R. Durem.—AdIa
"**F** is the fighting firetruck." See All around the town
"**F** was a fussy flamingo." Carolyn Wells.—BrLl
Fable. See "The mountain and the squirrel"
Fable ("Does everyone have to die? Yes, everyone") Merrill Moore.—DuS
The **fable** of the golden pear. Eve Merriam.—MeI
Fables
The ass and the lap-dog. R. S. Sharpe.—VrF
The ass in the lion's skin. Aesop.—ReO
The blind men and the elephant. J. G. Saxe.—BoH
The boy and the frogs. R. S. Sharpe.—VrF
Chanticleer and the fox. From The Canterbury tales. G. Chaucer.—ChT
The dog and the shadow. R. S. Sharpe.—VrF
The fable of the golden pear. E. Merriam.—MeI
The fox and the grapes. J. Lauren.—BoH
The fox and the rooster. E. Rees.—ArT-3
The frogs who wanted a king. J. Lauren.—BoH
The harnet and the bittle. J. Y. Akerman.—GrCt
The jewel on the dunghill. R. S. Sharpe.—VrF
The lion and the fox. E. Rees.—ArT-3
The lion and the mouse. R. S. Sharpe.—VrF
Little fable. R. Fuller.—CaD
"The mountain and the squirrel." R. W. Emerson.—BoGj—BoH
Fable.—ReO
The shepherd's dog and the wolf. J. Gay.—ReO
The wolf and the crane. E. Rees.—ArT-3
The wolf and the lioness. E. Rees.—ArT-3
Fabrizio, Ray
Birds.—SmM
Rabbits.—SmM
Spider webs.—SmM
"A **face** devoid of love or grace." Emily Dickinson.—DiPe
Face game. Unknown.—MoB
"The **face** of the dragonfly." Chisoku, tr. fr. the Japanese by R. H. Blyth.—LeMw
Faces
Conversation with myself. E. Merriam.—MeI
Curious something. W. Welles.—ArT-3
"A face devoid of love or grace." E. Dickinson.—DiPe
Face game. Unknown.—MoB
Faces. S. Teasdale.—LaC
"For beauty I am not a star." A. Euwer.—BrLl
Godmother. P. B. Morden.—ThA
"Heat waves." Issa.—LeOw
Phizzog. C. Sandburg.—ArT-3
"Portraits are to daily faces." E. Dickinson.—DiPe
"There is a garden in her face." T. Campion.—BoGj
"There was a young curate named Stone." F. H. Cozens.—BrLl
"There was a young lady whose chin." E. Lear.—ArT-3—BrLl
Limericks.—HoB
"There was an old person of Down." E. Lear.—BrLl
"Waiting in darkness." Unknown.—BeCs
Faces. Sara Teasdale.—LaC
Factories
"Factory windows are always broken." V. Lindsay.—LaC—LiP
Living among the toilers. H. Percikow.—LaC
The ropewalk. H. W. Longfellow.—LoPl
"The shopgirls leave their work." C. Reznikoff.—LaC
Smoke animals. R. B. Bennett.—LaPd
"**Factory** windows are always broken." Vachel Lindsay.—LaC—LiP
"**Fade** in the sound of summer music." See Notes for a movie script
The **faerie** queene, sels. Edmund Spenser
The garden of Proserpina.—GrCt
The mermaids.—GrCt
Sea monsters.—GrCt
Sleep after toil.—GrCt
A **faery** song. William Butler Yeats.—YeR
"The **faiery** beame upon you." See The gypsies metamorphos'd—Song
Failure
The fox and the grapes. J. Lauren.—BoH
"I took my power in my hand." E. Dickinson.—DiPe
The duel.—LiT
Nobody loses all the time. E. E. Cummings.—McWs
"Success is counted sweetest." E. Dickinson.—BoGj—DiPe
"**Fainter** and thin." See Midnight

"**Fair** are the Pleiades." See The Pleiades
"**Fair** daffodils, we weep to see." See To daffodils
"**Fair** fa' your honest, sonsie face." See Address to a haggis
"**Fair** ladies tall lovers." E. E. Cummings.—GrS
The **fair** maid. See "The fair maid who, the first of May"
"The **fair** maid who, the first of May." Mother Goose.—OpF
The fair maid.—ReOn
The first of May.—BrMg
Mother Goose rhymes, 34.—HoB
"**Fair** pledges of a fruitful tree." See To blossoms
Fairbun, Julie
The deserted house.—LeM
"**Faire** daffadills, we weep to see." See To daffodils
Fairies
Adventure. N. B. Turner.—HuS-3
The adventures of Oberon, king of the fairies, while searching for Queen Mab. From Nymphidia, the court of fairy. M. Drayton. —ReO
The adventures of Tom Bombadil, sels. J. R. R. Tolkien.—LiT (Complete)
Oliphaunt.—ClF
Perry-the-winkle.—ArT-3
Arethusa. P. B. Shelley.—CoD
The army of the Sidhe. Lady Gregory.—ThA
At dawn. R. Fyleman.—HoB
The bad kittens. E. J. Coatsworth.—ThA
Berries. W. De La Mare.—HoB
"The best game the fairies play." R. Fyleman. —ArT-3
The bugle song. From The princess. A. Tennyson.—HoB—HuS-3
Blow, bugle, blow.—GrCt
Song.—BlO
"The splendour falls on castle walls."—ArT-3—BoGj
The splendour falls.—CoR
The careless fairy. N. B. Turner.—HoB
Changeling. B. Young.—ThA
The child next door. R. Fyleman.—ThA
"Come unto these yellow sands." From The tempest. W. Shakespeare
Ariel's song.—BlO—BoGj
Could it have been a shadow. M. Shannon.—ArT-3—HuS-3
Crab-apple. Ethel Talbot.—ArT-3
XVIII. From The third book of ayres. T. Campion.—GrS
The elf and the dormouse. O. Herford.—ArT-3 —HoB—ThA
The elf singing. W. Allingham.—HuS-3
Elfin berries. R. Field.—AgH
An explanation of the grasshopper. V. Lindsay.—HuS-3
A faery song. W. B. Yeats.—YeR
Fairies ("I cannot see fairies") H. Conkling.—ArT-3—ThA
The fairies ("If ye will with Mab find grace") R. Herrick.—BlO
The fairies ("Up the airy mountain") W. Allingham.—BlO—CoR—GrCt—HoB—LaPd
"Up the airy mountain."—HuS-3
Fairies ("You can't see fairies unless you're good") M. Chute.—ThA
"The fairies have never a penny to spend." R. Fyleman.—HoB—HuS-3—ThA
Fairy dance. From A midsummer-night's dream. W. Shakespeare.—ShS
The fairy from the apple-seed. V. Lindsay.—LiP
Fairy-land. E. A. Poe.—PoP
The fairy ring. A. Young.—GrCt
Fairy thief. W. Welles.—BrSg
"Faith, I wish I were a leprechaun." M. Ritter.—ArT-3
The find. F. Ledwidge.—ThA
For a child named Katherine. L. T. Nicholl.—ThA
For a mocking voice. E. Farjeon.—ArT-3
From the hills of dream. W. Sharp.—ThA
The gnome. H. Behn.—ArT-3—LaPd
The goblin. Unknown.—ArT-3—LaPh
Goblin market. C. G. Rossetti.—CoD
A goblinade. F. P. Jaques.—ArT-3
The goblin's song. J. Telfer.—GrCt
Godmother. P. B. Morden.—ThA
The green fiddler. R. Field.—HoB
Have you watched the fairies. R. Fyleman.—ArT-3—ThA
The holiday. M. Stredder.—StF
How to tell goblins from elves. M. Shannon.—ArT-3
"I keep three wishes ready." A. Wynne.—ArT-3—HuS-3—LaPd—ThA
I'd love to be a fairy's child. R. Graves.—LaPd
The lame boy and the fairy. V. Lindsay.—LiP
Laughter. M. Waddington.—DoW
The little elf-man. J. K. Bangs.—ArT-3—HoB
I met a little elf man.—HuS-3
The little elf.—LaPd—ThA
The little green orchard. W. De La Mare.—ArT-3
The little land. R. L. Stevenson.—HuS-3
Little Orphant Annie. J. W. Riley.—CoBb—HoB—HuS-3
Lollocks. R. Graves.—GrCt
Long-nosed elf. Unknown.—DePp
The magic vine. Unknown.—BrSg
The man who hid his own front door. E. MacKinstry.—ArT-3
Midsummer eve. E. Farjeon.—FaA
Midsummer magic. I. O. Eastwick.—ArT-3
Never. W. De La Mare.—DeBg
Night dancers. T. Kennedy.—ThA
A nursery song. L. E. Richards.—HoB
The nymph complaining for the death of her fawn. A. Marvell.—ReO (sel.)
Of a spider. W. Thorley.—LaPd
Oread. H. D.—BoGj

"There came a day at summer's full." E. Dickinson.—DiPe
"Though the great waters sleep." E. Dickinson.—DiPe—PlE
"To lose one's faith surpasses." E. Dickinson. —DiPe
"We met as sparks—diverging flints." E. Dickinson.—DiPe
"We shall overcome." Unknown.—HiL—PlE
"**Faith**, I wish I were a leprechaun." Margaret Ritter.—ArT-3
"**Faith** is a fine invention." Emily Dickinson.—DiPe
The **faithless** flowers. Margaret Widdemer.—ThA
Faithless Nelly Gray. Thomas Hood.—BrSm
The **falcon** ("Lully, lulley; lully, lulley") See Corpus Christi carol
The **falcon** ("Why should my sleepy heart be taught") Elinor Wylie.—HaL
Falconry. See Falcons and falconry
Falcons and falconry
Corpus Christi carol. Unknown.—GrCt
The falcon.—SmM
Hawking. From Polyolbion. M. Drayton.—MoS
September. Folgore da San Geminiano.—MoS
The windhover. G. M. Hopkins.—PlE
Faldich, Anthony
Red.—BaH
Fall. See Autumn
Fall ("The geese flying south") Sally Andresen. —DuR
Fall ("The last of October") Aileen Fisher.—ArT-3—BrSg
The **fall** of the flowers. Yen Yun, tr. fr. the Chinese by Robert Kotewell and Norman L. Smith.—LeMw
The **fall** of the house of Usher, sel. Edgar Allan Poe
The haunted palace.—GrCt—PoP
The **fall** of the plum blossoms. Rankō.—ArT-3
Fall of the year. Aileen Fisher.—FiC
Fall surprises. Aileen Fisher.—FiIo
"**Fallen** into a dream, I could not rise." See Sailing to England
The **fallen** tree. Andrew Young.—CoBn
Falling in the creek. Iris Heke.—LeM
Falling leaves. Patricia Hubbell.—HoB
Falling snow ("See the pretty snowflakes") Unknown.—ArT-3—HoB
Falling snow ("Snow is falling, falling hard") Unknown, ad. fr. the Japanese by Charlotte B. DeForest.—DePp
The **falling** star. Sara Teasdale.—ArT-3—HuS-3 —LaPd—ThA
Fallis, Edwina
September.—ArT-3—BrSg
Wise Johnny.—ArT-3—BrSg
"The **fallow** deer." Conrad Aiken.—AiC
The **fallow** deer at the lonely house. Thomas Hardy.—BlO
The **false** fox. Unknown.—GrCt
"The **false** fox came unto our croft." See The false fox
False gods. Walter De La Mare.—PlE
False, or inconstancy. William Congreve.—CoBl
"**False** though she be to me and love." See False, or inconstancy
Falsehood. See Truthfulness and falsehood
Falsehood corrected. Elizabeth Turner.—VrF
"**Falsehood** of thee could I suppose." Emily Dickinson.—DiPe
Falstaff, Jake
Beautiful Sunday.—CoBn
Fame
"The beggar at the door for fame." E. Dickinson.—DiPe
"Fame is a bee." E. Dickinson.—DiPe
"Fame is the tint that scholars leave." E. Dickinson.—DiPe
The fortunes of the great. From The Canterbury tales. G. Chaucer.—ChT
"I think continually of those who were truly great." S. Spender.—PlE
I think continually of those.—GrCt
I was a phoebe. E. Dickinson.—ReBs
"I'm nobody. Who are you." E. Dickinson.—ArT-3—DiL—DiPe—LaPd
Let us now praise famous men. From Ecclesiasticus, Bible, Apocrypha.—GrCt
On the vanity of earthly greatness. A. Guiterman.—DuR
Popularity. R. Browning.—BrP
Questions of a studious working man. B. Brecht.—SmM
A song of greatness. M. Austin.—ArT-3—BrA —HoB
Stanzas written on the road between Florence and Pisa. G. G. Byron.—ByP
Vox populi. H. W. Longfellow.—LoPl
The white stag. E. Pound.—HaL
Who's who. W. H. Auden.—McWs
"**Fame** is a bee." Emily Dickinson.—DiPe
"**Fame** is the tint that scholars leave." Emily Dickinson.—DiPe
Familiar friends. James S. Tippett.—HoB—StF
Family. See also Children and childhood; Fathers and fatherhood; Home and family life; Married life; Mothers and motherhood; Relatives; also names of relatives, as Uncles
André. G. Brooks.—ArT-3—HoB
The cradle trap. L. Simpson.—LiT
"Diana Fitzpatrick Mauleverer James." A. A. Milne.—ArT-3
The dove says. Mother Goose.—BrMg
The family. Visvanath.—AlPi
The happy family. J. Ciardi.—CoO
House in St Petersburg. S. Burnshaw.—GrS
Manerathiak's song. Unknown.—DoW
"My parents kept me from children who were rough." S. Spender.—CaD
Rough.—HoL
Some families of my acquaintance. L. E. Richards.—CoO
Song for Naomi. I. Layton.—DoW

Family—*Continued*
"There was an old miser named Clarence." O. Nash.—BrLl
The **family.** Visvanath, tr. fr. the Hindi by Vidya Niwas Misra and Josephine Miles.—AlPi
Family life. See Home and family life
Famine
A description of famine. Unknown.—AlPi
The **fan.** Elizabeth Turner.—VrF
Fancy, sel. John Keats
"Thou shalt see the field-mouse peep."—ReO
The **fancy** ("With a bow to George Borrow's Lavengro") William Rose Benét.—MoS
Fandel, John
Indians.—BrA—DuR
Fanny and her cat. Unknown.—VrF
Fans
Ann's fan. E. Merriam.—MeC
The fan. E. Turner.—VrF
"Here comes." Issa.—IsF
Fanshawe, Catherine Maria
A riddle.—GrCt
Fantasy. Gerard De Nerval, tr. fr. the French by Geoffrey Wagner.—GrS
"**Far** above us where a jay." See Morning on the Lièvre
"**Far** and free o'er the lifting sea, the lapsing wastes and the waves that roam." See Return to New York
"**Far** and high." See Dinosaur air
Far away ("How far, today") David McCord.—McE
Far away ("Once a little boy") Elizabeth Jane Coatsworth.—CoSb
"**Far** away, and long ago." See The song of seven
"**Far** enough down is China, somebody said." See Digging for China
"**Far,** far down." See City afternoon
Far from Africa: Four poems. Margaret Danner.—BoA
"**Far** in a western brookland." See A Shropshire lad
"**Far** off, far off." See Song of the parrot
"The **far-off mountains** hide you from me." Unknown.—DoC
"**Far** out in the wilds of Oregon." See The nonpareil's grave
"**Far** spread, below." See The story of Vinland
Farber, Norma
The hatch.—HoL
Leaf and sun.—HoL
"**Fare** you well." See Farewell to summer
A **farewell.** Alfred Tennyson.—TeP
"**Farewell,** like a bee." Bashō, tr. fr. the Japanese by Harry Behn.—BeCs
Farewell to summer. Eleanor Farjeon.—FaA
Farewell to the farm. Robert Louis Stevenson.—ArT-3
Farewell to the warriors. Unknown, tr. fr. the Chippewa.—LeO
Farewells. See also Parting
Adieu. P. Lewenstein.—SmM
"Ae fond kiss, and then we sever." R. Burns.—BuPr
Coriolanus's farewell to his fellow-citizens as he goes into banishment. From Coriolanus. W. Shakespeare.—McWs
A farewell. A. Tennyson.—TeP
"Farewell, like a bee." Bashō.—BeCs
Farewell to summer. E. Farjeon.—FaA
Farewell to the farm. R. L. Stevenson.—ArT-3
Farewell to the warriors. Unknown.—LeO
Leave-taking. Unknown.—LeO
Parting. Wang Wei.—ArT-3—LeMw
Splinter. C. Sandburg.—ArT-3
Taking leave of a friend. Li T'ai-po.—HoL
There rolls the deep. From In memoriam. A. Tennyson.—TeP
To Lucasta, on going to the wars. R. Lovelace.—McWs
The true and tender wife. From Ramayana. Valmiki.—AlPi
Valedictory sonnet. W. Wordsworth.—WoP
Farjeon, Eleanor
After rain.—HoB
Aurora borealis.—FaT
B is for beanseed.—BrSg
Bedtime.—ArT-3—ReS
Bees in lavender.—FaA
Beggarman.—FaT
Big Bear and Little Bear.—FaT
The birds know.—FaA
Blind man's buff.—FaT
Blow the stars home.—LaPd
Boys' names.—ArT-3
Breakfast.—AgH
A carol for Christmas eve.—HoB
Carriage.—FaT
Castle.—FaT
"Cat."—BlO—CoB
Cats.—LaPd—StF
"Cherry pie black."—FaT
Cherry-stones.—AgH
"How many cherries."—FaT
Choosing.—ArT-3
Christmas stocking.—LaPh
Circus.—HoB
City streets and country roads.—ArT-3
Coach.—FaT
Cobbler, cobbler, mend my shoe.—FaT
Consequences.—FaT
Cottage.—FaT—StF
Cotton.—FaT
Cygnus.—FaT
Dancing.—HuS-3
The dewdrop.—FaA
"Do you know the muffin man."—FaT
Dog-star.—FaT
"Down, down."—ArT-3
A dragonfly.—FaA—LaPd
The earth.—FaT
Earth and sky.—BrSg
The ending of the year.—FaA
Enter November.—FaA
Evening star.—FaT
Farewell to summer.—FaA
Farm cart.—FaT
"First come was Cherrystones."—FaT

First signs.—FaA
The flower-seller.—BrSg
Follow-my-leader.—FaT
For a dance.—LaPh
For a mocking voice.—ArT-3
For autumn.—FaA
For Christmas day.—ArT-3
For snow.—FaA
Forfeits.—FaT
General Post.—FaT
Girls' names.—ArT-3
Halley's comet.—FaT
Hallowe'en.—FaA
Heigh-ho, April.—FaA
Here we go looby, looby, looby.—FaT
Here we go round the mulberry bush.—FaT
Hide-and-seek ("Tiptoe away, tiptoe away")—FaT
Hide-and-seek ("When little Jane lifts up her head")—FaT
"How many cherries." See Cherry-stones
Hunt the thimble.—FaT
The Hyades.—FaT
I sent a letter to my love.—FaT
I'm the king of the castle.—FaT
In the week when Christmas comes.—ArT-3—LaPd—LaPh
"Jill came from the fair."—ArT-3
Kiss-in-the-ring.—FaT
A kitten.—ArT-3
The lost star.—FaT
Lucky star.—FaT
Magical music.—FaT
Mansion.—FaT
May's song.—FaA
The meteors.—FaT
Midsummer eve.—FaA
"Mrs Peck-Pigeon."—ArT-3—HuS-3—LaPd
"Moon-come-out."—ArT-3
Moon rainbow.—FaT
Morning star.—FaT
Musical chairs.—FaT
Never.—FaT
Next year.—FaT
Night.—FaT
"The night will never stay."—HuS-3—LaP—TuW
Nuts in May.—FaT
O reaper.—FaA
The old shepherds.—FaT
Oranges and lemons.—FaT
Orion's belt.—FaT
"Over the garden wall."—HuS-3
Peep-primrose.—BrSg
Pegasus.—SmM
Pencil and paint.—LaPd
Pig-sty.—FaT
The planets.—FaT
The Pleiades.—FaT
Pole-star.—FaT
Poor man.—FaT
Postman's knock.—FaT
A prayer for little things.—StF
"Queen Cassiopeia."—FaT
Rags.—FaT
Rich man.—FaT
Ring-a-ring-a-roses.—FaT
Sailor.—FaT
Satin.—FaT
Saturn.—FaT
"The shepherd and the king."—ArT-3
Silk.—FaT
Skate and sled.—FaA
Soldier.—FaT
Some time.—FaT
"The sounds in the morning."—HoB
The Southern Cross.—FaT
Spelling bee.—FaT
The standing corn.—FaA
The star that watches the moon.—FaT
Strawberries.—AgH
"The swallows are homing."—FaA
Tailor.—FaT
There are big waves.—StF
Thief.—FaT
This year.—FaT
"Three little puffins."—ArT-3
"The tide in the river."—ArT-3—BlO—SmM
Tinker.—FaT
To any garden.—BrSg
To Beatrice and Sally.—FaT
Touch.—FaT
The trees and the wind.—FaA
Tug-of-war.—FaT
V is for vegetables.—BrSg
Victoria.—BlO
Welcome to the new year.—ThA
Wheelbarrow.—FaT
The white blackbirds.—FaA
White horses.—LaPd
Window-boxes.—BrSg
The zodiac.—FaT
Farley, Hilary-Anne
I love animals and dogs.—LeM
A little fish.—LeM
Sun goes up.—LeM
This is a poem.—LeM
Farm animals. See Animals; also names of farm animals, as Cows
Farm cart. Eleanor Farjeon.—FaT
Farm child. R. S. Thomas.—CaD—CoBn
Farm life. See also Country life; Fields; Harvests and harvesting; Plows and plowing; also names of farm products, as Wheat
"Ah, the peasant who." Hosokawa Yusai.—LeMw
All in the path of a power mower. R. Gillman.—DuS
Another little boy. A. and J. Taylor.—VrF
The anxious farmer. B. Johnson.—CoBn
April. N. Belting.—BeCm
The ballad of the boll weevil. Unknown.—HiL
The barnyard. M. Burnham.—ArT-3
Brown's descent; or, The willy nilly slide. R. Frost.—ArT-3
"The cock's on the house-top." Mother Goose.—OpF
Cock-crow.—BrMg

A **father** swings his child. W. D. Snodgrass.—McWs
Father to the man. John Knight.—PlE
"**Father,** who keepest." See A child's prayer at evening
Father William. See Alice's adventures in wonderland
Fathers and fatherhood
"As I went up by yonder hill." Unknown.—MoB
The aura. J. Dickey.—DuS
Automobile mechanics. D. W. Baruch.—ArT-3
"The beggar on the bridge." Issa.—LeOw
Bringing him up. Lord Dunsany.—CoBb
The bubble. K. Hopkins.—CaD
Cross. L. Hughes.—AdIa—BoA
Daddy. Mother Goose.—BrMg
Daddy fell into the pond. A. Noyes.—LaP—LaPd
The death of a father. H. S. Horsley.—VrF
Development. R. Browning.—BrP
"Each morning." From Hymn for Lanie Poo. L. Jones.—AdIa
Europe and America. D. Ignatow.—BrA
Father. F. M. Frost.—ArT-3—HuS-3
A father swings his child. W. D. Snodgrass.—McWs
First lesson. P. McGinley.—McWs
Fixer of midnight. R. Denney.—DuS
Forever. E. Merriam.—MeI
Full fathom five. From The tempest. W. Shakespeare.—GrCt—SmM
Ariel's dirge.—BoGj
Ariel's song.—BlO
A sea dirge.—CoSs
Growing up. K. Wilson.—DuS
"I will go with my father a-ploughing." J. Campbell.—ArT-3
The little boy lost ("Father, father, where are you going") W. Blake.—BlP
A little boy lost ("Nought loves another as itself") W. Blake.—BlP
The man of the house. D. Wagoner.—DuS
The mocking bird. Mother Goose.—BrMg
"My father died a month ago." Mother Goose.—MoB
Riches.—BrMg
"My father he died, but I can't tell you how." Unknown.—BlO
"Oh, no." M. M. Dodge.—CoBb
Peeking. A. Fisher.—FiIo
Piano practice. I. Serraillier.—CoBb
Rousecastle. D. Wright.—CaMb—CoSs
Self-sacrifice. H. Graham.—CoBb
Sohrab and Rustum. M. Arnold.—CoD
Son and father. C. Day-Lewis.—PlE
The stern parent. H. Graham.—CoBb—GrCt
A story for a child. B. Taylor.—CoB
Talking. A. Fisher.—FiIo
Those winter Sundays. R. E. Hayden.—AdIa—DuS
To my son. S. Sassoon.—McWs
"Were my father here." Issa.—LeOw
"When I had a little leisure." Wang Mou Fang.—LeMw
A wonderful man. A. Fisher.—FiIo
Fatigue
Fatigue. P. Bacon.—LaC
Fatigue. Peggy Bacon.—LaC
Faults and fears. See Love's labour's lost
Favorite eats. Carson McCullers.—AgH
The **fawn.** Edna St Vincent Millay.—CoB
The **fawn** in the snow. William Rose Benét.—ReO
"**Fawns** in the winter wood." See Ballet school
"**Fe,** fi, fo, fum." See "Fee, fi, fo, fum"
Fear
"Afraid? Of whom am I afraid." E. Dickinson.—DiPe
Americans are afraid of lizards. K. Shapiro.—BrA
The boy in the barn. H. Read.—CaD
Carmel Point. M. P. MacSweeney.—DuR
A charm. R. Herrick.—GrCt
Courage. From Julius Caesar. W. Shakespeare.—ShS
Deer at dusk. E. J. Coatsworth.—CoSb
The deserted house. J. Fairbun.—LeM
Do you fear the wind. H. Garland.—ArT-3—ThA
"Drums, drumming." B. Brown.—BaH
Eskimo chant. Unknown.—DoW
"There is joy in."—LeO
Faults and fears. From Love's labour's lost. W. Shakespeare.—ShS
"Fear no more the heat o' the sun." From Cymbeline. W. Shakespeare.—GrCt
Fear no more.—BoH—CoR
Fear when coming home through a dark country lane. P. Taylor.—LeM
Forgive us, O Lord. From Murder in the cathedral. T. S. Eliot.—PlE
Frighted by a cow. E. Turner.—VrF
A goblinade. F. P. Jaques.—ArT-3
Hark. W. De La Mare.—DeBg
"I years had been from home." E. Dickinson.—DiPe
In camera. T. Rajan.—AlPi
In the night. J. Stephens.—StS
In waste places. J. Stephens.—StS
The little coward. A. and J. Taylor.—VrF
A little girl lost. W. Blake.—BlP
Manerathiak's song. Unknown.—DoW
Moonlight. B. H. Nance.—BrA
"My parents kept me from children who were rough." S. Spender.—CaD
Rough.—HoL
Nursery nonsense. D'A. W. Thompson.—CoO
Ode to Hengist and Horsa. R. Jeffers.—GrS
Okefenokee swamp. D. W. Hicky.—BrA
"One need not be a chamber to be haunted." E. Dickinson.—DiPe
The panther possible. W. D. Barney.—DuS
Paper men to air hopes and fears. R. Francis.—DuS
Perry-the-winkle. From The adventures of Tom Bombadil. J. R. R. Tolkien.—ArT-3

Fear—*Continued*
A reasonable affliction. M. Prior.—BrSm
"A skeleton once in Khartoum. Unknown.—BrLl—BrSm
Song, on reading that the cyclotron has produced cosmic rays, blasted the atom into twenty-two particles, solved the mystery of the transmutation of elements and devil knows what. S. Hoffenstein.—BrSm
A spell. From The old wives' tale. G. Peele.—GrCt
The superstitious ghost. A. Guiterman.—BrSm
"Terror in the house does roar." W. Blake.—BlP
Variations 9. From Theme and variations. J. Stephens.—StS
Variations 13. From Theme and variations. J. Stephens.—StS
What the girl said. Kapilar.—AlPi
"When I hoped, I recollect." E. Dickinson.—DiL
The wind has wings. Unknown.—DoW
Yet the lean beast plays. E. J. Coatsworth.—CoDh
You've got to be taught. From South Pacific. O. Hammerstein II.—BrA
"**Fear** death?—to feel the fog in my throat." See Prospice
"**Fear** is, where is no cause." See Theme and variations—Variations 13
Fear no more. See Cymbeline—"Fear no more the heat o' the sun"
"**Fear** no more the heat o' the sun." See Cymbeline
"The **fear** was on the cattle, for the gale was on the sea." See Mulholland's contract
Fear when coming home through a dark country lane. Patricia Taylor.—LeM
"The **fearful** night sinks." See Hymn to the sun
Fearing, Bruce
Some brown sparrows.—CoB—DuR
Fearing, Kenneth
Art review.—DuS
Dirge.—HiL
"A **feast** being spread in springtime." See Her birthday
Feast of Lanterns
"Ching-a-ring-a-ring-ching, Feast of Lanterns." Mother Goose.—OpF
The **feather.** Walter De La Mare.—DeBg
"A **feather,** a feather." See The feather
"A **feather** from the whippowil." Emily Dickinson
Pine bough.—DiL
"**Feather** on feather." See Snow in spring
Feather or fur. John Becker.—ArT-3
"The **feathers** of the willow." See Song
The **features.** Mother Goose.—BrMg
February
The brook in February. C. G. D. Roberts.—CoBn—DoW
February ("Put the pine tree in its pot by the doorway") N. Belting.—BeCm
February ("The sun is coming") N. Belting.—BeCm
February twilight. S. Teasdale.—LaP—LaPd—ThA
February ("Put the pine tree in its pot by the doorway") Natalia Belting.—BeCm
February ("The sun is coming") Natalia Belting.—BeCm
February twilight. Sara Teasdale.—LaP—LaPd—ThA
"**Fee,** fi, fo, fum." Mother Goose.—BrF
"Fe, fi, fo, fum."—BrSm
The giant.—BrMg
"The **feeble** plant." Issa, tr. fr. the Japanese by R. H. Blyth.—LeOw
Feet
"As I was going out one day." Unknown.—CoO
Bump. Bang. Bump. J. Ciardi.—CiYk
Feet ("Feet are special things") M. C. Livingston.—HoB
Feet ("Feet of snails") A. Fisher.—FiC
Feet ("There are things") D. Aldis.—HoB
"I know a place." M. C. Livingston.—HoB
Upon her feet. R. Herrick.—SmM
Feet ("Feet are special things") Myra Cohn Livingston.—HoB
Feet ("Feet of snails") Aileen Fisher.—FiC
Feet ("There are things") Dorothy Aldis.—HoB
"**Feet** are special things." See Feet
"**Feet** of snails." See Feet
Feld, M. D.
Villanelle.—MoS
Felicia Ropps. Gelett Burgess.—CoBb
Felix Randal. Gerard Manley Hopkins.—CoR
"**Felix** Randal the farrier, O he is dead then? My duty all ended." See Felix Randal
A **feller** I know. Mary Austin.—BrA
"A **fellow** who slaughtered two toucans." Unknown.—BrLl
"The **fenceposts** wear marshmallow hats." See Snow
Fences
Knotholes. D. McCord.—McAd
Mending wall. R. Frost.—BrA
"The pickety fence." D. McCord.—McE
Riding a fence. K. Fraser.—FrS
Feng Yen-chi
Her birthday.—LeMw
Fergus and the druid. William Butler Yeats.—LiT
Ferguson, Sir Samuel
Dear dark head.—CoBl
Ferlinghetti, Lawrence
Fortune.—DuR—LaC
Fern hill. Dylan Thomas.—BoGj—CoR
Ferns
The ferns. G. Baro.—SmM
The **ferns.** Gene Baro.—SmM
Ferries
Ferry-boats. J. S. Tippett.—ArT-3
"Ferry me across the water." C. G. Rossetti.—BoGj—GrCt—LaPd

Recuerdo. E. St V. Millay.—BrA—CoBl—HiL
Ferril, Thomas Hornsby
House in Denver.—BrA
Swallows.—DuR
Ferry boats. See Ferries
Ferry-boats. James S. Tippett.—ArT-3
"**Ferry** me across the water." Christina Georgina Rossetti.—BoGj—GrCt—LaPd
Festivals. See Fairs
"**Fetch** me my tweezers and my comb." See Sutra-krtanga—In praise of celibacy
"**Few** are my books, but my small few have told." See Lovely dames
"A **few** flies." Issa, tr. fr. the Japanese by Nobuyuki Yuasa.—IsF
A **few** things explained. Pablo Neruda, tr. by Ben Belitt.—LiT (sel.)
"**Fhairshon** swore a feud." See The massacre of the Macpherson
The **fickle** wind. Cindy Schonhaut.—LeM
The **fiddler** ("I wander up and down here, and go from street to street") Ann and Jane Taylor.—VrF
A **fiddler** ("Once was a fiddler. Play could he") Walter De La Mare.—HaL
"The **fiddler** and his wife." Mother Goose.—OpF
The **fiddler** of Dooney. William Butler Yeats.—ArT-3—YeR
Fidelity. William Wordsworth.—ClF
Field, Eugene
The duel.—ArT-3—HoB—HuS-3—ReS
A leap-year episode. at.—CoBl
The little peach.—AgH—BrSm
The Sioux.—BoGj
Song.—ArT-3—LaPh
Wynken, Blynken, and Nod.—HoB—HuS-3
Field, Michael
"Bury her at even."—SmM
Field, Rachel (Lyman)
Acrobat. See A circus garland
The animal store.—ArT-3—HuS-3—LaP—LaPd
Blue flowers.—BrSg
A charm for spring flowers.—ArT-3—TuW
A circus garland, sels.—HuS-3 (Complete)
Acrobat
The elephant
The girl on the milk-white horse
The performing seal
City lights.—LaP—LaPd
Cranberry road.—ThA
Doorbells.—ArT-3—HuS-3
The elephant. See A circus garland
Elfin berries.—AgH
A fire.—AgH
The florist shop.—BrSg
The flower-cart man.—BrSg—LaC
General store.—HoB—HuS-3—TuW
The girl on the milk-white horse. See A circus garland
The green fiddler.—HoB
The ice-cream man.—HoB
"I'd like to be a lighthouse."—LaP—LaPd
The little rose tree.—ArT-3—BrSg
Manhattan lullaby.—BrA—LaC
New Year's day.—ArT-3—LaPh
The performing seal. See A circus garland
Picnic day.—ArT-3
Pushcart row.—BrSg
The quiet child.—ReS
"A road might lead to anywhere." See Roads
Roads.—HuS-3—LaPd
"A road might lead to anywhere."—StF
Skyscrapers.—HuS-3
Snow in the city.—ArT-3—LaP
Some people.—LaPd
"Something told the wild geese."—ArT-3—CoB—HoL—HuS-3—LaPd—SmM—TuW
A summer morning.—ArT-3—HoB—HuS-3—LaPd
Taxis.—ArT-3—LaP
The thorn trees.—BrSg
Vegetables.—BrSg
Whistles.—ArT-3—HuS-3
The **field** daisy. Ann and Jane Taylor.—VrF
"A **field** in sunshine is a field." See Psalm of the fruitful field
The **field** mouse. William Sharp.—CoB—ReS
"A **field** of cloud." See Upside down
Field of long grass. A. J. M. Smith.—CoBl
The **field** of the mice and the marigold. Etain Mary Clarke.—LeM
Fields, James T. (Thomas)
The alarmed skipper.—CoSs
Fields, Julia
Madness one Monday evening.—HaK—LiT
No time for poetry.—BoA
Fields
In fields of summer. G. Kinnell.—CoBn
Lives. H. Reed.—CoBn
Meadow morning. A. Fisher.—FiI
Meadow of hay. A. Fisher.—FiI
Mountain meadows. M. Keller.—CoBn
On a windy day. A. Fisher.—FiI
Psalm of the fruitful field. A. M. Klein.—DoW
Question in a field. L. Bogan.—HoL
The standing corn. E. Farjeon.—FaA
White fields. J. Stephens.—CoBn—StS
Winter field. A. E. Coppard.—ReBs
The **fields** abroad with spangled flowers. Unknown.—GrCt
"The **fields** abroad with spangled flowers are gilded." See The fields abroad with spangled flowers
"The **fields** are wrapped in silver snow." See The Christmas present
"The **fields** from Islington to Marybone." See Jerusalem I
"**Fife** and drum." Kathleen Fraser.—FrS
Fife tune. John Manifold.—BoGj—HoL—McWs
Fifteen. William Stafford.—DuR
"**Fifteen** churches lie here." See At Dunwich
"**Fifteen** men on the dead man's chest." See Derelict
"**Fifteen** or twenty feet below." See The anchorage
Fifth of November. K. W. Gransden.—CaD

The **fifth** sense. Patricia Beer.—CaMb
Fifty faggots. Edward Thomas.—ThG
Fifty stanzas for a thief, sel. Bilhana, tr. fr. the Sanskrit by E. Powys Mathers
"Even now."—AlPi
"**Fifty** stories more to fall." See Rhyme of rain
Fights
"The lion and the unicorn." Mother Goose.—BrF—BrMg—MoB—OpF
The massacre of the Macpherson. W. E. Aytoun.—GrCt
"Punch and Judy." Mother Goose.—BrMg
Riding together. W. Morris.—ClF
"There once were two cats of Kilkenny." Mother Goose.—BrLl
The cats of Kilkenny.—LaP
The Kilkenny cats.—BrMg—BrSm
To sparrows fighting. W. H. Davies.—ReBs
"Tweedledum and Tweedledee." Mother Goose.—BrMg—OpF
Figures of speech. David McCord.—McAd
"**File** into yellow candle light, fair choristers of King's. See Sunday morning, King's Cambridge
"A **filing-cabinet** of human lives." See Apartment house
Finch, Francis Miles
The blue and the gray.—HiL
Nathan Hale.—HiL
Finch, Robert
Peacock and nightingale.—CoB
Finches
Epitaph on Lady Ossory's bullfinch. H. Walpole.—GrCt—ReO
A goldfinch. W. De La Mare.—DeBg—ReBs
Yellow flutterings. J. Keats.—CoB
The **find.** Francis Ledwidge.—ThA
Finder, please return to Henry Thoreau. Elizabeth Jane Coatsworth.—CoDh
"**Finding** the feathers of a bird." See A summer wish—A dead bird
"The **finest** thing in London is the bobby." See The London bobby
Finger game. Unknown.—MoB
Finger-play poems. See also Nursery play
Birds on a stone. Mother Goose.—ReOn
Two birds.—BrMg
"Brow, brow, brenty." Unknown.—MoB
Finger game. Unknown.—MoB
"Little Boy Blue, come blow your horn." Mother Goose.—HuS-3—OpF
"Billy Boy Blue, come blow me your horn."—GrT
Boy Blue.—BrMg
"Little Boy Blue."—ReMg
"Little Boy Blue, come blow up your horn."—WiMg
Mother Goose rhymes, 3.—HoB
"This little cow eats grass." Unknown.—WyC
"This little pig had a rub-a-dub." Mother Goose.—BrMg
"This little pig went to market." Mother Goose.—BrMg—HuS-3—OpF—WiMg
Mother Goose rhymes, 36.—HoB
Thumb and finger game. Unknown.—MoB
"Two little dicky birds." Mother Goose.—WiMg
Fingers. See also Finger-play poems
Abigail's fingers. M. O'Neill.—OnF
City fingers. M. O'Neill.—OnF
Country fingers. M. O'Neill.—OnF
The fingers. Mother Goose.—BrMg
Greedy fingers. M. O'Neill.—OnF
Grown-up fingers. M. O'Neill.—OnF
Kevin's fingers. M. O'Neill.—OnF
Lisa's fingerprints. M. O'Neill.—OnF
Mark's fingers. M. O'Neill.—OnF
Mimi's fingers. M. O'Neill.—OnF
My fingers. M. O'Neill.—OnF
Newborn fingers. M. O'Neill.—OnF
Old fingers. M. O'Neill.—OnF
Paul's fingers. M. O'Neill.—OnF
Sarah's fingers. M. O'Neill.—OnF
"Tall and thin." Mother Goose.—OpF
Thumbprint. E. Merriam.—MeI
The **fingers.** Mother Goose.—BrMg
Fingers in the nesting box. Robert Graves.—CoB
Finis ("Night is come") Henry Newbolt.—ArT-3
Finis ("Now that our love has drifted") Waring Cuney.—BoA
"**Finite** to fail, but infinite to venture." Emily Dickinson.—DiPe
Finkel, Donald
Hunting song.—CaMb—CoB—DuR—WeP
Finn, Hugh
Beetle.—CoB
Fiorello H. LaGuardia. Eve Merriam.—MeIv
Fire. See also Fireplaces
Adolphus Elfinstone. G. Burgess.—CoBb
"Ashes denote that fire was." E. Dickinson.—DiPe
Autumn fires. R. L. Stevenson.—ArT-3—BrSg
Banking coal. J. Toomer.—BoH
Coals. W. De La Mare.—DeBg
Earthy anecdote. W. Stevens.—BoGj
"An emerald is as green as grass." C. G. Rossetti.—ArT-3
"F is the fighting firetruck." From All around the town. P. McGinley.—LaP
Fire ("Flickering flames of gold and red") J. Craik.—LeM
Fire ("I am fire. You know me") Pat Taylor.—LeM
The fire ("Loud roared the flames") W. De La Mare.—DeBg
A fire ("Why does a fire eat big sticks of wood") R. Field.—AgH
Fire and ice. R. Frost.—HoL
"Fire, fire, said Mrs Dyer." Mother Goose.—OpF
Fire.—BrMg
"Fire, fire, said the town crier."—ReMg
The fire of drift-wood. H. W. Longfellow.—LoPl
The fire of London. From Annus mirabilis. J. Dryden.—GrCt
Jeremiah. Mother Goose.—BrMg
Playing with fire. A. and J. Taylor.—VrF

"You cannot put a fire out." E. Dickinson.—DiPe
"You light the fire." Bashō.—LeMw
Fire. See "Fire, fire, said Mrs Dyer"
Fire ("Flickering flames of gold and red") Jill Craik.—LeM
Fire ("I am fire. You know me") Pat Taylor.—LeM
The **fire** ("Loud roared the flames") Walter De La Mare.—DeBg
A **fire** ("Why does a fire eat big sticks of wood") Rachel Field.—AgH
Fire and ice. Robert Frost.—HoL
"**Fire,** fire, said Mrs Dyer." Mother Goose.—OpF
Fire.—BrMg
"Fire, fire, said the town crier."—ReMg
"**Fire,** fire, said the town crier." See "Fire, fire, said Mrs Dyer"
Fire-flies. See Fireflies
Fire Island walking song. Eugene F. Kinkead.—CoB
The **fire** of drift-wood. Henry Wadsworth Longfellow.—LoPl
The **fire** of London. See Annus mirabilis
"**Fire** of the autumn turns to red and gold." See Foam flowers
"The **fire,** with well-dried logs supplied." See Marmion—Christmas time
Fireflies
"The beggar on the bridge." Issa.—IsF—LeOw
"Chasing the fireflies." K. Mizumura.—MiI
"Come out, fireflies." Issa.—LeOw
Fireflies. W. Welles.—ReS
"The fireflies flit." Issa.—IsF
Fireflies in the garden. R. Frost.—ReO—WeP
Firefly ("A little light is going by") E. M. Roberts.—BoGj—LaPd
The firefly ("The rain") Li T'ai-po.—LeMw
Firefly party. Unknown.—DePp
"The first firefly (it was off)." Issa.—LeOw
"The first firefly (why do you)." Issa.—IsF
"A giant firefly." Issa.—LeI
Glowworm. D. McCord.—McE
"In our house." Issa.—IsF—LeOw
The lights. E. J. Coatsworth.—CoSb
"Over the deepest." Shiyo.—BeCs
She-goat and glow-worm. C. Morgenstern.—ReO
Shooting stars. G. N. Crowell.—HoB
"That stone." Issa.—IsF
"There's a fire in the forest." W. W. E. Ross.—DoW
"Waiting in darkness." Unknown.—BeCs
Fireflies. Winifred Welles.—ReS
"The **fireflies** flit." Issa, tr. fr. the Japanese by R. H. Blyth.—IsF
Fireflies in the garden. Robert Frost.—ReO—WeP
Firefly ("A little light is going by") Elizabeth Madox Roberts.—BoGj—LaPd
The **firefly** ("The rain") Li T'ai-po, tr. fr. the Chinese by Henry H. Hart.—LeMw
"**Firefly,** airplane, satellite, star." See Back yard, July night
Firefly party. Unknown, ad. fr. the Japanese by Charlotte B. DeForest.—DePp
Fireplaces
Ballade by the fire. E. A. Robinson.—BoH
The hearth of Urien. W. Barnes.—GrCt
Fireworks
Fireworks ("Not guns, not thunder, but a flutter of clouded drums") B. Deutsch.—DuR
Fireworks ("People in a field with light and noise") E. Kroll.—DuS
Fireworks ("They rise like sudden fiery flowers") J. Reeves.—BrSg—LaPh
Fourth of July night. D. Aldis.—ArT-3—LaPh
The pinwheel's song. J. Ciardi.—LaPd
"**Fireworks.**" See Skywriting
Fireworks ("Not guns, not thunder, but a flutter of clouded drums") Babette Deutsch.—DuR
Fireworks ("People in a field with light and noise") Ernest Kroll.—DuS
Fireworks ("They rise like sudden fiery flowers") James Reeves.—BrSg—LaPh
First and last. David McCord.—McAd
"**First,** April, she with mellow showers." See The four sweet months
The **first** Christmas eve. Harry Behn.—BeG
"**First** come was Cherrystones." Eleanor Farjeon.—FaT
"The **first** day of Christmas my true love sent to me." See The twelve days of Christmas
First day of summer. Eve Merriam.—MeI
First epistle of Paul to the Corinthians, sel. Bible, New Testament
Charity.—HuS-3
First fight. Vernon Scannell.—SmM
"The **first** firefly (it was off)." Issa, tr. fr. the Japanese by R. H. Blyth.—LeOw
"The **first** firefly (why do you)." Issa, tr. fr. the Japanese by R. H. Blyth.—IsF
First flame. Samuel Daniel.—CoBl
"The **first** hour was a word the color of dawn." See Spring morning—Santa Fe
"**First** I am frosted." Mary Austin
Rhyming riddles.—ArT-3
"**First** in a carriage." See Punctuality
First-ing. Aileen Fisher.—FiIo
First lesson ("Lie back, daughter, let your head") Philip Booth.—MoS
First lesson ("The thing to remember about fathers is, they're men") Phyllis McGinley.—McWs
First love. John Clare.—GrCt
"The **first** man holds it in his hands." See Song of the sun and moon
"The **first** of all my dreams was of." E. E. Cummings.—GrS
The **first** of May. See "The fair maid who, the first of May"
"**First** paint a cage." See How to paint the portrait of a bird
The **first** rainbow. Ilo Orleans.—HoB
First sight. Philip Larkin.—CoBn—ReO
First signs. Eleanor Farjeon.—FaA

First snow ("Lighter than thistledown") Ivy O. Eastwick.—ArT-3
First snow ("Snow makes whiteness where it falls") Marie Louise Allen.—ArT-3
"**First** snowstorm romp." See Haiku
First song. Galway Kinnell.—BoGj
First song of the thunder. Unknown, tr. fr. the Navajo.—LeO
"The **first** speaker said." See Paper men to air hopes and fears
The **first** spring morning. Robert Bridges.—CoBn —SmM
The **first** Thanksgiving day. Margaret Junkin Preston.—HiL
"**First** the heel." Unknown.—MoB
"**First** there were two of us, then there were three of us." See The storm
"**First** time I saw little weevil he was on the western plain." See The ballad of the boll weevil
"**First** when Maggie was my care." See Whistle o'er the lave o't
"**First** you choose a husband." See Make-believe wedding procession
"**First,** you think they are dead." See Lobsters in the window
Fish. See also names of fish, as Starfish
Alas, alack. W. De La Mare.—ArT-3
All the fishes far below. E. J. Coatsworth.—CoSb
"A cloud shimmering." Shurin.—BeCs
The crayfish. R. Wallace.—CoB
The donkey and the fluke. E. Merriam.—MeC
Eating fish. G. Johnston.—DoW
Fish ("A fish dripping") W. W. E. Ross.—CoB
The fish ("I caught a tremendous fish") E. Bishop.—BoGj—CoB
The fish ("In a cool curving world he lies") R. Brooke.—ReO (sel.)
The fish counter at Bonneville. W. Stafford.—BrA
Fish crier. C. Sandburg.—BrA
Fish story. R. Armour.—DuR
The fish, the man, and the spirit. L. Hunt.—GrCt
The fish and the man.—CoR (sel.)
A fish answers.—ReO (sel.)—SmM (sel.)
To a fish.—SmM (sel.)
The fish with the deep sea smile. M. W. Brown.—LaPd
Fishes ("Little fishes in a brook") Mother Goose.—BrMg
The fishes ("Oh, a ship she was rigg'd, and ready for sea") Unknown.—CoSs
The fishes and the poet's hands. F. Yerby.—BoA
"Fishie, fishie, in the brook." Mother Goose.—OpF
A fishy square dance. E. Merriam.—MeI
The flattered flying fish. E. V. Rieu.—ArT-3—BrSm—LaPd
The flying fish. J. Gray.—GrCt
Golden fishes. Mother Goose.—BrF—BrMg
The hen and the carp. I. Serraillier.—CoB
Her heards be thousand fishes. From Colin Clout's come home again. E. Spenser.—GrCt
The huge leviathan. From Visions of the world's vanity. E. Spenser.—GrCt
Humpty Dumpty's poem. From Through the looking-glass. L. Carroll.—BlO
Humpty Dumpty's recitation.—GrCt
I caught a fish. B. Murray.—StF
The jellyfish ("Domelike top, speckled comets converging") G. Davis.—LeM
A jellyfish ("Visible, invisible") Marianne Moore.—WeP
A little fish. H. A. Farley.—LeM
"The little fish cries." D. Recht.—LeM
The little fish that would not do as it was bid. A. and J. Taylor.—VrF
Night song of the fish. C. Morgenstern.—CoB
Over the green sands. P. Bennett.—CoB
The pike ("And nigh this toppling reed, still as the dead") E. Blunden.—ReO (sel.)
The pike ("I take it he doesn't think at all") J. Bruce.—MoS
Poor little fish. J. Ciardi.—CiYk
The silver fish. S. Silverstein.—CoSs
Skeleton. S. Barry.—LeM
"The sun's perpendicular rays." W. L. Mansel. —GrCt
"There once was a corpulent carp." C. Wells. BrLl
To a fish of the brook. J. Wolcot.—CoB
"A trout leaps high." Onitsura.—LeMw
Two million two hundred thousand fishes. D. Marcus.—LeM
Undersea fever. W. Cole.—CoSs
"Wash well the fresh fish, wash well the fresh fish." Unknown.—MoB
Fish ("A fish dripping") W. W. E. Ross.—CoB
The **fish** ("I caught a tremendous fish") Elizabeth Bishop.—BoGj—CoB
The **fish** ("In a cool curving world he lies") Rupert Brooke.—ReO (sel.)
The **fish** ("When I was very little") Elizabeth Jane Coatsworth.—CoSb
The **fish** and the man. See The fish, the man, and the spirit
A **fish** answers. See The fish, the man, and the spirit
The **fish** counter at Bonneville. William Stafford. —BrA
Fish crier. Carl Sandburg.—BrA
"A **fish** dripping." See Fish
Fish story. Richard Armour.—DuR
The **fish,** the man, and the spirit. Leigh Hunt.—GrCt
The fish and the man.—CoR (sel.)
A fish answers.—ReO (sel.)—SmM (sel.)
To a fish.—SmM (sel.)
The **fish** with the deep sea smile. Margaret Wise Brown.—LaPd
Fishback, Margaret
Hell's bells.—BrSm
Fisher, Aileen
About caterpillars.—FiI

After a bath.—StF
After the rain is over.—FiI
Airlift.—FiI
All-day sucker.—FiIo
All winter.—FiC
As soon as it's fall.—FiC
Aspen leaves.—FiI
At Christmas time.—FiIo
At Mount Vernon.—HoB
At night.—FiC
At the end of the field.—FiC
Autumn bluebirds.—FiC
Autumn leaves.—FiI
Bedtime ("Father")—FiIo
Bedtime ("Ladybugs haven't a house to sweep")—FiC
Before breakfast.—FiIo
Beneath the snowy trees.—FiI
Best of all.—FiC
Bird talk.—HoB
Birthday.—FiIo
Birthday cake.—LaPd
Birthday present.—FiC
Bluebird.—FiI
Busy summer.—FiI
Butterfly tongues.—FiI
Butterfly wings.—FiI
Buzzy old bees.—FiI
A cane.—FiIo
Caterpillars.—FiC
Christmas cookies.—AgH
Christmas mouse.—LaPh
Christmas tree.—FiIo—LaPd—LaPh
Climbing.—ArT-3—FiI
Clouds.—FiI
Coaster wagon.—FiIo
Come along.—FiIo
Comma in the sky.—FiI
Company.—FiIo
Company clothes.—FiIo
Consolation.—FiIo
Counting petals.—FiC
Cracker time.—FiC
A cricket.—FiC
Daddy longlegs.—FiI
The daffodils.—FiC
Dandelions everywhere.—FiC
December.—LaPh
December bird.—LaPh
Deer mouse.—FiC
Down.—FiIo
Dreams.—FiIo
Dressing.—FiIo
A drink.—FiIo
The ducklings.—FiC
Easter morning.—LaPh
Fairy tale.—FiIo
Fall.—ArT-3—BrSg
Fall of the year.—FiC
Fall surprises.—FiIo
Feet.—FiC
First-ing.—FiIo
Flowers at night.—BrSg—FiI
For instance.—FiIo
Francie and I.—FiIo
Freckles.—FiIo
"The frog and I."—FiIo
The frog's lament.—FiI
Frosted-window world.—FiIo
Going barefoot, sel.
June.—LaP—LaPd
Going down the street.—FiIo
Going south so soon.—FiC
Goldfish.—FiIo
Good night.—FiIo
Grasses.—FiC
Grasshoppers.—FiC
Growing.—FiIo
The handiest nose.—FiC
Hideout.—FiI
Holes of green.—FiI
"I like fall."—LaPh
"I like it when it's mizzly."—LaPd
"If I were my mother."—FiIo
I'll be a baker.—FiIo
"In one door."—FiIo
In the dark of night.—FiC
In the treetops.—FiI
Jack-o'-lantern.—LaPh
Jelly beans.—FiIo
June. See Going barefoot
Jungles of grass.—FiC
The kite.—FiI
Knowing.—FiIo
Like a bug.—FiC
Little talk.—LaP
Looking through space.—FiI
May day.—LaPh
Meadow morning.—FiI
Meadow of hay.—FiI
Meanie.—FiIo
Measles.—FiIo
Moles.—FiC
Mother's party.—FiIo
Mouse roads.—FiI
Music box.—FiIo
My dog Ginger.—FiIo
New dollhouse.—FiIo
New neighbors.—FiIo
Night sky.—FiI
"Nobody's nicer."—FiIo
Old Man Moon.—FiI
On a windy day.—FiI
On an autumn night.—FiI
On the wing.—FiI
On time.—FiC
Open house.—FiI
Peeking.—FiIo
Peeking in.—FiIo
Picnics.—FiIo
Pine music.—FiC
Plans.—FiIo
"Please to have a little rain."—FiI
Pussy willows ("Close your eyes")—FiI
Pussy willows ("Every spring the pussy willows")—FiC
Raccoons.—LaP—LaPd
The race.—FiIo

Song of the fishermen. Unknown.—LeO
Tarpon. L. Lieberman.—DuS
"There was a young angler of Worthing." Unknown.—BrLl
The three fishers. C. Kingsley.—CoSs
We'll go to sea no more. Unknown.—CoSs—GrCt
The fishermen's song.—MoB (sel.)
Wharf. M. C. Livingston.—LiC
"When a jolly young fisher named Fisher." Unknown.—BrLl
The **fishermen's** song. See We'll go to sea no more
The **fisher's** boy. Henry David Thoreau.—GrCt
The **fisher's** life. Unknown.—GrCt
Fishes ("Little fishes in a brook") Mother Goose. —BrMg
The **fishes** ("Oh, a ship she was rigg'd, and ready for sea") Unknown.—CoSs
The **fishes** and the poet's hands. Frank Yerby.—BoA
"**Fishie**, fishie, in the brook." Mother Goose.—OpF
Fishing. See Fishermen and fishing
Fishing ("One day our skiff was loaded") Edward Nevzaroff.—BaH
Fishing ("We were a noisy crew; the sun in heaven") See The prelude
"**Fishing** for snakes." Richard Eberhart.—LiT
A **fishy** square dance. Eve Merriam.—MeI
Fit only for Apollo. Francis Beaumont.—GrCt
Fitch, Robert
High brow.—MoS
Fitts, Dudley
Flowers: For Heliodora. tr.—GrS
Heat. tr.—HoL
The sower. tr.—HoL
Fitz-Geffry, Charles
Holy transportations, sel.
Take frankincense, O God.—GrCt
Take frankincense, O God. See Holy transportations
Fitzgerald, Edward
"Myself when young did eagerly frequent." See The rubaiyát of Omar Khayyám
"Oh Thou, who man of baser earth didst make." See The rubaiyát of Omar Khayyám
The rubaiyát of Omar Khayyám, sels.
"Myself when young did eagerly frequent." tr.—PlE
"Oh Thou, who man of baser earth didst make." tr.—PlE
"Think, in this batter'd caravanserai"
From The rubaiyát of Omar Khayyám. tr.—GrCt
"Yet ah, that spring should vanish with the rose." tr.—TuW
Then from a ruin. tr.—ReBs
Think, in this batter'd caravanserai." See The rubaiyát of Omar Khayyám
"Yet ah, that spring should vanish with the rose." See The rubaiyát of Omar Khayyám
Fitzgerald, F. Scott
"There'd be an orchestra." See Thousand-and-first ship
Thousand-and-first ship, sel.
"There'd be an orchestra."—BoGj
Fitzgerald, Robert
Adulescentia.—MoS (sel.)
Chorus. See Oedipus at Colonus
Cobb would have caught it.—DuS—LiT—MoS
Oedipus at Colonus, sel.
Chorus.—GrS
Five. Clare Tringress.—StF
Five eyes. Walter De La Mare.—CoB
Five hens. See "There was an old man who lived in Middle Row"
Five little chickens. See The chickens ("Said the first little chicken")
"**Five** little children." See Five
"**Five** little girls, sitting on a form." See At school
"**Five** little goblins went to town." See The holiday
"**Five** little monkeys." See The monkeys and the crocodile
"**Five** little pussy-cats, invited out to tea." See The cats' tea-party
"**Five** little pussy cats sitting in a row." Mother Goose.—OpF
Five little sisters. Kate Greenaway.—GrT
"**Five** little sisters walking in a row." See Five little sisters
"**Five** minutes, five minutes more, please." See Bedtime
"**Five** shadows in heavy motion, lumbering half-seen." See Tarpon
"**Five** years have past; five summers, with the length." See Lines composed a few miles above Tintern abbey, on revisiting the banks of the Wye during a tour, July 13, 1798
Fixer of midnight. Revel Denney.—DuS
The **flag** goes by. Henry Holcomb Bennett.—ArT-3
Flagg, James Montgomery
"There is an old fellow named Mark."—BrLl
Flags—Confederate States of America
The bonnie blue flag. A. C. Ketchum.—HiL
Flags—United States
The flag goes by. H. H. Bennett.—ArT-3
The star-spangled banner. F. S. Key.—HiL
Flags. Gwendolyn Brooks.—BoA
"**Flags** of the Pacific." See The wedding of the rose and the lotus
"**Flame** flower, day-torch, Mauna Loa." See Lines to a nasturtium
Flame-heart. Claude McKay.—BoA
"A **flame-like** flower." See Nasturtium
The **flaming** terrapin, sel. Roy Campbell
"Out of the ark's grim hold."—CoB (sel.)—ReO
Flamingos
"F was a fussy flamingo." C. Wells.—BrLl
Flanders
In Flanders fields. J. McCrae.—ThA
"The old houses of Flanders." F. M. Hueffer. —PaH

Flannan isle. Wilfrid Wilson Gibson.—BlO—CoSs
Flapper. D. H. Lawrence.—CoBl
"**Flash** goes the lightning." See Clouds in a wild storm
"A **flash** of lightning." Buson, tr. fr. the Japanese by R. H. Blyth.—LeI
"The **flashing** and golden pageant of California." See Song of the redwood-tree
The **flat.** Laurence Lieberman.—DuS
The **flattered** flying fish. E. V. Rieu.—ArT-3—BrSm—LaPd
The **flattered** lightning bug. See Archy and Mehitabel. D. Marquis.—CoB
Flattery
The flattered flying fish. E. V. Rieu.—ArT-3—BrSm—LaPd
The flattered lightning bug. From Archy and Mehitabel. D. Marquis.—CoB
Idle fyno. Unknown.—GrCt
Flax
"At the end of my yard there is a vat." Unknown.—GrCt
The **flea.** Carmen Bernos de Gasztold, tr. fr. the French by Rumer Godden.—GaC
"A **flea** and a fly in a flue." Unknown.—BrLl
The fly and the flea.—McWs
Fleas
The flea. C. B. de Gasztold.—GaC
"A flea and a fly in a flue." Unknown.—BrLl
The fly and the flea.—McWs
"For you fleas too." Issa.—IsF
"I borrowed my cottage." Issa.—IsF
"My hut is so small." Issa.—IsF
"One two three (father caught a flea)." Unknown.—CoO
Flecker, James Elroy
Brumana.—PaH
The golden journey to Samarkand.—BoGj (sel.)—PaH
The old ships.—CoR—PaH
Santorin.—BoGj
Stillness.—BoGj
To a poet a thousand years hence.—GrCt
Fleeing to safety. Rajiv Chettur.—LeM
"**Fleet.**" See The gazelle
The **fleet.** See King Henry V
"**Fleet** and fair." See The long road—Gazelles and unicorns
Fleming, Elizabeth
Toadstools.—StF
Who's in.—BlO—ClF—ThA
Wild animals.—HuS-3
Fletcher, John
"Cast our caps and cares away."—SmM
Funeral song.—GrCt
Music. See "Orpheus with his lute made trees"
"Orpheus with his lute made trees."—GrCt
Music.—ClF
See also Beaumont, Frances, jt. au.
Fletcher, John Gould
Clouds across the canyon.—PaH
Down the Mississippi.—BrA (sel.)—PaH
Lincoln.—ThA
The skaters.—MoS
The walk on the beach.—CoBl
Flett, Mary
Kindness.—LeM
Flicker. David McCord.—McAd
"**Flickering** flames of gold and red." See Fire
Flies
"After a flock of flies." Issa.—LeOw
"As a diversion." Issa.—IsF
"Busy, curious, thirsty fly." Unknown.—ClF
"Come flies." Issa.—IsF
The cure. A. Noyes.—CoB
"Don't kill." Issa.—IsF
"A few flies." Issa.—IsF
"A flea and a fly in a flue."—Unknown.—BrLl
The fly and the flea.—McWs
Fly ("A fly buzzes up the pane") E. J. Coatsworth.—CoDh
The fly ("Little fly") W. Blake.—BlO—BlP
The fly ("Lord, shall I always go in black") C. B. de Gasztold.—GaC
"I heard a fly buzz when I died." E. Dickinson.—DiPe
"If things were better." Issa.—BeCs
In a garden. A. P. Herbert.—CoB
The little fly. Unknown.—LeO
"Off with you." Issa.—IsF
The old lady who swallowed a fly. Unknown.—BrSm
"One man and one fly." Issa.—BeCs
Table. D. McCord.—McE
A trapped fly. R. Herrick.—HoL
The amber bead.—GrCt
Flight ("All day long the clouds go by") George Johnston.—DoW
Flight ("Like a glum cricket") James Tate.—LaC
The **flight** ("Look back with longing eyes and know that I will follow") Sara Teasdale.—CoBl
Flight ("You know the sitting on the train not-knowing feeling") Steve Allen.—DuS
The **flight** of birds. John Clare.—CoB
Flight of the roller-coaster. Raymond Souster.—DoW
Flint, Roland
August from my desk.—BrA—DuR
"A **flock** of little boats." Samuel Menashe.—SmM
"A **flock** of sheep that leisurely pass by." See To sleep
"A **flock** of swallows have gone flying south." See August 28
"**Flocks** of birds have flown high and away." See The Ching-Ting mountain
Flodden, Battle of, 1513
Flodden. From Marmion. W. Scott.—ClF
Flodden. See Marmion
The **flood.** See Metamorphoses
"The **flood** had ended." See The first rainbow
Floods
Ballad of the flood. E. Muir.—CaMb
The flood. From Metamorphoses. Ovid.—GrCt
The history of the flood. J. Heath-Stubbs.—CaMb

"You cannot put a fire out." E. Dickinson.—DiPe
Florence, Italy
The old bridge at Florence. H. W. Longfellow.—LoPl—PaH
Florida
Florida road worker. L. Hughes.—DuS
Florida road worker. Langston Hughes.—DuS
The **florist** shop. Rachel Field.—BrSg
"**Florist** shops are beautiful." See The florist shop
"The **flour-capped** waves." See On the beach
"**Flour** of England, fruit of Spain." Mother Goose.—BrMg
"**Flow** down, cold rivulet, to the sea." See A farewell
"**Flow** gently, sweet Afton, among thy green braes." See Sweet Afton
Flower, Robin
The monk and his cat. tr.—ReO
"The tiny bird." tr.—ReBs
The tree of life. tr.—ReBs
Wrens of the lake. tr.—ReBs
"A **flower**." See The poem of ten ones
The **flower** ("Once in a golden hour") Alfred Tennyson.—TeP
The **flower** ("The wind is half the flower") Diane Cairns.—LeM
The **flower** and the lady, about getting up. Ann and Jane Taylor.—VrF
The **flower-cart** man. Rachel Field.—BrSg—LaC
The **flower-fed** buffaloes. Vachel Lindsay.—ArT-3—BoGj—BrA—CoB—GrCt—LiP
"The **flower-fed** buffaloes of the spring." See The flower-fed buffaloes
"**Flower** in the crannied wall." Alfred Tennyson.—CoBn—TeP
A **flower** lullaby. Unknown, ad. fr. the Japanese by Charlotte B. DeForest.—DePp
The **flower-pot** man. William Darton, rev. by Ann and Jane Taylor.—VrF
The **flower-seller.** Eleanor Farjeon.—BrSg
"The **flower-seller's** fat and she wears a big shawl." See The flower-seller
Flower song. Unknown, ad. fr. the Japanese by Charlotte B. DeForest.—DePp
"A **flower** was offer'd to me." See My pretty rose tree
The **flowering** forest. Edith Sitwell.—GrS
Flowers. See also Gardeners; Gardens and gardening; Plants; Trees; also names of flowers, as Roses
Adieu. P. Lewenstein.—SmM
"After the bells hummed." Bashō.—BeCs
Afternoon on a hill. E. St V. Millay.—ArT-3—ClF—HuS-3—LaPd
As a flower I come. Sundaram.—AlPi
At Easter time. L. E. Richards.—HoB
"The autumn breeze." Issa.—LeOw
The blossom. W. Blake.—BlP—BoGj
Blue flowers. R. Field.—BrSg
The broken-hearted gardener. Unknown.—GrCt
A charm for spring flowers. R. Field.—ArT-3—TuW
A contemplation upon flowers. H. King.—CoBn
Counting petals. A. Fisher.—FiC
A cut flower. K. Shapiro.—CoBn
The death of the flowers. W. C. Bryant.—CoBn
Early spring. M. Chute.—BrSg
The end of summer. E. St V. Millay.—CoBn
The faithless flowers. M. Widdemer.—ThA
The fall of the flowers. Yen Yun.—LeMw
"The feeble plant." Issa.—LeOw
The florist shop. R. Field.—BrSg
The flower ("Once in a golden hour") A. Tennyson.—TeP
The flower ("The wind is half the flower") D. Cairns.—LeM
The flower and the lady, about getting up. A. and J. Taylor.—VrF
The flower-cart man. R. Field.—BrSg—LaC
"Flower in the crannied wall." A. Tennyson.—CoBn—TeP
A flower lullaby. Unknown.—DePp
The flower-pot man. W. Darton.—VrF
The flower-seller. E. Farjeon.—BrSg
Flower song. Unknown.—DePp
Flowers. H. Behn.—BrSg
Flowers at night. A. Fisher.—BrSg—FiI
Flowers by the sea. W. C. Williams.—BoGj—HoL
Flowers: For Heliodora. Meleager of Gadara.—GrS
"Flowers for sale." Unknown.—WyC
"Flowers look like balls of wool." P. White.—LeM
Garden song. A. Guiterman.—BrSg—ThA
"Ha, the butterfly." Unknown.—LeI
A happy lover. From In memoriam. A. Tennyson.—TeP
"I bought." Issa.—IsF
I call and I call. R. Herrick.—GrCt
"I have lost my dewdrop, cries the flower." R. Tagore.—LeMf
I have loved flowers. R. Bridges.—BoGj
The idle flowers. R. Bridges.—CoBn—GrCt
In memoriam, Easter, 1915. E. Thomas.—ThG
"In one petal of this flower." Hirotsugu.—BaS
"In the eternal." Ki no Tomsnori.—BaS
"The infant flower opens its bud and cries." R. Tagore.—LeMf
"I've nothing else to bring, you know." E. Dickinson
With flowers.—SmM
Landscape as metal and flowers. W. T. Scott.—BoGj—BrA
"Let's ride." Issa.—LeOw
"The lily has an air." C. G. Rossetti.—BrSg
Locked out. R. Frost.—LiT
Lodged. R. Frost.—BrSg
The magic flower. D. Marcus.—LeM

"The **fog** comes in with a big sound." See The sounding fog
"**Fog** is a puff of smoke." See Fog
Fog, the magician. Melville Cane.—ThA
Foley, J. W.
The salvation of Texas Peters.—BrSm
Folgore da San Geminiano
September.—MoS
Folk song. Unknown.—BrSm
Folk tune. Richard Wilbur.—BrA
"The **folk** who live in backward town." Mary Ann Hoberman.—ArT-3—CoO
Folklore. See also Ballads—Old English and Scottish; Cowboys—Songs; Legends; Mythology—Greek and Roman; also names of folk heroes, as Henry, John
Folk song. Unknown.—BrSm
Folk tune. R. Wilbur.—BrA
Mountain medicine. E. E. Long.—BrA
Follen, Eliza Lee
The little kittens.—ArT-3
"**Follow,** follow, follow." James Stephens.—StS
"**Follow** my gabelory man." See The gabelory man
Follow-my-leader. Eleanor Farjeon.—FaT
Follow sleep, fall asleep. Sochi Raut Roy, tr. fr. the Oriya by Jyotirmoy Datta.—AlPi
"**Follow** sleep then, fall asleep." See Follow sleep, fall asleep
Follow the leader ("Follow the leader away in a row") Harry Behn.—ArT-3
Follow the leader ("Whatever he does, you have to do too") Kathleen Fraser.—FrS
"**Follow** the leader away in a row." See Follow the leader
"**Follow** your leader." See Follow-my-leader
Following the music. Hilda I. Rostron.—StF
Fong, Debra
"Birds are flying past me."—BaH
Fooba wooba John. Unknown.—CoO
Food. Marchette Chute.—AgH—LaC
Food and eating. See also Cooks and cooking; also names of foods, as Cakes and cookies
Address to a haggis. R. Burns.—BuPr
Aiken Drum. Unknown.—BlO
"There came a man to our town."—MoB (sel.)
Algy. Unknown.—BrSm
"Amelia mixed the mustard." A. E. Housman. —LiT
Animal crackers. C. Morley.—HoB—ThA
"Apple pie, pudding, and pancakes." Mother Goose.—OpF
Archbishop Tait. Unknown.—GrCt
Baby Toodles. J. S. Newman.—CoBb
"Bananas and cream." D. McCord.—McE
The bean eaters. G. Brooks.—HaK
"Beautiful soup, so rich and green." From Alice's adventures in wonderland. L. Carroll.—BlO
Beautiful soup.—SmM
Turtle soup.—ClF
"The boy stood in the supper-room." Unknown.—CoO
Bread and cherries. W. De La Mare.—BrSg
Breakfast. E. Farjeon.—AgH
Bring us in good ale. Unknown.—ClF
"By the light of the next room." Issa.—LeOw
A catch. M. A. Hoberman.—AgH
Celery. O. Nash.—HoB
"Charley Wag, Charley Wag." Mother Goose. —AgH—OpF
"Charlie Wag."—BrMg
"Cheese and bread." Unknown.—MoB
"A cheese that was aged and gray." Unknown.—BrLl
Cherry-stones. E. Farjeon.—AgH
The chickens. Unknown.—StF
Five little chickens.—LaPd
The Christmas pudding. Unknown.—ArT-3—LaPh
Commissary report. S. King.—BrSm
Company. A. Fisher.—FiIo
The contrary waiter. E. Parker.—CoO
Corn. E. Antin.—BrSg
Cracker time. A. Fisher.—FiC
The cupboard. W. De La Mare.—ArT-3—StF
Davy Dumpling. Mother Goose.—BrMg
"Deedle deedle dumpling, my son John." Mother Goose.—OpF
The pasty.—BrMg
"Deprived of other banquet." E. Dickinson.—DiPe
Dilly, dilly. Unknown.—AgH
"A diner while dining at Crewe." Unknown. —BrLl
"I raised a great hullabaloo."—LaPd
"Do you know the muffin man." E. Farjeon. —FaT
"Eat at pleasure." Mother Goose.—AgH
Eat-it-all Elaine. K. Starbird.—LaPd
"Eating a meal." Issa.—LeOw
Eating fish. G. Johnston.—DoW
Fairy tale. A. Fisher.—FiIo
Favorite eats. C. McCullers.—AgH
A fire. R. Field.—AgH
Fishes. Mother Goose.—BrMg
"Flour of England, fruit of Spain." Mother Goose.—BrMg
Folk song. Unknown.—BrSm
Food. M. Chute.—AgH—LaC
For instance. A. Fisher.—FiIo
From the sublime to the ridiculous to the sublimely ridiculous to the ridiculously sublime. J. Prelutsky.—CoO
General Monk. Mother Goose.—BrMg
"The giraffe and the woman." L. E. Richards. —LaPd
The greedy boy. E. Turner.—VrF
Greedy Tom. Unknown.—AgH—StF
"Hannah Bantry, in the pantry." Mother Goose.—OpF
"Hannah Bantry."—AgH—BrMg
"He who has never known hunger." E. J. Coatsworth.—ArT-3

Food and eating—*Continued*
"Hie, hie, says Anthony." Mother Goose.—OpF
Hie, hie.—ReOn
"Hokey pokey winkey wum." Mother Goose.—OpF
Horses chawin' hay. H. Garland.—HuS-3
Hot cake. Shu Hsi.—ClF (sel.)
"Hunger is bad." Unknown.—DoC
Hunting prayer. Unknown.—LeO
"I do not know." Unknown.—DoC
The ice-cream man. R. Field.—HoB
If we didn't have to eat. N. Waterman.—AgH
In Schrafft's. W. H. Auden.—McWs
"Isabel Jones & Curabel Lee." D. McCord.—McE
Jack and Roger. B. Franklin.—GrCt
"Jack Sprat could eat no fat." Mother Goose.—OpF—ReMg—WiMg
Jack Sprat.—BrMg
The life of Jack Sprat, his wife, and his cat.—VrF
Mother Goose rhymes, 11.—HoB
Jam. D. McCord.—McE
January. M. Sendak.—AgH
"Jean, Jean, Jean." Unknown.—MoB
"Jelly Jake and Butter Bill." L. F. Jackson.—CoBb
Johan the monk. Unknown.—LiT
"John Bull, John Bull." Mother Goose.—OpF
John Bull.—BrMg
"L was a lachrymose leopard." C. Wells.—BrLl
Little Billie. W. M. Thackeray.—BlO—BrSm—CoSs
"A little cock sparrow sat on a green tree." Mother Goose.—WiMg
A little cock sparrow.—BrMg
The little girl and the turkey. D. Aldis.—AgH
"Little Jack Horner." Mother Goose.—HuS-3—OpF—WiMg
Jack Horner.—BrMg
Mother Goose rhymes, 7.—HoB
"Little King Boggen, he built a fine hall." Mother Goose.—HuS-3
Little King Boggen.—ReOn
"Little Miss Tuckett." Mother Goose.—OpF
"A little old man of Derby." Mother Goose.—ReMg
Man of Derby.—BrMg
"Little snail, little snail (with your hard)." Unknown.—WyC
Little Thomas. F. G. Evans.—CoBb
Mary. W. De La Mare.—DeBg
Master Jack's song. L. E. Richards.—AgH
A matter of taste. E. Merriam.—AgH
Millions of strawberries. G. Taggard.—ArT-3—DuR
Miss T. W. De La Mare.—ArT-3—BoGj—LaPd
Modifications. R. Koertge.—DuS
Mother's biscuits. F. Quenneville.—DuR
Mouths. D. Aldis.—AgH
Mummy slept late and daddy fixed breakfast. J. Ciardi.—ArT-3—LaPd
"My aunt kept turnips in a flock." R. Jarrell.—AgH
"My mother said that I must go." Unknown.—MoB
Neighborly. V. A. Storey.—ArT-3
Old Joe Jones. L. E. Richards.—AgH
The old man from Dunoon. Unknown.—SmM
Old woman of Exeter. Unknown.—VrF
Oodles of noodles. L. and J. L. Hymes, Jr.—AgH
"An oyster from Kalamazoo." Unknown.—BrLl
Pancakes. C. G. Rossetti.—ClF
At home.—AgH
"Pease-porridge hot." Mother Goose.—ArT-3—BrMg—WiMg
Mother Goose rhymes, 39.—HoB
"Pease-porridge hot, pease-porridge cold."—OpF
Peculiar. E. Merriam.—MeC
Perry-the-winkle. From The adventures of Tom Bombadil. J. R. R. Tolkien.—ArT-3
Pete's sweets. E. Merriam.—MeC
Picnics ("Picnics in a box are nice") A. Fisher.—FiIo
Picnics ("Sunshine and weiners and pickles and ham") M. Chute.—AgH
Poll Parrot. Mother Goose.—BrMg
"Polly put the kettle on." Mother Goose.—GrT—OpF
Polly.—BrMg
Ponjoo. W. De La Mare.—BrSm
"Pretty Futility." E. J. Coatsworth.—AgH
"The principal food of the Sioux." Unknown.—BrLl
"Pussy cat ate the dumplings." Mother Goose.—OpF
Pussy cat.—BrMg
"The Queen of Hearts she made some tarts." Mother Goose.—OpF
Mother Goose rhymes, 13.—HoB (sel.)
"The Queen of Hearts."—BrF—BrMg—WiMg
"R is for the restaurant." From All around the town. P. McGinley.—ArT-3
"Red-currant jelly." M. M. Stephenson.—StF
A rhyme for Shrove Tuesday. Unknown.—ClF
Rice pudding. A. A. Milne.—CoBb—MiC
"Robin and Bobbin, two big-bellied men." Mother Goose.—OpF
"Robbin and Bobbin."—AgH
Robin the Bobbin.—BrMg
"Round about, round about, applety pie." Mother Goose.—OpF
"Said a bad little youngster named Beauchamp." C. Wells.—BrLl
Setting the table. D. Aldis.—ArT-3—HuS-3
Slumber party. C. McCullers.—AgH
Some little bug. R. Atwell.—BrSm
Song for a hot day. E. J. Coatsworth.—HuS-3
Song in praise of paella. C. W. V. Wordsworth.—AgH

Staying overnight. A. Fisher.—FiIo
The story of Augustus who would not have any soup. H. Hoffmann.—AgH—BoGj—BrSm—CoBb
The story of Augustus.—ArT-3
The sweet tooth. K. Pyle.—AgH—CoBb
Table manners. G. Burgess.—CoBb
A ternarie of littles, upon a pipkin of jellie sent to a lady. R. Herrick.—BoGj
"There is an old cook in N. Y." Unknown.—BrLl
"There once was a bonnie Scotch laddie." Unknown.—BrLl
"There once was a finicky ocelot." E. Merriam.—BrLl
"There once was a pious young priest." Unknown.—BrLl
"There once was a provident puffin." O. Herford.—BrLl
"There was a young lady named Perkins." Unknown.—BrLl
"There was a young lady of Corsica." E. Lear.—BrLl—GrCt
"There was a young lady of Poole." E. Lear.—AgH
"There was a young person named Tate." C. Wells.—BrLl
"There was an old man from the Rhine." Unknown.—BrLl
"There was an old man of the coast." E. Lear.—AgH
"There was an old man of the east." E. Lear.—AgH
"There was an old man who said, Please." E. V. Knox.—BrLl
"There was an old person of Dean." E. Lear.—AgH—BlO—BrLl
Limericks.—HoB
"There was an old person of Ewell." E. Lear.—AgH
"There was an old person of Sparta." E. Lear.—AgH
"There was an old person whose habits." E. Lear
Limericks.—HoB
"There was an old woman (and what do you think)." Mother Goose.—OpF
"There was an old woman who lived in the fens." W. De La Mare.—AgH
"There were three ghostesses." Mother Goose.—CoO
Ghostesses.—GrCt
Three ghostesses.—AgH—BrMg
"There's a girl out in Ann Arbor, Mich." Unknown.—BrLl
"There's a lady in Kalamazoo." W. Bellamy.—BrLl
"There's nothing in afternoon tea." G. Burgess.—BrLl
This is just to say. W. C. Williams.—BoGj—DuR—LiT
"This little morsel of morsels here." From A child's day. W. De La Mare.—AgH
"A thousand hairy savages." S. Milligan.—CoO
To a poor old woman. W. C. Williams.—HoL—LiT
"To bed, to bed." Mother Goose.—OpF
Bedtime.—BrMg
Let's go to bed.—GrCt—ReS
"To sleep easy at night." Mother Goose.—AgH
How to sleep easy.—BrMg
To the bat. Mother Goose.—BrMg
The toad-eater. R. Burns.—BuPr
Tomato time. M. C. Livingston.—AgH—BrSg
"Two girls of twelve or so at a table." C. Reznikoff.—LaC
The two old bachelors. E. Lear.—BrSm
Two robins. Mother Goose.—BrMg
"A very grandiloquent goat." C. Wells.—BrLl
Virginia. P. McGinley.—AgH
The visitor. K. Pyle.—CoBb
"The voice of the glutton I heard with disdain." A. and J. Taylor.—VrF
A vote for vanilla. E. Merriam.—MeI
The vulture. H. Belloc.—AgH
"The waiter said: Try the ragout." Unknown.—BrLl
"A wee little boy has opened a store." Unknown.—WyC
"When good King Arthur ruled this land." Mother Goose.—OpF
Good King Arthur.—BrF
King Arthur.—BrMg
When in Rome. M. Evans.—BoA
"When Jacky's a good boy." Mother Goose.—OpF
Cakes and custard.—BrMg
Reward.—AgH
Willy Wood. Unknown.—AgH
"Wine and cakes for gentlemen." Mother Goose.—ReMg
Wine and cakes.—BrMg—VrF
Wish at meal-time. J. Farrar.—HoB
"Yokie pokie." Unknown.—MoB
"The **food** pits are empty." See May-June
"A **foolish** rhythm turns in my idle head." See A tune
Fools
Another song of a fool. W. B. Yeats.—ReO
Cromek speaks. W. Blake.—BlP
The dunce. Mother Goose.—BrMg
In the poppy field. J. Stephens.—StS
Madman's song. E. Wylie.—HaL—ThA
Moon folly. F. S. Davis.—ThA
Revelations. S. A. Brown.—HaK
"Simple Simon met a pieman."—HuS-3—OpF—ReMg—WiMg
The history of Simple Simon.—VrF
Mother Goose rhymes, 49.—HoB
Simple Simon.—BrMg
"Some people admire the work of a fool." W. Blake.—BlP
The song of the mad prince. W. De La Mare.—BoGj—SmM

Fools—*Continued*
The song of wandering Aengus. W. B. Yeats. —ArT-3—BlO—BoGj—CoBl—GrS—HaL—HoL—McWs—SmM—ThA—YeR
"There was an old woman, as I've heard tell." Mother Goose.—ArT-3
Mother Goose rhymes, 55.—HoB
"There was a little woman as I've heard tell."—OpF
Two songs of a fool. W. B. Yeats.—ReO
Village portrait. T. W. Duncan.—ThA
"When I was a little boy (I had but little wit)." Mother Goose.—ReOn
The simpleton.—BrMg
"You say their pictures well painted be." W. Blake.—BlP
Fools gaze at painted courts. See Polyolbion
"**Fools** gaze at painted courts, to th' country let me go." See Polyolbion—Fools gaze at painted courts
Foot, fin or feather. See Psalm CXLVII
Foot patting. Mother Goose.—BrMg
Foot races. See Races and racing—Foot
Football
Cheers. E. Merriam.—DuR—MeI
The dangers of foot-ball. From Trivia. J. Gay. —MoS
Football. W. Mason.—MoS
Football song. W. Scott.—MoS
Heaps on heaps. From A match at football. M. Concanen.—MoS
"In the beginning was the." L. Murchison.—MoS
The man from Inversnaid. R. F. Murray.—MoS
The passer. G. Abbe.—DuS—MoS
Second half. D. McCord.—MoS
Settling some old football scores. M. Bishop. —MoS
Ties. D. Stuart.—DuS
Football. Walt Mason.—MoS
Football song. Walter Scott.—MoS
Foote, Samuel
The great panjandrum.—BlO
Footprints. See also Animal tracks
Steps. R. Heckman.—BaH
White fields. J. Stephens.—CoBn—StS
"**Footprints** now on bread or cake." See To a child with eyes
"The **footsteps** of a hundred years." See The founders of Ohio
For a child named Katherine. Louise Townsend Nicholl.—ThA
For a dance. Eleanor Farjeon.—LaPh
For a dead kitten. Sara Henderson Hay.—DuR
"**For** a domestic, gentle pet." See Advice to children
For a lady I know. Countee Cullen.—AdIa—BrSm—HaK
Four epitaphs.—BoA
For a little girl that did not like to be washed. Ann and Jane Taylor.—VrF
For a marriage of St Catherine. Dante Gabriel Rossetti.—GrS
For a mocking voice. Eleanor Farjeon.—ArT-3
For a mouthy woman. Countee Cullen.—BrSm
For a pessimist. Countee Cullen.—BrSm
"**For,** all day, we drag our burden tiring." See The cry of the children
For all sorts and conditions. Norman Nicholson. —PlE
"**For** all the joys of harvest." Elfrida Vipont.—BrSg
For Anne. Leonard Cohen.—CoBl
For Anne Gregory. William Butler Yeats.—McWs—YeR
For Annie. Edgar Allan Poe.—PoP
For autumn. Eleanor Farjeon.—FaA
"**For** beauty I am not a star." Anthony Euwer. —BrLl
For Christmas day. Eleanor Farjeon.—ArT-3
"**For** dinner at Donna's." See Staying overnight
"**For** do but note a wild and wanton herd." See The merchant of Venice—The power of music
For E. McC. Ezra Pound.—MoS
"**For** England, when with fav'ring gale." See By the deep nine
"**For** every parcel I stoop down to seize." See The armful
"**For** every sip the hen says grace." See Grace
"**For** every thing that moves and lives." See Psalm CXLVII—Foot, fin or feather
"**For** God has not given us the spirit of fear." See Second Timothy
"**For** God's sake, let us sit upon the ground." See King Richard II—Of the death of kings
For Hanukkah. H. N. Bialik, tr. fr. the Hebrew by Jessie E. Sampter.—ArT-3
"**For** hours the princess would not play or sleep." See The yak
"**For** I am rightful fellow of their band." See Mentors
"**For** I will consider my cat Jeoffry." See My cat Jeoffry
For instance. Aileen Fisher.—FiIo
"**For** iron winter held her firm." See Tardy spring
For Jim, Easter eve. Anne Spencer.—BoA
For John Keats. Countee Cullen.—HaK
Four epitaphs.—BoA
"**For** lo, the sea that fleets about the land." See Orchestra—The dancing sea
"**For,** lo, the winter is past." See The song of Solomon—The song of songs
"**For** Malcolm's eyes, when they broke." See A poem for black hearts
"**For** many, many days together." See Riding together
For Mopsa. Walter De La Mare.—DeBg
For my grandmother. Countee Cullen
Four epitaphs.—BoA
For my people. Margaret Walker.—AdIa—BoA—HaK
"**For** my people everywhere singing their slave songs repeatedly." See For my people
For Paul Laurence Dunbar. Countee Cullen.—HaK

Epitaphs: For Paul Laurence Dunbar.—BoH
Four epitaphs.—BoA
For sleep, or death. Ruth Pitter.—SmM
For snow. Eleanor Farjeon.—FaA
For the bicentenary of Isaac Watts. Norman Nicholson.—PlE
"**For** the dim regions whence my fathers came." See Outcast
For the Earth God. Unknown, tr. fr. the Dahomean by Frances Herskovits.—PlE
For the one who would take man's life in his hands. Delmore Schwartz.—HiL
"**For** the second shot." See The Zen archer
For the sisters of the Hôtel Dieu. A. M. Klein. —DoW
For the time being: A Christmas oratorio, sel. W. H. Auden
"He is the way."—PlE
"**For** them the sun shines ever in full might." See Life after death
"**For** they who fashion songs must live too close to pain." See Weltschmerz
"**For** want of a nail." Mother Goose.—ReMg
A nail.—BrMg
"**For** want of gruel or food, life will not depart." Unknown, tr. fr. Vedda.—LeO
"**For** you fleas too." Issa, tr. fr. the Japanese by R. H. Blyth.—IsF
"**Forbidden** fruit a flavor has." Emily Dickinson. —DiPe
Ford, Ford Madox (Ford Madox Hueffer)
Lullaby.—ReS
The unwritten song.—ReS
The **forecast.** Dan Jaffe.—DuR
Foreign children. Robert Louis Stevenson.—BoGj—HoB
Foreign missions in battle array. Vachel Lindsay.—LiP
A **foreigner** comes to earth on Boston Common. Horace Gregory.—PlE
Foreigners
Foreign children. R. L. Stevenson.—BoGj—HoB
Immigrants. N. B. Turner.—BrA
Forest magic. Claudia Lewis.—LeP
Foresters. See Forests and forestry
Forests and forestry. See also Lumbering; Trees
"Alone in the greenwood must I roam." Unknown.—MoB
Autumn woods. J. S. Tippett.—ArT-3—HoB—StF
"Black spruce and Norway pine." From The river. P. Lorentz.—BrA
The dark forest. E. Thomas.—ThG
Evening over the forest. B. Mayor.—ClF
Forest magic. C. Lewis.—LeP
Harmony. E. J. Coatsworth.—CoDh
"In the redwood forest." C. Lewis.—LeP
Lives. H. Reed.—CoBn
Staying alive. D. Wagoner.—CoBn—DuS
Stopping by woods on a snowy evening. R. Frost.—ArT-3—BoGj—CoBn—HuS-3—LaPd
"There's a fire in the forest." W. W. E. Ross. —DoW
To the wayfarer. Unknown.—ArT-3
"Walking in the forest." S. Bahe.—BaH
The way through the woods. R. Kipling.—HuS-3—McWs
What do we plant. H. Abbey.—ArT-3
The wood of flowers. J. Stephens.—LaPd—StS
The woodlands. W. Barnes.—CoBn
Forever. Eve Merriam.—MeI
Forfeits. Eleanor Farjeon.—FaT
Forget it. David McCord.—McAd
"**Forget** six counties overhung with smoke." See Chaucer's Thames
Forgive my guilt. Robert P. Tristram Coffin.—DuR
"**Forgive,** O Lord, my little jokes on Thee." Robert Frost.—PlE
Forgive us, O Lord. See Murder in the cathedral
"**Forgive** us, O Lord, we acknowledge ourselves as type of the common man." See Murder in the cathedral—Forgive us, O Lord
Forgiveness. See also Charity; Kindness
"Forgive, O Lord, my little jokes on Thee." R. Frost.—PlE
Forgiveness. E. Sewell.—PlE
"Oh Thou, who man of baser earth didst make." From The rubáiyát of Omar Khayyám. O. Khayyám.—PlE
"Of God we ask one favor." E. Dickinson.—PlE
Susan and Patty. E. Turner.—VrF
Forgiveness. Elizabeth Sewell.—PlE
Forman, Susan
Trees.—LeM
Former barn lot. Mark Van Doren.—HaL—LaPd
The **forsaken.** Duncan Campbell Scott.—DoW (sel.)
The **forsaken** merman. Matthew Arnold.—BlO—CoSs—SmM
Fort, Paul
The sailor and the shark.—SmM
"The **fort** by the oak tree there." See The Fort of Rathangan
Fort Louisburg, Nova Scotia
Louisburg. Unknown.—HiL
Fort of Rathangan
The Fort of Rathangan. Berchan.—GrCt
The old Fort of Rathangan.—HoL
The **Fort** of Rathangan. Berchan, tr. fr. the Irish by Kuno Meyer.—GrCt
The old Fort of Rathangan.—HoL
"The **fort** over against the oak-wood." See The Fort of Rathangan
Forts. See names of forts, as Fort Louisburg
Fortune. See Success
Fortune. Lawrence Ferlinghetti.—DuR—LaC
"**Fortune** has its cookies to give out." See Fortune
Fortune telling
All your fortunes we can tell ye. From Masque of gipsies. B. Jonson.—GrCt
Beggarman. E. Farjeon.—FaT
Carriage. E. Farjeon.—FaT
Castle. E. Farjeon.—FaT

Fortune telling—*Continued*
"Cherry pie black." E. Farjeon.—FaT
Cherry-stones ("How many cherries") E. Farjeon.—AgH
"How many cherries."—FaT
Cherry stones ("Tinker, tailor, soldier, sailor") Mother Goose.—BrMg
Coach. E. Farjeon.—FaT
Cottage. E. Farjeon.—FaT—StF
Cotton. E. Farjeon.—FaT
"Elysium is as far as to." E. Dickinson.—DiPe
Farm cart. E. Farjeon.—FaT
Mansion. E. Farjeon.—FaT
Never. E. Farjeon.—FaT
Next year. E. Farjeon.—FaT
"One I love, two I love." Mother Goose.—WiMg
Pig-sty. E. Farjeon.—FaT
Pips in the fire. Mother Goose.—ReOn
Poor man. E. Farjeon.—FaT
Rags. E. Farjeon.—FaT
Rich man. E. Farjeon.—FaT
Sailor. E. Farjeon.—FaT
Satin. E. Farjeon.—FaT
Silk. E. Farjeon.—FaT
Soldier. E. Farjeon.—FaT
Some time. E. Farjeon.—FaT
Tailor. E. Farjeon.—FaT
Thief. E. Farjeon.—FaT
This year. E. Farjeon.—FaT
Tinker. E. Farjeon.—FaT
Wheelbarrow. E. Farjeon.—FaT
The **fortunes** of the great. See The Canterbury tales
Forty singing seamen. Alfred Noyes.—HoB
Foss, Sam Walter
The coming American.—BrA (sel.)
Fossils. James Stephens.—StS
Foster, Clifton Roderick
"I feel a bit happier."—LeM
Foster, Glennis
Hills.—LeM
Night and noises.—LeM
Foster, Mavis Ruth
Spider.—LeM
Foster, Stephen Collins
Old dog Tray.—CoB
Foul shot. Edwin A. Hoey.—DuR
The **founders** of Ohio. William Henry Venable.—HiL
The **fountain** ("The sea hath tempered it; the mighty sun") Mu'tamid, tr. fr. the Arabian by Dulcie L. Smith.—HoL
The **fountain** ("We talked with open heart, and tongue") William Wordsworth.—WoP
"The **fountain** is dry at the Plaza." See The lady is cold
Fountains
A drink. A. Fisher.—FiIo
The fountain ("The sea hath tempered it; the mighty sun") Mu'tamid.—HoL
The fountain ("We talked with open heart, and tongue") W. Wordsworth.—WoP
"The **fountains** mingle with the river." See Love's philosophy
"**Four-and-twenty** Highlandmen." Unknown.—MoB
"**Four-and-twenty** mermaids." Unknown.—MoB
"**Four** and twenty tailors went to kill a snail." Mother Goose.—WiMg
Snail hunters.—BrMg
Four birds. Unknown.—GrCt
Four children. Mother Goose.—BrMg
"**Four** ducks on a pond." William Allingham.—BlO—DuR
Four glimpses of night. Frank Marshall Davis.—BoA
The **four** horses. James Reeves.—CoB
400-meter freestyle. Maxine W. Kumin.—MoS
Four little ducks. David McCord.—McAd
"**Four** o'clock strikes." See Out of school
Four questions addressed to his excellency, the prime minister. James P. Vaughn.—BoA
Four sheets to the wind and a one-way ticket to France, 1933. Conrad Kent Rivers.—AdIa—BoA
"**Four** stiff-standers." Mother Goose.—BrMg—GrCt—OpF
Riddle.—BrF
The **four** sweet months. Robert Herrick.—TuW
The **four** winds. Shirley Gash.—LeM
The **four** Zoas. William Blake.—BlP (sel.)
Fourth of July
Fireworks ("People in a field with light and noise") E. Kroll.—DuS
Fireworks ("They rise like sudden fiery flowers") J. Reeves.—BrSg—LaPh
Fourth of July. H. Behn.—BeG
Fourth of July night. D. Aldis.—ArT-3—LaPh
Grandfather Watts's private Fourth. H. C. Bunner.—ArT-3
"I asked my mother for fifteen cents." Unknown.—ArT-3
Fourth of July. Harry Behn.—BeG
Fourth of July night. Dorothy Aldis.—ArT-3—LaPh
The **fox** and the grapes. Joseph Lauren.—BoH
The **fox** and the rooster. Ennis Rees.—ArT-3
"The **fox** at midnight in the city square." See Concrete trap
"The **fox** came lolloping, lolloping." See Hunting song
"The **fox-coloured** pheasant enjoyed his peace." Peter Levi.—CaD
"The **fox** drags its wounded belly." See January
"The **fox** he came lolloping, lolloping." See Hunting song
Fox hunting. See Hunters and hunting
A **fox** jumped up. See The fox's foray
"A **fox** jumped up one winter's night." See The fox's foray
The **fox** rhyme. Ian Serraillier.—CoB—SmM
"The **fox** set out in hungry plight." See The fox's foray
"The **fox**, the ape, the humble-bee." See Love's labour's lost—Another riddle

"A **fox** went out in a hungry plight." See The fox's foray
Foxes
As soon as it's fall. A. Fisher.—FiC
The ballad of red fox. M. W. La Follette.—HaL
Chanticleer and the fox. From The Canterbury tales. G. Chaucer.—ChT
Concrete trap. E. J. Coatsworth.—CoB
The false fox. Unknown.—GrCt
Four little foxes. L. Sarett.—ArT-3—BoH—CoB—DuR—LaPd
The fox and the grapes. J. Lauren.—BoH
The fox and the rooster. E. Rees.—ArT-3
The fox rhyme. I. Serraillier.—CoB—SmM
The fox's foray. Mother Goose.—BrMg
A fox jumped up.—SmM
Mister Fox.—BlO
A visit from Mr Fox.—HuS-3
The hunt. L. Kent.—CoB
Hunting song. D. Finkel.—CaMb—CoB—DuR—WeP
January. R. S. Thomas.—CoB
The lion and the fox. E. Rees.—ArT-3
The little fox. M. Edey.—ArT-3
Night of wind. F. M. Frost.—ArT-3
Of foxes. B. Y. Williams.—CoB
Reynard the fox. J. Masefield.—ReO (sel.)
Tatterdemalion. P. Bennett.—CoB
The terrible robber men. P. Colum.—HaL
The three foxes. A. A. Milne.—BoGj—HuS-3—MiC
The trap. W. Beyer.—DuR
The vixen. J. Clare.—CoB
Young Reynard. G. Meredith.—CoB
Foxgloves (Flower)
Foxgloves. T. Hughes.—HaL
Foxgloves. Ted Hughes.—HaL
"**Foxgloves** on the." See Foxgloves
The **fox's** foray. Mother Goose.—BrMg
A fox jumped up.—SmM
Mister Fox.—BlO
A visit from Mr Fox.—HuS-3
Fra Lippo Lippi. Robert Browning.—BrP
Fragment ("The cataract, whirling to the precipice") John Clare.—CoBn
Fragment ("I would to heaven that I were so much clay") See Don Juan
Fragment of a bylina. Alexander Sergeyevich Pushkin, tr. fr. the Russian by Jane Harrison and Hope Mirrlees.—LiT
Fragment of a sleepy song. Sydney Dobell.—ReS
Fragment of an English opera. Alfred Edward Housman.—LiT
France
The Bartholdi statue. J. G. Whittier.—HiL
France. From The prelude. W. Wordsworth.—WoP
France—History. See also European war, 1914-1919; French and Indian war, 1755-1763; Naval battles; Warships; World war, 1939-1945; also names of battles, as Waterloo, Battle of, 1815
Aux Tuileries 1790. E. J. Coatsworth.—CoDh
The ballad of banners. J. Lehmann.—CaMb
French revolution. W. Wordsworth.—WoP
Hervé Riel. R. Browning.—CoSs
Hohenlinden. T. Campbell.—CoR—GrCt
Incident of the French camp. R. Browning.—BrP—CoR
Louisburg. Unknown.—HiL
"Oh, the mighty king of France." Mother Goose.—OpF
France. See The prelude. William Wordsworth
Francie and I. Aileen Fisher.—FiIo
"**Francie** said when she was three." See Francie and I
Francis, Colin
Tony O.—BlO
Francis, Joseph G.
"A lion emerged from his lair."—BrLl
"Said a sheep to her child, My dear Ruth."—BrLl
Francis, of Assisi, Saint (about)
A foreigner comes to earth on Boston Common. H. Gregory.—PlE
Saint Francis. J. P. Bishop.—PlE
"Saint Francis and Saint Benedight." W. Cartwright.—PlE
A house blessing.—GrCt
The sermon of St Francis. H. W. Longfellow.—LoPl
The voice of St Francis of Assisi. V. Lindsay.—LiP
Francis, Robert
The base stealer.—ArT-3—BoGj—DuR—MoS
Blue winter.—HoL
Eagle plain.—BrA
High diver.—MoS
"The mouse whose name is Time."—HaL
Night train.—ArT-3—HaL
The orb weaver.—DuS—ReO
Paper men to air hopes and fears.—DuS
Pitcher.—DuS—MoS
Preparation.—DuR
Sailboat, your secret.—MoS
"Sing a song of juniper."—HaL
Skier.—HoL—MoS
Summons.—DuR
That dark other mountain.—MoS
Francis Jammes: A prayer to go to Paradise with the donkeys. See Prayer to go to Paradise with the donkeys
Frankel, Doris
Song of the truck.—BrA
Frankenberg, Lloyd
The night of the full moon.—CoBl
Franklin, Benjamin
Jack and Roger.—GrCt
Franklin, Benjamin (about)
Benjamin Franklin ("Ben Franklin munched a loaf of bread while walking down the street") R. C. and S. V. Benét.—ArT-3
Benjamin Franklin ("Every day, every day") E. Merriam.—MeIv

Franklin, Benjamin (about)—*Continued*
On the death of Benjamin Franklin. P. Freneau.—HiL
Fraser, Hermia
The rousing canoe song.—DoW
Fraser, Kathleen
Balloon.—FrS
Blindman's buff.—FrS
Blowing bubbles.—FrS
Broom balancing.—FrS
"Catch the wooden fish."—FrS
Dolls.—FrS
"Fife and drum."—FrS
Flying a ribbon.—FrS
Follow the leader.—FrS
Hobbyhorse.—FrS
Hoops.—FrS
Jacks.—FrS
King of the mountain.—FrS
Knocking over castles made with marbles.—FrS
Make-believe christening.—FrS
Make-believe wedding procession.—FrS
Marbles.—FrS
Mud pie.—FrS
Parade.—FrS
Piggyback.—FrS
Playing with a pet bird.—FrS
Rattle.—FrS
Riding a barrel.—FrS
Riding a fence.—FrS
Running the gauntlet.—FrS
Shouting into a barrel.—FrS
Somersaults & headstands.—FrS
Stilts.—FrS
Swinging on a rail.—FrS
Tip-cat.—FrS
Tree climbing.—FrS
Tug of war.—FrS
Turn yourself around.—FrS
Waterwings.—FrS
Which hand.—FrS
"Who am I going to choose."—FrS
Wrestling.—FrS
Frater ave atque vale. Alfred Tennyson.—GrCt—TeP
Frazee-Bower, Helen (Helen Frazee Bower)
I bid you keep some few small dreams.—ThA
Freckles
Freckles. A. Fisher.—FiIo
Freckles. Aileen Fisher.—FiIo
"**Fred.**" See Fred's bed
Fred. David McCord.—ArT-3
Freddy the rat perishes. See Archy and Mehitabel
Frederick Douglass ("Susan B. Anthony led him onto the platform") Eve Merriam.—MeIv
Frederick Douglass ("When it is finally ours, this freedom, this liberty, this beautiful") Robert E. Hayden.—AdIa—BoA—HaK
Fred's bed. Eve Merriam.—MeC
Freedom. See Liberty
The **freedom** of the moon. Robert Frost.—HoL
Freeman, John
It was the lovely moon.—CoBn
Stone trees.—CoBn
Freeman, Mary E. (Eleanor) Wilkins (Mary E. Wilkins)
"The ostrich is a silly bird."—ArT-3
Freight boats. James S. Tippett.—HuS-3
The **freight** train. Rowena Bastin Bennett.—LaP—LaPd
French and Indian war, 1754-1763
Braddock's fate, with an incitement to revenge. S. Tilden.—HiL
Brave Wolfe. Unknown.—HiL
French revolution. William Wordsworth.—WoP
Freneau, Philip
The Indian burying ground.—HiL
On the death of Benjamin Franklin.—HiL
"**Fresh** from the dewy hill, the merry year." See Song
"**Fresh** spring, the herald of love's mighty king." Edmund Spenser.—GrCt
"**Fret** not thyself because of evildoers." See Psalms—Psalm 37
The **friar.** See Maid Marian
Friars
The friar. From Maid Marian. T. L. Peacock.—MoS
The ghosts. T. L. Peacock.—SmM
The grey monk. W. Blake.—BlP
Johan the monk. Unknown.—LiT
The legend beautiful. From Tales of a wayside inn. H. W. Longfellow.—LoPl
The monk and his cat. Unknown.—ReO
The prologue. From The Canterbury tales. G. Chaucer.—ChT
"Whan that Aprille with his shoures sote."—GrCt
Soliloquy of the Spanish cloister. R. Browning.—BrP—CoD
Friday, Ann
The wish.—LaPh
"A **Friday** night's dream on a Saturday told." Mother Goose.—OpF
Friedlaender, V. H.
Planting trees.—CoBn
The **friend.** A. A. Milne.—MiC
"**Friend,** I have lost the way." See The way
A **friend** in the garden. Juliana Horatia Ewing.—BrSg—HuS-3
"**Friend** of Ronsard, Nashe, and Beaumont." See On a birthday
The **friendly** beasts. Unknown.—LaPh
"The **friendly** cow all red and white." See The cow
A **friendly** mouse. Harry Behn.—BeG
The **friendly** rock. Susan Nichols Pulsifer.—LaP
Friends. See Friendship
Friendship
Auld lang syne. R. Burns.—BuPr
Bound no'th blues. L. Hughes.—BoA
The chums. T. Roethke.—DuS
"Elysium is as far as to." E. Dickinson.—DiPe
Epistle to James Smith. R. Burns.—BuPr

A feller I know. M. Austin.—BrA
The friend. A. A. Milne.—MiC
A girl speaks to her playmate. Unknown.—AlPi
"In our house." Issa.—IsF—LeOw
King Solomon. E. Merriam.—MeC
Parting. Wang Wei.—ArT-3—LeMw
Piggyback. K. Fraser.—FrS
Rattle. K. Fraser.—FrS
Taking leave of a friend. Li T'ai-po.—HoL
"To become a chief's favorite." Unknown.—DoC
Two friends. D. Ignatow.—DuS
"Under the cherry-blossoms." Issa.—IsF
Villains. Abhinanda.—AlPi
Wrestling. K. Fraser.—FrS
"A **friendship** where one cannot act without restraint." See Villains
Frietchie, Barbara (about)
Barbara Frietchie. J. G. Whittier.—HiL
Frighted by a cow. Elizabeth Turner.—VrF
Fringed gentians. Amy Lowell.—ThA
"The **frog.**" Issa, tr. fr. the Japanese by R. H. Blyth.—LeI
The **frog** ("Be kind and tender to the frog") Hilaire Belloc.—BoGj—HoB
The **frog** ("How nice to be") Conrad Aiken.—AiC
The **frog** ("What a wonderful bird the frog are") Unknown.—CoO
"The **frog** and I." Aileen Fisher.—FiIo
"A **frog** he would a-wooing go." See The love-sick frog
Frog in a bog. David McCord.—McAd
"The **frog** looks as if." Issa, tr. fr. the Japanese by Nobuyuki Yuasa.—IsF
"**Frog-school** competing." Shiki, tr. fr. the Japanese by Harry Behn.—BeCs
"**Froggie,** froggie." Unknown.—WyC
Frogs. See also Toads; Tree toads
"Among the leaves of grass." Issa.—LeOw
"Be brave." Issa.—IsF
"Bending over." Issa.—IsF
The boy and the frogs. R. S. Sharpe.—VrF
Boy with frogs. S. Kahn.—DuR
Bullfrog. T. Hughes.—CaD—CoB
Cheers. E. Merriam.—DuR—MeI
"Day darken, frogs say." Buson.—BeCs
"A drop of rain." Issa.—ArT-3—LeI
"Excuse me." Issa.—IsF
"The frog." Issa.—LeI
The frog ("Be kind and tender to the frog") H. Belloc.—BoGj—HoB
The frog ("How nice to be") C. Aiken.—AiC
The frog ("What a wonderful bird the frog are") Unknown.—CoO
"The frog and I." A. Fisher.—FiIo
Frog in a bog. D. McCord.—McAd
"The frog looks as if." Issa.—IsF
"Frog-school competing." Shiki.—BeCs
"Froggie, froggie." Unknown.—WyC
Frogs. B. Bose.—AlPi
Frogs at school. G. Cooper.—HoB
The frogs' call. Unknown.—DePp
The frog's lament. A. Fisher.—FiI
"Frogs squatting this way." Issa.—IsF
The frogs' wedding. E. J. Coatsworth.—CoSb
The frogs who wanted a king. J. Lauren.—BoH
"A giant frog and I." Issa.—IsF
Grandfather frog. L. S. Bechtel.—ArT-3
"Ho, for the May rains." Sanpu.—BeCs
"Hopping frog, hop here and be seen." C. G. Rossetti.—BlO
Hyla brook. R. Frost.—CoBn
In the bayou. D. Marquis.—BrA
"In the spring the chirping." Onitsura.—BeCs
A legend of Okeefinokee. L. E. Richards.—HoB
The love-sick frog. Mother Goose.—BrMg
The marriage of the frog and the mouse. Unknown.—ReO
"No doubt the boss." Issa.—IsF
"An old silent pond." Bashō.—BeCs
On an autumn night. A. Fisher.—FiI
"On how to sing." Shiki.—LeI
"Our Mr Toad." D. McCord.—ArT-3
"The right honorable." Issa.—IsF
"Serenely poised." Issa.—IsF
The song of the frog. Unknown.—DePp
The spring. R. Fyleman.—HuS-3
"A tadpole, a baby slyful tadpole." W. M. Taylor.—LeM
"There dwelt a puddy in a well." Unknown.—MoB
"There was a jolly frog in the river did swim, O." Unknown.—OpF
"When spring is gone, none." Yayu.—BeCs
"With that voice." Issa.—LeMw
Frogs. Buddhadeva Bose, tr. fr. the Bengali by the author.—AlPi
"The **frogs** and the serpents each had a football team." See Cheers
Frogs at school. George Cooper.—HoB
The **frogs'** call. Unknown, ad. fr. the Japanese by Charlotte B. DeForest.—DePp
"**Frogs** in the marsh and frogs in the stream." See Canticle of spring
"The **frogs** in the pond are calling, calling." See The frogs' call
"**Frogs** jump." See Jump or jiggle
The **frog's** lament. Aileen Fisher.—FiI
"**Frogs** squatting this way." Issa, tr. fr. the Japanese by R. H. Blyth.—IsF
The **frogs'** wedding. Elizabeth Jane Coatsworth.—CoSb
"The **frogs** were living happy as could be." See The frogs who wanted a king
The **frogs** who wanted a king. Joseph Lauren.—BoH
Froissart, Jean
Rondel.—HoL
The **frolic** mariners of Devon. See Britannia's pastorals
From a childhood. Rainer Maria Rilke, tr. fr. the German by C. F. MacIntyre.—GrS

"**From** a city window, 'way up high." See Motor cars
"**From** a mountain of fallen leaves." Kazue Mizumura.—MiI
From a 19th century Kansas painter's notebook. Dave Etter.—DuS
From a railway carriage. Robert Louis Stevenson.—ArT-3—LaPd
From a very little sphinx, sel. Edna St V. Millay
"Wonder where this horseshoe went."—ArT-3
The horseshoe.—HuS-3
"**From** all the jails the boys and girls." Emily Dickinson.—DiPe
From an airplane. Harry Behn.—BeG
From Cadillac mountain. Elizabeth Jane Coatsworth.—CoDh
"**From** camp to camp, through the foul womb of night." See King Henry V—Before Agincourt
"**From** childhood's hour I have not been." See Alone
"**From** far, from eve and morning." See A Shropshire lad
"**From** ghoulies and ghosties." See An old Cornish litany
"**From** gods of other men, fastidious heart." See False gods
"**From** Grant's grave Galena." See Old Dubuque
"**From** groves of spice." See Cradle song
From hawk and kite. James Stephens.—StS
"**From** low to high doth dissolution climb." See Mutability
From my study at the mouth of the valley. Ch'ien Ch'i, tr. fr. the Chinese by Witter Bynner and Kiang Kang-hu.—LeMw
"**From** old Fort Walla Walla and the Klickitats." See In the Oregon country
"**From** the blood of Medusa." See Pegasus
"**From** the cavern of my mind." See Mnemonic for spelunking
From the dark tower. Countee Cullen.—AdIa—HaK
"**From** the dark woods that breathe of fallen showers." See The zebras
"**From** the desert I come to thee." See Bedouin song
"**From** the forest of the night." See Lunar moth
"**From** the hag and hungry goblin." See Tom o' Bedlam's song
"**From** the high deck of Santa Fe's El Capitan." See A siding near Chillicothe
From the hills of dream. William Sharp.—ThA
"**From** the skewer O the blood O on my skin dripped down." Unknown, tr. fr. the Andamanese.—LeO
From the sublime to the ridiculous to the sublimely ridiculous to the ridiculously sublime. Jack Prelutsky.—CoO
"**From** the top of a bridge." See The river is a piece of sky
From Thee to Thee. Solomon Ibn Gabirol, tr. fr. the Hebrew by Israel Abrahams.—PlE
"**From** Victoria I can go." See Victoria
"**From** Wibbleton to Wobbleton is fifteen miles." See Wibbleton and Wobbleton
"**From** you have I been absent in the spring." See Sonnets. William Shakespeare
Frontier and pioneer life. See also Cowboys; Cowboys—Songs; Indians of the Americas; United States—History—Colonial period; United States—History—Westward movement
Buffalo dusk. C. Sandburg.—ArT-3—LaPd—ReO
Conquest. E. J. Coatsworth.—BrA
The wilderness is tamed.—HuS-3
Daniel Boone. A. Guiterman.—HuS-3
The flower-fed buffaloes. V. Lindsay.—ArT-3—BoGj—BrA—CoB—GrCt—LiP
The founders of Ohio. W. H. Venable.—HiL
The King's highway. J. S. McGroarty.—PaH
Moonlight. B. H. Nance.—BrA
The Oregon trail: 1851. J. Marshall.—HuS-3
The pioneer. A. Guiterman.—ArT-3
Pioneer rat. E. J. Coatsworth.—CoSb
The pioneer woman—in the North country. E. Tietjens.—BrA
Trail breakers. J. Daugherty.—BrA
Walthena. E. Peck.—BrA
Frost, Frances M.
Beach fire.—ArT-3
Christmas eve legend.—HoB
Christmas in the woods.—ArT-3 (sel.)
Clover for breakfast.—HuS-3
Dandelions.—ArT-3
Father.—ArT-3—HuS-3
Green afternoon.—ArT-3
Green hill neighbors.—ArT-3
Kentucky birthday: February 12, 1816.—HoB
The little whistler.—ArT-3—HoB—HuS-3—LaPd
Night of wind.—ArT-3
Night plane.—ArT-3—LaPd
Nocturne.—CoBn
River night.—LaC
Sniff.—ArT-3
Trains at night.—ArT-3
Valentine for earth.—ArT-3—HoB
White season.—ArT-3—CoB
Winter feast.—BrSg
Frost, Robert
Acquainted with the night.—GrCt—LaC—LaPd
After apple-picking.—CoR
The armful.—LiT
Blue-butterfly day.—BrSg
Brown's descent; or, The willy-nilly slide.—ArT-3
"But God's own descent." See Kitty Hawk
"But outer space."—LiT
Come in.—CoBn
A considerable speck.—CoB
The cow in apple time.—ReO
Departmental; or, The end of my ant Jerry.—DuS—McWs
Design.—HoL
Dust of snow.—ArT-3—LaPd—ReBs—ThA—TuW

Fire and ice.—HoL
Fireflies in the garden.—ReO—WeP
"Forgive, O Lord, my little jokes on Thee."—PlE
The freedom of the moon.—HoL
Gathering leaves.—BrSg—HaL
The gift outright.—BrA
Good hours.—GrS
Hyla brook.—CoBn
Kitty Hawk, sel.
"But God's own descent."—PlE
The last word of a bluebird.—ArT-3—BoGj—HuS-3—TuW
Locked out.—LiT
Lodged.—BrSg
Looking for a sunset bird in winter.—ReBs
Love and a question.—CaMb
Mending wall.—BrA
A minor bird.—HaL
The mountain.—PaH
My November guest.—BoH
Neither out far nor in deep.—GrCt
Nothing gold can stay.—BoH
Now close the windows.—HaL
October.—BoGj
On looking up by chance at the constellations.—LiT
Once by the Pacific.—PaH
The pasture.—ArT-3—BoGj—CoB—HuS-3—LaP—LaPd—ThA
A patch of old snow.—DuR—LaC
A peck of gold.—BoH—LaPd
Questioning faces.—CoB
The road not taken.—GrCt
The rose family.—CoBl
The runaway.—ArT-3—BoGj—CoB—HoB—HuS-3—LaPd
The secret sits.—HaL
A soldier.—HiL
The sound of trees.—BoH
Stopping by woods on a snowy evening.—ArT-3—BoGj—CoBn—HuS-3—LaPd
To the thawing wind.—HaL
Tree at my window.—BoH—CoBn
Unharvested.—CoBn
A young birch.—CoBn
Frost
December. T. W. Ramsey.—SmM
"The deer." Issa.—IsF
"Did we abolish frost." E. Dickinson.—DiPe
Frost ("The frost moved up the window-pane") E. J. Pratt.—DoW
Frost ("Frost on my window") G. Johnston.—DoW
Frost ("What swords and spears, what daggers bright") W. H. Davies.—CoBn
The frost ("Young man") Tzu Yeh.—LeMw
The frost pane. D. McCord.—HuS-3—McE
Frosted-window world. A Fisher.—FiIo
Hard frost. A. Young.—CoBn
Jack Frost. C. E. Pike.—StF
"When the frost lies white." Unknown.—BaS
"The white chrysanthemum." Mitsune.—BaS
Frost ("The frost moved up the window-pane") E. J. Pratt.—DoW
Frost ("Frost on my window") George Johnston.—DoW
Frost ("What swords and spears, what daggers bright") William Henry Davies.—CoBn
The **frost** ("Young man") Tzu Yeh, tr. fr. the Chinese by Henry H. Hart.—LeMw
"**Frost** called to water, Halt." See Hard frost
"**Frost** flowers on the window glass." See A valentine
"The **frost** is here." See The window—Winter
"**Frost** is the quietest thing that grows." See December
"The **frost** moved up the window-pane." See Frost
"**Frost** on my window." See Frost
The **frost** pane. David McCord.—HuS-3—McE
Frosted-window world. Aileen Fisher.—FiIo
A **frosty** night. Robert Graves.—CaMb
"**Frozen** are the gutters, frozen are the gardens." See Skate and sled
"The **frozen** river is drifted deep with snow." See In the evening I walk by the river
Fruit. See also Orchards; also names of fruits, as Apples
Poisonous fruit. E. Turner.—VrF
Frutta di mare. Geoffrey Scott.—CoSs—GrCt—GrS
"**Fueled.**" Marcie Hans.—DuR
Fujiwara, Lady
"It was I who did command."—BaS
Fujiwara no Okikaze
"With voice unceasing."—BaS
Fujiwara no Tadamichi
"As I row over the plain."—BaS
Full fathom five. See The tempest
"**Full** fathom five thy father lies." See The tempest—Full fathom five
The **full** heart. Robert Nichols.—CoBn
"**Full** merrily the humble-bee doth sing." See Troilus and Cressida—The humble-bee
"The **full** moon." Issa, tr. fr. the Japanese by R. H. Blyth.—LeOw
Full moon ("No longer throne of a goddess to whom we pray") Robert E. Hayden.—HaK
Full moon ("One night as Dick lay fast asleep") Walter De La Mare.—ArT-3—CoBn
"The **full** moon whispered to the world." John Rathe.—LeM
"**Full** of oatmeal." See Miss Norma Jean Pugh, first grade teacher
Full of the moon. Karla Kuskin.—LaP—LaPd
Fuller, Ethel Romig
Proof.—ThA
"Wind is a cat."—ThA
Fuller, Mary Jo
Encountering.—BaH
This old countryside.—BaH
Fuller, Roy
Little fable.—CaD
Nino, the wonder dog.—CaD
Fun in a garret.—Emma C. Dowd.—ArT-3
Fun with my shadow. Clare Tringress.—StF

Funeral song. John Fletcher.—GrCt
Funerals. See also Death; Grief; Laments
The ballad of the light-eyed little girl. G. Brooks.—LiT
Burial. M. Van Doren.—CaMb
The burial of Sir John Moore. C. Wolfe.—CoR
The burial of Sir John Moore after Corunna.—GrCt
"Bury her at even." M. Field.—SmM
"Bury the great duke." From Ode on the death of the Duke of Wellington. A. Tennyson.—TeP
Cat's funeral. E. V. Rieu.—ArT-3—McWs
Death of the cat. I. Serraillier.—CoB
The duke of Grafton. Unknown.—GrCt
Funeral song. J. Fletcher.—GrCt
Go down death. J. W. Johnson.—BoA
Invocation. H. Johnson.—BoA
Jerry Jones. Unknown.—BrSm
The jilted funeral. G. Burgess.—BrSm
"Lingle, lingle, lang tang." Unknown.—MoB
Madrigal macabre. S. Hoffenstein.—BrSm
On a politician. H. Belloc.—BrSm—McWs
On seeing a pompous funeral for a bad husband. Unknown.—BrSm
The rebel. M. Evans.—AdIa—BoA
"A silly young man named Hyde." Unknown.—BrLl—BrSm
"Who killed Cock Robin." Mother Goose.—OpF
The death and burial of Cock Robin.—BrMg—VrF
You'd say it was a funeral. J. Reeves.—BrSm
"**Funny,** how Felicia Ropps." See Felicia Ropps
Funya no Asayasu. See Bunya no Asayasu
Funya no Yasuhide
"Although both grasses and trees."—BaS
The **fur** coat. James Stephens.—StS
Furniture. See names of furniture, as Beds
A **furrier.** Unknown, at. to William Darton.—VrF
Furriers
A furrier. Unknown.—VrF
The **furrows** of the unicorn. Elizabeth Jane Coatsworth.—CoDh
"The **furrows** of the unicorn are crooked." See The furrows of the unicorn
Furry bear. A. A. Milne.—HuS-3—MiC
"**Furry** grandfather sleeps." See December
Furubito
"Will it go crying."—BaS
"**Futile** to chide the stinging shower." See Perspectives
Futility. Wilfred Owen.—HoL
"**Fuzzy** wuzzy, creepy crawly." Lillian Schulz Vanada.—ArT-3
Fyfe, Anne
Sparrows.—LeM
Fyleman, Rose
At dawn.—HoB
"The best game the fairies play."—ArT-3
The birthday child.—LaPh
The chickens.—ArT-3
The child next door.—ThA
The dentist.—ArT-3
"The fairies have never a penny to spend."—HoB—HuS-3—ThA
The goblin. tr.—ArT-3—LaPh
Have you watched the fairies.—ArT-3—ThA
Husky hi. tr.—ArT-3
If only.—HuS-3
In the park.—HuS-3
Jonathan. tr.—ArT-3
Mice.—HuS-3—LaPd—ThA
Mrs Brown.—ArT-3
Momotara. tr.—ArT-3
My donkey. tr.—ArT-3
My policeman.—HoB
The new neighbor.—ArT-3
October.—BrSg
Shop windows.—ArT-3
The singing fairy.—HoB—ReS
Singing-time.—ArT-3
The spring.—HuS-3
Very lovely.—ArT-3
Yesterday in Oxford street.—ArT-3—LaPd

G

G., Suzanne
The sea.—LeM
The **gabelory** man. Mother Goose.—ReOn
Gabirol, Solomon Ibn
From Thee to Thee.—PlE
Gabriel
The crusader. D. Parker.—BrSm
Gág, Wanda
The A B C bunny.—ArT-3
"**Gaily** bedight." See Eldorado
Galahad, Sir (about)
Sir Galahad. A. Tennyson.—TeP
Gale, Norman
Bartholomew.—ThA
The **gallant** highwayman. James De Mille.—DoW
The **gallant** weaver. Robert Burns.—BuH
Gallantly within the ring. John Hamilton Reynolds.—MoS
The **gallery.** Andrew Marvell.—GrS
"**Galloping** galloping galloping galloping." See All of a sudden
The **gallows.** Edward Thomas.—CoB—ThG
The **gals** o' Dublin town. Unknown.—CoSs
Galuppi. Baldassare (about)
A toccata of Galuppi's. R. Browning.—BrP
Galway races. Unknown.—MoS
The **game** of chess. Ezra Pound.—LiT
Games. See also Finger-play poems; Nursery play; also names of games, as Baseball
"A dis, a dis, a green grass." Mother Goose.—MoB
Green grass.—BrMg—ReOn
Alligoshee. Mother Goose.—BrMg
"The best games the fairies play." R. Fyleman.—ArT-3

Blind man's buff ("Blind man, blind man") Mother Goose.—BrMg
Blind man's buff ("Blindman! Blindman! Blundering about") E. Farjeon.—FaT
Blindman's buff ("With a scarf around his eyes") K. Fraser.—FrS
Blindman's in. W. De La Mare.—DeBg
"Catch the wooden fish." K. Fraser.—FrS
Cobbler, cobbler, mend my shoe. E. Farjeon. —FaT
Consequences. E. Farjeon.—FaT
"Coo-coo-roo of the girls." Unknown.—DoC
"Dab a pin in my lottery book." Unknown.—MoB
"Do you know the muffin man." E. Farjeon.—FaT
Flying a ribbon. K. Fraser.—FrS
Follow-my-leader. E. Farjeon.—FaT
Follow the leader ("Follow the leader away in a row") H. Behn.—ArT-3
Follow the leader ("Whatever he does, you have to do too") K. Fraser.—FrS
Forfeits. E. Farjeon.—FaT
The gabelory man. Mother Goose.—ReOn
"Gee lee, gu lu, turn the cake." Unknown.—WyC
General Post. E. Farjeon.—FaT
Here we go looby, looby, looby. E. Farjeon. —FaT
"Here wo go round by jinga-ring." Mother Goose.—OpF
"Here wo go round the jing-a-ring."—MoB
The merry-ma-tanza.—ReOn
Here wo go round the mulberry bush. E. Farjeon.—FaT
"Here's a poor widow from Sandisland." Unknown.—MoB
Hide-and-seek ("Tiptoe away, tiptoe away") E. Farjeon.—FaT
Hide and seek ("When I am alone, and quite alone") A. B. Shiffrin.—StF
Hide-and-seek ("When little Jane lifts up her head") E. Farjeon.—FaT
Hoops. K. Fraser.—FrS
"How many miles to Babylon." Mother Goose. —OpF—ReMg—TuW
Babylon.—BrMg—GrCt
"How many miles to Glasgow Lea." Unknown.—MoB
Hunt the thimble. E. Farjeon.—FaT
I sent a letter to my love. E. Farjeon.—FaT
I'm the king of the castle. E. Farjeon.—FaT
"I've a kisty." Unknown.—MoB
Jacks. K. Fraser.—FrS
King of the castle. Mother Goose.—BrMg
King of the mountain. K. Fraser.—FrS
Kiss-in-the-ring. E. Farjeon.—FaT
Knocking over castles made with marbles. K. Fraser.—FrS
Lady of the land. Mother Goose.—ReOn
"London bridge is broken down."—Mother Goose.—OpF
London bridge.—BrMg—GrCt
Magical music. E. Farjeon.—FaT
Marbles. K. Fraser.—FrS
"Matthew, Mark, Luke, John." Mother Goose. —MoB
Pick-a-back.—BrMg
Midnight raffle. L. Hughes.—LaC
The mulberry bush. Mother Goose.—BrMg
Musical chairs. E. Farjeon.—FaT
Nuts in May. E. Farjeon.—FaT
"Oh, what is Jeannie weeping for." Unknown. —MoB
Oranges and lemons. E. Farjeon.—FaT
"A peacock feather." Unknown.—WyC
"Pease-porridge hot." Mother Goose.—ArT-3 —BrMg—WiMg
Mother Goose rhymes, 39.—HoB
"Pease-porridge hot, pease-porridge cold." —OpF
Pop goes the weasel. Mother Goose.—BrMg
"Up and down the city road."—OpF
Postman's knock. E. Farjeon.—FaT
Queen Nefertiti. Unknown.—SmM
The rape of the lock, sel. A. Pope
The playing cards.—GrCt
"Rats in the garden, catch 'em Towser." Mother Goose.—OpF
Run, boys, run.—BrF—BrMg
"Ring a ring a pinkie." Unknown.—MoB
Ring-a-ring-a-roses. E. Farjeon.—FaT
"Ring-a-ring o' (or a) roses (a pocket full of posies)." Mother Goose.—BrMg—GrT—OpF
"Round and round the butter dish." Mother Goose.—OpF
Rules of contrary. Mother Goose.—ReOn
Running the gauntlet. K. Fraser.—FrS
Shuttlecocks. K. Greenaway.—GrT
Singing game ("And it's baking, Bessy Bell") Unknown.—MoB
Singing game ("Cam you by the salmon fishers") Unknown.—MoB
Singing game ("The farmer in his den") Unknown.—MoB
Singing game ("Here comes Gentle Robin") Unknown.—MoB
Singing game ("Here is a lass with a golden ring") Unknown.—MoB
Singing game ("In and out the dusty bluebells") Unknown.—MoB
Singing game ("Johnnie Johnson's ta'en a notion") Unknown.—MoB
Singing game ("Oats and beans and barley grows") Unknown.—MoB
Singing game ("One o'clock the gun went off") Unknown.—MoB
Singing game ("Roses up and roses down") Unknown.—MoB
"So you be a roller." Unknown.—WyC
"Song of the carousel." C. Lewis.—LeP
Song of the playing ball. From Shilappadakaram. I. Adigal.—AlPi
Spelling bee. E. Farjeon.—FaT
"Tip and toe." Unknown.—MoB
Tip-cat. K. Fraser.—FrS
"Tit, tat, toe." Mother Goose.—BrMg

I have an orchard. From The tragedy of Dido. C. Marlowe.—GrCt
In a garden. A. P. Herbert.—CoB
"January brings the snow." S. Coleridge.—ArT-3
The garden year.—HuS-3
Jardins sous la pluie. J. Redwood-Anderson.—ClF (sel.)
"Little garden at the gate." Issa.—IsF—LeOw
"Little seeds we sow in spring." E. H. Minarik.—BrSg
Lodged. R. Frost.—BrSg
"Mary, Mary, quite contrary." Mother Goose.—BrSg—HuS-3—OpF—ReMg—WiMg
Contrary Mary.—BrMg
Mother Goose rhymes, 2.—HoB
Midnight in the garden. Li Shang-yin.—LeMw
"Midways of a walled garden." From Golden wings. W. Morris.—GrCt
My garden. W. H. Davies.—CoBn
"Over the garden wall." E. Farjeon.—HuS-3
"This season our tunnips was red." D. McCord.—BrLl
The three cherry trees. W. De La Mare.—GrS
To any garden. E. Farjeon.—BrSg
To three small rabbits in a burrow. M. Kennedy.—CoB
Trouble in the greenhouse. M. M. Dodge.—BrSg
Gardner, Isabella
The masked shrew.—CoB
Roundelay.—HoL
Garfield, James Abram (about)
Garfield's murder. Unknown.—HiL
Garfield's murder. Unknown.—HiL
Gargi, Balwant
Silence. tr.—AlPi
A village girl. tr.—AlPi
Garland, Hamlin
Do you fear the wind.—ArT-3—ThA
Horses chawin' hay.—HuS-3
The passing of the buffalo.—HuS-3
Plowing: A memory.—HuS-3
The plowman of today.—HuS-3
"**Garlands** for queens may be." Emily Dickinson.—DiPe
Garrett, George
The March problem.—HoL
Saints.—PlE
Garrison, Theodosia (Pickering)
The poplars.—HuS-3
Young love.—CoBl
Gars
The gar. C. G. Bell.—BrA
Garstin, Crosbie
Fog.—CoSs
Garthwaite, Jimmy. See Garthwaite, Wymond (Bradbury)
Garthwaite, Wymond (Bradbury)
Night watchmen.—ReS
Garton, Desmond
"The birds are singing music."—LeM
"The **gas** was on in the Institute." See A Shropshire lad. John Betjeman
Gascoigne, George
The praise of Philip Sparrow.—ReO
Gasetsu
The iris.—ArT-3
Gash, Shirley
The four winds.—LeM
Seagull.—LeM
Gasztold, Carmen Bernos de
The bear.—GaC
The beaver.—GaC
The camel.—GaC—ReO
The centipede.—GrC
The flea.—GaC
The fly.—GaC
The gazelle.—GaC
The gnat.—GaC
The hedgehog.—GaC
The ladybird.—GaC
The lamb.—GaC
The lion.—GaC
"Little song."—GaC
The lizard.—GaC
The mole.—GaC
The mother hen.—GaC
The oyster.—GaC
The parrot.—GaC
The peacock.—GaC
The prayer of the butterfly.—LiT
The prayer of the cat.—ArT-3—LaPd
The prayer of the cock.—ArT-3
The prayer of the donkey.—ArT-3
The prayer of the goldfish.—LaPd
The prayer of the little ducks.—ArT-3—LaPd
The prayer of the little pig.—LiT
The prayer of the mouse.—LaPd
The prayer of the old horse.—LaPd
The prayer of the ox.—LiT—McWs
The seagull.—GaC
The snail.—GaC
The spider.—GaC
The starfish.—GaC
The swallow.—GaC—ReBs
The toad.—GaC
The whale.—GaC
"**Gather** ye rose-buds while ye may." See To the virgins to make much of time
Gathering leaves. Robert Frost.—BrSg—HaL
"**Gathering** the strength." See Poem
Gatti, Sarah
"It's a sunny, sunny day today."—LeM
The **gaudy** flower. Ann and Jane Taylor.—GrT
Gautier, Judith
By the river.—GrS
Gay, John
Black-eyed Susan.—CoR—CoSs
The dangers of foot-ball. See Trivia
Fly-fishing. See Rural sports
Rural sports, sel.
Fly-fishing.—MoS
The shepherd's dog and the wolf.—ReO
Three children sliding. at.—BrMg
Trivia, sel.
The dangers of foot-ball.—MoS

Gay, Zhenya
Upside down.—HoB
"When a goose meets a moose."—ArT-3
"The world is full of wonderful smells."—ArT-3
"**Gay** comes the singer." Unknown, tr. fr. the Latin by Helen Waddell.—SmM
"**Gay** go up and gay go down." See "Oranges and lemons"
Gay Head, Massachusetts
Gay Head. N. Abeel.—PaH
Gay Head. Neilson Abeel.—PaH
"**Gay** little girl-of-the-diving-tank." See At the carnival
"**Gaze** not on swans, in whose soft breast." See Beauty extolled
The **gazelle.** Carmen Bernos de Gasztold, tr. fr. the French by Rumer Godden.—GaC
Gazelles. See Antelopes
Gazelles and unicorns. See The long road
Gazinta. Eve Merriam.—MeI
"**Gee** lee, gu lu, turn the cake." Unknown.—WyC
"**Gee** up, Needy, to the fair." Mother Goose.—OpF
Geese
"An accomplished acrobat." Issa.—IsF
"Beyond the temple." Shiki.—BeCs
Blackthorn. Mother Goose.—ReOn
Fall. S. Andresen.—DuR
The false fox. Unknown.—GrCt
The fox's foray. Mother Goose.—BrMg
A fox jumped up.—SmM
Mister Fox.—BlO
A visit from Mr Fox.—HuS-3
"Go and tell Aunt Nancy." Unknown.—BlO
The old grey goose.—GrCt
Goose feathers. Mother Goose.—BrMg
"Goosey, goosey, gander." Mother Goose.—GrT—OpF—ReMg—WiMg
Goosey gander.—BrMg
Mother Goose rhymes, 56.—HoB
Grey goose. Unknown.—DuR
"Grey goose and gander." Mother Goose.—ReOn
Goose and gander.—GrCt
"Here's a string of wild geese." Unknown.—MoB
I, too, I, too. J. H. Wheelock.—SmM
"Old Mother Goose, when." Mother Goose.—WiMg
Old Mother Goose and the golden egg.—BrMg
"Out of the sky, geese." Soin.—BeCs
"Something told the wild geese." R. Field.—ArT-3—CoB—HoL—HuS-3—LaPd—SmM—TuW
To the snow. Mother Goose.—BrF—BrMg
Wild geese. E. Chipp.—ArT-3
Wild geese flying. Unknown.—DePp
"The wild geese returning." Tsumori Kunimoto.—BaS—LaPd—LeMw
Wild goose. C. Heath.—DuR
"Wild goose, O wild goose." Issa.—LeOw
Will this wind bring you. E. J. Coatsworth.—CoSb
"The **geese** flying south." See Fall
Gehrig, Lou (about)
To Lou Gehrig. J. Kieran.—MoS
Geltman, Helen
Are we their equals.—LeM
Gems. See Precious stones
The **general.** Siegfried Sassoon.—McWs
General Monk. Mother Goose.—BrMg
General Post. Eleanor Farjeon.—FaT
General store. Rachel Field.—HoB—HuS-3—TuW
"**General** Washington? He's around." See At Mount Vernon
General William Booth enters into heaven. Vachel Lindsay.—LiP
Generosity. Virginia Brasier.—HuS-3
Genesis. Elizabeth Jane Coatsworth.—CoDh
Genghis Khan (about)
The tower of Genghis Khan. H. Allen.—PaH
Gentians
Bavarian gentians. D. H. Lawrence.—BoGj
Fringed gentians. A. Lowell.—ThA
"**Gentle** as a feather." See Breeze
"**Gentle** Jane once chanced to sit." See The swift bullets
Gentle name. Selma Robinson.—ThA
"The **gentle** winds blow." See June
"The **gentlemen's** sticks swing extra high." See Sunday
"**Gently** dip, but not too deep." See The old wives' tale—Celenta at the well of life
"**Gently,** gently, the wind blows." Kazue Mizumura.—MiI
"**Gently** I stir a white feather fan." See In the mountains on a summer day
Geometry. See Mathematics
George, Bernice
My people.—BaH
George, Stefan
Augury.—GrS
George. Dudley Randall.—HaK
"**George-Hector.**" See The emancipation of George-Hector (a colored turtle)
George Moses Horton, myself. George Moses Horton.—HaK
"**George** the First was always reckoned." See The Georges
"**George** the Third." See George III
George III, King of England
George III. E. C. Bentley.—McWs
George III. E. C. Bentley.—McWs
The **Georges.** Walter Savage Landor.—GrCt
Georgia
Georgia dusk. J. Toomer.—BoA—HaK
Georgia towns. D. W. Hicky.—BrA
In the marble quarry. J. Dickey.—BrA
Nocturne: Georgia coast. D. W. Hicky.—BrA
O Daedalus, fly away home. R. E. Hayden.—AdIa—BoH
On passing two Negroes on a dark country road somewhere in Georgia. C. K. Rivers.—AdIa
Georgia dusk. J. Toomer.—BoA—HaK

Georgia towns. Daniel Whitehead Hicky.—BrA
The **Georgics**, sel. Virgil
  The chariot race, tr. fr. the Latin by Smith Palmer Bovie.—MoS
Georgie Porgie. See "Georgie Porgie, pudding and pie"
"**Georgie** Porgie, pudding and pie." Mother Goose.—OpF—ReMg—WiMg
  Georgie Porgie.—BrMg
Geography
  Physical geography. L. T. Nicholl.—LiT
Geology
  A serio-comic elegy. R. Whately.—BrSm
  Star-swirls. R. Jeffers.—DuS
The **Geraldine**'s cloak. James Stephens.—StS
Germs
  Some little bug. R. Atwell.—BrSm (sel.)
Geronimo. Ernest McGaffey.—HiL
Gershwin, Ira
  Embraceable you. See Girl crazy
  Girl crazy, sel.
    Embraceable you.—CoBl
Get this garbage out of my life. Paul Goggins.—BaH
Get up and bar the door. Unknown.—ArT-3—BlO—HoB—LaPd
Get up, blues. James A. Emanuel.—BoA—LiT
"**Get** up, get up for shame. The blooming morn." See Corinna's going a-Maying
Get up or you'll be late for school, silly. John Ciardi.—CiYk
"**Getting** colder." Issa, tr. fr. the Japanese by R. H. Blyth.—LeOw
Getting up. Rose Burgunder.—ArT-3
Getting-up time. Unknown, ad. fr. the Japanese by Charlotte B. DeForest.—DePp
Getting wood. John Tritt.—BaH
Geysers
  Clock time by the geyser. J. White.—BrSm
Ghazal. Jigar Morabandi, tr. fr. the Urdu by Rahm Ali Alhashmi.—AlPi
Ghettoes
  Childhood. H. Percikow.—LaC
  Taught me purple. E. T. Hunt.—LaC
Ghose, Zulfikar
  The rise of Shivaji.—CaMb
Ghosts
  The admiral's ghost. A. Noyes.—ArT-3
  At the keyhole. W. De La Mare.—BlO
  Cape Horn gospel. J. Masefield.—CoSs
  The cat. J. P. Brennan.—BrSm
  Daniel Webster's horses. E. J. Coatsworth.—BrA—CoDh
  Emperors of the island. D. Abse.—CaD
  The fall of the house of Usher, sel. E. A. Poe
    The haunted palace.—GrCt—PoP
  Flannan isle. W. W. Gibson.—BlO—CoSs
  A garden at night. J. Reeves.—HoB
  The garden seat. T. Hardy.—BoGj
  The ghost-chase. W. De La Mare.—DeBg
  The ghost of Roger Casement. W. B. Yeats.—YeR
  The ghost of the buffaloes. V. Lindsay.—LiP
  A ghost story. Unknown.—DePp
  The ghost that Jim saw. B. Harte.—BrSm
  The ghostly father. P. Redgrove.—CaMb
  Ghosts ("A cold and starry darkness moans") H. Behn.—BeG
  The ghosts ("In life three ghostly friars were we") T. L. Peacock.—SmM
  The ghost's song. Unknown.—BlO—MoB
    The cauld lad's song.—GrCt
  The great auk's ghost. R. Hodgson.—BrSm
  Hallowe'en. E. Farjeon.—FaA
  Hangman's tree. L. Z. White.—BrA
  Helen of Tyre. H. W. Longfellow.—GrS
  The horseman. W. De La Mare.—ArT-3—BoGj—LaP
  I saw a ghost. J. Boilleau.—ArT-3
  Lowery cot. L. A. G. Strong.—CaD
  "Lydia is gone this many a year." L. W. Reese.—BoGj
  Mary's ghost. T. Hood.—SmM
  Meet-on-the-road. Unknown.—BlO
  A meeting. From Encounters with a Doppelganger. G. D. Painter.—SmM
  Mentors. G. Brooks.—HaK
  Molly Means. M. Walker.—BoA—HaK
  Nothing. W. De La Mare.—DeBg
  "O, Pearlin Jean." Unknown.—MoB
  October. N. Belting.—BeCm
  An old Cornish litany. Unknown.—BrSm (sel.)
  The old wife and the ghost. J. Reeves.—BrSm—HoB—LaPd
  Ophelia. A. Rimbaud.—GrCt
  The parklands. S. Smith.—CaMb
  The phantom horsewoman. T. Hardy.—GrS
  The shepherd's hut. A. Young.—CaD
  Sir Roderick's song. From Ruddigore. W. S. Gilbert.—BrSm
  "A skeleton once in Khartoum." Unknown.—BrLl—BrSm
  The small phantom. W. De La Mare.—DeBg
  Southern mansion. A. Bontemps.—AdIa—BoA—BrA—HaK
  Spooks. N. Crane.—BrSm
  The superstitious ghost. A. Guiterman.—BrSm
  "There are men in the village of Erith." Unknown.—BrLl
    The village of Erith.—GrCt
  "There were three ghostesses." Mother Goose.—CoO
    Ghostesses.—GrCt
    Three ghostesses.—AgH—BrMg
  To a persistent phantom. F. Horne.—BoA
  The two old women of Mumbling hill. J. Reeves.—BrSm
  The two wives. Daniel Henderson.—BrSm
  Waltzing Matilda. A. B. Paterson.—GrCt
  What then. W. B. Yeats.—YeR
  The wife of Usher's well. Unknown.—ArT-3—GrCt
  "A wife was sitting at her reel ae night." Unknown.—BlO
    The strange visitor.—GrCt—MoB
  The wind has wings. Unknown.—DoW
Giants
  August. N. Belting.—BeCm

Giants—*Continued*
The ballad of Sir Thopas. From The Canterbury tales. G. Chaucer.—ChT
Big Goliath, little David. E. Merriam.—MeC
"But can see there, and laughing there." G. Brooks.—HaK
"Fee, fi, fo, fum." Mother Goose.—BrF
"Fe, fi, fo, fum."—BrSm
The giant.—BrMg
Giant Bonaparte. Mother Goose.—BrMg
The history of Jack the giant killer. Unknown. —VrF
In the orchard. J. Stephens.—CoR—HaL
Momotara. Unknown.—ArT-3
The ogre entertains. E. J. Coatsworth.—CoDh
The redwoods. L. Simpson.—BrA
Gibbons, Stella
Lullaby for a baby toad.—CoB—ReS
The **ghost-chase.** Walter De La Mare.—DeBg
"**Ghost-grey** the fall of night." See A robin
The **ghost** of Roger Casement. William Butler Yeats.—YeR
The **ghost** of the buffaloes. Vachel Lindsay.—LiP
A **ghost** story. Unknown, ad. fr. the Japanese by Charlotte B. DeForest.—DePp
The **ghost** that Jim saw. Bret Harte.—BrSm
Ghostesses. See "There were three ghostesses"
The **ghostly** father. Peter Redgrove.—CaMb
Ghosts ("A cold and starry darkness moans") Harry Behn.—BeG
The **ghosts** ("In life three ghostly friars were we") Thomas Love Peacock.—SmM
The **ghost's** song. Unknown.—BlO—MoB
The cauld lad's song.—GrCt
"A **ghoulish** old fellow in Kent." Morris Bishop. —BrSm
The **giant.** See "Fee, fi, fo, fum"
Giant Bonaparte. Mother Goose.—BrMg
"The **giant** cactus is ripe in the desert." See July
"A **giant** firefly." Issa, tr. fr. the Japanese by Harold G. Henderson.—LeI
"A **giant** frog and I." Issa, tr. fr. the Japanese by Nobuyuki Yuasa.—IsF
Giant Thunder. James Reeves.—CoBn—SmM
"**Giant** Thunder, striding home." See Giant Thunder
Gibney, Somerville
Tired.—GrT
Gibson, Lydia
Goats.—CoB
Gibson, Walker
Advice to travelers.—DuR
Athletes.—MoS
The circus ship Euzkera.—CoSs
The mountains.—MoS
The umpire.—MoS
Vacationer.—MoS
Gibson, Wilfrid Wilson
Flannan isle.—BlO—CoSs
Luck.—CoSs—SmM
The parrots.—CoR
The ponies.—CoB
The wind and the rain.—ClF
The **giddy** girl. Elizabeth Turner.—VrF
The **gift** outright. Robert Frost.—BrA
Gifts and giving. See also Charity; Thankfulness
And you, Helen. E. Thomas.—ThG
The Bartholdi statue. J. G. Whittier.—HiL
The bead mat. W. De La Mare.—DeBg
Billy Taylor. Unknown.—ReOn
Birthday present. A. Fisher.—FiC
Coal for Mike. B. Brecht.—LiT
Generosity. V. Brasier.—HuS-3
Gifts for a good boy. Unknown.—DePp
The gifts of the animals to man. From Shepherd song. P. Sidney.—ReO
Giving and taking. J. Kirkup.—PlE
"I had three little sisters across the sea." Unknown.—MoB
"I have found out a gift for my fair." From A pastoral ballad. W. Shenstone.—ReBs
I will give my love an apple. Unknown.—BlO
If I were to own. E. Thomas.—ThG
"If your mother has set out to fish." Unknown.—DoC
"I'll gie you a pennyworth o' preens." Unknown.—MoB
"In one petal of this flower." Hirotsugu.—BaS
In the imperative mood. J. Stephens.—StS
"It's all I have to bring to-day." E. Dickinson.—DiPe
Little girl. Mother Goose.—BrMg
"Little maid, little maid, where have you been." Mother Goose.—OpF
The mockingbird. Mother Goose.—BrMg
Night song at Amalfi. S. Teasdale.—BoH
Nursery rhyme of innocence and experience C. Causley.—BoGj—CaD
Oblation. A. C. Swinburne.—CoBl
Of giving. A. Guiterman.—ArT-3
On the gift of a cloak. Hugo of Orleans, known as Primas.—LiT
"One blessing had I, than the rest." E. Dickinson.—DiPe
Otto. G. Brooks.—LaPd—LaPh
Parting gift. E. Wylie.—HaL
Presents ("I have counted every present with my name") M. C. Livingston.—LiC
Presents ("I wanted a rifle for Christmas") M. Chute.—LaP—LaPh
"Pretty maid, pretty maid." Mother Goose.—OpF
Reflections on a gift of watermelon pickle received from a friend called Felicity. J. Tobias.—DuR
A rhyme for Shrove Tuesday. Unknown.—ClF
Runes IX. H. Nemerov.—DuS
St Martin and the beggar. T. Gunn.—CaMb
Seven gifts. Unknown.—DePp
The singing leaves. J. R. Lowell.—HuS-3
Six rows of pins. Unknown.—ReOn
A ternarie of littles, upon a pipkin of jellie sent to a lady. R. Herrick.—BoGj

The **gnat.** Carmen Bernos de Gasztold, tr. fr. the French by Rumer Godden.—GaC
Gnats
The gnat. C. B. de Gasztold.—GaC
The gnats. O. Tchernine.—SmM
The **gnats.** Odette Tchernine.—SmM
"The **gnats** are dancing in the sun." See The gnats
The **gnome.** Harry Behn.—ArT-3—LaPd
Gnomes. See Fairies
Gnus. See Antelopes
"**Go,** and be gay." See To my son
"**Go** and tell Aunt Nancy." Unknown.—BlO
The old grey goose.—GrCt
"**Go** count the stars." See Counting
Go down Death. James Weldon Johnson.—BoA
Go down, Moses. Unknown.—PlE
Go fly a saucer. David McCord.—LiT
"**Go,** for they call you, shepherd, from the hill." See The scholar gipsy
"**Go,** go." See No man on any moon
"**Go,** go, go." Unknown.—MoB
"**Go,** go, my naughty girl, and kiss." See The little girl that beat her sister
"**Go,** lovely rose." See Song
"**Go** now, my song." Andrew Young.—GrCt
"**Go** perfect into peace." See Sleep and dreams
"**Go** roll a prairie up like cloth." See The merry miner
"**Go** seeker, if you will, throughout the land." See Burning in the night
"**Go,** soul, the body's guest." See The lie
Go thou to Rome. See Adonais
"**Go** thou to Rome,—at once the paradise." See Adonais—Go thou to Rome
"**Go** through the gates with closed eyes." See Close your eyes
Go to bed. Mother Goose.—GrCt—ReOn—ReS
Bed.—BrMg
"**Go** to bed first." See Go to bed
"**Go** to bed, Tom." Mother Goose.—OpF
"**Go** to the shine that's on a tree." Richard Eberhart.—HoL—LiT
"**Go** to the western gate, Luke Havergal." See Luke Havergal
The **goat** paths. James Stephens.—BoGj—ReO—StS
The **goatherd.** Grace Hazard Conkling.—ArT-3
Goats
April. Y. Winters.—CoB—DuR
The bicycle. J. Harasymowicz.—DuS
The goat paths. J. Stephens.—BoGj—ReO—StS
The goatherd. G. H. Conkling.—ArT-3
The goats ("One two three four") C. Aiken.—AiC
Goats ("Today I saw, lying in the shade") L. Gibson.—CoB
Nosegay for a young goat. W. Welles.—CoB
She-goat and glow-worm. C. Morgenstern.—ReO
To be sung by a small boy who herds goats. Y. Winters.—WeP
"A very grandiloquent goat." C. Wells.—BrLl
The **goats** ("One two three four") Conrad Aiken.—AiC
Goats ("Today I saw, lying in the shade") Lydia Gibson.—CoB
The **goblin.** Unknown, tr. fr. the French by Rose Fyleman.—ArT-3—LaPh
"The **goblin** has a wider mouth." See How to tell goblins from elves
"A **goblin** lives in our house, in our house, in our house." See The goblin
Goblin market. Christina Georgina Rossetti.—CoD
A **goblinade.** Florence Page Jaques.—ArT-3
Goblins. See Fairies
"**Goblins** on the doorstep." See This is Halloween
The **goblin's** song. James Telfer.—GrCt
God. See also Faith; Hymns; Jesus Christ; Psalms
Abt Vogler. R. Browning.—BrP
Adon 'Olam. Unknown.—PlE
"All things bright and beautiful." C. F. Alexander.—HoB
"And the Lord was not in the whirlwind." From Visitations: VII. L. MacNeice.—PlE
"And the old women gathered." M. Evans.—HaK
As kingfishers catch fire. G. M. Hopkins.—PlE
"At the round earth's imagin'd corners, blow." J. Donne.—PlE
Blow your trumpets, angels.—GrCt
"Batter my heart, three person'd God." J. Donne.—PlE
Bermudas. A. Marvell.—GrCt—HiL
Bessie Bobtail. J. Stephens.—StS
Birkett's eagle. D. S. Howard.—CaMb
The book of Thel. W. Blake.—BlP (sel.)
Thel's motto.—GrCt (sel.)
The burning bush. N. Nicholson.—PlE
"But God's own descent." From Kitty Hawk. Robert Frost.—PlE
Caliban on Setebos; or, Natural theology in the island. R. Browning.—BrP
Cat and mouse. T. Hughes.—PlE
A chant out of doors. M. Wilkinson.—ThA
Chiliasm. R. Eberhart.—PlE
The collar. G. Herbert.—PlE
"Comfort ye, comfort ye my people." From Isaiah, Bible, Old Testament.—PlE
Composed on a May morning, 1838. W. Wordsworth.—WoP
Conversation in Avila. P. McGinley.—PlE
The cosmic fabric. Y. Polonsky.—PlE
The creditor. L. MacNeice.—PlE
"Curse God and die, you said to me." From J. B. A. MacLeish.—PlE
Didymus. L. MacNeice.—PlE
"Discovering God is waking one morning." J. L'Heureux.—CoBn
The divine image. W. Blake.—BlP
The everlasting gospel. W. Blake.—BlP (sel.)
False gods. W. De La Mare.—PlE
"Flower in the crannied wall." A. Tennyson.—CoBn—TeP

God—*Continued*
Foot, fin or feather. From Psalm CXLVII. C. Smart.—ReO
For a child named Katherine. L. T. Nicholl. —ThA
From Thee to Thee. S. I. Gabirol.—PlE
"Fueled." M. Hans.—DuR
"The giver of life." Unknown.—PlE
Giving and taking. J. Kirkup.—PlE
God giveth all things. Unknown.—HoB
"God, is, like, scissors." J. G. Villa.—PlE
God leads the way. Cleanthes.—PlE
"God made man, and man makes money." Unknown.—OpF
"God makes ducks." G. Wall.—LeM
God's world. E. St V. Millay.—TuW
A good-night ("Close now thine eyes, and rest secure") F. Quarles.—ReS
Good night ("On tip-toe comes the gentle dark") D. M. Pierce.—ArT-3
The great magicians. C. D. Lewis.—PlE
Hap. T. Hardy.—PlE
"He put the belt around my life." E. Dickinson.—DiPe
Huswifery. E. Taylor.—PlE
"I marvel at the ways of God." E. B. White. —McWs
I need no sky. W. Bynner.—PlE
"I rose up at the dawn of day." W. Blake.—BlP
"I see the moon." Mother Goose.—ArT-3—ReS—SmM
The moon.—BrMg
"I thank you God for most this amazing." E. E. Cummings.—PlE
"I went down into the desert." V. Lindsay.—LiP
"I wonder." J. Lawton.—LeM
I wonder why. E. V. Lee.—BaH
In a dark time. T. Roethke.—PlE
The Indian upon God. W. B. Yeats.—YeR
Invocation. L. Isaac of Berditshev.—PlE
Irony. J. Stephens.—StS
"Is God dead." M. Radcliffe.—LaC
Jerusalem. W. Blake.—BlP (sel.)
The lamb. W. Blake.—BlP—BoGj—CoB—HoB —PlE
"Like many footlights burned the red." E. Dickinson.—DiPe
Lines written in her breviary. Saint Theresa. —PlE
The little boy found. W. Blake.—BlP
Little children. T. N. Tsosie.—BaH
The little vagabond. W. Blake.—BlP
"Lord—Thine the day." Dag Hammarskjöld.—PlE
The making of birds. K. Tynan.—ReBs
Man is God's nature. R. Eberhart.—PlE
The merry policeman. J. Stephens.—StS
Milton. W. Blake.—BlP (sel.)
Jerusalem.—PlE (sel.)
"Mock on, mock on Voltaire, Rousseau." W. Blake.—BlP
Mulholland's contract. R. Kipling.—CoSs
"My, fellowship, with, God." J. G. Villa.—PlE
"No coward soul is mine." E. Brontë.—PlE
"O Many Named Beloved." S. Menashe.—SmM
Oh, our manhood's prime vigor. From Saul. R. Browning.—BrP
"Of God we ask one favor." E. Dickinson.—PlE
The old repair man. F. Johnson.—BoA
On another's sorrow. W. Blake.—BlP
On being brought from Africa to America. P. Wheatley.—HaK
The 151st psalm. K. Shapiro.—PlE
The orphan. A. and J. Taylor.—GrT
Pennsylvania station. L. Hughes.—BoA—HaK
Personal. L. Hughes.—BoA
Pied beauty. G. M. Hopkins.—BoGj—HoL—PlE—SmM
The preacher: Ruminates behind the sermon. G. Brooks.—LiT
Proof ("If radio's slim fingers") E. R. Fuller. —ThA
The proof ("Shall I love God for causing me to be") R. Wilbur.—PlE
The prophet. A. S. Pushkin.—PlE
The pulley. G. Herbert.—PlE
Redemption. G. Herbert.—PlE
Remember now thy Creator. From Ecclesiastes, Bible, Old Testament.—GrCt
"The ribs and terrors of the whale." H. Melville.—PlE
Son and father. C. D. Lewis.—PlE
The song of Solomon, sels. Bible, Old Testament
Awake.—BrSg
"I am the rose of Sharon."—GrCt
The song of songs.—ArT-3
"For, lo, the winter is past."—LaP—LaPd—TuW
Sonnet. W. Wordsworth.—WoP
It is a beauteous evening.—GrCt (sel.)
"The spirit walking in the sky takes care of us." Unknown.—LeO
Spring. W. Cornish.—CoBn—GrCt
Stranger. T. Merton.—PlE
Theologians. W. De La Mare.—PlE
Third enemy speaks. C. D. Lewis.—PlE
This is a poem. H. A. Farley.—LeM
"Thou art indeed just, Lord, if I contend." G. M. Hopkins.—PlE
"Though the great waters sleep." E. Dickinson.—DiPe—PlE
"Thy voice is on the rolling air." From In memoriam. A. Tennyson.—TeP
The tiger. W. Blake.—ArT-3—CoB—CoR—GrCt—ReO—TuW
The tyger.—BlO—BlP—PlE
To a snowflake. F. Thompson.—CoBn
The triumph of doubt. J. P. Bishop.—PlE
Two somewhat different epigrams. L. Hughes. —HaK
Vice versa. C. Morgenstern.—ReO
The voice of God. J. Stephens.—StS

"The way my ideas think me." J. G. Villa.—PlE
We are all workmen. R. M. Rilke.—PlE
What Tomas said in a pub. J. Stephens.—StS
"What will you do, God, when I die." R. M. Rilke.—PlE
When Mahalia sings. Q. Prettyman.—AdIa
"While sitting here looking toward the stars." L. Curry.—BaH
"Wild nights. Wild nights." E. Dickinson.—DiPe
Wmffre the sweep. R. Humphries.—PlE
Yet do I marvel. C. Cullen.—AdIa—BoA
"**God** and the devil still are wrangling." See For a mouthy woman
"**God** and the fairies, be true, be true." See For a child named Katherine
"**God** be in my head." Unknown.—PlE—SmM
Hymnus.—GrCt
"**God** be in my hede." See "God be in my head"
"**God** bless our meat." See An old grace
"**God** bless the master of this house." Mother Goose.—HuS-3
Christmas carol.—ArT-3
"**God** gave a loaf to every bird." Emily Dickinson.—DiPe
"**God** gave all men all earth to love." See Sussex
God giveth all things. Unknown.—HoB
"**God** guard me from those thoughts men think." See A prayer for old age
"**God** is a proposition." See Third enemy speaks
"**God,** is, like, scissors." José Garcia Villa.—PlE
"**God** is the old repair man." See The old repair man
"**God,** keep all claw-denned alligators." See Prayer for reptiles
God leads the way. Cleanthes, tr. fr. the Greek by C. C. Martindale.—PlE
"**God** made Him birds in a pleasant humour." See The making of birds
"**God** made man, and man makes money." Unknown.—OpF
"**God** made the bees." Unknown.—BlO
"**God** makes ducks." Gary Wall.—LeM
"**God** moves in a mysterious way." See Light shining out of darkness
"**God** of grave nights." See A chant out of doors
"**God** rest you, merry Innocents." See A carol for children
"**God,** we don't like to complain." See Caliban in the coal mines
"**God** who created me." See Prayer
"The **god** would come, the god would go." See Man is God's nature
Godden, Rumer
The bear. tr.—GaC
The beaver. tr.—GaC
The camel. tr.—GaC—ReO
The centipede. tr.—GaC
The flea. tr.—GaC
The fly. tr.—GaC
The gazelle. tr.—GaC
The gnat. tr.—GaC
The hedgehog. tr.—GaC
The ladybird. tr.—GaC
The lamb. tr.—GaC
The lion. tr.—GaC
"Little song." tr.—GaC
The lizard. tr.—GaC
The mole. tr.—GaC
The mother hen. tr.—GaC
The oyster. tr.—GaC
The parrot. tr.—GaC
The peacock. tr.—GaC
The prayer of the butterfly. tr.—LiT
The prayer of the cat. tr.—ArT-3—LaPd
The prayer of the cock. tr.—ArT-3
The prayer of the donkey. tr.—ArT-3
The prayer of the goldfish. tr.—LaPd
The prayer of the little ducks. tr.—ArT-3—LaPd
The prayer of the little pig. tr.—LiT
The prayer of the mouse. tr.—LaPd
The prayer of the old horse. tr.—LaPd
The prayer of the ox. tr.—LiT—McWs
The seagull. tr.—GaC
The snail. tr.—GaC
The spider. tr.—GaC
The starfish. tr.—GaC
The swallow. tr.—GaC—ReBs
The toad. tr.—GaC
The whale. tr.—GaC
The **goddess.** Theodore De Banville, tr. fr. the French by Stuart Merrill.—GrS
"**Godfrey** Gordon Gustavus Gore." William Brighty Rands.—ArT-3—CoBb—HoB
Godley, Elizabeth
Extremely naughty children.—CoBb
Godmother. Phyllis B. Morden.—ThA
Godmothers
Godmother. P. B. Morden.—ThA
God's-acre. Henry Wadsworth Longfellow.—LoPl
Gods and goddesses. See also Mythology—Greek and Roman; also names of gods and goddesses, as Neptune; Diana
Arjuna's paean to Krishna. From Bhagavad Gita. Unknown.—AlPi
The goddess. T. De Banville.—GrS
"I do not know much about gods; but I think that the river." From The dry salvages. T. S. Eliot.—ArT-3
"The noise of passing feet." Unknown.—LeO
The old gods. E. Muir.—PlE
There are no gods. Euripides.—PlE
To Agni. From Rig Veda. Unknown.—AlPi
To entertain divine Zenocrate. From Tamburlaine the Great. C. Marlowe.—GrCt
To the Maruts. From Rig Veda. Unknown.—AlPi
"**God's** angry man, His crotchety scholar." See The thunderer
God's world. Edna St Vincent Millay.—TuW
Goedicke, Patricia
Jack and the beanstalk.—DuS
"**Goes** round the mud." Mother Goose.—BrMg

Goethals, George Washington (about)
Goethals, the prophet engineer. P. MacKaye. —HuS-3
Goethals, the prophet engineer. Percy MacKaye. —HuS-3
Goggins, Paul
Get this garbage out of my life.—BaH
"**Goin'** down the road, Lawd." See Bound no'th blues
Going away. Myra Cohn Livingston.—LiC
Going barefoot, sel. Aileen Fisher
June.—LaP—LaPd
"**Going** by Daly's shanty I heard the boys within." See The emigrants
Going down the street. Aileen Fisher.—FiIo
"**Going** home by lamplight across Boston Common." See A revivalist in Boston
Going south so soon. Aileen Fisher.—FiC
"**Going,** the wild things of our land." See The passing of the buffalo
Going to bed ("The babe was in the cradle laid") Elizabeth Turner.—ReS—VrF
Going to bed ("Down upon my pillow warm") Ann and Jane Taylor.—VrF
Going to bed ("Go to bed late") Mother Goose. —BrMg
Going to bed ("I'm always told to hurry up") Marchette Chute.—HoB—LaP—LaPd
"**Going** to bed late." See Going to bed
Going to St Ives. See "As I was going to St Ives"
Going to school. Elizabeth Turner.—VrF
"**Going** to school." Eve Merriam.—MeC
Going too far. Mildred Howells.—ArT-3
Gold (Color)
Black and gold. N. B. Turner.—ArT-3—LaPh
Nothing gold can stay. R. Frost.—BoH
What is gold. M. O'Neill.—OnH
Gold (Metal). See also Money
A peck of gold. R. Frost.—BoH—LaPd
September. N. Belting.—BeCm
Song of young men working in gold mines. Unknown.—DoC
"**Gold** as an infant's humming dream." See Long summer
"**Gold** dust in the sky." See Valentine greetings
Gold-fish. See Goldfish
"**Gold** is a metal." See What is gold
"**Gold** locks, and black locks." See The barber's
"**Gold** on her head, and gold on her feet." See The eve of Crécy
The **golden** bird. James Stephens.—StS
The **golden** city of St Mary. John Masefield.—BoH—PaH
"The **golden** crocus reaches up." See The crocus
"The **golden** eve is all astir." See Theme and variations—Theme
Golden fishes. Mother Goose.—BrF—BrMg
Golden gates. Unknown.—BrSm
The **golden** hive. Harry Behn.—ArT-3—BeG
The **golden** journey to Samarkand. James Elroy Flecker.—BoGj (sel.)—PaH
The **golden** net. William Blake.—GrS
Golden slumbers. See Pleasant comedy of patient Grissell—A cradle song
"**Golden** slumbers kiss your eyes." See Pleasant comedy of patient Grissell—A cradle song
The **golden** tickseed. Gustav Davidson.—BoH
The **Golden** Vanity. Unknown.—BlO—CoSs
Golden wings, sels. William Morris
"Midways of a walled garden."—GrCt
The Song of Jehane du Castel Beau.—GrCt
"**Gold** wings across the sea." See Golden wings —The song of Jehane du Castel Beau
Goldenhair. See Chamber music—"Lean out of the window"
"The **goldenrod** is yellow." See September
A **goldfinch.** Walter De La Mare.—DeBg—ReBs
Goldfinches. See Finches
Goldfish
Goldfish. A. Fisher.—FiIo
The prayer of the goldfish. C. B. de Gasztold. —LaPd
Goldfish. Aileen Fisher.—FiIo
Goldsmith, Oliver
An elegy on the death of a mad dog.—BrSm —CoR
Golf
Afforestation. E. A. Wodehouse.—MoS
The ball and the club. F. Lindsay.—MoS
The city of golf. R. F. Murray.—MoS
Golfers. I. Layton.—MoS
Mullion. A. P. Herbert.—MoS
One down. R. Armour.—MoS
A public nuisance. R. Arkell.—MoS
Seaside golf. J. Betjeman.—MoS
"They say that ex-President Taft." Unknown. —BrLl
Golfers. Irving Layton.—MoS
Golgotha
Golgotha is a mountain. A. Bontemps.—BoA
Golgotha is a mountain. Arna Bontemps.—BoA
"**Golgotha** is a mountain, a purple mound." See Golgotha is a mountain
Golino, Carlo L.
The little trumpet. tr.—LiT
Goll, Claire
"Since my birth." tr.—HoL
Goll, Yvan
"Since my birth."—HoL
Gone ("Bright sun, hot sun, oh, to be") Walter De La Mare.—DeBg
Gone ("Where's the Queen of Sheba") Walter De La Mare.—BoGj
Gone forever. Barriss Mills.—DuR
"**Gone,** gone again." Edward Thomas.—ThG
"**Gone** the snowdrop—comes the crocus." See Come—gone
"**Gone** the wild day." See Interval
"**Gone** were but the winter." See Spring quiet
"**Gone** while your tastes were keen to you." See For E. McC.
Gonzalez y Contreras, Gilberto
Heat.—HoL
"**Good** afternoon, Sir Smasham Uppe." See Sir Smasham Uppe

Good and bad. Unknown, ad. fr. the Japanese by Charlotte B. DeForest.—DePp
"**Good** and bad are in my heart." See The twins
Good and bad children. Robert Louis Stevenson.—BlO—CoBb
Good advice. Unknown, tr. fr. the German by Louis Untermeyer.—ArT-3
"**Good-by,** good-by to summer." See Robin Redbreast
"**Good** children ought to be indulg'd." See A visit to Chelsea college
"**Good** children, when they're sent to school." See Going to school
"**Good** Christians all, both great and small, I pray you lend an ear." See The Avondale mine disaster
The **good** earth. Kathy Itta.—BaH
Good Friday
Good Friday. Unknown.—GrCt
"Hot cross buns." Mother Goose.—WiMg
Good Friday.—BrMg
Good Friday. See "Hot cross buns"
Good Friday ("Christ made a trance on Friday view") Unknown.—GrCt
The **good** girl. Elizabeth Turner.—VrF
"**Good** glory, give a look at Sporting Beasley." See Sporting Beasley
Good hours. Robert Frost.—GrS
The **good** Joan. Lizette Woodworth Reese.—ArT-3—ThA
Good King Arthur. See "When good King Arthur ruled this land"
Good King Wenceslas. Unknown.—CoO
"**Good** King Wenceslas looked out." See Good King Wenceslas
"**Good** lady." See A Negro peddler's song
"**Good** little boys should never say." See Politeness
The **good** little girl. A. A. Milne.—CoBb
"**Good** manners may in seven words be found." See Of courtesy
Good men. Bhartrhari, tr. fr. the Sanskrit by D. H. H. Ingalls.—AlPi
Good morning. Muriel Sipe.—ArT-3
"**Good** morning; good morning, the general said." See The general
Good-morning poems. See Wake-up poems
"**Good** morning to you, Lord of the world." See Invocation
"**Good** news to tell." See The corner
A **good-night** ("Close now thine eyes, and rest secure") Francis Quarles.—ReS
Good night ("Good night. Good night") Victor Hugo.—ArT-3
Good night ("On tip-toe comes the gentle dark") Dorothy Mason Pierce.—ArT-3
Good night ("This day's done") Aileen Fisher.—FiIo
"**Good** night. Good night." See Good night
Good-night poems. See also Bed-time
A good-night ("Close now thine eyes, and rest secure") F. Quarles.—ReS
Good night ("Good night. Good night") V. Hugo.—ArT-3
Good night ("On tip-toe comes the gentle dark") D. M. Pierce.—ArT-3
Good night ("This day's done") A. Fisher.—FiO
Goodnight. Mother Goose.—BrMg
Last song. J. Guthrie.—ArT-3—LaPd
Twilight song. J. Hunter-Duvar.—DoW
"**Good** night, sweet prince." See Meditation at Elsinore
"**Good** night, sweet repose." See Goodnight
"**Good** people all, of every sort." See An elegy on the death of a mad dog
A **good** play. Robert Louis Stevenson.—ArT-3
The **good** scholar. Elizabeth Turner.—VrF
"**Good** seamen strike with skill." See Catching a whale
"A **good** sword and a trusty hand." See The song of the western men
Good taste. Christopher Logue.—CaD
"**Good,** to forgive." See La Saisiaz—Prologue
"A **good** world it is, indeed." Issa, tr. fr. the Japanese by Lewis Mackenzie.—LeMw
Goode, Michael
April 4, 1968.—BaH
Me.—BaH
Goodge, W. T.
Daley's dorg Wattie.—CoB
Goodman, Amy
The night.—LeM
Goodman, Paul
Our Lucy, 1956-1960.—CoB
Goodness. See Conduct of life
"**Goodness** gracious sakes alive." See Tardiness
Goodnight. Mother Goose.—BrMg
Goodson, Michael
"Silent logs floating."—LeM
The **Goole** captain. Leonard Clark.—CaD
"The **Goops** they lick their fingers." See Table manners
Goose and gander. See "Grey goose and gander"
Goose feathers. Mother Goose.—BrMg
Goosey gander. See "Goosey, goosey, gander"
"**Goosey,** goosey, gander." Mother Goose.—GrT—OpF—ReMg—WiMg
Goosey gander.—BrMg
Mother Goose rhymes, 56.—HoB
"**Goosey,** goosey, gander, where shall I wander." See "Goosey, goosey, gander"
Gore-Booth, Eva
The little waves of Breffny.—PaH
"The **gorilla** lay on his back." See Au jardin des plantes
Gorillas. See Monkeys
Gospel according to Matthew, sel. Bible, New Testament
The Lord's prayer.—PlE
A **gospel** of beauty, sels. Vachel Lindsay.—LiP (Complete)
I. The proud farmer
II. The Illinois village
III. On the building of Springfield

Gossip
Gossip. L. D. Robertson.—ThA
"Gossip grows like weeds." Hitomaro.—BaS
"Hush, my child." Unknown.—DoC
"It costs little Gossip her income for shoes." Mother Goose.—OpF
"Miss One, Two, Three, could never agree." Mother Goose.—OpF
The talking bird; or, Dame Trudge and her parrot. Unknown.—VrF
The two old women of Mumbling hill. J. Reeves.—BrSm
Gossip. Lexie Dean Robertson.—ThA
"**Gossip** grows like weeds." Hitomaro, tr. fr. the Japanese by Kenneth Rexroth.—BaS
Gotlieb, Phyllis
"How and when and where and why."—DoW
Gottlieb, H. J.
Angler's choice.—DuR
Gould, Alice Lawry
Small rain.—ThA
Gould, Elizabeth
Red in autumn.—StF
Gould, Gerald
Wander-thirst.—ArT-3—ClF (sel.)—PaH
Government
An appointment. W. B. Yeats.—YeR
The statesman's holiday. W. B. Yeats.—YeR
Govoni, Corrado
The little trumpet.—LiT
"**Gr-r-r**—there go, my heart's abhorrence." See Soliloquy of the Spanish cloister
"**Grab** tight to its handle." See Rattle
Grace
Grace for light. M. O'Neill.—ThA
Grace. Walter De La Mare.—DeBg
Grace at meals
A child's grace. R. Herrick.—PlE
Another grace for a child.—BoGj
Grace before meals.—GrT
Grace before meat.—GrCt
Grace for a child.—SmM
Grace. W. De La Mare.—DeBg
"Madam Pussie's coming hame." Unknown.—MoB
An old grace. Unknown.—ClF
Grace for light. Moira O'Neill.—ThA
"**Graceful** and sure with youth, the skaters glide." See The skaters
"**Gracefullest** leaper, the dappled fox-cub." See Young Reynard
The **gracious** and the gentle thing. Robert P. Tristram Coffin.—ReO
Graham, Al
Interplanetary limerick.—BrLl
Graham, D. L.
Soul.—HaK
Graham, Harry
Aunt Eliza.—GrCt—McWs
The bath.—BrSm
A children's don't.—CoBb (sel.)
Quiet fun.—BrSm
Self-sacrifice.—CoBb
The stern parent.—CoBb—GrCt
Graham, James, Marquis of Montrose
Verses composed on the eve of his execution. —GrCt
Graham, James, Marquis of Montrose (about)
Verses composed on the eve of his execution. J. Graham.—GrCt
Grahame, Kenneth
Ducks' ditty. See The wind in the willows
The song of Mr Toad. See The wind in the willows
The wind in the willows, sels.
Ducks' ditty.—ArT-3—BoGj—CoB—LaP—LaPd—TuW
The song of Mr Toad.—BoGj
Grain. See names of grain, as Wheat
"The **grand** old duke of York." See Oh, the brave old duke of York
"The **grand** road from the mountain goes shining to the sea." See The little waves of Breffny
Granada, Spain
The road to Granada. A. Ketchum.—PaH
Grandad's pipe. Ian Serraillier.—StF
"**Grandam,** one night, as we did sit at supper." See King Richard III—Slow flowers, fast weeds
"**Grandfa'** Grig." See Grig's pig
Grandfather frog. Louise Seaman Bechtel.—ArT-3
"**Grandfather** Watts used to tell us boys." See Grandfather Watts's private Fourth
Grandfather Watts's private Fourth. Henry Cuyler Bunner.—ArT-3
"**Grandfather** wrote from Valley Forge." See Prophecy in flame
Grandfathers
A cane. A. Fisher.—FiIo
Grandad's pipe. I. Serraillier.—StF
Grandfather Watts's private Fourth. H. C. Bunner.—ArT-3
My old grandfather. J. Alumasa.—LeM
Outdistanced. L. Rubin.—DuS
Poor grandpa. R. C. O'Brien.—BrSm
Similia similibus. J. H. Morgan.—BrSm
The unemployed blacksmith. J. Woods.—McWs
"The **grandfathers** were instructed." See July
Grandmothers
"Amy Elizabeth Ermyntrude Annie." Q. S. Hopper.—ArT-3
The cupboard. W. De La Mare.—ArT-3—StF
For my grandmother. C. Cullen
Four epitaphs.—BoA
"Grandmother's garden." J. S. Tippett.—BrSg
Irish grandmother. K. Edelman.—BrA
Lineage. M. Walker.—HaK
Little girl. Mother Goose.—BrMg
"Little maid, little maid, where have you been." Mother Goose.—OpF
"Me and my grannie." Unknown.—MoB
Old Dubuque. D. Etter.—BrA
When grandmama was young. E. J. Coatsworth.—CoSb

"When we went out with grandmamma." K. Greenaway.—GrT
"**Grandmother's** garden." James S. Tippett.—BrSg
"**Grandpa** died on his vacation." See Poor grandpa
"**Granny,** I saw a witch go by." See Halloween
Gransden, K. W.
Fifth of November.—CaD
Grant, Ulysses Simpson (about)
The aged stranger. B. Harte.—BrA
Achilles Deatheridge. E. L. Masters.—BrA
Grantchester, England
The old vicarage, Grantchester. R. Brooke.—PaH (sel.)
Grapes
The fox and the grapes. J. Lauren.—BoH
Grapes. A. Pushkin.—HoL
Grapes. Alexander Pushkin, tr. fr. the Russian by Babette Deutsch and Avrahm Yarmolinsky.—HoL
"The **grapes** are ripe, the frost is near." See Pastoral X
Grass
The grass. W. Cardwell.—LeM
The grass on the mountain. Unknown.—BoH—BrA
"The grass so little has to do." E. Dickinson.—DiPe
Grasses. A. Fisher.—FiC
Jungles of grass. A. Fisher.—FiC
Little folks in the grass. A. Wynne.—ThA
"The pampas grass." Issa.—LeMw
Spring grass. C. Sandburg.—BoH
To turn back. J. Haines.—CoBn
The **grass.** Warren Cardwell.—LeM
"The **grass** is a rug for the trees to." See Trees
The **grass** on the mountain. Unknown, tr. fr. the Paiute Indian by Mary Austin.—BoH—BrA
"The **grass** people bow." See To turn back
"The **grass** seems to dance." See The grass
"The **grass** so little has to do." Emily Dickinson.—DiPe
Grasses. Aileen Fisher.—FiC
"**Grasshopper.**" See The grasshopper
"**Grasshopper** (be the keeper)." Issa, tr. fr. the Japanese by R. H. Blyth.—IsF
"**Grasshopper** (do not trample)." Issa, tr. fr. the Japanese by R. H. Blyth.—LeI
The **grasshopper** ("Down") David McCord.—McE
The **grasshopper** ("Grasshopper") Conrad Aiken.—AiC
The **grasshopper** ("Voice of the summerwind") Alfred Tennyson.—TeP
The **grasshopper** and the cricket. Leigh Hunt.—CoB
Grasshopper Green. Unknown.—HoB—StF
"**Grasshopper** Green is a comical chap." See Grasshopper Green
"The **grasshopper,** the grasshopper." See An explanation of the grasshopper
Grasshoppers
The butterfly's ball and the grasshopper's feast. W. Roscoe.—VrF
An explanation of the grasshopper. V. Lindsay.—HuS-3
"Grasshopper (be the keeper)." Issa.—IsF
"Grasshopper (do not trample)." Issa.—LeI
The grasshoper ("Down") D. McCord.—McE
The grasshopper ("Grasshopper") C. Aiken.—AiC
The grasshopper ("Voice of the summerwind") A. Tennyson.—TeP
The grasshopper and the cricket. L. Hunt.—CoB
Grasshopper Green. Unknown.—HoB—StF
Grasshoppers ("Did ever you hear") A. Fisher.—FiC
Grasshoppers ("Grasshoppers go in many a thrumming spring") J. Clare.—CoB
The limbs of the pin oak tree. From Some short poems. W. Stafford.—DuS
"Little Miss Tuckett." Mother Goose.—OpF
My grasshopper. M. C. Livingston.—BrSg
On the grasshopper and cricket. J. Keats.—CoB
On the grasshopper and the cricket.—ReO
"R-p-o-p-h-e-s-s-a-g-r." E. E. Cummings.—CoB
Grasshoppers ("Did ever you hear") Aileen Fisher.—FiC
Grasshoppers ("Grasshoppers go in many a thrumming spring") John Clare.—CoB
"**Grasshoppers** go in many a thrumming spring." See Grasshoppers
Gratitude. See Thankfulness
The **grave.** Unknown.—GrCt
The **gravedigger.** Bliss Carman.—CoBn
Graves, Benny
A boy.—LeM
Hurting.—LeM
Graves, John Woodcock
John Peel.—MoS
Graves, Robert
Allie.—BoGj—CaD—HaL
Apples and water.—CaD
Dead cow farm.—LiT
Fingers in the nesting box.—CoB
Flying crooked.—HoL—ReO
A frosty night.—CaMb
Henry and Mary.—BoGj—CaD—HaL
I'd love to be a fairy's child.—LaPd
In the wilderness.—PlE
Lollocks.—GrCt
Love without hope.—CoBl—GrCt—GrS
The pumpkin.—BrSg—LaPd
The six badgers.—BoGj—CoB
Star-talk.—BoGj—CoBn
Symptoms of love.—DuS
To walk on hills.—MoS
Traveller's curse after misdirection.—HoL
The two witches.—CaD
Vain and careless.—CaD—HaL

Graves, Robert—*Continued*
Warning to children.—BlO
The young cordwainer.—CaMb
Graves. See Tombs
Graveyard. Robert P. Tristram Coffin.—BrA
Graveyards. See Cemeteries
"**Gravity**—what's that." See Some short poems—The limbs of the pin oak tree
Gray, John
The flying fish.—GrCt
Gazelles and unicorns. See The long road
The long road, sel.
Gazelles and unicorns.—GrCt
Gray, Thomas
Ode on the spring, sel.
The peopled air.—ReO
The peopled air. See Ode on the spring
Gray (Color)
What is gray. M. O'Neill.—OnH
"The **gray** fox for the mountains." See Of foxes
"**Gray** is the color of an elephant." See What is gray
"The **gray** sea and the long black land." See Meeting at night
The **gray** squirrel. Humbert Wolfe.—BoGj—CoB
Great A. Mother Goose.—BrMg
"**Great** A, little a." See Great A
The **great** auk's ghost. Ralph Hodgson.—BrSm
"The **great** auk's ghost rose on one leg." See The great auk's ghost
The **great** black crow. Philip James Bailey.—CoB
Great Diocletian. Abraham Cowley.—GrCt (sel.)
"**Great-grandmother** talks by the hour to me." See Irish grandmother
"**Great,** grey caravans moving in the night." See Caravans
Great Lakes
Autumn squall: Lake Erie. L. I. Russo.—BrA
The Great Lakes suite. J. Reaney.—DoW
The **Great** Lakes suite. James Reaney.—DoW
The **great** magicians. C. Day-Lewis.—PlE
The **great** news. John Ciardi.—CiYk
"The **great** Pacific railway." See The railroad cars are coming
The **great** panjandrum. Samuel Foote.—BlO
The **Great** Silkie of Sule Skerry. Unknown.—GrCt
"**Great** things are done when men and mountains meet." William Blake.—BlP
"**Great** wave of youth, ere you be spent." See Sew the flags together
"A **great** while ago, there was a schoolboy." See Old gray squirrel
"**Great,** wide, beautiful, wonderful world." See The wonderful world
The **greater** mystery. John Myers O'Hara.—PaH
The **greatest** city. Walt Whitman.—LaC
Greece
Hellas. P. B. Shelley.—GrCt (sel.)
The isles of Greece. From Don Juan. G. G. Byron.—ByP—CoR—GrCt—PaH (sel.)
Greece—History
The fifth sense. P. Beer.—CaMb
The oracles. A. E. Housman.—CoR
Greed. See Selfishness
Greed. Peggy Bennett.—CoB
The **greedy** boy. Elizabeth Turner.—VrF
Greedy fingers. Mary O'Neill.—OnF
"**Greedy** fingers are hungry to." See Greedy fingers
"**Greedy** little sparrow." See Birds in the garden
Greedy Tom. Unknown.—AgH—StF
The **Greek** anthology, sel. Krinagoras
"This torch, still burning in my hand." tr. fr. the Greek by Kenneth Rexroth.—MoS
The **Greek** anthology, sel. Unknown
"I saw no doctor, but, feeling queer inside." tr. fr. the Greek by Humbert Wolfe.—BrSm
Greek mythology. See Mythology—Greek and Roman
Green, Mary McB.
Aeroplane.—ArT-3
Green (Color)
"The sea in the dusk." Bashō.—BeCs
Song to green. E. J. Coatsworth.—CoDh
What is green. M. O'Neill.—HoB—OnH
Green afternoon. Frances M. Frost.—ArT-3
"**Green** as a seedling the one lane shines." See City traffic
Green broom. Unknown.—BlO
"**Green,** brown, or gray, old bottle-shards." See Bits of glass
Green candles. Humbert Wolfe.—SmM
"**Green** cheeses, yellow laces." See Turn, cheeses, turn
"The **green** elm with the one great bough of gold." See October
"**Green-eyed** Care." See Old cat Care
The **green** fiddler. Rachel Field.—HoB
"**Green** fly, it's difficult to see." See In a garden
Green grass. See "A dis, a dis, a green grass"
Green, green is El Aghir. Norman Cameron.—CaMb
"**Green** grow the leaves." See The hawthorn tree
"**Green** grow the rashes, O." Robert Burns.—BuPr
Green hill neighbors. Frances M. Frost.—ArT-3
"A **green** hobgoblin." See A goblinade
"**Green** is like time, green creeps, green springs." See Song to green
"**Green** is the grass." See What is green
The **green** linnet. William Wordsworth.—WoP
"A **green** little boy in a green little way." See Verdancy
"**Green** little vaulter in the sunny grass." See The grasshopper and the cricket
"**Green** mistletoe." See Winter
Green moth. Winifred Welles.—ArT-3—HoB—ReS
Green park dreams. Myra Cohn Livingston.—LiC
"**Green** peas, mutton pies." Unknown.—MoB
Green rain. Mary Webb.—CoBn—TuW
The **green** roads. Edward Thomas.—ThG
"The **green** roads that end in the forest." See The green roads
"**Green** snake, when I hung you round my neck." See To the snake

Green song. Philip Booth.—CoBn
A **green** stream. Wang Wêi, tr. fr. the Chinese by Witter Bynner and Kiang Kang-hu.—MoS
Green weeds. James Stephens.—StS
Greenaway, Kate
As I was walking.—GrT
At school.—GrT
Baby mine.—GrT
Bowl away.—GrT
The butcher's boy.—GrT
The cats have come to tea.—GrT
Five little sisters.—GrT
Higgledy, piggledy. See "Higgledy, piggledy, see how they run"
"Higgledy, piggledy, see how they run."—ArT-3
Higgledy, piggledy.—GrT
"Jump—jump—jump."—ArT-3—StF
The little jumping girls.—GrT
"Little Blue Shoes."—ArT-3
The little jumping girls. See "Jump—jump—jump"
Little wind. See "Little wind, blow on the hill-top"
"Little wind, blow on the hill-top."—ArT-3
Little wind.—BoGj—LaP
Manners.—GrT
My house is red.—GrT
"Oh, Susan Blue."—ArT-3
Susan Blue.—GrT
On the bridge.—GrT
"Prince Finikin and his mamma."—GrT
"Ring the bells—ring."—GrT
Sailor's dance.—GrT
"School is over."—ArT-3—GrT
Shuttlecocks.—GrT
Susan Blue. See "Oh, Susan Blue"
The tea party.—GrT
Three bad children.—GrT
Three little girls.—GrT
To baby.—GrT
To mystery land.—GrT
Tommy and Jimmy.—GrT
"Tommy was a silly boy."—ArT-3
"The twelve Miss Pelicoes."—GrT
Under rose arches.—GrT
Under the window.—GrT
The wedding bells.—GrT
"When we went out with grandmamma."—GrT
When you and I grow up.—GrT
Wishes.—GrT—HoB
Greenleaf, J. T.
It was shut.—CoO
"A **greensweet** breathing." See The cow
The **greenwood.** W. L. Bowles.—ClF (sel.)
Greetings. See also Wake-up poems
And once. M. C. Livingston.—LiC
Good morning. M. Sipe.—ArT-3
"How do you do, neighbor." Mother Goose.—OpF
"I went to Noke." Mother Goose.—OpF
In this hotel. E. Carnevali.—GrS
"A joyful chant." Unknown.—LeO
Little puss. Unknown.—VrF
Mr Cromek. W. Blake.—GrCt
The new Colossus. E. Lazarus.—BoH—BrA
An old Christmas greeting. Unknown.—ArT-3
"One misty moisty morning." Mother Goose.—ArT-3—BrMg—HuS-3—LaPd—OpF—ReOn
How do you do.—GrCt
Stepping westward. W. Wordsworth.—WoP
Gregor, Arthur
Blackout.—GrS
Gregory, Horace
Elizabeth at the piano.—GrS
A foreigner comes to earth on Boston Common.—PlE
Gregory, Lady (Isabella Augusta)
The army of the Sidhe.—ThA
Donall Oge: The grief of a girl's heart. tr.—CoBl
The grief of a girl's heart.—GrCt
The grief of a girl's heart. See Donall Oge: Grief of a girl's heart
Gregory, Yvonne
Christmas lullaby for a new-born child.—BoA
Gregory Griggs. See "Gregory Griggs, Gregory Griggs"
"**Gregory** Griggs, Gregory Griggs." Mother Goose.—OpF
Gregory Griggs.—BrMg
Grenville, Sir Richard (about)
The Revenge. A. Tennyson.—CoD—TeP
"**Grey** as a guinea-fowl is the rain." See Kitchen song
"**Grey** as a mouse." See The adventures of Tom Bombadil—Oliphaunt
"The **grey** cat's kittled in Charlie's wig." Unknown.—MoB
Grey goose. Unknown.—DuR
"**Grey** goose and gander." Mother Goose.—ReOn
Goose and gander.—GrCt
The **grey** monk. William Blake.—BlP
"The **grey** quails were bunched together." Unknown, tr. fr. the Pima.—LeO
Grief. See also Laments; Melancholy
Adjuration. C. E. Wheeler.—BoA
Ah fading joy. J. Dryden.—GrCt
Calm is the morn. From In memoriam. A. Tennyson.—GrCt—TeP
Cares and joys. From King Henry VI. W. Shakespeare.—ShS
The carousel. G. C. Oden.—BoA—HaK
The chamber over the gate. H. W. Longfellow.—LoPl
The cross of snow. H. W. Longfellow.—LoPl
The debt. P. L. Dunbar.—BoA—BoH—HaK
The despairing lover. W. Walsh.—CoBl
"Dip down upon the northern shore." From In memoriam. A. Tennyson.—TeP
"Do not believe your Shakespeare's grief." From The argument. C. Aiken.—ReO
Donall Oge: Grief of a girl's heart. Unknown.—CoBl
The grief of a girl's heart.—GrCt
The dove. W. Barnes.—ReBs

Grief—*Continued*
From the dark tower. C. Cullen.—AdIa—HaK
Grieve not for me. Unknown.—BrSm
A happy lover. From In memoriam. A. Tennyson.—TeP
"I can wade grief." E. Dickinson.—DiPe
"I sometimes hold it half a sin." From In memoriam. A. Tennyson.—TeP
If the stars should fall. S. Allen.—AdIa
"If there be sorrow." M. Evans.—HaK
"I'll come back—and the things of me that." L. Hale.—BaH
"In less than two and twenty years." Asclepiades of Samos.—HoL
Infant sorrow. W. Blake.—BlP
Mad song. W. Blake.—BlP
Mock at sorrow. From King Richard II. W. Shakespeare.—ShS
Mose. S. A. Brown.—HaK
My November guest. R. Frost.—BoH
October journey. M. Walker.—AdIa—BoA
On another's sorrow. W. Blake.—BlP
"Out in the marsh reeds." Tsurayuki.—BaS
The paradox. P. L. Dunbar.—HaK
The pig-tale. From Sylvie and Bruno. L. Carroll.—ReO
The playmate. W. De La Mare.—DeBg
The return. Unknown.—LeMw
Snowflakes. H. W. Longfellow.—GrCt
Snow-flakes.—LoPl
Song for someone who is absent. Unknown.—DoC
Song of the earth. E. J. Coatsworth.—CoDh
Sonnet. W. Wordsworth.—WoP
"Sorrow is the only faithful one." O. Dodson.—AdIa—BoA
Spring and fall: To a young child. G. M. Hopkins.—BoGj—GrCt
Trifle. G. D. Johnson.—BoA—BoH
Weltschmerz. F. Yerby.—BoA
What hope is here. From In memoriam. A. Tennyson.—TeP
"When I am in grief." Yamanoue no Okura.—LeMw
When my light is low. From In memoriam. A. Tennyson.—TeP
"A widow bird sate mourning for her love." From Charles IV. P. B. Shelley.—BlO
Song from Charles IV.—SmM
Written in very early youth. W. Wordsworth.—WoP
The **griesly** wife. John Manifold.—CaMb
Grieve not for me. Unknown.—BrSm
"**Grieve** not for me my husband dear." See Grieve not for me
Griffins
Yet gentle will the griffin be. V. Lindsay.—HuS-3—LaPd—ThA
Grig's pig. Mother Goose.—BrMg
Grigson, Geoffrey
Life half lived. tr.—GrCt
Grilikhes, Alexandra
The runner.—MoS
"**Grill** me some bones, said the cobbler." See At the keyhold
"**Grim** Cotton Mather." See Cotton Mather
Grimké, Angeline W.
The black finger.—BoA
To Clarissa Scott Delany.—BoA
Grist mills. See Mills
Grizzly. Bret Harte.—CoB—ReO
Grizzly bear. Mary Austin.—ArT-3—BoGj—LaP—LaPd
"The **grizzly** bear is huge and wild." See Infant innocence
The **grocer.** Unknown, at. to William Darton.—VrF
Grocery shops
The grocer. Unknown.—VrF
"Nauty pauty." Mother Goose.—AgH
Jack-a-Dandy.—BrMg
"The **groggy** fighter on his knees." See Athletes
Grongar hill. John Dyer.—ClF (sel.)—GrCt
Ground hog day. See Candelmas day
Ground hog day. Marnie Pomeroy.—CoB
Ground hogs. See Woodchucks
Grouse
"The bonnie moor-hen." Unknown.—MoB
"The moorhens are chirping." Issa.—LeOw
Ptarmigan ("O ptarmigan, O ptarmigan") D. McCord.—McAd
The ptarmigan ("The ptarmigan is strange") Unknown.—CoB
Grover, Alliene
"See this beautiful rainy day."—LeM
"**Grow** old along with me." See Rabbi Ben Ezra
Growing. Aileen Fisher.—FiIo
"**Growing** in the vale." Christina Georgina Rossetti.—ArT-3
Sweet Daffadowndilly.—HoB
Growing up
A certain age. P. McGinley.—DuS
Development. R. Browning.—BrP
Fast run in the junkyard. J. Nichols.—DuS
Fishermen. J. A. Emanuel.—BoH
George. D. Randall.—HaK
Growing. A. Fisher.—FiIo
Growing up ("A big Jack, cutting outward toward blue") K. Wilson.—DuS
Growing up ("I'm growing very big and tall") E. K. Wallace.—ThA
Growing up ("When I was seven") H. Behn.—LaPd—LaPh
Grownups. M. Duskin.—LeM
Happy birthday to me. E. Merriam.—MeC
Here I am. Ann Morrissett.—CoBl
Hey, ho, the wind and the rain. From Twelfth night. W. Shakespeare.—ShS
A lazy thought. E. Merriam.—LaC
Lesson. H. Behn.—BrSg
Peggy Mitchell. J. Stephens.—StS
The question. K. Kuskin.—LaPd
A spike of green. B. Baker.—BrSg
"Take the curious case of Tom Pettigrew." D. McCord.—BrLl
Tommy. G. Brooks.—BrSg
Tomorrow. M. C. Livingston.—LiC

"When I was a little boy (my mammy)." Mother Goose.—OpF—TuW
The big boy.—BrMg
When you and I grow up. K. Greenaway.—GrT
Growing up ("A big Jack, cutting outward toward blue") Keith Wilson.—DuS
Growing up ("I'm growing very big and tall") Edna Kingsley Wallace.—ThA
Growing up ("When I was seven") Harry Behn.—LaPd—LaPh
"**Growltiger** was a Bravo Cat, who lived upon a barge." See Growltiger's last stand
Growltiger's last stand. T. S. Eliot.—CoR
Grown-up fingers. Mary O'Neill.—OnF
"**Grown-up** fingers are used to what they do." See Grown-up fingers
Grownups. Marc Duskin.—LeM
"**Grownups** are silly." See Grownups
"The **Guardian** Prince of Albion burns in his nightly tent." See America
The **guest.** Unknown.—PlE
"A **guest** for whom I did not care." See Lines scratched in wet cement
Guests
Autobiographical fragment. K. Amis.—CaD
The guest. Unknown.—PlE
The hostess. Wang Mou Fang.—LeMw
Lines scratched in wet cement. E. Jacobson.—BrSm
Guinea-pigs
"There was a little guinea-pig." Mother Goose.—OpF
Guha, Naresh
A little girl, Rumi's fancy.—AlPi
Guineas
Life. A. Kreymborg.—CoB
Guiteau, Charles (about)
Garfield's murder. Unknown.—HiL
Guiterman, Arthur
The ambiguous dog.—CoB
Ancient history.—DuR—McWs
The bat.—CoB
Belsnickel.—CoBb
"The cautious collapsible cow."—BrLl
Daniel Boone.—HuS-3
The dog's cold nose.—CoB
Eight oars and a coxswain.—MoS
Garden song.—BrSg—ThA
Habits of the hippopotamus.—ArT-3
House blessing.—ArT-3
Lament for the Alamo.—BrA
The London bobby.—PaH
Mexican serenade.—CoBl
Mule song.—CoB
Ode to the amoeba.—DuS
Of courtesy.—ArT-3
Of giving.—ArT-3
Of quarrels.—ArT-3
On the vanity of earthly greatness.—DuR
The pioneer.—ArT-3
Song of hate for eels.—CoB
The starlighter.—ThA
The superstitious ghost.—BrSm
What the gray cat sings.—LiT—ReS
"A **gull** rides on the ripples of a dream." See A walk in late summer
Gulls
Gull. W. J. Smith.—ArT-3
"A lone gull." K. Mizumura.—MiI
A question. Unknown.—DePp
"The sea gull curves his wings." E. J. Coatsworth.—ArT-3
Sea gull.—CoB
Seagull ("As I watch over") S. Gash.—LeM
The seagull ("A hole in the cliffs") C. B. de Gasztold.—GaC
Seagulls ("Two medicos, immaculate in gray") F. H. Savage.—DuS
Seagulls ("We have no time for bridges") P. Hubbell.—LaPd
A talisman. Marianne Moore.—BoGj—HoL
Three seagulls. Unknown.—DePp
A walk in late summer. T. Roethke.—ReO (sel.)
"A **gull's** ghostly call." Stephen Hopkins.—LeM
"The **gun** explodes them." See The sprinters
"The **gun** full swing the swimmer catapults and cracks." See 400-meter freestyle
Gunn, Thom
Jesus and his mother.—PlE
The produce district.—DuS
St Martin and the beggar.—CaMb
Gunpowder plot day. See "Please to remember"
Guns. See also Arms and armor; Hunters and hunting
Naming of parts. H. Reed.—BoGj
A parting shot. C. Day-Lewis.—CaD
The returned volunteer to his rifle. H. Melville.—HiL
"There was a little man, and he had a little gun." Mother Goose.—ReMg
The little man.—BrMg
"There was a little man."—OpF
Guthrie, A. B., Jr.
Twin Lakes hunter.—DuR
Guthrie, James
Last song.—ArT-3—LaPd
Guy Fawkes day
Fifth of November. K. W. Gransden.—CaD
"Please to remember." Mother Goose.—ReMg
Gunpowder plot day.—BrMg
Gyôdai
"The blind sparrow."—LeI
"Leaf falling on leaf."—BeCs
Gypsies. See Gipsies
The **gypsies** metamorphos'd, sel. Ben Jonson
Song.—GrS
"The **gypsies** they came to my lord Cassilis' yett." See Jackie Faa
"A **gypsy**, a gypsy." See Being gypsy
Gypsy Jane. William Brighty Rands.—ArT-3

H

H. D., pseud. See D., H., pseud.
"**Ha,** the butterfly." Unknown, tr. fr. the Japanese by Lafcadio Hearn.—LeI

"**Ha'** we lost the goodliest fere o' all." See Ballad of the Goodly Fere
"**Ha,** whare ye gaun, ye crowlan ferlie." See To a louse, on seeing one on a lady's bonnet at church
Habit
The elephant; or, The force of habit. A. E. Housman.—LiT
Habits of the hippopotamus. Arthur Guiterman.—ArT-3
Rabbits. R. Fabrizio.—SmM
Habits of the hippopotamus. Arthur Guiterman. —ArT-3
"**Had** I but plenty of money, money enough and to spare." See Up at a villa—down in the city
"**Had** I had the power I would have stretched." See Waves against a dog
"**Had** I not seen the sun." Emily Dickinson.—DiPe
"**Had** I the heavens' embroidered cloths." See He wishes for the cloths of heaven
"**Had** they not come in the year of the morning star." See Montezuma's song
Hadas, Moses
The breed of athletes. tr.—MoS
Hadley, L. M.
The rainbow fairies.—StF
"**Hadst** thou stayed, I must have fled." See Tales of a wayside inn—The legend beautiful
Haft, Larry
Household problems.—LeM
The **hag.** Robert Herrick.—BlO—SmM
"The **hag** is astride." See The hag
Haida Indians. See Indians of the Americas—Haida
Haidée. See Don Juan
Haiku. David Lippa.—LeM
Hail
"Hail." Issa.—LeMw
"**Hail.**" Issa, tr. fr. the Japanese by R. H. Blyth. —LeMw
Hail, Bishop Valentine. See An epithalamium on the Lady Elizabeth and Count Palatine being married on St Valentine's day
"**Hail,** Bishop Valentine, whose day this is." See An epithalamium on the Lady Elizabeth and Count Palatine being married on St Valentine's day—Hail, Bishop Valentine
"**Hail,** comely and clean. Hail, young child." See Second shepherds' play—The shepherds at Bethlehem
"**Hail,** let happiness come." See Blessings upon an infant
Hail to the sons of Roosevelt. Vachel Lindsay. —LiP
"**Hail** to thee, blithe spirit." See To a skylark
"**Hail,** ye indomitable heroes, hail." See The Crimean war heroes
"**Hail,** young lion, I would say a word." See Epigram
"**Haily** Paily." Unknown.—MoB
Haines, John
If the owl calls again.—CoBn
To turn back.—CoBn
Hair
Boy with his hair cut short. M. Rukeyser.—CoR
For Anne Gregory. W. B. Yeats.—McWs—YeR
"Gregory Griggs, Gregory Griggs." Mother Goose.—OpF
Gregory Griggs.—BrMg
"Haily Paily." Unknown.—MoB
The hairy dog. H. Asquith.—ArT-3—HoB—HuS-3—LaP—LaPd
"Hickety, pickety, i-silikety, pompalorum jig." Mother Goose.—OpF
"I'd rather have fingers than toes." G. Burgess.—BrLl
"In New Orleans there lived a young Creole." Unknown.—BrLl
Little people, M. C. Livingston.—LiC
"On the top of the hill." Unknown.—WyC
"A puppy whose hair was so flowing." O. Herford.—BrLl
"Queen, Queen Caroline." Mother Goose.—OpF
Queen Caroline.—BrMg
"Riddle me, riddle me (what is that)." Mother Goose.—OpF
Tiny Eenanennika. W. De La Mare.—DeBg
A tragic story. A. von Chamisso.—HoB
"V is a vain virtuoso." O. Herford.—BrLl
The **hairy** dog. Herbert Asquith.—ArT-3—HoB—HuS-3—LaP—LaPd
Hakutsú
"O pine tree standing."—BaS
Hale, Leonard
"Everybody laugh."—BaH
"I'll come back—and the things of me that." —BaH
Hale, Robert Beverly
The big nasturtiums.—CoBn
Denise.—CoB
Hale, Sarah Josepha (Buell)
"Mary had a little lamb."—OpF—WiMg
Mary's lamb.—BrMg
Mary's lamb. See "Mary had a little lamb"
Hale, Nathan (about)
Nathan Hale. F. M. Finch.—HiL
"**Half** a dozen white loaves lie." See The loaves
"**Half** a league, half a league." See The charge of the Light Brigade
Half moon. Federico García Lorca, tr. fr. the Spanish by W. S. Merwin.—LiT
"**Half** of my life is gone, and I have let." See Mezzo cammin
"**Half** the time they munched the grass, and all the time they lay." See Cows
Halfway down. A. A. Milne.—MiC
"**Halfway** down the stair." See Halfway down
"**Halfway** through shaving, it came." See Gone forever
Halkin, Simon
Kibbutz Sabbath. tr.—PlE

Hall, Donald
By the Exeter river.—CaMb
Detroit.—BrA
The man in the dead machine.—DuS
A second stanza for Dr Johnson.—BrSm
The stump.—DuR
Transcontinent.—DuR—LaC
Valentine.—CoBl—DuR
The windows.—DuS
Hall, Hazel
Two sewing.—ThA
Hall, John
An epicurean ode.—GrS
Hallam, Arthur Henry (about)
In memoriam, sels. A. Tennyson
Calm is the morn.—GrCt—TeP
"Dip down upon the northern shore."—TeP
A happy lover.—TeP
"I envy not in any moods."—TeP
"I sometimes hold it half a sin."—TeP
"I trust I have not wasted breath."—TeP
I wage not any feud.—TeP
My Lord and King.—GrCt—TeP
Now fades the last.—TeP
"Oh yet we trust that somehow good."—PlE
Oh yet we trust.—TeP
Ring out, wild bells.—ArT-3—LaPh—TeP
Strong Son of God.—PlE
Prologue.—TeP
There rolls the deep.—TeP
What hope is here.—TeP
When my light is low.—TeP
Hallelujah. Alfred Edward Housman.—BrSm
"**Hallelujah,** was the only observation." See Hallelujah
Halley's comet. Eleanor Farjeon.—FaT
Hallowe'en
Black and gold. N. B. Turner.—ArT-3—LaPh
The hag. R. Herrick.—BlO—SmM
Hallowe'en ("Bolt and bar the front door") M. Capes.—ThA
Hallowe'en ("Broomsticks and witches") M. Chute.—LaPh
Halloween ("Granny, I saw a witch go by") M. A. Lawson.—ArT-3
Hallowe'en ("On Hallowe'en the old ghosts come") E. Farjeon.—FaA
Halloween ("Ruth says apples have learned to bob") J. Ciardi.—ArT-3
Halloween ("The sky was yellow") I. O. Eastwick.—HoB—LaPh
Hallowe'en ("Tonight is the night") H. Behn. —ArT-3—HuS-3—LaPd—LaPh
Hallowe'en ("Who's that creature who's wearing a mask") M. A. Hoberman.—HoB
"Haly on a cabbage-stalk." Unknown.—MoB
"Hey-how for Hallowe'en." Unknown.—MoB
The witches.—GrCt
Jack-o'-lantern. A. Fisher.—LaPh
Mrs Elsinore. M. C. Livingston.—LiC
October magic. M. C. Livingston.—LaPd—LaPh
Pumpkins. D. McCord.—McAd
The ride-by-nights. W. De La Mare.—ArT-3
Theme in yellow. C. Sandburg.—ArT-3—HuS-3
"This is Hallowe'en." Unknown.—MoB
This is Halloween. D. B. Thompson.—ArT-3—LaPh
What am I. D. Aldis.—HuS-3—LaPh
What night would it be. J. Ciardi.—LaPd—LaPh
The witch. D. McCord.—McE
Hallowe'en ("Bolt and bar the front door") Molly Capes.—ThA
Hallowe'en ("Broomsticks and witches") Marchette Chute.—LaPh
Halloween ("Granny, I saw a witch go by") Marie A. Lawson.—ArT-3
Hallowe'en ("On Hallowe'en the old ghosts come") Eleanor Farjeon.—FaA
Halloween ("Ruth says apples have learned to bob") John Ciardi.—ArT-3
Halloween ("The sky was yellow") Ivy O. Eastwick.—HoB—LaPh
Hallowe'en ("Tonight is the night") Harry Behn. —ArT-3—HuS-3—LaPd—LaPh
Hallowe'en ("Who's that creature who's wearing a mask") Mary Ann Hoberman.—HoB
"**Haly** on a cabbage-stalk." Unknown.—MoB
Hamburger, Michael
April day: Binsey.—CaD
Changing the wheel. tr.—HoL
Children's crusade 1939. tr.—CaMb
Iron. tr.—HoL
To the sun. tr.—CoBn
"**Hamelin** town's in Brunswick." See The Pied Piper of Hamelin
Hamilton, John
Cold blows the wind.—ClF (sel.)
Hamilton, W.
Playtime.—GrT
Hamlet (about)
Meditation at Elsinore. E. J. Coatsworth.—CoDh
Hamlet, sels. William Shakespeare
Ophelia's death.—GrCt
Ophelia's song.—GrCt
"Some say that ever 'gainst that season comes."—ArT-3
Christmas.—GrCt
Hammarskjöld, Dag
"Lord—Thine the day."—PlE
The **hammers.** Ralph Hodgson.—BoGj
Hammerstein, Oscar, II
South Pacific, sel.
You've got to be taught.—BrA
You've got to be taught. See South Pacific
Hammira-mahakavya, sel. Nayacandra Suri, tr. fr. the Sanskrit by A. L. Basham
Radhadevi's dance.—AlPi
Hammock. David McCord.—McAd

Hammond, Eleanor
The magic window.—StF
A valentine.—ArT-3
Han-shan
"Cold Mountain is full of weird sights."—LeMw
The **hand** that signed the paper. Dylan Thomas.—McWs
"The **hand** that signed the paper felled a city." See The hand that signed the paper
"A **handful** of red sand, from the hot clime." See Sand of the desert in an hour-glass
The **handiest** nose. Aileen Fisher.—FiC
Hands
"After a flock of flies." Issa.—LeOw
The hand that signed the paper. D. Thomas.—McWs
Hands of a brown woman. F. M. Davis.—BoH
"The hands they were made to assist." A. Euwer.—BrLl
"In the falling snow." R. Wright
Hokku: "In the falling snow."—AdIa
Hokku poems.—BoA
On a hand. H. Belloc.—CoBl
"Warm, hands, warm." Mother Goose.—OpF
Which hand. K. Fraser.—FrS
Hands of a brown woman. Frank Marshall Davis.—BoH
"The **hands** they were made to assist." Anthony Euwer.—BrLl
"A **handsome** young noble of Spain." Unknown.—BrLl
Handwriting
Look at your copy. E. Turner.—VrF
Hang Fu. Elizabeth Jane Coatsworth.—CoDh
Hangings
Hangman's tree. L. Z. White.—BrA
King Charles upon the scaffold. From An Horatian ode upon Cromwell's return from Ireland. A. Marvell.—GrCt
A rope for Harry Fat. J. K. Baxter.—CaMb
The salvation of Texas Peters. J. W. Foley.—BrSm
Samuel Hall. Unknown.—GrCt
Shameful death. W. Morris.—GrCt—GrS
Hangman's tree. Lillian Zellhoefer White.—BrA
Hanks, Nancy (about)
I saw a ghost. J. Boilleau.—ArT-3
Nancy Hanks. R. C. and S. V. Benét.—ArT-3—HuS-3
Nancy Hanks, mother of Abraham Lincoln. V. Lindsay.—HiL
A reply to Nancy Hanks. J. Silberger.—ArT-3
"**Hannah** Bantry." See "Hannah Bantry, in the pantry"
"**Hannah** Bantry, in the pantry." Mother Goose.—OpF
"Hannah Bantry."—AgH—BrMg
Hans, Marcie
"Fueled."—DuR
Hansi. Harry Behn.—BeG
Hanukkah. See Jews
Hap. Thomas Hardy.—PlE
"**Hap** and row, hap and row." Unknown.—MoB
"**Happened** that the moon was up before I went to bed." See Mockery
"A **ha'penny** here, and a ha'penny there." Unknown.—MoB
Happiness
Afternoon on a hill. E. St V. Millay.—ArT-3—ClF—HuS-3—LaPd
Ah fading joy. J. Dryden.—GrCt
Another little boy. A. and J. Taylor.—VrF
"Are not the joys of morning sweeter." W. Blake.—BlP
"A bird in the air, a fish in the sea." Mother Goose.—OpF
Cares and joys. From King Henry VI. W. Shakespeare.—ShS
"Cast our caps and cares away." J. Fletcher.—SmM
Cottage boy. M. Elliott.—VrF
Dance. J. Stephens.—StS
The darkling thrush. T. Hardy.—CoR
"A drunkard cannot meet a cork." E. Dickinson.—DiPe
Ecstasy. R. A. Taylor.—GrS
Eskimo chant. Unknown.—DoW
"There is joy in."—LeO
Eternity. W. Blake.—BlP
First song. G. Kinnell.—BoGj
The fisher's life. Unknown.—GrCt
"From all the jails the boys and girls." E. Dickinson.—DiPe
Gladde things. Unknown.—ArT-3
The glory. E. Thomas.—ThG
Happiness. A. A. Milne.—ArT-3—MiC
The happy family. J. Ciardi.—CoO
The happy farmer. Tse Nan.—LeMw
The happy hedgehog. E. V. Rieu.—CoB
Happy thought. R. L. Stevenson.—ArT-3—HuS-3
Happy wind. W. H. Davies.—SmM
Heaven. L. Hughes.—ArT-3
"Hey nonny no." Unknown.—GrCt
"How gray the rain." E. J. Coatsworth.—ArT-3
"How happy is the little stone." E. Dickinson.—DiPe
"I can wade grief." E. Dickinson.—DiPe
I thought it was Tangiers I wanted. L. Hughes.—BoH
"Immured the whole of life." E. Dickinson.—DiPe
In youth is pleasure. R. Wever.—GrCt
Infant joy. W. Blake.—BlP—BoGj—TuW
"It is a lonesome glee." E. Dickinson.—DiPe
A jamboree for j. E. Merriam.—MeI
"Jog on, jog on, the foot-path way." From The winter's tale. W. Shakespeare.—ArT-3—BrSg—TuW
The merry heart.—ShS
Jolly miller. From Love in a village. I. Bickerstaffe.—BrMg
"There was a jolly miller once."—OpF—WiMg
"A joyful chant." Unknown.—LeO

King Solomon. E. Merriam.—MeC
"Merry are the bells, and merry would they ring." Mother Goose.—OpF
Merry are the bells.—ArT-3
The merry country lad. From The passionate shepherd. N. Breton.—ReO
Minuette. J. Stephens.—StS
"Mother shake the cherry-tree." C. G. Rossetti.—ArT-3
"My heart is all happy." Unknown.—LeO
My poem. E. Hewell.—LeM
"No matter how grouchy you're feeling." A. Euwer.—BrLl
On a reed. J. Stephens.—StS
On the hills. E. J. Coatsworth.—CoDh
The pleasures of merely circulating. W. Stevens.—HaL
Prologue. From La saisiaz. R. Browning.—BrP
Recuerdo. E. St V. Millay.—BrA—CoBl—HiL
Resolution and independence. W. Wordsworth.—CoBn (sel.)—WoP
Rhapsody. W. S. Braithwaite.—BoA—BoH
Rulers: Philadelphia. F. Johnson.—BrA
Serendipity. E. Merriam.—GrCt
Song ("Again rejoicing Nature sees") R. Burns. —CoBn
Song ("Memory, hither come") W. Blake.—BlP
Sonnet. W. Wordsworth.—WoP
The spring. W. Barnes.—CoBn
"Standing or sitting." Unknown.—BaS
This happy day. H. Behn.—ArT-3
Thrice happy he. W. Drummond, of Hawthornden.—CoBn
" 'Tis so much joy. 'Tis so much joy." E. Dickinson.—DiPe
"To wake alive, in this world." Unknown.—LeMw
"What happiness." Buson.—LeMw
"When I was young." Unknown.—LeO
"Who never wanted,—maddest joy." E. Dickinson.—DiL—DiPe
Why isn't the world happy. R. Lewis.—BaH
The wood of flowers. J. Stephens.—LaPd—StS
Happiness. A. A. Milne.—ArT-3—MiC
"The **happiness** of hedgehogs." See The happy hedgehog
"**Happy** and gay." See The ass and the lap-dog
Happy birthday to me. Eve Merriam.—MeC
The **happy** family. John Ciardi.—CoO
The **happy** farmer. Tse Nan, tr. fr. the Chinese by Henry H. Hart.—LeMw
The **happy** hedgehog. E. V. Rieu.—CoB
"**Happy** is the bride in the green." See The frogs' wedding
A **happy** lover. See In memoriam
"A **happy** lover who has come." See In memoriam—A happy lover
Happy thought. Robert Louis Stevenson.—ArT-3 —HuS-3
Happy wind. William Henry Davies.—SmM
Harasymowicz, Jerzy
The bicycle.—DuS
The **harbor.** Carl Sandburg.—HoL
"**Hard** by the lilied Nile I saw." See A crocodile
"**Hard** from the southeast blows the wind." Elizabeth Jane Coatsworth.—ArT-3
Hard frost. Andrew Young.—CoBn
"**Hard** old gray eyes, no pity." See The rancher
Hardship
Dust bowl. R. A. Davis.—AdIa
Hardy, Thomas
Afterwards.—CoBn—GrCt
And there was a great calm.—GrCt
Birds at winter nightfall.—ReBs
The blinded bird.—CoB—PlE
The darkling thrush.—CoR
The fallow deer at the lonely house.—BlO
The garden seat.—BoGj
Hap.—PlE
In the mind's eye.—GrS
Lines to a movement in Mozart's E-flat symphony.—CoBl
The night of Trafalgár.—GrCt
The phantom horsewoman.—GrS
The Roman road.—BoGj
The sacrilege.—CoD
Snow in the suburbs.—BoGj—CoBn
To the moon.—CoBn—GrCt
Weathers.—BlO—SmM—TuW
"When I set out for Lyonnesse."—PaH
The **hare.** Walter De La Mare.—ArT-3—TuW
The **hare** and the tortoise. Ian Serraillier.—CoB
Harebell ("Harebell! Harebell") John Buxton.—SmM
The **harebell** ("In the clear summer sunshine, hour by hour") Walter De La Mare.—DeBg
"**Harebell!** Harebell." See Harebell
Harebells
Harebell ("Harebell! Harebell") J. Buxton.—SmM
The harebell ("In the clear summer sunshine, hour by hour") W. De La Mare.—DeBg
Hares. See Rabbits
Hares at play. John Clare.—ReO
Hargrove, Leon
"Where am I going."—BaH
Hark. Walter De La Mare.—DeBg
"**Hark,** hark." See "Hark, hark, the dogs do bark"
"**Hark,** hark, the dogs do bark." Mother Goose. —ArT-3—OpF—ReMg—WiMg
The beggars.—BrMg
"Hark, hark."—BrF
Mother Goose rhymes, 23.—HoB
Hark, hark, the lark. See Cymbeline—"Hark, hark, the lark at heaven's gate sings"
"**Hark,** hark, the lark at heaven's gate sings." See Cymbeline
"**Hark** the herald angels sing." See On Dean Inge
"**Hark!** They cry! I hear by that." See Yolp, yolp, yolp, yolp
"**Hark,** when on hill and dale." See Ballad of the nightingale
Harlem
Harlem gallery. M. B. Tolson.—HaK (sel.)

Harlem—*Continued*
Harlem night song. L. Hughes.—LaC
Harlem sounds: Hallelujah corner. W. Browne.—BoA
Juke box love song. L. Hughes.—AdIa
Lenox avenue mural. L. Hughes.—BoA
Dream deferred.—LaC
Sketches of Harlem. David Henderson.—HaK
Sonnet to a Negro in Harlem. H. Johnson.—BoA
Stars. L. Hughes.—LaC
The still voice of Harlem. C. K. Rivers.—AdIa—HaK
The train runs late to Harlem. C. K. Rivers.—AdIa
Harlem gallery. Melvin B. Tolson.—HaK (sel.)
Harlem night song. Langston Hughes.—LaC
Harlem sounds: Hallelujah corner. William Browne.—BoA
Harmony. Elizabeth Jane Coatsworth.—CoDh
The **harnet** and the bittle. J. Y. Akerman.—GrCt
"A **harnet** zet in a hollur tree." See The harnet and the bittle
"The **harp** that once through Tara's halls." Thomas Moore.—CoR
Harper, Frances Ellen Watkins
The slave auction.—HaK
Harps
Enitharmon's song. From Vala. W. Blake.—GrCt
"The harp that once through Tara's halls." T. Moore.—CoR
King David. W. De La Mare.—LiT
The minstrel boy. T. Moore.—ClF—CoR
Harriet Beecher Stowe. Paul Laurence Dunbar.—HaK
Harrington, Helen
Is this life.—BaH
Life.—BaH
Harris, Max
The Tantanoola tiger.—CaMb
Harrison, Frances
At St Jerome.—DoW
Harrison, Jane and Mirrlees, Hope
Fragment of a bylina. trs.—LiT
Harrison, Jim
Dead doe.—HoL
Harrison, Phillip
"People talks."—BaH
Harrison, Susan
"How can the sea be dark and gray."—LeM
Harrison, William Henry (about)
Old Tippecanoe. Unknown.—HiL
Harrow-on-the-hill, England
Harrow-on-the-hill. J. Betjeman.—CaD
Harrow-on-the-hill. John Betjeman.—CaD
Hart, Henry H.
At Feng Ting temple. tr.—LeMw
Butterflies. tr.—LeMw
Calm of evening. tr.—LeMw
Discovery. tr.—LeMw
The firefly. tr.—LeMw
The frost. tr.—LeMw
The happy farmer. tr.—LeMw
The hermit. tr.—LeMw
The hostess. tr.—LeMw
Night at Yen Chou. tr.—LeMw
The poem of ten ones. tr.—LeMw
Returning. tr.—LeMw
Riding at daybreak. tr.—LeMw
The temple bells of Yun Sui. tr.—LeMw
"When I had a little leisure." tr.—LeMw
The **hart.** See "The hart he loves the high wood"
Hart and hare. See "The hart he loves the high wood"
"The **hart** he loves the high wood." Mother Goose.—OpF—ReMg
The hart.—BrMg
Hart and hare.—ReOn
Harte, (Francis) Bret
The aged stranger.—BrA
Chicago.—HiL
The ghost that Jim saw.—BrSm
Grizzly.—CoB—ReO
Relieving guard.—CoR
Harvest. Mother Goose.—BrMg—BrSg
Harvest home. Herbert Read.—SmM
"The **harvest** is finished. Winter stays its coming." See October
Harvests and harvesting
After apple-picking. R. Frost.—CoR
Aftermath. H. W. Longfellow.—LoPl
August from my desk. R. Flint.—BrA—DuR
Characterization. Yogesvara.—AlPi
"Come flies." Issa.—IsF
"For all the joys of harvest." E. Vipont.—BrSg
Harvest. Mother Goose.—BrMg—BrSg
Harvest home. H. Read.—SmM
Hee haw. Mother Goose.—ReOn
Hurrahing in harvest. G. M. Hopkins.—CoBn—GrCt
January. N. Belting.—BeCm
November. N. Belting.—BeCm
O reaper. E. Farjeon.—FaA
Real property. H. Monro.—CoBn
Reapers. J. Toomer.—HaK
The ripe and bearded barley. Unknown.—CoBn—GrCt
The solitary reaper. W. Wordsworth.—BlO—CoR—WoP
Unharvested. R. Frost.—CoBn
"We must overcome the east wind." Unknown.—DoC
"Willy boy, Willy boy, where are you going." Mother Goose.—HuS-3—OpF
Hay making.—BrMg
Harvey, Frederick William
The boy with the little bare toes.—StF
Ducks.—CoB (sel.)
"**Has** anybody seen my Mopser." See The bandog
"**Has** anybody seen my mouse." See Missing
"**Has** he got it in his left hand." See Which hand
"**Has** no one said those daring." See Two years later
Hashin
Loneliness.—LiT
"**Hast** thou given the horse strength." See Job

Haste, Gwendolen
Montana wives.—BrA
The **hatch.** Norma Farber.—HoL
Hate
"Bruadar and Smith and Glinn." D. Hyde.—McWs
Coriolanus's farewell to his fellow-citizens as he goes into banishment. From Coriolanus. W. Shakespeare.—McWs
Crooked-heart. J. Stephens.—StS
A glass of beer. J. Stephens.—McWs—StS
Hate ("The cries of hate are as loud as drums") M. Classé.—BaH
Hate ("My enemy came nigh") J. Stephens.—StS
Hatred. G. B. Bennett.—BoA
Hypocrites. Monk.—BaH
"I had no time to hate, because." E. Dickinson.—DiPe
I wish my tongue were a quiver. L. A. Mackay.—McWs
Impossibilities to his friend. R. Herrick.—GrS
Jake hates all the girls. E. E. Cummings.—DuS
My enemy. L. Curry.—BaH
Samuel Hall. Unknown.—GrCt
Soliloquy of the Spanish cloister. R. Browning.—BrP—CoD
Sporus. From Epistle to Dr Arbuthnot. A. Pope.—GrCt
Tit for tat. Unknown.—McWs
The twins. J. Stephens.—StS
When I loved you. T. Moore.—HoL
To ________.—CoBl
The world I see. M. Evans.—HaK
You've got to be taught. From South Pacific. O. Hammerstein, II.—BrA
Hate ("The cries of hate are as loud as drums") Margaret Classé.—BaH
Hate ("My enemy came nigh") James Stephens.—StS
Hatred. Gwendolyn B. Bennett.—BoA
Hats
"A charming old lady of Settle." E. Lear.—BrLl
The hatter. Unknown.—VrF
A memory. L. A. G. Strong.—CaD
"Mr Spats." S. Silverstein.—CoO
My hat. S. Smith.—SmM
The Quangle Wangle's hat. E. Lear.—HoB
A second stanza for Dr Johnson. D. Hall.—BrSm
"There was a young lady whose bonnet." Unknown.—BrLl
"There was an old lady of Durban." Unknown.—BrLl
"There was an old person of Fratton." Unknown.—BrLl
"When first my Jamie he came to the town." Unknown.—MoB
White cap. Mother Goose.—BrMg
"**Hats** off." See The flag goes by
The **hatter.** Unknown, at. to William Darton.—VrF
Hatteras calling. Conrad Aiken.—CoBn
The **haughty** snail-king. Vachel Lindsay.—HaL
Haul away Joe. Unknown.—CoSs
The **haunted** oak. Paul Laurence Dunbar.—HaK
The **haunted** palace. See The fall of the house of Usher
Havasupai Indians. See Indians of the Americas—Havasupai
"**Have** done, you men and women all." See The animals in the ark
"**Have** pity on us, Power just and severe." See Prayer
"**Have** you any gooseberry wine." See Mazilla and Mazura
"**Have** you been catching of fish, Tom Noddy." See Tit for tat
"**Have** you ever felt like nobody." See Being nobody
"**Have** you ever seen a rail." See Swinging on a rail
"**Have** you got a brook in your little heart." Emily Dickinson
The brook of the heart.—CoBl
"**Have** you had your tonsils out." See The new neighbor
"**Have** you heard of the wonderful one-hoss shay." See The deacon's masterpiece; or, The wonderful one-hoss shay
"**Have** you no weathervane." See Straws
"**Have** you not seen them fighting for the lead." See The chariot race
"**Have** you seen a little dog anywhere about." See My dog
"**Have** you seen Old Lovell." Unknown.—BrSg
"**Have** you seen the lights of London how they twinkle, twinkle, twinkle." See Parliament hill
Have you watched the fairies. Rose Fyleman.—ArT-3—ThA
"**Have** you watched the fairies when the rain is done." See Have you watched the fairies
Haven. Donald Jeffrey Hayes.—BoA
"**Having** attained success in business." See Robert Whitmore
"**Having** been tenant long to a rich Lord." See Redemption
Having climbed to the topmost peak of the Incense-burner mountain. Po Chü-i, tr. fr. the Chinese by Arthur Waley.—MoS
"**Having** finished the Blue-plate special." See In Schrafft's
"**Having** lived a Coney Island life." See A Coney Island life
"**Having** read the inscriptions." See Wang Peng's recommendation for improving the people
Having words. Eve Merriam.—MeI
Havre de Grace, France
"As I went down by Havre de Grace." E. Wylie.—PaH
Hawes, Stephen
Epitaph of Graunde Amoure. See The palace of pleasure
The palace of pleasure, sel.
Epitaph of Graunde Amoure.—GrCt

The **hawk.** Harold Witt.—DuS
Hawk roosting. Ted Hughes.—ReO
Hawker, Robert Stephen
The mystic magi.—GrCt
The song of the western men.—CoR
"The **hawker** cried, Bing-tang-hoo-loo." See Several people
Hawking. See Polyolbion
Hawks
From hawk and kite. J. Stephens.—StS
The hawk. H. Witt.—DuS
Hawk roosting. T. Hughes.—ReO
Hurt hawks. R. Jeffers.—CoB
The penniless hawk. Unknown.—DePp
The rabbit. E. St V. Millay.—CoB
"The sea hawk hunting." Taigi.—BeCs
Shiva. R. Jeffers.—GrS
Hawkshawe, Anne (or Hawkshaw, Ann) (Aunt Effie, pseud.)
Dame Duck's lecture.—StF
The **hawthorn.** Unknown.—GrCt
A **hawthorn** berry. Mary Webb.—TuW
The **hawthorn** tree. Mother Goose.—ReOn
Hawthorn trees
Green rain. M. Webb.—CoBn—TuW
The hawthorn. Unknown.—GrCt
A hawthorn berry. M. Webb.—TuW
The hawthorn tree. Mother Goose.—ReOn
The wicked hawthorn tree. W. B. Yeats.—YeR
Hay, Sara Henderson
The builders.—DuR
For a dead kitten.—DuR
Pigeon English.—ReBs
Hay
An argument against the empirical method. From Some short poems. W. Stafford.—GrCt
Hay for the horses. G. Snyder.—DuS
The haystack. A. Young.—CaD
"How cool cut hay smells." Boncho.—BeCs
"Load of hay." Mother Goose.—TuW
Meadow of hay. A. Fisher.—FiI
A song. R. Hodgson.—BoGj
"Willy boy, Willy boy, where are you going." Mother Goose.—HuS-3—OpF
Hay making.—BrMg
Hay for the horses. Gary Snyder.—DuS
Hay making. See "Willy boy, Willy boy, where are you going"
Hayden, Robert E.
A ballad of remembrance.—AdIa—BoA
The ballad of Sue Ellen Westerfield.—HaK
The diver.—DuS—HaK
Frederick Douglass.—AdIa—BoA—HaK
Full moon.—HaK
Middle passage.—AdIa—BoA
Mourning poem for the queen of Sunday.—DuS
O Daedalus, fly away home.—AdIa—BoH
Runagate runagate.—AdIa
Summertime and the living.—HaK
Those winter Sundays.—AdIa—DuS
Veracruz.—BoA
The whipping.—AdIa
Witch doctor.—BoA
Haydn, Franz Joseph (about)
"There was a composer named Haydn." Unknown.—BrLl
Hayes, Donald Jeffrey
Alien.—BoA
Appoggiatura.—BoA
Benediction.—BoA
Haven.—BoA
Night.—ReS (sel.)
Pastourelle.—BoA
Poet.—BoA
Threnody.—BoA
Hayes, Evelyn
Garden-lion.—GrCt
Hays, H. R.
Ballad of the soldier. tr.—LiT
Coal for Mike. tr.—LiT
The coming star. tr.—LiT
The mask of evil. tr.—LiT
My voice. tr.—LiT
Of swimming in lakes and rivers. tr.—MoS
To Miss Rápida. tr.—LiT
Winter song. tr.—LiT
With the roses. tr.—LiT
The **haystack.** Andrew Young.—CaD
Hayward, Max and Reavey, George
Brooklyn bridge. trs.—LiT
Hazardous occupations. Carl Sandburg.—HoL
Hazo, Samuel
Challenge.—MoS
"**He** ate and drank the precious words." Emily Dickinson.—DiPe
"**He** brought a team from Inversnaid." See The man from Inversnaid
"**He** came." See A legend of Paul Bunyan
"**He** came all so still." Unknown.—TuW
"**He** came from Malta; and Eumêlus says." See A Maltese dog
"**He** came in silvern armor, trimmed with black." See Sonnet I
"**He** captured light and caged it in a glass." See And yet fools say
"**He** clasps the crag with crooked hands." See The eagle
"**He** climbed up the candlestick." Unknown.—WyC
"**He** climbed up the peak." See High brow
"**He** climbs the wind above green clouds of pine." See Wild goose
"**He** debated whether." See Arthur Ridgewood, M.D.
"**He** did not come just one day: he did not come just two days." See What her friend said
"**He** did not come to woo U Nu." See Just dropped in
"**He** did not wear his scarlet coat." See The ballad of Reading gaol
"**He** dines alone surrounded by reflections." See Witch doctor
"**He** dumped her in the wheelbarrow." See Wheelbarrow
"**He** fell in a sweeping arc." See Malfunction
"**He** found my being, set it up." Emily Dickinson.—DiPe

"**He** gazed at her with his whole soul." See Dark eyes at Forest Hills
"**He** had a falcon on his wrist." See Love me, love my dog
"**He** had driven half the night." See Hay for the horses
"**He,** he, he." See Touch
"**He** is always standing there." See My policeman
He is like the lotus. See Book of the dead
"**He** is murdered upright in the day." See Vaticide
"**He** is not John the gardener." See A friend in the garden
"**He** is running like a wasp." See Pole vault
"**He** is that fallen lance that lies as hurled." See A soldier
"**He** is the way." See For the time being: A Christmas oratorio
"**He** is white as Helvellyn when winter is well in." See The white rabbit
"**He** let go." See Take-off
"The **he-lizard** is crying." See The lizard is crying
"**He** lost it over the dark gray hills." See Lost
"**He** mends the shoes." See Cobbler
"**He** never spoke a word to me." See Simon the Cyrenian speaks
"**He** never used to notice me." See The policeman
"**He** nothing common did or mean." See An Horatian ode upon Cromwell's return from Ireland—King Charles upon the scaffold
"**He,** of his gentleness." See In the wilderness
"**He** played by the river when he was young." See Washington
"**He** put the belt around my life." Emily Dickinson.—DiPe
"**He** ran all down the meadow, that he did." See The boy with the little bare toes
"**He** ran right out of the woods to me." See The story of the baby squirrel
He remembers forgotten beauty. William Butler Yeats.—YeR
"**He** rises and begins to round." See The lark ascending
"**He** rocked the boat." See Ezra Shank
"**He** rolls in the orchard: he is stained with moss." See The child in the orchard
"**He** rubbed his eyes and wound the silver horn." See Little Boy Blue
"**He** said, Do not point your gun." See A parting shot
"**He** sang of life, serenely sweet." See The poet
"**He** sat upon the rolling deck." See Sailor
"**He** seemed to know the harbour." See The shark
"**He** sent so many." See Manhattan epitaphs: Lawyer
"**He** shot at Lee Wing." Unknown.—BrSm
"**He** snuggles his fingers." See After winter
"**He** spent his childhood hours in a den." See The dreamer
"**He** stands in rags upon the heaving prow." See Jonah
"**He** stoops above the clumsy snare." See The snare
"**He** struggled to kiss her. She struggled the same." See An original love-story
"**He** swings down like the flourish of a pen." See Skier
"**He** talked, and as he talked." See The storyteller
"**He** that is down needs fear no fall." See The pilgrim's progress—The shepherd boy sings in the valley of humiliation
"**He** that is slow to anger is better than the mighty." See Proverbs, Bible, Old Testament
"**He** that lies at the stock." See Three a-bed
"**He** that would thrive." Mother Goose.—OpF
Advice.—BrMg
"**He** there does now enjoy eternal rest." See The faerie queene—Sleep after toil
"**He** thought he saw a buffalo." See Sylvie and Bruno—A strange wild song
"**He** used to wake to him." See The aura
"**He** walked through the woods." See The walk
"**He** walks still upright from the root." See Upon Appleton house—The hewel, or woodpecker
"**He** walks, the enchanter, on his sea of glass." See Antichrist
"**He** was a man as hot as whiskey." See Andrew Jackson
"**He** was a rat, and she was a rat." Unknown.—BlO
What became of them.—SmM
"**He** was as old as old could be." See Danny Murphy
"**He** was caged up." See Madman
"**He** was found by the Bureau of Statistics to be." See The unknown citizen
"**He** was the half-wit of that prairie town." See Village portrait
"**He** went to fix the awning." See Fixer of midnight
"**He** went to the wood and caught it." Mother Goose.—BrMg
"**He** who bathes among crocodiles." Unknown, tr. fr. the Zulu.—LeO
"**He** who bends to himself a joy." See Eternity
"**He** who has lost a tooth." See Ditty for a child losing his first tooth
"**He** who has never known hunger." Elizabeth Jane Coatsworth.—ArT-3
He wishes for the cloths of heaven. William Butler Yeats.—HoL—ThA—YeR
"**He** with body waged a fight." See Supernatural songs—IX. The four ages of man
"**He** wore his coffin for a hat." See For a pessimist
Headlam, Walter
Life after death. tr.—PlE
"The **headlights** raced; the moon, death-faced." See The child on the curbstone

Heads
"As I was going out one day." Unknown.—CoO
The happy family. J. Ciardi.—CoO
The hatter. Unknown.—VrF
"Mr Spats." S. Silverstein.—CoO
Someone lost his head at bedtime but he got it back. J. Ciardi.—CiYk
"The **head's** the court of knowledge, reason, wit." See The hatter
"The **headwaiter** says." See In this hotel
A **health** unto his majesty. Jeremy Savile.—GrCt
Heaney, Seamus
Blackberry-picking.—CoBn
"**Heap** on more wood, the wind is chill." See Marmion—Christmas time
Heaps on heaps. See A match at football
"**Hear** from the forest the cry of a deer." See A hunted deer
"**Hear** the sledges with the bells." See The bells
"**Hear** the voice of the bard." See Introduction to the Songs of experience
Hearing
The fifth sense. P. Beer.—CaMb
"Old woman, old woman, shall we go a-shearing." Mother Goose.—ArT-3
Mother Goose rhymes, 48.—HoB
The old woman.—BrMg
Hearing the cuckoo. John Heath-Stubbs.—CaD
"**Hearing** the hawk squeal in the high sky." See The rabbit
Hearing the wind at night. May Swenson.—CoBn
Hearn, Lafcadio
"Ha, the butterfly." tr.—LeI
Hearst, James S.
Voices.—ThA
The **heart** of Midlothian, sel. Walter Scott
Proud Maisie.—BlO—GrCt
Heartbeat of democracy. Virginia Brasier.—HuS-3
"The **hearth** has forgotten cooking." See A description of famine
The **hearth** of Urien. William Barnes.—GrCt
"**Hearts** were made to give away." Annette Wynne.—ArT-3
Heat
Heat. G. Gonzalez y Contreras.—HoL
Heavy is the heat. E. J. Coatsworth.—CoDh
Heat. Gilberto Gonzalez y Contreras, tr. fr. the Spanish by Dudley Fitts.—HoL
"The **heat** of yesterday transformed the city into." See A kingdom of clouds
"**Heat** waves." Issa, tr. fr. the Japanese.—LeOw
Heath, Curtis
Wild goose.—DuR
Heath-Stubbs, John
A charm against the toothache.—CaD—SmM
Hearing the cuckoo.—CaD
The history of the flood.—CaMb
Heaven
The bells of heaven. R. Hodgson.—BoGj—CoB—PlE—ThA
Besides that. J. Stephens.—StS
A blackbird suddenly. J. Auslander.—ArT-3—TuW
The crusader. D. Parker.—BrSm
Earth and sky. Euripides.—PlE
Epitaph for any New Yorker. C. Morley.—BrSm
For a lady I know. C. Cullen.—AdIa—BrSm—HaK
Four epitaphs.—BoA
For a mouthy woman. C. Cullen.—BrSm
General William Booth enters into heaven. V. Lindsay.—LiP
The golden city of St Mary. J. Masefield.—BoH—PaH
He wishes for the cloths of heaven. W. B. Yeats.—Hol—ThA—YeR
Heaven. L. Hughes.—ArT-3
Heaven and earth. James I, King of England.—GrCt
Heriger, Bishop of Mainz. Unknown.—LiT
Hunchback girl: She thinks of heaven. G. Brooks.—HaK
"I give you the end of a golden string." W. Blake.—BlP
"Immured the whole of life." E. Dickinson.—DiPe
"It troubled me as once I was." E. Dickinson.—DiPe
The kingdom of God. F. Thompson.—PlE
Life after death. Pindar.—PlE
The marriage of heaven and hell. W. Blake.—BlP (sel.)
"Musicians wrestle everywhere." E. Dickinson.—DiPe
"No matter where the saints abide." E. Dickinson.—DiPe
On a puritanicall lock-smith. W. Camden.—BrSm
On looking up by chance at the constellations. R. Frost.—LiT
Peace. H. Vaughan.—GrCt—PaH—PlE
Prayer to go to Paradise with the donkeys. F. Jammes.—CoB—ReO
Francis Jammes: A prayer to go to Paradise with the donkeys.—ArT-3—PlE
Running to paradise. W. B. Yeats.—HaL—YeR
"Some keep the Sabbath going to church." E. Dickinson.—DiPe
Sporting Beasley. S. A. Brown.—HaK
Swing low, sweet chariot. Unknown.—BrA
Tell me, O swan. Kabir.—AlPi
"Who has not found the heaven—below." E. Dickinson.—DiPe
Heaven. Langston Hughes.—ArT-3
Heaven and earth. James I, King of England.—GrCt
"**Heaven** is." See Heaven
"The **heaven** is bright." Unknown.—WyC
"**Heaven** is in my hand, and I." See A blackbird suddenly
The **heavens.** See Psalms—Psalm 19
"The **heavens** declare the glory of God." See Psalms—Psalm 19

Heavy is the heat. Elizabeth Jane Coatsworth.—CoDh
"**Heavy** is the heat, heavy and solid." See Heavy is the heat
Heckman, Rachel
Steps.—BaH
Hector Protector. Mother Goose.—BrMg
"**Hector** Protector was dressed all in green." See Hector Protector
Hector the dog. Kate Barnes.—CoB
"**He'd** had enough of lying in the furze." See The ghostly father
"**He'd** have given me rolling lands." See The choice
"**He'd** play, after the bawdy songs and blues." See When de saints go ma'chin' home
Hedge, F. H.
"A mighty fortress is our God." tr.—PlE
The **hedgehog** ("The hedgehog, from his hollow root") See The shepherd's calendar
Hedgehog ("Twitching the leaves just where the drainpipe clogs") Anthony Thwaite.—CaD
The **hedgehog** ("Yes, Lord, I prick") Carmen Bernos de Gasztold, tr. fr. the French by Rumer Godden.—GaC
"The **hedgehog,** from his hollow root." See The shepherd's calendar—The hedgehog
Hedgehogs. See Porcupines
Hee haw. Mother Goose.—ReOn
"**Heigh-ho.**" See Heigh-ho, April
"**Heigh-ho.**" Elizabeth Jane Coatsworth.—CoSb
Heigh-ho, April. Eleanor Farjeon.—FaA
Heigh ho the holly. See As you like it—"Blow, blow, thou winter wind"
The **height** of the ridiculous. Oliver Wendell Holmes.—HuS-3
Heine, Heinrich
The kings from the east.—GrCt
Heitler, Susan
Candles.—LeM
Heke, Iris
Falling in the creek.—LeM
Helen of Tyre. Henry Wadsworth Longfellow.—GrS
"**Helen,** thy beauty is to me." See To Helen
Hell
"The caverns of the grave I've seen." W. Blake.—BlP
A curt addendum. Unknown.—BrSm
For a mouthy woman. C. Cullen.—BrSm
Heriger, Bishop of Mainz. Unknown.—LiT
Joshua Hight. Unknown.—BrSm
Lord Waterford. Unknown.—GrCt
The marriage of heaven and hell. W. Blake.—BlP (sel.)
Hellas. Percy Bysshe Shelley.—GrCt (sel.)
"**Hello,** you, are you a ghost." See A ghost story
Hell's bells. Margaret Fishback.—BrSm
"**Helmet** and rifle, pack and overcoat." See The battle
Helpfulness. See Service
"**Helter-skelter.**" Issa, tr. fr. the Japanese by R. H. Blyth.—IsF
Helton, Roy
Lonesome water.—BrA
Hemans, Felicia Dorothea (Felicia Dorothea Brown)
The landing of the Pilgrim Fathers.—ArT-3—HiL
Hempseed, Isabell
Rufty and Tufty.—StF
Hempseed. Mother Goose.—ReOn
"**Hempseed I** set." See Hempseed
The **hen** and the carp. Ian Serraillier.—CoB
"**Hence** loathed melancholy." See L'allegro
Henderson, Daniel
St Swithin.—BrSm
The two wives.—BrSm
Henderson, David
Sketches of Harlem.—HaK
Henderson, Harold G.
"A giant firefly." tr.—LeI
"Insects. Do not cry." tr.—LeMw
"Little gray cuckoo." tr.—LeMw
Loneliness. tr.—LiT
"On how to sing." tr.—LeI
On the road to Nara. tr.—ArT-3
"Play about, do." tr.—LeMw
"A trout leaps high." tr.—LeMw
Winter. tr.—LiT
Henderson, Rose
March dreams.—ThA
Hengist, Jute chief (about)
Ode to Hengist and Horsa. R. Jeffers.—GrS
Henniker-Heaton, Peter J.
Post early for space.—BrA
Henry IV, of Navarre, King of France (about)
Birth of Henri Quatre. E. J. Coatsworth.—CoDh
Henry V, King of England (about)
Henry's address to his troops. From King Henry V. W. Shakespeare.—McWs
Henry VI, King of England (about)
A king is dead. From King Henry VI. W. Shakespeare.—GrCt
Henry, John (about)
John Henry ("John Henry told his captain") Unknown.—BoH
John Henry ("John Henry was a little baby") Unknown.—HoB
John Henry ("When John Henry was a little boy") Unknown.—HiL
John Henry ("When John Henry was about three days old") Unknown.—BrA
Strange legacies. S. A. Brown.—HaK
Henry and Mary. Robert Graves.—BoGj—CaD—HaL
Henry King, who chewed bits of string, and was early cut off in dreadful agonies. Hilaire Belloc.—BrSm
Henry Thoreau. Eve Merriam.—MeIv
Henry Ward Beecher. See "The Reverend Henry Ward Beecher"
"**Henry** was a young king." See Henry and Mary

Henry's address to his troops. See King Henry V
Hens. See Chickens
The **hens.** Elizabeth Madox Roberts.—ArT-3—BoGj—CoB—HuS-3—LaPd—ThA—TuW
Hen's nest. John Clare.—ReO
Her birthday. Feng Yen-chi, tr. fr. the Chinese by Ch'n Ta-kao.—LeMw
"**Her** hand which touched my hand she moved away." See On a hand
Her heards be thousand fishes. See Colin Clout's come home again
"**Her** losses make our gains ashamed." Emily Dickinson.—DiPe
"**Her** pa committed suicide." See Such a pleasant familee
"**Her** pinched grey body." See Supper
"**Her** pretty feet." See Upon her feet
"**Her** sight is short, she comes quite near." See Jenny Wren
"**Her** skin is like dusk on the eastern horizon." See Karintha
Herbert, A. (Alan) P. Patrick)
The centipede.—CoB
The chameleon.—CoB
In a garden.—CoB
Mullion.—MoS
The oyster.—CoB
What is love.—CoBl (sel.)
Herbert, George
The collar.—PlE
Love.—GrCt
Peace.—GrCt
The pilgrimage.—GrCt
The pulley.—PlE
Redemption.—PlE
Herbs
Ballad of the rosemary. P. McGinley.—McWc
The rock. Unknown.—GrCt
The **herd** boy. Lu Yu, tr. fr. the Chinese by Arthur Waley.—GrCt—LeMw
Herding lambs. Ruth Pitter.—CaD
Herdsmen
The herd boy. Lu Yu.—GrCt—LeMw
Spanish Johnny. W. S. Cather.—McWs
To be sung by a small boy who herds goats. Y. Winters.—WeP
"**Here.**" See The castle yonder
"**Here** a little child I stand." See A child's grace
"**Here** a pretty baby lies." See Upon a child
"**Here,** a sheer hulk, lies poor Tom Bowling." See Tom Bowling
"**Here** again, she said, is March the third." See March the third
"**Here** am I, little jumping Joan." Mother Goose. —GrT
Jumping Joan.—BrMg
Little jumping Joan.—ArT-3
"**Here** am I where you see me." See River's song
Here and now. Catherine Cater.—BoA
"**Here** are crocuses, white, gold, grey." See O dear me
"**Here** are no signs of festival." See African Christmas
"**Here** are some flowers to remember me by." See Adieu
"**Here** are sweet peas, on tiptoe for a flight." See I stood tiptoe on a little hill
"**Here** come I." See Hogmanay
"**Here** come real stars to fill the upper skies." See Fireflies in the garden
"**Here** comes." Issa, tr. fr. the Japanese by Nobuyuki Yuasa.—IsF
"**Here** comes another, bumping over the sage." See Tumbleweed
"**Here** comes Gentle Robin." See Singing game
"**Here** comes little Fred." See Little Freddy
"**Here** comes the elephant." See The elephant
"**Here** comes the old man with his flowers to sell." See The flower-pot man
"**Here** comes Varge." See Varge
"**Here** did sway the eltrot flow'rs." See Times o' year
"**Here** from the field's edge we survey." See Highway: Michigan
"**Here** he lies moulding." See Epitaph
"**Here** Holy Willie's sair worn clay." See Epitaph on Holy Willie
"**Here,** houses close their sleepy window eyes." See Arizona village
"**Here** houses rise so straight and tall." See Tall city
Here I am. Ann Morrissett.—CoBl
"**Here** I am dwelling. Go now to Radha." See Gita Govinda—Krishna's longing
"**Here** I am with my rabbit." See The rabbit man
"**Here** I go round." See Rules of contrary
"**Here** I go up in my swing." See Swing song
"**Here** I lie outside the chancel door." See Outside the chancel door
"**Here** in a quiet and dusty room they lie." See The seed shop
"**Here,** in my rude log cabin." See The battle of New Orleans
"**Here** in the newspaper—the wreck of the East Bound." See It's here in the
"**Here** in the sand, where someone laid him down." See Cruciform
"**Here** in the scuffled dust." See A father swings his child
"**Here** in this book, collected for you." William Cole.—CoBb
"**Here,** in this little bay." Coventry Patmore.—CoBn
"**Here** in this sequestered close." See A garden song
"**Here** is a lass with a golden ring." See Singing game
"**Here** is a long and silent street." See The street
"**Here** is a place that is no place." See Madhouse
"**Here** is a world which slowed the hands of time." See Okefenokee swamp
"**Here** is an apple, ripe and red." See Dividing
"**Here** is how I eat a fish." See Eating fish
"**Here** is the old fly, more eager than the rest." See Monologue of a dying man

"**Here** is the perfect picture of them all." See Shilappadakarom—The lover's song
"**Here** is the spinner, the orb weaver." See The orb weaver
"**Here** lies." See Tombstone
"**Here** lies a little bird." See A bird's epitaph
"**Here** lies a man who was killed by lightning." See At Great Torrington, Devon
"**Here** lies a piece of Christ; a star in dust." See Epitaph for a godly man's tomb
"**Here** lies a poor woman who was always tired." See On a tired housewife
"**Here** lies John Bun." See John Bun
"**Here** lies John Coil." See John Coil
"**Here** lies John Knott." See Epitaph on John Knott
"**Here** lies Johnie Pigeon." See Epitaph on John Dove, innkeeper
"**Here** lies Lester Moore." See At Boot Hill in Tombstone, Arizona
Here lies my wife. John Dryden.—BrSm
"**Here** lies my wife: here let her lie." See Here lies my wife
"**Here** lies, neatly wrapped in sod." See Epitaph for a postal clerk
"**Here** lies our sovereign lord the king." See Impromptu on Charles II
"**Here** lies resting, out of breath." See Little elegy
"**Here** lies the body of Anna." See In memory of Anna Hopewell
"**Here** lies the body of Cassie O'Lang." See Cassie O'Lang
"**Here** lies the Reverend Jonathan Doe." See On the Reverend Jonathan Doe
"**Here** lies, whom hound did ne'er pursue." See Epitaph on a hare
"**Here** on my breast have I bled." See War song
"**Here** on our rock-away horse we go." See Johnny's by-low song
"**Here** on the mellow hill." See Autumn scene
"**Here** on this bridge let's sit on this railing." See Three seagulls
"**Here,** richly, with ridiculous display." See On a politician
Here she is. Mary Britton Miller.—ArT-3
"**Here** she lies—in bed of spice." See Upon a maid
"**Here** something stubborn comes." See Seed leaves
"**Here** the formal times are surrendered." See Looking in the album
"**Here** the horse-mushrooms make a fairy ring." See The fairy ring
"**Here** the young lover, on his elbow raised." See The corner of the field
"**Here** upon the prairie." See The prairie battlements
"**Here** we are; in the darkness." See The mine
"**Here** we come a-caroling." Unknown.—ArT-3
"**Here** we come a-piping." Unknown.—BlO
Here we go looby, looby, looby. Eleanor Farjeon.—FaT
"**Here** we go round by jinga-ring." Mother Goose.—OpF
"Here we go round the jing-a-ring."—MoB
The merry-ma-tanza.—ReOn
"**Here** we go round the jing-a-ring." See "Here we go round by jinga-ring"
"**Here** we go round the mulberry bush." See The mulberry bush
Here we go round the mulberry bush. Eleanor Farjeon.—FaT
"**Here** we go up, up, up." Unknown.—VrF
"**Here** where the wild ducks." Taniha Ōmé.—BaS
"**Here** you have morning bursting buds." See The golden hive
"**Here's** a curmudgeon." See Who's here
"**Here's** a health unto his majesty." See A health unto his majesty
"**Here's** a poor widow from Babylon." See Lady of the land
"**Here's** a poor widow from Sandisland." Unknown.—MoB
"**Here's** a string of wild geese." Unknown.—MoB
"**Here's** a thing and a very pretty thing." See Forfeits
"**Here's** an example from." See The example
"**Here's** Corporal Bull." Mother Goose.—OpF
Corporal Bull.—BrMg
"**Here's** little Jim Nast of Pawtucket." Hugh Lofting.—BrLl
"**Here's** my baby's bread and milk." See Breakfast and puss
"**Here's** November." See Enter November
"**Here's** Sulky Sue." Mother Goose.—OpF
Sulky Sue.—BrMg
"**Here's** the mail, sort it quick." See A sure sign
"**Here's** the tailor with his sheers." Unknown.—VrF
"**Here's** the tender coming." See The press-gang
"**Here's** to Nelson's memory." Robert Browning.—BrP
"**Here's** to thee." See "Here's to thee, good apple tree"
"**Here's** to thee, good apple tree." Mother Goose.—OpF
Apples.—BrMg
"Here's to thee."—BlO
Twelfth night.—TuW
"**Here's** to thee, old apple tree." See "Here's to thee, good apple tree"
Herford, Oliver
"E is the egotist dread."—BrLl
Earth. See "If this little world to-night"
The elf and the dormouse.—ArT-3—HoB—ThA
"I heard a bird sing."—ArT-3—CoB—LaP—LaPd—ThA
"If this little world to-night."—BrSm
Earth.—DuR
Kitten's night thoughts.—HoB
Lèse majesté.—CoB
"O is an optimist glad."—BrLl
"P's a poetical bore."—BrLl
"A puppy whose hair was so flowing."—BrLl
"Said an envious, erudite ermine."—BrLl

Herford, Oliver—*Continued*
"Said the condor, in tones of despair."—BrLl
"Said the snail to the tortoise: You may."—BrLl
"A tapir who lived in Malay."—BrLl
"There once was a provident puffin."—BrLl
"There was once a giraffe who said, What."—BrLl
The untutored giraffe.—BrSm (sel.)
"V is a vain virtuoso."—BrLl
"**Heriger.**" See Heriger, Bishop of Mainz
Heriger, Bishop of Mainz. Unknown, tr. fr. the Latin by Helen Waddell.—LiT
Heritage
Heritage ("I want to see the slim palm trees") G. B. Bennett.—BoA
Heritage ("What is Africa to me") C. Cullen.—BoA
The inheritance. Unknown.—StF
Legacy ("I had a rich old great-aunt") N. B. Turner.—ThA
Legacy ("The year has made her will: she left to me") C. Morley.—DuR
Lineage. M. Walker.—HaK
"My father died a month ago." Mother Goose.—MoB
Riches.—BrMg
"My father he died, but I still can't tell you how." Unknown.—BlO
Our heritage. J. Stuart.—BrA
Strange legacies. S. A. Brown.—HaK
Three acres of land. Mother Goose.—BrMg
The twins. J. Stephens.—StS
Heritage ("I want to see the slim palm trees") Gwendolyn B. Bennett.—BoA
Heritage ("What is Africa to me") Countee Cullen.—BoA
The **hermit.** Hsu Pen, tr. fr. the Chinese by Henry H. Hart.—LeMw
Hermits
The hermit. Hsu Pen.—LeMw
Hernton, Calvin C.
Madhouse.—AdIa—HaK
"Young Negro poet."—HaK
Herod, King of the Jews (about)
Innocent's song. C. Causley.—CaD
The **heroes.** Louis Simpson.—DuS
Heroes and heroines
B stands for bear. From A moral alphabet. H. Belloc.—BrSm
The Crimean war heroes. W. S. Landor.—McWs
Death of an aircraft. C. Causley.—CaMb
The heroes. L. Simpson.—DuS
How they brought the good news from Ghent to Aix. R. Browning.—ArT-3—BrP—CoR—HuS-3
Incident of the French camp. R. Browning.—BrP—CoR
Litany of the heroes. V. Lindsay.—LiP
Negro hero. G. Brooks.—HaK
"Now that he is safely dead." C. W. Hines, Jr.—BoH
"One dream all heroes." Bashō.—BeCs
A song of greatness. M. Austin.—ArT-3—BrA—HoB
"There was a young man named Achilles." E. M. Robinson.—BrLl
Heroism. See Heroes and heroines
Heron, Leila
Rain.—LeM
The **heron.** See Bird cage
"The **heron** flew east, the heron flew west." See The knight in the bower
"The **heron** stands in water where the swamp." See The heron
Herons
Boy into heron. C. Randall.—SmM
Egret dyke. Wang Wei.—LeMw
Egrets. Judith Wright.—BoGj
The heron. From Bird cage. T. Roethke.—CoB—HoL—LaPd—ReBs
"The herons on Bo island." E. Shane.—CoB
"If the white herons." Chiyo.—BeCs
The knight in the bower. Unknown.—GrCt
"Lightning flickering." Bashō.—BeCs
"Like a wave crest." Emperor Uda.—BaS
"With the evening breeze." Buson.—LeI
"The **herons** on Bo island." Elizabeth Shane.—CoB
Herrick, Robert
The amber bead. See A trapped fly
Another grace for a child. See A child's grace
Ceremonies for Christmas.—ArT-3
A charm.—GrCt
A child's grace.—PlE
Another grace for a child.—BoGj
Grace before meals.—GrT
Grace before meat.—GrCt
Grace for a child.—SmM
A Christmas caroll, sung to the king in the presence at White-hall.—BoGj
A conjuration, to Electra.—GrS
Corinna's going a-Maying.—CoBn
The fairies.—BlO
The four sweet months.—TuW
Grace before meals. See A child's grace
Grace before meat. See A child's grace
Grace for a child. See A child's grace
The hag.—BlO—SmM
His cavalier.—BoGj
His grange; or, Private wealth.—BoGj
How marigolds came yellow.—GrCt
How roses came red.—GrCt
I call and I call.—GrCt
Impossibilities to his friend.—GrS
"Instead of neat inclosures." See An ode of the birth of our Saviour
An ode of the birth of our Saviour, sel.
"Instead of neat inclosures."—GrCt
On himself.—GrCt
A ternarie of littles, upon a pipkin of jellie sent to a lady.—BoGj
Thanksgiving to God, for his house.—GrCt
To blossoms.—CoBn—SmM
To daffadills. See To daffodils
To daffodils.—CoBn—HoL
To daffadills.—BoGj

To musique, to becalme his fever.—BoGj
To the virgins, to make much of time.—GrCt
To violets.—TuW
A trapped fly.—HoL
The amber bead.—GrCt
Upon a child.—SmM
Upon a maid.—GrCt
Upon her feet.—SmM
Upon Julia's clothes.—GrCt—HoL
The white island.—GrCt
Herrick, Robert (about)
On himself. R. Herrick.—GrCt
Herschberger, Ruth
The bat.—DuR
Hershenson, Miriam
"Husbands and wives."—DuR—LaC
Herskovits, Frances
For the Earth God. tr.—PlE
"The giver of life." tr.—PlE
To destiny. tr.—PlE
Hervé Riel. Robert Browning.—CoSs
"**He's** a lion-hearted man." See Mr Zoo
"**He's** bought a bed and a table too." See Mary Ann
"**He's** nothing much but fur." See A kitten
"**He's** reddish." See My dog Ginger
Hesiod (about)
Hesiod, 1908. A. Mair.—GrS
Hesoid, 1908. Alexander Mair.—GrS
Hesperus. James Stephens.—StS
"**Hesperus,** the day is gone." See The evening star
The **hewel,** or woodpecker. See Upon Appleton house
Hewell, Ethel
My poem.—LeM
Hewison, R. J. P.
"A scientist living at Staines."—BrLl
Hexameter and pentameter. Unknown.—GrCt
"**Hey,** cocky doo." Unknown.—MoB
"**Hey** dan dilly dow." Unknown.—MoB
"**Hey** diddle diddle." See "Hey, diddle, diddle, the cat and the fiddle"
"**Hey** diddle diddle (the physicists)." See Rhymes for a modern nursery
"**Hey,** diddle, diddle, the cat and the fiddle." Mother Goose.—ArT-3
The cat and the fiddle.—BrMg—OpF
"Hey diddle diddle."—HuS-3—WiMg
Mother Goose rhymes, 17.—HoB
"**Hey** diddle dinkety poppety pet." Mother Goose.—OpF
"**Hey** ding a ding, and ho ding a ding." Mother Goose.—OpF
Hey, ho, the wind and the rain. See Twelfth night
"**Hey-how** for Hallow'en." Unknown.—MoB
The witches.—GrCt
"**Hey,** little dog, don't bark at me." See The tea roaster
"**Hey** my kitten, my kitten." Unknown.—MoB
"**Hey,** my lad, ho, my lad." See Welcome to the new year
"**Hey** nonny no." Unknown.—GrCt
"**Hey** the dusty miller." See The dusty miller
"**Hey,** the little postman." See The postman
Heyward, DuBose
Dusk.—PaH
Evening in the Great Smokies.—PaH
New England landscape.—PaH
Heywood, Thomas
Matin song. See The rape of Lucrece
Pack, clouds, away. See The rape of Lucrece—Matin song
"Pack, clouds, away, and welcome day." See The rape of Lucrece—Matin song
The rape of Lucrece, sel.
Matin song.—TuW
Pack, clouds, away.—ReBs
"Pack clouds, away, and welcome, day."—BlO
Hiawatha
The song of Hiawatha, sels. H. W. Longfellow
Hiawatha's childhood.—ArT-3
Hiawatha's sailing.—LoPl
Hiawatha's childhood. See The song of Hiawatha
Hiawatha's sailing. See The song of Hiawatha
Hibernation
"How and when and where and why." P. Gotlieb.—DoW
Hiccoughs
"Hiccup, hiccup." Unknown.—MoB
"**Hiccup,** hiccup." Unknown.—MoB
"**Hick-a-more,** hack-a-more." Mother Goose.—ArT-3
Mother Goose rhymes, 29.—HoB
"**Hickety,** bickety, pease scone." Unknown.—MoB
"**Hickety,** pickety, i-silikety, pompalorum jig." Mother Goose.—OpF
"**Hickety,** pickety, my black hen." Mother Goose.—OpF—ReMg—WiMg
"Higgledy, piggledy, my black hen."—ArT-3—HuS-3
Mother Goose rhymes, 18.—HoB
My black hen.—BrMg
"**Hickory,** dickory, dock." Mother Goose.—BrMg—OpF—ReMg—WiMg
Mother Goose rhymes, 16.—HoB
Hicky, Daniel Whitehead
Georgia towns.—BrA
Nocturne: Georgia coast.—BrA
Okefenokee swamp.—BrA
Polo player.—ThA
The river boats.—BrA
A ship for Singapore.—ThA
To an aviator.—ThA
Who pilots ships.—ThA
Hide and seek ("Tiptoe away, tiptoe away") Eleanor Farjeon.—FaT
Hide and seek ("When I am alone, and quite alone") A. B. Shiffrin.—StF
Hide-and-seek ("When little Jane lifts up her head") Eleanor Farjeon.—FaT
"**Hide** not, hide not." See The rousing canoe song
"**Hide** of a leopard and hide of a deer." See The giraffe
Hideout. Aileen Fisher.—FiI

Hiding
Hideout. A. Fisher.—FiI
Hiding. D. Aldis.—ArT-3—HoB
The rabbit. E. M. Roberts.—ArT-3—BrSg—CoB—HoB—LaP—TuW
"A strange place." P. Rake.—LeM
Hiding. Dorothy Aldis.—ArT-3—HoB
Hie away. See Waverley—"Hie away, hie away"
"**Hie** away, hie away." See Waverley
Hie, hie. See "Hie, hie, says Anthony"
"**Hie,** hie, says Anthony." Mother Goose.—OpF
Hie, hie.—ReOn
"**Hie** to the market, Jenny come trot." See Jenny
Hiebert, Paul
Steeds.—DoW
Higgins, F. R.
Cradle song.—ReS
Higgledy, piggledy. See "Higgledy, piggledy, see how they run"
"**Higgledy,** piggledy, my black hen." See "Hickety, pickety, my black hen"
"**Higgledy,** piggledy, see how they run." Kate Greenaway.—ArT-3
Higgledy, piggledy.—GrT
Higglety, pigglety. See "Higglety, pigglety, pop"
"**Higglety,** pigglety, pop." Mother Goose.—StF
Higglety, pigglety.—BrMg
"**High** adventure." See Maps
"**High** and proud on the barnyard fence." See Chanticleer
High brow. Robert Fitch.—MoS
High diver. Robert Francis.—MoS
"**High,** high in the branches." See The ferns
"**High** on a mountain." Bashō, tr. fr. the Japanese by Harry Behn.—BeCs
"**High** on a slope in New Guinea." See The man in the dead machine
"**High** on a stilt-raised bed above the reeds." See Boy into heron
"**High** on the southern wall the clock." See The coming forth by day of Osiris Jones
High wheat country. Elijah L. Jacobs.—BrA
The **high** wind. See "Arthur O'Bower has broken his band"
"**Higher** than a house." Mother Goose.—ArT-3—BrMg
Highland Mary. Robert Burns.—BuPr
"**Highlandman,** Highlandman." Unknown.—MoB
"**Highty tighty, paradighty.**" Mother Goose.—BrMg—GrCt
Highway: Michigan. Theodore Roethke.—DuS
The **highwayman.** Alfred Noyes.—ArT-3—CoBl
Highwaymen. See Crime and criminals
Highways. See also Roads and trails
Highway: Michigan. T. Roethke.—DuS
The King's highway. J. S. McGroarty.—PaH
The long black grave. E. J. Coatsworth.—CoDh
On the expressway. R. Dana.—LaC
The **hike.** Neil Weiss.—MoS
Hill, Brian
Ophelia. tr.—GrCt
Hill, Diane
"Slowly melting, slowly dying."—LeM
Hill, Geoffrey
In memory of Jane Fraser.—CaD
Hill, Leslie Pinckney
So quietly.—AdIa
Hill, Mabel B.
"There was a wee girl named Estella."—BrLl
Hill, Pati
The dormouse.—CoB
The **hill.** Rupert Brooke.—CoBl
"A **hill** full, a hole full." Mother Goose.—ArT-3
"The **hill** is bare. I only find." See Katty Gollagher
The **hill** of vision. James Stephens.—ClF (sel.)
Hill people. Harriet Gray Blackwell.—BrA
"The **hill** was higher every year." See Model T
Hills. See also Mountains
Afternoon on a hill. E. St V. Millay.—ArT-3—ClF—HuS-3—LaPd
At St Jerome. F. Harrison.—DoW
Grongar hill. J. Dyer.—ClF (sel.)—GrCt
Hill people. H. G. Blackwell.—BrA
Hills ("The hills are going somewhere") H. Conkling.—HuS-3
Hills ("Scrub hills") G. Foster.—LeM
"The hills are like shouts of children." R. Tagore.—LeMf
In the hills. Wang Wei.—HoL
On the hills. E. J. Coatsworth.—CoDh
The painted hills of Arizona. E. Curran.—PaH
There is an eminence. W. Wordsworth.—WoP
"There was an old woman (lived under a hill and if)." Mother Goose.—GrT—OpF
Under a hill.—BrMg
To a young girl leaving the hill country. A. Bontemps.—HaK
To walk on hills. R. Graves.—MoS
Hills ("The hills are going somewhere") Hilda Conkling.—HuS-3
Hills ("Scrub hills") Glennis Foster.—LeM
"The **hills** are going somewhere." See Hills
"The **hills** are like shouts of children." Rabindranath Tagore.—LeMf
"The **hills** are wroth; the stones have scored you bitterly." See To a young girl leaving the hill country
"**Hills** surround the ancient kingdom; they never change." See The city of stones
Hillyer, Robert (Silliman)
Bobwhite.—CoB
Book of the dead, sel.
He is like the lotus. tr.—PlE
He is like the lotus. See Book of the dead
Lullaby.—DuR—HaL—ReS
Lunar moth.—ReO
Moo.—CoB
A pastoral.—CoBn
Pastoral X.—HaL
"The plants stand silent round me." tr.—HoL
The termites.—ReO
Hind, Gertrude
The donkey.—CoB
Hine, Al
Christmas 1945.—HiL

Hines, Carl Wendell, Jr.
"Now that he is safely dead."—BoH
Two jazz poems.—BoA—DuR (sel.)—HaK
"**Hinx,** minx." Mother Goose.—BrMg—ReOn
"**Hinx,** minx, the old witch winks." See "Hinx, minx"
"**Hippety** hop to the barber shop." Mother Goose.—ArT-3
Hippity hop to bed. Leroy F. Jackson.—ArT-3—ReS
Hippopotami
Advice to children. C. Wells.—CoO
Habits of the hippopotamus. A. Guiterman.—ArT-3
The hippopotamus. G. R. Durston.—ArT-3
I had a hippopotamus. P. Barrington.—CoB
Rose's calf. P. Bennett.—CoB
The **hippopotamus.** Georgia Roberts Durston.—ArT-3
"The **hippopotamus** has calved beside her pool." See Rose's calf
"The **hippopotamus** is strong." See Habits of the hippopotamus
Hirohito, Emperor of Japan
A memory.—ThA
Hiroshige
"Two ducks swim to the shore."—LeMw
Hiroshima
Dirge for the new sunrise. E. Sitwell.—PlE
Hirotsugu
"In one petal of this flower."—BaS
"**His** art is eccentricity, his aim." See Pitcher
"**His** bill an auger is." Emily Dickinson.—DiPe
"**His** black tongue flickers." See Gila monster
"**His** bridle hung around the post." See Horse
"**His** brother said that pain was what he knew." See Traction: November 22, 1963
His cavalier. Robert Herrick.—BoGj
"**His** chosen comrades thought at school." See What then
His Excellency, General Washington. Phillis Wheatley.—HaK
"**His** eyes are mournful, but the long lined palm." See Creatures in the zoo—Ape
"**His** father died." Unknown.—MoB
"**His** feathers are burnished gold." See Rooster
"**His** friends went off and left Him dead." See The resurrection
"**His** golden arrow is tipped with hawk's feathers." See Border songs
"**His** golden locks time hath to silver turned." See The old knight
His grange; or, Private wealth. Robert Herrick.—BoGj
"**His** massive dignity—sixteen." See Horse and hammer
"**His** name it is Pedro-Pablo-Ignacio-Juan." See A feller I know
"**His** nose is short and scrubby." See My dog
"**His** pole with pewter basons hung." See The barber
"**His** proper name was Peter Sweet." See The reformed pirate
"**His** sister named Lucy O'Finner." Lewis Carroll.—BrLl
"**His** small feet." See Dragonfly
"**His** spirit in smoke ascended to high heaven." See The lynching
"**His** tail is remarkably long." See Mixed beasts—The kangarooster
"**His** weary glance, from passing by the bars." See The panther
"**Hist** whist." E. E. Cummings.—LiT
History
Litany of the heroes. V. Lindsay.—LiP
Sand of the desert in an hour-glass. H. W. Longfellow.—LoPl
History—Ancient
Address to a mummy. H. Smith.—CoR
After reading translations of ancient texts on stone and clay. C. Reznikoff.—GrS
Ancient history. A. Guiterman.—DuR—McWs
The destruction of Jerusalem by the Babylonian hordes. I. Rosenberg.—GrS
To my son Parker, asleep in the next room. B. Kaufman.—HaK
Vision of Belshazzar. G. G. Byron.—ByP—CoR
The **history** of Jack the giant killer. Unknown.—VrF
The **history** of little Tom Tucker. Unknown.—VrF
The **history** of Sam the sportsman, and his gun, also, of his wife Joan. Unknown.—VrF
The **history** of Simple Simon. See "Simple Simon met a pieman"
The **history** of the flood. John Heath-Stubbs.—CaMb
Hitomaro
"Because the treetops of the peak."—LeMw
"Gossip grows like weeds."—BaS
"In the empty mountains."—BaS
"In the ocean of the sky."—LeMw
"On the sea of heaven the waves of cloud arise."—BaS
Hits and runs. Carl Sandburg.—MoS
"**Ho,** for taxis green or blue." See Taxis
"**Ho,** for the May rains." Sanpu, tr. fr. the Japanese by Harry Behn.—BeCs
"**Ho,** for the Pirate Don Durk of Dowdee." See Pirate Don Durk of Dowdee
"**Ho,** ho, ho, ho." See Caw
"**Ho,** my hand is this." See Prayer to the moon
Ho P'ei Yu
The poem of ten ones.—LeMw
"**Ho** starling, quarrelsome swaggerer, you up there on the gable." See Spring song
Hobbies
"A certain young gallant named Robbie." Unknown.—BrLl
My brother Bert. T. Hughes.—CoBb
The **hobbit,** sels. J. R. R. Tolkien
Dwarves' song.—LiT
"Roads go ever ever on."—ArT-3
The stone troll.—LiT

Hobbyhorse. Kathleen Fraser.—FrS
Hobby-horses
Hobbyhorse. K. Fraser.—FrS
"I had a little hobby horse." Mother Goose.—MoB
Mother Goose rhymes, 58.—HoB
Hoberman, Mary Ann
The birthday bus.—ArT-3
A catch.—AgH
"The folk who live in backward town."—ArT-3—CoO
Hallowe'en.—HoB
Hoddley, poddley. Mother Goose.—BrMg
"**Hoddley,** poddley, puddle and fogs." See Hoddley, poddley
"**Hoddy** doddy." Mother Goose.—OpF
Hodgins, Hannah
The scared clouds.—LeM
Hodgman, Jennifer
"A leaf crashes gently to the ground."—LeM
Hodgson, Ralph
"And every sky was blue and rain." See To deck a woman
The bells of heaven.—BoGj—CoB—PlE—ThA
The bull.—ReO (sel.)
Eve.—SmM
The great auk's ghost.—BrSm
The hammers.—BoGj
A song.—BoGj
Stupidity street.—CoB—HaL—LaPd—ThA
"Time, you old gipsy man."—PaH
To deck a woman, sel.
"And every sky was blue and rain."—HaL
A wood song.—BoGj
Hoey, Edwin A.
Foul shot.—DuR
Hoffenstein, Samuel
Madrigal macabre.—BrSm
Progress.—HiL
Song, on reading that the cyclotron has produced cosmic rays, blasted the atom into twenty-two particles, solved the mystery of the transmutation of elements and devil knows what.—BrSm
When you're away.—CoBl
"Your little hands."—CoBl
Hoffman, Charles Fenno
Monterey.—HiL
Hoffman, Daniel
"Three jovial gentlemen."—CaMb
Hoffmann, (August) Heinrich
Slovenly Peter.—CoBb
The story of Augustus. See The story of Augustus who would not have any soup
The story of Augustus who would not have any soup.—AgH—BoGj—BrSm—CoBb
The story of Augustus.—ArT-3
The story of Johnny Head-in-air.—ArT-3—CoBb
"**Hog** butcher for the world." See Chicago
Hogg, James
A boy's song.—BlO
The skylark.—CoB
Hogg, Robert
Song.—DoW
Hogmanay
Hogmanay ("Here come I") Unknown.—MoB
Hogmanay ("Here comes in Judas") Unknown.—MoB
"Rise up, goodwife, and shake your feathers." Unknown.—MoB
Hogmanay ("Here come I") Unknown.—MoB
Hogmanay ("Here comes in Judas") Unknown.—MoB
Hogs. See Pigs
Hohenlinden, Battle of, 1800
Hohenlinden. T. Campbell.—CoR—GrCt
Hohenlinden. Thomas Campbell.—CoR—GrCt
"**Hokey** pokey winkey wum." Mother Goose.—OpF
"**Hold** fast to dreams." See Dreams
Hold fast your dreams. Louise Driscoll.—ArT-3
"**Hold** her softly, not for long." See At a child's baptism
Hölderlin, J. C. F.
Life half lived.—GrCt
Holding hands. Lenore M. Link.—ArT-3—LaP
"A **hole** in the cliffs." See The seagull
Holes of green. Aileen Fisher.—FiI
The **holiday** ("Five little goblins went to town") M. Stredder.—StF
Holiday ("Where are you going") Ella Young.—ArT-3
Holiday ("You sunburn'd sicklemen, of August weary") See The tempest
Holidays. See also names of holidays, as Christmas; Fourth of July
Holiday. From The tempest. W. Shakespeare.—ShS
Miss Jones. H. Behn.—BeG
Once upon a great holiday. A. Wilkinson.—DoW
Sir Roderick's song. From Ruddigore. W. S. Gilbert.—BrSm
Holland
The character of Holland. A. Marvell.—GrCt (sel.)
A Dutch picture. H. W. Longfellow.—LoPl
Going too far. M. Howells.—ArT-3
"**Holland,** that scarce deserves the name of land." See The character of Holland
Hollo, Anselm
Bicycles. tr.—LiT
The **Hollow** Land. William Morris.—GrCt
"The **hollow** winds begin to blow." See Signs of rain
Holly. See Holly trees
"The **holly** and the ivy." Unknown.—GrCt
"The **holly** berry that burns so red." See Legend of the holly
"**Holly** Springs in Mississippi." See Ida B. Wells
Holly trees
"But give me holly, bold and jolly." C. G. Rossetti.—ArT-3
"The holly and the ivy." Unknown.—GrCt
Legend of the holly. P. McGinley.—McWc
Hollyhocks
"All day in gray rain." Bashō.—BeCs

Holman, M. Carl
And on this shore.—BoA
Letter across doubt and distance.—BoA
Mr Z.—HaK
Notes for a movie script.—BoA—HaK
Song.—BoA—HaK
Three brown girls singing.—HaK
Holmes, George S.
And yet fools say.—ArT-3
Holmes, John
Carry me back.—BrA
Map of my country.—BrA
Old men and young men.—McWs
Rhyme of rain.—LaC
Short history of man.—McWs
Two kinds: Bold and shy.—McWs
Holmes, Oliver Wendell
A ballad of the Boston tea-party.—HiL
The ballad of the oysterman.—SmM
Brother Jonathan's lament for Sister Caroline. —HiL
The deacon's masterpiece; or, The wonderful one-hoss shay.—HuS-3
The height of the ridiculous.—HuS-3
Henry Ward Beecher. See "The Reverend Henry Ward Beecher"
Intramural aestivation, or summer in town, by a teacher of Latin.—GrCt
The last leaf.—BoH
Old Ironsides.—CoSs—HiL
"The Reverend Henry Ward Beecher."—BrLl
Henry Ward Beecher.—GrCt
The **holy** fair. Robert Burns.—BuPr
"**Holy** Gabriel, holy man." See The gabelory man
Holy sonnets, sel. John Donne
Death be not proud.—GrCt
Sonnet.—HoL
Holy Thursday
Holy Thursday ("Is this a holy thing to see") W. Blake.—BlP
Holy Thursday ("'Twas on a Holy Thursday, their innocent faces clean") W. Blake.—BlP
Holy Thursday ("Is this a holy thing to see") William Blake.—BlP
Holy Thursday ("'Twas on a Holy Thursday, their innocent faces clean") William Blake. —BlP
Holy transportations, sel. Charles Fitz-Geffry
Take frankincense, O God.—GrCt
Holy Willie's prayer. Robert Burns.—BuPr
Home. See Home and family life
Home ("A home is a place to live") Elijah Montgomery.—BaH
The **home** ("I paced alone on the road across the field") Rabindranath Tagore.—BoGj
Home ("Not the end: but there's nothing more") Edward Thomas.—ThG
Home and family life. See also Family; Homesickness; Housekeepers and housekeeping
After the winter. C. McKay.—AdIa
At St Jerome. F. Harrison.—DoW
"Be quiet, my baby." Unknown.—DoC
Blessings upon an infant. Unknown.—DoC
"Buy me a milking pail." Unknown.—MoB
"Children." Issa.—IsF
"Children when they're very sweet." J. Ciardi. —CoBb
The children's hour. H. W. Longfellow.—TuW
Daddy. C. Begay.—BaH
"Dear little baby." Unknown.—WyC
"A few flies." Issa.—IsF
For instance. A. Fisher.—FiIo
Fragment of an English opera. A. E. Housman.—LiT
"God bless the master of this house." Mother Goose.—HuS-3
Christmas carol.—ArT-3
"Hap and row, hap and row." Unknown.—MoB
The hearth of Urien. W. Barnes.—GrCt
Home ("A home is a place to live") E. Montgomery.—BaH
The home ("I paced alone on the road across the field") R. Tagore.—BoGj
Home ("Not the end: but there's nothing more") E. Thomas.—ThG
Household problems. L. Haft.—LeM
I like. C. Tringress.—StF
"I saw green banks of daffodils." From Home thoughts in Laventi. E. W. Tennant.—ArT-3
"I years had been from home." E. Dickinson. —DiPe
Kid in the park. L. Hughes.—LaC
The letter. E. Turner.—VrF
The mad family. Mother Goose.—BrF—BrMg
The memory-filled house. M. White.—LeM
Mrs Brown. R. Fyleman.—ArT-3
Modifications. R. Koertge.—DuS
The mother's song. Unknown.—LeO
Mummy slept late and daddy fixed breakfast. J. Ciardi.—ArT-3—LaPd
My home. J. Saltwater.—BaH
"My old home." Issa.—LeOw
Oh, joyous house. R. Janzen.—LeM
Oh stay at home. A. E. Housman.—McWs
"O such a hurry-burry." Unknown.—MoB
"On a very high mountain." Unknown.—WyC
One home. W. Stafford.—BrA
Our polite parents. C. Wells.—CoBb
Pain for a daughter. A. Sexton.—McWs
The rescue. H. Summers.—CaD
The return ("At fifteen I joined the army") Unknown.—LeMw
Return ("Sometimes the moment comes for the return") Elizabeth Jane Coatsworth.—CoDh
Sailing homeward. Chan Fang-shēng.—ArT-3 —LeM—ThA
"Saint Francis and Saint Benedight." Unknown.—PlE
So run along and play. D. McCord.—ArT-3
So still. A. Fisher.—FiIo
Such a pleasant familee. W. Irwin.—BrSm
"Tho' I get home how late—how late." E. Dickinson.—DiL

Home and family life—*Continued*
Those winter Sundays. R. E. Hayden.—AdIa —DuS
"The warm of heart shall never lack a fire." E. J. Coatsworth.—ArT-3
"What does the bee do." C. G. Rossetti.—ArT-3
Where. W. De La Mare.—DeBg
"A **home** is a place to live." See Home
Home-thoughts, from abroad. Robert Browning. —BrP—CoBn—PaH
Home-thoughts, from the sea. Robert Browning. —BrP
Home thoughts in Laventi, sel. E. Wyndham Tennant
"I saw green banks of daffodils."—ArT-3
Homer
Iliad, sel.
Night encampment outside Troy.—CoR
Night encampment outside Troy. See Iliad
Homer (about)
On first looking into Chapman's Homer. J. Keats.—CoR—GrCt
Homesickness
Ballad. H. Treece.—CaD
Longing for the south country. Li Yu.—LeMw
Sunday: New Guinea. K. Shapiro.—BrA
The tropics in New York. C. McKay.—BoA—BoH—HaK
The yellow bird. Unknown.—ReBs
"An **honest** man what loves his trade." See Industrious Carpenter Dan
Honesty. See Truthfulness and falsehood
Honey. See also Bees
"A dish full of all kinds of flowers." Unknown.—OpF
"The pedigree of honey." E. Dickinson.—DiPe
"**Honey.**" See Sister Lou
Honey-bees. See King Henry V
Honor
Honor among scamps. V. Lindsay.—LiP
Honor among scamps. Vachel Lindsay.—LiP
Hood, Thomas
Dust to dust.—BrSm
Faithless Nelly Gray.—BrSm
Mary's ghost.—SmM
No.—BlO—GrCt—McWs
Queen Mab.—HuS-3
Sally Simpkin's lament.—BrSm
To Minerva.—GrCt
"**Hoolie,** the bed'll fall." Unknown.—MoB
The **hoopee.** John Becker.—CoB
"The **hoopee** is a nasty bird." See The hoopee
Hoops. Kathleen Fraser.—FrS
"**Hooroo,** hooroo, won't it be fun." See Beggarman
"A **hop,** a skip, and off you go." See Dancing
"**Hop** out of my way." Chora, tr. fr. the Japanese by Harry Behn.—BeCs
"The **hop-poles** stand in cones." See The midnight skaters
Hope
After winter. S. Brown.—BoH
Dark testament. P. Murray.—BoA
The darkling thrush. T. Hardy.—CoR
Hope. W. Shenstone.—CoBn (sel.)
"Hope is a subtle glutton." E. Dickinson.—DiPe
"Hope is the thing with feathers." E. Dickinson.—ArT-3—DiL
Paper men to air hopes and fears. R. Francis. —DuS
"When I hoped, I recollect." E. Dickinson.—DiL
Work without hope. S. T. Coleridge.—CoBn
Hope. William Shenstone.—CoBn (sel.)
"**Hope** is a crushed stalk." See Dark testament
"**Hope** is a subtle glutton." Emily Dickinson.—DiPe
"**Hope** is the thing with feathers." Emily Dickinson.—ArT-3—DiL
Hopi Indians. See Indians of the Americas—Hopi
Hopkins, Gerard Manley
As kingfishers catch fire.—PlE
Binsey poplars felled 1879.—CoBn
The cuckoo.—CoB
Felix Randal.—CoR
Hurrahing in harvest.—CoBn—GrCt
"I am like a slip of comet."—LiT
Pied beauty.—BoGj—HoL—PlE—SmM
Spring.—CoBn
Spring and fall: To a young child.—BoGj—GrCt
"The stars were packed so close that night." —LiT
"Thou art indeed just, Lord, if I contend."—PlE
A vision of the mermaids.—GrCt (sel.)
The windhover.—PlE
The wreck of the Deutschland.—LiT (sel.)
Hopkins, John Henry
We three kings.—LaPh (sel.)
Hopkins, Kenneth
The bubble.—CaD
Hopkins, Stephen
"A gull's ghostly call."—LeM
Hopper, Queenie Scott
"Amy Elizabeth Ermyntrude Annie."—ArT-3
"**Hopping** frog, hop here and be seen." Christina Georgina Rossetti.—BlO
Hoppity. A. A. Milne.—ArT-3—HoB—MiC
Horan, Robert
Little city.—CoB
An **Horatian** ode upon Cromwell's return from Ireland, sel. Andrew Marvell
King Charles upon the scaffold.—GrCt
Horne, Frank
Kid stuff.—BoA—BoH—HaK—LiT
Notes found near a suicide, sels.—BoA (Complete)
To James.—BoH—HaK
Symphony.—BoA
To a persistent phantom.—BoA
To James. See Notes found near a suicide

Hornets
The harnet and the bittle. J. Y. Akerman.—GrCt
The **horns.** Elizabeth Jane Coatsworth.—CoDh
"The **horns,** the hunting horns, there's game afoot." See The horns
The **horny-goloch.** Unknown.—CoB
Earwig.—MoB
"The **horny-goloch** is an awesome beast." See The horny-goloch
Horsa, Jute leader
Ode to Hengist and Horsa. R. Jeffers.—GrS
Horsbrugh, Wilma
Old Mr Bows.—CoO
Horse ("His bridle hung around the post") Elizabeth Madox Roberts.—CoB
The **horse** ("The horse moves") William Carlos Williams.—ReO—WeP
The **horse** ("I will not change my horse with any that treads") See King Henry V
The **horse** ("Round-hoof'd, short-jointed, fetlocks shag and long)" See Venus and Adonis—The horse of Adonis
"**Horse** after horse." Issa, tr. fr. the Japanese by Nobuyuki Yuasa.—IsF
Horse and hammer. Peter Kane Dufault.—CoB
"**Horse** and hattock." See The witch's broomstick spell
Horse and rider. Wey Robinson.—MoS
Horse-chestnut time. Kaye Starbird.—LaPd
"The **horse** in the field." See Shadows
"The **horse** moves." See The horse
The **horse** of Adonis. See Venus and Adonis
Horse racing. See Rides and riding—Horse
"A **horse** would tire." Elizabeth Jane Coatsworth.—ArT-3
The **horseman** ("I heard a horseman") Walter De La Mare.—ArT-3—BoGj—LaP
The **horseman** ("There was a horseman rode so fast") Walter De La Mare.—DeBg—SmM
Horses. See also Rides and riding—Horse
All of a sudden. E. J. Coatsworth.—CoSb
At Amberley Wild Brooks. A. Young.—ReO
At grass. P. Larkin.—CaD—MoS
The bell of Atri. From Tales of a wayside inn. H. W. Longfellow.—LoPl
"The black and the brown." Unknown.—MoB
A blessing. James Wright.—DuS
The blood horse. B. Cornwall.—CoB
The broncho that would not be broken. V. Lindsay.—ArT-3—CoB—CoR—LiP
Carriage. E. Farjeon.—FaT
"A certain young gallant named Robbie." Unknown.—BrLl
The child in the orchard. E. Thomas.—ThG
Clouds. J. Reaney.—DoW
Elegy on Willie Nicol's mare. R. Burns.—BuPr
"A farmer went trotting upon his grey mare." Mother Goose.—ArT-3
"A farmer went riding."—OpF—HuS-3
The mischievous raven.—BrF—BrMg
Foal. M. B. Miller.—ArT-3—CoB—LaPd
The four horses. J. Reeves.—CoB
"A gigantic beauty of a stallion, fresh and responsive to my caresses." From Song of myself. W. Whitman.—CoB—LaPd
"Go, go, go." Unknown.—MoB
"Hast thou given the horse strength." From Job, Bible, Old Testament.—GrCt
The war horse.—CoB
Hay for the horses. G. Snyder.—DuS
Hobbyhorse. K. Fraser.—FrS
Horse ("His bridle hung around the post") E. M. Roberts.—CoB
The horse ("The horse moves") W. C. Williams.—ReO—WeP
The horse ("I will not change my horse with any that treads") From King Henry V. W. Shakespeare.—CoB
"Horse after horse." Issa.—IsF
Horse and hammer. P. K. Dufault.—CoB
Horse and rider. W. Robinson.—MoS
The horse of Adonis. From Venus and Adonis. W. Shakespeare.—ClF
The horse.—ShS
The horseman ("I heard a horseman") W. De La Mare.—ArT-3—BoGj—LaP
The horseman ("There was a horseman rode so fast") W. De La Mare.—DeBg—SmM
Horses ("The long whip lingers") L. MacNeice.—CaD
The horses ("Red horse") E. J. Coatsworth.—CoSb
Horses chawin' hay. H. Garland.—HuS-3
"The horses of the sea." C. G. Rossetti.—BoGj
Horses on the Camargue. R. Campbell.—CaD—ReO
"How joyous his neigh." Unknown.—LeO
"I had a little pony." Mother Goose.—BlO—HuS-3—MoB—OpF
The bad rider.—BrMg
"I lost my mare in Lincoln lane." Mother Goose.—ReMg
In the blueberry bushes. E. J. Coatsworth.—CoSb
"John Cook had a little grey mare." Mother Goose.—WiMg
John Cook.—BlO
John Cook's mare.—ReOn
The leap of Roushan Beg. From Birds of passage. H. W. Longfellow.—HuS-3
Little nag. Mother Goose.—BrMg
"Little sparrow." Issa.—LeOw
Moss. Mother Goose.—ReOn
"A mother horse." Issa.—LeMw
"My horse clip-clopping." Bashō.—BeCs
Night clouds. A. Lowell.—ThA
Noonday Sun. K. and B. Jackson.—ArT-3
Nottamun town. Unknown.—BlO
Old Smokie. Unknown.—LaP
"On a rainy spring day." Issa.—IsF
"On the bridge." Issa.—IsF
"One white foot, buy him." Mother Goose.—OpF
Orchard. R. Stone.—CoB
Pain for a daughter. A. Sexton.—McWs

Horses—*Continued*
The ponies. W. W. Gibson.—CoB
Pony clouds. P. Hubbell.—ArT-3
The power of music. From The merchant of Venice. W. Shakespeare.—ShS
The prancing pony. Unknown.—DePp
The prayer of the old horse. C. B. de Gasztold.—LaPd
The runaway. R. Frost.—ArT-3—BoGj—CoB—HoB—HuS-3—LaPd
"Shoe the horse." E. J. Coatsworth.—CoSb
Steeds. P. Hiebert.—DoW
"Step aside, step aside." Issa.—IsF
Stopping by woods on a snowy evening. R. Frost.—ArT-3—BoGj—CoBn—HuS-3—LaPd
"There was a man who went to the fair." Mother Goose.—OpF
"There was a young prince of Bombay." W. Parke.—BrLl
The three horses. I. O. Eastwick.—HoB
To the four courts, please. J. Stephens.—StS
"Trot along, pony." M. Edey.—ArT-3
"Trot, trot, horsie." Unknown.—MoB
"Up a hill hurry me not." Unknown.—OpF
The white horse. Tu Fu.—GrCt
White horses. E. Farjeon.—LaPd
Wild horse. H. Allen.—LeM
Horses ("The long whip lingers") Louis MacNeice.—CaD
The **horses** ("Red horse") Elizabeth Jane Coatsworth.—CoSb
Horses chawin' hay. Hamlin Garland.—HuS-3
"The **horses** of the sea." Christina Georgina Rossetti.—BoGj
Horses on the Camargue. Roy Campbell.—CaD—ReO
"The **horses,** the pigs." See Familiar friends
The **horseshoe.** See From a very little sphinx—"Wonder where this horseshoe went"
Horseshoes. See also Blacksmiths and blacksmithing
Foot patting. Mother Goose.—BrMg
"For want of a nail." Mother Goose.—ReMg
A nail.—BrMg
"Pitty Patty Polt." Mother Goose.—StF
"Shoe the horse." E. J. Coatsworth.—CoSb
"Wonder where this horseshoe went." From From a very little sphinx. E. St V. Millay.—ArT-3
The horseshoe.—HuS-3
Horsley, Henry Sharpe
The death of a father.—VrF
The death of a mother.—VrF
Idleness.—VrF
On politeness.—VrF
The orphans.—VrF
The poor cripple girl.—VrF
School.—VrF
A visit to Chelsea college.—VrF
A visit to Newgate.—VrF
A visit to the blind asylum.—VrF
A visit to the lunatic asylum.—VrF
The watchman.—VrF
Horton, George Moses
George Moses Horton, myself.—HaK
On liberty and slavery.—HaK
Horton, George Moses (about)
George Moses Horton, myself. G. M. Horton.—HaK
Hosokawa Yusai
"Ah, the peasant who."—LeMw
Hospitality
Hospitality. W. McClintic.—CoB
The hostess. Wang Mou Fang.—LeMw
Hospitality. Winona McClintic.—CoB
The **host** of the air. William Butler Yeats.—LiT—YeR
The **hostess.** Wang Mou Fang, tr. fr. the Chinese by Henry H. Hart.—LeMw
Hot cake. Shu Hsi, tr. by Arthur Waley.—ClF (sel.)
Hot cockles. Mother Goose.—ReOn
"**Hot** cross buns." Mother Goose.—WiMg
Good Friday.—BrMg
"The **hot** sun has ripened the corn." See August
A **hot-weather** song. Don Marquis.—HuS-3
Hotels. See Inns and taverns
"The **hototogisu** is singing." Issa, tr. fr. the Japanese by R. H. Blyth.—IsF
"**Hound** yellow, light of tread—the cunning foe." See An englyn on a yellow greyhound
Hourigan, Marie
Breeze.—LeM
The **hours.** See King Henry VI
"**Hours** are leaves of life." Susan Morrison.—LeM
"The **hours** of night were passing." See Midnight in the garden
The **house** ("The ancestral house talks to me. Wherever I move") Rajlukshmee Debee, tr. fr. the Bengali by the author.—AlPi
The **house** ("A lane at the end of Old Pilgrim street") Walter De La Mare.—DeBg
House ("Shall I sonnet-sing you about myself") Robert Browning.—BrP
A **house** blessing. See "Saint Francis and Saint Benedight"
House blessing ("Bless the four corners of this house") Arthur Guiterman.—ArT-3
The **house** cat. Annette Wynne.—HuS-3
"The **house** cat sits." See The house cat
The **house** dog's grave. Robinson Jeffers.—CoB
"The **house** frames hang like spider webs." See Construction
"A **house** full." See "A house full, a hole full"
"A **house** full, a hole full." Mother Goose.—BrMg
"A house full."—OpF—ReOn
House in Denver. Thomas Hornsby Ferril.—BrA
House in St Petersburg. Stanley Burnshaw.—GrS
"A **house** like a man all lean and coughing." See Even numbers
The **house** of dream. Walter De La Mare.—DeBg
"The **house** of the mouse." Lucy Sprague Mitchell.—ArT-3

The **house** on the hill. Edwin Arlington Robinson.—BoGj—BoH
The **house** plants. Elizabeth Jane Coatsworth.—CoSb
"The **house** plants always have." See The house plants
The **house** that Jack built. See "This is the house that Jack built"
The **house** with nobody in it. Joyce Kilmer.—HuS-3—ThA
"The **house** was haunted like spear." See Murder
Household problems. Larry Haft.—LeM
"The **housekeeper** in bombazine is rattling of her keys." See Mansion
Housekeepers and housekeeping. See also Servants
The cares of a caretaker. W. Irwin.—CoO
"Cock a doodle doodle do (cock a doodle dandy)." Unknown.—StF
Dust. S. K. Russell.—BrSm—DuR
"I had a little wife." Mother Goose.—OpF
Lines scratched in wet cement. E. Jacobson.—BrSm
Little Thomas. F. G. Evans.—CoBb
"Old Mother Shuttle." Mother Goose.—WiMg
Mother Shuttle.—BrMg
On a tired housewife. Unknown.—SmM
Portrait by a neighbor. E. St V. Millay.—ArT-3—HaL—LaPd—ThA—TuW
"Robin he married a wife in the west." Unknown.—OpF
Housekeeping. See Housekeepers and housekeeping
Houses
Animals' houses. J. Reeves.—StF
Apartment house. G. Raftery.—BrA—DuR—LaC
"The autumn moon." Issa.—IsF
Bam, bam, bam. E. Merriam.—LaPd—MeC
"Be a good boy." Issa.—LeOw
"A beautiful kite." Issa.—IsF—LeOw
The builders. S. H. Hay.—DuR
The cabin. E. J. Coatsworth.—CoDh
Candy house. E. J. Coatsworth.—CoSb
The chair house. E. J. Coatsworth.—CoSb
Construction. P. Hubbell.—LaC
Cottage. E. Farjeon.—FaT—StF
The deserted house ("I am afraid") J. Fairbun.—LeM
The deserted house ("Life and thought have gone away") A. Tennyson.—TeP
Even numbers. C. Sandburg.—LaC
From my study at the mouth of the valley. Ch'ien Ch'i.—LeMw
"The full moon." Issa.—LeOw
The goblin. Unknown.—ArT-3—LaPh
The house ("The ancestral house talks to me. Wherever I move") R. Debee.—AlPi
The house ("A lane at the end of Old Pilgrim street") W. De La Mare.—DeBg
House ("Shall I sonnet-sing you about myself") R. Browning.—BrP
House blessing. A. Guiterman.—ArT-3
House in St Petersburg. S. Burnshaw.—GrS
"The house of the mouse." L. S. Mitchell.—ArT-3
The house on the hill. E. A. Robinson.—BoGj—BoH
The house with nobody in it. J. Kilmer.—HuS-3—ThA
The hut. R. Pitter.—CaD
"I know some lonely houses off the road." E. Dickinson.—DiL
"In our house." Issa.—IsF—LeOw
Love in a life. R. Browning.—BrP
The man of the house. D. Wagoner.—DuS
Mansion. E. Farjeon.—FaT
"A measuring worm." Issa.—IsF
"My hut is so small." Issa.—IsF
"Now to be good if you'll begin." Unknown.—VrF
Oh, joyous house. R. Janzen.—LeM
"The old houses of Flanders." F. M. Hueffer.—PaH
The old woman of the roads. P. Colum.—HuS-3—ThA
On an overgrown hill. E. J. Coatsworth.—CoDh
Rabbit and lark. J. Reeves.—StF
"Round my hut." Issa.—LeOw
"Saint Francis and Saint Benedight." W. Cartwright.—PlE
A house blessing.—GrCt
"Since my house burned down." Masahide.—BeCs
"A single mat." Issa.—IsF
Song for a little house. C. Morley.—HuS-3—LaP
Southern mansion. A. Bontemps.—AdIa—BoA—BrA—HaK
Squares and angles. A. Storni.—LaC
A tale. E. Thomas.—GrCt
Tall city. S. N. Pulsifer.—LaC
The termites. R. Hillyer.—ReO
Thanksgiving to God, for his house. R. Herrick.—GrCt
"This is the house that Jack built." Mother Goose.—HuS-3—OpF
The house that Jack built.—BrMg
"Today also, today also." Issa.—LeOw
The treehouse. J. A. Emanuel.—BoH
Vacant house. J. DeL. Bonnette.—DuS
Visitors. A. Fisher.—FiIo
"Whose cottage." Issa.—LeOw
"The **houses** are haunted." See Disillusionment of ten o'clock
"**Houses,** houses,—Oh, I know." See Where
"**Houses** in a row, houses in a row." See Squares and angles
The **housewife.** Balamani Amma, tr. fr. the Malayalam by the author.—AlPi
Housman, Alfred Edward
"Amelia mixed the mustard."—LiT
"As I was walking slowly."—LiT

Housman, Alfred Edward—*Continued*
Away with bloodshed.—BrSm
"Away with bloodshed, I love not such." —LiT
"Away with bloodshed, I love not such." See Away with bloodshed
Easter hymn.—PlE
The elephant; or, The force of habit.—LiT
"Far in a western brookland." See A Shropshire lad
Fragment of an English opera.—LiT
"From far, from eve and morning." See A Shropshire lad
Hallelujah.—BrSm
Infant innocence.—GrCt
Inhuman Henry; or, Cruelty to fabulous animals.—CoBb
Into my heart. See A Shropshire lad—"Into my heart an air that kills"
"Into my heart an air that kills." See A Shropshire lad
Loveliest of trees. See A Shropshire lad
"Loveliest of trees, the cherry now." See A Shropshire lad—Loveliest of trees
"O billows bounding far."—CoBn
"Oh see how thick the goldcup flowers." See A Shropshire lad
Oh stay at home.—McWs
Oh, when I was in love. See A Shropshire lad
The oracles.—CoR
The shades of night.—GrCt
A Shropshire lad, sels.
"Far in a western brookland."—PaH
"From far, from eve and morning."—HoL
"Into my heart an air that kills."—GrCt
Into my heart.—BoGj
Loveliest of trees.—BlO—CoBn—HuS-3—SmM—TuW
"Loveliest of trees, the cherry now."—GrCt
"Oh see how thick the goldcup flowers." —CoBl
Oh, when I was in love.—McWs
To an athlete dying young.—MoS
"When I was one-and-twenty."—BoH—CoBl—HoL
"Stars, I have seen them fall."—GrCt
To an athlete dying young. See A Shropshire lad
"We'll to the woods no more."—HaL
"When I was one-and-twenty." See A Shropshire lad
Hovey, Richard
Love in the winds.—CoBl
The sea gypsy.—CoSs—LaPd
The **how** and the why. Alfred Tennyson.—TeP
"**How** and when and where and why." Phyllis Gotlieb.—DoW
"**How** beastly the bourgeois is." D. H. Lawrence.—GrCt
"**How** beautiful new fingers are." See Newborn fingers
"**How** brave, how faithful, and how frightening." See Winter morning
"**How** bravely morning-glory vines." See Morning-glories
"**How** bright on the blue." See The kite
"**How** can a deep love seem deep love." Tu Mu, tr. fr. the Chinese by Witter Bynner and Kiang Kang-hu.—LeMw
"**How** can I, that girl standing there." See Politics
"**How** can the sea be dark and gray." Susan Harrison.—LeM
"**How** charming are the women's songs as they husk the winter rice." See Characterization
"**How** clear, how keen, how marvellously bright." See November 1
"**How** cold is an empty room." See Song for someone who is absent
"**How** cool cut hay smells." Boncho, tr. fr. the Japanese by Harry Behn.—BeCs
"**How** deep is his duplicity who in a flash." See High diver
"**How** delightful, at sunset, to loosen the boat." See The excursion
"**How** did the party go in Portman square." See Juliet
How do I love thee. See Sonnets from the Portuguese—"How do I love thee? Let me count the ways"
"**How** do I love thee? Let me count the ways." See Sonnets from the Portuguese
"**How** do robins build their nests." See What robin told
"**How** do you amuse." See Ditto marks; or, How do you amuse a muse
How do you do. See "One misty moisty morning"
"**How** do you do, neighbor." Mother Goose.—OpF
"**How** do you know it's spring." Margaret Wise Brown.—BrSg
"**How** do you like to go up in a swing." See The swing
"**How** doth the little busy bee." See Little busy bee
"**How** doth the little crocodile." See Alice's adventures in wonderland
"**How** far, today." See Far away
"**How** fearful." See King Lear—The sea
"**How** fits his umber coat." Emily Dickinson.—DiPe
"**How** go the ladies, how go they." Mother Goose.—OpF
"**How** goes it, turtle." See The long black grave
"**How** goes the night." Unknown, tr. fr. the Chinese by Helen Waddell.—LeMw
"**How** gracious, how benign, is solitude." See The prelude—Summer vacation
"**How** gray the rain." Elizabeth Jane Coatsworth.—ArT-3
"**How** happy, how affectionate they are." Issa, tr. fr. the Japanese by R. H. Blyth.—LeOw
"**How** happy is the little stone." Emily Dickinson.—DiPe
"**How** hard is my fortune." See The convict of Clonmel

"How, how, he said. Friend Chang, I said." See The Chinese nightingale
"How I yearn to be." Okura.—BaS
"How in heaven's name did Columbus get over." See Columbus
"How is the gold become dim." See The lamentations of Jeremiah
"How joyous his neigh." Unknown, tr. fr. the Navajo.—LeO
How little I was. Myra Cohn Livingston.—LiC
"How little I was then." See How little I was
"How long, how long must I regret." See The lost tribe
"How long, O lion, hast thou fleshless lain." See The lion's skeleton
"How long shall I pine for love." See Pining for love
"How lost is the little fox at the borders of night." See Night of wind
"How lovely." Issa, tr. fr. the Japanese by R. H. Blyth.—LeI—LeMw
"How lovely is the standing corn." See The standing corn
How many birds. Unknown.—ReOn
"How many cherries." See Cherry-stones
"How many dawns, chill from his rippling rest." See To Brooklyn bridge
"How many days has my baby to play." Mother Goose.—ArT-3
"How many hundreds for my sake have died." See Riddle
"How many miles to Babylon." Mother Goose. —OpF—ReMg—TuW
Babylon.—BrMg—GrCt
"How many miles to Glasgow Lea." Unknown. —MoB
"How many miles to Mylor." A. L. Rowse.—CaD
"How many times." See Waiting
"How many times these low feet staggered." Emily Dickinson.—DiPe
How marigolds came yellow. Robert Herrick.—GrCt
"How much." Issa, tr. fr. the Japanese by R. H. Blyth.—LeOw
"How much living have you done." See The poet speaks
"How much the present moment means." Emily Dickinson.—DiPe
"How much wood would a wood-chuck chuck." Mother Goose.—ArT-3—HuS-3
"How must it feel." See The seal
"How nice to be." See The frog
"How pure, how beautiful, how fine." See Reflections dental
"How pleasant to know Mr Lear." Edward Lear.—GrCt
Mr Lear.—TuW
"How ran lithe monkeys through the leaves." See Walker in Nicaragua—Monkeys
How roses came red. Robert Herrick.—GrCt
"How sad I was." See Longing for the south country
"How sad it is to be alone." See Alone
"How sad this road." Mitsune.—BaS
How Samson bore away the gates of Gaza. Vachel Lindsay.—LiP
"How shall I begin my songs." See Medicine song
"How shall I seek the origin? where find." See The prelude—School-time
"How should I your true love know." See Hamlet—Ophelia's song
"How soft a caterpillar steps." Emily Dickinson. —DiL
"How stately stand yon pines upon the hill." See The ancient mansion—Spring to winter
"How still." See Sea calm
"How still it is here in the woods. The trees." See Solitude
"How still the bells in steeples stand." Emily Dickinson.—DiL—DiPe
"How straight it flew, how long it flew." See Seaside golf
How strange it is. Claudia Lewis.—LeP
"How strange it seems. These Hebrews in their graves." See The Jewish cemetery at Newport
"How sweet a thought." See A hawthorn berry
"How sweet I roam'd from field to field." See Song
"How sweet is the shepherd's sweet lot." See The shepherd
"How sweet the moonlight sleeps upon this bank." See The merchant of Venice—Night music
"How sweet, when weary, dropping on a bank." See Summer
"How the great moon crushes the cloud." Ishikawa, tr. fr. the Japanese by Chi Hwang Chu and Edna Worthley Underwood.—LeMw
How the sun rose. See "I'll tell you how the sun rose"
How they bite. Unknown.—MoS
How they brought the good news from Ghent to Aix. Robert Browning.—ArT-3—BrP—CoR—HuS-3
How time consumeth all earthly things. Thomas Proctor.—GrCt
How to eat a poem. Eve Merriam.—AgH—DuR —MeI
How to paint the portrait of a bird. Jacques Prévert, tr. by Paul Dehn.—SmM
How to sleep easy. See "To sleep easy at night"
How to sow beans. Unknown.—BrSg
How to tell goblins from elves. Monica Shannon. —ArT-3
How to tell the wild animals. Carolyn Wells.—ArT-3
"How will he hear the bell at school." See Mutterings over the crib of a deaf child
"How will you manage." Princess Daihaku.—BaS
"How would it be." See Butterfly wings
Howard, Dorothy
The knifesmith.—SmM
Howard, Dorothy S.
Birkett's eagle.—CaMb

Wisdom.—ArT-3
Without benefit of declaration.—BoA
Youth.—BoH—BrA—LiT
Hughes, Richard
Old cat Care.—ReS
Hughes, Ted
Bullfrog.—CaD—CoB
Cat and mouse.—PlE
Crag Jack's apostasy.—PlE
Foxgloves.—HaL
Hawk roosting.—ReO
My brother Bert.—CoBb
An otter.—CaD (sel.)
September.—GrS
Two wise generals.—CaMb
Hugo, Victor (Marie, Vicomte)
Be like the bird.—ArT-3
Good night.—ArT-3
Hugo of Orleans (Primas)
On the gift of a cloak.—LiT
Hull, R. F. C.
Vice versa. tr.—ReO
Hulme, T. E.
Autumn.—HaL—SmM
"The **hum** of either army stilly sounds." See King Henry V—Before Agincourt
The **human** abstract. William Blake.—BlP
Human body. See Body, Human
The **human** image, sel. William Blake
London.—GrCt
Human race. See Man
The **human** race. Walter Raleigh.—McWs
Human things. Howard Nemerov.—CoBn
The **humble-bee.** See Troilus and Cressida
"**Humble** in dress and low in state." See Cottage boy
Humility
"I am nobody." R. Wright
Hokku poems.—BoA
"I will bow and be simple." Unknown.—PlE
"If humility and purity be not in the heart." From The rock. T. S. Eliot.—ArT-3
"I'm nobody. Who are you." E. Dickinson.—ArT-3—DiL—DiPe—LaPd
In place of a curse. J. Ciardi.—DuS
Mary. W. Blake.—BlP
The shepherd boy sings in the valley of humiliation. From The pilgrim's progress. J. Bunyan.—PlE
The violet. J. Taylor.—HoB
Wisdom. L. Hughes.—ArT-3
Humming bird. See "A route of evanescence"
Humming birds
Garden song. A. Guiterman.—BrSg—ThA
The hummingbird. M. Kennedy.—CoB
"A route of evanescence." E. Dickinson.—DiPe
Humming bird.—DiL
Song of hummingbird. Unknown.—LeO
The **hummingbird.** Mary Kennedy.—CoB
Humorists
The height of the ridiculous. O. W. Holmes.—HuS-3
Humphrey, Gillian
Winter.—LeM
Humphries, Rolfe
Aeneid, sels.
The boat race. tr.—MoS
The boxing match. tr.—MoS
The boat race. See Aeneid
The boxing match. See Aeneid
The creation. See Metamorphoses
Metamorphoses, sel.
The creation. tr.—ClF
Polo grounds.—MoS
Wmffre the sweep.—PlE
Humpty Dumpty. See "Humpty Dumpty sat on a wall . . . (all the king's horses)"
"**Humpty** Dumpty and his brother." Mother Goose.—OpF
"**Humpty** Dumpty ligs in t' beck." Mother Goose.—OpF
"**Humpty** Dumpty sat on a spoon." Mother Goose.—OpF
"**Humpty** Dumpty sat on a wall . . . (all the king's horses)." Mother Goose.—GrT—OpF—WiMg
Humpty Dumpty.—BrMg
Mother Goose rhymes, 25.—HoB
"**Humpty** Dumpty sat on a wall . . . (four score men)." Mother Goose.—HuS-3—OpF
"**Humpty** Dumpty sat on the wall." See Mother Goose, circa 2054
"**Humpty** Dumpty went to town." Mother Goose.—OpF
Humpty Dumpty's poem. See Through the looking-glass
Humpty Dumpty's recitation. See Through the looking-glass—Humpty Dumpty's poem
Hunc, said he. See "There was a lady loved a swine"
Hunchback girl: She thinks of heaven. Gwendolyn Brooks.—HaK
Hunchbacks
Hunchback girl: She thinks of heaven. G. Brooks.—HaK
"A **hundred** autumns he has wheeled." See Crow
Hung, William
Overnight in the apartment by the river. tr.—GrCt
"**Hung** be the heavens with black, yield day to night." See King Henry VI—A king is dead
Hunger
"Babies are crying." P. John.—BaH
A description of famine. Unknown.—AlPi
The forsaken. D. C. Scott.—DoW (sel.)
"Hunger is bad." Unknown.—DoC
"I do not know." Unknown.—DoC
"I had been hungry all the years." E. Dickinson.—DiPe
"I have given up singing about men." Unknown.—DoC
Is this life. H. Harrington.—BaH
Life. H. Harrington.—BaH
Navajo rug. B. J. Lee.—BaH

Hunger—*Continued*
Poem to hunger. E. J. Coatsworth.—CoDh
"A small hungry child." Bashō.—BeCs
Song for the lazy. Unknown.—DoC
Street window. C. Sandburg.—LaC
Yet the lean beast plays. E. J. Coatsworth.—CoDh
"**Hunger** every second of the day." See Is this life
"**Hunger** is bad." Unknown.—DoC
"A **hungry** dog some meat had seized." See The dog and the shadow
"A **hungry** owl hoots." Jōsō, tr. fr. the Japanese by Harry Behn.—BeCs
"**Hungry** tree." Nathan Altshuler.—LeM
Hunt, Evelyn Tooley
Taught me purple.—LaC
Hunt, (James Henry) Leigh
The fish and the man. See The fish, the man, and the spirit
A fish answers. See The fish, the man, and the spirit
The fish, the man, and the spirit.—GrCt
The fish and the man.—CoR (sel.)
A fish answers.—ReO (sel.)—SmM (sel.)
To a fish.—SmM (sel.)
The grasshopper and the cricket.—CoB
To a fish. See The fish, the man, and the spirit
The **hunt.** Louis Kent.—CoB
Hunt the thimble. Eleanor Farjeon.—FaT
A **hunted** deer. Unknown, ad. fr. the Japanese by Charlotte B. DeForest.—DePp
Hunter-Duvar, John
Twilight song.—DoW
Hunter, John
Tree.—LeM
The **hunter.** Ogden Nash.—CoB—MoS
"The **hunter** crouches in his blind." See The hunter
Hunter trials. John Betjeman.—CaD
Hunters and hunting. See also Falcons and falconry
A-hunting we will go. Mother Goose.—ReOn
"All in green went my love riding." E. E. Cummings.—BoGj—MoS
Badger. J. Clare.—ClF (sel.)—CoB
The ballad of red fox. M. W. La Follette.—HaL
Beagles. W. R. Rodgers.—MoS
"The clear note." Issa.—IsF
Contest. F. Victor.—MoS
Deer hunt. J. Jerome.—DuR
Done for. W. De La Mare.—BlO—DeBg
"Four and twenty tailors went to kill a snail." Mother Goose.—WiMg
Snail hunters.—BrMg
Fragment of a bylina. A. S. Pushkin.—LiT
The friar. From Maid Marian. T. L. Peacock.—MoS
Growing up. K. Wilson.—DuS
The history of Sam the sportsman, and his gun, also, of his wife Joan. Unknown.—VrF
The horns. E. J. Coatsworth.—CoDh
The hunt. L. Kent.—CoB
A hunted deer. Unknown.—DePp
The hunter. O. Nash.—CoB—MoS
Hunter trials. J. Betjeman.—CaD
Hunter's song ("In the bush, in the deep forest") Unknown.—DoC
Hunter's song ("The toils are pitch'd, and the stakes are set") From The lady of the lake. W. Scott.—ReO
Hunting. J. Aluskak.—BaH
The hunting of the wren. Unknown.—MoB
Hunting prayer. Unknown.—LeO
"I do not know."—DoC
Hunting song ("Comes the deer to my singing") Unknown.—LeO
Hunting song ("The fox came lolloping, lolloping") D. Finkel.—CaMb—CoB—DuR—WeP
Hunting song ("Hurry, there went the game") Unknown.—LeO
Hunting song ("Something I've killed, and I lift up my voice") Unknown.—LeO
Hunting song ("Up, up, ye dames and lasses gay") S. T. Coleridge.—BlO
Hunting song ("Waken, lords and ladies gay") W. Scott.—MoS
"The hunting tribes of air and earth." From Rokeby. W. Scott.—ReO
The huntsmen. W. De La Mare.—ArT-3—HuS-3
"Jack, Jack Joe." Mother Goose.—OpF
John Peel. J. W. Graves.—MoS
Landscape, deer season. B. Howes.—BoGj
The Lincolnshire poacher. Unknown.—MoS
"A little cock sparrow sat on a green tree." Mother Goose.—WiMg
A little cock sparrow.—BrMg
"Luther Leavitt is a whale hunter." A. Brower.—BaH
"A man went a-hunting at Rygate." Mother Goose.—BrLl
Manerathiak's song. Unknown.—DoW
"The men of valor." Akahito.—BaS
Moose hunting. T. Willis.—BaH
"My bow, its lower part, I drew back." Unknown.—LeO
My heart's in the Highlands. R. Burns.—BuH (sel.)—BuPr—ClF—MoS
"My heart's in the Highlands, my heart is not here."—BlO—PaH
The night hunt. T. MacDonagh.—CoB—CoR
O what if the fowler. C. Dalmon.—CoB—ReBs
Old Blue. Unknown.—MoS
An old song. E. Thomas.—ThG
The old squire. W. S. Blunt.—MoS
One-eyed gunner. Mother Goose.—ReOn
Orion's belt. E. Farjeon.—FaT
Paddling song. Unknown.—LeO
Prayer to the moon. Unknown.—LeO
"Robin-a-Bobbin." Mother Goose.—BrMg
"Robin-a-Bobin bent his bow."—ReMg
The rousing canoe song. H. Fraser.—DoW
A runnable stag. J. Davidson.—CoB—MoS—ReO
Sport. W. H. Davies.—CoB

Hymes, Lucia and James L., Jr
Oodles of noodles.—AgH
Tombstone.—ArT-3
Hymn ("Lord, by whose breath all souls and seeds are living") Andrew Young.—PlE
Hymn ("The words of hymns abruptly plod") Louise Townsend Nicholl.—PlE
Hymn for Lanie Poo, sel. LeRoi Jones
"Each morning."—AdIa
Hymn to Diana. See Cynthia's revels
Hymn to God my God, in my sickness. John Donne.—GrCt
Hymn to the night. Henry Wadsworth Longfellow.—LoPl
Hymn to the sun. Unknown, tr. fr. the Fang.—LeO
Hymn written after Jeremiah preached to me in a dream. Owen Dodson.—BoA—HaK
A **hymne** to God the Father. John Donne.—PlE
Hymns
Battle hymn of the republic. J. W. Howe.—HiL—PlE
The cable hymn. J. G. Whittier.—HiL
Child's evening hymn. S. Baring-Gould.—ReS
Concord hymn. R. W. Emerson.—BrA—HiL—HuS-3—PaH—TuW
Cradle hymn. M. Luther.—ArT-3—HoB—LaPh
Easter hymn. A. E. Housman.—PlE
Evening hymn. E. M. Roberts.—ArT-3
For the Earth God. Unknown.—PlE
Hymn ("Lord, by whose breath all souls and seeds are living") A. Young.—PlE
Hymn ("The words of hymns abruptly plod") L. T. Nicholl.—PlE
Hymn to God my God, in my sickness. J. Donne.—GrCt
Hymn to the night. H. W. Longfellow.—LoPl
Hymn to the sun. Unknown.—LeO
Hymn written after Jeremiah preached to me in a dream. O. Dodson.—BoA—HaK
A hymne to God the Father. J. Donne.—PlE
Johnny Appleseed's hymn to the sun. V. Lindsay.—LiP
Light shining out of darkness. W. Cowper.—PlE
"A mighty fortress is our God." M. Luther.—PlE
"O God, our help in ages past." I. Watts.—PlE
The song of creation. From Rig Veda. Unknown.—AlPi
"The spacious firmament on high." J. Addison.—PlE
Hymns and spiritual songs, sel. Christopher Smart
Christmas day.—GrCt
Hymnus. See "God be in my head"
Hypocrites. Monk.—BaH

I

"**I.**" See Night practice
"**I.**" See Status symbol
"I always let Peter." See A drink
"I always paint pictures." See From a 19th century Kansas painter's notebook
"I always take my judgment from a fool." See Cromek speaks
"I am . . ." See The station
I am. Hilda Conkling.—ArT-3
"I am a black man, soul and all." Brenda J. Lewis.—BaH
"I am a broken-hearted milkman, in grief I'm arrayed." See Polly Perkins
"I am a gentleman in a dust-coat trying." See Piazza piece
"I am a little black boy." See Black is beautiful
"I am a Navajo, the Navajos are my people." See My people
"I am a nice nice boy." Martin O'Connor.—LeM
"I am a pretty wench." See A pretty wench
"I am a quiet gentleman." See The tired man
"I am a sea shell flung." See Frutta di mare
"I am a soul in the world: in." See The invention of comics
"I am a trombone. By the chinaberry tree." See New Orleans
"I am a wanderer, I shall die stretched out." Unknown, tr. fr. the Lamba.—LeO
"I am a young girl." See Young girl: Annam
"I am afoot with my vision." See Song of myself
"I am afraid." See The deserted house
"I am any man's suitor." See The how and the why
"I am blind. All that I can see." See Mimi's fingers
"I am cold and alone." See The boy fishing
"I am come to make thy tomb." See The duchess of Malfi
"I am fainty." See My feelings
"I am fevered with the sunset." See The sea gypsy
"I am fire. You know me." See Fire
"I am glad daylong for the gift of song." See Rhapsody
"I am he that walks with the tender and growing night." See Song of myself
"I am his highness' dog at Kew." See Engraved on the collar of a dog, which I gave to his royal highness
"I am Lake Superior." See The Great Lakes suite
"I am like a flag by far spaces surrounded." See Presentiment
"I am like a slip of comet." Gerard Manley Hopkins.—LiT
"I am monarch of all I survey." See The solitude of Alexander Selkirk
"I am nobody." Richard Wright
Hokku poems.—BoA
"I am not an old China hand." See But no
"I am of Shropshire, my shins be sharp." See A Shropshire lad
"I am Paul Bunyan." See Vacation
"I am poor and old and blind." See Belisarius
"I am poor brother Lippo, by your leave." See Fra Lippo Lippi

"I am Queen Anne, of whom 'tis said." See Queen Anne
"I am rich." See On wealth
I am Rose. Gertrude Stein.—SmM
"I am Rose my eyes are blue." See I am Rose
"I am round like a ball." Unknown
Riddles.—StF
"I am sad because the sun is setting and night is drawing near." See On visiting a clear spring
"I am so little and grey." See The prayer of the mouse
"I am that merry wanderer of the night." See A midsummer-night's dream—Puck's song
"I am the ancient apple-queen." See Pomona
"I am the dancer of the wood." See The spirit of the birch
"I am the king." See King of the mountain
"I am the magical mouse." See The magical mouse
"I am the maker." See The ancient elf
"I am the man who made the knife." See The knifesmith
"I am the mother of sorrows." See The paradox
"I am the pure lotus." See Book of the dead—He is like the lotus
"I am the queerest sort of boy the world has ever seen." See The contrary boy
"I am the rose of Sharon." See The song of Solomon
"I am the sister of him." See Little
"I am the star of mariners." See Pole-star
I am tired of the wind. John Smith.—SmM
"I am tired of the wind leaning against me." See I am tired of the wind
"I am tired of work; I am tired of building up somebody else's civilization." See Tired
"I am unjust, but I can strive for justice." See Why I voted the socialist ticket
I am waiting. Vanessa C. Howard.—BaH
"I am waiting for the sun." See I am waiting
"I am willowy boughs." See I am
"I am within as white as snow." Unknown.—GrCt
"I am writer." James Stephens.—StS
"I and Pangur Ban, my cat." See The monk and his cat
"I arise from dreams of thee." See Indian serenade
"I arise from rest with movements swift." Unknown, tr. fr. the Eskimo.—LeO
"I ask you this." See Prayer
"I asked a seagull on the bay." See A question
"I asked her, Is Aladdin's lamp." See The sorceress
"I asked him how old he was." Issa, tr. fr. the Japanese by Nobuyuki Yuasa.—IsF
"I asked my mother for fifteen cents." Unknown.—ArT-3
"I asked no other thing." Emily Dickinson.—DiPe
"I asked the heaven of stars." See Night song at Amalfi
"I ate my sandwich on the rocks." See Ants and sailboats
"I bear, in sign of love." See Shepherdess' valentine
"I being silent, the woods began to sing." See Harmony
"I believe a leaf of grass is no less than the journey-work of the stars." See Song of myself
"I believe one day when." Margaret Classé.—BaH
"I bent again unto the ground." See The voice of God
"I bet with every wind that blew." Emily Dickinson.—DiPe
I bid you keep some few small dreams. Helen Frazee-Bower.—ThA
I bless this man. See Nemea 11
"I bless this man for Agesilas, his father." See Nemea 11—I bless this man
"I blew myself a bubble." See The bubble
"I borrowed my cottage." Issa, tr. fr. the Japanese by R. H. Blyth.—IsF
"I borrowed the wayside shrine." Issa, tr. fr. the Japanese.—LeOw
"I bought." Issa, tr. fr. the Japanese by Nobuyuki Yuasa.—IsF
"I broke my heart because of you, my dear." See Literary love
"I built a castle in the sand." See The sandcastle
"I buried you deeper last night." See To a persistent phantom
"I busy too, the little boy." See A world to do
I call and I call. Robert Herrick.—GrCt
"I call, I call. Who do ye call." See I call and I call
"I came from under the earth." Unknown, tr. fr. the Melanesian.—LeO
"I came to look, and lo." See The fall of the plum blossoms
"I came to the new world empty-handed." See North star shining
"I can hear banjos." See Slave quarter
"I can jump, jump, jump." See You do it too
"I can play." See Lamplighter barn
"I can prick your finger." See Riddles
"I can remember looking cross-lots from." See House in Denver
"I can wade grief." Emily Dickinson.—DiPe
"I can walk on this." Unknown
Riddles.—StF
"I cannot give you the Metropolitan tower." See Parting gift
"I cannot see fairies." See Fairies
I cannot tell. Deborah Crawford.—BaH
"I cannot tell when it's going to rain." See I cannot tell
"I can't bite." See The frog's lament
"I Carolyn Jackson am a pure-blooded Negro in soul and mind." See I don't mind
I caught a fish. Bertram Murray.—StF
"I caught a little fish one day." See I caught a fish
"I caught a tremendous fish." See The fish

"I caught this morning morning's minion." See The windhover
"I celebrate myself." See Song of myself
"I cleaned." Issa, tr. fr. the Japanese by Nobuyuki Yuasa.—IsF
"I climbed, one day." See Mountain fantasy
"I climbed up on the merry-go-round." See Merry-go-round
"I come from haunts of coot and hern." See The brook
"I come more softly than a bird." Mary Austin
Rhyming riddle.—CoBn
Rhyming riddles.—ArT-3
"I could eat it." Issa, tr. fr. the Japanese by R. H. Blyth.—LeMw
"I could have painted pictures like that youth's." See Pictor ignotus
"I could love her with a love so warm." See The world is a mighty ogre
"I could not prove the years had feet." Emily Dickinson.—DiPe
"I could take the Harlem night." See Juke box love song
"I dance and dance without any feet." See Spells
"I die, I die, the mother said." See The grey monk
"I died for beauty, but was scarce." Emily Dickinson.—DiPe
"I dig and dig." See The mole
"I do not know." See Hunting prayer
"I do not know much about gods; but I think that the river." See The dry salvages
"I do not like thee, Doctor Fell." See Doctor Fell
"I do not like to go to bed." See Sleepy Harry
"I do not see the hummingbird." See The hummingbird
"I don't believe in 'ristercrats." See My sort o' man
"I don't know any more what it used to be." See A girl
"I don't know why." Myra Cohn Livingston.—BrSg
"I don't know why I'm so crazy." See Why
"I don't like bees." See Bees
I don't mind. Carolyn Jackson.—LeM
"I don't much exactly quite care." David McCord.—BrLl
"I doubt, I doubt." Mother Goose.—ReOn
"I doubt not God is good, well-meaning, kind." See Yet do I marvel
I dream a world. Langston Hughes.—BoA—BoH
"I dream a world where man." See I dream a world
"I dream, and I dream." See Known of old
I dream of a place. Walter De La Mare.—DeBg
"I dream of a place where I long to live always." See I dream of a place
"I dreamed all my fortitude screamed." See Letter across doubt and distance
"I dreamed of war-heroes, of wounded war heroes." See The heroes
"I dreamed Ted Williams." See Dream of a baseball star
"I dreamed the fairies wanted me." See Crabapple
"I dreamt a dream the other night." See Lowlands
"I dreamt a dream, what can it mean." See The angel
"I dreamt I heard the grass grow." See Cornwall
"I drew a rabbit. John erased him." See Pad and pencil
"I dwell apart." See The hermit
"I dwell in possibility." Emily Dickinson.—DiPe
"I dwelt alone." See Eulalie—A song
"I eat from the dish of the world." See Look
I envy not in any moods. See In memoriam
"I envy seas whereon he rides." Emily Dickinson.—DiPe
"I fancied once that all places looked beautiful." See Waves of thought
"I feel." See Splish splosh
"I feel a bit happier." Clifton Roderick Foster.—LeM
"I feel cold." See A winter night
"I feel myself in need." See George Moses Horton, myself
"I feel relaxed and still." Karen Anderson.—LeM
"I feel so exceedingly lazy." See A hot-weather song
"I feel very sorry for." See Not any more
"I felt a cleavage (or cleaving) in my mind." Emily Dickinson.—DiL—DiPe
"I flew my kite." See Kite
I found. Myra Cohn Livingston.—BrSg
"I found a ball of grass among the hay." See Mouse's nest
"I found a dimpled spider, fat and white." See Design
"I found a four-leaf clover." See I found
"I found myself one day." See The hatch
"I found the phrase to every thought." Emily Dickinson.—DiPe
"I gather thyme upon the sunny hills." See Immalee
"I gave myself to him." Emily Dickinson.—DiPe
"I gazed upon the cloudless moon." Emily Brontë.—GrCt
"I give you now Professor Twist." See The purist
"I give you the end of a golden string." William Blake.—BlP
"I go out in the grey evening." See An evening air
"I got pocketed behind 7X-3824." See Ambition
"I got those sad old weary blues." See Too blue
"I grew single and sure." See Independence
"I, guest to ogres, naturally understand." See The ogre entertains
"I ha' seen them 'mid the clouds on the heather." See The white stag
"I had a beginning but shall have no end." See Stone angel
I had a boat. Mary Coleridge.—SmM
"I had a boat and the boat had wings." See I had a boat
"I had a dog (whose name was Buff)." See Buff

"I have just seen a beautiful thing." See The black finger
"I have known nights rain-washed and crystal-clear." See Wisdom
"I have legs." See Riddles
"I have long legs." Mother Goose.—OpF
"I have looked him round and looked him through." See Nora Criona
"I have lost my dewdrop, cries the flower." Rabindranath Tagore.—LeMf
I have loved flowers. Robert Bridges.—BoGj
"I have loved flowers that fade." See I have loved flowers
"I have no dog, but it must be." See My dog
"I have no happiness in dreaming of Brycelinde." See Under the moon
"I have no life but this." Emily Dickinson.—DiPe
"I have no name." See Infant joy
"I have no wings, but yet I fly." Mary Austin
Rhyming riddles.—ArT-3
"I have not been as Joshua when he fought." See Three helpers in battle
"I have searched my thesaurus through." See Be my non-valentine
"I have seen." See Mary Tudor
"I have seen many old fingers." See Old fingers
"I have seen old ships sail like swans asleep." See The old ships
"I have seen the birds of paradise." See The birds of paradise
"I have some sympathy for that cat." See At the lion's cage
"I have something to tell you." See Two friends
"I have sown beside all waters in my day." See A blackman talks of reaping
"I have sown upon the fields." See The idle flowers
"I have taken that vow." See The red-haired man's wife
"I have teeth." See Riddles
I have twelve oxen. Unknown.—GrCt
"I have twelve oxen that be fair and brown." See I have twelve oxen
"I have two dashing, prancing steeds." See Steeds
"I have wished a bird would fly away." See A minor bird
"I have wrapped my dreams in a silken cloth." Countee Cullen.—ThA
"I haven't a palace." See Any bird
"I hear." See Thunder
"I hear a sudden cry of pain." See The snare
I hear America singing. Walt Whitman.—ArT-3—BrA—HoB—HuS-3—WhA
"I hear America singing, the varied carols I hear."—LaPd
"I hear America singing, the varied carols I hear." See I hear America singing
"I hear leaves drinking rain." See The rain
I hear the crane. See Du Bartas his divine weeks
"I hear the engine pounding." See The ways of trains
"I heard a bird at break of day." See Overtones
"I heard a bird at dawn." See The rivals
"I heard a bird sing." Oliver Herford.—ArT-3—CoB—LaP—LaPd—ThA
"I heard a cow low, a bonnie cow low." Unknown.—MoB
"I heard a fly buzz when I died." Emily Dickinson.—DiPe
"I heard a horseman." See The horseman
"I heard a linnet courting." Robert Bridges.—ReO
"I heard a mouse." See The mouse
"I heard a thousand blended notes." See Lines written in early spring
"I heard an angel singing." William Blake.—BlP
"I heard Immanuel singing." Vachel Lindsay.—LiP
"I heard it in the valley." Annette Wynne.—ThA
"I heard the bells on Christmas day." See Christmas bells
"I heard the old, old men say." See The old men admiring themselves in the water
"I heard the trailing garments of the night." See Hymn to the night
"I heard the wild geese flying." See Wild geese
"I heard the wind coming." See Hearing the wind at night
"I held a jewel in my fingers." Emily Dickinson.—DiL—DiPe
"I hope the old Romans." See Ancient history
"I imagine him still with heavy brow." See Beethoven's death mask
"I jump. I bite." See The flea
"I keep three wishes ready." Annette Wynne.—ArT-3—HuS-3—LaPd—ThA
"I kissed a kiss in youth." See Scintilla
"I knew an old lady." See Antique shop
"I know." See October magic
"I know a bank whereon the wild thyme blows." See A midsummer-night's dream
"I know a busy fisherman." See Sky net
"I know a cow who says, How now." See Oddity land
"I know a funny little man." See Mr Nobody
"I know a girl." See The canal bank
"I know a Jew fish crier down on Maxwell street, with a." See Fish crier
"I know a large dune rat whose first name is Joe." See Fire Island walking song
"I know a little cupboard." See The cupboard
"I know a little pussy." See Pussy willow song
"I know a moon door in the Forbidden City." See Moon door
"I know a place." See A boy's place
"I know a place." Myra Cohn Livingston.—HoB
"I know a place, in the ivy on a tree." See The bird's nest
I know all this when gipsy fiddles cry. Vachel Lindsay.—LiP
"I know an old lady who swallowed a fly." See The old lady who swallowed a fly
"I know and you know and Billy knows, too." See Please don't tell him
"I know her by her angry air." See Kate

"I know I shall remember." See The cathedral of St Louis
"I know my body's of so frail a kind." See Nosce teipsum—I know myself a man
I know myself a man. See Nosce teipsum
"I know not how to speak to thee, girl—damselle." See Love song
"I know now." See I thought it was Tangiers I wanted
"I know some lonely houses off the road." Emily Dickinson.—DiL
"I know someone who is so slow." See Someone slow
"I know someone who lives at the zoo." See Come to think of it
"I know that I shall meet my fate." See An Irish airman foresees his death
"I know the language of the ocean." See Someday
"I know the trusty almanac." See May-day
"I know what the caged bird feels, alas." See Sympathy
"I know where I'd get." See Asses
"I leant upon a coppice gate." See The darkling thrush
"I learned today the world is round." See The road to China
I like. Clare Tringress.—StF
"I like a mouse." See Wild animals
"I like cake that is brown with spice." See Spice cake
"I like days." See December
"I like days in winter." See Winter walk
"I like fall." Aileen Fisher.—LaPh
"I like it when it's mizzly." Aileen Fisher.—LaPd
"I like my fingers." See Mark's fingers
"I like that ancient Saxon phrase, which calls." See God's-acre
"I like the birds because." Zachary White.—BaH
"I like the circling proud old family beech." See Beech
"I like the hunting of the hare." See The old squire
"I like the people who keep shops." See Shops
"I like the whistle of trains at night." See Trains at night
"I like the woods." See Autumn woods
"I like the word, space." See Space
"I like white ones." See Jelly beans
"I like wrestling with Herbie because." See Wrestling
"I like to feel my father's whiskers." See Whiskers
"I like to go to the stable after supper." See White cat
"I like to have a home life in the house." See Afterwards
"I like to move. There's such a feeling." See Moving
"I like to ride in my uncle's plane." See Flying
"I like to see." See The clown
"I like to see a thunder storm." See Rhyme
"I like to see it lap the miles." Emily Dickinson.—DiL—DiPe—LaPd
"I like to stay at home and put." See I like
"I like to walk." See Crows
"I live all alone, and I am a young girl." See The garden of bamboos
"I live among workers." See Living among the toilers
"I lived among great houses." See The statesman's holiday
"I longed to win the spelling bee." See Why I did not reign
"I look on the specious electrical light." See A rhyme about an electrical advertising sign
"I looked for universal things; perused." See The prelude—Residence at Cambridge
"I looked from my window and there." See Seen by moonlight
"I looked in the mirror." Beatrice Schenk De Regniers.—LaPd
"I looked out at the lilac." See The sparrow bush
"I looked over Jordan, and what did I see." See Swing low, sweet chariot
"I loosed an arrow from my bow." See Crookedheart
"I lost my mare in Lincoln lane." Mother Goose.—ReMg
"I lost the love of heaven above." See A vision
I love animals and dogs. Hilary-Anne Farley.—LeM
"I love animals and dogs and everything." See I love animals and dogs
"I love at early morn, from new-mown swath." See Summer images
"I love every stock and stone." See An American in England
"I love little pussy." Jane Taylor.—ArT-3—OpF
  "I love little pussy, her coat is so warm."—WiMg
  Kindness.—BrMg
"I love little pussy, her coat is so warm." See "I love little pussy"
"I love noodles. Give me oodles." See Oodles of noodles
"I love octopussy, his arms are so long." See Mixed beasts—The octopussycat
"I love rain." See Rain
"I love roads." See Roads
"I love the fitful gust that shakes." See Autumn
"I love the jocund dance." See Song
"I love the juice, but the sun goes up; I see the stars." See Sun goes up
"I love the winding trail." See The trail
I love the world. Paul Wollner.—LeM
"I love to rise in a summer morn." See The school boy
"I love to wallow in the mud." See The rhinoceros
"I love you, big world." See I love the world
"I love you first because your face is fair." See V-letter
"I loved my friend." See Poem

"I thought I heard the captain say." See Leave her, Johnny
"I thought I saw an angel flying low." See Nocturne at Bethesda
"I thought I saw white clouds, but no." See Lilies
I thought it was Tangiers I wanted. Langston Hughes.—BoH
"I thought no more was needed." See A song
"I thought of thee, my partner and my guide." See After-thought
"I thought that nature was enough." Emily Dickinson.—DiPe
"I throw myself to the left." See Dance of the animals
"I told the sun that I was glad." See The sun
"I told them a thousand times if I told them once." See The builders
I, too. See "I, too, sing America"
I, too, I, too. John Hall Wheelock.—SmM
"I, too, sing America." Langston Hughes.—AdIa
I, too.—BoA—HaK
I took a little stick. Elizabeth Jane Coatsworth. —CoSb
"I took a reed and blew a tune." See The find
"I took money and bought flowering trees." See Planting flowers on the eastern embankment
"I took my foot in my hand." Unknown.—MoB
"I took my power in my hand." Emily Dickinson.—DiPe
The duel.—LiT
"I travell'd on, seeing the hill, where lay." See The pilgrimage
"I travelled among unknown men." William Wordsworth.—WoP
"I trust I have not wasted breath." See In memoriam
"I try to grab sunlight." See Kevin's fingers
"I turned my back when in the pot they tossed." See Walthena
"I twist your arm." See A deux
I wage not any feud. See In memoriam
"I wage not any feud with death." See In memoriam—I wage not any feud
"I wake in the morning early." See Singing-time
"I walk alone." See Love song
"I walk down the garden-paths." See Patterns
"I walked by chance." See Discovery
"I walked in my clogs on Salisbury plain." See Soldier
"I walked out in my coat of pride." See The fur coat
"I wander down on Clinton street south of Polk." See Clinton south of Polk
"I wander thro' each charter'd street." See London
"I wander up and down here, and go from street to street." See The fiddler
I wandered lonely. See The daffodils
"I wandered lonely as a cloud." See The daffodils
"I want to become like one of those." See The boy
"I want to climb the santol tree." See A wish
"I want to die while you love me." Georgia Douglass Johnson.—BoA—HaK
I want to go wandering. Vachel Lindsay.—LiP—PaH
"I want to go wandering. Who shall declare." See I want to go wandering
I want to know. John Drinkwater.—HoB
"I want to know why when I'm late." See I want to know
"I want to learn to whistle." See Whistles
"I want to see the slim palm trees." See Heritage
I want you to meet. David McCord.—McE
"I wanted a rifle for Christmas." See Presents
"I warn you once, I warn you twice." See Johnny Rover
"I warned the parents, you know." See Father to the man
I was a phoebe. Emily Dickinson.—ReBs
"I was a phoebe—nothing more." See I was a phoebe
"I was about to go, and said so." See Loneliness
"I was angry with my friend." See A poison tree
"I was appointed guardian by." See The merry policeman
"I was ashamed. I dared not lift my eyes." See Shame
"I was bat seven year alld." See The laily worm and the machrel of the sea
"I was born in Illinois." See Alexander Campbell—My fathers came from Kentucky
"I was but seven year auld." See The laily worm and the machrel of the sea
"I was chopping wood when I heard it, wild and clear." See Chain
"I was frightened, for a wind." See The secret
"I was hiding in the crooked apple tree." See The apple tree
"I was in a hooker once, said Karlssen." See Cape Horn gospel
"I was not apprenticed nor ever dwelt in famous Lincolnshire." See An old song
"I was playing with my hoop along the road." See The turn of the road
"I was the chief of the race—he had stricken my father dead." See The voyage of Maeldune
"I was the first fruit of the battle of Missionary Ridge." See The Spoon River anthology—Knowlt Hoheimer
"I was thy neighbour once, thou rugged pile." See Elegiac stanzas, suggested by a picture of Peele castle, in a storm, painted by Sir George Beaumont
"I was very scared." See Falling in the creek
"I was walking there along the hill." See Thorn song
"I was with Grant, the stranger said." See The aged stranger
"I washed my face in water." Unknown.—GrCt
"I watch you travel slowly down the mountains." See Parting

"I wouldn't want a whistle." See A whistle
"I wrote some lines once on a time." See The height of the ridiculous
"I years had been from home." Emily Dickinson.—DiPe
IBM cards
Epitaph. L. Mellichamp.—BrSm
Ice
"As I was going o'er London bridge." Mother Goose.—BrMg
Candy house. E. J. Coatsworth.—CoSb
Fire and ice. R. Frost.—HoL
Ice ("When it is the winter time") D. Aldis. —ArT-3
Ice ("When winter scourged the meadow and the hill") C. G. D. Roberts.—CoBn—DoW
The ice king. A. B. Demille.—DoW
Ice storm. E. J. Coatsworth.—CoSb
Improvisations: Light and snow.—CoBl (sel.) —CoBn (sel.)
"Lives in winter." Mother Goose.—ArT-3
"Slowly melting, slowly dying." D. Hill.—LeM
Three children sliding. Mother Goose.—BrMg
"Why." Onitsura.—LeMw
Ice ("When it is the winter time") Dorothy Aldis.—ArT-3
Ice ("When winter scourged the meadow and the hill") Charles G. D. Roberts.—CoBn—DoW
"**Ice** built, ice bound, and ice bounded." See Alaska
"**Ice** cream and cake are my favorite eats." See Favorite eats
The **ice-cream** man. Rachel Field.—HoB
The **ice** king. A. B. Demille.—DoW
Ice-skaters. Elder Olson.—MoS
Ice storm. Elizabeth Jane Coatsworth.—CoSb
The **icebound** swans. Unknown, tr. fr. the Gaelic by Sean O'Faolain.—ReO
Iceland
The broken oar. H. W. Longfellow.—LoPl
June. N. Belting.—BeCm
"The **icicles** beneath our eaves." See Candy house
"**Ickle** ockle, blue bockle." See A pretty maid
"**I'd** like a different dog." See Dogs and weather
"**I'd** like, above all, to be one of those." See The boy
"**I'd** like to be a dentist with a plate upon the door." See The dentist
"**I'd** like to be a lighthouse." Rachel Field.—LaP—LaPd
"**I'd** like to be walking the Cranberry road." See Cranberry road
I'd love to be a fairy's child. Robert Graves.—LaPd
"**I'd** often seen before." See The sheaf
"**I'd** rather have fingers than toes." Gelett Burgess.—BrLl
Ida B. Wells. Eve Merriam.—MeIv
Idea, sel. Michael Drayton
"Since there's no help, come, let us kiss and part."—CoBl
Ideals. See also Ambition; Conduct of life; Dreams
Excelsior. H. W. Longfellow.—LoPl
Identification
Identity parade. Unknown.—SmM
Identity parade. Unknown.—SmM
"An **idle** child is e'er despis'd." See Idleness
The **idle** flowers. Robert Bridges.—CoBn—GrCt
Idle fyno. Unknown.—GrCt
Idleness
"Elsie Marley is grown so fine." Mother Goose.—GrT—OpF
Elsie Marley.—BrMg—CoBb
The gipsies. A. and J. Taylor.—VrF
A hot-weather song. D. Marquis.—HuS-3
Idleness. H. S. Horsley.—VrF
An immorality. E. Pound.—BoGj—McWs
Au jardin des plantes. J. Wain.—CoB
"Lazy duck, that sit in the coal-nooks." Unknown.—MoB
Lazy Lou. M. M. Dodge.—CoBb
"Lazy Zany Addlepate." Unknown.—OpF
Leisure. W. H. Davies.—ArT-3—CoBn—SmM —TuW
The lotos-eaters. A. Tennyson.—ClF (sel.)—GrCt (sel.)—PaH (sel.)—TeP
The ne'er-do-well. A. M. Sampley.—DuR
"Nothing to do." S. Silverstein.—CoBb
The old beggar man. A. and J. Taylor.—VrF
One little boy. A. and J. Taylor.—VrF
"Robin and Richard (were two pretty men)." Mother Goose.—BrMg—OpF
The sluggard. Lucilius.—MoS
"Sluggardy-guise, sluggardy-guise." Unknown. —OpF
Song for the lazy. Unknown.—DoC
Spring fever. E. Merriam.—MeI
Sunday at the end of summer. H. Nemerov. —CoBn
Sunning. J. S. Tippett.—ArT-3—DuR
"There was an old man (and he lived in the west)." Unknown.—MoB
Tired Tim. W. De La Mare.—ArT-3—ReS
"What a wonderful." Shiki.—BeCs
Where's Mary. I. O. Eastwick.—ArT-3
Idleness. Henry Sharpe Horsley.—VrF
"**Idly** my ship glides." Otsuji, tr. fr. the Japanese by Harry Behn.—BeCs
Idolatry. Arna Bontemps.—BoA
Idylls of the king, sels. Alfred Tennyson
Blow trumpet.—TeP
If love be love.—TeP
Morte d' Arthur.—CoD—TeP
Rain, rain, and sun.—TeP
If. See "If all the seas were one sea"
"**If** a jackal bothers you, show him a hyena." Unknown.—DoC
"**If** a pig wore a wig." Christina Georgina Rossetti.—HoB
"**If** all the pens that ever poets held." See Tamburlaine the Great
"**If** all the seas were one sea." Mother Goose.—HuS-3—OpF
If.—BrMg

"If things were better." Issa, tr. fr. the Japanese by Harry Behn.—BeCs
"If this life-saving rock should fail." See On Middleton Edge
"If this little world to-night." Oliver Herford.—BrSm
Earth.—DuR
"If thou must love me, let it be for naught." See Sonnets from the Portuguese
If we didn't have to eat. Nixon Waterman.—AgH
If we must die. Claude McKay.—AdIa—HaK
"If we must die—let it not be like hogs." See If we must die
"If we want to tell a lie." Unknown.—DoC
"If when the wind blows." See Daniel Webster's horses
"If wishes were horses." Mother Goose.—BrMg—OpF—WiMg
"If wishes were horses, beggars would ride."—ReMg
Mother Goose rhymes, 32.—HoB
"If wishes were horses, beggars would ride." See "If wishes were horses"
"If ye fear to be affrighted." See A charm
"If ye gae up to yon hill-top." See The Tarbolton lasses
"If ye will with Mab find grace." See The fairies
"If you add a tittle." See Tittle and jot, jot and tittle
"If you are hungry." See Song for the lazy
"If you are knightly on your daily way." See Serendipity
"If you are tender to them." Issa, tr. fr. the Japanese by R. H. Blyth.—IsF
"If you awake at midnight and hear a horse's feet." See A smuggler's song
"If you become the moon, my love." See Song of Ranga
If you came. Ruth Pitter.—CaD
"If you came to my secret glade." See If you came
"If you can hang on to what Joany said." See The witch
"If you can, now and then, will you remember me." See Now and then
"If you chance to be crossing." Unknown.—WyC
"If you ever, ever, ever meet a grizzly bear." See Grizzly bear
"If you had been owned by a fat old king." See Fourth of July
"If you hurry so." See Miss Rápida
"If you love me, pop and fly." See Pips in the fire
"If you promise me a rose." See Promise me a rose
If you should fall, don't forget this. John Ciardi.—CiYk
If you should go. Countee Cullen.—BoH
"If you should meet a crocodile." Unknown.—LaPd
"If you should see a man walking." See Voice in the crowd
"If you trap the moment before it's ripe." William Blake.—BlP
"If you were a bird." See December bird
"If you were an animal inside the zoo." See Inside the zoo
"If you were coming in the fall." Emily Dickinson.—DiPe
"If you will tell me why the fen." See I may, I might, I must
"If your mother has set out to fish." Unknown.—DoC
Ignatow, David
The bagel.—DuS
Europe and America.—BrA
Two friends.—DuS
"**Ignore** dull days; forget the showers." See Lesson from a sun-dial
Iliad, sel. Homer
Night encampment outside Troy, tr. fr. the Greek by Alfred Tennyson.—CoR
"**Ilka** day." See Cock and hen
I'll be a baker. Aileen Fisher.—FiIo
"**I'll** be a baker and run a bakery shop." See I'll be a baker
"**I'll** be an otter, and I'll let you swim." See Otters
"**I'll** build a house of arrogance." See Haven
"**I'll** come as a flower to you." See As a flower I come
"**I'll** come back—and the things of me that." Leonard Hale.—BaH
"**I'll** find me a spruce." See Christmas tree
"**I'll** gie you a pennyworth o' preens." Unknown.—MoB
"**I'll** give you a pin to stick in your thumb." Unknown.—MoB
"**I'll** haunt this town, though gone the maids and men." See The dream of all the Springfield writers
"**Ill** on a journey." Issa, tr. fr. the Japanese.—LeOw
"**I'll** sing ye a story o' trouble an' woe that'll cause ye to shudder an' shiver." See The Chinese bumboatman
"**I'll** sing you a true song of Billy the Kid." See Billy the Kid
"**I'll** tell thee everything I can." See Through the looking-glass
"**I'll** tell you a story." Mother Goose.—ReMg
Jack a Nory.—BrMg
"**I'll** tell you a tale to-night." See The admiral's ghost
"**I'll** tell you how matters stand with me." See A few things explained
"**I'll** tell you how the sun rose." Emily Dickinson.—DiL—DiPe—LaPd
How the sun rose.—HuS-3
I'll walk the tightrope. Margaret Danner.—HaK
"**I'll** walk the tightrope that's been stretched for me." See I'll walk the tightrope
I'll wear a shamrock. Mary Carolyn Davies.—ArT-3
Illinois
First song. G. Kinnell.—BoGj

In a desert town. Lionel Stevenson.—BrA—HuS-3
"**In** a dream last night." See Iron
"**In** a far away northern county in the placid pastoral region." See The ox-tamer
In a garden. A. P. Herbert.—CoB
In a gondola, sel. Robert Browning
"The moth's kiss, first."—BrP
"**In** a gorge titanic." See Ula Masondo's dream
"**In** a gust of wind the white dew." Bunya (or Funya) no Asayasu, tr. fr. the Japanese by Kenneth Rexroth.—BaS—LeMw
"**In** a herber green, asleep where as I lay." See In youth is pleasure
"**In** a matchbox." See A cricket
"**In** a meadow of hay." See Meadow of hay
"**In** a milkweed cradle." See Baby seeds
In a million years. Claudia Lewis.—LeP
"**In** a mirage I filled my pitcher." Vindra Karandikar, tr. fr. the Marathi by R. P. Sirkar. —AlPi
"**In** a pitcher I have." See Spanish folk song
"**In** a puddle left from last week's rain." See Discovery
"**In** a quiet watered land, a land of roses." See The dead at Clonmacnois
"**In** a shoe box stuffed in an old nylon stocking." See The meadow mouse
"**In** a small bitterness of wind." See Young Argonauts
In a spring still not written of. Robert Wallace. —CoBn
"**In** an envelope marked personal." See Personal
"**In** an old plum tree." See A winter's dream
"**In** and out the bushes, up the ivy." See The chipmunk's song
"**In** and out the dusty bluebells." See Singing game
"**In** any kind of woodland." See Aspen leaves
"**In** April, when these orchards blow." See Blackbirds
"**In** Armoric, sometimes called Brittany." See The Canterbury tales—The rocks of Brittany
"**In** Baltimore there lived a boy." See The boy who laughed at Santa Claus
"**In** Breughel's great picture, The Kermess." See The dance
"**In** broad daylight, and at noon." See Daylight and moonlight
"**In** California there are." See In California there are two hundred and fifty six religions
In California there are two hundred and fifty six religions. Richard E. Albert.—DuS
"**In** candent ire the solar splendor flames." See Intramural aestivation, or summer in town, by a teacher of Latin
In camera. Tilottama Rajan.—AlPi
"**In** Cecina the solacing words were over a portal." See Italian excursion
"**In** college once I climbed the tree." See Sickle pears
"**In** dark fens of the Dismal swamp." See The slave in the Dismal swamp
In dispraise of the moon. Mary Coleridge.—CoBn
In distrust of merits. Marianne Moore.—PlE
"**In** dog-days plowmen quit their toil." See The swimmer
"**In** drowsy fit." See Coals
"**In** dulci jubilo." John Wedderburn.—GrCt
"**In** early spring when Samuel plows." See Corn
"**In** every house on every street." See At Christmas time
"**In** February when few gusty flakes." See Ground hog day
In fields of summer. Galway Kinnell.—CoBn
In Flanders fields. John McCrae.—ThA
"**In** Flanders fields the poppies blow." See In Flanders fields
"**In** form and feature, face and limb." See The twins
"**In** futurity." See The little girl lost
In Glencullen. John M. Synge.—ReBs
"**In** grapes I know there may be seeds." See Answering your question
"**In** Han's old mill his three black cats." See Five eyes
"**In** heaven a spirit doth dwell." See Israfel
"**In** his sea lit." See The double-play
"**In** his travels, the elephant." See Elephant
"**In** holy fathers' lives of old." See Johan the monk
In honour of Taffy Topaz. Christopher Morley. —ArT-3
"**In** January." See January
"**In** just." See Chanson innocente
"**In** lands I never saw, they say." Emily Dickinson.—DiPe
"**In** less than two and twenty years." Asclepiades of Samos, tr. fr. the Greek by William and Mary Wallace.—HoL
"**In** life three ghostly friars were we." See The ghosts
"**In** Little Rock the people bear." See The Chicago Defender sends a man to Little Rock, Fall, 1967
"**In** London there I was bent." See London lackpenny
In Louisiana. Albert Bigelow Paine.—BrA
"**In** love, if love be love, if love be ours." See Idylls of the king—If love be love
"**In** Maine the dead." See Lost graveyards
In marble halls. See "In marble halls as white as milk"
"**In** marble halls as white as milk." Mother Goose.—BrMg—GrCt—HuS-3—OpF
In marble halls.—ReOn-SmM
"**In** Mauchline there dwells six proper young belles." See The belles of Mauchline
"**In** May, when sea winds pierced our solitudes." See The rhodora
"**In** mediaeval Rome, I know not where." See Morituri salutamus—A Roman legend
In memoriam, sels. Alfred Tennyson
Calm is the morn.—GrCt—TeP
"Dip down upon the northern shore."—TeP
A happy lover.—TeP
"I envy not in any moods."—TeP
"I sometimes hold it half a sin."—TeP
"I trust I have not wasted breath."—TeP

"In the darkness east of Chicago, the sky burns over the plumbers' nightmares." See A valedictory to Standard Oil of Indiana
"In the dawn of day." Issa, tr. fr. the Japanese by R. H. Blyth.—IsF
"In the depot and the darkened day." See Depot in a river town
"In the desert sand." Nelson Leonard.—BaH
"In the dream." Issa, tr. fr. the Japanese.—LeOw
"In the drinking-well." See Aunt Eliza
In the dumps. See "We're all in the dumps"
"In the dying of the daylight." See The small phantom
"In the eastern quarter dawn breaks, the stars flicker pale." See Cockcrow song
"In the empty mountains." Hitomaro, tr. fr. the Japanese by Kenneth Rexroth.—BaS
"In the eternal." Ki no Tomonori, tr. fr. the Japanese by Kenneth Rexroth.—BaS
In the evening. Gilbert Keith Chesterton.—LiT
"In the evening." Minamoto no Tsunenobu, tr. fr. the Japanese by Kenneth Rexroth.—BaS
"In the evening calm the cranes search for prey." Unknown.—BaS
"In the evening glow." Kazue Mizumura.—MiI
In the evening I walk by the river. Hsiu Ouyang, tr. fr. the Chinese by Kenneth Rexroth.—LeMw
"In the falling snow." Richard Wright
Hokku: "In the falling snow."—AdIa
Hokku poems.—BoA
"In the family drinking well." See Sister Nell
"In the far corner." See The blackbird
In the fashion. A. A. Milne.—LaP
In the fields. Charlotte Mew.—CoBn—SmM
"In the fields of spring." Unknown.—BaS
"In the forest a fir." See Forest magic
"In the gloom of whiteness." See Snow
"In the grass." See Little folks in the grass
"In the gray evening." See The garden hose
"In the greenest of our valleys." See The fall of the house of Usher—The haunted palace
"In the grey wastes of dread." See Horses on the Camargue
"In the harbour, in the island, in the Spanish seas." See Trade winds
"In the heel of my thumb." See Thumbprint
"In the high trees—many doleful winds." See The liberator
In the hills. Wang Wei, tr. fr. the Chinese by Robert Payne.—HoL
"In the hole of a heel of an old brown stocking." See Stocking fairy
"In the hollow tree, in the old gray tower." See The owl
"In the house." See Teevee
In the imperative mood. James Stephens.—StS
"In the June twilight, we looked without knowing why." See The bats
"In the land of the Tao-chou." See The people of Tao-chou
"In the land of the Bumbley Boo." See The land of the Bumbley Boo
In the late afternoon. Elizabeth Jane Coatsworth.—CoDh
"In the leafy treetops." Yakamochi.—BaS
"In the long, sleepless watches of the night." See The cross of snow
"In the mandrill." See The mandrill
In the marble quarry. James Dickey.—BrA
"In the market-place of Bruges stands the belfry old and brown." See The belfry of Bruges
"In the May evening." See The old ones
In the mind's eye. Thomas Hardy.—GrS
"In the monotonous heat." See Dialogue
"In the morning I'm always sleepy." See Myself
"In the morning, in the dark." See The night hunt
"In the morning the city." See City: San Francisco
"In the mountain village." Minamoto no Morotada, tr. fr. the Japanese by Kenneth Rexroth.—BaS
In the mountains on a summer day. Li T'ai-po, tr. fr. the Chinese by Arthur Waley.—MoS
In the night. James Stephens.—StS
"In the night while everybody is sleeping." See My imagination
"In the northern hemisphere." See Kangaroo
"In the northwest wind." Kazue Mizumura.—MiI
"In the ocean of the sky." Hitomaro, tr. fr. the Japanese by Arthur Waley.—LeMw
In the orchard. James Stephens.—CoR—HaL
In the Oregon country. William Stafford.—BrA
"In the other gardens." See Autumn fires
"In the pale summertime, when far above you." See Of swimming in lakes and rivers
In the park. Rose Fyleman.—HuS-3
"In the pond in the park." See Water picture
In the poppy field. James Stephens.—StS
"In the proud land of the Navajos." See The proud Navajo
"In the queer light, in twilight." See The young man in April
In the red. James Stephens.—StS
"In the redwood forest." Claudia Lewis.—LeP
"In the ribs of an ugly school building." See Three brown girls singing
"In the scented bud of the morning-O." See The daisies
"In the sedge a tiny song." See The warbler
"In the shade of the thicket." Issa, tr. fr. the Japanese.—LeOw
"In the shadow of Old South Church the turn of spring is." See A foreigner comes to earth on Boston Common
"In the shadow of the tall bamboos." See The temple bells of Yun Sui
"In the silent night." Jill Yokomizo.—BaH
"In the sky." See How strange it is
"In the small New England places." See Graveyard
"In the southern village the boy who minds the ox." See The herd boy
In the spring ("In the spring a fuller crimson comes upon the robin's breast") See Locksley hall

In the spring ("Let's go, let's go") Unknown, ad. fr. the Japanese by Charlotte B. DeForest. —DePp

"**In** the spring a fuller crimson comes upon the robin's breast." See Locksley hall—In the spring

"**In** the spring, in the morning." See Herding lambs

"**In** the spring of the year, in the spring of the year." See The spring and the fall

"**In** the springtime, the warm time, the soft time." See Fragment of a bylina

"**In** the squdgy river." See The hippopotamus

"**In** the still dark depths." See At night

"**In** the streets I have just left." Charles Reznikoff.—LaC

"**In** the sweet month of May (when the fields)." See A pleasant walk

"**In** the time of wild roses." See Bab-Lock-Hythe

In the treetops. Aileen Fisher.—FiI

"**In** the undergrowth." See About the bloath

"**In** the upper garden there is no end of trees." See Two songs of spring wandering

"**In** the village churchyard she lies." See In the churchyard at Cambridge

"**In** the walled world of darkness and his fever." See Child with malaria

In the week when Christmas comes. Eleanor Farjeon.—ArT-3—LaPd—LaPh

"**In** the wicked afternoon." See Abracadabra

"**In** the wide and rocky pasture where the cedar trees are gray." See Connecticut road song

"**In** the wild October night-time, when the wind raved round the land." See The night of Trafalgar

In the wilderness. Robert Graves.—PlE

"**In** the winter the rabbits match their pelts to the earth." See White season

"**In** the winter time we go." See White fields

"**In** the wintry grove." Issa, tr. fr. the Japanese by R. H. Blyth.—LeOw

"**In** the woods a piece of sky." See Bluebird

"**In** the year of our Lord eighteen hundred and six." See The Irish Rover

"**In** these days of indigestion." See Some little bug

"**In** 'thirty-nine, in Poland." See Children's crusade 1939

"**In** this dehydrated time of digests, pills." See Runes IX

"**In** this fleeting world." Issa, tr. fr. the Japanese. —LeOw

"**In** this green month when resurrected flowers." See Memorial wreath

In this hotel. Emanuel Carnevali.—GrS

"**In** this jungle." Myra Cohn Livingston.—LiC

"**In** this short life." Emily Dickinson.—DiPe

"**In** this summer month which blasts all hope." See Summer

"**In** this, the city of my discontent." See Springfield magical

"**In** this water, clear as air." See The pool in the rock

"**In** this world, the isle of dreams." See The white island

In three days. Robert Browning.—BrP

"**In** through the window a sea-mustang brought me." See Doctor Mohawk

"**In** tight pants, tight skirts." See The young ones, flip side

In time of crisis. Raymond Richard Patterson.—AdIa

"**In** time of silver rain." Langston Hughes.—ArT-3

"**In** time the drummers beat their drums, the lutanists plucked their lutes." See Hammira-mahakavya—Radhadevi's dance

"**In** town you have expensive clocks." See Town and country

In waste places. James Stephens.—StS

"**In** Westminster not long ago." See The rat-catcher's daughter

In which Roosevelt is compared to Saul. Vachel Lindsay.—LiP

In winter. Robert Wallace.—CoBn

"**In** winter I get up at night." See Bed in summer

"**In** winter time our flower store." See Winter flower store

"**In** winter, when it's cold out." See Baseball note

"**In** winter, when the fields are white." See Through the looking-glass—Humpty Dumpty's poem

"**In** winter when the nights are long." See The beggar wind

"**In** wintry midnight, o'er a stormy main." Petrarch, tr. fr. the Italian by William Barnes. —GrCt

"**In** with the luck." Issa, tr. fr. the Japanese by Nobuyuki Yuasa.—IsF

"**In** Xanadu did Kubla Khan." See Kubla Khan

"**In** your next letter I wish you'd say." See Letter to N. Y.

"**In** youth from rock to rock I went." See To the daisy

"**In** youth have I known one with whom the earth." See Stanzas

In youth is pleasure. Robert Wever.—GrCt

Incantation to Oedipus. See Oedipus

Incense. Vachel Lindsay.—LiP

The **Inchcape** rock. Robert Southey.—GrCt

Incident. Countee Cullen.—AdIa—HoB—HoL—ThA

Incident of the French camp. Robert Browning. —BrP—CoR

Inconsistent. Mark Van Doren.—CoBl

Independence

Close your eyes. A. Bontemps.—BoA—HaK

Independence. J. Stephens.—StS

Lone dog. I. R. McLeod.—ArT-3—CoB—LaPd —ThA

Revelations. S. A. Brown.—HaK

Independence. James Stephens.—StS

Independence day. See Fourth of July

The jazz of this hotel. V. Lindsay.—BoH
A lady comes to an inn. E. J. Coatsworth.—ArT-3—CoDh
"On a rainy spring day." Issa.—IsF
"R is for the restaurant." From All around the town. P. McGinley.—ArT-3
The rabbits' song outside the tavern. E. J. Coatsworth.—ArT-3
Tarantella. H. Belloc.—PaH—ThA
Inhuman Henry; or, Cruelty to fabulous animals. Alfred Edward Housman.—CoBb
Innisfree (Lake)
The lake isle of Innisfree. W. B. Yeats.—ArT-3—CoR—PaH—ThA—YeR
Innocence
Infant innocence. A. E. Housman.—GrCt
"Two girls of twelve or so at a table." C. Reznikoff.—LaC
Innocent's song. Charles Causley.—CaD
Innuendo. David McCord.—McAd
The **innumerable** Christ. Hugh MacDiarmid.—PlE
Insanity
Madhouse. C. C. Hernton.—AdIa—HaK
Madman ("He was caged up") B. O'Shea.—LeM
A madman ("A madman lives in a very special house") S. Dawson.—LeM
"Much madness is divinest sense." E. Dickinson.—DiPe
Divinest sense.—HoL
Tom o' Bedlam's song. Unknown.—GrCt
A visit to the lunatic asylum. H. S. Horsley.—VrF
An **inscription** by the sea. Edwin Arlington Robinson.—CoSs—GrCt
Inscription for an old bed. William Morris.—ReS
Inscriptions. See also Epitaphs
An inscription by the sea. E. A. Robinson.—CoSs—GrCt
Inscription for an old bed. W. Morris.—ReS
The new Colossus. E. Lazarus.—BoH—BrA
"The **insect** world, now sunbeams higher climb." See March
Insects. See also names of insects, as Ants
"All kinds of cicadas singing." Issa.—IsF
"Because the treetops of the peak." Hitomaro.—LeMw
Bedtime. A. Fisher.—FiC
Daddy longlegs. A. Fisher.—FiI
"Even among insects, in this world." Issa.—IsF
The flattered lightning bug. From Archy and Mehitabel. D. Marquis.—CoB
"I said to a bug in the sink." J. Ciardi.—BrLl
"Insects are crying." Issa.—LeOw
"Insects. Do not cry." Issa.—LeMw
"Insects on a bough." Issa.—IsF
Interlude III. K. Shapiro.—DuR
"The lightning bug has wings of gold." Unknown.—LaC
Like a bug. A. Fisher.—FiC
Little folks in the grass. A. Wynne.—ThA
Little talk. A. Fisher.—LaP
The minimal. T. Roethke.—LiT
Stay-at-home. A. Fisher.—FiC
"**Insects** are crying." Issa, tr. fr. the Japanese.—LeOw
"**Insects.** Do not cry." Issa, tr. fr. the Japanese by Harold G. Henderson.—LeMw
"**Insects** on a bough." Issa, tr. fr. the Japanese by R. H. Blyth.—IsF
Inside a poem. Eve Merriam.—ArT-3—MeI
"The **inside** of a whirlpool." See Warning
Inside the zoo. Eve Merriam.—MeC
Insouciance. John W. Dickson.—DuS
"**Instead** of neat inclosures." See An ode of the birth of our Saviour
"**Instead** of the Puritans landing on Plymouth Rock." See Thoughts for St Stephen
Instruction in the art. Philip Booth.—MoS
"**Insured** for every accident." See Epitaph
Interlude III. Karl Shapiro.—DuR
Interplanetary limerick. Al Graham.—BrLl
Interval. Edward Thomas.—ThG
"**Intery,** mintery, cutery-corn." Mother Goose.—ArT-3—TuW
A counting-out rhyme.—ClF
"Intry, mintry, cutry, corn."—HuS-3
Intimations of immortality. See Ode: Intimations of immortality from recollections of early childhood
Into my heart. See A Shropshire lad—"Into my heart an air that kills"
"**Into** my heart an air that kills." See A Shropshire lad
"**Into** my heart's treasury." See The coin
"**Into** that stricken hour the hunted had gathered." See Vaticide
"**Into** the acres of the newborn state." See A gospel of beauty—The proud farmer
"**Into** the basin put the plums." See The Christmas pudding
"**Into** the endless dark." See City lights
"**Into** the scented woods we'll go." See Green rain
"**Into** what would I like to change myself." See Songs in praise of the chief
Intramural aestivation, or summer in town, by a teacher of Latin. Oliver Wendell Holmes.—GrCt
Introduction ("Come, peep at London's famous town") William Darton, rev. by Ann and Jane Taylor.—VrF
Introduction ("Piping down the valleys wild") See The piper
Introduction to Songs of innocence. See The piper
Introduction to the Songs of experience. William Blake.—BlP
The poet's voice.—GrCt
The **intruder.** James Reeves.—LaPd
"**Intry,** mintry, cutry, corn." See "Intery, mintery, cutery-corn"
The **invention** of comics. L. Jones.—BoA
Inventions. See Inventors and inventions

Inventors and inventions
Alexander Graham Bell did not invent the telephone. R. P. T. Coffin.—ArT-3
And yet fools say. G. S. Holmes.—ArT-3
"Young Frankenstein's robot invention." B. Braley.—BrLl
The **invisible** man. Conrad Kent Rivers.—HaK
"**Inviting,** rippling waters." Margaret Bendig.—LeM
Invocation ("American muse, whose strong and diverse heart") See John Brown's body
Invocation ("Good morning to you, Lord of the world") Levi Isaac of Berdichev, tr. by Olga Marx.—PlE
Invocation ("Let me be buried in the rain") Helene Johnson.—BoA
Invocations
Invocation ("American muse, whose strong and diverse heart") From John Brown's body. S. V. Benét.—BrA
Invocation ("Good morning to you, Lord of the world") Levi Isaac of Berdichev.—PlE
Invocation ("Let me be buried in the rain") H. Johnson.—BoA
The **invoice.** Robert Creeley.—DuS
Iowa
Iowa farmer. M. Walker.—HaK
Iowa farmer. Margaret Walker.—HaK
Ipecacuanha. George Canning.—GrCt
Ipsey Wipsey. Mother Goose.—BrMg
"**Ipsey** Wipsey spider." See Ipsey Wipsey
Ireland
The bells of Shandon. Father Prout.—CoR—GrCt—PaH
"Come gather round me, Parnellites." W. B. Yeats.—YeR
"Come gather round me, players all." From Three songs to the one burden. W. B. Yeats.—YeR
The dead at Clonmacnois. T. W. Rolleston.—PaH
"The harp that once through Tara's halls." T. Moore.—CoR
"I took my foot in my hand." Unknown.—MoB
Irish. E. J. O'Brien.—LaPh—ThA
Irish grandmother. K. Edelman.—BrA
An Irish legend. P. McGinley.—McWc
The little waves of Breffny. E. Gore-Booth.—PaH
Red Hanrahan's song about Ireland. W. B. Yeats.—YeR
September 1913. W. B. Yeats.—YeR
Springtime in Donegal. M. R. Stevenson.—HuS-3
A strong wind. A. Clarke.—CoBn
The voyage of Maeldune. A. Tennyson.—TeP
The wild swans at Coole. W. B. Yeats.—GrCt—PaH—YeR
Ireland—History
The Fort of Rathangan. Berchan.—GrCt
The old Fort of Rathangan.—HoL
The **iris.** Gasetsu.—ArT-3
Irises
The iris. Gasetsu.—ArT-3
Irises. P. Colum.—CoBn
Irises. Padraic Colum.—CoBn
Irish
I'll wear a shamrock. M. C. Davies.—ArT-3
Irish. E. J. O'Brien.—LaPh—ThA
An Irish airman foresees his death. W. B. Yeats.—BoGj—HoL—YeR
Irish grandmother. K. Edelman.—BrA
The Irish Rover. Unknown.—CoSs
Under Ben Bulben.—YeR (sel.)
Irish. Edward J. O'Brien.—LaPh—ThA
An **Irish** airman foresees his death. William Butler Yeats.—BoGj—HoL—YeR
Irish grandmother. Katherine Edelman.—BrA
An **Irish** legend. Phyllis McGinley.—McWc
"**Irish** poets, learn your trade." See Under Ben Bulben
The **Irish** Rover. Unknown.—CoSs
Iron (Metal)
Iron. B. Brecht.—HoL
Red iron ore. Unknown.—ArT-3
Iron. Bertolt Brecht, tr. fr. the German by Michael Hamburger.—HoL
Irony. James Stephens.—StS
Iroquois Indians. See Indians of the Americas—Iroquois
Irrigation. See In my mother's house
Irritable song. Russell Atkins.—BoA
Irwin, Wallace (Hashimura Togo, pseud.)
The battle of Clothesline bay.—CoSs
Blow me eyes.—CoBl
Captain Pink of the Peppermint.—CoSs
The cares of a caretaker.—CoO
The dutiful mariner.—CoSs
Industrious Carpenter Dan.—CoSs
Meditations of a mariner.—CoSs
A nautical extravagance.—HuS-3
The powerful eyes o' Jeremy Tait.—CoSs
The rhyme of the chivalrous shark.—BrSm
Science for the young.—BrSm (sel.)—CoBb
The sea serpant.—CoB
Such a pleasant familee.—BrSm
"**Is** a caterpillar ticklish." See Only my opinion
"**Is** God dead." Martin Radcliffe.—LaC
"**Is** it coffee for breakfast." See Breakfast
"**Is** it so far from thee." See The chamber over the gate
"**Is** it for naught that where the tired crowds see." See The town of American visions
"**Is** it the wind of the dawn that I hear in the pine overhead." See Becket—Duet
"**Is** John Smith within." See The blacksmith
"**Is** Mary in the dairy." See Where's Mary
"**Is** not this hearth, where goats now feed." See The hearth of Urien
"**Is** not this mountain like a flower." Rabindranath Tagore.—LeMf
"**Is** Oz." See Oz
"**Is** that an angel." See Waterwings
Is the moon tired. Christina Georgina Rossetti.—HuS-3

"Is the moon tired? She looks so pale." See Is the moon tired
"Is there a bolt that can avail to shut up love." See Kural—Love
"Is there a cause why we should wake the dead." See The yew-tree
"Is there anybody there, said the traveler." See The listeners
"Is there for honest poverty." See A man's a man for a' that
"Is this a holy thing to see." See Holy Thursday
"Is this dancing sunlight." See Symphony
"Is this it, then." Issa, tr. fr. the Japanese.—LeOw
Is this life. Helen Harrington.—BaH
Is this someone you know. John Ciardi.—CiYk
Isabel. Unknown, tr. fr. the French by George Lanigan.—DoW
"Isabel Jones & Curabel Lee." David McCord.—McE
"Isabel met an enormous bear." See Adventures of Isabel
"Isabel of the lily-white hand." See Isabel
Isabella. Unknown.—ReOn
"Isabella, Isabella, Isabella, farewell." See Isabella
Isaiah, sels. Bible, Old Testament
"But they that wait upon the Lord shall renew their strength."—ArT-3
"Comfort ye, comfort ye my people."—PlE
"The wolf also shall dwell with the lamb."—LaPd
"Isaiah, the country-boy, marched against the jazz." See Babylon, Babylon, Babylon the great
Iscariot, Judas
The sacrifice. G. W. Barrax.—HaK
Ise, Lady
"The spring rain (which hangs)."—BaS
"The rains of spring."—ArT-3
Ishikawa
"How the great moon crushes the cloud."—LeMw
The island, sel. Francis Brett Young
Atlantic Charter, A. D. 1620-1942.—ArT-3—BrA
The island. Christopher Morley.—PaH
Islands
Ballad of the Western Island in the North country. Unknown.—GrS
Emperors of the island. D. Abse.—CaD
Flannan isle. W. W. Gibson.—BlO—CoSs
Les isles d' Amerique. E. J. Coatsworth.—CoDh
Sketch for an island. E. J. Coatsworth.—CoDh
Staffa. J. Keats.—GrS
To an isle in the water. W. B. Yeats.—SmM—YeR
Tristan de cunha. R. Campbell.—CoR
When dawn comes to the city. C. McKay.—BoH—LaC
The isles of Greece. See Don Juan
"The isles of Greece, the isles of Greece." See Don Juan—The isles of Greece
"Isn't it." See Epigram
"Isn't it strange some people make." See Some people
Israfel. Edgar Allan Poe.—PoP
Issa
"An accomplished acrobat."—IsF
"After a flock of flies."—LeOw
"The aged dog."—IsF
"Ah, to be."—IsF—LeOw
"All kinds of cicadas singing."—IsF
"All the while."—IsF
"Along the cold post road."—IsF
"Among the leaves of grass."—LeOw
"As a diversion."—IsF
"As one of us."—LeOw
"As we grow old."—LeOw
"At the altar."—IsF
"At the flower-vase."—IsF
"At the morning exhibition."—IsF
"The autumn breeze."—LeOw
"An autumn evening (a man)."—LeOw
"An autumn evening (it is)."—LeOw
"The autumn moon."—IsF
"The autumn wind (the shadow)."—LeOw
"The autumn wind (there are)."—LeOw
"Be a good boy."—LeOw
"Be brave."—IsF
"A beautiful kite."—IsF—LeOw
"The beggar on the bridge."—IsF—LeOw
"Bending over."—IsF
"A branch of willow."—IsF
"The Buddha."—IsF
"A butterfly came."—LeOw
"By the light of the next room."—LeOw
"The cherry-blossoms (they have)."—IsF
"The child sobs."—IsF—LeOw
"The child sways on the swing."—LeMw
"Children."—IsF
"Clear, cold water."—LeOw
"The clear note."—IsF
"Click, clack."—LeOw
"Come."—IsF
"Come and play with me."—LeOw
"Come flies."—IsF
"Come on, owl."—LeI
"Come out, fireflies."—LeOw
"The cool breeze."—IsF—LeOw
"The coolness."—LeOw
"Country bumpkin."—LeOw
"Crawl, laugh."—LeOw
"The crow."—IsF
"A day of spring."—LeOw
"The deer."—IsF
"Dewdrops on the grass."—LeOw
"The dogs."—IsF
"Don't kill."—IsF
"The dragon-fly."—IsF
"A drop of rain."—ArT-3—LeI
"The ears of barley, too."—IsF
"Eating a meal."—LeOw
"Even among insects, in this world."—IsF

"Whose is it then."—IsF
"Wild goose, O wild goose."—LeOw
"The wind gives us."—LeOw
"With feeble steps."—LeOw
"With that voice."—LeMw
"The woodpecker."—LeOw
"The world of dew."—LeOw
"A world of short-lived dew."—LeOw
"The wren."—IsF—LeOw
"It ain't no use to grumble and complain." See Rain
"It can be so tedious, a bore." See Moods of rain
"It costs little Gossip her income for shoes." Mother Goose.—OpF
"It does not happen. That love, removes." See Audubon, drafted
"It doesn't always have to rhyme." See Inside a poem
"It doesn't hurt no place when I'm sad." See Hurting
"It dropped so low in my regard." Emily Dickinson.—DiPe
"It fell about the Martinmas time." See Get up and bar the door
"It happen'd that a little snail." See The selfish snails
It happens once in a while. Myra Cohn Livingston.—LiC
"It has eyes and a nose." Unknown.—WyC
It is a beauteous evening. See Sonnet ("It is a beauteous evening, calm and free")
"It is a beauteous evening, calm and free." See Sonnet
"It is a cold and snowy night. The main street is deserted." See Driving to town late to mail a letter
"It is a curious thing that you." See The kangaroo
"It is a lonesome glee." Emily Dickinson.—DiPe
"It is a new America." See Brown river, smile
"It is a pleasure." Tachibana Akemi, tr. fr. the Japanese by Donald Keene.—LeMw
"It is a wonder foam is so beautiful." See Spray
"It is an ancient mariner." See The rime of the ancient mariner
"It is blue-butterfly day here in spring." See Blue-butterfly day
"It is dangerous for a woman to defy the gods." See Letter to my sister
"It is evening, Senlin says, and in the evening." See Senlin: A biography—Senlin
"It is hard, inland." See In winter
"It is hot today, dry enough for cutting grain." See August from my desk
"It is hunger who says to the gull." See Poem to hunger
"It is in October, a favorite season." See Elegy for a nature poet
"It is late last night the dog was speaking of you." See Donall Oge: Grief of a girl's heart
"It is man who counts." Unknown.—DoC
"It is memory speaking, preternaturally clear." See Elizabeth at the piano
"It is natural to be gloomy now and then." See Don't bomb human nature out of existence
"It is nice to read." Onitsura, tr. fr. the Japanese by Harry Behn.—BeCs
It is not far. See Night ("Stars over snow")
"It is not growing like a tree." See To the immortal memory of that noble pair, Sir Lucius Cary and Sir H. Morison
"It is portentous, and a thing of state." See Abraham Lincoln walks at midnight
"It is raining." Lucy Sprague Mitchell.—ArT-3
"It is said that many a king in troubled Europe would sell." See Rulers: Philadelphia
"It is so still in the house." See The mother's song
"It is the evening hour." See To Mary: It is the evening hour
"It is the first mild day of March." See To my sister
"It is the little brown hour of twilight." See In the evening
"It is the picnic with Ruth in the spring." See The picnic
"It is the tears of the earth." Rabindranath Tagore.—LeMf
"It is there that our hearts are set." Unknown.—LeO
It is time. Ted Joans.—HaK
"It is time for the United States to spend money on education." See It is time
"It is time. The geese fly overhead, returning." See March
"It is time to cock your hay and corn." See Hee haw
It is time, you know. John Ciardi.—CiYk
"It is very dark." See Winter night
"It isn't the cough." Unknown.—BrSm
"It lay, dark in the corner of the field." See Suicide pond
"It lies in the groove." Noelene Qualthrough.—LeM
"It little profits that an idle king." See Ulysses
"It lives there." See Tomorrow
"It makes no difference abroad." Emily Dickinson.—DiPe
"It may not be Saint Anthony hated devils." See And laughter sounded
"It might be just beginning." See This thing called space
"It ought to come in April." See Wearing of the green
"It rained." See The lime avenue
"It rained in the night." Jorge Carrera Andrade, tr. fr. the Spanish by Muna Lee de Muñoz Marín.—HoL
"It rains, it hails, it batters, it blows." Unknown.—OpF
"It really gives me heartfelt pain." See Maria Jane
"It seems like a giant bite—holding me tight." See Get this garbage out of my life
"It seems to me, said Booker T." See Booker T. and W. E. B.

"It's just an old alley cat." See The stray cat
"It's lemonade, it's lemonade, it's daisy." See April
"It's lemonading time again." See Lemonade
"It's my birthday." See Happy birthday to me
"It's never too early." See Advertisement for a divertissement
"It's no joke at all, I'm not that sort of poet." See The confession
"It's not a bit windy." See Toadstools
"It's not very far to the edge of town." See Adventure
"It's once I courted as pretty a lass." See An unkind lass
It's raining. Mother Goose.—BrMg
"It's raining again in the Southwest—wet." See Rain in the Southwest
"It's raining big." See Rain of leaves
"It's raining, it's hailing." See Old Smokie
"It's raining, it's raining." See It's raining
"It's raining, raining all around." See Rain
"It's seven incense boxes." See Seven gifts
"It's silly for the day to be so long." Issa, tr. fr. the Japanese.—LeOw
"It's so nice to be out today." See The weather
"It's springtime in Donegal." See Springtime in Donegal
"It's such a little thing to weep." Emily Dickinson.—DiPe
"It's such a static reference; looking." See Epistrophe
"Its sudden dash from the huddled trees." See The death of a squirrel in McKinley park
"It's there you'll see confectioners with sugar sticks and dainties." See Galway races
"It's time, autumn said to the hollyhocks." See Warning
"It's very hard to be polite." See Under-the-table manners
"It's watering time." See Rain
"It's wonderful dogs they're breeding now." See Tim, an Irish terrier
Itta, Kathy
The good earth.—BaH
My town.—BaH
The wind.—BaH
Itylus
Itylus. A. C. Swinburne.—GrCt
Itylus. Algernon Charles Swinburne.—GrCt
"I've a kisty." Unknown.—MoB
"I've an ingle, shady ingle, near a dusky bosky dingle." See Midsummer jingle
"I've caught a fish." See A catch
"I've changed my ways a little; I cannot now." See The house dog's grave
"I've found something." Unknown.—MoB
"I've got a mule, her name is Sal." See The Erie canal
"I've had my supper." See In the dark
"I've just come from a place." Bashō, tr. fr. the Japanese by R. H. Blyth.—LeI
"I've known rivers." See The Negro speaks of rivers
"I've looked in all the places." See Early spring
"I've never sailed the Amazon." See Rolling down to Rio
"I've nothing else to bring, you know." Emily Dickinson
With flowers.—SmM
"I've noticed how the woolly lamb." See All wool
"I've often heard my mother say." See The unknown color
"I've only seen him." See Whippoorwill
"I've seen a little girl, mamma." See Playing with fire
"I've seen caravans." See Caravans
"I've seen one flying saucer. Only when." See Go fly a saucer
"I've seen you where you never were." Mother Goose.—OpF
"I've stayed in the front yard all my life." See A song in the front yard
"I've swallowed a fly, cried Marjorie Fry." See The cure
"I've taken it down." See The box
"I've tried the new moon tilted in the air." See The freedom of the moon
"I've watched the clouds by day and night." See Watching clouds
"I've watched you now a full half-hour." See To a butterfly
Ivory. David McCord.—McAd
Ivy
"The holly and the ivy." Unknown.—GrCt
"I have a little sister (she lives)." Mother Goose.—OpF
The ivy green. From The Pickwick papers. C. Dickens.—CoBn
The **ivy** green. See The Pickwick papers
Izembō
A shower.—ArT-3
Izen
"These flowers of the plum."—LeMw

J

J. B, sel. Archibald MacLeish
"Curse God and die, you said to me."—PlE
Jabberwocky. See Through the looking-glass
Jack. See "Jack be nimble"
Jack-a-Dandy. See "Nauty pauty"
Jack a Nory. See "I'll tell you a story"
"**Jack** and Gye." Mother Goose.—BrMg
"**Jack** and Jill." See "Jack and Jill went up the hill"
Jack and Jill and old Dame Dob. See "Jack and Jill went up the hill"
"**Jack** and Jill went up the hill." Mother Goose. —HuS-3—OpF—WiMg
"Jack and Jill."—GrT
Jack and Jill and old Dame Dob.—BrMg
Jack and Roger. Benjamin Franklin.—GrCt
Jack and the beanstalk. Patricia Goedicke.—DuS

"**Jack** be nimble." Mother Goose.—ArT-3—HuS-3—WiMg
Jack.—BrMg
"**Jack**, eating rotten cheese, did say." See Jack and Roger
Jack Frost. Cecily E. Pike.—StF
Jack Horner. See "Little Jack Horner"
"**Jack-in-the-pulpit**: Where are you, Jack." See Spring talk
"**Jack**, Jack Joe." Mother Goose.—OpF
Jack-o'-lantern. Aileen Fisher.—LaPh
"**Jack-o'-lantern**, jack-o'-lantern." See Jack-o'-lantern
Jack-o'-lanterns. See Hallowe'en
"**Jack** Parker was a cruel boy." See The cruel boy
Jack Sprat. See "Jack Sprat could eat no fat"
"**Jack** Sprat could eat no fat." Mother Goose.—OpF—ReMg—WiMg
Jack Sprat.—BrMg
The life of Jack Sprat, his wife, and his cat.—VrF
Mother Goose rhymes, 11.—HoB
Jack the piper. See "As I was going up the hill"
Jack was every inch a sailor. Unknown.—DoW
Jackie Faa. Unknown.—GrCt
Jacks. Kathleen Fraser.—FrS
"**Jacks** look like stars." See Jacks
Jackson, Andrew (about)
Andrew Jackson. M. Keller.—BrA
The statue of old Andrew Jackson. V. Lindsay.—LiP
Jackson, Carolyn
I don't mind.—LeM
Jackson, Debbie
The conquered one.—BaH
Jackson, Helen Hunt (H. H., pseud.; Helen Hunt; Saxe Holme, pseud.)
October's bright blue weather.—HoB
September.—BoGj—HoB—HuS-3
Jackson, Kathryn
Things of summer.—BrSg
Jackson, Kathryn and Byron
Noonday Sun.—ArT-3
Open range.—ArT-3
Jackson, Kenneth
Arran. tr.—GrCt
Jackson, Leroy F.
Hippity hop to bed.—ArT-3—ReS
"Jelly Jake and Butter Bill."—CoBb
Polly Picklenose.—CoBb
Jackson, Mahalia (about)
When Mahalia sings. Q. Prettyman.—AdIa
Jackson, Sara
Lily McQueen.—CoBl
Jackson, Thomas Jonathan (Stonewall) (about)
The brigade must not know, sir. Unknown.—HiL
"**Jacky**, come give me thy fiddle." See Jacky's fiddle
Jacky Jingle. See "Now what do you think"
Jacky's fiddle. Mother Goose.—ReOn
Jacob Tonson, his publisher. John Dryden.—GrCt
Jacobs, Elijah L.
High wheat country.—BrA
Saturday in the county seat.—BrA
Jacobson, Ethel
Atomic courtesy.—BrSm
Lines scratched in wet cement.—BrSm
"The **jade** faces of the girls on Yueh stream." See The women of Yueh
Jaffe, Dan
The forecast.—DuR
Jaffe, Lee
Someone.—LeM
"A **jagged** mountain." See From an airplane
"**Jake** hates." See Jake hates all the girls
Jake hates all the girls. E. E. Cummings.—DuS
Jam. David McCord.—McE
Jamboree. David McCord.—McAd
A **jamboree** for j. Eve Merriam.—MeI
James and the giant peach. Roald Dahl.—CoB (sel.)
James I, King of England
Heaven and earth.—GrCt
James, Jesse (about)
Jesse James ("It was on a Wednesday night, the moon was shining bright") Unknown.—McWs
Jesse James ("Jesse James was a man, and he had a robber band") Unknown.—BrA
Jesse James ("Jesse James was a two-gun man") W. R. Benét.—HiL
James, Johnson
"Cruel winter wind."—BaH
James Honeyman. W. H. Auden.—CaMb—SmM
"**James** Honeyman was a silent child." See James Honeyman
"**James**, James." See Disobedience
Jammes, Francis
Francis Jammes: A prayer to go to Paradise with the donkeys. See Prayer to go to Paradise with the donkeys
Prayer to go to Paradise with the donkeys.—CoB—ReO
Francis Jammes: A prayer to go to Paradise with the donkeys.—ArT-3—PlE
Jammes, Francis (about)
Prayer to go to Paradise with the donkeys. F. Jammes.—CoB—ReO
Francis Jammes: A prayer to go to Paradise with the donkeys.—ArT-3—PlE
Jane, do be careful. Irene Page.—CoBb
Janine
"The darkness darts. The moon curls up."—LeM
Janosco, Beatrice
The garden hose.—DuR
To a tidelands oil pump.—DuS
January
January ("The days are short") J. Updike.—LaPd
January ("The fox drags its wounded belly") R. S. Thomas.—CoB
January ("In January") M. Sendak.—AgH
January ("The mountain passes are deep in snow") N. Belting.—BeCm

January ("A snow may come as quietly") E. J. Coatsworth.—HoB
January ("The summer corn ripens") N. Belting.—BeCm
January ("Under low grey sky") C. Lewis.—LeP
January ("The days are short") John Updike.—LaPd
January ("The fox drags its wounded belly") R. S. Thomas.—CoB
January ("In January") Maurice Sendak.—AgH
January ("The mountain passes are deep in snow") Natalia Belting.—BeCm
January ("A snow may come as quietly") Elizabeth Jane Coatsworth.—HoB
January ("The summer corn ripens") Natalia Belting.—BeCm
January ("Under low grey sky") Claudia Lewis. —LeP
"**January** brings the snow." Sara Coleridge.—ArT-3
The garden year.—HuS-3
Janzen, Richard
Oh, joyous house.—LeM
Japan
February. N. Belting.—BeCm
In a bar near Shibuya station, Tokyo. P. Engle.—BrA
The jingo and the minstrel. V. Lindsay.—LiP
Momotara. Unknown.—ArT-3
Japanese
"A globe-trotting man from St Paul." F. G. Christgau.—BrLl
In a bar near Shibuya station, Tokyo. P. Engle.—BrA
"The **Japanese** next to me at the bar." See In a bar near Shibuya station, Tokyo
Jaques, Florence Page
A goblinade.—ArT-3
There once was a puffin.—ArT-3—StF
Jardins sous la pluie. John Redwood-Anderson. —ClF (sel.)
Jarrell, Randall
The bat baby. See Bats
Bats.—DuS—ReO—WeP
The bat baby.—McWs (sel.)
The bird of night.—ReBs
The chipmunk's song.—LaPd
The lost world.—LiT (sel.)
The mockingbird.—LiT—ReO
"My aunt kept turnips in a flock."—AgH
Jaszi, Jean
Lullaby.—HoB
Jayadeva
Gita Govinda, sel.
Krishna's longing.—AlPi
Krishna's longing. See Gita Govinda
Jays
August 28. D. McCord.—McE
Blue jay. H. Conkling.—CoB—ReBs
"Crazy jay blue." E. E. Cummings.—CoB
"If the jay would stop." M. C. Livingston.—LiC
It happens once in a while. M. C. Livingston. —LiC
Squirrel with jays. R. Souster.—CoB
Jazz
Elegy for a jazz musician. E. Kroll.—DuS
Jazz fantasia. C. Sandburg.—LaC
The jazz of this hotel. V. Lindsay.—BoH
Two jazz poems. C. W. Hines, Jr.—BoA—DuR (sel.)—HaK
Jazzonia. L. Hughes.—BoA—HaK
Jazz fantasia. Carl Sandburg.—LaC
The **jazz** of this hotel. Vachel Lindsay.—BoH
Jazzonia. Langston Hughes.—BoA—HaK
"**Jealous** girls these sometimes were." See How marigolds came yellow
Jealousy
Anashuya and Vijaya. W. B. Yeats.—LiT
Birthday party. E. J. Coatsworth.—CoDh
Green weeds. J. Stephens.—StS
How marigolds came yellow. R. Herrick.—GrCt
Jealousy. W. Davenant.—CoBl
The laboratory. R. Browning.—BrP
My pretty rose tree. W. Blake.—BlP
Jealousy. William Davenant.—CoBl
"**Jean,** Jean, Jean." Unknown.—MoB
Jeffers, Robinson
Ascent to the Sierras.—PaH
The house dog's grave.—CoB
Hurt hawks.—CoB
The maid's thought.—CoBl
Ode to Hengist and Horsa.—GrS
Salmon-fishing.—MoS
Shine, Republic.—BrA
Shiva.—GrS
Star-swirls.—DuS
Jefferson, Thomas (about)
The death of Jefferson. H. Butterworth.—HiL
"Thomas Jefferson." R. C. and S. V. Benét.—ArT-3
"**Jellicle** cats come out to-night." See The song of the Jellicles
Jelly beans. Aileen Fisher.—FiIo
"**Jelly** Jake and Butter Bill." Leroy F. Jackson. —CoBb
The **jellyfish** ("Domelike top, speckled comets converging") Glenn Davis.—LeM
A **jellyfish** ("Visible, invisible") Marianne Moore. —WeP
Jemima. See "There was a little girl, and she had a little curl"
Jemmy Dawson. See "Brave news is come to town"
Jenkins, Brooks
Loneliness.—DuR
Jenkins, J.
The spider.—LeM
Jenner, Edward
Signs of rain.—CoBn
"**Jennie,** come tie my." See The bonnie cravat
Jennings, Elizabeth
Santa Maria Maggiore, Rome.—CaD
The visitation.—CaMb
Jenny. Mother Goose.—BrMg

"**Jill** came from the fair." Eleanor Farjeon.—ArT-3
The **jilted** funeral. Gelett Burgess.—BrSm
The **jilted** nymph. Thomas Campbell.—CoBl
"**Jim** and I as children played together." See Oh lucky Jim
Jim Jay. Walter De La Mare.—SmM
Jim, who ran away from his nurse, and was eaten by a lion. Hilaire Belloc.—BrSm—CoBb—GrCt
Jiménez, Juan Ramón
  The coming star.—LiT
  My voice.—LiT
  To Miss Rápida.—LiT
  Winter song.—LiT
  With the roses.—LiT
"**Jimmy** the Mowdy." See Greedy Tom
Jingle bells. Mother Goose.—BrMg
"**Jingle** bells, jingle bells." See Jingle bells
The **jingo** and the minstrel. Vachel Lindsay.—LiP
Jippy and Jimmy. Laura E. Richards.—ArT-3
"**Jippy** and Jimmy were two little dogs." See Jippy and Jimmy
Jittery Jim. William Jay Smith.—CoBb
Joan of Arc (about)
  The good Joan. L. W. Reese.—ArT-3—ThA
Joans, Ted
  It is time.—HaK
  Lester Young.—BoA
  Voice in the crowd.—BoA—HaK
Joass, Lynette
  "Dark, dark night."—LeM
Job (about)
  Job. E. Sewell.—PlE
  "My soul is weary of my life." From Job, Bible, Old Testament.—PlE
Job, sels. Bible, Old Testament
  "Hast thou given the horse strength."—GrCt
    The war horse.—CoB
  "Man that is born of a woman."—GrCt
  "My soul is weary of my life."—PlE
Job. Elizabeth Sewell.—PlE
"**Jock** plays them rants so lively." Unknown.—MoB
Joe. David McCord.—ArT-3—HoB—McE
"**Jog** on, jog on, the foot-path way." See The winter's tale
Johan the monk. Unknown, tr. fr. the Latin by George F. Whicher.—LiT
John, Pricilla
  "Babies are crying."—BaH
John, Saint, the Baptist (about)
  In the wilderness. R. Graves.—PlE
  Saint John. E. J. Coatsworth.—CoDh
  Saint John the Baptist. W. Drummond, of Hawthornden.—PlE
John Anderson my jo. Robert Burns.—BuH—BuPr
"**John** Anderson, my jo, John." See John Anderson, my jo
John Barleycorn: A ballad. Robert Burns.—BuPr
"**John** Brown of Ossawatomie spake on his dying day." See Brown of Ossawatomie
John Brown's body, sels. Stephen Vincent Benét
  Invocation.—BrA
  "It was noon when the company marched to the railroad station"
    From John Brown's body.—HiL
  Robert E. Lee.—BrA
  "There was a girl I used to go with."—HaL
  "Three elements."—PlE
"**John** Brown's body lies a-mouldering in the grave." See Glory hallelujah; or, John Brown's body
John Bull. See "John Bull, John Bull"
"**John** Bull, John Bull." Mother Goose.—OpF
  John Bull.—BrMg
John Bun. Unknown.—BrSm
John Coil. Unknown.—BrSm
John Cook. See "John Cook had a little grey mare"
"**John** Cook had a little grey mare." Mother Goose.—WiMg
  John Cook.—BlO
  John Cook's mare.—ReOn
"**John** Cook he had a little grey mare." See "John Cook had a little grey mare"
John Cook's mare. See "John Cook had a little grey mare"
John Deth, sel. Conrad Aiken
  "With myriad voices grass was filled."—ReO
"**John** Gilpin was a citizen." See The diverting history of John Gilpin
"**John** had." See Happiness
John Henry ("John Henry told his captain") Unknown.—BoH
John Henry ("John Henry was a little baby") Unknown.—HoB
John Henry ("When John Henry was a little boy") Unknown.—HiL
John Henry ("When John Henry was about three days old") Unknown.—BrA
"**John** Henry told his captain." See John Henry
"**John** Henry was a little baby." See John Henry
John James Audubon. Rosemary Carr and Stephen Vincent Benét.—HiL
"**John,** John, and his sister, Susan." See Fly away
John L. Sullivan, the strong boy of Boston. Vachel Lindsay.—LiP
John Peel. John Woodcock Graves.—MoS
"**John** Smith's a very good man." Unknown.—MoB
"**Johnnie** Crack and Flossie Snail." See Under Milk Wood
"**Johnnie** Johnson's ta'en a notion." See Singing game
"**Johnnie** Norrie." Mother Goose.—BrMg
"**Johnnie** Scott was awful thin." See Colter's candy
Johnny. Emma Rounds.—BrSm
Johnny Appleseed. Rosemary Carr and Stephen Vincent Benét.—HoB

Jones, John Luther (about)
Casey Jones. Unknown.—BlO—HiL—McWs
Jones, LeRoi
As a possible lover.—BoA
Audubon, drafted.—HaK
"Each morning." See Hymn for Lanie Poo
The end of man is his beauty.—BoA
Epistrophe.—HaK
Hymn for Lanie Poo, sel.
"Each morning."—AdIa
The invention of comics.—BoA
A poem for black hearts.—AdIa
Preface to a twenty volume suicide note.—BoA—HaK
Snake eyes.—HaK
Jones, Valerie Lorraine
"One stormy night."—BaH
Jonson, Ben
All your fortunes we can tell ye. See Masque of gipsies
Cynthia's revels, sel.
Hymn to Diana.—GrCt
Epitaph on Elizabeth, L. H.—HoL
The gypsies metamorphos'd, sel.
Song.—GrS
Hymn to Diana. See Cynthia's revels
"It is not growing like a tree." See To the immortal memory of that noble pair, Sir Lucius Cary and Sir H. Morison
Lovel's song.—HoL
Masque of gipsies, sel.
All your fortunes we can tell ye.—GrCt
Mother Maudlin the witch. See The sad shepherd
The sad shepherd, sel.
Mother Maudlin the witch.—GrCt
Slow, slow, fresh fount.—GrCt
Song. See The gypsies metamorphos'd
Song to Celia.—BoH
To the immortal memory of that noble pair, Sir Lucius Cary and Sir H. Morison, sel.
"It is not growing like a tree."—GrCt
To the memory of my beloved; the author Mr William Shakespeare.—GrCt (sel.)
Witches' charm.—BlO
Joralemon street. Patricia Hubbell.—LaC
Jörgensen, Johannes
"The plants stand silent round me."—HoL
Jōsa
Crocuses.—ArT-3
"**Joseph** was an old man." See The cherry-tree carol
"**Joseph** West had been told." See The good scholar
Joshi, Umashankar
The washerman.—AlPi
Joshua Hight. Unknown.—BrSm
Jōsō
"Bent down by a storm."—BeCs
"A hungry owl hoots."—BeCs
"That duck, bobbing up."—BeCs
Winter.—LiT
The **journey.** Walter De La Mare.—DeBg
Journey of the Magi. T. S. Eliot.—PlE
Joy. See Happiness
"A **joy** of apple blossoms." See May morning
Joyce, James
All day I hear. See Chamber music—The noise of waters
"All day I hear the noise of waters." See Chamber music—The noise of waters
Chamber music, sels.
"Lean out of the window."—CoBl—HaL
Goldenhair.—GrCt—ThA
"My love is in a light attire."—HaL
The noise of waters.—ArT-3
All day I hear.—HoL
"All day I hear the noise of waters."—LiT
"Strings in the earth and air."—HaL
Goldenhair. See Chamber music—"Lean out of the window"
"In the dark pine-wood."—CoBl
"Lean out of the window." See Chamber music
"My love is in a light attire." See Chamber music
The noise of waters. See Chamber music
On the beach at Fontana.—LiT
"Strings in the earth and air." See Chamber music
"A **joyful** chant." Unknown, fr. the Trobriand islands.—LeO
"**J's** the jumping jay-walker." See All around the town
Judgment day
Saint Peter relates an incident of the Resurrection day. J. W. Johnson.—HaK
When the saints go marchin' in. Unknown.—PlE
Jug and mug. David McCord.—McE
"**Jug,** aren't you fond of mug." See Jug and mug
"**Jugglers** keep six bottles in the air." See Hazardous occupations
Juke box love song. Langston Hughes.—AdIa
Juliana. Unknown, tr. fr. the Latin by George F. Whicher.—CoBl
"**Juliana,** one sweet spring." See Juliana
Juliet. Hilaire Belloc.—CoBl
Julius Caesar, sel. William Shakespeare
Courage.—ShS
Julius Caesar and the honey-bee. Charles Tennyson Turner.—ReO
July
Back yard, July night. W. Cole.—CoBn
July ("The giant cactus is ripe in the desert") N. Belting.—BeCm
July ("The grandfathers were instructed") N. Belting.—BeCm
July storm. E. J. Coatsworth.—CoDh
Weekend stroll. F. Cornford.—CoBn
July ("The giant cactus is ripe in the desert") Natalia Belting.—BeCm
July ("The grandfathers were instructed") Natalia Belting.—BeCm
July storm. Elizabeth Jane Coatsworth.—CoDh
Jumble jingle. Laura E. Richards.—CoO

K

Kennedy, X. J.
Epitaph for a postal clerk.—BrSm
"King Tut."—LiT
Little elegy.—BoGj
Rondeau.—McWs
Kenneth Yasuda
The cuckoo. tr.—LeMw
"The nightingales sing." tr.—LeI
Skylark. tr.—LeMw
Kent, Louis
The hunt.—CoB
"**Kentish** Sir Byng stood for his king." See Cavalier tunes—Marching along
Kentucky
Kivers. A. Cobb.—BrA
My fathers came from Kentucky. From Alexander Campbell. V. Lindsay.—BrA—LiP
Uncle Ambrose. J. Still.—BrA
Walthena. E. Peck.—BrA
Kentucky birthday: February 12, 1816. Frances M. Frost.—HoB
Kenward, Jean
A dressmaker.—SmM
"Old Mother Minchin."—SmM
Snail, moon and rose.—SmM
"**Kepe** well x, and flee fro vii." See Ten commandments, seven deadly sins, and five wits
Kershaw, Linda
Creep.—LeM
Kershaw, S.
"I saw a green beetle climb crippled grass."—LeM
Ketchum, Annie Chambers
The bonnie blue flag.—HiL
Ketchum, Arthur
The road to Granada.—PaH
The spirit of the birch.—ThA
Kevin's fingers. Mary O'Neill.—OnF
"**Kevin's** whispers." See Whispers
Key, Francis Scott
The star-spangled banner.—HiL
The **key** of the kingdom. See This is the key
Keyser, Gustave
Absolutes.—DuR
Khayyám, Omar. See Omar Khayyám
Ki no Tomonori
"In the eternal."—BaS
Kiang Kang-hu. See Bynner, Witter and Kiang Kang-hu
Kibbutz Sabbath. Levi Ben Amittai, tr. by Simon Halkin.—PlE
Kid in the park. Langston Hughes.—LaC
Kid stuff. Frank Horne.—BoA—BoH—HaK—LiT
Kidd, William (about)
Captain Kidd. R. C. and S. V. Benét.—HiL—TuW
Kids. See Some short poems
Kieran, John
To Lou Gehrig.—MoS
Kikaku
"A baby warbler."—BeCs
"Behind me the moon."—BeCs
"Poor crying cricket."—BeCs
"This fall of new snow."—BeCs
Kikuriō
Daffodils.—ArT-3
The **Kilkenny** cats. See "There once were two cats of Kilkenny"
Killdees
Killdees. H. Behn.—BeG
Killdees. Harry Behn.—BeG
"**Killdees** rush out." See Killdees
Kilmer, Aline
Song against children.—ThA
Kilmer, Joyce
Easter.—ArT-3—LaPd—LaPh
The house with nobody in it.—HuS-3—ThA
Kilroy. Peter Viereck.—HiL
"**Kind** reader, Jack makes you a bow." See The history of Jack the giant killer
Kindness. See also Animals—Care; Service; Sympathy
"Be kind." Unknown.—LeO
"Jack and Gye." Mother Goose.—BrMg
Kindness. M. Flett.—LeM
War is kind. S. Crane.—HiL
"The warm of heart shall never lack a fire." E. J. Coatsworth.—ArT-3
Kindness. See "I love little pussy"
Kindness ("A loving arm") Mary Flett.—LeM
Kindness to animals. See Animals—Care
Kindness to animals ("Little children, never give") Unknown.—ClF
Kindness to animals ("Riddle cum diddle cum dido") Laura E. Richards.—ArT-3—StF
King Arthur. See Arthur, King (about)
King, Ben
The pessimist.—BlO—SmM
That cat.—CoB
King, E. L. M.
Robin's song.—ArT-3
King, Edith
The duck.—HuS-3
The rabbit.—HuS-3
King, Henry, Bishop of Chichester
A contemplation upon flowers.—CoBn
King, Martin Luther (about)
April 4, 1968. M. Goode.—BaH
King, Paul. See De Coccola, Raymond and King, Paul
King, Ronald
The desert.—BaH
King, Stoddard
Commissary report.—BrSm
Étude géographique.—BrA
"**King** and queen of Cantelon." See "How many miles to Babylon"
King Arthur. See "When good King Arthur ruled this land"
"**King** Arthur's men have come again." Vachel Lindsay.—LiP
"The **king** asked." See The king's breakfast
"**King** Charles, and who'll do him right now." See Cavalier tunes—Give a rouse
King Charles upon the scaffold. See An Horatian ode upon Cromwell's return from Ireland
King David. Walter De La Mare.—LiT

"**King** David and King Solomon." J. B. Naylor. —SmM
"**King** David was a sorrowful man." See King David
"**King** Fisher courted Lady Bird." See Sylvie and Bruno concluded—The king-fisher song
The **king-fisher** song. See Sylvie and Bruno concluded
King Henry IV, sel. William Shakespeare
Sleep.—ShS
King Henry V, sels. William Shakespeare
Before Agincourt.—GrCt
Before battle.—ShS
The fleet.—ShS
Henry's address to his troops.—McWs
Honey-bees.—CoB
The horse.—CoB
A muse of fire.—GrCt
Peace and war.—ShS
King Henry VI, sels. William Shakespeare
Cares and joys.—ShS
Comparisons.—ShS
The hours.—ShS
A king is dead.—GrCt
Protection.—ShS
The shepherd's life.—ShS
A **king** is dead. See King Henry VI
King Lear, sels. William Shakespeare
The sea.—ShS
The storm.—ShS
"With hey, ho, the wind and the rain."—ArT-3
King of the castle. Mother Goose.—BrMg
King of the mountain. Kathleen Fraser.—FrS
"The **king** of yellow butterflies." Vachel Lindsay. —CoB
King Richard II, sels. William Shakespeare
England.—ShS
This England.—PaH
Mock at sorrow.—ShS
Of the death of kings.—GrCt
King Richard III, sels. William Shakespeare
A dream of wrecks.—GrCt
Slow flowers, fast weeds.—ShS
Wise song.—ShS
King Rufus. Y. Y. Segal, tr. fr. the Yiddish by A. M. Klein.—DoW
"The **king** sent for his wise men all." See W
"The **king** sent his lady on the first Yule day." See "The twelve days of Christmas"
"The **king** sits in Dumferling (or Dunfermline or Dumferlin) town (or toun)." See Sir Patrick Spens
King Solomon. Eve Merriam.—MeC
"**King** Solomon, before his palace gate." See Tales of a wayside inn—Azrael
"**King** Solomon was such a wise old king." See King Solomon
King Stephen. See Othello
"**King** Stephen was a worthy peer." See Othello —King Stephen
"**King** Tut." X. J. Kennedy.—LiT
"The **king** walked in his garden green." See The three singing birds
"The **king** was on his throne." See Vision of Belshazzar
A **kingdom** of clouds. Maura Copeland.—LeM
The **kingdom** of God. Francis Thompson.—PlE
"The **kingdoms** fall in sequence, like the waves on the shore." See The sparrow's skull
The **kingfisher.** See Upon Appleton house
"The **kingfisher.**" Tori, tr. fr. the Japanese by R. H. Blyth.—LeMw
Kingfishers
The king-fisher song. From Sylvie and Bruno concluded. L. Carroll.—BlO
"The kingfisher." Tori.—LeMw
The kingfisher. From Upon Appleton house. A. Marvell.—GrCt
One kingfisher and one yellow rose. E. Brennan.—ReBs
Kings. See Kings and rulers
Kings and rulers. See also Princes and princesses; also names of kings and rulers, as David, King of Israel
The Akond of Swat. E. Lear.—BrLl—SmM
Alas, poor queen. M. Angus.—GrS
The Bourbons at Naples. E. J. Coatsworth.—CoDh
"A Briton who shot at his king." D. Ross.—BrSm
Buckingham palace. A. A. Milne.—LaPd—MiC
The cap and bells. W. B. Yeats.—GrCt—YeR
"Cast our caps and cares away." J. Fletcher. —SmM
A curse for kings. V. Lindsay.—LiP
The emperor's bird's-nest. H. W. Longfellow. —ReBs
Emperors of the island. D. Abse.—CaD
The empresses. E. J. Coatsworth.—CoDh
Fergus and the druid. W. B. Yeats.—LiT
The Georges. W. S. Landor.—GrCt
Gone. W. De La Mare.—BoGj—DeBg
Good King Wenceslas. Unknown.—CoO
Hector Protector. Mother Goose.—BrMg
Henry and Mary. R. Graves.—BoGj—CaD—HaL
The ice king. A. B. Demille.—DoW
Jonathan Bing. B. C. Brown.—ArT-3—LaP—LaPd
King Rufus. Y. Y. Segal.—DoW
King Stephen. From Othello. W. Shakespeare. —ShS
The king's breakfast. A. A. Milne.—MiC
The knifesmith. D. Howard.—SmM
Moon door. M. Kennedy.—CoBl
Nahautl poem. Unknown.—HoL
"Oh, the mighty king of France." Mother Goose.—OpF
Of the death of kings. From King Richard II. W. Shakespeare.—GrCt
"Old King Cole was a merry old soul." Mother Goose.—OpF
Mother Goose rhymes, 62.—HoB
"Old King Cole."—BrMg—WiMg
"Old Sir Simon the king." Mother Goose.—BrF
Sir Simon the king.—BrMg

Kings and rulers—*Continued*
Ozymandias. P. B. Shelley.—CoR—PaH
"Pretty maid, pretty maid." Mother Goose.—OpF
Queen Anne. Unknown.—GrCt
"Queen Cassiopeia." E. Farjeon.—FaT
Queen Mab ("A little fairy comes at night") T. Hood.—HuS-3
Queen Mab ("O, then I see Queen Mab hath been with you") From Romeo and Juliet. W. Shakespeare.—ShS
"Queen Mary, Queen Mary, my age is sixteen." Unknown.—MoB
Queen Mary's men. Unknown.—MoB
Queen Nefertiti. Unknown.—SmM
The queen of fairies. Unknown.—SmM
"The Queen of Hearts she made some tarts." Mother Goose.—OpF
Mother Goose rhymes, 13.—HoB (sel.)
"The Queen of Hearts."—BrF—BrMg—WiMg
"Queen, Queen Caroline." Mother Goose.—OpF
Queen Caroline.—BrMg
Queens. J. M. Synge.—GrCt
A reply from the Akond of Swat. E. T. Schef-fauer.—BrLl
Rulers: Philadelphia. F. Johnson.—BrA
The shepherd's life. From King Henry VI. W. Shakespeare.—ShS
"Sing a song of sixpence." Mother Goose.—BrF—BrMg—HuS-3—OpF—SmM—WiMg
Mother Goose rhymes, 61.—HoB
Songs in praise of the chief. Unknown.—DoC
"Into what would I like to change myself"
"O great chief"
Tartary. W. De La Mare.—ThA
Teddy bear. A. A. Milne.—MiC
A threnody. G. T. Lanigan.—DoW
"To become a chief's favorite." Unknown.—DoC
"When good King Arthur ruled this land." Mother Goose.—OpF
Good King Arthur.—BrF
King Arthur.—BrMg
Who knows. V. Lindsay.—LiP
You shall be queen. Mother Goose.—BrMg
The **king's** breakfast. A. A. Milne.—MiC
The **kings** from the east. Heinrich Heine.—GrCt
The **King's** highway. John S. McGroarty.—PaH
"The **king's** on his castle." See I'm the king of the castle
Kingsley, Charles
Alton Locke, sel.
The sands of Dee.—BlO—ClF—CoSs
The sands of Dee. See Alton Locke
A song of a doll. See The water babies
The three fishers.—CoSs
The tide river.—CoBn
The water babies, sel.
A song of a doll.—GrT
Kinkead, Eugene F.
Fire Island walking song.—CoB
Kinnell, Galway
First song.—BoGj
In fields of summer.—CoBn
On Hardscrabble mountain.—DuS
Spring oak.—CoBn
Kiowa Indians. See Indians of the Americas—Kiowa
Kiph. Walter De La Mare.—ArT-3—DeBg
Kipling, Rudyard
The ballad of east and west.—ArT-3
"Cities and thrones and powers."—BoGj
The gipsy trail.—PaH
The jungle book, sel.
Seal lullaby.—ArT-3—ReS
The seal's lullaby.—McWs
The law of the jungle. See The second jungle book
Mulholland's contract.—CoSs
Rolling down to Rio.—PaH
Seal lullaby. See The jungle book
The seal's lullaby. See The jungle book—Seal lullaby
The second jungle book, sel.
The law of the jungle.—HoB—ReO
The secret of the machines.—HuS-3
Skating.—MoS
A smugglers' song.—BlO
Song of the galley-slaves.—GrCt
Sussex.—PaH
"There was once a small boy in Quebec."—BrLl
The way through the woods.—HuS-3—McWs
The wet litany.—GrS
Kirkman, Martin
Calcutta, tr.—AlPi
Kirkup, James
The eve of Christmas.—CaD
Giving and taking.—PlE
The lonely scarecrow.—BlO—CaD—LaPd
The nature of love.—PlE
Wild Wilbur.—CaD
The Zen archer.—PlE
The **kiss.** Thomas Moore.—CoBl
Kiss-in-the-ring. Eleanor Farjeon.—FaT
"**Kiss** me and comfort my heart." See The beggar's valentine
Kissin'. Unknown.—CoBl
Kissing
"Come here, my beloved." Unknown.—DoC
Confession. Charles d'Orleans.—GrCt
Earth and the kisses of men. E. J. Coatsworth.—CoDh
"Georgie Porgie, pudding and pie." Mother Goose.—OpF—ReMg—WiMg
Georgie Porgie.—BrMg
The kiss. T. Moore.—CoBl
Kissin'. Unknown.—CoBl
The look. S. Teasdale.—BoH—CoBl
"The moth's kiss, first." From In a gondola. R. Browning.—BrP
"She frowned and called him Mr." Unknown.—BrLl
Sing jigmijole. Mother Goose.—BrMg
Summum bonum. R. Browning.—CoBl

"There once was a maiden of Siam." Unknown.—BrLl
Trip upon trenchers. Mother Goose.—ReOn
A sad song.—BrMg
"Wine and cakes for gentlemen." Mother Goose.—ReMg
Wine and cakes.—BrMg
Kitagaki, Lynn
"Birds."—BaH
Kitchen song. Edith Sitwell.—CaD
The **kite** ("How bright on the blue") Harry Behn.—ArT-3
Kite ("I flew my kite") David McCord.—LaPd
A **kite** ("I often sit and wish that I") Unknown. —ArT-3—HoB
The **kite** ("What do you see where you ride, kite") Aileen Fisher.—FiI
A **kite** is a victim. Leonard Cohen.—MoS
"A **kite** is a victim you are sure of." See A kite is a victim
Kites
"A beautiful kite." Issa.—IsF—LeOw
"Coming along the mountain path." Taigi.—LeMw
"It has eyes and a nose." Unknown.—WyC
The kite ("How bright on the blue") H. Behn. —ArT-3
Kite ("I flew my kite") D. McCord.—LaPd
A kite ("I often sit and wish that I") Unknown.—ArT-3—HoB
The kite ("What do you see where you ride, kite") A. Fisher.—FiI
A kite is a victim. L. Cohen.—MoS
Someone asked me. J. Ciardi.—CiYk
"The tight string broke and." Kubonta.—BeCs
"Two little sisters went walking one day." Unknown.—WyC
"What a pretty kite." Issa.—BeCs
"Wind, wind." K. Mizumura.—MiI
Kites (Birds)
From hawk and kite. J. Stephens.—StS
"A **kitten.**" Issa, tr. fr. the Japanese by Nobuyuki Yuasa.—IsF
A **kitten** ("He's nothing much but fur") Eleanor Farjeon.—ArT-3
The **kitten** ("The trouble with a kitten is") Ogden Nash.—CoB
The **kitten** and the falling leaves. William Wordsworth.—BlO—CoB
Kittens. See Cats
"**Kittens** have paws they don't have pawses." See Just because
Kitten's night thoughts. Oliver Herford.—HoB
Kitty Hawk, sel. Robert Frost
"But God's own descent."—PlE
"**Kitty,** kitty, pretty thing." See A cat called Little Bell
Kivers. Ann Cobb.—BrA
Kiyowara Fukayabu
"Because the mist."—BaS
Kiyowara no Fukayabu
Late snowflakes.—LeMw
Klamath Indians. See Indians of the Americas—Klamath
Klein, A. M.
Bandit.—DoW
For the sisters of the Hôtel Dieu.—DoW
King Rufus. tr.—DoW
Orders.—DoW
Psalm of the fruitful field.—DoW
Klein, Jocelyn
"Many shiver."—LeM
The **Klondike.** Edwin Arlington Robinson.—HiL
The **knife-grinder's** budget. Unknown.—VrF
The **knifesmith.** Dorothy Howard.—SmM
Knight, John
Father to the man.—PlE
"A **knight** came riding from the East." Unknown.—BlO
The **knight** in the bower. Unknown.—GrCt
The **knight** of the burning pestle, sel. Francis Beaumont and John Fletcher
The month of May.—GrCt
Knighthood. See Knights and knighthood
Knights and knighthood. See also Arthur, King; Chivalry; Romance
The ballad of Sir Thopas. From The Canterbury tales. G. Chaucer.—ChT
Childe Roland to the dark tower came. R. Browning.—BrP—CoD
Eldorado. E. A. Poe.—PaH—PoP
The enchanted knight. E. Muir.—CaD
"Fast rode the knight." S. Crane.—LiT
Flowers in the valley. Unknown.—BlO—GrS
"I'll tell thee everything I can." From Through the looking-glass. L. Carroll.—AgH
"A knight came riding from the East." Unknown.—BlO
The knight's tomb. S. T. Coleridge.—ClF
Lochinvar. From Marmion. W. Scott.—CoR—HuS-3
"Midways of a walled garden." From Golden wings. W. Morris.—GrCt
"O, where are you going." Unknown.—MoB
The old knight. G. Peele.—GrCt
The outlandish knight. Unknown.—BrSm
The prologue. From The Canterbury tales. G. Chaucer.—ChT
"Whan that Aprille with his shoures sote."—GrCt
The rocks of Brittany. From The Canterbury tales. G. Chaucer.—ChT
Shameful death. W. Morris.—GrCt—GrS
"Sir Eglamour that worthy knight." Unknown. —BlO
Sir Galahad. A. Tennyson.—TeP
The song of Jehane du Castel Beau. From Golden wings. W. Morris.—GrCt
Three knights. Mother Goose.—ReOn
Three knights from Spain. Unknown.—BlO
The three ravens. Unknown.—GrCt
Tom. O. Sitwell.—CaD
Unfinished knews item. E. Merriam.—MeI
The wandering knight's song. J. G. Lockhart. —GrCt
Knights and ladies. See Knights and knighthood
Knights of the Round Table. See Arthur, King; Knights and knighthood

The **knight's** tomb. Samuel Taylor Coleridge.—ClF
Knister, Raymond
White cat.—DoW
Knitting
Beg parding. Unknown.—CoO—GrCt
Knives
The knifesmith. D. Howard.—SmM
Knocking over castles made with marbles. Kathleen Fraser.—FrS
Knotholes. David McCord.—McAd
Knowing. Aileen Fisher.—FiIo
Knowledge
The child in the orchard. E. Thomas.—ThG
Circles. From The people, yes. C. Sandburg.—BrA
Discovery. H. Behn.—BeG
Giles Johnson, Ph.D. F. M. Davis.—HaK
Good men. Bhartrhari.—AlPi
I know myself a man. From Nosce teipsum. J. Davies.—GrCt
Limits. R. W. Emerson.—ReO
A little learning. From An essay on criticism. A. Pope.—GrCt
Much knowledge, little reason. From Nosce teipsum. J. Davies.—GrCt
Sext. W. H. Auden.—LiT (sel.)
Song of a woman abandoned by the tribe because she is too old to keep up with their migration. Unknown.—HoL
Under the rose. W. De La Mare.—DeBg
"When land is gone and money spent." Mother Goose.—ReMg
You know who. J. Ciardi.—CiYk
The Zebra Dun. Unknown.—HuS-3
Knowlt Hoheimer. See The Spoon River anthology
Known of old. Walter De La Mare.—DeBg
Knox, E. V.
"There was an old man who said, Please."—BrLl
Kodo
The cuckoo.—LeMw
Koertge, Ron
Modifications.—DuS
Koka
"Searching for the visitor's shoes."—LeMw
Korea bound, 1952. William Childress.—BrA
Korean war. See United States—History—Korean war
Koriyama, Naoshi
Unfolding bud.—DuR
Korostylev, Vadim
Baby camel.—CoB
Kotewell, Robert and Smith, Norman L.
The fall of the flowers. trs.—LeMw
"Only be willing to search for poetry, and there will be poetry." trs.—LeMw
Only be willing to search for poetry.—LaPd
"Whose are this pond and house." trs.—LeMw
Koyo
"O moon, why must you."—BeCs
The **kraken.** Alfred Tennyson.—TeP
Krakens
The kraken. A. Tennyson.—TeP
Krasnoff, Barbara
Rain dance.—LeM
Kreymborg, Alfred
City sparrow.—LaC
Epigram.—CoBl
Life.—CoB
Manhattan epitaphs: Lawyer.—LaC
Vista.—CoBl—SmM
Krinagoras
The Greek anthology, sel.
"This torch, still burning in my hand."—MoS
"This torch, still burning in my hand." See The Greek anthology
Krishna
Arjuna's paean to Krishna. From Bhagavad Gita. Unknown.—AlPi
Krishna's longing. From Gita Govinda. Jayadeva.—AlPi
Krishna's longing. See Gita Govinda
Kroll, Ernest
Elegy for a jazz musician.—DuS
Fireworks.—DuS
The snowy owl.—CoB
Ku-Klux. Madison Cawein.—HiL
Ku Klux Klan
Ku-Klux. M. Cawein.—HiL
Kubla Khan. Samuel Taylor Coleridge.—BoGj—CoR—GrCt—McWs (sel.)—PaH
Kubonta
"The tight string broke and."—BeCs
Kulasrestha, Mahendra
L and S.—AlPi
Kumin, Maxine W.
400-meter freestyle.—MoS
May 10th.—CoBn
The microscope.—DuR
The sound of night.—CoBn
Kunitz, Stanley
A waltzer in the house.—CoB—WeP
Kural, sel. Tiruvalluvar
Love.—AlPi
Kuramoto, Paul
Clouds.—LeM
Kurdish shepherds. Alan Ross.—CaD
Kurds
Kurdish shepherds. A. Ross.—CaD
Kuskin, Karla
The balloon.—LaPd
Catherine.—LaPd
Full of the moon.—LaP—LaPd
Lewis has a trumpet.—LaPd
Me, Alexander Soames.—ArT-3
The question.—LaPd
The seasons.—BrSg
The snake.—BrSg—LaP
Spring.—LaPd
Tiptoe.—ArT-3—LaPd
Very early.—LaPd
The witches' ride.—LaPd—LaPh

Kyorai
"Puffed by a wind, sails."—BeCs
Kyoroku
"Voices."—LeI
Kyoshi
"Lightly a new moon."—BeCs

L

L and S. Mahendra Kulasrestha.—AlPi
"**L** is for lovable Lena." Unknown.—BrLl
"**L** was a lachrymose leopard." Carolyn Wells.—BrLl
La belle dame sans merci. John Keats.—BoGj—BoH—CoD—GrCt—GrS—SmM
La Saisiaz, sel. Robert Browning
Prologue.—BrP
La tour du sorcier. Osbert Sitwell.—CaD
Labor. See Work
Labor day. See Work
The **laboratory.** Robert Browning.—BrP
Laborers. See Work
La Crosse, Wisconsin
La Crosse at ninety miles an hour. R. Eberhart.—BrA
La Crosse at ninety miles an hour. Richard Eberhart.—BrA
"**Ladies** and gentlemen come to supper." Mother Goose.—ReMg
The **lady.** Elizabeth Jane Coatsworth.—CoDh
"A **lady** and kids are out of food." See Navajo rug
The **lady** and the bear. Theodore Roethke.—BoGj
The **lady** and the swine. See "There was a lady loved a swine"
Lady-birds. See Beetles
"**Lady** bug, lady bug (fly away, do)." Unknown.—WyC
Lady bugs. See Beetles
"A **lady** came to a bear by a stream." See The lady and the bear
"**Lady** Clara Vere de Vere." Alfred Tennyson.—TeP
Lady Clare. Alfred Tennyson.—HuS-3—TeP
A **lady** comes to an inn. Elizabeth Jane Coatsworth.—ArT-3—CoDh
Lady Geraldine's courtship. Elizabeth Barrett Browning.—CoD
"**Lady,** I cannot act, though I admire." See The tramp's refusal
The **lady** is cold. E. B. White.—PaH
"**Lady,** Lady Landers." See Ladybird
Lady lost. John Crowe Ransom.—ReO
"**Lady,** lovely lady." See Vain and careless
The **lady** of Shalott. Alfred Tennyson.—HuS-3—TeP
The **lady** of the lake, sel. Walter Scott
Hunter's song.—ReO
Lady of the land. Mother Goose.—ReOn
"A **lady** red upon the hill." Emily Dickinson
The waking year.—CoBn
"A **lady** there was of Antigua." Cosmo Monkhouse.—BrLl
Lady, three white leopards. See Ash Wednesday
"**Lady,** three white leopards sat under a juniper tree." See Ash Wednesday—Lady, three white leopards
The **ladybird** ("Dear God") Carmen Bernos de Gasztold, tr. fr. the French by Rumer Godden.—GaC
Ladybird ("Lady, Lady Landers") Unknown.—MoB
"**Ladybird,** ladybird (fly away home)." Mother Goose.—BrMg—SmM
Mother Goose rhymes, 57.—HoB
"**Ladybird,** ladybird (where do you hide)." Ivy O. Eastwick.—BrSg
"**Ladybird,** ladybird." Mother Goose.—BrMg—SmM
Mother Goose rhymes, 57.—HoB
Ladybirds. See Beetles
"**Ladybugs** haven't a house to sweep." See Bedtime
"**Laegaire,** son of the king of Connacht." See The army of the Sidhe
La Fayette. Dolly Madison.—HiL
Lafayette, Marquis de (about)
La Fayette. D. Madison.—HiL
La Follette, Melvin Walker
The ballad of red fox.—HaL
La Guardia, Fiorello Henry (about)
Fiorello H. La Guardia. E. Merriam.—MeIv
The **laily** worm and the machrel of the sea. Unknown.—GrCt—ReO
Laing, Dilys
Dance of burros.—CoB
"The **lake.**" See Keep away
The **lake** ("In spring of youth it was my lot") Edgar Allan Poe.—PoP
The **lake** ("Rippling green and gold and brown") Harry Behn.—BeG
The **lake** isle of Innisfree. William Butler Yeats.—ArT-3—CoR—PaH—ThA—YeR
Lakes. See also Great Lakes
By a lake in Minnesota. James Wright.—BrA
"Clear is the bottom of the lake." Yakamochi.—BaS
Conversation by Loch Ness. E. J. Coatsworth.—CoDh
Egrets. Judith Wright.—BoGj
Ensnare the clouds. E. J. Coatsworth.—CoDh
Keep away. E. J. Coatsworth.—CoDh
The lake ("In spring of youth it was my lot") E. A. Poe.—PoP
The lake ("Rippling green and gold and brown") H. Behn.—BeG
A legend of Okeefinokee. L. E. Richards.—HoB
Suicide pond. K. McLaughlin.—DuS
Water picture. M. Swenson.—CoBn—LaC
The winter lakes. W. Campbell.—CoBn

Laksmidhara
Late winter.—AlPi
Lal, P.
"All these hurt." tr.—AlPi
Arjuna's paean to Krishna. See Bhagavad Gita
Bhagavad Gita, sels.
Arjuna's paean to Krishna. tr.—AlPi
Who is the man of poise. tr.—AlPi
The rendezvous.—AlPi
Rig Veda, sels.
The song of creation. tr.—AlPi
To Agni. tr.—AlPi
To the dawn. tr.—AlPi
To the Maruts. tr.—AlPi
To the waters. tr.—AlPi
To the wind. tr.—AlPi
The song of creation. See Rig Veda
"Time a river." tr.—AlPi
To Agni. See Rig Veda
To the dawn. See Rig Veda
To the Maruts. See Rig Veda
To the waters. See Rig Veda
To the wind. See Rig Veda
Who is the man of poise. See Bhagavad Gita
The **lamb** ("Little lamb, who made thee") William Blake.—BlP—BoGj—CoB—HoB—PlE
The **lamb** ("A spindle on four legs") Carmen Bernos de Gasztold, tr. fr. the French by Rumer Godden.—GaC
Lambs. See also Sheep
Herding lambs. R. Pitter.—CaD
The lamb ("Little lamb, who made thee") W. Blake.—BlP—BoGj—CoB—HoB—PlE
The lamb ("A spindle on four legs") C. B. de Gasztold.—GaC
The lambs of Grasmere, 1860. C. G. Rossetti. —CoB
The little lambs. Unknown.—VrF
"Mary had a little lamb." S. J. Hale.—OpF—WiMg
Mary's lamb.—BrMg
Tame animals I have known. N. Waterman.—CoO
Woolly lambkins. C. G. Rossetti.—HuS-3
The **lambs** of Grasmere, 1860. Christina Georgina Rossetti.—CoB
"**Lambs** that learn to walk in snow." See First sight
"A **lame** boy." See The lame boy and the fairy
The **lame** boy and the fairy. Vachel Lindsay.—LiP
A **lament.** Percy Bysshe Shelley.—GrCt
Lament for the Alamo. Arthur Guiterman.—BrA
Lament for the makaris. William Dunbar.—GrCt
A **lament** for the priory of Walsingham. Unknown.—GrCt (sel.)
"**Lament** in rhyme, lament in prose." See Poor Mailie's elegy
The **lament** of the mole-catcher. Osbert Sitwell. —CoB
The **lamentations** of Jeremiah, sel. Bible, Old Testament
"How is the gold become dim."—GrCt
Laments. See also Death
The black man's lament; or, How to make sugar. A. Opie.—VrF
Cowboy's lament. Unknown.—GrCt—HiL
"As I walked out in the streets of Laredo."—McWs
David's lament. From The second book of Samuel, Bible, Old Testament.—GrCt
A dirge ("Call for the robin red-breast and the wren") From The white devil. J. Webster. —BlO
Call for the robin-redbreast.—GrCt
Dirge ("1-2-3 was the number he played but to-day the number came 3-2-1") K. Fearing. —HiL
A dirge ("Rough wind, that moanest loud") P. B. Shelley.—GrCt
A dirge ("Why were you born when the snow was falling") C. G. Rossetti.—GrCt
Dirge for a bad boy. E. V. Rieu.—CoBb
Dirge for the new sunrise. E. Sitwell.—PlE
An elegy for a dead child in the street. R. Rao.—AlPi
Elegy for a dead soldier. K. Shapiro.—HiL
Elegy for a jazz musician. E. Kroll.—DuS
Elegy for a nature poet. H. Nemerov.—CoBn
Elegy for Jog. J. Ciardi.—DuR
Elegy in a country churchyard. G. K. Chesterton.—McWs
An elegy on the death of a mad dog. O. Goldsmith.—BrSm—CoR
Elegy on Willie Nicol's mare. R. Burns.—BuPr
The frog's lament. A. Fisher.—FiI
Full fathom five. From The tempest. W. Shakespeare.—GrCt—SmM
Ariel's dirge.—BoGj
Ariel's song.—BlO
A sea dirge.—CoSs
Go thou to Rome. From Adonais. P. B. Shelley.—GrCt
"How is the gold become dim." From The lamentations of Jeremiah, Bible, Old Testament.—GrCt
A lament. P. B. Shelley.—GrCt
Lament for the Alamo. A. Guiterman.—BrA
Lament for the makaris. W. Dunbar.—GrCt
A lament for the priory of Walsingham. Unknown.—GrCt (sel.)
The lament of the mole-catcher. O. Sitwell.—CoB
Little elegy ("Here lies resting, out of breath") X. J. Kennedy.—BoGj
Little elegy ("Withouten you") E. Wylie.—HaL
Lycidas. J. Milton.—GrCt
A lyke-wake dirge. Unknown.—GrCt—PlE
Mourning poem for the queen of Sunday. R. E. Hayden.—DuS
Poor Mailie's elegy. R. Burns.—BuPr
Request for requiems. L. Hughes.—BrSm
Requiem. R. L. Stevenson.—BoH—ClF—SmM
Sally Simpkin's lament. T. Hood.—BrSm
The sea ritual. G. Darley.—GrS

A serio-comic elegy. R. Whately.—BrSm
Threnody ("Let happy throats be mute") D. J. Hayes.—BoA
Threnody ("Only quiet death") W. Cuney.—BoA
A threnody ("What, what, what") G. T. Lanigan.—DoW
Lamplighter barn. Myra Cohn Livingston.—ArT-3
Lampman, Archibald
Among the millet.—DoW
Morning on the Lièvre.—MoS
Solitude.—CoBn
Lamps
Aladdin. J. R. Lowell.—CoR
A song of always. E. Rosenzweig.—ArT-3—ThA
"**Lamps** burn all the night." See The fifth sense
L'an trentiesme de mon eage. Archibald MacLeish.—GrS
Lancaster county tragedy. W. Lowrie Kay.—BrSm
Lancelot, Sir (Lancelot du Lac) (about)
The lady of Shalott. A. Tennyson.—HuS-3—TeP
The **land** of counterpane. Robert Louis Stevenson.—HoB—HuS-3
The **land** of dreams. William Blake.—BlP
The **land** of heart's desire. William Butler Yeats.—PaH
"The **land** of running horses, fair." See Oedipus at Colonus—Chorus
The **land** of story-books. Robert Louis Stevenson.—ArT-3
The **land** of the Bumbley Boo. Spike Milligan.—StF
Land of the free. Archibald MacLeish.—BrA (sel.)
The sound track.—LiT (sel.)
"The **land**, that, from the rule of kings." See The Bartholdi statue
"The **land** was ours before we were the land's." See The gift outright
"The **land** was white." Unknown.—GrCt
Landeweer, Elizabeth
Dakota badlands.—BrA
The **landing** of the Pilgrim Fathers. Felicia Dorothea Hemans.—ArT-3—HiL
Landlords
Lord Waterford. Unknown.—GrCt
Landor, Walter Savage
The Crimean war heroes.—McWs
A critic.—GrCt
The gardener and the mole.—ReO
The Georges.—GrCt
I strove with none.—GrCt
Night airs. See Night airs and moonshine
Night airs and moonshine.—GrCt
Night airs.—CoBn
On music.—BoGj
A reply to lines by Thomas Moore.—GrCt (sel.)
Rose Aylmer.—CoR
Some of Wordsworth.—GrCt
Stand close around.—GrCt
Landscape as metal and flowers. Winfield Townley Scott.—BoGj—BrA
Landscape, deer season. Barbara Howes.—BoGj
Landscapes, sels. T. S. Eliot
Cape Ann.—BoGj—CaD—HoL
New Hampshire.—HaL
"**Landscapes** dissolve in rain." See March weather
"A **lane** at the end of Old Pilgrim street." See The house
Lang, Andrew
The last chance.—MoS
Langford, Margaret
You do it too.—StF
Langland, Joseph
War.—DuS
Langley, Timothy
The concrete mixer.—LeM
Language. See also Words
"As I was laying on the green." Unknown.—McWs
Cecilia. Unknown.—DoW
A cliché. E. Merriam.—MeI
Figures of speech. D. McCord.—McAd
Innuendo. D. McCord.—McAd
Just because. D. McCord.—CoO—McE
Latin. Unknown.—GrCt
Love song. R. Whittemore.—BrA
O-u-g-h. D. McCord.—McAd
Scat scitten. D. McCord.—McE
Singular indeed. D. McCord.—McAd
Story for an educated child. P. McGinley.—McWc
Sum, es, est. Unknown.—GrCt
"There was an old maid from Peru." Unknown.—BrLl
The **languishing** moon. See With how sad steps, O moon
Lanier, Sidney
Song of the Chattahoochee.—BrA—CoBn
The story of Vinland.—HiL
Lanigan, George T.
Isabel. tr.—DoW
A threnody.—DoW
"The **lanky** hank of a she in the inn over there." See A glass of beer
A **lantern.** Walter De La Mare.—DeBg
"A **lantern** lighted me to bed." See A lantern
Lanterns
Brown's descent; or, The willy-nilly slide. R. Frost.—ArT-3
A lantern. W. De La Mare.—DeBg
Lanty Leary. Samuel Lover.—CoBl—GrCt
Lape, Fred
Biddy.—CoB
Litter of pigs.—CoB
Sheep shearing.—CoB
"**Lapped** in the light and heat of noon." See The orchard
Lapwings. See Peewees
Larcom, Lucy
The brown thrush.—HoB

"**Large** towns, small towns." See Our largest and smallest cities
"The **lariat** snaps; the cowboy rolls." See The closing of the rodeo
The **lark** ascending. George Meredith.—ReO (sel.)
The **lark** in the morning. See "As I was a-walking"
"The **lark** is but a bumpkin fowl." See Kenilworth—The bonny, bonny owl
"The **lark** now leaves his wat'ry nest." William Davenant.—GrCt
Larkin, Philip
At grass.—CaD—MoS
Days.—SmM
First sight.—CoBn—ReO
Larks
"Above the mountain." Shiki.—BeCs
Address to a lark singing in winter. From Address to a lark. J. Clare.—ReBs
Answer to a child's question. S. T. Coleridge. —BlO—CoB—ReBs
"As I was a-walking." Unknown.—ReBs
The lark in the morning.—GrCt
The crow and the lark. From The merchant of Venice. W. Shakespeare.—ShS
"Frog-school competing." Shiki.—BeCs
"Hark, hark, the lark at heaven's gate sings." From Cymbeline. W. Shakespeare.—BlO
Hark, hark, the lark.—GrCt—SmM
"High on a mountain." Bashō.—BeCs
"Horse after horse." Issa.—IsF
The lark ascending. G. Meredith.—ReO (sel.)
"The lark now leaves his wat'ry nest." W. Davenant.—GrCt
Lo, here the gentle lark. From Venus and Adonis. W. Shakespeare.—GrCt
On a birthday. J. M. Synge.—GrCt
"On how to sing." Shiki.—LeI
Rabbit and lark. J. Reeves.—StF
The skylark ("Bird of the wilderness") J. Hogg.—CoB
Skylark ("Singing clear and loud") Seien.—LeMw
Skylark ("Up in the lift go we") Unknown.—MoB
Spring song. A. Fisher.—FiC
To a sky-lark ("Up with me, up with me into the clouds") W. Wordsworth.—WoP
To a skylark ("Hail to thee, blithe spirit") P. B. Shelley.—CoR
Upon the lark and the fowler. J. Bunyan.—CoB
"Voices." Kyoroku.—LeI
"Who is't now we hear." From Alexander and Campaspe. J. Lyly.—ReBs
"**Larkspur** and hollyhock." See Names
La Rue, M.
Wind, waves, and sails.—CoSs
Lasanta, Miriam
Confidence.—BaH
"Leave me alone, I would always shout."—BaH
"The trees are a beautiful sight."—BaH
A **lass** wi' a tocher. Robert Burns.—BuPr
"The **last** and greatest herald of heaven's King." See Saint John the Baptist
The **last** chance. Andrew Lang.—MoS
"**Last** fall I saw the farmer follow." See Preparation
The **last** leaf. Oliver Wendell Holmes.—BoH
"**Last** May, a braw wooer cam doun the lang glen." See The braw wooer
"**Last** night a freezing cottontail." See Twin Lakes hunter
"**Last** night a sword-light in the sky." See Stone trees
"**Last** night a thunderstorm went by." See The storm
"**Last** night, ah, yesternight, betwixt her lips and mine." See Non sum qualis eram bonae sub regno Cynarae
"**Last** night along the river banks." See The boats are afloat
"**Last** night at black midnight I woke with a cry." See The ghost of the buffaloes
"**Last** night did Christ the Sun rise from the dark." See Easter Sunday
"**Last** night I dreamed a ghastly dream." See Ballad of the flood
"**Last** night I heard a rat-tat-too." See Rain riders
"**Last** night in the open shippen." See Christmas day
"**Last** night the cold wind and the rain blew hard." See Sunday at the end of summer
"**Last** night, while we were fast asleep." See New Year's day
"The **last** of October." See Fall
The **last** ride together. Robert Browning.—BrP
"The **last** snow is going." See Spring
Last song. James Guthrie.—ArT-3—LaPd
Last song of Sitting Bull. Unknown, tr. fr. the Teton Sioux.—LeO
The **last** word of a bluebird. Robert Frost.—ArT-3—BoGj—HuS-3—TuW
"**Last** year the war was in the northeast." See War
"**Last** year we fought by the head-stream of the Sang-kan." See The nefarious war
Lat take a cat. See The Canterbury tales—Phoebus and the crow
"**Lat** take a cat, and fostre him well with milk." See The Canterbury tales—Phoebus and the crow
"**Late** August, given heavy rain and sun." See Blackberry-picking
Late corner. Langston Hughes.—HaK
Late last night. Unknown.—BrSm
"**Late** last night I slew my wife." See Late last night
"**Late** lies the wintry sun a-bed." See Wintertime
Late October. Elizabeth Jane Coatsworth.—CoSb
Late snowflakes. Kiyowara no Fukayabu, tr. fr. the Japanese by Curtis Hidden Page.—LeMw

"**Late** that mad Monday evening." See Madness one Monday evening
Late winter. Laksmidhara, tr. fr. the Sanskrit by Daniel H. H. Ingalls.—AlPi
"**Lately**, I've become accustomed to the way." See Preface to a twenty volume suicide note
The **latest** decalogue. Arthur Hugh Clough.—GrCt
Latin. Unknown.—GrCt
"**Latin** is a dead language." See Latin
Lattimore, Richmond
The crabs.—DuS
I bless this man. See Nemea 11
Nemea 11, sel.
I bless this man. tr.—MoS
A siding near Chillicothe.—BrA
Lau, D. C.
Name or person. tr.—SmM
Laudate dominum. See Psalms—Psalm 150
Laughing song. William Blake.—ArT-3—BlP—BoGj
Laughing time. William Jay Smith.—HoB
Laughter
American laughter. K. A. Robinson.—BrA
The boy who laughed at Santa Claus. O. Nash.—CoBb
Danny Murphy. J. Stephens.—CoR—StS
Early supper. B. Howes.—BoGj
"Everybody laugh." L. Hale.—BaH
Laughing song. W. Blake.—ArT-3—BlP—BoGj
Laughing time. W. J. Smith.—HoB
Laughter. M. Waddington.—DoW
Why. M. C. Livingston.—LiC
Laughter. Miriam Waddington.—DoW
"**Laughter** of children brings." See Early supper
The **launch** in miniature. Mary Elliott.—VrF
Laundresses and laundrymen. See Laundry
Laundromat. David McCord.—McAd
Laundry
"Can you wash your father's shirt." Mother Goose.—OpF
"Down by the river." Mother Goose.—BrMg
Laundromat. D. McCord.—McAd
Monday. Unknown.—StF
"The old woman must stand at the tub, tub, tub." Mother Goose.—OpF
Our washing machine. P. Hubbell.—HoB
The shepherd's hut. A. Young.—CaD
"They that wash on Monday." Mother Goose.—BlO—OpF
The washerman. U. Joshi.—AlPi
Windy wash day. D. Aldis.—ArT-3—LaP
Laundrymen. See Laundry
Laurance, Annabel
My brain.—LeM
Lauren, Joseph
The fox and the grapes.—BoH
The frogs who wanted a king.—BoH
Lavender (Flower)
Bees in lavender. E. Farjeon.—FaA
"**Lavender's** blue, diddle, diddle." Mother Goose.—OpF
Law
The harnet and the bittle. J. Y. Ackerman.—GrCt
The law of the jungle. From The second jungle book. R. Kipling.—HoB—ReO
The **law** of the jungle. See The second jungle book
Lawrence, D. H.
Aware.—CoBn
Ballad of another Ophelia.—GrCt
Bavarian gentians.—BoGj
Flapper.—CoBl
"How beastly the bourgeois is."—GrCt
In a boat.—CoBl
Kangaroo.—ReO
A living.—CoB
The mosquito knows.—ReO
New moon.—CoBn
River roses.—GrS
The sea.—CoBn
Sea-weed.—CoBn
Snake.—ArT-3—CoB
Spray.—CoBn
Spring morning.—CoBl
Talk.—ClF
"**Lawsamassy,** for heaven's sake." See Lucy Lake
Lawson, Marie A.
Halloween.—ArT-3
Lawton, Jewell
"I wonder."—LeM
Lawyers
The briefless barrister. J. G. Saxe.—BrSm
Manhattan epitaphs: Lawyer. A. Kreymborg.—LaC
"**Lay** doon yer little heidie." Unknown.—OpF
"**Lay** me on an anvil, O God." See Prayers of steel
The **lay** of the last minstrel. Walter Scott.—PaH (sel.)
Layton, Irving
The bull calf.—CoB
Golfers.—MoS
Song for Naomi.—DoW
"A spider danced a cosy jig."—DoW
Lazarus, Emma
The new Colossus.—BoH—BrA
Laziness. See Idleness
"**Lazy** and slow, through the snags and trees." See In the bayou
"**Lazy** ducks, that sit in the coal-nooks." Unknown.—MoB
Lazy Lou. Mary Mapes Dodge.—CoBb
"**Lazy** Lou, Lazy Lou." See Lazy Lou
"**Lazy** sheep, pray tell me why." See The sheep
A **lazy** thought. Eve Merriam.—LaC
"**Lazy** Zany Addlepate." Unknown.—OpF
Lea, Gordon
When I learned to whistle.—LeM
"**Lead** me, O God, and thou my destiny." See God leads the way
The **leaden-eyed.** Vachel Lindsay.—LiP
Leaf and sun. Norma Farber.—HoL
"A **leaf** crashes gently to the ground." Jennifer Hodgman.—LeM

"There was an old person of Ware"
Limericks.—HoB
"There was an old person whose habits"
Limericks.—HoB
The two old bachelors.—BrSm
Lear, Edward (about)
"How pleasant to know Mr Lear." E. Lear.—GrCt
Mr Lear.—TuW
A reply from the Akond of Swat. E. T. Scheffauer.—BrLl
Learning to go alone. Ann and Jane Taylor.—VrF
Leaso, Maresala
Stillness.—LeM
"The **least** of breezes." Onitsura, tr. fr. the Japanese by Harry Behn.—BeCs
"**Leathery,** wry, and rough." See Rodeo
Leave her, Johnny. Unknown.—SmM
"**Leave** me alone, I would always shout." Miriam Lasanta.—BaH
Leave-taking. Unknown, tr. fr. the Quechura.—LeO
Leaves
Among the leaves. E. J. Coatsworth.—CoSb
Autumn leaves. A. Fisher.—FiI
The city of falling leaves. A. Lowell.—ArT-3
Cottonwood leaves. B. Clark.—ArT-3
The dead ones. M. C. Livingston.—LiC
Down. A. Fisher.—FiIo
"Down, down." E. Farjeon.—ArT-3
Falling leaves. P. Hubbell.—HoB
"From a mountain of fallen leaves." K. Mizumura.—MiI
Gathering leaves. R. Frost.—BrSg—HaL
Ice storm. E. J. Coatsworth.—CoSb
In the college of surgeons. J. Stephens.—HaL
The kitten and the falling leaves. W. Wordsworth.—BlO—CoB
Leaf and sun. N. Farber.—HoL
"A leaf crashes gently to the ground." J. Hodgman.—LeM
"A leaf looks prickly and sharp." Peter Johnson.—LeM
Leaves ("The leaves fall") P. Walker.—LaPd
The leaves ("The leaves had a wonderful frolic") Unknown.—StF
The leaves ("Leaves of the summer, lovely summer's pride") W. Barnes.—CoBn—GrCt
Leaves ("One, two, and three") C. Cullen.—BoH
Looking up at leaves. B. Howes.—CoBn
The minimal. T. Roethke.—LiT
November night. A. Crapsey.—HoL
Oak leaves. E. J. Coatsworth.—HuS-3
October. R. Fyleman.—BrSg
October wind. D. McCord.—McAd
October's party. G. Cooper.—HoB
Rain of leaves. A. Fisher.—FiI
The singing leaves. J. R. Lowell.—HuS-3
"Watch long enough, and you will see the leaf." C. Aiken.—HoL
"The wind gives us." Issa.—LeOw
Leaves ("The leaves fall") Paul Walker.—LaPd
The **leaves** ("The leaves had a wonderful frolic") Unknown.—StF
The **leaves** ("Leaves of the summer, lovely summer's pride") William Barnes.—CoBn—GrCt
Leaves ("One, two, and three") Countee Cullen.—BoH
The **leaves** are green. Unknown.—ReOn
"The **leaves** are green, the nuts are brown." See The leaves are green
"The **leaves** are puppets." See Falling leaves
"The **leaves** are uncurling." See Spring
"**Leaves** fall." See The city of falling leaves
"The **leaves** fall." See Leaves
"The **leaves** had a wonderful frolic." See The leaves
"The **leaves** have left without a warning." See The seasons
"**Leaves** make a slow." See Spring rain
"**Leaves** of the summer, lovely summer's pride." See The leaves
Leavetaking. Eve Merriam.—LaPd—MeI
Lebanon
"As I came down from Lebanon." C. Scollard.—PaH
Lechlitner, Ruth
Kansas boy.—BrA—DuR
LeCron, Helen Cowles
Little Charlie Chipmunk.—ArT-3
Ledoux, Louis V.
Slumber song.—ReS
Ledwidge, Francis
August.—GrS
The find.—ThA
The shadow people.—ThA
To a linnet in a cage.—CoR
Lee, Alan S.
The child in school. tr.—LeMw
The return. tr.—LeMw
Lee, Betty Jane
Navajo rug.—BaH
Lee, Estelita Vanessa
I wonder why.—BaH
Lee, Laurie
Day of these days.—CoBn
Long summer.—CoBn
Lee, Robert E. (about)
Robert E. Lee. From John Brown's body. S. V. Benét.—BrA
Leeuwenhoek, Anton (about)
The microscope. M. W. Kumin.—DuR
"**Left** and right and swing around." See Dance
Legacy ("I had a rich old great-aunt") Nancy Byrd Turner.—ThA
Legacy ("The year has made her will: she left to me") Christopher Morley.—DuR
Le Gallienne, Richard
Brooklyn bridge at dawn.—ArT-3
"A caravan from China comes."—ThA
"I meant to do my work to-day."—ArT-3—LaP—ThA
London beautiful.—PaH
Legend. John V. A. Weaver.—BrA

The **legend** beautiful. See Tales of a wayside inn
A **legend** from Russia. Phyllis McGinley.—McWc
A **legend** of Okeefinokee. Laura E. Richards.—HoB
A **legend** of Paul Bunyan. Arthur S. Bourinot.—BrA
The **legend** of Rabbi Ben Levi. See Tales of a wayside inn
The **legend** of the cat. Phyllis McGinley.—McWc
Legend of the holly. Phyllis McGinley.—McWc
Legends. See also Mythology
  Ballad of the nightingale. P. McGinley.—McWc
  Ballad of the robin. P. McGinley.—McWc
  Ballad of the rosemary. P. McGinley.—McWc
  Ballad of the two tapsters. V. Watkins.—CaMb
  The birthday. P. McGinley.—McWc
  The canticle of the bees. P. McGinley.—McWc
  Christmas eve legend. F. M. Frost.—HoB
  Gluskap's hound. T. G. Roberts.—DoW
  An Irish legend. P. McGinley.—McWc
  Legend. J. V. A. Weaver.—BrA
  The legend beautiful. From Tales of a wayside inn. H. W. Longfellow.—LoPl
  A legend from Russia. P. McGinley.—McWc
  A legend of Okeefinokee. L. E. Richards.—HoB
  A legend of Paul Bunyan. A. S. Bourinot.—BrA
  The legend of Rabbi Ben Levi. From Tales of a wayside inn. H. W. Longfellow.—LoPl
  The legend of the cat. P. McGinley.—McWc
  Legend of the holly. P. McGinley.—McWc
  The night. P. McGinley.—McWc
  The pine tree. P. McGinley.—McWc
  A Roman legend. From Morituri salutamus. H. W. Longfellow.—LoPl
  Santa Maria Maggiore, Rome. E. Jennings.—CaD
  Santorin. J. E. Flecker.—BoGj
  The stars' story. P. McGinley.—McWc
  The stork. P. McGinley.—McWc
  Story for an educated child. P. McGinley.—McWc
  The voyage of Maeldune. A. Tennyson.—TeP
  Why the owl wakes at night. P. McGinley.—McWc
Lehmann, John
  The ballad of banners.—CaMb
  This excellent machine.—DuS
Leigh, Henry Sambrooke
  The twins.—ArT-3—BrSm
Leishman, J. B.
  The boy. tr.—SmM
Leisure. William Henry Davies.—ArT-3—CoBn—SmM—TuW
Leland, Charles Godfrey (Hans Breitmann, pseud.)
  El capitan-general.—CoSs
Lemonade. David McCord.—McAd
Lemons
  Lemons and apples. M. Neville.—ArT-3
Lemons and apples. Mary Neville.—ArT-3
Lemont, Jessie
  The panther. tr.—ReO
Lenore. Edgar Allan Poe.—PoP
Lenox avenue mural. Langston Hughes.—BoA
  Dream deferred.—LaC
Lenski, Lois
  People.—LaC
Lent
  Lady, three white leopards. From Ash Wednesday. T. S. Eliot.—GrS
  A rhyme for Shrove Tuesday. Unknown.—ClF
Leonard, Nelson
  "In the desert sand."—BaH
Leonard, William Ellery
  The ass in the lion's skin. tr.—ReO
Leopards
  The dalliance of the leopards. Unknown.—HoL
  "L was a lachrymose leopard." C. Wells.—BrLl
  Little Katy. Unknown.—BrSm
Les isles d'Amérique. Elizabeth Jane Coatsworth.—CoDh
Les Saintes-Maries-de-la-Mer. Alan Ross.—CaD
Lèse majesté. Oliver Herford.—CoB
Lessing, Gotthold Ephraim
  On Fell.—BrSm
The **lesson** ("Letters twenty-six you see") Unknown.—GrT
Lesson ("To plant a seed and watch it grow") Harry Behn.—BrSg
Lesson from a sun-dial. Unknown, tr. fr. the German by Louis Untermeyer.—ArT-3
Lester, Julius
  "Around the church." See Poems
  "As we got." See Poems
  "The man who tried to." See Poems
  Poems, sels.
    "Around the church."—HaK
    "As we got."—HaK
    "The man who tried to."—HaK
    "She should be."—HaK
    "Spring dawn."—HaK
    "With its fog-shroud the."—HaK
  "She should be." See Poems
  "Spring dawn." See Poems
  "With its fog-shroud the." See Poems
Lester Young. Ted Joans.—BoA
Let all things pass away. William Butler Yeats.—GrCt
"**Let** feasting begin in the wild camp." See Border songs
"**Let** happy throats be mute." See Threnody
Let her give her hand. Unknown.—CoBl
"**Let** her give her hand, her glove." See Let her give her hand
Let it be forgotten. Sara Teasdale.—BoH
"**Let** it be forgotten, as a flower is forgotten." See Let it be forgotten
"**Let** it rain." See The engineer
"**Let** me be buried in the rain." See Invocation
"**Let** me but do my work from day to day." See Work

"**Let** me shoot a small bird for my younger brother." See Cradle song for a boy
"**Let** no man see my girl." See Inconsistent
"**Let** no one suppose." James Reeves.—CoB
"**Let** not our town be large, remembering." See A gospel of beauty—On the building of Springfield
"**Let** not young souls be smothered out before." See The leaden-eyed
"**Let** nothing disturb thee." See Lines written in her breviary
"**Let** Sporus tremble—What? that thing of silk." See Epistle to Dr Arbuthnot—Sporus
"**Let** the knowing speak." See Adjuration
"**Let** the limerick form be rehoised." See Leaning on a limerick
"**Let** the man who has and doesn't give." See In the imperative mood
"**Let** the rain kiss you." See April rain song
"**Let** them bestow on every airth a limb." See Verses composed on the eve of his execution
"**Let** us be quiet for a while." See The petal of a rose
"**Let** us go, then, exploring." Virginia Woolf.—CoBn
"**Let** us move the stone gentleman to the toadstool wood." See The stone gentleman
"**Let** us not look upon." See Prayer
Let us now praise famous men. See Ecclesiasticus
"**Let** us now praise famous men, and our fathers that begat us." See Ecclesiasticus—Let us now praise famous men
"**Let** us walk in the white snow." See Velvet shoes
"**Let** us who live in leafy cage." See Leaf and sun
Let ye then my birds alone. See Summer evening
"**Let's** contend no more, Love." See A woman's last word
"**Let's** go, let's go." See In the spring
"**Let's** go see old Abe." See Lincoln monument: Washington
Let's go to bed. See "To bed, to bed"
"**Let's** go to bed, says Sleepy-head." See "To bed, to bed"
"**Let's** listen to the crickets." See Mountain summer
"**Let's** ride." Issa, tr. fr. the Japanese.—LeOw
The **letter.** Elizabeth Turner.—VrF
Letter across doubt and distance. M. Carl Holman.—BoA
Letter to my sister. Anne Spencer.—BoA
Letter to N. Y. Elizabeth Bishop.—McWs
Letters and letter writing
I sent a letter to my love. E. Farjeon.—FaT
The letter. E. Turner.—VrF
Letter across doubt and distance. M. C. Holman.—BoA
Letter to my sister. A. Spencer.—BoA
Letter to N. Y. E. Bishop.—McWs
"This is my letter to the world." E. Dickinson.—DiL—DiPe
"The way I read a letter's—this." E. Dickinson.—DiL
Young girl: Annam. P. Colum.—HaL
Letters found near a suicide. See Notes found near a suicide
Letters of the alphabet. See Alphabet
"**Letters** twenty-six you see." See The lesson
Letts, Winifred M.
Shops.—ThA
Tim, an Irish terrier.—CoB
Lettuce
Soliloquy of a tortoise on revisiting the lettuce beds after an interval of one hour while supposed to be sleeping in a clump of blue hollyhocks. E. V. Rieu.—ArT-3—BrSg—CoB—McWs
"**Leveling** his pole like some quixotic lance." See Challenge
Levertov, Denise
The rainwalkers.—DuS
A solitude.—DuS
To the snake.—CoB
Levi Isaac of Berdichev
Invocation.—PlE
Levi, Peter
"The fox-coloured pheasant enjoyed his peace."—CaD
—and Milner-Gulland, Robin
On a bicycle. trs.—LiT (sel.)
Schoolmaster. trs.—LiT
Zima junction. trs.—LiT (sel.)
Levy, Newman
Midsummer jingle.—CoBn
The revolving door.—BrSm
Lewenstein, Paul
Adieu.—SmM
Lewis, Brenda J.
"I am a black man, soul and all."—BaH
Lewis, Claudia
Blue.—LeP
Dinosaur air.—LeP
The dome of night.—LeP
"A drove of rams and ewes and woolly lambs." See Two poems
Earth, moon, and sun.—LeP
Eclipse.—LeP
Forest magic.—LeP
How strange it is.—LeP
In a million years.—LeP
"In the redwood forest."—LeP
January.—LeP
Listen to the unheard.—LeP
Mountain fantasy.—LeP
Mountain summer.—LeP
No man on any moon.—LeP
"On a winter day."—LeP
Sea magic.—LeP
"Sheep of plush, push." See Two poems
"Song of the carousel."—LeP
Space.—LeP
A thousand stones.—LeP
"Three skies."—LeP
To the young locust tree outside the window.—LeP

Lewis, Claudia—*Continued*
Two poems.—LeP
I. "A drove of rams and ewes and woolly lambs"
II. "Sheep of plush, push"
A way of looking.—LeP
Wheels.—LeP
Lewis, Emily
My dog.—StF
Lewis, Ramona
Why isn't the world happy.—BaH
"**Lewis** and Clark." Rosemary Carr and Stephen Vincent Benét.—HuS-3
Lewis and Clark expedition
"Lewis and Clark." R. C. and S. V. Benét.—HuS-3
Lewis has a trumpet. Karla Kuskin.—LaPd
L'Heureux, John
"Discovering God is waking one morning."—CoBn
Li Shang-yin
Midnight in the garden.—LeMw
Li T'ai-po (Li Po or Rihaku)
At Feng Ting temple.—LiMw
"Blue water . . . a clear moon."—LeMw
The Ching-Ting mountain.—LiT
The firefly.—LeMw
The fisherman.—LeMw
Girls on the Yueh river.—GrCt
In the mountains on a summer day.—MoS
Name or person.—SmM
The nefarious war.—LiT
On visiting a clear spring.—LeMw
The river-merchant's wife: A letter.—BoH—CoBl—LiT
Taking leave of a friend.—HoL
To his friend, Wei.—LiT (sel.)
War.—GrCt
The women of Yueh.—HoL
Li Yu
Longing for the south country.—LeMw
The **liberator.** Wu-ti, tr. fr. the Chinese by Arthur Waley.—ReBs
Liberty
"Alone in the greenwood must I roam." Unknown.—MoB
Beehive. J. Toomer.—AdIa
Birds. R. Fabrizio.—SmM
Conversation on V. O. Dodson.—HaK
The daybreakers. A. Bontemps.—AdIa—BoA
Frederick Douglass. R. E. Hayden.—AdIa—BoA—HaK
The freedom of the moon. R. Frost.—HoL
From the dark tower. C. Cullen.—AdIa—HaK
The golden bird. J. Stephens.—StS
Harlem gallery. M. B. Tolson.—HaK (sel.)
"The harp that once through Tara's halls." T. Moore.—CoR
Harriet Beecher Stowe. P. L. Dunbar.—HaK
Heartbeat of democracy. V. Brasier.—HuS-3
Korea bound, 1952. W. Childress.—BrA
Land of the free. A. MacLeish.—BrA (sel.)
The sound track.—LiT (sel.)
The liberator. Wu-ti.—ReBs
The minstrel boy. T. Moore.—ClF—CoR
Minuette. J. Stephens.—StS
"No rack can torture me." E. Dickinson.—DiPe
Of old sat freedom. A. Tennyson.—TeP
On liberty and slavery. G. M. Horton.—HaK
On the extinction of the Venetian republic. W. Wordsworth.—PaH—WoP
The proclamation. J. G. Whittier.—HiL
"Quickly fly away." Issa.—IsF
Refugee in America. L. Hughes.—BoH—BrA
Runagate runagate. R. E. Hayden.—AdIa
Shine, Republic. R. Jeffers.—BrA
The slave in the Dismal swamp. H. W. Longfellow.—LoPl
Stanzas. G. G. Byron.—ByP
Status symbol. M. Evans.—AdIa
Sympathy. P. L. Dunbar.—AdIa—BoA
To a linnet in a cage. F. Ledwidge.—CoR
To my son Parker, asleep in the next room. B. Kaufman.—HaK
To the Right Honorable William, Earl of Dartmouth. P. Wheatley.—HaK (sel.)
We're free. C. Williams.—BaH
Why I am a liberal. R. Browning.—BrP
Libraries. See Books and reading
Lice
"A louse crept out of my lady's shift." G. Bottomley.—GrCt
To a louse, on seeing one on a lady's bonnet at church. R. Burns.—BuH—BuPr—CoB
The **lie.** Walter Raleigh.—GrCt
"**Lie** back, daughter, let your head." See First lesson
"**Lie** still, my newly married wife." See The griesly wife
Lieberman, Laurence
The flat.—DuS
Tarpon.—DuS
The **lien.** Adelaide Love.—ThA
Lies. Yevgeny Yevtushenko.—DuS
Life
All thoughts, all creeds. A. Tennyson.—TeP
Are we their equals. H. Geltman.—LeM
"As I went down by Havre de Grace." E. Wylie.—PaH
Ballade by the fire. E. A. Robinson.—BoH
Beehive. J. Toomer.—AdIa
Being nobody. K. Crawford.—LeM
The birds of America. J. Broughton.—BrA
Boy with his hair cut short. M. Rukeyser.—CoR
The breath of life. J. Stephens.—StS
"Busy, curious, thirsty fly." Unknown.—ClF
But no. E. J. Coatsworth.—CoDh
Calm after storm. F. Yerby.—BoA
Carving away in the mist. M. Padgaonkar.—AlPi
The cauld lad's song. Unknown.—GrCt
Circle one. O. Dodson.—BoH—HaK
Cold are the crabs. E. Lear.—BoGj
Compensation. P. L. Dunbar.—BoA
A Coney Island life. J. L. Weil.—BrA—DuR—CoSs

Life—*Continued*
Solace. C. S. Delany.—BoA
A song in the front yard. G. Brooks.—AdIa—BoH
Song of an unlucky man. Unknown.—DoC
The soul's dark cottage. From Of the last verses in the book. E. Waller.—GrCt
The subway. C. K. Rivers.—HaK
"Surgeons must be very careful." E. Dickinson.—DiPe
Symphony. F. Horne.—BoA
"That I did always love." E. Dickinson.—DiPe
"There was a young man of Cadiz." Unknown.—BrLl
"Three jovial gentlemen." D. Hoffman.—CaMb
Tired. F. Johnson.—AdIa—HaK
To Satch. S. Allen.—BoA—HaK
American Gothic.—AdIa
To Satch; or, American Gothic.—MoS
The tree of life. Unknown.—ReBs
The treehouse. J. A. Emanuel.—BoA—BoH
The Trosachs. W. Wordsworth.—WoP
Vain is the glory of the sky. W. Wordsworth.—WoP
Vastness. A. Tennyson.—TeP
Warning. L. Rubin.—DuS
We real cool. G. Brooks.—AdIa—BoH—LaC
What the tramp said. J. Stephens.—StS
What then. W. B. Yeats.—YeR
"While it is alive, until death touches it." E. Dickinson.—DiPe
Who's who. W. H. Auden.—McWs
The wicked hawthorn tree. W. B. Yeats.—YeR
"A woman is a branchy tree." J. Stephens.—StS
The world is too much with us. W. Wordsworth.—GrCt—WoP
"The world turns and the world changes." From The rock. T. S. Eliot.—ArT-3
Your world. G. D. Johnson.—BoA—BoH
Life—Life and death
After-thought. W. Wordsworth.—WoP
Afterwards. T. Hardy.—CoBn—GrCt
Beware. From The tempest. W. Shakespeare.—ShS
Black water and bright air. C. Carrier.—MoS
Celenta at the well of life. From The old wives' tale. G. Peele.—BlO
The voice from the well of life speaks to the maiden.—GrCt
A cherry fair. Unknown.—GrCt
"Dark, dark night." L. Joass.—LeM
Design. R. Frost.—HoL
"Dewdrops on the grass." Issa.—LeOw
Dirge. K. Fearing.—HiL
The doves of my eyes. G. P. Mohanty.—AlPi
Elegy. C. Tichborne.—GrCt
Fly. E. J. Coatsworth.—CoDh
Follow sleep, fall asleep. S. R. Roy.—AlPi
"From far, from eve and morning." From A Shropshire lad. A. E. Housman.—HoL
The goddess. T. De Banville.—GrS
Good taste. C. Logue.—CaD
Hap. T. Hardy.—PlE
"Her losses make our gains ashamed." E. Dickinson.—DiPe
"I am like a slip of comet." G. M. Hopkins.—LiT
"I have no life but this." E. Dickinson.—DiPe
"In snow thou comest." E. Dickinson.—DiPe
Interlude III. K. Shapiro.—DuR
Irritable song. R. Atkins.—BoA
Long I have loved to stroll. T'ao Ch'ien.—GrCt
"Man that is born of a woman." From Job, Bible, Old Testament.—GrCt
Much knowledge, little reason. From Nosce teipsum. J. Davies.—GrCt
The noble. From The prelude. W. Wordsworth.—GrCt
Nobody loses all the time. E. E. Cummings.—McWs
Notes found near a suicide, sels. F. Horne.—BoA (Complete)
To James.—BoA—BoH—HaK
Out, out, brief candle. From Macbeth. W. Shakespeare.—GrCt
The passionate man's pilgrimage. W. Raleigh.—GrCt
The pilgrimage. G. Herbert.—GrCt
"Rain or hail." E. E. Cummings.—DuS
The reckoning. N. L. Madgett.—HaK
Review from Staten island. G. C. Oden.—HaK
The rubaiyát of Omar Khayyám, sels. O. Khayyám
"Myself when young did eagerly frequent."—PlE
"Oh Thou, who man of baser earth didst make."—PlE
"Think, in this batter'd caravanserai"
From The rubaiyát of Omar Khayyám.—GrCt
"Yet ah, that spring should vanish with the rose."—TuW
"She dwelt among the untrodden ways." W. Wordsworth.—WoP
"Since feeling is first." E. E. Cummings.—DuS
Slow, slow, fresh fount. B. Jonson.—GrCt
Song, on reading that the cyclotron has produced cosmic rays, blasted the atom into twenty-two particles, solved the mystery of the transmutation of elements and devil knows what. S. Hoffenstein.—BrSm
Three years she grew. W. Wordsworth.—WoP
" 'Tis so much joy. 'Tis so much joy." E. Dickinson.—DiPe
To daffodils. R. Herrick.—CoBn—HoL
To daffadills.—BoGj
To night. J. B. White.—CoR
Vitae summa brevis spem nos vetat incohare longam. E. Dowson.—GrCt
"Watch long enough, and you will see the leaf." C. Aiken.—HoL
"We wish to be joyful." Unknown.—DoC
The world's a sea. F. Quarles.—GrCt
Life—Morality. See Conduct of life
"Life." Teddy Blake.—BaH

Life ("A crust of bread and a corner to sleep in") Paul Laurence Dunbar.—BoA
Life ("I met four guinea hens today") Alfred Kreymborg.—CoB
Life ("Poverty and hunger in my backyard") Helen Harrington.—BaH
Life after death. Pindar, tr. fr. the Greek by Walter Headlam.—PlE
"**Life** and thought have gone away." See The deserted house
Life half lived. J. C. F. Hölderlin, tr. fr. the German by Geoffrey Grigson.—GrCt
"**Life** has loveliness to sell." See Barter
Life in a love. Robert Browning.—BrP
"**Life** is a dream." See A dream
Life is motion. Wallace Stevens.—MoS
"**Life** is seldom if ever dull." See Gull
The **life** of Jack Sprat, his wife, and his cat. See "Jack Sprat could eat no fat"
"The **life** that tied too tight escapes." Emily Dickinson.—DiPe
"**Life** was a narrow lobby, dark." See For the bicentenary of Isaac Watts
"The **life** we have is very great." Emily Dickinson.—DiPe
"**Life** with yon lambs, like day, is just begun." See Composed on a May morning, 1838
"**Life** would be an easy matter." See If we didn't have to eat
"The **lifeguard's** whistle organized our swimming." See The river
"**Lift** your arms to the stars." John Hall Wheelock.—CoBl
Ligeia, sel. Edgar Allan Poe
  The conqueror worm.—PoP
"A **light** exists in spring." Emily Dickinson.—DiPe
Light for a bride. Unknown, ad. fr. the Japanese by Charlotte B. DeForest.—DePp
The **light-house-keeper's** white-mouse. John Ciardi.—LaPd
"**Light** of morning around her like a sash of glory." See Petrarch for Laura
"A **light** shines bright." See Light for a bride
Light shining out of darkness. William Cowper.—PlE
"**Lighter** than thistledown." See First snow
Lighthearted William. William Carlos Williams.—HaL
"**Lighthearted** William twirled." See Lighthearted William
Lighthouses
  The Eddystone light. Unknown.—CoSs
  Flannan isle. W. W. Gibson.—BlO—CoSs
  "I'd like to be a lighthouse." R. Field.—LaP—LaPd
  The light-house-keeper's white-mouse. J. Ciardi.—LaPd
"**Lightless,** unholy, eldritch thing." See The bat
"**Lightly** a new moon." Kyoshi, tr. fr. the Japanese by Harry Behn.—BeCs
"**Lightly,** O lightly, we bear her along." See Palanquin bearers
Lightning
  At Great Torrington, Devon. Unknown.—BrSm
  "Beyond the dark trees." Shiki.—BeCs
  "I never speak a word." M. Austin
    Rhyming riddles.—ArT-3
"A **lightning** bug got." See Archy and Mehitabel—The flattered lightning bug
"The **lightning** bug has wings of gold." Unknown.—LaC
"**Lightning** flickering." Bashō, tr. fr. the Japanese by Harry Behn.—BeCs
The **lights.** Elizabeth Jane Coatsworth.—CoSb
Lights and lighting. See also Candles; Lamps; Lanterns; Lighthouses
  And yet fools say. G. S. Holmes.—ArT-3
  Blessing for light. Unknown.—ThA
  City in summer. M. C. Livingston.—LiC
  "Eight are the lights." I. Orleans.—ThA
  Grace for light. M. O'Neill.—ThA
  Late corner. L. Hughes.—HaK
  Parliament hill. H. H. Bashford.—ThA
"The **lights** from the parlour and kitchen shone out." See Escape at bedtime
The **lights** in the sky are stars. Kenneth Rexroth.—LiT (sel.)
Lights out. Edward Thomas.—ThG
The **lightship.** Josephine Johnson.—ThA
Like a bug. Aileen Fisher.—FiC
"**Like** a cliff." See Pirate
"**Like** a gaunt, scraggly pine." See Lincoln
"**Like** a glum cricket." See Flight
"**Like** a small gray." See The gray squirrel
"**Like** a tall woman walking across the hayfield." See July storm
"**Like** a wave crest." Emperor Uda, tr. fr. the Japanese by Kenneth Rexroth.—BaS
"**Like** a white cat." See Moonlight
"**Like** acrobats on a high trapeze." Mary O'Neill.—OnH
"**Like** an echo." See Seascape
"**Like** an invader, not a guest." See Winter—Winter's troops
"**Like** any merchant in a store." See The ticket agent
"**Like** any school-girl." See Kanya-Kumari
Like arrows. Elizabeth Jane Coatsworth.—CoSb
"**Like** as the waves make towards the pebbled shore." See Sonnets. William Shakespeare
"**Like** cats, the sand dunes doze." See Evening at the seashore
"**Like** mighty footlights burned the red." Emily Dickinson.—DiPe
"**Like** my cupped hands." Tsurayuki.—BaS
"**Like** rain it sounded till it curved." Emily Dickinson.—DiPe
"**Like** Sieur Montaigne's distinction." See Golfers
"**Like** two doves we left my town." Unknown, tr. fr. the Quechua.—LeO
A **likeness.** Robert Browning.—BrP
Likes and dislikes
  Afterwards. G. Stein.—HaL (sel.)
  Animal crackers. C. Morley.—HoB—ThA
  Autumn woods. J. S. Tippett.—ArT-3—HoB—StF

"F was a fussy flamingo." C. Wells.—BrLl
"A fellow who slaughtered two toucans." Unknown.—BrLl
"A flea and a fly in a flue." Unknown.—BrLl
The fly and the flea.—McWs
"For beauty I am not a star." A. Euwer.—BrLl
"A girl who weighed many an oz." Unknown.—BrLl
"A globe-trotting man from St Paul." F. G. Christgau.—BrLl
"The hands they were made to assist." A. Euwer.—BrLl
"A handsome young noble of Spain." Unknown.—BrLl
"Here's little Jim Nast of Pawtucket." H. Lofting.—BrLl
"His sister named Lucy O'Finner." L. Carroll.—BrLl
"I don't much exactly quite care." D. McCord.—BrLl
"I said to a bug in the sink." J. Ciardi.—BrLl
"I wish that my room had a floor." G. Burgess.—LaP
Relativity and levitation.—BrLl
"I'd rather have fingers than toes." G. Burgess.—BrLl
"An important young man of Quebec." J. H. Pitman.—BrLl
"In New Orleans there lived a young Creole." Unknown.—BrLl
Interplanetary limerick. A. Graham.—BrLl
"It's been a bad year for the moles." D. McCord.—BrLl
"L is for lovable Lena." Unknown.—BrLl
"L was a lachrymose leopard." C. Wells.—BrLl
"A lady there was of Antigua." C. Monkhouse.—BrLl
Leaning on a limerick. E. Merriam.—MeI
A limerick in blank verse. W. S. Gilbert.—BrLl
"A limerick shapes to the eye." D. McCord.—BrLl
"The limerick's lively to write." D. McCord.—BrLl
"A lion emerged from his lair." J. G. Francis.—BrLl
"A little boy down in Natchez." Unknown.—BrLl
"M is for mournful Miss Molly." I. F. Bellows.—BrLl
"A man went a-hunting at Rygate." Mother Goose.—BrLl
"A man who was fond of his skunk." D. McCord.—BrLl
"A medical student named Elias." Unknown.—BrLl
Mistress Towl. Unknown.—VrF
"A modern composer named Brahms." Unknown.—BrLl
"A mouse in her room woke Miss Dowd." Unknown.—BrLl
"A musical lady from Ga." Unknown.—BrLl
"A new servant maid named Maria." Unknown.—BrLl
"No matter how grouchy you're feeling." A. Euwer.—BrLl
"O is an optimist glad." O. Herford.—BrLl
"Of a sudden the great prima-donna." P. West.—BrLl
"An old lady living in Worcester." Unknown.—BrLl
The old man from Dunoon. Unknown.—SmM
Old woman of Bath. Unknown.—VrF
Old woman of Croydon. Unknown.—VrF
Old woman of Ealing. Unknown.—VrF
Old woman of Exeter. Unknown.—VrF
Old woman of Gosport. Unknown.—VrF
Old woman of Harrow. Unknown.—VrF
Old woman of Lynn. Unknown.—VrF
On Monsieur Coué. C. C. Inge.—BrLl
On the poet O'Shaughnessy. D. G. Rossetti.—GrCt
"One day I went out to the zoo." G. T. Johnson.—BrLl
"An opera star named Maria." Unknown.—BrLl
"An oyster from Kalamazoo." Unknown.—BrLl
"Pa followed the pair to Pawtucket." Unknown.—BrLl
"A pirate who hailed from Nertskinski." Unknown.—BrLl
"The poor benighted Hindoo." C. Monkhouse.—BrLl
"The principal food of the Sioux." Unknown.—BrLl
"P's a poetical bore." O. Herford.—BrLl
"A puppy whose hair was so flowing." O. Herford.—BrLl
"A rather polite man of Hawarden." Unknown.—BrLl
A reply from the Akond of Swat. E. T. Scheffauer.—BrLl
"The Reverend Henry Ward Beecher." O. W. Holmes.—BrLl
Henry Ward Beecher.—GrCt
"Said a bad little youngster named Beauchamp." C. Wells.—BrLl
"Said a boy to his teacher one day." Unknown.—BrLl
"Said a crow in the top of a tree." J. Ciardi.—BrLl
"Said a foolish young lady of Wales." L. Reed.—BrLl
"Said a sheep to her child, My dear Ruth." J. G. Francis.—BrLl
"Said an envious, erudite ermine." O. Herford.—BrLl
"Said Mrs Isosceles Tri." C. B. Burgess.—BrLl
"Said the condor, in tones of despair." O. Herford.—BrLl
"Said the snail to the tortoise: You may." O. Herford.—BrLl
"A scientist living at Staines." R. J. P. Hewison.—BrLl

"There was a young lady of Harwich." Unknown.—BrLl
"There was a young lady of Kent." Unknown.—BrLl
"There was a young lady of Niger." Unknown.—BrLl—BrSm—LaPd
"There was a young lady of Oakham." Unknown
Two limericks.—CoBb
"There was a young lady of Ryde." Unknown.—BrSm—LaPd
"There was a young lady of station." L. Carroll.—BrLl
"There was a young lady whose bonnet." Unknown.—BrLl
"There was a young man at the War Office." J. W. Churton.—BrLl
"There was a young man from the city." Unknown.—BrLl
"There was a young man from Trinity." Unknown.—BrLl
"There was a young man, let me say." D. McCord.—BrLl
"There was a young man named Achilles." E. M. Robinson.—BrLl
"There was a young man of Bengal." Unknown.—BrLl
"There was a young man of Cadiz." Unknown.—BrLl
"There was a young man of Calcutta." Unknown.—BrLl
"There was a young man of Herne bay." Unknown.—BrLl
"There was a young man so benighted." Unknown.—BrLl
"There was a young man who was bitten." Unknown.—BrLl
"There was a young person called Smarty." Unknown.—BrLl
"There was a young person named Tate." C. Wells.—BrLl
"There was a young poet of Kew." Unknown.—BrLl
"There was a young prince of Bombay." W. Parke.—BrLl
"There was a young woman of Ayr." Unknown.—BrLl
"There was an old hag of Malacca." Unknown.—BrLl
"There was an old lady named Carr." Unknown.—BrLl
"There was an old lady named Crockett." W. J. Smith.—BrLl—BrSm
"There was an old lady of Brooking." Unknown.—BrLl
"There was an old lady of Rye." Unknown.—BrLl
"There was an old lady of Steen." Unknown.—BrLl
"There was an old lady who said." Unknown.—BrLl
"There was an old maid from Peru." Unknown.—BrLl
"There was an old man from Peru." Unknown.—LaPd
"There was an old man from the Rhine." Unknown.—BrLl
"There was an old man of Blackheath." Unknown.—BrLl—LaP—LaPd
"There was an old man of Calcutta." O. Nash.—BrLl
"There was an old man of Khartoum." Unknown.—BrLl
"There was an old man of Nantucket." Unknown.—BrLl
"There was an old man of Tarentum." Unknown.—BrLl
"There was an old man of the Cape." R. L. Stevenson.—BrLl
"There was an old man, of wherever." D. McCord.—BrLl
"There was an old man who cried Boo." D. McCord.—BrLl
"There was an old man who said, Do." Unknown.—BrLl
"There was an old man who said, Gee." Unknown.—BrLl
"There was an old man who said, Please." E. V. Knox.—BrLl
"There was an old miser named Clarence." O. Nash.—BrLl
"There was an old person of Durban." Unknown.—BrLl
"There was an old person of Fratton." Unknown.—BrLl
"There was an old soldier of Bister." Unknown.—BrLl
"There was once a giraffe who said, What." O. Herford.—BrLl
"There was once a most charming young miss." Unknown.—BrLl
"There was once a small boy in Quebec." R. Kipling.—BrLl
"There was once a young man of Oporta." L. Carroll.—BrLl
"There's a dowager near Sneden Landing." Unknown.—BrLl
"There's a girl out in Ann Arbor, Mich." Unknown.—BrLl
"There's a lady in Kalamazoo." W. Bellamy.—BrLl
"There's a tiresome young man in Bay Shore." Unknown.—BrLl
"There's a tune, said a sly Bengalese." J. Bennett.—BrLl
"There's a very mean man of Belsize." Unknown.—BrLl
"There's nothing in afternoon tea." G. Burgess.—BrLl
"They say that ex-President Taft." Unknown.—BrLl
Thief. Unknown.—CoBb
"This season our tunnips was red." D. McCord.—BrLl
"Though a young man of football physique." Unknown.—BrLl

The dream of all the Springfield writers.—LiP
The eagle that is forgotten.—LiP
Epilogue to the adventures while preaching the gospel of beauty.—LiP
Euclid.—HoL—LiT
An explanation of the grasshopper.—HuS-3
"Factory windows are always broken."—LaC —LiP
The fairy from the apple-seed.—LiP
The flower-fed buffaloes.—ArT-3—BoGj—BrA —CoB—GrCt—LiP
Foreign missions in battle array.—LiP
General William Booth enters into heaven.—LiP
The ghost of the buffaloes.—LiP
A gospel of beauty, sels.—LiP (Complete)
I. The proud farmer
II. The Illinois village
III. On the building of Springfield
Hail to the sons of Roosevelt.—LiP
The haughty snail-king.—HaL
Honor among scamps.—LiP
How Samson bore away the gates of Gaza.—LiP
"I heard Immanuel singing."—LiP
I know all this when gipsy fiddles cry.—LiP
I want to go wandering.—LiP
"I went down into the desert."—LiP
The Illinois village. See A gospel of beauty
In praise of Johnny Appleseed.—HuS-3—LiP
In which Roosevelt is compared to Saul.—LiP
Incense.—LiP
An Indian summer day on the prairie.—HuS-3
The jazz of this hotel.—BoH
The jingo and the minstrel.—LiP
John L. Sullivan, the strong boy of Boston.—LiP
Johnny Appleseed speaks of the apple-blossom amaranth that will come to this city.—LiP
Johnny Appleseed's hymn to the sun.—LiP
Johnny Appleseed's ship comes in.—LiP
Johnny Appleseed's wife from the palace of Eve.—LiP
Kalamazoo.—PaH
The kallyope yell.—LiP
Kansas.—PaH
"King Arthur's men have come again."—LiP
"The king of yellow butterflies."—CoB
The lame boy and the fairy.—LiP
The leaden-eyed.—LiP
The lion.—BrSm
Litany of the heroes.—LiP
The little turtle.—ArT-3—BoGj—HoB—HuS-3 —LaPd—ThA
Love and law.—LiP
Mark Twain and Joan of Arc. See Three poems about Mark Twain
The merciful hand.—LiP
"The moon's the north wind's cooky."—HoB—HuS-3—LaP—LaPd—ThA
"The mouse that gnawed the oak-tree down." —HaL—LiP
My fathers came from Kentucky. See Alexander Campbell
The mysterious cat.—ArT-3—BoGj—GrCt—HuS-3—ThA
Nancy Hanks, mother of Abraham Lincoln.—HiL
A net to snare the moonlight.—LiP
Niagara.—LiP
The North star whispers to the blacksmith's son.—LiP
On the building of Springfield. See A gospel of beauty
"On the road to nowhere."—LiP
Our mother Pocahontas.—LiP
Parvenu.—LiP
The potatoes' dance.—HoB—ThA
The prairie battlements.—LiP
Prologue. See Rhymes to be traded for bread
The proud farmer. See A gospel of beauty
The raft. See Three poems about Mark Twain
A rhyme about an electrical advertising sign. —LiP
A rhymed address to all renegade Campbellites, exhorting them to return. See Alexander Campbell
Rhymes to be traded for bread, sel.
Prologue.—LiP
Roosevelt.—LiP
The Santa Fe trail.—LiP
The sea serpent chantey.—LiP
Sew the flags together.—LiP
Shantung; or, The empire of China is crumbling down.—LiP
So much the worse for Boston.—LiP (sel.)
The sorceress.—LaPd
The soul of a spider.—LiP
The soul of the city receives the gift of the Holy Spirit.—LiP
Springfield magical.—LiP
The Springfield of the far future.—LiP
The statue of old Andrew Jackson.—LiP
Sunset.—ReS
Three poems about Mark Twain.—LiP
I. The raft
II. When the Mississippi flowed in Indiana
III. Mark Twain and Joan of Arc
The town of American visions.—LiP
The tramp's refusal.—LiP
The traveler.—LiP
Two old crows.—HaL
The unpardonable sin.—LiP
The voice of St Francis of Assisi.—LiP
The wedding of the rose and the lotus.—LiP
What the hyena said.—LiP
When Peter Jackson preached in the old church.—LiP
When the Mississippi flowed in Indiana. See Three poems about Mark Twain
Where is the real non-resistant.—LiP
Who knows.—LiP
Why I voted the socialist ticket.—LiP
The would-be merman.—LiP

Lindsay, Vachel (Nichols)—*Continued*
Written in a year when many of my people died. See Alexander Campbell
Yet gentle will the griffin be.—HuS-3—LaPd—ThA
Lindsay, Vachel (Nicholas) (about)
Doctor Mohawk. V. Lindsay.—LiP
Epilogue to the adventures while preaching the gospel of beauty. V. Lindsay.—LiP
"The **line** and plummet guide the tool." See The bricklayer
"A **line** in long array where they wind betwixt green islands." See Cavalry crossing a ford
Line-up for yesterday. Ogden Nash.—MoS
Lineage. Margaret Walker.—HaK
Lines and squares. A. A. Milne.—MiC
Lines composed a few miles above Tintern abbey, on revisiting the banks of the Wye during a tour, July 13, 1798. William Wordsworth.—WoP
Lines scratched in wet cement. Ethel Jacobson.—BrSm
Lines supposed to have been addressed to Fanny Brawne. John Keats.—CoBl
Lines to a movement in Mozart's E-flat symphony. Thomas Hardy.—CoBl
Lines to a nasturtium. Anne Spencer.—BoA
Lines written in early spring. William Wordsworth.—WoP
Lines written in her breviary. Saint Theresa, tr. fr. the Spanish by Henry Wadsworth Longfellow.—PlE
Lines written in Windsor forest. Alexander Pope.—GrS
"**Lingle,** lingle, lang tang." Unknown.—MoB
Link, Lenore M.
Holding hands.—ArT-3—LaP
Link rhymes. See Build-on rhymes
Linnets
The green linnet. W. Wordsworth.—WoP
"I heard a linnet courting." R. Bridges.—ReO
To a linnet in a cage. F. Ledwidge.—CoR
Within the bush. From A rose-bud, by my early walk. R. Burns.—ReBs
The **lion** ("The lion is a kingly beast") Vachel Lindsay.—BrSm
The **lion** ("The lion is a lordly thing") Conrad Aiken.—AiC
Lion ("The lion, ruler over all the beasts") William Jay Smith.—CoB—WeP
The **lion** ("The lion walks behind his bars") Herbert Asquith.—LiT
The **lion** ("Lord, I am king") Carmen Bernos de Gasztold, tr. fr. the French by Rumer Godden.—GaC
The **lion** ("Oh, weep for Mr and Mrs Bryan") Ogden Nash.—BrSm
The **lion** and the fox. Ennis Rees.—ArT-3
The **lion** and the mouse. Richard Scrafton Sharpe.—VrF
"The **lion** and the unicorn." Mother Goose.—BrF—BrMg—MoB—OpF
"A **lion** emerged from his lair." Joseph G. Francis.—BrLl
"A **lion** has a tail and a very fine tail." See In the fashion
"The **lion** heart, the ounce gave active might." See Shepherd song—The gifts of the animals to man
"**Lion-hunger,** tiger leap." See The way of Cape Race
"The **lion** is a kingly beast." See The lion
"The **lion** is a lordly thing." See The lion
"The **lion** ramps around the cage." See Lèse majesté
"The **lion,** ruler over all the beasts." See Lion
"A **lion** too old to have any heart." See The lion and the fox
"The **lion** walks behind his bars." See The lion
Lions
The ass in the lion's skin. Aesop.—ReO
At the lion's cage. P. K. Dufault.—CoB
The captive lion. W. H. Davies.—CoB
Daniel. V. Lindsay.—GrCt—LiP
The Daniel jazz.—SmM
Epigram. Viryamitra.—AlPi
"A handsome young noble of Spain." Unknown.—BrLl
In waste places. J. Stephens.—StS
Inhuman Henry; or, Cruelty to fabulous animals. A. E. Housman.—CoBb
Jim, who ran away from his nurse, and was eaten by a lion. H. Belloc.—BrSm—CoBb—GrCt
Lesè majesté. O. Herford.—CoB
The lion ("The lion is a kingly beast") V. Lindsay.—BrSm
The lion ("The lion is a lordly thing") C. Aiken.—AiC
Lion ("The lion, ruler over all the beasts") W. J. Smith.—CoB—WeP
The lion ("The lion walks behind his bars") H. Asquith.—LiT
The lion ("Lord, I am king") C. B. de Gasztold.—GaC
The lion ("Oh, weep for Mr and Mrs Bryan") O. Nash.—BrSm
The lion and the fox. E. Rees.—ArT-3
The lion and the mouse. R. S. Sharpe.—VrF
"The lion and the unicorn." Mother Goose.—BrF—BrMg—MoB—OpF
"A lion emerged from his lair." J. G. Francis.—BrLl
The lion's skeleton. C. T. Turner.—ReO
The little girl found. W. Blake.—BlP
Why no one pets the lion at the zoo. J. Ciardi.—DuR
The wolf and the lioness. E. Rees.—ArT-3
The **lion's** skeleton. Charles Tennyson Turner.—ReO
Lippa, David
Haiku.—LeM
Lisa's fingerprints. Mary O'Neill.—OnF
"**Listen.**" See November night
"**Listen** here, Joe." See Without benefit of declaration
"**Listen,** lords, in good intent." See The Canterbury tales—The ballad of Sir Thopas

"**Listen**, Miranda is playing magical music." See Magical music
"**Listen**, my children, and you shall hear." See Tales of a wayside inn—Paul Revere's ride
"**Listen.** The wind is still." See Spring thunder
"**Listen** to me there have." See Archy and Mehitabel—Freddy the rat perishes
Listen to the unheard. Claudia Lewis.—LeP
"**Listen**, what stillness." Bashō, tr. fr. the Japanese by Harry Behn.—BeCs
The **listeners.** Walter De La Mare.—HuS-3
Lister, R. P.
The albatross.—CoSs
The rhinoceros.—CoB
The **litany** of the dark people. Countee Cullen. —PlE
Litany of the heroes. Vachel Lindsay.—LiP
Literary love. Harry Kemp.—BoH
Literature: The god, its ritual. Merrill Moore.—DuS
Litter of pigs. Fred Lape.—CoB
Little, Malcolm (Malcolm X) (about)
A poem for black hearts. L. Jones.—AdIa
Little. Dorothy Aldis.—ArT-3
"A **little** after twilight." See The stranger
"**Little** bat, quick little bat." See A round trip
"**Little** beast behind the rafter." See Hospitality
The **little** beggar girl. Ann and Jane Taylor.—VrF
"**Little** Betty Blue." Mother Goose.—GrT—HuS-3 —OpF
Little Big Horn, Battle of, 1876
Custer's last charge. F. Whittaker.—HiL
Little Billee. William Makespeace Thackeray.—BlO—BrSm—CoSs
"**Little** Billy Breek." Mother Goose.—BrMg
"**Little** bird flitting." Bashō, tr. fr. the Japanese by Harry Behn.—BeCs
"**Little** bird, your leg is hurt." See Playing with a pet bird
The **little** black boy. William Blake.—BlP
The **little** black dog. Mother Goose.—BrMg
"The **little** black dog ran round the house." See The little black dog
The **little** black hen. A. A. Milne.—MiC
"A **little** black thing among the snow." See The chimney sweeper.
Little Blue Ben. Mother Goose.—BrMg
"**Little** Blue Ben, who lives in the glen." See Little Blue Ben
"**Little** Blue Shoes." Kate Greenaway.—ArT-3
"**Little** Bo-peep." See "Little Bo-peep has lost her sheep"
"**Little** Bo-peep has lost her sheep." Mother Goose.—HuS-3—WiMg
"Little Bo-peep."—BrMg—OpF
"**Little** Bob Robin." Mother Goose.—ReOn
The **little** boy. See "Little boy, little boy, where were you born"
The **little** boy ("There was a little boy went into a barn") Mother Goose.—BrMg
"**Little** Boy Blue." See "Little Boy Blue, come blow your horn"
Little Boy Blue. John Crowe Ransom.—WeP
"**Little** Boy Blue, come blow up your horn." See "Little Boy Blue, come blow your horn"
"**Little** Boy Blue, come blow your horn." Mother Goose.—HuS-3—OpO
"Billy Boy Blue, come blow me your horn."—GrT
Boy Blue.—BrMg
"Little Boy Blue."—ReMg
"Little Boy Blue, come blow up your horn."—WiMg
Mother Goose rhymes, 3.—HoB
"A **little** boy down in Natchez." Unknown.—BrLl
The **little** boy found. William Blake.—BlP
"The **little** boy is fishing." See The fisherman
"**Little** boy kneels at the foot of the bed." See Vespers
"**Little** boy, little boy, where were you born." Mother Goose.—OpF
The little boy.—BrMg—ReOn
The **little** boy lost ("Father, father, where are you going") William Blake.—BlP
A **little** boy lost ("Nought loves another as itself") William Blake.—BlP
"The **little** boy lost in the lonely fen." See The little boy found
"A **little** boy stood on the corner." See December
"A **little** boy wandering alone in the night." See The boy in the barn
"**Little** boys and little maidens." See Little catkins
Little boys of Texas. Robert P. Tristram Coffin. —BrSm
"The **little** boys of Texas prance." See Little boys of Texas
"The **little** bridge goes hop-across." See Bridges
Little brother's secret. Katherine Mansfield.—ArT-3—ThA
"**Little** brown boy." See Poem
"**Little** brown brother, oh, little brown brother." See Baby seed song
Little busy bee. Isaac Watts.—HuS-3
"The **little** caterpillar creeps." See Cocoon
Little catkins. Alexander Blok, tr. fr. the Russian by Babette Deutsch.—PlE
Little Charlie Chipmunk. Helen Cowles LeCron. —ArT-3
"**Little** Charlie Chipmunk was a talker. Mercy me." See Little Charlie Chipmunk
"A **little** child." Issa, tr. fr. the Japanese by Nobuyuki Yuasa.—LeMw
"**Little** child, good child, go to sleep." See Evening song
Little children. Tom Nakai Tsosie.—BaH
"**Little** children, never give." See Kindness to animals
"**Little** children, run along." See Little children
Little city. Robert Horan.—CoB
A **little** cock sparrow. See "A little cock sparrow sat on a green tree"
"A **little** cock sparrow sat on a green tree." Mother Goose.—WiMg
A little cock sparrow.—BrMg

"A **little** colt—broncho, loaned to the farm." See The broncho that would not be broken
The **little** coward. Ann and Jane Taylor.—VrF
"**Little** Dicky Dilver." See Dicky Dilver
The **little** donkey. Unknown.—VrF
Little donkey close your eyes. Margaret Wise Brown.—LaP—LaPd
"**Little** donkey on the hill." See Little donkey close your eyes
"A **little** egg." Tina Anthony.—LeM
Little elegy ("Here lies resting, out of breath") X. J. Kennedy.—BoGj
Little elegy ("Withouten you") Elinor Wylie.—HaL
The **little** elf. See The little elf-man
The **little** elf-man. John Kendrick Bangs.—ArT-3—HoB
  I met a little elf man.—HuS-3
  The little elf.—LaPd—ThA
"**Little** eyes see pretty things." Unknown.—WyC
Little fable. Roy Fuller.—CaD
"A **little** fairy comes at night." See Queen Mab
"**Little** Fairy Flitabout had such a craze for fleetness." See The careless fairy
Little Fanny. Unknown.—VrF
A **little** fish. Hilary-Anne Farley.—LeM
"The **little** fish cries." David Recht.—LeM
"A **little** fish swims in the water." See A little fish
The **little** fish that would not do as it was bid. Ann and Jane Taylor.—VrF
"**Little** fishes in a brook." See Fishes
"The **little** flowers came through the ground." See At Easter time
"**Little** fly." See The fly
The **little** fly. Unknown, tr. fr. the Yaqui.—LeO
Little folks in the grass. Annette Wynne.—ThA
The **little** fox. Marion Edey.—ArT-3
Little Freddy. Unknown.—VrF
"**Little** garden at the gate." Issa, tr. fr. the Japanese by R. H. Blyth.—IsF—LeOw
"**Little** General Monk." See General Monk
A **little** girl. See "When I was a little girl (about seven years old)"
"A **little** girl (dressed)." Mother Goose.—OpF
Little girl ("Little girl, little girl") Mother Goose.—BrMg
The **little** girl and the turkey. Dorothy Aldis.—AgH
The **little** girl found. William Blake.—BlP
"**Little** girl, little girl." See Little girl
A **little** girl lost ("Children of the future age") William Blake.—BlP
The **little** girl lost ("In futurity") William Blake.—BlP
A **little** girl, Rumi's fancy. Naresh Guha, tr. fr. the Bengali by Jyotirmoy Datta.—AlPi
"The **little** girl said." See The little girl and the turkey
The **little** girl that beat her sister. Ann and Jane Taylor.—VrF
"The **little** goat." See April
"**Little** gray cuckoo." Bashō, tr. fr. the Japanese by Harold G. Henderson.—LeMw
"**Little** gray tree." See The little maple
"A **little** green bird sat on a fence rail." Mother Goose
  Mother Goose rhymes, 22.—HoB
The **little** green orchard. Walter De La Mare.—ArT-3
Little Gustava. Celia Thaxter.—HoB
"**Little** Gustava sits in the sun." See Little Gustava
Little husband.—BrMg—VrF
"**Little** Indian, Sioux or Crow." See Foreign children
"**Little** Jack Dandersprat." Mother Goose.—OpF
  My first suitor.—BrMg
"**Little** Jack Dandy-prat." See "Little Jack Dandersprat"
"**Little** Jack Horner." Mother Goose.—HuS-3—OpF—WiMg
  Jack Horner.—BrMg
  Mother Goose rhymes, 7.—HoB
"**Little** Jenny Wren." See "Jenny Wren fell sick"
"The **little** Jesus came to town." See A Christmas folk-song
Little John Bottlejohn. Laura E. Richards.—LaPd
"**Little** John Bottlejohn lived on the hill." See Little John Bottlejohn
"**Little** Johnny-jump-up said." See Wise Johnny
The **little** jumping girls. See "Jump—jump—jump"
Little jumping Joan. See "Here am I, little jumping Joan"
Little Katy. Unknown.—BrSm
"**Little** Katy wandered where." See Little Katy
Little King Boggen. See "Little King Boggen, he built a fine hall"
"**Little** King Boggen, he built a fine hall." Mother Goose.—HuS-3
  Little King Boggen.—ReOn
The **little** kittens. Eliza Lee Follen.—ArT-3
"**Little** lad, little lad." Mother Goose.—GrT—TuW
"**Little** Lady Wren." Tom Robinson.—ArT-3
"**Little** lamb, who made thee." See The lamb
The **little** lambs. Unknown.—VrF
The **little** land. Robert Louis Stevenson.—HuS-3
A **little** learning. See An essay on criticism
"A **little** learning is a dang'rous thing." See An essay on criticism—A little learning
"A **little** light is going by." See Firefly
"A **little** madness in the spring." Emily Dickinson.—DiPe
A **little** maid. Mother Goose.—BrMg
"**Little** maid, little maid, where have you been." Mother Goose.—OpF
"**Little** maid, pretty maid, whither goest thou." Mother Goose.—OpF
  The milkmaid.—BrMg
The **little** man. See "There was a little man, and he had a little gun"
The **little** man and the little maid. See Memoirs of the little man and the little maid

"**Little** man in coal pit." See Putting on a nightgown
The **little** maple. Charlotte Zolotow.—BrSg
"The **little** men of meadow land." See Adventure
"**Little** Miss Moon." Unknown, ad. fr. the Japanese by Charlotte B. DeForest.—DePp
"**Little** Miss Muffet (crouched)." See Rhymes for a modern nursery
"**Little** Miss Muffet." Mother Goose.—BrMg—HuS-3—OpF—WiMg
  Mother Goose rhymes, 4.—HoB
"**Little** Miss Tuckett." Mother Goose.—OpF
Little moppet. See "I had a little moppety, I put it in my pockety"
A **little** morning music. Delmore Schwartz.—CoBn
"A **little** mountain spring I found." See The spring
"**Little** mouse in gray velvet." See Mouse
Little nag. Mother Goose.—BrMg
"**Little** Nancy Etticoat." Mother Goose.—BrMg—GrCt—HuS-3
  "Little Nanny Etticoat."—ArT-3
  Mother Goose rhymes, 30.—HoB
"**Little** Nanny Etticoat." See "Little Nancy Etticoat"
"The **little** newt." See The newt
The **little** nut tree. See "I had a little nut tree; nothing would it bear"
"A **little** old man of Derby." Mother Goose.—ReMg
  Man of Derby.—BrMg
"A **little** old woman." See Behind the waterfall
"**Little** one, come to my knee." See A story for a child
Little Orphant Annie. James Whitcomb Riley.—CoBb—HoB—HuS-3
"**Little** Orphant Annie's come to our house to stay." See Little Orphant Annie
"**Little** park that I pass through." See Ellis park
The **little** peach. Eugene Field.—AgH—BrSm
"A **little** peach in the orchard grew." See The little peach
Little people. Myra Cohn Livingston.—LiC
"**Little** people, thin people, dance on my arm." See Little people
"**Little-Plum-Tree** village." Issa, tr. fr. the Japanese by R. H. Blyth.—IsF
"**Little** Poll Parrot." See Poll Parrot
"**Little** Pollie Pillikins." See A—apple pie
"**Little** Polly Flinders." Mother Goose.—OpF
  Polly Flinders.—BrMg
"The **little** priest of Felton." See The brave priest
"**Little** Prince Carl he stole away." See What the Lord High Chamberlain said
Little puss. Unknown.—VrF
Little rain. Elizabeth Madox Roberts.—ArT-3—BrSg
The **little** red sled. Jocelyn Bush.—ArT-3
"**Little** Robin Redbreast (sat upon a rail)." Mother Goose.—HuS-3
Little Rock, Arkansas
  The Chicago Defender sends a man to Little Rock, Fall, 1967. G. Brooks.—BoA
The **little** rose tree. Rachel Field.—ArT-3—BrSg
"A **little** saint." See Porcupine
"A **little** saint best fits a little shrine." See A ternarie of littles, upon a pipkin of jellie sent to a lady
"A **little** seed." See Maytime magic
"**Little** seeds we sow in spring." Else Holmelund Minarik.—BrSg
The **little** sempstress. Mary Elliott.—VrF
"**Little** sister, come away." See Come and play in the garden
"**Little** snail." See Snail
Little snail. Hilda Conkling.—ArT-3
"**Little** snail, little snail (with your hard)." Unknown.—WyC
"**Little** song." Carmen Bernos de Gasztold, tr. fr. the French by Rumer Godden.—GaC
A **little** song of life. Lizette Woodworth Reese.—ThA
"**Little** sparrow." Issa, tr. fr. the Japanese by R. H. Blyth.—LeOw
A **little** squirrel. Unknown.—ArT-3
Little star. See The star ("Twinkle, twinkle, little star")
"**Little** stilts are for learning to keep your balance on." See Stilts
Little talk. Aileen Fisher.—LaP
"**Little** Tee-wee." See Tee-wee's boat
Little things, Importance of
  "For want of a nail." Mother Goose.—ReMg
    A nail.—BrMg
  A ternarie of littles, upon a pipkin of jellie sent to a lady. R. Herrick.—BoGj
  Trifle. G. D. Johnson.—BoA—BoH
Little things. James Stephens.—ArT-3—BoGj—CoB—LaPd—PlE—StS
"**Little** things that run and quail." See Little things
Little Thomas. F. Gwynne Evans.—CoBb
"**Little** Tog Dogget." See Colly my cow
"**Little** Tom Tickleby." See Tom Tickleby and his nose
"**Little** Tommy Tittlemouse." Mother Goose.—OpF—ReMg
  Tommy Tittlemouse.—BrMg
"**Little** Tommy Tucker." Mother Goose.—OpF—WiMg
  Tommy Tucker.—BrMg
"**Little** tree." See Chanson innocente
Little Trotty Wagtail. John Clare.—BlO
"**Little** Trotty Wagtail, he went in the rain." See Little Trotty Wagtail
The **little** trumpet. Corrado Govoni, tr. fr. the Italian by Carlo L. Golino.—LiT
The **little** turtle. Vachel Lindsay.—ArT-3—BoGj—HoB—HuS-3—LaPd—ThA
The **little** vagabond. William Blake.—BlP
The **little** waves of Breffny. Eva Gore-Booth.—PaH
The **little** whistler. Frances M. Frost.—ArT-3—HoB—HuS-3—LaPd

"Lo, here the gentle yak, weary of rest." See Bird thou never wert
"Lo, I have opened unto you the wide gates of my being." See Psalm to my belovèd
"Lo, in a valley peopled thick with trees." See The dying crane
"Lo, in the mute, mid wilderness." See Nepenthe—The unicorn
"Lo, sweeten'd with the summer light." See The lotos-eaters
"Lo, the bat with leathern wing." See Songs from an island in the moon
"Lo, the moon's self." See One word more—Phases of the moon
"Lo, 'tis a gala night." See Ligeia—The conqueror worm
"Load of hay." Mother Goose.—TuW
The **loaves.** Ronald Everson.—DoW
Lob-lie-by-the-fire. Walter De La Mare.—DeBg
Lobster cove shindig. Lillian Morrison.—CoBn
The **lobster** quadrille. See Alice's adventures in wonderland
Lobsters
Conversion. J. T. Lillie.—CoB
The lobster quadrille. From Alice's adventures in wonderland. L. Carroll.—HoB
The mock turtle's song.—GrCt
Lobsters in the window. W. D. Snodgrass.—DuS
Lobsters in the window. W. D. Snodgrass.—DuS
Localities. Carl Sandburg.—BrA
"The **Loch** Achray was a clipper tall." See The yarn of the Loch Achray
Lochinvar. See Marmion
"**Lock** the dairy door." See Cock and hen
"**Locked** arm in arm they cross the way." See Tableau
Locked out. Robert Frost.—LiT
Lockhart, John Gibson
The wandering knight's song.—GrCt
Locksley hall, sel. Alfred Tennyson
In the spring.—CoBn—TeP
Locomotives. See Railroads
Locust trees
To the young locust tree outside the window. C. Lewis.—LeP
Locusts (Insect)
"Listen, what stillness." Bashō.—BeCs
Lodged. Robert Frost.—BrSg
Lofting, Hugh
"Here's little Jim Nast of Pawtucket."—BrLl
Picnic.—BoGj
The **lofty** sky. Edward Thomas.—ThG
"**Log,** bog, and frog." See Frog in a bog
Logan, John
The brothers: Two Saltimbanques.—DuS
The picnic.—CoBl—DuS
Logic
The deacon's masterpiece; or, The wonderful one-hoss shay. O. W. Holmes.—HuS-3
Logue, Christopher
Good taste.—CaD
"**Lola.**" See Balcony
Lollocks. Robert Graves.—GrCt
London, England
Buckingham palace. A. A. Milne.—LaPd—MiC
The fire of London. From Annus mirabilis. J. Dryden.—GrCt
"Hey diddle dinkety poppety pet." Mother Goose.—OpF
"I'll give you a pin to stick in your thumb." Unknown.—MoB
Introduction. W. Darton.—VrF
London ("I wander thro' each charter'd street") W. Blake.—BlP—GrCt (sel.)
London ("There souls of men are bought and sold") From The human image. W. Blake. —GrCt
London beautiful. R. LeGallienne.—PaH
The London bobby. A. Guiterman.—PaH
"London bridge is broken down." Mother Goose.—OpF
London bridge.—BrMg—GrCt
London, 1802. W. Wordsworth.—WoP
London lackpenny. Unknown.—GrCt
London rain. N. B. Turner.—ThA
London snow. R. Bridges.—CoBn—GrCt
"Mother and father and Uncle Dick." Mother Goose.—OpF
The smoking stick.—BrMg
On London bridge, and the stupendous sight, and structure thereof. J. Howell.—GrCt
"Oranges and lemons." Mother Goose.—BrMg —OpF—SmM—WiMg
London bells.—GrCt
Parliament hill. H. H. Bashford.—ThA
Poverty in London. From London. S. Johnson. —GrCt
"See-saw, Jack in the hedge." Mother Goose. —OpF
"See-saw, sacradown." Mother Goose.—OpF
"See-saw, sacaradown."—ReMg
To the city of London. W. Dunbar.—GrCt
Troynovant. T. Dekker.—GrCt
Yesterday in Oxford street. R. Fyleman.—ArT-3—LaPd
London, sel. Samuel Johnson
Poverty in London.—GrCt
London ("I wander thro' each charter'd street") William Blake.—BlP—GrCt (sel.)
London ("There souls of men are bought and sold") See The human image
London beautiful. Richard LeGallienne.—PaH
London bells. See "Oranges and lemons"
The **London** bobby. Arthur Guiterman.—PaH
London bridge. See "London bridge is broken down"
"**London** bridge is broken down." Mother Goose. —OpF
London bridge.—BrMg—GrCt
London, 1802. William Wordsworth.—WoP
"**London,** I heard one say, no more is fair." See London beautiful
London lackpenny. Unknown.—GrCt
London rain. Nancy Byrd Turner.—ThA
London snow. Robert Bridges.—CoBn—GrCt
"**London,** thou art of townes A per se." See To the city of London

"**London,** to thee I do present the merry month of May." See The knight of the burning pestle—The month of May
Lone dog. Irene Rutherford McLeod.—ArT-3—CoB—LaPd—ThA
"**Lone** flower, hemmed in with snows, and white as they." See To a snowdrop
"A **lone** gull." Kazue Mizumura.—MiI
Loneliness
Alone. K. Mann.—BaH
"Birds are flying past me." D. Fong.—BaH
The conquered one. D. Jackson.—BaH
Desert. L. Hughes.—HaK
"Eating a meal." Issa.—LeOw
"An empty bed." S. Silon.—LeM
"For you fleas too." Issa.—IsF
The forsaken merman. M. Arnold.—BlO—CoSs—SmM
The garden of bamboos. Unknown.—CoBl
"In my loneliness." Ryōzen.—BaS
"It is a lonesome glee." E. Dickinson.—DiPe
Kid in the park. L. Hughes.—LaC
The land of heart's desire. W. B. Yeats.—PaH
Loneliness ("I was about to go, and said so") B. Jenkins.—DuR
Loneliness ("No sky at all") Hashin.—LiT
The lonely boy. Unknown.—DePp
Nicholas Nye. W. De La Mare.—BlO—CoB—HoB—ReO
Now in the stillness. E. J. Coatsworth.—CoDh
Oh lady. S. Menashe.—SmM
On a lonely spray. J. Stephens.—StS
The path of the lonely ones. G. E. Varela.—BaH
The preacher: Ruminates behind the sermon. G. Brooks.—LiT
A sad song about Greenwich village. F. Park.—LaC
This old countryside. M. J. Fuller.—BaH
"Turned towards the moon." Yakamochi.—BaS
"Upon the mountain edge." Emperor Okamoto.—BaS
What she said. M. Kantan.—AlPi
"While I stay alone." Unknown.—BaS
Young girl: Annam. P. Colum.—HaL
Loneliness ("I was about to go, and said so") Brooks Jenkins.—DuR
Loneliness ("No sky at all") Hashin, tr. fr. the Japanese by Harold G. Henderson.—LiT
"**Lonely** and ugly." See The toad
The **lonely** boy. Unknown, ad. fr. the Japanese by Charlotte B. DeForest.—DePp
"A **lonely** lake, a lonely shore." See The loon
"**Lonely** little question mark." See Kid in the park
The **lonely** scarecrow. James Kirkup.—BlO—CaD—LaPd
"A **lonely,** sickly old man." See Casual lines
"A **lonely** task it is to plow." See Plowing: A memory
"The **lonely** troll he sat on a stone." See The adventures of Tom Bombadil—Perry-the-winkle
Lonesome water. Roy Helton.—BrA
Long, Elizabeth-Ellen
Mountain medicine.—BrA
"**Long** ago, long ago." See Ballad of the robin
The **long** black grave. Elizabeth Jane Coatsworth.—CoDh
"The **long** canoe." See Lullaby
"The **long,** gray moss that softly swings." See In Louisiana
"A **long** green swell." See Chill of the eve
Long I have loved to stroll. T'ao Ch'ien, tr. fr. the Chinese by William Acker.—GrCt
"**Long** I have loved to stroll among the hills and marshes." See Long I have loved to stroll
Long Island, New York
Bonac. J. H. Wheelock.—PaH
Long, long ago. Unknown.—ArT-3—LaPd—LaPh
"**Long** long pillows of lavender-flower." See Bees in lavender
"**Long** man legless, came to the door staffless." Mother Goose.—OpF
"The **long** night." Shiki, tr. fr. the Japanese by R. H. Blyth.—LeMw
Long-nosed elf. Unknown, ad. fr. the Japanese by Charlotte B. DeForest.—DePp
"**Long** poles support the branches of the orchards in New Hampshire." See Apples in New Hampshire
The **long** road, sel. John Gray
Gazelles and unicorns.—GrCt
"The **long-rolling.**" See The main-deep
Long sleep. David Short.—LeM
The **long** small room. Edward Thomas.—ThG
"The **long** small room that showed willows in the west." See The long small room
Long summer. Laurie Lee.—CoBn
A **long** time ago. Unknown.—CoSs
"A **long** time, many years, we've had these wars." See On a certain engagement south of Seoul
Long trip. Langston Hughes.—ArT-3
"The **long** whip lingers." See Horses
"A **long** white barn." Unknown.—GrCt
"**Long** years ago I blazed a trail." See The pioneer
Longfellow, Henry Wadsworth
Aftermath.—LoPl
The arrow and the song.—LoPl
The arsenal at Springfield.—LoPl
Azrael. See Tales of a wayside inn
The belfry of Bruges.—PaH
Belisarius.—LoPl
The bell of Atri. See Tales of a wayside inn
Birds of passage, sel.
The leap of Roushan Beg.—HuS-3
The broken oar.—LoPl
The building of the ship.—LoPl
The chamber over the gate.—LoPl
Chaucer.—LoPl
The children's hour.—TuW
Christmas bells.—LaPh (sel.)
The cross of snow.—LoPl
Dante.—LoPl

The day is done.—LoPl
Daybreak.—LoPl
Daylight and moonlight.—LoPl
Divina commedia.—LoPl
A Dutch picture.—LoPl
The emperor's bird's-nest.—ReBs
Evangeline, sel.
Prologue.—LoPl
Excelsior.—LoPl
The fire of drift-wood.—LoPl
God's-acre.—LoPl
Helen of Tyre.—GrS
Hiawatha's childhood. See The song of Hiawatha
Hiawatha's sailing. See The song of Hiawatha
Hymn to the night.—LoPl
In the churchyard at Cambridge.—LoPl
Jemima. See "There was a little girl, and she had a little curl"
The Jewish cemetery at Newport.—LoPl—PaH
The leap of Roushan Beg. See Birds of passage
The legend beautiful. See Tales of a wayside inn
The legend of Rabbi Ben Levi. See Tales of a wayside inn
Lines written in her breviary. tr.—PlE
Mezzo cammin.—LoPl
Michael Angelo, A fragment.—LoPl (sel.)
Morituri salutamus, sel.
A Roman legend.—LoPl
My lost youth.—BoGj—CoR—LoPl—PaH
Nature.—CoBn
The occultation of Orion.—LoPl
The old bridge at Florence.—LoPl—PaH
Paul Revere's ride. See Tales of a wayside inn
Prologue. See Evangeline
The rainy day.—LoPl
A Roman legend. See Morituri salutamus
Rondel. tr.—HoL
The ropewalk.—LoPl
Sand of the desert in an hour-glass.—LoPl
Seaweed.—LoPl
Serenade. See The Spanish student
The sermon of St Francis.—LoPl
The slave in the Dismal swamp.—LoPl
The slave singing at midnight.—LoPl
Snow-flakes. See Snowflakes
Snowflakes.—GrCt
Snow-flakes.—LoPl
The song of Hiawatha, sels.
Hiawatha's childhood.—ArT-3—HuS-3
Hiawatha's sailing.—LoPl
The sound of the sea.—LoPl
The Spanish student, sel.
Serenade.—LoPl
Tales of a wayside inn, sels.
Azrael.—LoPl
The bell of Atri.—LoPl
The legend beautiful.—LoPl
The legend of Rabbi Ben Levi.—LoPl
Paul Revere's ride.—ArT-3—HiL—HuS-3—LoPl
"There was a little girl, and she had a little curl." at.—OpF—WiMg
Jemima.—BlO—CoBb
Mother Goose rhymes, 15.—HoB
"The tide rises, the tide falls."—CoSs—GrCt—LoPl
The tides.—LoPl
To the driving cloud.—GrCt—LoPl
The village blacksmith.—HuS-3—LoPl—TuW
Vox populi.—LoPl
The warden of the Cinque ports.—LoPl
The warning.—LoPl
The wreck of the Hesperus.—LoPl
Longfellow, Henry Wadsworth (about)
The cross of snow. H. W. Longfellow.—LoPl
Mezzo cammin. H. W. Longfellow.—LoPl
Longing for the south country. Li Yu, tr. fr. the Chinese by Ch'u Ta-kao.—LeMw
"**Longing** pleases me like sweet fragrance." Unknown.—DoC
Look ("I eat from the dish of the world") John Smith.—SmM
The **look** ("Strephon kissed me in the spring") Sara Teasdale.—BoH—CoBl
"**Look** ahead, look astern, look the weather and the lee." See The coasts of high Barbary
"**Look** at me." See Here I am
"**Look** at the eyes look from my tail." See Peacock and nightingale
"**Look** at this village boy, his head is stuffed." See Farm child
Look at your copy. Elizabeth Turner.—VrF
"**Look** back with longing eyes and know that I will follow." See The flight
Look, Edwin. Edna St Vincent Millay.—BoGj
"**Look,** Edwin. Do you see that boy." See Look, Edwin
"**Look** how the wild geese fly and fly." See Wild geese flying
"**Look.** Look, the spring is come." See The first spring morning
"**Look** one way and the sun is going down." See The mockingbird
"**Look** over there." See Mountains on mountains
"**Look** out how you use proud words." See Primer lesson
"**Look** out, look out." See Jack Frost
"**Look,** says the catkin." See Time for rabbits
"**Look** snail." Issa, tr. fr. the Japanese by R. H. Blyth.—IsF—LeOw
"**Look,** we don't give a hoot if Zippo-Fasteners have gone to war." See Memorial to the great big beautiful self-sacrificing advertisers
"**Look,** what thy soul holds dear, imagine it." See King Richard II—Mock at sorrow
Looking for a sunset bird in winter. Robert Frost.—ReBs
Looking in the album. Vern Rutsala.—DuS
Looking through space. Aileen Fisher.—FiI
Looking up at leaves. Barbara Howes.—CoBn
Loomis, Charles Battell
"A teacher whose spelling's unique."—BrLl

The **loon.** Lew Sarett.—BoH
"A **loon** I thought it was." Unknown, tr. fr. the Chippewa.—LeO
Loons
Chain. P. Petrie.—CoB
The loon. L. Sarett.—BoH
"A loon I thought it was." Unknown.—LeO
Three. E. J. Coatsworth.—CoSb
"**Loping** along on the day's patrol." See The sheepherder
"The **loping** in the darkness, here, now there." See Death of a dog
Lorca, Federico García
Balcony.—LiT
Ballad of the little square.—LiT
Half moon.—LiT
The lizard is crying.—LiT
Song.—SmM
Silly song.—LiT
Song. See The lizard is crying
"**Lord.**" See The prayer of the butterfly
"**Lord.**" See The prayer of the little pig
"**Lord** (I am the cat)." See The prayer of the cat
"**Lord,** by whose breath all souls and seeds are living." See Hymn
"**Lord,** confound this surly sister." See The curse
"**Lord,** do not be displeased." See The camel
Lord, have mercy on us. Thomas Nashe.—GrCt
"**Lord,** I am king." See The lion
The **Lord** is my shepherd. See Psalms—Psalm 23
"The **Lord** is my shepherd; I shall not want." See Psalms—Psalm 23
"**Lord,** Lord—these miracles, the streets, all say." See Stone too can pray
"The **Lord** of all, who reigned supreme." See Adon 'Olam
Lord of jesters, prince of fellows. Peggy Bennett.—CoB
Lord Randal. Unknown.—ClF
"**Lord,** shall I always go in black." See The fly
"**Lord,** the Roman hyacinths are blooming in bowls and." See A song for Simeon
"**Lord**—Thine the day." Dag Hammarskjöld, tr. by W. H. Auden and Leif Sjöberg.—PlE
"**Lord,** thou hast been our dwelling place." See Psalms—Psalm 90
"**Lord,** thou hast given me a cell." See Thanksgiving to God, for his house
Lord Ullin's daughter. Thomas Campbell.—CoR
Lord Waterford. Unknown.—GrCt
"**Lord** Waterford is dead, says the Shan Van Vocht." See Lord Waterford
"**Lord,** when I look at lovely things which pass." See In the fields
"**Lord,** who has inlaid." See The lizard
"**Lord,** you try for a little while." See The snail
"**Lord,** your deep has closed over me." See The starfish
"**Lord's** lost Him His mockingbird." See Mourning poem for the queen of Sunday
The **Lord's** prayer. See Gospel according to Matthew
Lorentz, Pare
"Black spruce and Norway pine." See The river
"Down the Yellowstone, the Milk, the White and Cheyenne." See The river
The river, sels.
"Black spruce and Norway pine."—BrA
"Down the Yellowstone, the Milk, the White and Cheyenne."—BrA
Loss. Paul Éluard, tr. fr. the French by Patricia Terry.—HoL
Loss of the Royal George. William Cowper.—CoSs
On the loss of the Royal George.—CoR
Lost ("Desolate and lone") Carl Sandburg.—DuR—LaPd
Lost ("He lost it over the dark gray hills") Eve Recht.—LeM
Lost ("I have a little turtle") David McCord.—McE
Lost ("I shall remember chuffs the train") Harry Behn.—BeG
The **lost** cat. E. V. Rieu.—ArT-3—CoB
Lost graveyards. Elizabeth Jane Coatsworth.—CoDh
The **lost** leader. Robert Browning.—BrP
A **lost** snowflake. Unknown, ad. fr. the Japanese by Charlotte B. DeForest.—DePp
The **lost** son. Theodore Roethke.—LiT (sel.)
The **lost** star. Eleanor Farjeon.—FaT
The **lost** tribe. Ruth Pitter.—HoL
The **lost** world. Randall Jarrell.—LiT (sel.)
The **lotos-eaters.** Alfred Tennyson.—ClF (sel.)—GrCt (sel.)—PaH (sel.)—TeP
"**Loud** he sang the psalm of David." See The slave singing at midnight
"**Loud** nights and the creaking." See Night and noises
A **loud** proud someone. J. Ciardi.—CiYk
"**Loud** rairs the blast amang the woods." See Cold blows the wind
"**Loud** roared the flames." See The fire
"**Louis** is leading the crusade from the loftiest of motives." See Romanesque frieze
Louisburg. Unknown.—HiL
Louisiana
In Louisiana. A. B. Paine.—BrA
"A **louse** crept out of my lady's shift." Gordon Bottomley.—GrCt
L'Ouverture, Toussaint. See Toussaint L'Ouverture
"**Lovable** she is, and tractable, though wild." See Characteristics of a child three years old
Love, Adelaide
The lien.—ThA
Love, George
The noonday April sun.—AdIa
Love. See also Romance
Adam's curse. W. B. Yeats.—YeR
"Ae fond kiss, and then we sever." R. Burns.—BuPr
"All in green went my love riding." E. E. Cummings.—BoGj—MoS

All the way. W. De La Mare.—DeBg
"All your young beauty is to me." Unknown. —LeO
Alone. W. De La Mare.—GrCt
An amulet. S. Menashe.—SmM
Anacreontics. A. Tennyson.—TeP
Anashuya and Vijaya. W. B. Yeats.—LiT
"And every sky was blue and rain." From To deck a woman. R. Hodgson.—HaL
And on this shore. M. C. Holman.—BoA
"The angel that presided o'er my birth." W. Blake.—BlP
April's amazing meaning. G. Dillon.—CoBl
As a flower I come. Sundaram.—AlPi
As a possible lover. L. Jones.—BoA
"As birds are fitted to the boughs." L. Simpson.—CoBl—HoL
As when emotion too far exceeds its cause. G. C. Oden.—BoA—HaH
"As you came from the holy land." W. Raleigh.—GrCt
Audubon, drafted. L. Jones.—HaK
"Ay, waukin, O." R. Burns.—BuPr
The bait. J. Donne.—MoS
Balade. G. Chaucer.—GrCt
The ballad of Sue Ellen Westerfield. R. E. Hayden.—HaK
Baptist. S. Menashe.—SmM
The bead mat. W. De La Mare.—DeBg
"Being your slave, what should I do but tend." W. Shakespeare
Sonnet LVII.—CoBl
The belles of Mauchline. R. Burns.—BuH
A birthday. C. G. Rossetti.—BlO—CoBl
Bleeberrying. J. Denwood.—CaMb
The blossoming of love. Dharmakirti.—AlPi
"Bobby Shaftoe's gone to sea." Mother Goose. —MoB—WiMg
Bobby Shaftoe.—BrMg
Mother Goose rhymes, 1.—HoB
Brown penny. W. B. Yeats.—CoBl—YeR
The buds. J. Stephens.—StS
Buttered pippin-pies. J. Davies of Hereford. —GrCt
By Sandy waters. J. Stuart.—BrA
By the river. J. Gautier.—GrS
The captive bird of paradise. R. Pitter.—GrS
Casabianca. E. Bishop.—GrS
The clod and the pebble. W. Blake.—BlP
The cloud messenger. Kalidasa.—AlPi (sel.)
Come down, O maid. From The princess. A. Tennyson.—TeP
"Come here, my beloved." Unknown.—DoC
Come hither, my dear one. J. Clare.—CoBl
"Come into the garden, Maud." From Maud. A. Tennyson.—CoBl—TeP
Come loose every sail to the breeze. Unknown. —CoSs
A conjuration, to Electra. R. Herrick.—GrS
The constant lover. J. Suckling.—HoL
"Out upon it, I have loved."—CoBl
Could be. L. Hughes.—LaC
Crooked-heart. J. Stephens.—StS
The crystal cabinet. W. Blake.—BlP
"Curse God and die, you said to me." From J. B. A. MacLeish.—PlE
Dagonet's canzonet. E. Rhys.—GrS
The dalliance of the leopards. Unknown.—HoL
De gustibus. R. Browning.—BrP
Deaf and dumb. R. Browning.—BrP
Dear dark head. S. Ferguson.—CoBl
The despairing lover. W. Walsh.—CoBl
A deux. W. Wood.—CoBl
"Devouring time, blunt thou the lion's paws." From Sonnets. W. Shakespeare.—GrCt
Sonnet.—HoL
Dialogue. From As you like it. W. Shakespeare.—McWs
Down by the Salley gardens. W. B. Yeats.—CoBl
A dream within a dream. E. A. Poe.—GrCt (sel.)—PoP
Drunken lover. O. Dodson.—BoA
Duet. From Becket. A. Tennyson.—GrS
Dulce ridentem. S. V. Benét.—HaL
The dusty miller. R. Burns.—BuH
"Eight o'clock bells are ringing." Unknown.—MoB
XVIII. From The third book of ayres. T. Campion.—GrS
Embraceable you. From Girl crazy. I. Gershwin.—CoBl
An epicurean ode. J. Hall.—GrS
Epigram. A. Kreymborg.—CoBl
Eulalie—A song. E. A. Poe.—PoP
The eve of Crécy. W. Morris.—GrS
Eve speaks to Adam. From Paradise lost. J. Milton.—GrCt
"Even for the space of a flash." Unknown.—BaS
"Even now." From Fifty stanzas for a thief. Bilhana.—AlPi
An expostulation. I. Bickerstaffe.—CoBl
The fable of the golden pear. E. Merriam.—MeI
"Fair ladies tall lovers." E. E. Cummings.—GrS
False, or inconstancy. W. Congreve.—CoBl
"The far-off mountains hide you from me." Unknown.—DoC
Field of long grass. A. J. M. Smith.—CoBl
First flame. S. Daniel.—CoBl
First love. J. Clare.—GrCt
"The first of all my dreams was of." E. E. Cummings.—GrS
Flags. G. Brooks.—BoA
Flapper. D. H. Lawrence.—CoBl
The flight. S. Teasdale.—CoBl
Flowers: For Heliodora. Meleager of Gadara. —GrS
For Anne. L. Cohen.—CoBl
For Anne Gregory. W. B. Yeats.—McWs—YeR
For Mopsa. W. De La Mare.—DeBg
"Fresh spring, the herald of love's mighty king." E. Spenser.—GrCt

Love song for Nneka. Unknown.—DoC
"Love to faults is always blind." W. Blake.—BlP
Lovelight. G. D. Johnson.—BoA
Lovel's song. B. Jonson.—HoL
Lovely dames. W. H. Davies.—GrS
A lover and his lass. From As you like it. W. Shakespeare.—ShS
The lover praises his lady's bright beauty. S. O'Sheel.—CoBl
The lover tells of the rose in his heart. W. B. Yeats.—YeR
The lover to the Thames of London, to favour his lady passing thereon. G. Turberville.—GrCt
The lover's song. From Shilappadakaram. I. Adigal.—AlPi
Love's philosophy. P. B. Shelley.—CoBl
The lowest trees have tops. E. Dyer.—HoL
A modest love.—CoBl
Lowlands. Unknown.—GrCt
"Maid of Athens, ere we part." G. G. Byron.—ByP
The maid's thought. R. Jeffers.—CoBl
March weather. S. Barker.—HoL
Mary Hynes. J. Stephens.—StS
Mary Morison. R. Burns.—BuPr
Matin song. From The rape of Lucrece. T. Heywood.—TuW
"Pack, clouds, away."—ReBs
"Pack, clouds, away, and welcome, day."—BlO
Meditation at Elsinore. E. J. Coatsworth.—CoDh
Meeting at night. R. Browning.—BrP—CoBl—HoL—TuW
Misconceptions. R. Browning.—BrP
Miss Cherry. W. De La Mare.—DeBg
Moon door. M. Kennedy.—CoBl
"The moth's kiss, first." From In a gondola. R. Browning.—BrP
"Music, when soft voices die." P. B. Shelley.—BoH
"My heart is all happy." Unknown.—LeO
My Lord and King. From In memoriam. A. Tennyson.—GrCt—TeP
"My love." Ono no Yoshiki.—HoL
"My love is in a light attire." From Chamber music. J. Joyce.—HaL
"My mistress' eyes are nothing like the sun." From Sonnets. W. Shakespeare
Sonnet CXXX.—BoH—CoBl
My star. R. Browning.—BrP
The nature of love. J. Kirkup.—PlE
"Never pain to tell thy love." W. Blake.—BlP
"Never seek to tell thy love."—CoBl
Nicoletta. W. De La Mare.—DeBg
The night of the full moon. L. Frankenberg.—CoBl
Night ride. H. Read.—CoBl
Night song at Amalfi. S. Teasdale.—BoH
The night wind. E. Brontë.—CoR—GrCt
Non sum qualis eram bonae sub regno Cynarae. E. Dowson.—CoBl
Nora Criona. J. Stephens.—StS
Now. R. Browning.—BrP
Now silent falls. W. De La Mare.—GrS
Now sleeps the crimson petal. From The princess. A. Tennyson.—GrCt—TeP
O Daedalus, fly away home. R. E. Hayden.—AdIa—BoH
"Oh dear, what can the matter be." Mother Goose.—McWs—OpF
What can the matter be.—BrMg
O mistress mine. From Twelfth night. W. Shakespeare.—CoBl
Song.—BoGj
Song from Twelfth night.—HoL
"O were my love yon lilac fair." R. Burns.—GrCt
"O wert thou in the cauld blast." R. Burns.—BuPr
Oh, when I was in love. From A Shropshire lad. A. E. Housman.—McWs
Oblation. A. C. Swinburne.—CoBl
"Of a' the airts the wind can blaw." R. Burns.—BuPr
An old song. E. Thomas.—ThG
On a hand. H. Belloc.—CoBl
On Lydia distracted. P. Ayres.—GrS
On the beach at Fontana. J. Joyce.—LiT
Orpheus' dream. E. Muir.—GrS
Papago love song. Unknown.—HoL
The passionate shepherd to his love. C. Marlowe.—CoBl—McWs
A pavane for the nursery. W. J. Smith.—BoGj—CoBl
Perspectives. D. Randall.—BoA
Petrarch for Laura. C. McAllistair.—GrS
The picnic. J. Logan.—CoBl—DuS
Pierrot. S. Teasdale.—CoBl
A Poe-'em of passion. C. F. Lummis.—BrSm
Poem ("I loved my friend") L. Hughes.—LiT
Poem ("Little brown boy") H. Johnson.—BoA
The poet speaks. G. D. Johnson.—BoA
Poet to his love. M. Bodenheim.—CoBl
Polly Perkins. Unknown.—CoBl
Portrait of a girl. From Priapus and the pool. C. Aiken.—BoGj
Preludes for Memnon. C. Aiken.—CoBl (sel.)
A proverb. Unknown.—CoBl
The puritan's ballad. E. Wylie.—CoBl
Pursuit of love. Unknown.—GrCt
Put out my eyes. R. M. Rilke.—HoL
Rainy song. M. Eastman.—BoH
A red, red rose. R. Burns.—ArT-3—BoH—BuH—BuPr—CoBl—GrCt
Renouncement. A. Meynell.—CoBl
The river-merchant's wife: A letter. Li T'ai-po.—BoH—CoBl—LiT
"The road looks longer as I go to meet her." Unknown.—LeO
Rondel. J. Froissart.—HoL
Rose Aylmer. W. S. Landor.—CoR
The rose family. R. Frost.—CoBl
"Roses are red." Mother Goose.—BrMg
The rose is red.—HuS-3
Sailing to England. D. Moraes.—AlPi

Vastness. A. Tennyson.—TeP
Vista. A. Kreymborg.—CoBl—SmM
The walk on the beach. J. G. Fletcher.—CoBl
A waltz in the afternoon. B. Bentley.—CoBl
"We learned the whole of love." E. Dickinson.—DiPe
Were you on the mountain. Unknown.—CoBl
What is love. A. P. Herbert.—CoBl (sel.)
What the girl said. Kapilar.—AlPi
What the lover said. A. Nanmullaiyar.—AlPi
When. From The window. A. Tennyson.—TeP
"When I am not with you." S. Teasdale.—CoBl
When I loved you. T. Moore.—HoL
To——.—CoBl
"When I was one-and-twenty." From A Shropshire lad. A. E. Housman.—BoH—CoBl—HoL
"When trout swim down Great Ormond street." From Priapus and the pool. C. Aiken.—HoL—McWs
When you are old. W. B. Yeats.—BoGj—CoBl—YeR
"While it is alive, until death touches it." E. Dickinson.—DiPe
Who goes with Fergus. W. B. Yeats.—BoGj
Who is Silvia. From Two gentlemen of Verona. W. Shakespeare.—CoBl
Why so pale and wan. From Aglaura. J. Suckling.—CoBl
"Why was Cupid a boy." W. Blake.—BlP
"A widow bird sate mourning for her love." From Charles IV. P. B. Shelley.—BlO
Song from Charles IV.—SmM
William Bond. W. Blake.—BlP
Winter. S. Wingfield.—CoBl
Wisdom. F. Yerby.—BoA
Without name. P. Murray.—BoA
A woman's last word. R. Browning.—BrP
The world is a mighty ogre. F. Johnson.—BoA
You are a part of me. F. Yerby.—BoA
You'll love me yet. From Pippa passes. R. Browning.—BrP
Young girl: Annam. P. Colum.—HaL
Young love ("Within my bed, the whole night thru") T. Garrison.—CoBl
Young love ("The world is cold and gray and wet") S. Teasdale.—CoBl
The young man in April. R. Brooke.—CoBl
Love—Courtship. See Courtship
Love—Fulfillment
A decade. A. Lowell.—CoBl
Psalm to my belovèd. E. Tietjens.—CoBl
The seaman's happy return. Unknown.—GrCt
True love. P. Sidney.—GrCt
Love—Humor
Amo amas. J. O'Keefe.—CoBl—GrCt
Faithless Nelly Gray. T. Hood.—BrSm
Lanty Leary. S. Lover.—CoBl—GrCt
Literary love. H. Kemp.—BoH
Love song. D. Parker.—McWs
"Old woman, old woman, shall we go a-shearing." Mother Goose.—ArT-3
Mother Goose rhymes, 48.—HoB
The old woman.—BrMg
An original love-story. Unknown.—CoBl
Song. J. Manifold.—CoBl
Sorrows of Werther. W. M. Thackeray.—BrSm
When one loves tensely. D. Marquis.—CoBl
When you're away. S. Hoffenstein.—CoBl
"Your little hands." S. Hoffenstein.—CoBl
Love—Maternal. See Mothers and motherhood
Love—Love and death
Aghadoe. J. Todhunter.—CoBl
Annabel Lee. E. A. Poe.—CoR—HuS-3—PoP
Bridal ballad. E. A. Poe.—PoP
The burnt bridge. L. MacNeice.—GrS
Come night, come Romeo. From Romeo and Juliet. W. Shakespeare.—CoBl
Compensation. P. L. Dunbar.—BoA
Discordants. C. Aiken.—CoBl
Faithless Nelly Gray. T. Hood.—BrSm
For Annie. E. A. Poe.—PoP
The garden of love. W. Blake.—BlP
"The glory of the day was in her face." J. W. Johnson.—AdIa
Highland Mary. R. Burns.—BuPr
I have loved flowers. R. Bridges.—BoGj
"I want to die while you love me." G. D. Johnson.—BoA—HaK
In the mind's eye. T. Hardy.—GrS
The juniper tree. W. Watson.—CoBl—DoW
The lady of Shalott. A. Tennyson.—HuS-3—TeP
Lanty Leary. S. Lover.—CoBl
The last ride together. R. Browning.—BrP
Lenore. E. A. Poe.—PoP
Lines supposed to have been addressed to Fanny Brawne.—CoBl
Luke Havergal. E. A. Robinson.—GrS
"Never more will the wind." H. D.—GrS
Patterns. A. Lowell.—BoH—CoBl
The phantom horsewoman. T. Hardy.—GrS
Porphyria's lover. R. Browning.—BrP
The raven. E. A. Poe.—BoGj—PoP
The sleeper. E. A. Poe.—PoP
Song for a dark girl. L. Hughes.—AdIa
"Strange fits of passion have I known." W. Wordsworth.—WoP
Tears, idle tears. From The princess. A. Tennyson.—TeP
To Ann Scott-Moncrieff. E. Muir.—GrS
To Helen. E. A. Poe.—PoP
To Mary: It is the evening hour. J. Clare.—GrCt
To one in paradise. From The assignation. E. A. Poe.—PoP
The two April mornings. W. Wordsworth.—WoP
Ulalume—A ballad. E. A. Poe.—PoP
When I am dead. C. G. Rossetti.—CoBl
The yew-tree. Unknown.—GrCt
The young cordwainer. R. Graves.—CaMb
Love—Plaints and protests
An apple gathering. C. G. Rossetti.—CoBl

Love—Plaints and protests—*Continued*
Ballad of the Western Island in the North country. Unknown.—GrS
The banks o' Doon. R. Burns.—BuPr—CoBl
Bedouin song. B. Taylor.—CoBl
Black-eyed Susan. J. Gay.—CoR—CoSs
The broken-hearted gardener. Unknown.—GrCt
"Do you remember that night." G. Petrie.—CoBl
Do you remember the night.—GrS
I pass in silence. J. Clare.—CoBl
I sought you. J. H. Wheelock.—CoBl
Now and then. S. Muktibodh.—AlPi
Pining for love. F. Beaumont.—CoBl
Souvenirs. D. Randall.—HaK
Spring night. S. Teasdale.—CoBl
"When I asked for him at Entoto, he was towards Akaki." Unknown.—DoC
Love—Tragedy of love
Ballad of another Ophelia. D. H. Lawrence.—GrCt
The cap and bells. W. B. Yeats.—GrCt—YeR
Donall Oge: Grief of a girl's heart. Unknown.—CoBl
The grief of a girl's heart.—GrCt
Early one morning. Unknown.—GrCt
Finis. W. Cuney.—BoA
"In a mirage I filled my pitcher." V. Karandikar.—AlPi
"In wintry midnight, o'er a stormy main." Petrarch.—GrCt
Love without hope. R. Graves.—CoBl—GrCt—GrS
Mariana. A. Tennyson.—TeP
Ophelia's song. From Hamlet. W. Shakespeare.—GrCt
Parting after a quarrel. E. Tietjens.—CoBl
The rock. Unknown.—GrCt
The sacrilege. T. Hardy.—CoB
So shuts the marigold her leaves. From Britannia's pastorals. W. Browne.—GrCt
The song of Jehane du Castel Beau. From Golden wings. W. Morris.—GrCt
The spring and the fall. E. St V. Millay.—CoBl
To shades of underground. T. Campion.—GrCt
A tune. A. Symons.—CoBl
What her friend said. Varumulaiyaritti.—AlPi
What she said. M. Kantan.—AlPi
With how sad steps, O moon. P. Sidney.—GrCt
The languishing moon.—CoBn
Love—Wedded love. See Married life
Love ("Is there a bolt that can avail to shut up love") See Kural
Love ("Love bade me welcome: yet my soul drew back") George Herbert.—GrCt
Love ("Love lives beyond") John Clare.—GrCt
Love and a question. Robert Frost.—CaMb
Love and law. Vachel Lindsay.—LiP
Love at sea. Algernon Charles Swinburne.—GrS
"**Love** bade me welcome: yet my soul drew back." See Love
"**Love** comes quietly." Robert Creeley.—CoBl
"**Love** has crept out of her sealèd heart." See Flapper
Love in a life. Robert Browning.—BrP
Love in a valley, sel. George Meredith
The white owl.—GrCt
Love in a village, sel. Isaac Bickerstaffe
Jolly Miller.—BrMg
"There was a jolly miller once."—OpF—WiMg
Love in the winds. Richard Hovey.—CoBl
"**Love** is a universal migraine." See Symptoms of love
"**Love** is and was my Lord and King." See My Lord and King
"**Love** is anterior to life." Emily Dickinson.—DiPe
"**Love** is done when love's begun." Emily Dickinson.—DiPe
Love is enough. William Morris.—CoBl
"**Love** is enough: though the world be a-waning." See Love is enough
"**Love** is like a lamb, and love is like a lion." Thomas Middleton.—CoBl
"**Love** is not all: it is not meat nor drink." See Sonnet XXX
"**Love,** leave me like the light." See If you should go
"**Love,** love, what wilt thou with this heart of mine." See Rondel
Love lyric. Unknown, tr. fr. the Ancient Egyptian by Noel Stock.—HoL
Love me, love my dog. Isabella V. Crawford.—DoW
Love on the mountain. Thomas Boyd.—CoBl
Love poem ("My clumsiest dear, whose hands shipwreck vases") John Frederick Nims.—McWs
Love poem ("When we are in love, we love the grass") Robert Bly.—CoBl
"**Love** seeketh not itself to please." See The clod and the pebble
The **love-sick** frog. Mother Goose.—BrMg
Love song ("I know not how to speak to thee, girl—damselle") Reed Whittemore.—BrA
Love song ("I walk alone") Unknown, tr. fr. the Zulu.—LeO
Love song ("My own dear love, he is strong and bold") Dorothy Parker.—McWs
Love song for Nneka. Unknown.—DoC
The **love** song of J. Alfred Prufrock, sel. T. S. Eliot
"The yellow fog that rubs its back upon the window-pane."—ArT-3
Yellow fog.—HaL
"**Love** to faults is always blind." William Blake.—BlP
Love under the republicans—or democrats. Ogden Nash.—McWs
"**Love,** why have you led me here." See The young cordwainer

Love without hope. Robert Graves.—CoBl—GrCt—GrS
"**Love** without hope, as when the young bird-catcher." See Love without hope
Lovelace, Richard
To Lucasta, on going to the wars.—McWs
Loveliest of trees. See A Shropshire lad
"**Loveliest** of trees, the cherry now." See A Shropshire lad—Loveliest of trees
Lovelight. Georgia Douglas Johnson.—BoA
Loveliness. Hilda Conkling.—ArT-3
"**Loveliness** that dies when I forget." See Loveliness
Lovel's song. Ben Jonson.—HoL
"**Lovely** are the curves of the white owl sweeping." See Love in a valley—The white owl
Lovely dames. William Henry Davies.—GrS
"**Lovely** hill-torrents are." See Song
Lover, Samuel
Lanty Leary.—CoBl—GrCt
A **lover** and his lass. See As you like it
The **lover** praises his lady's bright beauty. Shaemas O'Sheel.—CoBl
The **lover** tells of the rose in his heart. William Butler Yeats.—YeR
The **lover** to the Thames of London, to favour his lady passing thereon. George Turberville.—GrCt
"**Lovers** lie around in it." See Stuff
"**Lovers,** O lovers, listen to my call." See Epilogue to the adventures while preaching the gospel of beauty
The **lover's** song. See Shilappadakaram
Love's labour's lost, sels. William Shakespeare
Another riddle.—ShS
Faults and fears.—ShS
"When icicles hang by (or on) the wall."—BoGj—CoR—TuW
Winter.—BlO—CoBn—GrCt—ShS
Wit's pedlar.—ShS
The **loves** of the plants, sel. Erasmus Darwin
Stay thy soft murmuring.—ReO
Love's philosophy. Percy Bysshe Shelley.—CoBl
"**Love's** the boy stood on the burning deck." See Casabianca
"A **loving** arm." See Kindness
"The **low** beating of the tom-toms." See African dance
"A **low** range of mountains, towards them I am running." Unknown, tr. fr. the Papago.—LeO
Lowell, Amy
The city of falling leaves.—ArT-3
A decade.—CoBl
Fringed gentians.—ThA
Night clouds.—ThA
Patterns.—BoH—CoBl
Points of view.—HaL
Sea shell.—BoH—HuS-3
Texas.—BrA
—and Ayscough, Florence
The excursion. trs.—MoS
Lowell, James Russell
Aladdin.—CoR
A day in June. See The vision of Sir Launfal
The singing leaves.—HuS-3
The vision of Sir Launfal, sel.
A day in June.—HuS-3
Lowell, Robert
As a plane tree by the water.—GrS
Christmas eve under Hooker's statue.—HiL
The mouth of the Hudson.—BrA—LaC
The Quaker graveyard in Nantucket.—PaH
Lowery cot. L. A. G. Strong.—CaD
The **lowest** trees have tops. Edward Dyer.—HoL
A modest love.—CoBl
"The **lowest** trees have tops, the ant her gall." See The lowest trees have tops
Lowlands. Unknown.—GrCt
Lowry, H. D.
The spring will come.—CoBn
Loyalty
Fidelity. W. Wordsworth.—ClF
The star in the hills. W. Stafford.—DuS
Lozada, Enrique
The pier.—LeM
Lu Lun
Border songs.—LeMw
Lu Yu
The herd boy.—GrCt—LeMw
The peddler of spells.—LeMw
Lucan
The coracle. See Pharsalia
Pharsalia, sel.
The coracle.—GrCt
Lucas, Edward Verrall
Carpenter.—HuS-3
The conjuror.—HoB
Stamp battalion.—HuS-3
Lucas, F. L.
Beleaguered cities.—ClF (sel.)
The dolphin's tomb. tr.—ReO
Sleep upon the world. See Vesper
Vesper. tr.—ReO
Sleep upon the world.—GrCt
Lucifer in the train. Adrienne Cecile Rich.—PlE
Lucilius
The boxer's face.—MoS
The sluggard.—MoS
The world's worst boxer.—MoS
Luck
"In with the luck." Issa.—IsF
Luck. W. W. Gibson.—CoSs—SmM
Lucky star. E. Farjeon.—FaT
Midnight raffle. L. Hughes.—LaC
Oh lucky Jim. Unknown.—GrCt
Pins. Mother Goose.—BrMg
Song of an unlucky man. Unknown.—DoC
Luck. Wilfrid Wilson Gibson.—CoSs—SmM
Lucky star. Eleanor Farjeon.—FaT
"**Lucky** the living child, born in a land." See American child
Lucretia Mott. Eve Merriam.—MeIv
Lucy and Dicky. Elizabeth Turner.—VrF

"Willow leaves murmur, hua-la-la." Unknown. —WyC
Wynken, Blynken, and Nod. E. Field.—HoB —HuS-3
"You spotted snakes with double tongue." From A midsummer-night's dream. W. Shakespeare.—BlO
Song.—SmM
Lullaby ("Baby swimming down the river") Unknown, tr. fr. the Kiowa.—LeO
Lullaby ("Bedtime's come fu' little boys") Paul Laurence Dunbar.—HoB
Lullaby ("The long canoe") Robert Hillyer.—DuR—HaL—ReS
Lullaby ("Lullaby, oh lullaby") Christina Georgina Rossetti.—HoB
Lullaby ("The moon and the stars and the wind in the sky") Jean Jaszi.—HoB
Lullaby ("The rook's nests do rock on the treetop") William Barnes.—ReS
Lullaby ("Sleep, sleep, sleep") Unknown, tr. fr. the Zuni.—LeO
Lullaby ("We've watched all about the upland fallows") Ford Madox Ford.—ReS
Lullaby for a baby toad. Stella Gibbons.—CoB—ReS
"**Lullaby**, lullaby, baby dear." See Sleeping
"**Lullaby**, lullaby, slumberland bound." See A dream party
"**Lullaby**, oh lullaby." See Lullaby
"**Lulled** by La Belle Dame Sans Merci he lies." See The enchanted knight
Lully. Walter De La Mare.—DeBg
"**Lully**, lulley; lully, lulley." See Corpus Christi carol
Lummis, Charles Fletcher
A Poe-'em of passion.—BrSm
Lunar moth. Robert Hillyer.—ReO
Luther, Martin
Ane sang of the birth of Christ, with the tune of baw lula low.—GrCt
Cradle hymn.—ArT-3—HoB—LaPh
"A mighty fortress is our God."—PlE
"**Luther** Leavitt is a whale hunter." Alfred Brower.—BaH
Lutz, Gertrude May
African sunrise.—DuR
Lycidas. John Milton.—GrCt
"**Lydia** is gone this many a year." Lizette Woodworth Reese.—BoGj
Lydia Sherman. Unknown.—BrSm
"**Lydia** Sherman is plagued with rats." See Lydia Sherman
"**Lying** in bed in the dark, I hear the bray." See Weather ear
"**Lying** in the sun." Ian Johnson.—LeM
A **lyke-wake** dirge. Unknown.—GrCt—PlE
Lyly, John
Alexander and Campaspe, sel.
"Who is't now we hear."—ReBs
What bird so sings.—BlO
"Who is't now we hear." See Alexander and Campaspe
The **lynching**. Claude McKay.—AdIa
Lynchings
Between the world and me. R. Wright.—AdIa —BoA
The haunted oak. P. L. Dunbar.—HaK
The lynching. C. McKay.—AdIa
So quietly. L. P. Hill.—AdIa
Song for a dark girl. L. Hughes.—AdIa
When the drive goes down. D. Malloch.—BrA —HuS-3
Lyrebirds
Lyrebirds. Judith Wright.—BoGj
Lyrebirds. Judith Wright.—BoGj

M

M., Alex
Dancing.—LeM
"**M** is for mournful Miss Molly." Isabel Frances Bellows.—BrLl
M., singing. Louise Bogan.—BoGj
McAllistair, Claire
Petrarch for Laura.—GrS
Macavity: The mystery cat. T. S. Eliot.—ArT-3 —CoB—LiT—SmM
"**Macavity's** a mystery cat; he's called the Hidden Paw." See Macavity: The mystery cat
Macbeth, sels. William Shakespeare
Out, out, brief candle.—GrCt
Witches' song.—McWs
Song of the witches.—ShS
McCall, Linden
"I stand under the naked tree."—LeM
McClintic, Winona
Hospitality.—CoB
McDonogh day in New Orleans. Marcus B. Christian.—BoA
"The **mackerel's** cry." Mother Goose.—ReOm
Macleod, Fiona, pseud. See Sharp, William
McCord, David
All day long.—McAd
Answering your question.—McAd
Ants and sailboats.—McAd
Any day now.—BrSm
August 28.—McE
"Bananas and cream."—McE
Beech.—McAd
Boo moo.—McAd
"Books fall open."—McAd
Bridges.—McAd
Bumblebee.—McAd
The cellar hole.—McAd
Cities and science. See Poet always next but one
The clouds.—McAd
Cocoons.—McE
Come Christmas.—McAd—McE
"Consider this odd little snail."—BrLl
Corinna.—McAd

MacFadden, David
Elephant.—DoW
McGaffey, Ernest
Geronimo.—HiL
McGahey, Jeanne
Oregon winter.—BrA—DuR
McGinley, Phyllis
The adversary.—McWs
All around the town, sels.
"B's the bus."—ArT-3
"C is for the circus."—ArT-3
"E is the escalator."—ArT-3
"F is the fighting firetruck."—ArT-3—LaP
"J's the jumping jay-walker."—ArT-3
"P's the proud policeman."—ArT-3
"Q is for the quietness."—LaC
"R is for the restaurant."—ArT-3
"U is for umbrellas."—ArT-3
"V is for the vendor."—BrSg
"W is for windows."—ArT-3
Ballad of the nightingale.—McWc
Ballad of the robin.—McWc
Ballad of the rosemary.—McWc
The birthday.—McWc
"B's the bus." See All around the town
"C is for the circus." See All around the town
The canticle of the bees.—McWc
A certain age.—DuS
Conversation in Avila.—PlE
"E is the escalator." See All around the town
"F is the fighting firetruck." See All around the town
First lesson.—McWs
An Irish legend.—McWc
"J's the jumping jay-walker." See All around the town
A legend from Russia.—McWc
The legend of the cat.—McWc
Legend of the holly.—McWc
The new order.—BrA
The night.—McWc
The old feminist.—HiL
The pine tree.—McWc
"P's the proud policeman." See All around the town
"Q is for the quietness." See All around the town
"R is for the restaurant." See All around the town
Reflections dental.—DuR
Reflections outside of a gymnasium.—MoS
Star-spangled ode.—HiL
The stars' story.—McWc
The stork.—McWc
Story for an educated child.—McWc
The thunderer.—PlE
Trinity place.—LaC
"U is for umbrellas." See All around the town
"V is for the vendor." See All around the town
Virginia.—AgH
"W is for windows." See All around the town
Why the owl wakes at night.—McWc
McGregor, Bruce
A teacher.—LeM
McGroarty, John S.
The King's highway.—PaH
Machinery. See also names of machines, as Steam shovels
The misery of mechanics. P. Booth.—DuS
Nightmare number three. S. V. Benét.—McWs
The secret of the machines. R. Kipling.—HuS-3
Machwe, P.
"The earth is not an old woman." tr.—AlPi
MacIntyre, C. F.
From a childhood. tr.—GrS
McIntyre, Philip, Jr.
The rabbit.—LeM
McKay, Claude
After the winter.—AdIa
America.—BoH
Flame-heart.—BoA
If we must die.—AdIa—BoA—HaK
The lynching.—AdIa
Outcast.—BoA
St Isaac's church, Petrograd.—BoA—HaK
Spring in New Hampshire.—BoH—HaK
The tropics in New York.—BoA—BoH—HaK
When dawn comes to the city.—BoH—LaC
The white house.—BoA
Mackay, L. A.
I wish my tongue were a quiver.—McWs
MacKaye, Percy
Goethals, the prophet engineer.—HuS-3
Mackenzie, Lewis
"Come on, owl." tr.—LeI
"Even as the snow fell." tr.—LeMw
"A good world it is, indeed." tr.—LeMw
"Sleeping, waking." tr.—LeMw
"The snow thaws." tr.—LeMw
"Under the willow." tr.—LeMw
Mackie, Albert D.
Molecatcher.—CoB
MacKinstry, Elizabeth
The man who hid his own front door.—ArT-3
McKuen, Rod
Twenty-five.—DuS
McLaughlin, Kathy
Suicide pond.—DuS
MacLeish, Archibald
America was promises.—BrA (sel.)
American letter.—BrA (sel.)
Ars poetica.—BoH
Conquistador.—HiL (sel.)
"Curse God and die, you said to me." See J. B.
The end of the world.—McWs
Immortal autumn.—GrS
J. B., sel.
"Curse God and die, you said to me."—PlE
L'an trentiesme de mon eage.—GrS
Land of the free.—BrA (sel.)
The sound track.—LiT (sel.)
Men.—BrA
Poem in prose.—McWs
The snow fall.—HaL
The sound track. See Land of the free

MacLeish, Archibald—*Continued*
The too-late born.—BoGj
Where the hayfields were.—HaL
McLennan, William
Cecilia. tr.—DoW
McLeod, Irene Rutherford
Lone dog.—ArT-3—CoB—LaPd—ThA
McMahon, M. J.
The nonpareil's grave.—MoS
MacNeice, Louis
"And the Lord was not in the whirlwind." See Visitations: VII
Bar-room matins.—PlE
The burnt bridge.—GrS
Clowns.—CaD
The creditor.—PlE
Didymus.—PlE
Glass falling.—CaD
Horses.—CaD
Prayer in mid-passage.—PlE
The streets of Laredo.—CaMb—GrCt
Visitations: VII, sel.
"And the Lord was not in the whirlwind."—PlE
MacSweeney, Margaret Phyllis
Carmel Point.—DuR
McWebb, Elizabeth Upham
At Mrs Appleby's.—ArT-3—HuS-3
"The **mackerel's** cry." Mother Goose.—ReOn
Mad as the mist and snow. William Butler Yeats.—GrCt
The **mad** family. Mother Goose.—BrF—BrMg
The **mad** man. Mother Goose.—BrMg
There was a man.—SmM
"**Mad** Patsy said, he said to me." See In the poppy field
Mad song. William Blake.—BlP
"**Madam,** I present you with six rows of pins." See Six rows of pins
"**Madam,** I will give you a new lace cap." Unknown.—OpF
"**Madam** Pussie's coming hame." Unknown.—MoB
"**Madame** Mouse trots." Edith Sitwell.—CaD—HaL
Madeira
Madeira from the sea. S. Teasdale.—PaH
Madeira from the sea. Sara Teasdale.—PaH
Madgett, Naomi Long
The reckoning.—HaK
Trinity: A dream sequence.—HaK (sel.)
Madhouse. Calvin C. Hernton.—AdIa—HaK
Madison, Dolly
La Fayette.—HiL
Madman ("He was caged up") Bill O'Shea.—LeM
A **madman** ("A madman lives in a very special house") Stephen Dawson.—LeM
"A **madman** lives in a very special house." See A madman
Madman's song. Elinor Wylie.—HaL—ThA
Madness one Monday evening. Julia Fields.—HaK—LiT
Madrigal macabre. Samuel Hoffenstein.—BrSm
"**Maggie** and Milly and Molly and May." E. E. Cummings.—HaL
The **magi.** See On the morning of Christ's Nativity
Magic. See also Enchantment
Aladdin. J. R. Lowell.—CoR
Aladdin and the jinn. V. Lindsay.—LiP
The bad kittens. E. J. Coatsworth.—ThA
Behind the waterfall. W. Welles.—ArT-3—HuS-3
Crab-apple. E. Talbot.—ArT-3
Fit only for Apollo. F. Beaumont.—GrCt
Forest magic. C. Lewis.—LeP
How little I was. M. C. Livingston.—LiC
Incantation to Oedipus. From Oedipus. J. Dryden.—GrS
Kiph. W. De La Mare.—ArT-3—DeBg
Legend. J. V. A. Weaver.—BrA
The little trumpet. C. Govoni.—LiT
A magic carpet. T. Weiss.—WeP
The magic flower. D. Marcus.—LeM
The magic vine. Unknown.—BrSg
The magic window. E. Hammond.—StF
The magical mouse. K. Patchen.—HaL—WeP
The magnifying glass. W. De La Mare.—BlO—DeBg
Maytime magic. M. Watts.—BrSg
Merlin and the gleam. A. Tennyson.—TeP
Midsummer magic. I. O. Eastwick.—ArT-3
Night magic. A. J. Burr.—ThA
Sea magic. C. Lewis.—LeP
Songs accompanying healing magic. Unknown.—DoC
"I sweep this hut"
"This is a root"
The sorceress. V. Lindsay.—LaPd
A spell. From The old wives' tale. G. Peele.—GrCt
Spells. J. Reeves.—SmM
Tillie. W. De La Mare.—ArT-3
A true story. J. Smith.—SmM
Western magic. M. Austin.—BrA
"When I set out for Lyonnesse." T. Hardy.—PaH
The witch's broomstick spell. Unknown.—GrCt
A witch's spell. Unknown.—GrCt
A **magic** carpet. Theodore Weiss.—WeP
The **magic** flower. Danny Marcus.—LeM
The **magic** vine. Unknown.—BrSg
The **magic** window. Eleanor Hammond.—StF
The **magical** mouse. Kenneth Patchen.—HaL—WeP
Magical music. Eleanor Farjeon.—FaT
"**Magnificent** snow." Temmu.—BaS
The **magnifying** glass. Walter De La Mare.—BlO—DeBg
Magicians
The conjurer. E. V. Lucas.—HoB
The great magicians. C. Day-Lewis.—PlE
The two magicians. Unknown.—GrCt
Magnifying glasses
The magnifying glass. W. De La Mare.—BlO—DeBg

"**Magpie,** magpie, chatter and flee." Mother Goose.—OpF
To the magpie.—BrMg
"**Magpie,** magpie, flutter and flee." See "Magpie, magpie, chatter and flee"
"The **magpie** singing his delight." David Campbell.—ReBs
"The **magpie.** The magpie. Here underneath." Unknown, tr. fr. the Tewa.—LeO
Magpies
As black as ink. Mother Goose.—ReOn
A charm against a magpie. Unknown.—GrCt
"I saw eight magpies in a tree." Mother Goose. —OpF
"Magpie, magpie, chatter and flee." Mother Goose.—OpF
To the magpie.—BrMg
"The magpie singing his delight." D. Campbell.—ReBs
"The magpie. The magpie. Here underneath." Unknown.—LeO
"A pie (or pye) sat on a pear tree." Mother Goose.—BlO—GrCt—OpF
Mahabharata, sel. Unknown
Precepts.—AlPi
Mahapatra, Godavaris
"If I die tomorrow."—AlPi
Mahoney, Francis Sylvester. See Prout, Father, pseud.
Maid Marian, sel. Thomas Love Peacock
The friar.—MoS
"**Maid** of Athens, ere we part." George Gordon Byron.—ByP
"The **maiden** caught me in the wild." See The crystal cabinet
"A **maiden** caught stealing a dahlia." See Thief
The **maiden** makeles. Unknown.—GrCt
"The **maiden** ran away to fetch the clothes." See Deluge
The **maid's** thought. Robinson Jeffers.—CoBl
"**Maids** to bed, and cover coal." See The bellman's song
Mail service. See also Letters and letter writing; Mailmen
Aunt Maud. Unknown.—BrSm
Driving to town late to mail a letter. R. Bly.—CoBn
Epitaph for a postal clerk. X. J. Kennedy.—BrSm
The night mail. W. H. Auden.—GrCt
The pony express. D. B. Thompson.—BrA
Post early for space. P. J. Henniker-Heaton.—BrA
Stamp battalion. E. V. Lucas.—HuS-3
V-letter. K. Shapiro.—HiL
Mailmen
"Eight o'clock." C. G. Rossetti.—ArT-3
The postman. L. E. Richards.—ArT-3
Postman's knock. E. Farjeon.—FaT
The **main-deep.** James Stephens.—StS
Maine
Lost graveyards. E. J. Coatsworth.—CoDh
Maine. P. Booth.—BrA
This is my country. R. P. T. Coffin.—PaH
Maine. Philip Booth.—BrA
Mair, Alexander
Hesiod, 1908.—GrS
"**Majestic** tomes, you are the tomb." See Epitaph on the proofreader of the Encyclopedia Britannica
Major, Clarence
Celebrated return.—BoA
"**Make** a joyful noise unto the Lord, all ye lands." See Psalms—Psalm 100
Make-believe christening. Kathleen Fraser.—FrS
Make-believe wedding procession. Kathleen Fraser.—FrS
"**Make** me thy spinning wheel of use for thee." See Huswifery
"**Make** no mistake: if He rose at all." See Seven stanzas at Easter
"**Make** three-fourths of a cross." Mother Goose. —BrMg
"**Make** up your mind snail." Richard Wright
Hokku poems.—BoA
"**Making** his way through the crowd." Issa, tr. fr. the Japanese by R. H. Blyth.—IsF—LeOw
The **making** of birds. Katherine Tynan.—ReBs
Malam, Charles
Steam shovel.—DuR
Malcolm X. See Little, Malcolm
The **Maldive** shark. Herman Melville.—CoB
Malfunction. Richard E. Albert.—DuS
Mallard. Rex Warner.—CoB
Malloch, Douglas
When the drive goes down.—BrA—HuS-3
Malta
A Maltese dog. Tymnès.—ArT-3
The dog from Malta.—CoB
A **Maltese** dog. Tymnès, tr. fr. the Greek by Edmund Blunden.—ArT-3
The dog from Malta.—CoB
"**Mama.**" See Silly song
"**Mama**—a girl—wears a new hat." See Make-believe christening
"**Mamie.** Mamie." See We're free
"**Mamma** had ordered Ann, the maid." See The sash
"**Mamma,** shall we visit Miss Hammond to-day." See Disappointment
Man. See also Woman
Apostrophe to man. E. St V. Millay.—DuS
As kingfishers catch fire. G. M. Hopkins.—PlE
The bird-man. W. H. Davies.—SmM
Color. E. Merriam.—MeI
Composed on a May morning, 1838. W. Wordsworth.—WoP
The conqueror worm. From Ligeia. E. A. Poe. —PoP
Cruciform. W. Welles.—HoL
Dark affections. From The merchant of Venice. W. Shakespeare.—ShS
A divine image ("Cruelty has a human heart") W. Blake.—BlP—GrCt
The divine image ("To mercy, pity, peace, and love") W. Blake.—BlP

Man—*Continued*
The everlasting gospel. W. Blake.—BlP (sel.)
The fish, the man, and the spirit. L. Hunt.—GrCt
The fish and the man.—CoR (sel.)
A fish answers.—ReO (sel.)—SmM (sel.)
To a fish.—SmM (sel.)
"Flower in the crannied wall." A. Tennyson.—CoBn—TeP
The human race. W. Raleigh.—McWs
"I marvel at the ways of God." E. B. White.—McWs
The intruder. J. Reeves.—LaPd
"It is man who counts." Unknown.—DoC
Jerusalem. W. Blake.—BlP (sel.)
Lines written in early spring. W. Wordsworth.—WoP
Man and cows. A. Young.—CaD
Man is God's nature. R. Eberhart.—PlE
"Man that is born of a woman." From Job, Bible, Old Testament.—GrCt
Meditatio. E. Pound.—ArT-3—DuR—HaL
Milton. W. Blake.—BlP (sel.)
Jerusalem.—PlE (sel.)
IX. The four ages of man. From Supernatural songs. W. B. Yeats.—YeR
Oh, our manhood's prime vigor. From Saul. R. Browning.—BrP
"One man and one fly." Issa.—BeCs
"Pity this busy monster, manunkind." E. E. Cummings.—HoL
Rural dumpheap. M. Cane.—BrA
"The seasons were appointed and the times." N. Belting.—BeCm
Short history of man. J. Holmes.—McWs
The song of Quoodle. G. K. Chesterton.—BoGj
The term. W. C. Williams.—DuR—LaC—LiT
"There was a young lady of station." L. Carroll.—BrLl
"A thing which fades." Ono no Komachi.—BaS
To the moon. T. Hardy.—CoBn—GrCt
Two somewhat different epigrams. L. Hughes.—HaK
Univac to Univac. L. B. Salomon.—DuS
A wind blows. E. J. Coatsworth.—CoDh
"A woman is a branchy tree." J. Stephens.—StS
Man and cows. Andrew Young.—CaD
"The **man** bent over his guitar" See The man with the blue guitar
"A **man** came slowly from the setting sun." See The death of Cuchulain
The **man** from Inversnaid. Robert Fuller Murray.—MoS
"The **man** in the corner." See Fatigue
The **man** in the dead machine. Donald Hall.—DuS
"The **man** in the moon (came tumbling down)." Mother Goose
Mother Goose rhymes, 44.—HoB
"The **man** in the moon (looked out)." Mother Goose.—BrMg—ReS
"The **man** in the moon drinks claret." Mother Goose.—BrMg
The **man** in the onion bed. John Ciardi.—CoO
A **man** in the wilderness. See "A man in the wilderness asked me"
"A **man** in the wilderness asked me." Mother Goose.—OpF
A man in the wilderness.—BrMg
"**Man** is a bird." See The bird-man
A **man** is buried where the cold winds blow. Dan G. Matumeak.—BaH
Man is God's nature. Richard Eberhart.—PlE
"**Man** lives by his sweat but the bird works harder." See Yet the lean beast plays
Man of Derby. See "A little old man of Derby"
A **man** of double deed. Mother Goose.—BrMg
There was a man.—SmM
The **man** of the house. David Wagoner.—DuS
Man of Thessaly. Mother Goose.—BrMg
A **man** of words. See "A man of words and not of deeds"
"A **man** of words and not of deeds." Mother Goose.—BlO—ReMg
A man of words.—ReOn
"A **man** said to me at the fair." See The market
"The **man** that hath no music in himself." See The merchant of Venice—Dark affections
"**Man** that is born of a woman." See Job
"A **man** was sitting underneath a tree." See Seumas Beg
"A **man** went a-hunting at Rygate." Mother Goose.—BrLl
"A **man** went down to Panama." See Goethals, the prophet engineer
The **man** who hid his own front door. Elizabeth MacKinstry.—ArT-3
"The **man** who tried to." See Poems
"A **man** who was fond of his skunk." David McCord.—BrLl
The **man** with naught. See "There was a man and he had naught"
The **man** with the blue guitar. Wallace Stevens.—LiT (sel.)
The **man** with the hoe. Edwin Markham.—BoH—PlE
Manatees
Columbus and the mermaids. E. J. Coatsworth.—CoDh
The **mandrill.** Conrad Aiken.—AiC
Manerathiak's song. Unknown, tr. fr. the Eskimo by Raymond De Coccola and Paul King.—DoW
Mangan, James Clarence
Siberia.—CoR
The time of the Barmacides.—CoR
Manhattan. Morris Abel Beer.—BrA
Manhattan epitaphs: Lawyer. Alfred Kreymborg.—LaC
Manhattan lullaby. Rachel Field.—BrA—LaC
Manhole covers. Karl Shapiro.—BoGj—BoH—BrA
Manifold, John
Fife tune.—BoGj—HoL—McWs
The griesly wife.—CaMb
Song.—CoBl
Mann, Kathie
Alone.—BaH

Manners. See Etiquette
Manners. Kate Greenaway.—GrT
"**Manners** in the dining room." Mother Goose.—AgH
The **manoeuvre.** William Carlos Williams.—HaL
The **manor** farm. Edward Thomas.—ClF (sel.)
Manovinoda
Autumn.—AlPi
A **man's** a man for a' that. Robert Burns.—BoH—BuPr
Mansei
"To what shall I compare."—BaS
Mansel, W. L.
"The sun's perpendicular rays."—GrCt
Mansfield, Katherine, pseud. (Kathleen Beauchamp)
Little brother's secret.—ArT-3—ThA
Mansion. Eleanor Farjeon.—FaT
Manual system. Carl Sandburg.—ArT-3
"**Many** a hearth upon our dark globe sighs after many a vanish'd face." See Vastness
"**Many** a long, long year ago." See The alarmed skipper
"**Many** a tree is found in the wood." See A salute to trees
"**Many** arms." See Pine
"**Many** fair ev'nings, many flow'rs." See The shower
"The **many-handed** octopus." See The octopus
"**Many** love music but for music's sake." See On music
"**Many-maned** scud-thumper, tub." See Winter ocean
"**Many** shiver." Jocelyn Klein.—LeM
The **map.** G. C. Oden.—BoA
Map of my country. John Holmes.—BrA
"A **map** of my native country is all edges." See Map of my country
"The **map** shows me where it is you are. I." See A private letter to Brazil
The **maple.** Elizabeth Jane Coatsworth.—CoSb
"The **maple** is a dainty maid." See Autumn fancies
Maple trees
The little maple. C. Zolotow.—BrSg
The maple. E. J. Coatsworth.—CoSb
"Swift cloud shadows." Shusen.—BeCs
The **mapmaker** on his art. Howard Nemerov.—DuS
Maps
The map. G. C. Oden.—BoA
Map of my country. J. Holmes.—BrA
The mapmaker on his art. H. Nemerov.—DuS
Maps. D. B. Thompson.—ArT-3
Maps. Dorothy Brown Thompson.—ArT-3
Marabandi, Jigar
Ghazal.—AlPi
Marbles. Kathleen Fraser.—FrS
March, Joseph Moncure
City autumn.—LaC
March
March ("Awake to the cold light") H. Crane.—CoBn
March ("A blue day") E. J. Coatsworth.—LaPd
March ("The insect world, now sunbeams higher climb") J. Clare.—ReO
March ("It is time. The geese fly overhead, returning") N. Belting.—BeCm
March ("The wind is big enough") M. C. Livingston.—LiC
March ("Winter has packed her brown garments") N. Belting.—BeCm
March dreams. R. Henderson.—ThA
March in New Mexico. E. J. Coatsworth.—CoDh
The March problem. G. Garrett.—HoL
March the third. E. Thomas.—ThG
March weather. S. Barker.—HoL
March wind. H. Behn.—BeG
Written in March. W. Wordsworth.—ArT-3—BoGj—CoBn—TuW—WoP
March.—HoB
March ("Awake to the cold light") Hart Crane.—CoBn
March ("A blue day") Elizabeth Jane Coatsworth.—LaPd
March ("The cock is crowing") See Written in March
March ("The insect world, now sunbeams higher climb") John Clare.—ReO
March ("It is time. The geese fly overhead, returning") Natalia Belting.—BeCm
March ("The wind is big enough") Myra Cohn Livingston.—LiC
March ("Winter has packed her brown garments") Natalia Belting.—BeCm
March dreams. Rose Henderson.—ThA
March in New Mexico. Elizabeth Jane Coatsworth.—CoDh
"**March,** march a-way." See Playtime
The **March** problem. George Garrett.—HoL
March the third. Edward Thomas.—ThG
March weather. Shirley Barker.—HoL
March wind. Harry Behn.—BeG
"**March** winds and April showers." Mother Goose.—BrSg
Spring.—BrMg
Marching. See also Parades
"Fife and drum." K. Fraser.—FrS
Marching along. From Cavalier tunes. R. Browning.—BrP
Marching song. R. L. Stevenson.—ArT-3
Marching along. See Cavalier tunes
Marching song. Robert Louis Stevenson.—ArT-3
"**Marcia** and I went over the curb." See Millions of strawberries
Marcus, Danny
The magic flower.—LeM
Two million two hundred thousand fishes.—LeM
"**Marcus,** the sluggard, dreamed he ran a race." See The sluggard
Mardhekar, B. S.
Poem.—AlPi
Mardi gras
A ballad of remembrance. R. E. Hayden.—AdIa—BoA

"The **mare** roamed soft about the slope." See Orchard
"**Márgarét,** are you grieving." See Spring and fall: To a young child
"**Margaret** mentioned Indians." See Indians
Maria Jane. Alfred Scott-Gatty.—CoBb
"**Maria** was a careless child." See Careless Maria
Mariana. Alfred Tennyson.—TeP
"**Maria's** aunt, who lived in town." See The fan
Marigolds
Five little sisters. K. Greenaway.—GrT
How marigolds came yellow. R. Herrick.—GrCt
"**Mariana's** gone, and now I sit." See Britannia's pastorals—So shuts the marigold her leaves
Mariners' carol. W. S. Merwin.—PlE
Marion, Francis (about)
Song of Marion's men. W. C. Bryant.—HiL
Marjorie's almanac. Thomas Bailey Aldrich.—BrSg
Mark Twain and Joan of Arc. See Three poems about Mark Twain
The **market.** James Stephens.—StS
The **market** man. John Ratti.—DuS
Markets and marketing. See also Shops and shopkeepers
Artichoke. P. Neruda.—LiT
"As I was going to Banbury." Mother Goose.—OpF
Banbury fair.—BrMg
"As I was going to sell my butter." Mother Goose.—OpF
"As I was going to sell my eggs." Mother Goose.—OpF
Bandy legs.—BrMg
A boy went walking. Unknown.—StF
"Father and mother and Uncle John." Mother Goose.—OpF
Goblin market. C. G. Rossetti.—CoD
The holiday. M. Stredder.—StF
In the bazaars of Hyderabad. S. Naidu.—AlPi—ThA
Jenny. Mother Goose.—BrMg
The market man. J. Ratti.—DuS
My brother. D. Aldis.—HoB
Shopping for meat in winter. O. Williams.—HoL
"There was an old woman as I've heard tell." Mother Goose.—ArT-3
Mother Goose rhymes, 55.—HoB
The story of the little woman.—BrMg
"There was a little woman as I've heard tell."—OpF—SmM
"To market, to market, a gallop, a trot." Mother Goose.—OpF
"To market, to market, to buy a fat pig." Mother Goose.—ArT-3—HuS-3—OpF
"To market, to market to buy a plum bun." Mother Goose.—OpF
To market.—BrMg
Markham, Edwin
The man with the hoe.—BoH—PlE
Mark's fingers. Mary O'Neill.—OnF
Marlowe, Christopher
"Ah, Faustus." See The tragical history of Dr Faustus
The bloody conquests of mighty Tamburlaine. See Tamburlaine the Great
Elegies, sel.
To verse let kings give place. tr.—GrCt
I have an orchard. See The tragedy of Dido
"If all the pens that ever poets held." See Tamburlaine the Great
The Jew of Malta, sel.
Mine argosy from Alexandria.—GrCt
Mine argosy from Alexandria. See The Jew of Malta
The passionate shepherd to his love.—CoBl—McWs
A spell of invisibility. See The tragical history of Dr Faustus
Tamburlaine the Great, sels.
The bloody conquests of mighty Tamburlaine.—GrCt
"If all the pens that ever poets held."—GrCt
To entertain divine Zenocrate.—GrCt
To entertain divine Zenocrate. See Tamburlaine the Great
To verse let kings give place. See Elegies
The tragedy of Dido, sel.
I have an orchard.—GrCt
The tragical history of Dr Faustus, sels.
"Ah Faustus"
From Dr Faustus.—GrCt
A spell of invisibility.—GrCt
Marlowe, Christopher (about)
Christopher Marlowe. From To Henry Reynolds, of poets and poesy. M. Drayton.—GrCt
Marmion, sels. Walter Scott
Christmas time.—ClF
"Heap on more wood, the wind is chill."—ArT-3
Flodden.—ClF
Lochinvar.—CoR—HuS-3
Marquis, Don (Donald Robert Perry Marquis)
Archy and Mehitabel, sels.
The flattered lightning bug.—CoB
Freddy the rat perishes.—LaC
Pete at the seashore.—CoB
Short course in natural history.—CoB
The flattered lightning bug. See Archy and Mehitabel
Freddy the rat perishes. See Archy and Mehitabel
A hot-weather song.—HuS-3
In the bayou.—BrA
Mrs Swartz.—HiL
"Noah an' Jonah an' Cap'n John Smith."—CoSs
Pete at the seashore. See Archy and Mehitabel
Short course in natural history. See Archy and Mehitabel
When one loves tensely.—CoBl
Marr, J. R.
A girl speaks to her playmate. tr.—AlPi

Married life—*Continued*
"My little old man and I fell out." Mother Goose.—ReMg
Squabbles.—BrMg
My singing aunt. J. Reeves.—BrSm
"Needles and pins, needles and pins." Mother Goose
Mother Goose rhymes, 33.—HoB
"Now what do you think." Mother Goose.—OpF
Jacky Jingle.—BrMg
Oh lucky Jim. Unknown.—GrCt
"O, when I was a wee thing." Unknown.—MoB
The old-marrieds. G. Brooks.—BoA
Old Sam's wife. Unknown.—GrCt
On the wife of a parish clerk.—BrSm
"Old wife, old wife." Unknown.—MoB
"On Saturday night I lost my wife." Mother Goose.—OpF
Saturday night.—BrMg
On seeing a pompous funeral for a bad husband. Unknown.—BrSm
On the death of a wife. Unknown.—LeO
Patient Griselda. From The Canterbury tales. G. Chaucer.—ChT
"Peter, Peter, pumpkin-eater." Mother Goose.—WiMg
Mother Goose rhymes, 9.—HoB
Peter.—BrMg
Phoebus and the crow. From The Canterbury tales. G. Chaucer.—ChT
Lat take a cat.—GrCt (sel.)
Take any bird.—ReO (sel.)
Poem in prose. A. MacLeish.—McWs
"The Quaker's wife sat down to bake." Unknown.—MoB
A reasonable affliction. M. Prior.—BrSm
The red-haired man's wife. J. Stephens.—StS
The river merchant's wife: A letter. Li T'ai-po.—BoH—CoBl—LiT
"Robin he married a wife in the west." Unknown.—OpF
"She rose to his requirement, dropped." E. Dickinson.—DiPe
The story of Constance. From The Canterbury tales. G. Chaucer.—ChT
"Stranger call this not." Unknown.—BrSm
Teevee. E. Merriam.—MeC
"There was a wee wifie rowed (or row't) up in a blanket." Mother Goose.—MoB—OpF
"There was an old man who lived in a wood." Mother Goose.—HuS-3
This spot. Unknown.—BrSm
The tired man. A. Wickham.—SmM
Tommy O'Linn. Mother Goose.—BrMg
The true and tender wife. From Ramayana. Valmiki.—AlPi
The turtledoves. A. Fisher.—FiC
The two wives. Daniel Henderson.—BrSm
Wasn't it you. K. R. Narasimhaswamy.—AlPi
Wedding procession, from a window. J. A. Emanuel.—HaK
"When I was a little boy (I lived)." Mother Goose.—ReMg
A sad story.—BrMg
Whistle o'er the lave o't. R. Burns.—BuPr
Wife and husband. C. Day.—LeM
Wills. J. G. Saxe.—BrSm
"Within this grave do lie." Unknown.—BrSm
You'd say it was a funeral. J. Reeves.—BrSm
Marryat, A.
Waking.—GrT
Marryat, Frederick
The old navy.—CoSs
The **marsh.** W. D. Snodgrass.—CoBn
Marshall, James
The Oregon trail: 1851.—HuS-3
Martial (Marcus Valerius Martialis)
Doctor Fell.—BrMg—GrCt
"I do not like thee, Dr Fell."—ReMg
"I do not like thee, Dr Fell." See Doctor Fell
A **martial** mouse. Samuel Butler.—ReO
"A **Martian** named Harrison Harris." See Interplanetary limerick
Martin, I. L.
At the tennis clinic.—MoS
Dark eyes at Forest Hills.—MoS
Martin, Saint
St Martin and the beggar. T. Gunn.—CaMb
"**Martin** sat young upon his bed." See St Martin and the beggar
Martindale, C. C.
God leads the way. tr.—PlE
Martins
Children of the wind. From The people, yes. C. Sandburg.—HuS-3
These children of the wind.—ReBs
Martul, Stefan
Splish splash.—LeM
Marvell, Andrew
Bermudas.—GrCt—HiL
Carrying their coracles. See Upon Appleton house
The character of Holland.—GrCt (sel.)
Cromwell dead. See A poem upon the death of Oliver Cromwell
The gallery.—GrS
The garden.—CoBn (sel.)—GrCt (sel.)
The hewel, or woodpecker. See Upon Appleton house
An Horation ode upon Cromwell's return from Ireland, sel.
King Charles upon the scaffold.—GrCt
King Charles upon the scaffold. See An Horatian ode upon Cromwell's return from Ireland
The kingfisher. See Upon Appleton house
The nymph complaining for the death of her fawn.—ReO (sel.)
A poem upon the death of Oliver Cromwell, sel.
Cromwell dead.—GrCt
Upon Appleton house, sels.
Carrying their coracles.—GrCt

The hewel, or woodpecker.—GrCt
The woodpecker.—ReBs
The kingfisher.—GrCt
The woodpecker. See Upon Appleton house—The hewel, or woodpecker
Marx, Olga
Invocation. tr.—PlE
Mary II, Queen of England (about)
Orange lilies. J. Reaney.—DoW
Mary, Queen of Scots (about)
Alas, poor queen. M. Angus.—GrS
Mary, Virgin (about)
Jesus and his mother. T. Gunn.—PlE
The maiden makeles. Unknown.—GrCt
The seven virgins. Unknown.—GrCt
The visitation. E. Jennings.—CaMb
Mary ("Mary. Mary. Mary") Walter De La Mare.—DeBg
Mary ("Sweet Mary, the first time she ever was there") William Blake.—BlP
Mary Ann. Joseph Tabrar.—CoBl
"**Mary** Ann, Mary Ann." Mother Goose.—OpF
"**Mary** had a little bird." See The canary
"**Mary** had a little lamb." Sarah Josepha Hale.—OpF—WiMg
Mary's lamb.—BrMg
"**Mary** has a thingamajig clamped on her ears." See Manual system
Mary Hynes. James Stephens.—StS
"**Mary** is a gentle name." See Gentle name
"**Mary.** Mary. Mary." See Mary
"**Mary,** Mary, quite contrary." Mother Goose.—BrSg—HuS-3—OpF—ReMg—WiMg
Contrary Mary.—BrMg
Mother Goose rhymes, 2.—HoB
Mary Morison. Robert Burns.—BuPr
Mary Tudor. Elizabeth Jane Coatsworth.—CoDh
"**Mary's** eyes are blue as azure." Shelley Silverstein.—CoBl
Mary's ghost. Thomas Hood.—SmM
Mary's lamb. See "Mary had a little lamb"
Masahide
"Since my house burned down."—BeCs
Masefield, John
A ballad of John Silver.—CoSs
Cape Horn gospel.—CoSs
Captain Stratton's fancy.—CoSs
Cargoes.—ArT-3—CoR—CoSs—ThA
The emigrant.—ClF
The golden city of St Mary.—BoH—PaH
Posted as missing.—BlO
Reynard the fox.—ReO (sel.)
Roadways.—PaH
Sea fever.—ArT-3—CoSs—HoB—Hus-3—LaPd—ThA
Trade winds.—BoH—ClF
A wanderer's song.—TuW
The yarn of the Loch Achray.—CoSs
The **mask** of evil. Bertolt Brecht, tr. fr. the German by H. R. Hays.—LiT
The **masked** shrew. Isabella Gardner.—CoB
Masks
Beethoven's death mask. S. Spender.—LiT
The mask of evil. B. Brecht.—LiT
Mason, Bronwyn
The mine.—LeM
Mason, Sarah
War.—LeM
Mason, Walt
Football.—MoS
Masque of gipsies, sel. Ben Jonson
All your fortunes we can tell ye.—GrCt
The **masque** of the twelve months, sel. at. to George Chapman
"Shine out, fair sun, with all your heat."—GrCt
The **massacre** of the innocents. William Jay Smith.—PlE
The **massacre** of the Macpherson. William Edmonstone Aytoun.—GrCt
"**Master** I have, and I am his man." Mother Goose.—ArT-3
Master Jack's song. Laura E. Richards.—AgH
Masters, Edgar Lee
Achilles Deatheridge.—BrA
Anne Rutledge. See The Spoon River anthology
Knowlt Hoheimer. See The Spoon River anthology
The new world.—BrA (sel.)
The Spoon River anthology, sels.
Anne Rutledge.—BrA—HiL
Knowlt Hoheimer.—HoL
The village atheist.—PlE
The village atheist. See The Spoon River anthology
Masters, Edgar Lee (about)
The prairie battlements. V. Lindsay.—LiP
Masters, Marcia
April.—DuR
Masters, in this hall. William Morris.—GrCt
A **match** at football, sel. Matthew Concanen
Heaps on heaps.—MoS
Mathematics. See also Arithmetic
Euclid. V. Lindsay.—HoL—LiT
"Said Mrs Isosceles Tri." C. B. Burgess.—BrLl
"There was a young man from Trinity." Unknown.—BrLl
"There was an old man who said, Do." Unknown.—BrLl
"There was an old man who said, Gee." Unknown.—BrLl
Mather, Cotton (about)
Cotton Mather. R. C. and S. V. Benét.—HiL
Mathers, E. Powys
The dalliance of the leopards. tr.—HoL
Dates. See Thousand and one nights
"Even now." See Fifty stanzas for a thief
Fifty stanzas for a thief, sel.
"Even now." tr.—AlPi
The garden of bamboos. tr.—CoBl
A proverb. tr.—CoBl
Thousand and one nights, sel.
Dates. tr.—HoL
Mathias, Eileen
Zoo manners.—StF

Matilda ("Matilda got her stockings wet") F. Gwynne Evans.—CoBb
Matilda ("Matilda told such dreadful lies") Hilaire Belloc.—BlO
"**Matilda** got her stockings wet." See Matilda
"**Matilda** told such dreadful lies." See Matilda
Matin song. See The rape of Lucrece
A **matter** of taste. Eve Merriam.—AgH
"**Matthew,** Mark, Luke, and John (bless)." See Prayer before sleeping
"**Matthew,** Mark, Luke, and John (hold my horse)." See "Matthew, Mark, Luke, John"
"**Matthew,** Mark, Luke, John." Mother Goose.—MoB
Pick-a-back.—BrMg
Matumeak, Dan G.
A man is buried where the cold winds blow.—BaH
Mauch, J.
Circuit through the hills. tr.—AlPi
Evening at the seashore. tr.—AlPi
Maud, sels. Alfred Tennyson
"Come into the garden, Maud."—CoBl—TeP
"See what a lovely shell."—BoGj
From Maud.—CoBn
May, Darcy
Clouds in a wild storm.—LeM
May
By a chapel as I came. Unknown.—GrCt
Corinna's going a-Maying. R. Herrick.—CoBn
The crazy woman. G. Brooks.—BoH—LiT
"The fair maid who, the first of May." Mother Goose.—OpF
The fair maid.—ReOn
The first of May.—BrMg
Mother Goose rhymes, 34.—HoB
The fields abroad with spangled flowers. Unknown.—GrCt
For a dance. E. Farjeon.—LaPh
In praise of May. Unknown.—ReBs
Marjorie's almanac. T. B. Aldrich.—BrSg
May ("Mother o' blossoms, and ov all") W. Barnes.—GrCt
May ("Night is almost gone") N. Belting.—BeCm
May ("The Seven Stars are shining again") N. Belting.—BeCm
May day ("A delicate fabric of bird song") S. Teasdale.—CoBn
May day ("So soft came the breath") M. C. Livingston.—BrSg
May day ("Winter rose, and in one night fled away") J. Reeves.—CaD
May day ("You heard the screen door open") A. Fisher.—LaPh
May-June ("The food pits are empty") N. Belting.—BeCm
May-June ("In the beginning man did not have cattle") N. Belting.—BeCm
May morning. E. J. Coatsworth.—CoSb
The May queen. A. Tennyson.—TeP
May 10th. M. W. Kumin.—CoBn
"May wind is busy." K. Mizumura.—MiI
May's song. E. Farjeon.—FaA
Memory. T. B. Aldrich.—CoBn
The month of May. From The knight of the burning pestle. F. Beaumont and J. Fletcher.—GrCt
Nuts in May. E. Farjeon.—FaT
The old ones. F. Bellerby.—CaD
The Padstow night song. Unknown.—GrCt
A pleasant walk. Unknown.—VrF
Québec May. E. Birney.—DoW
Song: On May morning. J. Milton.—CoBn
On a May morning.—ClF (sel.)
"There is but one May in the year." C. G. Rossetti.—ArT-3
May ("Mother o' blossoms, and ov all") William Barnes.—GrCt (sel.)
May ("Night is almost gone") Natalia Belting.—BeCm
May ("The Seven Stars are shining again") Natalia Belting.—BeCm
May day. See May
May-day, sels. Ralph Waldo Emerson
"I know the trusty almanac."—ReBs
"Why chidest thou the tardy spring."—ReBs
May day ("A delicate fabric of bird song") Sara Teasdale.—CoBn
May day ("So soft came the breath") Myra Cohn Livingston.—BrSg
May day ("Winter rose, and in one night fled away") James Reeves.—CaD
May day ("You heard the screen door open") Aileen Fisher.—LaPh
"**May-day,** delightful day." See In praise of May
May-June ("The food pits are empty") Natalia Belting.—BeCm
May-June ("In the beginning man did not have cattle") Natalia Belting.—BeCm
May morning. Elizabeth Jane Coatsworth.—CoSb
The **May** queen. Alfred Tennyson.—TeP
May 10th. Maxine W. Kumin.—CoBn
"**May** the gravediggers not bury me." Unknown—DoC
"**May** they stumble, stage by stage." See Traveller's curse after misdirection
"**May** wind is busy." K. Mizumura.—MiI
Mayakovsky, Vladimir
Brooklyn bridge.—LiT
"**Maybe** it's so." See Snail's pace
Mayor, Beatrice
Evening over the forest.—ClF
May's song. Eleanor Farjeon.—FaA
Maytime magic. Mabel Watts.—BrSg
Mazilla and Mazura. Unknown.—GrCt
Me ("As long as I live") Walter De La Mare.—DeBg—HuS-3
Me ("Who's me, a little black boy") Michael Goode.—BaH
Me, Alexander Soames. Karla Kuskin.—ArT-3
"**Me** and my grannie." Unknown.—MoB
Me and the mule. Langston Hughes.—AdIa
"**Me** father was the keeper of the Eddystone light." See The Eddystone light
"**Me** oh my, said the tiny, shiny ant." See Big little boy

Meader, Susan
A thundery day.—LeM
"A **meadow** lark came back one day." See Spring song
Meadow larks. See Larks
Meadow morning. Aileen Fisher.—FiI
The **meadow** mouse. Theodore Roethke.—McWs—ReO
Meadow of hay. Aileen Fisher.—FiI
"**Meadowlarks.**" See When spring appears
Meadows. See Fields
Meals. See Breakfast; Dinner; Supper
Meanie. Aileen Fisher.—FiIo
The **meaning** of atman. See Upanishads
"**Meare's** milk and deer's milk." See A witch's spell
Measles. Aileen Fisher.—FiIo
"A **measuring** worm." Issa, tr. fr. the Japanese by Nobuyuki Yuasa.—IsF
Meat. See Food and eating
Meddlesome Matty. Ann and Jane Taylor.—GrT
"A **medical** student named Elias." Unknown.—BrLl
Medicine
Ipecacuanha. G. Canning.—GrCt
Medicine song. Unknown.—LeO
Mountain medicine. E. E. Long.—BrA
Medicine song. Unknown, tr. fr. the Navajo.—LeO
Meditatio. Ezra Pound.—ArT-3—DuR—HaL
Meditation at Elsinore. Elizabeth Jane Coatsworth.—CoDh
Meditations of a mariner. Wallace Irwin.—CoSs
Meditations of a tortoise dozing under a rose-tree near a bee hive at noon while a dog scampers about and a cuckoo calls from a distant wood. E. V. Rieu.—ArT-3—CoB
"**Meet** Ladybug." See I want you to meet
"**Meet** me my love, meet me my love." See The juniper tree
Meet-on-the-road. Unknown.—BlO
Meeting ("Over the grass a hedgehog came") Clifford Dyment.—CoB (sel.)
A **meeting** ("When George began to climb all unawares") See Encounters with a Doppelganger
Meeting at night. Robert Browning.—BrP—CoBl—HoL—TuW
Meeting the Easter bunny. Rowena Bastin Bennett.—ArT-3
Meetings
Meeting ("Over the grass a hedgehog came") C. Dyment.—CoB (sel.)
A meeting ("When George began to climb all unawares") From Encounters with a Doppelganger. G. D. Painter.—SmM
The rendezvous. P. Lal.—AlPi
The reunion. O. Dodson.—BoH
Meg Merrilies. John Keats.—ArT-3—BlO—ClF—HuS-3—SmM
Meigs, Mildred Plew (Mildred Plew Merryman)
Abraham Lincoln.—ArT-3
Johnny Fife and Johnny's wife.—ArT-3
Pirate Don Durk of Dowdee.—ArT-3—HoB—LaPd
Silver ships.—ArT-3
Meisetsu
"A river leaping."—BeCs
Melancholy
"At twilight." E. J. Coatsworth.—CoDh
The day is done. H. W. Longfellow.—LoPl
Don't bomb human nature out of existence. J. Tagliabue.—DuS
Get up, blues. J. A. Emanuel.—BoA—LiT
Hurting. B. Graves.—LeM
King David. W. De La Mare.—LiT
"M is for mournful Miss Molly." I. F. Bellows.—BrLl
On visiting a clear spring. Li T'ai-po.—LeMw
The path of the lonely ones. G. E. Varela.—BaH
Prologue. From Evangeline. H. W. Longfellow.—LoPl
The rainy day. H. W. Longfellow.—LoPl
Resolution and independence. W. Wordsworth.—CoBn (sel.)—WoP
Roman wall blues. W. H. Auden.—SmM
"Over the heather the wet wind blows."—CaD
Song ("Again rejoicing Nature sees") R. Burns.—CoBn
Song ("Dressed up in my melancholy") M. C. Holman.—BoA—HaK
Song ("Memory, hither come") W. Blake.—BlP
Theme with variations. J. Stephens.—StS (sel.)
To a nightingale. J. Keats.—GrCt
Too blue. L. Hughes.—DuR
"We're all in the dumps." Mother Goose.—BlO
In the dumps.—BrMg
What the tramp said. J. Stephens.—StS
"When I hoped, I recollect." E. Dickinson.—DiL
"The **melancholy** days are come, the saddest of the year." See The death of the flowers
Melanesia
September. N. Belting.—BeCm
Meleager of Gadara
Flowers: For Heliodora.—GrS
Mellichamp, Leslie
Epitaph.—BrSm
"**Mellow** the moonlight to shine is beginning." See A spinning-wheel song
Melville, Herman
Always with us—the black preacher.—ReBs
The Maldive shark.—CoB
The returned volunteer to his rifle.—HiL
"The ribs and terrors in the whale."—PlE
Running the batteries.—HiL
Shiloh, A requiem.—BrA—PaH
The tuft of kelp.—GrCt
Memoirs of the little man and the little maid. Unknown, at. to Charles Sidley.—VrF
The little man and the little maid.—BrMg
Memorabilia. Robert Browning.—BrP
Memoranda. William Dickey.—DuS

Outward show.—ShS
The power of music.—ShS
Merchants. See Shops and shopkeepers
The **merciful** hand. Vachel Lindsay.—LiP
Mercy. See Sympathy
Mercy. See The merchant of Venice
Meredith, George
The lark ascending.—ReO (sel.)
Love in a valley, sel.
The white owl.—GrCt
The sweet o' the year.—CoBn
Tardy spring.—ClF (sel.)
The white owl. See Love in a valley
Young Reynard.—CoB
Meredith, William Tucker
Farragut.—HiL
Merlin and the gleam. Alfred Tennyson.—TeP
The **mermaid.** Unknown.—CoSs
The **mermaidens.** Laura E. Richards.—HuS-3
The **mermaids** ("And now they nigh approachèd to the stead") See The faerie queene
Mermaids ("Leagues, leagues over") Walter De La Mare.—DeBg
Mermaids and mermen
Blow, ye winds. Unknown.—CoSs
Bonum omen. W. De La Mare.—DeBg
Cape Horn gospel. J. Masefield.—CoSs
Columbus and the mermaids. E. J. Coatsworth. —CoDh
The Eddystone light. Unknown.—CoSs
The forsaken merman. M. Arnold.—BlO—CoSs —SmM
"Four-and-twenty mermaids." Unknown.— MoB
In place of a curse. J. Ciardi.—DuS
Little John Bottlejohn. L. E. Richards.—LaPd
Madness one Monday evening. J. Fields.—HaK —LiT
The mermaid. Unknown.—CoSs
The mermaidens. L. E. Richards.—HuS-3
The mermaids ("And now they nigh approachèd to the stead") From The faerie queene. E. Spenser.—GrCt
Mermaids ("Leagues, leagues over") W. De La Mare.—DeBg
Song by Lady Happy, as a sea-goddess. M. Cavendish.—GrS
Song of the mermaids. G. Darley.—GrCt
A vision of the mermaids. G. M. Hopkins.— GrCt (sel.)
The would-be merman. V. Lindsay.—LiP
Mermen. See Mermaids and mermen
Merriam, Eve
Aa couple of doublles.—MeI
Advertisement for a divertissement.—MeI
Alligator on the escalator.—LaC—MeC
Ann's fan.—MeC
Backwards.—MeC
Bam, bam, bam.—LaPd—MeC
Be my non-valentine.—MeI
Benjamin Franklin.—MeIv
Beware of the doggerel.—MeI
Beware, or be yourself.—MeI
Big Goliath, little David.—MeC
Big little boy.—MeC
Catch a little rhyme.—LaPd—MeC
"A chameleon, when he's feeling blue."—BrLl
Cheers.—DuR—MeI
City traffic.—LaC—LaPd—MeI
A cliché.—MeI
Color.—MeI
A commercial for spring.—MeI
Conversation with myself.—MeI
Couplet countdown.—MeI
Dick's trick.—MeC
Ding, ding.—MeC
Ditto marks; or, How do you amuse a muse. —MeI
The donkey and the fluke.—MeC
Double trouble.—MeI
The egotistical orchestra.—MeI
Elizabeth Blackwell.—MeIv
End of winter.—MeI
The fable of the golden pear.—MeI
Fiorello H. LaGuardia.—MeIv
First day of summer.—MeI
A fishy square dance.—MeI
Forever.—MeI
Frederick Douglass.—MeIv
Fred's bed.—MeC
Gazinta.—MeI
"Going to school."—MeC
Happy birthday to me.—MeC
Having words.—MeI
Henry Thoreau.—MeIv
How to eat a poem.—AgH—DuR—MeI
I, says the poem.—ArT-3—MeI
Ida B. Wells.—MeIv
Inside a poem.—ArT-3—MeI
Inside the zoo.—MeC
A jamboree for j.—MeI
June's tune.—MeC
King Solomon.—MeC
A lazy thought.—LaC
Leaning on a limerick.—MeI
Leavetaking.—LaPd—MeI
Lucretia Mott.—MeIv
A matter of taste.—AgH
Metaphor.—MeI
Methuselah.—MeI
Mr Zoo.—MeI
Mnemonic for spelunking.—MeI
Mona Lisa.—MeI
Night song.—MeC
A number of numbers.—MeC
Nym and graph.—MeI
Ollie's polly.—MeC
On our way.—MeC
One, two, three—gough.—MeI
Onomatopoeia.—MeI
Onomatopoeia II.—MeI
Oz.—DuR—MeI
Peculiar.—MeC
Pete's sweets.—MeC
Quatrain.—MeI
Schenectady.—MeC

Montezuma's song. E. J. Coatsworth.—CoDh
Meyer, Kuno
The Fort of Rathangan. tr.—GrCt
The old Fort of Rathangan.—HoL
The old Fort of Rathangan. See The Fort of Rathangan
Meyers, Bert
Porcupine.—CoB
Meynell, Alice
The rainy summer.—BoGj—GrS
Renouncement.—CoBl
Meynell, Francis
Chimes.—TuW
Mezzo cammin. Henry Wadsworth Longfellow. —LoPl
Mice
Birthday cake. A. Fisher.—LaPd
The brave priest. Mother Goose.—BrMg
Cat and mouse. T. Hughes.—PlE
Cat asks mouse out. S. Smith.—CaD
"The cattie sat in the kiln-ring." Unknown.—MoB
Christmas mouse. A. Fisher.—LaPh
The city mouse and the garden mouse. C. G. Rossetti.—ArT-3—HoB—HuS-3
"The city mouse lives in a house."—BrSg
Cruel clever cat. G. Taylor.—GrCt
"Dame Trot and her cat." Mother Goose.—StF
Dame Trot.—BrMg
Dark kingdom. E. J. Coatsworth.—CoB
Deer mouse. A. Fisher.—FiC
The field mouse. W. Sharp.—CoB—ReS
A friendly mouse. H. Behn.—BeG
"He climbed up the candlestick." Unknown.—WyC
"Hickory, dickory, dock." Mother Goose.—BrMg—OpF—ReMg—WiMg
Mother Goose rhymes, 16.—HoB
Hospitality. W. McClintic.—CoB
"The house of the mouse." L. S. Mitchell.—ArT-3
"I saw a ship a-sailing." Mother Goose.—ArT-3—HuS-3—ReMg—WiMg
I saw a ship.—CoSs—SmM
Mother Goose rhymes, 60.—HoB
A ship a-sailing.—BrMg
"In our house." Issa.—IsF—LeOw
In the dark of night. A. Fisher.—FiC
"It's been a bad year for the moles." D. McCord.—BrLl
Lancaster county tragedy. W. L. Kay.—BrSm
Lèse majesté. O. Herford.—CoB
The light-house-keeper's white-mouse. J. Ciardi.—LaPd
The lion and the mouse. R. S. Sharpe.—VrF
Little fable. R. Fuller.—CaD
"A little white mouse." M. Thomas.—LeM
The love-sick frog. Mother Goose.—BrMg
"Madame Mouse trots." E. Sitwell.—CaD—HaL
The magical mouse. K. Patchen.—HaL—WeP
The marriage of the frog and the mouse. Unknown.—ReO
A martial mouse. S. Butler.—ReO
The meadow mouse. T. Roethke.—McWs—ReO
Mice. R. Fyleman.—HuS-3—LaPd—ThA
Missing. A. A. Milne.—LaP—LaPd
The mouse ("Hush") M. M. Stephenson.—StF
The mouse ("I heard a mouse") E. J. Coatsworth.—ArT-3—CoB—ReS—ThA
Mouse ("Little mouse in gray velvet") H. Conkling.—ArT-3—HuS-3
"A mouse in her room woke Miss Dowd." Unknown.—BrLl
The mouse in the wainscot. I. Serraillier.—CoB—LaPd
Mouse roads. A. Fisher.—FiI
"The mouse that gnawed the oak-tree down." V. Lindsay.—HaL—LiP
Mouses's nest. J. Clare.—CoB—GrCt
The mousetrap. C. Morgenstern.—ReO
"Mousie, mousie, come to me." Unknown.—MoB
Of the mean and sure estate. T. Wyatt.—ReO (sel.)
The old wife and the ghost. J. Reeves.—BrSm—HoB—LaPd
The old woman. B. Potter.—BoGj—LaPd
The old woman and the mouse. Mother Goose. —BrMg
Poll Parrot. Mother Goose.—BrMg
The prayer of the mouse. C. B. de Gasztold.—LaPd
"Pretty John Watts." Mother Goose.—OpF
Rats and mice.—ReOn
The prince. W. De La Mare.—DeBg
"Six little mice sat down to spin." Mother Goose.—OpF
Six little mice.—BrMg—SmM—StF
Spinning song. E. Sitwell.—CaD
Supper. W. De La Mare.—DeBg
"There was a wee bit mousikie (or moosikie)." Mother Goose.—BlO—MoB—OpF
"Three blind mice, see how they run." Mother Goose.—OpF—WiMg
Three blind mice.—BrMg
Three mice. C. D. Cole.—StF
Tickling game. Unknown.—MoB
To a mouse. R. Burns.—BuH—BuPr—CoB—ReO
The two old bachelors. E. Lear.—BrSm
A waltzer in the house. S. Kunitz.—CoB—WeP
Who scans the meadow. A. Fisher.—FiI
Mice. Rose Fyleman.—HuS-3—LaPd—ThA
"**Mice** are the citizens of a dark kingdom." See Dark kingdom
Michael Angelo, A fragment. Henry Wadsworth Longfellow.—LoPl (sel.)
Michie, James
Arizona nature myth.—SmM
Michigan
Highway: Michigan. T. Roethke.—DuS
Mick. James Reeves.—CoB
"**Mick** my mongrel-o." See Mick
The **microscope.** Maxine W. Kumin.—DuR
Microscopes
"Faith is a fine invention." E. Dickinson.—DiPe

Microscopes—*Continued*
The microscope. M. W. Kumin.—DuR
Mid-country blow. Theodore Roethke.—CoBn
Middle age
Mezzo cammin. H. W. Longfellow.—LoPl
Prayer in mid-passage. L. MacNeice.—PlE
Middle ages. See Arthur, King; Crusades; Knights and knighthood; Minstrels and troubadours
Middle passage. Robert E. Hayden.—AdIa—BoA
Middleton, Christopher
She-goat and glow-worm. tr.—ReO
Middleton, Richard
The carol of the poor children.—SmM
Middleton, Thomas
"Love is like a lamb, and love is like a lion."—CoBl
Midnight.—BlO—ReS
"The **midges** dance aboon the burn." Robert Tannahill.—CoBn
"**Midget** Eenanennika." See Tiny Eenanennika
Midnight ("Fainter and thin") James Stephens.—StS
Midnight ("Midnight's bell goes ting, ting, ting, ting, ting") Thomas Middleton.—BlO—ReS
Midnight in the garden. Li Shang-yin, tr. by Arthur Christy.—LeMw
"**Midnight** is no time for." See No time for poetry
"The **midnight** plane with its riding lights." See Night plane
Midnight raffle. Langston Hughes.—LaC
The **midnight** skaters. Edmund Blunden.—BoGj
Midnight was come. See The complaint of Henrie, Duke of Buckingham
"**Midnight** was come, and every vital thing." See The complaint of Henrie, Duke of Buckingham—Midnight was come
"**Midnight's** bell goes ting, ting, ting, ting, ting." See Midnight
Midsummer. Sybil Horatia Calverley.—ReBs
Midsummer eve. Eleanor Farjeon.—FaA
"**Midsummer** eve, a year ago, my mother she commanded." See Midsummer magic
Midsummer jingle. Newman Levy.—CoBn
Midsummer magic. Ivy O. Eastwick.—ArT-3
A **midsummer-night's** dream, sels. William Shakespeare
Fairy dance.—ShS
"I know a bank whereon the wild thyme blows."—CoBn
"Now the hungry lion roars."—GrCt
The ousel cock.—SmM
"Over hill, over dale."—BlO
Fairy's song.—ShS
Puck's song.—ShS
Song for goblins.—ShS
Sunrise on the sea.—GrCt
"You spotted snakes with double tongue."—BlO
Song.—SmM
A **midsummer** song. Richard Watson Gilder.—CoBn
"**Midways** of a walled garden." See Golden wings
Midwest town. Ruth Delong Peterson.—BrA
Midwife cat. Mark Van Doren.—ReO
"The **midwife** laid her hand on his thick skull." See Absalom and Achitopel—Thomas Shadwell the poet
"A **mighty** fortress is our God." Martin Luther, tr. fr. the German by F. H. Hedge.—PlE
A **mighty** runner, variation of a Greek theme. Edwin Arlington Robinson.—MoS
"The **mighty** thoughts of an old world." Thomas Lovell Beddoes.—BoGj
Song.—GrS
Migration—Birds. See Birds—Migration
"A **mile** behind is Gloucester town." See Gloucester moors
Miles, Josephine
The family. tr.—AlPi
Sale.—DuS
Since I left the ocean. tr.—AlPi
Milk and milking
"Bonnie lady." Unknown.—MoB
Buttercup cow. E. Rendall.—ArT-3
"Cushy cow, bonny, let down thy milk." Mother Goose.—HuS-3—OpF—ReMg
Milking.—BrMg
Jenny. Mother Goose.—BrMg
"Little maid, pretty maid, whither goest thou." Mother Goose.—OpF
The milkmaid.—BrMg
Milk for the cat. H. Monro.—BlO—CoB—SmM
Milking time. E. M. Roberts.—BoGj—HoB
The strangers. A. A. Brown.—DoW
White cat. R. Knister.—DoW
Milk for the cat. Harold Monro.—BlO—CoB—SmM
The **milk** maid. See "Where are you going (to) my pretty maid"
The **milk-white** dove. Unknown.—GrCt
"**Milk-white** moon, put the cows to sleep." Carl Sandburg.—HuS-3
Milking. See "Cushy cow, bonny, let down thy milk"
Milking time. Elizabeth Madox Roberts.—BoGj—HoB
The **milkmaid.** See "Little maid, pretty maid, where goest thou"
Milkmaids
"Little maid, pretty maid, whither goest thou." Mother Goose.—OpF
The milkmaid.—BrMg
"Where are you going (to) my pretty maid." Mother Goose.—OpF—WiMg
The milk maid.—BrMg
The **milkman.** See "Milkman, milkman, where have you been"
"**Milkman,** milkman, where have you been." Mother Goose.—OpF
The milkman.—BrMg
Milkmen
"Milkman, milkman, where have you been." Mother Goose.—OpF
The milkman.—BrMg
Polly Perkins. Unknown.—CoBl
Milky Way
"How lovely." Issa.—LeI—LeMw

Milne, A. (Alan) A. (Alexander)—*Continued*
Disobedience.—MiC
The engineer.—MiC
The friend.—MiC
Furry bear.—HuS-3—MiC
The good little girl.—CoBb
Halfway down.—MiC
Happiness.—ArT-3—MiC
Hoppity.—ArT-3—HoB—MiC
In the dark.—MiC
In the fashion.—LaP
The king's breakfast.—MiC
Lines and squares.—MiC
The little black hen.—MiC
Missing.—LaP—LaPd
Puppy and I.—ArT-3—LaPd
Rice pudding.—CoBb—MiC
Sneezles.—MiC
Swing song.—MiC
Teddy bear.—MiC
The three foxes.—BoGj—HuS-3—MiC
Us two.—ArT-3—MiC
Vespers.—MiC
Milne, Ewart
Diamond cut diamond.—ArT-3—CoB
Milner-Gulland, Robin. See Levi, Peter and Milner-Gulland, Robin
Milosevic, Peter
Murder.—LeM
Milton, John
Arms and the Muse, sel.
When the assault was intended to the city.—CoR
At a vacation exercise, sel.
Rivers arise: A fragment.—GrCt
Death of Samson. See Samson Agonistes
Eve speaks to Adam. See Paradise lost
Expulsion from Paradise. See Paradise lost
Lycidas.—GrCt
The magi. See On the morning of Christ's Nativity
The moon and the nightingale. See Paradise lost
On a May morning. See Song: On May morning
On his blindness.—GrCt
On the morning of Christ's Nativity, sel.
The magi.—GrCt
Paradise lost, sels.
Eve speaks to Adam.—GrCt
Expulsion from Paradise.—GrCt
The moon and the nightingale.—GrCt
Satan journeys to the Garden of Eden.—GrCt
Standing on earth.—GrCt
"What though the field be lost."—PlE
Rivers arise: A fragment. See At a vacation exercise
Samson Agonistes, sel.
Death of Samson.—GrCt
Satan journeys to the Garden of Eden. See Paradise lost
Song: On May morning.—CoBn
On a May morning.—ClF (sel.)
Standing on earth. See Paradise lost
"What though the field be lost." See Paradise lost
When the assault was intended to the city. See Arms and the Muse
Milton, John (about)
London, 1802. W. Wordsworth.—WoP
Milton. W. Blake.—BlP (sel.)
Jerusalem.—PlE(sel.)
On his blindness. J. Milton.—GrCt
Milton. William Blake.—BlP (sel.)
Jerusalem.—PlE (sel.)
"**Milton,** thou shouldst be living at this hour." See London, 1802
Mimi's fingers. Mary O'Neill.—OnF
Minamoto no Morotada
"In the mountain village."—BaS
Minamoto no Sanetoma
"If only the world."—BaS
Minamoto no Shitagō
"When I count."—BaS
Minamoto no Tsunenobu
"In the evening."—BaS
Minarik, Else Holmelund
"Little seeds we sow in spring."—BrSg
Mind. See also Wisdom
A considerable speck. R. Frost.—CoB
"I felt a cleavage (or cleaving) in my mind." E. Dickinson.—DiL—DiPe
Memory. T. B. Aldrich.—CoBn
Twenty-five. R. McKuen.—DuS
The **mine.** Bronwyn Mason.—LeM
Mine argosy from Alexandria. See The Jew of Malta
"**Mine** enemy is growing old." Emily Dickinson —DiPe
"**Mine** eyes have seen the glory of the coming of the Lord." See Battle hymn of the republic
"**Mine** was a midwest home—you can keep your world." See One home
Miners. See Mines and mining
Mines and mining
The Avondale mine disaster. Unknown.—HiL
A ballad of a mine. R. Skelton.—CaMb
Caliban in the coal mines. L. Untermeyer.—LaPd
Childhood. M. Walker.—HaK
The collier. V. Watkins.—CaD
In the marble quarry. J. Dickey.—BrA
The Klondike. E. A. Robinson.—HiL
The merry miner. Unknown.—HuS-3
The mine. B. Mason.—LeM
The mule in the mines. Unknown.—GrCt
Song of young men working in gold mines Unknown.—DoC
"**Mingled.**" See Subway rush hour
The **minimal.** Theodore Roethke.—LiT
The **minister.** Fenton Johnson.—HaK
"The **minister** in the pulpit." Unknown.—CoO—MoB
Ministers of the gospel
An answer to the parson. W. Blake.—BlP
The bishop orders his tomb at Saint Praxed' church. R. Browning.—BrP

Doctor Foster. Mother Goose.—BrMg
Heriger, Bishop of Mainz. Unknown.—LiT
The minister. F. Johnson.—HaK
"The minister in the pulpit." Unknown.—CoO—MoB
On the Reverend Jonathan Doe. Unknown.—GrCt
The preacher: Ruminates behind the sermon. G. Brooks.—LiT
A revivalist in Boston. A. C. Rich.—PlE
"Tell me, ladies, if you can." Mother Goose.—OpF
Miniver Cheevy. Edwin Arlington Robinson.—GrCt
"**Miniver** Cheevy, child of scorn." See Miniver Cheevy
Minnesota
By a lake in Minnesota. James Wright.—BrA
"**Minnie** and Mattie." Christina Georgina Rossetti.—ArT-3—BoGj
Minor, Carlton
The gleaming stream.—BaH
"The sea was calm."—BaH
A **minor** bird. Robert Frost.—HaL
The **minstrel** boy. Thomas Moore.—ClF—CoR
"The **minstrel** boy to the war is gone." See The minstrel boy
Minstrels and troubadours
The banjo player. F. Johnson.—HaK
The minstrel boy. T. Moore.—ClF—CoR
Minstrel's song. Unknown.—DoC
Minstrel's song. Unknown.—DoC
Minuette. James Stephens.—StS
"**Mips** and ma the mooly moo." See Praise to the end
Miracles
Miracles. From Song of myself. W. Whitman.—HuS-3—LiT—SmM
The shape called star. L. T. Nicholl.—HoL
Miracles. See Song of myself
"**Miraculously,** through prayer to Saint Anthony." See Adulescentia
Mirage. Richard Church.—SmM
Mirages
Mirage. R. Church.—SmM
Mirrlees, Hope. See Harrison, Jane and Mirrlees, Hope
The **mirror.** William H. Davies.—ThA
"The **mirror** in my mother's room." See The two mirrors
Mirror, mirror. Deborah Ensign.—LeM
"**Mirrored** in the waters of the Kamunabi river." Prince Atsumi.—BaS
Mirrors. See also Reflections (Mirrored)
"I've seen you where you never were." Mother Goose.—OpF
The mirror. W. H. Davies.—ThA
Mirror, mirror. D. Ensign.—LeM
The two mirrors. E. J. Coatsworth.—CoSb
The **mischievous** raven. See "A farmer went trotting upon his gray mare"
Misconceptions. Robert Browning.—BrP
Misdirection. Eleanor Slater.—ThA
Misers
One good turn deserves another. Unknown.—BrSm
"There was an old miser named Clarence." O. Nash.—BrLl
The **misery** of mechanics. Philip Booth.—DuS
"The **misery** of mechanics, back." See The misery of mechanics
The **misfortunes** of Elphin, sel. Thomas Love Peacock
The war song of Dinas Vawr.—McWs
Misra, Gopal Chandra
Music of stones.—AlPi
Misra, Vidya Niwas
Evening clouds. tr.—AlPi
The family. tr.—AlPi
"**Miss Agnes** had two or three dolls, and a box." See The hoyden
"**Miss** Ann saw a man." See The new penny
"**Miss** Bell was almost six years old." See The dunce
Miss Cherry. Walter De La Mare.—DeBg
"**Miss** Helen Slingsby was my maiden aunt." See Aunt Helen
"**Miss** Helen was always too giddy to heed." See The giddy girl
"**Miss** J. Hunter Dunn, Miss J. Hunter Dunn." See A subaltern's love-song
Miss Jones. Harry Behn.—BeG
"**Miss** Lucy was a charming child." See Lucy and Dicky
"**Miss** Lucy Wright, though not so tall." See Drawing teeth
"**Miss** Lydia Banks, though very young." See The good girl
Miss Norma Jean Pugh, first grade teacher. Mary O'Neill.—ArT-3
"**Miss** One, Two, Three, could never agree." Mother Goose.—OpF
Miss Peggy. Elizabeth Turner.—VrF
Miss Sophia. Elizabeth Turner.—VrF
"**Miss** Sophy, one fine sunny day." See Miss Sophia
Miss T. Walter De La Mare.—ArT-3—BoGj—LaPd
"The **missel-thrush.**" Andrew Young.—ReBs
Missel thrush. Walter De La Mare.—DeBg
Missing. A. A. Milne.—LaP—LaPd
Missing commas. See "I saw a fishpond all on fire"
Missing commas. See "I saw a pack of cards gnawing on a bone"
Missing commas. See "I saw a peacock with a fiery tail"
Mississippi river
Down the Mississippi. J. G. Fletcher.—BrA (sel.)—PaH
The river, sels. P. Lorentz
"Black spruce and Norway pine."—BrA
"Down the Yellowstone, the Milk, the White and Cheyenne."—BrA
Mist. See also Fog
"A hill full, a hole full." Mother Goose.—ArT-3
Misty moor. Mother Goose.—ReOn

Mist—*Continued*
"The morning mist." G. Mohanty.—LeM
"One misty moisty morning." Mother Goose.—ArT-3—BrMg—HuS-3—LaPd—OpF—ReOn
How do you do.—GrCt
"The **mist** condenses." See A warm winter day
"A **mist** was driven down the British channel." See The warden of the Cinque ports
Mr Cromek. William Blake.—GrCt
"**Mr** East gave a feast." See Mr East's feast
Mr East's feast. Mother Goose.—AgH
Mister Fox. See The fox's foray
Mr Kartoffel. James Reeves.—CoO—SmM
"**Mr** Kartoffel's a whimsical man." See Mr Kartoffel
Mr Lear. See "How pleasant to know Mr Lear"
"**Mr** Lear, I'm the Akond of Swat." See A reply from the Akond of Swat
Mr Mixup tells a story. David McCord.—McAd
Mr Nobody. Unknown.—HuS-3
Mr Potts. Harry Behn.—BeG
Mister Punchinello. Unknown.—CoO
Mr Pyme. Harry Behn.—ArT-3—LaPd
Mister Rusticap. See "As I went over Lincoln bridge"
Mr Spade and Mr Pail. David McCord.—McAd
"**Mr** Spade and Mr Pail and Mr Henry Digger." See Mr Spade and Mr Pail
"**Mr** Spats." Shelley Silverstein.—CoO
"**Mister** Thomas Jones." See Bringing him up
"**Mr** Turtledove and wife." See The turtledoves
Mr Z. M. Carl Holman.—HaK
Mr Zoo. Eve Merriam.—MeI
"**Mrs** Binns." See A dressmaker
Mrs Brown. Rose Fyleman.—ArT-3
Mrs Elsinore. Myra Cohn Livingston.—LiC
Mrs Gilfillan. James Reeves.—LiT
"**Mrs** Lombardi's month-old son is dead." See Italian extravaganza
"**Mistress** Mary, quite contrary." See "Mary, Mary, quite contrary"
Mrs Mason. See "Mrs Mason broke a basin"
"**Mrs** Mason bought a basin." See "Mrs Mason broke a basin"
"**Mrs** Mason broke a basin." Mother Goose.—OpF
Mrs Mason.—ReOn
Mrs Mason's basin.—BrF—BrMg
Mrs Mason's basin. See "Mrs Mason broke a basin"
"**Mrs** Mouse." See Cat asks mouse out
"**Mrs** Peck-Pigeon." Eleanor Farjeon.—ArT-3—HuS-3—LaPd
Mrs Snipkin and Mrs Wobblechin. Laura E. Richards.—ArT-3—HuS-3
"**Mrs** Spider." Myra Cohn Livingston.—LaPd
Mrs Swartz. Don Marquis.—HiL
Mistress Towl. Unknown.—VrF
"**Mrs** Wolf did lots of bragging." See The wolf and the lioness
"**Misty-moisty** was the morn." See "One misty moisty morning"
Misty moor. Mother Goose.—ReOn
"**Misunderstood** and largely mispronounced." See Water ouzel
Mitchell, Adrian
The elephant knocked the ground.—SmM
Stuff.—SmM
Mitchell, Lucy Sprague
"The house of the mouse."—ArT-3
"It is raining."—ArT-3
Mitchell, Ruth Comfort
The vinegar man.—ThA
Mites
A considerable speck. R. Frost.—CoB
Mithraic emblems, sel. Roy Campbell
To the sun.—PlE
Mitra, Premendra
The soul of birds.—AlPi
Mitsune
"How sad this road."—BaS
"The white chrysanthemum."—BaS
The **mitten** song. Marie Louise Allen.—ArT-3
Mittens. See also Gloves
The mitten song. M. L. Allen.—ArT-3
Presents. M. Chute.—LaP—LaPh
"Three little kittens." Mother Goose.—BrMg
"**Mix** a pancake." See Pancakes
"**Mix** them." See Christmas cookies
Mixed beasts, sels. Kenyon Cox
The bumblebeaver.—ArT-3
The kangarooster.—ArT-3
The octopussycat.—ArT-3
Mizumura, Kazue
"Cat's whiskers."—MiI
"Chasing the fireflies."—MiI
"From a mountain of fallen leaves."—MiI
"Gently, gently, the wind blows."—MiI
"Huddled starlings."—MiI
"I may be a boy."—MiI
"I see the wind."—MiI
"In the evening glow."—MiI
"In the northwest wind."—MiI
"A lone gull."—MiI
"May wind is busy."—MiI
"Once again."—MiI
"Raging wind."—MiI
"Snowflakes drift."—MiI
"Waiting for the children."—MiI
"While the last wind of winter."—MiI
"Wind, wind."—MiI
Mnemonic for spelunking. Eve Merriam.—MeI
Mobile. David McCord.—McAd
Mobiles.
Mobile. D. McCord.—McAd
"**Mobs** are like the Gulf Stream." See The would-be merman
Mock at sorrow. See King Richard II
"**Mock** on, mock on Voltaire, Rousseau." William Blake.—BlP
The **mock** turtle's song. See Alice's adventures in wonderland—The lobster quadrille
Mockery. Katherine Dixon Riggs.—ThA
The **mocking** bird. Mother Goose.—BrMg
Mocking birds
A legend of Okeefinokee. L. E. Richards.—HoB

The mocking bird. Mother Goose.—BrMg
The mockingbird. R. Jarrell.—LiT—ReO
The **mockingbird.** Randall Jarrell.—LiT—ReO
Model T. Adrien Stoutenburg.—DuS
"**A** modern composer named Brahms." Unknown. —BrLl
A **modern** dragon. Rowena Bastin Bennett.—ArT-3—LaPd
"**Modest** and needy is my destiny in thy world, O God." See Kibbutz Sabbath
A **modest** love. See The lowest trees have tops
"The **modest** rose puts forth a thorn." See The lilly
Modifications. Ron Koertge.—DuS
Moffitt, John
"To look at any thing."—DuR
Mohanty, G. P.
The doves of my eyes.—AlPi
Mohanty, Geeta
"The morning mist."—LeM
Pearls on the grass.—LeM
Mohanty, J. M.
The doves of my eyes. tr.—AlPi
"**Moist,** glaucous." See The oyster
"The **moistened** osier of the hoary willow." See Pharsalia—The coracle
The **mole** ("I dig and dig") Carmen Bernos de Gasztold, tr. fr. the French by Rumer Godden.—GaC
The **mole** ("The mole—it may have been vole: I can't distinguish") Roy Daniells.—DoW
The **mole** ("Think a moment") Ilo Orleans.—BrSg
"The **mole**—it may have been vole: I can't distinguish." See The mole
Molecatcher. Albert D. Mackie.—CoB
Moles (Animals)
A dead mole. A. Young.—CoB
The eagle and the mole. E. Wylie.—ReO
"Fat father robin." D. McCord.—McE
The gardener and the mole. W. S. Landor.—ReO
"It's been a bad year for the moles." D. McCord.—BrLl
The lament of the mole-catcher. O. Sitwell.—CoB
The mole ("I dig and dig") C. B. de Gasztold. —GaC
The mole ("The mole—it may have been vole: I can't distinguish") R. Daniells.—DoW
The mole ("Think a moment") I. Orleans.—BrSg
Molecatcher. A. D. Mackie.—CoB
Moles. A. Fisher.—FiC
Moles. Aileen Fisher.—FiC
Moll-in-the-Wad. Mother Goose.—BrMg
"**Moll-in-the-Wad** and I fell out." See Moll-in-the-Wad
"**Mollis** abuti." Jonathan Swift.—GrCt
Molly Means. Margaret Walker.—BoA—HaK
Molly Pitcher. Laura E. Richards.—HiL
A **moment** please. Samuel Allen.—AdIa—BoA—HaK
Momotara. Unknown, tr. fr. the Japanese by Rose Fyleman.—ArT-3
Mona Lisa. Eve Merriam.—MeI
Monday. Unknown.—StF
"**Monday's** child is fair of face." Mother Goose. —HuS-3—WiMg
Mother Goose rhymes, 35.—HoB
A week of birthdays.—BrMg
"**Monday's** the fast." Unknown.—MoB
Money. See also Wealth
If only. R. Fyleman.—HuS-3
Kitchen song. E. Sitwell.—CaD
"Lucy Locket lost her pocket." Mother Goose. —OpF
Lucy and Kitty.—BrMg
Moll-in-the-Wad. Mother Goose.—BrMg
"Your plack and my plack." Unknown.—MoB
Monk, pseud. (Tom Burns)
Hypocrites.—BaH
I often wonder.—BaH
"Memories are great great things."—BaH
The **monk** and his cat. Unknown, tr. fr. the Gaelic by Robin Flower.—ReO
"**Monkey** monkey moo." See So many monkeys
Monkeys
Ape. From Creatures in the zoo. B. Deutsch.—DuS
Au jardin des plantes. J. Wain.—CoB
"A barber who lived in Batavia." Unknown.—BrLl
Black monkeys. R. Ainsworth.—StF
Come to think of it. J. Ciardi.—CiYk
"The long night." Shiki.—LeMw
Lord of jesters, prince of fellows. P. Bennett.—CoB
The mandrill. C. Aiken.—AiC
Monkeys ("How ran lithe monkeys through the leaves") From Walker in Nicaragua. J. Miller.—ReO
The monkeys ("Sing a song of monkeys") E. O. Thompson.—ArT-3
Monkeys ("Two little creatures") P. Colum.—CoB
The monkeys and the crocodile. L. E. Richards.—ArT-3—BrSm—HoB—LaP
Paddling song. Unknown.—LeO
The ship of Rio. W. De La Mare.—ArT-3—LaP—LaPd
So many monkeys. M. Edey.—ArT-3
Swell people. C. Sandburg.—HaL
When monkeys eat bananas. D. McCord.—McAd
Monkeys ("How ran little monkeys through the leaves") See Walker in Nicaragua
The **monkeys** ("Sing a song of monkeys") Edith Osborne Thompson.—ArT-3
Monkeys ("Two little creatures") Padraic Colum. —CoB
The **monkeys** and the crocodile. Laura E. Richards.—ArT-3—BrSm—HoB—LaP
"**Monkeys** in a forest." See Where
"The **monkeys** shiver in the wind." See Late winter

"I am round like a ball." Unknown
Riddles.—StF
"I gazed upon the cloudless moon." E. Brontë.—GrCt
"I see the moon." Mother Goose.—ArT-3—ReS—SmM
The moon.—BrMg
In dispraise of the moon. M. Coleridge.—CoBn
"In Mornigan's park there is a deer." Unknown.—GrCt
"In my delight to see." Unknown.—BaS
Is the moon tired. C. G. Rossetti.—HuS-3
It was the lovely moon. J. Freeman.—CoBn
January ("The mountain passes are deep in snow") N. Belting.—BeCm
January ("The summer corn ripens") N. Belting.—BeCm
July ("The giant cactus is ripe in the desert") N. Belting.—BeCm
July ("The grandfathers were instructed") N. Belting.—BeCm
June ("The gentle winds blow") N. Belting.—BeCm
June ("There is no night") N. Belting.—BeCm
"Lightly a new moon." Kyoshi.—BeCs
"Little Miss Moon." Unknown.—DePp
"The man in the moon (came tumbling down)." Mother Goose
Mother Goose rhymes, 44.—HoB
"The man in the moon (looked out)." Mother Goose.—BrMg—ReS
"The man in the moon drinks claret." Mother Goose.—BrMg
March ("It is time. The geese fly overhead, returning") N. Belting.—BeCm
March ("Winter has packed her brown garments") N. Belting.—BeCm
May ("Night is almost gone") N. Belting.—BeCm
May ("The Seven Stars are shining again") N. Belting.—BeCm
May-June ("The food pits are empty") N. Belting.—BeCm
May-June ("In the beginning man did not have cattle") N. Belting.—BeCm
"Milk-white moon, put the cows to sleep." C. Sandburg.—HuS-3
Mockery. K. D. Riggs.—ThA
Moon ("I have a white cat whose name is Moon") W. J. Smith.—LaPd
Moon ("Moon, moon") Mother Goose.—BrMg
The moon and the nightingale. From Paradise lost. J. Milton.—GrCt
"The moon cannot fight." Unknown.—LeO
"Moon-come-out." E. Farjeon.—ArT-3
Moon folly. F. S. Davis.—ThA
"Moon, for what do you wait." R. Tagore.—LeMf
"The moon in the water." Ryôta.—LeI
"The moon is distant from the sea." E. Dickinson.—DiPe
"Moon, O mother moon, O mother moon." Unknown.—LeO
"The moon over the mountains." Issa.—IsF
Moon rainbow. E. Farjeon.—FaT
Moon song. H. Conkling.—ThA
"The moon was but a chin of gold." E. Dickinson
The moon.—HoB
Moonlight ("Like a white cat") M. E. Uschold.—HuS-3
Moonlight ("My father hated moonlight") Berta Hart Nance.—BrA
A moonlight night. Liu Fang-p'ing.—LeMw
Moonlit apples. J. Drinkwater.—CoBn
The moon's funeral. H. Belloc.—ThA
"The moon's the north wind's cooky." V. Lindsay.—HoB—HuS-3—LaP—LaPd—ThA
"Mother moon, bless baby." Unknown.—LeO
Mountain fantasy. C. Lewis.—LeP
A net to snare the moonlight. V. Lindsay.—LiP
New moon. D. H. Lawrence.—CoBn
"New moon, come out, give water for us." Unknown.—LeO
Night. P. Hubbell.—LaPd
Night airs and moonshine. W. S. Landor.—GrCt
Night airs.—CoBn
The night of the full moon. L. Frankenberg.—CoBl
No man on any moon. C. Lewis.—LeP
November ("Cold flings itself out of the north") N. Belting.—BeCm
November ("The crops are in from the fields") N. Belting.—BeCm
"Now the moon goes down." Buson.—BeCs
O Lady Moon. C. G. Rossetti.—ReS
"O moon, why must you." Koyo.—BeCs
"Oh, my sun, my moon." Unknown.—LeO
October ("The harvest is finished. Winter stays its coming") N. Belting—BeCm
October ("The villages stand on the lake-edge") N. Belting.—BeCm
The old man in the moon. Unknown.—ReS
Old Man Moon. A. Fisher.—FiI
"On Saturday night I lost my wife." Mother Goose.—OpF
Saturday night.—BrMg
Phases of the moon. From One word more. R. Browning.—GrCt
The pinwheel's song. J. Ciardi.—LaPd
Prayer to the moon. Unknown.—LeO
A pretty thing. A. and J. Taylor.—VrF
Riddle #29: The moon and the sun. Unknown.—BoGj
Running moon. E. J. Coatsworth.—CoSb
"The seasons were appointed, and the times." N. Belting.—BeCm
September ("Beyond the Shining mountains") N. Belting.—BeCm
September ("The dry fingers of the sun have wiped up the dampness around the grass roots") N. Belting.—BeCm
"She has put the child to sleep." Issa.—LeOw

Moore, Carol
"Waves slap on the shore."—LeM
Moore, Clement C.
A visit from St Nicholas.—ArT-3—HoB—HuS-3
Moore, Sir John (about)
The burial of Sir John Moore. C. Wolfe.—CoR
The burial of Sir John Moore after Corunna.—GrCt
Moore, Marianne
I may, I might, I must.—McWs
In distrust of merits.—PlE
A jellyfish.—WeP
Silence.—HoL—McWs
A talisman.—BoGj—HoL
What are years.—PlE
The wood-weasel.—ReO
Moore, Merrill
Fable.—DuS
Literature: The god, its ritual.—DuS
What she did in the morning, I wouldn't know, she was seated there in the midst of her resilient symptoms, always.—DuS
Moore, Richard
Willy.—DuS
Moore, Rosalie
Catalogue.—DuR
Moore, Thomas
Child's song. See A garden song
A garden song.—CoBn
Child's song.—SmM
"The harp that once through Tara's halls."—CoR
I have a fawn.—ClF
The kiss.—CoBl
The minstrel boy.—ClF—CoR
"The time I've lost in wooing."—CoBl
" 'Tis the last rose of summer."—CoBn
To——. See When I loved you
When I loved you.—HoL
To——. —CoBl
Moore, Thomas (about)
A reply to lines by Thomas Moore. W. S. Landor.—GrCt (sel.)
To Thomas Moore. G. G. Byron.—ByP
"The **moorhens** are chirping." Issa, tr. fr. the Japanese.—LeOw
Moose hunting. Tommy Willis.—BaH
Moraes, Dom
Sailing to England.—AlPi
A **moral** alphabet, sel. Hilaire Belloc
B stands for bear.—BrSm
Morden, Phyllis B.
Godmother.—ThA
"**More** beautiful than the remarkable moon and her noble light." See To the sun
Morels. William Jay Smith.—CoBn
Morgan, John Hunt
Similia similibus.—BrSm
Morgenstern, Christian
The mousetrap.—ReO
Night song of the fish.—CoB
She-goat and glow-worm.—ReO
Vice versa.—ReO
Morituri salutamus, sel. Henry Wadsworth Longfellow
A Roman legend.—LoPl
Morley, Christopher
Animal crackers.—HoB—ThA
Epitaph for any New Yorker.—BrSm
Epitaph on the proofreader of the Encyclopaedia Britannica.—BrSm
In honour of Taffy Topaz.—ArT-3
The island.—PaH
Legacy.—DuR
Nursery rhymes for the tender-hearted, sel.
"Scuttle, scuttle, little roach."—CoB
The old swimmer.—MoS
The plumpuppets.—ArT-3—ReS
"Scuttle, scuttle, little roach." See Nursery rhymes for the tender-hearted
Smells, Junior.—ArT-3—BoH—HoB
Song for a little house.—HuS-3—LaP
Thoughts for St Stephen.—BrSm
"The **morn** of life is past." See Old dog Tray
Morning. See also Wake-up poems
Alba. D. Walcott.—BoGj
The angler's reveille. H. Van Dyke.—HuS-3
"Are not the joys of morning sweeter." W. Blake.—BlP
"Are you too proud to kiss me." R. Tagore.—LeMf
"As I was a-walking." Unknown.—ReBs
The lark in the morning.—GrCt
At dawn. R. Fyleman.—HoB
Awaken. S. Bingham.—LeM
Beautiful Sunday. J. Falstaff.—CoBn
Before breakfast. E. J. Coatsworth.—CoSb
"The birds are singing music." D. Garton.—LeM
"The black turkey gobbler, under the east, the middle of his tail." Unknown.—LeO
Chanticleer. K. Tynan.—ArT-3—TuW
The child's morning. W. T. Scott.—DuR
Cock-crow. E. Thomas.—ThG
Cockcrow song. Unknown.—LeMw
Cold blows the wind. J. Hamilton.—ClF
Dawn ("An angel, robed in spotless white") P. L. Dunbar.—BoA
Dawn ("A thrush is tapping a stone") G. Bottomley.—ReBs
"A dawn wind blows." S. Morrison.—LeM
"Day." From Pippa passes. R. Browning.—BrP
Day of these days. L. Lee.—CoBn
Daybreak ("After the dark of night") W. De La Mare.—DeBg
Daybreak ("Dawn? blinks fawn") D. McCord.—McAd
Daybreak ("Daybreak comes first") C. Sandburg.—LaPd
Daybreak ("A wind came up out of the sea") H. W. Longfellow.—LoPl
"Discovering God is waking one morning." J. L'Heureux.—CoBn
Ducks at dawn. J. S. Tippett.—ArT-3
Early astir. H. Read.—CaD
The early morning. H. Belloc.—CoBn
Early one morning. E. Thomas.—ThG

Morton, David
Old ships.—HuS-3—TuW
Morwitz, Ernst. See Valhope, Carol Hope and Morwitz, Ernst
Mose. Sterling A. Brown.—HaK
"**Mose** is black and evil." See Mose
Moses (about)
"The angels came a-mustering." Unknown.—PlE
The burning bush. N. Nicholson.—PlE
Go down, Moses. Unknown.—PlE
Moses. E. J. Coatsworth.—CoDh
The murder of Moses. K. Shapiro.—PlE
Moses, W. R.
Big dam.—BrA
Moses ("Moses supposes his toeses are roses") Mother Goose.—BrMg
Moses ("Plainly then, he was a desert man") Elizabeth Jane Coatsworth.—CoDh
"**Moses** supposes his toeses are roses." See Moses
The **mosquito.** John Updike.—DuS
"A **mosquito** bit me." Issa, tr. fr. the Japanese by Nobuyuki Yuasa.—IsF
The **mosquito** knows. D. H. Lawrence.—ReO
"The **mosquito** knows full well, small as he is." See The mosquito knows
Mosquitoes
"All the while." Issa.—IsF
August. N. Belting.—BeCm
"I borrowed my cottage." Issa.—IsF
The mosquito. J. Updike.—DuS
"A mosquito bit me." Issa.—IsF
The mosquito knows. D. H. Lawrence.—ReO
"The mosquitoes." Issa.—IsF
"Swatted out." Issa.—IsF
"The **mosquitoes.**" Issa, tr. fr. the Japanese by R. H. Blyth.—IsF
Moss, Howard
Traction: November 22, 1963.—BrA
Moss. Mother Goose.—ReOn
"**Moss** was a little man." See Moss
"**Mossy** clear water." Issa, tr. fr. the Japanese.—LeOw
"**Most** chivalrous fish of the ocean." See The rhyme of the chivalrous shark
The **most-sacred** mountain. Eunice Tietjens.—PaH
"**Most** she touched me by her muteness." Emily Dickinson.—ReBs
"The **most** stupendous show they ever gave." See The circus ship Euzkera
Moth. Kenneth Slade Alling.—HoL
"A **moth** ate a word. To me it seemed." See Book-moth
"A **moth** flies round the window." John Bairstow.—LeM
"**Mother** and father and Uncle Dick." Mother Goose.—OpF
The smoking stick.—BrMg
"The **mother** cow looked up and great surprise." See Green afternoon
"**Mother** dear." Unknown.—DoC
"**Mother** gets funny ideas." See For instance

Mother Goose
A, apple pie. See "A was an apple pie"
"A was an apple-pie."—OpF
A, apple pie.—BrMg—GrT
Mother Goose rhymes, 38.—HoB
The tragical death of A apple-pye.—VrF
"A dis, a dis, a green grass."—MoB
Green grass.—BrMg—ReOn
Advice. See "He that would thrive"
A-hunting we will go.—ReOn
All work and no play.—BrMg
Alligoshee.—BrMg
"Andy Pandy, fine and dandy."—OpF
"Anna Mariar she sat on the fire."—BrMg—OpF
Anne.—ReOn
"An apple for the king."—ReOn
"Apple pie, pudding, and pancakes."—OpF
The apple tree. See "As I went up the apple tree"
Apples. See "Here's to thee, good apple tree"
"Around the rick, around the rick."—BrMg
"Arthur O'Bower has broken his band."—OpF
The high wind.—GrCt
Wind.—MoB
As black as ink.—ReOn
"As high as a castle."—OpF
"As I walk'd by myself."—GrCt—ReOn
By myself.—BrMg
"As I was going by Charing cross."—BlO—OpF
"As I was going o'er London bridge."—BrMg
"As I was going o'er Tipple Tine."—OpF
"As I went over Tipple Tyne."—GrCt
"As I was going to Banbury."—OpF
Banbury fair.—BrMg
"As I was going to St Ives."—HuS-3—OpF—ReMg—WiMg
Going to St Ives.—BrMg
Mother Goose rhymes, 26.—HoB
"As I was going to sell my butter."—OpF
"As I was going to sell my eggs."—OpF
Bandy legs.—BrMg
"As I was going up Pippen hill." See "As I went up Pippin hill"
"As I was going up the hill."—OpF
Jack the piper.—GrCt
"As I was walking in a field of wheat."—BrMg—OpF
"As I went over Lincoln bridge."—OpF
Mister Rusticap.—BrMg
"As I went over the water."—SmM
Two little blackbirds."—BrMg
"As I went over Tipple Tyne." See "As I was going o'er Tipple Tine"
"As I went through the garden gap"
Mother Goose rhymes, 31.—HoB
"As I went to Bonner."—ReMg
A strange pig.—BrMg
"As I went up a slippery gap."—OpF
Uncle Davy.—BrMg
"As I went up Pippin hill."—BlO
"As I was going up Pippen hill."—OpF
Pippen hill.—BrMg

Mother Goose—*Continued*
"As I went up the apple tree."—OpF
The apple tree.—BrMg
"As light as a feather."—OpF
"As round as a biscuit."—OpF
"As round as a butter bowl."—OpF
"As round as a marble."—OpF
"As round as a saucer."—OpF
"As round as an apple." See "As round as an apple, as deep as a cup"
"As round as an apple (as sharp as a lance)." —OpF
"As round as an apple, as deep as a cup."—ArT-3
"As round as an apple."—BrMg
"As the days lengthen."—ReOn
"As Tommy Snooks and Bessie Brooks."—WiMg
"Tommy and Bessy."—BrMg
"As white as milk (as soft as silk)."—OpF
"As white as milk, as black as coal."—OpF
At Brill. See "At Brill on the hill"
"At Brill on the hill."—OpF
At Brill.—BrMg
Brill.—ReOn
"Baa, baa, black sheep."—ArT-3—BrMg—HuS-3—OpF—WiMg
Mother Goose rhymes, 21.—HoB
"Baby and I."—BrMg
Babylon. See "How many miles to Babylon"
The bad rider. See "I had a little pony"
Bagpipes. See "Puss came dancing out of the barn"
Banbury fair. See "As I was going to Banbury"
Bandy legs. See "As I was going to sell my eggs"
Barber, barber. See "Barber, barber, shave a pig"
"Barber, barber, shave a pig."—OpF—ReMg
Barber, barber.—BrMg
Mother Goose rhymes, 20.—HoB
Barney Bodkin.—ReOn
"A bear went over the mountain."—HuS-3
Bed. See Go to bed
Bedtime. See "To bed, to bed"
Bedtime ("Come, let's to bed")—BrMg
Bedtime ("Down with the lambs")—BrMg
The beggars. See "Hark, hark, the dogs do bark"
Beggars rhyme. See Christmas ("Christmas is coming, the geese are getting fat")
"Bell horses, bell horses, what time of day."—ArT-3
Race starting.—BrMg
Belle isle.—ReOn
"Betty Botter bought some butter."—OpF
Betty Botter's batter.—BrMg
Betty Botter's batter. See "Betty Botter bought some butter"
The big boy. See "When I was a little boy (my mammy)"
"Billy Boy Blue, come blow me your horn." See "Little Boy Blue, come blow your horn"
"A bird in the air, a fish in the sea."—OpF
"Birds of a feather flock together."—ReMg
The birds of the air.—ReOn
Birds on a stone.—ReOn
Two birds.—BrMg
"Black I am and much admired."—BrMg
"Black within, and red without."—BrMg
Mother Goose rhymes, 27.—HoB
The blacksmith.—ReOn
Blackthorn.—ReOn
"Bless you, bless you, burnie-bee."—OpF
Blind man's buff.—BrMg
"Blow, wind, blow." See "Blow wind, blow, and go mill, go"
"Blow wind, blow, and go mill, go."—ArT-3—HuS-3—OpF
"Blow, wind, blow."—BrMg
The windmill.—VrF
Bobby Shaftoe. See "Bobby Shaftoe's gone to sea"
"Bobby Shaftoe's gone to sea."—MoB—WiMg
Bobby Shaftoe.—BrMg
Mother Goose rhymes, 1.—HoB
"Bobbie Shafto's gone to sea." See "Bobby Shaftoe's gone to sea"
The bonnie cravat.—ArT-3
"Bonny lass, canny lass."—OpF
Booman.—ReOn
Bow-wow.—BrMg
"Bow, wow, wow."—ArT-3—HuS-3—OpF
Tom Tinker's dog.—BrMg
Boy Blue. See "Little Boy Blue, come blow your horn"
Boys and girls. See "What are little boys made of"
"Boys and girls come out to play." See "Girls and boys, come out to play"
Brandy hill.—ReOn
"Brave news is come to town."—OpF
"Braw news is come to town."—MoB
Jemmy Dawson.—BrMg
The brave old duke of York. See "Oh, the brave old duke of York"
The brave priest.—BrMg
"Braw news is come to town." See "Brave news is come to town"
Brill. See "At Brill on the hill"
The broad water.—ReOn
"Bryan O'Lynn and his wife and his wife's mother."—OpF
Buff.—BrMg
By myself. See "As I walk'd by myself"
"Bye baby bunting."—ArT-3—HuS-3—OpF—WiMg
Mother Goose rhymes, 40.—HoB
Rabbit skin.—BrMg
Cakes and custard. See "When Jacky's a good boy"
"Can you wash your father's shirt."—OpF
"Careful Katie cooked a crisp and crinkly cabbage."—OpF
The carrion crow. See "A carrion crow sat on an oak"

"A carrion crow sat on an oak."—BlO—ReMg—SmM
The carrion crow.—BrMg
The cat and the fiddle. See "Hey, diddle, diddle, the cat and the fiddle"
"A cat came fiddling out of a barn."—HuS-3—WiMg
Mother Goose rhymes, 45.—HoB
"The cat sat asleep by the side of the fire."—OpF
Catch him, crow.—BrF—BrMg
The cats of Kilkenny. See "There once were two cats of Kilkenny"
Caution. See "Mother, may I go out to swim"
Charley. See "Charley, Charley"
Charley Barley.—BrMg
"Charley, Charley."—WiMg
Charley.—BrF
"Charley Wag, Charley Wag."—AgH—OpF
"Charlie Wag."—BrMg
"Charlie Wag." See "Charley Wag, Charley Wag"
Charlie Warlie.—BrMg
"Cheese and bread for gentlemen."—OpF
Cherry stones.—BrMg
Chicken come clock.—ReOn
"Ching-a-ring-a-ring-ching, Feast of Lanterns."—OpF
Christmas. See "Christmas comes but once a year"
Christmas ("Christmas is coming, the geese are getting fat")—ArT-3—BrMg
Beggar's rhyme.—LaPh
Christmas carol. "See God bless the master of this house"
"Christmas comes but once a year."—ReMg
Christmas.—BrMg
Churning. See "Come, butter, come"
"Clothed in yellow, red, and green."—BrMg
The coachman. See "Up at Piccadilly, oh"
Cobbler, cobbler. See "Cobbler, cobbler, mend my shoe"
"Cobbler, cobbler, mend my shoe."—WiMg
Cobbler, cobbler.—BrMg
"Cock-a-doodle-do." See "Cock a doodle doo (my dame)"
"Cock a doodle doo (my dame)."—BrMg
"Cock-a-doodle-do."—ReMg
Cock and hen.—BrMg
What the cock and hen say.—ReOn
Cock-crow. See "The cock's on the house-top"
"The cock doth crow."—ArT-3
Cock Robin.—ReOn
"Cocks crow in the morn."—ArT-3—ReMg
"The cock's on the house-top."—OpF
Cock-crow.—BrMg
Colly my cow.—ReOn
"Come, butter, come."—HuS-3
Churning.—BrMg
"Come here to me, my merry, merry men."—OpF
The recruiting sergeant.—BrMg
Contrary Mary. See "Mary, Mary, quite contrary"
Corporal Bull. See "Here's Corporal Bull"
A cottage in Fife. See "In a cottage in Fife"
A counting-out rhyme. See "Intery, mintery, cutery-corn"
The crooked man. See "There was a crooked man, and he went a crooked mile"
"Cross-patch."—BrMg—GrCt—WiMg
The crows. See "On the first of March"
Cruel Tom.—ReOn
The cuckoo. See "The cuckoo is a merry bird"
Cuckoo, cherry tree.—BrMg
"The cuckoo comes in April."—OpF
"The cuckoo is a merry bird."—OpF
The cuckoo.—CoB—GrCt
"Curly Locks, Curly Locks." See "Curly Locks, Curly Locks, wilt thou be mine"
"Curly Locks, Curly Locks, wilt thou be mine."—WiMg
"Curly Locks, Curly Locks."—BrMg
"Cushy cow, bonny, let down thy milk."—HuS-3—OpF—ReMg
Milking.—BrMg
Daddy.—BrMg
"Daffadowndilly." See "Daffy-down-dilly has now come to town"
Daffy-down-dilly. See "Daffy-down-dilly has now come to town"
"Daffy-down-dilly has new come to town." See "Daffy-down-dilly has now come to town"
"Daffy-down-dilly has now come to town."—OpF—ReMg
"Daffadowndilly."—ArT-3
Daffy-down-dilly.—BrMg—BrSg
Mother Goose rhymes, 5.—HoB
"Dame get up and bake your pies."—WiMg
Dame Trot. See "Dame Trot and her cat"
"Dame Trot and her cat."—StF
Dame Trot.—BrMg
"Dance to your daddie." See "Dance to your daddy"
"Dance to your daddy."—BrMg—MoB
"Dance to your daddie."—ArT-3
"Dancy-diddlety-poppety-pin."—OpF
Davy Dumpling.—BrMg
Days in the month. See "Thirty days hath September"
The death and burial of Cock Robin. See "Who killed Cock Robin"
"Deedle deedle dumpling, my son John."—OpF
The pasty.—BrMg
The Derby ram.—BrMg
The devil.—BrMg
"Dickery, dickery, dare."—OpF—WiMg
The flying pig.—BrMg
Dicky Dilver.—BrMg
Diddle, diddle, dumpling. See "Diddle, diddle, dumpling, my son John"
"Diddle, diddle, dumpling, my son John."—HuS-3—OpF—WiMg
Diddle, diddle, dumpling.—BrMg
Mother Goose rhymes, 14.—HoB
"Diddle-me-diddle-me-dandy-O."—OpF

Mother Goose—*Continued*
"A dillar, a dollar." See "A diller, a dollar, a ten o'clock scholar"
"A diller, a dollar." See "A diller, a dollar, a ten o'clock scholar"
"A diller, a dollar, a ten o'clock scholar."—ArT-3
"A dillar, a dollar."—WiMg
"A diller, a dollar."—OpF—ReMg
Mother Goose rhymes, 12.—HoB
Ten o'clock scholar.—BrMg
"Ding, dong, bell." See "Ding, dong, bell, pussy's in the well"
"Ding, dong, bell, pussy's in the well."—OpF
"Ding, dong, bell."—ArT-3—BrMg—ReMg—WiMg
Mother Goose rhymes, 8.—HoB
"Doctor Faustus was a good man."—ReMg
Doctor Foster. See "Doctor Foster went to Gloucester (in a shower)"
Doctor Foster ("Old Doctor Foster")—BrMg
"Doctor Foster went to Gloster." See "Doctor Foster went to Gloucester (in a shower)"
"Doctor Foster went to Gloucester (in a shower)."—OpF
Doctor Foster.—BrMg—CoO
"Doctor Foster went to Gloster."—WiMg
The donkey. See "Donkey, donkey, old and grey"
The donkey. See "If I had a donkey"
"Donkey, donkey, do not bray."—OpF
"Donkey, donkey, old and grey."—OpF
The donkey.—BrMg
The dove says.—BrMg
"Down by the river."—BrMg
The dunce.—BrMg
Dusty miller.—BrMg
"O the dusty miller."—MoB
"Eaper Weaper, chimney sweeper."—ReMg
"Eat at pleasure."—AgH
Elder belder.—ReOn
"Elizabeth, Elspeth, Betsy, and Bess."—OpF
Elsie Marley. See "Elsie Marley's grown so fine"
"Elsie Marley is grown so fine."—GrT—OpF
Elsie Marley.—BrMg—CoBb
The fair maid. See "The fair maid who, the first of May"
"The fair maid who, the first of May."—OpF
The fair maid.—ReOn
The first of May.—BrMg
Mother Goose rhymes, 34.—HoB
"A farmer went riding." See "A farmer went trotting upon his gray mare"
"A farmer went trotting upon his gray mare."—ArT-3
"A farmer went riding."—HuS-3—OpF
The mischievous raven.—BrF—BrMg
"Father and mother and Uncle John."—OpF
"Fe, fi, fo, fum." See "Fee, fi, fo, fum"
The features.—BrMg
"Fee, fi, fo, fum."—BrF
"Fe, fi, fo, fum."—BrSm
The giant.—BrMg
"The fiddler and his wife."—OpF
The fingers.—BrMg
Fire. See "Fire, fire, said Mrs Dyer"
"Fire, fire, said Mrs Dyer."—OpF
Fire.—BrMg
"Fire, fire, said the town crier."—ReMg
"Fire, fire, said the town crier." See "Fire, fire, said Mrs Dyer"
"The first day of Christmas my true love sent to me." See The twelve days of Christmas
The first of May. See "The fair maid who, the first of May"
Fishes.—BrMg
"Fishie, fishie, in the brook."—OpF
Five hens. See "There was an old man who lived in Middle Row"
"Five little pussy cats sitting in a row."—OpF
"Flour of England, fruit of Spain."—BrMg
The flying pig. See "Dickery, dickery, dare"
Foot patting.—BrMg
"For want of a nail."—ReMg
A nail.—BrMg
"Four and twenty tailors went to kill a snail."—WiMg
Snail hunters.—BrMg
Four children.—BrMg
"Four stiff-standers."—BrMg—GrCt—OpF
Riddle.—BrF
A fox jumped up. See The fox's foray
The fox's foray.—BrMg
A fox jumped up.—SmM
Mister Fox.—BlO
A visit from Mr Fox.—HuS-3
"A Friday night's dream on a Saturday told."—OpF
The gabelory man.—ReOn
"Gee up, Neddy, to the fair."—OpF
General Monk.—BrMg
Georgie Porgie. See "Georgie Porgie, pudding and pie"
"Georgie Porgie, pudding and pie."—OpF—ReMg—WiMg
Georgie Porgie.—BrMg
Ghostesses. See "There were three ghostesses"
The giant. See "Fee, fi, fo, fum"
Giant Bonaparte.—BrMg
Ginger. See "Ginger, Ginger, broke the winder"
"Ginger, Ginger, broke the winder."—OpF
Ginger.—BrMg
"A girl in the army."—BrMg
"The girl in the land."—BrMg—ReOn
"Girls and boys." See "Girls and boys, come out to play"
"Girls and boys, come out to play."—ArT-3—GrT—HuS-3—OpF—WiMg
"Boys and girls come out to play."—BrMg—SmM
"Girls and boys."—AgH
Go to bed.—GrCt—ReOn—ReS
Bed.—BrMg
"Go to bed, Tom."—OpF
"God bless the master of this house."—HuS-3
Christmas carol.—ArT-3

Mother Goose—*Continued*
How do you do. See "One misty moisty morning"
"How do you do, neighbor."—OpF
"How go the ladies, how go they."—OpF
"How many days has my baby to play."—ArT-3
"How many miles to Babylon."—OpF—ReMg—TuW
Babylon.—BrMg—GrCt
"How much wood would a wood-chuck chuck."—ArT-3—HuS-3
How to sleep easy. See "To sleep easy at night"
Humpty Dumpty. See "Humpty Dumpty sat on a wall . . . (all the king's horses)"
"Humpty Dumpty and his brother."—OpF
"Humpty Dumpty ligs in t' beck."—OpF
"Humpty Dumpty sat on a spoon."—OpF
"Humpty Dumpty sat on a wall . . . (all the king's horses)."—GrT—OpF—WiMg
Humpty Dumpty.—BrMg
Mother Goose rhymes, 25.—HoB
"Humpty Dumpty sat on a wall . . . (four score men)."—HuS-3—OpF
"Humpty Dumpty went to town."—OpF
Hunc, said he. See "There was a lady loved a swine"
Hurly burly.—ReOn
Hush-a-ba, birdie. See "Hush-a-ba, birdie, croon, croon"
"Hush-a-ba, birdie, croon, croon."—MoB
Hush-a-ba, birdie.—ReS
Scottish lullaby.—BrMg
Hush-a-bye. See "Hush-a-bye, baby, on the tree top"
"Hush-a-bye, baby, on the tree top."—HuS-3—OpF—WiMg
Hush-a-bye.—BrMg
"I doubt, I doubt."—ReOn
"I had a little cow (hey-diddle)."—OpF
"I had a little cow and to save her."—OpF
"I had a little dog (and his name was Bluebell)."—OpF
"I had a little hobby horse."—MoB
Mother Goose rhymes, 58.—HoB
"I had a little moppet." See "I had a little moppety, I put it in my pockety"
"I had a little moppety, I put it in my pockety."—OpF
"I had a little moppet."—ReOn
Little moppet.—BrMg
"I had a little nut tree." See "I had a little nut-tree; nothing would it bear"
"I had a little nut-tree; nothing would it bear."—HuS-3—ReMg
"I had a little nut tree."—OpF—SmM
The little nut tree.—BrF—BrMg
Mother Goose rhymes, 59.—HoB
"I had a little pony."—BlO—HuS-3—MoB—OpF
The bad rider.—BrMg
"I had a little wife."—OpF
"I have a little sister (she lives)."—OpF
"I have a little sister, they call her Peep-peep."—ArT-3—BrMg—HuS-3
One eye.—ReOn
"I have long legs."—OpF
"I lost my mare in Lincoln lane."—ReMg
"I saw a fishpond all on fire."—GrCt—OpF
Missing commas.—BrMg
"I saw a pack of cards gnawing a bone."—OpF
Missing commas.—BrMg
I saw a peacock. See "I saw a peacock with a fiery tail"
"I saw a peacock with a fiery tail."—BlO—MoB—OpF
I saw a peacock.—GrCt—SmM
Missing commas.—BrMg
I saw a ship. See "I saw a ship a-sailing"
"I saw a ship a-sailing."—ArT-3—HuS-3—ReMg—WiMg
I saw a ship.—CoSs—SmM
Mother Goose rhymes, 60.—HoB
A ship a-sailing.—BrMg
"I saw eight magpies in a tree."—OpF
"I see the moon."—ArT-3—ReS—SmM
The moon.—BrMg
"I went to Noke."—OpF
"I went up the high hill."—OpF
Where I went.—BrMg
If. See "If all the seas were one sea"
"If all the seas were one sea."—HuS-3—OpF
If.—BrMg
If all the world. See "If all the world were paper"
"If all the world were apple pie."—ReMg
"If all the world were paper."—AgH—BlO—OpF—WiMg
If all the world.—BrMg
"If I had a donkey."—OpF
The donkey.—BrMg
"If I had a donkey that wouldn't go."—WiMg
"If I had a donkey that wouldn't go." See "If I had a donkey"
"If I had gold in goupins."—OpF
"If 'ifs' and 'ans' were pots and pans."—OpF
"If wishes were horses."—BrMg—OpF—WiMg
"If wishes were horses, beggars would ride."—ReMg
Mother Goose rhymes, 32.—HoB
"If wishes were horses, beggars would ride." See "If wishes were horses"
"I'll tell you a story."—ReMg
Jack a Nory.—BrMg
"I'm called by the name of a man."—BrMg
"In a cottage in Fife."—OpF—WiMg
A cottage in Fife.—BrMg
In marble halls. See "In marble halls as white as milk"
"In marble halls as white as milk."—BrMg—GrCt—HuS-3—OpF
In marble halls.—ReOn—SmM
"In spring I look gay."—BrMg—OpF
In the dumps. See "We're all in the dumps"

"Intery, mintery, cutery-corn."—ArT-3—TuW
A counting-out rhyme.—ClF
"Intry, mintry, cutry, corn."—HuS-3
"Intry, mintry, cutry, corn." See "Intery, mintery, cutery-corn"
Ipsey Wipsey.—BrMg
"It costs little Gossip her income for shoes."—OpF
"It was on a merry time."—OpF
It's raining.—BrMg
"I've seen you where you never were."—OpF
Jack. See "Jack be nimble"
Jack-a-Dandy. See "Nauty pauty"
Jack a Nory. See "I'll tell you a story"
"Jack and Gye."—BrMg
"Jack and Jill." See "Jack and Jill went up the hill"
Jack and Jill and old Dame Dob. See "Jack and Jill went up the hill"
"Jack and Jill went up the hill."—HuS-3—OpF—WiMg
"Jack and Jill."—GrT
Jack and Jill and old Dame Dob.—BrMg
"Jack be nimble."—ArT-3—HuS-3—WiMg
Jack.—BrMg
Jack Horner. See "Little Jack Horner"
"Jack, Jack Joe."—OpF
Jack Sprat. See "Jack Sprat could eat no fat"
"Jack Sprat could eat no fat."—OpF—ReMg—WiMg
Jack Sprat.—BrMg
The life of Jack Sprat, his wife, and his cat.—VrF
Mother Goose rhymes, 11.—HoB
Jack the piper. See "As I was going up the hill"
Jacky Jingle. See "Now what do you think"
Jacky's fiddle.—ReOn
Jemima. See "There was a little girl, and she had a little curl"
Jemmy Dawson. See "Brave news is come to town"
Jenny.—BrMg
"Jenny Wren fell sick."—ReO—SmM
Mother Goose rhymes, 24.—HoB
Robin and Jenny.—BrMg
Jeremiah.—BrMg
Jeremiah Obadiah. See "Jeremiah Obadiah, puff, puff, puff"
"Jeremiah Obadiah, puff, puff, puff."—OpF
Jeremiah Obadiah.—BrMg
"Jerry Hall."—BrMg
Jingle bells.—BrMg
John Bull. See "John Bull, John Bull"
"John Bull, John Bull."—OpF
John Bull.—BrMg
John Cook. See "John Cook had a little grey mare"
"John Cook had a little grey mare."—WiMg
John Cook.—BlO
John Cook's mare.—ReOn
John Cook's mare. See "John Cook had a little grey mare"
"Johnnie Norrie."—BrMg
Johnny Armstrong.—ReOn
"Johnny, come lend me your fiddle." See "Johnny shall have a new bonnet"
Johnny Rover.—ReOn
"Johnny shall have a new bonnet."—GrT
"Johnny, come lend me your fiddle."—MoB
Jolly red nose. See "Nose, nose, jolly red nose"
Jolly Welchman. See "Taffy was a Welshman"
Jumping Joan. See "Here am I, little jumping Joan"
The key of the kingdom. See This is the key
The Kilkenny cats. See "There once were two cats of Kilkenny"
King Arthur. See "When good King Arthur ruled this land"
King of the castle.—BrMg
"Ladies and gentlemen come to supper."—ReMg
The lady and the swine. See "There was a lady loved a swine"
Lady of the land.—ReOn
"Ladybird, ladybird (fly away home)."—BrMg—SmM
Mother Goose rhymes, 57.—HoB
"Lavender's blue, diddle, diddle."—OpF
Let's go to bed. See "To bed, to bed"
The life of Jack Sprat, his wife, and his cat. See "Jack Sprat could eat no fat"
"The lion and the unicorn."—BrF—BrMg—MoB—OpF
"Little Betty Blue."—GrT—HuS-3—OpF
"Little Billy Breek."—BrMg
The little black dog.—BrMg
Little Blue Ben.—BrMg
"Little Bo-peep." See "Little Bo-peep has lost her sheep"
"Little Bo-peep has lost her sheep."—HuS-3—WiMg
"Little Bo-peep."—BrMg—OpF
"Little Bob Robin."—ReOn
The little boy. See "Little boy, little boy, where were you born"
"Little Boy Blue." See "Little Boy Blue, come blow your horn"
"Little Boy Blue, come blow up your horn." See "Little Boy Blue, come blow your horn"
"Little Boy Blue, come blow your horn."—HuS-3—OpF
"Billy Boy Blue, come blow me your horn."—GrT
Boy Blue.—BrMg
"Little Boy Blue."—ReMg
"Little Boy Blue, come blow up your horn."—WiMg
Mother Goose rhymes, 3.—HoB
"Little boy, little boy, where were you born."—OpF
The little boy.—BrMg—ReOn
A little cock sparrow. See "A little cock sparrow sat on a green tree"
"A little cock sparrow sat on a green tree."—WiMg
A little cock sparrow.—BrMg

"Pussy-cat, pussy-cat, where have you been." —HuS-3—OpF—WiMg
Mother Goose rhymes, 19.—HoB
Pussy-cat.—BrMg
"Pussy-cat, pussy-cat."—ArT-3
"Pussy cat sits beside the fire."—OpF
Putting on a nightgown.—BrMg
Queen Caroline. See "Queen, Queen Caroline"
"The Queen of Hearts." See "The Queen of Hearts she made some tarts"
"The Queen of Hearts she made some tarts." —OpF
Mother Goose rhymes, 13.—HoB (sel.)
"The Queen of Hearts."—BrF—BrMg—WiMg
"Queen, Queen Caroline."—OpF
Queen Caroline.—BrMg
The rabbit man.—BrMg
Rabbit skin. See "Bye baby bunting"
Race starting. See "Bell horses, bell horses, what time of day"
Rain.—ArT-3—BrMg
"Rain before seven."—BrMg—ReMg
"Rain, rain, go away (come again)."—ArT-3
To the rain.—BrMg
"Rain, rain, go away (this is mother's washing day)."—OpF
"Rain, rain, go to Spain."—WiMg
A rat. See "There was a rat, for want of stairs"
"Rat a tat tat, who is that."—OpF
Rats and mice. See "Pretty John Watts"
"Rats in the garden, catch 'em Towser."—OpF
Run, boys, run.—BrF—BrMg
The recruiting sergeant. See "Come here to me, my merry, merry men"
Red stockings.—BrMg
Reward. See "When Jacky's a good boy"
Riches. See "My father died a month ago"
"A riddle, a riddle, as I suppose."—ArT-3
"Riddle me, riddle me (what is that)."—OpF
"Riddle me, riddle me ree (a little man)."—BrMg
"Riddle-me riddle-me riddle-me-ree (perhaps you)"
Mother Goose rhymes, 28.—HoB
Ride a cock-horse. See "Ride a cock-horse to Banbury cross (to see a fair or fine lady)"
"Ride a cock-horse to Banbury cross (to buy or see little Johnny)."—GrT—OpF
"Ride a cock-horse to Banbury cross (to see a fair or fine lady)."—ArT-3—HuS-3—OpF—ReMg—WiMg
Ride a cock-horse.—BrMg
"Ride a cock-horse to Banbury cross (to see what Tommy)."—OpF
Mother Goose rhymes, 41.—HoB
Ride away. See "Ride away, ride away"
"Ride away, ride away."—ArT-3
Ride away.—BrMg—StF
"Rindle, randle."—OpF
"Ring-a-ring o' or a roses."—BrMg—GrT—OpF
The riot.—BrMg
"Roast beef and marshmallows."—OpF
"Robbin and Bobbin." See "Robin and Bobbin, two big-bellied men"
Robert Rowley. See "Robert Rowley rolled a round roll 'round"
"Robert Rowley rolled a round roll 'round."—HuS-3
Robert Rowley.—ReOn
"Robin-a-Bobbin."—BrMg
"Robin-a-Bobin bent his bow."—ReMg
"Robin-a-Bobin bent his bow." See "Robin-a-Bobbin"
"Robin and Bobbin, two big-bellied men."—OpF
"Robbin and Bobbin."—AgH
Robin the Bobbin.—BrMg
Robin and Jenny. See "Jenny Wren fell sick"
"Robin and Richard (were two pretty men)."—BrMg—OpF
"Robin the Bobbin." See "Robin and Bobbin, two big-bellied men"
"Rock-a-boo babby, babbies is bonny."—OpF
Rock-a-bye. See "Rock-a-bye, baby (thy cradle)"
"Rock-a-bye, baby (thy cradle)."—GrT
Rock-a-bye.—BrMg
The rose is red. See "Roses are red"
"Roses are red."—BrMg
The rose is red.—HuS-3
"Round about, round about, applety pie."—OpF
"Round and round the butter dish."—OpF
Round apples.—ReOn
"Rub-a-dub-dub."—OpF—ReMg
Three men in a tub.—BrMg
The rugged rock.—BrMg
Rules of contrary.—ReOn
Run, boys, run. See "Rats in the garden, catch 'em Towser"
"Runs all day and never walks."—ArT-3
A sad song. See Trip upon trenchers
A sad story. See "When I was a little boy (I lived)"
Sally.—BrF—BrMg
Saturday night. See "On Saturday night I lost my wife"
Scottish lullaby. See "Hush-a-ba birdie, croon, croon"
See-saw. See "See-saw, Margery Daw (Jacky or Johnny shall have a new master)"
"See-saw, Jack in the hedge."—OpF
"See-saw, Margery Daw (Jacky or Johnny shall have a new master)."—OpF—WiMg
See-saw.—BrMg
"See-saw, Margery Daw (sold her bed)."—BrMg —OpF
"See-saw, sacaradown." See "See-saw sacradown"
"See-saw, sacradown."—OpF
"See-saw, sacaradown."—ReMg
Sea shells. See "She sells sea-shells on the sea shore"
"Send daddy home."—OpF

"There was a man who went to the fair."—OpF
There was a monkey.—BrMg
"There was a rat, for want of stairs."—ReMg
A rat.—BrMg
"There was a thing a full month old."—BrMg
"There was a wee bit mousikie (or moosikie)."—BlO—MoB—OpF
"There was a wee wifie rowed (or row't) up in a blanket."—MoB—OpF
"There was an old man (and he had a calf)."—BrMg
"There was an old man who lived in a wood."—HuS-3
"There was an old man who lived in Middle Row."—OpF
Five hens.—BrMg
"There was an old woman (and she sold puddings and pyes)."—AgH
"There was an old woman (and what do you think)."—OpF
"There was an old woman (lived under a hill and if)."—GrT—OpF
Under a hill.—BrMg
"There was an old woman as I've heard tell."—ArT-3
Mother Goose rhymes, 55.—HoB
The story of the little woman.—BrMg
"There was a little woman as I've heard tell."—OpF—SmM
"There was an old woman in Surrey"
Mother Goose rhymes, 47.—HoB
"There was an old woman lived under some stairs."—OpF
"There was an old woman tossed up in a basket."—HuS-3—OpF—ReMg—WiMg
Mother Goose rhymes, 53.—HoB
An old woman.—BrMg
Sweeping the sky.—LaPd
"There was an old woman who lived in a shoe."—HuS-3—OpF—ReMg—WiMg
Mother Goose rhymes, 52.—HoB
"There was an owl lived in an oak (whiskey, whaskey, weedle)." See "There was an owl lived in an oak (wisky, wasky, weedle)"
"There was an owl lived in an oak (the more he heard)."—OpF
"There was an owl lived in an oak (wisky, wasky, weedle)."—OpF
"There was an owl lived in an oak (whiskey, whaskey, weedle)."—ReMg
"There were three cooks of Colebrook."—OpF
Three cooks.—BrMg
"There were three ghostesses."—CoO
Ghostesses.—GrCt
Three ghostesses.—AgH—BrMg
"There were three jovial huntsmen." See "There were three jovial Welshmen"
"There were three jovial Welshmen."—BlO
"There were three jovial huntsmen."—HuS-3
Three jovial huntsmen.—SmM
The three jovial Welshmen.—BrMg
"There were two crows sat on a stone."—MoB—OpF
"They that wash on Monday."—BlO—OpF
The thirteen days. See The twelve days of Christmas
Thirteen Yule days. See The twelve days of Christmas
"Thirty days hath September."—HuS-3—WiMg
Days in the month.—BrMg
"Thirty white horses."—BrMg—OpF—ReOn
"Thirty white horses upon a red hill."—ArT-3
"Twenty white horses."—HuS-3
"Thirty white horses upon a red hill." See "Thirty white horses"
"This is the house that Jack built."—HuS-3—OpF
The house that Jack built.—BrMg
This is the key.—BlO
The key of the kingdom.—BrMg
"This is the way the ladies ride."—ArT-3—BrMg—WiMg
"This land was white."—BrMg
"This little pig had a rub-a-dub."—BrMg
"This little pig said, I want some corn."—OpF
"This little pig went to market."—BrMg—HuS-3—OpF—WiMg
Mother Goose rhymes, 36.—HoB
Three a-bed.—BrMg
Three acres of land.—BrMg
Three bad ones.—CoBb
Three blind mice. See "Three blind mice, see how they run"
"Three blind mice, see how they run."—OpF—WiMg
Three blind mice.—BrMg
Three children sliding.—BrMg
Three cooks. See "There were three cooks of Colebrook"
"Three crooked cripples."—ReOn
Three ghostesses. See "There were three ghostesses"
Three jovial huntsmen. See "There were three jovial Welshmen"
The three jovial Welshmen. See "There were three jovial Welshmen"
Three knights.—ReOn
"Three little kittens."—BrMg
Three men in a tub. See "Rub-a-dub-dub"
"Three wise men of Gotham."—OpF—WiMg
The wise men of Gotham.—BrMg
Three young rats.—BrMg—GrCt—SmM
Tickly, tickly.—BrMg
"Tit, tat, toe."—BrMg
"To bed, to bed."—OpF
Bedtime.—BrMg
Let's go to bed.—GrCt—ReS
To market. See "To market, to market, to buy a plum bun"
"To market, to market, a gallop, a trot."—OpF
"To market, to market, to buy a fat pig."—ArT-3—HuS-3—OpF

Love on the mountain. T. Boyd.—CoBl
"A low range of mountains, towards them I am running." Unknown.—LeO
Morning prayer. Unknown.—DoC
The most-sacred mountain. E. Tietjens.—PaH
The mountain. R. Frost.—PaH
"The mountain and the squirrel." R. W. Emerson.—BoGj—BoH
Fable.—ReO
Mountain fantasy. C. Lewis.—LeP
Mountain meadows. M. Keller.—CoBn
Mountain summer. C. Lewis.—LeP
Mountains ("Mountains are the high places") From In my mother's house. A. N. Clark.—HuS-3
The mountains ("The mountains? Rising from some wet ravine") W. Gibson.—MoS
Mountains on mountains. Unknown.—DePp
November 1. W. Wordsworth.—WoP
On Hardscrabble mountain. G. Kinnell.—DuS
On the road to Nara. Bashō.—ArT-3
The paps of Dana. J. Stephens.—StS
"A river leaping." Meisetsu.—BeCs
Slieve Gua. Unknown.—GrCt
Tehachapi mountains. M. C. Livingston.—LiC
Water and shadow. M. Zaturenska.—GrS
Mountains ("Mountains are the high places") See In my mother's house
The **mountains** ("The mountains? Rising from some wet ravine") Walker Gibson.—MoS
"**Mountains** and plains." See Winter
"**Mountains** are moving, rivers." See The redwoods
"**Mountains** are the high places." See In my mother's house—Mountains
"**Mountains** cover the white sun." See At Heron lodge
Mountains on mountains. Unknown, ad. fr. the Japanese by Charlotte B. DeForest.—DePp
"The **mountains**? Rising from some wet ravine." See The mountains
"The **mountains** stand, and stare around." See The paps of Dana
"**Mounted** on Kyrat strong and fleet." See Birds of passage—The leap of Roushan Beg
Mourning poem for the queen of Sunday. Robert E. Hayden.—DuS
The **mouse** ("Hush") M. M. Stephenson.—StF
The **mouse** ("I heard a mouse") Elizabeth Jane Coatsworth.—ArT-3—CoB—ReS—ThA
Mouse ("Little mouse in gray velvet") Hilda Conkling.—ArT-3—HuS-3
"A **mouse** goes out." See In the dark of night
"A **mouse** in her room woke Miss Dowd." Unknown.—BrLl
The **mouse** in the wainscot. Ian Serraillier.—CoB—LaPd
"The **mouse** like halting clockwork, in the light." See Little fable
Mouse roads. Aileen Fisher.—FiI
"The **mouse** that gnawed the oak tree down." Vachel Lindsay.—HaL
"A **mouse**, whose martial value has so long." See A martial mouse
"The **mouse** whose name is Time." Robert Francis.—HaL
Mouse's nest. John Clare.—CoB—GrCt
The **mousetrap.** Christian Morgenstern, tr. fr. the German by W. D. Snodgrass.—ReO
"**Mousie,** mousie, come to me." Unknown.—MoB
The **mouth** and the body. Phillip Mwanikih.—LeM
The **mouth** of the Hudson. Robert Lowell.—BrA—LaC
Mouths
The mouth and the body. P. Mwanikih.—LeM
Mouths. D. Aldis.—AgH
The sad story of a little boy that cried. Unknown.—CoBb
Mouths. Dorothy Aldis.—AgH
"**Move** him in the sun." See Futility
Moving
Moving ("Bookshelves empty, tables lampless, walls") R. Wallace.—DuS
Moving ("I like to move. There's such a feeling") E. Tietjens.—ArT-3
Moving ("Bookshelves empty, tables lampless, walls") Robert Wallace.—DuS
Moving ("I like to move. There's such a feeling") Eunice Tietjens.—ArT-3
"**Moving** from left to right, the light." See View of the capitol from the Library of Congress
Mowing. See Farm life; Harvests and harvesting
Much ado about nothing, sel. William Shakespeare
Sigh no more.—CoBl
"**Much** have I roved by Sandy river." See By Sandy waters
"**Much** have I travell'd in the realms of gold." See On first looking into Chapman's Homer
Much knowledge, little reason." See Nosce teipsum
"**Much** madness is divinest sense." Emily Dickinson.—DiPe
Divinest sense.—HoL
Mud
"I know a place." M. C. Livingston.—HoB
Mud. P. C. Boyden.—ArT-3
Mud pie. K. Fraser.—FrS
Mud. Polly Chase Boyden.—ArT-3
"**Mud** in the road and wind in my hair." See And a big black crow is cawing
"**Mud** is very nice to feel." See Mud
Mud pie. Kathleen Fraser.—FrS
"**Muddy** meek river, oh, it was splendid sport." See Big dam
"**Muffle** the wind." See Orders
Muhlenberg, William
"Carol, brothers, carol."—ArT-3
Muir, A.
Old friends.—CoB
Muir, Edwin
Antichrist.—PlE
Ballad of the flood.—CaMb
The enchanted knight.—CaD

The bagpipe man. N. B. Turner.—ArT-3
The banjo player. F. Johnson.—HaK
"A boy who played tunes on a comb." Unknown.—BrLl
Carry me back. J. Holmes.—BrA
Chamber music, sels. J. Joyce
"Lean out of the window."—CoBl—HaL
Goldenhair.—GrCt—ThA
"My love is in a light attire."—HaL
The noise of waters.—ArT-3
All day I hear.—HoL
"All day I hear the noise of waters."—LiT
"Strings in the earth and air."—HaL
Dark affections. From The merchant of Venice. W. Shakespeare.—ShS
Daybreak in Alabama. L. Hughes.—BrA
Death song of a song maker. Unknown.—LeO
Discordants. C. Aiken.—CoBl
Elegy for a jazz musician. E. Kroll.—DuS
Elizabeth at the piano. H. Gregory.—GrS
The find. F. Ledwidge.—ThA
First song. G. Kinnell.—BoGj
Following the music. H. I. Rostron.—StF
Harlem sounds: Hallelujah corner. W. Browne.—BoA
Israfel. E. A. Poe.—PoP
Jazz fantasia. C. Sandburg.—LaC
The jazz of this hotel. V. Lindsay.—BoH
Jazzonia. L. Hughes.—BoA—HaK
"Jock plays them rants so lively." Unknown.—MoB
King Solomon. E. Merriam.—MeC
Lester Young. T. Joans.—BoA
A little morning music. D. Schwartz.—CoBn
M., singing. L. Bogan.—BoGj
Magical music. E. Farjeon.—FaT
The man with the blue guitar. W. Stevens.—LiT (sel.)
"A modern composer named Brahms." Unknown.—BrLl
Music of stones. G .C. Misra.—AlPi
"Music, when soft voices die." P. B. Shelley.—BoH
Musician. L. Bogan.—BoGj
"Musicians wrestle everywhere." E. Dickinson.—DiPe
"My music." Unknown.—LeO
Night music. From The merchant of Venice. W. Shakespeare.—ShS
On a reed. J. Stephens.—StS
On music. W. S. Landor.—BoGj
"Orpheus with his lute made trees." J. Fletcher.—GrCt
Music.—ClF
Pierrot. S. Teasdale.—CoBl
Pine music. A. Fisher.—FiC
A piper. S. O'Sullivan.—ArT-3—LaPd
Poem. H. Johnson.—BoA
The post captain. C. E. Carryl.—CoSs
The power of music. From The merchant of Venice. W. Shakespeare.—ShS
"Puss came dancing out of a (or the) barn." Mother Goose.—OpF
Bagpipes.—BrMg
Request for requiems. L. Hughes.—BrSm
A short note. E. Merriam.—MeI
Slave quarter. C. Carmer.—ThA
Song from a country fair. L. Adams.—BoGj
Stanzas for music. G. G. Byron.—ByP
Starry night I. E. Merriam.—MeI
Summer concert. R. Whittemore.—BrA
"There once was a corpulent carp." C. Wells.—BrLl
"There was a composer named Bong." Unknown.—BrLl
"There was a composer named Haydn." Unknown.—BrLl
"There was a composer named Liszt." Unknown.—BrLl
"There was an old lady of Steen." Unknown.—BrLl
"There was an old man with a gong." E. Lear
Limericks.—BoGj
"There'd be an orchestra." From Thousand-and-first ship. F. S. Fitzgerald.—BoGj
To musique, to becalme his fever. R. Herrick.—BoGj
A toccata of Galuppi's. R. Browning.—BrP
T'other little tune. Mother Goose.—ReOn
Variations for two pianos. D. Justice.—DuS
View of the capitol from the Library of Congress. E. Bishop.—BrA
When de saints go ma'chin' home. S. A. Brown.—BoA
"When I had a little leisure." Wang Mou Fang.—LeMw
Yardbird's skull. O. Dodson.—AdIa—BoA
Music box. Aileen Fisher.—FiIo
"**Music** I heard with you was more than music." See Discordants
Music of stones. Gopal Chandra Misra, tr. fr. the Oriya by the author.—AlPi
"**Music,** when soft voices die." Percy Bysshe Shelley.—BoH
Musical chairs. Eleanor Farjeon.—FaT
"The **musical** chairs, O the musical chairs." See Musical chairs
Musical instruments. See also names of musical instruments, as Pianos
The egotistical orchestra. E. Merriam.—MeI
Music box. A. Fisher.—FiIo
"A **musical** lady from Ga." Unknown.—BrLl
Musician. Louise Bogan.—BoGj
Musicians. See Music and musicians
"**Musicians** wrestle everywhere." Emily Dickinson.—DiPe
Mutability. William Wordsworth.—WoP
Mu'tamid, King of Seville
The fountain.—HoL
Mutterings over the crib of a deaf child. James Wright.—DuS
Mwanikih, Phillip
The mouth and the body.—LeM

"My fingers have felt all the." See Paul's fingers
"My fingers know hay." See Country fingers
My first suitor. See "Little Jack Dandersprat"
"My first thought was, he lied in every word." See Childe Roland to the dark tower came
"My flowers shall not perish." Unknown, tr. fr. the Aztec.—LeO
My garden. William Henry Davies.—CoBn
"My garden seeds are coming up." See Spring planting
"My ghostly fadir, I me confess." See Confession
My gift. See A Christmas carol ("In the bleak mid-winter")
"My good blade carves the casques of men." See Sir Galahad
"My grandfather died and he left me a cow." Unknown.—OpF
"My grandfather was an unemployed blacksmith." See The unemployed blacksmith
"My grandmothers were strong." See Lineage
My grasshopper. Myra Cohn Livingston.—BrSg
"My grasshopper died." See My grasshopper
"My hair is gray, but not with years." See The prisoner of Chillon
My hat. Stevie Smith.—SmM
"My heart aches, and a drowsy numbness pains." See To a nightingale
"My heart fills up with beauty, as I stand." See Gay Head
"My heart is all happy." Unknown, tr. fr. the Pygmy.—LeO
"My heart is like a singing bird." See A birthday
My heart leaps up. See "My heart leaps up when I behold"
"My heart leaps up when I behold." William Wordsworth.—ArT-3—BoH
My heart leaps up.—LaP—WoP
The rainbow.—CoR
"My heart would be faithless." See Fingers in the nesting box
My heart's in the Highlands. Robert Burns.—BuH (sel.)—BuPr—ClF—MoS
"My heart's in the Highlands, my heart is not here."—BlO—PaH
"My heart's in the Highlands, my heart is not here." See My heart's in the Highlands
My home. Jones Saltwater.—BaH
"My home is a haven for one who enjoys." See Our dumb friends
"My honored sir, before you pick yourself." See The windmill addresses Don Quixote
"My horse clip-clopping." Bashō, tr. fr. the Japanese by Harry Behn.—BeCs
My house is red. Kate Greenaway.—GrT
"My house is red—a little house." See My house is red
"My hut is so small." Issa, tr. fr. the Japanese by R. H. Blyth.—IsF
My imagination. Mary Petla.—BaH
"My joy, my jockey, my Gabriel." George Barker.—CaD
"My kitten thinks." See Christmas tree
"My lad, you're so full of your fun and your slaughter." See Angling
"My lady Wind, my lady Wind." Mother Goose.—OpF
The wind.—BrMg
"My land is fair for any eyes to see." Jesse Stuart.—ArT-3
My last duchess. Robert Browning.—BrP
"My life closed twice before its close." Emily Dickinson.—DiPe
"My life had stood a loaded gun." Emily Dickinson.—DiPe
"My life is like a stroll along the beach." See The fisher's boy
"My light thou art, without thy glorious sight." See To his mistress
"My little Charles is afraid of the dark." See Hark
My little dog. See "Oh where, oh where has my little dog gone"
"My little golden sister." Unknown.—WyC
"My little old man and I fell out." Mother Goose.—ReMg
Squabbles.—BrMg
"My little snowman has a mouth." See Snowman
"My little son." See The hostess
"My long two-pointed ladder's sticking through a tree." See After apple-picking
My Lord and King. See In memoriam
My lost youth. Henry Wadsworth Longfellow.—BoGj—CoR—LoPl—PaH
"My love." Ono no Yoshiki, tr. fr. the Japanese by Arthur Waley.—HoL
"My love came up from Barnegat." See The puritan's ballad
"My love comes down from the mountain." See Love on the mountain
"My love has left me has gone from me." See Souvenirs
"My love is in a light attire." See Chamber music
"My maid Mary." Mother Goose.—BrMg—OpF
"My mammy was a wall-eyed goat." Unknown.—GrCt
My mammy's maid. Mother Goose.—BrMg
"My mill grinds pepper and spice." See Two mills
"My mind lets go a thousand things." See Memory
"My mistress' eyes are nothing like the sun." See Sonnets. William Shakespeare
My mother. Teddy Kee.—BaH
"My mother bore me in an inland town." See Sea born
"My mother bore me in the southern wild." See The little black boy
"My mother groan'd; my father wept." See Infant sorrow
"My mother has the prettiest tricks." See Song for my mother
"My mother is old and gray." See My mother
"My mother said, I never should." Mother Goose.—BlO—BrMg
"My mother said that I never should."—OpF

"**My** zipper suit is bunny brown." See My zipper suit
Myself. Lula Ahsoak.—BaH
"**Myself** when young did eagerly frequent." See The rubaiyát of Omar Khayyám
The **mysterious** cat. Vachel Lindsay.—ArT-3—BoGj—GrCt—HuS-3—ThA
"**Mysterious** night, when our first parent knew." See To night
"**Mystery:** Catherine the bride of Christ." See For a marriage of St Catherine
The **mystic** magi. Robert Stephen Hawker.—GrCt
Mythology—Australian
The bunyip. D. Stewart.—ReO
Mythology—Greek and Roman
Arethusa. P. B. Shelley.—CoD
Atalanta's race. W. Morris.—CoD
The centaur. M. Swenson.—DuS
The centaurs. J. Stephens.—CoB—StS
Chorus. From Oedipus at Colonus. R. Fitzgerald.—GrS
A conjuration, to Electra. R. Herrick.—GrS
The crackling twig. J. Stephens.—StS
Dido my dear, alas, is dead. From Shepheardes calendar. E. Spenser.—GrCt
Dog-star. E. Farjeon.—FaT
Europa. W. Plomer.—CaMb
"The Fates." E. J. Coatsworth.—CoDh
The garden of Proserpina. From The faerie queene. E. Spenser.—GrCt
The Hyades. E. Farjeon.—FaT
Hymn to Diana. From Cynthia's revels. B. Jonson.—GrCt
In praise of Neptune. T. Campion.—CoBn
Incantation to Oedipus. From Oedipus. J. Dryden.—GrS
Itylus. A. C. Swinburne.—GrCt
O Daedalus, fly away home. R. E. Hayden.—AdIa—BoH
The occultation of Orion. H. W. Longfellow.—LoPl
Oread. H. D.—BoGj
Orion. D. McCord.—McAd
Orion's belt. E. Farjeon.—FaT
Orpheus' dream. E. Muir.—GrS
"Orpheus with his lute made trees." J. Fletcher.—GrCt
Pegasus. E. Farjeon.—SmM
Philomela. J. C. Ransom.—GrCt
The Pleiades. E. Farjeon.—FaT
Pomona. W. Morris.—HoL
Proserpine. From The garden of Proserpine. A. C. Swinburne.—GrCt
"Queen Cassiopeia." E. Farjeon.—FaT
Song of the syrens. W. Browne.—GrCt
To Minerva. T. Hood.—GrCt
To the Muses. W. Blake.—BlP—GrCt

N

Nadaud, Gustave
Carcassonne.—PaH
Nadkarni, D. G.
Now and then. tr.—AlPi
Nahuatl poem. Unknown, tr. fr. the Nahuatl by William Carlos Williams.—HoL
Naidu, Sarojini
Cradle song.—ThA
In the bazaars of Hyderabad.—AlPi—ThA
Palanquin bearers.—ThA
A **nail.** See "For want of a nail"
Nakatsukasa, Lady
"If it were not for the voice."—BaS
"A **naked** sun—a yellow sun." See Omen
Naladiyar, sel. Unknown, tr. fr. the Tamil by A. L. Basham
Observations.—AlPi
Name or person. Li T'ai-po, tr. fr. the Chinese by D. C. Lau.—SmM
Names. See also Christenings
American names. S. V. Benét.—BrA—PaH
And off he went just as proud as you please. J. Ciardi.—CiYk
Answering your question. D. McCord.—McAd
Boys' names. E. Farjeon.—ArT-3
Dialogue. From As you like it. W. Shakespeare.—McWs
"Diana Fitzpatrick Mauleverer James." A. A. Milne.—ArT-3
Epitaph on John Knott. Unknown.—BrSm—GrCt
"Excuse me." E. L. Dailey.—BaH
Gentle name. S. Robinson.—ThA
Georgia towns. D. W. Hicky.—BrA
Girls' names. E. Farjeon.—ArT-3
Indian names. L. H. Sigourney.—BrA
John Bun. Unknown.—BrSm
Names. D. Aldis.—BrSg—HoB
Names from the war. B. Catton.—BrA
The naming of cats. T. S. Eliot.—WeP
Naming of parts. H. Reed.—BoGj
On Samuel Pease. Unknown.—BrSm
Ptarmigan. D. McCord.—McAd
Pudden Tame. Unknown.—GrCt
Schenectady. E. Merriam.—MeC
Signatures. C. T. Stevenson.—BrA
"There was a king met a king." Mother Goose.—OpF
"There was a man, his name was Dob." Mother Goose.—OpF
Walthena. E. Peck.—BrA
Young Sammy. D. McCord.—McAd
Names. Dorothy Aldis.—BrSg—HoB
Names from the war. Bruce Catton.—BrA
The **naming** of cats. T. S. Eliot.—WeP
"The **naming** of cats is a difficult matter." See The naming of cats
Naming of parts. Henry Reed.—BoGj
Nance, Berta Hart
Moonlight.—BrA
Nancy Hanks. Rosemary Carr and Stephen Vincent Benét.—ArT-3—HuS-3
Nancy Hanks, mother of Abraham Lincoln. Vachel Lindsay.—HiL
Nanmullaiyar, Allur
What the lover said.—AlPi

Nantucket
The Quaker graveyard in Nantucket. R. Lowell.—PaH
"**Naow** whin Oi wuz a little boy an' so me mother told me." See Haul away Joe
Naples, Italy
The Bourbons at Naples. E. J. Coatsworth.—CoDh
Napoleon Bonaparte I, Emperor of France (about)
Incident of the French camp. R. Browning.—BrP—CoR
Narasimhaswamy, K. R.
Wasn't it you.—AlPi
Narihira
"Can it be that there is no moon."—BaS
"I have always known."—BaS
"A **narrow** fellow in the grass." Emily Dickinson.—BoGj—CoB—DiL—DiPe—LiT—ReO
The snake.—WeP
Nash, Ogden
Adventures of Isabel.—BrSm (sel.)—LaP (sel.)—LaPd (sel.)
The boy who laughed at Santa Claus.—CoBb
"A bugler named Dougal MacDougal."—BrLl
Edouard.—McWs
The buses headed for Scranton.—McWs
A carol for children.—PlE
Celery.—HoB
The cow.—CoB
Decline and fall of a Roman umpire.—MoS
Edouard. See "A bugler named Dougal MacDougal"
The hunter.—CoB—MoS
The kitten.—CoB
Line-up for yesterday.—MoS
The lion.—BrSm
Love under the republicans—or democrats.—McWs
Lucy Lake.—BrSm
The octopus.—ArT-3—McWs
The ostrich.—CoB
The panther.—CoB—HoB
The purist.—BoGj—BrSm
The sniffle.—McWs
The termite.—BrSm
"There was an old man of Calcutta."—BrLl
"There was an old miser named Clarence."—BrLl
Nashe (or Nash), Thomas
Lord, have mercy on us.—GrCt
Spring.—BlO—CoBn—TuW
Nashookpuk, Sally
Whale hunting.—BaH
Nasturtium. Mary Britton Miller.—BrSg
Nasturtiums
The big nasturtiums. R. B. Hale.—CoBn
Lines to a nasturtium. A. Spencer.—BoA
Nasturtium. M. B. Miller.—BrSg
Nathan, L. E.
Evening clouds. tr.—AlPi
Spring wind. tr.—AlPi
Nathan Hale. Francis Miles Finch.—HiL
A **nation's** strength. Ralph Waldo Emerson.—BrA (sel.)
The **nativity** chant. Walter Scott.—GrCt
Nature. See also Country life; Wayfaring life
"All I could see from where I stood." From Renascence. E. St V. Millay.—LaPd
Among the leaves. E. J. Coatsworth.—CoSb
"Are not the mountains, waves, and skies, a part." From Childe Harold's pilgrimage. G. G. Byron.—CoBn
Arizona nature myth. J. Michie.—SmM
Arran. Unknown.—GrCt
At Carmel. M. Austin.—BrA
"At the time when blossoms." Unknown.—LeMw
The book of Kells. H. Nemerov.—PlE
The breath of life. J. Stephens.—StS
Busy summer. A. Fisher.—FiI
Buzzy old bees. A. Fisher.—FiI
A chant out of doors. M. Wilkinson.—ThA
Come hither, my dear one. J. Clare.—CoBl
Composed upon Westminster bridge, September 3, 1802. W. Wordsworth.—ArT-3—GrCt—PaH—WoP
The cosmic fabric. Y. Polonsky.—PlE
Dark Danny. I. O. Eastwick.—ArT-3
Discovery. H. Behn.—BeG
Doffing the bonnet. J. Stephens.—StS
Elegy for a nature poet. H. Nemerov.—CoBn
The flower and the lady, about getting up. A. and J. Taylor.—VrF
The full heart. R. Nichols.—CoBn
"Garlands for queens may be." E. Dickinson.—DiPe
Give me the splendid silent sun. W. Whitman.—CoBn
"Go to the shine that's on a tree." R. Eberhart.—HoL—LiT
The golden hive. H. Behn.—ArT-3—BeG
The greater mystery. J. M. O'Hara.—PaH
Green song. P. Booth.—CoBn
Hope. W. Shenstone.—CoBn (sel.)
"The hunting tribes of air and earth." From Rokeby. W. Scott.—ReO
"I bet with every wind that blew." E. Dickinson.—DiPe
I cannot tell. D. Crawford.—BaH
"I don't know why." M. C. Livingston.—BrSg
"I know a bank whereon the wild thyme blows." From A midsummer-night's dream. W. Shakespeare.—CoBn
"I meant to do my work to-day." R. Le Gallienne.—ArT-3—LaP—ThA
I need no sky. W. Bynner.—PlE
"I saw a green beetle climb crippled grass." S. Kershaw.—LeM
"I taste a liquor never brewed." E. Dickinson.—DiL—DiPe
"I thought that nature was enough." E. Dickinson.—DiPe
Interval. E. Thomas.—ThG
"It makes no difference abroad." E. Dickinson.—DiPe

"It's all I have to bring to-day." E. Dickinson. —DiPe
Keeper's wood. F. T. Prince.—SmM
Legacy. N. B. Turner.—ThA
Lines composed a few miles above Tintern abbey, on revisiting the banks of the Wye during a tour, July 13, 1798. W. Wordsworth.—WoP
Lines written in early spring. W. Wordsworth. —WoP
"A little madness in the spring." E. Dickinson. —DiPe
The maid's thought. R. Jeffers.—CoBl
The marsh. W. S. Snodgrass.—CoBn
May 10. M. W. Kumin.—CoBn
Me. W. De La Mare.—DeBg—HuS-3
Meadow morning. A. Fisher.—FiI
"The midges dance aboon the burn." R. Tannahill.—CoBn
Naming of parts. H. Reed.—BoGj
Nature. H. W. Longfellow.—CoBn
Nothing gold can stay. R. Frost.—BoH
Now fades the last. From In memoriam. A. Tennyson.—TeP
"Of a' the airts the wind can blaw." R. Burns. —BuPr
"Of gold and jewels I have not any need." Yuan Chieh.—LeMw
On a wet day. F. Sacchetti.—CoBn
"One night as I did wander." R. Burns.—BuH
"Only be willing to search for poetry, and there will be poetry." Yuan Mei.—LeMw
Only be willing to search for poetry.—LaPd
Or hounds to follow on a track. E. J. Coatsworth.—CoSb
"The plants stand silent round me." J. Jörgensen.—HoL
The poem of ten ones. Ho P'ei Yu.—LeMw
"Poor bird." W. De La Mare.—DeBg
Prelude. J. M. Synge.—CoBn—GrCt
Proem. M. Cawein.—CoBn
Resolution and independence. W. Wordsworth.—CoBn (sel.)—WoP
Rural dumpheap. M. Cane.—BrA
St Swithin. Daniel Henderson.—BrSm
Seed leaves. R. Wilbur.—CoBn
Seeds. W. De La Mare.—ArT-3—BrSg—HuS-3
The signature of all things. K. Rexroth.—CoBn (sel.)
The Simplon pass. W. Wordsworth.—WoP
"The sky is low, the clouds are mean." E. Dickinson.—DiPe
Beclouded.—CoBn
A small migration. H. Behn.—BeG
"A soft sea washed around the house." E. Dickinson.—DiL—DiPe
"Some keep the Sabbath going to church." E. Dickinson.—DiPe
Sonnet. W. Wordsworth.—WoP
Spring. G. M. Hopkins.—CoBn
Stanzas. E. A. Poe.—PoP
Stay thy soft murmuring. From The loves of the plants. E. Darwin.—ReO
Summer. J. Davidson.—CoBn
Supper. W. De La Mare.—DeBg
The sweet o' the year. G. Meredith.—CoBn
Talking in their sleep. E. M. Thomas.—CoBn
Thanatopsis. W. C. Bryant.—CoBn
Three years she grew. W. Wordsworth.—WoP
Thrice happy he. W. Drummond, of Hawthornden.—CoBn
"Through lane it lay—thro' bramble." E. Dickinson.—DiL
Through lane it lay.—GrS
To a child with eyes. M. Van Doren.—HaL
To M. H. W. Wordsworth.—WoP
The Trosachs. W. Wordsworth.—WoP
Ula Masondo's dream. W. Plomer.—CaMb
The valley of unrest. E. A. Poe.—PoP
Village portrait. T. W. Duncan.—ThA
The voice of God. J. Stephens.—StS
Waves of thought. Panikkar.—AlPi
"When I hoped, I recollect." E. Dickinson.—DiL
When in the darkness. A. Tennyson.—TeP
Where. W. De La Mare.—DeBg
Work without hope. S. T. Coleridge.—CoBn
Nature. Henry Wadsworth Longfellow.—CoBn
"**Nature** brings forth her fruits and flow'rs." See The tambour worker
The **nature** of love. James Kirkup.—PlE
"**Nature's** decorations glisten." See Hymns and spiritual songs—Christmas day
"**Nature's** first green is gold." See Nothing gold can stay
Naughty Sam. Elizabeth Turner.—VrF
A **nautical** ballad. See Davy and the goblin
A **nautical** extravagance. Wallace Irwin.—HuS-3
"**Nauty** pauty." Mother Goose.—AgH
Jack-a-Dandy.—BrMg
"**Nauty** pauty Jack-a-Dandy." See "Nauty pauty"
The **Navajo.** Elizabeth Jane Coatsworth.—BrA
Navajo Indians. See Indians of the Americas—Navajo
Navajo rug. Betty Jane Lee.—BaH
Naval battles. See also Warships
The ballad of the Billycock. A. C. Deane.—CoSs
The battle of Clothesline bay. W. Irwin.—CoSs
The battle of the Baltic. T. Campbell.—CoR
The cruise of the Monitor. G. H. Boker.—HiL
The death of Admiral Benbow. Unknown.—BlO
Loss of the Royal George. W. Cowper.—CoSs
On the loss of the Royal George.—CoR
The night of Trafalgar. T. Hardy.—GrCt
The old navy. F. Marryat.—CoSs
The Revenge. A. Tennyson.—CoD—TeP
Navin (Balakrishna Sharma)
Since I left the ocean.—AlPi
"**Nay** but you, who do not love her." See Song
"**Nay,** by Saint Jamy." See The taming of the shrew—A riddle
"**Nay,** ninny, shut those sleepy eyes." See Lully

The Negro speaks of rivers. L. Hughes.—AdIa—BoA—BrA—LiT
No images. W. Cuney.—BoA—BoH
North star shining, sels. H. H. Swift
"I came to the new world empty-handed." —BrA
"My name was legion."—BrA
O black and unknown bards. J. W. Johnson.—BoA
O Daedalus, fly away home. R. E. Hayden.—AdIa—BoH
October journey. M. Walker.—AdIa—BoA
Old Lem. S. A. Brown.—AdIa
On being brought from Africa to America. P. Wheatley.—HaK
On passing two Negroes on a dark country road somewhere in Georgia. C. K. Rivers.—AdIa
1 black foot + 1 black foot = 2 black feet. G. Solomon.—BaH
Outcast. C. McKay.—BoA
The party. P. L. Dunbar.—BoA
Poem. H. Johnson.—BoA
A poem for black hearts. L. Jones.—AdIa
The proclamation. J. G. Whittier.—HiL
The rebel. M. Evans.—AdIa—BoA
The road. H. Johnson.—BoA
Robert Whitmore. F. M. Davis.—HaK
Sadie's playhouse. M. Danner.—HaK
Saint Peter relates an incident of the Resurrection day. J. W. Johnson.—HaK
Salute. O. Pitcher.—HaK
Simon the Cyrenian speaks. C. Cullen.—BoA
Sister Lou. S. A. Brown.—BoA
Sketches of Harlem. David Henderson.—HaK
So quietly. L. P. Hill.—AdIa
Song for a dark girl. L. Hughes.—AdIa
A song in the front yard. G. Brooks.—AdIa—BoH
Sonnet to a Negro in Harlem. H. Johnson.—BoA
"Sorrow is the only faithful one." D. Owen.—AdIa—BoA
Soul. D. L. Graham.—HaK
Status symbol. M. Evans.—AdIa
Stevedore. L. M. Collins.—BoA
The still voice of Harlem. C. K. Rivers.—AdIa—HaK
Strange legacies. S. A. Brown.—HaK
A strange meeting. W. H. Davies.—BlO
Strong men. S. A. Brown.—BoH
Summertime and the living. R. E. Hayden.—HaK
These beasts and the Benin bronze. M. Danner.—HaK
Three brown girls singing. M. C. Holman.—Hak
Tired. F. Johnson.—AdIa—HaK
To Richard Wright. C. K. Rivers.—AdIa
To the Right Honorable William, Earl of Dartmouth. P. Wheatley.—HaK (sel.)
We real cool. G. Brooks.—AdIa—BoH—LaC
"We shall overcome." Unknown.—HiL—PlE
We wear the mask. P. L. Dunbar.—AdIa—BoA—BoH
We're free. C. Williams.—BaH
When de saints go ma'chin' home. S. A. Brown.—BoA
"Where am I going." L. Hargrove.—BaH
The whipping. R. E. Hayden.—AdIa
The white house. C. McKay.—BoA
Yet do I marvel. C. Cullen.—AdIa—BoA
"Young Negro poet." C. C. Hernton.—HaK
Neighborly. Violet Alleyn Storey.—ArT-3
Neighbors
"And now you live dispersed on ribbon roads." From The rock. T. S. Eliot.—ArT-3
The child next door. R. Fyleman.—ThA
Mending wall. R. Frost.—BrA
Neighborly. V. A. Storey.—ArT-3
Neighbors. Tu Fu.—LeMw
The new neighbor. R. Fyleman.—ArT-3
New neighbors. A. Fisher.—FiIo
"O moon, why must you." Koyo.—BeCs
Portrait by a neighbor. E. St V. Millay.—ArT-3—HaL—LaPd—ThA—TuW
Neighbors. Tu Fu, tr. fr. the Chinese by Chi Hwang Chu and Edna Worthley Underwood.—LeMw
Neither hook nor line. John Bunyan.—MoB
Neither out far nor in deep. Robert Frost.—GrCt
Nell Flaherty's drake. Unknown.—ReO
Nelson, Horatio (about)
The admiral's ghost. A. Noyes.—ArT-3
"Here's to Nelson's memory." R. Browning.—BrP
Nelson, Lowry, Jr
You were shattered. tr.—LiT (sel.)
Nemea 11, sel. Pindar
I bless this man, tr. fr. the Greek by Richmond Lattimore.—MoS
Nemerov, Howard
At the airport.—DuS—McWs
The book of Kells.—PlE
Elegy for a nature poet.—CoBn
Human things.—CoBn
The mapmaker on his art.—DuS
Redeployment.—HiL
Runes IX.—DuS
Sunday at the end of summer.—CoBn
Trees.—CoBn
Nepenthe, sels. George Darley
The phoenix.—GrCt
The unicorn.—GrCt
Neptune
In praise of Neptune. T. Campion.—CoBn
"**Neptune** and Mars in council sat." See Louisburg
Neruda, Pablo
Artichoke.—LiT
Diver.—LiT
A few things explained.—LiT (sel.)
Nesbit, Edith (Edith Nesbit Bland)
Baby seed song.—HoB—ThA
Nesbit, Wilbur D.
"Who hath a book."—ArT-3

A **net** to snare the moonlight. Vachel Lindsay.—LiP
Nettles
Nettles. Mother Goose.—ReOn
Tall nettles. E. Thomas.—GrCt—ThG
Nettles. Mother Goose.—ReOn
"**Nettles** grow in an angry bush." See Nettles
Nevada
"Dogs have as much right as people in Nevada." H. Witt.—DuS
Vacation. W. Stafford.—BrA
Never ("Never, wailed the wind") Eleanor Farjeon.—FaT
Never ("Take me, or leave me—I'm not thine") Walter De La Mare.—DeBg
"**Never** again rejoicing in the surges that I sunder." See The dolphin's tomb
"**Never** get up till the sun gets up." Unknown.—DoC
"**Never** mind the day we left, or the way the women clung to us." See The Klondike
"**Never** more will the wind." H. D.—GrS
"**Never** pain to tell thy love." William Blake.—BlP
"Never seek to tell thy love."—CoBl
"**Never** saw him." See The Negro
"**Never** seek to tell thy love." See "Never pain to tell thy love"
"**Never** shall a young man." See For Anne Gregory
"**Never** talk down to a glowworm." See Glowworm
"**Never,** wailed the wind." See Never
Never weather-beaten sail. Thomas Campion.—GrCt
"**Never** weather-beaten sail more willing bent to shore." See Never weather-beaten sail
Neville, Mary
Lemons and apples.—ArT-3
Nevzoroff, Edward
Fishing.—BaH
The **new** baby calf. Edith H. Newlin.—ArT-3
The **new** book. Elizabeth Turner.—VrF
New dollhouse. Aileen Fisher.—FiIo
The **new** Colossus. Emma Lazarus.—BoH—BrA
New England
Brown's descent; or, The willy-nilly slide. R. Frost.—ArT-3
Clipper ships and captains. R. C. and S. V. Benét.—HuS-3
Covered bridge. R. P. T. Coffin.—BrA
Graveyard. R. P. T. Coffin.—BrA
New England landscape. D. Heyward.—PaH
Square-toed princes. R. P. T. Coffin.—BrA
New England landscape. DuBose Heyward.—PaH
New Guinea
Sunday: New Guinea. K. Shapiro.—BrA
New Hampshire
Apples in New Hampshire. M. Gilchrist.—CoBn
New Hampshire. From Landscapes. T. S. Eliot.—HaL
Spring in New Hampshire. C. McKay.—BoH—HaK
New Hampshire. See Landscapes
New Jersey
Legend. J. V. A. Weaver.—BrA
New Mexico
March in New Mexico. E. J. Coatsworth.—CoDh
New Mexico. P. C. Boyden.—ArT-3
The railroad cars are coming. Unknown.—BrA
Santos: New Mexico. M. Sarton.—PlE
The sound of morning in New Mexico. R. S. Kelley.—BrA
New Mexico. Polly Chase Boyden.—ArT-3
New moon. D. H. Lawrence.—CoBn
"**New** moon, come out, give water for us." Unknown, tr. fr. the Bushman.—LeO
"The **new** moon hangs like an ivory bugle." See The penny whistle
"The **new** moon, of no importance." See New moon
The **new** neighbor. Rose Fyleman.—ArT-3
New neighbors. Aileen Fisher.—FiIo
The **new** order. Phyllis McGinley.—BrA
New Orleans, Louisiana
The cathedral of St Louis. C. Carmer.—ThA
Dialect quatrain. M. B. Christian.—BoA
McDonogh day in New Orleans. M. B. Christian.—BoA
New Orleans. H. Carruth.—BrA
New Orleans, Battle of, 1815
The battle of New Orleans. T. D. English.—HiL
Farragut. W. T. Meredith.—HiL
New Orleans. Hayden Carruth.—BrA
The **new** pastoral, sel. Thomas Buchanan Read
Blennerhassett's island.—HiL
The **new** penny. Elizabeth Turner.—VrF
"A **new** servant maid named Maria." Unknown.—BrLl
New shoes. Alice Wilkins.—ArT-3
"**New** shoes, new shoes." See Choosing shoes
A **new** song to sing about Jonathan Bing. Beatrice Curtis Brown.—CoO
The **new** world ("There was a strange and unknown race") Paul Engle.—BrA (sel.)
The **new** world ("This America is an ancient land") Edgar Lee Masters.—BrA (sel.)
New year
"Ah, to be." Issa.—IsF—LeOw
"Dip down upon the northern shore." From In memoriam. A. Tennyson.—TeP
"God bless the master of this house." Mother Goose.—HuS-3
Christmas carol.—ArT-3
New Year's day. R. Field.—ArT-3—LaPh
Queen Mary's men. Unknown.—MoB
Ring out, wild bells. From In memoriam. A. Tennyson.—ArT-3—LaPh—TeP
Welcome to the new year. E. Farjeon.—ThA
"You'll find whenever the new year comes." Unknown.—WyC
New Year's day. Rachel Field.—ArT-3—LaPh
New York (City)
All around the town, sels. P. McGinley
"B's the bus."—ArT-3

"C is for the circus."—ArT-3
"E is the escalator."—ArT-3
"F is the fighting firetruck."—ArT-3—LaP
"J's the jumping jay-walker."—ArT-3
"P's the proud policeman."—ArT-3
"Q is for the quietness."—LaC
"R is for the restaurant."—ArT-3
"U is for umbrellas."—ArT-3
"V is for the vendor."—BrSg
"W is for windows."—ArT-3
Broadway: Twilight. T. Prideaux.—LaC
Brooklyn bridge. V. Mayakovsky.—LiT
Central park tourney. M. Weston.—BrA—DuR—LaC
Epistrophe. L. Jones.—HaK
Epitaph for any New Yorker. C. Morley.—BrSm
The lady is cold. E. B. White.—PaH
Letter to N. Y. E. Bishop.—McWs
Manhattan. M. A. Beer.—BrA
Manhattan lullaby. R. Field.—BrA—LaC
My city. J. W. Johnson.—BoH
Return to New York. J. H. Wheelock.—PaH
Review from Staten island. G. C. Oden.—HaK
Rhyme of rain. J. Holmes.—LaC
A sad song about Greenwich village. F. Park.—LaC
The stone. P. Blackburn.—DuS
Trinity place. P. McGinley.—LaC
The tropics in New York. C. McKay.—BoA—BoH—HaK
When dawn comes to the city. C. McKay.—BoH—LaC
New Zealand
May-June. N. Belting.—BeCm
Newbolt, Sir Henry
Drake's drum.—CoSs
Finis.—ArT-3
Newborn fingers. Mary O'Neill.—OnF
Newlin, Edith H.
The new baby calf.—ArT-3
Tiger-cat Tim.—ArT-3
Newman, Joseph S.
Baby Toodles.—CoBb
Newport, Rhode Island
The Jewish cemetery at Newport. H. W. Longfellow.—LoPl—PaH
News
"Brave news is come to town." Mother Goose.—OpF
"Braw news is come to town."—MoB
Jemmy Dawson.—BrMg
How they brought the good news from Ghent to Aix. R. Browning.—ArT-3—BrP—CoR—HuS-3
It's here in the. R. Atkins.—BoA
Unfinished knews item. E. Merriam.—MeI
"What's the news of the day." Mother Goose.—OpF
What's the news.—BrMg
Newsome, Mary Effie Lee
The baker's boy.—AgH
Morning light the dew-drier.—BoA
Newspapers
A patch of old snow. R. Frost.—DuR—LaC
The **newt**. David McCord.—ArT-3
Newton, Mary Leslie
Queen Anne's lace.—ThA
Newts. See Salamanders
"The **next** best thing to Christmas." See Birthday
"**Next** Marlowe, bathed in the Thespian springs." See To Henry Reynolds, of poets and poesy—Christopher Marlowe
"**Next** to of course God America I." E. E. Cummings.—BrA—HiL
Next year. Eleanor Farjeon.—FaT
Nez, Irene Ellen
A dream.—BaH
Nez, Justin
"Sun, God of living."—BaH
Niagara. Vachel Lindsay.—LiP
Niagara falls
Niagara. V. Lindsay.—LiP
"A **nice** old lady by the sea." See The cares of a caretaker
Nicholas, Saint. See Santa Claus
Nicholas Nye. Walter De La Mare.—BlO—CoB—HoB—ReO
Nicholl, Louise Townsend
For a child named Katherine.—ThA
Hymn.—PlE
Physical geography.—LiT
The shape called star.—HoL
Nichols, Grace
Alaska.—BaH
Nichols, Jeannette
Fast run in the junkyard.—DuS
Nichols, Robert
The full heart.—CoBn
Nicholson, Norman
The burning bush.—PlE
For all sorts and conditions.—PlE
For the bicentenary of Isaac Watts.—PlE
The motion of the earth.—LiT
"An old man sat in a waterfall."—CaD
Weather ear.—CaD
Nicoletta. Walter De La Mare.—DeBg
Night
Acquainted with the night. R. Frost.—GrCt—LaC—LaPd
At night. A. Fisher.—FiC
"At night may I roam." Unknown.—LeO
"At the time that turned the heat of the earth." Unknown.—LeO
"At the time when the earth became hot." Unknown.—LeO
Back yard, July night. W. Cole.—CoBn
"Blue water . . . a clear moon." Li T'ai-po.—LeMw
Check. J. Stephens.—ArT-3—HaL—ReS—StS—ThA
Night was creeping.—HuS-3
A child's prayer at evening. C. G. D. Roberts.—ReS
Come night, come Romeo. From Romeo and Juliet. W. Shakespeare.—CoBl
"Dark fills the sky with his big black cloak." B. Dinsdale.—LeM

Turn of the night. E. J. Coatsworth.—CoDh
"Turning from watching." Shiki.—BeCs
Visit. E. Recht.—LeM
Waiting. Unknown.—LeMw
Wanderer's night song. M. Bacon.—ReS
"The water bug is drawing the shadows of evening." Unknown.—LeO
What's night to me. S. Gilford.—LeM
Windy nights. R. L. Stevenson.—ArT-3—BoGj—HoB—TuW
Winter night ("Blow, wind, blow") M. F. Butts.—ArT-3
A winter night ("I feel cold") J. F. Velez.—BaH
Winter night ("It is very dark") H. Behn.—BeG
A winter night ("It was a chilly winter's night") W. Barnes.—GrCt
Winter night ("A tree may be laughter in the spring") C. Hutchison.—ArT-3
The **night** ("As I curl up to go to sleep") Amy Goodman.—LeM
Night ("Night can be a gypsy") Eleanor Farjeon.—FaT
The **night** ("The night creeps in") Myra Cohn Livingston.—HoB—LaPd
Night ("Night gathers itself into a ball of dark yarn") See The windy city
Night ("Night is a purple pumpkin") Patricia Hubbell.—LaPd
Night ("Night like purple flakes of snow") Donald Jeffrey Hayes.—ReS (sel.)
The **night** ("On the night that Christ was born") Phyllis McGinley.—McWc
Night ("The snow is white, the wind is cold") Mary Frances Butts.—ReS
Night ("Stars over snow") Sara Teasdale.—ArT-3—ThA
It is not far.—HuS-3
Night ("The sun descending in the west") William Blake.—BlP—BrSg (sel.)—CoBn—ReS (sel.)
Night airs. See Night airs and moonshine
Night airs and moonshine. Walter Savage Landor.—GrCt
Night airs.—CoBn
"**Night** airs that make tree-shadows walk, and sheep." See Night airs and moonshine
Night and noises. Glennis Foster.—LeM
Night at Yen Chou. Chou Shang Ju, tr. fr. the Chinese by Henry H. Hart.—LeMw
"**Night** can be a gypsy." See Night
Night clouds. Amy Lowell.—ThA
"The **night** creeps in." See The night
Night crow. Theodore Roethke.—HoL—ReBs
Night dancers. Thomas Kennedy.—ThA
Night encampment outside Troy. See Iliad
"The **night** flowers for me." See Starry night II
"**Night** gathers itself into a ball of dark yarn." See The windy city—Night
"**Night** held me as I scrawled and scrambled near." See The Turkish trench dog
The **night** hunt. Thomas MacDonagh.—CoB—CoR
Night in early spring. Elizabeth Jane Coatsworth.—CoSb
"**Night** is a beautiful thing." See What's night to me
"**Night** is a purple pumpkin." See Night
"**Night** is almost gone." See May
"**Night** is come." See Finis
"The **night** is darkening round me." Emily Brontë.—HoL
Night journey. Theodore Roethke.—BoH—BrA
"**Night** like purple flakes of snow." See Night
Night magic. Amelia Josephine Burr.—ThA
The **night** mail. W. H. Auden.—GrCt
Night music. See The merchant of Venice
The **night** of the full moon. Lloyd Frankenberg.—CoBl
Night of the scorpion. Nissim Ezekiel.—AlPi
The **night** of Trafalgar. Thomas Hardy.—GrCt
Night of wind. Frances M. Frost.—ArT-3
"The **night** opens the flower in secret." Rabindranath Tagore.—LeMf
A **night-piece** ("The sky is overcast") William Wordsworth.—WoP
Night piece ("What I know") Elizabeth Jane Coatsworth.—CoDh
Night plane. Frances M. Frost.—ArT-3—LaPd
Night practice. May Swenson.—LiT
Night ride. Herbert Read.—CoBl
"**Night** scarcely settles about one star." See Northern summer
Night sky. Aileen Fisher.—FiI
Night song ("Hushaby, hushaby, hushaby") Eve Merriam.—MeC
Night song ("On moony nights the dogs bark shrill") Frances Cornford.—CoB
Night song at Amalfi. Sara Teasdale.—BoH
Night song of the fish. Christian Morgenstern.—CoB
"The **night** the green moth came for me." See Green moth
Night thought of a tortoise suffering from insomnia on a lawn. E. V. Rieu.—ArT-3—CoB
Night time. Paul Wisdom.—LeM
Night train ("Across the dim frozen fields of night") Robert Francis.—ArT-3—HaL
Night train ("A train at night") Adrien Stoutenburg.—LaPd
"The **night** was coming very fast." See The hens
Night was creeping. See Check
"The **night** was creeping on the ground." See Check
"The **night** was thick and hazy." See Davy and the goblin—Robinson Crusoe's story
Night watchmen. Wymond Garthwaite.—ReS
"The **night** will never stay." Eleanor Farjeon.—HuS-3—LaP—TuW
The **night** wind. Emily Brontë.—CoR—GrCt
Night wind in spring. Elizabeth Jane Coatsworth.—CoDh
Nightingale, Madeleine
The scissor-man.—ArT-3
The **nightingale.** Monroe Stearns.—ArT-3
Nightingales
Ballad of the nightingale. P. McGinley.—McWc
The Chinese nightingale. V. Lindsay.—LiP
Echo. W. De La Mare.—DeBg

The first rainbow. I. Orleans.—HoB
The history of the flood. J. Heath-Stubbs.—CaMb
A long time ago. Unknown.—CoSs
Noah ("They gathered around and told him not to do it") R. Daniells.—DoW
Noah ("When old Noah stared across the floods") S. Sassoon.—ClF
"Noah an' Jonah an' Cap'n John Smith." D. Marquis.—CoSs
Noah and the rabbit. H. Chesterman.—ReO
Old Noah's ark. Unknown.—CoB
"Out of the ark's grim hold." From The flaming terrapin. R. Campbell.—CoB (sel.)—ReO
Parley of beasts. H. MacDiarmid.—ReO

Noah ("They gathered around and told him not to do it") Roy Daniells.—DoW
Noah ("When old Noah stared across the floods") Siegfried Sassoon.—ClF
"**Noah** an' Jonah an' Cap'n John Smith." Don Marquis.—CoSs
Noah and the rabbit. Hugh Chesterman.—ReO
"**Noah** of old three babies had." Mother Goose.—OpF
Nobility
"Lady Clara Vere de Vere." A. Tennyson.—TeP
The noble. From The prelude. W. Wordsworth.—GrCt
The toad-eater. R. Burns.—BuPr
The **noble.** See The prelude.
"**Nobly,** nobly Cape Saint Vincent to the Northwest died away." See Home-thoughts, from the sea
"**Nobody** gives it to you." Myra Cohn Livingston.—LiC
"**Nobody** knows from whence he came." See Mr Potts
Nobody loses all the time. E. E. Cummings.—McWs
"**Nobody,** nobody told me." See Under the rose
"**Nobody** planted roses, he recalls." See Summertime and the living
"**Nobody** teaches." See Knowing
"**Nobody** wanted this infant born." See Burial
"**Nobody's** nicer." Aileen Fisher.—FiIo
Nobuyuki Yuasa
"An accomplished acrobat." tr.—IsF
"All the while." tr.—IsF
"Along the cold post road." tr.—IsF
"Be brave." tr.—IsF
"Bending over." tr.—IsF
"A branch of willow." tr.—IsF
"The Buddha." tr.—IsF
"A child stretched forth." tr.—LeMw
"Children." tr.—IsF
"The clear note." tr.—IsF
"Come." tr.—IsF
"Come flies." tr.—IsF
"The deer." tr.—IsF
"Don't kill." tr.—IsF
"A drop of rain." tr.—ArT-3—LeI
"Excuse me." tr.—IsF
"A few flies." tr.—IsF
"The frog looks as if." tr.—IsF
"A giant frog and I." tr.—IsF
"Here comes." tr.—IsF
"Horse after horse." tr.—IsF
"I asked him how old he was." tr.—IsF
"I bought." tr.—IsF
"I cleaned." tr.—IsF
"I punished my child." tr.—IsF
"In with the luck." tr.—IsF
"A kitten." tr.—IsF
"Leaping the torrent." tr.—IsF
"A little child." tr.—LeMw
"A measuring worm." tr.—IsF
"A mosquito bit me." tr.—IsF
"A mother horse." tr.—LeMw
"On a rainy spring day." tr.—IsF
"On the bridge." tr.—IsF
"On the porch." tr.—IsF
"Quickly fly away." tr.—IsF
"The rat-a-tat-tat." tr.—IsF
"The right honorable." tr.—IsF
"Serenely poised." tr.—IsF
"A single mat." tr.—IsF
"Softly." tr.—LeMw
"Step aside, step aside." tr.—IsF
"A thousand." tr.—IsF—LeOw
"We are forever talking." tr.—IsF
"A weeping child." tr.—LeMw
Nocturne. Frances M. Frost.—CoBn
Nocturne at Bethesda. Arna Bontemps.—BoA
Nocturne: Georgia coast. Daniel Whitehead Hicky.—BrA
Nod. Walter De La Mare.—ReS
Noel, Henry
Beauty extolled.—GrCt
Noël. Unknown.—LaPh
Noffke, Ngaire
"I shook his hand."—LeM
Nōin
"After the storm."—BaS
"As now I come."—BaS
Noise. See Sounds
"**Noise** of hammers once I heard." See The hammers
"The **noise** of passing feet." Unknown, tr. fr. the Chippewa.—LeO
The **noise** of waters. See Chamber music
"**Noises** coming down the stairs." See Rest hour
"The **noisiest** bird that ever grew." See The bugle-billed bazoo
Non sum qualis eram bonae sub regno Cynarae. Ernest Dowson.—CoBl
"**Nona** poured oil on the water and saw the eye." See The evil eye
"**None** can experience stint." Emily Dickinson.—DiPe
The **nonny.** James Reeves.—CoB
"The **nonny-bird** I love particularly." See The nonny
The **nonpareil's** grave. M. J. McMahon.—MoS

Nonsense. See also Limericks; Mother Goose; also entries under Carroll, Lewis; Lear, Edward; Richards, Laura E.
Adventures of Isabel. O. Nash.—BrSm (sel.)—LaP (sel.)—LaPd (sel.)
Alas, alack. W. De La Mare.—ArT-3
"As I was going out one day." Unknown.—CoO
"As I was walking slowly." A. E. Housman.—LiT
"As I went by by Humbydrum." Unknown.—MoB
"As I went up the humber jumber." Unknown.—OpF
As to the restless brook. J. K. Bangs.—CoO
At the bottom of the well. L. Untermeyer.—BoGj
Beg parding. Unknown.—CoO—GrCt
"Beware, my child." S. Silverstein.—CoO—LaPd
The boar and the dromedar. H. Beissel.—DoW
Boston Charlie. W. Kelly.—BoGj
The bugle-billed bazoo. J. Ciardi.—BoH
The cares of a caretaker. W. Irwin.—CoO
The contrary waiter. E. Parker.—CoO
Cow. W. J. Smith.—CoO
Dinky. T. Roethke.—CoO—LiT
Donkey riding. Unknown.—DoW—StF
Don't ever seize a weasel by the tail. J. Prelutsky.—CoO
Eeka, neeka. W. De La Mare.—DeBg
"The folk who live in backward town." M. A. Hoberman.—ArT-3—CoO
Fooba wooba John. Unknown.—CoO
"Four-and-twenty Highlandmen." Unknown.—MoB
The frog. Unknown.—CoO
From the sublime to the ridiculous to the sublimely ridiculous to the ridiculously sublime. J. Prelutsky.—CoO
Good King Wenceslas. Unknown.—CoO
The great panjandrum. S. Foote.—BlO
The happy family. J. Ciardi.—CoO
A hot-weather song. D. Marquis.—HuS-3
"A hurrying man he always was." Unknown.—WyC
I love animals and dogs. H. A. Farley.—LeM
"I wish that my room had a floor." G. Burgess.—LaP
Relativity and levitation.—BrLl
"If a pig wore a wig." C. G. Rossetti.—HoB
Intramural aestivation, or summer in town, by a teacher of Latin. O. W. Holmes.—GrCt
It was shut. J. T. Greenleaf.—CoO
Jim Jay. W. De La Mare.—SmM
"Johnnie Crack and Flossie Snail." From Under Milk Wood. D. Thomas.—BoGj—CaD—HaL—LaPd
Jonathan Bing. B. C. Brown.—ArT-3—LaP—LaPd
Just because. D. McCord.—CoO—McE
Just dropped in. W. Cole.—BoGj
"King Tut." X. J. Kennedy.—LiT
The lady and the bear. T. Roethke.—BoGj
The land of the Bumbley Boo. S. Milligan.—StF
"Lo, the bat with leathern wing." From Songs from an island in the moon. W. Blake.—LiT
"The minister in the pulpit." Unknown.—CoO—MoB
Mr Kartoffel. J. Reeves.—CoO—SmM
Mr Mixup tells a story. D. McCord.—McAd
"Mr Spats." S. Silverstein.—CoO
"Mollis abuti." J. Swift.—GrCt
The monotony song. T. Roethke.—LiT
A nautical ballad. From Day and the goblin. C. E. Carryl.—HuS-3
A nautical extravagance. W. Irwin.—HuS-3
A new song to sing about Jonathan Bing. B. C. Brown.—CoO
A nonsense song. S. V. Benét.—TuW
Nottamun town. Unknown.—BlO
Nursery nonsense. D'A. W. Thompson.—CoO
Nursery rhyme. W. H. Auden.—GrS
Oddity land. E. Anthony.—HoB
"On the Ning Nang Nong." S. Milligan.—CoO—StF
"Outside my door, I heard someone say." Unknown.—WyC
Peterhof. E. Wilson.—BoGj
A pig tale. J. Reeves.—LaP—SmM
Praise to the end. T. Roethke.—LiT (sel.)
The ptarmigan. Unknown.—CoB
Pudden Tame. Unknown.—GrCt
A reunion in Kensington. S. J. Cohen.—SmM
A second stanza for Dr Johnson. D. Hall.—BrSm
The shades of night. A. E. Housman.—GrCt
Silly song. F. G. Lorca.—LiT
Sir Smashum Uppe. E. V. Rieu.—CoO
The sniffle. O. Nash.—McWs
Song of the pop-bottlers. M. Bishop.—McWs
Stately verse. Unknown.—ArT-3
"Tam o the linn came up the gate." Unknown.—MoB
Tame animals I have known. N. Waterman.—CoO
There once was a puffin. F. P. Jaques.—ArT-3—StF
"A thousand hairy savages." S. Milligan.—CoO
"Three little puffins." E. Farjeon.—ArT-3
'Tis midnight. Unknown.—CoO
Tragedy. W. Cheney.—CoO
The train pulled in the station. Unknown.—CoO
Two or three. J. Keats.—SmM
"Way down south where bananas grow." Unknown.—CoO
"We're all in the dumps." Mother Goose.—BlO
In the dumps.—BrMg
What someone told me about Bobby Link. J. Ciardi.—AgH—CiYk
What's in the cupboard. Unknown.—GrCt
"When a goose meets a moose." Z. Gay.—ArT-3
Where. W. De La Mare.—DeBg
The zobo bird. F. A. Collymore.—BoGj

A **nonsense** song. Stephen Vincent Benét.—TuW
The **noonday** April sun. George Love.—AdIa
Noonday Sun. Kathryn and Byron Jackson.—ArT-3
Nootka Indians. See Indians of the Americas—Nootka
Nora Criona. James Stephens.—StS
Norris, Leslie
The ballad of Billy Rose.—CaMb
Norsemen
"O'er the wild gannet's bath." G. Darley.—CoSs—GrCt
The story of Vinland. S. Lanier.—HiL
The Vikings. Unknown.—GrCt
North, Christopher (about)
To Christopher North. A. Tennyson.—TeP
North Carolina
Report from the Carolinas. H. Bevington.—BrA (sel.)
North Dakota
August from my desk. R. Flint.—BrA—DuR
North star shining, sels. Hildegarde Hoyt Swift
"I came to the new world empty-handed."—BrA
"My name was legion."—BrA
The **North** star whispers to the blacksmith's son. Vachel Lindsay.—LiP
"The **North** star whispers: You are one." See The North star whispers to the blacksmith's son
The **north** wind. See "The north wind doth blow"
"The **north** wind doth blow." Mother Goose.—BlO—HuS-3—OpF—ReMg—SmM—WiMg
The north wind.—BrMg
Northern lights
Aurora borealis. E. Farjeon.—FaT
Northern summer. Harry Behn.—BeG
Norton, M. D. Herter
The boy. tr.—LiT
The carousel. tr.—LiT
Presentiment. tr.—LiT
Nosce teipsum, sels. John Davies
I know myself a man.—GrCt
Much knowledge, little reason.—GrCt
"**Nose**, nose, jolly red nose." Mother Goose, at. to Francis Beaumont and John Fletcher.—ClF
Jolly red nose.—BrMg
Nosegay for a young goat. Winifred Welles.—CoB
Noses
The dog's cold nose. A. Guiterman.—CoB
The dong with a luminous nose. E. Lear.—GrCt
The handiest nose. A. Fisher.—FiC
"Nose, nose, jolly red nose." Mother Goose.—ClF
Jolly red nose.—BrMg
Old woman of Lynn. Unknown.—VrF
"Peter White." Mother Goose.—OpF
Peter White's nose.—BrMg
Polly Picklenose. L. F. Jackson.—CoBb
"There was a young lady of Kent." Unknown.—BrLl
"There was a young lady whose nose." E. Lear.—BrLl
Limericks.—HoB
"There was an old man in a barge." E. Lear.—BrLl
"There was an old man of West Drumpet." E. Lear.—BrLl
"There was an old man on whose nose." E. Lear
Limericks.—HoB
"There was an old man with a nose." E. Lear.—BrLl
Tom Tickleby and his nose. L. E. Richards.—CoO
"**Not** a drum was heard, not a funeral note." See The burial of Sir John Moore
"**Not** a man is stirring." See Riding at daybreak
"**Not** Aladdin magian." See Staffa
"**Not** all of them must suffer. Some." See Saints
"**Not** always sure what things called sins may be." See Forgive my guilt
Not any more. Dorothy Aldis.—HoB
"**Not** as Black Douglas, bannered, trumpeted." See Two wise generals
"**Not** bad, but miserable." See War
"**Not** born to the forest are we." See Twelfth night: Song of the camels
"**Not** every man has gentians in his house." See Bavarian gentians
"**Not** gold, but only man can make." See A nation's strength
"**Not** greatly moved with awe am I." See The two deserts
"**Not** guns, not thunder, but a flutter of clouded drums." See Fireworks
Not in vain. See "If I can stop one heart from breaking"
"**Not** like the brazen giant of Greek fame." See The new Colossus
Not me. Shelley Silverstein.—CoB
Not ragged-and-tough. Unknown.—GrCt
"**Not** the end: but there's nothing more." See Home
"**Not** the whole warbling grove in concert heard." See To the cuckoo
"**Not** to shift with weather or with tides." See A question of weather
"**Not** what you get, but what you give." See Of giving
"**Not** with a club the heart is broken." Emily Dickinson.—DiPe
"**Not** with my hands." See Benediction
"**Not** writ in water, nor in mist." See For John Keats
Notes for a movie script. M. Carl Holman.—BoA—HaK
Notes found near a suicide, sels. Frank Horne.—BoA (Complete)
To James.—BoA—BoH—HaK
Notes on a track meet. David McCord.—MoS
Nothing. Walter De La Mare.—DeBg
Nothing-at-all. Mother Goose.—BrMg
"**Nothing** at all more delicate and charming." See Dance of burros

Nothing gold can stay. Robert Frost.—BoH
"**Nothing** happens only once." See Circle one
"**Nothing** if not utterly in death." See So
"**Nothing** is so beautiful as spring." See Spring
"**Nothing,** nothing can keep me from my love." See Love lyric
"**Nothing** sings from these orange trees." See On watching the construction of a skyscraper
"**Nothing** that is shall perish utterly." See Michael Angelo, A fragment
"**Nothing** to do." Shelley Silverstein.—CoBb
"**Nothing** to do but work." See The pessimist
Nothing will die. Alfred Tennyson.—TeP
"**Nothing** would sleep in that cellar, dank as a ditch." See Root cellar
Nottamun town. Unknown.—BlO
"**Nought** loves another as itself." See A little boy lost
November
The crazy woman. G. Brooks.—BoH—LiT
Enter November. E. Farjeon.—FaA
My November guest. R. Frost.—BoH
No. T. Hood.—BlO—GrCt—McWs
November ("The birds have all flown") C. Gluck.—LeM
November ("Cold flings itself out of the north") N. Belting.—BeCm
November ("The crops are in from the fields") N. Belting.—BeCm
November ("November's days are thirty") E. Thomas.—ThG
November ("Trees worry in November") M. C. Livingston.—LiC
"November bares the robin's nest." D. McCord.—McAd
November day. E. Averitt.—DuR
November glow. H. I. Rostron.—StF
November night. A. Crapsey.—HoL
November ("The birds have all flown") Charles Gluck.—LeM
November ("Cold flings itself out of the north") Natalia Belting.—BeCm
November ("The crops are in from the fields") Natalia Belting.—BeCm
November ("November's days are thirty") Edward Thomas.—ThG
November ("Trees worry in November") Myra Cohn Livingston.—LiC
"**November** bares the robin's nest." David McCord.—McAd
November day. Eleanor Averitt.—DuR
November glow. Hilda I. Rostron.—StF
"**November** is a cold month." See November glow
November night. Adelaide Crapsey.—HoL
November 1. William Wordsworth.—WoP
"**November's** days are thirty." See November
Now. Robert Browning.—BrP
Now and then. Sharatchandra Muktibodh, tr. fr. the Marathi by D. G. Nadkarni.—AlPi
"**Now** are the autumn days hospitable to wild geese." See Autumn
"**Now** are you a marsupial." See Are you a marsupial
"**Now** as I was young and easy under the apple boughs." See Fern hill
"**Now** as the river fills with ice." See Crew cut
"**Now** as the train bears west." See Night journey
"**Now** came still ev'ning on, and twilight gray." See Paradise lost—The moon and the nightingale
Now close the windows. Robert Frost.—HaL
"**Now** close the windows and hush all the fields." See Now close the windows
"**Now** come to think of it, you say." See Figures of speech
"**Now** crouch, ye kings of greatest Asia." See Tamburlaine the Great—The bloody conquests of mighty Tamburlaine
"**Now** do you know of Avalon." See The jingo and the minstrel
"**Now** does the golden tickseed bloom its last." See The golden tickseed
"**Now** every breath of air." See The trees and the wind
Now fades the last. See In memoriam
"**Now** fades the last long streak of snow." See In memoriam—Now fades the last
Now fall asleep. Elizabeth Jane Coatsworth.—ReS
"**Now** fayre, fayrest of every fayre." See To the Princess Margaret Tudor
"**Now** from the dark, a deeper dark." See Calling in the cat
"**Now** hand in hand, you little maidens, walk." See Spring
"**Now** his nose's bridge is broken, one eye." See On Hurricane Jackson
"**Now** I am going out." Issa, tr. fr. the Japanese by R. H. Blyth.—LeOw
"**Now** I am young and credulous." See Wisdom cometh with the years
"**Now** I can see." See The birds
"**Now** I go down here and bring up a moon." See Auctioneer
"**Now** I lay me down to sleep." Mother Goose.—SmM
A prayer.—BrMg
"**Now** I will fashion the tale of a fish." See Physiologus—The whale
"**Now** if you're good while I'm away." See Gifts for a good boy
"**Now,** in the night, all music haunts us here." See Johnny Appleseed speaks of the apple-blossom amaranth that will come to this city
Now in the stillness. Elizabeth Jane Coatsworth.—CoDh
"**Now** in the stillness and the aloneness." See Now in the stillness
"**Now,** innocent, within the deep." See M., singing
"**Now** into the saddle, and over the grass." See The pony express
"**Now** is the hour between midnight and the first false dawn." See Turn of the night
"**Now** is the ox-eyed daisy out." See June
"**Now** it is spring." Yakamochi.—BaS

"**Now** let the generations pass." See Shantung; or, The empire of China is crumbling down
"**Now** let us speak of cowboys who on swift." See Wild West
"**Now** lighted windows climb the dark." See Manhattan lullaby
"**Now**—more near ourselves than we." E. E. Cummings.—WeP
"**Now**, my fair'st friend." See The winter's tale—Some flowers o' the spring
"**Now** one and all, you roses." See A wood song
"**Now**, pray, where are you going, said Meet-on-the-Road." See Meet-on-the-Road
"**Now** rouses earth, so long quiescent." See Spring
"**Now**, said the sun, when winter had gone." See The sun's frolic
Now silent falls. Walter De La Mare.—GrS
"**Now** silent falls the clacking mill." See Now silent falls
"**Now** sleep the mountain-summits, sleep the glens." See Vesper
Now sleeps the crimson petal. See The princess
"**Now** sleeps the crimson petal, now the white." See The princess—Now sleeps the crimson petal
"**Now** that he is safely dead." Carl Wendell Hines, Jr.—BoH
"**Now** that he's left the room." See Univac to Univac
"**Now** that I am dressed I'll go." See Peadar Og goes courting
"**Now** that I, tying thy glass mask tightly." See The laboratory
"**Now** that our love has drifted." See Finis
"**Now** that the winter's gone, the earth has lost." See The youthful spring
"**Now** the bright morning star, day's harbinger." See Song: On May morning
"**Now** the day is over." See Child's evening hymn
"**Now** the frog, all lean and weak." See The sweet o' the year
"**Now** the hungry lion roars." See A midsummer-night's dream
"**Now** the moon goes down." Buson, tr. fr. the Japanese by Harry Behn.—BeCs
"**Now** the rich cherry, whose sleek wood." See Country summer
"**Now** the small birds come to feast." See Winter feast
"**Now** the snow is vanished clean." See Québec May
"**Now** the sudden shower's done." See Thunder pools
"**Now** the winds are riding by." See And it was windy weather
"**Now** the year's let loose; it skips like a feckless child." See April day: Binsey
"**Now** this is the law of the jungle—as old and as true as the sky." See The second jungle book—The law of the jungle
"**Now** to be good if you'll begin." Unknown.—VrF
"**Now** to th' ascent of that steep savage hill." See Paradise lost—Satan journeys to the Garden of Eden
"**Now** touch the air softly." See A pavane for the nursery
"**Now**, 'twas twenty-five or thirty years since Jack first saw the light." See Jack was every inch a sailor
"**Now** what do you think." Mother Goose.—OpF
  Jacky Jingle.—BrMg
"**Now** what in the world shall we dioux." See The Sioux
"**Now** where's a song for our small dear." See The unwritten song
"**Now** with a sigh November comes to the brooding land." See Autumn in Carmel
"**Now** would I tread my darkness down." See When I am dead
Nowell sing we. Unknown.—GrCt
"**Nowell** sing we now and some." See Nowell sing we
"**Nowhere** are we safe." See Hymn written after Jeremiah preached to me in a dream
Noyes, Alfred
  The admiral's ghost.—ArT-3
  The cure.—CoB
  Daddy fell into the pond.—LaP—LaPd
  Edinburgh.—PaH
  Forty singing seamen.—HoB
  The highwayman.—ArT-3—CoBl
  Old gray squirrel.—CoSs
  Slumber song.—ReS (sel.)
  A song of Sherwood.—ArT-3—ThA
A **number** of numbers. Eve Merriam.—MeC
"**Nuns** fret not at their convent's narrow room." See Sonnet
Nurse outwitted. Mary Elliott.—VrF
The **nursery**. See The coming forth by day of Osiris Jones
Nursery nonsense. D'Arcy Wentworth Thompson.—CoO
Nursery play
  Catch him, crow. Mother Goose.—BrF—BrMg
  "Dance to your daddy." Mother Goose.—BrMg—MoB
    "Dance to your daddie."—ArT-3
  "Diddle-me-diddle-me-dandy-O." Mother Goose.—OpF
  Face game. Unknown.—MoB
  "A farmer went trotting upon his gray mare." Mother Goose.—ArT-3
    "A farmer went riding."—HuS-3—OpF
    The mischievous raven.—BrF—BrMg
  "Father and mother and Uncle John." Mother Goose.—OpF
  The features. Mother Goose.—BrMg
  Foot patting. Mother Goose.—BrMg
  "Hey my kitten, my kitten." Unknown.—MoB
  "I had a little hobby-horse." Mother Goose.—MoB
    Mother Goose rhymes, 58.—HoB
  "I had a little manikin, I set him on my thumbikin." Unknown.—MoB

O

"**O** blackbird, sing me something well." See The blackbird
"**O** blackbird, what a boy you are." See Vespers
"**O** blest unfabled incense tree." See Nepenthe—The phoenix
"**O** blithe new-comer. I have heard." See To the cuckoo
"**Oh,** blithely shines the bonny sun." See We'll go to sea no more
"**O,** but I saw a solemn sight." See The wicked hawthorn tree
"**O** butterfly." Chiyo-ni, tr. fr. the Japanese by R. H. Blyth.—LeMw
"**O** can you sew cushions." Unknown.—MoB
O captain, my captain. Walt Whitman.—CoR—HiL—HuS-3
"**O** captain, my captain, our fearful trip is done." See O captain, my captain
O cat of carlish kind. See Philip (or Phylip) Sparrow—The cursing of the cat
"**O** clear and musical." See The bird
"**O** come, let us sing unto the Lord." See Psalms—Psalm 95
"**Oh** come, my joy, my soldier boy." See Ballad
"**O** come to my master, cries honest old Tray." Ann and Jane Taylor.—VrF
"**O** come with me into this moonlight world." See The night of the full moon
"**O** crocodile." See The crocodile
"**O** crows take care, beware." See A warning to crows
"**O** cuckoo, shall I call thee bird." See To the cuckoo
O Daedalus, fly away home. Robert E. Hayden.—AdIa—BoH
Oh dear. Mother Goose.—BrMg
"**Oh,** dear, how will it end." See To mystery land
"**Oh** dear, I must wear my red slippers to-day." See Dancing
O dear me. Walter De La Mare.—ArT-3—SmM
"**Oh** dear, oh. My cake's all dough." Mother Goose.—OpF
"**Oh** dear, what can the matter be." Mother Goose.—McWs—OpF
What can the matter be.—BrMg
"**O** death, rock me on sleep." at. to Anne Boleyn.—GrCt
"**O** early one morning I walked out like Agag." See The streets of Laredo
"**Oh,** east is east, and west is west, and never the twain shall meet." See The ballad of east and west
"**Oh,** fair to see." Christina Georgina Rossetti.—ArT-3
"**Oh,** fatal stroke, —must hope expire." See The death of a father
"**O** father's gone to market town, he was up before the day." See A midsummer song
"**O** fie, Master Edward, I feel much surprise." See The crying child
"**O** fireflies dear." See Firefly party
"**O** fish, come." See Song of the fishermen
"**O** foolish ducklings." Buson, tr. fr. the Japanese by Harry Behn.—BeCs
"**O** for a muse of fire, that would ascend." See King Henry V—A muse of fire
"**O** for a voice like thunder, and a tongue." See Prologue intended for a dramatic piece of King Edward the Fourth
"**Oh** Galuppi, Baldassare, this is very sad to find." See A toccata of Galuppi's
"**Oh,** gipsies, proud and stiff-necked and perverse." See I know all this when gipsy fiddles cry
"**O** give thanks unto the Lord; for he is good." See Psalms—Psalm 136
"**O** God (forever I turn)." See The prayer of the goldfish
"**Oh,** God of dust and rainbows, help us see." See Two somewhat different epigrams
"**O** God, our help in ages past." Isaac Watts.—PlE
"**O** God, who made me." See The prayer of the donkey
"**O** goody, it's coming, the circus parade." See The circus parade
"**O** great chief." See Songs in praise of the chief
"**O** great mountain, you chief." See Morning prayer
"**O,** happy wind, how sweet." See Happy wind
"**Oh** Harry, Harry, hold me close." See The catipoce
"**O** have you seen the Shah." See A-hunting we will go
"**O** hawk in the sky there." See The penniless hawk
"**O** holy virgin, clad in purest white." See To morning
"**Oh,** how I love to skip alone." See Skipping along alone
"**Oh,** how it makes me giggle." See Merry thoughts
"**Oh,** how shall I get it, how shall I get it." See The egg
"**O,** how this spring of love resembleth." See Two gentlemen of Verona—This spring of love
"**Oh,** hush thee, my baby, the night is behind us." See The jungle book—Seal lullaby
"**O** hushed October morning mild." See October
"**Oh,** I have walked in Kansas." See Kansas
"**O,** I say, you Joe." See Songs from an island in the moon
"**Oh,** I went down to Framingham." See Spooks
"**Oh** I wish the sun was bright in the sky." See The terrible robber men
"**Oh,** if you were a little boy." See Wishes
"**Oh,** I'm a good old rebel, that's what I am." See The rebel
"**Oh** I'm being eaten by a boa constrictor." See Boa constrictor
"**Oh,** I'm so sleepy, I'll lie down to rest." See Tired
"**O** is an optimist glad." Oliver Herford.—BrLl

"**O** she looked out of the window." See The two magicians
"**Oh**, she walked unaware of her own increasing beauty." See She walked unaware
"**Oh** Shenandoah, I long to hear you." See Shenandoah
"**Oh**, she's mean." See Mrs Elsinore
"**Oh**, silver tree." See Jazzonia
"**O** sing unto the Lord a new song." See Psalms —Psalm 98
"**Oh**, sister Susan, come, pray come." See Susan and Patty
"**O**, sixteen hundred and ninety one." See The two witches
"**Oh** sky, you look so drear." See Earth and sky
"**O** soft embalmer of the still midnight." See To sleep
"**Oh**, soldier, soldier, will you marry me." See "Soldier, soldier, won't you marry me"
"**Oh**, some are fond of red wine, and some are fond of white." See Captain Stratton's fancy
"**Oh** some have killed in angry love." See A rope for Harry Fat
"**O** spread agen your leaves an' flow'rs." See The woodlands
Oh stay at home. Alfred Edward Housman.—McWs
"**Oh** stay at home, my lad, and plough." See Oh stay at home
"**O** such a hurry-burry." Unknown.—MoB
"**O** sun and skies and clouds of June." See October's bright blue weather
"**O** sun, O sun." Unknown, tr. fr. the Gabon Pygmie.—LeO
"**Oh**, sure am I when come to die." See Old friends
"**Oh**, Susan Blue." Kate Greenaway.—ArT-3
Susan Blue.—GrT
"**O**, sweep of stars over Harlem streets." See Stars
"**Oh**, talk not to me of a name great in story." See Stanzas written on the road between Florence and Pisa
"**Oh**, that I were." Mother Goose.—BrMg
"**Oh**, that my young life were a lasting dream." See Dreams
"**O** the barberry bright, the barberry bright." See Song against children
"**Oh**, the brave old duke of York." Mother Goose. —OpF
The brave old duke of York.—BrMg
"The grand old duke of York."—ArT-3
"O, the grand old duke of York."—WiMg
"**Oh**, the brown Missouri mule has a copper-plated throat." See Mule song
"**Oh**, the cuckoo, he is a royal bird." See Cuckoo's palace
"**O** the dusty miller." See Dusty miller
"**Oh** the falling snow." See For snow
"**O**, the grand old duke of York." See "Oh, the brave old duke of York"
"**O** the green glimmer of apples in the orchard." See Ballad of another Ophelia
"**Oh**, the little roses." See New dollhouse
"**O** the little rusty dusty miller." See Dusty miller
"**Oh**, the men who laughed the American laughter." See American laughter
"**Oh**, the mighty king of France." Mother Goose. —OpF
"**O**, the mill, mill, O." Unknown.—MoB
"**O** the raggedy man. He works fer pa." See The raggedy man
"**Oh**, the shambling sea is a sexton old." See The gravedigger
"**Oh**, the slimy, squirmy, slithery eel." See Song of hate for eels
"**O** the spring will come." See The spring will come
"**O**, the train pulled in the station." See The train pulled in the station
"**O**, then, I see Queen Mab hath been with you." See Romeo and Juliet—Queen Mab
"**Oh** there is blessing in this gentle breeze." See The prelude—Childhood
"**Oh**, there once was a puffin." See There once was a puffin
"**O** there was a woman, and she was a widow." See Flowers in the valley
"**Oh**, these spring days." See On the road to Nara
"**Oh**, they built the ship Titanic, and they built her strong and true." See The Titanic
"**O** Thou my monster, Thou my guide." See Prayer in mid-passage
"**O** Thou, that in the heavens does dwell." See Holy Willie's prayer
"**O** thou, that sit'st upon a throne." See A song to David
"**O** thou, whatever title suit thee." See Address to the deil
"**Oh** Thou, who man of baser earth didst make." See The rubaiyát of Omar Khayyám
"**O** thou, who passest thro' our vallies in." See To summer
"**O** thou with dewy locks, who lookest down." See To spring
"**Oh** to be in England." See Home-thoughts, from abroad
"**Oh**, to be in England now that April's there." See Home-thoughts, from abroad
"**Oh**, to have a little house." See The old woman of the roads
O-u-g-h. David McCord.—McAd
"**Oh**, weep for Mr and Mrs Bryan." See The lion
"**O** were my love yon lilac fair." Robert Burns.—GrCt
"**O**, were you on the mountain, or saw you my love." See Were you on the mountain
"**O** wert thou in the cauld blast." Robert Burns. —BuPr
"**Oh**, what a blessing is the sight." See A visit to the blind asylum
"**Oh**, what a pleasure for the animals." See Genesis
"**Oh.** What a worrit." See The mother hen
"**O** what can ail thee, knight-at-arms." See La belle dame sans merci

"**O** what has made that sudden noise." See The ghost of Roger Casement
"**Oh**, what have you got for dinner, Mrs Bond." See Dilly dilly
"**Oh**, what if the Easter bunny." See What if
O what if the fowler. Charles Dalmon.—CoB—ReBs
"**O** what if the fowler my blackbird has taken." See O what if the fowler
"**Oh**, what is Jeannie weeping for." Unknown.—MoB
"**Oh**, what is that comes gliding in." See Sally Simpkin's lament
"**O** what is that sound which so thrills the ear." W. H. Auden.—CaD—GrS
"**Oh**, what shall my blue eyes go see." See To baby
"**O** what's the rhyme to porringer." Unknown.—MoB
"**O** what's the weather in a beard." See Dinky
"**O**, when I was a wee thing." Unknown.—MoB
Oh, when I was in love. See A Shropshire lad
"**Oh** when I was in love with you." See A Shropshire lad—Oh, when I was in love
"**Oh** when the early morning at the seaside." See East Anglian bathe
"**O** when the saints go marchin' in." See When the saints go marchin' in
"**O** when 'tis summer weather." See The greenwood
"**O**, where are you going." Unknown.—MoB
"**O**, where are you going, Goodspeed and Discovery." See Southern ships and settlers
"**Oh** where are you going? says Milder to Malder." See The cutty wren
"**O** where hae ye been, Lord Randal, my son." See Lord Randal
"**O** where is tiny Hewe." See The goblin's song
"**Oh** where, oh where has my little dog gone." Mother Goose.—WiMg
My little dog.—BrMg
"**O** whistle an' I'll come to ye, my lad." Robert Burns.—BuPr—CoBl
"**Oh**, who is lost to-night." See Fireflies
"**O** why do you walk through the fields in gloves." See To a fat lady seen from the train
"**O** wild west wind, thou breath of autumn's being." See Ode to the west wind
"**O** Willie brew'd a peck o' maut." See Willie brew'd a peck o' maut
"**O**, wilt thou go wi' me, sweet Tibbie Dunbar." See Sweet Tibbie Dunbar
"**O** wind, why do you never rest." Christina Georgina Rossetti.—ArT-3
"**O** winter, bar thine adamantine doors." See To winter
"**O** words are lightly spoken." See The rose tree
"**O** world, I cannot hold thee close enough." See God's world
"**O** world invisible, we view thee." See The kingdom of God
"**O** world. O life. O time." See A lament
"**Oh** would you know why Henry sleeps." See Inhuman Henry; or, Cruelty to fabulous animals
"**O** ye that look on ecstasy." See Ecstasy
"**O** ye wha are sae guid yoursel'." See Address to the unco good
"**O** yellow bird, yellow bird." See The yellow bird
Oh yet we trust. See In memoriam—"Oh yet we trust that somehow good"
"**O** yet we trust that somehow good." See In memoriam
"**O**, you are like the tender cotton worms." Unknown, tr. fr. the Manipuries.—LeO
"**O** you who lose the art of hope." See A gospel of beauty—The Illinois village
"**O**, young Lochinvar is come out of the west." See Marmion—Lochinvar
"**O** young mariner." See Merlin and the gleam
The **oak**. Alfred Tennyson.—TeP
"**Oak**. I am the rooftree and the keel." See Tapestry trees
Oak leaves. Elizabeth Jane Coatsworth.—HuS-3
Oak trees
The haunted oak. P. L. Dunbar.—HaK
The limbs of the pin oak tree. From Some short poems. W. Stafford.—DuS
The oak. A. Tennyson.—TeP
Oak leaves. E. J. Coatsworth.—HuS-3
Spring oak. G. Kinnell.—CoBn
The stump. D. Hall.—DuR
"**Oats** and beans and barley grows." See Singing game
Obedience. See also Behavior
Dangerous sport. E. Turner.—VrF
The giddy girl. E. Turner.—VrF
Jim, who ran away from his nurse, and was eaten by a lion. H. Belloc.—BrSm—CoBb—GrCt
The law of the jungle. From The second jungle book. R. Kipling.—HoB—ReO
The little fish that would not do as it was bid. A. and J. Taylor.—VrF
"The moon is distant from the sea." E. Dickinson.—DiPe
"My mother said I never should." Mother Goose.—BlO—BrMg
"My mother said that I never should."—OpF
Playing with fire. A. and J. Taylor.—VrF
Silly Willy. R. L. B.—BrSm
Tardiness. G. Burgess.—CoBb
The **obedient** child. Mary Elliott.—VrF
Oblation. Algernon Charles Swinburne.—CoBl
Obrien, Edward J.
Irish.—LaPh—ThA
O'Brien, R. C.
Poor grandpa.—BrSm
Observations. See Naladiyar
The **occultation** of Orion. Henry Wadsworth Longfellow.—LoPl
Ocean
After the sea ship. W. Whitman.—CoSs

Alien. D. J. Hayes.—BoA
The anchorage. P. Wilson.—CoSs
"As I row over the plain." Fujiwara no Tadamichi.—BaS
Augury. S. George.—GrS
"Break, break, break." A. Tennyson.—BlO—BoGj—TeP
Brightness. Unknown.—BeG
"By the sandy water I breathe the odor of the sea." Unknown.—LeO
By the sea. C. G. Rossetti.—CoBn
The cares of a caretaker. W. Irwin.—CoO
Carmel Point. M. P. MacSweeney.—DuR
The city in the sea. E. A. Poe.—GrS—PoP
The dancing sea. From Orchestra. J. Davies.—GrCt
"Doth not a Tenarif, or higher hill." From Anatomy of the world: The first anniversary. J. Donne.—GrCt
"An everywhere of silver." E. Dickinson.—DiPe
Exiled. E. St V. Millay.—PaH
The fisher's boy. H. D. Thoreau.—GrCt
Flowers by the sea. W. C. Williams.—BoGj—HoL
The flying fish. J. Gray.—GrCt
The flying sea. R. Mortimer.—LeM
The gravedigger. B. Carman.—CoBn
Her heards be thousand fishes. From Colin Clout's come home again. E. Spenser.—GrCt
"Here, in this little bay." C. Patmore.—CoBn
Home-thoughts, from the sea. R. Browning.—BrP
"How can the sea be dark and gray." S. Harrison.—LeM
"I started early, took my dog." E. Dickinson.—DiL—DiPe
"If all the seas were one sea." Mother Goose.—HuS-3—OpF
    If.—BrMg
In praise of Neptune. T. Campion.—CoBn
In winter. R. Wallace.—CoBn
An inscription by the sea. E. A. Robinson.—CoSs—GrCt
Lobster cove shindig. L. Morrison.—CoBn
Long trip. L. Hughes.—ArT-3
Madness one Monday evening. J. Fields.—HaK—LiT
The main-deep. J. Stephens.—StS
"The moon is distant from the sea." E. Dickinson.—DiPe
Mountain fantasy. C. Lewis.—LeP
"O billows bounding far." A. E. Housman.—CoBn
The ocean. From Childe Harold's pilgrimage. G. G. Byron.—CoSs
    Deep and dark blue ocean.—GrCt
Oread. H. D.—BoGj
"Out fishing on the ocean." B. Pollock.—LeM
The pool in the rock. W. De La Mare.—ClF
Sailing homeward. Chan Fang-shēng.—ArT-3—LeM—ThA
Sam. W. De La Mare.—ArT-3—CoSs
Santorin. J. E. Flecker.—BoGj
The sea ("How fearful") From King Lear. W. Shakespeare.—ShS
The sea ("The sea is a hungry dog") J. Reeves.—CoSs
The sea ("The untamed sea is human") S. Shoenblum.—LeM
The sea ("You, you are all unloving, loveless, you") D. H. Lawrence.—CoBn
Sea born. H. Vinal.—BoH
Sea calm. L. Hughes.—HaL—LiT
Sea fever. J. Masefield.—ArT-3—CoSs—HuB—HuS-3—LaPd—ThA
The sea gypsy. R. Hovey.—CoSs—LaPd
"The sea in the dusk." Bashō.—BeCs
Sea lullaby. E. Wylie.—CoBn
Sea magic. C. Lewis.—LeP
Sea monsters. From The faerie queene. E. Spenser.—GrCt
The sea serpant. W. Irwin.—CoB
The sea serpent chantey. V. Lindsay.—LiP
Sea shell. A. Lowell.—BoH—HuS-3
"The sea was calm." C. Minor.—BaH
Sea-weed. D. H. Lawrence.—CoBn
Seascape. B. J. Esbensen.—ArT-3
Seaside golf. J. Betjeman.—MoS
Seaweed. H. W. Longfellow.—LoPl
Shanty. D. Wright.—CaD
The shell. J. Stephens.—CoBn—StS
Since I left the ocean. Navin.—AlPi
Slave of the moon. M. Yarmon.—LeM
Someday. M. C. Livingston.—LiC
The sound of the sea. H. W. Longfellow.—LoPl
Storm at sea. W. Davenant.—CoR
Sunrise on the sea. From A midsummer-night's dream. W. Shakespeare.—GrCt
"The sun's perpendicular rays." W. L. Mansel.—GrCt
Sunset on the sea. L. Ubell.—LeM
"There's a tiresome young man in Bay Shore." Unknown.—BrLl
"The tide rises, the tide falls." H. W. Longfellow.—CoSs—GrCt—LoPl
Trade winds. J. Masefield.—BoH—ClF
Undersea. M. Chute.—LaP
Undersea fever. W. Cole.—CoSs
The uses of ocean. O. Seaman.—CoSs
Voices. J. S. Hearst.—ThA
Wander-thirst. G. Gould.—ArT-3—ClF (sel.)—PaH
A wanderer's song. J. Masefield.—TuW
"We rowed into fog." Shiki.—BeCs
We'll go to sea no more. Unknown.—CoSs—GrCt
    The fishermen's song.—MoB (sel.)
Whale at twilight. E. J. Coatsworth.—CoDh
Who pilots ships. D. W. Hicky.—ThA
Winter ocean. J. Updike.—CoSs
"The world below the brine." W. Whitman.—CoBn

The **ocean.** See Childe Harold's pilgrimage

Oceania

May. N. Belting.—BeCm

"**O'Driscoll** drove with a song." See The host of the air
Odysseus. See Ulysses
Oedipus (about)
Chorus. From Oedipus at Colonus. R. Fitzgerald.—GrS
Incantation to Oedipus. From Oedipus. J. Dryden.—GrS
Oedipus, sel. John Dryden
Incantation to Oedipus.—GrS
Oedipus at Colonus, sel. Robert Fitzgerald
Chorus.—GrS
"**O'er** golden sands my waters flow." See The enchanted spring
"**O'er** the wild gannet's bath." George Darley.—CoSs—GrCt
Of a spider. Wilfrid Thorley.—LaPd
"**Of** a sudden the great prima-donna." Paul West.—BrLl
"**Of** a' the airts the wind can blaw." Robert Burns.—BuPr
Of all the barbarous middle ages. See Don Juan
"**Of** all the barbarous middle ages, that." See Don Juan—Of all the barbarous middle ages
"**Of** all the birds from east to west." See Chanticleer
"**Of** all the birds that I do know." See The praise of Philip Sparrow
"**Of** all the birds that rove and sing." See Jenny Wren
"**Of** all the gay birds that e'er I did see." Mother Goose.—OpF
The owl.—BrMg
"**Of** all the rides since the birth of time." See Skipper Ireson's ride
"**Of** all the songs that birds sing." See Roosters and hens
"**Of** all the souls that stand create." Emily Dickinson.—DiPe
"**Of** all the sounds despatched abroad." Emily Dickinson.—DiPe
"**Of** animals' houses." See Animals' houses
"**Of** Brussels it was not." Emily Dickinson.—DiPe
"**Of** course I tried to tell him." See Poets hitchhiking on the highway
"**Of** course there were sweets." See Conversation about Christmas
Of courtesy. Arthur Guiterman.—ArT-3
"**Of** everykune tre." See The hawthorn
Of foxes. B. Y. Williams.—CoB
Of giving. Arthur Guiterman.—ArT-3
"**Of** gladde things there be four, ay four." See Gladde things
"**Of** God we ask one favor." Emily Dickinson.—PlE
"**Of** gold and jewels I have not any need." Yuan Chieh, tr. fr. the Chinese by Arthur Waley.—LeMw
"**Of** Jonathan Chapman." See Johnny Appleseed
"**Of** living creatures most I prize." See Butterfly
"**Of** Nelson and the North." See The battle of the Baltic
"**Of** Neptune's empire let us sing." See In praise of Neptune
"**Of** old Goody Trudge and her talkative bird." See The talking bird; or, Dame Trudge and her parrot
Of old sat freedom. Alfred Tennyson.—TeP
"**Of** old sat freedom on the heights." See Of old sat freedom
Of quarrels. Arthur Guiterman.—ArT-3
Of swimming in lakes and rivers. Bertolt Brecht, tr. fr. the German by H. R. Hays.—MoS
"**Of** the birds that fly in the farthest sea." See The flying fish
Of the death of kings. See King Richard II
Of the last verses in the book, sel. Edmund Waller
The soul's dark cottage.—GrCt
Of the mean and sure estate. Thomas Wyatt.—ReO (sel.)
"**Of** the myriad afflictions that beset Hellas." See The breed of athletes
"**Of** the three wise men." See Carol of the brown king
"**Of** what use are twigs." Buson, tr. fr. the Japanese by Harry Behn.—BeCs
"**Of** white and tawny, black as ink." See Variation on a sentence
O'Faolain, Sean
The icebound swans. tr.—ReO
"**Off** the coast of Hispaniola." See Columbus and the mermaids
"**Off** with you." Issa, tr. fr. the Japanese by R. H. Blyth.—IsF
Offshore. Philip Booth.—MoS
"**Oft** have I seen at some cathedral door." See Divina commedia
"**Oft** I had heard of Lucy Gray." See Lucy Gray; or, Solitude
"**Often** I think of the beautiful town." See My lost youth
The **ogre** entertains. Elizabeth Jane Coatsworth.—CoDh
O'Hara, John Myers
The greater mystery.—PaH
O'Higgins, Myron
Sunset horn.—BoA
Vaticide.—AdIa—HaK
Ohio
The founders of Ohio. W. H. Venable.—HiL
Oil
To a tidelands oil pump. B. Janosco.—DuS
A valedictory to Standard Oil of Indiana. D. Wagoner.—DuS
Ojibway Indians. See Indians of the Americas—Ojibway
Okamoto, Emperor
"Upon the mountain edge."—BaS
Okamoto Kanoko
"As the stately stork."—LeMw
O'Keefe (or O'Keeffe), Adelaide
"The dog will come when he is called."—BlO
O'Keefe, John
Amo amas.—CoBl—GrCt
Okefenokee swamp
Okefenokee swamp. D. W. Hicky.—BrA
Okefenokee swamp. Daniel Whitehead Hicky.—BrA

Oklahoma
Earthy anecdote. W. Stevens.—BoGj
Okura
"Come, companions."—BaS
"How I yearn to be."—BaS
"One of us may feel."—BaS
Old Abram Brown. Mother Goose.—ReOn
"**Old** Abram Brown is dead and gone." See Old Abram Brown
"**Old** Adam, the carrion crow." See Song
Old age. See also Birthdays; Childhood recollections; Youth and age
"The aged dog." Issa.—IsF
The ageing athlete. N. Weiss.—MoS
"As I was walking slowly." A. E. Housman.—LiT
"As we grow old." Issa.—LeOw
The bean eaters. G. Brooks.—HaK
By the Exeter river. D. Hall.—CaMb
California winter. K. Shapiro.—BrA (sel.)
Casual lines. Su Shih.—LeMw
The dutiful mariner. W. Irwin.—CoSs
The eastern gate. Unknown.—LeMw
"I'll tell thee everything I can." From Through the looking-glass. L. Carroll.—AgH
"In my old age." Issa.—LeOw
The last leaf. O. W. Holmes.—BoH
Old Dan'l. L. A. G. Strong.—ClF—SmM
Old fingers. M. O'Neill.—OnF
Old man. J. Siegal.—LeM
"An old man sat in a waterfall." N. Nicholson.—CaD
The old men admiring themselves in the water. W. B. Yeats.—BoGj—LiT—YeR
The old ones. F. Bellerby.—CaD
A prayer for old age. W. B. Yeats.—YeR
Rabbi Ben Ezra. R. Browning.—BrP
A Roman legend. From Morituri salutamus. H. W. Longfellow.—LoPl
Song from a country fair. L. Adams.—BoGj
Song of a woman abandoned by the tribe because she is too old to keep up with their migration. Unknown.—HoL
Spring and fall: To a young child. G. M. Hopkins.—BoGj—GrCt
"That time of year thou mayst in me behold." From Sonnets. W. Shakespeare.—GrCt
"To be old." Teika.—BaS
To the four courts, please. J. Stephens.—StS
Too old to work. J. Glazer.—HiL
Two friends. D. Ignatow.—DuS
Uncle Ambrose. J. Still.—BrA
When you are old. W. B. Yeats.—BoGj—CoBl—YeR
"With feeble steps." Issa.—LeOw
Old age. See Thera-gatha and Theri-gatha
The **old** beggar man. Ann and Jane Taylor.—VrF
"**Old** Ben Bailey." See Done for
"**Old** Billy, poor man." See The knife-grinder's budget
Old Blue ("I had a dog and his name was Blue") Unknown.—MoS
Old Blue ("Old Blue was tough") Robert P. Tristram Coffin.—ReO
"**Old** Blue was tough." See Old Blue
Old Boniface. Mother Goose.—BrMg
"**Old** Boniface he loved good cheer." See Old Boniface
The **old** bridge. Hilda Conkling.—ThA
The **old** bridge at Florence. Henry Wadsworth Longfellow.—LoPl—PaH
"The **old** bridge has a wrinkled face." See The old bridge
"The **old** brown thorn-trees break in two high over Cummen Strand." See Red Hanrahan's song about Ireland
"**Old** Capting Pink of the Peppermint." See Captain Pink of the Peppermint
"**Old** castles on the cliff arise." See Grongar hill
Old cat Care. Richard Hughes.—ReS
Old chairs. Mother Goose.—BrMg
An **old** Christmas greeting. Unknown.—ArT-3
An **old** Cornish litany. Unknown.—BrSm (sel.)
"An **old** dame to the blacksmith went." Unknown.—VrF
Old Dan'l. L. A. G. Strong.—ClF—SmM
"**Old** Doctor Foster." See Doctor Foster
"The **old** doctor has at last retired to his room." See Johnsonia
"**Old** dog lay in the summer sun." See Sunning
Old dog Tray. Stephen Collins Foster.—CoB
Old Dubuque. Dave Etter.—BrA
"**Old** Euclid drew a circle." See Euclid
"**Old** Farmer Giles." Mother Goose.—BrMg
The **old** feminist. Phyllis McGinley.—HiL
Old fingers. Mary O'Neill.—OnF
The **old** Fort of Rathangan. See The Fort of Rathangan
Old friends. A. Muir.—CoB
The **old** gods. Edwin Muir.—PlE
"**Old** gods and goddesses who have lived so long." See The old gods
An **old** grace. Unknown.—ClF
Old gray squirrel. Alfred Noyes.—CoSs
The **old** grey goose. See "Go and tell Aunt Nancy"
"**Old** haggard wind has." See November day
"The **old** houses of Flanders." Ford Madox Hueffer.—PaH
Old Ironsides. See Warships
Old Ironsides. Oliver Wendell Holmes.—CoSs—HiL
Old Jack Noman. Edward Thomas.—BlO
Old Jake Sutter. Kaye Starbird.—ArT-3
"**Old** Jake Sutter has a cabin-hut." See Old Jake Sutter
Old Joe Jones. Laura E. Richards.—AgH
"**Old** Joe Jones and his old dog Bones." See Old Joe Jones
"**Old** Jumpety-Bumpety-Hop-and-Go-One." See The kangaroo
"**Old** King Cole." See "Old King Cole was a merry old soul"
"**Old** King Cole was a merry old soul." Mother Goose.—OpF
Mother Goose rhymes, 62.—HoB
"Old King Cole."—BrMg—WiMg
The **old** knight. George Peele.—GrCt

"An **old** lady living in Worcester." Unknown.—BrLl
The **old** lady who swallowed a fly. Unknown.—BrSm
"**Old** lame Bridget doesn't hear." See The shadow people
Old Lem. Sterling A. Brown.—AdIa
Old man. Jessica Siegal.—LeM
The **old** man from Dunoon. Unknown.—SmM
"**An** old man in a lodge within a park." See Chaucer
The **old** man in the moon. Unknown.—ReS
Old Man Moon. Aileen Fisher.—FiI
"**Old** man, once sturdy as a mountain." See Old man
"An **old** man sat in a waterfall." Norman Nicholson.—CaD
"An **old** man selling charms in a cranny of the town wall." See The peddler of spells
"An **old** man whose black face." See The rain-walkers
"The **old** man's words—something had skittered the cattle." See The panther possible
The **old-marrieds.** Gwendolyn Brooks.—BoA
"**Old** Meg she was a gipsy." See Meg Merrilies
The **old** men admiring themselves in the water. William Butler Yeats.—BoGj—LiT—YeR
Old men and young men. John Holmes.—McWs
"**Old** men are full of zest and information." See Old men and young men
Old Mr Bows. Wilma Horsbrugh.—CoO
"**Old** Mr Chang, I've heard it said." Unknown.—WyC
"**Old** Molly Means was a hag and a witch." See Molly Means
"The **old** moon is tarnished." See Sea lullaby
Old Mother Goose and the golden egg. See "Old Mother Goose, when"
"**Old** Mother Goose, when." Mother Goose.—WiMg (sel.)
  Old Mother Goose and the golden egg.—BrMg
"**Old** Mother Hubbard." See "Old Mother Hubbard, she went to the cupboard"
Old Mother Hubbard and her dog. See "Old Mother Hubbard, she went to the cupboard"
"**Old** Mother Hubbard, she went to the cupboard." Mother Goose.—OpF
  Mother Goose rhymes, 54.—HoB
  Mother Hubbard and her dog.—VrF
  "Old Mother Hubbard."—HuS-3—WiMg
  Old Mother Hubbard and her dog.—BrMg
"**Old** Mother Minichin." Jean Kenward.—SmM
"**Old** Mother Shuttle." Mother Goose.—WiMg
  Mother Shuttle.—BrMg
"**Old** Mother Twitchett had (or has) but one eye." Mother Goose.—ArT-3—BrMg
The **old** navy. Frederick Marryat.—CoSs
"**Old** Noah once he built an ark." See Old Noah's ark
Old Noah's ark. Unknown.—CoB
"**Old,** old cars, rusting away." See Scrapyard
The **old** ones. Frances Bellerby.—CaD
"**Old** Peter Prairie-Dog." See Prairie-dog town
"The **old** priest Peter Gilligan." See The ballad of Father Gilligan
"**Old** Quin Queeribus." Nancy Byrd Turner.—ArT-3—BrSg
The **old** repair man. Fenton Johnson.—BoA
Old Roger. See "Old Roger is dead and laid in his grave"
"**Old** Roger is dead and laid in his grave." Mother Goose.—OpF
  Old Roger.—BrMg
"An **old** sad man who catches moles." See The lament of the mole-catcher
The **old** sailor. Walter De La Mare.—DeBg
Old Sam's wife. Unknown.—GrCt
  On the wife of a parish clerk.—BrSm
"**Old** Saturn lolls in heaven." See Saturn
"An **old** seadog on a sailor's log." See The powerful eyes o' Jeremy Tait
The **old** shepherds. Eleanor Farjeon.—FaT
Old shepherd's prayer. Charlotte Mew.—PlE
The **old** ships ("I have seen old ships sail like swans asleep") James Elroy Flecker.—CoR—PaH
Old ships ("There is a memory stays upon old ships") David Morton.—HuS-3—TuW
"An **old** silent pond." Bashō, tr. fr. the Japanese by Harry Behn.—BeCs
"An **old** silver church in a forest." See Poet to his love
"**Old** Sir Simon the king." Mother Goose.—BrF
  Sir Simon the king.—BrMg
Old Smokie. Unknown.—LaP
An **old** song ("I was not apprenticed nor ever dwelt in famous Lincolnshire") Edward Thomas.—ThG
An **old** song ("The sun set, the wind fell, the sea") Edward Thomas.—ThG
The **old** squire. Wilfrid Scawen Blunt.—MoS
The **old** sweet dove of Wiveton. Stevie Smith.—ReO
The **old** swimmer. Christopher Morley.—MoS
The **old** tailor. Walter De La Mare.—DeBg
Old tennis player. Gwendolyn Brooks.—MoS
"**Old** Tillie Turveycombe." See Tillie
Old Tippecanoe. Unknown.—HiL
"**Old** Tom Bombadil was a merry fellow." See The adventures of Tom Bombadil
The **old** tree. Andrew Young.—BoGj
The **old** vicarage, Grantchester. Rupert Brooke. —PaH (sel.)
"**Old** woman, old woman, shall we go a-shearing." Mother Goose.—ArT-3
  Mother Goose rhymes, 48.—HoB
  The old woman.—BrMg
"The **old** West, the old time." See Spanish Johnny
The **old** wife and the ghost. James Reeves.—BrSm—HoB—LaPd
"**Old** wife, old wife." Unknown.—MoB
The **old** wives' tale, sels. George Peele
  Celenta at the well of life.—BlO
    The voice from the well of life speaks to the maiden.—GrCt
  A spell.—GrCt

"On Easter morn at early dawn." See Meeting the Easter bunny
"On either side the river lie." See The lady of Shalott
On Fell. Gotthold Ephraim Lessing.—BrSm
On first looking into Chapman's Homer. John Keats.—CoR—GrCt
"On Hallowe'en the old ghosts come." See Hallowe'en
On Hardscrabble mountain. Galway Kinnell.—DuS
On himself. Robert Herrick.—GrCt
On his blindness. John Milton.—GrCt
"On his bow-back he hath a battle set." See Venus and Adonis—The boar
"On his death-bed poor Lubin lies." See A reasonable affliction
"On how to sing." Shiki, tr. fr. the Japanese by Harold G. Henderson.—LeI
On Hurricane Jackson. Alan Dugan.—MoS
On killing a tree. Gieve Patel.—AlPi
On liberty and slavery. George Moses Horton.—HaK
"On Linden, when the sun was low." See Hohenlinden
"On little Harry's christ'ning day." Mary Elliott.—VrF
On London bridge, and the stupendous sight, and structure thereof. James Howell.—GrCt
On looking up by chance at the constellations. Robert Frost.—LiT
On Lydia distracted. Philip Ayres.—GrS
On Middleton Edge. Andrew Young.—MoS
"On midsummer eve." See Midsummer eve
On Monsieur Coué. Charles Cuthbert Inge.—BrLl
"On moonlight bushes." See Nightingales
"On moony nights the dogs bark shrill." See Night song
On music. Walter Savage Landor.—BoGj
"On my wall hangs a Japanese carving." See The mask of evil
"On ochre walls in ice-formed caves shaggy Neanderthals marked their place in time." See To my son Parker, asleep in the next room
"On old Cold Crendon's windy tops." See Reynard the fox
"On old slashed spruce boughs." See On Hardscrabble mountain
On our way. Eve Merriam.—MeC
On passing two Negroes on a dark country road somewhere in Georgia. Conrad Kent Rivers.—AdIa
On politeness. Henry Sharpe Horsley.—VrF
"On powdery wings the white moths pass." See A garden at night
On Rome. See Childe Harold's pilgrimage
On Samuel Pease. Unknown.—BrSm
"On Saturday night." See Here we go looby, looby, looby
"On Saturday night I lost my wife." Mother Goose.—OpF
Saturday night.—BrMg
"On Saturday night shall be my care." Mother Goose.—OpF
On seeing a pompous funeral for a bad husband. Unknown.—BrSm
"On still black waters where the stars lie sleeping." See Ophelia
"On summer eves with wild delight." See Childhood—Bat
"On summer nights." See City in summer
"On summer nights." Tsurayuki.—BaS
On the army of Spartans, who died at Thermopylae. Simonides of Ceos.—GrCt
On the beach. Colin Parker.—LeM
On the beach at Fontana. James Joyce.—LiT
"On the beach at night." Walt Whitman.—GrCt
"On the bridge." Issa, tr. fr. the Japanese by Nobuyuki Yuasa.—IsF
On the bridge. Kate Greenaway.—GrT
On the building of Springfield. See A gospel of beauty
"On the cheerful village green." See The village green
On the death of a wife. Unknown, tr. fr. the Dama.—LeO
On the death of Benjamin Franklin. Philip Freneau.—HiL
On the Duchess of Gordon's reel dancing. Robert Burns.—BuPr
On the expressway. Robert Dana.—LaC
On the extinction of the Venetian republic. William Wordsworth.—PaH—WoP
"On the fine wire of her whine she walked." See The mosquito
"On the first cold fall days the little pigs." See Litter of pigs
"On the first of March." Mother Goose.—MoB—OpF
The crows.—BrMg
On the gift of a cloak. Hugo of Orleans, known as Primas, tr. fr. the Latin by George F. Whicher.—LiT
On the grasshopper and cricket. John Keats.—CoB
On the grasshopper and the cricket.—ReO
On the grasshopper and the cricket. See On the grasshopper and cricket
"On the grassy banks." See Woolly lambkins
"On the great streams the ships may go." See The canoe speaks
On the hills. Elizabeth Jane Coatsworth.—CoDh
"On the Indo-Pak frontier." See A snapshot
"On the last Mayday morning my cat brought." See Cats
On the loss of the Royal George. See Loss of the Royal George
On the morning of Christ's Nativity, sel. John Milton
The magi.—GrCt
"On the mountain peak, called Going-To-The-Sun." See The apple-barrel of Johnny Appleseed
"On the night that Christ was born." See The night

"**Once** we were wayfarers, then seafarers, then airfarers." See Post early for space
"**Once** when the snow of the year was beginning to fall." See The runaway
"**One,** a shrill voice." See One, two, three
The **one** answer. Unknown.—LaPd
1 black foot + 1 black foot = 2 black feet. George Solomon.—BaH
"**One** black monkey swinging on a tree." See Black monkeys
"**One** blessing had I, than the rest." Emily Dickinson.—DiPe
One bowl, one bottle. Mother Goose.—ReOn
"**One** cannot have enough." See Soliloquy of a tortoise on revisiting the lettuce beds after an interval of one hour while supposed to be sleeping in a clump of blue hollyhocks
"**One** cold winter morning." See Two million two hundred thousand fishes
"**One** day a boy went walking." See A boy went walking
"**One** day Abigail said." See Abigail's fingers
"**One** day as I walked by Crocodile mansions." See The Goole captain
"**One** day I listened to the earth." See Listen to the unheard
"**One** day I might feel." See Lemons and apples
"**One** day I saw a downy duck." See Good morning
"**One** day I saw some birds." See The birds
"**One** day I went out to the zoo." G. T. Johnson. —BrLl
"**One** day on our village in the month of July." See Death of an aircraft
"**One** day our skiff was loaded." See Fishing
"**One** day there reached me from the street." See The goatherd
"**One** dignity delays for all." Emily Dickinson.—DiPe
One down. Richard Armour.—MoS
"**One** dream all heroes." Bashō, tr. fr. the Japanese by Harry Behn.—BeCs
"**One-ery,** two-ery-tickery, seven." Mother Goose. —BrMg
"**One** evening when the sun was low." See The big Rock Candy mountains
One eye. See "I have a little sister, they call her Peep-peep"
One-eyed gunner. Mother Goose.—ReOn
"**One** for the money." Mother Goose.—HuS-3
"**One** for the mouse, one for the crow." See How to sow beans
One good turn deserves another. Unknown.—BrSm
"**One** had a lovely face." See Memory
One home. William Stafford.—BrA
The **151st** psalm. Karl Shapiro.—PlE
The **one** I always get. Myra Cohn Livingston.—LiC
"**One** I love, two I love." Mother Goose.—WiMg
"**One** is a number that may be conceited." See A number of numbers
"**One** is amazed." See Unfolding bud
One king-fisher and one yellow rose. Eileen Brennan.—ReBs
"**One** little." See A counting rhyme
One little boy. Ann and Jane Taylor.—VrF
"**One** little dicky-bird." See Ten little dicky-birds
"**One** little duck." See Four little ducks
"**One** man and one fly." Issa, tr. fr. the Japanese by Harry Behn.—BeCs
"**One** misty moisty morning." Mother Goose.—ArT-3—BrMg—HuS-3—LaPd—OpF—ReOn
How do you do.—GrCt
"**One** morning a weasel came swimming." See The weasel
"**One** morning in spring." See Fife tune
"**One** morning in the month of June." See The royal fisherman
"**One** mouse adds up to many mice." See Singular indeed
"**One** must have a mind of winter." See The snow man
"**One** need not be a chamber to be haunted." Emily Dickinson.—DiPe
"**One** nice summer day I heard a sound." See Whoops a daisy
"**One** night as Dick lay fast asleep." See Full moon
"**One** night as I did wander." Robert Burns.—BuH
"**One** night came on a hurricane." See The sailor's consolation
"**One** night I dreamed." See The dream
"**One** o'clock the gun went off." See Singing game
"**One** of the nicest beds I know." See Autumn leaves
"**One** of us may feel." Okura.—BaS
One old ox. See "One old Oxford ox opening oysters"
"**One** old ox opening oysters." See "One old Oxford ox opening oysters"
"**One** old Oxford ox opening oysters." Mother Goose.—OpF
One old ox.—GrCt
"**One** road leads to London." See Roadways
"**One** scene as I bow to pour her coffee." See Vacation
"**One** star fell and another as we walked." See Preludes for Memnon
"**One** stormy night." Valerie Lorraine Jones.—BaH
"**One** summer night a little raccoon." See Raccoon
"**One** summer's day a fox was passing through." See The fox and the grapes
"**One** thing you left with us, Jack Johnson." See Strange legacies
"**One** thread of truth in a shuttle." Unknown.—DoC
"**One** to make ready." See The start
"**One,** two." See "One, two, buckle my shoe"
"**One,** two (what shall I do)." Ruth Ainsworth.—StF
"**One,** two, and three." See Leaves

"**One,** two, buckle my shoe." Mother Goose.—HuS-3—WiMg
Mother Goose rhymes, 37.—HoB
"One, two."—ArT-3—BrMg—OpF
"**One** two three (father caught a flea)." Unknown.—CoO
One, two, three ("One, a shrill voice") Narendra Kumar Sethi.—AlPi
"**One** two three four." See The goats
"**One,** two, three, four (Mary at the cottage door)." Mother Goose.—OpF
"**1,** 2, 3, 4, 5 (I caught a hare alive)." Mother Goose.—ArT-3
"**One,** two, three, four, five (once I caught a fish)." Mother Goose.—BrMg—OpF—SmM—WiMg
One, two, three—gough. Eve Merriam.—MeI
"**1-2-3** was the number he played but to-day the number came 3-2-1." See Dirge
"**One** ugly trick has often spoil'd." See Meddlesome Matty
"**One** very nice day I went to the pier." See The pier
"**One** white foot, buy him." Mother Goose.—OpF
"**One** without looks in tonight." See The fallow deer at the lonely house
One word more, sel. Robert Browning
Phases of the moon.—GrCt
O'Neill, Mary
Abigail's fingers.—OnF
City fingers.—OnF
"The colors live."—OnH
Country fingers.—OnF
Greedy fingers.—OnF
Grown-up fingers.—OnF
Kevin's fingers.—OnF
"Like acrobats on a high trapeze."—OnH
Lisa's fingerprints.—OnF
Mark's fingers.—OnF
Mimi's fingers.—OnF
Miss Norma Jean Pugh, first grade teacher.—ArT-3
My fingers.—OnF
Newborn fingers.—OnF
Old fingers.—OnF
Paul's fingers.—OnF
Sarah's fingers.—OnF
What is black.—OnH
What is blue.—OnH
What is brown.—OnH
What is gold.—OnH
What is gray.—OnH
What is green.—HoB—OnH
What is orange.—OnH
What is pink.—OnH
What is purple.—OnH
What is red.—OnH
What is white.—OnH
What is yellow.—OnH
O'Neill, Moira, pseud. (Nesta Higginson Skrine)
Grace for light.—ThA
O'Neill, W.
"With a hop, and a skip, and a jump."—StF
"**One's** none." Mother Goose.—OpF—ReOn
Onions
The man in the onion bed. J. Ciardi.—CoO
Onitsura
"At last, in sunshine."—BeCs
"A day of spring."—LeI
"Even stones under."—BeCs
"In spring the chirping."—BeCs
"It is nice to read."—BeCs
"The least of breezes."—BeCs
"A trout leaps high."—LeMw
"Why."—LeMw
"**Only.**" See Snow country
Only be willing to search for poetry. See "Only be willing to search for poetry, and there will be poetry"
"**Only** be willing to search for poetry, and there will be poetry." Yuan Mei, tr. fr. the Chinese by Robert Kotewell and Norman L. Smith.—LeMw
Only be willing to search for poetry.—LaPd
"**Only** in the wilderness where no man may live." See A wind blows
Only my opinion. Monica Shannon.—ArT-3—HuS-3
"The **only** news I know." Emily Dickinson.—DiPe
"**Only** quiet death." See Threnody
"**Only** the dim-witted say it's evening." See What she said
"**Only** the prism's obstruction shows aright." See Deaf and dumb
"**Only** the sound remains." See The mill-water
Ono no Komachi
"A thing which fades."—BaS
Ono no Yoshiki
"My love."—HoL
Onomatopoeia. Eve Merriam.—MeI
Onomatopoeia II. Eve Merriam.—MeI
Ontei
"Brightly the sun shines."—BeCs
Oodles of noodles. Lucia and James L. Hymes, Jr.—AgH
"An **open** door says, Come in." See Doors
Open house. Aileen Fisher.—FiI
Open range. Kathryn and Byron Jackson.—ArT-3
Open the door. Marion Edey.—ArT-3
"**Open** the door and who'll come in." See Open the door
"An **opera** star named Maria." Unknown.—BrLl
Ophelia. Arthur Rimbaud, tr. fr. the French by Brian Hill.—GrCt
Ophelia's death. See Hamlet
Ophelia's song. See Hamlet
Opie, Amelia
The black man's lament; or, How to make sugar.—VrF
The **opossum.** Marnie Pomeroy.—CoB
Opossums
The opossum. M. Pomeroy.—CoB
The **opportune** overthrow of Humpty Dumpty. Guy Wetmore Carryl.—CoBb
Optimism. See also Happiness; Laughter; Success
Epilogue. From Asolando. R. Browning.—BrP

Otters
An otter. T. Hughes.—CaD (sel.)
Otters. P. Colum.—ReO
River-mates.—CoB
Otters. Padraic Colum.—ReO
River-mates.—CoB
Otto. Gwendolyn Brooks.—LaPd—LaPh
"**Our** balloon man has balloons." See The balloon man
"**Our** band is few, but true and tried." See Song of Marion's men
"**Our** barn roof has three lovely holes." See Three lovely holes
"**Our** birth is but a sleep and a forgetting." See Ode: Intimations of immortality from recollections of early childhood
"**Our** bugles sang truce, for the night-cloud had lowered." See The soldier's dream
Our circus. Laura Lee Randall.—ArT-3
Our country. Harry Behn.—BeG
"**Our** dog is not stupid, but stubborn, and so." See Hansi
Our dumb friends. Ralph Wotherspoon.—CoB
"**Our** Father which art in heaven." See Gospel according to Matthew—The Lord's prayer
"**Our** fathers were fellows of substance and weight." See Commissary report
"**Our** favorite sons are fools." See Jack and the beanstalk
"**Our** flesh was a battle-ground." See The litany of the dark people
"**Our** great." See Clocks and watches
"**Our** hammock swings between two trees." See Hammock
"**Our** hearts go by green-cliffed Kinsale." See The island
Our heritage. Jesse Stuart.—BrA
"**Our** history is grave noble and tragic." See Men
"**Our** journey had advanced." Emily Dickinson.—DiL—DiPe
Our largest and smallest cities. Nettie Rhodes.—LaC
"**Our** little boat." See Patterns of life
"**Our** little kinsmen after rain." Emily Dickinson.—DiPe
"**Our** little mobile hangs and swings." See Mobile
"**Our** little nurse with pleasure eyes." See The tender nurse
"**Our** lives are Swiss." Emily Dickinson.—DiL—DiPe
Our Lucy, 1956-1960. Paul Goodman.—CoB
"**Our** Mr Toad." David McCord.—ArT-3
Our mother Pocahontas. Vachel Lindsay.—LiP
"**Our** moulting days are in their twilight stage." See Far from Africa: Four poems
Our polite parents. Carolyn Wells.—CoBb
"**Our** purses shall be proud, our garments poor." See The taming of the shrew—Appearances
"**Our** share of night to bear." Emily Dickinson.—DiPe
"**Our** ship is leaving Portsmouth town." See Sea chanty
"**Our** skipping ropes lie silent." See Ten o'clock
"**Our** walk was far among the ancient trees." See To M. H.
Our washing machine. Patricia Hubbell.—HoB
"**Our** washing machine went whisity whirr." See Our washing machine
"**Our** window is a magic frame." See The magic window
"**Our** world's a ball, this causes day and night." See The tallow-chandler
The **ousel** cock. See A midsummer-night's dream
"The **ousel** cock so black of hue." See A midsummer-night's dream—The ousel cock
"**Out** beyond the sunset, could I but find the way." See The golden city of St Mary
"**Out** fishing on the ocean." Bretton Pollock.—LeM
"**Out** in a world of death, far to the northward lying." See The winter lakes
Out in the dark. Edward Thomas.—ThG
"**Out** in the dark over the snow." See Out in the dark
"**Out** in the dark something complains." See Cradle song
"**Out** in the marsh reeds." Tsurayuki, tr. fr. the Japanese by Kenneth Rexroth.—BaS
Out in the wood. Clinton Scollard.—ThA
"**Out** in the wood today, oh, such a wonder." See Out in the wood
"**Out** of a northern city's bay." See The cruise of the Monitor
Out of blindness. Leslie B. Blades.—DuS
"**Out** of his cottage to the sun." See Old Dan'l
"**Out** of me, unworthy and unknown." See The Spoon River anthology
"**Out** of one wintry." Ransetsu, tr. fr. the Japanese by Harry Behn.—BeCs
Out of school. Hal Summers.—CaD
"**Out** of the ark's grim hold." See The flaming terrapin
"**Out** of the bosom of the air." See Snowflakes
"**Out** of the cleansing night of stars and tides." See Brooklyn bridge at dawn
Out of the cradle endlessly rocking, sel. Walt Whitman
Two guests from Alabama.—ReO
"**Out** of the dark." See Tracks in the snow
"**Out** of the delicate dream of the distance an emerald emerges." See Madeira from the sea
"**Out** of the earth." See I sing for the animals
"**Out** of the factory chimney, tall." See Smoke animals
"**Out** of the hills of Habersham." See Song of the Chattahoochee
"**Out** of the living word." See The book of Kells
"**Out** of the night and the north." See The train dogs
"**Out** of the northeast." See The white horse
"**Out** of the sky, geese." Soin, tr. fr. the Japanese by Harry Behn.—BeCs
"**Out** of the trees." See Fall of the year
"**Out** of the wood of thoughts that grows by night." See Cock-crow
"**Out** of us all." See Words

"**Out** of your whole life give but a moment." See Now
"**Out** on the desert dry and hot." See My home
Out, out, brief candle. See Macbeth
"**Out** they came from Liberty, out across the plains." See The Oregon trail: 1851
"**Out** upon it. I have loved." See The constant lover
"**Out** we go." See First-ing
"**Out** West is windy." See New Mexico
"**Out** West, they say, a man's a man; the legend still persists." See Étude géographique
"**Out** with the mountain moon, stinging clear." See Mill valley
"**Out** with the tide, beneath the morning sun." See The lightship
Outcast. Claude McKay.—BoA
Outdistanced. Larry Rubin.—DuS
Outdoor life. See Adventure and adventurers; Country life; Gipsies; Nature; Roads and trails; Wayfaring life; also names of outdoor sports, as Hunters and hunting
Outer space. See Space and space travel
The **outlandish** knight. Unknown.—BrSm
"An **outlandish** knight came out of the North." See The outlandish knight
Outlaws. See Crime and criminals
"The **outlook** wasn't brilliant for the Mudville nine that day." See Casey at the bat
"**Outside** Bristol Rovers football ground." See The ballad of Billy Rose
"**Outside** my door, I heard someone say." Unknown.—WyC
Outside the chancel door. Unknown.—BrSm
Outward. Louis Simpson.—LiT
Outward show. See The merchant of Venice
Ouzels
"The tiny bird." Unknown.—ReBs
The water ousel. M. Webb.—TuW
Water ouzel. D. McCord.—CoB
"**Over** dusty daisies." See Summer
"**Over** hill, over dale." See A midsummer-night's dream
"**Over** New England now, the snow." See Nocturne
"**Over** rock and wrinkled ground." See Beagles
"**Over** the bleak and barren snow." See Tony O
"**Over** the borders, a sin without pardon." See Keepsake mill
"**Over** the climbing meadows." See Dandelions
"**Over** the darkness." See Snail, moon and rose
"**Over** the deepest." Shiyo, tr. fr. the Japanese by Harry Behn.—BeCs
"**Over** the eye behind the moon's cloud." See Raison d'être
"**Over** the fields to Shottery, fresh with a wet-green scent." See The path to Shottery
"**Over** the garden wall." Eleanor Farjeon.—HuS-3
"**Over** the grass a hedgehog came." See Meeting
Over the green sands. Peggy Bennett.—CoB
"**Over** the heather the wet wind blows." See Roman wall blues
"**Over** the hills." See The witches' ride
"**Over** the ice-bright mountain." See Brightness
"**Over** the ice she flies." See Skating
"**Over** the land freckled with snow half-thawed." See Thaw
"**Over** the meadow." See Airlift
"**Over** the mountains." See Trains
"**Over** the oily swell it heaved, it rolled." See Fog
"**Over** the river." See Ferry-boats
"**Over** the river and through the wood." See Thanksgiving day
"**Over** the sea." See Virginia
"**Over** the shoulders and slopes of the dune." See The daisies
"**Over** the sun-darkened river sands calls the." Unknown, tr. fr. the aboriginal of Australia. —LeO
"**Over** the warts on the bumpy." See Sadie's playhouse
"**Over** the west side of this mountain." See Lyre-birds
"**Over** the wintry." Soseki, tr. fr. the Japanese by Harry Behn.—BeCs—LaPd
"**Over** this hearth—my father's seat." See The returned volunteer to his rifle
"**Overhead** the tree-tops meet." See Pippa passes
Overheard on a saltmarsh. Harold Monro.—ArT-3 —BoGj—DuR—McWs—ThA
Overnight in the apartment by the river. Tu Fu, tr. fr. the Chinese by William Hung.—GrCt
"**Overnight,** very." See Mushrooms
Overtones. William Alexander Percy.—BoH
Ovid (Publius Ovidius Naso)
The creation. See Metamorphoses
Elegies, sel.
To verse let kings give place.—GrCt
The flood. See Metamorphoses
Metamorphoses, sels.
The creation.—ClF
The flood.—GrCt
The phoenix self-born.—GrCt
The phoenix self-born. See Metamorphoses
To verse let kings give place. See Elegies
Owen
Wild spurs.—LeM
Owen, Wilfred
Anthem for doomed youth.—BoH—GrCt
Futility.—HoL
The **owl.** See "Of all the gay birds that e'er I did see"
The **owl.** See "A wise old owl lived in an oak"
The **owl** ("Downhill I came, hungry, and yet not starved") Edward Thomas.—GrCt—ReBs—ThG
The **owl** ("In the hollow tree, in the old gray tower") Barry Cornwall.—CoB
The **owl** ("The owl that lives in the old oak tree") William Jay Smith.—LaPd
The **owl** ("To whit") Conrad Aiken.—AiC
The **owl** ("When cats run home and light is come") Alfred Tennyson.—BlO—TuW
Song: The owl.—BoGj—TeP
The **owl** and the pussy-cat. Edward Lear.—ArT-3 —BlO—BoGj—HoB—HuS-3—LaPd—SmM—StF

"The **owl** and the pussy-cat went to sea." See The owl and the pussy-cat
"**Owl,** crevice-sitter." Unknown, tr. fr. the Sotho. —LeO
"The **owl** hooted and told of the morning star." Unknown, tr. fr. the Yuma.—LeO
"The **owl** is abroad, the bat and the toad." See Witches' charm
"The **owl** that hunts." See Why the owl wakes at night
"The **owl** that lives in the old oak tree." See The owl
Owls
The aziola. P. B. Shelley.—GrS
The barn owl. S. Butler.—SmM
The bird of night. R. Jarrell.—ReBs
The bonny, bonny owl. From Kenilworth. W. Scott.—ReBs
The canal bank. J. Stephens.—StS
"Come on, owl." Issa.—LeI
Hansi. H. Behn.—BeG
"A hungry owl hoots." Jōsō.—BeCs
If the owl calls again. J. Haines.—CoBn
The little boy. Mother Goose.—BrMg
The little fox. M. Edey.—ArT-3
Mistress Towl. Unknown.—VrF
"O owl." Issa.—IsF
"Of all the gay birds that e'er I did see." Mother Goose.—OpF
The owl.—BrMg
The owl ("Downhill I came, hungry, and yet not starved") E. Thomas.—GrCt—ReBs—ThG
The owl ("In the hollow tree, in the old gray tower") B. Cornwall.—CoB
The owl ("The owl that lives in the old oak tree") W. J. Smith.—LaPd
The owl ("To whit") C. Aiken.—AiC
The owl ("When cats run home and light is come") A. Tennyson.—BlO—TuW
Song: The owl.—BoGj—TeP
The owl and the pussy-cat. E. Lear.—ArT-3—BlO—BoGj—HoB—HuS-3—LaPd—SmM—StF
"Owl, crevice-sitter." Unknown.—LeO
"The owl hooted and told of the morning star." Unknown.—LeO
Owls talking. D. McCord.—CoB
Questioning faces. R. Frost.—CoB
Second song. A. Tennyson.—TeP
The snowy owl. E. Kroll.—CoB
Sweet Suffolk owl. Unknown.—GrCt
Then from a ruin. Farid-uddin Attar.—ReBs
"There was an old man of Dumbree." E. Lear. —BrLl
"There was an old person of Crowle." E. Lear.—BrLl
"There was an owl lived in an oak (the more he heard)." Mother Goose.—OpF
"There was an owl lived in an oak (wisky, wasky, weedle)." Mother Goose.—OpF
"There was an owl lived in an oak (whiskey, whaskey, weedle)."—ReMg
The white owl. From Love in a valley. G. Meredith.—GrCt
Why the owl wakes at night. P. McGinley.—McWc
"A wise old owl lived in an oak." Mother Goose.—WiMg
The owl.—BrMg
Owls talking. David McCord.—CoB
The **ox-tamer.** Walt Whitman.—CoB
Oxen. See Cattle
The **oyster** ("Moist, glaucous") Carmen Bernos de Gasztold, tr. fr. the French by Rumer Godden.—GaC
The **oyster** ("The oyster takes no exercise") A. P. Herbert.—CoB
"An **oyster** from Kalamazoo." Unknown.—BrLl
"The **oyster** takes no exercise." See The oyster
Oysters
The oyster ("Moist, glaucous") C. B. de Gasztold.—GaC
The oyster ("The oyster takes no exercise") A. P. Herbert.—CoB
"An oyster from Kalamazoo." Unknown.—BrLl
"There's a lady in Kalamazoo." W. Bellamy.—BrLl
Oz. David McCord.—McAd
Oz. [ounce] Eve Merriam.—DuR—MeI
Ozymandias. Percy Bysshe Shelley.—CoR—PaH

P

"**Pa** followed the pair to Pawtucket." Unknown. —BrLl
Pacific ocean
Once by the Pacific. R. Frost.—PaH
Pack, clouds, away. See The rape of Lucrece—Matin song
"**Pack,** clouds, away, and welcome, day." See The rape of Lucrece—Matin song
Pad and pencil. David McCord.—McAd—McE
"The **paddle** with staccato feet." See Pigeons
Paddling song. Unknown, tr. fr. the Bantu.—LeO
"**Paddling** we saw that turtle, saw its eyes open." Unknown, tr. fr. the aboriginal of Australia. —LeO
"**Paddy** on the railway." Unknown.—MoB
Padgaonkar, Mangesh
Carving away in the mist.—AlPi
The **Padstow** night song. Unknown.—GrCt
Page, Curtis Hidden
"Gladly I'll live in a poor mountain hut." tr.—LeMw
"I wonder in what fields today." tr.—LeMw
Late snowflakes. tr.—LeMw
Shadows. tr.—LeMw
"There is a trinity of loveliest things." tr.—LeMw
Waiting. tr.—LeMw
Page, Irene
Jane, do be careful.—CoBb
Page, P. K.
The crow.—DoW
Paget-Fredericks, Joseph
Alone.—HuS-3

Pai Ta-shun
"The days and months do not last long."—LeMw
Pain
"After great pain, a formal feeling comes." E. Dickinson.—DiL
"All these hurt." Vainateya.—AlPi
Pain for a daughter. A. Sexton.—McWs
"Pain has an element of blank." E. Dickinson.—DiPe
The swift bullets. C. Wells.—BrSm
"There was a faith healer of Deal." Unknown.—BrLl
"An unpopular youth of Cologne." Unknown.—BrLl
Pain for a daughter. Anne Sexton.—McWs
"**Pain** has an element of blank." Emily Dickinson.—DiPe
Paine, Albert Bigelow
In Louisiana.—BrA
Painted desert
The Painted desert. H. Behn.—BeG
The **Painted** desert. Harry Behn.—BeG
The **painted** hills of Arizona. Edwin Curran.—PaH
Painter, George D.
Encounters with a Doppelganger, sel.
A meeting.—SmM
A meeting. See Encounters with a Doppelganger
Paintings and pictures
Absolutes. G. Keyser.—DuR
The dance. W. C. Williams.—BoGj
A Dutch picture. H. W. Longfellow.—LoPl
Elegiac stanzas, suggested by a picture of Peele castle, in a storm, painted by Sir George Beaumont. W. Wordsworth.—WoP
A likeness. R. Browning.—BrP
"Portraits are to daily faces." E. Dickinson.—DiPe
Snow pictures. A. Fisher.—FiIo
Paiute Indians. See Indians of the Americas—Paiute
The **palace** of pleasure, sel. Stephen Hawes
Epitaph of Graunde Amoure.—GrCt
Palaces
Buckingham palace. A. A. Milne.—LaPd—MiC
The hammers. R. Hodgson.—BoGj
The haunted palace. From The fall of the house of Usher. E. A. Poe.—GrCt—PoP
Palanquin bearers. Sarojini Naidu.—ThA
Palanquins
Palanquin bearers. E. Naidu.—ThA
"**Pale,** beyond porch and portal." See The garden of Proserpine—Proserpine
"**Palmström** hasn't a crumb in the house." See The mousetrap
"The **pampas** grass." Issa, tr. fr. the Japanese by R. H. Blyth.—LeMw
Panama canal
A song of Panama. D. Runyan.—HiL
Panama Pacific exposition
The wedding of the rose and the lotus. V. Lindsay.—LiP
Pancakes. Christina Georgina Rossetti.—ClF
At home.—AgH
Panigeo, Hazel F.
"When I see."—BaH
Panikkar
Waves of thought.—AlPi
Pansies
Wise Johnny. E. Fallis.—ArT-3—BrSg
"**Pansies,** lilies, kingcups, daisies." See To the small celandine
The **panther** ("His weary glance, from passing by the bars") Rainer Maria Rilke, tr. fr. the German by Jessie Lemont.—ReO
The **panther** ("The panther is like a leopard") Ogden Nash.—CoB—HoB
"The **panther** is like a leopard." See The panther
"**Panther** lies next to Wharncliffe." See Appalachian front
The **panther** possible. William D. Barney.—DuS
Panthers
The panther ("His weary glance, from passing by the bars") R. M. Rilke.—ReO
The panther ("The panther is like a leopard") O. Nash.—CoB—HoB
The panther possible. W. D. Barney.—DuS
"**Papa,** said Eugene, is a daisy a book." See The daisy
Papago Indians. See Indians of the Americas—Papago
Papago love song. Unknown, tr. fr. the Papago Indians by Mary Austin.—HoL
Paper
"If all the world were paper." Mother Goose.—AgH—BlO—OpF—WiMg
If all the world.—BrMg
Metaphor. E. Merriam.—MeI
The term. W. C. Williams.—DuR—LaC—LiT
Paper boats. Rabindranath Tagore.—BoH—ThA
Paper men to air hopes and fears. Robert Francis.—DuS
The **paps** of Dana. James Stephens.—StS
Parachutes
Malfunction. R. E. Albert.—DuS
Parade. Kathleen Fraser.—FrS
"A **parade.** A parade." See Parade
Parades
The circus parade. O. B. Miller.—ArT-3
The flag goes by. H. H. Bennett.—ArT-3
Parade. K. Fraser.—FrS
Paradise. See Heaven
Paradise lost, sels. John Milton
Eve speaks to Adam.—GrCt
Expulsion from Paradise.—GrCt
The moon and the nightingale.—GrCt
Satan journeys to the Garden of Eden.—GrCt
Standing on earth.—GrCt
"What though the field be lost."—PlE
The **paradox** ("I am the mother of sorrows") Paul Laurence Dunbar.—HaK
A **paradox** ("Though we boast of modern progress as aloft we proudly soar") Unknown.—BrSm
"**Pardon** me, lady, but I wanta ast you." See Drug store

Parents and parenthood. See Family; Fathers and fatherhood; Home and family life; Mothers and motherhood
Paris, France
Four sheets to the wind and a one-way ticket to France, 1933. C. K. Rivers.—AdIa—BoA
Look, Edwin. E. St V. Millay.—BoGj
Montmartre. L. Hughes.—HaK
Park, Frances
A sad song about Greenwich Village.—LaC
The **park.** James S. Tippett.—ArT-3
"The **park** is filled with night and fog." See Spring night
"The **park** is green and quiet." Charles Reznikoff.—LaC
Parke, Walter
"There was a young prince of Bombay."—BrLl
Parker, Charles (about)
Yardbird's skull. O. Dodson.—AdIa—BoA
Parker, Colin
On the beach.—LeM
Parker, Dorothy
The choice.—CoBl
The crusader.—BrSm
Experience.—CoBl
Love song.—McWs
Men.—CoBl
Résumé.—BrSm—DuR
Parker, Edgar
The contrary waiter.—CoO
The **parklands.** Stevie Smith.—CaMb
Parks
Central park tourney. M. Weston.—BrA—DuR—LaC
A city park. A. Brody.—LaC
Ellis park. H. Hoyt.—ThA
Green park dream. M. C. Livingston.—LiC
In the park. R. Fyleman.—HuS-3
Kid in the park. L. Hughes.—LaC
The park. J. S. Tippett.—ArT-3
"The park is green and quiet." C. Reznikoff.—LaC
Water picture. M. Swenson.—CoBn—LaC
Parley of beasts. Hugh MacDiarmid.—ReO
Parliament hill. Henry Howarth Bashford.—ThA
Parmar, Pramila
Shadow.—LeM
Parodies
The ballad of Sir Thopas. From The Canterbury tales. G. Chaucer.—ChT
Casabianca. E. Bishop.—GrS
Father William. From Alice's adventures in wonderland. L. Carroll.—BoGj—LaP (sel.)—LaPd (sel.)
You are old, Father William.—HoB
"You are old, Father William, the young man said."—ArT-3
"How doth the little crocodile." From Alice's adventures in wonderland. L. Carroll.—ArT-3—BlO—BrSm—HoB—LaP
The lobster quadrille. From Alice's adventures in wonderland. L. Carroll.—HoB
The mock turtle's song.—GrCt
The man from Inversnaid. R. F. Murray.—MoS
The new order. P. McGinley.—BrA
A Poe-'em of passion. C. F. Lummis.—BrSm
The shades of night. A. E. Housman.—GrCt
Winter trees. C. Diekmann.—MoS
The **parrot.** Carmen Bernos de Gasztold, tr. fr. the French by Rumer Godden.—GaC
Parrots
"Clothed in yellow, red, and green." Mother Goose.—BrMg
The donkey and the fluke. E. Merriam.—MeC
"Never get up till the sun gets up." Unknown.—DoC
Ollie's polly. E. Merriam.—MeC
The parrot. C. B. de Gasztold.—GaC
The parrots. W. W. Gibson.—CoR
Poll Parrot. Mother Goose.—BrMg
Song of the parrot. E. J. Coatsworth.—HuS-3
The talking bird; or, Dame Trudge and her parrot. Unknown.—VrF
The **parrots.** Wilfrid Wilson Gibson.—CoR
"The **parson,** his wife." Unknown.—OpF
Parsons, Mary Catherine
My valentine.—ArT-3
"**Partake** as doth the bee." Emily Dickinson.—DiPe
Parties
The butterfly's ball and the grasshopper's feast. W. Roscoe.—VrF
Mother's party. A. Fisher.—FiIo
The party. P. L. Dunbar.—BoA
Slumber party. C. McCullers.—AgH
"There was a young man so benighted." Unknown.—BrLl
"There was a young person called Smarty." Unknown.—BrLl
Un-birthday party. A. Fisher.—FiIo
Waiting. J. Reeves.—StF
Parting. See also Farewells
A dream within a dream. E. A. Poe.—GrCt (sel.)—PoP
The eastern gate. Unknown.—LeMw
The Geraldine's cloak. J. Stephens.—StS
If you should go. C. Cullen.—BoH
Isabella. Unknown.—ReOn
"It was a' for our rightfu' king." R. Burns.—BuPr
Leavetaking. E. Merriam.—LaPd—MeI
"Like my cupped hands." Tsurayuki.—BaS
"Maid of Athens, ere we part." G. G. Byron.—ByP
Parting. Wang Wei.—ArT-3—LeMw
Parting after a quarrel. E. Tietjens.—CoBl
Parting at morning. R. Browning.—BrP
Parting gift. E. Wylie.—HaL
"Since there's no help, come, let us kiss and part." From Idea. M. Drayton.—CoBl
Parting. Wang Wei, tr. fr. the Chinese by Arthur Waley.—ArT-3—LeMw
Parting after a quarrel. Eunice Tietjens.—CoBl
Parting at morning. Robert Browning.—BrP
Parting gift. Elinor Wylie.—HaL

A **parting** shot. C. Day-Lewis.—CaD
Partridges and quails
Bobwhite. R. Hillyer.—CoB
"The grey quail were bunched together." Unknown.—LeO
The **party.** Paul Laurence Dunbar.—BoA
Parvenu. Vachel Lindsay.—LiP
The **passer.** George Abbe.—DuS—MoS
The **passing** of the buffalo. Hamlin Garland.—HuS-3
"A **passing** shower." Unknown.—BaS
"**Passing** through huddled and ugly walls." See The harbor
The **passionate** man's pilgrimage. Walter Raleigh.—GrCt
The **passionate** shepherd, sel. Nicholas Breton
The merry country lad.—ReO
The **passionate** shepherd to his love. Christopher Marlowe.—CoBl—McWs
Past. See Time—Past
A **pastoral.** Robert Hillyer.—CoBn
A **pastoral** ballad, sel. William Shenstone
"I have found out a gift for my fair."—ReBs
Pastoral X. Robert Hillyer.—HaL
Pastourelle. Donald Jeffrey Hayes.—BoA
The **pasture.** Robert Frost.—ArT-3—BoGj—CoB—HuS-3—LaP—LaPd—ThA
"**Pasture,** stone wall, and steeple." See Question in a field
The **pasty.** See "Deedle deedle dumpling, my son John"
Pat-a-cake. See "Pat-a-cake, pat-a-cake, baker's man"
"**Pat-a-cake,** pat-a-cake, baker's man." Mother Goose.—HuS-3—OpF—ReMg—WiMg
Pat-a-cake.—BrMg
"The **Patagonian.**" See Archy and Mehitabel—Short course in natural history
A **patch** of old snow. Robert Frost.—DuR—LaC
Patchen, Kenneth
An easy decision.—DuS—HaL
The magical mouse.—HaL—WeP
A trueblue gentleman.—ReO
"**Patches** and patches." Mother Goose.—OpF
Patel, Gieve
On killing a tree.—AlPi
Patel, Harji
The sleepy day.—LeM
Paterson, Andrew Barton
Waltzing Matilda.—GrCt
The **path.** Edward Thomas.—ThG
The **path** of the lonely ones. Guillermo E. Varela.—BaH
The **path** of the padres. Edith D. Osborne.—BrA
The **path** to Shottery. Cornelia Otis Skinner.—ThA
Patience. See also Perseverance
"Courage has a crimson coat." N. B. Turner.—ThA
"He that is slow to anger is better than the mighty." From Proverbs, Bible, Old Testament.—ArT-3
Patient Griselda. From The Canterbury tales. G. Chaucer.—ChT
The tired man. A. Wickham.—SmM
Patient Griselda. See The Canterbury tales
Patmore, Coventry
"Here, in this little bay."—CoBn
The two deserts.—CoBn
The year's round.—BrSg
Patrick, Saint (about)
I'll wear a shamrock. M. C. Davies.—ArT-3
Wearing of the green. A. Fisher.—LaPh
Patrick, Michael
"When spring comes."—LeM
The **patriot.** Robert Browning.—BrP
Patriotism. See also Fourth of July; Heroes and heroines; Memorial day; Veteran's day; also names of countries, as England; United States
The lay of the last minstrel. W. Scott.—PaH (sel.)
The patriot. R. Browning.—BrP
Patroness. Gerald William Barrax.—HaK
"The **pattering** rain dances." See Rain dance
Patterns. Amy Lowell.—BoH—CoBl
Patterns of life. Elizabeth Jane Coatsworth.—CoDh
Patterson, Raymond Richard
In time of crisis.—AdIa
Paul Revere's ride. See Tales of a wayside inn
Paul's fingers. Mary O'Neill.—OnF
A **pavane** for the nursery. William Jay Smith.—BoGj—CoBl
"The **pawn-shop** man knows hunger." See Street window
Pawnee Indians. See Indians of the Americas—Pawnee
Payne, Robert
In the hills. tr.—HoL
"A piece of colored cloud shines on the stone well." tr.—LeMw
The women of Yueh. tr.—HoL
The yellow bird. tr.—ReBs
Paz, Octavio
The street.—LaC
Peace. See also Memorial Day; Veteran's day
An answer to the parson. W. Blake.—BlP
"Eternity's low voice." M. Van Doren.—PlE
The fox and the rooster. E. Rees.—ArT-3
The hand that signed the paper. D. Thomas.—McWs
I am waiting. V. C. Howard.—BaH
"I heard an angel singing." W. Blake.—BlP
The jingo and the minstrel. V. Lindsay.—LiP
Lady, three white leopards. From Ash Wednesday. T. S. Eliot.—GrS
The occultation of Orion. H. W. Longfellow.—LoPl
Peace ("My soul, there is a countrie") H. Vaughan.—GrCt—PaH—PlE
Peace ("Sweet peace where dost thou dwell? I humbly crave") G. Herbert.—GrCt
Peace and war. From King Henry V. W. Shakespeare.—ShS

Peace—*Continued*
Peace on earth. W. C. Williams.—HaL
Sunset horn. M. O'Higgins.—BoA
"The wolf also shall dwell with the lamb." From Isaiah, Bible, Old Testament.—McWs
"The world was meant to be peaceful." V. Bryant.—BaH
Peace ("My soul, there is a countrie") Henry Vaughan.—GrCt—PaH—PlE
Peace ("Sweet peace, where dost thou dwell? I humbly crave") George Herbert.—GrCt
Peace and war. See King Henry V
Peace on earth. William Carlos Williams.—HaL
"**Peach** blossom after rain." Unknown, tr. fr. the Chinese by Helen Waddell.—LeMw
Peach tree with fruit. Padraic Colum.—CoBn
Peaches
"Keep straight down this block." R. Wright
Hokku poems.—BoA
The little peach. E. Field.—AgH—BrSm
"Peach blossom after rain." Unknown.—LeMw
Peach tree with fruit. P. Colum.—CoBn
Peacock, Thomas Love
The friar. See Maid Marian
The ghosts.—SmM
Maid Marian, sel.
The friar.—MoS
The misfortunes of Elphin, sel.
The war song of Dinas Vawr.—McWs
The war song of Dinas Vawr. See The misfortunes of Elphin
The **peacock**. Carmen Bernos de Gasztold, tr. fr. the French by Rumer Godden.—GaC
Peacock and nightingale. Robert Finch.—CoB
"A **peacock** feather." Unknown.—WyC
Peacocks
"All the night o'er and o'er." Unknown.—MoB
"I saw a peacock with a fiery tail." Mother Goose.—BlO—MoB—OpF
I saw a peacock.—GrCt—SmM
Missing commas.—BrMg
The peacock. C. B. de Gasztold.—GaC
Peacock and nightingale. R. Finch.—CoB
Swell people. C. Sandburg.—HaL
Truth. W. Cowper.—CoB (sel.)
Peadar Og goes courting. James Stephens.—CoBl
Peake, Charlotte M. A. See Shotaro Kimura and Peake, Charlotte M. A.
Pearce, W.
By the deep nine.—GrCt
"**Pearl** avenue runs past the high-school lot." See Ex-basketball player
Pearls among swine. Peggy Bennett.—CoB
Pearls on the grass. Geeta Mohanty.—LeM
Pears
The fable of the golden pear. E. Merriam.—MeI
"Pretty Futility." E. J. Coatsworth.—AgH
Sickle pears. O. Dodson.—BoA
Someone had a helping hand. J. Ciardi.—CiYk
Peasants
Cottage boy. M. Elliott.—VrF
"The **peasants** of Calabria." See Earth and the kisses of men
"**Pease-porridge** hot." Mother Goose.—ArT-3—BrMg—WiMg
Mother Goose rhymes, 39.—HoB
"Pease-porridge hot, pease porridge cold."—OpF
"**Pease-porridge** hot, pease porridge cold." See "Pease-porridge hot"
Peck, Elizabeth
Between the walls of the valley.—BrA
Walthena.—BrA
A **peck** of gold. Robert Frost.—BoH—LaPd
Peculiar. Eve Merriam.—MeC
The **peddler** of spells. Lu Yu, tr. fr. the Chinese by Arthur Waley.—LeMw
Peddlers and venders
Aunt Jane Allen. F. Johnson.—AdIa
The balloon man. D. Aldis.—ArT-3
Bread and cherries. W. De La Mare.—BrSg
Ding, ding. E. Merriam.—MeC
"Do you know the muffin man." E. Farjeon.—FaT
Fish crier. C. Sandburg.—BrA
The flower-cart man. R. Field.—BrSg—LaC
The flower-pot man. W. Darton.—VrF
The flower-seller. E. Farjeon.—BrSg
"Flowers for sale." Unknown.—WyC
"Hot cross buns." Mother Goose.—WiMg
Good Friday.—BrMg
The ice-cream man. R. Field.—HoB
The knife-grinder's budget. Unknown.—VrF
Lemonade. D. McCord.—McAd
A Negro peddler's song. F. Johnson.—BoA
Old chairs. Mother Goose.—BrMg
Old Joe Jones. L. E. Richards.—AgH
The orphans. H. S. Horsley.—VrF
The peddler of spells. Lu Yu.—LeMw
The pedlar. From The winter's tale. W. Shakespeare.—ShS
The pedlar's caravan. W. B. Rands.—BlO
Pushcart row. R. Field.—BrSg
The rabbit man. Mother Goose.—BrMg
The ratcatcher's daughter. Unknown.—GrCt
The scissor-man. M. Nightingale.—ArT-3
Strawberries. E. Farjeon.—AgH
"There was an old woman (and she sold puddings and pyes)." Mother Goose.—AgH
"There was an old woman lived under some stairs." Mother Goose.—OpF
"V is for the vendor." From All around the town. P. McGinley.—BrSg
"Will you buy syboes." Unknown.—MoB
Wit's pedlar. From Love's labour's lost. W. Shakespeare.—ShS
"The **pedigree** of honey." Emily Dickinson.—DiPe
Pedigrees. See Ancestry
The **pedlar.** See The winter's tale
Pedlars. See Peddlers and venders
The **pedlar's** caravan. William Brighty Rands.—BlO
Peeking. Aileen Fisher.—FiIo
Peeking in. Aileen Fisher.—FiIo
Peel, Arthur J.
Shadows.—ThA

Peele, George
Celenta at the well of life. See The old wives' tale
The old knight.—GrCt
The old wives' tale, sels.
Celenta at the well of life.—BlO
The voice from the well of life speaks to the maiden.—GrCt
A spell.—GrCt
A spell. See The old wives' tale
The voice from the well of life speaks to the maiden. See The old wives' tale—Celenta at the well of life
Peep-primrose. Eleanor Farjeon.—BrSg
Peewees
I was a phoebe. E. Dickinson.—ReBs
O lapwing. W. Blake.—GrCt—ReBs
Two pewits. E. Thomas.—ThG
Peg. Mother Goose.—BrMg
"**Peg** Nicholson was a good bay mare." See Elegy on Willie Nicol's mare
Pegasus
Pegasus. E. Farjeon.—SmM
Pegasus. Eleanor Farjeon.—SmM
Peggy Mitchell. James Stephens.—StS
Pelicans
"The reason for the pelican." J. Ciardi.—HoB—LaP—LaPd
"A wonderful bird is the pelican." D. L. Merritt.—BrLl
Pelleas and Ettarre, sel. Alfred Tennyson
A rose, but one.—TeP
Pencil and paint. Eleanor Farjeon.—LaPd
Pennies
"As round as a marble." Mother Goose.—OpF
The **penniless** hawk. Unknown, ad. fr. the Japanese by Charlotte B. DeForest.—DePp
Pennsylvania Dutch
Lancaster county tragedy. W. L. Kay.—BrSm
"**Pennsylvania** Dutch mouse." See Lancaster county tragedy
Pennsylvania station. Langston Hughes.—BoA—HaK
"The **Pennsylvania** station in New York." See Pennsylvania station
"A **penny** is heavier than the shrew." See The masked shrew
The **penny** whistle. Edward Thomas.—ThG
Peonies
"Farewell, like a bee." Bashō.—BeCs
"The peony." Buson.—LeMw
"The **peony.**" Buson, tr. fr. the Japanese by R. H. Blyth.—LeMw
People
Bird talk. A. Fisher.—HoB
The Bourbons at Naples. E. J. Coatsworth.—CoDh
"Color—caste—denomination." E. Dickinson.—PlE
Counting. F. Johnson.—BoA
Encountering. M. J. Fuller.—BaH
Faces. S. Teasdale.—LaC
Going down the street. A. Fisher.—FiIo
The greatest city. W. Whitman.—LaC
Hill people. H. G. Blackwell.—BrA
"How beastly the bourgeois is." D. H. Lawrence.—GrCt
In a million years. C. Lewis.—LeP
The lost world. R. Jarrell.—LiT (sel.)
No man on any moon. C. Lewis.—LeP
"The noise of passing feet." Unknown.—LeO
"People (happy, sad)." O. Rock.—BaH
The people ("The ants are walking under the ground") E. M. Roberts.—ArT-3—BoGj
People ("Tall people, short people") L. Lenski.—LaC
"People are few." Issa.—IsF—LeMw
"People talks." P. Harrison.—BaH
People who must. C. Sandburg.—LaC—LaPd
Question in a field. L. Bogan.—HoL
Several people. Pien Chih-lin.—LeMw
"The show is not the show." E. Dickinson.—DiPe
Some people. R. Field.—LaPd
Swell people. C. Sandburg.—HaL
Then as now. W. De La Mare.—DeBg—LiT
Those who go forth before daylight. C. Sandburg.—HuS-3
Trees. H. Nemerov.—CoBn
The unknown citizen. W. H. Auden.—DuS
Wang Peng's recommendation for improving the people. P. Eldridge.—BrSm
"We human beings." Issa.—IsF
"When wilt thou save the people." E. Elliott.—PlE
Who's in. E. Fleming.—BlO—ClF—ThA
Wonder wander. L. Kandel.—DuR
People—Portraits. See also Boys and boyhood; Girls and girlhood
The prologue. From The Canterbury tales. G. Chaucer.—ChT
"Whan that Aprille with his shoures sote."—GrCt
A true story. J. Smith.—SmM
"You really resemble." Unknown.—DoC
People—Portraits—Men
Jacob Tonson, his publisher. J. Dryden.—GrCt
Lighthearted William. W. C. Williams.—HaL
Miniver Cheevy. E. A. Robinson.—GrCt
Mr Pyme. H. Behn.—ArT-3—LaPd
"O my, you should have seen Colquhoun." Unknown.—MoB
Old Jake Sutter. K. Starbird.—ArT-3
Sporus. From Epistle to Dr Arbuthnot. A. Pope.—GrCt
Uncle Ambrose. J. Still.—BrA
People—Portraits—Women
Appoggiatura. D. J. Hayes.—BoA
At the carnival. A. Spencer.—HaK
A ballad of the mulberry road. E. Pound.—HaL
Bessie Bobtail. J. Stephens.—StS
Deirdre. J. Stephens.—StS
The gallery. A. Marvell.—GrS
Girls on the Yueh river. Li T'ai-po.—GrCt
The infanta. E. J. Coatsworth.—CoDh
Kate. A. Tennyson.—TeP

People—Portraits—Women—*Continued*
A lady comes to an inn. E. J. Coatsworth.—ArT-3—CoDh
Mary Tudor. E. J. Coatsworth.—CoDh
No images. W. Cuney.—BoA—BoH
Portrait by a neighbor. E. St V. Millay.—ArT-3—HaL—LaPd—ThA—TuW
Proletarian portrait. W. C. Williams.—LaC
"She was a phantom of delight." W. Wordsworth.—WoP
The stone-breaker. Nirala.—AlPi
"Woman, your soul is misshapen." Unknown.—DoC
Young woman at a window. W. C. Williams.—LaC
People—Size
Big Goliath, little David. E. Merriam.—MeC
Big little boy. E. Merriam.—MeC
Colter's candy. Unknown.—MoB
The cruel naughty boy. Unknown.—CoBb
"A girl who weighed many an oz." Unknown.—BrLl
"A globe-trotting man from St Paul." F. G. Christgau.—BrLl
"His sister named Lucy O'Finner." L. Carroll.—BrLl
If you should fall, don't forget this. J. Ciardi.—CiYk
"It is not growing like a tree." From To the immortal memory of that noble pair, Sir Lucius Cary and Sir H. Morison. B. Jonson.—GrCt
"Jerry Hall." Mother Goose.—BrMg
The little elf-man. J. K. Bangs.—ArT-3—HoB
I met a little elf man.—HuS-3
The little elf.—LaPd—ThA
Mrs Snipkin and Mrs Wobblechin. L. E. Richards.—ArT-3—HuS-3
Old woman of Bath. Unknown.—VrF
Slow flowers, fast weeds. From King Richard III. W. Shakespeare.—ShS
"Some credulous chroniclers tell us." J. W. Riley.—BrLl
"There was a young lady from Lynn." Unknown.—BrLl
The young lady of Lynn.—GrCt
"There was an old man, who when little." E. Lear.—BrLl
"There was once a young man of Oporta." L. Carroll.—BrLl
The wee, wee man. Unknown.—MoB
"**People** (living)." See Encountering
"**People** (happy, sad)." Orville Rock.—BaH
The **people** ("The ants are walking under the ground") Elizabeth Madox Roberts.—ArT-3—BoGj
People ("Tall people, short people") Lois Lenski.—LaC
"The **people** along the sand." See Neither out far nor in deep
"**People** always say to me." See The question
"**People** are few." Issa, tr. fr. the Japanese by R. H. Blyth.—IsF—LeMw
"**People** buy a lot of things." Annette Wynne.—LaPd
"**People** in a field with light and noise." See Fireworks
The **people** of Tao-chou. Po Chü-i, tr. fr. the Chinese by Arthur Waley.—GrCt
"**People** talks." Phillip Harrison.—BaH
"**People** that I meet and pass." See Faces
"The **people** who allege that we." See The uses of ocean
People who must. Carl Sandburg.—LaC—LaPd
The **people**, yes, sels. Carl Sandburg
All one people.—BrA
Children of the wind.—HuS-3
These children of the wind.—ReBs
Circles.—BrA
"They have yarns."—BrA
American yarns.—HuS-3
The **peopled** air. See Ode on the spring
Pepys, Samuel (about)
Birthday party. E. J. Coatsworth.—CoDh
Percikow, Henri
Childhood.—LaC
Living among the toilers.—LaC
Percy, William Alexander
Overtones.—BoH
Perfection
The deacon's masterpiece; or, The wonderful one-hoss shay. O. W. Holmes.—HuS-3
"**Perfection**, of a kind, was what he was after." See Epitaph on a tyrant
The **performing** seal. See A circus garland
Perfume
"The bottle of perfume that Willie sent." Unknown.—BrLl
"Essential oils are wrung." E. Dickinson.—DiPe
Perhaps. Bob Kaufman.—HaK
"**Perhaps** our age has driven us indoors." See The forecast
Perleberg, Max
An enjoyable evening in the village near the lake. tr.—LeMw
Permanence
"All things of earth have an end, and in the midst." Unknown.—LeO
"As for this world." Semimaru.—BaS
"By word laid low." Unknown.—GrCt
Earth upon earth. Unknown.—GrCt
The Fort of Rathangan. Berchan.—GrCt
The old Fort of Rathangan.—HoL
Gone. W. De La Mare.—BoGj—DeBg
The greatest city. W. Whitman.—LaC
The hammers. R. Hodgson.—BoGj
The hearth of Urien. W. Barnes.—GrCt
How time consumeth all earthly things. T. Proctor.—GrCt
The ivy green. From The Pickwick papers. C. Dickens.—CoBn
A lament for the priory of Walsingham. Unknown.—GrCt (sel.)
Let all things pass away. W. B. Yeats.—GrCt
Ozymandias. P. B. Shelley.—CoR—PaH
The wind and the rain. W. W. Gibson.—ClF

Perrins walk. Harry Behn.—BeG
Perry-the-winkle. See The adventures of Tom Bombadil
Perseverance
Conquest. G. D. Johnson.—BoA—BoH
I may, I might, I must. Marianne Moore.—McWs
The lion and the mouse. R. S. Sharpe.—VrF
"The mouse that gnawed the oak-tree down." V. Lindsay.—HaL—LiP
"We shall overcome." Unknown.—HiL—PlE
Persia
Sohrab and Rustum. M. Arnold.—CoD
Persia—History
The oracles. A. E. Housman.—CoR
Personal. Langston Hughes.—BoA
Perspectives. Dudley Randall.—BoA
Peru
Peruvian dance song. Unknown.—LeO
Peruvian dance song. Unknown, tr. fr. the Ayacucho.—LeO
Pessimism. See also Failure; Optimism
For a pessimist. C. Cullen.—BrSm
The pessimist. B. King.—BlO—SmM
The **pessimist.** Ben King.—BlO—SmM
The **petal** of a rose. James Stephens.—StS
"**Pete.**" See Pete's sweets
Pete at the seashore. See Archy and Mehitabel
Pete at the zoo. Gwendolyn Brooks.—HaL—LaPd
"**Pete** Rousecastle the sailor's son." See Rousecastle
Peter. See "Peter, Peter, pumpkin-eater"
Peter and John. Elinor Wylie.—CaMb
"**Peter** Jackson was a-preaching." See When Peter Jackson preached in the old church
"**Peter,** Peter, pumpkin-eater." Mother Goose.—WiMg
Mother Goose rhymes, 9.—HoB
Peter.—BrMg
"**Peter** Piper picked a peck of pickled (or pickling) pepper." See Peter Piper's practical principles of plain and perfect pronunciation
Peter Piper's practical principles of plain and perfect pronunciation. Unknown.—VrF
"Peter Piper picked a peck of pickled (or pickling) pepper."—BrMg—HuS-3—OpF—WrMg
Mother Goose rhymes, 43.—HoB
Peter the Great, Czar of Russia
Peterhof. E. Wilson.—BoGj
"**Peter,** walking with his mother." See The orphans
"**Peter** White." Mother Goose.—OpF
Peter White's nose.—BrMg
"**Peter** White will ne'er go right." See "Peter White"
Peter White's nose. See "Peter White"
Peterhof. Edmund Wilson.—BoGj
Peters, Edmund W.
Bicycalamity.—MoS
Peterson, Denise
"This is a world full of Negroes and whites." —BaH
Peterson, Ruth Delong
Midwest town.—BrA
Pete's sweets. Eve Merriam.—MeC
Petla, Mary
My imagination.—BaH
Petrarch (Francesco Petrarca)
"In wintry midnight, o'er a stormy main."—GrCt
Petrarch for Laura. Claire McAllistair.—GrS
Petrie, George
"Do you remember that night."—CoBl
Do you remember the night.—GrS
Do you remember the night. See "Do you remember that night"
Petrie, Paul
Chain.—CoB
Pets. See also names of animals, as Dogs
Advice to children. C. Wells.—CoO
A child's pet. W. H. Davies.—CoB
Consolation. A. Fisher.—FiIo
The death and dying words of poor Mailie. R. Burns.—BuPr
Lost. D. McCord.—McE
My brother Bert. T. Hughes.—CoBb
The pets ("Colm had a cat") R. Farren.—ReO
Pets ("Once we had a little retriever") D. Pettiward.—CoB
Playing with a pet bird. K. Fraser.—FrS
Poor Mailie's elegy. R. Burns.—BuPr
The python. H. Belloc.—BrSm
Two songs of a fool. W. B. Yeats.—ReO
The **pets** ("Colm had a cat") Robert Farren.—ReO
Pets ("Once we had a little retriever") Daniel Pettiward.—CoB
"**Pets** are the hobby of my brother Bert." See My brother Bert
Pettiward, Daniel
Pets.—CoB
"**Pew,** pew." See The milk-white dove
Phantom. Samuel Taylor Coleridge.—GrS
The **phantom** horsewoman. Thomas Hardy.—GrS
Phantoms. See Ghosts
"The **Pharaoh** of the Exodus is eight feet tall." See After reading translations of ancient texts on stone and clay
Pharsalia, sel. Lucan
The coracle, tr. fr. the Latin by Walter Raleigh.—GrCt
Phases of the moon. See One word more
The **pheasant.** Robert P. Tristram Coffin.—ArT-3—DuR
"A **pheasant** cock sprang into view." See The pheasant
Pheasants
"From a mountain of fallen leaves." K. Mizumura.—MiI
The pheasant. R. P. T. Coffin.—ArT-3—DuR
Philadelphia, Pennsylvania
Rulers: Philadelphia. F. Johnson.—BrA
Philip (or Phylip) Sparrow, sel. John Skelton
The cursing of the cat.—ReO
O cat of carlish kind.—GrCt

Philippians, sel. Bible, New Testament
"Whatsoever things are true."—ArT-3
Philippine islands
On a soldier fallen in the Philippines. W. V. Moody.—HiL
"**Phillis** is my only joy." See Phillis
Philomela. John Crowe Ransom.—GrCt
Phizzog. Carl Sandburg.—ArT-3
"**Phlebas** the Phoenician, a fortnight dead." See The waste land—Death by water
Phoebus
Phoebus and the crow. From The Canterbury tales. G. Chaucer.—ChT
Lat take a cat.—GrCt (sel.)
Take any bird.—ReO (sel.)
Phoebus and the crow. See The Canterbury tales
Phoenix
"I saw a phoenix in the wood alone." From The visions of Petrarch. E. Spenser.—GrCt
The phoenix ("O blest unfabled incense tree") From Nepenthe. G. Darley.—GrCt
The phoenix ("Some say the phoenix dwells in Aethiopia") S. Sassoon.—GrCt
The phoenix self-born. From Metamorphoses. Ovid.—GrCt
The **phoenix** ("O blest unfabled incense tree") See Nepenthe
The **phoenix** ("Some say the phoenix dwells in Aethiopia") Siegfried Sassoon.—GrCt
The **phoenix** self-born. See Metamorphoses
Photographers and photography
Looking in the album. V. Rutsala.—DuS
"No pleasant task this picture to take." M. Elliott.—VrF
Physical geography. Louise Townsend Nicholl.—LiT
Physiologus, sel.
The whale. Unknown, tr. fr. the Old English by Charles W. Kennedy.—ReO
Piano after war. Gwendolyn Brooks.—BoA—HaK
Piano practice. Ian Serraillier.—CoBb
Pianos
If all the unplayed pianos. W. T. Scott.—DuS
Piano after war. G. Brooks.—BoA—HaK
Piano practice. I. Serraillier.—CoBb
Variations for two pianos. D. Justice.—DuS
Piazza piece. John Crowe Ransom.—GrS
Pick-a-back. See "Matthew, Mark, Luke, John"
"**Pick**, crow, pick, and have no fear." Mother Goose.—OpF
"**Pick** up a stick up." See Jumble jingle
"**Pickaxes,** pickaxes swinging today." See Bam, bam, bam
"The **pickety** fence." David McCord.—McE
The **Pickwick** papers, sel. Charles Dickens
The ivy green.—CoBn
Picnic ("Ella, fella") Hugh Lofting.—BoGj
The **picnic** ("It is the picnic with Ruth in the spring") John Logan.—CoBl—DuS
The **picnic** ("We brought a rug for sitting on") Dorothy Aldis.—ArT-3
Picnic day. Rachel Field.—ArT-3
Picnics
Beach fire. F. M. Frost.—ArT-3
Picnic ("Ella, fella") H. Lofting.—BoGj
The picnic ("It is the picnic with Ruth in the spring") J. Logan.—CoBl—DuS
The picnic ("We brought a rug for sitting on") D. Aldis.—ArT-3
Picnic day. R. Field.—ArT-3
Picnics ("Picnics in a box are nice") A. Fisher.—FiIo
Picnics ("Sunshine and weiners and pickles and ham") M. Chute.—AgH
Picnics ("Picnics in a box are nice") Aileen Fisher.—FiIo
Picnics ("Sunshine and weiners and pickles and ham") Marchette Chute.—AgH
"**Picnics** in a box are nice." See Picnics
Pictor ignotus. Robert Browning.—BrP
Pictures. See Paintings and pictures
Pidgeon, Linda
The sunbeams.—LeM
The **pie.** See "Who made the pie"
"A **pie** (or pye) sat on a pear tree." Mother Goose.—BlO—GrCt—OpF
"A **piece** of colored cloud shines on the stone well." Chien Hsu, tr. by Robert Payne.—LeMw
"**Piecemeal** the summer dies." See Exeunt
Pied beauty. Gerard Manley Hopkins.—BoGj—HoL—PlE—SmM
The **Pied** Piper of Hamelin. Robert Browning.—ArT-3—BrP—GrT—HoB—HuS-3
"Rats."—CoB (sel.)
Pien Chih-lin
Several people.—LeMw
The **pier.** Enrique Lozada.—LeM
Pierce, Dorothy Mason
Good night.—ArT-3
Sprinkling.—ArT-3
Pierrot. Sara Teasdale.—CoBl
"**Pierrot** stands in the garden." See Pierrot
Pies
A-apple pie. W. De La Mare.—DeBg
"A was an apple-pie." Mother Goose.—OpF
A, apple pie.—BrMg—GrT
Mother Goose rhymes, 38.—HoB
The tragical death of A apple-pye.—VrF
"As I went up the apple tree." Mother Goose.—OpF
The apple tree.—BrMg
"Baby and I." Mother Goose.—BrMg
Buttered pippin-pies. J. Davies of Hereford.—GrCt
"Cherry pie black." E. Farjeon.—FaT
"Dame, get up and bake your pies." Mother Goose.—WiMg
Mud pie. K. Fraser.—FrS
"Punch and Judy." Mother Goose.—BrMg
"Rindle, randle." Mother Goose.—OpF
"Sing a song of sixpence." Mother Goose.—BrF—BrMg—HuS-3—OpF—SmM—WiMg
Mother Goose rhymes, 61.—HoB
Table. D. McCord.—McE
"There was an old lady of Brooking." Unknown.—BrLl
"There was an old lady of Rye." Unknown.—BrLl

Trouble with pies. D. McCord.—McAd
"Who made the pie." Mother Goose.—OpF
The pie.—BrMg
Pig-sty. Eleanor Farjeon.—FaT
A **pig** tale ("Poor Jane Higgins") James Reeves.—LaP—SmM
The **pig-tale** ("There was a pig that sat alone") See Sylvie and Bruno
"**Pigalle.**" See Montmartre
Pigeon English. Sara Henderson Hay.—ReBs
Pigeon playmates. Unknown, ad. fr. the Japanese by Charlotte B. DeForest.—DePp
Pigeons
The ballad of the light-eyed little girl. G. Brooks.—LiT
Cecilia. Unknown.—DoW
Counting out. Unknown.—MoB
The dove. W. Barnes.—ReBs
The dove says. Mother Goose.—BrMg
The dove's song. Unknown.—StF
The milk-white dove. Unknown.—GrCt
"Mrs Peck-Pigeon." E. Farjeon.—ArT-3—HuS-3—LaPd
The old sweet dove of Wiveton. S. Smith.—ReO
A parting shot. C. Day-Lewis.—CaD
Pigeon English. S. H. Hay.—ReBs
Pigeon playmates. Unknown.—DePp
Pigeons. R. Kell.—SmM
Real estate. M. C. Livingston.—LiC
"See how the doves flutter and huddle." Unknown.—DoC
Song. J. Keats.—BlO—CoB
I had a dove.—ReBs
Song of fixed accord. W. Stevens.—ReO
Trinity place. P. McGinley.—LaC
The turtledoves. A. Fisher.—FiC
Two pigeons. Mother Goose.—BrMg
"Two pigeons flying high." Mother Goose.—OpF
The white dove. Mother Goose.—ReOn
Wren and dove. Unknown.—MoB
Pigeons. Richard Kell.—SmM
"**Pigeons** and crows, take care of your toes." Unknown.—OpF
"The **pigeons** own the building." See Real estate
"The **pigeons** that peck at the grass in Trinity churchyard." See Trinity place
Piggyback. Kathleen Fraser.—FrS
Pigs
As I looked out. Unknown.—StF
"As I went to Bonner." Mother Goose.—ReMg
A strange pig.—BrMg
"Barber, barber, shave a pig." Mother Goose.—OpF—ReMg
Barber, barber.—BrMg
Mother Goose rhymes, 20.—HoB
The boar and the dromedar. H. Beissel.—DoW
"A carrion crow sat on an oak." Mother Goose.—BlO—ReMg—SmM
The carrion crow.—BrMg
A counting rhyme. M. M. Stephenson.—StF
"Dickery, dickery, dare." Mother Goose.—OpF—WiMg
The flying pig.—BrMg
"From the skewer O the blood O on my skin dripped down." Unknown.—LeO
Grig's pig. Mother Goose.—BrMg
"If a pig wore a wig." C. G. Rossetti.—HoB
Litter of pigs. F. Lape.—CoB
Pearls among swine. P. Bennett.—CoB
Pig-sty. E. Farjeon.—FaT
A pig tale ("Poor Jane Higgins") J. Reeves.—LaP—SmM
The pig-tale ("There was a pig that sat alone") From Sylvie and Bruno. L. Carroll.—ReO
Pigs. W. De La Mare.—DeBg
The prayer of the little pig. C. B. de Gasztold.—LiT
The story of the old woman and her pig. Mother Goose.—BrMg
"There was a lady loved a swine." Mother Goose.—OpF
Hunc, said he.—GrCt
The lady and the swine.—BrF—BrMg
"This little pig had a rub-a-dub." Mother Goose.—BrMg
"This little pig said, I want some corn." Mother Goose.—OpF
"This little pig went to market." Mother Goose.—BrMg—HuS-3—OpF—WiMg
Mother Goose rhymes, 36.—HoB
"Tom, Tom, the piper's son (stole a pig)." Mother Goose.—OpF—WiMg
Tom.—BrMg
The unknown color. C. Cullen.—BoH
The visitor. K. Pyle.—CoBb
"Whose little pigs are these, these, these." Mother Goose.—OpF
Pigs. Walter De La Mare.—DeBg
Pike, Cecily E.
Jack Frost.—StF
The **pike** ("And nigh this toppling reed, still as the dead") Edmund Blunden.—ReO (sel.)
The **pike** ("I take it he doesn't think at all") John Bruce.—MoS
The **pilgrim** ("The sword sang on the barren heath") William Blake.—ArT-3
The sword and the sickle.—GrCt
"The sword sung on the barren heath."—BlP
The **pilgrim** ("Who would true valour see") See The pilgrim's progress
Pilgrim Fathers. See Thanksgiving day; United States—History—Colonial period
The **pilgrimage.** George Herbert.—GrCt
Pilgrims
The Canterbury tales, sels. G. Chaucer
The ballad of Sir Thopas.—ChT
Chanticleer and the fox.—ChT
The fortunes of the great.—ChT
Patient Griselda.—ChT
Phoebus and the crow.—ChT
Lat take a cat.—GrCt (sel.)
Take any bird.—ReO (sel.)
The prologue.—ChT
"Whan that Aprille with his shoures sote."—GrCt
The rocks of Brittany.—ChT

Pilgrims—*Continued*
The Canterbury Tales, sels.—*Continued*
The story of Constance.—ChT
Three men in search of death.—ChT
The wily chemist.—ChT
The pilgrim ("The sword sang on the barren heath") W. Blake.—ArT-3
The sword and the sickle.—GrCt
"The sword sung on the barren heath."—BlP
The pilgrim ("Who would true valour see") From The pilgrim's progress. J. Bunyan.—ArT-3—ClF
Riding together. W. Morris.—ClF
The **pilgrim's** progress, sels. John Bunyan
The pilgrim.—ArT-3—ClF
The shepherd boy sings in the valley of humiliation.—PlE
Pilots and piloting. See Aviators
Pima Indians. See Indians of the Americas—Pima
"A **pin** to see the poppet-show." See The poppet-show
"A **pin** to see the puppet show." Unknown.—MoB
"**Pin** wheels whirling round." See Fourth of July night
Pindar
Life after death.—PlE
Nemea 11, sel.
I bless this man.—MoS
Pine. Myra Cohn Livingston.—LiC
Pine bough. See "A feather from the whippowil"
The **pine** bough ("I saw a thing, and stopped to wonder") Richard Aldridge.—HoL
"The **pine** has a harp." See Pine music
Pine music. Aileen Fisher.—FiC
The **pine** tree. Phyllis McGinley.—McWc
Pine trees
"A feather from the whippowil." E. Dickinson
Pine bough.—DiL
"In the dark pine-wood." J. Joyce.—CoBl
"The least of breezes." Onitsura.—BeCs
"O pine tree standing." Hakutsú.—BaS
Pine. M. C. Livingston.—LiC
The pine bough. R. Aldridge.—HoL
Pine music. A. Fisher.—FiC
The pine tree. P. McGinley.—McWc
"When I see the pine trees." Unknown.—BaS
"The **pine** was mortal, once, like other trees." See The pine tree
Pining for love. Francis Beaumont.—CoBl
Pink (Color)
What is pink. M. O'Neill.—OnH
"What is pink? a rose is pink." C. G. Rossetti.—ArT-3
What is pink.—BoGj—BrSg—HuS-3
"**Pink** is the color of a rose." See What is pink
"**Pink,** small, and punctual." Emily Dickinson.—DiPe
Pins
A dressmaker. J. Kenward.—SmM
"Needles and pins, needles and pins." Mother Goose
Mother Goose rhymes, 33.—HoB
Pins. Mother Goose.—BrMg
Pins. Mother Goose.—BrMg
The **Pinta,** the Nina and the Santa Maria; and many other cargoes of light. John Tagliabue.—BrA
The **pinwheel's** song. John Ciardi.—LaPd
The **pioneer.** Arthur Guiterman.—ArT-3
Pioneer life. See Frontier and pioneer life
Pioneer rat. Elizabeth Jane Coatsworth.—CoSb
The **pioneer** woman—in the North country. Eunice Tietjens.—BrA
"**Pip,** pop, flippety flop." See The song of the cornpopper
A **piper** ("A piper in the streets today") Seumas O'Sullivan.—ArT-3—LaPd
The **piper** ("Piping down the valleys wild") William Blake.—CoR—HoB—LaP—LaPd
Introduction.—BoGj—ClF
Introduction to Songs of innocence.—ArT-3—BlP—SmM
Piping down the valleys.—HuS-3
"A **piper** in the streets to-day." See A piper
Pipers
"As I was going up the hill." Mother Goose.—OpF
Jack the piper.—GrCt
The host of the air. W. B. Yeats.—LiT—YeR
The Pied Piper of Hamelin. R. Browning.—ArT-3—BrP—GrT—HoB—HuS-3
"Rats."—CoB (sel.)
A piper ("A piper in the streets to-day") S. O'Sullivan.—ArT-3—LaPd
The piper ("Piping down the valleys wild") W. Blake.—CoR—HoB—LaP—LaPd
Introduction.—BoGj—ClF
Introduction to Songs of innocence.—ArT-3—BlP—SmM
Piping down the valleys.—HuS-3
"Tom, Tom, the piper's son (he learnt to play)." Mother Goose.—GrT—ReMg
"Tom he was a piper's son."—ArT-3—OpF
Pipes
Grandad's pipe. I. Serraillier.—StF
Piping down the valleys. See The piper
Pippa passes, sels. Robert Browning
"All service ranks the same with God."—BrP
"Day."—BrP
"Oh day, if I squander a wavelet of thee."—BrP
"Overhead the tree-tops meet."—BrP
"The year's at the spring."—BrP—HoB
Pippa's song.—BoGj—LaPd
Song.—TuW
You'll love me yet.—BrP
Pippa's song. See Pippa passes—"The year's at the spring"
Pippen hill. See "As I went up Pippin hill"
Pips in the fire. Mother Goose.—ReOn
Pirate. Samuel Menashe.—SmM

Pirate Don Durk of Dowdee. Mildred Plew Meigs.—ArT-3—HoB—LaPd
Pirate story. Robert Louis Stevenson.—ArT-3
"A **pirate** who hailed from Nertskinski." Unknown.—BrLl
Pirates. See also names of pirates, as Kidd, Captain
The battle of Clothesline bay. W. Irwin.—CoSs
The Chinese bumboatman. Unknown.—CoSs
The coasts of high Barbary. Unknown.—BlO
Derelict. Y. E. Allison.—CoSs
El capitan-general. C. G. Leland.—CoSs
Pirate. S. Menashe.—SmM
Pirate Don Durk of Dowdee. M. P. Meigs.—ArT-3—HoB—LaPd
Pirate story. R. L. Stevenson.—ArT-3
"A pirate who hailed from Nertskinski." Unknown.—BrLl
The post captain. C. E. Carryl.—CoSs
The reformed pirate. T. G. Roberts.—DoW
The Salcombe seaman's flaunt to the proud pirate. Unknown.—GrCt
The **pit** of bliss. James Stephens.—StS
"**Pit,** pat, well-a-day." Mother Goose.—ReMg
Pitcher, Molly (about)
Molly Pitcher. L. E. Richards.—HiL
Pitcher, Oliver
Raison d'être.—BoA—HaK
Salute.—HaK
Pitcher. Robert Francis.—DuS—MoS
"A **pitcher** of thoughts." See Silence
"**Pitiful** these crying swans to-night." See The icebound swans
Pitman, J. H.
"An important young man of Quebec."—BrLl
Pitter, Ruth
The bat.—CaD—CoB
The captive bird of paradise.—GrS
For sleep, or death.—SmM
Herding lambs.—CaD
The hut.—CaD
If you came.—CaD
The lost tribe.—HoL
The sparrow's skull.—PlE
The viper.—CaD
The weed.—SmM
"**Pitter** patter, falls the rain." See The umbrella brigade
Pittsburgh, Pennsylvania
Pittsburgh. W. Bynner.—BrA
Pittsburgh. Witter Bynner.—BrA
"**Pitty** Patty Polt." Mother Goose.—StF
"**Pity** this busy monster, manunkind." E. E. Cummings.—HoL
"**Pity** would be no more." See The human abstract
Places. See also names of places, as San Francisco
Places. S. Teasdale.—PaH
"Step lightly on this narrow spot." E. Dickinson.—DiPe
"A strange place." P. Rake.—LeM
Places. Sara Teasdale.—PaH
"**Places** I love come back to me like music." See Places
Plain talk for a pachyderm. Peggy Bennett.—CoB
"**Plainly** then, he was a desert man." See Moses
Plains. See Prairies
The **plaint** of the camel. See Davy and the goblin
"A **planet** doesn't explode of itself, said drily." See Earth
Planets. See also Moon; Stars; World
Interplanetary limerick. A. Graham.—BrLl
Looking through space. A. Fisher.—FiI
The planets. E. Farjeon.—FaT
Two views of the planet earth. H. Behn.—BeG
Valentine for earth. F. M. Frost.—ArT-3—HoB
The **planets.** Eleanor Farjeon.—FaT
Plans. Aileen Fisher.—FiIo
Planting flowers on the eastern embankment. Po Chü-i, tr. fr. the Chinese by Arthur Waley.—CoBn
The **planting** of the apple tree. William Cullen Bryant.—HuS-3
Planting trees. V. H. Friedlaender.—CoBn
Plants and planting. See also names of plants, as Dandelions
Crow in springtime. E. J. Coatsworth.—CoSb
The house plants. E. J. Coatsworth.—CoSb
Lesson. H. Behn.—BrSg
"The plants stand silent round me." J. Jörgensen.—HoL
Spring planting. M. Chute.—BrSg
Tommy. G. Brooks.—BrSg
"The **plants** stand silent round me." Johannes Jörgensen, tr. fr. the Danish by Robert Hillyer.—HoL
Plath, Sylvia
Mushrooms.—CoBn—SmM
"**Plato** told." See Plato told him
Plato told him. E. E. Cummings.—BrA—HiL
Play. See also Counting-out rhymes; Finger-play poems; Games; Nursery play; Playmates
All work and no play. Mother Goose.—BrMg
Allie. R. Graves.—BoGj—CaD—HaL
"An apple for the king." Mother Goose.—ReOn
At the sea-side. R. L. Stevenson.—ArT-3
Baby playing. R. C. Clarke.—LeM
The ball poem. J. Berryman.—LaC (sel.)
Blowing bubbles. K. Fraser.—FrS
Bowl away. K. Greenaway.—GrT
The box. M. C. Livingston.—LiC
Broom balancing. K. Fraser.—FrS
The butterbean tent. E. M. Roberts.—BoGj—BrSg—HuS-3
The cellar hole. D. McCord.—McAd
The centaur. M. Swenson.—DuS—LiT
The chair house. E. J. Coatsworth.—CoSb
Coaster wagon. A. Fisher.—FiIo
Come along. A. Fisher.—FiIo
Come and play in the garden. J. Taylor.—GrT
Come out with me. A. A. Milne.—MiC
Creep. L. Kershaw.—LeM
Dick's trick. E. Merriam.—MeC

Tommy and Jimmy. K. Greenaway.—GrT
Tree climbing. K. Fraser.—FrS
Turn yourself around. K. Fraser.—FrS
Two million two hundred thousand fishes. D. Marcus.—LeM
"Upon the beach." I. Orleans.—ArT-3
Upside down ("A field of clouds") R. Burgunder.—ArT-3
Upside down ("Some day when you're out of town") Z. Gay.—HoB
Us two. A. A. Milne.—ArT-3—MiC
The village green. A. and J. Taylor.—GrT
The voyage of Jimmy Poo. J. A. Emanuel.—BoA
Waiting. A. Fisher.—FiIo
What to do. W. Wise.—ArT-3
Where go the boats. R. L. Stevenson.—ArT-3—BoGj—HoB
White cap. Mother Goose.—BrMg
Whoops a daisy. T. Carr.—LeM
"The wind blows the rain into our faces." C. Reznikoff.—LaC
"With a hop, and a skip, and a jump." W. O'Neill.—StF
The worm. E. M. Roberts.—BrSg—HoB
You do it too. M. Langford.—StF

"**Play** about, do." Ransetsu, tr. fr. the Japanese by Harold G. Henderson.—LeMw
"**Play** on the seashore." See Shore
"**Play** the St Louis Blues." See Request for requiems
Playing. Pauline Costello.—LeM
The **playing** cards. See The rape of the lock
"**Playing** upon the hill the centaurs were." See The centaurs
Playing with a pet bird. Kathleen Fraser.—FrS
Playing with fire. Ann and Jane Taylor.—VrF
The **playmate.** Walter De La Mare.—DeBg
Playmates
Binker. A. A. Milne.—MiC
A girl speaks to her playmate. Unknown.—AlPi
Pigeon playmates. Unknown.—DePp
The playmate. W. De La Mare.—DeBg
Playtime. W. Hamilton.—GrT
Pleasant comedy of patient Grissell, sel. Thomas Dekker
A cradle song.—BlO
Golden slumbers.—SmM
A **pleasant** ride. Unknown.—VrF
A **pleasant** walk. Unknown.—VrF
Please. John Ciardi.—CiYk
"**Please** don't kill my antelope." Unknown, tr. fr. the Bushman.—LeO
Please don't tell him. John Ciardi.—CiYk
"**Please** God, take care of little things." See A prayer for little things
Please tell this someone to take care. John Ciardi.—CiYk
"**Please** to have a little rain." Aileen Fisher.—FiI
"**Please** to remember." Mother Goose.—ReMg
Gunpowder plot day.—BrMg
"**Pleasure** it is." See Spring
"**Pleasures** newly found are sweet." See To the same flower
The **pleasures** of merely circulating. Wallace Stevens.—HaL
The **Pleiades.** Eleanor Farjeon.—FaT
Plomer, William
Europa.—CaMb
Plotz, Sarah
"Eastward I stand, mercies I beg." tr.—PlE
Ploughing on Sunday. Wallace Stevens.—BoGj—SmM—WeP
Ploughs. See Plows and plowing
Plovers
"A thousand." Issa.—IsF—LeOw
Plowing: A memory. Hamlin Garland.—HuS-3
The **plowman** of today. Hamlin Garland.—HuS-3
Plows and plowing
"As I was a-walking." Unknown.—ReBs
The furrows of the unicorn. E. J. Coatsworth.—CoDh
The lark in the morning. Unknown.—GrCt
Ploughing on Sunday. W. Stevens.—BoGj—SmM—WeP
Plowing: A memory. H. Garland.—HuS-3
The plowman of today. H. Garland.—HuS-3
"Sitting on the stone, O crab." Unknown.—LeO
To a mountain daisy. R. Burns.—BuPr
Winter field. A. E. Coppard.—ReBs
"The **plum** blossoms have opened." Unknown.—BaS
Plum trees
"Even stones under." Onitsura.—BeCs
The fall of the plum blossoms. Rankō.—ArT-3
"Steal this one." Issa.—IsF
"These flowers of the plum." Izen.—LeMw
Wild plum. O. Johns.—BoH
"**Plumed** in sacred tufts of smoke." See The Blackfoot chieftains.
"The **plump,** the pompous bosomed bird." See Pigeon English
The **plumpuppets.** Christopher Morley.—ArT-3—ReS
Plums
To a poor old woman. W. C. Williams.—HoL—LiT
Plymouth Rock
Thoughts for St Stephen. C. Morley.—BrSm
Po Chü-i
"Each time that I look at a fine landscape."—LeMw
Having climbed to the topmost peak of the Incense-burner Mountain.—MoS
The people of Tao-chow.—GrCt
Planting flowers on the eastern embankment.—CoBn
The red cockatoo.—GrCt—ReO
The **pobble.** Edward Lear.—BlO
"The **pobble** who has no toes." See The pobble
Pocahontas (about)
Our mother Pocahontas. V. Lindsay.—LiP
Pocahontas. W. M. Thackeray.—BrA—HiL
Pocahontas. William Makepeace Thackeray.—BrA—HiL

Pockets
"Keep a poem in your pocket." B. S. De Regniers.—LaPd
Pockets. S. A. Williams.—StF
"Timothy Dan." J. D. Sheridan.—StF
Pockets. Susan Adger Williams.—StF
Poe, Edgar Allan
Al Aaraaf, sel.
Song from Al Aaraaf.—PoP
Alone.—PoP
Annabel Lee.—CoR—HuS-3—PoP
The assignation, sel.
To one in paradise.—PoP
The bells.—BoH—PoP
Bridal ballad.—PoP
The city in the sea.—GrS—PoP
The coliseum.—PoP
The conqueror worm. See Ligeia
Dream-land.—PoP
A dream within a dream.—GrCt (sel.)—PoP
Dreams.—PoP
Eldorado.—PaH—PoP
An enigma.—PoP
Eulalie—A song.—PoP
Fairy-land.—PoP
The fall of the house of Usher, sel.
The haunted palace.—GrCt—PoP
For Annie.—PoP
The haunted palace. See The fall of the house of Usher
Israfel.—PoP
The lake.—PoP
Lenore.—PoP
Ligeia, sel.
The conqueror worm.—PoP
The raven.—BoGj—PoP
Romance.—PoP
The sleeper.—PoP
Song from Al Aaraaf. See Al Aaraaf
Song of triumph.—PoP
Sonnet—Silence.—PoP
Sonnet—To science.—PoP
Stanzas.—PoP
To Helen ("Helen, thy beauty is to me").—CoBl—GrCt—PoP
To Helen ("I saw thee once—once only—years ago").—PoP
To my mother.—PoP
To one in paradise. See The assignation
Ulalume—A ballad.—PoP
The valley of unrest.—PoP
A **Poe-'em** of passion. Charles Fletcher Lummis.—BrSm
Poem ("As the cat") William Carlos Williams.—CoB—DuR—HaL—LaPd
Poem ("Gathering the strength") B. S. Mardhekar, tr. fr. the Marathi by Dilip Chitre.—AlPi
Poem ("I loved my friend") Langston Hughes.—LiT
Poem ("Little brown boy") Helene Johnson.—BoA
A **poem** for black hearts. LeRoi Jones.—AdIa
Poem in June. Milton Acorn.—DoW
Poem in October. Dylan Thomas.—CaD
Poem in prose. Archibald MacLeish.—McWs
"This **poem** is for my wife." See Poem in prose
The **poem** of ten ones. Ho P'ei Yu, tr. fr. the Chinese by Henry H. Hart.—LeMw
"A **poem** rarely has to shout." See What did you say
"A **poem** should be palpable and mute." See Ars poetica
Poem to be read at 3 A.M. Donald Justice.—DuS
A **poem** to delight my friends who laugh at science-fiction. Edwin Rolfe.—HiL
Poem to hunger. Elizabeth Jane Coatsworth.—CoDh
A **poem** upon the death of Oliver Cromwell, sel. Andrew Marvell
Cromwell dead.—GrCt
Poems, sels. Julius Lester
"Around the church."—HaK
"As we got."—HaK
"She should be."—HaK
"Spring dawn."—HaK
"The man who tried to."—HaK
"With its fog-shroud the."—HaK
Poems. Peter Kelso.—LeM
Poems for my brother Kenneth, VII. Owen Dodson.—AdIa
The **poet** ("He sang of life, serenely sweet") Paul Laurence Dunbar.—HaK
Poet ("No rock along the road but knows") Donald Jeffrey Hayes.—BoA
A **poet** ("A poet.—He hath put his heart to school") William Wordsworth.—WoP
Poet always next but one, sel. David McCord
Cities and science.—BrA
The **poet** and his song. Paul Laurence Dunbar.—BoH
"A **poet.**—He hath put his heart to school." See A poet
The **poet** speaks. Georgia Douglas Johnson.—BoA
Poet to his love. Maxwell Bodenheim.—CoBl
Poetry. See Poets and poetry
"The **poetry** of earth is never dead." See On the grasshopper and cricket
Poets and critics. Alfred Tennyson.—TeP
Poets and poetry. See also names of poets, as Lear, Edward; also names of verse forms, as Limericks
An apology for the bottle volcanic. V. Lindsay.—LiP
An argument. V. Lindsay.—LiP
Ars poetica. A. MacLeish.—BoH
Arthur Ridgewood, M.D. F. M. Davis.—HaK
"The autumn breeze is blowing." Buson.—LeMw
The balloon. A. Tennyson.—CoR
Beware of the doggerel. E. Merriam.—MeI
The broken oar. H. W. Longfellow.—LoPl
Catch a little rhyme. E. Merriam.—LaPd—MeC
A coat. W. B. Yeats.—YeR
Compensation. P. L. Dunbar.—BoA
The confession. Wen Yi-tuo.—GrCt

Couplet countdown. E. Merriam.—MeI
"A decrepit old gas man named Peter." Unknown.—BrLl
Dunbar. A. Spencer.—HaK
"Each time that I look at a fine landscape." Po Chü-i.—LeMw
Elegy for a nature poet. H. Nemerov.—CoBn
An enigma. E. A. Poe.—PoP
Epistle to James Smith. R. Burns.—BuPr
The fishes and the poet's hands. F. Yerby.—BoA
For Mopsa. W. De La Mare.—DeBg
The golden journey to Samarkand. J. E. Flecker.—BoGj (sel.)—PaH
Gone forever. B. Mills.—DuR
Hexameter and pentameter. Unknown.—GrCt
How to eat a poem. E. Merriam.—AgH—DuR—MeI
I, says the poem. E. Merriam.—ArT-3—MeI
"If all the pens that ever poets held." From Tamburlaine the Great. C. Marlowe.—GrCt
In a spring still not written of. R. Wallace.—CoBn
In the red. J. Stephens.—StS
Inside a poem. E. Merriam.—ArT-3—MeI
Introduction to the Songs of experience. W. Blake.—BlP
  The poet's voice.—GrCt
Invocation. From John Brown's body. S. V. Benét.—BrA
"It is a pleasure." Tachibana Akemi.—LeMw
"Keep a poem in your pocket." B. S. De Regniers.—LaPd
Leaning on a limerick. E. Merriam.—MeI
"The limerick's lively to write." D. McCord.—BrLl
Literary love. H. Kemp.—BoH
Literature: The god, its ritual. Merrill Moore.—DuS
"Little song." C. B. de Gasztold.—GaC
The market. J. Stephens.—StS
Mona Lisa. E. Merriam.—MeI
A muse of fire. From King Henry V. W. Shakespeare.—GrCt
No time for poetry. J. Fields.—BoA
The North star whispers to the blacksmith's son. V. Lindsay.—LiP
O black and unknown bards. J. W. Johnson.—BoA
"Only be willing to search for poetry, and there will be poetry." Yuan Mei.—LeMw
  Only be willing to search for poetry.—LaPd
The piper. W. Blake.—CoR—HoB—LaP—LaPd
  Introduction.—BeGj—ClF
  Introduction to Songs of innocence.—ArT-3—BlP—SmM
  Piping down the valleys.—HuS-3
The pit of bliss. J. Stephens.—StS
Poems. P. Kelso.—LeM
The poet ("He sang of life, serenely sweet") P. L. Dunbar.—HaK
Poet ("No rock along the road but knows") D. J. Hayes.—BoA
A poet ("A poet.—He hath put his heart to school") W. Wordsworth.—WoP
The poet and his song. P. L. Dunbar.—BoH
The poet speaks. G. D. Johnson.—BoA
Poets and critics. A. Tennyson.—TeP
Poets hitchhiking on the highway. G. Corso.—DuR
"The poets light but lamps." E. Dickinson.—DiPe
The poet's song. A. Tennyson.—TeP
Popularity. R. Browning.—BrP
Praise. R. M. Rilke.—GrCt
Proem. M. Cawein.—CoBn
Prologue. From Rhymes to be traded for bread. V. Lindsay.—LiP
"P's a poetical bore." O. Herford.—BrLl
Quatrain. E. Merriam.—MeI
Resolution and independence. W. Wordsworth.—CoBn (sel.)—WoP
Rhapsody. W. S. Braithwaite.—BoA—BoH
Rhymes. Y. Y. Segal.—DoW
Sarasvati. J. Stephens.—StS
Seaweed. H. W. Longfellow.—LoPl
"Some limericks—most of them, reely." D. McCord.—BrLl
Some uses for poetry. E. Merriam.—MeI
Standing on earth. From Paradise lost. J. Milton.—GrCt
"There was a young bard of Japan." Unknown.—BrLl
"There was a young poet of Kew." Unknown.—BrLl
This is a poem. H. A. Farley.—LeM
"This was a poet—it is that." E. Dickinson.—DiPe
Thomas Shadwell the poet. From Absalom and Achitopel. J. Dryden.—GrCt
To a poet a thousand years hence. J. E. Flecker.—GrCt
To a poet, who would have me praise certain bad poets, imitators of his and mine. W. B. Yeats.—YeR
To Minerva. T. Hood.—GrCt
To the Muses. W. Blake.—BlP—GrCt
To verse let kings give place. From Elegies. Ovid.—GrCt
Trees. H. Nemerov.—CoBn
Under Ben Bulben. W. B. Yeats.—YeR (sel.)
Unfolding bud. N. Koriyama.—DuR
Valedictory sonnet. W. Wordsworth.—WoP
The voice of the ancient bard. W. Blake.—BlP
Voice in the crowd. T. Joans.—BoA—HaK
Vox populi. H. W. Longfellow.—LoPl
W. J. Reeves.—GrCt
The washerman. U. Joshi.—AlPi
Weltschmerz. F. Yerby.—BoA
What did you say. E. Merriam.—MeI
What hope is here. From In memoriam. A. Tennyson.—TeP
What then. W. B. Yeats.—YeR
When the assault was intended to the city. From Arms and the Muse. J. Milton.—CoR
Words. E. Thomas.—ThG

"The **poor** little bee." Unknown, tr. fr. the Ka-ni-ga.—LeO
Poor little fish. John Ciardi.—CiYk
Poor Mailie's elegy. Robert Burns.—BuPr
Poor man. Eleanor Farjeon.—FaT
"A **poor** man went to hang himself." See One good turn deserves another
"**Poor** Martha Snell has gone away." See Epitaph on Martha Snell
"**Poor** old Jonathan Bing." See Jonathan Bing
"A **poor** old widow, something past her prime." See The Canterbury tales—Chanticleer and the fox
"**Poor** Peter was burnt by the poker one day." See Dangerous sport
"**Poor** soul, the center of my sinful earth." See Sonnets. William Shakespeare
"**Poor** stubborn sheep, why do you struggle." See Sheep shearing
"**Poor** tired Tim. It's sad for him." See Tired Tim
"**Pop** bottles pop-bottles." See Song of the pop-bottlers
Pop goes the weasel. Mother Goose.—BrMg
  "Up and down the city road."—OpF
Popcorn. See Corn and cornfields
"**Popcorn** peanuts clams and gum." See Bar-room matins
Pope, Alexander
  Engraved on the collar of a dog, which I gave to his royal highness.—GrCt
  Epistle to Dr Arbuthnot, sels.
    Sporus.—GrCt
    Why did I write.—GrCt
  An essay on criticism, sel.
    A little learning.—GrCt
  Lines written in Windsor forest.—GrS
  A little learning. See An essay on criticism
  The playing cards. See The rape of the lock
  The rape of the lock, sel.
    The playing cards.—GrCt
  Sporus. See Epistle to Dr Arbuthnot
  Why did I write. See Epistle to Dr Arbuthnot
Pope, Alexander (about)
  Why did I write. From Epistle to Dr Arbuthnot. A. Pope.—GrCt
Popham, Ivor
  The child.—PlE
The **poplar.** Richard Aldington.—BoH
The **poplar** field. William Cowper.—CoR—GrCt
Poplar trees
  Binsey poplars felled 1879. G. M. Hopkins.—CoBn
  The poplar. R. Aldington.—BoH
  The poplar field. W. Cowper.—CoR—GrCt
  The poplars. T. Garrison.—HuS-3
The **poplars.** Theodosia Garrison.—HuS-3
"The **poplars** are felled, farewell to the shade." See The poplar field
"**Poplars** are standing there still as death." See Southern mansion
The **poppet-show.** Unknown.—ReOn
Poppies
  In Flanders fields. J. McCrae.—ThA
  In the poppy field. J. Stephens.—StS
  "Just simply alive." Issa.—LeI
  "Making his way through the crowd." Issa.—IsF—LeOw
  The valley of white poppies. W. Sharp.—ThA
Popularity. Robert Browning.—BrP
Porcupine. Bert Meyers.—CoB
Porcupines
  "As I went over Lincoln bridge." Mother Goose.—OpF
    Mister Rusticap.—BrMg
  The happy hedgehog. E. V. Rieu.—CoB
  The hedgehog ("The hedgehog, from his hollow root") From The shepherd's calendar. J. Clare.—ReO
  Hedgehog ("Twitching the leaves just where the drainpipe clogs") A. Thwaite.—CaD
  The hedgehog ("Yes, Lord, I prick") C. B. de Gasztold.—GaC
  "Little Billy Breek." Mother Goose.—BrMg
  Meeting. C. Dyment.—CoB (sel.)
  Porcupine. B. Meyers.—CoB
"**Poring** on Caesar's death with earnest eye." See Julius Caesar and the honey-bee
"**Porky** & porkie." E. E. Cummings.—LiT
Porphyria's lover. Robert Browning.—BrP
Porpoises. See Dolphins
Portland, Maine
  My lost youth. H. W. Longfellow.—BoGj—CoR—LoPl—PaH
Portrait. See "Buffalo Bill's"
Portrait by a neighbor. Edna St Vincent Millay.—ArT-3—HaL—LaPd—ThA—TuW
Portrait of a girl. See Priapus and the pool
"**Portraits** are to daily faces." Emily Dickinson.—DiPe
Possessions. See Wealth
The **post** captain. Charles Edward Carryl.—CoSs
Post early for space. Peter J. Henniker-Heaton.—BrA
Postal service. See Mail service
Posted as missing. John Masefield.—BlO
The **postman.** Laura E. Richards.—ArT-3
"**Postman's** at the door." See Postman's knock
Postman's knock. Eleanor Farjeon.—FaT
Postmen. See Mailmen
Potatoes
  "Have you seen Old Lovell." Unknown.—BrSg
  The potatoes' dance. V. Lindsay.—HoB—ThA
The **potatoes'** dance. Vachel Lindsay.—HoB—ThA
Pots and pans
  "Hoddy doddy." Mother Goose.—OpF
Potter, Beatrix
  The old woman.—BoGj—LaPd
Pottery
  Anecdote of the jar. W. Stevens.—HoL
  Bible stories. L. W. Reese.—ThA
  Jug and mug. D. McCord.—McE
  "Mrs Mason broke a basin." Mother Goose
    Mrs Mason.—ReOn
    Mrs Mason's basin.—BrF—BrMg
  November. N. Belting.—BeCm

Prayer ("Let us not look upon") Witter Bynner.—PlE
A **prayer** ("Sun, my relative") Unknown.—LeO
Prayer before sleeping. Unknown.—ReS
A **prayer** for little things. Eleanor Farjeon.—StF
A **prayer** for old age. William Butler Yeats.—YeR
Prayer for reptiles. Patricia Hubbell.—LaPd
Prayer in mid-passage. Louis MacNeice.—PlE
"**Prayer** is the little implement." Emily Dickinson.—DiPe
The **prayer** of the butterfly. Carmen Bernos de Gasztold, tr. fr. the French by Rumer Godden.—LiT
The **prayer** of the cat. Carmen Bernos de Gasztold, tr. fr. the French by Rumer Godden.—ArT-3—LaPd
The **prayer** of the cock. Carmen Bernos de Gasztold, tr. fr. the French by Rumer Godden.—ArT-3
The **prayer** of the donkey. Carmen Bernos de Gasztold, tr. fr. the French by Rumer Godden.—ArT-3
The **prayer** of the goldfish. Carmen Bernos de Gasztold, tr. fr. the French by Rumer Godden.—LaPd
The **prayer** of the little ducks. Carmen Bernos de Gasztold, tr. fr. the French by Rumer Godden.—ArT-3—LaPd
The **prayer** of the little pig. Carmen Bernos de Gasztold, tr. fr. the French by Rumer Godden.—LiT
The **prayer** of the mouse. Carmen Bernos de Gasztold, tr. fr. the French by Rumer Godden.—LaPd
The **prayer** of the old horse. Carmen Bernos de Gasztold, tr. fr. the French by Rumer Godden.—LaPd
The **prayer** of the ox. Carmen Bernos de Gasztold, tr. fr. the French by Rumer Godden.—LiT—McWs
Prayer to go to Paradise with the donkeys. Francis Jammes, tr. fr. the French by Alan Conder.—CoB; tr. fr. the French by Richard Wilbur.—ReO
  Francis Jammes: A prayer to go to Paradise with the donkeys, tr. fr. the French by Richard Wilbur.—ArT-3—PlE
Prayer to the moon. Unknown, tr. fr. the Bushman.—LeO
Prayer to the sun god. See Indian songs
"**Prayer** unsaid, and mass unsung." See The sea ritual
Prayers. See also Grace; Hymns
  "All the while." Issa.—IsF
  "At least to pray is left, is left." E. Dickinson.—DiPe
  "At the round earth's imagin'd corners, blow." J. Donne.—PlE
    Blow your trumpets, angels.—GrCt
  The bear. C. B. de Gasztold.—GaC
  The beaver. C. B. de Gasztold.—GaC
  "Because I am poor." Unknown.—LeO
  Blessing for light. Unknown.—ThA
  "Bruadar and Smith and Glinn." D. Hyde.—McWs
  Caliban in the coal mines. L. Untermeyer.—LaPd
  The camel. C. B. de Gasztold.—GaC—ReO
  The centipede. C. B. de Gasztold.—GaC
  Child's prayer. M. L. Duncan.—GrT
  A child's prayer at evening. C. G. D. Roberts.—ReS
  The curse. J. M. Synge.—GrCt
  "Dear Father." M. W. Brown.—LaPd
  "Eastward I stand, mercies I beg." Unknown.—PlE
  "Every morning when I wake." From Under Milk Wood. D. Thomas.—HaL
  The flea. C. B. de Gasztold.—GaC
  The fly. C. B. de Gasztold.—GaC
  For all sorts and conditions. N. Nicholson.—PlE
  For sleep, or death. R. Pitter.—SmM
  Forgive us, O Lord. From Murder in the cathedral. T. S. Eliot.—PlE
  The gazelle. C. B. de Gasztold.—GaC
  The gnat. C. B. de Gasztold.—GaC
  "God be in my head." Unknown.—PlE—SmM
    Hymnus.—GrCt
  "Goosey, goosey, gander." Mother Goose.—GrT—OpF—ReMg—WiMg
    Goosey gander.—BrMg
    Mother Goose rhymes, 56.—HoB
  The hedgehog. C. B. de Gasztold.—GaC
  The Hollow Land. W. Morris.—GrCt
  Holy Willie's prayer. R. Burns.—BuPr
  Hunting prayer. Unknown.—LeO
    "I do not know."—DoC
  "I will bow and be simple." Unknown.—PlE
  An imprecation against foes and sorcerers. From Atharva Veda. Unknown.—AlPi
  Kibbutz Sabbath. Levi Ben Amittai.—PlE
  The ladybird. C. B. de Gasztold.—GaC
  The lamb. C. B. de Gasztold.—GaC
  The lion. C. B. de Gasztold.—GaC
  The litany of the dark people. C. Cullen.—PlE
  The lizard. C. B. de Gasztold.—GaC
  Lord, have mercy on us. T. Nashe.—GrCt
  The Lord's prayer. From Gospel according to Matthew, Bible, New Testament.—PlE
  The mole. C. B. de Gasztold.—GaC
  "Moon, O mother moon, O mother moon." Unknown.—LeO
  Morning prayer. Unknown.—DoC
  The mother hen. C. B. de Gasztold.—GaC
  "My period had come for prayer." E. Dickinson.—PlE
  Never weather-beaten sail. T. Campion.—GrCt
  "Now I lay me down to sleep." Mother Goose.—SmM
    A prayer.—BrMg
  An old Cornish litany. Unknown.—BrSm (sel.)
  Old Sam's wife. Unknown.—GrCt
    On the wife of a parish clerk.—BrSm
  Old shepherd's prayer. C. Mew.—PlE

Prayers—*Continued*
The oyster. C. B. de Gasztold.—GaC
The peacock. C. B. de Gasztold.—GaC
Prayer ("God who created me") H. C. Beeching.—MoS
Prayer ("Have pity on us, Power just and severe") J. H. Wheelock.—PlE
Prayer ("I ask you this") L. Hughes.—PlE
Prayer ("Let us not look upon") W. Bynner.—PlE
A prayer ("Sun, my relative") Unknown.—LeO
Prayer before sleeping. Unknown.—ReS
A prayer for little things. E. Farjeon.—StF
A prayer for old age. W. B. Yeats.—YeR
Prayer for reptiles. P. Hubbell.—LaPd
Prayer in mid-passage. L. MacNeice.—PlE
"Prayer is the little implement." E. Dickinson.—DiPe
The prayer of the butterfly. C. B. de Gasztold.—LiT
The prayer of the cat. C. B. de Gasztold.—ArT-3—LaPd
The prayer of the cock. C. B. de Gasztold.—ArT-3
The prayer of the donkey. C. B. de Gasztold.—ArT-3
The prayer of the goldfish. C. B. de Gasztold.—LaPd
The prayer of the little ducks. C. B. de Gasztold.—ArT-3—LaPd
The prayer of the little pig. C. B. de Gasztold.—LiT
The prayer of the mouse. C. B. de Gasztold.—LaPd
The prayer of the old horse. C. B. de Gasztold.—LaPd
The prayer of the ox. C. B. de Gasztold.—LiT—McWs
Prayer to go to Paradise with the donkeys. F. Jammes.—CoB—ReO
Francis Jammes: A prayer to go to Paradise with the donkeys.—ArT-3—PlE
Prayer to the moon. Unknown.—LeO
Prayer to the sun god. From Indian songs. L. Mertins.—HuS-3
Prayers of steel. C. Sandburg.—LaC—LaPd
The seagull. C. B. de Gasztold.—GaC
The snail. C. B. de Gasztold.—GaC
Song of the sky loom. Unknown.—LeO
The spider. C. B. de Gasztold.—GaC
The starfish. C. B. de Gasztold.—GaC
Stone too can pray. C. Aiken.—PlE—SmM
"Sun, God of living." J. Nez.—BaH
The swallow. C. B. de Gasztold.—GaC—ReBs
"There was a rat, for want of stairs." Mother Goose.—ReMg
A rat.—BrMg
"This little cloud, and this." Unknown.—DoC
"Three elements." From John Brown's body. S. V. Benét.—PlE
To Agni. From Rig Veda. Unknown.—AlPi
To destiny. Unknown.—PlE
To secure victory in battle. From Atharva Veda. Unknown.—AlPi
To the dawn. From Rig Veda. Unknown.—AlPi
To the Maruts. From Rig Veda. Unknown.—AlPi
To the waters. From Rig Veda. Unknown.—AlPi
To the wind. From Rig Veda. Unknown.—AlPi
The toad. C. B. de Gasztold.—GaC
Verses composed on the eve of his execution. J. Graham.—GrCt
Vespers. A. A. Milne.—MiC
"We pray that the beetles appear." Unknown.—LeO
The wet litany. R. Kipling.—GrS
The whale. C. B. de Gasztold.—GaC
"When I pray." M. Classé.—BaH
"When wilt thou save the people." E. Elliott.—PlE
The world's a sea. F. Quarles.—GrCt
The wreckers' prayer. T. G. Roberts.—CoSs
Prayers of steel. Carl Sandburg.—LaC—LaPd
The **preacher**: Ruminates behind the sermon. Gwendolyn Brooks.—LiT
Preachers. See Ministers of the gospel; Sermons
Precepts. See Mahabharata
Precious stones
"An emerald is as green as grass." C. G. Rossetti.—ArT-3
" 'Tis little I could care for pearls." E. Dickinson.—DiPe
Prediction. Barbara Juster Esbensen.—ArT-3
Preface to a twenty volume suicide note. LeRoi Jones.—BoA—HaK
"**Prefer** the cherry when the fruit hangs thick." See Under the boughs
Prejudice. Georgia Douglas Johnson.—BoA
Prejudices. See Likes and dislikes
The **prelude,** sels. William Wordsworth
Books.—WoP
Childhood.—WoP
Fishing.—MoS
France.—WoP
The noble.—GrCt
Residence at Cambridge.—WoP
School-time.—WoP
Skating.—MoS
Summer vacation.—WoP
Prelude ("Still south I went and west and south again") John M. Synge.—CoBn—GrCt
Prelude ("The winter evening settles down") See Prelude I
Prelude I. T. S. Eliot.—ArT-3
Prelude.—CaD—LaC
Preludes for Memnon. Conrad Aiken.—CoBl (sel.)
Prelutsky, Jack
Don't ever seize a weasel by the tail.—CoO
From the sublime to the ridiculous to the sublimely ridculous to the ridiculously sublime.—CoO
Preparation. Robert Francis.—DuR
Presentiment
Presentiment. R. M. Rilke.—LiT

"Presentiment is that long shadow on the lawn." E. Dickinson.—DiL—DiPe
Presentiment.—HoL
Presentiment. See "Presentiment is that long shadow on the lawn"
Presentiment ("I am like a flag by far spaces surrounded") Rainer Maria Rilke, tr. fr. the German by M. D. Herter Norton.—LiT
"**Presentiment** is that long shadow on the lawn." Emily Dickinson.—DiL—DiPe
Presentiment.—HoL
Presents ("I have counted every present with my name") Myra Cohn Livingston.—LiC
Presents ("I wanted a rifle for Christmas") Marchette Chute.—LaP—LaPh
Presidents. See names of presidents, as Lincoln, Abraham
Press, John
African Christmas.—CaD
The **press-gang.** Unknown.—GrCt
Preston, Margaret Junkin
The first Thanksgiving day.—HiL
Pretty cow. Ann Taylor.—HuS-3
The cow.—VrF
"**Pretty** flower, tell me why." See The flower and the lady, about getting up
"**Pretty** Futility." Elizabeth Jane Coatsworth.—AgH
"**Pretty** John Watts." Mother Goose.—OpF
Rats and mice.—ReOn
A **pretty** maid. Mother Goose.—BrMg
"**Pretty** maid, pretty maid." Mother Goose.—OpF
"**Pretty** Miss Jones enjoys valentines." See Miss Jones
Pretty Polly. Byron Herbert Reece.—CoBl
"**Pretty** Polly goes dressed in red." See Pretty Polly
"A **pretty** sneaking knave I knew." See Mr Cromek
A **pretty** thing. Ann and Jane Taylor.—VrF
A **pretty** wench. Mother Goose.—BrMg
Prettyman, Quandra
When Mahalia sings.—AdIa
Prévert, Jacques
How to paint the portrait of a bird.—SmM
Priapus and the pool, sels. Conrad Aiken
Atlantis.—GrS
Portrait of a girl.—BoGj
"When trout swim down Great Ormond street." —HoL—McWs
Pride and vanity. See also Conceit
And off he went just as proud as you please. J. Ciardi.—CiYk
"Are you too proud to kiss me." R. Tagore.—LeMf
Belisarius. H. W. Longfellow.—LoPl
Chanticleer and the fox. From The Canterbury tales. G. Chaucer.—ChT
"E is the egotist dread." O. Herford.—BrLl
Epitaph for a grim woman. P. Eden.—McWs
The flattered flying fish. E. V. Rieu.—ArT-3—BrSm—LaPd
Mehitabel. D. Marquis.—CoB
The flattered lightning bug. From Archy and
The fur coat. J. Stephens.—StS
The gaudy flower. A. and J. Taylor.—GrT
Haven. D. J. Hayes.—BoA
"I shook his hand." N. Noffke.—LeM
In Schrafft's. W. H. Auden.—McWs
King Stephen. From Othello. W. Shakespeare. —ShS
"Leave me alone, I would always shout." M. Lasanta.—BaH
A loud proud someone. J. Ciardi.—CiYk
The mysterious cat. V. Lindsay.—ArT-3—BoGj —GrCt—HuS-3—ThA
Nahuatl poem. Unknown.—HoL
On the vanity of earthly greatness. A. Guiterman.—DuR
One little boy. A. and J. Taylor.—VrF
Poor little fish. J. Ciardi.—CiYk
Primer lesson. C. Sandburg.—HuS-3—TuW
Proud Maisie. From The heart of Midlothian. W. Scott.—BlO—GrCt
Remember now thy Creator. From Ecclesiastes, Bible, Old Testament.—GrCt
"Saw you Eppie Marley, honey." Unknown.—MoB
Someone made me proud of you. J. Ciardi.—CiYk
Sporting Beasley. S. A. Brown.—HaK
Two kinds: Bold and shy. J. Holmes.—McWs
Vain and careless. R. Graves.—CaD—HaL
"When I was small, a woman died." E. Dickinson.—DiPe
Prideaux, Tom
Broadway: Twilight.—LaC
Priest, Alan
"Under the misty sky of the early spring." tr. —LeMw
Priests
The ballad of Father Gilligan. W. B. Yeats.—McWs—PlE—YeR
The brave priest. Mother Goose.—BrMg
The ghostly father. P. Redgrove.—CaMb
The King's highway. J. S. McGroarty.—PaH
The path of the padres. E. D. Osborne.—BrA
The prologue. From The Canterbury tales. G. Chaucer.—ChT
"Whan that Aprille with his shoures sote." —GrCt
"There once was a pious young priest." Unknown.—BrLl
"The wolf has come." Unknown.—WyC
Primas. See Hugo of Orleans
Primer lesson. Carl Sandburg.—HuS-3—TuW
Primer of consequences. Virginia Brasier.—BrSm
Primroses
Peep-primrose. E. Farjeon.—BrSg
Prince, F. T.
Keeper's wood.—SmM
The **prince.** Walter De La Mare.—DeBg
"**Prince** Absalom and Sir Rotherham Redde." See Evening
"**Prince** Finikin and his mamma." Kate Greenaway.—GrT

Princes and princesses
After all and after all. M. C. Davies.—ArT-3—ThA
After ever happily; or, The princess and the woodcutter. I. Serraillier.—CoBl
The prince. W. De La Mare.—DeBg
The princess of Scotland. R. A. Taylor.—GrS
The song of the mad prince. W. De La Mare.—BoGj—SmM
"There was a young prince of Bombay." W. Parke.—BrLl
To the Princess Margaret Tudor. W. Dunbar.—GrS
What the Lord High Chamberlain said. V. W. Cloud.—CoBb
The yak. V. Sheard.—DoW
The **princess,** sels. Alfred Tennyson
The bugle song.—HoB—HuS-3
Blow, bugle, blow.—GrCt
Song.—BlO
"The splendor falls on castle walls."—ArT-3—BoGj
The splendour falls.—CoR
Come down, O maid.—TeP
Now sleeps the crimson petal.—GrCt—TeP
Sweet and low.—BlO—HoB—HuS-3—TeP
A cradle song.—CoSs
Song.—SmM
Tears, idle tears.—TeP
The **princess** of Scotland. Rachel Annand Taylor.—GrS
Princesses. See Princes and princesses
"The **principle** food of the Sioux." Unknown.—BrLl
Pringle, Thomas
Afar in the desert.—ReO (sel.)
Printers and printing
Address from the printer to his little readers. Unknown.—VrF
Epitaph on the proofreader of the Encyclopedia Britannica. C. Morley.—BrSm
"The land was white." Unknown.—GrCt
Prior, Matthew
A reasonable affliction.—BrSm
The **prisoner** of Chillon. George Gordon Byron.—CoD
Prisoners. See Prisons and prisoners
Prisons and prisoners
The ballad of Reading gaol. O. Wilde.—CoD
The house plants. E. J. Coatsworth.—CoSb
The prisoner of Chillon. G. G. Byron.—CoD
A visit to Newgate. H. S. Horsley.—VrF
Women of Syracuse. E. J. Coatsworth.—CoDh
Pritam, Amrita
Silence.—AlPi
A **private** letter to Brazil. G. C. Oden.—BoA—HaK
The **proclamation.** John Greenleaf Whittier.—HiL
"**Procne,** Philomela, and Itylus." See Philomela
Proctor, Thomas
How time consumeth all earthly things.—GrCt
The **produce** district. Thom Gunn.—DuS
Proem. Madison Cawein.—CoBn
Professions. See names of professions, as Doctors
Progress
Progress ("There are two ways now") E. Agnew.—BrA
Progress ("They'll soon be flying to Mars, I hear") S. Hoffenstein.—HiL
Progress ("There are two ways now") Edith Agnew.—BrA
Progress ("They'll soon be flying to Mars, I hear") Samuel Hoffenstein.—HiL
The **progress** of the soul, sel. John Donne
The whale.—GrCt
"The **prohibition** agents came." See Mrs Swartz
Proletarian portrait. William Carlos Williams.—LaC
Prologue ("Even the shrewd and bitter") See Rhymes to be traded for bread
Prologue ("Good, to forgive") See La Saisiaz
Prologue ("Strong Son of God, immortal love") See In memoriam—Strong Son of God
Prologue ("This is the forest primeval. The murmuring pines and the hemlocks") See Evangeline
The **prologue** ("Whan that Aprille with his shoures sote") See The Canterbury tales
Prologue intended for a dramatic piece of King Edward the Fourth. William Blake.—BlP
Promise me a rose. Bob Merrill.—CoBl
Pronunciation
O-u-g-h. D. McCord.—McAd
One, two, three—gough. E. Merriam.—MeI
Proof ("If radio's slim fingers") Ethel Romig Fuller.—ThA
The **proof** ("Shall I love God for causing me to be") Richard Wilbur.—PlE
Propeller. Philip Booth.—DuS
Propellers
Propeller. P. Booth.—DuS
Prophecy in flame. Frances Minturn Howard.—BrA
The **prophet.** Alexander Sergeyevich Pushkin, tr. fr. the Russian by Babette Deutsch.—PlE
Prophets
The prophet. A. S. Pushkin.—PlE
A **proposal.** Mother Goose.—BrMg
Proserpine
The garden of Proserpina. From The faerie queene. E. Spenser.—GrCt
Proserpine. From The garden of Proserpine. A. C. Swinburne.—GrCt
Proserpine. See The garden of Proserpine
Prospice. Robert Browning.—BrP
Protection. See King Henry VI
Prothalamion. Edmund Spenser.—GrCt
"The **proud** Aegyptian queen, her Roman guest." See And she washed his feet with her tears, and wiped them with the hairs of her head
The **proud** farmer. See A gospel of beauty
"**Proud** in a cloud of sun." See Deer
Proud Maisie. See The heart of Midlothian
"**Proud** Maisie is in the wood." See The heart of Midlothian—Proud Maisie
"**Proud** men." See The kallyope yell

The **proud** Navajo. Phillip Kee.—BaH
Prout, Father, pseud. (Francis Sylvester Mahoney)
The bells of Shandon.—CoR—GrCt—PaH
A **proverb.** Unknown, tr. fr. the Turkish by E. Powys Mathers.—CoBl
Proverbs. See also Superstitions
"Birds of a feather flock together." Mother Goose.—ReMg
"But they that wait upon the Lord shall renew their strength." From Isaiah, Bible, Old Testament.—ArT-3
"Cast thy bread upon the waters." From Ecclesiastes, Bible, Old Testament.—ArT-3
Day-dreamer. Unknown.—ArT-3
"Eat at pleasure." Mother Goose.—AgH
"For God hath not given us the spirit of fear." From Second Timothy, Bible, New Testament.—ArT-3
Good advice. Unknown.—ArT-3
"He that is slow to anger is better than the mighty." From Proverbs, Bible, Old Testament.—ArT-3
"He who has never known hunger." E. J. Coatsworth.—ArT-3
"If a jackal bothers you, show him a hyena." Unknown.—DoC
Lesson from a sun-dial. Unknown.—ArT-3
The marriage of heaven and hell. W. Blake.—BlP
Motto. Unknown.—ArT-3
Observations. From Naladiyar. Unknown.—AlPi
Of courtesy. A. Guiterman.—ArT-3
Of giving. A. Guiterman.—ArT-3
Of quarrels. A. Guiterman.—ArT-3
A proverb. Unknown.—CoBl
"A pullet in the pen." Mother Goose.—AgH
Short sermon. Unknown.—ArT-3
Similia similibus. J. H. Morgan.—BrSm
"A soft answer turneth away wrath." From Proverbs, Bible, Old Testament.—ArT-3
A merry heart.—HuS-3
"To sleep easy at night." Mother Goose.—AgH
How to sleep easy.—BrMg
"Wilful waste brings woeful want." Mother Goose.—AgH
Proverbs, sels. Bible, Old Testament
"He that is slow to anger is better than the mighty."—ArT-3
"A soft answer turneth away wrath."—ArT-3
A merry heart.—HuS-3
"**Prr.**" See Sparrows
"**P's** a poetical bore." Oliver Herford.—BrLl
"**P's** the proud policeman." See All around the town
Psalm 19. See Psalms
Psalm 23. See Psalms
Psalm 24. See Psalms
Psalm 37. See Psalms
Psalm 90. See Psalms
Psalm 95. See Psalms
Psalm 98. See Psalms
Psalm 100. See Psalms
Psalm 103. See Psalms
Psalm 107. See Psalms
Psalm 136. See Psalms
Psalm 147. See Psalms
Psalm 150. See Psalms
Psalm of the fruitful field. A. M. Klein.—DoW
Psalm CXLVII, sel. Christopher Smart
Foot, fin or feather.—ReO
Psalm to my belovèd. Eunice Tietjens.—CoBl
Psalms, sels. Bible, Old Testament
Psalm 19
The heavens.—GrCt
Psalm 23.—ArT-3
The Lord is my shepherd.—HuS-3
Psalm 24.—ArT-3
The earth is the Lord's.—PlE
Psalm 37.—ArT-3
Psalm 90
"Lord, thou hast been our dwelling place." —PlE
Psalm 95.—HoB
Psalm 98
"O sing unto the Lord a new song."—PlE
Psalm 100.—ArT-3—HoB
Psalm 103.—ArT-3
Psalm 107
They that go down to the sea.—GrCt
Psalm 136.—HoB
Psalm 147.—ArT-3
Psalm 150.—ArT-3
Laudate dominum.—GrCt
Psychological prediction. Virginia Brasier.—CoBb
Ptarmigan ("O ptarmigan, O ptarmigan") David McCord.—McAd
The **ptarmigan** ("The ptarmigan is strange") Unknown.—CoB
"The **ptarmigan** is strange." See The ptarmigan
A **public** nuisance. Reginald Arkell.—MoS
Puck's song. See A midsummer-night's dream
Pudden Tame. Unknown.—GrCt
"**Puffed** by a wind, sails." Kyorai, tr. fr. the Japanese by Harry Behn.—BeCs
"A **pullet** in the pen." Mother Goose.—AgH
The **pulley.** George Herbert.—PlE
Pulsifer, Susan Nichols
The friendly rock.—LaP
The sounding fog.—LaPd
Tall city.—LaC
Pumas
"A Boston boy went out to Yuma." D. D.—BrSm
The **pumpkin.** Robert Graves.—BrSg—LaPd
Pumpkins
Coach. E. Farjeon.—FaT
The pumpkin. R. Graves.—BrSg—LaPd
Pumpkins ("At the end of the garden") J. Cotton.—CoBn
Pumpkins ("October sun for miles and miles and miles") D. McCord.—McAd
Theme in yellow. C. Sandburg.—ArT-3—HuS-3
Pumpkins ("At the end of the garden") John Cotton.—CoBn

Pumpkins ("October sun for miles and miles and miles") David McCord.—McAd
"**Punch** and Judy." Mother Goose.—BrMg
Punctuality
Punctuality. Mother Goose.—BrMg
Punctuality. Mother Goose.—BrMg
Punctuation
Ditto marks; or, How do you amuse a muse. E. Merriam.—MeI
"I saw a fishpond all on fire." Mother Goose. —GrCt—OpF
Missing commas.—BrMg
"I saw a pack of cards gnawing a bone." Mother Goose.—OpF
Missing commas.—BrMg
"I saw a peacock with a fiery tail." Mother Goose.—BlO—MoB—OpF
I saw a peacock.—GrCt—SmM
Missing commas.—BrMg
Punishment. See also Retribution
The ballad of Reading gaol. O. Wilde.—CoD
The crying child. E. Turner.—VrF
Dirge for a bad boy. E. V. Rieu.—CoBb
"Doctor Faustus was a good man." Mother Goose.—ReMg
"Don't-care didn't care." Unknown.—BlO
The dunce ("Miss Bell was almost six years old") E. Turner.—VrF
The dunce ("This is a sight to give us pain") M. Elliott.—VrF
"Here's the tailor with his sheers." Unknown. —VrF
The hoyden. E. Turner.—VrF
"I punished my child." Issa.—IsF
Improper words. E. Turner.—VrF
"Little Polly Flinders." Mother Goose.—OpF—WiMg
Polly Flinders.—BrMg
Matilda. H. Belloc.—BlO
The opportune overthrow of Humpty Dumpty. G. W. Carryl.—CoBb
Quarrelsome children. E. Turner.—VrF
Rebecca. H. Belloc.—DuR—TuW
The sash. E. Turner.—VrF
Self-sacrifice. H. Graham.—CoBb
"Speak roughly to your little boy." From Alice's adventures in wonderland. L. Carroll.—BlO
The dutchess' lullaby.—CoBb
What someone said when he was spanked on the day before his birthday. J. Ciardi.—CiYk
The whipping. R. E. Hayden.—AdIa
The **puppet** play. Padraic Colum.—CoR
Puppets and puppetry
"A pin to see the puppet show." Unknown.—MoB
The poppet-show. Unknown.—ReOn
"Punch and Judy." Mother Goose.—BrMg
The puppet play. P. Colum.—CoR
Puppy. Robert L. Tyler.—DuR
Puppy and I. A. A. Milne.—ArT-3—LaPd
"The **puppy** asleep." Issa, tr. fr. the Japanese by R. H. Blyth.—LeI
"A **puppy** whose hair was so flowing." Oliver Herford.—BrLl
Purdy, Alfred
The rattlesnake.—DoW
Purification. Unknown, tr. fr. the Pima by Harry Behn.—BeG
The **purist.** Ogden Nash.—BoGj—BrSm
Puritans
The puritan's ballad. E. Wylie.—CoBl
Thoughts for St Stephen. C. Morley.—BrSm
The **puritan's** ballad. Elinor Wylie.—CoBl
Purple (Color)
What is purple. M. O'Neill.—OnH
"**Purple,** yellow, red, and green." Mother Goose. —BrMg
Pursuit of love. Unknown.—GrCt
Pushcart row. Rachel Field.—BrSg
Pushkin, Alexander Sergeyevich
Fragment of a bylina.—LiT
Grapes.—HoL
The prophet.—PlE
"**Puss** came dancing out of the barn." Mother Goose.—OpF
Bagpipes.—BrMg
"**Pussicat,** wussicat, with a white foot." Mother Goose.—OpF
"**Pussy** at the fireside." See "Pussy at the fireside suppin' up brose"
"**Pussy** at the fireside suppin' up brose." Mother Goose.—OpF
"Pussy at the fireside."—SmM
Pussy cat. See "Pussy cat ate the dumplings"
Pussy-cat. See "Pussy-cat, pussy-cat, where have you been"
"**Pussy** cat ate the dumplings." Mother Goose.—OpF
Pussy cat.—BrMg
"**Pussy** cat mew jumped over a coal." Mother Goose.—OpF
"**Pussy-cat,** pussy-cat." See "Pussy-cat, pussy-cat, where have you been"
"**Pussy-cat,** pussy-cat, where have you been." Mother Goose.—HuS-3—OpF—WiMg
Mother Goose rhymes, 19.—HoB
Pussy-cat.—BrMg
"Pussy-cat, pussy-cat."—ArT-3
"**Pussy** cat sits beside the fire." Mother Goose.—OpF
"**Pussy** has a whiskered face." Christina Georgina Rossetti.—ArT-3
"**Pussy,** pussy baudrons." Unknown.—MoB
Pussy willow song. Unknown.—CoO
Pussy willows. See Willow trees
Pussy willows ("Close your eyes") Aileen Fisher. —FiI
Pussy willows ("Every spring the pussy willows") Aileen Fisher.—FiC
Put out my eyes. Rainer Maria Rilke, tr. fr. the German by Babette Deutsch.—HoL
"**Put** out my eyes, and I can see you still." See Put out my eyes
"**Put** the pine tree in its pot by the doorway." See February

"**Put** the rubber mouse away." See For a dead kitten
"**Put** your head, darling, darling, darling." See Dear dark head
Putting on a nightgown. Mother Goose.—BrMg
Pygmies
"But can see there, and laughing there." G. Brooks.—HaK
Dance of the animals. Unknown.—DoC—LeO
"Moon, O mother moon, O mother moon." Unknown.—LeO
Pyle, Katherine
The sweet tooth.—AgH—CoBb
The visitor.—CoBb
The **python.** Hilaire Belloc.—BrSm
"A **python** I should not advise." See The python

Q

"**Q** is for the quietness." See All around the town
Quack. Walter De La Mare.—ArT-3—CoB—DeBg
"**Quack.** Quack." See Ducks at dawn
"**Quadroon** mermaids, Afro angels, black saints." See A ballad of remembrance
Quails. See Partridges and quails
The **Quaker** graveyard in Nantucket. Robert Lowell.—PaH
Quakers
The Quaker graveyard in Nantucket. R. Lowell.—PaH
"The Quaker's wife sat down to bake." Unknown.—MoB
"The **Quaker's** wife sat down to bake." Unknown.—MoB
"The **quality** of mercy is not strained." See The merchant of Venice—Mercy
"The **quality** of these trees, green height; of the sky, shining; of water, a clear flow; of the rock, hardness." See Shine, Republic
Qualthrough, Noelene
"It lies in the groove."—LeM
The **Quangle** Wangle's hat. Edward Lear.—HoB
Quarles, Francis
A good-night.—ReS
The world's a sea.—GrCt
Quarrels and quarreling. See also Fights
Mrs Snipkin and Mrs Wobblechin. L. E. Richards.—ArT-3—HuS-3
"Mother dear." Unknown.—DoC
"My little old man and I fell out." Mother Goose.—ReMg
Squabbles.—BrMg
Of quarrels. A. Guiterman.—ArT-3
Parting after a quarrel. E. Tietjens.—CoBl
Quarrelsome children. E. Turner.—VrF
Quarrelsome children. Elizabeth Turner.—VrF
Quatrain. Eve Merriam.—MeI
Quebec, Canada
Québec May. E. Birney.—DoW
Québec May. Earle Birney.—DoW
Quechua Indians. See Indians of the Americas—Quechua
"**Queen,** and huntress, chaste, and fair." See Cynthia's revels—Hymn to Diana
Queen Anne. Unknown.—GrCt
"**Queen** Anne, Queen Anne, has washed her lace." See Queen Anne's lace
Queen Anne's lace
Queen Anne's lace. M. L. Newton.—ThA
Queen Anne's lace. Mary Leslie Newton.—ThA
Queen Caroline. See "Queen, Queen Caroline"
"**Queen** Cassiopeia." Eleanor Farjeon.—FaT
"A **queen** lived in the South." See Dagonet's canzonet
Queen Mab ("A little fairy comes at night") Thomas Hood.—HuS-3
Queen Mab ("O, then, I see Queen Mab hath been with you") See Romeo and Juliet
"**Queen** Mary, Queen Mary, my age is sixteen." Unknown.—MoB
Queen Mary's men. Unknown.—MoB
Queen Nefertiti. Unknown.—SmM
The **queen** of fairies. Unknown.—SmM
"The **Queen** of Hearts." See "The Queen of Hearts she made some tarts"
"The **Queen** of Hearts she made some tarts." Mother Goose.—OpF
Mother Goose rhymes, 13.—HoB (sel.)
"The Queen of Hearts."—BrF—BrMg—WiMg
"The **Queen** of Sheba met Tom Smith." See Consequences
"The **queen** of Sheba was a true romantic." See Dedicated to her highness
"The **queen** only embroiders. She cannot read." See Aux Tuileries 1790
"**Queen,** Queen Caroline." Mother Goose.—OpF
Queen Caroline.—BrMg
Queens. See Kings and rulers
Queens. John M. Synge.—GrCt
"**Queer** are the ways of a man I know." See The phantom horsewoman
Quennell, Peter
Small birds.—ReBs
Quenneville, Freda
Mother's biscuits.—DuR
A **question** ("I asked a seagull on the bay") Unknown, ad. fr. the Japanese by Charlotte B. DeForest.—DePp
The **question** ("People always say to me") Karla Kuskin.—LaPd
Question in a field. Louise Bogan.—HoL
A **question** of weather. K. C. Katrak.—AlPi
Questioning faces. Robert Frost.—CoB
Questions of a studious working man. Bertolt Brecht, tr. fr. the German by Yvonne Kapp.—SmM
"**Quick.** Grab the baby, the precious pet." See Short history of man
"**Quickly** fly away." Issa, tr. fr. the Japanese by Nobuyuki Yuasa.—IsF
The **quiet** child. Rachel Field.—ReS
Quiet fun. Harry Graham.—BrSm

"**Quiet** mist, the milk of dreams." See Evening star
Quiet woods. See Two gentlemen of Verona
"**Quietly** and softly it came." See The dew
"**Quietness** clings to the air." See The snow fall
"The **quietude** of a soft wind." See The creditor
"**Quilly-quo.**" See Snowman
Quilts
Kivers. A. Cobb.—BrA
"**Quinquireme** of Nineveh from distant Ophir." See Cargoes
"**Quite** unexpectedly as Vasserot." See The end of the world

R

"**R** is for the restaurant." See All around the town
"**R-p-o-p-h-e-s-s-a-g-r.**" E. E. Cummings.—CoB
Rabbi Ben Ezra. Robert Browning.—BrP
"**Rabbi** Ben Levi, on the Sabbath, read." See Tales of a wayside inn—The legend of Rabbi Ben Levi
The **rabbit** ("Brown bunny sits inside his burrow") Edith King.—HuS-3
The **rabbit** ("Hearing the hawk squeal in the high sky") Edna St Vincent Millay.—CoB
The **rabbit** ("I see a rabbit drinking at a stream") Philip McIntyre, Jr.—LeM
The **rabbit** ("When they said the time to hide was mine") Elizabeth Madox Roberts.—ArT-3—BrSg—CoB—HoB—LaP—TuW
Rabbit and lark. James Reeves.—StF
A **rabbit** as king of the ghosts. Wallace Stevens.—ReO
The **rabbit** man. Mother Goose.—BrMg
"The **rabbit** sits upon the green." See Vice versa
Rabbit skin. See "Bye baby bunting"
Rabbits
The A B C bunny. Wanda Gág.—ArT-3
Adventure. N. B. Turner.—HuS-3
"And timid, funny, brisk little bunny." C. G. Rossetti.—ArT-3
As soon as it's fall. A. Fisher.—FiC
Done for. W. De La Mare.—BlO—DeBg
Epitaph on a hare. W. Cowper.—BlO—CoB
The hare. W. De La Mare.—ArT-3—TuW
The hare and the tortoise. I. Serraillier.—CoB
Hares at play. J. Clare.—ReO
Meeting the Easter bunny. R. B. Bennett.—ArT-3
Noah and the rabbit. H. Chesterman.—ReO
The old squire. W. S. Blunt.—MoS
The rabbit ("Brown bunny sits inside his burrow") E. King.—HuS-3
The rabbit ("Hearing the hawk squeal in the high sky") E. St V. Millay.—CoB
The rabbit ("I see a rabbit drinking at a stream") P. McIntyre, Jr.—LeM
The rabbit ("When they said the time to hide was mine") E. M. Roberts.—ArT-3—BrSg—CoB—HoB—LaP—TuW
Rabbit and lark. J. Reeves.—StF
A rabbit as king of the ghosts. W. Stevens.—ReO
The rabbit man. Mother Goose.—BrMg
Rabbits. R. Fabrizio.—SmM
The rabbits' song outside the tavern. E. J. Coatsworth.—ArT-3
Rapid reading. D. McCord.—McAd
The snare. J. Stephens.—ArT-3—BlO—CoB—LaP—LaPd—McWs—SmM—StS—ThA
"So have I seen some fearful hare maintain." From Annus mirabilis. J. Dryden
Annus mirabilis.—CoB
A story in the snow. P. R. Crouch.—ArT-3
"There was an old person whose habits." E. Lear
Limericks.—HoB
Time for rabbits. A. Fisher.—FiC—LaPh
To a starved hare in the garden in winter. C. T. Turner.—SmM
To three small rabbits in a burrow. M. Kennedy.—CoB
Twin Lakes hunter. A. B. Guthrie, Jr.—DuR
Two songs of a fool. W. B. Yeats.—ReO
Vice versa. C. Morgenstern.—ReO
What if. M. C. Livingston.—LiC
The white rabbit. E. V. Rieu.—SmM
White season. F. M. Frost.—ArT-3—CoB
Why rabbits jump. Unknown.—DePp
Rabbits. Ray Fabrizio.—SmM
"**Rabbits** and foxes." See As soon as it's fall
"**Rabbits** and squirrels." See The reason
"**Rabbits** have fur." See Rabbits
The **rabbits'** song outside the tavern. Elizabeth Jane Coatsworth.—ArT-3
Raccoon. William Jay Smith.—ArT-3
Raccoons
Mill valley. M. C. Livingston.—LiC
Raccoon. W. J. Smith.—ArT-3
Raccoons. A. Fisher.—LaP—LaPd
"There once was a knowing raccoon." M. M. Dodge.—BrLl
Raccoons. Aileen Fisher.—LaP—LaPd
The **race.** Aileen Fisher.—FiIo
Race relations
All one people. From The people, yes. C. Sandburg.—BrA
America. C. McKay.—BoH
Award. R. Durem.—AdIa
The ballad of Sue Ellen Westerfield. R. E. Hayden.—HaK
Black is a soul. J. White.—AdIa
A black man talks of reaping. A. Bontemps.—AdIa—BoA—BoH—HaK
The black man's lament; or, How to make sugar. A. Opie.—VrF
Black Narcissus. G. W. Barrax.—HaK
Brown river, smile. J. Toomer.—BoA
The Chicago Defender sends a man to Little Rock, Fall, 1967. G. Brooks.—BoA
Circles. From The people, yes. C. Sandburg.—BrA
Color. E. Merriam.—MeI
Common dust. G. D. Johnson.—BoA
Cross. L. Hughes.—AdIa—BoA

Dark symphony. M. B. Tolson.—BoA
Daybreak in Alabama. L. Hughes.—BrA
Dialect quatrain. M. B. Christian.—BoA
The emancipation of George-Hector (a colored turtle). M. Evans.—BoA
Encountering. M. J. Fuller.—BaH
For a lady I know. C. Cullen.—AdIa—BrSm—HaK
Four epitaphs.—BoA
Hypocrites. Monk.—BaH
I don't mind. C. Jackson.—LeM
I dream a world. L. Hughes.—BoA—BoH
"I, too, sing America." L. Hughes.—AdIa
I, too.—BoA—HaK
Incident. C. Cullen.—AdIa—HoB—HoL—ThA
Is this life. H. Harrington.—BaH
"Leave me alone, I would always shout." M. Lasanta.—BaH
The lynching. C. McKay.—AdIa
Me and the mule. L. Hughes.—AdIa
Mr Z. M. C. Holman.—HaK
A moment please. S. Allen.—AdIa—BoA—HaK
My mother. T. Kee.—BaH
Negro hero. G. Brooks.—HaK
Old Lem. S. A. Brown.—AdIa
Outcast. C. McKay.—BoA
A poem for black hearts. L. Jones.—AdIa
Prejudice. G. D. Johnson.—BoA
Salute. O. Pitcher.—HaK
So quietly. L. P. Hill.—AdIa
Status symbol. M. Evans.—AdIa
Strong men. S. A. Brown.—BoH
Tableau. C. Cullen.—BrA—HaK
"This is a world full of Negroes and whites." D. Peterson.—BaH
Tired. F. Johnson.—AdIa—HaK
To Richard Wright. C. K. Rivers.—AdIa—BoA
We wear the mask. P. L. Dunbar.—AdIa—BoA—BoH
We're free. C. Williams.—BaH
"What will become." B. Brown.—BaH
"Where am I going." L. Hargrove.—BaH
Where, when, which. L. Hughes.—HaK
The white house. C. McKay.—BoA
Why. J. F. Velez.—BaH
"Why do the white man lie." L. Curry.—BaH
Why isn't the world happy. R. Lewis.—BaH
Why prejudice. B. Chase.—BaH
The world I see. M. Evans.—HaK
You've got to be taught. From South Pacific. O. Hammerstein, II.—BrA
Race starting. See "Bell horses, bell horses, what time of day"
Races and racing
The hare and the tortoise. I. Serraillier.—CoB
Races and racing—Boat
The boat race. From Aeneid. Virgil.—MoS
Races and racing—Bicycle
Bicycalamity. E. W. Peters.—MoS
Races and racing—Chariot
The chariot race. From The Georgics. Virgil.—MoS
Races and racing—Foot
Atalanta's race. W. Morris.—CoD
"Bell horses, bell horses, what time of day." Mother Goose.—ArT-3
Race starting.—BrMg
A mighty runner, variation of a Greek theme. E. A. Robinson.—MoS
Notes on a track meet. D. McCord.—MoS
"One for the money." Mother Goose.—HuS-3
Runner ("All visible, visibly") W. H. Auden.—MoS
The runner ("On a flat road runs the well-train'd runner") W. Whitman.—MoS
The runner ("Suddenly with intense") A. Grilikhes.—MoS
The sluggard. Lucilius.—MoS
The sprinters. L. Murchison.—MoS
The start. Unknown.—MoS
"This torch, still burning in my hand." From The Greek anthology. Krinagoras.—MoS
To James. From Notes found near a suicide. F. Horne.—BoA—BoH—HaK
Races and racing—Horse
At Galway races. W. B. Yeats.—MoS
At grass. P. Larkin.—CaD—MoS
Galway races. Unknown.—MoS
Morning workout. B. Deutsch.—MoS
Racing. See Races and racing
Radcliffe, Martin
"Is God dead."—LaC
Radhadevi's dance. See Hammira-mahakavya
Radio
Proof. E. R. Fuller.—ThA
Raffel, Burton
On watching the construction of a skyscraper. —DuR—LaC
Riddle #29: The moon and the sun. tr.—BoGj
The **raft.** See Three poems about Mark Twain
Raftery, Gerald
Apartment house.—BrA—DuR—LaC
"**Ragged** and tough." See Not ragged-and-tough
The **raggedy** man. James Whitcomb Riley.—HoB—HuS-3
The **raggle,** taggle gypsies. Unknown.—ArT-3—HuS-3
The wraggle taggle gypsies.—McWs
"**Raging** wind." Kazue Mizumura.—MiI
Rags. Eleanor Farjeon.—FaT
Ragweeds
The ragwort. J. Clare.—GrCt
The **ragwort.** John Clare.—GrCt
"**Ragwort,** thou humble flower with tattered leaves." See The ragwort
Raha, Asokbijay
Conjecture.—AlPi
The **railroad** cars are coming. Unknown.—BrA
"The **railroad** track is miles away." See Travel
Railroadmen. See Railroads
Railroads
Casey Jones. Unknown.—BlO—HiL—McWs
Coal for Mike. B. Brecht.—LiT
Continental crossing. D. B. Thompson.—BrA
Crossing. P. Booth.—BrA—DuR
Crossing Kansas by train. D. Justice.—DuR
Depot in a river town. M. Williams.—DuS
Engine. J. S. Tippett.—HoB

Moods of rain. V. Scannell.—CoBn
"New moon, come out, give water for us." Unknown.—LeO
"O owl." Issa.—IsF
"On a rainy spring day." Issa.—IsF
On a wet day. F. Sacchetti.—CoBn
Pearls on the grass. G. Mohanty.—LeM
"Please to have a little rain." A. Fisher.—FiI
Rain ("Dancing dancing down the street") E. Young.—ArT-3
The rain ("I hear leaves drinking rain") W. H. Davies.—ArT-3—BrSg
Rain ("I love rain") L. Heron.—LeM
Rain ("I woke in the swimming dark") W. De La Mare.—DeBg
Rain ("It ain't no use to grumble and complain") J. W. Riley.—CoBn
Rain ("It's raining, raining all around") P. Williams.—LeM
Rain ("It's watering time") R. Drillich.—LeM
Rain ("Rain falls gently down") B. Eng.—BaH
Rain ("Rain hits over and over") A. Stoutenburg.—LaPd
Rain ("Rain is") M. Taylor.—BaH
Rain ("The rain is raining all around") R. L. Stevenson.—ArT-3—BoGj—HoB—HuS-3
Rain ("Rain on the green grass") Mother Goose. —ArT-3—BrMg
Rain ("The rain screws up its face") A. K. Smith.—LeM
"Rain before seven." Mother Goose.—BrMg—ReMg
Rain chant. From Indian songs. L. Mertins.—HuS-3
Rain dance. B. Krasnoff.—LeM
Rain in the night. A. J. Burr.—ArT-3—ThA
Rain in the Southwest. R. S. Kelley.—BrA
"Rain is leaking in." Issa.—IsF
"Rain, rain, go away (come again)." Mother Goose.—ArT-3
To the rain.—BrMg
"Rain, rain, go away (this is mother's washing day)." Mother Goose.—OpF
"Rain, rain, go to Spain." Mother Goose.—WiMg
"Rain, rain, rattle stanes." Unknown.—MoB
Rain riddle. Unknown.—DePp
Rain riders. C. Scollard.—ArT-3
"The rain showers down." Unknown.—LeO
Rain sizes. J. Ciardi.—HuS-3
Rain-walking. M. C. Livingston.—LiC
"Rain went sweeping on." Sho-U.—BeCs
Raindrops. K. Dickinson.—LeM
"The rains of spring." Lady Ise.—ArT-3
The rainwalkers. D. Levertov.—DuS
The rainy day. R. Tagore.—AlPi
Rainy song. M. Eastman.—BoH
The rainy summer. A. Meynell.—BoGj—GrS
The reason. D. Aldis.—ArT-3
Rhyme of rain. J. Holmes.—LaC
The rhyme of the rain machine. F. W. Clarke. —CoBn
Run in the rain. A. Fisher.—FiIo
"See this beautiful rainy day." A. Grover.—LeM
"She should be." From Poems. J. Lester.—HaK
A shower ("Shower came") Izembō.—ArT-3
The shower ("Waters above: Eternal springs") H. Vaughan.—ClF (sel.)—CoBn—GrCt
Signs of rain. E. Jenner.—CoBn
Small rain. A. L. Gould.—ThA
The song of the rain. Unknown.—LeO
Splish splosh. S. Martul.—LeM
"Spring rain (everything)." Chiyo-ni.—LeMw
"Spring rain (a few)." Issa.—LeOw
"The spring rain (which hangs)." Lady Ise.—BaS
Spring rain ("Leaves make a slow") H. Behn. —ArT-3
Spring rain ("The storm came up so very quick") M. Chute.—ArT-3—LaP
Sudden storm. E. J. Coatsworth.—CoSb
Summer rain ("A shower, a sprinkle") E. Merriam.—LaPd
Summer rain ("Through morning rain") Lin Keng.—LeMw
Summer shower. See "A drop fell on the apple tree"
Summer shower ("Thundering, shimmering, silvery gray") S. Robinson.—ThA
"A sunshiny shower." Mother Goose.—ReMg
"There is an umbrella." V. Cokeham.—LeM
This is a night. E. J. Coatsworth.—CoDh
"This little cloud, and this." Unknown.—DoC
"This lizard, with body poised." Unknown.—LeO
Thunder pools. R. P. T. Coffin.—HaL
A thundery day. S. Meader.—LeM
"U is for umbrellas." From All around the town. P. McGinley.—ArT-3
The umbrella brigade. L. E. Richards.—ArT-3
Very lovely. R. Fyleman.—ArT-3
"Waiting for the children." K. Mizumura.—MiI
"We must overcome the east wind." Unknown. —DoC
Weather. E. Merriam.—MeC
What to do. W. Wise.—ArT-3
"When it rains." A. Fisher.—FiI
"When the dew is on the grass." Mother Goose.—ReMg
Who likes the rain. C. D. Bates.—ArT-3—StF
"Who loves the rain." F. Shaw.—ThA
"Whose town did you leave." R. Wright
Hokku poems.—BoA
The wind and the rain. W. W. Gibson.—ClF
Wind weather. V. Brasier.—HuS-3
Winter rain. C. G. Rossetti.—CoBn
"With hey, ho, the wind and the rain." From King Lear. W. Shakespeare.—ArT-3
"The **rain**." See The firefly
Rain ("Dancing dancing down the street") Ella Young.—ArT-3
The **rain** ("I hear leaves drinking rain") William Henry Davies.—ArT-3—BrSg
Rain ("I love rain") Leila Heron.—LeM

Rain ("I woke in the swimming dark") Walter De La Mare.—DeBg
Rain ("It ain't no use to grumble and complain") James Whitcomb Riley.—CoBn
Rain ("It's raining, raining all around") Pat Williams.—LeM
Rain ("It's watering time") Richard Drillich.—LeM
Rain ("Rain falls gently down") Betty Eng.—BaH
Rain ("Rain hits over and over") Adrien Stoutenburg.—LaPd
Rain ("Rain is") Marcus Taylor.—BaH
Rain ("The rain is raining all around") Robert Louis Stevenson.—ArT-3—BoGj—HoB—HuS-3
Rain ("Rain on the green grass") Mother Goose.—ArT-3—BrMg
Rain ("The rain screws up its face") Adrian Keith Smith.—LeM
"**Rain** before seven." Mother Goose.—BrMg—ReMg
"The **rain** begins. This is no summer rain." See Oregon winter
Rain chant. See Indian songs
"The **rain** comes in sheets." See Sudden storm
"**Rain** comes in various sizes." See Rain sizes
Rain dance. Barbara Krasnoff.—LeM
"**Rain** falls gently down." See Rain
"The **rain** had fallen, the poet arose." See The poet's song
"**Rain** hits over and over." See Rain
Rain in the night. Amelia Josephine Burr.—ArT-3—ThA
Rain in the Southwest. Reeve Spencer Kelley.—BrA
"**Rain** is." See Rain
"The **rain** is clinging to the round rose-cheek." See After rain
"**Rain** is leaking in." Issa, tr. fr. the Japanese by R. H. Blyth.—IsF
"The **rain** is raining all around." See Rain
"The **rain** of a night and a day and a night." See After rain
Rain of leaves. Aileen Fisher.—FiI
"**Rain** on the green grass." See Rain
"**Rain** or hail." E. E. Cummings.—DuS
Rain, rain, and sun. See Idylls of the king
"**Rain,** rain, and sun, a rainbow in the sky." See Idylls of the king—Rain, rain, and sun
"**Rain,** rain, go away (come again)." Mother Goose.—ArT-3
  To the rain.—BrMg
"**Rain,** rain, go away (this is mother's washing day)." Mother Goose.—OpF
"**Rain,** rain, go to Spain." Mother Goose.—WiMg
"**Rain,** rain, rattle stanes." Unknown.—MoB
Rain riddle. Unknown, ad. fr. the Japanese by Charlotte B. DeForest.—DePp
Rain riders. Clinton Scollard.—ArT-3
"The **rain** screws up its face." See Rain
"The **rain** set early in to-night." See Porphyria's lover
"The **rain** showers down." Unknown, tr. fr. the Yoruba.—LeO
Rain sizes. John Ciardi.—HuS-3
"The **rain** to the wind said." See Lodged
Rain-walking. Myra Cohn Livingston.—LiC
"**Rain** went sweeping on." Sho-U, tr. fr. the Japanese by Harry Behn.—BeCs
The **rainbow.** See "My heart leaps up when I behold"
The **rainbow** ("I saw the lovely arch") Walter De La Mare.—ArT-3
The **rainbow** fairies. L. M. Hadley.—StF
"**Rainbow** round the moon." See Moon rainbow
Rainbows
  "As we got." From Poems. J. Lester.—HaK
  "Boats sail on the rivers." C. G. Rossetti.—ArT-3—HoB—HuS-3
  The first rainbow. I. Orleans.—HoB
  "How gray the rain." E. J. Coatsworth.—ArT-3
  Moon rainbow. E. Farjeon.—FaT
  "My heart leaps up when I behold." W. Wordsworth.—ArT-3—BoH
    My heart leaps up.—LaP—WoP
    The rainbow.—CoR
  "Purple, yellow, red and green." Mother Goose.—BrMg
  The rainbow. W. De La Mare.—ArT-3
  The rainbow fairies. L. M. Hadley.—StF
  Skipping ropes. D. Aldis.—HuS-3
  Two somewhat different epigrams. L. Hughes.—HaK
"The **rainbows** all lie crumpled on these hills." See The painted hills of Arizona
"A **raindrop** fell down on a dormouse's nose." See The dormouse
Raindrops. Ken Dickinson.—LeM
"**Raindrops** shimmer down dirty glass." See Raindrops
"**Raining,** raining." See Rain in the night
"The **rains** have come, and frogs are full of glee." See Frogs
"The **rains** of spring." Lady Ise, tr. fr. the Japanese by Olive Beaupré Miller.—ArT-3
The **rainwalkers.** Denise Levertov.—DuS
The **rainy** day ("The day is cold, and dark, and dreary") Henry Wadsworth Longfellow.—LoPl
The **rainy** day ("Sullen clouds are gathering fast over") Rabindranath Tagore, tr. fr. the Bengali by the author.—AlPi
Rainy song. Max Eastman.—BoH
The **rainy** summer. Alice Meynell.—BoGj—GrS
Raison d'être. Oliver Pitcher.—BoA—HaK
Rajan, Tilottama
  In camera.—AlPi
Rake, Peter
  "A strange place."—LeM
Raleigh, Sir Walter (1552-1618)
  "As you came from the holy land."—GrCt
  The coracle. See Pharsalia
  Even such is time.—GrCt
  The lie.—GrCt
  Pharsalia, sel.
    The coracle. tr.—GrCt
  The passionate man's pilgrimage.—GrCt

"Lydia is gone this many a year."—BoGj
The white fury of the spring.—GrS
Reeves, Claude
Down on Roberts' farm.—HiL
Reeves, James
Animals' houses.—StF
The black pebble.—LaPd
The catipoce.—CoB
Cows.—BlO—CoB—StF
The doze.—CoB
Fireworks.—BrSg—LaPh
The four horses.—CoB
A garden at night.—HoB
Giant Thunder.—CoBn—SmM
The intruder.—LaPd
"Let no one suppose."—CoB
May day.—CaD
Mick.—CoB
Mr Kartoffel.—CoO—SmM
Mrs Gilfillan.—LiT
My singing aunt.—BrSm
The nonny.—CoB
The old wife and the ghost.—BrSm—HoB—LaPd
A pig tale.—LaP—SmM
Rabbit and lark.—StF
Run a little.—StF
The sea.—CoSs
Slowly.—BlO
The snail.—BlO—BrSg—CoB
Spells.—SmM
The stone gentleman.—CaD
The three singing birds.—LaPd
The two old women of Mumbling hill.—BrSm
W.—GrCt
Waiting.—StF
You'd say it was a funeral.—BrSm
Reflection ("Beauty is a lily") Lew Sarett.—ThA
Reflection ("I sought to make fair autumn yet more fair") Tomonori, tr. fr. the Japanese by Shotaro Kimura and Charlotte M. A. Peake. —LeMw
Reflections (Mirrored)
The lost star. E. Farjeon.—FaT
The mirror. W. H. Davies.—ThA
Reflection ("Beauty is a lily") L. Sarett.—ThA
Reflection ("I sought to make fair autumn yet more fair") Tomonori.—LeMw
Walking by the stream. Hsin Ch'i-chi.—LeMw
Water picture. M. Swenson.—CoBn—LaC
Reflections dental. Phyllis McGinley.—DuR
Reflections on a gift of watermelon pickle received from a friend called Felicity. John Tobias.—DuR
Reflections outside of a gymnasium. Phyllis McGinley.—MoS
The **reformed** pirate. Theodore Goodridge Roberts.—DoW
Refugee in America. Langston Hughes.—BoH—BrA
"**Refuses.**" See Old tennis player
"**Refusing** to fall in love with God, he gave." See Didymus
"**Regarding** a door." David Antin.—DuS
Rege
Steel.—AlPi
"A **regular** country toad—pebbly." See Ungainly things
Reindeer. See Deer
Relatives. See also names of relatives, as Uncles
"Everybody says." D. Aldis.—ThA
The lost tribe. R. Pitter.—HoL
Relativity and levitation. See "I wish that my room had a floor"
"**Relentless** press of little things." See The lien
Relieving guard. Bret Harte.—CoR
Religion
Baptism. C. G. Bell.—BrA
Brahma. R. W. Emerson.—PlE
Daniel. V. Lindsay.—GrCt—LiP
The Daniel jazz.—SmM
Foreign missions in battle array. V. Lindsay.—LiP
The greater mystery. J. M. O'Hara.—PaH
The holy fair. R. Burns.—BuPr
"I'm ceded, I've stopped being theirs." E. Dickinson.—DiPe
In California there are two hundred and fifty six religions. R. E. Albert.—DuS
Incense. V. Lindsay.—LiP
Lady, three white leopards. From Ash Wednesday. T. S. Eliot.—GrS
The minister. F. Johnson.—HaK
"Some keep the Sabbath going to church." E. Dickinson.—DiPe
The story of Constance. From The Canterbury tales. G. Chaucer.—ChT
Sunday: New Guinea. K. Shapiro.—BrA
Through the varied patterned lace. M. Danner.—HaK
When Peter Jackson preached in the old church. V. Lindsay.—LiP
The Zen archer. J. Kirkup.—PlE
"**Remember** he was poor and country-bred." See Abraham Lincoln
Remember now thy Creator. See Ecclesiastes
"**Remember** now thy Creator in the days of thy youth." See Ecclesiastes—Remember now thy Creator
Remembrance
"I held a jewel in my fingers." E. Dickinson. —DiL—DiPe
"Remembrance has a rear and front." E. Dickinson.—DiPe
"**Remembrance** has a rear and front." Emily Dickinson.—DiPe
Reminiscence II. See "I saw the wind today"
Renascence, sel. Edna St Vincent Millay
"All I could see from where I stood."—LaPd
Rendall, Elizabeth
Buttercup cow.—ArT-3
The **rendezvous.** P. Lal.—AlPi
Renouncement. Alice Meynell.—CoBl
"**Repeat** that, repeat." See The cuckoo
Repentance
Johan the monk. Unknown.—LiT

A **reply** from the Akond of Swat. Ethel Talbot Scheffauer.—BrLl
A **reply** to lines by Thomas Moore. Walter Savage Landor.—GrCt (sel.)
A **reply** to Nancy Hanks. Julius Silberger.—ArT-3
Report from the Carolinas. Helen Bevington.—BrA (sel.)
Reptiles. See also Crocodiles; Lizards; Snakes
Prayer for reptiles. P. Hubbell.—LaPd
Request for requiems. Langston Hughes.—BrSm
Requiem. Robert Louis Stevenson.—BoH—ClF—SmM
Requiems. See Laments
The **rescue.** Hal Summers.—CaD
Residence at Cambridge. See The prelude. William Wordsworth
Resnick, Seymour
Squares and angles. tr.—LaC
Resolution and independence. William Wordsworth.—CoBn (sel.)—WoP
Response. Bob Kaufman.—HaK
Rest hour. George Johnston.—DoW
"The **restless** sea is calling, and I would be away." See Voices
Résumé. Dorothy Parker.—BrSm—DuR
The **resurrection.** Jonathan Brooks.—BoA
Resurrection day. See Judgment day
"**Retire,** my daughter." See Fragment of an English opera
Retribution. See also Punishment
The ballad of Semmerwater. W. Watson.—BlO
Bishop Hatto. R. Southey.—GrCt
The boy who laughed at Santa Claus. O. Nash.—CoBb
The debt. P. L. Dunbar.—BoA—BoH—HaK
The Inchcape rock. R. Southey.—GrCt
Inhuman Henry; or, Cruelty to fabulous animals. A. E. Housman.—CoBb
Little Thomas. F. G. Evans.—CoBb
The sacrilege. T. Hardy.—CoD
The story of Augustus who would not have any soup. H. Hoffmann.—AgH—BoGj—BrSm—CoBb
The story of Augustus.—ArT-3
The **return** ("At fifteen I joined the army") Unknown, tr. by Alan S. Lee.—LeMw
Return ("Sometimes the moment comes for the return") Elizabeth Jane Coatsworth.—CoDh
Return to New York. John Hall Wheelock.—PaH
"**Return** to the most human, nothing less." See Santos: New Mexico
The **returned** volunteer to his rifle. Herman Melville.—HiL
Returning. Ch'en Fu, tr. fr. the Chinese by Henry H. Hart.—LeMw
The **reunion.** Owen Dodson.—BoH
A **reunion** in Kensington. S. J. Cohen.—SmM
Reveilles. See Wake-up poems
Revelation. Leonard Clark.—SmM
Revelations. Sterling A. Brown.—HaK
Revenge
The sisters. A. Tennyson.—TeP
The voyage of Maeldune. A. Tennyson.—TeP
The **Revenge.** Alfred Tennyson.—CoD—TeP
Revere, Paul (about)
Paul Revere. From Tales of a wayside inn. H. W. Longfellow.—ArT-3—HiL—HuS-3—LoPl
"The **Reverend** Henry Ward Beecher." Oliver Wendell Holmes.—BrLl
Henry Ward Beecher.—GrCt
The **reverie** of poor Susan. William Wordsworth.—WoP
Review from Staten island. G. C. Oden.—HaK
A **revivalist** in Boston. Adrienne Cecile Rich.—PlE
Revolution. See United States—History—Revolution
Reward. See "When Jacky's a good boy"
Rexroth, Kenneth
"After the storm." tr.—BaS
"As I row over the plain." tr.—BaS
The boats are afloat. tr.—LeMw
"Gossip grows like weeds." tr.—BaS
The Greek anthology, sel.
"This torch, still burning in my hand." tr.—MoS
"I have always known." tr.—BaS
"I wish I were close." tr.—LiT
"If only the world." tr.—BaS
"In a gust of wind the white dew." tr.—BaS—LeMw
"In the empty mountains." tr.—BaS
"In the eternal." tr.—BaS
"In the evening." tr.—BaS
In the evening I walk by the river. tr.—LeMw
"In the mountain village." tr.—BaS
The lights in the sky are stars.—LiT (sel.)
"Like a wave crest." tr.—BaS
"Out in the marsh reeds." tr.—BaS
The signature of all things.—CoBn (sel.)
South wind. tr.—ArT-3—LeM
"This torch, still burning in my hand." See The Greek anthology
"When I went out." tr.—BaS—LeMw
Reynard the fox. John Masefield.—ReO (sel.)
Reynolds, John Hamilton
Gallantly within the ring.—MoS
Reznikoff, Charles
After reading translations of ancient texts on stone and clay.—GrS
The English in Virginia.—GrS
"In the streets I have just left."—LaC
"The park is green and quiet."—LaC
"The shopgirls leave their work."—LaC
"Two girls of twelve or so at a table."—LaC
"The wind blows the rain into our faces."—LaC
Rhapsody. William Stanley Braithwaite.—BoA—BoH
The **rhinoceros** ("Beware lest you should get a toss") Conrad Aiken.—AiC
The **rhinoceros** ("I love to wallow in the mud") R. P. Lister.—CoB
The **rhinoceros** ("Rhinoceros, your hide looks all undone") Hilaire Belloc.—GrCt
"**Rhinoceros,** your hide looks all undone." See The rhinoceros

Rhinoceroses
The rhinoceros ("Beware lest you should get a toss") C. Aiken.—AiC
The rhinoceros ("I love to wallow in the mud") R. P. Lister.—CoB
The rhinoceros ("Rhinoceros, your hide looks all undone") H. Belloc.—GrCt
"**Rhoda-in-rags.**" See Rags
Rhodes, Nettie
Our largest and smallest cities.—LaC
The **rhodora.** Ralph Waldo Emerson.—CoBn
Rhodoras
The rhodora. R. W. Emerson.—CoBn
Rhyme (about)
Catch a little rhyme. E. Merriam.—LaPd—MeC
Jamboree. D. McCord.—McAd
"O what's the rhyme to porringer." Unknown. —MoB
Rhymes. Y. Y. Segal.—DoW
W. J. Reeves.—GrCt
Rhyme. Elizabeth Jane Coatsworth.—CoSb
A **rhyme** about an electrical advertising sign. Vachel Lindsay.—LiP
"A **rhyme** for ham? Jam." See Jamboree
A **rhyme** for Shrove Tuesday. Unknown.—ClF
Rhyme of rain. John Holmes.—LaC
The **rhyme** of the ancient mariner. See The rime of the ancient mariner
The **rhyme** of the chivalrous shark. Wallace Irwin.—BrSm
The **rhyme** of the rain machine. F. W. Clarke.—CoBn
A **rhymed** address to all renegade Campbellites, exhorting them to return. See Alexander Campbell
Rhymes. Y. Y. Segal, tr. fr. the Yiddish by Miriam Waddington.—DoW
Rhymes for a modern nursery, sels. Paul Dehn
"Hey diddle diddle (the physicists)."—DuR
"In a cavern, in a canyon."—BrSm
"Little Miss Muffet (crouched)."—BrSm—DuR
Rhymes to be traded for bread, sel. Vachel Lindsay
Prologue.—LiP
Rhys, Ernest
Dagonet's canzonet.—GrS
"The **ribs** and terrors in the whale." Herman Melville.—PlE
Rice
Characterization. Yogesvara.—AlPi
December. N. Belting.—BeCm
Rice pudding. A. A. Milne.—CoBb—MiC
"The seed of all song." Bashō.—BeCs
"A small hungry child." Bashō.—BeCs
"Washing my rice hoe." Buson.—BeCs
"The **rice-cutting** moons have gone." See December
Rice pudding. A. A. Milne.—CoBb—MiC
Rich, Adrienne Cecile
Lucifer in the train.—PlE
A revivalist in Boston.—PlE
Rich days. William Henry Davies.—CoBn
Rich man. Eleanor Farjeon.—FaT
"**Rich** or poor or low or high." See Lucky star
"**Richard** has been sent to bed." See Dirge for a bad boy
Richards, Laure E. (Elizabeth)
Antonio.—ArT-3—LaPd
At Easter time.—HoB
The buffalo.—CoO
The egg.—ArT-3
Eletelephony.—ArT-3—BoGj—HoB—LaPd
"The giraffe and the woman."—LaPd
Jippy and Jimmy.—ArT-3
Johnny's by-low song.—HoB
Jumble jingle.—CoO
Kindness to animals.—ArT-3—StF
A legend of Okeefinokee.—HoB
Little John Bottlejohn.—LaPd
Master Jack's song.—AgH
The mermaidens.—HuS-3
Merry thoughts.—CoO
Mrs Snipkin and Mrs Wobblechin.—ArT-3—HuS-3
Molly Pitcher.—HiL
The monkeys and the crocodile.—ArT-3—BrSm—HoB—LaP
A nursery song.—HoB
Old Joe Jones.—AgH
The postman.—ArT-3
Some families of my acquaintance.—CoO
Some fishy nonsense.—ArT-3—StF
The song of the cornpopper.—HoB
Talents differ.—ArT-3
Tom Tickleby and his nose.—CoO
The umbrella brigade.—ArT-3
Was she a witch.—LaPd—LaPh
Riches. See Wealth
Riches. See "My father died a month ago"
Riches ("The countless gold of a merry heart") William Blake.—BlP
"**Rick** draws rabbits on the snow." See Snow pictures
Riddle ("How many hundreds for my sake have died") Unknown.—VrF
A **riddle** ("Nay by Saint Jamy") See The taming of the shrew
A **riddle** ("'Twas in heaven pronounced, and 'twas muttered in hell") Catherine Maria Fanshawe.—GrCt
Riddle ("What is it cries without a mouth") Elizabeth Jane Coatsworth.—CoSb
"A **riddle,** a riddle, as I suppose." Mother Goose. —ArT-3
"**Riddle** cum diddle cum dido." See Kindness to animals
A **riddle** from the Old English. Unknown.—GrCt
"**Riddle** me, riddle me (what is that)." Mother Goose.—OpF
"**Riddle** me, riddle me ree (a little man)." Mother Goose.—BrMg
"**Riddle-me** riddle-me riddle-me-ree (perhaps you)." Mother Goose
Mother Goose rhymes, 28.—HoB
Riddle #29: The moon and the sun. Unknown, tr. fr. the Old English by Burton Raffel.—BoGj

"The **riddle** we can guess." Emily Dickinson.—DiPe
Riddles
Aeiou. J. Swift.—BlO
"An altered look about the hills." E. Dickinson.—DiL—DiPe
Another riddle. From Love's labour's lost. W. Shakespeare.—ShS
"Around the rick, around the rick." Mother Goose.—BrMg
As black as ink. Mother Goose.—ReOn
"As high as a castle." Mother Goose.—OpF
"As I was going o'er London bridge." Mother Goose.—BrMg
"As I was going o'er Tipple Tine." Mother Goose.—OpF
"As I went over Tipple Tyne."—GrCt
"As I was going to St Ives." Mother Goose.—HuS-3—OpF—ReMg—WiMg
Going to St Ives.—BrMg
Mother Goose rhymes, 26.—HoB
"As I was walking in a field of wheat." Mother Goose.—BrMg—OpF
"As I went over Lincoln bridge." Mother Goose.—OpF
Mister Rusticap.—BrMg
"As I went over London bridge." Unknown.—GrCt
"As I went through the garden gap." Mother Goose
Mother Goose rhymes, 31.—HoB
"As light as a feather." Mother Goose.—OpF
"As round as a biscuit." Mother Goose.—OpF
"As round as a butter bowl." Mother Goose.—OpF
"As round as a marble." Mother Goose.—OpF
"As round as a saucer." Mother Goose.—OpF
"As round as an apple (as sharp as a lance)." Mother Goose.—OpF
"As round as an apple, as deep as a cup." Mother Goose.—ArT-3
"As round as an apple."—BrMg
"As white as milk (as soft as silk)." Mother Goose.—OpF
"As white as milk, as black as coal." Mother Goose.—OpF
"At the end of my yard there is a vat." Unknown.—GrCt
"Black I am and much admired." Mother Goose.—BrMg
"Black within, and red without." Mother Goose.—BrMg
Mother Goose rhymes, 27.—HoB
"A bright red flower he wears on his head." Unknown.—WyC
The broad water. Mother Goose.—ReOn
"Brothers and sisters have I none." Unknown.—OpF
"Clothed in yellow, red, and green." Mother Goose.—BrMg
"Come a riddle, come a riddle." Unknown.—MoB
"A dish full of all kinds of flowers." Unknown.—OpF
"Drab habitation of whom." E. Dickinson.—DiPe
"Elizabeth, Elspeth, Betsy and Bess." Mother Goose.—OpF
An enigma. E. A. Poe.—PoP
"An everywhere of silver." E. Dickinson.—DiPe
"Farther in summer than the birds." E. Dickinson.—DiPe
"The fiddler and his wife." Mother Goose.—OpF
"First I am frosted." M. Austin
Rhyming riddles.—ArT-3
"Flour of England, fruit of Spain." Mother Goose.—BrMg
"Four stiff-standers." Mother Goose.—BrMg—GrCt—OpF
Riddle.—BrF
"Goes round the mud." Mother Goose.—BrMg
"A ha'penny here, and a ha'penny there." Unknown.—MoB
"He went to the wood and caught it." Mother Goose.—BrMg
"Hick-a-more, hack-a-more." Mother Goose.—ArT-3
Mother Goose rhymes, 29.—HoB
"Higher than a house." Mother Goose.—ArT-3—BrMg
"Highty tighty, paradighty." Mother Goose.—BrMg—GrCt
"A hill full, a hole full." Mother Goose.—ArT-3
"His bill an auger is." E. Dickinson.—DiPe
"Hoddy doddy." Mother Goose.—OpF
"A house full, a hole full." Mother Goose.—BrMg
"A house full."—OpF—ReOn
The how and the why. A. Tennyson.—TeP
How many birds. Unknown.—ReOn
"Humpty Dumpty sat on a wall . . . (all the king's horses)." Mother Goose.—GrT—OpF—WiMg
Humpty Dumpty.—BrMg
Mother Goose rhymes, 25.—HoB
"I am round like a ball." Unknown
Riddles.—StF
"I am within as white as snow." Unknown.—GrCt
"I can walk on this." Unknown
Riddles.—StF
"I come more softly than a bird." M. Austin
Rhyming riddle.—CoBn
Rhyming riddles.—ArT-3
"I had three little sisters across the sea." Unknown.—MoB
"I have a little sister (she lives)." Mother Goose.—OpF
"I have a little sister they call her Peep-peep." Mother Goose.—ArT-3—BrMg—HuS-3
One eye.—ReOn
"I have long legs." Mother Goose.—OpF
"I have no wings, but yet I fly." M. Austin
Rhyming riddles.—ArT-3

"I like to see it lap the miles." E. Dickinson.—DiL—DiPe—LaPd
"I never speak a word." M. Austin
Rhyming riddles.—ArT-3
"I washed my face in water." Unknown.—GrCt
"If Dick's father is John's son." Unknown.—OpF
"I'm called by the name of a man." Mother Goose.—BrMg
"In marble halls as white as milk." Mother Goose.—BrMg—GrCt—HuS-3—OpF
In marble halls.—ReOn—SmM
"In Mornigan's park there is a deer." Unknown.—GrCt
"In spring I look gay." Mother Goose.—BrMg—OpF
"It has eyes and a nose." Unknown.—WyC
"It sifts from leaden sieves." E. Dickinson.—DiPe
"I've seen you where you never were." Mother Goose.—OpF
"The land was white." Unknown.—GrCt
"Little Billy Breek." Mother Goose.—BrMg
"A little girl (dressed)." Mother Goose.—OpF
"Little Nancy Etticoat." Mother Goose.—BrMg—GrCt—HuS-3
"Little Nanny Etticoat."—ArT-3
Mother Goose rhymes, 30.—HoB
"Lives in winter." Mother Goose.—ArT-3
"Long man legless, came to the door staffless." Mother Goose.—OpF
"A long white barn." Unknown.—GrCt
"My boat is turned up at both ends." Unknown.—WyC
"Noah of old three babies had." Mother Goose.—OpF
"Old Mr Chang, I've heard it said." Unknown.—WyC
"Old Mother Twitchett had (or has) but one eye." Mother Goose.—ArT-3—BrMg
"On yonder hill there is a red deer." Unknown.—GrCt
"The parson, his wife." Unknown.—OpF
"Patches and patches." Mother Goose.—OpF
"Purple, yellow, red, and green." Mother Goose.—BrMg
Rain riddle. Unknown.—DePp
Rat riddles. C. Sandburg.—LaC
Riddle ("How many hundreds for my sake have died") Unknown.—VrF
A riddle ("Nay, by Saint Jamy") From The taming of the shrew. W. Shakespeare.—ShS
A riddle ("'Twas in heaven pronounced, and 'twas muttered in hell") C. M. Fanshawe.—GrCt
Riddle ("What is it cries without a mouth") E. J. Coatsworth.—CoSb
"A riddle, a riddle, as I suppose." Mother Goose.—ArT-3
A riddle from the Old English. Unknown.—GrCt
"Riddle me, riddle me (what is that)." Mother Goose.—OpF
"Riddle me, riddle me ree (a little man)." Mother Goose.—BrMg
"Riddle-me riddle-me riddle-me-ree (perhaps you)." Mother Goose
Mother Goose rhymes, 28.—HoB
Riddle #29: The moon and the sun. Unknown.—BoGj
"The riddle we can guess." E. Dickinson.—DiPe
Riddles. R. Ainsworth.—StF
"A route of evanescence." E. Dickinson.—DiPe
Humming bird.—DiL
"Runs all day and never walks." Mother Goose.—ArT-3
"She slept beneath a tree." E. Dickinson.—DiPe
"A son just born." M. B. Miller.—ArT-3
"Tall and thin." Mother Goose.—OpF
"Tell me, ladies, if you can." Mother Goose.—OpF
"There was a king met a king." Mother Goose.—OpF
"There was a man who went to the fair." Mother Goose.—OpF
"There was a thing a full month old." Mother Goose.—BrMg
"There were three sisters in a hall." Unknown.—OpF
"There's a wee, wee house." Unknown.—MoB
"These are the days when birds come back." E. Dickinson.—DiPe
"Thirty white horses." Mother Goose.—BrMg—OpF—ReOn
"Thirty white horses upon a red hill."—ArT-3
"Twenty white horses."—HuS-3
"This being's most despised by man." Unknown.—OpF
"This is the tree." Unknown.—MoB
"This land was white." Mother Goose.—BrMg
"Twelve pairs hanging high." Mother Goose
Mother Goose rhymes, 51.—HoB
"Two brothers we are." Mother Goose.—BrMg
"Two legs sat upon three legs." Mother Goose.—BrMg—OpF
Two legs.—ReOn
A walnut. Mother Goose.—BrMg
"Wee man o' leather." Unknown.—GrCt
What am I. D. Aldis.—HuS-3—LaPh
"What has feet like plum blossoms." Unknown.—WyC
"White bird featherless." Unknown.—GrCt—ReOn
"A white bird floats down through the air." Unknown.—GrCt
"Without a bridle or a saddle." Mother Goose.—OpF
"You can see me in the country." Unknown
Riddles.—StF
Riddles. Ruth Ainsworth.—StF
Ride a cock-horse. See "Ride a cock-horse to Banbury cross (to see a fair or fine lady)"

Sir Smashum Uppe.—CoO
Soliloquy of a tortoise on revisiting the lettuce beds after an interval of one hour while supposed to be sleeping in a clump of blue hollyhocks.—ArT-3—BrSg—CoB—McWs
Tony the turtle.—ArT-3
Two people.—CoBb
The unicorn.—CoB
The white rabbit.—SmM
Rig Veda, sels. Unknown, tr. fr. the Sanskrit by P. Lal
The song of creation.—AlPi
To Agni.—AlPi
To the dawn.—AlPi
To the Maruts.—AlPi
To the waters.—AlPi
To the wind.—AlPi
Riggs, Katherine Dixon
Mockery.—ThA
Riggs, Lynn
Spring morning—Sante Fe.—PaH
"The **right** honorable." Issa, tr. fr. the Japanese by Nobuyuki Yuasa.—IsF
The **rigs** o' barley. Robert Burns.—BuPr
Rihaku. See Li T'ai-po
Riley, James Whitcomb
Little Orphant Annie.—CoBb—HoB—HuS-3
The raggedy man.—HoB—HuS-3
Rain.—CoBn
"Some credulous chroniclers tell us."—BrLl
A wee little worm.—LaPd
When the frost is on the punkin.—CoBn
Rilke, Rainer Maria
The boy.—LiT—SmM
The carousel.—LiT
From a childhood.—GrS
The panther.—ReO
Praise.—GrCt
Presentiment.—LiT
Put out my eyes.—HoL
We are all workmen.—PlE
"What will you do, God, when I die."—PlE
Rimbaud, Arthur
Ophelia.—GrCt
The **rime** of the ancient mariner. Samuel Taylor Coleridge.—CoR—CoSs (sel.)
"**Rindle,** randle." Mother Goose.—OpF
"**Ring** a ring a pinkie." Unknown.—MoB
Ring-a-ring-a-roses. Eleanor Farjeon.—FaT
"**Ring-a-ring** o' (or a) roses (a pocket full of posies)." Mother Goose.—BrMg—GrT—OpF
"**Ring** around the world." Annette Wynne.—ArT-3—HuS-3
"The **ring** is on my hand." See Bridal ballad
Ring out, wild bells. See In memoriam
"**Ring** out, wild bells to the wild sky." See In memoriam—Ring out, wild bells
"**Ring** the bells, ring." See The dunce
"**Ring** the bells—ring." Kate Greenaway.—GrT
Rings (Jewelry)
The two wives. Daniel Henderson.—BrSm
Rio de Janeiro
Rolling down to Rio. R. Kipling.—PaH
The **riot.** Mother Goose.—BrMg
The **ripe** and bearded barley. Unknown.—CoBn—GrCt
"**Ripe,** ripe strawberries." See Strawberries
"**Rippling** green and gold and brown." See The lake
Rippo
"There is a trinity of loveliest things."—LeMw
The **rise** of Shivaji. Zulfikar Ghose.—CaMb
"**Rise** up, goodwife, and shake your feathers." Unknown.—MoB
"**Rise** up, rise up." See The trumpet
Ritter, Margaret
"Faith, I wish I were a leprechaun."—ArT-3
The **rivals.** James Stephens.—ReBs—StS—ThA
The **river,** sels. Pare Lorentz
"Black spruce and Norway pine."—BrA
"Down the Yellowstone, the Milk, the White and Cheyenne."—BrA
The **river.** Dabney Stuart.—DuS
The **river** boats. Daniel Whitehead Hicky.—BrA
The **river** is a piece of sky. John Ciardi.—ArT-3—HuS-3—LaPd
"A **river** leaping." Meisetsu, tr. fr. the Japanese by Harry Behn.—BeCs
River-mates. See Otters
The **river-merchant's** wife: A letter. Li T'ai-po, tr. fr. the Chinese by Ezra Pound.—BoH—CoBl—LiT
River night. Frances Frost.—LaC
River roses. D. H. Lawrence.—GrS
River skater. Winifred Welles.—MoS
River travel. Ts'ui Hao, tr. fr. the Chinese by Arthur Christy.—LeMw
Rivers, Conrad Kent
Four sheets to the wind and a one-way ticket to France, 1933.—AdIa—BoA
The invisible man.—HaK
On passing two Negroes on a dark country road somewhere in Georgia.—AdIa
The still voice of Harlem.—AdIa—HaK
The subway.—HaK
To Richard Wright.—AdIa—BoA
The train runs late to Harlem.—AdIa
Rivers. See also names of rivers, as Chattahoochee river
American child. P. Engle.—BrA
The banks o' Doon. R. Burns.—BuPr—CoBl
Big dam. W. R. Moses.—BrA
The Bothie of Tober-na-Vuolich. A. H. Clough.—CoBn (sel.)
By Sandy waters. J. Stuart.—BrA
Detroit. D. Hall.—BrA
A green stream. Wang Wei.—MoS
"I do not know much about gods; but I think that the river." From The dry salvages. T. S. Eliot.—ArT-3
In the evening I walk by the river. Hsiu Ou-yang.—LeMw
La Crosse at ninety miles an hour. R. Eberhart.—BrA
Lives. H. Reed.—CoBn
Morning on the Lièvre. A. Lampman.—MoS

"**Roaming** the lonely wilds." See The soul of birds
"**Roaring,** clanking." See Broadway: Twilight
"**Roast** beef and marshmallows." Mother Goose. —OpF
"**Robbin** and Bobbin." See "Robin and Bobbin, two big-bellied men"
Robbins, Martin
Spring is a looping-free time.—MoS
Robbins, Patricia
Chucklehead.—ArT-3
Robert E. Lee. See John Brown's body
Robert Gould Shaw. Paul Laurence Dunbar.—HaK
Robert of Lincoln. William Cullen Bryant.—CoB —HoB
Robert Rowley. See "Robert Rowley rolled a round roll 'round"
"**Robert** Rowley rolled a round roll 'round." Mother Goose.—HuS-3
Robert Rowley.—ReOn
Robert Whitmore. Frank Marshall Davis.—HaK
Roberts, Sir Charles G. (George) D. (Douglas)
The brook in February.—CoBn—DoW
A child's prayer at evening.—ReS
Ice.—CoBn—DoW
Roberts, Elizabeth Madox
The butterbean tent.—BoGj—BrSg—HuS-3
Christmas morning.—HuS-3
The cornfield.—BoGj
Crescent moon.—ArT-3
Evening hymn.—ArT-3
Firefly.—BoGj—LaPd
The hens.—ArT-3—BoGj—CoB—HuS-3—LaPd —ThA—TuW
Horse.—CoB
Little rain.—ArT-3—BrSg
Milking time.—BoGj—HoB
Mumps.—LaP
The people.—ArT-3—BoGj
The rabbit.—ArT-3—BrSg—CoB—HoB—LaP—TuW
The star.—ReS
Strange tree.—CoBn—HoB—ThA
The twins.—ArT-3
Water noises.—CoBn—ThA
The woodpecker.—ArT-3—HoB—HuS-3—LaP
The worm.—BrSg—HoB
Roberts, Theodore Goodridge
Gluskap's hound.—DoW
The reformed pirate.—DoW
The wreckers' prayer.—CoSs
Robertson, Lexie Dean
Gossip.—ThA
The **robin.** See "The robin is the one"
A **robin** ("Ghost-grey the fall of night") Walter De La Mare.—GrCt—ReBs
"**Robin-a-Bobbin.**" Mother Goose.—BrMg
"Robin-a-Bobin bent his bow."—ReMg
"**Robin-a-Bobin** bent his bow." See "Robin-a-Bobbin"
"A **robin** and a robin's son." See Two robins
"**Robin** and Bobbin, two big-bellied men." Mother Goose.—OpF
"Robbin and Bobbin."—AgH
Robin the Bobbin.—BrMg
The **robin** and child. Ann and Jane Taylor.—VrF
Robin and Jenny. See "Jenny Wren fell sick"
"**Robin** and Richard (were two pretty men)." Mother Goose.—BrMg—OpF
"The **robin** and the redbreast." See The robin and the wren
"The **robin** and the wren." See Four birds
The **robin** and the wren. Unknown.—BlO
"The **robin** came to the wren's nest." Unknown. —MoB
"**Robin** he married a wife in the west." Unknown.—OpF
Robin Hood
Robin Hood and Allin-a-Dale. Unknown.—HoB
Robin Hood and Little John. Unknown.—HuS-3
Robin Hood and the Bishop of Hereford. Unknown.—BlO
Robin Hood and the ranger. Unknown.—HuS-3
Robin Hood rescuing the widow's three sons. Unknown.—ArT-3
Song. A. Munday.—BlO
A song of Sherwood. A. Noyes.—ArT-3—ThA
Robin Hood and Allin-a-Dale. Unknown.—HoB
Robin Hood and Little John. Unknown.—HuS-3
Robin Hood and the Bishop of Hereford. Unknown.—BlO
Robin Hood and the ranger. Unknown.—HuS-3
Robin Hood rescuing the widow's three sons. Unknown.—ArT-3
"The **robin** is the one." Emily Dickinson
The robin.—ReBs
Robin Redbreast ("Good-by, good-by to summer") William Allingham.—HoB—ReBs
Robin Redbreast ("Welcome Robin with thy greeting") Unknown.—CoB
Robin Redbreast's testament. Unknown.—MoB
"**Robin,** Robin Redbreast (cutty, cutty wran)." Unknown.—MoB
"**Robin,** Robin Redbreast (sits upon a rail)." Unknown.—MoB
Robin the Bobbin. See "Robin and Bobbin, two big-bellied men"
"**Robin** the Bobbin, the big-bellied Ben." See "Robin and Bobbin, two big-bellied men"
Robins
All on a Christmas morning. E. J. Coatsworth. —CoSb
Always with us—the black preacher. H. Melville.—ReBs
Ballad of the robin. P. McGinley.—McWc
Before breakfast. E. J. Coatsworth.—CoSb
The cat and the bird. G. Canning.—GrCt—ReBs
Cock Robin. Mother Goose.—ReOn
"Deprived of other banquet." E. Dickinson.—DiPe
"Fat father robin." D. McCord.—McE

"**Romance,** who loves to nod and sing." See Romance
Romanesque frieze. Elizabeth Jane Coatsworth. —CoDh
Rome
On Rome. From Childe Harold's pilgrimage. G. G. Byron.—ByP
A Roman legend. From Morituri salutamus. H. W. Longfellow.—LoPl
Roman wall blues. W. H. Auden.—SmM
"Over the heather the wet wind blows." —CaD
Santa Maria Maggiore, Rome. E. Jennings.—CaD
Two in the Campagna. R. Browning.—BrP—CoBl
When in Rome. M. Evans.—BoA
The wind and the rain. W. W. Gibson.—ClF
Rome—History
The Roman road. T. Hardy.—BoGj
Romeo and Juliet, sels. William Shakespeare
Come night, come Romeo.—CoBl
Queen Mab.—ShS
Rondeau. X. J. Kennedy.—McWs
Rondel. Jean Froissart, tr. fr. the French by Henry Wadsworth Longfellow.—HoL
"The **roofs** are shining from the rain." See April
"The **rook's** nests do rock on the tree-top." See Lullaby
"**Room** after room." See Love in a life
"The **room** was low and small and kind." See Bible stories
Rooms
The country bedroom. F. Cornford.—BlO
The long small room. E. Thomas.—ThG
The nursery. From The coming forth by day of Osiris Jones. C. Aiken.—HaL
"**Roon,** roon, rosie." Unknown.—MoB
Roosevelt, Theodore (about)
Hail to the sons of Roosevelt. V. Lindsay.—LiP
In which Roosevelt is compared to Saul. V. Lindsay.—LiP
Roosevelt. V. Lindsay.—LiP
Roosevelt. Vachel Lindsay.—LiP
Rooster. Fyodor Belkin, tr. fr. the Russian by Babette Deutsch.—CoB
"A **rooster** had flown high up in a tree." See The fox and the rooster
Roosters and hens. Harry Behn.—BeG
Root cellar. Theodore Roethke.—CoBn—HoL
Roots
"In the redwood forest." C. Lewis.—LeP
Root cellar. T. Roethke.—CoBn—HoL
"Roots are the branches down in the earth." R. Tagore.—LeMf
Split the stones. E. J. Coatsworth.—CoDh
"**Roots** are the branches down in the earth." Rabindranath Tagore.—LeMf
"The **roots** of trees go everywhere." See Split the stones
A **rope** for Harry Fat. James K. Baxter.—CaMb
"The **rope** she is stout an' the rope she is strong." See Tug-of-war
Ropes
A rope for Harry Fat. J. K. Baxter.—CaMb
The ropewalk. H. W. Longfellow.—LoPl
Tug-of-war. K. Fraser.—FrS
The **ropewalk.** Henry Wadsworth Longfellow.—LoPl
"**Rosalind** is your love's name." See As you like it—Dialogue
Roscoe, William
The butterfly's ball and the grasshopper's feast.—VrF
Rose Aylmer. Walter Savage Landor.—CoR
A **rose-bud,** by my early walk, sel. Robert Burns
Within the bush.—ReBs
A **rose,** but one. See Pelleas and Ettarre
"A **rose,** but one, none other rose had I." See Pelleas and Ettarre—A rose, but one
Rose-cheeked Laura. Thomas Campion.—GrS
"**Rose-cheeked** Laura, come." See Rose-cheeked Laura
The **rose** family. Robert Frost.—CoBl
"The **rose** is a rose." See The rose family
The **rose** is red. See "Roses are red"
"The **rose** is red, the rose is white." See Tuppence ha'penny farden
The **rose** on the wind. James Stephens.—StS
The **rose** tree. William Butler Yeats.—YeR
"**Rosemary,** lily, lilac tree." See Ballad of the rosemary
"**Rosemary,** Rosemary, let down your hair." See A nonsense song
Rosenberg, Isaac
The destruction of Jerusalem by the Babylonian hordes.—GrS
Rosenzweig, Efraim
Dreidel song.—ArT-3
A song of always.—ArT-3—ThA
Roses
The bees' song. W. De La Mare.—McWs
Big wind. T. Roethke.—BoGj
"Esssential oils are wrung." E. Dickinson.—DiPe
How roses came red. R. Herrick.—GrCt
The little rose tree. R. Field.—ArT-3—BrSg
My pretty rose tree. W. Blake.—BlP
One kingfisher and one yellow rose. E. Brennan.—ReBs
"Partake as doth the bee." E. Dickinson.—DiPe
River roses. D. H. Lawrence.—GrS
A rose, but one. From Pelleas and Ettarre. A. Tennyson.—TeP
The rose family. R. Frost.—CoBl
The rose tree. W. B. Yeats.—YeR
Roses and thorns. S. G. Betai.—AlPi
"A sepal, petal, and a thorn." E. Dickinson.—BrSg
The sick rose. W. Blake.—BlP—GrCt
Snail, moon and rose. J. Kenward.—SmM
Song. E. Waller.—BoGj
Thorn song. Unknown.—DePp
"'Tis the last rose of summer." T. Moore.—CoBn
Tuppence ha'penny farden. Mother Goose.—BrMg

Under rose arches. K. Greenaway.—GrT
White rose. S. Sitwell.—GrS
With the roses. J. R. Jiménez.—LiT
Roses and thorns. Sunderji G. Betai, tr. fr. the Gujarati by the author.—AlPi
"**Roses** are red." Mother Goose.—BrMg
The rose is red.—HuS-3
Rose's calf. Peggy Bennett.—CoB
"**Roses** up and roses down." See Singing game
Ross, Abram Bunn
Two in bed.—ArT-3
Ross, Alan
Kurdish shepherds.—CaD
Les Saintes-Maries-de-la-Mer.—CaD
Ross, David
"A Briton who shot at his king."—BrSm
Ross, Mrs David. See Sipe, Muriel
Ross, W. W. E. (Eustace)
The diver.—DoW
Fish.—CoB
"The snake trying."—CoB
"There's a fire in the forest."—DoW
The walk.—MoS
Rossetti, Christina Georgina
"All the bells were ringing."—ArT-3
"And timid, funny, brisk little bunny."—ArT-3
The animals mourn with Eve. See Eve
An apple gathering.—CoBl
At home. See Pancakes
A birthday.—BlO—CoBl
"Boats sail on the rivers."—ArT-3—HoB—HuS-3
"Brown and furry."—BrSg
Caterpillar.—BoGj—CoB—HoB—HuS-3—LaP
"But give me holly, bold and jolly."—ArT-3
By the sea.—CoBn
Caterpillar. See "Brown and furry"
A Christmas carol.—GrCt
My gift.—LaPh (sel.)
The city mouse and the garden mouse.—ArT-3—HoB—HuS-3
"The city mouse lives in a house."—BrSg
"The city mouse lives in a house." See The city mouse and the garden mouse
Clouds.—HuS-3—LaP
"White sheep, white sheep."—ArT-3
"The days are clear."—ArT-3
A dirge.—GrCt
"Eight o'clock."—ArT-3
"An emerald is as green as grass."—ArT-3
Eve, sel.
The animals mourn with Eve.—ReO
"Ferry me across the water."—BoGj—GrCt—LaPd
Goblin market.—CoD
"Growing in the vale."—ArT-3
Sweet Daffadowndilly.—HoB
"Hopping frog, hop here and be seen."—BlO
"The horses of the sea."—BoGj
"Hurt no living thing."—BrSg—LaPd
"If a pig wore a wig."—HoB
Immalee.—BlO—CoBn
Is the moon tired.—HuS-3
The lambs of Grasmere, 1860.—CoB
"The lily has an air."—BrSg
Lullaby.—HoB
"Minnie and Mattie."—ArT-3—BoGj
"Mother shake the cherry-tree."—ArT-3
My gift. See A Christmas carol
"Oh, fair to see."—ArT-3
O Lady Moon.—ReS
"O wind, why do you never rest."—ArT-3
Pancakes.—ClF
At home.—AgH
"Pussy has a whiskered face."—ArT-3
"Rushes in a watery place."—GrCt—LaPd
Sea-sand and sorrow.—GrCt
"Sing in the silent sky."—ReBs
"Sing me a song."—HoB
Sing song.—StF
The sound of the wind. See "The wind has such a rainy sound"
Spring quiet.—CoBn—ReBs
Summer.—CoBn
The swallow.—HuS-3
Sweet Daffadowndilly. See "Growing in the vale"
"There is but one May in the year."—ArT-3
Twilight calm.—CoBn
"What does the bee do."—ArT-3
What is pink. See "What is pink? a rose is pink"
"What is pink? a rose is pink."—ArT-3
What is pink.—BoGj—BrSg—HuS-3
When I am dead.—CoBl
"White sheep, white sheep." See Clouds
"Who has seen the wind."—BlO—BoGj—HuS-3—LaPd
The wind.—HoB
The wind. See "Who has seen the wind"
"The wind has such a rainy sound."—ArT-3
The sound of the wind.—BlO
Winter rain.—CoBn
Woolly lambkins.—HuS-3
"Wrens and robins in the hedge."—ArT-3
Rossetti, Dante Gabriel
For a marriage of St Catherine.—GrS
On a wet day. tr.—CoBn
On the poet O'Shaughnessy.—GrCt
September. tr.—MoS
Sestina. tr.—GrS
Tom Agnew, Bill Agnew.—GrCt
Rostron, Hilda I.
Autumn's passing.—StF
Following the music.—StF
November glow.—StF
"The **rosy** mouth and rosy toe." See A bunch of roses
"A **rosy** shield upon its back." See The dead crab
Roth, Dan
War.—DuR
"The **rotten-wooded** willow." Suguwara no Michizane.—BaS
"**Rou-cou** spoke the dove." See Song of fixed accord
Rough. See "My parents kept me from children who were rough"

"**Rough** wind, that moanest loud." See A dirge
The **round.** Philip Booth.—CoBn
"**Round** about, round about, applety pie." Mother Goose.—OpF
"**Round** about the cauldron go." See Macbeth—Witches' song
"**Round** about the porridge pot." Unknown.—MoB
"**Round** and round the butter dish." Mother Goose.—OpF
"**Round** and round the rugged rock." See The rugged rock
Round apples. Mother Goose.—ReOn
"**Round** apples, round apples." See Round apples
"**Round** goes the mill." See The millstream
"**Round-hoofed,** short-jointed, fetlocks shag and long." See Venus and Adonis—The horse of Adonis
"**Round** my hut." Issa, tr. fr. the Japanese by R. H. Blyth.—LeOw
"**Round** the cape of a sudden came the sea." See Parting at morning
"**Round** the Maypole dance about." See For a dance
"**Round** the yard, a thousand ways." See Farm yard at evening
A **round** trip. Unknown, ad. fr. the Japanese by Charlotte B. DeForest.—DePp
Roundelay. Isabella Gardner.—HoL
Rounds, Emma
Johnny.—BrSm
Rousecastle. David Wright.—CaMb—CoSs
The **rousing** canoe song. Hermia Fraser.—DoW
Rousseau, Jean Jacques (about)
"Mock on, mock on Voltaire, Rousseau." W. Blake.—BlP
"A **route** of evanescence." Emily Dickinson.—DiPe
Humming bird.—DiL
"**Rover** killed the goat." See Brave Rover
"**Row,** row, row your boat." Unknown.—MoS
"**Row** (us) out from Desenzano, to your Sirmione row." See Frater ave atque vale
"**Rowing,** I reach'd a rock—the sea was low." See A vision of the mermaids
Rowse, A. L.
"How many miles to Mylor."—CaD
Roy, Sochi Raut
Follow sleep, fall asleep.—AlPi
The **royal** fisherman. Unknown.—GrCt
"A **royal** train." See The peacock
"**Rub-a-dub-dub.**" Mother Goose.—OpF—ReMg
Three men in a tub.—BrMg
Rubadiri, James D.
Stanley meets Mutesa.—BoH
The **rubaiyát** of Omar Khayyám, sels. Omar Khayyám, tr. fr. the Persian by Edward Fitzgerald
"Myself when young did eagerly frequent."—PlE
"Oh Thou, who man of baser earth didst make."—PlE
"Think, in this batter'd caravanserai"
From The rubaiyát of Omar Khayyám.—GrCt
"Yet, ah, that spring should vanish with the rose."—TuW
"The **rubber** man." See Diver
Rubin, Larry
Outdistanced.—DuS
Warning.—DuS
Ruddigore, sel. William Schwenck Gilbert
Sir Roderic's song.—BrSm
Rudolph is tired of the city. Gwendolyn Brooks.—LaPd
Rufty and Tufty. Isabell Hempseed.—StF
"**Rufty** and Tufty were two little elves." See Rufty and Tufty
The **rugged** rock. Mother Goose.—BrMg
"A **rugged** star, a wreath of root." See The shape called star
Ruggeri, Agnes O'Gara
To the city in the snow.—ThA
Rugs
Navajo rug. B. J. Lee.—BaH
"A **ruin**—yet what ruin, from its mass." See Childe Harold's pilgrimage—On Rome
Rukeyser, Muriel
Boy with his hair cut short.—CoR
The street. tr.—LaC
Rulers. See Kings and rulers
Rulers: Philadelphia. Fenton Johnson.—BrA
Rules of contrary. Mother Goose.—ReOn
The **Rum** Tum Tugger. T. S. Eliot.—ArT-3—LaPd
"The **Rum** Tum Tugger is a curious cat." See The Rum Tum Tugger
Rumination. Richard Eberhart.—HoL—SmM
"The **Rummy-jums,** the Rummy-jums." See Some families of my acquaintance
"A **rumpled** sheet." See The term
Run a little. James Reeves.—StF
"**Run** a little this way." See Run a little
"**Run** away engine." See Runaway engine
Run, boys, run. See "Rats in the garden, catch 'em Towser"
Run in the rain. Aileen Fisher.—FiIo
Run, kitty, run. Wymond Garthwaite.—CoBb
Runagate runagate. Robert E. Hayden.—AdIa
The **runaway,** sel. James Whaler
Boy in a pond.—ReO
The **runaway.** Robert Frost.—ArT-3—BoGj—CoB—HoB—HuS-3—LaPd
Runaway engine. Molly Clarke.—StF
Runes IX. Howard Nemerov.—DuS
A **runnable** stag. John Davidson.—CoB—MoS—ReO
Runner ("All visible, visibly") W. H. Auden.—MoS
The **runner** ("On a flat road runs the well-train'd runner") Walt Whitman.—MoS
The **runner** ("Suddenly with intense") Alexandra Grilikhes.—MoS
Runners and running. See Races and racing—Foot

"**Running** along a bank, a parapet." See The path
Running moon. Elizabeth Jane Coatsworth.—CoSb
Running the batteries. Herman Melville.—HiL
Running the gauntlet. Kathleen Fraser.—FrS
Running to paradise. William Butler Yeats.—HaL—YeR
"**Runs** all day and never walks." Mother Goose.—ArT-3
"**Runs** falls rises stumbles on from darkness into darkness." See Runagate runagate
Runyon, (Alfred) Damon
A song of Panama.—HiL
Rural dumpheap. Melville Cane.—BrA
Rural sports, sel. John Gay
Fly-fishing.—MoS
"**Rushes** in a watery place." Christina Georgina Rossetti.—GrCt—LaPd
Russell, Ivy
Tails.—StF
Russell, Sydney King
Dust.—BrSm—DuR
Russia
A legend from Russia. P. McGinley.—McWc
Russo, Lola Ingres
Autumn squall: Lake Erie.—BrA
"The **rusty** spigot." See Onomatopoeia
"**Ruth** and Johnnie." Unknown.—BrSm
"**Ruth** says apples have learned to bob." See Halloween
Rutledge, Anne (about)
Anne Rutledge. From The Spoon River anthology. E. L. Masters.—BrA—HiL
Rutsala, Vern
Looking in the album.—DuS
Sunday.—DuS
Rye, Anthony
Birds must sing.—SmM
Ryôta
"The moon in the water."—LeI
Ryōzen
"In my loneliness."—BaS

S

Sacchetti, Franco
On a wet day.—CoBn
Sackville, Thomas, Earl of Dorset (Lord Buckhurst)
The complaint of Henrie, Duke of Buckinghame, sel.
Midnight was come.—ReO
Midnight was come. See The complaint of Henrie, Duke of Buckinghame
The **sacrifice.** Gerald William Barrax.—HaK
The **sacrilege.** Thomas Hardy.—CoD
"The **sad** bells sound." See Strangers
Sad memories, sel. Charles Stuart Calverley
The cat.—GrCt
The **sad** shepherd, sel. Ben Jonson
Mother Maudlin the witch.—GrCt
A **sad** song. See Trip upon trenchers
A **sad** song about Greenwich village. Frances Park.—LaC
A **sad** story. See "When I was a little boy (I lived)"
The **sad** story of a little boy that cried. Unknown.—CoBb
"The **saddest** noise, the sweetest noise." Emily Dickinson.—ClF (sel.)
Sadie's playhouse. Margaret Danner.—HaK
"**Safe** in their alabaster chambers." Emily Dickinson.—DiL—DiPe
"The **saffron** moth." See Moth
Safety
Danger. E. J. Coatsworth.—CoSb
Fleeing to safety. R. Chettur.—LeM
"J's the jumping jay-walker." From All around the town. P. McGinley.—ArT-3—LaP
The mole. R. Daniells.—DoW
Sagittarius
Southdown summer.—PaH
"**Said** a bad little youngster named Beauchamp." Carolyn Wells.—BrLl
"**Said** a boy to his teacher one day." Unknown.—BrLl
"**Said** a crow in the top of a tree." John Ciardi.—BrLl
"**Said** a foolish young lady of Wales." Langford Reed.—BrLl
"**Said** a sheep to her child, My dear Ruth." Joseph G. Francis.—BrLl
"**Said** an envious, erudite ermine." Oliver Herford.—BrLl
"**Said** Big Bear to Little Bear." See Big Bear and Little Bear
"**Said** Billy to Willy." See And off he went just as proud as you please
"**Said** Jeremy Jonathan Joseph Jones." See The rhyme of the rain machine
"**Said** Mr Smith, I really cannot." See Bones
"**Said** Mrs Isosceles Tri." Clinton Burgess Brooks.—BrLl
"**Said** Peter the Great to a Great Dane." See Peterhof
"**Said** the birds of America." See The birds of America
"**Said** the condor, in tones of despair." Oliver Herford.—BrLl
"**Said** the duck to the kangaroo." See The duck and the kangaroo
"**Said** the first little chicken." See The chickens
"**Said** the shark to the flying fish over the phone." See The flattered flying fish
"**Said** the snail to the tortoise: You may." Oliver Herford.—BrLl
"**Said** the table to the chair." See The table and the chair
"**Said** the wind to the moon." See The wind and the moon

Saigyo Hōshi
"Since I am convinced."—BaS
"Startled."—BaS
Sailboat, your secret. Robert Francis.—MoS
"**Sailboat,** your secret, with what dove-and-serpent." See Sailboat, your secret
Sailing homeward. Chan Fang-shēng.—ArT-3—LeM—ThA
Sailing to England. Dom Moraes.—AlPi
Sailor ("He sat upon the rolling deck") Langston Hughes.—BoH
Sailor ("My sweetheart's a sailor") Eleanor Farjeon.—FaT
The **sailor** and the shark. Paul Fort, tr. fr. the French by Frederick York Powell.—SmM
"The **sailor** in his sailboat, homeward bound." See Vacationer
Sailors. See Seamen
The **sailor's** consolation. Charles Dibdin.—CoSs—HuS-3
Sailor's dance. Kate Greenaway.—GrT
Sailors on leave. Owen Dodson.—BoA
A **sailor's** yarn. James Jeffrey Roche.—CoSs
Saint Agnes' eve
The eve of St Agnes. J. Keats.—CoD
"**St** Agnes eve—ah, bitter chill it was." See The eve of St Agnes
"**St** Dunstan, as the story goes." See The devil
Saint Francis. John Peale Bishop.—PlE
"**Saint** Francis and Saint Benedight." William Cartwright.—PlE
A house blessing.—GrCt
St Isaac's church, Petrograd. Claude McKay.—BoA—HaK
St Jerome, Canada
At St Jerome. F. Harrison.—DoW
Saint John. Elizabeth Jane Coatsworth.—CoDh
Saint John the Baptist. William Drummond, of Hawthornden.—PlE
St Louis, Missouri
Sunset. S. Teasdale.—PaH
St Martin and the beggar. Thom Gunn.—CaMb
Saint Nicholas. See Santa Claus
"**Saint** Patrick, slave to Milcho of the herds." See The proclamation
Saint Patrick's day. See Patrick, Saint
"**St** Patrick's day is with us." See I'll wear a shamrock
Saint Peter relates an incident of the Resurrection day. James Weldon Johnson.—HaK
Stephen, Saint (about)
The cutty wren. Unknown.—ReOn
Thoughts for St Stephen. C. Morley.—BrSm
St Swithin. Daniel Henderson.—BrSm
St Swithin's day. See Swithin, Saint
Saint Valentine's day
Be my non-valentine. E. Merriam.—MeI
The beggar's valentine. V. Lindsay.—LiP
Hail, Bishop Valentine. From An epithalamium on the Lady Elizabeth and Count Palatine being married on St Valentine's day. J. Donne.—GrCt
"Hearts were made to give away." A. Wynne.—ArT-3
"I bear, in sign of love." From Shepherdess' valentine. F. Andrewes.—ReBs
"Mary's eyes are blue as azure." S. Silverstein.—CoBl
My valentine. M. C. Parsons.—ArT-3
A sure sign. N. B. Turner.—ArT-3
To my valentine. Unknown.—LaPh
Valentine ("Chipmunks jump, and") D. Hall.—CoBl—DuR
A valentine ("Frost flowers on the window glass") E. Hammond.—ArT-3
Valentine greetings. K. Sexton.—LaPh
Valentine's day. A. Fisher.—LaPh
The vinegar man. R. C. Mitchell.—ThA
Saints. See also names of saints, as Francis, of Assisi, Saint
Bonny Saint John. Unknown.—MoB
Les Saintes-Maries-de-la-Mer. A. Ross.—CaD
"No matter where the saints abide." E. Dickinson.—DiPe
Saints. G. Garrett.—PlE
Santos: New Mexico. M. Sarton.—PlE
Saints. George Garrett.—PlE
Sakeagak, Thea Faye
Whales.—BaH
Salamanders
The newt. D. McCord.—ArT-3
The **Salcombe** seaman's flaunt to the proud pirate. Unknown.—GrCt
Sale. Josephine Miles.—DuS
"The **sale** began—young girls were there." See The slave auction
Sallie. Walter De La Mare.—DeBg
Sally. Mother Goose.—BrF—BrMg
Sally and Manda. Alice B. Campbell.—LaP
"**Sally** and Manda are two little lizards." See Sally and Manda
Sally Birkett's ale. Unknown.—GrCt
"**Sally** go round the sun." See Sally
"**Sally,** having swallowed cheese." See Cruel clever cat
Sally Simpkin's lament. Thomas Hood.—BrSm
Salmon-fishing. Robinson Jeffers.—MoS
Salomon, Louis B.
Univac to Univac.—DuS
Salt Lake City, Utah
Salt Lake City. H. Carruth.—BrA
Salt Lake City. Hayden Carruth.—BrA
Saltus, Francis
The sphinx speaks.—PaH
Saltwater, Jones
My home.—BaH
Salute. Oliver Pitcher.—HaK
A **salute** to trees. Henry Van Dyke.—HuS-3
The **salvation** of Texas Peters. J. W. Foley.—BrSm
Sam. Walter De La Mare.—ArT-3—CoSs
"**Sam,** shut the shutter, Mother Hyde." See It was shut
Samarkand
The golden journey to Samarkand. J. E. Flecker.—BoGj (sel.)—PaH
The **same** old law. See Song of myself

"**Sammy** Smith would drink and eat." See The greedy boy
Samoa
June. N. Belting.—BeCm
Sampley, Arthur M.
The ne'er-do-well.—DuR
Sampter, Jessie E.
Blessings for Chanukah.—ArT-3
For Hanukkah. tr.—ArT-3
Samson (about)
Death of Samson. From Samson Agonistes. J. Milton.—GrCt
The fortunes of the great. From The Canterbury tales. G. Chaucer.—ChT
How Samson bore away the gates of Gaza. V. Lindsay.—LiP
Samson. E. J. Coatsworth.—CoDh
The warning. H. W. Longfellow.—LoPl
Samson. Elizabeth Jane Coatsworth.—CoDh
Samson Agonistes, sel. John Milton
Death of Samson.—GrCt
Samuel Hall. Unknown.—GrCt
Sand
"I can walk on this." Unknown
Riddles.—StF
Sand of the desert in an hour-glass. H. W. Longfellow.—LoPl
"**Sand** drums of the desert." See The desert
Sand of the desert in an hour-glass. Henry Wadsworth Longfellow.—LoPl
"**Sand,** shovel and shingle." See The concrete mixer
Sandburg, Carl
All one people. See The people, yes
American yarns. See The people, yes—"They have yarns"
Arithmetic.—BoH—DuR
Auctioneer.—LaPd
Bee song.—LaPd
Buffalo dusk.—ArT-3—LaPd—ReO
Chicago.—PaH
Children of the wind. See The people, yes
Circles. See The people, yes
City number.—LaC
Clinton south of Polk.—BrA
Daybreak.—LaPd
The dinosaur bones.—DuS
Doors.—HaL
Even numbers.—LaC
Fish crier.—BrA
Fog.—ArT-3—HoB—HuS-3—LaP—ThA
The harbor.—HoL
Hazardous occupations.—HoL
Hits and runs.—MoS
Jazz fantasia.—LaC
Localities.—BrA
Lost.—DuR—LaPd
Manual system.—ArT-3
"Milk-white moon, put the cows to sleep."—HuS-3
Night. See The windy city
People who must.—LaC—LaPd
The people, yes, sels.
All one people.—BrA
Children of the wind.—HuS-3
These children of the wind.—ReBs
Circles.—BrA
"They have yarns."—BrA
American yarns.—HuS-3
Phizzog.—ArT-3
Prayers of steel.—LaC—LaPd
Primer lesson.—HuS-3—TuW
Rat riddles.—LaC
Sandpipers.—ReBs
Sketch.—BoH
Splinter.—ArT-3
Spring grass.—BoH
Stars.—LiT
Street window.—LaC
Summer stars.—HaL
Swell people.—HaL
Theme in yellow.—ArT-3—HuS-3
These children of the wind. See The people, yes—Children of the wind
"They have yarns." See The people, yes
Those who go forth before daylight.—HuS-3
To Beachey, 1912.—ArT-3
The windy city, sel.
Night.—LaC
Worms and the wind.—ReO
Sandburg, Carl (about)
Babylon, Babylon, Babylon the great. V. Lindsay.—LiP
The **sandcastle.** M. M. Stephenson.—StF
The **sandhill** crane. Mary Austin.—ArT-3—CoB
"**Sandman's** coming—childhood echoes." See Slumber song
The **sandpiper.** Celia Thaxter.—HoB
Sandpipers
The sandpiper. C. Thaxter.—HoB
Sandpipers. C. Sandburg.—ReBs
Sandpipers. Carl Sandburg.—ReBs
The **sands** of Dee. See Alton Locke
"**Sandy,** quo he, lend me your mill." Unknown. —MoB
San Francisco
City: San Francisco. L. Hughes.—BrA
City.—LaP—LaPd
Trip: San Francisco. L. Hughes.—BrA
Sangster, Charles
The rapid.—DoW
San Juan, Puerto Rico
Tennis in San Juan. R. Denney.—MoS
"**Sank** through easeful." See The diver
Sanpu
"Ho, for the May rains."—BeCs
Sansom, Clive
The dustman.—StF
Santa Claus
Belsnickel. A. Guiterman.—CoBb
The boy who laughed at Santa Claus. O. Nash.—CoBb
Conversation between Mr and Mrs Santa Claus. R. B. Bennett.—ArT-3
A visit from St Nicholas. C. C. Moore.—ArT-3 —HoB—HuS-3
"**Santa** Claus comes when you're good." See Belsnickel

Santa Fe, New Mexico
Santa Fe west. H. Behn.—BeG
Spring morning—Santa Fe. L. Riggs.—PaH
Santa Fe trail
The Santa Fe trail. V. Lindsay.—LiP
The **Santa** Fe trail. Vachel Lindsay.—LiP
Santa Fe west. Harry Behn.—BeG
Santa Maria Maggiore, Rome. Elizabeth Jennings.—CaD
Santaro
"Children are the children of the wind."—LeMw
Santorin. James Elroy Flecker.—BoGj
Santos, Tomas
A wish.—LeM
Santos: New Mexico. May Sarton.—PlE
Sappho
"The moon has set."—GrCt
Sarah Byng. Hilaire Belloc.—BoGj
"**Sarah** Cynthia Sylvia Stout." Shelley Silverstein.—CoBb
Sarah's fingers. Mary O'Neill.—OnF
"**Sarah's** fingers are long and thin." See Sarah's fingers
Sarasvati. James Stephens.—StS
Sarett, Lew
Blacktail deer.—CoB
Brittle world.—ThA
Four little foxes.—ArT-3—BoH—CoB—DuR—LaPd
Impasse.—CoB
The loon.—BoH
Reflection.—ThA
The sheepherder.—BrA
Sargent, William D.
Wind-wolves.—ArT-3
Sarto, Andrea del (about)
Andrea del Sarto. R. Browning.—BrP
Sarton, May
Santos: New Mexico.—PlE
The **sash.** Elizabeth Turner.—VrF
Sassoon, Siegfried
At the grave of Henry Vaughan.—PlE
Everyone sang.—HaL—SmM
The general.—McWs
Noah.—ClF
The phoenix.—GrCt
To my son.—McWs
Satan journeys to the Garden of Eden. See Paradise lost
Satin. Eleanor Farjeon.—FaT
"The **satin** mice creaking last summer's grass." Robert P. Tristram Coffin.—ReO
Satoru Sato
Pole vault. tr.—MoS
Saturday. See Days of the week—Saturday
Saturday in the county seat. Elijah L. Jacobs.—BrA
Saturday night. See "On Saturday night I lost my wife"
Saturday's child. Countee Cullen.—BoH—HaK
Saturn
Saturn. E. Farjeon.—FaT
Saturn. Eleanor Farjeon.—FaT
Satyarthi, Devendra
"The earth is not an old woman."—AlPi
Satyrs
The crackling twig. J. Stephens.—StS
"A **saucer** holds a cup." Emily Dickinson.—DiL
Saul, sel. Robert Browning
Oh, our manhood's prime vigor.—BrP
Savage, Frances Higginson
Seagulls.—DuS
Saville, Jeremy
A health unto his majesty.—GrCt
"**Saw** a flea kick a tree." See Fooba wooba John
"**Saw** you Eppie Marley, honey." Unknown.—MoB
Saws
Similia similibus. J. H. Morgan.—BrSm
Sawyer, Ruth
On Christmas morn. See Words from an old Spanish carol
Words from an old Spanish carol.—LaPh
On Christmas morn.—LaPd
Saxe, John Godfrey
The blind men and the elephant.—BoH
The briefless barrister.—BrSm
Wills.—BrSm
Say not. See "Say not the struggle naught availeth"
"**Say** not the struggle naught availeth." Arthur Hugh Clough.—PlE
Say not.—TuW
"**Say** the snow drifted down." See Santa Maria Maggiore, Rome
"**Say,** where have you been, Frank—say, where have you been." See The old man in the moon
Sayings. See Proverbs
"**Says** A, give me a good large slice." See A curious discourse that passed between the twenty-five letters at dinner-time
"**Says-so** is in a woe of shuddered." See Irritable song
Says Tom to me. David McCord.—McAd
"**Says** Tom to me: I slept the sleep of the just." See Says Tom to me
"**Says** Tweed to Till." See The two rivers
Scandinavia. See also Denmark; Norway; Norsemen
December. N. Belting.—BeCm
Scannell, Vernon
First fight.—SmM
Moods of rain.—CoBn
"A **scarecrow.**" Issa, tr. fr. the Japanese.—LeOw
Scarecrows
"In my old age." Issa.—LeOw
The lonely scarecrow. J. Kirkup.—BlO—CaD—LaPd
"Pigeons and crows, take care of your toes." Unknown.—OpF
"A scarecrow." Issa.—LeOw
"There once was a scarecrow named Joel." D. McCord.—BrLl
The **scared** clouds. Hannah Hodgins.—LeM
The **scarred** girl. James Dickey.—DuS

"The **scars** take us back to places we have been." See Memoranda
Scat scitten. David McCord.—McE
"**Scattering** evil with light." See Rig Veda—To Agni
"A **scent** of ripeness from over a wall." See Unharvested
Scheffauer, Ethel Talbot
A reply from the Akond of Swat.—BrLl
Schenectady, New York
Schenectady. E. Merriam.—MeC
Schenectady. Eve Merriam.—MeC
Schevill, James
What are the most unusual things you find in garbage cans.—DuS
The **scholar** gipsy. Matthew Arnold.—GrCt
The **scholars.** William Butler Yeats.—YeR
Schonhaut, Cindy
The fickle wind.—LeM
School. See also Teachers and teaching
At school. K. Greenaway.—GrT
The child in school. Unknown.—LeMw
"A collegiate damsel named Breeze." Unknown.—BrLl
"A diller, a dollar, a ten o'clock scholar." Mother Goose.—ArT-3
"A dillar, a dollar."—WiMg
"A diller, a dollar."—OpF—ReMg
Mother Goose rhymes, 12.—HoB
Ten o'clock scholar.—BrMg
Frogs at school. G. Cooper.—HoB
"Going to school." E. Merriam.—MeC
Going to school. E. Turner.—VrF
The good scholar. E. Turner.—VrF
"It lies in the groove." N. Qualthrough.—LeM
Look at your copy. E. Turner.—VrF
"Mary had a little lamb." S. J. Hale.—OpF—WiMg
Mary's lamb.—BrMg
"A medical student named Elias." Unknown. —BrLl
Miss Norma Jean Pugh, first grade teacher. M. O'Neill.—ArT-3
Out of school. H. Summers.—CaD
Physical geography. L. T. Nicholl.—LiT
The scholar gipsy. M. Arnold.—GrCt
The scholars. W. B. Yeats.—YeR
School ("Children are sent to school to learn") H. S. Horsley.—VrF
School ("Within the neat cottage, beside the tall tree") A. and J. Taylor.—VrF
The school boy. W. Blake.—BlP—CoBn
The school-girl in 1820. W. Upton.—VrF
"School is over." K. Greenaway.—ArT-3—GrT
"The school servant." Suifu.—LeMw
School-time. From The prelude. W. Wordsworth.—WoP
September ("Brownie, it isn't my fault") A. Fisher.—FiIo
September ("When winds die down at dawn") H. Behn.—BeG
Sniff. F. M. Frost.—ArT-3
Three brown girls singing. M. C. Holman.—HaK
Timothy Winters. C. Causley.—SmM
"The wind was bringing me to school." J. Snyder.—LeM
School ("Children are sent to school to learn") Henry Sharpe Horsley.—VrF
School ("Within the neat cottage, beside the tall tree") Ann and Jane Taylor.—VrF
The **school** boy. William Blake.—BlP—CoBn
The **school-girl** in 1820. William Upton.—VrF
"**School** is over." Kate Greenaway.—ArT-3—GrT
"The **school** servant." Suifu, tr. fr. the Japanese by R. H. Blyth.—LeMw
School-time. See The prelude. William Wordsworth
Schoolmaster. Yevgeny Yevtushenko, tr. fr. the Russian by Robin Milner-Gulland and Peter Levi.—LiT
"**Schott** and Willing did engage." See The duel
Schultz, Dodi
"My old maid aunt."—DuS
Schwartz, Delmore
The deceptive present, the phoenix year.—CoBn
For the one who would take man's life in his hands.—HiL
A little morning music.—CoBn
Science
Cities and science. From Poet always next but one. D. McCord.—BrA
"Faith is a fine invention." E. Dickinson.—DiPe
James Honeyman. W. H. Auden.—CaMb—SmM
Science for the young. W. Irwin.—BrSm (sel.) —CoBb
"A scientist living at Staines." R. J. P. Hewison.—BrLl
Sonnet—To science. E. A. Poe.—PoP
The washerman. U. Joshi.—AlPi
Science for the young. Wallace Irwin.—BrSm (sel.)—CoBb
"**Science,** true daughter of old time thou art." See Sonnet—To science
"A **scientist** living at Staines." R. J. P. Hewison. —BrLl
Scintilla. William Stanley Braithwaite.—BoA
"A **scissor.**" See Double trouble
The **scissor-man.** Madeleine Nightingale.—ArT-3
Scissors
Double trouble. E. Merriam.—MeI
Scissors-grinders
The scissor-man. M. Nightingale.—ArT-3
Scollard, Clinton
"As I came down from Lebanon."—PaH
Out in the wood.—ThA
Rain riders.—ArT-3
"**Scores** of years ago." See Halley's comet
"**Scorn** not the sonnet; critic, you have frowned." See Sonnet
Scorpions
Night of the scorpion. N. Ezekiel.—AlPi
On Fell. G. E. Lessing.—BrSm

Scotland. See also Ballads—Old English and Scottish; Dialect—Scottish
The banks o' Doon. R. Burns.—BuPr—CoBl
"Highlandman, Highlandman." Unknown.—MoB
My heart's in the Highlands. R. Burns.—BuH (sel.)—BuPr—ClF—MoS
"My heart's in the Highlands, my heart is not here."—BlO—PaH
The princess of Scotland. R. A. Taylor.—GrS
Sweet Afton. R. Burns.—BuPr
Afton water.—CoBn
The Tarbolton lasses. R. Burns.—BuPr
"There once was a bonnie Scotch laddie." Unknown.—BrLl
Scotland—History. See also names of battles, as Bannockburn, Battle of, 1314
Flodden. From Marmion. W. Scott.—ClF
"It was a' for our rightfu' king." R. Burns.—BuPr
Scots, wha hae. R. Burns.—BuPr
To the Princess Margaret Tudor. W. Dunbar.—GrS
Scots, wha hae. Robert Burns.—BuPr
"**Scots,** wha hae wi' Wallace bled." See Scots, wha hae
Scott, Duncan Campbell
The forsaken.—DoW (sel.)
Scott-Gatty, Alfred
Maria Jane.—CoBb
Scott, Geoffrey
Frutta di mare.—CoSs—GrCt—GrS
Scott, Sir Walter
The bonny, bonny owl. See Kenilworth
Christmas time. See Marmion
Flodden. See Marmion
Football song.—MoS
Gin by pailfuls.—GrCt
"Heap on more wood, the wind is chill." See Marmion—Christmas time
The heart of Midlothian, sel.
Proud Maisie.—BlO—GrCt
Hie away. See Waverley—"Hie away, hie away"
"Hie away, hie away." See Waverley
Hunter's song. See The lady of the lake
Hunting song.—MoS
"The hunting tribes of air and earth." See Rokeby
Kenilworth, sel.
The bonny, bonny owl.—ReBs
The lady of the lake, sel.
Hunter's song.—ReO
The lay of the last minstrel.—PaH (sel.)
Lochinvar. See Marmion
Marmion, sels.
Christmas time.—ClF
"Heap on more wood, the wind is chill."—ArT-3
Flodden.—ClF
Lochinvar.—CoR—HuS-3
The nativity chant.—GrCt
Proud Maisie. See The heart of Midlothian
Rokeby, sel.
"The hunting tribes of air and earth."—ReO
Waverley, sel.
"Hie away, hie away."—ArT-3
Hie away.—SmM
Scott, Winfield Townley
The child's morning.—DuR
If all the unplayed pianos.—DuS
Landscape as metal and flowers.—BoGj—BrA
Two lives and others.—DuR
Scottish lullaby. See "Hush-a-ba birdie, croon, croon"
Scottus, Sedulius
Easter Sunday.—LiT
Scovell, E. J.
The boy fishing.—ClF—SmM
Scrapyard. Michael Benson.—LeM
"**Scrub** hills." See Hills
"**Scrunch.**" See The dead ones
Sculptors. See Sculpture and sculpturing
Sculpture and sculpturing. See also Statues
Ozymandias. P. B. Shelley.—CoR—PaH
These beasts and the Benin bronze. M. Danner.—HaK
"**Scum** of clergymen, clergy's dregs." See On the gift of a cloak
"**Scuttle,** scuttle, little roach." See Nursery rhymes for the tender-hearted
Sea. See Ocean
The **sea** ("How fearful") See King Lear
The **sea** ("On the way I saw the sea") Suzanne G.—LeM
The **sea** ("The sea is a hungry dog") James Reeves.—CoSs
The **sea** ("The untamed sea is human") Susan Shoenblum.—LeM
The **sea** ("You, you are all unloving, loveless, you") D. H. Lawrence.—CoBn
"The **sea** awoke at midnight from its sleep." See The sound of the sea
Sea born. Harold Vinal.—BoH
Sea calm. Langston Hughes.—HaL—LiT
Sea chanty. Abe Burrows.—CoSs
A **sea** dirge. See The tempest—Full fathom five
Sea fever. John Masefield.—ArT-3—CoSs—HoB—HuS-3—LaPd—ThA
Sea gull. See "The sea gull curves his wings"
"The **sea** gull curves his wings." Elizabeth Jane Coatsworth.—ArT-3
Sea gull.—CoB
Sea gulls. See Gulls
Sea gulls. Frances Higginson Savage.—DuS
The **sea** gypsy. Richard Hovey.—CoSs—LaPd
"The **sea** hath tempered it; the mighty sun." See The fountain
"The **sea** hawk hunting." Taigi, tr. fr. the Japanese by Harry Behn.—BeCs
"The **sea** in the dusk." Bashō, tr. fr. the Japanese by Harry Behn.—BeCs
"The **sea** is a hungry dog." See The sea
"The **sea** is a wilderness of waves." See Long trip

"The **sea** is calm to-night." See Dover beach
"The **sea** is enormous, but calm with evening and sunset." See Whale at twilight
Sea life. See Ocean; Seamen
Sea love. Charlotte Mew.—CoBl
Sea lullaby. Elinor Wylie.—CoBn
Sea magic. Claudia Lewis.—LeP
Sea monsters. See The faerie queene
The **sea** ritual. George Darley.—GrS
"The **sea** rolls by." See The flying sea
"The **sea** rushes up." See Slave of the moon
Sea-sand and sorrow. Christina Georgina Rossetti.—GrCt
The **sea** serpant. Wallace Irwin.—CoB
The **sea** serpent chantey. Vachel Lindsay.—LiP
Sea serpents
The sea serpant. W. Irwin.—CoB
The sea serpent chantey. V. Lindsay.—LiP
Sea shell. Amy Lowell.—BoH—HuS-3
"**Sea** shell, sea shell." See Sea shell
Sea shells. See Shells
Sea shells. See "She sells sea-shells on the sea shore"
"The **sea** was calm." Carlton Minor.—BaH
Sea-weed. D. H. Lawrence.—CoBn
"**Sea-weed** sways and sways and swirls." See Sea-weed
Seafaring life. See Ocean; Seamen
Seagull ("As I watch over") Shirley Gash.—LeM
The **seagull** ("A hole in the cliffs") Carmen Bernos de Gasztold, tr. fr. the French by Rumer Godden.—GaC
Seagulls. Patricia Hubbell.—LaPd
The **seal** ("How must it feel") Conrad Aiken.—AiC
Seal ("See how he dives") William Jay Smith.—CoB—DuR
Seal lullaby. See The jungle book
Seals (Animals)
The Great Silkie of Sule Skerry. Unknown.—GrCt
The performing seal. From A circus garland. R. Field.—HuS-3
The seal ("How must it feel") C. Aiken.—AiC
Seal ("See how he dives") W. J. Smith.—CoB—DuR
Seal lullaby. From The jungle book. R. Kipling.—ArT-3—ReS
The seal's lullaby.—McWs
The seals. D. Aldis.—ArT-3
The **seals.** Dorothy Aldis.—ArT-3
"The **seals** all flap." See The seals
The **seal's** lullaby. See The jungle book—Seal lullaby
Seaman, Owen
The uses of ocean.—CoSs
The **seaman's** happy return. Unknown.—GrCt
Seamen. See also Naval battles; Ocean; Ships
The alarmed skipper. J. T. Fields.—CoSs
The albatross. R. P. Lister.—CoSs
"As I went up the garden." Unknown.—MoB—StF
The ballad of Kon-Tiki. I. Serraillier.—CoSs
The battle of Clothesline bay. W. Irwin.—CoSs
Billy Taylor. Unknown.—ReOn
Black-eyed Susan. J. Gay.—CoR—CoSs
Blow me eyes. W. Irwin.—CoBl
Blow, ye winds. Unknown.—CoSs
By the deep nine. W. Pearce.—GrCt
Cape Horn gospel. J. Masefield.—CoSs
Captain Pink of the Peppermint. W. Irwin.—CoSs
Captain Stratton's fancy. J. Masefield.—CoSs
Cecilia. Unknown.—DoW
The Chinese bumboatman. Unknown.—CoSs
Christmas at sea. R. L. Stevenson.—CoSs
Clipper ships and captains. R. C. and S. V. Benét.—HuS-3
Come loose every sail to the breeze. Unknown.—CoSs
The dutiful mariner. W. Irwin.—CoSs
El capitan-general. C. G. Leland.—CoSs
"Finite to fail, but infinite to venture." E. Dickinson.—DiPe
The fishes. Unknown.—CoSs
Fog. C. Garstin.—CoSs
Forty singing seamen. A. Noyes.—HoB
"The fox-coloured pheasant enjoyed his peace." P. Levi.—CaD
The frolic mariners of Devon. From Britannia's pastorals. W. Browne.—GrCt
The gals o' Dublin town. Unknown.—CoSs
The golden city of St Mary. J. Masefield.—BoH—PaH
The Golden Vanity. Unknown.—BlO—CoSs
The Goole captain. L. Clark.—CaD
Haul away Joe. Unknown.—CoSs
Hervé Riel. R. Browning.—CoSs
Industrious Carpenter Dan. W. Irwin.—CoSs
The Irish Rover. Unknown.—CoSs
Isabel. Unknown.—DoW
Jack was every inch a sailor. Unknown.—DoW
The Jumblies. E. Lear.—ArT-3—BlO—BoGj—GrCt—HuS-3—SmM
Leave her, Johnny. Unknown.—SmM
Little Billee. W. M. Thackeray.—BlO—BrSm—CoSs
Luck. W. W. Gibson.—CoSs—SmM
Mariners' carol. W. S. Merwin.—PlE
Meditations of a mariner. W. Irwin.—CoSs
The mermaid. Unknown.—CoSs
Mulholland's contract. R. Kipling.—CoSs
A nautical ballad. From Davy and the goblin. C. E. Carryl.—HuS-3
A nautical extravagance. W. Irwin.—HuS-3
Nursery rhyme of innocence and experience. C. Causley.—BoGj—CaD
Old gray squirrel. A. Noyes.—CoSs
The old sailor. W. De La Mare.—DeBg
An old song. E. Thomas.—ThG
Pole-star. E. Farjeon.—FaT
The post captain. C. E. Carryl.—CoSs
The powerful eyes o' Jeremy Tait. W. Irwin.—CoSs
The press gang. Unknown.—GrCt
The puritan's ballad. E. Wylie.—CoBl

"The days and months do not last long." Pai Ta-shan.—LeMw
The deceptive present, the phoenix year. D. Schwartz.—CoBn
"Did we abolish frost." E. Dickinson.—DiPe
"Each season, more lovely." Yakamochi.—BaS
Eskimo chant. Unknown.—DoW
"There is joy in."—LeO
Going south so soon. A. Fisher.—FiC
"How do you know it's spring." M. W. Brown. —BrSg
"I heard a bird sing." O. Herford.—ArT-3—CoB—LaP—LaPd—ThA
"In the spring the chirping." Onitsura.—BeCs
Life half lived. J. C. F. Hölderlin.—GrCt
"Little seeds we sow in spring." E. H. Minarik.—BrSg
"March winds and April showers." Mother Goose.—BrSg
Spring.—BrMg
The ripe and bearded barley. Unknown.—CoBn—GrCt
The seasons. K. Kuskin.—BrSg
"The seasons were appointed, and the times." N. Belting.—BeCm
Solace. C. S. Delany.—BoA
"Spring is almost gone." Buson.—BeCs
"Spring is showery, flowery, bowery." Mother Goose.—OpF
Spring to winter. From The ancient mansion. G. Crabbe.—GrCt
Times o' year. W. Barnes.—CoBn
Upside down. R. Burgunder.—ArT-3
"When the Milky Way you spy." Unknown.—WyC
Wild peaches. E. Wylie.—PaH
Winter night. C. Hutchison.—ArT-3
The year's round. C. Patmore.—BrSg
The **seasons.** Karla Kuskin.—BrSg
"The **seasons** were appointed, and the times." Natalia Belting.—BeCm
Seaweed. Henry Wadsworth Longfellow.—LoPl
The **second** book of Samuel, sel. Bible, Old Testament
David's lament.—GrCt
The **second** coming. William Butler Yeats.—PlE
Second half. David McCord.—MoS
The **second** jungle book, sel. Rudyard Kipling
The law of the jungle.—HoB—ReO
Second shepherds' play, sel. Unknown
The shepherds at Bethlehem.—GrCt
Second song. Alfred Tennyson.—TeP
A **second** stanza for Dr Johnson. Donald Hall.—BrSm
Second Timothy, sel. Bible, New Testament
"For God hath not given us the spirit of fear." —ArT-3
The **secret** ("I was frightened, for a wind") James Stephens.—StS
The **secret** ("We have a secret, just we three") Unknown.—ArT-3—HoB
The **secret** of the machines. Rudyard Kipling.—HuS-3
The **secret** sits. Robert Frost.—HaL
The **secret** song. Margaret Wise Brown.—LaP—LaPd
Secrets
Little brother's secret. K. Mansfield.—ArT-3—ThA
Lyrebirds. Judith Wright.—BoGj
Please don't tell him. J. Ciardi.—CiYk
The secret ("I was frightened, for a wind") J. Stephens.—StS
The secret ("We have a secret, just we three") Unknown.—ArT-3—HoB
The secret sits. R. Frost.—HaL
The secret song. M. W. Brown.—LaP—LaPd
"The skies can't keep their secret." E. Dickinson.—DiL
The **secular** masque, sel. John Dryden
"All, all of a piece throughout."—GrCt
Sedge-warblers. Edward Thomas.—ReBs (sel.)
Sedley, Sir Charles
To Phillis.—CoBl
"**See** a pin and pick it up." See Pins
"**See** an old unhappy bull." See The bull
"**See,** here are the gipsy-folks, boiling their pot." See The gipsies
"**See** how from far upon the eastern road." See On the morning of Christ's Nativity—The magi
"**See** how he dives." See Seal
"**See** how the doves flutter and huddle." Unknown.—DoC
"**See,** Lord (my coat)." See The prayer of the old horse
"**See** Master Proud-Face." See Won't
See saw. See "See-saw, Margery Daw (Jacky or Johnny shall have a new master)"
"**See-saw,** down in my lap." See White cap
"**See-saw,** Jack in the hedge." Mother Goose.—OpF
"**See-saw,** Margery Daw (Jacky or Johnny shall have a new master)." Mother Goose.—OpF—WiMg
See saw.—BrMg
"**See-saw,** Margery Daw (sold her bed)." Mother Goose.—BrMg—OpF
"**See-saw** sacaradown." See "See-saw sacradown"
"**See-saw,** sacradown." Mother Goose.—OpF
"See-saw, sacaradown."—ReMg
"**See** the kitten on the wall." See The kitten and the falling leaves
"**See** the pretty snowflakes." See Falling snow
"**See** the stars, love." See In a boat
"**See** these piles of marbles." See Knocking over castles made with marbles
"**See,** they are clearing the sawdust course." See A circus garland—The girl on the milk-white horse
"**See** this beautiful rainy day." Alliene Grover.—LeM
"**See** what a lovely shell." See Maud
"**See,** Will, 'ere's a go." Unknown.—GrCt
"**See** yonder cloud." See Substantiations
Seed leaves. Richard Wilbur.—CoBn

"The **seed** of all song." Bashō, tr. fr. the Japanese by Harry Behn.—BeCs
The **seed** shop. Muriel Stuart.—CoBn
Seeds
The anxious farmer. B. Johnson.—CoBn
Baby seed song. E. Nesbit.—HoB—ThA
Baby seeds. Unknown.—BrSg
Doffing the bonnet. J. Stephens.—StS
Elm seed blizzard. D. McCord.—McAd
The flower. A. Tennyson.—TeP
The golden tickseed. G. Davidson.—BoH
Hempseed. Mother Goose.—ReOn
Lesson. H. Behn.—BrSg
"Little seeds we sow in spring." E. H. Minarik.—BrSg
The magic vine. Unknown.—BrSg
Maytime magic. M. Watts.—BrSg
Seed leaves. R. Wilbur.—CoBn
The seed shop. M. Stuart.—CoBn
Seeds ("The seeds I sowed") W. De La Mare.—ArT-3—BrSg—HuS-3
Seeds ("Seeds know just the way to start") A. Fisher.—FiC
Spring planting. M. Chute.—BrSg
"There was a young farmer of Leeds." Unknown.—BrLl
Tillie. W. De La Mare.—ArT-3
Tommy. G. Brooks.—BrSg
Waiting. H. Behn.—ArT-3—BrSg
Seeds ("The seeds I sowed") Walter De La Mare.—ArT-3—BrSg—HuS-3
Seeds ("Seeds know just the way to start") Aileen Fisher.—FiC
"The **seeds** I sowed." See Seeds
"**Seeds** know just the way to start." See Seeds
Seeger, Alan
"I have a rendezvous with death."—HiL
"**Seeing** the plum tree I thought of the Western Island." See Ballad of the Western Island in the North country
Seen by moonlight. Elizabeth Jane Coatsworth.—CoSb
"**Seen** from the moon in any phase, this twisting." See Two views of the planet earth
Segal, Y. Y.
King Rufus.—DoW
Rhymes.—DoW
Seien
Skylark.—LeMw
Sekula, Irene
Mother Goose, circa 2054.—BrSm
"**Seldom** we find, says Solomon Don Dunce." See An enigma
Self
"As I walk'd by myself." Mother Goose.—GrCt—ReOn
By myself.—BrMg
As kingfishers catch fire. G. M. Hopkins.—PlE
Confidence. M. Lasanta.—BaH
Conversation with myself. E. Merriam.—MeI
"Everybody says." D. Aldis.—ThA
"Everything that I can spy." J. Stephens.—StS
I am Rose. G. Stein.—SmM
"I asked no other thing." E. Dickinson.—DiPe
"I could not prove the years had feet." E. Dickinson.—DiPe
"I looked in the mirror." B. S. De Regniers.—LaPd
"Maggie and Milly and Molly and May." E. E. Cummings.—HaL
Me ("As long as I live") W. De La Mare.—DeBg—HuS-3
Me ("Who's me, a little black boy") M. Goode.—BaH
My feelings. P. Thompson.—LeM
Myself. L. Ahsoak.—BaH
Preludes for Memnon. C. Aiken.—CoBl
The sorceress. V. Lindsay.—LaPd
Thumbprint. E. Merriam.—MeI
To a louse, on seeing one on a lady's bonnet at church. R. Burns.—BuP—BuPr—CoB
To what shore would you cross. Kabir.—AlPi
"Want to be someone." H. R. Yazzie.—BaH
Wishes. E. K. Wallace.—ThA
"The **self-applauding** bird, the peacock, see." See Truth
Self-sacrifice. Harry Graham.—CoBb
The **selfish** snails. Ann and Jane Taylor.—VrF
Selfishness
The ballad of Semmerwater. W. Watson.—BlO
The dog and the shadow. R. S. Sharpe.—VrF
Greed. P. Bennett.—CoB
The greedy boy. E. Turner.—VrF
Greedy-fingers. M. O'Neill.—OnF
Greedy Tom. Unknown.—AgH—StF
Ipecacuanha. G. Canning.—GrCt
The selfish snails. A. and J. Taylor.—VrF
The sweet tooth. K. Pyle.—AgH—CoBb
Willy Wood. Unknown.—AgH
Selkirk, Alexander (about)
The solitude of Alexander Selkirk. W. Cowper.—CoR
Sellers, Gillian
"Summer is golden."—LeM
Semimaru
"As for this world."—BaS
Sen, Samar
An evening air.—AlPi
"**Send** daddy home." Mother Goose.—OpF
"**Send** peace on all the lands and flickering corn." See Anashuya and Vijaya
Sendak, Maurice
January.—AgH
Senlin. See Senlin: A biography
Senlin: A biography, sel. Conrad Aiken
Senlin.—HaL
Sennacherib
The destruction of Sennacherib. G. G. Byron.—ByP
Senses. See also names of senses, as Sight
Curious something. W. Welles.—ArT-3
The fifth sense. P. Beer.—CaMb
"Little eyes see pretty things." Unknown.—WyC
Things of summer. K. Jackson.—BrSg
The **sensitive** figure. Elizabeth Turner.—VrF
"**Sent** as a present from Annam." See The red cockatoo

"A **sepal**, petal, and a thorn." Emily Dickinson. —BrSg
September
September ("And in September, O what keen delight") Folgore da San Geminiano.—MoS
September ("Beyond the Shining mountains") N. Belting.—BeCm
September ("Brownie, it isn't my fault") A. Fisher.—FiIo
September ("The dry fingers of the sun have wiped up the dampness around the grass roots") N. Belting.—BeCm
September ("The goldenrod is yellow") H. H. Jackson.—BoGj—HoB—HuS-3
September ("A road like brown ribbon") E. Fallis.—ArT-3—BrSg
September ("We sit late, watching the dark slowly unfold") T. Hughes.—GrS
September ("When winds die down at dawn") H. Behn.—BeG
September ("And in September, O what keen delight") Folgore da San Geminiano, tr. fr. the Latin by Dante Gabriel Rossetti.—MoS
September ("Beyond the Shining mountains") Natalia Belting.—BeCm
September ("Brownie it isn't my fault") Aileen Fisher.—FiIo
September ("The dry fingers of the sun have wiped up the dampness around the grass roots") Natalia Belting.—BeCm
September ("The goldenrod is yellow") Helen Hunt Jackson.—BoGj—HoB—HuS-3
September ("A road like brown ribbon") Edwina Fallis.—ArT-3—BrSg
September ("We sit late, watching the dark slowly unfold") Ted Hughes.—GrS
September ("When winds die down at dawn") Harry Behn.—BeG
September 1913. William Butler Yeats.—YeR
"**September** was when it began." See The coming of the plague
Serenade. See The Spanish student
Serendipity. Eve Merriam.—MeI
"**Serenely** poised." Issa, tr. fr. the Japanese by Nobuyuki Yuasa.—IsF
A **serio-comic** elegy. Richard Whately.—BrSm
The **sermon** of St Francis. Henry Wadsworth Longfellow.—LoPl
Sermons
Go down death. J. W. Johnson.—BoA
How Samson bore away the gates of Gaza. V. Lindsay.—LiP
The sermon of St Francis. H. W. Longfellow. —LoPl
The **serpent.** Theodore Roethke.—LiT
Serpents. See Sea serpents; Snakes
Serraillier, Ian
After ever happily; or, The princess and the woodcutter.—CoBl
The ballad of Kon-Tiki.—CoSs
Death of the cat.—CoB
The fox rhyme.—CoB—SmM
Grandad's pipe.—StF
The hare and the tortoise.—CoB
The hen and the carp.—CoB
The mouse in the wainscot.—CoB—LaPd
Piano practice.—CoBb
The squirrel.—CoB
The tickle rhyme.—CoO—LaP
Servants. See also Housekeepers and housekeeping
The dust man. W. Darton.—VrF
The dustman. C. Sansom.—StF
For a lady I know. C. Cullen.—AdIa—BrSm—HaK
Four epitaphs.—BoA
My mammy's maid. Mother Goose.—BrMg
"A new servant maid named Maria." Unknown.—BrLl
Polly Perkins. Unknown.—CoBl
The raggedy man. J. W. Riley.—HoB—HuS-3
"The school servant." Suifu.—LeMw
Service, Robert W.
The cremation of Sam McGee.—ArT-3—BrSm
The shooting of Dan McGrew.—DoW
Service. See also Charity; Gifts and giving; Heroes and heroines; Kindness
"All service ranks the same with God." From Pippa passes. R. Browning.—BrP
The ballad of Father Gilligan. W. B. Yeats.—McWs—PlE—YeR
Incantation to Oedipus. From Oedipus. J. Dryden.—GrS
On his blindness. J. Milton.—GrCt
Someone had a helping hand. J. Ciardi.—CiYk
Three helpers in battle. M. Coleridge.—PlE
To a child. W. Wordsworth.—WoP
"**Serving** no haughty muse, my hands have here." See Valedictory sonnet
Sestina. Dante, tr. fr. the Italian by Dante Gabriel Rossetti.—GrS
"**Set** back your watches—this is Mountain Time." See Continental crossing
"**Set** your watch, the weather said." See On time
Sethi, Narendra Kumar
One, two, three.—AlPi
The **setting** of the sun. Maura Copeland.—LeM
Setting the table. Dorothy Aldis.—ArT-3—HuS-3
Settling some old football scores. Morris Bishop. —MoS
Seumas Beg. James Stephens.—BlO—CoR
"**Seven** around the moon go up." See The pinwheel's song
"**Seven** dog-days we let pass." See Queens
Seven gifts. Unknown, ad. fr. the Japanese by Charlotte B. DeForest.—DePp
Seven stanzas at Easter. John Updike.—PlE
"The **Seven** Stars are shining again." See May
"**Seven** sweet notes." See Echo
The **seven** virgins. Unknown.—GrCt
Several people. Pien Chih-lin, tr. fr. the Chinese by Harold Acton and Ch'en Shih-Hsiang.—LeMw
The **Severn.** See The baron's war
Severn river
The Severn. From The baron's war. M. Drayton.—GrCt
Sew the flags together. Vachel Lindsay.—LiP

Sewell, Elizabeth
Forgiveness.—PlE
Job.—PlE
Sewing
The little sempstress. M. Elliott.—VrF
The tambour worker. Unknown.—VrF
Sext. W. H. Auden.—LiT (sel.)
Sexton, Anne
Pain for a daughter.—McWs
Sexton, Kathryn
Valentine greetings.—LaPh
Seymour, William Kean
Cortez.—SmM
Sh. James S. Tippett.—ArT-3
"**Sh,** says mother." See Sh
"The **shade** once swept about your boughs." See The fallen tree
The **shades** of night. Alfred Edward Housman.—GrCt
"The **shades** of night were falling fast." See Excelsior
"The **shades** of night were falling fast." See The shades of night
Shadow ("My shadow is very bad and foolish") Pramila Parmar.—LeM
The **shadow** ("When the last of gloaming's gone") Walter De La Mare.—DeBg—HoB
Shadow dance. Ivy O. Eastwick.—ArT-3—LaP
"A **shadow** is floating through the moonlight." See The bird of night
The **shadow** people. Francis Ledwidge.—ThA
Shadows
The clouds that are so light. E. Thomas.—ThG
Could it have been a shadow. M. Shannon.—ArT-3—HuS-3
The dog and the shadow. R. S. Sharpe.—VrF
Fun with my shadow. C. Tringress.—StF
My shadow. R. L. Stevenson.—ArT-3—HuS-3—LaP—LaPd
Shadow ("My shadow is very bad and foolish") P. Parmar.—LeM
The shadow ("When the last of gloaming's gone") W. De La Mare.—HoB
Shadow dance. I. O. Eastwick.—ArT-3—LaP
Shadows ("A dark, elusive shadow") A. J. Peel.—ThA
Shadows ("The horse in the field") W. De La Mare.—DeBg
Shadows ("The moon is risen, and without a sound") Unknown.—LeMw
Water and shadow. M. Zaturenska.—GrS
The weaving. H. L. Cook.—ThA
Shadows ("A dark, elusive shadow") Arthur J. Peel.—ThA
Shadows ("The horse in the field") Walter De La Mare.—DeBg
Shadows ("The moon is risen, and without a sound") Unknown, tr. fr. the Japanese by Curtis Hidden Page.—LeMw
"**Shadows** are long on Soldiers Field." See Second half
"**Shadows** of clouds." See Clouds across the canyon
"The **shadows** of the ships." See Sketch
Shadwell, Thomas (about)
Thomas Shadwell the poet. From Absalom and Achitophel. J. Dryden.—GrCt
"**Shaggy,** and lean, and shrewd, with pointed ears." See The woodman's dog
"**Shake** hands with Hector the dog, for Hector is." See Hector the dog
"**Shake** off your heavy trance." See Fit only for Apollo
Shakespeare, William
Another riddle. See Love's labour's lost
Antony and Cleopatra, sel.
Clouds.—ShS
Appearances. See The taming of the shrew
Ariel's dirge. See The tempest—Full fathom five
Ariel's song. See The tempest—"Come unto these yellow sands"
Ariel's song. See The tempest—Full fathom five
Ariel's song. See The tempest—Where the bee sucks
As you like it, sels.
"Blow, blow, thou winter wind."—GrCt
Heigh ho the holly.—ShS
Dialogue.—McWs
A lover and his lass.—ShS
"Under the greenwood tree."—ArT-3—CoBn—ShS—TuW
Before Agincourt. See King Henry V
Before battle. See King Henry V—Before Agincourt
"Being your slave what should I do but tend." See Sonnets
Beware. See The tempest
"Blow, blow, thou winter wind." See As you like it
The boar. See Venus and Adonis
Cares and joys. See King Henry VI
Christmas. See Hamlet—"Some say that ever 'gainst that season"
Clouds. See Antony and Cleopatra
Come night, come Romeo. See Romeo and Juliet
"Come unto these yellow sands." See The tempest
Comparisons. See King Henry VI
Coriolanus, sel.
Coriolanus's farewell to his fellow-citizens as he goes into banishment.—McWs
Coriolanus's farewell to his fellow-citizens as he goes into banishment. See Coriolanus
Courage. See Julius Caesar
The crow and the lark. See The merchant of Venice
Cymbeline, sels.
"Fear no more the heat o' the sun."—GrCt
Fear no more.—BoH—CoR
"Hark, hark, the lark at heaven's gate sings."—BlO
Hark, hark, the lark.—GrCt—SmM
"Daffodils." See The winter's tale
Dark affections. See The merchant of Venice

Who is Silvia. See Two gentlemen of Verona
Winter. See Love's labour's lost—"When icicles hang (or on) the wall"
The winter's tale, sels.
"Daffodils."—ArT-3—BrSg—TuW
"Jog on, jog on, the foot-path way."—ArT-3
The merry heart.—ShS
The pedlar.—ShS
Some flowers o' the spring.—GrCt
Wise song. See King Richard III
Witches' song. See Macbeth
"With hey, ho, the wind and the rain." See King Lear
Wit's pedlar. See Love's labour's lost
"You spotted snakes with double tongue." See A midsummer-night's dream
Shakespeare, William (about)
The path to Shottery. C. O. Skinner.—ThA
To the memory of my beloved; the author Mr William Shakespeare. B. Jonson.—GrCt (sel.)
"**Shall** I love God for causing me to be." See The proof
"**Shall** I sonnet-sing you about myself." See House
"**Shall** I tell you who will come." See Words from an old Spanish carol
"**Shall** I, wasting in despair." George Wither.—CoBl
"**Shall** we gather our nuts in May, Maureen." See Nuts in May
"**Shall** we tell a last tale." Unknown.—OpF
Shame. James Stephens.—StS
Shameful death. William Morris.—GrCt—GrS
Shamrocks
I'll wear a shamrock. M. C. Davies.—ArT-3
Shane, Elizabeth
"The herons on Bo island."—CoB
Hush song.—ThA
Shanks, Edward
The storm.—CoBn
Shannon, Monica
Could it have been a shadow.—ArT-3—HuS-3
Country trucks.—ArT-3
How to tell goblins from elves.—ArT-3
Only my opinion.—ArT-3—HuS-3
The tree toad.—ArT-3
Shanties. See Work songs
Shantung; or, The empire of China is crumbling down. Vachel Lindsay.—LiP
"**Shanty** of the singing sailor." See Shanty
The **shape** called star. Louise Townsend Nicholl.—HoL
"The **shape** of a rat." See The lost son
Shapiro, Karl
Americans are afraid of lizards.—BrA
California winter.—BrA (sel.)
A cut flower.—CoBn
Elegy for a dead soldier.—HiL
Interlude III.—DuR
Manhole covers.—BoGj—BoH—BrA
The murder of Moses.—PlE
The 151st psalm.—PlE
Sunday: New Guinea.—BrA
V-letter.—HiL
The **shark.** E. J. Pratt.—DoW
Sharks
About the teeth of sharks. J. Ciardi.—CoB
"A daring young lady of Guam." Unknown.—BrLl
The flattered flying fish. E. V. Rieu.—ArT-3—BrSm—LaPd
Harlem gallery. M. B. Tolson.—HaK (sel.)
The Maldive shark. H. Melville.—CoB
The powerful eyes o' Jeremy Tait. W. Irwin.—CoSs
The rhyme of the chivalrous shark. W. Irwin.—BrSm
The sailor and the shark. P. Fort.—SmM
Sally Simpkin's lament. T. Hood.—BrSm
The shark. E. J. Pratt.—DoW
Sharma, Nalin Vilochan
Evening at the seashore.—AlPi
Sharp, William (Fiona Macleod, pseud.)
The field mouse.—CoB—ReS
From the hills of dream.—ThA
Hushing song.—ThA
The valley of white poppies.—ThA
"**Sharp** as sword of Saracen." See Epitaph for a grim woman
Sharpe, Richard Scrafton
The ass and the lap-dog.—VrF
The boy and the frogs.—VrF
The dog and the shadow.—VrF
The jewel on the dunghill.—VrF
The lion and the mouse.—VrF
"The **shattered** water made a misty din." See Once by the Pacific
Shaw, Frances
"Who loves the rain."—ThA
Shaw, Isabel
Christmas chant.—LaPh
Shaw, Robert Gould (about)
Robert Gould Shaw. P. L. Dunbar.—HaK
She. Theodore Roethke.—CoBl
"**She,** a stone-breaker." See The stone-breaker
"**She** bids you on the wanton rushes lay you down." See King Henry IV—Sleep
"**She** caught a butterfly." See Patroness
"**She** counted her cherries and wept a salt tear." See Next year
"**She** does not know." See No images
"**She** drove in the dark to leeward." See The wreck of the Deutschland
"**She** dwelt among the untrodden ways." William Wordsworth.—WoP
"**She** even thinks that up in heaven." See For a lady I know
"**She** frowned and called him Mr." Unknown.—BrLl
She-goat and glow-worm. Christian Morgenstern, tr. fr. the German by Christopher Middleton.—ReO
"**She** goes but softly, but she goeth sure." See Upon the snail

"**She** grew up in bedeviled southern wilderness." See The ballad of Sue Ellen Westerfield
"**She** had a name among the children." See A cat
"**She** had corn flowers in her hair." See Gypsy Jane
"**She** had not held her secret long enough." See The visitation
"**She** had opened an immense hole in the soft ground." See The goddess
"**She** has gone,—she has left us in passion and pride." See Brother Jonathan's lament for Sister Caroline
"**She** has not found herself a hard pillow." See To Clarissa Scott Delany
"**She** has put the child to sleep." Issa, tr. fr. the Japanese by R. H. Blyth.—LeOw
"**She** is the sky." See Mary Hynes
"**She** kiltit up her kirtle weel." See On the Duchess of Gordon's reel dancing
"**She** lives in a garret." See A sad song about Greenwich Village
"**She** rose to his requirement, dropped." Emily Dickinson.—DiPe
"**She** sells sea-shells on the sea shore." Mother Goose.—OpF
Sea shells.—BrMg
"**She** should be." See Poems
She sights a bird. See "She sights a bird, she chuckles"
"**She** sights a bird, she chuckles." Emily Dickinson
She sights a bird.—ReO
"**She** sits with." See Young woman at a window
"**She** slept beneath a tree." Emily Dickinson.—DiPe
"**She** sweeps with many-colored brooms." Emily Dickinson.—DiL—DiPe
"**She** that goes to the well." Unknown.—MoB
"**She** told the story, and the whole world wept." See Harriet Beecher Stowe
"**She** took a last and simple meal when there were none to see her steal." See The lost cat
She walked unaware. Patrick MacDonogh.—CoBl
She walks in beauty. George Gordon Byron.—ByP—CoR
"**She** walks in beauty, like the night." See She walks in beauty
"**She** was a phantom of delight." William Wordsworth.—WoP
"**She** was a stately lady." See Changeling
"**She** was skilled in music and the dance." See Alas, poor queen
"**She** wrote him a letter." See I sent my love a letter
The **sheaf.** Andrew Young.—GrCt
Sheard, Virna
Exile.—CoB
The yak.—DoW
Sheba, Queen of (about)
Dedicated to her highness. E. J. Coatsworth.—CoDh
Sheep. See also Lambs
All wool. A. F. Brown.—ArT-3
An answer to the parson. W. Blake.—BlP
"Baa, baa, black sheep." Mother Goose.—ArT-3—BrMg—HuS-3—OpF—WiMg
Mother Goose rhymes, 21.—HoB
A child's pet. W. H. Davies.—CoB
Clouds. C. G. Rossetti.—HuS-3—LaP
"White sheep, white sheep."—ArT-3
The death and dying words of poor Mailie. R. Burns.—BuPr
The Derby ram. Mother Goose.—BrMg
First sight. P. Larkin.—CoBn—ReO
Impasse. L. Sarett.—CoB
"Little Bo-peep has lost her sheep." Mother Goose.—HuS-3—WiMg
"Little Bo-peep."—BrMg—OpF
Poor Mailie's elegy. R. Burns.—BuPr
"Said a sheep to her child, My dear Ruth." J. G. Francis.—BrLl
The sheep ("Lazy sheep, pray tell me why") A. Taylor.—HoB
Sheep ("When I was once in Baltimore") W. H. Davies.—ClF—ReO
Sheep shearing. F. Lape.—CoB
The shepherd's dog and the wolf. J. Gay.—ReO
The sleepy song. J. D. D. Bacon.—HuS-3—ThA
Slumber song. L. V. Ledoux.—ReS
"There was an old man of Khartoum." Unknown.—BrLl
Two poems. C. Lewis.—LeP
I. "A drove of rams and ewes and woolly lambs"
II. "Sheep of plush, push"
"When the white pinks begin to appear." Mother Goose.—OpF
The **sheep** ("Lazy sheep, pray tell me why") Ann Taylor.—HoB
Sheep ("When I was once in Baltimore") William Henry Davies.—ClF—ReO
"**Sheep** of plush, push." See Two poems
Sheep shearing. Fred Lape.—CoB
The **sheepherder.** Lew Sarett.—BrA
"The **sheets** were frozen hard, and they cut the naked hand." See Christmas at sea
The **shell.** James Stephens.—CoBn—StS
"**She'll** come at dusky first of day." See August
Shelley, Percy Bysshe
Adonais, sel.
Go thou to Rome.—GrCt
Arethusa.—CoD
The aziola.—GrS
Charles IV, sel.
"A widow bird sate mourning for her love."—BlO
Song from Charles IV.—SmM
A dirge.—GrCt
Evening: Ponte al Mare, Pisa.—ClF (sel.)
Go thou to Rome. See Adonais
Hellas.—GrCt (sel.)
Indian serenade.—CoBl

A lament.—GrCt
Love's philosophy.—CoBl
"Music, when soft voices die."—BoH
Ode to the west wind.—CoBn
Ozymandias.—CoR—PaH
Song from Charles IV. See Charles IV—"A widow bird sate mourning for her love"
Summer and winter.—CoBn
To a skylark.—CoR
To the moon.—CoBn—SmM
"A widow bird sate mourning for her love." See Charles IV
Shelley, Percy Bysshe (about)
The fishes and the poet's hands. F. Yerby.—BoA
Memorabilia. R. Browning.—BrP
Shellfish. See names of shellfish, as Lobsters
Shells
Frutta di mare. G. Scott.—CoSs—GrCt—GrS
Sea shell. A. Lowell.—BoH—HuS-3
"See what a lovely shell." From Maud. A. Tennyson.—BoGj
From Maud.—CoBn
"She sells sea-shells on the sea shore." Mother Goose.—OpF
Sea shells.—BrMg
The shell. J. Stephens.—CoBn—StS
Shelton, Peter
Singing.—LeM
Shenandoah. Unknown.—BrA
Shenstone, William
Hope.—CoBn (sel.)
"I have found out a gift for my fair." See A pastoral ballad
A pastoral ballad, sel.
"I have found out a gift for my fair."—ReBs
Shepheardes calendar, sel. Edmund Spenser
Dido my dear, alas, is dead.—GrCt
The **shepherd** ("How sweet is the shepherd's sweet lot") William Blake.—ArT-3—BlP
The **shepherd** ("When I was out one morning") Walter De La Mare.—DeBg
"The **shepherd** and the king." Eleanor Farjeon.—ArT-3
The **shepherd** boy sings in the valley of humiliation. See The pilgrim's progress
"The **shepherd** boy was David." See Big Goliath, little David
Shepherd song, sel. Philip Sidney
The gifts of the animals to man.—ReO
Shepherdess' valentine, sel. Francis Andrewes
"I bear, in sign of love."—ReBs
Shepherdesses. See Shepherds and shepherdesses
Shepherds and shepherdesses
Dido my dear, alas, is dead. From Shepheardes calendar. E. Spenser.—GrCt
Fidelity. W. Wordsworth.—ClF
The fifth sense. P. Beer.—CaMb
Herding lambs. R. Pitter.—CaD
Kurdish shepherds. A. Ross.—CaD
Little Boy Blue. J. C. Ransom.—WeP
"Little Boy Blue, come blow your horn." Mother Goose.—HuS-3—OpF
"Billy Boy Blue, come blow me your horn."—GrT
Boy Blue.—BrMg
"Little Boy Blue."—ReMg
"Little Boy Blue, come blow up your horn."—WiMg
Mother Goose rhymes, 3.—HoB
Nod. W. De La Mare.—ReS
The old shepherds. E. Farjeon.—FaT
Old shepherd's prayer. C. Mew.—PlE
The passionate shepherd to his love. C. Marlowe.—CoBl—McWs
Perrin's walk. H. Behn.—BeG
The sheepherder. L. Sarett.—BrA
The shepherd ("How sweet is the shepherd's sweet lot") W. Blake.—ArT-3—BlP
The shepherd ("When I was out one morning") W. De La Mare.—DeBg
"The shepherd and the king." E. Farjeon.—ArT-3
The shepherd boy sings in the valley of humiliation. From The pilgrim's progress. J. Bunyan.—PlE
The shepherd's hut. A. Young.—CaD
The shepherd's life. From King Henry VI. W. Shakespeare.—ShS
The sky. Mother Goose.—BrMg
The **shepherds** at Bethlehem. See Second shepherds' play
The **shepherd's** calendar, sel. John Clare
The hedgehog.—ReO
The **shepherd's** dog and the wolf. John Gay.—ReO
The **shepherd's** hut. Andrew Young.—CaD
The **shepherd's** life. See King Henry VI
Sherburne, Edward
And she washed his feet with her tears, and wiped them with the hairs of her head.—GrCt
Sheridan, John D.
"Timothy Dan."—StF
Sherman, Frank Dempster
The snow-bird.—ArT-3
Sherwood forest, England
A song of Sherwood. A. Noyes.—ArT-3—ThA
"**Sherwood** in the twilight, is Robin Hood awake." See A song of Sherwood
Shiffrin, A. B.
Hide and seek.—StF
Shigeyoshi Obata
"Blue water . . . a clear moon." tr.—LeMw
The Ching-Ting mountain. tr.—LiT
The nefarious war. tr.—LiT
To his friend, Wei. tr.—LiT (sel.)
Shiki
"Above the mountain."—BeCs
"Above the water."—BaS
"Beyond the dark trees."—BeCs
"Beyond the temple."—BeCs
"Frog-school competing."—BeCs
"The long night."—LeMw

Shirley, James
"The glories of our blood and state."—GrCt
Upon his mistress dancing.—McWs
Shiva. Robinson Jeffers.—GrS
Shiro Murano
Pole vault.—MoS
Shiyo
"Over the deepest."—BeCs
Sho-U
"Rain went sweeping on."—BeCs
"**Shock-headed** Peter. There he stands." See Slovenly Peter
"**Shoe** a little horse." See Foot patting
Shoe-makers. See Shoemakers
"**Shoe** the horse." Elizabeth Jane Coatsworth.—CoSb
Shoemakers. See also Boots and shoes
At the keyhole. W. De La Mare.—BlO
The cobbler ("Crooked heels") E. A. Chaffee.—ArT-3
Cobbler ("He mends the shoes") P. Bacon.—LaC
The cobbler ("Wandering up and down one day") Unknown.—StF
"Cobbler, cobbler, mend my shoe." Mother Goose.—WiMg
Cobbler, cobbler.—BrMg
Cobbler, cobbler, mend my shoe. E. Farjeon.—FaT
The young cordwainer. R. Graves.—CaMb
Shoenblum, Susan
The sea.—LeM
Shoes. See Boots and shoes
Shoes. Tom Robinson.—ArT-3
The **shooting** of Dan McGrew. Robert W. Service.—DoW
Shooting star. Aileen Fisher.—FiI
Shooting stars. Grace Noll Crowell.—HoB
Shop windows. Rose Fyleman.—ArT-3
"The **shopgirls** leave their work." Charles Reznikoff.—LaC
Shopkeepers. See Shops and shopkeepers
Shopping. See Markets and marketing; Peddlers and venders; Shops and shopkeepers
Shopping for meat in winter. Oscar Williams.—HoL
Shops. Winifred M. Letts.—ThA
Shops and shopkeepers. See also names of shops and shopkeepers, as Barbers and barbershops
The animal store. R. Field.—ArT-3—HuS-3—LaP—LaPd
Antique shop. C. Carmer.—ThA
Could be. L. Hughes.—LaC
Drug store. J. V. A. Weaver.—HiL
Emma's store. D. Aldis.—LaC
Felicia Ropps. G. Burgess.—CoBb
The florist shop. R. Field.—BrSg
General store. R. Field.—HoB—HuS-3—TuW
"Hey diddle dinkety poppety pet." Mother Goose.—OpF
The revolving door. N. Levy.—BrSm
Sale. J. Miles.—DuS
The seed shop. M. Stuart.—CoBn
Shop windows.—ArT-3
Shops. W. M. Letts.—ThA
Street window. C. Sandburg.—LaC
Sunday. E. J. Coatsworth.—BrA—LaC
"A wee little boy has opened a store." Unknown.—WyC
Winter flower store. D. Aldis.—BrSg
Shore. See Seashore
Shore. Mary Britton Miller.—ArT-3
Short, David
Long sleep.—LeM
Short course in natural history. See Archy and Mehitabel
Short history of man. John Holmes.—McWs
"The **short** night." Issa, tr. fr. the Japanese.—LeOw
A **short** note. Eve Merriam.—MeI
Short sermon. Unknown, tr. fr. the German by Louis Untermeyer.—ArT-3
Short song. Mother Goose.—BrMg
Shoson Yasuda
"Ah, the peasant who." tr.—LeMw
"As the stately stork." tr.—LeMw
"When I am in grief." tr.—LeMw
Shoshone Indians. See Indians of the Americas—Shoshone
Shotaro Kimura and Peake, Charlotte M. A.
Foam flowers. trs.—LeMw
Reflection. trs.—LeMw
"**Should** auld acquaintances be forgot." See Auld lang syne
"**Should** I sing a requiem, as the trap closes." See Perhaps
"**Should** you, my lord, while you pursue my song." See To the Right Honorable William, Earl of Dartmouth
Shouting into a barrel. Kathleen Fraser.—FrS
"The **show** is not the show." Emily Dickinson.—DiPe
"**Show** me again the time." See Lines to a movement in Mozart's E-flat symphony
A **shower** ("Shower came") Izembō, tr. fr. the Japanese by Olive Beaupré Miller.—ArT-3
The **shower** ("Waters above. Eternal springs") Henry Vaughan.—ClF (sel.)—CoBn—GrCt
"A **shower,** a sprinkle." See Summer rain
"**Shower** came." See A shower
"The **showman** comes with his box of dolls." See The puppet play
Shrews
The masked shrew. I. Gardner.—CoB
"The **shrimp** said to the lobster." See Conversion
"The **shrimping** boats are late today." See Nocturne: Georgia coast
Shrimps
Conversion. J. T. Lillie.—CoB
Nocturne: Georgia coast. D. W. Hicky.—BrA
A **Shropshire** lad, sels. Alfred Edward Housman
"Far in a western brookland."—PaH
"From far, from eve and morning."—HoL
"Into my heart an air that kills."—GrCt
Into my heart.—BoGj

Silence ("My father used to say") Marianne Moore.—HoL—McWs
Silence ("A pitcher of thoughts") Amrita Pritam, tr. fr. the Panjabi by Balwant Gargi.—AlPi
Silence ("Under a low sky") William Carlos Williams.—ReBs
Silence ("When I meet you, I greet you with a stare") Anna Wickham.—CoBl
The **silent** generation. Louis Simpson.—HiL
"**Silent** logs floating." Michael Goodson.—LeM
"**Silent** nymph, with curious eye." See Grongar hill
The **silent** snake. Unknown.—ArT-3
"**Silently** licking his gold-white paw." See A cat
Silk. Eleanor Farjeon.—FaT
Silkin, John
  Death of a bird.—CaD
"The **silly** bit chicken." Unknown.—MoB
Silly Sallie. Walter De La Mare.—BlO—DeBg
"**Silly** Sallie. Silly Sallie." See Silly Sallie
Silly song. Federico Garciá Lorca, tr. fr. the Spanish by Harriet De Onis.—LiT
Silly Willy. R. L. B.—BrSm
"A **silly** young fellow named Hyde." Unknown. —BrLl—BrSm
Silon, Stephie
  "An empty bed."—LeM
Silver, John (about)
  A ballad of John Silver. J. Masefield.—CoSs
Silver (Color)
  Silver. W. De La Mare.—ArT-3—CoBn—HoB—HuS-3—ReS
  Washed in silver. J. Stephens.—StS
Silver. Walter De La Mare.—ArT-3—CoBn—HoB—HuS-3—ReS
"**Silver** bark of beech, and sallow." See Counting-out rhyme
The **silver** fish. Shelley Silverstein.—CoSs
"A **silver-scaled** dragon with jaws flaming red." See The toaster
Silver ships. Mildred Plew Meigs.—ArT-3
"The **silver** swanne (or swan) who living had no note." Unknown.—GrCt—GrS
Silverstein, Shelley
  About the bloath.—CoB
  "Beware, my child."—CoO—LaPd
  Boa constrictor.—CoO
  The clam.—CoB
  "Mary's eyes are blue as azure."—CoBl
  "Mr Spats."—CoO
  Not me.—CoB
  "Nothing to do."—CoBb
  "Sarah Cynthia Sylvia Stout."—CoBb
  The silver fish.—CoSs
  Think of eight numbers.—CoBb
  When the sline comes to dine.—CoB
Simeon (about)
  A song for Simeon. T. S. Eliot.—PlE
Simile: Willow and ginkgo. Eve Merriam.—MeI
Similia similibus. John Hunt Morgan.—BrSm
"**Simon** Danz has come home again." See A Dutch picture
Simon the Cyrenian
  Simon the Cyrenian speaks. C. Cullen.—BoA
Simon the Cyrenian speaks. Countee Cullen.—BoA
Simonides of Ceos
  On the army of Spartans, who died at Thermopylae.—GrCt
"A **simple** child." See We are seven
Simple Simon. See "Simple Simon met a pieman"
"**Simple** Simon met a pieman." Mother Goose.—HuS-3—OpF—ReMg—WiMg
  The history of Simple Simon.—VrF
  Mother Goose rhymes, 49.—HoB
  Simple Simon.—BrMg
The **simpleton.** See "When I was a little boy (I had but little wit)"
The **Simplon** pass. William Wordsworth.—WoP
Simpson, Joan Murray
  Spring song.—SmM
Simpson, Louis
  "As birds are fitted to the boughs."—CoBl—HoL
  The battle.—DuS
  Carentan O Carentan.—CaMb
  The cradle trap.—LiT
  The heroes.—DuS
  Outward.—LiT
  The redwoods.—BrA
  The silent generation.—HiL
Sin
  "There was one I met upon the road." S. Crane.—PlE
  The unpardonable sin. V. Lindsay.—LiP
"**Since** all the riches of this world." William Blake.—BlP
"**Since** congress with your mistress will be short." See The blossoming of love
"**Since** feeling is first." E. E. Cummings.—DuS
"**Since** I am coming to that holy room." See Hymn to God my God, in my sickness
"**Since** I am convinced." Saigyo Hōshi.—BaS
Since I left the ocean. Navin, tr. fr. the Hindi by Josephine Miles.—AlPi
"**Since** my birth." Yvan Goll, tr. fr. the French by Claire Goll.—HoL
"**Since** my house burned down." Masahide, tr. fr. the Japanese by Harry Behn.—BeCs
"**Since** that this thing we call the world." See An epicurean ode
"**Since** there's no help, come, let us kiss and part." See Idea
Sincerity. See Conduct of life
"**Sing** a song of juniper." Robert Francis.—HaL
"**Sing** a song of kittens." Elizabeth Jane Coatsworth.—CoSb
"**Sing** a song of laughter." See The giraffe and the woman
"**Sing** a song of monkeys." See The monkeys
"**Sing** a song of picnics." See Picnic day
"**Sing** a song of scissor men." See The scissorman

Three brown girls singing. M. C. Holman.—HaK
To a skylark. P. B. Shelley.—CoR
"To hear an oriole sing." E. Dickinson.—DiPe
Two sparrows. H. Wolfe.—SmM
"When a man's body is young." Unknown.—LeO
When Mahalia sings. Q. Prettyman.—AdIa
Winter song. J. R. Jiménez.—LiT
"A young lady sings in our choir." Unknown.—BrLl
Singing. Peter Shelton.—LeM
The **singing** cat. Stevie Smith.—CaD
The **singing** fairy. Rose Fyleman.—HoB—ReS
Singing game ("And it's baking, Bessy Bell") Unknown.—MoB
Singing game ("Cam you by the salmon fishers") Unknown.—MoB
Singing game ("The farmer in his den") Unknown.—MoB
Singing game ("Here comes Gentle Robin") Unknown.—MoB
Singing game ("Here is a lass with a golden ring") Unknown.—MoB
Singing game ("In and out the dusty bluebells") Unknown.—MoB
Singing game ("Johnnie Johnson's ta'en a notion") Unknown.—MoB
Singing game ("Oats and beans and barley grows") Unknown.—MoB
Singing game ("One o'clock, the gun went off") Unknown.—MoB
Singing game ("Roses up and roses down") Unknown.—MoB
Singing games. See Games; Nursery play
The **singing** leaves. James Russell Lowell.—HuS-3
"**Singing.** Singing." See Winter song
Singing-time. Rose Fyleman.—ArT-3
"A **single** man stands like a bird-watcher." See The mouth of the Hudson
"A **single** mat." Issa, tr. fr. the Japanese by Nobuyuki Yuasa.—IsF
Singular indeed. David McCord.—McAd
The **Sioux.** Eugene Field.—BoGj
Sioux Indians. See Indians of the Americas—Sioux
Sipe, Muriel (Mrs David Ross)
Good morning.—ArT-3
"**Sir.**" See Four questions addressed to his excellency, the prime minister
"**Sir** Eglamour, that worthy knight." Unknown.—BlO
Sir Galahad. Alfred Tennyson.—TeP
Sir Patrick Spence. See Sir Patrick Spens
Sir Patrick Spens. Unknown.—BlO—BoGj—HoB
The ballad of Sir Patrick Spens.—CoR
Sir Patrick Spence.—ArT-3—CoSs
Sir Roderic's song. See Ruddigore
Sir Simon the king. See "Old Sir Simon the king"
Sir Smashum Uppe. E. V. Rieu.—CoO
"**Sir,** when I flew to seize the bird." See Beau's reply
Sirius
Dog-star. E. Farjeon.—FaT
Sirkar, R. P.
Carving away in the mist. tr.—AlPi
"In a mirage I filled my pitcher." tr.—AlPi
Then go at once. tr.—AlPi
Sister Lou. Sterling A. Brown.—BoA
Sister Nell. Unknown.—CoBb
"**Sister** Simplicitie." See Fragment of a sleepy song
"**Sister,** sister, go to bed." See Brother and sister
Sisters. See Brothers and sisters
The **sisters.** Alfred Tennyson.—TeP
Sit up when you sit down. John Ciardi.—CiYk
"**Sitting.**" Tom Nakai Tsosie.—BaH
Sitting Bull
Last song of Sitting Bull. Unknown.—LeO
"**Sitting** on the stone, O crab." Unknown, tr. fr. Pullayas of Kerala.—LeO
Sitwell, Edith
Dirge for the new sunrise.—PlE
Evening.—CaMb
The flowering forest.—GrS
Kitchen song.—CaD
"Madame Mouse trots."—CaD—HaL
Spinning song.—CaD
"When cold December."—McWs
Sitwell, Osbert
Aubade: Dick the donkey boy.—CaD
The lament of the mole-catcher.—CoB
La tour du sorcier.—CaD
Tom.—CaD
Winter the huntsman.—BlO—ClF
Sitwell, Sacheverell
The lime avenue.—HaL
White rose.—GrS
The **six** badgers. Robert Graves.—BoGj—CoB
"**Six** feet beneath." See Jerry Jones
Six little mice. See "Six little mice sat down to spin"
"**Six** little mice sat down to spin." Mother Goose.—OpF
Six little mice.—BrMg—SmM—StF
"**Six** little sheep." See Impasse
Six rows of pins. Unknown.—ReOn
Size. See also People—Size
The magnifying glass. W. De La Mare.—BlO—DeBg
Night magic. A. J. Burr.—ThA
Rain sizes. J. Ciardi.—HuS-3
Runes IX. H. Nemerov.—DuS
"A saucer holds a cup." E. Dickinson.—DiL
A visit from abroad. J. Stephens.—HaL
"Way down south where bananas grow." Unknown.—CoO
Sjöberg, Leif. See Auden, W. H. and Sjöberg, Leif
Skate and sled. Eleanor Farjeon.—FaA
The **skaters** ("Black swallows swooping or gliding") John Gould Fletcher.—MoS
The **skaters** ("Graceful and sure with youth, the skaters glide") John Williams.—MoS

"**Sky.**" See African sunrise
"**Sky.**" See Blue
"The **sky.**" See Snowstorm
The **sky** ("Red sky at night") Mother Goose.—BrMg
The **sky** ("The sky at night is like a big city") Unknown, tr. fr. the Ewe.—LeO
"The **sky** above us here is open again." See Traveling storm
"The **sky** at night is like a big city." See The sky
"The **sky** has the oldest voice." See Voice of the sky
"The **sky** is low, the clouds are mean." Emily Dickinson.—DiPe
  Beclouded.—CoBn
"The **sky** is overcast." See A night-piece
Sky-larks. See Larks
"The **sky**, lazily disdaining to pursue." See Georgia dusk
"The **sky** looks bigger." See Night sky
Sky net. Aileen Fisher.—FiI
"The **sky** unfolding its blanket to free." See Morning workout
"The **sky** was." See Song
"The **sky** was yellow." See Halloween
The **skylark** ("Bird of the wilderness") James Hogg.—CoB
Skylark ("Singing clear and loud") Seien, tr. fr. the Japanese by Kenneth Yasuda.—LeMw
Skylark ("Up in the lift go we") Unknown.—MoB
Skylarks. See Larks
"The **skyline** of New York does not excite me." See Review from Staten island
Skyscrapers
  On watching the construction of a skyscraper. B. Raffel.—DuR—LaC
  Skyscrapers. R. Field.—HuS-3
Skyscrapers. Rachel Field.—HuS-3
Skywriting. Eve Merriam.—MeI
Slater, Eleanor
  Misdirection.—ThA
The **slave** and the iron lace. Margaret Danner.—BoA
The **slave** auction. Frances Ellen Watkins Harper.—HaK
The **slave** in the Dismal swamp. Henry Wadsworth Longfellow.—LoPl
Slave of the moon. Mary Yarmon.—LeM
Slave quarter. Carl Carmer.—ThA
The **slave** singing at midnight. Henry Wadsworth Longfellow.—LoPl
Slavery
  Harriet Beecher Stowe. P. L. Dunbar.—HaK
  London. From The human image. W. Blake.—GrCt
  Middle passage. R. E. Hayden.—AdIa—BoA
  On liberty and slavery. G. M. Horton.—HaK
  The people of Tao-chow. Po Chü-i.—GrCt
  The proclamation. J. G. Whittier.—HiL
  Runagate runagate. R. E. Hayden.—AdIa
  The slave and the iron lace. M. Danner.—BoA
  The slave auction. F. E. W. Harper.—HaK
  The slave in the Dismal swamp. H. W. Longfellow.—LoPl
  Slave quarter. C. Carmer.—ThA
  The slave singing at midnight. H. W. Longfellow.—LoPl
  Song of the galley-slaves. R. Kipling.—GrCt
  Song of the son. J. Toomer.—BoA—HaK
  Southern mansion. A. Bontemps.—AdIa—BoA—BrA—HaK
  Strong men. S. A. Brown.—BoH
  To the Right Honorable William, Earl of Dartmouth. P. Wheatley.—HaK (sel.)
  "Why should I care for the men of Thames." W. Blake.—BlP—GrCt
Sleds and sleighs
  The little red sled. J. Bush.—ArT-3
  Skate and sled. E. Farjeon.—FaA
Sleep. See also Bed-time; Dreams; Lullabies
  After apple-picking. R. Frost.—CoR
  "All animals like me." R. Souster.—DoW
  Asleep. E. J. Coatsworth.—CoSb
  Bedtime. A. Fisher.—FiC
  Beware. From The tempest. W. Shakespeare.—ShS
  Birds asleep. M. C. Livingston.—LiC
  "I borrowed my cottage." Issa.—IsF
  "I borrowed the wayside shrine." Issa.—LeOw
  "I feel relaxed and still." K. Anderson.—LeM
  Lights out. E. Thomas.—ThG
  Mad song. W. Blake.—BlP
  "The mosquitoes." Issa.—IsF
  Night piece. E. J. Coatsworth.—CoDh
  Nod. W. De La Mare.—ReS
  Now fall asleep. E. J. Coatsworth.—ReS
  Old Boniface. Mother Goose.—BrMg
  On bell-ringers. Voltaire.—BrSm
  Peace on earth. W. C. Williams.—HaL
  Peeking. A. Fisher.—FiIo
  Says Tom to me. D. McCord.—McAd
  Serenade. From The Spanish student. H. W. Longfellow.—LoPl
  Sleep ("She bids you on the wanton rushes lay you down") From King Henry IV. W. Shakespeare.—ShS
  Sleep ("Sleep is a god too proud to wait in palaces") A. Cowley.—GrCt (sel.)
  Sleep and dreams. P. Kelso.—LeM
  "Sleep brings pearl necklaces, do not cry, baby." Unknown.—LeO
  Sleep is a reconciling. Unknown.—GrCt
  The sleeper. E. A. Poe.—PoP
  "A sleeper from the Amazon." Unknown.—BrLl
  Sleepy John. C. Tringress.—StF
  Slumber party. C. McCullers.—AgH
  Summons. R. Francis.—DuR
  Tired. S. Gibney.—GrT
  To sleep ("A flock of sheep that leisurely pass by") W. Wordsworth.—WoP
  To sleep ("O soft embalmer of the still midnight") J. Keats.—GrCt
  "To sleep easy at night." Mother Goose.—AgH
    How to sleep easy.—BrMg

Sleep—*Continued*
Tommy Trot. Mother Goose.—BrMg
Tree-sleeping. R. P. T. Coffin.—HaL
Two in bed. A. B. Ross.—ArT-3
Vesper. Alcman of Sparta.—ReO
Sleep upon the world.—GrCt
"When a man's body is young." Unknown.—LeO
Young love. T. Garrison.—CoBl
Sleep ("She bids you on the wanton rushes lay you down") See King Henry IV
Sleep ("Sleep is a god too proud to wait in palaces") Abraham Cowley.—GrCt (sel.)
Sleep after toil. See The faerie queene
Sleep and dreams. Peter Kelso.—LeM
"**Sleep**, baby, sleep." Unknown.—HoB
Nurse's song.—SmM
"**Sleep** brings pearl necklaces, do not cry, baby." Unknown, tr. fr. the Mikiris.—LeO
"**Sleep** is a god too proud to wait in palaces." See Sleep
Sleep is a reconciling. Unknown.—GrCt
"**Sleep** late with your dream." See Poems for my brother Kenneth, VII
"**Sleep**, little one, sleep for me." See Response
"**Sleep**, my child." See Lullaby for a baby toad
"**Sleep**, sleep, beauty bright." See A cradle song
"**Sleep**, sleep, little one, close your eyes, sleep, little one." Unknown, tr. fr. the Bagon Pygmie.—LeO
"**Sleep**, sleep, sleep." See Lullaby
"**Sleep** softly . . . eagle forgotten . . . under the stone." See The eagle that is forgotten
Sleep upon the world. See Vesper
The **sleeper**. Edgar Allan Poe.—PoP
"A **sleeper** from the Amazon." Unknown.—BrLl
Sleeping. Unknown.—GrT
"**Sleeping**, waking." Issa, tr. fr. the Japanese by Lewis Mackenzie.—LeMw
The **sleepy** day. Harji Patel.—LeM
Sleepy Harry. Ann and Jane Taylor.—GrT—VrF
Sleepy John. Clare Tringress.—StF
The **sleepy** song. Josephine Dodge Daskam Bacon.—HuS-3—ThA
Sleepy sparrows. Unknown, ad. fr. the Japanese by Charlotte B. DeForest.—DePp
Sleepyhead. Walter De La Mare.—ArT-3
Sleighs. See Sleds and sleighs
Sliding. Myra Cohn Livingston.—ArT-3
Slieve Gua. Unknown.—GrCt
"**Slieve** Gua, craggy and black wolf-den." See Slieve Gua
"The **slithergadee** has crawled out of the sea." See Not me
The **sloth**. Theodore Roethke.—CoB—WeP
Sloths
The sloth. T. Roethke.—CoB—WeP
Slovenly Peter. Heinrich Hoffmann.—CoBb
"**Slow** creatures, slow." See Death
Slow flowers, fast weeds. See King Richard III
"The **slow** freight wriggles along the rail." See The freight train
Slow, slow, fresh fount. Ben Jonson.—GrCt
"**Slow**, slow, fresh fount, keep time with my salt tears." See Slow, slow, fresh fount
Slow spring. Sydney Tremayne.—SmM
Slowly. James Reeves.—BlO
"**Slowly** I smoke and hug my knee." See Ballade by the fire
"**Slowly** melting, slowly dying." Diane Hill.—LeM
"**Slowly**, sedately, Indian file." See Ducks at twilight
"**Slowly**, silently, now the moon." See Silver
"**Slowly** the moon is rising out of the ruddy haze." See Aware
"**Slowly** the night blooms, unfurling." See Flowers of darkness
"**Slowly** the tide creeps up the land." See Slowly
"**Slowly** ticks the big clock." See The big clock
The **sluggard**. Lucilius, tr. fr. the Greek by Humbert Wolfe.—MoS
"**Sluggardy-guise**, sluggardy-guise." Unknown.—OpF
"A **slumber** did my spirit seal." William Wordsworth.—WoP
Slumber party. Carson McCullers.—AgH
Slumber song ("Drowsily come the sheep") Louis V. Ledoux.—ReS
Slumber song ("Sandman's coming—childhood echoes") Alfred Noyes.—ReS (sel.)
"A **sly**, false-hearted canon came one day." See The Canterbury tales—The wily alchemist
"A **small** and pompous alderman." See Tatterdemalion
"**Small** as a fox and like." See Our Lucy, 1956-1960
Small birds. Peter Quennell.—ReBs
"**Small** birds who sweep into a tree." See Small birds
"A **small** boy when asked to spell yacht." Unknown.—BrLl
"A **small** boy who lived in Iquique." Unknown—BrLl
"The **small**, green leaf." See Theme and variations—Variations 8
"A **small** hungry child." Bashō, tr. fr. the Japanese by Harry Behn.—BeCs
A **small** migration. Harry Behn.—BeG
The **small** phantom. Walter De La Mare.—DeBg
Small rain. Alice Lawry Gould.—ThA
"**Small** service is true service while it lasts." See To a child
"**Small** shining drop, no lady's ring." See The dewdrop
Smart, Christopher
"Beauteous, yea beauteous more than these." See A song to David
Christmas day. See Hymns and spiritual songs
Foot, fin or feather. See Psalm CXLVII
Hymns and spiritual songs, sel.
Christmas day.—GrCt
My cat Jeoffry.—BlO—CoB—GrCt
Psalm CXLVII, sel.
Foot, fin or feather.—ReO

A song to David.—GrCt
"Beauteous, yea beauteous more than these."—PlE (sel.)
The stars.—GrCt (sel.)
"The **smear** of blue peat smoke." See The shepherd's hut
Smells, Junior. Christopher Morley.—ArT-3—BoH—HoB
The **smile.** William Blake.—BlP
Smith, A. J. M.
Field of long grass.—CoBl
Smith, Adrian Keith
Rain.—LeM
Smith, Dulcie L.
The fountain. tr.—HoL
Smith, Horace
Address to a mummy.—CoR
Smith, John
I am tired of the wind.—SmM
Look.—SmM
A true story.—SmM
Smith, John (about)
"Noah an' Jonah an' Cap'n John Smith." D. Marquis.—CoSs
Pocahontas. W. M. Thackeray.—BrA—HiL
Smith, Norman L. See Kotewell, Robert and Smith, Norman L.
Smith, Stevie
Cat asks mouse out.—CaD
My hat.—SmM
Nipping pussy's feet in fun.—CaD—SmM
The old sweet dove of Wiveton.—ReO
The parklands.—CaMb
The singing cat.—CaD
Smith, William Jay
Butterfly.—ArT-3—BoGj
The closing of the rodeo.—HoL—McWs—MoS
Cow.—CoO
Dog.—BoGj
Gull.—ArT-3
Jittery Jim.—CoBb
Laughing time.—HoB
Lion.—CoB—WeP
The massacre of the innocents.—PlE
Moon.—LaPd
Morels.—CoBn
The owl.—LaPd
A pavane for the nursery.—BoGj—CoBl
Raccoon.—ArT-3
Seal.—CoB—DuR
"There was an old lady named Crockett."—BrLl—BrSm
The toaster.—AgH—ArT-3—DuR
Waves.—CoSs
Winter morning.—CoBn
Smoke
"A house full, a hole full." Mother Goose.—BrMg
"A house full."—OpF—ReOn
"The smoke." Issa.—LeOw
Smoke animals. R. B. Bennett.—LaPd
"The **smoke.**" Issa, tr. fr. the Japanese by R. H. Blyth.—LeOw
Smoke animals. Rowena Bastin Bennett.—LaPd
The **smoking** stick. See "Mother and father and Uncle Dick"
Smoky mountains
Evening in the Great Smokies. D. Heyward.—PaH
A **smugglers'** song. Rudyard Kipling.—BlO
"The **snail.**" Issa, tr. fr. the Japanese by R. H. Blyth.—IsF
The **snail** ("At sunset, when the night-dews fall") James Reeves.—BlO—BrSg
Snail ("Little snail") Langston Hughes.—ArT-3—BrSg—McWs
The **snail** ("Lord, you try for a little while") Carmen Bernos de Gasztold, tr. fr. the French by Rumer Godden.—GaC
The **snail** ("The snail is very odd and slow") Grace Hazard Conkling.—BrSg
Snail ("Snail upon the wall") John Drinkwater.—BoGj
The **snail** ("To grass, or leaf, or fruit, or wall") William Cowper.—CoB
Snail hunters. See "Four and twenty tailors went to kill a snail"
"The **snail** is very odd and slow." See The snail
Snail, moon and rose. Jean Kenward.—SmM
"**Snail,** snail, put out your horns." See To the snail
"**Snail** upon the wall." See Snail
Snails
"Consider this odd little snail." D. McCord.—BrLl
The fairy ring. A. Young.—GrCt
"Four-and-twenty Highlandmen." Unknown.—MoB
"Four and twenty tailors went to kill a snail." Mother Goose.—WiMg
Snail hunters.—BrMg
The garden snail. R. Wallace.—CoB
The haughty snail-king. V. Lindsay.—HaL
"Highty tighty, paradighty." Mother Goose.—BrMg—GrCt
"Johnnie Crack and Flossie Snail." From Under Milk Wood. D. Thomas.—BoGj—CaD—HaL—LaPd
Little snail. H. Conkling.—ArT-3
"Little snail, little snail (with your hard)." Unknown.—WyC
"Look, snail." Issa.—IsF—LeOw
"Make up your mind snail." R. Wright
Hokku poems.—BoA
"A red morning sky." Issa.—LeI
"Said the snail to the tortoise: You may." O. Herford.—BrLl
The selfish snails. A. and J. Taylor.—VrF
"The snail." Issa.—IsF
The snail ("At sunset, when the night-dews fall") J. Reeves.—BlO—BrSg—CoB
Snail ("Little snail") L. Hughes.—ArT-3—BrSg—McWs
The snail ("Lord, you try for a little while") C. B. de Gasztold.—GaC

"In the falling snow." R. Wright
Hokku: "In the falling snow."—AdIa
Hokku poems.—BoA
"In the northwest wind." K. Mizumura.—MiI
"It sifts from leaden sieves." E. Dickinson.—DiPe
"It was I who did command." Lady Fujiwara.—BaS
January. E. J. Coatsworth.—HoB
"Just being here." Issa.—IsF—LeOw
Late snowflakes. Kiyowara no Fukayabu.—LeMw
London snow. R. Bridges.—CoBn—GrCt
A lost snowflake. Unknown.—DePp
"Magnificent snow." Temmu.—BaS
"A mountain village." Shiki.—BeCs
On a night of snow. E. J. Coatsworth.—CoB—DuR
"On a winter day." C. Lewis.—LeP
A patch of old snow. R. Frost.—DuR—LaC
The pine bough. R. Aldridge.—HoL
Prediction. B. J. Esbensen.—ArT-3
Santa Maria Maggiore, Rome. E. Jennings.—CaD
Snow ("The fenceposts wear marshmallow hats") D. Aldis.—ArT-3
On a snowy day.—LaPd
The snow ("In no way that I chose to go") C. Dyment.—SmM
Snow ("In the gloom of whiteness") E. Thomas.—ThG
Snow ("The men of the East") Unknown.—MoB
Snow ("The snow fell softly all the night") A. Wilkins.—ArT-3
The snow ("The sun that brief December day") From Snow-bound. J. G. Whittier.—HuS-3
Snow ("There's a chime in the glitter of the snow") K. Orendurff.—LeM
Snow advent. J. Auslander.—ThA
Snow country. D. Etter.—BrA
The snow fall. A. MacLeish.—HaL
"Snow fell until dawn." Rokwa.—BeCs
Snow harvest. A. Young.—ClF—CoBn
Snow in spring. I. O. Eastwick.—LaPd
Snow in the city. R. Field.—ArT-3—LaP
Snow in the suburbs. T. Hardy.—BoGj—CoBn
The snow lies light. W. W. Christman.—ReBs (sel.)
Snow pictures. A. Fisher.—FiIo
"The snow thaws." Issa.—LeMw
Snow toward evening. M. Cane.—ArT-3—LaPd
Snowball wind. A. Fisher.—FiI
The snowflake. W. De La Mare.—DeBg
Snowflakes ("I once thought that snowflakes were feathers") M. Chute.—LaP—LaPd
Snowflakes ("Out of the bosom of the air") H. W. Longfellow.—GrCt
Snow-flakes.—LoPl
Snowflakes ("Sometime this winter if you go") D. McCord.—McAd
"Snowflakes drift." K. Mizumura.—MiI
Snowman ("My little snowman has a mouth") D. McCord.—McE
Snowman ("Quilly-quo") Unknown.—DePp
The snowman ("We look out of the window") R. Ainsworth.—StF
The snowstorm ("Announced by all the trumpets of the sky") R. W. Emerson.—CoBn
"Announced by all the trumpets of the sky."—ArT-3 (sel.)
Snowstorm ("The sky") A. Fisher.—FiI
Snowstorm ("What a night. The wind howls, hisses, and but stops") J. Clare.—CoBn
Song for snow. E. J. Coatsworth.—McWs
Stopping by woods on a snowy evening. R. Frost.—ArT-3—BoGj—CoBn—HuS-3—LaPd
A story in the snow. P. R. Crouch.—ArT-3
Thaw. E. Thomas.—HoL—ReBs—ThG
"There was once a small boy in Quebec." R. Kipling.—BrLl
"This fall of new snow." Kikaku.—BeCs
To a snowflake. F. Thompson.—CoBn
"To be old." Teika.—BaS
To the city in the snow. A. O'Gara Ruggeri.—ThA
To the snow. Mother Goose.—BrF—BrMg
Tracks in the snow ("Out of the dark") E. J. Coatsworth.—HoB
Tracks in the snow ("Wherever fox or cat or crow") E. J. Coatsworth,—CoSb
Velvet shoes. E. Wylie.—ArT-3—BoGj—HuS-3—ThA
"We are forever talking." Issa.—IsF
"Well, now, let's be off." Issa.—IsF
When snow will come. E. J. Coatsworth.—CoSb
"White bird featherless." Unknown.—GrCt—ReOn
"A white bird floats down through the air." Unknown.—GrCt
White fields. J. Stephens.—CoBn—StS
White morning. A. Fisher.—FiIo
Winter day. A. Fisher.—FiIo
The wonderful weaver. G. Cooper.—HoB
"You light the fire." Bashō.—LeMw
"The **snow**." See Vista
Snow ("The fenceposts wear marshmallow hats") Dorothy Aldis.—ArT-3
On a snowy day.—LaPd
The **snow** ("In no way that I chose to go") Clifford Dyment.—SmM
Snow ("In the gloom of whiteness") Edward Thomas.—ThG
Snow ("The men of the East") Unknown.—MoB
Snow ("The snow fell softly all the night") Alice Wilkins.—ArT-3
The **snow** ("The sun that brief December day") See Snow-bound
Snow ("There's a chime in the glitter of the snow") Karen Orendurff.—LeM
Snow advent. Joseph Auslander.—ThA
The **snow-bird.** Frank Dempster Sherman.—ArT-3
Snow-birds. See Snowbirds

Soap bubbles
"As light as a feather." Mother Goose.—OpF
Blowing bubbles. K. Fraser.—FrS
The bubble. K. Hopkins.—CaD
"A **soapship** went a-rocking." See The voyage of Jimmy Poo
Socialism
Why I voted the socialist ticket. V. Lindsay.—LiP
"A **soft** answer turneth away wrath." See Proverbs, Bible, Old Testament
"**Soft-footed** stroller from the herbless wood." See To a starved hare in the garden in winter
"A **soft** sea washed around the house." Emily Dickinson.—DiL—DiPe
Soft wings. James Stephens.—StS
"**Softly.**" Issa, tr. fr. the Japanese by Nobuyuki Yuasa.—LeMw
"**Softly** along the road of evening." See Nod
"**Softly,** drowsily." See A child's day
Sohrab and Rustum. Matthew Arnold.—CoD
"The **soiled** city oblongs stand sprawling." See City number
"**Soiled** clouds hang." See A thundery day
Soin
"Out of the sky, geese."—BeCs
Solace. Clarissa Scott Delany.—BoA
A **soldier** ("He is that fallen lance that lies as hurled") Robert Frost.—HiL
Soldier ("I walked in my clogs on Salisbury plain") Eleanor Farjeon.—FaT
The **soldier** and the maid. See "Soldier, soldier, won't you marry me"
"**Soldier,** soldier, won't you marry me." Mother Goose.—BlO
"Oh, soldier, soldier, will you marry me."—OpF
The soldier and the maid.—BrMg
The **soldier's** dream. Thomas Campbell.—CoR
Soldiers. See also Memorial day; War; also names of wars, as European war, 1914-1918; also names of battles, as Waterloo, Battle of, 1815
And on this shore. M. C. Holman.—BoA
Anthem for doomed youth. W. Owen.—BoH—GrCt
Apples and water. R. Graves.—CaD
The army of the Sidhe. Lady Gregory.—ThA
Azrael. From Tales of a wayside inn. H. W. Longfellow.—LoPl
Ballad. H. Treece.—CaD
Ballad of the soldier. B. Brecht.—LiT
Buckingham palace. A. A. Milne.—LaPd—MiC
Camptown. J. Ciardi.—HiL
Carentan O Carentan. L. Simpson.—CaMb
Cavalry crossing a ford. W. Whitman.—GrCt—WhA
"Come here to me, my merry, merry men." Mother Goose.—OpF
The recruiting sergeant.—BrMg
Elegy for a dead soldier. K. Shapiro.—HiL
Faithless Nelly Gray. T. Hood.—BrSm
Farewell to the warriors. Unknown.—LeO
Fife tune. J. Manifold.—BoGj—HoL—McWs
The general. S. Sassoon.—McWs
General Monk. Mother Goose.—BrMg
Henry's address to his troops. From King Henry V. W. Shakespeare.—McWs
"Here's Corporal Bull." Mother Goose.—OpF
Corporal Bull.—BrMg
"Hey ding a ding, and ho ding a ding." Mother Goose.—OpF
Hugh Selwyn Mauberley. E. Pound.—HiL
"I have a rendezvous with death." A. Seeger. —HiL
In a bar near Shibuyu Station, Tokyo. P. Engle.—BrA
"It's jolly." E. E. Cummings.—HiL
Kilroy. P. Viereck.—HiL
Naming of parts. H. Reed.—BoGj
Oh stay at home. A. E. Housman.—McWs
"Oh, the brave old duke of York." Mother Goose.—OpF
The brave old duke of York.—BrMg
The grand old duke of York.—ArT-3
"O, the grand old duke of York"—WiMg
"Oh, the mighty king of France." Mother Goose.—OpF
"O what is that sound which so thrills the ear." W. H. Auden.—CaD—GrS
On a certain engagement south of Seoul. H. Carruth.—BrA
On a soldier fallen in the Philippines. W. V. Moody.—HiL
The press-gang. Unknown.—GrCt
Relieving guard. B. Harte.—CoR
Roman wall blues. W. H. Auden.—SmM
"Over the heather the wet wind blows." —CaD
Shiloh, A requiem. H. Melville.—BrA—PaH
A soldier ("He is that fallen lance that lies as hurled") R. Frost.—HiL
Soldier ("I walked in my clogs on Salisbury plain") E. Farjeon.—FaT
"Soldier, soldier, won't you marry me." Mother Goose.—BlO
"Oh, soldier, soldier, will you marry me." —OpF
The soldier and the maid.—BrMg
The soldier's dream. T. Campbell.—CoR
"A stopwatch and an ordnance map." S. Spender.—CaMb
"Success is counted sweetest." E. Dickinson.—BoGj—DiPe
Two wise generals. T. Hughes.—CaMb
A visit to Chelsea college. H. S. Horsley.—VrF
War is kind. S. Crane.—HiL
"We be soldiers three." Unknown.—GrCt
When Johnny comes marching home. P. S. Gilmore.—HiL
"Who saw the Forty-second." Unknown.—MoB
Soliloquy of a tortoise on revisiting the lettuce beds after an interval of one hour while supposed to be sleeping in a clump of blue hollyhocks. E. V. Rieu.—ArT-3—BrSg—CoB —McWs

Soliloquy of the Spanish cloister. Robert Browning.—BrP—CoD
The **solitary** reaper. William Wordsworth.—BlO—CoR—WoP
Solitude. See also Loneliness; Silence
Alone ("The abode of the nightingale is bare") W. De La Mare.—GrCt
Alone ("From childhood's hour I have not been") E. A. Poe.—PoP
Alone ("I never had walked quite so far") J. Paget-Fredericks.—HuS-3
A boy's place. R. Burgunder.—LaPd
The dreamer. W. Childress.—DuS
The goat paths. J. Stephens.—BoGj—ReO—StS
The lake. E. A. Poe.—PoP
The lake isle of Innisfree. W. B. Yeats.—ArT-3—CoR—PaH—ThA—YeR
The little land. R. L. Stevenson.—HuS-3
Looking up at leaves. B. Howes.—CoBn
Love song. Unknown.—LeO
Lucy Gray; or, Solitude. W. Wordsworth.—WoP
"The moon has set." Sappho.—GrCt
Pastourelle. D. J. Hayes.—BoA
Quiet woods. From Two gentlemen of Verona. W. Shakespeare.—ShS
"She dwelt among the untrodden ways." W. Wordsworth.—WoP
The solitary reaper. W. Wordsworth.—BlO—CoR—WoP
"Solitude." E. Merriam.—MeI
A solitude ("A blind man. I can stare at him") D. Levertov.—DuS
Solitude ("How still it is here in the woods. The trees") A. Lampman.—CoBn
Solitude ("Wish, and it's thine, the changeling piped") W. De La Mare.—DeBg
The solitude of Alexander Selkirk. W. Cowper.—CoR
A winter night. W. Barnes.—GrCt
"**Solitude.**" Eve Merriam.—MeI
A **solitude** ("A blind man. I can stare at him") Denise Levertov.—DuS
Solitude ("How still it is here in the woods. The trees") Archibald Lampman.—CoBn
Solitude ("Wish, and it's thine, the changeling piped") Walter De La Mare.—DeBg
The **solitude** of Alexander Selkirk. William Cowper.—CoR
Solomon, King of Israel (about)
Dedicated to her highness. E. J. Coatsworth.—CoDh
"King David and King Solomon." J. B. Naylor.—SmM
King Solomon. E. Merriam.—MeC
Solomon, George
1 black foot + 1 black foot = 2 black feet.—BaH
"**Solomon** Grundy." Mother Goose.—BrMg—WiMg
"A **somber** dragon." See Thunder dragon
"**Sombre** and rich, the skies." See By the statue of King Charles at Charing cross
"**Some** are in prison; some are dead." See The chums
"**Some** are teethed on a silver spoon." See Saturday's child
"**Some** birds leave." See Stay-at-homes
Some brown sparrows. Bruce Fearing.—CoB—DuR
"**Some** brown sparrows who live." See Some brown sparrows
Some cook. John Ciardi.—AgH—LaP—LaPd
"**Some** credulous chroniclers tell us." James Whitcomb Riley.—BrLl
"**Some** day." See What someone said when he was spanked on the day before his birthday
Some day. Elizabeth Jane Coatsworth.—CoSb
"**Some** day, ere she grows too antique." Unknown.—BrLl
"**Some** day our town will grow old." See The Springfield of the far future
"**Some** day, when trees shed their leaves." See After the winter
"**Some** day when you're out of town." See Upside down
"**Some** days my thoughts are just cocoons—all cold, and dull and blind." See Days
Some families of my acquaintance. Laura E. Richards.—CoO
Some fishy nonsense. Laura E. Richards.—ArT-3—StF
"**Some** flowers close their petals." See Flowers at night
Some flowers o' the spring. See The winter's tale
"**Some** gain a universal fame." See A ballade of lawn tennis
"**Some** haystacks don't even have any needle." See Some short poems—An argument against the empirical method
"**Some** horses run in the field." See Hobby-horse
"**Some** keep the Sabbath going to church" Emily Dickinson.—DiPe
"**Some** limericks—most of them, reely." David McCord.—BrLl
Some little bug. Roy Atwell.—BrSm (sel.)
"**Some** men break your heart in two." See Experience
"**Some** men live for warlike deeds." See John James Audubon
"**Some** night I think if you should walk with me." See The lover praises his lady's bright beauty
"**Some** of the cowboys I know best." See Calling all cowboys
Some of Wordsworth. Walter Savage Landor.—GrCt
Some one. Walter De La Mare.—ArT-3—HuS-3—LaPd—StF—ThA
Someone.—HoB
"**Some** one is always sitting there." See The little green orchard
Some people. Rachel Field.—LaPd
"**Some** people admire the work of a fool." William Blake.—BlP
"**Some** people hang portraits up." See A likeness

"**Some** primal termite knocked on wood." See The termite
"**Some** say I have my mother's nose." See Lisa's fingerprints
"**Some** say kissin's ae sin." See Kissin'
"**Some** say, that ever 'gainst that season comes." See Hamlet
"**Some** say the phoenix dwells in Aethiopia." See The phoenix
"**Some** say the sun is a golden earring." Natalia Belting.—LaPd
"**Some** say the world will end in fire." See Fire and ice
Some short poems, sels. William Stafford.—DuS
An argument against the empirical method
Comfort
Kids
The limbs of the pin oak tree
Star guides
"**Some** things are very dear to me." See Sonnet II
Some time. Eleanor Farjeon.—FaT
"**Some** time, some time." See Some time
Some uses for poetry. Eve Merriam.—MeI
"**Some** want a vault, some want a grave." See Madrigal macabre
"**Some** years ago you heard me sing." See Sarah Byng
"**Somebody** else can be captain." See Ding, ding
"**Somebody** up in the rocky pasture." See The ant village
"**Somebody** was mistaken." See All-day sucker
"**Someday.**" See Skipping ropes
Someday. Myra Cohn Livingston.—LiC
"**Someday** I'm going to have a store." See General store
"**Somehow,** flowers." See Counting petals
Someone ("And she looked at me") Lee Jaffe.—LeM
Someone ("Some one came knocking") See Some one
"**Someone** about." See Please
"**Someone** about as big as a bump." See Sit up when you sit down
"**Someone**—and I mean you, my sweet." See Bump. Bang. Bump
Someone asked me. John Ciardi.—CiYk
Someone at my house said. John Ciardi.—CiYk
"**Someone** big and someone small." See If you should fall, don't forget this
"**Someone** came knocking." See Some one
"**Someone** fast and someone slow." See Someone showed me the right way to run away
Someone had a helping hand. John Ciardi.—CiYk
"**Someone** heard the whole town saying." See The great news
"**Someone**—I forget just who." See Someone made me proud of you
"**Someone** I knew was very proud." See A loud proud someone
"**Someone** I know." See Please tell this someone to take care
"**Someone** I know—and he's very near." See Get up or you'll be late for school, silly
"**Someone** I know had a helping hand." See Someone had a helping hand
"**Someone** I met." See It is time, you know
Someone lost his head at bedtime but he got it back. John Ciardi.—CiYk
Someone made me proud of you. John Ciardi.—CiYk
"**Someone** prepared this mighty show." Emily Dickinson.—DiPe
"**Someone** said." See Someone lost his head at bedtime but he got it back
Someone showed me the right way to run away. John Ciardi.—CiYk
Someone slow. John Ciardi.—CiYk
"**Someone** under a chestnut tree." See Can someone tell me why
"**Someone** up in a tree—that tree." See Someone was up in that tree
Someone was up in that tree. John Ciardi.—CiYk
"**Someone** whom no man can see." See Eyes are lit up
"**Someone's** playing with a bottle." See Baby playing
Somersaults. See Play
Somersaults & headstands. Kathleen Fraser.—FrS
"**Something** befell." See At the bottom of the well
"**Something** inspires the only cow of late." See The cow in apple time
"**Something** I've killed, and I lift up my voice." See Hunting song
"**Something** strange I do not comprehend." See Literature: The god, its ritual
"**Something** there is that doesn't love a wall." See Mending wall
"**Something** told the wild geese." Rachel Field.—ArT-3—CoB—HoL—HuS-3—LaPd—TuW
"**Sometime** this winter if you go." See Snowflakes
"**Sometime** we see a cloud that's dragonish." See Antony and Cleopatra—Clouds
"**Sometimes.**" See Automobile mechanics
"**Sometimes.**" See Song of the thunders
Sometimes. Eve Merriam.—MeC
"**Sometimes** goldfinches one by one will drop." See Yellow flutterings
"**Sometimes** he was cool like an eternal." See Lester Young
"**Sometimes** I dip my pen and find the bottle full of fire." See An apology for the bottle volcanic
"**Sometimes** I feel like I will never stop." See To Satch
"**Sometimes** I share things." See Sometimes
"**Sometimes** I think how lovely it would be." See An enchanted garden
"**Sometimes** in the summer." See Sprinkling
"**Sometimes** the moment comes for the return." See Return
"**Sometimes** the rain falls straight." See Rain riddle

Song of myself, sels. Walt Whitman
Animals.—CoB
"I think I could turn and live with animals."—LaPd
Song of myself.—LiT—SmM
"A gigantic beauty of a stallion, fresh and responsive to my caresses."—CoB—LaPd
"I am afoot with my vision."—CoB
"I am he that walks with the tender and growing night.—GrCt
"I believe a leaf of grass is no less than the journey-work of the stars."—ArT-3—LaPd
"I celebrate myself"
Song of myself.—WhA
Miracles.—HuS-3—LiT—SmM
The same old law.—ReO
A **song** of Panama. Damon Runyon.—HiL
The **song** of Quoodle. Gilbert Keith Chesterton.—BoGj
Song of Ranga, sel. Unknown
"If you become the moon, my love."—LeO
The **song** of seven. Walter De La Mare.—DeBg
A **song** of Sherwood. Alfred Noyes.—ArT-3—ThA
The **song** of Solomon, sels. Bible, Old Testament
Awake.—BrSg
"I am the rose of Sharon."—GrCt
The song of songs.—ArT-3
"For, lo, the winter is past."—LaP—LaPd—TuW
The **song** of songs. See The song of Solomon
"The **song** of the aged mother which shook the heavens with wrath." See The four Zoas
Song of the brook. See The brook
Song of the builders. Jessie Wilmore Murton.—BrA
Song of the butterfly. Unknown, tr. fr. the Chippewa.—LeO
"**Song** of the carousel." Claudia Lewis.—LeP
Song of the Chattahoochee. Sidney Lanier.—BrA—CoBn
The **song** of the cornpopper. Laura E. Richards.—HoB
Song of the earth. Elizabeth Jane Coatsworth.—CoDh
Song of the fishermen. Unknown, tr. fr. the Mbundu.—LeO
Song of the four little shell-animals. Unknown, tr. fr. the Quileute.—LeO
The **song** of the frog. Unknown, ad. fr. the Japanese by Charlotte B. DeForest.—DePp
Song of the galley-slaves. Rudyard Kipling.—GrCt
The **song** of the Jellicles. T. S. Eliot.—BlO—LiT—McWs
The **song** of the mad prince. Walter De La Mare.—BoGj—SmM
Song of the mermaids. George Darley.—GrCt
The **song** of the old mother. William Butler Yeats.—HaL—YeR
Song of the open road. Walt Whitman.—WhA
"Afoot and light-hearted, I take to the open road."—ArT-3
Song of the parrot. Elizabeth Jane Coatsworth.—HuS-3
Song of the playing ball. See Shilappadakaram
Song of the pop-bottlers. Morris Bishop.—McWs
The **song** of the rain. Unknown, tr. fr. the Bushman.—LeO
Song of the redwood-tree. Walt Whitman.—PaH (sel.)
"The **song** of the saw." See Busy carpenters
Song of the sky loom. Unknown, tr. fr. the Tewa.—LeO
Song of the son. Jean Toomer.—BoA—HaK
Song of the sun and moon. Unknown, tr. fr. the Navajo.—LeO
Song of the syrens. William Browne.—GrCt
Song of the thunders. Unknown, tr. fr. the Chippewa.—LeO
Song of the truck. Doris Frankel.—BrA
The **song** of the western men. Robert Stephen Hawker.—CoR
The **song** of the wind bell. Ch'en Meng-chia, tr. fr. the Chinese by Harold Acton and Ch'en Shih-hsiang.—LeMw
Song of the witches. See Macbeth—Witches' song
Song of triumph. Edgar Allan Poe.—PoP
The **song** of wandering Aengus. William Butler Yeats.—ArT-3—BlO—BoGj—CoBl—GrS—HaL—HoL—McWs—SmM—ThA—YeR
Song of young men working in gold mines. Unknown.—DoC
Song: On May morning. John Milton.—CoBn
On a May morning.—ClF (sel.)
Song, on reading that the cyclotron has produced cosmic rays, blasted the atom into twenty-two particles, solved the mystery of the transmutation of elements and devil knows what. Samuel Hoffenstein.—BrSm
"The **song** that I'm going to sing." See The crafty farmer
Song: The owl. See The owl ("When cats run home and light is come")
Song to Celia. Ben Jonson.—BoH
Song to cloud. Harry Behn.—BeG
A **song** to David. Christopher Smart.—GrCt
"Beauteous, yea beauteous more than these."—PlE (sel.)
Song to green. Elizabeth Jane Coatsworth.—CoDh
Songs accompanying healing magic. Unknown.—DoC
"I sweep this hut"
"This is a root"
Songs from an island in the moon, sels. William Blake
"Lo, the bat with leathern wing."—LiT
"O, I say, you Joe."—LiT
Songs in praise of the chief. Unknown.—DoC
"Into what would I like to change myself"
"O great chief"
Sonic boom. John Updike.—DuR
Sonnet ("Devouring time, blunt thou the lion's paws") See Sonnets. William Shakespeare

Sonnet ("It is a beauteous evening calm and free") William Wordsworth.—WoP
It is a beauteous evening.—GrCt (sel.)
Sonnet ("Nuns fret not at their convent's narrow room") William Wordsworth.—WoP
Sonnet ("Scorn not the sonnet; critic, you have frowned") William Wordsworth.—WoP
Sonnet ("The stars are mansions built by nature's hand") William Wordsworth.—WoP
Sonnet ("Surprised by joy—impatient as the wind") William Wordsworth.—WoP
Sonnet ("Where are we to go when this is done") Alfred A. Duckett.—BoA
Sonnet LVII. See Sonnets—"Being your slave, what should I do but tend"
Sonnet I. Gwendolyn B. Bennett.—BoA
Sonnet CXXX. See Sonnets—"My mistress' eyes are nothing like the sun"
Sonnet—Silence. Edgar Allan Poe.—PoP
Sonnet XXX ("Love is not all: it is not meat nor drink") Edna St Vincent Millay.—CoBl
Sonnet to a Negro in Harlem. Helene Johnson.—BoA
Sonnet—To science. Edgar Allan Poe.—PoP
Sonnet XXIX. See Sonnets—"When, in disgrace with fortune and men's eyes"
Sonnet II. Gwendolyn B. Bennett.—BoA
Sonnets (about)
An enigma. E. A. Poe.—PoP
Sonnet ("Nuns fret not at their convent's narrow room") W. Wordsworth.—WoP
Sonnet ("Scorn not the sonnet; critic, you have frowned") W. Wordsworth.—WoP
Sonnets, sels. William Shakespeare
"Being your slave, what should I do but tend"
Sonnet LVII.—CoBl
"Devouring time, blunt thou the lion's paws."—GrCt
Sonnet.—HoL
"From you have I been absent in the spring."—GrCt
"Like as the waves make towards the pebbled shore."—GrCt
"My mistress' eyes are nothing like the sun"
Sonnet CXXX.—BoH—CoBl
"Poor soul, the center of my sinful earth."—PlE
"That time of year thou mayest in me behold."—GrCt
"When, in disgrace with fortune and men's eyes"
Sonnet XXIX.—CoBl
Sonnets from the Portuguese, sels. Elizabeth Barrett Browning
"How do I love thee? Let me count the ways."—CoBl
How do I love thee.—BoH
"If thou must love me, let it be for naught."—CoBl
"The **soote** season, that bud and bloom forth brings." See Spring
The **sorceress.** Vachel Lindsay.—LaPd
Sorrow. See Grief
"**Sorrow** is the only faithful one." Owen Dodson.—AdIa—BoA
"**Sorrow** on the acres." See Winter field
Sorrows of Werther. William Makepeace Thackeray.—BrSm
"The **sort** of girl I like to see." See The Olympic girl
Soseki
"Butterfly, these words."—BeCs
"Over the wintry."—BeCs—LaPd
Soul. See also Death and immortality; Immortality
Ballad of the little square. F. G. Lorca.—LiT
The devil's bag. J. Stephens.—LiT
The meaning of atman. From Upanishads. Unknown.—AlPi
"No rack can torture me." E. Dickinson.—DiPe
"Of all the souls that stand create." E. Dickinson.—DiPe
"Poor soul, the center of my sinful earth." From Sonnets. W. Shakespeare.—PlE
Soul. D. L. Graham.—HaK
The soul of a spider. V. Lindsay.—LiP
The soul of birds. P. Mitra.—AlPi
The soul of the city receives the gift of the Holy Spirit. V. Lindsay.—LiP
"The soul selects her own society." E. Dickinson.—DiL—DiPe
"The soul unto itself." E. Dickinson.—DiPe
"Soul, wilt thou toss again." E. Dickinson.—DiPe
The souling song. Unknown.—GrS
Souls. F. S. Davis.—ThA
The soul's dark cottage. From Of the last verses in the book. E. Waller.—GrCt
Squares and angles. A. Storni.—LaC
"Woman, your soul is misshapen." Unknown. DoC
Soul. D. L. Graham.—HaK
"A **soul,** a soul, a soul cake." See The souling song
The **soul** of a spider. Vachel Lindsay.—LiP
The **soul** of birds. Premendra Mitra, tr. fr. the Bengali by Lila Ray.—AlPi
The **soul** of the city receives the gift of the Holy Spirit. Vachel Lindsay.—LiP
"The **soul** selects her own society." Emily Dickinson.—DiL—DiPe
"The **soul** unto itself." Emily Dickinson.—DiPe
"**Soul,** wilt thou toss again." Emily Dickinson.—DiPe
The **souling** song. Unknown.—GrS
Souls. Fannie Stearns Davis.—ThA
The **soul's** dark cottage. See Of the last verses in the book
"The **soul's** dark cottage, batter'd and decay'd." See Of the last verses in the book—The soul's dark cottage
"A **sound-alike.**" See Nym and graph
"**Sound** from hearing disconnects." See Elegy for a jazz musician
The **sound** of morning in New Mexico. Reeve Spencer Kelley.—BrA

The **sound** of night. Maxine W. Kumin.—CoBn
The **sound** of the sea. Henry Wadsworth Longfellow.—LoPl
The **sound** of the wind. See "The wind has such a rainy sound"
The **sound** of trees. Robert Frost.—BoH
"**Sound** the flute." See Spring
The **sound** track. See Land of the free
The **sounding** fog. Susan Nichols Pulsifer.—LaPd
Sounds
The bugle-billed bazoo. J. Ciardi.—HoB
Bump. Bang. Bump. J. Ciardi.—CiYk
Dan Dunder. J. Ciardi.—CoBb
Flight. J. Tate.—LaC
Galoshes. R. W. Bacmeister.—ArT-3
Harlem sounds: Hallelujah corner. W. Browne. —BoA
Hearing the wind at night. M. Swenson.—CoBn
"In quiet night." M. C. Livingston.—LiC
In the night. J. Stephens.—StS
A loud proud someone. J. Ciardi.—CiYk
Music box. A. Fisher.—FiIo
"The noise of passing feet." Unknown.—LeO
The noise of waters. From Chamber music. J. Joyce.—ArT-3
All day I hear.—HoL
"All day I hear the noise of waters."—LiT
November night. A. Crapsey.—HoL
"O what is that sound that so thrills the ear." W. H. Auden.—CaD—GrS
On bell-ringers. Voltaire.—BrSm
"On the Ning Nang Nong." S. Milligan.—CoO—StF
Peeking. A. Fisher.—FiIo
"Q is for the quietness." From All around the town. P. McGinley.—LaC
Rest hour. G. Johnston.—DoW
"A scientist living at Staines." R. J. P. Hewison.—BrLl
Sh. J. S. Tippett.—ArT-3
The shell. J. Stephens.—CoBn—StS
Sonic boom. J. Updike.—DuR
The sound of morning in New Mexico. R. S. Kelley.—BrA
The sound of night. M. W. Kumin.—CoBn
The sound of the sea. H. W. Longfellow.—LoPl
The sound of trees. R. Frost.—BoH
The sounding fog. S. N. Pulsifer.—LaPd
"The sounds in the morning." E. Farjeon.—HoB
"Stillness." Chora.—LeI
Water noises. E. M. Roberts.—CoBn—ThA
Whispers. A. Fisher.—FiIo
"The wind has such a rainy sound." C. G. Rossetti.—ArT-3
The sound of the wind.—BlO
"The **sounds** in the morning." Eleanor Farjeon.—HoB
Souster, Raymond
"All animals like me."—DoW
Dog, midwinter.—CoB
Flight of the roller-coaster.—DoW
Squirrel with jays.—CoB
Summer afternoon.—CoBn
The worm.—DoW
South Carolina
Report from the Carolinas. H. Bevington.—BrA (sel.)
The **South** Country. Hilaire Belloc.—PaH
South Dakota
Dakota badlands. E. Landeweer.—BrA
"**South** of the bridge on Seventeenth." See Fifteen
South Pacific, sel. Oscar Hammerstein II
You've got to be taught.—BrA
South wind. Tu Fu, tr. fr. the Chinese by Kenneth Rexroth.—ArT-3—LeM
Southbound on the freeway. May Swenson.—BrA—DuR
Southdown summer. Sagittarius.—PaH
"**Southeast,** and storm, and every weathervane." See Hatteras calling
The **Southern** Cross. Eleanor Farjeon.—FaT
Southern mansion. Arna Bontemps.—AdIa—BoA—BrA—HaK
Southern ships and settlers. Rosemary Carr and Stephen Vincent Benét.—BrA
Southey, Robert
Bishop Hatto.—GrCt
The Inchcape rock.—GrCt
Winter portrait.—CoBn
Souvenirs. Dudley Randall.—HaK
"The **sow** came in with the saddle." See The riot
The **sower.** R. Olivares Figueroa, tr. fr. the Spanish by Dudley Fitts.—HoL
Sowing. Edward Thomas.—ClF—ThG
Space ("I like the word, space") Claudia Lewis. —LeP
Space ("In the air, instruments circle") William Burford.—HoL
Space and space travel
"But outer space." R. Frost.—LiT
The dome of night. C. Lewis.—LeP
How strange it is. C. Lewis.—LeP
"If this little world to-night." O. Herford.—BrSm
Earth.—DuR
Interplanetary limerick. A. Graham.—BrLl
Looking through space. A. Fisher.—FiI
No man on any moon. C. Lewis.—LeP
Outward. L. Simpson.—LiT
Post early for space. P. J. Henniker-Heaton.—BrA
Space ("I like the word, space") C. Lewis.—LeP
Space ("In the air, instruments circle") W. Burford.—HoL
This thing called space. M. C. Livingston.—LiC
"Three skies." C. Lewis.—LeP
Valentine for earth. F. M. Frost.—ArT-3—HoB
"**Space,** and the twelve clean winds of heaven." See The most-sacred mountain

"The **spacious** firmament on high." Joseph Addison.—PlE
"**Spades** take up leaves." See Gathering leaves
Spain
The emperor's bird's-nest. H. W. Longfellow. ReBs
Evening. W. J. Turner.—PaH
A few things explained. P. Neruda.—LiT (sel.)
Spanish Johnny. W. S. Cather.—McWs
Spain—History. See also United States—History —War with Spain
Conquistador. A. MacLeish.—HiL (sel.)
"The **spangled** pandemonium." Palmer Brown.—Art-3
"A **spaniel,** Beau, that fares like you." See On a spaniel, called Beau, killing a young bird
Spanish folk song. Unknown, tr. fr. the Spanish by S. De Madariaga.—ClF
Spanish Johnny. Willa Sibert Cather.—McWs
"A **Spanish** sculptor named Cherino." See Who has seen the wind
The **Spanish** student, sel. Henry Wadsworth Longfellow
Serenade.—LoPl
"A **spark** in the sun." Harry Behn.—BeCs—BrSg
The **sparrow** bush. Elizabeth Jane Coatsworth.—CoSb
"**Sparrow,** in the cherry-tree." See The child and the sparrow
Sparrows
"At last, in sunshine." Onitsura.—BeCs
"At the morning exhibition." Issa.—IsF
"The blind sparrow." Gyôdai.—LeI
The child and the sparrow. T. Westwood.—ReBs
City sparrow. A. Kreymborg.—LaC
"Come." Issa.—IsF
"Come and play with me." Issa.—LeOw
The cursing of the cat. From Philip (or Phylip) Sparrow. J. Skelton.—ReO
O cat of carlish kind.—GrCt
"A day of spring." Onitsura.—LeI
"An exhausted sparrow." Issa.—IsF—LeOw
"If you are tender to them." Issa.—IsF
Let ye then my birds alone. From Summer evening. J. Clare.—ReBs
"A little cock sparrow sat on a green tree." Mother Goose.—WiMg
A little cock sparrow.—BrMg
"Little sparrow." Issa.—LeOw
The praise of Philip Sparrow. G. Gascoigne.—ReO
Sleepy sparrows. Unknown.—DePp
Some brown sparrows. B. Fearing.—CoB—DuR
The sparrow bush. E. J. Coatsworth.—CoSb
Sparrows. A. Fyfe.—LeM
Sparrows or butterflies. Unknown.—DePp
The sparrow's skull. R. Pitter.—PlE
"Step aside, step aside." Issa.—IsF
To sparrows fighting. W. H. Davies.—ReBs
Two sparrows. H. Wolfe.—SmM
"Who killed Cock Robin." Mother Goose.—OpF
The death and burial of Cock Robin.—BrMg—VrF
Sparrows. Anne Fyfe.—LeM
"A **sparrow's** on a willow twig." See Sparrows or butterflies
Sparrows or butterflies. Unknown, ad. fr. the Japanese by Charlotte B. DeForest.—DePp
The **sparrow's** skull. Ruth Pitter.—PlE
Spartans
On the army of Spartans, who died at Thermopylae. Simonides of Ceos.—GrCt
"**Speak** gently, spring, and make no sudden sound." See Four little foxes
"**Speak** of the birds, he lifts a listening finger." See The blind man
"**Speak** roughly to your little boy." See Alice's adventures in wonderland
"**Speaking** of Joe, I should have said." See Fred
"A **speck** that would have been beneath my sight." See A considerable speck
"A **speck** went blowing up against the sky." See A visit from abroad
"A **speckled** cat and a tame hare." See Two songs of a fool
Spectacles (Eye-glasses)
"Without a bridle or a saddle." Mother Goose.—OpF
Speech
"Could any mortal lip divine." E. Dickinson.—DiPe
"The girl in the lane." Mother Goose.—BrMg—ReOn
Improper words. E. Turner.—VrF
"There was a young man of Calcutta." Unknown.—BrLl
Ululation. E. Merriam.—MeI
Speed
Ambition. M. Bishop.—BrA
Hell's bells. M. Fishback.—BrSm
Highway: Michigan. T. Roethke.—DuS
"Said the snail to the tortoise: You may." O. Herford.—BrLl
Slowly. J. Reeves.—BlO
Snail's pace. A. Fisher.—FiI
Someone showed me the right way to run away. J. Ciardi.—CiYk
"There was a young lady of Bright." A. H. R. Buller.—ArT-3—BrLl
To Miss Rápida. J. R. Jiménez.—LiT
A **spell.** See The old wives' tale
A **spell** of invisibility. See The tragical history of Dr Faustus
A **spell** of weather. Eve Merriam.—MeI
Spelling
"A boy at Sault Ste. Marie." Unknown.—BrLl
O-u-g-h. D. McCord.—McAd
One, two, three—gough. E. Merriam.—MeI
"A small boy when asked to spell yacht." Unknown.—BrLl
Spelling bee. E. Farjeon.—FaT

Spiders—*Continued*
"The spider holds a silver ball." E. Dickinson.—DiL
Tightrope walker. A. Fisher.—FiIo
Upon a spider catching a fly. E. Taylor.—ReO
A **spike** of green. Barbara Baker.—BrSg
"**Spin** a coin, spin a coin." See Queen Nefertiti
"**Spin,** spin, spin." See The spinners
Spinach
"There was an old woman (who lived at Greenwich)." W. De La Mare.—BrSg
"A **spindle** on four legs." See The lamb
The **spinners.** Unknown, ad. fr. the Japanese by Charlotte B. DeForest.—DePp
Spinning
"The cattie sat in the kiln-ring." Unknown.—MoB
"Cross-patch." Mother Goose.—BrMg—GrCt—WiMg
"My wheelie goes round." Unknown.—MoB
The spinners. Unknown.—DePp
Spinning song. E. Sitwell.—CaD
A spinning-wheel song. J. F. Waller.—CoBl
The spinning-wheel.—GrCt
A tale. Mother Goose.—BrMg
Spinning song. Edith Sitwell.—CaD
The **spinning-wheel.** See A spinning-wheel song
A **spinning-wheel** song. John Francis Waller.—CoBl
The spinning-wheel.—GrCt
Spinsterhood
"My old maid aunt." D. Schultz.—DuS
What she did in the morning, I wouldn't know, she was seated there in the midst of her resilient symptoms, always. Merrill Moore.—DuS
Spire, Andre
Spring.—CoBl
The **spirit** of the birch. Arthur Ketchum.—ThA
"The **spirit** walking in the sky takes care of us." Unknown, tr. fr. the Ojibway.—LeO
Spirits. See Ghosts
Spirituals. See Negro spirituals
"The **splendor** falls on castle walls." See The princess—The bugle song
"The **splendor** of spring slowly, slowly departs—but whither." See The fall of the flowers
The **splendour** falls. See The princess—The bugle song
Splinter. Carl Sandburg.—ArT-3
Splish splosh. Stefan Martul.—LeM
Split the stones. Elizabeth Jane Coatsworth.—CoDh
Spooks. Nathalia Crane.—BrSm
The **Spoon** River anthology, sels. Edgar Lee Masters
Anne Rutledge.—BrA—HiL
Knowlt Hoheimer.—HoL
The village atheist.—PlE
Sport. William Henry Davies.—CoB
Sporting Beasley. Sterling A. Brown.—HaK
Sports. See Athletes and athletics; Games; also names of games, as Baseball; also names of sports, as Fishermen and fishing
"A **sporty** young man in St Pierre." Ferdinand G. Christgau.—BrLl
Sporus. See Epistle to Dr Arbuthnot
"**Sprawled** on the crates and sacks in the rear of the truck." See Green, green is El Aghir
Spray. D. H. Lawrence.—CoBn
"**Spread,** said toast to butter." See Jam
Spring. See also April; March; May; Seasons
"Above the water." Shiki.—BaS
After the winter. C. McKay.—AdIa
After winter. S. Brown.—BoH
And a big black crow is cawing. E. J. Coatsworth.—CoSb
"And every sky was blue and rain." From To deck a woman. R. Hodgson.—HaL
"As I was a-walking." Unknown.—ReBs
"As now I come." Nōin.—BaS
At Mrs Appleby's. E. M. McWebb.—ArT-3—HuS-3
A bird song in the ravine. Wang Wei.—LeMw
The birds know. E. Farjeon.—FaA
Birds must sing. A. Rye.—SmM
Blue-butterfly day. R. Frost.—BrSg
The boats are afloat. Chu Hsi.—LeMw
"The bridge of dreams." Teika.—BaS
The buds. J. Stephens.—StS
But these things also. E. Thomas.—ThG
"Can it be that there is no moon." Narihira.—BaS
Canticle of spring. H. Behn.—BeG
Ceremony. H. Behn.—BeG
A charm for spring flowers. R. Field.—ArT-3—TuW
Come, come away. From The merry beggars. R. Brome.—ReBs
Come—gone. W. De La Mare.—DeBg
A commercial for spring. E. Merriam.—MeI
The country in spring. Lin Keng.—LeMw
Crow in springtime. E. J. Coatsworth.—CoSb
"The day before April." M. C. Davies.—ThA
"A day of spring (in the garden)." Onitsura.—LeI
"A day of spring (twilight)." Issa.—LeOw
"The days are clear." C. G. Rossetti.—ArT-3
December. S. Vanderbilt.—LaC
"Do those girls set out." Tsurayuki.—BaS
Early spring ("I've looked in all the places") M. Chute.—BrSg
Early spring ("Once more the heavenly power") A. Tennyson.—TeP
The enchanted spring. G. Darley.—CoBn
End of winter. E. Merriam.—MeI
"Even as the snow fell." Issa.—LeMw
The fall of the flowers. Yen Yun.—LeMw
First-ing. A. Fisher.—FiIo
First signs. E. Farjeon.—FaA
The first spring morning. R. Bridges.—CoBn—SmM
"The flowers to the tree's root." Sūtoku.—BaS
Four little foxes. L. Sarett.—ArT-3—BoH—CoB—DuR—LaPd
The four sweet months. R. Herrick.—TuW
"Fresh spring, the herald of love's mighty king." E. Spenser.—GrCt

"From you have I been absent in the spring." From Sonnets. W. Shakespeare.—GrCt
"Gay comes the singer." Unknown.—SmM
Green song. P. Booth.—CoBn
"Here we come a-piping." Unknown.—BlO
"I feel a bit happier." C. R. Foster.—LeM
"I heard it in the valley." A. Wynne.—ThA
I took a little stick. E. J. Coatsworth.—CoSb
"If it were not for the voice." Lady Nakatsukasa.—BaS
In a spring still not written of. R. Wallace.—CoBn
"In just." From Chanson innocente. E. E. Cummings.—DuR
"In the eternal." Ki no Tomonori.—BaS
In the fields. C. Mew.—CoBn—SmM
"In the fields of spring." Unknown.—BaS
In the spring ("In the spring a fuller crimson comes upon the robin's breast") From Locksley hall. A. Tennyson.—CoBn—TeP
In the spring ("Let's go, let's go") Unknown.—DePp
"In time of silver rain." L. Hughes.—ArT-3
"It is nice to read." Onitsura.—BeCs
"A lady red upon the hill." E. Dickinson
The waking year.—CoBn
"A light exists in spring." E. Dickinson.—DiPe
"A little madness in the spring." E. Dickinson.—DiPe
A lover and his lass. From As you like it. W. Shakespeare.—ShS
May day. M. C. Livingston.—BrSg
"Mirrored in the waters of the Kamunabi river." Atsumi.—BaS
A moonlight night. Liu Fang-p'ing.—LeMw
Night in early spring. E. J. Coatsworth.—CoSb
Night wind in spring. E. J. Coatsworth.—CoDh
Now fades the last. From In memoriam. A. Tennyson.—TeP
"Now it is spring." Yakamochi.—BaS
"O owl." Issa.—IsF
"Oh see how thick the goldcup flowers." From A Shropshire lad. A. E. Housman.—CoBl
Old Dan'l. L. A. G. Strong.—ClF—SmM
"On a rainy spring day." Issa.—IsF
On the road to Nara. Bashō.—ArT-3
On time. A. Fisher.—FiC
"Once again." K. Mizumura.—MiI
Out in the wood. C. Scollard.—ThA
"Out of one wintry." Ransetsu.—BeCs
The penny whistle. E. Thomas.—ThG
The peopled air. From Ode on the spring. T. Gray.—ReO
"The plum blossoms have opened." Unknown.—BaS
Raccoons. A. Fisher.—LaP—LaPd
"The rains of spring." Lady Ise.—ArT-3
Robin's song. E. L. M. King.—ArT-3
Rondeau. X. J. Kennedy.—McWs
"The rotten-wooded willow." Suguwara no Michizane.—BaS
"The saddest noise, the sweetest noise." E. Dickinson.—ClF (sel.)
Slow spring. S. Tremayne.—SmM
Snow in spring. I. O. Eastwick.—LaPd
Song. E. E. Cummings.—McWs
The song of Solomon, sels. Bible, Old Testament
Awake.—BrSg
"I am the rose of Sharon."—GrCt
The song of songs.—ArT-3
"For lo, the winter is past."—LaP—LaPd—TuW
Spring ("The alder by the river") C. Thaxter.—HoB
Spring ("I'm shouting") K. Kuskin.—LaPd
Spring ("The last snow is going") H. Behn.—ArT-3—LaP
Spring ("The leaves are uncurling") M. Chute.—BrSg
Spring ("Nothing is so beautiful as spring") G. M. Hopkins.—CoBn
Spring ("Now hand in hand, you little maidens, walk") A. Spire.—CoBl
Spring ("Now rouses earth, so long quiescent") M. Bishop.—McWs
Spring ("Pleasure it is") W. Cornish.—CoBn—GrCt
Spring ("The soote season, that bud and bloom forth brings") H. Howard.—ReO
Spring ("Sound the flute") W. Blake.—ArT-3—BlP—HoB
Spring ("Spring, the sweet spring, is the year's pleasant king") T. Nashe.—BlO—CoBn—TuW
Spring ("When I woke up this morning") C. Wilson.—BaH
The spring ("When wintry weather's all a-done") W. Barnes.—CoBn
"Spring comes on the world." E. Dickinson.—DiPe
"Spring dawn." From Poems. J. Lester.—HaK
"Spring departing." Bashō.—LeMw
Spring fever. E. Merriam.—MeI
"Spring goeth all in white." R. Bridges.—CoBn—GrCt
Spring grass. C. Sandburg.—BoH
Spring in New Hampshire. C. McKay.—BoH—HaK
Spring is a looping-free time. M. Robbins.—MoS
"The spring lingers on." R. Wright
Hokku poems.—BoA
Spring morning. D. H. Lawrence.—CoBl
Spring morning—Santa Fe. L. Riggs.—PaH
Spring oak. G. Kinnell.—CoBn
Spring quiet. C. G. Rossetti.—CoBn—ReBs
"Spring rain (everything)." Chiyo-ni.—LeMw
"Spring rain (a few)." Issa.—LeOw
"The spring rain (which hangs)." Lady Ise.—BaS
Spring rain ("Leaves make a slow") H. Behn.—ArT-3
Spring rain ("The storm came up so very quick") M. Chute.—ArT-3—LaP
Spring reminiscence. C. Cullen.—BoH
Spring song ("Ho starling, quarrelsome swaggerer, you up there on the gable") J. M. Simpson.—SmM

Spring song ("Spring is coming, spring is coming") William Blake.—BrSg
Spring talk. David McCord.—McAd
"**Spring,** the sweet spring, is the year's pleasant king." See Spring
Spring thunder. Mark Van Doren.—BoH
Spring to winter. See The ancient mansion
"**Spring** tried and tried, but could not make." See I took a little stick
The **spring** will come. H. D. Lowry.—CoBn
Spring wind. Kedar Nath Agrawal, tr. fr. the Hindi by L. E. Nathan.—AlPi
Springfield, Illinois
After reading the sad story of the fall of Babylon. V. Lindsay.—LiP
The dream of all the Springfield writers. V. Lindsay.—LiP
Johnny Appleseed speaks of the apple-blossom amaranth that will come to this city. V. Lindsay.—LiP
On the building of Springfield. From A gospel of beauty. V. Lindsay.—LiP
The soul of the city receives the gift of the Holy Spirit. V. Lindsay.—LiP
Springfield magical. V. Lindsay.—LiP
The Springfield of the far future. V. Lindsay. LiP
The town of American visions. V. Lindsay.—LiP
Springfield, Massachusetts
The arsenal at Springfield. H. W. Longfellow. —LoPl
Springfield magical. Vachel Lindsay.—LiP
The **Springfield** of the far future. Vachel Lindsay.—LiP
Springs (Water)
On visiting a clear spring. Li T'ai-po.—LeMw
The pasture. R. Frost. ArT-3—BoGj—CoB—HuS-3—LaP—LaPd—ThA
The spring. R. Fyleman.—HuS-3
"**Spring's** blue water gushes down the hill." See The country in spring
Springtime in Donegal. Mabel Rose Stevenson. —HuS-3
Sprinklers (Water)
Sprinkling. D. M. Pierce.—ArT-3
Sprinkling. Dorothy Mason Pierce.—ArT-3
The **sprinters.** Lee Murchison.—MoS
Spruce trees
Beneath the snowy trees. A. Fisher.—FiI
"**Spruce** up, O baggy elephant." See Plain talk for a pachyderm
Squabbles. See "My little old man and I fell out"
Square-toed princes. Robert P. Tristram Coffin.—BrA
Squares and angles. Alfonsina Storni, tr. fr. the Spanish by Seymour Resnick.—LaC
Squash (Game)
Civilities. T. Whitbread.—MoS
"**Squawking** they rise from reeds into the sun." See Mallard
Squire, Sir J. (John) C. (Collings or Collins)
The discovery. See There was an Indian
There was an Indian.—BrA
The discovery.—ClF
The **squirrel** ("Among the fox-red fallen leaves I surprised him. Snap") Ian Serraillier.—CoB
The **squirrel** ("Whisky, frisky") Unknown.—ArT-3—HoB—HuS-3—LaPd
The **squirrel** ("The winds they did blow") Mother Goose.—BrMg
"The **squirrel** in his shirt stands there." Unknown, tr. fr. the Navajo.—LeO
Squirrel in sunshine. William Cowper.—CoB
"The **squirrel** is the curliest thing." See The curliest thing
Squirrel with jays. Raymond Souster.—CoB
Squirrels
An appointment. W. B. Yeats.—YeR
Chucklehead. P. Robbins.—ArT-3
The curliest thing. Unknown.—StF
The death of a squirrel in McKinley park. G. W. Barrax.—HaK
Fred. D. McCord.—ArT-3
The gray squirrel. H. Wolfe.—BoGj—CoB
Joe. D. McCord.—ArT-3—HoB—McE
Little Charlie Chipmunk. H. C. LeCron.—ArT-3
A little squirrel. Unknown.—ArT-3
"The mountain and the squirrel." R. W. Emerson.—BoGj—BoH
Fable.—ReO
"A saucer holds a cup." E. Dickinson.—DiL
The squirrel ("Among the fox-red fallen leaves I surprised him. Snap") I. Serraillier.—CoB
The squirrel ("Whisky, frisky") Unknown.—ArT-3—HoB—HuS-3—LaPd
The squirrel ("The winds they did blow") Mother Goose.—BrMg
"The squirrel in his shirt stands there." Unknown.—LeO
Squirrel in sunshine. W. Cowper.—CoB
Squirrel with jays. R. Souster.—CoB
The story of the baby squirrel. D. Aldis.—ArT-3
Ten little squirrels. Mother Goose.—StF
To a squirrel at Kyle-Na-No. W. B. Yeats.—BlO—CoB—LaPd
To a winter squirrel. G. Brooks.—BoH
"The **staff** slips from the hand." See Outward
Staffa. John Keats.—GrS
Stafford, William
An argument against the empirical method. See Some short poems
Comfort. See Some short poems
Fifteen.—DuR
The fish counter at Bonneville.—BrA
In the Oregon country.—BrA
Kids. See Some short poems
The limbs of the pin oak tree. See Some short poems
One home.—BrA

Stafford, William—*Continued*
Some short poems, sels.—DuS
An argument against the empirical method
Comfort
Kids
The limbs of the pin oak tree
Star guides
Star guides. See Some short poems
The star in the hills.—DuS
Traveling through the dark.—DuS
Vacation.—BrA
Stairs
Halfway down. A. A. Milne.—MiC
"Johnnie Norrie." Mother Goose.—BrMg
Stamp battalion. Edward Verrall Lucas.—HuS-3
Stamps
Stamp battalion. E. V. Lucas.—HuS-3
"A **stamp's** a tiny, flimsy thing." See Stamp battalion
Stand close around. Walter Savage Landor.—GrCt
"**Stand** close around, ye Stygian set." See Stand close around
"**Stand** still, true poet that you are." See Popularity
The **standing** corn. Eleanor Farjeon.—FaA
Standing on earth. See Paradise lost
"**Standing** on earth, not rapt above the pole." See Paradise lost—Standing on earth
"**Standing** or sitting." Unknown.—BaS
Stanley, Sir Henry Morton (about)
Stanley meets Mutesa. J. D. Rubadiri.—BoH
Stanley meets Mutesa. James D. Rubadiri.—BoH
Stanzas ("Could love for ever") George Gordon Byron.—ByP
Stanzas ("In youth have I known one with whom the earth") Edgar Allan Poe.—PoP
Stanzas ("When a man hath no freedom to fight for at home") George Gordon Byron.—ByP
Stanzas for music. George Gordon Byron.—ByP
Stanzas to Augusta. George Gordon Byron.—ByP
Stanzas written in passing the Ambracian gulf. George Gordon Byron.—ByP
Stanzas written on the road between Florence and Pisa. George Gordon Byron.—ByP
The **star** ("O little one away so far") Elizabeth Madox Roberts.—ReS
The **star** ("Twinkle, twinkle, little star") Jane Taylor.—ArT-3—BrMg—HoB
Little star.—HuS-3
"Twinkle, twinkle, little star."—SmM
"**Star** bright, star-light." See "Star-light, star-bright"
Star guides. See Some short poems
"A **star** hit in the hills behind our house." See The star in the hills
The **star** in the hills. William Stafford.—DuS
"The **star** is in the orange tree." See The coming star
Star light. See "Star-light, star-bright"
"**Star-light,** star-bright." Mother Goose.—ArT-3—TuW
"Star bright, star-light."—HuS-3
Star light.—BrMg
The **star-spangled** banner. Francis Scott Key.—HiL
Star-spangled ode. Phyllis McGinley.—HiL
Star-swirls. Robinson Jeffers.—DuS
Star-talk. Robert Graves.—BoGj—CoBn
The **star** that watches the moon. Eleanor Farjeon.—FaT
"A **star-white** sky." See Witches
Starbird, Kaye
"Don't ever cross a crocodile."—ArT-3—LaPd
Eat-it-all Elaine.—LaPd
Flying.—LaPd
Horse-chestnut time.—LaPd
Old Jake Sutter.—ArT-3
Starfish
The starfish ("Lord, your deep has closed over me") C. B. de Gasztold.—GaC
The starfish ("Triangles are commands of God") R. P. T. Coffin.—LiT
The **starfish** ("Lord, your deep has closed over me") Carmen Bernos de Gasztold, tr. fr. the French by Rumer Godden.—GaC
The **starfish** ("Triangles are commands of God") Robert P. Tristram Coffin.—LiT
"**Stark** day corrodes the silver of the dream." See Trinity: A dream sequence
The **starlighter.** Arthur Guiterman.—ThA
"**Starling** in my cherry-tree." See This year
Starlings
"Fluttering helplessly." T. Boughton.—LeM
"Huddled starlings." K. Mizumura.—MiI
The manoeuvre. W. C. Williams.—HaL
Spring song. J. M. Simpson.—SmM
Starlings. M. Webb.—TuW
Starlings. Mary Webb.—TuW
The **starry** nevers. Elizabeth Jane Coatsworth.—CoSb
Starry night I. Eve Merriam.—MeI
Starry night II. Eve Merriam.—MeI
Stars
At the bottom of the well. L. Untermeyer.—BoGj
Big Bear and Little Bear. E. Farjeon.—FaT
Blue stars and gold. J. Stephens.—StS
Caliban in the coal mines. L. Untermeyer.—LaPd
Come in. R. Frost.—CoBn
The coming star. J. R. Jiménez.—LiT
Counting. F. Johnson.—BoA
Cygnus. E. Farjeon.—FaT
Daisies. A. Young.—BoGj
Dog-star. E. Farjeon.—FaT
The dome of night. C. Lewis.—LeP
The earth. E. Farjeon.—FaT
El hombre. W. C. Williams.—HoL
Escape at bedtime. R. L. Stevenson.—ArT-3—ReS
The evening star ("Hesperus, the day is gone") J. Clare.—GrCt
Evening star ("Quiet mist, the milk of dreams") E. Farjeon.—FaT

The falling star. S. Teasdale.—ArT-3—HuS-3—LaPd—ThA
February twilight. S. Teasdale.—LaP—LaPd—ThA
The flowering forest. E. Sitwell.—GrS
Hesperus. J. Stephens.—StS
"Higher than a house." Mother Goose.—ArT-3—BrMg
The Hyades. E. Farjeon.—FaT
"I have a little sister, they call her Peep-peep." Mother Goose.—ArT-3—BrMg—HuS-3
One eye.—ReOn
"I have lost my dewdrop, cries the flower." R. Tagore.—LeMf
If the stars should fall. S. Allen.—AdIa
"If this little world to-night." O. Herford.—BrSm
Earth.—DuR
In a boat. D. H. Lawrence.—CoBl
In a million years. C. Lewis.—LeP
It is not far. S. Teasdale.—HuS-3
The lights in the sky are stars. K. Rexroth.—LiT (sel.)
The lost star. E. Farjeon.—FaT
Lucky star. E. Farjeon.—FaT
Moon song. H. Conkling.—ThA
The morning star ("Cold, clear, and blue, the morning heaven") E. Brontë.—GrCt
Morning star ("Was then the morning too bright for him") E. Farjeon.—FaT
My star. R. Browning.—BrP
Night ("Night is a purple pumpkin") P. Hubbell.—LaPd
Night ("Stars over snow") S. Teasdale.—ThA
It is not far.—HuS-3
The North star whispers to the blacksmith's son. V. Lindsay.—LiP
The old shepherds. E. Farjeon.—FaT
On looking up by chance at the constellations. R. Frost.—LiT
"On the beach at night." W. Whitman.—GrCt
Orion. D. McCord.—McAd
Orion's belt. E. Farjeon.—FaT
"The owl hooted and told of the morning star." Unknown.—LeO
The Pleiades. E. Farjeon.—FaT
Polar star. Unknown.—LeO
Pole-star. E. Farjeon.—FaT
"Queen Cassiopeia." E. Farjeon.—FaT
"The seasons were appointed, and the times." N. Belting.—BeCm
The shape called star. L. T. Nicholl.—HoL
Shooting star. A. Fisher.—FiI
Shooting stars. G. N. Crowell.—HoB
Sonnet. W. Wordsworth.—WoP
The Southern Cross. E. Farjeon.—FaT
The star ("O little one away so far") E. M. Roberts.—ReS
The star ("Twinkle, twinkle, little star") J. Taylor.—ArT-3—BrMg—HoB
Little star.—HuS-3
"Twinkle, twinkle, little star."—SmM
Star guides. From Some short poems. W. Stafford.—GrCt
The star in the hills. W. Stafford.—DuS
"Star-light, star-bright." Mother Goose.—ArT-3—TuW
"Star bright, star-light."—HuS-3
Star light.—BrMg
Star-swirls. R. Jeffers.—DuS
Star-talk. R. Graves.—BoGj—CoBn
The star that watches the moon. E. Farjeon.—FaT
The starlighter. A. Guiterman.—ThA
Starry night I. E. Merriam.—MeI
Starry night II. E. Merriam.—MeI
Stars ("Alone in the night") S. Teasdale.—ArT-3—HoB—ThA
Stars ("And then") F. S. Edsall.—ThS
Stars ("O, sweep of stars over Harlem streets") L. Hughes.—LaC
Stars ("The stars are too many to count") C. Sandburg.—LiT
The stars ("Stars of the superior class") C. Smart.—GrCt (sel.)
"Stars, I have seen them fall." A. E. Housman.—GrCt
The stars' story. P. McGinley.—McWc
"The stars were packed so close that night." G. M. Hopkins.—LiT
Summer stars. C. Sandburg.—HaL
Tired. F. Johnson.—AdIa—HaK
To Beatrice and Sally. E. Farjeon.—FaT
To the evening star. W. Blake.—BlP—CoBn—GrCt—GrS
"Tonight in the sky." Issa.—LeOw
Until we built a cabin. A. Fisher.—ArT-3
"When I heard the learn'd astronomer." W. Whitman.—HoL
Stars ("Alone in the night") Sara Teasdale.—ArT-3—HoB—ThA
Stars ("And then") Florence Small Edsall.—ThA
Stars ("O, sweep of stars over Harlem streets") Langston Hughes.—LaC
Stars ("The stars are too many to count") Carl Sandburg.—LiT
The **stars** ("Stars of the superior class") Christopher Smart.—GrCt (sel.)
"The **stars** are everywhere to-night." See Daisies
"The **stars** are mansions built by nature's hand." See Sonnet
"The **stars** are too many to count." See Stars
"**Stars**, I have seen them fall." Alfred Edward Housman.—GrCt
"**Stars** of the summer night." See The Spanish student—Serenade
"**Stars** of the superior class." See The stars
"**Stars** over snow." See Night
The **stars'** story. Phyllis McGinley.—McWc
"The **stars** were packed so close that night." Gerard Manley Hopkins.—LiT
The **start.** Unknown.—MoS
"**Starter.**" See Notes on a track meet
"**Startled.**" Saigyo Hōshi.—BaS

"**State** street is lonely today. Aunt Jane Allen has driven." See Aunt Jane Allen
Stately verse. Unknown.—ArT-3
Staten island
Review from Staten island. G. C. Oden.—HaK
States (of U.S.). See also names of states, as Alabama
Stately verse. Unknown.—ArT-3
The **statesman's** holiday. William Butler Yeats.—YeR
The **station.** John Rathe.—LeM
Statue of Liberty
The Bartholdi statue. J. G. Whittier.—HiL
The new Colossus. E. Lazarus.—BoH—BrA
The **statue** of old Andrew Jackson. Vachel Lindsay.—LiP
Statues. See also Sculpture and sculpturing; Statue of Liberty
A boy looking at big David. M. Swenson.—LiT
"An old man sat in a waterfall." N. Nicholson.—CaD
The statue of old Andrew Jackson. V. Lindsay.—LiP
The stone gentleman. J. Reeves.—CaD
Status symbol. Mari Evans.—AdIa
Stay-at-home. Aileen Fisher.—FiC
Stay-at-homes. Aileen Fisher.—FiI
"**Stay** for a while over the thickets, haunted by the girls of the hill-folk." See The cloud messenger
Stay thy soft murmuring. See The loves of the plants
"**Stay** thy soft murmuring waters, gentle rill." See The loves of the plants—Stay thy soft murmuring
Staying alive. David Wagoner.—CoBn—DuS
"**Staying** alive in the woods is a matter of calming down." See Staying alive
Staying overnight. Aileen Fisher.—FiIo
"**Steal** this one." Issa, tr. fr. the Japanese by R. H. Blyth.—IsF
Steam shovel. Charles Malam.—DuR
Steam shovels
Steam shovel. C. Malam.—DuR
"The **steamboat** is a slow poke." See Boats
Stearns, Monroe
Afternoon.—ArT-3
The nightingale.—ArT-3
Steeds. Paul Hiebert.—DoW
Steel
Prayers of steel. C. Sandburg.—LaC—LaPd
Steel. Rege, tr. fr. the Marathi by the author.—AlPi
"**Steer,** hither steer, your wingèd pines." See Song of the syrens
Stein, Gertrude
Afterwards.—HaL (sel.)
I am Rose.—SmM
"**Step** aside, step aside." Issa, tr. fr. the Japanese by Nobuyuki Yuasa.—IsF
"**Step** in the ring and kiss." See Kiss-in-the-ring
"**Step** lightly on this narrow spot." Emily Dickinson.—DiPe
"**Step** to the garden from the cool-roomed house." See Weekend stroll
Stephens, James
The ancient elf.—StS
And it was windy weather.—ClF—StS
The apple tree.—LiT
Besides that.—StS
Bessie Bobtail.—StS
Blue stars and gold.—StS
The breath of life.—StS
The buds.—StS
The canal bank.—StS
The centaurs.—CoB—StS
Check.—ArT-3—HaL—ReS—StS—ThA
Night was creeping.—HuS-3
Chill of the eve.—StS
The coolin.—StS
The crackling twig.—StS
Crooked-heart.—StS
The daisies.—StS
Dance.—StS
Danny Murphy.—CoR—StS
Death.—StS
Deirdre.—StS
The devil's bag.—LiT
Doffing the bonnet.—StS
"Everything that I can spy."—StS
"Follow, follow, follow."—StS
Fossils.—StS
From hawk and kite.—StS
The fur coat.—StS
The Geraldine's cloak.—StS
A glass of beer.—McWs—StS
The goat paths.—BoGj—ReO—StS
The golden bird.—StS
Green weeds.—StS
Hate.—StS
Hesperus.—StS
The hill of vision.—ClF (sel.)
"I am writer."—StS
I wish.—StS
"If I had wings just like a bird."—StS
In the college of surgeons.—HaL
In the imperative mood.—StS
In the night.—StS
In the orchard.—CoR—HaL
In the poppy field.—StS
In the red.—StS
In waste places.—StS
Independence.—StS
Irony.—StS
Katty Gollagher.—StS
Little things.—ArT-3—BoGj—CoB—LaPd—PlE—StS
The main-deep.—StS
The market.—StS
Mary Hynes.—StS
The merry policeman.—StS
Midnight.—StS
Minuette.—StS
Night was creeping. See Check
Nora Criona.—StS
On a lonely spray.—StS
On a reed.—StS

"The wind begun (or began) to rock the grass." E. Dickinson.—DiL—DiPe
A thunder-storm.—CoBn
Storni, Alfonsina
Squares and angles.—LaC
A **story** for a child. Bayard Taylor.—CoB
Story for an educated child. Phyllis McGinley.—McWc
A **story** in the snow. Pearl Riggs Crouch.—ArT-3
The **story** of Augustus. See The story of Augustus who would not have any soup
The **story** of Augustus who would not have any soup. Heinrich Hoffmann.—AgH—BoGj—BrSm—CoBb
The story of Augustus.—ArT-3
The **story** of Constance. See The Canterbury tales
The **story** of Johnny Head-in-air. Heinrich Hoffmann.—ArT-3—CoBb
The **story** of the baby squirrel. Dorothy Aldis.—ArT-3
The **story** of the little woman. See "There was an old woman as I've heard tell"
The **story** of the old woman and her pig. Mother Goose.—BrMg
The **story** of Vinland. Sidney Lanier.—HiL
The **story-teller.** Mark Van Doren.—HaL
Story-telling
"I'll tell you a story." Mother Goose.—ReMg
Jack a Nory.—BrMg
Mr Mixup tells a story. D. McCord.—McAd
"Shall we tell a last tale." Unknown.—OpF
The story-teller. M. Van Doren.—HaL
"They have yarns." From The people, yes. C. Sandburg.—BrA
American yarns.—HuS-3
This story. M. C. Livingston.—LiC
Stoutenburg, Adrien
Channel U.S.A.—live.—BrA—HiL
Model T.—DuS
Night train.—LaPd
Rain.—LaPd
Reel one.—DuS
Stowe, Harriet Beecher (about)
Harriet Beecher Stowe. P. L. Dunbar.—HaK
"**Strampin'** the bent, like the Angel o' Daith." See Molecatcher
"**Strange** atoms we unto ourselves." See Lovelight
"**Strange** but true is the story." See Harlem gallery
"**Strange** fits of passion have I known." William Wordsworth.—WoP
"**Strange** it was." See The first Christmas eve
Strange legacies. Sterling A. Brown.—HaK
A **strange** meeting. William Henry Davies.—BlO
A **strange** pig. See "As I went to Bonner"
"A **strange** place." Peter Rake.—LeM
Strange tree. Elizabeth Madox Roberts.—CoBn—HoB—ThA
The **strange** visitor. See "A wife was sitting at her reel ae night"
A **strange** wild song. See Sylvie and Bruno
Stranger ("A little after twilight") Walter De La Mare.—DeBg
Stranger ("When no one listens") Thomas Merton.—PlE
"**Stranger** call this not." Unknown.—BrSm
"A **stranger** came to the door at eve." See Love and a question
The **strangers** ("Early this morning") Audrey Alexandra Brown.—DoW
Strangers ("The sad bells sound") Walter De La Mare.—DeBg
"The **strangest** thing." See Frosted-window world
Strawberries
Good taste. C. Logue.—CaD
Millions of strawberries. G. Taggard.—ArT-3—DuR
Strawberries. E. Farjeon.—AgH
Strawberries. Eleanor Farjeon.—AgH
Straws. Elizabeth Jane Coatsworth.—BrA
The **stray** cat. Eve Merriam.—MeC
"A **streak** across the sky." See The setting of the sun
Stredder, M.
The holiday.—StF
The **street.** Octavio Paz, tr. by Muriel Rukeyser.—LaC
"The **street** light." See Late corner
Street window. Carl Sandburg.—LaC
The **streetcleaner's** lament. Patricia Hubbell.—LaC
Streets. See also Highways; Roads and trails
Broadway: Twilight. T. Prideaux.—LaC
The child on the curbstone. E. Wylie.—LaC
Clinton south of Polk. C. Sandburg.—BrA
Could be. L. Hughes.—LaC
"In the streets I have just left." C. Reznikoff.—LaC
Joralemon street. P. Hubbell.—LaC
Late corner. L. Hughes.—HaK
Manhattan. M. A. Beer.—BrA
Stars. L. Hughes.—LaC
The street. O. Paz.—LaC
The streetcleaner's lament. P. Hubbell.—LaC
The streets of Laredo. L. MacNeice.—CaMb—GrCt
Water-front streets. L. Hughes.—LaC
Yesterday in Oxford street. R. Fyleman.—ArT-3—LaPd
The **streets** of Laredo. Louis MacNeice.—CaMb—GrCt
"**Streets** of the roaring town." See On a soldier fallen in the Philippines
"The **streets** that slept all afternoon in sun." See Camptown
"**Strength** leaves the hand I lay on this beech bole." See The beech
"**Strengthened** to live, strengthened to die for." See In distrust of merits
"**Strephon** kissed me in the spring." See The look
"**Strings** in the earth and air." See Chamber music
"**Strolling** on the bank of the Sabarmati." See The washerman

Strong, L. (Leonard) A. (Alfred) G. (George)
By the firelight.—CaD
Lowery cot.—CaD
A memory.—CaD
Old Dan'l.—ClF—SmM
Strong men. Sterling A. Brown.—BoH
Strong men, riding horses. Gwendolyn Brooks.—HaK
"**Strong** men, riding horses. In the west." See Strong men, riding horses
"**Strong-shouldered** mole." See A dead mole
Strong Son of God. See In memoriam
"**Strong** Son of God, immortal Love." See In memoriam—Strong Son of God
A **strong** wind. Austin Clarke.—CoBn
Struther, Jan
The cats.—CoB
Traveling America.—BrA
Struthill well. Unknown.—MoB
Stuart, Dabney
The river.—DuS
Ties.—DuS
Stuart, Jesse
By Sandy waters.—BrA
I sing America now.—BrA
"My land is fair for any eyes to see."—ArT-3
Our heritage.—BrA
Up silver stairsteps.—BrA
Stuart, Muriel
The seed shop.—CoBn
"**Stubborn** on her lips." See Steel
Stuff. Adrian Mitchell.—SmM
The **stump.** Donald Hall.—DuR
Stupidity street. Ralph Hodgson.—CoB—HaL—LaPd—ThA
Su Shih
Casual lines.—LeMw
A **subaltern's** love-song. John Betjeman.—McWs
Subramanyan, Ka Naa
Kanya-Kumari.—AlPi
Substantiations. Vallana, tr. fr. the Sanskrit by Daniel H. H. Ingalls.—AlPi
The **subway.** Conrad Kent Rivers.—HaK
Subway rush hour. Langston Hughes.—LaC
Subways
"Husbands and wives." M. Hershenson.—DuR—LaC
The subway. C. K. Rivers.—HaK
Subway rush hour. L. Hughes.—LaC
Success. See also Ambition; Fame; Service; Thrift
Robert Whitmore. F. M. Davis.—HaK
"Success is counted sweetest." E. Dickinson.—BoGj—DiPe
The train runs late to Harlem. C. K. Rivers.—AdIa
"Triumph may be of several kinds." E. Dickinson.—DiPe
What then. W. B. Yeats.—YeR
"**Success** is counted sweetest." Emily Dickinson.—BoGj—DiPe
"**Such** a morning it is when love." See Day of these days
Such a pleasant familee. Wallace Irwin.—BrSm
"**Such** a time of it they had." See Stanley meets Mutesa
Suckling, Sir John
Aglaura, sel.
Why so pale and wan.—CoBl
The constant lover.—HoL
"Out upon it, I have loved."—CoBl
"Out upon it, I have loved." See The constant lover
Why so pale and wan. See Aglaura
"**Sudden** refreshment came upon the school." See Physical geography
Sudden storm. Elizabeth Jane Coatsworth.—CoSb
"**Suddenly** the sky turned gray." See Snow toward evening
"**Suddenly** with intense." See The runner
Suffolk, England.
At Dunwich. A. Thwaite.—CaMb
Sugar
The black man's lament; or, How to make sugar. A. Opie.—VrF
Suguwara no Michizane
"The rotten-wooded willow."—BaS
Suicide
The briefless barrister. J. G. Saxe.—BrSm
"A cat in despondency sighed." Unknown.—BrLl
"The man who tried to." From Poems. J. Lester.—HaK
Notes found near a suicide, sels. F. Horne.—BoA (Complete)
To James.—BoH—HaK
One good turn deserves another. Unknown.—BrSm
Preface to a twenty volume suicide note. L. Jones.—BoA—HaK
Résumé. D. Parker.—BrSm—DuR
Sorrows of Werther. W. M. Thackeray.—BrSm
Suicide pond. K. McLaughlin.—DuS
Suicide pond. Kathy McLaughlin.—DuS
Suifu
"The school servant."—LeMw
"**Sukey,** you shall be my wife." See A proposal
Sulking. Ann and Jane Taylor.—VrF
Sulky Sue. See "Here's Sulky Sue"
"**Sullen** clouds are gathering fast over the black fringe of the forest." See The rainy day
Sullivan, John L. (about)
John L. Sullivan, the strong boy of Boston. V. Lindsay.—LiP
Sum, es, est. Unknown.—GrCt
"**Sum**—I am a gentleman." See Sum, es, est
"**Sumer** is icumen in." See The cuckoo song
Summer. See also August; July; June; Seasons
"As imperceptibly as grief." E. Dickinson.—DiPe
Bed in summer. R. L. Stevenson.—BoGj—HuS-3
Busy summer. A. Fisher.—FiI
"Cat's whiskers." K. Mizumura.—MiI
"Consulting summer's clock." E. Dickinson.—DiPe
Country summer. L. Adams.—BoGj

The cuckoo song. Unknown.—GrCt
"A drop fell on the apple tree." E. Dickinson
Summer shower.—CoBn
Dusk. E. Recht.—LeM
The end of summer. E. St V. Millay.—CoBn
Exeunt. R. Wilbur.—CoBn—HoL
Farewell to summer. E. Farjeon.—FaA
First day of summer. E. Merriam.—MeI
Fortune. L. Ferlinghetti.—DuR-LaC
The frost pane. D. McCord.—HuS-3—McE
The greenwood. W. L. Bowles.—ClF (sel.)
"Heigh-ho." E. J. Coatsworth.—CoSb
"I taste a liquor never brewed." E. Dickinson. —DiL—DiPe
In fields of summer. G. Kinnell.—CoBn
"In summer the rains come and the grass grows up." Unknown.—LeO
"In the leafy treetops." Yakamochi.—BaS
In the mountains on a summer day. Li T'ai-po.—MoS
"Let us go, then, exploring." V. Woolf.—CoBn
Long summer. L. Lee.—CoBn
"Lying in the sun." I. Johnson.—LeM
Midsummer. S. H. Calverley.—ReBs
Midsummer eve. E. Farjeon.—FaA
Midsummer jingle. N. Levy.—CoBn
A midsummer song. R. W. Gilder.—CoBn
Mountain summer. C. Lewis.—LeP
Northern summer. H. Behn.—BeG
"On a cool evening." Issa.—LeOw
"On summer nights." Tsurayuki.—BaS
The rainy summer. A. Meynell.—BoGj—GrS
"A soft sea washed around the house." E. Dickinson.—DiL—DiPe
"Someone prepared this mighty show." E. Dickinson.—DiPe
Southdown summer. Sagittarius.—PaH
"Summer." T. N. Tsosie.—BaH
Summer ("A butterfly") R. Aldington.—ClF
Summer ("Glow-worm-like the daisies peer") J. Davidson.—CoBn
Summer ("How sweet, when weary, dropping on a bank") J. Clare.—CoBn
Summer ("In this summer month which blasts all hope") Bana.—AlPi
Summer ("Over dusty daisies") H. Behn.—BeG
Summer ("Winter is cold-hearted") C. G. Rossetti.—CoBn
Summer afternoon. R. Souster.—CoBn
Summer and winter. P. B. Shelley.—CoBn
Summer days. A. Fisher.—FiC
Summer images. J. Clare.—GrCt
"Summer in the world." Bashō.—LeMw
"Summer is golden." G. Sellers.—LeM
A summer morning. R. Field.—ArT-3—HoB—HuS-3—LaPd
Summer rain. Lin Keng.—LeMw
Summer shower. S. Robinson.—ThA
Summer stars. C. Sandburg.—HaL
Summertime and the living. R. E. Hayden.—HaK
"There comes a warning like a spy." E. Dickinson.—DiPe
Things of summer. K. Jackson.—BrSg
The throstle. A. Tennyson.—CoB—CoBn—TeP
To summer. W. Blake.—BlP
Two times three. D. McCord.—McAd
The waking. T. Roethke.—McWs
"What happiness." Buson.—LeMw
Zummer stream. W. Barnes.—CoBn
"**Summer.**" Tom Nakai Tsosie.—BaH
Summer ("A butterfly") Richard Aldington.—ClF
Summer (Glow-worm-like the daisies peer") John Davidson.—CoBn
Summer ("How sweet, when weary, dropping on a bank") John Clare.—CoBn
Summer ("In this summer month which blasts all hope") Bana, tr. fr. the Sanskrit by D. H. H. Ingalls.—AlPi
Summer ("Over dusty daisies") Harry Behn.—BeG
Summer ("Winter is cold-hearted") Christina Georgina Rossetti.—CoBn
Summer afternoon. Raymond Souster.—CoBn
"The **summer** and autumn had been so wet." See Bishop Hatto
Summer and winter. Percy Bysshe Shelley.—CoBn
Summer concert. Reed Whittemore.—BrA
"The **summer** corn ripens." See January
Summer days. Aileen Fisher.—FiC
"**Summer** ends now; now, barbarous in beauty, the stooks arise." See Hurrahing in harvest
Summer evening, sel. John Clare
Let ye then my birds alone.—ReBs
Summer images. John Clare.—GrCt
"**Summer** in the world." Bashō, tr. fr. the Japanese by R. H. Blyth.—LeMw
"**Summer** is coming, summer is coming." See The throstle
"**Summer** is golden." Gillian Sellers.—LeM
"The **summer** is over." See October
"**Summer** is over, the old cow said." See Moo
A **summer** morning. Rachel Field.—ArT-3—HoB—HuS-3—LaPd
Summer rain ("A shower, a sprinkle") Eve Merriam.—LaPd
Summer rain ("Through morning rain") Lin Keng, tr. fr. the Chinese by Harold Acton and Ch'en Shih-hsiang.—LeMw
Summer shower. Selma Robinson.—ThA
Summer stars. Carl Sandburg.—HaL
"The **summer** that I was ten." See The centaur
Summer vacation. See The prelude. William Wordsworth
A **summer** wish, sel. Andrew Young
A dead bird.—CoB—ReBs
Summers, Hal
April fool.—CaD
Out of school.—CaD
The rescue.—CaD
"**Summers** and winters had come and gone—how many times." See To his friend, Wei
"**Summer's** flurry." See Autumn

"**Summer's** full of smelling things." See Things of summer
Summertime and the living. Robert E. Hayden. —HaK
Summons. Robert Francis.—DuR
Summum bonum. Robert Browning.—CoBl
Sun
African sunrise. G. M. Lutz.—DuR
"As round as a saucer." Mother Goose.—OpF
"As the sun came up, a ball of red." Unknown.—WyC
"The black turkey gobbler, under the east, the middle of his tail." Unknown.—LeO
"Blazing in gold and quenching in purple." E. Dickinson.—DiL—DiPe
The brave man. W. Stevens.—LiT
"Brightly the sun shines." Ontei.—BeCs
"A cautious crow flies." Bashō.—BeCs
Day moon. E. J. Coatsworth.—CoDh
The eagle. Unknown.—LeO
Earth, moon, and sun. C. Lewis.—LeP
Eclipse. C. Lewis.—LeP
Enitharmon's song. From Vala. W. Blake.—GrCt
February. N. Belting.—BeCm
Futility. W. Owen.—HoL
Give me the splendid silent sun. W. Whitman. —CoBn
"The giver of life." Unknown.—PlE
"Had I not seen the sun." E. Dickinson.—DiPe
"Hick-a-more, hack-a-more." Mother Goose.—ArT-3
Mother Goose rhymes, 29.—HoB
Hymn to the sun. Unknown.—LeO
"I washed my face in water." Unknown.—GrCt
"I'll tell you how the sun rose." E. Dickinson. —DiL—DiPe—LaPd
How the sun rose.—HuS-3
An Indian summer day on the prairie. V. Lindsay.—HuS-3
"It's a sunny, sunny day today." S. Gatti.—LeM
Johnny Appleseed's hymn to the sun. V. Lindsay.—LiP
Leaf and sun. N. Farber.—HoL
"Like mighty footlights burned the red." E. Dickinson.—DiPe
The little fly. Unknown.—LeO
Look. J. Smith.—SmM
"The moon cannot fight." Unknown.—LeO
"Moon-come-out." E. Farjeon.—ArT-3
"Moon, for what do you wait." R. Tagore.—LeMf
Morning prayer. Unknown.—DoC
The nature of love. J. Kirkup.—PlE
"Oh my sun, my moon." Unknown.—LeO
"O sun, O sun." Unknown.—LeO
Omen. B. Diop.—HoL
"On yonder hill there is a red deer." Unknown.—GrCt
A prayer. Unknown.—LeO
Prayer to the sun god. From Indian songs. L. Mertins.—HuS-3
"The red sun sinks low." Boncho.—BeCs
Riddle #29: The moon and the sun. Unknown.—BoGj
"The seasons were appointed, and the times." N. Belting.—BeCm
The setting of the sun. M. Copeland.—LeM
"She sweeps with many-colored brooms." E. Dickinson.—DiL—DiPe
"Some say the sun is a golden earring." N. Belting.—LaPd
Song of the sun and moon. Unknown.—LeO
The sun ("Every day coming") A. Fisher.—FiI
The sun ("I told the sun that I was glad") J. Drinkwater.—ArT-3—HuS-3
"Sun, God of living." J. Nez.—BaH
The sun is first to rise. E. J. Coatsworth.—HuS-3
"The sun is stuck." M. C. Livingston.—LiC
"Sun low in the west." Buson.—BeCs
The sun used to shine. E. Thomas.—ThG
The sunbeams. L. Pidgeon.—LeM
Sunrise and sun. H. Behn.—BeG
Sunrise on the sea. From A midsummer-night's dream. W. Shakespeare.—GrCt
The sun's frolic. C. Tringress.—StF
"The sun's perpendicular rays." W. L. Mansel.—GrCt
Sunset ("Hushed in the smoky haze of summer sunset") S. Teasdale.—PaH
Sunset ("The sun is an eagle old") V. Lindsay. —ReS
Sunset on the sea. L. Ubell.—LeM
Tailor's song. P. Dehn.—SmM
Theme. From Theme and variations. J. Stephens.—StS
There's nothing like the sun. E. Thomas.—ThG
This happy day. H. Behn.—ArT-3
To the sun ("More beautiful than the remarkable moon and her noble light") I. Bachman.—CoBn
To the sun ("Oh let your shining orb grow dim") From Mithraic emblems. R. Campbell.—PlE
Variations 8. From Theme and variations. J. Stephens.—StS
War. D. Roth.—DuR
"We have seen the sun." Tenchi.—BaS
"When I have seen the sun emerge." E. Dickinson.—DiPe
"White bird featherless." Unknown.—GrCt—ReOn
The **sun** ("Every day coming") Aileen Fisher.—FiI
The **sun** ("I told the sun that I was glad") John Drinkwater.—ArT-3—HuS-3
"**Sun** arose from a mist and the stops." See A small migration
"The **sun** became a small round moon." See Climbing in Glencoe
"The **sun** came out in April." C. Day-Lewis.—CaMb
"**Sun** comes, moon comes." See The window—When

"The **sun** descending in the west." See Night
"The **sun** does rise." See The ecchoing green
The **sun-flower.** See Ah, sun-flower
"**Sun,** God of living." Justin Nez.—BaH
"The **sun,** God's eye." See The nature of love
Sun goes up. Hilary-Anne Farley.—LeM
"The **sun** is a huntress young." See An Indian summer day on the prairie
"The **sun** is an eagle old." See Sunset
"The **sun** is coming." See February
The **sun** is first to rise. Elizabeth Jane Coatsworth.—HuS-3
"The **sun** is mine." See Song
"The **sun** is set; the swallows are asleep." See Evening: Ponte al Mare, Pisa
"The **sun** is stuck." Myra Cohn Livingston.—LiC
"**Sun** low in the west." Buson, tr. fr. the Japanese by Harry Behn.—BeCs
"**Sun,** my relative." See A prayer
"The **sun** rises." See In fields of summer
"The **sun** rises in south east corner of things." See A ballad of the mulberry road
"The **sun** says nothing." See Among the leaves
"The **sun** set, the wind fell, the sea." See An old song
"**Sun,** sun do you know." See Sunbeams
"The **sun,** that brave man." See The brave man
"The **sun** that brief December day." See Snow-bound—The snow
The **sun** used to shine. Edward Thomas.—ThG
"The **sun** used to shine while we two walked." See The sun used to shine
"The **sun** was leaning across the ground." See A friendly mouse
"The **sun** was shining on the sea." See Through the looking-glass—The walrus and the carpenter
"The **sun,** with his great eye." See Daisy's song
Sun Yun Feng
Riding at daybreak.—LeMw
Sunbeams. Linda Pidgeon.—LeM
Sundaram
As a flower I come.—AlPi
Sunday. See Days of the week—Sunday
Sunday ("The gentlemen's sticks swing extra high") E. B. White.—McWs
Sunday ("This is the day when all through the town") Elizabeth Jane Coatsworth.—BrA—LaC
Sunday ("Up early while everyone sleeps") Vern Rutsala.—DuS
"**Sunday** afternoon." See Veracruz
Sunday at Hampstead. James Thomson.—SmM (sel.)
Sunday at the end of summer. Howard Nemerov.—CoBn
Sunday morning. King's Cambridge. John Betjeman.—PlE
Sunday: New Guinea. Karl Shapiro.—BrA
"**Sunday** shuts down on this twentieth-century evening." See Boy with his hair cut short
"**Sunday** too my father got up early." See Those winter Sundays
Sundials
Lesson from a sun-dial. Unknown.—ArT-3
Sunflower. John Updike.—CoBn
"**Sunflower,** of flowers." See Sunflower
Sunflowers
Ah, sun-flower. W. Blake.—BlP
The sun-flower.—GrCt
Sunflower. J. Updike.—CoBn
"**Sunflowers.**" See Summer days
Sunning. James S. Tippett.—ArT-3—DuR
Sunrise and sun. Harry Behn.—BeG
Sunrise on the sea. See A midsummer-night's dream
"The **sunrise** tints the dew." See Crocuses
The **sun's** frolic. Clare Tringress.—StF
"The **sun's** perpendicular rays." W. L. Mansel.—GrCt
"The **sun's** rays." See The eagle
Sunset ("Hushed in the smoky haze of summer sunset") Sara Teasdale.—PaH
Sunset ("The sun is an eagle old") Vachel Lindsay.—ReS
"**Sunset** and evening star." See Crossing the bar
"The **sunset** bloomed" See Dusk
Sunset horn. Myron O'Higgins.—BoA
Sunset on the sea. Lori Ubell.—LeM
"**Sunshine** and rain." Mother Goose.—OpF
"**Sunshine** and weiners and pickles and ham." See Picnics
"**Sunshine,** forever." See Indian songs—Prayer to the sun god
"A **sunshiny** shower." Mother Goose.—ReMg
"**Superiority** to fate." Emily Dickinson.—DiPe
Supernatural. See Ghosts; Miracles; Witchcraft
Supernatural songs, sel. William Butler Yeats
IX. The four ages of man.—YeR
Superstitions
The eve of St Agnes. J. Keats.—CoD
The evil eye. J. Ciardi.—CaMb
Hee haw. Mother Goose.—ReOn
Moon rainbow. E. Farjeon.—FaT
Night of the scorpion. N. Ezekiel.—AlPi
Pins. Mother Goose.—BrMg
"She that goes to the well." Unknown.—MoB
The superstitious ghost. A. Guiterman.—BrSm
The **superstitious** ghost. Arthur Guiterman.—BrSm
Supper
Early supper. B. Howes.—BoGj
"If things were better." Issa.—BeCs
"Ladies and gentlemen come to supper." Mother Goose.—ReMg
"Little Tommy Tucker." Mother Goose.—OpF—WiMg
Tommy Tucker.—BrMg
"Madam Pussie's coming hame." Unknown.—MoB
Setting the table. D. Aldis.—ArT-3—HuS-3
Supper ("Her pinched grey body") W. De La Mare.—DeBg
Supper ("I supped where bloomed the red red rose") W. De La Mare.—DeBg
Supper ("Her pinched grey body") Walter De La Mare.—DeBg

Supper ("I supped where bloomed the red red rose") Walter De La Mare.—DeBg
"**Supported** by the yielding pillow." See The death of a mother
"**Suppose** that you have seen." See King Henry V—The fleet
"**Sure** my sparrows are my own." See Summer evening—Let ye then my birds alone
A **sure** sign. Nancy Byrd Turner.—ArT-3
"**Sure,** we can, said the man." See Heartbeat of democracy
"**Surely** that is not a man." See A circus garland —Acrobat
"**Surgeons** must be very careful." Emily Dickinson.—DiPe
Suri, Nayacandra
Hammira-mahakavya, sel.
Radhadevi's dance.—AlPi
Radhadevi's dance. See Hammira-mahakavya
"**Surprised** by joy—impatient as the wind." See Sonnet
Survival
Staying alive. D. Wagoner.—CoBn—DuS
Susan and Patty. Elizabeth Turner.—VrF
"**Susan** B. Anthony led him onto the platform." See Frederick Douglass
Susan Blue. See "Oh, Susan Blue"
"**Susie** boasted she could sing." See Meanie
Susie Mooney. Mother Goose.—ReOn
"**Susie's** galoshes." See Galoshes
Sussex, England
In Romney marsh. J. Davidson.—PaH
The South Country. H. Belloc.—PaH
Southdown summer. Sagittarius.—PaH
Sussex. R. Kipling.—PaH
Sussex. Rudyard Kipling.—PaH
Sūtoku
"The flowers to the tree's root."—BaS
Sutra-krtanga, sel. Unknown, tr. fr. the Sanskrit by A. L. Basham
In praise of celibacy.—AlPi
"The **swallow.**" Otsuyu, tr. fr. the Japanese by R. H. Blyth.—LeMw
The **swallow** ("Fly away, fly away over the sea") Christina Georgina Rossetti.—HuS-3
The **swallow** ("Who is quick, quick, quick") Carmen Bernos de Gasztold, tr. fr. the French by Rumer Godden.—GaC—ReBs
"**Swallow,** my sister, O sister swallow." See Itylus
Swallows
August 28. D. McCord.—McE
Itylus. A. C. Swinburne.—GrCt
"The swallow." Otsuyu.—LeMw
The swallow ("Fly away, fly away over the sea") C. G. Rossetti.—HuS-3
The swallow ("Who is quick, quick, quick") C. B. de Gasztold.—GaC—ReBs
The swallows ("All day—when early morning shone") A. Young.—CoB
Swallows ("The prairie wind blew harder than it could") T. H. Ferril.—DuR
"The swallows are homing." E. Farjeon.—FaA
The **swallows** ("All day—when early morning shone") Andrew Young.—CoB
Swallows ("The prairie wind blew harder than it could") Thomas Hornsby Ferril.—DuR
"The **swallows** and the butterflies." See When snow will come
"The **swallows** are homing." Eleanor Farjeon.—FaA
"**Swampstrife** and spatterdock." See The marsh
The **swan.** Mother Goose.—GrCt
Mother Goose rhymes, 42.—HoB
"**Swan** swam over the sea." See The swan
Swans
Cygnus. E. Farjeon.—FaT
"Down the stream the swans all glide." S. Milligan.—StF
The dying swan. Unknown.—GrCt
The icebound swans. Unknown.—ReO
A riddle from the Old English. Unknown.—GrCt
"The silver swanne (or swan) who living had no note." Unknown.—GrCt—GrS
"A son just born." M. B. Miller.—ArT-3
The swan. Mother Goose.—GrCt
Mother Goose rhymes, 42.—HoB
Swans at night. M. Gilmore.—CoB (sel.)
Tell me, O swan. Kabir.—AlPi
The wild swans at Coole. W. B. Yeats.—GrCt —PaH—YeR
Swans at night. Mary Gilmore.—CoB (sel.)
Sward, Robert
"By the swimming."—DuS
"**Swatted** out." Issa, tr. fr. the Japanese by R. H. Blyth.—IsF
"**Sweep,** sweep, sweep, sweep, cries little Jack." See The chimney sweeper
Sweeping the sky. See "There was an old woman tossed up in a basket"
"A **sweet,** a delicate white mouse." See A waltzer in the house
Sweet Afton. Robert Burns.—BuPr
Afton water.—CoBn
Sweet and low. See The princess
"**Sweet** and low, sweet and low." See The princess—Sweet and low
Sweet apple. James Stephens.—StS
"A **sweet** chubby fellow." William Darton, rev. by Ann and Jane Taylor.—VrF
A **sweet** country life. Unknown.—ReOn
"A **sweet** country life is to me both dear and charming." See A sweet country life
Sweet Daffadowndilly. See "Growing in the vale"
"**Sweet** dreams, form a shade." See A cradle song
"A **sweet** girl graduate, lean as a fawn." See Nancy Hanks, mother of Abraham Lincoln
"**Sweet** maiden of Passamaquoddy." James De Mille.—DoW
"**Sweet** Mary, the first time she ever was there." See Mary
The **sweet** o' the year. George Meredith.—CoBn

"**Sweet** peace, where dost thou dwell? I humbly crave." See Peace
Sweet peas
"Here are sweet peas, on tiptoe for a flight." From I stood tiptoe on a little hill. J. Keats. —BrSg
"**Sweet** Peridarchus was a prince." See The prince
"**Sweet** Sally took a carboard box." See The ballad of the light-eyed little girl
Sweet Suffolk owl. Unknown.—GrCt
"**Sweet** Suffolk owl, so trimly dight." See Sweet Suffolk owl
"**Sweet** Swan of Avon, what a sight it were." See To the memory of my beloved; the author Mr William Shakespeare
Sweet Tibbie Dunbar. Robert Burns.—BuH
The **sweet** tooth. Katherine Pyle.—AgH—CoBb
"A **sweet-tooth** was our Frederick." See The sweet tooth
"**Sweeter** than rough hair." See To be sung by a small boy who herds goats
Swell people. Carl Sandburg.—HaL
Swenson, May
A boy looking at big David.—LiT
Cat & the weather.—CoB
The centaur.—DuS—LiT
Hearing the wind at night.—CoBn
Night practice.—LiT
Southbound on the freeway.—BrA—DuR
Water picture.—CoBn—LaC
Swift, Hildegarde Hoyt
"I came to the new world empty-handed." See North star shining
"My name was legion." See North star shining
North star shining, sels.
"I came to the new world empty-handed." —BrA
"My name was legion."—BrA
Swift, Jonathan
Aeiou.—BlO
"Mollis abuti."—GrCt
"**Swift** as an arrow in the wind he goes." See Polo player
The **swift** bullets. Carolyn Wells.—BrSm
"**Swift** cloud shadows." Shusen, tr. fr. the Japanese by Harry Behn.—BeCs
"**Swift** things are beautiful." Elizabeth Jane Coatsworth.—ArT-3—DuR—HuS-3
The **swimmer.** John Crowe Ransom.—MoS
Swimmers. Louis Untermeyer.—MoS (sel.)
Swimming and diving. See also Bathing
"By the swimming." R. Sward.—DuS
Cold logic. B. Hutchinson.—MoS
"Come on in." Unknown.—MoS
The diver ("I would like to dive") W. W. E. Ross.—DoW
Diver ("The rubber man") P. Neruda.—LiT
The diver ("Sank through easeful") R. E. Hayden.—DuS—HaK
East Anglian bathe. J. Betjeman.—MoS
Ensnare the clouds. E. J. Coatsworth.—CoDh
First lesson. P. Booth.—MoS
400 meter freestyle. M. W. Kumin.—MoS
High diver. R. Francis.—MoS
"Inviting, rippling waters." M. Bendig.—LeM
Isabel. Unknown.—DoW
Little boys of Texas. R. P. T. Coffin.—BrSm
"Mother, may I go out to swim." Mother Goose.—OpF
Caution.—BrMg
O beautiful here. M. C. Livingston.—LiC
Of swimming in lakes and rivers. B. Brecht.—MoS
The old swimmer. C. Morley.—MoS
The river. D. Stuart.—DuS
A Shropshire lad. J. Betjeman.—CaMb
The swimmer. J. C. Ransom.—MoS
Swimmers. L. Untermeyer.—MoS (sel.)
Undersea fever. W. Cole.—CoSs
What someone told me about Bobby Link. J. Ciardi.—AgH—CiYk
Written after swimming from Sestos to Abydos. G. G. Byron.—ByP
Yes, by golly. Unknown.—MoS
Swinburne, Algernon Charles
Envoi.—BoGj
White butterflies.—LaPd
The garden of Proserpine, sel.
Proserpine.—GrCt
Itylus.—GrCt
Love at sea.—GrS
Oblation.—CoBl
Proserpine. See The garden of Proserpine
White butterflies. See Envoi
The **swing.** Robert Louis Stevenson.—ArT-3—BoGj—HoB—HuS-3—LaP—LaPd
"**Swing** high, Iscariot." See The sacrifice
Swing low, sweet chariot. Unknown.—BrA
"**Swing** low, sweet sun, like a gold hunter." See Tailor's song
Swing song ("Here I go up in my swing") A. A. Milne.—MiC
Swing song ("Oh, I've discovered") Harry Behn. —ArT-3
"**Swing** thee low in thy cradle soft." See Indian cradle song
Swinging
"The child sways on the swing." Issa.—LeMw
A father swings his child. W. D. Snodgrass.—McWs
The swing. R. L. Stevenson.—ArT-3—BoGj—HoB—HuS-3—LaP—LaPd
Swing song ("Here I go up in my swing") A. A. Milne.—MiC
Swing song ("Oh, I've discovered") H. Behn. —ArT-3
Swinging. Mother Goose.—BrMg
Swinging on a rail. K. Fraser.—FrS
"Waiting for the children." K. Mizumura.—MiI
The walnut tree. D. McCord.—McAd
Waterwings. K. Fraser.—FrS
Swinging. Mother Goose.—BrMg
Swinging on a rail. Kathleen Fraser.—FrS

Swiss
"Our lives are Swiss." E. Dickinson.—DiL—DiPe
Swithin, Saint (about)
St Swithin. Daniel Henderson.—BrSm
"**Swoop.** The egret dives into the red lotus blossoms." See Egret dyke
The **sword** and the sickle. See The pilgrim
"The **sword** sang on the barren heath." See The pilgrim
"The **sword** sung on the barren heath." See The pilgrim
Swords
The legend of Rabbi Ben Levi. From Tales of a wayside inn. H. W. Longfellow.—LoPl
The pilgrim. W. Blake.—ArT-3
The sword and the sickle.—GrCt
"The sword sung on the barren heath."—BlP
Sylvester, Joshua
Du Bartas his divine weeks, sel.
I hear the crane.—ReO
I hear the crane. See Du Bartas his divine weeks
Sylvie and Bruno, sels. Lewis Carroll
The pig-tale.—ReO
A strange wild song.—HuS-3
Sylvie and Bruno concluded, sel. Lewis Carroll
The king-fisher song.—BlO
Symonds, J. A.
There are no gods. tr.—PlE
Symons, Arthur
The gardener.—CoBn
A tune.—CoBl
Sympathy. See also Friendship; Kindness; Love
"I heard an angel singing." W. Blake.—BlP
La belle dame sans merci. J. Keats.—BoGj—BoH—CoD—GrCt—GrS—SmM
Lord, have mercy on us. T. Nashe.—GrCt
Mercy. From The merchant of Venice. W. Shakespeare.—BoH
"Poor fellow me." Unknown.—LeO
Sympathy. P. L. Dunbar.—AdIa—BoA
"Terror in the house does roar." W. Blake.—BlP
"There was one I met upon the road." S. Crane.—PlE
Sympathy. Paul Laurence Dunbar.—AdIa—BoA
Symphony. Frank Horne.—BoA
Symptoms of love. Robert Graves.—DuS
Synge, John M. (Millington)
The curse.—GrCt
In Glencullen.—ReBs
On a birthday.—GrCt
Prelude.—CoBn—GrCt
Queens.—GrCt
Winter.—SmM
Synge, John M. (about)
A memory. L. A. G. Strong.—CaD
Syracuse, Sicily
Syracuse. E. J. Coatsworth.—PaH
Women of Syracuse. E. J. Coatsworth.—CoDh
Syracuse. Elizabeth Jane Coatsworth.—PaH

T

Taalak, Nancy L.
The weather.—BaH
Tabb, John Banister (Father Tabb)
A bunch of roses.—ThA
Taber, Harry P.
"Wilhelmina Mergenthaler."—CoBb
Table. David McCord.—McE
The **table** and the chair. Edward Lear.—HoB—HuS-3
"**Table,** I've got my eye on you." See Table
Table manners. Gelett Burgess.—CoBb
Tableau. Countee Cullen.—BrA—HaK
Tables
Table. D. McCord.—McE
The table and the chair. E. Lear.—HoB—HuS-3
Tabrar, Joseph
Mary Ann.—CoBl
Tachibana Akemi
"It is a pleasure."—LeMw
"**Taddeo** Gaddi built me. I am old." See The old bridge at Florence
"A **tadpole,** a baby slyful tadpole." William Michael Taylor.—LeM
"A **tadpole** hasn't a pole at all." See First and last
Tadpoles. See Frogs; Toads; Tree toads
Taffy. See "Taffy was a Welshman"
"**Taffy** is a Welshman." See "Taffy was a Welshman"
"**Taffy,** the topaz-coloured cat." See In honour of Taffy Topaz
"**Taffy** was a Welshman." Mother Goose.—BrMg
Jolly Welchman.—VrF
Taffy.—CoBb
"Taffy is a Welshman."—OpF
Taft, William Howard (about)
"They say that ex-President Taft." Unknown.—BrLl
Taggard, Genevieve
Millions of strawberries.—ArT-3—DuR
Tagliabue, John
Don't bomb human nature out of existence.—DuS
Fast.—MoS
The Pinta, the Nina and the Santa Maria; and many other cargoes of light.—BrA
Tagore, Rabindranath
"Are you too proud to kiss me."—LeMf
"The bird-song is the echo of the morning light."—LeMf
"The bird wishes it were a cloud."—LeMf
"The cobweb pretends to catch dewdrops."—LeMf
"The hills are like shouts of children."—LeMf
The home.—BoGj
"I have lost my dewdrop, cries the flower."—LeMf
"I sit at my window this morning."—LeMf
"The infant flower opens its bud and cries."—LeMf
"Is not this mountain like a flower."—LeMf

"It is the tears of the earth."—LeMf
"Moon, for what do you wait."—LeMf
"The night opens the flower in secret."—LeMf
"Night's darkness is a bag."—LeMf
"The night's silence, like a deep lamp."—LeMf
On the seashore.—AlPi
Paper boats.—BoH—ThA
The rainy day.—AlPi
"Roots are the branches down in the earth."—LeMf
Tell me, O swan. tr.—AlPi
"Thoughts pass in my mind like flocks of ducks in the sky."—LeMf
To what shore would you cross. tr.—AlPi
"The trees come up to my window."—LeMf
Unfathomed past.—AlPi
Taigi
"Coming along the mountain path."—LeMw
"The sea hawk hunting."—BeCs
"A **tail** behind, a trunk in front." See The elephant; or, The force of habit
"A **tail** is such a useful thing." See Tails
Tailor. Eleanor Farjeon.—FaT
"The **tailor** of Bicester." Mother Goose.—BrMg
"A **tailor,** who sailed from Quebec." Mother Goose.—WiMg
Tailors
"A carrion crow sat on an oak." Mother Goose.—BlO—ReBg—SmM
The carrion crow.—BrMg
"Four-and-twenty Highlandmen." Unknown.—MoB
"Four and twenty tailors went to kill a snail." Mother Goose.—WiMg
Snail hunters.—BrMg
"Here's the tailor with his sheers." Unknown.—VrF
The old tailor. W. De La Mare.—DeBg
Tailor. E. Farjeon.—FaT
"The tailor of Bicester." Mother Goose.—BrMg
"A tailor, who sailed from Quebec." Mother Goose.—WiMg
Tailor's song. P. Dehn.—SmM
Tailor's song. Paul Dehn.—SmM
Tails
In the fashion. A. A. Milne.—LaP
Tails. I. Russell.—StF
Tails. Ivy Russell.—StF
Take any bird. See The Canterbury tales—Phoebus and the crow
"**Take** any bird, and put it in a cage." See The Canterbury tales—Phoebus and the crow
"**Take** as a gift." See Giving and taking
Take frankincense, O God. See Holy transportations
"**Take** frankincense, O God, take gold, O king." See Holy transportations—Take frankincense, O God
"**Take** me or leave me—I'm not thine." See Never
Take-off. Peter Thorpe.—DuS
"**Take** the curious case of Tom Pettigrew." David McCord.—BrLl
"**Take** this kiss upon the brow." See A dream within a dream
Taking leave of a friend. Li T'ai-po (Rihaku), tr. fr. the Japanese by Ezra Pound.—HoL
Taking off. Unknown.—ArT-3
"**Taking** pity on this scrag-end of the city." See One kingfisher and one yellow rose
Talbot, Ethel
Crab-apple.—ArT-3
A **tale** ("There once the walls") Edward Thomas.—GrCt
A **tale** ("There was an old woman sat spinning") Mother Goose.—BrMg
Talents
"The mountain and the squirrel." R. W. Emerson.—BoGj—BoH
Fable.—ReO
Talents differ. L. E. Richards.—ArT-3
Talents differ. Laura E. Richards.—ArT-3
Tales of a wayside inn, sels. Henry Wadsworth Longfellow
Azrael.—LoPl
The bell of Atri.—LoPl
The legend beautiful.—LoPl
The legend of Rabbi Ben Levi.—LoPl
Paul Revere's ride.—ArT-3—HiL—HuS-3—LoPl
A **talisman.** Marianne Moore.—BoGj—HoL
Talk. D. H. Lawrence.—ClF
Talking
Little talk. A. Fisher.—LaP
Talk. D. H. Lawrence.—ClF
Talking. A. Fisher.—FiIo
The talking bird; or, Dame Trudge and her parrot. Unknown.—VrF
Talking in their sleep. E. M. Thomas.—CoBn
"There was an owl lived in an oak (the more he heard)." Mother Goose.—OpF
Three little girls. K. Greenaway.—GrT
Talking. Aileen Fisher.—FiIo
The **talking** bird; or, Dame Trudge and her parrot. Unknown.—VrF
Talking in their sleep. Edith Matilda Thomas.—CoBn
"**Tall** and thin." Mother Goose.—OpF
Tall city. Susan Nichols Pulsifer.—LaC
Tall nettles. Edward Thomas.—GrCt—ThG
"**Tall** nettles cover up, as they have done." See Tall nettles
"**Tall** people, short people." See People
"**Tall,** with tow-hair, the texture of hide." See Aubade: Dick, the donkey boy
The **tallow-chandler.** Unknown, at. to William Darton.—VrF
Tam o' Shanter. Robert Burns.—BuPr
"**Tam** o the linn came up the gate." Unknown.—MoB
The **tambour** worker. Unknown, at. to William Darton.—VrF
Tamburlaine the Great, sels. Christopher Marlowe
The blood conquests of mighty Tamburlaine.—GrCt

"I love little pussy."—ArT-3—OpF
"I love little pussy, her coat is so warm." —WiMg
Kindness.—BrMg
"I love little pussy, her coat is so warm." See "I love little pussy"
Kindness. See "I love little pussy"
Little star. See The star
The star.—ArT-3—BrMg—HoB
Little star.—HuS-3
"Twinkle, twinkle, little star."—SmM
"Twinkle, twinkle, little star." See The star
The violet.—HoB
Taylor, Marcus
Rain.—BaH
Taylor, Pat
Fire.—LeM
Taylor, Patricia
Fear when coming home through a dark country lane.—LeM
Taylor, Rachel Annand
Ecstasy.—GrS
The princess of Scotland.—GrS
Taylor, William Michael
"A tadpole, a baby slyful tadpole."—LeM
Tchernine, Odette
The gnats.—SmM
Tea
"One two three (father caught a flea)." Unknown.—CoO
"Polly put the kettle on." Mother Goose.—GrT —OpF
Polly.—BrMg
The tea roaster. Unknown.—DePp
Tea parties
The cats have come to tea. K. Greenaway.—GrT
The cats' tea-party. F. E. Weatherly.—ArT-3
Manners. K. Greenaway.—GrT
"Prince Finikin and his mamma." K. Greenaway.—GrT
The tea party. K. Greenaway.—GrT
The **tea** party. Kate Greenaway.—GrT
The **tea** roaster. Unknown, ad. fr. the Japanese by Charlotte B. DeForest.—DePp
A **teacher.** Bruce McGregor.—LeM
"A **teacher** whose spelling's unique." Charles Battel Loomis.—BrLl
Teachers and teaching. See also School
The child in school. Unknown.—LeMw
"Doctor Faustus was a good man." Mother Goose.—ReMg
"John Smith's a very good man." Unknown.—MoB
The kiss. T. Moore.—CoBl
Miss Jones. H. Behn.—BeG
Miss Norma Jean Pugh, first grade teacher. M. O'Neill.—ArT-3
The purist. O. Nash.—BoGj—BrSm
"Said a boy to his teacher one day." Unknown.—BrLl
Schoolmaster. Y. Yevtushenko.—LiT
A serio-comic elegy. R. Whately.—BrSm
Sickle pears. O. Dodson.—BoA
"A small boy when asked to spell yacht." Unknown.—BrLl
A teacher. B. McGregor.—LeM
"A teacher whose spelling's unique." C. B. Loomis.—BrLl
You've got to be taught. From South Pacific. O. Hammerstein II.—BrA
"A **teacher's** got a temper." See A teacher
Teapots. See Pottery
"**Teapots** and quails." Edward Lear.—BoGj
Tears
Dust to dust. T. Hood.—BrSm
"It is the tears of the earth." R. Tagore.—LeMf
Tears, idle tears. From The princess. A. Tennyson.—TeP
"What will become." B. Brown.—BaH
Tears, idle tears. See The princess
"**Tears,** idle tears, I know not what they mean." See The princess—Tears, idle tears
Teasdale, Sara
April.—ArT-3—HuS-3—LaPd
Barter.—ThA
The coin.—ArT-3—ThA
Faces.—LaC
The falling star.—ArT-3—HuS-3—LaPd—ThA
February twilight.—LaP—LaPd—ThA
The flight.—CoBl
It is not far. See Night
Let it be forgotten.—BoH
The look.—BoH—CoBl
Madeira from the sea.—PaH
May day.—CoBn
Night.—ArT-3—ThA
It is not far.—HuS-3
Night song at Amalfi.—BoH
Pierrot.—CoBl
Places.—PaH
Spring night.—CoBl
Stars.—ArT-3—HoB—ThA
Sunset.—PaH
"When I am not with you."—CoBl
Winter solstice.—HoB
Young love.—CoBl
Teasing
"Annie Bolanny." Unknown.—GrCt
"Georgie Porgie, pudding and pie." Mother Goose.—OpF—ReMg—WiMg
Georgie Porgie.—BrMg
Growing up. E. K. Wallace.—ThA
Johnny Rover. Mother Goose.—ReOn
Meanie. A. Fisher.—FiIo
The monkeys and the crocodile. L. E. Richards.—ArT-3—BrSm—HoB—LaP
Silly Sallie. W. De La Mare.—BlO—DeBg
"Sticks and stones." Unknown.—MoB
The vinegar man. R. C. Mitchell.—ThA
Teddy bear ("A bear, however hard he tries") A. A. Milne.—MiC
Teddy bear ("I had to give Reginald a slap") Harry Behn.—ArT-3
Tee-wee's boat. Mother Goose.—BrMg

Teeth
Address to the toothache. R. Burns.—BuPr
A charm against the toothache. J. Heath-Stubbs.—CaD—SmM
Ditty for a child losing his first tooth. Unknown.—DoC
Drawing teeth. E. Turner.—VrF
"An old dame to the blacksmith went." Unknown.—VrF
Reflections dental. P. McGinley.—DuR
"There was an old man of Blackheath." Unknown.—BrLl—LaP—LaPd
"There was an old man of Tarentum." Unknown.—BrLl
"Thirty white horses." Mother Goose.—BrMg—OpF—ReOn
"Thirty white horses upon a red hill."—ArT-3
"Twenty white horses."—HuS-3
Teevee. Eve Merriam.—MeC
Tehachapi mountains. Myra Cohn Livingston.—LiC
Teika
"The bridge of dreams."—BaS
"To be old."—BaS
Telegram. William Wise.—ArT-3
Telegraph
Telegram. W. Wise.—ArT-3
Telegraph poles. P. Dehn.—SmM
Telegraph poles. Paul Dehn.—SmM
The **telephone** brought you back. Elizabeth Jane Coatsworth.—CoDh
"The **telephone** poles." See Crossing Kansas by train
Telephones
Alexander Graham Bell did not invent the telephone. R. P. T. Coffin.—ArT-3
Eletelephony. L. E. Richards.—ArT-3—BoGj—HoB—LaPd
Manual system. C. Sandburg.—ArT-3
The telephone brought you back. E. J. Coatsworth.—CoDh
Think of eight numbers. S. Silverstein.—CoBb
Telescopes
At the bottom of the well. L. Untermeyer.—BoGj
Television
Reflections dental. P. McGinley.—DuR
Teevee. E. Merriam.—MeC
The winning of the TV West. J. T. Alexander.—BoH—BrA
Telfer, James
The goblin's song.—GrCt
"**Tell** all my mourners." See Wake
"**Tell** all the truth but tell it slant." Emily Dickinson.—DiPe
"**Tell** me about that harvest field." See Real property
"**Tell** me, ladies, if you can." Mother Goose.—OpF
"**Tell** me not, Sweet, I am unkind." See To Lucasta, on going to the wars
"**Tell** me, O octopus, I begs." See The octopus
Tell me, O swan. Kabir, tr. fr. the Sanskrit by Rabindranath Tagore.—AlPi
"**Tell** me, O swan, your ancient tale." See Tell me, O swan
"**Tell** me, tell me, gentle robin." See The cat and the bird
"**Tell** them in Lacedaemon, passer-by." See On the army of Spartans, who died at Thermopylae
"**Telling** lies to the young is wrong." See Lies
Temmu
"Magnificent snow."—BaS
The **tempest,** sels. William Shakespeare
Beware.—ShS
"Come unto these yellow sands"
Ariel's song.—BlO—BoGj
Full fathom five.—GrCt—SmM
Ariel's dirge.—BoGj
Ariel's song.—BlO
A sea dirge.—CoSs
Holiday.—ShS
Where the bee sucks.—BlO—SmM
Ariel's song.—LaPd
Merrily, merrily.—ShS
"Where the bee sucks, there suck I."—ArT-3
The **temple** bells of Yun Sui. Yang Wan-li, tr. fr. the Chinese by Henry H. Hart.—LeMw
"The **temple** is clean." See A song of always
Temples
At Feng Ting temple. Li T'ai-po.—LeMw
Kanya-Kumari. K. N. Subramanyan.—AlPi
The lonely boy. Unknown.—DePp
"On the porch." Issa.—IsF
Ten commandments, seven deadly sins, and five wits. Unknown.—GrCt
Ten little dicky-birds. A. W. I. Baldwin.—StF
"**Ten** little Injuns." Mother Goose.—OpF
Ten little squirrels. Mother Goose.—StF
"**Ten** little squirrels sat on a tree." See Ten little squirrels
"**Ten** miles of flat land along the sea." See Sandpipers
Ten o'clock. Patricia Hubbell.—LaC
Ten o'clock scholar. See "A diller, a dollar, a ten o'clock scholar"
"**Ten,** one, sixty-eight, at the west Y on Coal avenue." See Crucifixion
"**Ten** thousand apricots bordering the river bank." See Two songs of spring wandering
Ten twice. David McCord.—McAd
"**Ten** years ago, who chased me madly at the Muttur fair." See Wasn't it you
Tenchi
"We have seen the sun."—BaS
The **tender** nurse. Mary Elliott.—VrF
"**Tenderly,** gently, the soft rain." See Jardins sous la pluie
Tennant, E. Wyndham
Home thoughts in Laventi, sel.
"I saw green banks of daffodils."—ArT-3
"I saw green banks of daffodils." See Home thoughts in Laventi

Tennessee
Anecdote of the jar. W. Stevens.—HoL
Tennis
Adulescentia. R. Fitzgerald.—MoS (sel.)
At the tennis clinic. I. L. Martin.—MoS
A ballade of lawn tennis. F. P. Adams.—MoS
Dark eyes at Forest Hills. I. L. Martin.—MoS
Old tennis player. G. Brooks.—MoS
The Olympic girl. J. Betjeman.—MoS
A snapshot for Miss Bricka who lost in the semi-final round of the Pennsylvania lawn tennis tournament at Haverford, July, 1960. R. Wallace.—MoS
A subaltern's love-song. J. Betjeman.—McWs
Tennis in San Juan. R. Denney.—MoS
Tennis in San Juan. Reuel Denney.—MoS
Tennyson, Alfred, Lord
All things will die.—TeP
All thoughts, all creeds.—TeP
Anacreontics.—TeP
The balloon.—CoR
Becket, sel.
Duet.—GrS
The blackbird.—TeP
Blow, bugle, blow. See The princess—The bugle song.
Blow trumpet. See Idylls of the king
"Break, break, break."—BlO—BoGj—TeP
The brook.—BlO—BoGj—ClF—CoBn
Song of the brook.—TeP
The bugle song. See The princess
"Bury the great duke." See Ode on the death of the Duke of Wellington
Calm is the morn. See In memoriam
The charge of the Light Brigade.—TeP
Come down, O maid. See The princess
"Come into the garden, Maud." See Maud
A cradle song. See The princess—Sweet and low
Crossing the bar.—TeP
The deserted house.—TeP
"Dip down upon the northern shore." See In memoriam
The dragon-fly. See The two voices
Duet. See Becket
The eagle.—BlO—BoGj—CoB—LaPd—TeP—TuW
Early spring.—TeP
A farewell.—TeP
The flower.—TeP
"Flower in the crannied wall."—CoBn—TeP
Frater ave atque vale.—GrCt—TeP
The grasshopper.—TeP
A happy lover. See In memoriam
The how and the why.—TeP
"I envy not in any moods." See In memoriam
"I sometimes hold it half a sin." See In memoriam
"I trust I have not wasted breath." See In memoriam
I wage not any feud. See In memoriam
Idylls of the king, sels.
Blow trumpet.—TeP
If love be love.—TeP
Morte d' Arthur.—CoD—TeP
Rain, rain, and sun.—TeP
If love be love. See Idylls of the king
In memoriam, sels.
Calm is the morn.—GrCt—TeP
"Dip down upon the northern shore."—TeP
A happy lover.—TeP
"I envy not in any moods."—TeP
"I sometimes hold it half a sin."—TeP
"I trust I have not wasted breath."—TeP
I wage not any feud.—TeP
My Lord and King.—GrCt—TeP
Now fades the last.—TeP
"Oh yet we trust that somehow good."—PlE
Oh yet we trust.—TeP
Ring out, wild bells.—ArT-3—LaPh—TeP
Strong Son of God.—PlE
Prologue.—TeP
There rolls the deep.—TeP
What hope is here.—TeP
When my light is low.—TeP
In the spring. See Locksley hall
Kate.—TeP
The kraken.—TeP
"Lady Clara Vere de Vere."—TeP
Lady Clare.—HuS-3—TeP
The lady of Shalott.—HuS-3—TeP
Locksley hall, sel.
In the spring.—CoBn—TeP
The lotos-eaters.—ClF (sel.)—GrCt (sel.)—PaH (sel.)—TeP
Mariana.—TeP
Maud, sels.
"Come into the garden, Maud."—CoBl—TeP
"See what a lovely shell."—BoGj
From Maud.—CoBn
The May queen.—TeP
Merlin and the gleam.—TeP
Morte d' Arthur. See Idylls of the king
My Lord and King. See In memoriam
Night encampment outside Troy. tr.—CoR
Nothing will die.—TeP
Now fades the last. See In memoriam
Now sleeps the crimson petal. See The princess
Oh yet we trust. See In memoriam—"Oh yet we trust that somehow good"
"Oh yet we trust that somehow good." See In memoriam
The oak.—TeP
Ode on the death of the Duke of Wellington, sel.
"Bury the great duke."—TeP
Of old sat freedom.—TeP
The owl.—BlO—TuW
Song: The owl.—BoGj—TeP

Tennyson, Alfred, Lord—*Continued*
Pelleas and Ettarre, sel.
A rose, but one.—TeP
Poets and critics.—TeP
The poet's song.—TeP
The princess, sels.
The bugle song.—HoB—HuS-3
Blow, bugle, blow.—GrCt
Song.—BlO
"The splendor falls on castle walls."—ArT-3—BoGj
The splendour falls.—CoR
Come down, O maid.—TeP
Now sleeps the crimson petal.—GrCt—TeP
Sweet and low.—BlO—HoB—HuS-3—TeP
A cradle song.—CoSs
Song.—SmM
Tears, idle tears.—TeP
Prologue. See In memoriam—Strong Son of God
Rain, rain, and sun. See Idylls of the king
The Revenge.—CoD—TeP
Ring out, wild bells. See In memoriam
A rose, but one. See Pelleas and Ettarre
Second song.—TeP
"See what a lovely shell." See Maud
Sir Galahad.—TeP
The sisters.—TeP
Song ("The splendor falls on castle walls") See The princess—The bugle song
Song ("Sweet and low, sweet and low") See The princess—Sweet and low
Song of the brook. See The brook
Song: The owl. See The owl
"The splendor falls on castle walls." See The princess—The bugle song
The splendour falls. See The princess—The bugle song
Strong Son of God. See In memoriam
Sweet and low. See The princess
Tears, idle tears. See The princess
There rolls the deep. See In memoriam
The throstle.—CoB—CoBn—TeP
To Christopher North.—TeP
To Virgil.—GrCt—TeP
The two voices, sel.
The dragon-fly.—ReO
Ulysses.—TeP
Vastness.—TeP
The voyage of Maeldune.—TeP
What hope is here. See In memoriam
When. See The window
When in the darkness.—TeP
When my light is low. See In memoriam
The window, sels.
When.—TeP
Winter.—TeP
Winter. See The window
"**Tenorio,** out for the strong-arm vote." See Brazilian happenings
"**Terence** McDiddler." Mother Goose.—BrMg
Teresa Li
A boatwoman. tr.—LeMw
Casual lines. tr.—LeMw
Teresa, of Avila, Saint (about)
Conversation in Avila. P. McGinley.—PlE
"**Teresa** was God's familiar. She often spoke." See Conversation in Avila
The **term.** William Carlos Williams.—DuR—LaC—LiT
The **termite.** Ogden Nash.—BrSm
Termites
The termite. O. Nash.—BrSm
The termites. R. Hillyer.—ReO
The **termites.** Robert Hillyer.—ReO
A **ternarie** of littles, upon a pipkin of jellie sent to a lady. Robert Herrick.—BoGj
Terrapins. See Turtles
The **terrible** robber men. Padraic Colum.—HaL
"**Terror** in the house does roar." William Blake.—BlP
Terry, Patricia
Loss. tr.—HoL
Terry, Steven
"The eye penetrates into the thoughts of others."—LeM
Tewa Indians. See Indians of the Americas—Tewa
Texas
Little boys of Texas. R. P. T. Coffin.—BrSm
Texas. A. Lowell.—BrA
Texas trains and trails. M. Austin.—ArT-3
Texas—History
The men of the Alamo. J. J. Roche.—HiL
Texas. Amy Lowell.—BrA
Texas trains and trails. Mary Austin.—ArT-3
Thackeray, William Makepeace
Little Billee.—BlO—BrSm—CoSs
Pocahontas.—BrA—HiL
Sorrows of Werther.—BrSm
A tragic story. tr.—HoB
Who misses or who wins.—MoS
Thames river
Bab-Lock-Hythe. L. Binyon.—MoS
Ballad of the two tapsters. V. Watkins.—CaMb
Chaucer's Thames.—ClF (sel.)
The lover to the Thames of London, to favour his lady passing thereon. G. Turberville.—GrCt
"Why should I care for the men of Thames." W. Blake.—BlP—GrCt
Thanatopsis. William Cullen Bryant.—CoBn
"**Thank** heaven, the crisis." See For Annie
"**Thank** You." See Thanksgiving
"**Thank** you, pretty cow, that made." See Pretty cow
Thankfulness. See also Thanksgiving day
Belisarius. H. W. Longfellow.—LoPl
"Blow, blow, thou winter wind." From As you like it. W. Shakespeare.—GrCt
Heigh ho the holly.—ShS
"For all the joys of harvest." E. Vipont.—BrSg
God giveth all things. Unknown.—HoB
Thanksgiving ("I thank you, God") L. Driscoll.—LaPh (sel.)
Thanksgiving ("Thank You") I. O. Eastwick.—BrSg

Thanksgiving to God, for his house. R. Herrick.—GrCt
A visit to the blind asylum. H. S. Horsley.—VrF
A visit to the lunatic asylum. H. S. Horsley.—VrF
Thanksgiving ("I thank you, God") Louise Driscoll.—LaPh (sel.)
Thanksgiving ("Thank You") Ivy O. Eastwick.—BrSg
Thanksgiving day. See also Thankfulness
The first Thanksgiving day. M. J. Preston.—HiL
The little girl and the turkey. D. Aldis.—AgH
Thanksgiving day. L. M. Child.—HuS-3—LaPh
Thanksgiving dinner. A. Fisher.—FiIo
"There once was a finicky ocelot." E. Merriam.—BrLl
Thanksgiving day. Lydia Maria Child.—HuS-3—LaPh
Thanksgiving dinner. Aileen Fisher.—FiIo
Thanksgiving to God, for his house. Robert Herrick.—GrCt
Thapar, Romila
The stone-breaker. tr.—AlPi
"**That** bright chimeric beast." Countee Cullen.—BoA
That cat. Ben King.—CoB
"**That** crafty cat, a buff-black Siamese." See Double Dutch
That dark other mountain. Robert Francis.—MoS
"**That** distance was between us." Emily Dickinson.—DiPe
"**That** duck, bobbing up." Jōsō, tr. fr. the Japanese by Harry Behn.—BeCs
"**That** force is lost." See Snake eyes
"**That** I did always love." Emily Dickinson—DiPe
"**That** is the way God made you." See To a winter squirrel
"**That** junkyard fell down the side of the hill." See Fast run in the junkyard
"**That** red fox." See The trap
"**That** stone." Issa, tr. fr. the Japanese by R. H. Blyth.—IsF
"**That** such have died enables us." Emily Dickinson.—DiPe
"**That** there is falsehood in his looks." See On Dr Babington's looks
"**That** time of year thou mayst in me behold." See Sonnets. William Shakespeare
"**That** vengeance I ask and cry." See Philip (or Phylip) Sparrow—The cursing of the cat
"**That** was once her casement." See In the mind's eye
"**That** was the year." See A poem to delight my friends who laugh at science-fiction
"**That's** my last duchess painted on the wall." See My last duchess
Thaw. Edward Thomas.—HoL—ReBs—ThG
Thaxter, Celia (Leighton)
Little Gustava.—HoB
The sandpiper.—HoB
Spring.—HoB
Thayer, Ernest Lawrence
Casey at the bat.—BoH—MoS
"**Their** learned kings bent down to chat with frogs." See Nursery rhyme
Their lonely betters. W. H. Auden.—BoGj—HaL
"**Their** quick feet pattered on the grass." See Night dancers
Thel's motto. See The book of Thel
Theme. See Theme and variations
Theme and variations, sels. James Stephens
Theme.—StS
Variations 8, 9, and 13.—StS
Theme in yellow. Carl Sandburg.—ArT-3—HuS-3
Theme with variations. James Stephens.—StS (sel.)
Then as now. Walter De La Mare.—DeBg—LiT
"**Then** as now; and now as then." See Then as now
"**Then** be ye glad, good people." See Noël
Then from a ruin. Farid-uddin Attar, tr. fr. the Persian by Edward Fitzgerald.—ReBs
"**Then** from a ruin where conceal'd he lay." See Then from a ruin
Then go at once. Vasant Bapat, tr. fr. the Marathi by R. P. Sirkar.—AlPi
"**Then** hey for a song of Sussex." See Southdown summer
"**Then** it was." See The prelude—France
"**Then** it was dusk in Illinois, the small boy." See First song
"**Then** strip, lads, and to it, though sharp be the weather." See Football song
"**Then** the Lord answered Job out of the whirlwind." See Job—"Hast thou given the horse strength"
"**Then,** the quick plunge into the cool, green dark." See Swimmers
Theologians. Walter De La Mare.—PlE
Theology
The blind men and the elephant. J. G. Saxe.—BoH
Caliban on Setebos; or, Natural theology in the island. R. Browning.—BrP
Theologians. W. De La Mare.—PlE
Thera-gatha and Theri-gatha, sel. Unknown, tr. fr. the Sanskrit by A. L. Basham
Old age.—AlPi
"**There** always is a noise when it is dark." See In the night
There are big waves. Eleanor Farjeon.—StF
"**There** are big waves and little waves." See There are big waves
"**There** are dealers in pictures named Agnew." See Tom Agnew, Bill Agnew
"**There** are lions and roaring tigers, and enormous camels and things." See At the zoo
"**There** are lots and lots of people who are always asking things." See The friend
"**There** are men in the village of Erith." Unknown.—BrLl
The village of Erith.—GrCt
"**There** are mushrooms in the paddock." See The wagon in the barn

"**There** are no fairy-folk in our Southwest." See Western magic.
There are no gods. Euripides, tr. fr. the Greek by J. A. Symonds.—PlE
"**There** are not many blossoms yet." See First signs
"**There** are people go to Carmel." See At Carmel
"**There** are plenty of sweeping, swinging, stinging, gorgeous things to shout about." See Bryan, Bryan, Bryan, Bryan
"**There** are rivers." See Wilderness rivers
"**There** are, some people say, no riches in the bush." See Minstrel's song
"**There** are some qualities—some incorporate things." See Sonnet—Silence
"**There** are strange things done in the midnight sun." See The cremation of Sam McGee
"**There** are the eagles crying, swooping from side to side." Unknown, tr. fr. the aboriginal of Australia.—LeO
"**There** are things." See Feet
"**There** are trails that a lad may follow." See Silver ships
"**There** are twelve months in all the year." See Robin Hood rescuing the widow's three sons
"**There** are two ripenings, one of sight." Emily Dickinson.—DiPe
"**There** are two ways now." See Progress
"**There** are words like Freedom." See Refugee in America
"**There** be none of beauty's daughters." See Stanzas for music
"**There** came a day at summer's full." Emily Dickinson.—DiPe
"**There** came a man to our town." See Aiken Drum
"**There** came a satyr creeping through the wood." See The crackling twig
"**There** came a wind like a bugle." Emily Dickinson.—DiPe
The storm.—SmM
"**There** came an old sailor." See The old sailor
"**There** comes a warning like a spy." Emily Dickinson.—DiPe
"**There** comes an end to summer." See To his mistress
"**There** dwelt a puddy in a well." Unknown.—MoB
"**There** dwelt an old woman at Exeter." See Old woman of Exeter
"**There** go the grownups." See A lazy thought
"**There** had been years of passion—scorching, cold." See And there was a great calm
"**There** he cast." See Angler's choice
"**There** in the bracken was the ominous spoor mark." See The Tantanoola tiger
"**There** is (one great society alone on earth)." See The prelude—The noble
"**There** is a bush that no one sees." See Here we go round the mulberry bush.
"**There** is a clouded city, gone to rest." See The Aztec city
"**There** is a cool river." See Detroit
"**There** is a fading time." Unknown.—BaS
"**There** is a garden in her face." Thomas Campion.—BoGj
"**There** is a hawk that is picking the birds out of our sky." See Shiva
There is a lady. Unknown.—CoBl
"**There** is a lady sweet and kind." See There is a lady
"**There** is a lion which has never roared." See The starry nevers
"**There** is a little garden path." See A garden path
"**There** is a melody for which I would surrender." See Fantasy
"**There** is a memory stays upon old ships." See Old ships
"**There** is a moment country children know." See Village before sunset
"**There** is a plain in western Italy." See The Canterbury tales—Patient Griselda
"**There** is a pleasure in the pathless woods." See Childe Harold's pilgrimage—The ocean
"**There** is a smile of love." See The smile
"**There** is a star that runs very fast." See Moon song
"**There** is a stream, I name not its name, lest inquisitive tourist." See The Bothie of Toberna-Vuolich
"**There** is a sudden little wind that grieves." See October wind
"**There** is a trinity of loveliest things." Rippo, tr. fr. the Japanese by Curtis Hidden Page.—LeMw
"**There** is a willow grows aslant a brook." See Hamlet—Ophelia's death
"**There** is a word." Emily Dickinson.—DiPe
"**There** is an animal known as skink." See Two from the zoo
There is an eminence. William Wordsworth.—WoP
"**There** is an eminence,—of these our hills." See There is an eminence
"**There** is an old cook in N. Y." Unknown.—BrLl
"**There** is an old fellow named Mark." James Montgomery Flagg.—BrLl
"**There** is an umbrella." V. Cokeham.—LeM
"**There** is but one May in the year." Christina Georgina Rossetti.—ArT-3
"**There** is joy in." See Eskimo chant
"**There** is music in me, the music of a peasant people." See The banjo player
"**There** is no beauty." See The world I see
"**There** is no frigate like a book." Emily Dickinson.—BoGj—DiL—DiPe
"**There** is no music now in all Arkansas." See Variations for two pianos
"**There** is no name for brother." See Hail to the sons of Roosevelt
"**There** is no night." See June
"**There** is no reason I can find." See To a cat
"**There** is no rhyme that is half so sweet." See Proem
There is power in a Union. Unknown.—HiL
"**There** is so much loveliness gone out of the world." See The triumph of doubt

"**There** is sweet music here that softer falls." See The lotos-eaters
"**There** is the story of a deserted island." See Emperors of the island
"**There** it was I saw what I shall never forget." See The fawn
"**There** liv'd an old woman of Lynn." See Old woman of Lynn
There lived a little man. Mother Goose.—StF
"**There** lived a sage in days of yore." See A tragic story
"**There** lived a wife at Usher's well." See The wife of Usher's well
"**There** lived an old man in a garret." See Nursery nonsense
"**There** mournful cypress grew in greatest store." See The faerie queene—The garden of Proserpina
"**There** once the walls." See A tale
"**There** once was a barber of Kew." Cosmo Monkhouse.—BrLl
"**There** once was a bonnie Scotch laddie." Unknown.—BrLl
"**There** once was a boy of Bagdad." Unknown.—BrLl
"**There** once was a corpulent carp." Carolyn Wells.—BrLl
"**There** once was a finicky ocelot." Eve Merriam.—BrLl
"**There** once was a frog." See A legend of Okeefinokee
"**There** once was a girl of New York." Cosmo Monkhouse.—BrLl
"**There** once was a knowing raccoon." Mary Mapes Dodge.—BrLl
"**There** once was a maiden of Siam." Unknown.—BrLl
"**There** once was a man in the moon." David McCord.—BrLl
"**There** once was a man, named Power." See Clock time by the geyser
"**There** once was a man who said, Why." Carolyn Wells.—BrLl
"**There** once was a man with a sneeze." Mary Mapes Dodge.—BrLl
"**There** once was a pious young priest." Unknown.—BrLl
"**There** once was a plesiosaurus." Unknown.—BrLl
"**There** once was a provident puffin." Oliver Herford.—BrLl
There once was a puffin. Florence Page Jaques.—ArT-3—StF
"**There** once was a scarecrow named Joel." David McCord.—BrLl
"**There** once was a stately giraffe." Margaret Vandegrift.—BrLl
"**There** once was a young man named Hall." See "There was a young fellow named Hall"
"**There** once was an arch armadillo." Carolyn Wells.—BrLl
"**There** once was an old man who said, Hush." Edward Lear.—BrLl
"**There** once were two cats of Kilkenny." Mother Goose.—BrLl
  The cats of Kilkenny.—LaP
  The Kilkenny cats.—BrMg—BrSm
There rolls the deep. See In memoriam
"**There** rolls the deep where grew the tree." See In memoriam—There rolls the deep
"**There** souls of men are bought and sold." See The human image—London
"**There** stands an old tinker, he's mending a pan." See The tinker
"**There** they stand, on their ends, the fifty faggots." See Fifty faggots
"**There** wanst was two cats at Kilkenny." See "There once were two cats of Kilkenny"
"**There** was a bee sat on a wall." Mother Goose.—ReMg
"**There** was a bird." See Jonathan Gentry—Tom's sleeping song
"**There** was a boy of other days." See Lincoln
"**There** was a boy who skinned his knees." See Is this someone you know
"**There** was a boy whose name was Jim." See Jim, who ran away from his nurse, and was eaten by a lion
"**There** was a bucket full of them. They spilled." See The crabs
"**There** was a captain-general who ruled in Vera Cruz." See El capitan-general
"**There** was a composer named Bong." Unknown.—BrLl
"**There** was a composer named Haydn." Unknown.—BrLl
"**There** was a composer named Liszt." Unknown.—BrLl
"**There** was a crooked man." See "There was a crooked man, and he went a crooked mile"
"**There** was a crooked man, and he went a crooked mile." Mother Goose.—HuS-3—LaP—WiMg
  The crooked man.—BrMg
  Mother Goose rhymes, 50.—HoB
  "There was a crooked man."—OpF—SmM
"**There** was a crow sat on a stone." Mother Goose.—ReMg
"**There** was a cruel naughty boy." See The cruel naughty boy
"**There** was a fairy once." See The singing fairy
"**There** was a faith healer of Deal." Unknown.—BrLl
"**There** was a fat man of Bombay." Mother Goose
  Mother Goose rhymes, 46.—HoB
"**There** was a fish who was born in a cup." See Poor little fish
"**There** was a giant by the orchard wall." See In the orchard
"**There** was a girl I used to go with." See John Brown's body
"**There** was a gray rat looked at me." See Rat riddles
"**There** was a horseman rode so fast." See The horseman

"**There** was a young angler of Worthing." Unknown.—BrLl
"**There** was a young bard of Japan." Unknown. —BrLl
"**There** was a young curate named Stone." F. H. Cozens.—BrLl
"**There** was a young farmer of Leeds." Unknown. —BrLl
"**There** was a young fellow named Hall." Unknown.—BrLl—SmM
"There once was a young man named Hall."—BrSm
"**There** was a young fellow named Weir." Unknown.—BrLl
"**There** was a young fellow of Ealing." Unknown.—BrLl
"**There** was a young fellow of Perth." Unknown. —BrLl
"**There** was a young girl, a sweet lamb." Unknown.—BrLl
"**There** was a young girl in the choir." Unknown. —BrLl
"**There** was a young girl of Asturias." Unknown
Two limericks.—CoBb
"**There** was a young girl of Majorca." Edward Lear.—BrLl
"**There** was a young lady from Lynn." Unknown. —BrLl
The young lady of Lynn.—GrCt
"**There** was a young lady from Woosester." Unknown.—BrLl
"**There** was a young lady named Perkins." Unknown.—BrLl
"**There** was a young lady named Ruth." Unknown.—BrLl
"**There** was a young lady named Wemyss." Unknown.—BrLl
"**There** was a young lady of Bright." A. H. Reginald Buller.—ArT-3—BrLl
"**There** was a young lady of Bute." Edward Lear
Nonsense verses.—HuS-3
"**There** was a young lady of Corsica." Edward Lear.—BrLl—GrCt
"**There** was a young lady of Harwich." Unknown.—BrLl
"**There** was a young lady of Kent." Unknown.—BrLl
"**There** was a young lady of Lynn." See "There was a young lady from Lynn"
"**There** was a young lady of Niger." Unknown.—BrLl—BrSm—LaPd
"**There** was a young lady of Norway." Edward Lear.—ArT-3—BrLl
Nonsense verses.—HuS-3
"**There** was a young lady of Oakham." Unknown
Two limericks.—CoBb
"**There** was a young lady of Poole." Edward Lear.—AgH
"**There** was a young lady of Russia." Edward Lear.—BrLl
"**There** was a young lady of Ryde." Unknown.—BrSm—LaPd
"**There** was a young lady of Spain." See A young lady of Spain
"**There** was a young lady of station." Lewis Carroll.—BrLl
"**There** was a young lady residing at Prague." Unknown.—CoO
"**There** was a young lady whose bonnet." Unknown.—BrLl
"**There** was a young lady whose chin." Edward Lear.—ArT-3—BrLl
Limericks.—HoB
"**There** was a young lady whose eyes." Edward Lear
Limericks.—BoGj
"**There** was a young lady whose nose." Edward Lear.—BrLl
Limericks.—HoB
"**There** was a young man at the War Office." J. W. Churton.—BrLl
"**There** was a young man from Port Jervis." See At the tennis clinic
"**There** was a young man from the city." Unknown.—BrLl
"**There** was a young man from Trinity." Unknown.—BrLl
"**There** was a young man, let me say." David McCord.—BrLl
"**There** was a young man named Achilles." Edwin Meade Robinson.—BrLl
"**There** was a young man of Bengal." Unknown. —BrLl
"**There** was a young man of Cadiz." Unknown.—BrLl
"**There** was a young man of Calcutta." Unknown.—BrLl
"**There** was a young man of Herne bay." Unknown.—BrLl
"**There** was a young man so benighted." Unknown.—BrLl
"**There** was a young man who was bitten." Unknown.—BrLl
"**There** was a young person called Smarty." Unknown.—BrLl
"**There** was a young person named Tate." Carolyn Wells.—BrLl
"**There** was a young person of Crete." Edward Lear.—BrLl
"**There** was a young poet of Kew." Unknown.—BrLl
"**There** was a young prince of Bombay." Walter Parke.—BrLl
"**There** was a young woman of Ayr." Unknown. —BrLl
"**There** was an archbishop named Tait." See Archbishop Tait
There was an Indian. J. C. Squire.—BrA
The discovery.—ClF
"**There** was an Indian, who had known no change." See There was an Indian
"**There** was an island in the sea." See Priapus and the pool—Atlantis
"**There** was an old crow (sat upon a clod)." See Short song

"**There** was an old person of Burton." Edward Lear.—BrLl
"**There** was an old person of Crowle." Edward Lear.—BrLl
"**There** was an old person of Dean." Edward Lear.—AgH—BlO—BrLl
Limericks.—HoB
"**There** was an old person of Diss." Edward Lear
Limericks.—BoGj
"**There** was an old person of Dover." See A double limerick or twiner
"**There** was an old person of Down." Edward Lear.—BrLl
"**There** was an old person of Durban." Unknown. —BrLl
"**There** was an old person of Ewell." Edward Lear.—AgH
"**There** was an old person of Fratton." Unknown. —BrLl
"**There** was an old person of Grange." Edward Lear.—BrLl
"**There** was an old person of Gretna." Edward Lear.—GrCt
"**There** was an old person of Ickley." Edward Lear.—BrLl
"**There** was an old person of Ischia." Edward Lear.—BrLl
"**There** was an old person of Shoreham." Edward Lear.—BrLl
"**There** was an old person of Skye." Edward Lear.—GrCt
"**There** was an old person of Sparta." Edward Lear.—AgH
"**There** was an old person of Ware." Edward Lear
Limericks.—HoB
"**There** was an old person whose habits." Edward Lear
Limericks.—HoB
"**There** was an old soldier of Bister." Unknown. —BrLl
"**There** was an old wife and she lived all alone." See The old wife and the ghost
"**There** was an old woman." See Berries
"**There** was an old woman (lived under a hill, she put)." See The old woman and the mouse
"**There** was an old woman." See Was she a witch
"**There** was an old woman (and she sold puddings and pyes)." Mother Goose.—AgH
"**There** was an old woman (and what do you think)." Mother Goose.—OpF
"**There** was an old woman (lived under a hill and if)." Mother Goose.—GrT—OpF
Under a hill.—BrMg
"**There** was an old woman (who lived at Greenwich)." Walter De La Mare.—BrSg
"**There** was an old woman and she went one." Unknown.—OpF
"**There** was an old woman as I've heard tell." Mother Goose.—ArT-3
Mother Goose rhymes, 55.—HoB
The story of the little woman.—BrMg
"There was a little woman as I've heard tell." —OpF—SmM
"**There** was an old woman called Nothing-at-all." See Nothing-at-all
"**There** was an old woman had three cows." See The old woman's three cows
"**There** was an old woman, her name was Peg." See Peg
"**There** was an old woman in Surrey." Mother Goose
Mother Goose rhymes, 47.—HoB
"**There** was an old woman lived under some stairs." Mother Goose.—OpF
"**There** was an old woman named Towl." See Mistress Towl
"**There** was an old woman of Bath." See Old woman of Bath
"**There** was an old woman of Croydon." See Old woman of Croydon
"**There** was an old woman of Ealing." See Old woman of Ealing
"**There** was an old woman of Gosport." See Old woman of Gosport
"**There** was an old woman of Harrow." See Old woman of Harrow
"**There** was an old woman sat spinning." See A tale
"**There** was an old woman tossed up in a basket." Mother Goose.—HuS-3—OpF—ReMg—WiMg
Mother Goose rhymes, 53.—HoB
An old woman.—BrMg
Sweeping the sky.—LaPd
"**There** was an old woman who lived in a shoe." Mother Goose.—HuS-3—OpF—ReMg—WiMg
Mother Goose rhymes, 52.—HoB
"**There** was an old woman who lived in the fens." Walter De La Mare.—AgH
"**There** was an owl lived in an oak (whiskey, whaskey, weedle)." See "There was an owl lived in an oak (wisky, wasky, weedle)"
"**There** was an owl lived in an oak (the more he heard)." Mother Goose.—OpF
"**There** was an owl lived in an oak (wisky, wasky, weedle)." Mother Goose.—OpF
"There was an owl lived in an oak (whiskey, whaskey, weedle)."—ReMg
"**There** was I and I was confused." See 1 black foot + 1 black foot = 2 black feet
"**There** was no sun." See Metamorphoses—The creation
"**There** was once a giraffe who said, What." Oliver Herford.—BrLl
"**There** was once a most charming young miss." Unknown.—BrLl
"**There** was once a nice little dog, Trim." See The dog Trim
"**There** was once a small boy in Quebec." Rudyard Kipling.—BrLl
"**There** was once a swing in a walnut tree." See The walnut tree

"**There**'s the Irishman Arthur O'Shaughnessy." See On the poet O'Shaughnessy
There's wisdom in women. Rupert Brooke.—CoBl
Theresa, Saint
Lines written in her breviary.—PlE
Thermopylae, Battle of, 480 B.C.
On the army of Spartans, who died at Thermopylae. Simonides of Ceos.—GrCt
"**Therus.**" See Onomatopoeia II
"**These** are the days when birds come back." Emily Dickinson.—DiPe
"**These** are the days when early." See Indian summer
"**These** are the Hyades." See The Hyades
"**These** are the saddest of possible words." See Baseball's sad lexicon
"**These** are the signs of the zodiac." See The zodiac
These beasts and the Benin bronze. Margaret Danner.—HaK
"**These** buildings are too close to me." See Rudolph is tired of the city
These children of the wind. See The people, yes —Children of the wind
"**These** clouds are soft fat horses." See Clouds
"**These** fell miasmic rings of mist." See Prejudice
"**These** flowers of the plum." Izen, tr. fr. the Japanese by R. H. Blyth.—LeMw
"**These** foreigners with strange and avid faces." See Immigrants
"**These** fought in any case." See Hugh Selwyn Mauberley
"**These**, in the dusk, are bars." See Telegraph poles
"**These** were our fields." See Dust bowl
"**They** are all gone away." See The house on the hill
"**They** are all gone into the world of light." Henry Vaughan.—DuS (sel.)
"**They** are at their places, straining." See Aeneid —The boat race
"**They** are cutting down the great plane trees at the end of the gardens." See The trees are down
"**They** are not given much to laughter." See Hill people
"**They** are not long, the weeping and the laughter." See Vitae summa brevis spem nos vetat incohare longam
"**They** are rattling breakfast plates in basement kitchens." See Morning at the window
"**They** are sleeping, these velvet elephants." See Tehachapi mountains
"**They** are unholy who are born." See Wild plum
"**They** argued on till dead of night." See Theologians
"**They** call me cruel. Do I know if mouse or songbird feels." See Sad memories—The cat
"**They** chose me from my brothers." See What am I
"**They** crashed among the spider nets." See Dolphins at Cochin
"**They** dance before they learn." See Some short poems—Kids
"**They** did not know this face." See Job
"**They** dragged you from homeland." See Strong men
"**They** eat beans mostly, this old yellow pair." See The bean eaters
"**They** fished and they fished." See The fish with the deep sea smile
"**They** gathered around and told him not to do it." See Noah
"**They** got pictures of V stamped on letter stamps." See Conversation on V
"**They** hail you as their morning star." See Men
"**They** have a king and officers of sorts." See King Henry V—Honey-bees
"**They** have gone." See Traveling song
"**They** have yarns." See The people, yes
"**They** haven't got no noses." See The song of Quoodle
"**They** hunt, the velvet tigers in the jungle." See India
"**They** landed and could." See The English in Virginia
"**They** left their Babylon bare." See The destruction of Jerusalem by the Babylonian hordes
"**They** looked for me." See Hideout
"**They** rise like sudden fiery flowers." See Fireworks
"**They** say one king is mad. Perhaps. Who knows." See Who knows
"**They** say that." See Color
"**They** say that ex-President Taft." Unknown.—BrLl
"**They** say that when they burned young Shelley's corpse." See The fishes and the poet's hand
"**They** say the war is over. But water still." See Redeployment
"**They** shut the road through the woods." See The way through the woods
"**They** slew a god in a valley." See Gluskap's hound
"**They** squat silhouetted against the hills." See Kurdish shepherds
"**They** take their stand, each rising." See Aeneid —The boxing match
"**They** tell me she is beautiful, my city." See Dusk
They that go down to the sea. See Psalms—Psalm 107
"**They** that go down to the sea in ships." See Psalms—Psalm 107
"**They** that wash on Monday." Mother Goose.—BlO—OpF
"**They** twitter gentle little rhymes." See Autumn bluebirds
"**They** walked in the green wood, wild snows, soft, unchilling." See The flowering forest
"**They** went to sea in a sieve, they did." See The Jumblies

"**This** dog barking at me now." See Dog, midwinter
This England. See King Richard II—England
"**This** evening so cold and chill." Shiki.—BaS
This excellent machine. John Lehmann.—DuS
"**This** excellent machine is neatly planned." See This excellent machine
"**This** face in the mirror." See Conversation with myself
"**This** face in the mirror." See A real dream
"**This** face you got." See Phizzog
"**This** fall of new snow." Kikaku, tr. fr. the Japanese by Harry Behn.—BeCs
"**This** feather-soft creature." See A goldfinch
"**This** fellow pecks up wit as pigeons pease." See Love's labour's lost—Wit's pedlar
"**This** gentleman the charming duck." See A trueblue gentleman
"**This** girl gave her heart to me." See Improvisations: Light and snow
"**This** great purple butterfly." See Another song of a fool
This happy day. Harry Behn.—ArT-3
"**This** is a baby Fanny cries." See Dressing a doll
"**This** is a day to be compared with lions." See Winter splendor
This is a night. Elizabeth Jane Coatsworth.—CoDh
"**This** is a night on which to pity cats." See This is a night
This is a poem. Hilary-Anne Farley.—LeM
"**This** is a poem about god looks after things." See This is a poem
"**This** is a root." See Songs accompanying healing magic
"**This** is a sight to give us pain." See The dunce
"**This** is a spray the bird clung to." See Misconceptions
"**This** is a world full of Negroes and whites." Denise Peterson.—BaH
"**This** is enchanted country, lies under a spell." See Bonac
"**This** is good New year's even-night." See Queen Mary's men
"**This** is Hallowe'en." Unknown.—MoB
This is Halloween. Dorothy Brown Thompson.—ArT-3—LaPh
This is just to say. William Carlos Williams.—BoGj—DuR—LiT
"**This** is little Tom Tucker." See The history of little Tom Tucker
This is my country. Robert P. Tristram Coffin.—PaH
"**This** is my country, bitter as the sea." See This is my country
"**This** is my letter to the world." Emily Dickinson.—DiL—DiPe
"**This** is my rock." David McCord.—HuS-3—LaPd—McE
"**This** is my tree." See Tree climbing
"**This** is Nevada, near the end of one." See You are on U.S. 40 headed west
"**This** is no case of petty right or wrong." Edward Thomas.—ThG
"**This** is so brisk, so fine a day." See Birth of Henri Quatre
"**This** is the arsenal. From floor to ceiling." See The arsenal at Springfield
"**This** is the day when all through the town." See Sunday
"**This** is the debt I pay." See The debt
"**This** is the football hero's moment of fame." See Settling some old football scores
"**This** is the forest primeval. The murmuring pines and the hemlocks." See Evangeline—Prologue
"**This** is the horrible tale of Paul." See The revolving door
"**This** is the house that Jack built." Mother Goose.—HuS-3—OpF
The house that Jack built.—BrMg
"**This** is the house where Jessie White." See Lowery cot
This is the key. Mother Goose.—BlO
The key of the kingdom.—BrMg
"**This** is the key of the kingdom." See This is the key
"**This** is the man that broke the barn." See Thumb and finger game
"**This** is the night mail crossing the border." See The night mail
"**This** is the night my ship comes in." See Johnny Appleseed's ship comes in
"**This** is the order of the music of the morning." See The Santa Fe trail
"**This** is the promise that hangs on the tree." See Christmas 1945
"**This** is the shape of the leaf, and this of the flower." See Portrait of a girl
"**This** is the sin against the Holy Ghost." See The unpardonable sin
"**This** is the song that the truck drivers hear." See Song of the truck
"**This** is the stagnant hour." See Drunken lover
"**This** is the tale that was told to me." See A sailor's yarn
"**This** is the tree." Unknown.—MoB
"**This** is the way the ladies ride." Mother Goose.—ArT-3—BrMg—WiMg
"**This** is the way the ladies ride (jimp and small)." Unknown.—MoB
"**This** is the way the wheels on the rails." See Santa Fe west
"**This** is the weather the cuckoo likes." See Weathers
"**This** is the week when Christmas comes." See In the week when Christmas comes
"**This** is their moment, when the brimming skies." See Evening in the Great Smokies
"**This** Kansas boy who never saw the sea." See Kansas boy
"**This** land grows the oldest living things." See California winter
"**This** land was white." Mother Goose.—BrMg

The combe.—ThG
The dark forest.—ThG
Digging.—ThG
Early one morning.—ThG
Fifty faggots.—ThG
The gallows.—CoB—ThG
The glory.—ThG
"Gone, gone again."—ThG
The green roads.—ThG
Home.—ThG
If I should ever by chance.—BoGj—ThG
"If I should ever by chance grow rich." —BlO
"If I should ever by chance grow rich." See If I should ever by chance
If I were to own.—ThG
In memoriam, Easter, 1915.—ThG
Interval.—ThG
Lights out.—ThG
The lofty sky.—ThG
The long small room.—ThG
The manor farm.—ClF (sel.)
March the third.—ThG
The mill-water.—ThG
"No one cares less than I."—ThG
November.—ThG
October.—ThG
Old Jack Noman.—BlO
An old song ("I was not apprenticed nor ever dwelt in famous Lincolnshire")—ThG
An old song ("The sun set, the wind fell, the sea")—ThG
Out in the dark.—ThG
The owl.—GrCt—ReBs—ThG
The path.—ThG
The penny whistle.—ThG
Roads.—ThG
Sedge-warblers.—ReBs (sel.)
Snow.—ThG
Song.—ThG
Sowing.—ClF—ThG
The sun used to shine.—ThG
A tale.—GrCt
Tall nettles.—GrCt—ThG
Thaw.—HoL—ReBs—ThG
There's nothing like the sun.—ThG
"This is no case of petty right or wrong."—ThG
The trumpet.—GrS—ThG
Two pewits.—ThG
The wasp trap.—ThG
What shall I give.—ThG
"Will you come."—BoGj—ThG
Words.—ThG
Thomas, Mona
"A little white mouse."—LeM
Thomas, R. S.
Alpine.—CoBn
A blackbird singing.—CoB
Cynddylan on a tractor.—CaD
A day in autumn.—CoBn
Farm child.—CaD—CoBn
January.—CoB
Thomas, Rosemary
East river.—BrA
Thomas of Hales
"Where is Paris and Heleyne."—GrCt
"**Thomas** Jefferson." Rosemary Carr and Stephen Vincent Benét.—ArT-3
Thomas Rymer and the queen of Elfland. Unknown.—GrCt
Thomas Shadwell the poet. See Absalom and Achitopel
"**Thomas** was a little glutton." See Little Thomas
Thompson, D'Arcy Wentworth
Nursery nonsense.—CoO
Thompson, Dorothy Brown
Arbor day.—BrSg
Continental crossing.—BrA
Maps.—ArT-3
The pony express.—BrA
This is Halloween.—ArT-3—LaPh
Thompson, Edith Osborne
The monkeys.—ArT-3
Thompson, Francis
The kingdom of God.—PlE
To a snowflake.—CoBn
Thompson, Irene
Caravans.—StF
Thompson, Paul
My feelings.—LeM
Thomson, James
Sunday at Hampstead.—SmM (sel.)
"**Thonah.** Thonah." See First song of the thunder
Thoreau, Henry David
The crow.—ReBs
The fisher's boy.—GrCt
What's the railroad.—HiL
Thoreau, Henry David (about)
Finder, please return to Henry Thoreau. E. J. Coatsworth.—CoDh
Henry Thoreau. E. Merriam.—MeIv
Thorley, Wilfrid
Of a spider.—LaPd
Thorn song. Unknown, ad. fr. the Japanese by Charlotte B. DeForest.—DePp
Thorn trees
The thorn trees. R. Field.—BrSg
The **thorn** trees. Rachel Field.—BrSg
"The **thorn** trees hold their berries high." See The thorn trees
Thorns
"He went to the wood and caught it." Mother Goose.—BrMg
Roses and thorns. S. G. Betai.—AlPi
Thorn song. Unknown.—DePp
Thornton, Patricia
The witch.—LeM
Thorpe, Peter
Take-off.—DuS
"**Those** dear little lambs, how pretty they look." See The little lambs
"**Those** things you have on the sides of your head." See Someone at my house said
Those who go forth before daylight. Carl Sandburg.—HuS-3

Those winter Sundays. Robert E. Hayden.—AdIa —DuS
"**Thou** art indeed just, Lord, if I contend." Gerard Manley Hopkins.—PlE
"**Thou** art the soul of a summer's day." See A song
"**Thou** dusky spirit of the wood." See The crow
"**Thou** fair-haired angel of the evening." See To the evening star
"**Thou** moon, that aidest us with thy magic might." See A charm
"**Thou** shalt have one God only; who." See The latest decalogue
"**Thou** shalt see the field-mouse peep." See Fancy
"**Thou** simple bird what mak'st thou here to play." See Upon the lark and the fowler
"**Thou** sorrow, venom elfe." See Upon a spider catching a fly
"**Thou** stately stream that with the swelling tide." See The lover to the Thames of London, to favour his lady passing thereon
"**Thou** that in fury with thy knotted tail." See The captive lion
"**Thou** wast that all to me, love." See The assignation—To one in paradise
"**Though** a young man of football physique." Unknown.—BrLl
"**Though** cherries and currants are stripp'd from the bough." See Nutting
"**Though** clock." See His grange; or, Private wealth
"**Though** I be now a grey, grey friar." See Maid Marian—The friar
"**Though** I speak with the tongues of men and of angels." See First epistle of Paul to the Corinthians—Charity
"**Though** my hands and face are black." See Charcoal burner
"**Though** the crocuses poke up their heads in the usual places." See Vernal sentiment
"**Though** the day of my destiny's over." See Stanzas to Augusta
"**Though** the fairies meet by night." See At dawn
"**Though** the great waters sleep." Emily Dickinson.—DiPe—PlE
"**Though** the sun has set." See Calm of evening
"**Though** three men dwell on Flannan isle." See Flannan isle
"**Though** we boast of modern progress as aloft we proudly soar." See A paradox
Thought. See also Mind
At the end of the field. A. Fisher.—FiC
"The autumn wind (there are)." Issa.—LeOw
Day-dreamer. Unknown.—ArT-3
Days. K. W. Baker.—ArT-3—ThA
"I found the phrase to every thought." E. Dickinson.—DiPe
Or hounds to follow on a track. E. J. Coatsworth.—CoSb
Ten twice. D. McCord.—McAd
Thought. From Dhamma-pada. Unknown.—AlPi
"A thought went up my mind today." E. Dickinson.—DiL
"Thoughts pass in my mind like flocks of ducks in the sky." R. Tagore.—LeMf
Waves of thought. Panikkar.—AlPi
Wondering. K. Windsor.—LeM
Thought. See Dhamma-pada
"A **thought** went up my mind today." Emily Dickinson.—DiL
"**Thoughtful** little Willie Frazer." See Science for the young
Thoughts for St Stephen. Christopher Morley.—BrSm
"**Thoughts** pass in my mind like flocks of ducks in the sky." Rabindranath Tagore.—LeMf
"A **thousand.**" Issa, tr. fr. the Japanese by Nobuyuki Yuasa.—IsF—LeOw
Thousand-and-first ship, sel. F. Scott Fitzgerald
"There'd be an orchestra."—BoGj
Thousand and one nights. Unknown
Dates.—HoL
"A **thousand** hairy savages." Spike Milligan.—CoO
A **thousand** stones. Claudia Lewis.—LeP
"**Thouzandz** of thornz there be." See The bees' song
Three. Elizabeth Jane Coatsworth.—CoSb
Three a-bed. Mother Goose.—BrMg
Three acres of land. Mother Goose.—BrMg
"**Three** ancient men in Bethlehem's cave." See The mystic magi
Three bad children. Kate Greenaway.—GrT
Three bad ones. Mother Goose.—CoBb
"**Three** big cats in a greenhouse." See Trouble in the greenhouse
Three blind mice. See "Three blind mice, see how they run"
"**Three** blind mice, see how they run." Mother Goose.—OpF—WiMg
Three blind mice.—BrMg
Three brown girls singing. M. Carl Holman.—HaK
The **three** cherry trees. Walter De La Mare.—GrS
Three children sliding. Mother Goose; also at. to John Gay.—BrMg
"**Three** children sliding on the ice." See Three children sliding
Three cooks. See "There were three cooks of Colebrook"
"**Three** crooked cripples." Mother Goose.—ReOn
The **three** deer. Elizabeth Jane Coatsworth.—CoDh
Three don'ts. Ivy O. Eastwick.—BrSg
"**Three** drunken roisterers of whom I tell." See The Canterbury tales—Three men in search of death
"**Three** elements." See John Brown's body
The **three** fishers. Charles Kingsley.—CoSs
"**Three** fishers went sailing out into the west." See The three fishers
The **three** foxes. A. A. Milne.—BoGj—HuS-3—MiC
Three ghostesses. See "There were three ghostesses"
Three helpers in battle. Mary Coleridge.—PlE

The **three** horses. Ivy O. Eastwick.—HoB
"**Three** horses came." See The three horses
"**Three** jolly gentlemen." See The huntsmen
"**Three** jovial gentlemen." Daniel Hoffman.—CaMb
Three jovial huntsmen. See "There were three jovial Welshmen"
The **three** jovial Welshmen. See "There were three jovial Welshmen"
Three knights. Mother Goose.—ReOn
Three knights from Spain. Unknown.—BlO
"**Three** little children sitting on the sand." See All, all a-lonely
"**Three** little ghostesses." See "There were three ghostesses"
Three little girls. Kate Greenaway.—GrT
"**Three** little girls were sitting on a rail." See Three little girls
"**Three** little kittens." Mother Goose.—BrMg
"**Three** little mice walked into town." See Three mice
"**Three** little puffins." Eleanor Farjeon.—ArT-3
Three lovely holes. Winifred Welles.—HuS-3
Three men in a tub. See "Rub-a-dub-dub"
Three men in search of death. See The Canterbury tales
Three mice. Charlotte Druitt Cole.—StF
"**Three** of us afloat in the meadow by the swing." See Pirate story
Three poems about Mark Twain. Vachel Lindsay.—LiP
I. The raft
II. When the Mississippi flowed in Indiana
III. Mark Twain and Joan of Arc
The **three** ravens. Unknown.—GrCt
Three seagulls. Unknown, ad. fr. the Japanese by Charlotte B. DeForest.—DePp
"**Three** ships they lay in Frisco bay." See A long time ago
The **three** singing birds. James Reeves..—LaPd
"**Three** skies." Claudia Lewis.—LeP
Three songs to the one burden, sel. William Butler Yeats
"Come gather round me, players all."—YeR
"**Three** strange men came to the inn." See A lady comes to an inn
"**Three** virgins at the break of day." See The golden net
"**Three** white stones." See Struthill well
"**Three** wise men of Gotham." Mother Goose.—OpF—WiMg
The wise men of Gotham.—BrMg
Three years she grew. William Wordsworth.—WoP
"**Three** years she grew in sun and shower." See Three years she grew
"The **three** young heifers were at summer supper." See The gracious and the gentle thing
Three young rats. Mother Goose.—BrMg—GrCt—SmM
"**Three** young rats with black felt hats." See Three young rats
Threnody ("Let happy throats be mute") Donald Jeffrey Hayes.—BoA
Threnody ("Only quiet death") Waring Cuney.—BoA
A **threnody** ("What, what, what") George T. Lanigan.—DoW
Thrice happy he. William Drummond, of Hawthornden.—CoBn
"**Thrice** happy he, who by some shady grove." See Thrice happy he
"**Thrice** tosse these oaken ashes in the ayre." See The third book of ayres—XVIII
Thrift
"He that would thrive." Mother Goose.—OpF
Advice.—BrMg
"There's a very mean man of Belsize." Unknown.—BrLl
"Wilful waste brings woeful want." Mother Goose.—AgH
The **throstle.** Alfred Tennyson.—CoB—CoBn—TeP
"**Through** and through the inspired leaves." See The book-worms
"**Through** cloudless skies, in silvery sheen." See Stanzas written in passing the Ambracian gulf
"**Through** Dangly woods the aimless doze." See The doze
"**Through** his iron glades." See Winter the huntsman
"**Through** hottest days the bobwhite sings." See Bobwhite
Through lane it lay. See "Through lane it lay—thro' bramble"
"**Through** lane it lay—thro' bramble." Emily Dickinson.—DiL
Through lane it lay.—GrS
"**Through** morning rain." See Summer rain
"**Through** the Appalachian valleys, with his kit." See Ballad of Johnny Appleseed
"**Through** the black, rushing smoke-bursts." See Empedocles on Etna—Callicles' song
"**Through** the gate, where nowhere and night begin." See At the airport
"**Through** the house give glimmering light." See A midsummer-night's dream—Fairy dance
Through the looking-glass, sels. Lewis Carroll
Humpty Dumpty's poem.—BlO
Humpty Dumpty's recitation.—GrCt
"I'll tell thee everything I can."—AgH
Jabberwocky.—ArT-3—BoGj—HoB
The walrus and the carpenter.—BlO—HoB—HuS-3
"The time has come, the walrus said."—ArT-3 (sel.)
"**Through** the parklands, through the parklands." See Parklands
"**Through** the revolving door." See Alligator on the escalator
Through the varied patterned lace. Margaret Danner.—HaK
"**Through** thick Arcadian woods a hunter went." See Atalanta's race
"**Throughout** the world." Unknown, tr. fr. the Winnebago.—LeO

"**Throwing** them up to the moon." Unknown, tr. fr. the Japanese by R. H. Blyth.—LeMw
"A **thrush** is tapping a stone." See Dawn
"**Thrush,** linnet, stare, and wren." See In Glencullen
Thrushes
  The brown thrush. L. Larcom.—HoB
  Come in. R. Frost.—CoBn
  The darkling thrush. T. Hardy.—CoR
  "The missel-thrush." A. Young.—ReBs
  Missel thrush. W. De La Mare.—DeBg
  The throstle. A. Tennyson.—CoB—CoBn—TeP
  The thrush's nest. J. Clare.—BlO—BoGj—SmM
  Two sparrows. H. Wolfe.—SmM
  Watching bird. L. O. Coxe.—CoB
The **thrush's** nest. John Clare.—BlO—BoGj—SmM
Thumb and finger game. Unknown.—MoB
Thumbprint. Eve Merriam.—MeI
"**Thumbs** in the thumb-place." See The mitten song
Thunder
  Dan Dunder. J. Ciardi.—CoBb
  First song of the thunder. Unknown.—LeO
  Giant Thunder. J. Reeves.—CoBn—SmM
  "I never speak a word." M. Austin
    Rhyming riddles.—ArT-3
  "Over the sun-darkened river sands calls the." Unknown.—LeO
  Song of the thunders. Unknown.—LeO
  Spring thunder. M. Van Doren.—BoH
  Thunder ("Call the cows home") W. De La Mare.—CoBn—DeBg
  Thunder ("I hear") G. Van Every.—LeM
  Thunder dragon. H. Behn.—BeG
  Thunder pools. R. P. T. Coffin.—HaL
  "The voice that beautifies the land." Unknown. —LeO
  "Winter's thunder." Mother Goose.—ReOn
Thunder ("Call the cows home") Walter De La Mare.—CoBn—DeBg
Thunder ("I hear") Glenys Van Every.—LeM
Thunder dragon. Harry Behn.—BeG
Thunder pools. Robert P. Tristram Coffin.—HaL
A **thunder-storm.** See "The wind begun (or began) to rock the grass"
The **thunderer.** Phyllis McGinley.—PlE
"**Thundering,** shimmering, silvery gray." See Summer shower
A **thundery** day. Susan Meader.—LeM
"**Thus** she sat weeping." See Eve—The animals mourn with Eve
"**Thus,** some tall tree that long hath stood." See On the death of Benjamin Franklin
"**Thus** sometimes hath the brightest day a cloud." See King Henry VI—Cares and joys
"**Thus** spake a man in days of old." See Irony
Thwaite, Anthony
  At Dunwich.—CaMb
  Dead and gone.—CaD
  Hedgehog.—CaD
"**Thy** need is great." See For the Earth God
"**Thy** tuwhits are lull'd, I wot." See Second song
"**Thy** voice is on the rolling air." See In memoriam
Tichborne, Chidiock
  Elegy.—GrCt
"**Tick-tock,** tick-tock." See Hang Fu
"**Tick-tock,** tick-tock." See Household problems
The **ticket** agent. Edmund Leamy.—HuS-3
The **tickle** rhyme. Ian Serraillier.—CoO—LaP
Tickling game ("Adam and Eve gaed up my sleeve") Unknown.—MoB
Tickling game ("There was a man") Unknown.—MoB
Tickling game ("There was a wee mouse") Unknown.—MoB
Tickly, tickly. Mother Goose.—BrMg
"**Tickly,** tickly, on your knee." See Tickly, tickly
"**Tide** be runnin' the great world over." See Sea love
"The **tide** in the river." Eleanor Farjeon.—ArT-3 —BlO—SmM
"The **tide** rises, the tide falls." Henry Wadsworth Longfellow.—CoSs—GrCt—LoPl
The **tide** river. Charles Kingsley.—CoBn
Tidelands
  To a tidelands oil pump. B. Janosco.—DuS
Tides
  A question. Unknown.—DePp
  "The tide in the river." E. Farjeon.—ArT-3—BlO—SmM
  "The tide rises, the tide falls." H. W. Longfellow.—CoSs—GrCt—LoPl
  The tides. H. W. Longfellow.—LoPl
The **tides.** Henry Wadsworth Longfellow.—LoPl
"**Tidewater** born he was, and ever." See The rivers remember
Tierney, Joseph Paul
  Donne redone.—BrSm
Ties. Dabney Stuart.—DuS
Tietjens, Eunice
  The most-sacred mountain.—PaH
  Moving.—ArT-3
  Parting after a quarrel.—CoBl
  The pioneer woman—in the North country.—BrA
  Psalm to my belovèd.—CoBl
The **tiger.** William Blake.—ArT-3—CoB—CoR—GrCt—ReO—TuW
  The tyger.—BlO—BlP—PlE
Tiger-cat Tim. Edith H. Newlin.—ArT-3
"**Tiger** Christ unsheathed his sword." See For the one who would take man's life in his hands
Tiger lily. David McCord.—BoGj—LaPd
"The **tiger** lily is a panther." See Tiger lily
"**Tiger,** tiger, burning bright." See The tiger
Tigers
  Good taste. C. Logue.—CaD
  Here she is. M. B. Miller.—ArT-3
  India. W. J. Turner.—BlO—LaPd
  The little girl found. W. Blake.—BlP
  The Tantanoola tiger. M. Harris.—CaMb
  "There was a young lady of Niger." Unknown. —BrLl—BrSm—LaPd
  "There was an old hag of Malacca." Unknown.—BrLl

To a young girl leaving the hill country. Arna Bontemps.—HaK
To an athlete dying young. See A Shropshire lad
To an aviator. Daniel Whitehead Hicky.—ThA
To an isle in the water. William Butler Yeats.—SmM—YeR
To Agni. See Rig Veda
To Ann Scott-Moncrieff. Edwin Muir.—GrS
To any garden. Eleanor Farjeon.—BrSg
To **autumn** ("O autumn, laden with fruit, and stained") William Blake.—BlP—CoBn
To autumn ("Season of mists and mellow fruitfulness") John Keats.—ClF (sel.)—CoBn—CoR
To baby. Kate Greenaway.—GrT
"**To** be a giant and keep quiet about it." See Trees
"**To** be not jealous, give not love." See Green weeds
"**To** be old." Teika.—BaS
To Beachey, 1912. Carl Sandburg.—ArT-3
To Beatrice and Sally. Eleanor Farjeon.—FaT
"**To** bed, to bed." Mother Goose.—OpF
Bedtime.—BrMg
Let's go to bed.—GrCt—ReS
To be carved on a stone at Thoor Ballylee. William Butler Yeats.—YeR
To be sung by a small boy who herds goats. Yvor Winters.—WeP
"**To** become a chief's favorite." Unknown.—DoC
"**To** Bethlem did they go, the shepherds three." See Masters, in this hall
To blossoms. Robert Herrick.—CoBn—SmM
To Brooklyn bridge. Hart Crane.—HiL—PaH
"**To** build." See The beaver
To Christopher North. Alfred Tennyson.—TeP
To Clarissa Scott Delany. Angeline W. Grimké.—BoA
To daffadills. See To daffodils
To daffodils. Robert Herrick.—CoBn—HoL
To daffadills.—BoGj
"**To-day** I saw the dragon-fly." See The two voices—The dragon-fly
"**To-day** I think." See Digging
"**To-day** I want the sky." See The lofty sky
To deck a woman, sel. Ralph Hodgson
"And every sky was blue and rain."—HaL
To destiny. Unknown, tr. fr. the Dahomean by Frances Herskovits.—PlE
"**To** drum-beat and heart-beat." See Nathan Hale
To entertain divine Zenocrate. See Tamburlaine the Great
"**To** every man." See The treehouse
"**To** every sacrifice you hasten together." See Rig Veda—To the Maruts
"**To** fight aloud is very brave." Emily Dickinson.—DiPe
"**To** fish for pearls in Lethe." See The great magicians
"**To** fling my arms wide." See Dream variation
"**To** give—and forgive." See Short sermon
"**To** grass, or leaf, or fruit, or wall." See The snail
"**To** have my name." See The bear
"**To** hear an oriole sing." Emily Dickinson.—DiPe
To Helen ("Helen, thy beauty is to me") Edgar Allan Poe.—CoBl—GrCt—PoP
To Helen ("I saw thee once—once only—years ago") Edgar Allan Poe.—PoP
To Henry Reynolds, of poets and poesy, sel. Michael Drayton
Christopher Marlowe.—GrCt
"**To** him who in the love of nature holds." See Thanatopsis
To his friend, Wei. Li T'ai-po, tr. fr. the Chinese by Shigeyoshi Obata.—LiT (sel.)
To his mistress ("My light thou art, without thy glorious sight") John Wilmot, Earl of Rochester.—CoBl
To his mistress ("There comes an end to summer") Ernest Dowson.—CoBl
"**To** Houston at Gonzales town, ride, Ranger, for your life." See The men of the Alamo
To James. See Notes found near a suicide
To Kate, skating better than her date. David Daiches.—MoS
"**To** live a life, free from gout, pain, and phthisic." See Athletic employment
"**To** look at any thing." John Moffitt.—DuR
"**To** lose one's faith surpasses." Emily Dickinson.—DiPe
To Lou Gehrig. John Kieran.—MoS
To Lucasta, on going to the wars. Richard Lovelace.—McWs
To M. H. William Wordsworth.—WoP
"**To** make a knothole." See Knotholes
To make a prairie. See "To make a prairie it takes a clover and one bee"
"**To** make a prairie it takes a clover and one bee." Emily Dickinson.—DiPe
To make a prairie.—BoH
"**To** make some bread you must have dough." See One, two, three—gough
To market. See "To market, to market, to buy a plum bun"
"**To** market, to market, a gallop, a trot." Mother Goose.—OpF
"**To** market, to market, to buy a fat pig." Mother Goose.—ArT-3—HuS-3—OpF
"**To** market, to market, to buy a plum bun." Mother Goose.—OpF
To market.—BrMg
To Mary: It is the evening hour. John Clare.—GrCt
"**To** Meath of the pastures." See A drover
"**To** mend their every hurt, to heal all their ills." See Mountain medicine
"**To** mercy, pity, peace, and love." See The divine image
To Minerva. Thomas Hood.—GrCt
To Miss Rápida. Juan Ramón Jiménez, tr. fr. the Spanish by H. R. Hays.—LiT
To Mistress Margaret Hussey. John Skelton.—BoGj
To morning. William Blake.—BlP
To musique, to calm his fever. Robert Herrick.—BoGj
To my mother. Edgar Allan Poe.—PoP

To my sister. William Wordsworth.—WoP
To my son. Siegfried Sassoon.—McWs
To my son Parker, asleep in the next room. Bob Kaufman.—HaK
To my valentine. Unknown.—LaPh
To mystery land. Kate Greenaway.—GrT
To night. Joseph Blanco White.—CoR
To one in paradise. See The assignation
"**To** paint without a palette." See Some uses for poetry
To Phillis. Charles Sedley.—CoBl
"**To** plant a seed and watch it grow." See Lesson
"**To** plant a tree! How small the twig." See Arbor day
To Richard Wright. Conrad Kent Rivers.—AdIa —BoA
To Satch. Samuel Allen.—BoA—HaK
American Gothic.—AdIa
To Satch; or, American Gothic.—MoS
To Satch; or, American Gothic. See To Satch
To secure victory in battle. See Atharva Veda
To see a nightingale. Unknown, ad. fr. the Japanese by Charlotte B. DeForest.—DePp
"**To** see the world in a grain of sand." See Auguries of innocence
To shades of underground. Thomas Campion.—GrCt
To sleep ("A flock of sheep that leisurely pass by") William Wordsworth.—WoP
To sleep ("O soft embalmer of the still midnight") John Keats.—GrCt
"**To** sleep easy all night." See "To sleep easy at night"
"**To** sleep easy at night." Mother Goose.—AgH
How to sleep easy.—BrMg
"**To** smash the simple atom." See Atomic courtesy
To sparrows fighting. William Henry Davies.—ReBs
To spring. William Blake.—BlP—CoBn
To summer. William Blake.—BlP
"**To** talk of the weather." Unknown.—MoB
To the bat. Mother Goose.—BrMg
To the city in the snow. Agnes O'Gara Ruggeri. —ThA
To the city of London. William Dunbar.—GrCt
To the cuckoo ("Cuckoo, cuckoo, what do you do") Mother Goose.—BrMg
To the cuckoo ("Not the whole warbling grove in concert heard") William Wordsworth.—WoP
To the cuckoo ("O blithe new-comer. I have heard") William Wordsworth.—WoP
To the cuckoo ("O cuckoo, shall I call thee bird") F. H. Townsend.—GrCt
To the daisy. William Wordsworth.—WoP
To the dawn. See Rig Veda
"**To** the dim light and the large circle of shade." See Sestina
To the driving cloud. Henry Wadsworth Longfellow.—GrCt—LoPl
To the evening star. William Blake.—BlP—CoBn —GrCt—GrS
To the four courts, please. James Stephens.—StS
To the immortal memory of that noble pair, Sir Lucius Cary and Sir H. Morison, sel. Ben Jonson
"It is not growing like a tree."—GrCt
To the magpie. See "Magpie, magpie, chatter and flee"
To the Maruts. See Rig Veda
To the memory of my beloved; the author Mr William Shakespeare. Ben Jonson.—GrCt (sel.)
To the moon ("Art thou pale for weariness") Percy Bysshe Shelley.—CoBn—SmM
To the moon ("What have you looked at, moon") Thomas Hardy.—CoBn—GrCt
To the Muses. William Blake.—BlP—GrCt
To the Princess Margaret Tudor. William Dunbar.—GrS
To the rain. See "Rain, rain, go away (come again)"
To the Right Honorable William, Earl of Dartmouth. Phillis Wheatley.—HaK (sel.)
To the same flower ("Pleasures newly found are sweet") William Wordsworth.—WoP
To the same flower ("With little here to do or see") William Wordsworth.—WoP
To the small celandine. William Wordsworth.—WoP
To the snail. Mother Goose.—BrMg
To the snake. Denise Levertov.—CoB
To the snow. Mother Goose.—BrF—BrMg
"**To** the sun." See Last song
To the sun ("More beautiful than the remarkable moon and her noble light") Ingeborg Bachmann, tr. by Michael Hamburger.—CoBn
To the sun ("Oh let your shining orb grow dim") See Mithraic emblems
To the terrestrial globe. William Schwenck Gilbert.—LiT
To the thawing wind. Robert Frost.—HaL
To the Virginian voyage. Michael Drayton.—HiL
To the virgins, to make much of time. Robert Herrick.—GrCt
To the waters. See Rig Veda
To the wayfarer. Unknown.—ArT-3
To the wind. See Rig Veda
To the young locust tree outside the window. Claudia Lewis.—LeP
"**To** this my song." Unknown, tr. fr. the Inca.—LeO
To Thomas Moore. George Gordon Byron.—ByP
To three small rabbits in a burrow. Mary Kennedy.—CoB
To Toussaint l'Ouverture. William Wordsworth. —WoP
"**To** town, to town." See Silk
To turn back. John Haines.—CoBn
To verse let kings give place. See Elegies
"**To** verse let kings give place, and kingly shows." See Elegies—To verse let kings give place
To violets. Robert Herrick.—TuW
To Virgil. Alfred Tennyson.—GrCt—TeP
"**To** wait an hour is long." Emily Dickinson.—DiPe

"**To** wake alive, in this world." Unknown, tr. fr. the Japanese by R. H. Blyth.—LeMw
"**To** walk abroad is, not with eyes." See Walking
To walk on hills. Robert Graves.—MoS
"**To** walk on hills is to employ legs." See To walk on hills
"**To** what shall I compare." Mansei.—BaS
To what shore would you cross. Kabir, tr. fr. the Sanskrit by Rabindranath Tagore.—AlPi
"**To** what shore would you cross, O." See To what shore would you cross
"**To** whit." See The owl
"**To-whit,** to-whit, to-whee." See Who stole the nest
"**To** whom do lions cast their gentle looks." See King Henry VI—Protection
To winter. William Blake.—BlP
"**To** zig-zag with the ant." See Summer afternoon
The **toad.** Carmen Bernos de Gasztold, tr. fr. the French by Rumer Godden.—GaC
The **toad-eater.** Robert Burns.—BuPr
"The **toad.** It looks as if." Issa, tr. fr. the Japanese by R. H. Blyth.—LeI
Toads. See also Frogs; Tree toads
A friend in the garden. J. H. Ewing.—BrSg—HuS-3
"Hop out of my way." Chora.—BeCs
Lullaby for a baby toad. S. Gibbons.—CoB—ReS
The song of Mr Toad. From The wind in the willows. K. Grahame.—BoGj
The toad. C. B. de Gasztold.—GaC
"The toad. It looks as if." Issa.—LeI
Ungainly things. R. Wallace.—DuS
Toadstools. See Mushrooms
Toadstools. Elizabeth Fleming.—StF
The **toaster.** William Jay Smith.—AgH—ArT-3—DuR
Toasters
The toaster. W. J. Smith.—AgH—ArT-3—DuR
Toasts
A health unto his majesty. J. Savile.—GrCt
To Thomas Moore. G. G. Byron.—ByP
Tobacco
"Make three-fourths of a cross." Mother Goose.—BrMg
Tobias, John
Reflections on a gift of watermelon pickle received from a friend called Felicity.—DuR
A **toccata** of Galuppi's. Robert Browning.—BrP
"**Today** also, today also." Issa, tr. fr. the Japanese.—LeOw
"**Today** I saw, lying in the shade." See Goats
"**Today** I walked on lion-colored hills." See On the hill
"**Today** I went to market with my mother." See My brother
"**Today** is the day of my departure." See Leave-taking
"**Today** six slender fruit trees stand." See Planting trees
"**Today** they cut down the oak." See The stump
"**Today** we have naming of parts. Yesterday." See Naming of parts
Todhunter, John
Aghadoe.—CoBl
Toe-play poems. See Finger-play poems
Toes
"I sits with my toes in the brook." Unknown.—OpF
Moses. Mother Goose.—BrMg
The pobble. E. Lear.—BlO
"**Together,** we looked down." See Wedding procession, from a window
"The **toils** are pitch'd, and the stakes are set." See The lady of the lake—Hunter's song
Tolkien, J. R. R.
The adventures of Tom Bombadil, sels.—LiT (Complete)
Oliphaunt.—ClF
Perry-the-winkle.—ArT-3
Dwarves' song. See The hobbit
The hobbit, sels.
Dwarves' song.—LiT
"Roads go ever ever on."—ArT-3
The stone troll.—LiT
Oliphaunt. See The adventures of Tom Bombadil
Perry-the-winkle. See The adventures of Tom Bombadil
"Roads go ever ever on." See The hobbit
The stone troll. See The hobbit
"**Toll** for the brave." See Loss of the Royal George
The **toll** taker. Patricia Hubbell.—ArT-3
Tolson, Melvin B.
African China.—HaK
Dark symphony.—BoA
Harlem gallery.—HaK (sel.)
Tom. Osbert Sitwell.—CaD
Tom Agnew, Bill Agnew. Dante Gabriel Rossetti.—GrCt
"**Tom** and Charles once took a walk." See Naughty Sam
Tom Bowling. Charles Dibdin.—CoSs
"**Tom** he was a piper's son." See "Tom, Tom, the piper's son (he learnt to play)"
Tom o' Bedlam's song. Unknown.—GrCt
"**Tom** Thumbkin." See The fingers
Tom Thumb's picture alphabet. Mother Goose.—BrMg
Tom Tickleby and his nose. Laura E. Richards.—CoO
Tom Tiddler's ground. Unknown.—MoB
"**Tom** tied a kettle to the tail of a cat." See Three bad ones
Tom Tinker's dog. See "Bow, wow, wow"
Tom Tinker's ground. Mother Goose.—ReOn
"**Tom** told his dog called Tim to beg." See Tom's little dog
"**Tom,** Tom, the piper's son (he learnt to play)." Mother Goose.—GrT—ReMg
"Tom, he was a piper's son."—ArT-3—OpF
"**Tom,** Tom, the piper's son (stole a pig)." Mother Goose.—OpF—WiMg
Tom.—BrMg

Tomato time. Myra Cohn Livingston.—AgH—BrSg
Tomatoes
Tomato time. M. C. Livingston.—AgH—BrSg
Tombs. See also Epitaphs
At the grave of Henry Vaughan. S. Sassoon.—PlE
"Bending over." Issa.—IsF
The bishop orders his tomb at Saint Praxed's church. R. Browning.—BrP
Booman. Mother Goose.—ReOn
"The caverns of the grave I've seen." W. Blake.—BlP
Dedication of the illustrations to Blair's grave. W. Blake.—BlP—GrCt
The dolphin's tomb. Anyte of Tegea.—ReO
The grave. Unknown.—GrCt
The gravedigger. B. Carman.—CoBn
The house dog's grave. R. Jeffers.—CoB
An inscription by the sea. E. A. Robinson.—CoSs—GrCt
Invocation. H. Johnson.—BoA
"Is this it, then." Issa.—LeOw
The knight's tomb. S. T. Coleridge.—ClF
"May the gravediggers not bury me." Unknown.—DoC
St Swithin. Daniel Henderson.—BrSm
A serio-comic elegy. R. Whately.—BrSm
"Stranger call this not." Unknown.—BrSm
This spot. Unknown.—BrSm
The valley of white poppies. W. Sharp.—ThA
Verdancy. Unknown.—BrSm
"Visiting the graves." Issa.—IsF—LeOw
Tombstone, Arizona
At Boot Hill in Tombstone, Arizona. Unknown.—BrSm
Tombstone. Lucia M. and James L. Hymes, Jr.—ArT-3
Tommy. Gwendolyn Brooks.—BrSg
Tommy and Bessy. See "As Tommy Snooks and Bessie Brooks"
Tommy and Jimmy. Kate Greenaway.—GrT
"**Tommy** O'Linn was a Scotsman born." See Tommy O'Linn
Tommy Tittlemouse. See "Little Tommy Tittlemouse"
Tommy Trot. Mother Goose.—BrMg
"**Tommy** Trot, a man of law." See Tommy Trot
Tommy Tucker. See "Little Tommy Tucker"
"**Tommy** was a silly boy." Kate Greenaway.—ArT-3
Tomonori
"The cherry tree blossomed. Black was my hair."—LeMw
Reflection.—LeMw
Tomorrow. Myra Cohn Livingston.—LiC
"**Tomorrow,** and tomorrow, and tomorrow." See Macbeth—Out, out, brief candle
"**Tomorrow's** Christmas day: three kinds of pies." See Trouble with pies
Tom's little dog. Walter De La Mare.—ArT-3—CoB—DeBg
Tom's sleeping song. See Jonathan Gentry
Tongue-twisters
"Betty Botter bought some butter." Mother Goose.—OpF
Betty Botter's batter.—BrMg
"A canner, exceedingly canny." C. Wells.—BrLl
"Careful Katie cooked a crisp and crinkly cabbage." Mother Goose.—OpF
"A certain young fellow named Beebee." Unknown.—BrLl
The duel. Unknown.—BrSm
"How much wood would a wood-chuck chuck." Mother Goose.—ArT-3—HuS-3
Jumble jingle. L. E. Richards.—CoO
Moses. Mother Goose.—BrMg
Not ragged-and-tough. Unknown.—GrCt
One bowl, one bottle. Mother Goose.—ReOn
Peter Piper's practical principles of plain and perfect pronunciation. Unknown.—VrF
"Peter Piper picked a peck of pickled (or pickling) pepper."—BrMg—HuS-3—OpF—WiMg
Mother Goose rhymes, 43.—HoB
"Robert Rowley rolled a round roll 'round." Mother Goose.—HuS-3
Robert Rowley.—ReOn
The rugged rock. Mother Goose.—BrMg
"She sells sea-shells on the sea shore." Mother Goose.—OpF
Sea shells.—BrMg
The swan. Mother Goose.—GrCt
Mother Goose rhymes, 42.—HoB
"There was a man, his name was Dob." Mother Goose.—OpF
"There was an old lady named Carr." Unknown.—BrLl
"Three crooked cripples." Mother Goose.—ReOn
The tutor. C. Wells.—McWs
"A twister of twists once twisted a twist." Unknown.—OpF
Twister twisting twine. J. Wallis.—GrCt
Tongues
Butterfly tongues. A. Fisher.—FiI
"**Tonight** a blackout. Twenty years ago." See Christmas eve under Hooker's statue
Tonight in Chicago. Unknown.—BrA
"**Tonight** in the sky." Issa, tr. fr. the Japanese.—LeOw
"**Tonight** in this town." Unknown, tr. fr. the Japanese by Harry Behn.—BeCs
"**Tonight** is the night." See Hallowe'en
"**Tonight,** then, is the night." See First fight
"**Tonight** when the hoar frost falls on the wood." See Christmas in the woods
Tony O. Colin Francis.—BlO
Tony the turtle. E. V. Rieu.—ArT-3
"**Tony** was a turtle." See Tony the turtle
Too blue. Langston Hughes.—DuR
"**Too** dense to have a door." See The haystack
"**Too** green the springing April grass." See Spring in New Hampshire
The **too-late** born. Archibald MacLeish.—BoGj

"**Too** much thought." See Day-dreamer
Too old to work. Joe Glazer.—HiL
Toomer, Jean
Banking coal.—BoH
Beehive.—AdIa
Brown river, smile.—BoA
Carma.—HaK (sel.)
Georgia dusk.—BoA—HaK
Karintha.—HaK (sel.)
Reapers.—HaK
Song of the son.—BoA—HaK
Torai
"A child stretched forth."—LeMw
Tori
"The kingfisher."—LeMw
The **tortoise** in eternity. Elinor Wylie.—HoL—ReO
Tortoises. See Turtles
T'other little tune. Mother Goose —ReOn
Toucans
"A fellow who slaughtered two toucans." Unknown.—BrLl
Touch, Sense of
Felicia Ropps. G. Burgess.—CoBb
Mud. P. C. Boyden.—ArT-3
My fingers. M. O'Neill.—OnF
To a fat lady seen from the train. F. Cornford.—BoGj
Touch. E. Farjeon.—FaT
Touch. Eleanor Farjeon.—FaT
"A **touch** of cold in the autumn night." See Autumn
Toulouse-Lautrec, Henri Marie Raymond de (about)
Ungainly things. R. Wallace.—DuS
"A **tourist** came in from Orbitville." See Southbound on the freeway
Toussaint L'Ouverture, Pierre Dominique (about)
To Toussaint l'Ouverture. W. Wordsworth.—WoP
"**Toussaint,** the most unhappy man of men." See To Toussaint l'Ouverture
"**Toward** the sea turning my troubled eye." See Visions of the world's vanity—The huge leviathan
The **tower** of Genghis Khan. Hervey Allen.—PaH
Towers
To be carved on a stone at Thoor Ballylee. W. B. Yeats.—YeR
Town and country ("In town you have expensive clocks") Unknown, ad. fr. the Japanese by Charlotte B. DeForest.—DePp
Town and country ("My child, the town's a fine place") Thomas Moult.—ClF
The **town** of American visions. Vachel Lindsay. —LiP
Towns. See also Cities and city life; also names of towns, as Jerusalem
Adlestrop. E. Thomas.—BlO—BoGj—PaH—ThG
Adventure. H. Behn.—ArT-3
Arizona village. R. S. Davieau.—BrA
Barrow. L. Adams.—BaH
"Coming along the mountain path." Taigi.—LeMw
Connecticut road song. A. H. Branch.—PaH
Courthouse square. H. Merrill.—BrA
Depot in a river town. M. Williams.—DuS
Driving to town late to mail a letter. R. Bly.—CoBn
"Every morning when I wake." From Under Milk Wood. D. Thomas.—HaL
Georgia towns. D. W. Hicky.—BrA
Green, green is El Aghir. N. Cameron.—CaMb
In a desert town. L. Stevenson.—BrA—HuS-3
Midwest town. R. D. Peterson.—BrA
The mountain. R. Frost.—PaH
My town. K. Itta.—BaH
People. L. Lenski.—LaC
Poem to be read at 3 A.M. D. Justice.—DuS
Saturday in the county seat. E. L. Jacobs.—BrA
A small migration. H. Behn.—BeG
Summer concert. R. Whittemore.—BrA
Town and country ("In town you have expensive clocks") Unknown.—DePp
Town and country ("My child, the town's a fine place") T. Moult.—ClF
Wibbleton and Wobbleton.—Mother Goose.—BrMg
Townsend, F. H.
To the cuckoo.—GrCt
Toys. See also Play; also names of toys, as Dolls
The box. M. C. Livingston.—LiC
The duel. E. Field.—ArT-3—HoB—HuS-3—ReS
Not any more. D. Aldis.—HoB
The sensitive figure. E. Turner.—VrF
Teddy bear. H. Behn.—ArT-3
Us two. A. A. Milne.—ArT-3—MiC
Track sports
Challenge. S. Hazo.—MoS
Notes on a track meet. D. McCord.—MoS
Pole vault. S. Murano.—MoS
"This torch, still burning in my hand." From The Greek anthology. Krinagoras.—MoS
Tracks, Animal. See Animal tracks
Tracks in the snow ("Out of the dark") Elizabeth Jane Coatsworth.—HoB
Tracks in the snow ("Wherever fox or cat or crow") Elizabeth Jane Coatsworth.—CoSb
Traction: November 22, 1963. Howard Moss.—BrA
Tractors
Cynddylan on a tractor. R. S. Thomas.—CaD
The plowman of today. H. Garland.—HuS-3
Trade winds. John Masefield.—BoH—ClF
Trades. See Occupations; also names of occupations, as Carpenters and carpentry
Trading
"His father died." Unknown.—MoB
"My father he died, but I can't tell you how." Unknown.—BlO
Traffic
Broadway: Twilight. T. Prideaux.—LaC
City traffic. E. Merriam.—LaC—LaPd—MeI

"There was a young lady of Bright." A. H. R. Buller.—BrLl
"There was a young lady residing at Prague." Unknown.—CoO
The ticket agent. E. Leamy.—HuS-3
Trains. R. Burgunder.—ArT-3
Travel ("I should like to rise and go") R. L. Stevenson.—ArT-3—BoH—PaH
"I should like to rise and go."—HuS-3
Travel ("The railroad track is miles away") E. St V. Millay.—ArT-3—BoH—LaP—LaPd—ThA
Traveling America. J. Struther.—BrA
Traveling song. Unknown.—BeG
Traveling through the dark. W. Stafford.—DuS
Traveller's curse after misdirection. R. Graves.—HoL
"Trot, trot, horsie." Unknown.—MoB
The unexplorer. E. St V. Millay.—HaL
Up silver stairsteps. J. Stuart.—BrA
Victoria. E. Farjeon.—BlO
Wheels. C. Lewis.—LeP
"Wild goose, O wild goose." Issa.—LeOw
You are on U. S. 40 headed west. V. White.—BrA
"You, north must go." Unknown.—StF
Travel ("I should like to rise and go") Robert Louis Stevenson.—ArT-3—BoH—PaH
"I should like to rise and go."—HuS-3
Travel ("The railroad track is miles away") Edna St Vincent Millay.—ArT-3—BoH—LaP—LaPd—ThA
The **traveler.** Vachel Lindsay.—LiP
"**Travelers** take heed for journeys undertaken in the dark." See October journey
Traveling America. Jan Struther.—BrA
"**Traveling** America, I am England-haunted." See Traveling America
"The **traveling** is over, dear." See Circuit through the hills
Traveling song. Unknown, tr. fr. the Papago by Harry Behn.—BeG
Traveling storm. Mark Van Doren.—ThA
Traveling through the dark. William Stafford.—DuS
"**Traveling** through the dark I found a deer." See Traveling through the dark
Traveller's curse after misdirection. Robert Graves.—HoL
"**Travelling,** a man met a tiger, so." See Good taste
"**Treading** a field I saw afar." See Death on a live wire
Treasure
Three men in search of death. From The Canterbury tales. G. Chaucer.—ChT
Tree. John Hunter.—LeM
A **tree** at dusk. Winifred Welles.—ThA
Tree at my window. Robert Frost.—BoH—CoBn
"**Tree** at my window, window tree." See Tree at my window
Tree climbing. Kathleen Fraser.—FrS
A **tree** design. Arna Bontemps.—BoH
"A **tree** frog trilling." Rogetsu, tr. fr. the Japanese by Harry Behn.—BeCs
"The **tree** has entered my hands." See A girl
"A **tree** is a base for poison ivy." Vicky Williams.—LeM
"A **tree** is more than a shadow." See A tree design
"A **tree** may be laughter in the spring." See Winter night
The **tree** of life. Unknown, tr. fr. the Irish by Robin Flower.—ReBs
"The **tree** of life with bloom unchanged." See The tree of life
Tree-sleeping. Robert P. Tristram Coffin.—HaL
"The **tree** still bends over the lake." See Winter
The **tree** toad. Monica Shannon.—ArT-3
"The **tree** toad is a creature neat." See The tree toad
Tree toads. See also Frogs; Toads
"A tree frog trilling." Rogetsu.—BeCs
The tree toad. M. Shannon.—ArT-3
Treece, Henry
Ballad.—CaD
The **treehouse.** James A. Emanuel.—BoA—BoH
Trees. See also Forests and forestry; also names of trees, as Oak trees
Afforestation. E. A. Wodehouse.—MoS
Arbor day. D. B. Thompson.—BrSg
Autumn fancies. Unknown.—HuS-3
Best of all. A. Fisher.—FiC
California winter. K. Shapiro.—BrA (sel.)
Ceremony. H. Behn.—BeG
City trees. E. St V. Millay.—BoH—LaC
Climbing. A. Fisher.—ArT-3—FiI
Counting-out rhyme. E. St V. Millay.—BoGj—DuR
"Every time I climb a tree." D. McCord.—ArT-3—LaP—LaPd—McE
The fallen tree. A. Young.—CoBn
A ghost story. Unknown.—DePp
Grongar hill. J. Dyer.—ClF (sel.)—GrCt
Hangman's tree. L. Z. White.—BrA
Hideout. A. Fisher.—FiI
Holes of green. A. Fisher.—FiI
"Hungry tree." N. Altshuler.—LeM
"I had a little nut-tree; nothing would it bear." Mother Goose.—HuS-3—ReMg
"I had a little nut tree."—OpF—SmM
The little nut tree.—BrF—BrMg
Mother Goose rhymes, 59.—HoB
"I stand under the naked tree." L. McCall.—LeM
"In spring I look gay." Mother Goose.—BrMg—OpF
In the treetops. A. Fisher.—FiI
November. M. C. Livingston.—LiC
The old tree. A. Young.—BoGj
"On a cool evening." Issa.—LeOw
On killing a tree. G. Patel.—AlPi
Open house. A. Fisher.—FiI
Planting trees. V. H. Friedlaender.—CoBn
A salute to trees. H. Van Dyke.—HuS-3
"Skinny Jim." M. C. Livingston.—LiC
Someone was up in that tree. J. Ciardi.—CiYk

Trees—*Continued*
Song. R. W. Dixon.—GrCt
The sound of trees. R. Frost.—BoH
Split the stones. E. J. Coatsworth.—CoDh
Stone trees. J. Freeman.—CoBn
Strange tree. E. M. Roberts.—CoBn—HoB—ThA
Tapestry trees. W. Morris.—CoBn
To the wayfarer. Unknown.—ArT-3
Tree. J. Hunter.—LeM
A tree at dusk. W. Welles.—ThA
Tree at my window. R. Frost.—BoH—CoBn
Tree climbing. K. Fraser.—FrS
A tree design. A. Bontemps.—BoH
"A tree is a base for poison ivy." V. Williams. —LeM
Tree-sleeping. R. P. T. Coffin.—HaL
Trees ("The grass is a rug for the trees to") S. Forman.—LeM
Trees ("To be a giant and keep quiet about it") H. Nemerov.—CoBn
Trees ("Trees are the kindest things I know") H. Behn.—ArT-3—HoB
Trees ("Trees just stand around all day") A. Fisher.—FiC
Trees ("The trees share their shade with") N. Dishman.—LeM
The trees and the wind. E. Farjeon.—FaA
"The trees are a beautiful sight." M. Lasanta. BaH
The trees are down. C. Mew.—CoBn
"The trees come up to my window." R. Tagore.—LeMf
The two old women of Mumbling hill. J. Reeves.—BrSm
"Under the greenwood tree." From As you like it. W. Shakespeare.—ArT-3—CoBn—ShS —TuW
Waiting. Unknown.—LeMw
What do we plant. H. Abbey.—ArT-3
Windy tree. A. Fisher.—FiI
Winter night. C. Hutchison.—ArT-3
The winter trees. C. Dyment.—ClF
A wish. T. Santos.—LeM
"The **trees**." See Stillness
Trees ("The grass is a rug for the trees to") Susan Forman.—LeM
Trees ("To be a giant and keep quiet about it") Howard Nemerov.—CoBn
Trees ("Trees are the kindest things I know") Harry Behn.—ArT-3—HoB
Trees ("Trees just stand around all day") Aileen Fisher.—FiC
Trees ("The trees share their shade with") Nelda Dishman.—LeM
"The **trees** along this city street." See City trees
The **trees** and the wind. Eleanor Farjeon.—FaA
"The **trees** are a beautiful sight." Miriam Lasanta.—BaH
The **trees** are down. Charlotte Mew.—CoBn
"**Trees** are full of holes." See Holes of green
"The **trees** are in their autumn beauty." See The wild swans at Coole
"**Trees** are short." See Best of all
"**Trees** are the kindest things I know." See Trees
"The **trees** come up to my window." Rabindranath Tagore.—LeMf
"**Trees** in the old days used to stand." See Carentan O Carentan
"**Trees** just stand around all day." See Trees
"The **trees** shadow stretches across the stream." See The gleaming stream
"The **trees** share their shade with." See Trees
"The **trees** stand hushed, on tiptoe for the sight." See Waiting
"**Trees** worry in November." See November
Tremayne, Sydney
Slow spring.—SmM
"**Trembling** I sit day and night, my friends are astonish'd at me." See Jerusalem
"**Triangles** are commands of God." See The starfish
"A **trick** that everyone abhors." See Rebecca
Trifle. Georgia Douglas Johnson.—BoA—BoH
Trifles. See Little things, Importance of
"The **trigger** will shoot and the dagger will strike." See Ballad of the soldier
Tringress, Clare
Five.—StF
Fun with my shadow.—StF
I like.—StF
Sleepy John.—StF
The sun's frolic.—StF
Trinity: A dream sequence. Naomi Long Madgett.—HaK (sel.)
Trinity place. Phyllis McGinley.—LaC
Trip: San Francisco. Langston Hughes.—BrA
Trip upon trenchers. Mother Goose.—ReOn
A sad song.—BrMg
"**Trip** upon trenchers and dance upon dishes." See Trip upon trenchers
Tristan da Cunha. Roy Campbell.—CoR
"**Trit** trot to Boston, trit trot to Lynn." Mother Goose.—OpF
Tritt, John
Getting wood.—BaH
"**Triumph** may be of several kinds." Emily Dickinson.—DiPe
The **triumph** of doubt. John Peale Bishop.—PlE
Trivia, sel. John Gay
The dangers of foot-ball.—MoS
Troilus and Cressida, sel. William Shakespeare
The humble-bee.—ShS
Trojan war
Night encampment outside Troy. From Iliad. Homer.—CoR
"**Troll** sat alone on his seat of stone." See The hobbit—The stone troll
"**Troop** home to silent grots and caves." See Song of the mermaids
"**Tropical** mid-day. Indolence." See Heat
Tropics
Heat. G. Gonzalez y Contreras.—HoL
The tropics in New York. C. McKay.—BoA—BoH—HaK
The **tropics** in New York. Claude McKay.—BoA —BoH—HaK
The **Trosachs.** William Wordsworth.—WoP

"**Trot** along, pony." Marion Edey.—ArT-3
"**Trot,** trot, horsie." Unknown.—MoB
Troubadours. See Minstrels and troubadours
Trouble in the greenhouse. Mary Mapes Dodge. —BrSg
"The **trouble** with a kitten is." See The kitten
Trouble with pies. David McCord.—McAd
Troubles. Dorothy Aldis.—HuS-3
Trousers
Double trouble. E. Merriam.—MeI
"A **trout** leaps high." Onitsura, tr. fr. the Japanese by Harold G. Henderson.—LeMw
Troynovant. Thomas Dekker.—GrCt
"**Troynovant** is now no more a city." See Troynovant
Trucks
Country trucks. M. Shannon.—ArT-3
Song of the truck. D. Frankel.—BrA
The **true** and tender wife. See Ramayana
True love. Philip Sidney.—GrCt
"**True** love is founded in rocks of remembrance." See Love and law
A **true** story. John Smith.—SmM
"**True** Thomas lay o'er yond grassy bank." See Thomas Rymer and the queen of Elfland
A **trueblue** gentleman. Kenneth Patchen.—ReO
"A **trumpet.**" See Lewis has a trumpet
The **trumpet.** Edward Thomas.—GrS—ThG
Trumpets
Lewis has a trumpet. K. Kuskin.—LaPd
The little trumpet. C. Govini.—LiT
The trumpet. E. Thomas.—GrS—ThG
"The **trunk** of a tree." See Climbing
"**Trust** not too much, fair youth, unto thy feature." See White primit falls
Truth. William Cowper.—CoB (sel.)
Truth will out. Peggy Bennett.—CoB
Truthfulness and falsehood
Falsehood corrected. E. Turner.—VrF
"I died for beauty, but was scarce." E. Dickinson.—DiPe
"If we want to tell a lie." Unknown.—DoC
The lie. W. Raleigh.—GrCt
Lies. Y. Yevtushenko.—DuS
On Dr Babington's looks. R. Burns.—BuPr
"One thread of truth in a shuttle." Unknown. —DoC
Someone. L. Jaffe.—LeM
"Tell all the truth but tell it slant." E. Dickinson.—DiPe
"There was a young lady named Ruth." Unknown.—BrLl
Voice in the crowd. T. Joans.—BoA—HaK
"Whatsoever things are true." From Philippians, Bible, New Testament.—ArT-3
Tse Nan
The happy farmer.—LeMw
Tso, Mae Verna
"The coyote sat."—BaH
Tsosie, Tom Nakai
Little children.—BaH
"My old mother stands."—BaH
"Ride along, my friend."—BaH
"Sitting."—BaH
"Summer."—BaH
"Walking."—BaH
Ts'ui Hao
River travel.—LeMw
Tsumori Kunimoto
"The wild geese returning."—BaS—LaPd—LeMw
Tsurayuki
"Do those girls set out."—BaS
"Like my cupped hands."—BaS
"My existence in the world has been."—BaS
"On summer nights."—BaS
"Out in the marsh reeds."—BaS
"With the spreading mists."—BaS
Tu Fu
After rain.—HoL
The excursion.—MoS
Neighbors.—LeMw
Overnight in the apartment by the river.—GrCt
South wind.—ArT-3—LeM
The white horse.—GrCt
Tu Mu
"How can a deep love seem deep love."—LeMw
The **tub.** George S. Chappell.—StF
Tubman, Harriet (about)
Runagate runagate. R. E. Hayden.—AdIa
Tudor, Mary, Queen of England (about)
Mary Tudor. E. J. Coatsworth.—CoDh
The **tuft** of kelp. Herman Melville.—GrCt
Tug of war ("No one is quite sure") Kathleen Fraser.—FrS
Tug-of-war ("The rope she is stout an' the rope she is strong") Eleanor Farjeon.—FaT
Tulips
"She slept beneath a tree." E. Dickinson.—DiPe
Tumbleweed. David Wagoner.—CoBn
Tumbleweeds
Tumbleweed. D. Wagoner.—CoBn
Tumbling Mustard. Malcolm Cowley.—BrA
"**Tumultuous** years bring their voice to your bosom." See Unfathomed past
"**Tuna** turn." See A fishy square dance
A **tune.** Arthur Symons.—CoBl
Tuppence ha'penny farden. Mother Goose.—BrMg
Turberville, George
The lover to the Thames of London, to favour his lady passing thereon.—GrCt
Turkeys
The little girl and the turkey. D. Aldis.—AgH
The **Turkish** trench dog. Geoffrey Dearmer.—CoB
Turn, cheeses, turn. Mother Goose.—ReOn
Turn of the night. Elizabeth Jane Coatsworth.—CoDh
The **turn** of the road. James Stephens.—LiT
Turn yourself around. Kathleen Fraser.—FrS
"**Turned** towards the moon." Yakamochi.—BaS
Turner, Charles Tennyson
Julius Caesar and the honey-bee.—ReO
The lion's skeleton.—ReO
To a starved hare in the garden in winter.—SmM

" '**Twas** in heaven pronounced, and 'twas muttered in hell." See A riddle
" '**Twas** in the middle of the night." See Mary's ghost
" '**Twas** in the year of forty-nine." See The whale
" '**Twas** just this time last year I died." Emily Dickinson.—DiPe
" '**Twas** mercy brought me from my pagan land." See On being brought from Africa to America
" '**Twas** midsummer; cooling breezes all the languid forests fanned." See The death of Jefferson
" '**Twas** on a Holy Thursday, their innocent faces clean." See Holy Thursday
" '**Twas** on a Sunday mornin', down 'cross the Southern sea." See Blow, ye winds
" '**Twas** on the Eastern Filigrees." See The dutiful mariner
" '**Twas** on the shores that round our coast." See The yarn of the Nancy Bell
" '**Twas** the frogge in the well." See The marriage of the frog and the mouse
" '**Twas** the night before Christmas, when all through the house." See A visit from St Nicholas
" '**Twas** the voice of the sweet dove." See The old sweet dove of Wiveton
Tweed and Till. See The two rivers
"**Tweedledum** and Tweedledee." Mother Goose. —BrMg—OpF
Twelfth night. See "Here's to thee, good apple tree"
Twelfth night, sels. William Shakespeare
  Hey, ho, the wind and the rain.—ShS
  O mistress mine.—CoBl
    Song.—BoGj
    Song from Twelfth night.—HoL
Twelfth night: Song of the camels. Elizabeth Jane Coatsworth.—BoH
The **twelve** days of Christmas. Mother Goose.—BrMg—LaPh
  "The first day of Christmas my true love sent to me."—OpF
  The thirteen days.—ReOn
  Thirteen Yule days.—MoB
  The Yule days.—GrCt
"**Twelve** good friends." See Peter and John
"The **twelve** Miss Pelicoes." Kate Greenaway.—GrT
"**Twelve** pairs hanging high." Mother Goose
  Mother Goose rhymes, 51.—HoB
"**Twelve** snails went walking after night." See The haughty snail-king
Twenty-five. Rod McKuen.—DuS
"**Twenty** froggies went to school." See Frogs at school
"**Twenty** white horses." See "Thirty white horses"
" '**Twere** a dree night, a dree night, as the squire's end drew nigh." See The dree night
"**Twice** five years." See The prelude.—Books
Twilight calm. Christina Georgina Rossetti.—CoBn
"**Twilight** came." See The lost star
Twilight song. John Hunter-Duvar.—DoW
Twin Lakes hunter. A. B. Guthrie, Jr.—DuR
"**Twin** streaks twice higher than cumulus." See Vapor trails
"**Twinkle,** twinkle, little star." See The star
Twins
  The twins ("Good and bad are in my heart") J. Stephens.—StS
  The twins ("In form and feature, face and limb") H. S. Leigh.—ArT-3—BrSm
  Twins ("Two little girls were standing there") Unknown.—DePp
  The twins ("The two-ones is the name for it") E. M. Roberts.—ArT-3
The **twins** ("Good and bad are in my heart") James Stephens.—StS
The **twins** ("In form and feature, face and limb") Henry Sambrooke Leigh.—ArT-3—BrSm
Twins ("Two little girls were standing there") Unknown, ad. fr. the Japanese by Charlotte B. DeForest.—DePp
The **twins** ("The two-ones is the name for it") Elizabeth Madox Roberts.—ArT-3
"**Twirl** about, dance about." See Dreidel song
"**Twirling** your blue skirts, travelling the sward." See Blue girls
"A **twister** of twists once twisted a twist." Unknown.—OpF
Twister twisting twine. John Wallis.—GrCt
"**Twitching** the leaves just where the drainpipe clogs." See Hedgehog
The **two** April mornings. William Wordsworth.—WoP
Two birds. See Birds on a stone
"**Two** birds." See L and S
Two birds flying. Unknown, ad. fr. the Japanese by Charlotte B. DeForest.—DePp
"**Two** birds were flying." See Two birds flying
"**Two-boots** in the forest walks." See The intruder
"**Two** boys stand at the end of the full train." See The brothers: Two Saltimbanques
"**Two** brothers there were of Sioux City." Unknown.—BrLl
"**Two** brothers we are." Mother Goose.—BrMg
"**Two** butterflies went out at noon." Emily Dickinson.—DiPe
"**Two** cats." See Diamond cut diamond
The **two** cats. Elizabeth Jane Coatsworth.—CoSb
"**Two** deep clear eyes." Walter De La Mare.—DeBg
The **two** deserts. Coventry Patmore.—CoBn
"**Two** ducks swim to the shore." Hiroshige.—LeMw
Two friends. David Ignatow.—DuS
Two from the zoo. Eve Merriam.—ArT-3
Two gentlemen of Verona, sels. William Shakespeare
  Quiet woods.—ShS
  The spring of love.—GrCt
  Time.—ShS
  Who is Silvia.—CoBl
"**Two** girls of twelve or so at a table." Charles Reznikoff.—LaC

Two guests from Alabama. See Out of the cradle endlessly rocking
Two in bed. Abram Bunn Ross.—ArT-3
Two in the Campagna. Robert Browning.—BrP —CoBl (sel.)
Two Indian boys. Joseph Leonard Concha.—BaH
Two jazz poems. Carl Wendell Hines, Jr.—BoA —DuR (sel.)—HaK
Two kinds: Bold and shy. John Holmes.—McWs
"**Two** leaps the water from its race." See The mill
Two legs. See "Two legs sat upon three legs"
"**Two** legs sat upon three legs." Mother Goose.—BrMg—OpF
Two legs.—ReOn
Two little blackbirds. See "As I went over the water"
"**Two** little clouds one summer's day." See The rainbow fairies
"**Two** little creatures." See Monkeys
"**Two** little dicky birds." Mother Goose.—WiMg
"**Two** little dogs sat by the fire." Mother Goose. —OpF
"**Two** little girls were standing there." See Twins
"**Two** little sisters had got leave." See The poor cripple girl
"**Two** little sisters went walking one day." Unknown.—WyC
Two lives and others. Winfield Townley Scott.—DuR
The **two** magicians. Unknown.—GrCt
"**Two** medicos, immaculate in gray." See Seagulls
Two million two hundred thousand fishes. Danny Marcus.—LeM
Two mills. Mother Goose.—BrMg
The **two** mirrors. Elizabeth Jane Coatsworth.—CoSb
The **two** nests. See Childhood. Francis Carlin
The **two** old bachelors. Edward Lear.—BrSm
"**Two** old bachelors were living in one house." See The two old bachelors
Two old crows. Vachel Lindsay.—HaL
"**Two** old crows sat on a fence rail." See Two old crows
"The **two** old trees on Mumbling hill." See The two old women of Mumbling hill
The **two** old women of Mumbling hill. James Reeves.—BrSm
"The **two-ones** is the name for it." See The twins
Two or three. John Keats.—SmM
"**Two** or three posies." See Two or three
"**Two** people." See Fast
Two people. E. V. Rieu.—CoBb
"**Two** people live in Rosamund." See Two people
Two pewits. Edward Thomas.—ThG
Two pigeons. Mother Goose.—BrMg
"**Two** pigeons flying high." Mother Goose.—OpF
Two poems. Claudia Lewis.—LeP
I. "A drove of rams and ewes and woolly lambs"
II. "Sheep of plush, push"
Two puppies. Unknown, ad. fr. the Japanese by Charlotte B. DeForest.—DePp
"**Two** respectable **rhymes**." See Rhymes
The **two** rivers. Unknown.—GrCt
Tweed and Till.—CoBn
"**Two** roads diverged in a yellow wood." See The road not taken
Two robins. Mother Goose.—BrMg
Two sewing. Hazel Hall.—ThA
Two somewhat different epigrams. Langston Hughes.—HaK
Two songs of a fool. William Butler Yeats.—ReO
Two songs of spring wandering. Wang Wei, tr. fr. the Chinese by Chan Yin-nan and Lewis C. Walmsley.—LeMw
Two sparrows. Humbert Wolfe.—SmM
"**Two** sparrows, feeding." See Two sparrows
"**Two** tapsters traded on Thames's side." See Ballad of the two tapsters
"**Two** thousand feet beneath our wheels." See Cockpit in the clouds
Two times three. David McCord.—McAd
"**Two** travellers of such a cast." See The chameleon
"**Two** twigs acting as a loom." See Dew on a spider web
Two views of the planet earth. Harry Behn.—BeG
The **two** voices, sel. Alfred Tennyson
The dragon-fly.—ReO
"**Two** wee birdies." See Finger play
Two wise generals. Ted Hughes.—CaMb
The **two** witches. Robert Graves.—CaD
The **two** wives. Daniel Henderson.—BrSm
Two years later. William Butler Yeats.—YeR
"**Two** yellow dandelion shields do not make spring." See Night wind in spring
" '**Twould** ring the bells of heaven." See The bells of heaven
The **tyger.** See The tiger
"**Tyger,** tyger, burning bright." See The tiger
Tyler, Robert L.
Puppy.—DuR
Tymnès
The dog from Malta. See A Maltese dog
A Maltese dog.—ArT-3
The dog from Malta.—CoB
Tynan, Katharine (Katharine Tynan Hinkson)
Chanticleer.—ArT-3—TuW
The making of birds.—ReBs
"**Type** of the antique Rome. Rich reliquary." See The coliseum
Tyrants
Epitaph on a tyrant. W. H. Auden.—HoL
The grey monk. W. Blake.—BlP
Tyre, Phoenicia
Helen of Tyre. H. W. Longfellow.—GrS
Tzu Yeh
The frost.—LeMw

U

"U is for umbrellas." See All around the town
Ubell, Lori
Sunset on the sea.—LeM

Uda
"Like a wave crest."—BaS
Ukō
"The nightingales sing."—LeI
Ula Masondo's dream. William Plomer.—CaMb
Ulalume—A ballad. Edgar Allan Poe.—PoP
Ululation. Eve Merriam.—MeI
Ulysses (about)
Return. E. J. Coatsworth.—CoDh
Ulysses. A. Tennyson.—TeP
Ulysses. Alfred Tennyson.—TeP
The **umbrella** brigade. Laura E. Richards.—ArT-3
Umbrellas
The elf and the dormouse. O. Herford.—ArT-3 —HoB—ThA
Nursery nonsense. D'A. W. Thompson.—CoO
Sudden storm. E. J. Coatsworth.—CoSb
"There was a wee girl named Estella." M. B. Hill.—BrLl
"U is for umbrellas." From All around the town. P. McGinley.—ArT-3
The umbrella brigade. L. E. Richards.—ArT-3
"You can see me in the country." Unknown Riddles.—StF
The **umpire** ("Everyone knows he's blind as a bat") Walker Gibson.—MoS
The **umpire** ("The umpire is a lonely man") Milton Bracker.—MoS
"The **umpire** is a lonely man." See The umpire
Un-birthday party. Aileen Fisher.—FiIo
Uncle Ambrose. James Still.—BrA
Uncle Davy. See "As I went up a slippery gap"
"**Uncle** Tiger just went out under the tree." See It happens once in a while
Uncles
"As I went up a slippery gap." Mother Goose. —OpF
Uncle Davy.—BrMg
Extremely naughty children. E. Godley.—CoBb
My singing aunt. J. Reeves.—BrSm
My uncle Jack. D. Amey.—LeM
Ponjoo. W. De La Mare.—BrSm
The sensitive figure. E. Turner.—VrF
The stone troll. From The hobbit. J. R. R. Tolkien.—LiT
A true story. J. Smith.—SmM
Uncle Ambrose. J. Still.—BrA
Zima junction. Y. Yevtushenko.—LiT (sel.)
Under a hill. See "There was an old woman (lived under a hill and if)"
"**Under** a lonely sky, a lonely tree." See On a lonely spray
"**Under** a low sky." See Silence
"**Under** a splintered mast." See A talisman
"**Under** a spreading chestnut-tree." See The village blacksmith
"**Under** a toadstool." See The elf and the dormouse
"**Under** all her topsails she trembled like a stag." See Posted as missing
Under Ben Bulben. William Butler Yeats.—YeR (sel.)
"**Under** his relentless eye." See Boy with frogs
"**Under** low grey sky." See January
Under Milk Wood, sels. Dylan Thomas
"Every morning when I wake."—HaL
"Johnnie Crack and Flossie Snail."—BoGj—CaD—HaL—LaPd
Under rose arches. Kate Greenaway.—GrT
"**Under** rose arches to Rose town." See Under rose arches
"**Under** the after-sunset sky." See Two pewits
Under the boughs. Gene Baro.—CoBn
"**Under** the cherry-blossoms." Issa, tr. fr. the Japanese by R. H. Blyth.—IsF
"**Under** the dawn I wake my two-wheel friend." See On a bicycle
"**Under** the force." See Fleeing to safety
Under the frontier post. Wang Chang-Ling, tr. fr. the Chinese by Rewi Alley.—GrCt
"**Under** the greenwood tree." See As you like it
"**Under** the ground." See Rabbit and lark
"**Under** the misty sky of the early spring." Shinsai, tr. fr. the Japanese by Alan Priest.—LeMw
Under the moon. William Butler Yeats.—PaH
"**Under** the rabbit there, I saw a tree." See Mr Mixup tells a story
Under the rose. Walter De La Mare.—DeBg
Under the round tower. William Butler Yeats.—GrS
"**Under** the sun." See The song of the rain
Under-the-table manners. Unknown.—StF
Under the trees. Aileen Fisher.—FiI
"**Under** the wide and starry sky." See Requiem
"**Under** the willow." Issa, tr. fr. the Japanese by Lewis Mackenzie.—LeMw
Under the window. Kate Greenaway.—GrT
"**Under** the window is my garden." See Under the window
"**Under** this sod and beneath these trees." See On Samuel Pease
Undersea. Marchette Chute.—LaP
Undersea fever. William Cole.—CoSs
"**Underwater** eyes, an eel's." See An otter
Underwood, Edna Worthley. See Chi Hwang Chu and Underwood, Edna Worthley
The **unemployed** blacksmith. John Woods.—McWs
The **unexplorer.** Edna St Vincent Millay.—HaL
Unfathomed past. Rabindranath Tagore, tr. fr. the Bengali by the author.—AlPi
Unfinished knews item. Eve Merriam.—MeI
Unfolding bud. Naoshi Koriyama.—DuR
Ungaretti, Giuseppe
You were shattered.—LiT (sel.)
Ungainly things. Robert Wallace.—DuS
Unharvested. Robert Frost.—CoBn
The **unicorn** ("Lo! in the mute, mid wilderness") See Nepenthe
The **unicorn** ("The unicorn stood, like a king in a dream") E. V. Rieu.—CoB
The **unicorn** ("While yet the morning star") Ella Young.—ArT-3
"The **unicorn** stood, like a king in a dream." See The unicorn

Unicorns
The furrows of the unicorn. E. J. Coatsworth. —CoDh
Gazelles and unicorns. From The long road. J. Gray.—GrCt
Inhuman Henry; or, Cruelty to fabulous animals. A. E. Housman.—CoBb
The lion and the unicorn. Mother Goose.—BrF —BrMg—MoB—OpF
Reflections on a gift of watermelon pickle received from a friend called Felicity. J. Tobias.—DuR
Senlin. From Senlin: A biography. C. Aiken.—HaL
The strangers. A. A. Brown.—DoW
The unicorn ("Lo! in the mute, mid wilderness") From Nepenthe. G. Darley.—GrCt
The unicorn ("The unicorn stood, like a king in a dream") E. V. Rieu.—CoB
The unicorn ("While yet the morning star") E. Young.—ArT-3
"The unicorn's hoofs." Unknown.—ReO
"The **unicorn's** hoofs." Unknown, tr. fr. the Chinese by Arthur Waley.—ReO
"**Unite,** unite, let us all unite." See The Padstow night song
United States. See also America; also names of states, as New Hampshire
All one people. From The people, yes. C. Sandburg.—BrA
America. C. McKay.—BoH
America for me. H. Van Dyke.—ThA
America the beautiful. K. L. Bates.—PlE
America was promises. A. MacLeish.—BrA (sel.)
American letter. A. MacLeish.—BrA (sel.)
American names. S. V. Benét.—BrA—PaH
The birds of America. J. Broughton.—BrA
The building of the ship. H. W. Longfellow.—LoPl
Burning in the night. T. Wolfe.—BrA
The coming American. S. W. Foss.—BrA (sel.)
Continental crossing. D. B. Thompson.—BrA
Eagle plain. R. Francis.—BrA
Europe and America. D. Ignatow.—BrA
I hear America griping. M. Bishop.—BrA
I hear America singing. W. Whitman.—ArT-3 —BrA—HoB—HuS-3—WhA
"I hear America singing, the varied carols I hear."—LaPd
I sing America now. J. Stuart.—BrA
"I, too, sing America." L. Hughes.—AdIa
I, too.—BoA—HaK
Invocation. From John Brown's body. S. V. Benét.—BrA
It is time. T. Joans.—HaK
Land of the free. A. MacLeish.—BrA (sel.)
The sound track.—LiT (sel.)
Localities. C. Sandburg.—BrA
Love song. R. Whittemore.—BrA
Map of my country. J. Holmes.—BrA
"My country need not change her gown." E. Dickinson.—BrA—DiPe
"My land is fair for any eyes to see." J. Stuart. —ArT-3
A nation's strength. R. W. Emerson.—BrA (sel.)
The new Colossus. E. Lazarus.—BoH—BrA
The new world ("There was a strange and unknown race") P. Engle.—BrA
The new world ("This America is an ancient land") E. L. Masters.—BrA
"Next to of course God America I." E. E. Cummings.—BrA—HiL
Night journey. T. Roethke.—BoH—BrA
Nocturne. F. M. Frost.—CoBn
Our country. H. Behn.—BeG
Our heritage. J. Stuart.—BrA
The path of the padres. E. D. Osborne.—BrA
The Pinta, the Nina and the Santa Maria; and many other cargoes of light. J. Tagliabue.—BrA
Shine, Republic. R. Jeffers.—BrA
Song of the redwood-tree. W. Whitman.—PaH (sel.)
Song of the truck. D. Frankel.—BrA
The star-spangled banner. F. S. Key.—HiL
Star-spangled ode. P. McGinley.—HiL
"They have yarns." From The people, yes. C. Sandburg.—BrA
American yarns.—HuS-3
Traveling America. J. Struther.—BrA
View of the capitol from the Library of Congress. E. Bishop.—BrA
Walthena. E. Peck.—BrA
"What is America." J. F. Velez.—BaH
United States—History
America. W. Blake.—BlP (sel.)
Channel U.S.A.—live. A Stoutenburg.—BrA—HiL
Down on Roberts' farm. C. Reeves.—HiL
The gift outright. R. Frost.—BrA
In the Oregon country. W. Stafford.—BrA
Men. A. MacLeish.—BrA
Middle passage. R. E. Hayden.—AdIa—BoA
North star shining, sels. H. H. Swift
"I came to the new world empty-handed." —BrA
"My name was legion."—BrA
Signatures. C. T. Stevenson.—BrA
Traction: November 22, 1963. H. Moss.—BrA
United States—History—Colonial period
The English in Virginia. C. Reznikoff.—GrS
The first Thanksgiving day. M. J. Preston.—HiL
Giles Corey. Unknown.—HiL
The landing of the Pilgrim Fathers. F. D. Hemans.—ArT-3—HiL
Southern ships and settlers. R. C. and S. V. Benét.—BrA
To the Virginian voyage. M. Drayton.—HiL
United States—History—Revolution
A ballad of the Boston tea-party. O. W. Holmes.—HiL
Concord hymn. R. W. Emerson.—BrA—HiL—HuS-3—PaH—TuW
Nathan Hale. F. M. Finch.—HiL
Paul Revere's ride. From Tales of a wayside inn. H. W. Longfellow.—ArT-3—HiL—HuS-3 —LoPl

Prophecy in flame. F. M. Howard.—BrA
Song of Marion's men. W. C. Bryant.—HiL
"Yankee Doodle came (or went) to town." Mother Goose.—HuS-3—OpF
Yankee Doodle.—BrMg—GrCt
United States—History—Burr conspiracy
Blennerhassett's island. From The new pastoral. T. B. Read.—HiL
United States—History—War of 1812
The battle of New Orleans. T. D. English.—HiL
The star-spangled banner. F. S. Key.—HiL
United States—History—War with Mexico
Lament for the Alamo. A. Guiterman.—BrA
The men of the Alamo. J. J. Roche.—HiL
Monterey. C. F. Hoffman.—HiL
United States—History—Civil war
Achilles Deatheridge. E. L. Masters.—BrA
The aged stranger. B. Harte.—BrA
The arsenal at Springfield. H. W. Longfellow.—LoPl
Barbara Frietchie. J. G. Whittier.—HiL
Battle hymn of the republic. J. W. Howe.—HiL—PlE
Bivouac on a mountain side. W. Whitman.—GrCt—LiT
The blue and the gray. F. M. Finch.—HiL
The brigade must not know, sir. Unknown.—HiL
Brother Jonathan's lament for Sister Caroline. O. W. Holmes.—HiL
Carry me back. J. Holmes.—BrA
The cruise of the Monitor. G. H. Boker.—HiL
Farragut. W. T. Meredith.—HiL
John Brown's body, sels. S. V. Benét
Invocation.—BrA
"It was noon when the company marched to the railroad station"
From John Brown's body.—HiL
Robert E. Lee.—BrA
"There was a girl I used to go with."—HaL
"Three elements."—PlE
Knowlt Hoheimer. From The Spoon River anthology. E. L. Masters.—HoL
Memorial wreath. D. Randall.—AdIa
Names from the war. B. Catton.—BrA
The returned volunteer to his rifle. H. Melville.—HiL
Robert Gould Shaw. P. L. Dunbar.—HaK
Runagate runagate. R. E. Hayden.—AdIa
Running the batteries. H. Melville.—HiL
They will look for a few words. N. B. Turner.—BrA
When Johnny comes marching home. P. S. Gilmore.—HiL
United States—History—Reconstruction
Ku-Klux. M. Cawein.—HiL
The rebel. I. Randolph.—HiL
United States—History—Westward movement. See also Cowboys; Frontier and pioneer life; Indians of the Americas
Conquest. E. J. Coatsworth.—BrA
The wilderness is tamed.—HuS-3
"Lewis and Clark." R. C. and S. V. Benét.—HuS-3
The Oregon trail: 1851. J. Marshall.—HuS-3
The passing of the buffalo. H. Garland.—HuS-3
The pony express. D. B. Thompson.—BrA
The railroad cars are coming. Unknown.—BrA
To the driving cloud. H. W. Longfellow.—GrCt—LoPl
Trail breakers. J. Daugherty.—BrA
United States—History—War with Spain
Cuba libra. J. Miller.—HiL
United States—History—World war I. See European war, 1914-1918
United States—History—World war II. See World war, 1939-1945
United States—History—Korean war
Korea bound, 1952. W. Childress.—BrA
On a certain engagement south of Seoul. H. Carruth.—BrA
Univac to Univac. Louis B. Salomon.—DuS
Universe. See World
An **unkind** lass. Mother Goose.—BrMg
The **unknown** citizen. W. H. Auden.—DuS
The **unknown** color. Countee Cullen.—BoH
"**Unknown,** she was the form I preferred." See Loss
Unknown soldier
Saint Peter relates an incident of the Resurrection day. J. W. Johnson.—HaK
"**Unless** there's one thing seen." See Your poem, man
The **unpardonable** sin. Vachel Lindsay.—LiP
"An **unpopular** youth of Cologne." Unknown.—BrLl
Unsatisfied yearning. Richard Kendall Munkittrick.—DuR
"The **untamed** sea is human." See The sea
Untermeyer, Louis
At the bottom of the well.—BoGj
Caliban in the coal mines.—LaPd
Day-dreamer. tr.—ArT-3
Good advice. tr.—ArT-3
Lesson from a sun-dial. tr.—ArT-3
Motto. tr.—ArT-3
Short sermon. tr.—ArT-3
Swimmers.—MoS (sel.)
Until we built a cabin. Aileen Fisher.—ArT-3
The **untutored** giraffe. Oliver Herford.—BrSm (sel.)
The **unwritten** song. Ford Madox Ford.—ReS
"**Up** a hill hurry me not." Unknown.—OpF
"**Up** and at them." See Danger
"**Up** and down the city road." See Pop goes the weasel
"**Up** and down the river." See River night
"**Up** and down the small streets, in which." See The widows
"**Up** and down, up and down." See After the salvo
"**Up** and down, up and down." See A midsummer-night's dream—Song for goblins
"**Up** and up, the Incense-burner peak." See Having climbed to the topmost peak of the Incense-burner mountain

V

Mountain summer. C. Lewis.—LeP
Poor grandpa. R. C. O'Brien.—BrSm
Summer vacation. From The prelude. W. Wordsworth.—WoP
Vacation ("I am Paul Bunyan") E. Merriam.—MeI
Vacation ("One scene as I bow to pour her coffee") W. Stafford.—BrA
Vacationer. W. Gibson.—MoS
Vacation ("I am Paul Bunyan") Eve Merriam.—MeI
Vacation ("One scene as I bow to pour her coffee") William Stafford.—BrA
"**Vacation** is over." See Leavetaking
Vacationer. Walker Gibson.—MoS
The **vagabond.** Robert Louis Stevenson.—PaH
Vagabonds. See Gipsies; Tramps; Wayfaring life
Vain and careless. Robert Graves.—CaD—HaL
Vain is the glory of the sky. William Wordsworth.—WoP
Vainateya
"All these hurt."—AlPi
Vala, sel. William Blake
Enitharmon's song.—GrCt
Valedictory sonnet. William Wordsworth.—WoP
A **valedictory** to Standard Oil of Indiana. David Wagoner.—DuS
Valentin, Delia
A storm at sea.—LeM
Valentine, Saint. See Saint Valentine's day
Valentine ("Chipmunks jump, and") Donald Hall.—CoBl—DuR
A **valentine** ("Frost flowers on the window glass") Eleanor Hammond.—ArT-3
Valentine for earth. Frances M. Frost. ArT-3—HoB
Valentine greetings. Kathryn Sexton.—LaPh
Valentines. See Saint Valentine's day
Valentine's day. Aileen Fisher.—LaPh
Valhope, Carol Hope and Morwitz, Ernst
Augury. trs.—GrS
Vallana
Substantiations.—AlPi
The **valley** of the black pig. William Butler Yeats.—GrCt
The **valley** of unrest. Edgar Allan Poe.—PoP
The **valley** of white poppies. William Sharp.—ThA
Valleys
Between the walls of the valley. E. Peck.—BrA
The combe. E. Thomas.—ThG
Come down, O maid. From The princess. A. Tennyson.—TeP
The valley of the black pig. W. B. Yeats.—GrCt
The valley of unrest. E. A. Poe.—PoP
The valley of white poppies. W. Sharp.—ThA
Valmiki
Ramayana, sel.
The true and tender wife.—AlPi
The true and tender wife. See Ramayana
Vanada, Lillian Schulz
"Fuzzy wuzzy, creepy crawly."—ArT-3
Vandegrift, Margaret, pseud. (Margaret Thompson Janvier)
"There once was a stately giraffe."—BrLl
Vanderbilt, Sanderson
December.—LaC
Van Doren, Mark
And then it rained.—CoBn
Burial.—CaMb
Chipmunk, chipmunk.—ReS
Crow.—ReO
Donkey.—PlE
"Down dip the branches."—ReS
"Eternity's low voice."—PlE
Former barn lot.—HaL—LaPd
Inconsistent.—CoBl
Jonathan Gentry, sel.
Tom's sleeping song.—HaL
Midwife cat.—ReO
No communication.—ReBs
Praise doubt.—PlE
Spring thunder.—BoH
The story-teller.—HaL
To a child with eyes.—HaL
Tom's sleeping song. See Jonathan Gentry
Traveling storm.—ThA
Van Dyke, Henry
America for me.—ThA
The angler's reveille.—HuS-3
A salute to trees.—HuS-3
Work.—ThA
Van Every, Glenys
Thunder.—LeM
Vanilla
A vote for vanilla. E. Merriam.—MeI
"**Vanilla,** vanilla, vanilla for me." See A vote for vanilla
Vanity. See Pride and vanity
"**Vanity,** saith the preacher, vanity." See The bishop orders his tomb at Saint Praxed's church
Vapor trails. Gary Snyder.—DuS
Varela, Guillermo E.
The path of the lonely ones.—BaH
Varge. Patricia Hubbell.—ArT-3
Variation on a sentence. Louise Bogan.—HoL
Variations 8, 9, and 13. See Theme and variations
Variations for two pianos. Donald Justice.—DuS
Varumulaiyaritti
What her friend said.—AlPi
Vasquez, Rosalia
The birds.—BaH
Vastness. Alfred Tennyson.—TeP
Vaticide. Myron O'Higgins.—AdIa—HaK
Vaughan, Henry
Peace.—GrCt—PaH—PlE
The shower.—ClF (sel.)—CoBn—GrCt
"They are all gone into the world of light."—GrCt (sel.)
A vision. See The world
The world, sel.
A vision.—HoL

Vaughan, Henry (about)
At the grave of Henry Vaughan. S. Sassoon.—PlE
Vaughn, James P.
Four questions addressed to his excellency, the prime minister.—BoA
So.—BoA
"**Vaunts** violoncello." See The egotistical orchestra
Vegetables. See also Gardens and gardening; also names of vegetables, as Potatoes
Artichoke. P. Neruda.—LiT
"This season our tunnips was red." D. McCord.—BrLl
V is for vegetables. E. Farjeon.—BrSg
Vegetables. R. Field.—BrSg
Vegetables. Rachel Field.—BrSg
Velez, Joseph Francis
"What is America."—BaH
Why.—BaH
A winter night.—BaH
Velvet shoes. Elinor Wylie.—ArT-3—BoGj—HuS-3—ThA
Venable, William Henry
The founders of Ohio.—HiL
Venders. See Peddlers and venders
"**Venerable** Mother Toothache." See A charm against the toothache
Venice, Italy
Beppo. G. G. Byron.—ByP
The city of falling leaves. A. Lowell.—ArT-3
On the extinction of the Venetian republic. W. Wordsworth.—PaH—WoP
Venus and Adonis, sels. William Shakespeare
The boar.—CoB
The horse of Adonis.—ClF
The horse.—ShS
Lo, here the gentle lark.—GrCt
Veracruz, Mexico
Veracruz. R. E. Hayden.—BoA
Veracruz. Robert E. Hayden.—BoA
Verdancy. Unknown.—BrSm
Vern. Gwendolyn Brooks.—ArT-3—LaC
Vernal sentiment. Theodore Roethke.—McWs
Verses composed on the eve of his execution. James Graham.—GrCt
"**Very** afraid." See The dalliance of the leopards
Very early. Karla Kuskin.—LaPd
"A **very** grandiloquent goat." Carolyn Wells.—BrLl
Very lovely. Rose Fyleman.—ArT-3
"**Very** old are the woods." See All that's past
"A **very** young lady." See Frighted by a cow
Vesey, Paul. See Allen, Samuel
Vesper. Alcman of Sparta, tr. fr. the Greek by F. L. Lucas.—ReO
Sleep upon the world. tr. by Thomas Campbell.—GrCt
Vespers ("Little boy kneels at the foot of the bed") A. A. Milne.—MiC
Vespers ("O blackbird, what a boy you are") T. E. Brown.—CoB
Vesuvian bay
Drifting. T. B. Read.—PaH
Veteran's day
Everyone sang. S. Sassoon.—HaL—SmM
"I have a rendezvous with death." A. Seeger.—HiL
In Flanders fields. J. McCrae.—ThA
Vice versa. Christian Morgenstern, tr. fr. the German by R. F. C. Hull.—ReO
Victor, Florence
Contest.—MoS
Victoria. Eleanor Farjeon.—BlO
"**Victoria,** Carlota, and Eugénie." See The empresses
Victory
Conversation on V. O. Dodson.—HaK
Song of triumph. E. A. Poe.—PoP
"Success is counted sweetest." E. Dickinson.—BoGj—DiPe
Viereck, Peter
Kilroy.—HiL
View of the capitol from the Library of Congress. Elizabeth Bishop.—BrA
Vikings. See Norsemen
The **Vikings.** Unknown.—GrCt
Villa, José Garcia
"God, is, like, scissors."—PlE
"My, fellowship, with, God."—PlE
"The way my ideas think me."—PlE
The **village** atheist. See The Spoon River anthology
Village before sunset. Frances Cornford.—CoBn
The **village** blacksmith. Henry Wadsworth Longfellow.—HuS-3—LoPl—TuW
A **village** girl. Mohan Singh, tr. fr. the Panjabi by Balwant Gargi.—AlPi
The **village** green. Ann and Jane Taylor.—GrT
Village life. See also Towns
At Dunwich. A. Thwaite.—CaMb
"In the mountain village." Minamoto no Morotada.—BaS
"Little-Plum-Tree village." Issa.—IsF
"A mountain village." Shiki.—BeCs
October. N. Belting.—BeCm
"There are men in the village of Erith." Unknown.—BrLl
The village of Erith.—GrCt
Village before sunset. F. Cornford.—CoBn
The village blacksmith. H. W. Longfellow.—HuS-3—LoPl—TuW
The village green. A. and J. Taylor.—GrT
Village portrait. T. W. Duncan.—ThA
The **village** of Erith. See "There are men in the village of Erith"
Village portrait. Thomas W. Duncan.—ThA
"The **villages** stand on the lake-edge." See October
Villains. Abhinanda, tr. fr. the Sanskrit by Daniel H. H. Ingalls.—AlPi
Villanelle. M. D. Feld.—MoS
Vinal, Harold
Sea born.—BoH
The **vinegar** man. Ruth Comfort Mitchell.—ThA
Vines. See also names of vines, as Ivy
The magic vine. Unknown.—BrSg

Violence
Away with bloodshed. A. E. Housman.—BrSm
"Away with bloodshed, I love not such." —LiT
The **violet.** Jane Taylor.—HoB
Violets
To violets. R. Herrick.—TuW
The violet. J. Taylor.—HoB
"When I went out." Akahito.—BaS—LeMw
"**Violets,** daffodils." Elizabeth Jane Coatsworth. —ArT-3
"**Violets** in April." See Blue flowers
Violinists. See Violins and violinists
Violins and violinists
"Cock a doodle doo (my dame)." Mother Goose.—BrMg
"Cock-a-doodle-do."—ReMg
The drowned lady. Unknown.—GrCt
The fiddler ("I wander up and down here, and go from street to street") A. and J. Taylor.—VrF
A fiddler ("Once was a fiddler. Play could he") W. De La Mare.—HaL
The fiddler of Dooney. W. B. Yeats.—ArT-3—YeR
The green fiddler. R. Field.—HoB
Jacky's fiddle. Mother Goose.—ReOn
"Old King Cole was a merry old soul." Mother Goose.—OpF
Mother Goose rhymes, 62.—HoB
"Old King Cole."—BrMg—WiMg
"Terence McDiddler." Mother Goose.—BrMg
The **viper.** Ruth Pitter.—CaD
Vipont, Elfrida
"For all the joys of harvest."—BrSg
Virgil (Publius Vergilius Maro)
Aeneid, sels.
The boat race.—MoS
The boxing match.—MoS
The boat race. See Aeneid
The boxing match. See Aeneid
The chariot race. See The Georgics
The Georgics, sel.
The chariot race.—MoS
Virgil (Publius Vergilius Maro) (about)
To Virgil. A. Tennyson.—GrCt—TeP
Virgin Mary. See Mary, Virgin
Virginia
The English in Virginia. C. Reznikoff.—GrS
To the Virginian voyage. M. Drayton.—HiL
Virginia. P. McGinley.—AgH
Virginia. Phyllis McGinley.—AgH
Virgins
The golden net. W. Blake.—GrS
The seven virgins. Unknown.—GrCt
Viryamitra
Epigram.—AlPi
"The **viscous** air, wheres'ere she fly." See Upon Appleton house—The kingfisher
"**Visible,** invisible." See A jellyfish
A **vision** ("I lost the love of heaven above") John Clare.—GrCt
A **vision** ("I saw eternity the other night") See The world
Vision of Belshazzar. George Gordon Byron.—ByP—CoR
"The **vision** of Christ that thou dost see." See The everlasting gospel
The **vision** of Sir Launfal, sel. James Russell Lowell
A day in June.—HuS-3
A **vision** of the mermaids. Gerard Manley Hopkins.—GrCt (sel.)
Visions. See also Dreams
An argument. V. Lindsay.—LiP
Kubla Khan. S. T. Coleridge.—BoGj—CoR—GrCt—McWs (sel.)—PaH
The legend beautiful. From Tales of a wayside inn. H. W. Longfellow.—LoPl
The occultation of Orion. H. W. Longfellow. —LoPl
Tony O. C. Francis.—BlO
A vision. From The world. H. Vaughan.—HoL
Vision of Belshazzar. G. G. Byron.—ByP—CoR
The **visions** of Petrarch, sel. Edmund Spenser
"I saw a phoenix in the wood alone."—GrCt
Visions of the world's vanity, sel. Edmund Spenser
The huge leviathan.—GrCt
Visit. Eve Recht.—LeM
A **visit** from abroad. James Stephens.—HaL
A **visit** from Mr Fox. See The fox's foray
A **visit** from St Nicholas. Clement C. Moore.—ArT-3—HoB—HuS-3
A **visit** to Chelsea college. Henry Sharpe Horsley.—VrF
A **visit** to Newgate. Henry Sharpe Horsley.—VrF
A **visit** to the blind asylum. Henry Sharpe Horsley.—VrF
A **visit** to the lunatic asylum. Henry Sharpe Horsley.—VrF
The **visitation.** Elizabeth Jennings.—CaMb
Visitations: VII, sel. Louis MacNeice
"And the Lord was not in the whirlwind."—PlE
"**Visiting** the graves." Issa, tr. fr. the Japanese by R. H. Blyth.—IsF—LeOw
The **visitor.** Katherine Pyle.—CoBb
Visitors. Aileen Fisher.—FiIo
Vista. Alfred Kreymborg.—CoBl—SmM
Visvanath
The family.—AlPi
Vitae summa brevis spem nos vetat incohare longam. Ernest Dowson.—GrCt
The **vixen.** John Clare.—CoB
Vocations. See also names of vocations, as Carpenters and carpentry
Sext. W. H. Auden.—LiT (sel.)
Vogler, Abbé Georg Joseph (about)
Abt Vogler. R. Browning.—BrP
The **voice.** Walter De La Mare.—DeBg
The **voice** from the well of life speaks to the maiden. See The old wives' tale—Celenta at the well of life
Voice in the crowd. Ted Joans.—BoA—HaK
The **voice** of God. James Stephens.—StS
"The **voice** of magic melody." See My singing aunt

The **voice** of St Francis of Assisi. Vachel Lindsay.—LiP
The **voice** of the ancient bard. William Blake.—BlP
"The **voice** of the glutton I heard with disdain." Ann and Jane Taylor.—VrF
"The **voice** of the last cricket." See Splinter
Voice of the sky. Aileen Fisher.—FiI
"**Voice** of the summerwind." See The grasshopper
"The **voice** that beautifies the land." Unknown, tr. fr. the Navajo.—LeO
Voices
My voice. J. R. Jiménez.—LiT
"A small boy who lived in Iquique." Unknown.—BrLl
Splinter. C. Sandburg.—ArT-3
The voice. W. De La Mare.—DeBg
Voice in the crowd. T. Joans.—BoA—HaK
The voice of God. J. Stephens.—StS
The voice of St Francis of Assisi. V. Lindsay. —LiP
The voice of the ancient bard. W. Blake.—BlP
"The voice of the glutton I heard with disdain." A. and J. Taylor.—VrF
Voice of the sky. A. Fisher.—FiI
"The voice that beautifies the land." Unknown.—LeO
Voices. J. S. Hearst.—ThA
"Voices." Kyoroku.—LeI
Whispers. A. Fisher.—FiIo
Voices. James S. Hearst.—ThA
"**Voices.**" Kyoroku, tr. fr. the Japanese by R. H. Blyth.—LeI
Voltaire (François Marie Arouet)
On bell-ringers.—BrSm
Voltaire (François Marie Arouet) (about)
"Mock on, mock on Voltaire, Rousseau." W. Blake.—BlP
A **vote** for vanilla. Eve Merriam.—MeI
Vox populi. Henry Wadsworth Longfellow.—LoPl
The **voyage** of Jimmy Poo. James A. Emanuel.—BoA
The **voyage** of Maeldune. Alfred Tennyson.—TeP
Voyages. See Adventure and adventurers; Seamen; Travel
Voznesensky, Andrei
Bicycles.—LiT
The **vulture.** Hilaire Belloc.—AgH
"The **vulture** eats between his meals." See The vulture
Vultures
The vulture. H. Belloc.—AgH

W

W. James Reeves.—GrCt
"**W** is for windows." See All around the town
Waddell, Helen
The Abbot Adam of Angers. tr.—LiT
Easter Sunday. tr.—LiT
"Gay comes the singer." tr.—SmM
Heriger, Bishop of Mainz. tr.—LiT
"How goes the night." tr.—LeMw
"Peach blossoms after rain." tr.—LeMw
Waddington, Miriam
Laughter.—DoW
Rhymes. tr.—DoW
"**Wae's** me, wae's me." See The ghost's song
Wagner, Geoffrey
Fantasy. tr.—GrS
The **wagon** in the barn. John Drinkwater.—ThA
"**Wagon** Wheel Gap is a place I never saw." See Localities
Wagoner, David
The man of the house.—DuS
Staying alive.—CoBn—DuS
Tumbleweed.—CoBn
A valedictory to Standard Oil of Indiana.—DuS
The words.—DuS
Wagons
Coaster wagon. A. Fisher.—FiIo
Wheels. C. Lewis.—LeP
"The **wagons** loom like blue caravans in the dusk." See Harvest home
Wain, John
Au jardin des plantes.—CoB
Confusions of the alphabet.—CaD
"**Wait,** Kate. You skate at such a rate." See To Kate, skating better than her date
"The **waiter** said: Try the ragout." Unknown.—BrLl
Waiters and waitresses
The contrary waiter. E. Parker.—CoO
Waiting ("Dreaming of honeycombs to share") Harry Behn.—ArT-3—BrSg
Waiting ("How many times") Aileen Fisher.—FiIo
Waiting ("The trees stand hushed, on tiptoe for the sight") Unknown, tr. fr. the Japanese by Curtis Hidden Page.—LeMw
Waiting ("Waiting, waiting, waiting") James Reeves.—StF
"**Waiting** for the children." Kazue Mizumura.—MiI
"**Waiting** in darkness." Unknown, tr. fr. the Japanese by Harry Behn.—BeCs
"**Waiting,** waiting, waiting." See Waiting
Wait's carol. Barbara Young.—ThA
Wake. Langston Hughes.—BrSm
"**Wake** up, little sparrows." See Sleepy sparrows
"**Wake** up, old sleepy." Bashō, tr. fr. the Japanese by Harry Behn.—BeCs
Wake-up poems. See also Morning
Chanticleer. J. Farrar.—ArT-3
The cock. Unknown.—VrF
"The cock doth crow." Mother Goose.—ArT-3
"Cocks crow in the morn." Mother Goose.—ArT-3—ReMg
"The ears of barley, too." Issa.—IsF
Get up or you'll be late for school, silly. J. Ciardi.—CiYk
Getting up. R. Burgunder.—ArT-3

"**Want** to run the gauntlet." See Running the gauntlet
War. See also Memorial day; Naval battles; Peace; Soldiers; Veteran's day; also names of wars and battles, as European war, 1914-1918; Bannockburn, Battle of, 1314; also subdivisions under countries, as United States—History—Civil war
After the salvo. H. Asquith.—LiT
"All, all of a piece throughout." From The secular masque. J. Dryden.—GrCt
Anthem for doomed youth. W. Owen.—BoH—GrCt
Apostrophe to man. E. St V. Millay.—DuS
At war. R. Atkins.—BoA
Belle isle. Mother Goose.—ReOn
The bloody conquests of mighty Tamburlaine. From Tamburlaine the Great. C. Marlowe. —GrCt
Border songs. Lu Lun.—LeMw
Celebrated return. C. Major.—BoA
Christmas eve under Hooker's statue. R. Lowell.—HiL
A curse for kings. V. Lindsay.—LiP
The dark hills. E. A. Robinson.—BoGj—BoH
Dead cow farm. R. Graves.—LiT
"Fast rode the knight." S. Crane.—LiT
A few things explained. P. Neruda.—LiT (sel.)
The hand that signed the paper. D. Thomas.—McWs
The heroes. L. Simpson.—DuS
In distrust of merits. Marianne Moore.—PlE
"It's jolly." E. E. Cummings.—HiL
James Honeyman. W. H. Auden.—CaMb—SmM
The minstrel boy. T. Moore.—ClF—CoR
The nefarious war. Li T'ai-po.—LiT
On a certain engagement south of Seoul. H. Carruth.—BrA
Overnight in the apartment by the river. Tu Fu.—GrCt
Peace and war. From King Henry V. W. Shakespeare.—ShS
Piano after war. G. Brooks.—BoA—HaK
The pilgrim. W. Blake.—ArT-3
The sword and the sickle.—GrCt
Plato told him. E. E. Cummings.—BrA—HiL
The press-gang. Unknown.—GrCt
Prologue intended for a dramatic piece of King Edward the Fourth. W. Blake.—BlP
Sailors on leave. O. Dodson.—BoA
A snapshot. H. Barua.—AlPi
Sonnet. A. A. Duckett.—BoA
"A stopwatch and an ordnance map." S. Spender.—CaMb
Sunset horn. M. O'Higgins.—BoA
This excellent machine. J. Lehmann.—DuS
To his friend, Wei. Li T'ai-po.—LiT (sel.)
To Lucasta, on going to the wars. R. Lovelace.—McWs
The too-late born. A. MacLeish.—BoGj
The trumpet. E. Thomas.—GrS—ThG
Two wise generals. T. Hughes.—CaMb
The unpardonable sin. V. Lindsay.—LiP
The valley of the black pig. W. B. Yeats.—GrCt
The voice of St Francis of Assisi. V. Lindsay. —LiP
War ("Dawn came slowly") D. Roth.—DuR
War ("Last year the war was in the northeast") Li T'ai-po.—DuW
War ("Not bad, but miserable") S. Mason.—LeM
War ("When my young brother was killed") J. Langland.—DuS
War is kind. S. Crane.—HiL
The white horse. Tu Fu.—GrCt
Without benefit of declaration. L. Hughes.—BoA
War ("Dawn came slowly") Dan Roth.—DuR
War ("Last year the war was in the northeast") Li T'ai-po, tr. fr. the Chinese by Rewi Alley.—DuW
War ("Not bad, but miserable") Sarah Mason.—LeM
War ("When my young brother was killed") Joseph Langland.—DuS
The **war** horse. See Job—"Hast thou given the horse strength"
War is kind. Stephen Crane.—HiL
War of 1812. See United States—History—War of 1812
War song. Unknown, tr. fr. the Ojibway.—LeO
The **war** song of Dinas Vawr. See The misfortunes of Elphin
War songs
Glory hallelujah; or, John Brown's body. Unknown.—HiL
The song of the western men. R. S. Hawker.—CoR
War song. Unknown.—LeO
The war song of Dinas Vawr. From The misfortunes of Elphin. T. L. Peacock.—McWs
"**War** war." See April 4, 1968
War with Mexico. See United States—History—War with Mexico
War with Spain. See United States—History—War with Spain
The **warbler.** Walter De La Mare.—DeBg
Warblers
"A baby warbler." Kikaku.—BeCs
Sedge-warblers. E. Thomas.—ReBs (sel.)
The warbler. W. De La Mare.—DeBg
The **warden** of the Cinque ports. Henry Wadsworth Longfellow.—LoPl
Ware, Eugene Fitch (Ironquill, pseud.)
The Aztec city.—PaH
"**Warm,** hands, warm." Mother Goose.—OpF
"**Warm** noon's joy spreads under the big leaved trees." See Calcutta
"The **warm** of heart shall never lack a fire." Elizabeth Jane Coatsworth.—ArT-3
A **warm** winter day. Julian Cooper.—CoBn
Warner, Rex
Mallard.—CoB
The **warning** ("Beware! The Israelite of old, who tore") Henry Wadsworth Longfellow.—LoPl

"**Water,** water, wall-flower, growing up so high." Unknown.—MoB
Waterfalls
Behind the waterfall. W. Welles.—ArT-3—HuS-3
Fragment. J. Clare.—CoBn
"An old man sat in a waterfall." N. Nicholson.—CaD
"The **waterfowl.**" Ginkō, tr. fr. the Japanese by R. H. Blyth.—LeMw
Waterloo, Battle of, 1815
Waterloo. From Childe Harold's pilgrimage. G. G. Byron.—ByP
Waterloo. See Childe Harold's pilgrimage
Waterman, Nixon
If we didn't have to eat.—AgH
Tame animals I have known.—CoO
"**Waters** above. Eternal springs." See The shower
Waterwings. Kathleen Fraser.—FrS
Watkins, Vernon
Ballad of the two tapsters.—CaMb
Cats. tr.—CoB
The collier.—CaD
The yew-tree.—PlE
Watson, Burton
"Cold Mountain is full of weird sights." tr.—LeMw
Watson, Wilfred
The juniper tree.—CoBl—DoW
Watson, Sir William
The ballad of Semmerwater.—BlO
Watts, Isaac
A cradle song.—HoB
Little busy bee.—HuS-3
"O God, our help in ages past."—PlE
Watts, Isaac (about)
For the bicentenary of Isaac Watts. N. Nicholson.—PlE
Watts, Mabel
Maytime magic.—BrSg
Watts, Marjorie Seymour
The policeman.—ArT-3
Waverley, sel. Walter Scott
"Hie away, hie away."—ArT-3
Hie away.—SmM
Waves. See also Ocean
"Each time a wave breaks." Nissha.—LeMw
Foam flowers. Yasuhide.—LeMw
"The horses of the sea." C. G. Rossetti.—BoGj
The little waves of Breffny. E. Gore-Booth.—PaH
A question. Unknown.—DePp
"Raging wind." K. Mizumura.—MiI
Spray. D. H. Lawrence.—CoBn
There are big waves. E. Farjeon.—StF
Waves. W. J. Smith.—CoSs
Waves against a dog. T. Baybars.—SmM
"Waves, coming up against the rocks." Unknown.—LeO
"Waves slap on the shore." C. Moore.—LeM
The way of Cape Race. E. J. Pratt.—DoW
Wind, waves, and sails. M. La Rue.—CoSs
Waves. William Jay Smith.—CoSs
Waves against a dog. Taner Baybars.—SmM
"**Waves,** coming up against the rocks." Unknown, tr. fr. the aboriginal of Australia.—LeO
"The **waves** of the ocean fight." See My rough sketch
Waves of thought. Panikkar, tr. fr. the Malayalam by the author.—AlPi
"**Waves** slap on the shore." Carol Moore.—LeM
"The **waves** that come down from the edge of the sky." See Waves
The **way.** Edwin Muir.—GrS—HaL
"The **way** a crow." See Dust of snow
"**Way** down south in Dixie." See Song for a dark girl
"**Way** down south where bananas grow." Unknown.—CoO
"The **way** I read a letter's—this." Emily Dickinson.—DiL
"The **way** my ideas think me." José Garcia Villa.—PlE
The **way** of Cape Race. E. J. Pratt.—DoW
A **way** of looking. Claudia Lewis.—LeP
The **way** through the woods. Rudyard Kipling.—HuS-3—McWs
Wayfaring life. See also Adventure and adventurers; Gipsies; Roads and trails
"At night may I roam." Unknown.—LeO
Ballads. H. Treece.—CaD
The gipsy trail. R. Kipling.—PaH
"I am a wanderer, I shall die stretched out." Unknown.—LeO
I know all this when gipsy fiddles cry. V. Lindsay.—LiP
I want to go wandering. V. Lindsay.—LiP—PaH
Old Jack Noman. E. Thomas.—BlO
Roadways. J. Masefield.—PaH
A ship for Singapore. D. W. Hicky.—ThA
Song of the open road. W. Whitman.—WhA
"Afoot and light-hearted, I take to the open road."—ArT-3
The song of wandering Aengus. W. B. Yeats.—ArT-3—BlO—BoGj—CoBl—GrS—HaL—HoL—McWs—SmM—ThA—YeR
To the wayfarer. Unknown.—ArT-3
Tumbling Mustard. M. Cowley.—BrA
The vagabond. R. L. Stevenson.—PaH
Voices. J. S. Hearst.—ThA
Wander-thirst. G. Gould.—ArT-3—ClF (sel.)—PaH
A wanderer's song. J. Masefield.—TuW
The **ways** of trains. Elizabeth Jane Coatsworth.—ArT-3—HoB
"**We** are a part of this rough land." See Our heritage
We are all workmen. Rainer Maria Rilke, tr. fr. the German by Babette Deutsch.—PlE
"**We** are all workmen: prentice, journeyman." See We are all workmen
"**We** are forever talking." Issa, tr. fr. the Japanese by Nobuyuki Yuasa.—IsF
"**We** are going to see the little crabs." See Song of the four little shell-animals
"**We** are in love's land to-day." See Love at sea
"**We** are light." See Laughter

"**We** walked along, while bright and red." See The two April mornings
"**We** walked in the sun on Joralemon street." See Joralemon street
"**We** watched the condors winging towards the moon." See Condors
We wear the mask. Paul Laurence Dunbar.—AdIa—BoA—BoH
"**We** wear the mask that grins and lies." See We wear the mask
"**We** went out on an Easter morning." See Easter morning
"**We** were a noisy crew; the sun in heaven." See The prelude—Fishing
"**We** were all passengers in that motorcade." See Channel U.S.A.—live
"**We** were camped on the plains at the head of the Cimarron." See The Zebra Dun
"**We** were hangin' Rustler Murphy for the stealin' of a horse." See The salvation of Texas Peters
"**We** were just three." See Three
"**We** were not many, we who stood." See Monterey
"**We** were schooner-rigged and rakish, with a long and lissome hull." See A ballad of John Silver
"**We** were taken from the ore bed and the mine." See The secret of the machines
"**We** were two daughters of one race." See The sisters
"**We** were very tired, we were very merry." See Recuerdo
"**We** who are old, old and gay." See A faery song
"**We,** who play under the pines." See The rabbits' song outside the tavern
"**We** who with songs beguile your pilgrimage." See The golden journey to Samarkand
"**We** will go to the wood, says Robin to Bobbin." See The wren hunt
"**We** wish to be joyful." Unknown.—DoC
"**We** wouldn't need straws for bottles." See Butterfly tongues
Wealth
Any bird. I. Orleans.—BrSg
Appalachian front. R. L. Weeks.—BrA
"Before I got my eye put out." E. Dickinson.—DiPe
"The day will bring some lovely thing." G. N. Crowell.—ArT-3
"The fairies have never a penny to spend." R. Fyleman.—HoB—HuS-3—ThA
"God gave a loaf to every bird." E. Dickinson.—DiPe
The golden hive. H. Behn.—ArT-3—BeG
His grange; or, Private wealth. R. Herrick.—BoGj
Hope. W. Shenstone.—CoBn (sel.)
"I had been hungry all the years." E. Dickinson.—DiPe
I hear America griping. M. Bishop.—BrA
"I rose up at the dawn of day." W. Blake.—BlP
If I should ever by chance. E. Thomas.—BoGj—ThG
"If I should every by chance grow rich."—BlO
"If I were to own." E. Thomas.—ThG
King Solomon. E. Merriam.—MeC
A man's a man for a' that. R. Burns.—BoH—BuPr
Minstrel's song. Unknown.—DoC
"My father died a month ago." Mother Goose.—MoB
Riches.—BrMg
"My grandfather died and he left me a cow." Unknown.—OpF
"None can experience stint." E. Dickinson.—DiPe
Of all the barbarous middle ages. From Don Juan. G. G. Byron.—ByP
"Of gold and jewels I have not any need." Yuan Chieh.—LeMw
On wealth. Unknown.—DoC—LeO
Real property. H. Monro.—CoBn
Rich man. E. Farjeon.—FaT
Riches. W. Blake.—BlP
"Since all the riches of this world." W. Blake.—BlP
Song. R. Hogg.—DoW
The soul of a spider. V. Lindsay.—LiP
"Timothy Dan." J. D. Sheridan.—StF
" 'Tis little I could care for pearls." E. Dickinson.—DiPe
A wee little worm. J. W. Riley.—LaPd
"A **wealthy** dromedar." See The boar and the dromedar
Weapons. See Arms and armor; also names of weapons, as Guns
"**Wearied** arm and broken sword." See Pocahontas
Wearing of the green. Aileen Fisher.—LaPh
The **weasel.** Unknown.—GrCt
Weasels
Don't ever seize a weasel by the tail. J. Prelutsky.—CoO
"O foolish ducklings." Buson.—BeCs
The weasel. Unknown.—GrCt
The wood-weasel. Marianne Moore.—ReO
Weather. See also Clouds; Dew; Fog; Mist; Rain; Rainbows; Seasons; Snow; Storms; Weather vanes; Wind
April fool. H. Summers.—CaD
"As the days lengthen." Mother Goose.—ReOn
But no. E. J. Coatsworth.—CoDh
Dogs and weather. W. Welles.—ArT-3—HuS-3
The forecast. D. Jaffe.—DuR
From a 19th century Kansas painter's notebook. D. Etter.—DuS
Glass falling. L. MacNeice.—CaD
Ipsey Wipsey. Mother Goose.—BrMg
"January brings the snow." Sara Coleridge.—ArT-3
The garden year.—HuS-3
Lighthearted William. W. C. Williams.—HaL
"The mackerel's cry." Mother Goose.—ReOn
March weather. S. Barker.—HoL

Weeks, Robert Lewis
Appalachian front.—BrA
"**Weep** no more, nor grieve, nor sigh." See The playmate
"**Weep** not, weep not." See Go down death
"**Weep,** weep, ye woodmen, wail." See Song
"**Weep** you no more, sad fountains." See Sleep is a reconciling
Weeping cherry trees. Unknown, ad. fr. the Japanese by Charlotte B. DeForest.—DePp
"A **weeping** child." Issa, tr. fr. the Japanese by Nobuyuki Yuasa.—LeMw
"**Weight** distributed." See One down
Weil, James L.
A Coney Island life.—BrA—CoSs—DuR
Weiss, Neil
The ageing athlete.—MoS
The hike.—MoS
Weiss, Theodore
A magic carpet.—WeP
A world to do.—GrS
Welchmen
"Taffy was a Welshman."—BrMg
Jolly Welchman.—VrF
Taffy.—CoBb
"Taffy is a Welshman."—OpF
"There were three jovial Welshmen." Mother Goose.—BlO
"There were three jovial huntsmen."—HuS-3
Three jovial huntsmen.—SmM
The three jovial Welshmen.—BrMg
"**Welcome,** maids of honor." See To violets
"**Welcome,** precious stone of the night." See Welcome to the moon
"**Welcome** robin with thy greeting." See Robin Redbreast
Welcome to the moon. Unknown.—CoBn—GrCt
Welcome to the new year. Eleanor Farjeon.—ThA
"**Welcome** to you rich autumn days." See Rich days
We'll go no more a-roving. See "So we'll go no more a roving"
We'll go to sea no more. Unknown.—CoSs—GrCt
The fishermen's song.—MoB (sel.)
"**Well,** hello down there." Issa, tr. fr. the Japanese by Harry Behn.—BeCs
"A **well-known** knavish knight with knobby knees." See Unfinished knews item
"**Well,** now, let's be off." Issa, tr. fr. the Japanese by R. H. Blyth.—IsF
"**Well** old spy." See Award
"**Well,** son, I'll tell you." See Mother to son
"**We'll** to the woods no more." Alfred Edward Housman.—HaL
Welles, Winifred
The angel in the apple tree.—HuS-3
Behind the waterfall.—ArT-3—HuS-3
Cruciform.—HoL
Curious something.—ArT-3
Dogs and weather.—ArT-3—HuS-3
Fairy thief.—BrSg
Fireflies.—ReS
Green moth.—ArT-3—HoB—ReS
Nosegay for a young goat.—CoB
River skater.—MoS
Skipping along alone.—ArT-3
Stocking fairy.—ArT-3—HoB
Three lovely holes.—HuS-3
A tree at dusk.—ThA
Winter morning.—HoL
Wellington, Arthur Wellesley, First Duke of (about)
"Bury the great duke." From Ode on the death of the Duke of Wellington. A. Tennyson.—TeP
The warden of the Cinque ports. H. W. Longfellow.—LoPl
Wells, Carolyn
Advice to children.—CoO
"A canner, exceedingly canny."—BrLl
The careless niece.—BrSm
"F was a fussy flamingo."—BrLl
How to tell the wild animals.—ArT-3
"L was a lachrymose leopard."—BrLl
Our polite parents.—CoBb
"Said a bad little youngster named Beauchamp."—BrLl
The swift bullets.—BrSm
"There once was a corpulent carp."—BrLl
"There once was a man who said, Why."—BrLl
"There once was an arch armadillo."—BrLl
"There was a young person named Tate."—BrLl
The tutor.—McWs
"A very grandiloquent goat."—BrLl
Wells, Ida B. (about)
Ida B. Wells. E. Merriam.—MeIv
Wells
"As I went by my little pig-sty." Unknown.—OpF
"As round as an apple, as deep as a cup." Mother Goose.—ArT-3
"As round as an apple."—BrMg
At the bottom of the well. L. Untermeyer.—BoGj
Aunt Eliza. H. Graham.—GrCt—McWs
"The coolness." Issa.—LeOw
"A doctor fell in a deep well." Unknown.—BrSm
The grasshopper. D. McCord.—McE
Little Willie. Unknown.—BrSm
Piano practice. I. Serraillier.—CoBb
"Riddle-me riddle-me riddle-me-ree (perhaps you)." Mother Goose
Mother Goose rhymes, 28.—HoB
"She that goes to the well." Unknown.—MoB
Sister Nell. Unknown.—CoBb
Struthill well. Unknown.—MoB
Weltschmerz. Frank Yerby.—BoA
Wen Yi-tuo
The confession.—GrCt
Wen Yi-tuo (about)
The confession. Wen Yi-tuo.—GrCt
"**Went** into a shoestore to buy a pair of shoes." See Sale

"**We're** all in the dumps." Mother Goose.—BlO
In the dumps.—BrMg
We're free. Carolyn Williams.—BaH
"**We're** having a lovely time today." See Fun in a garret
"**Were** my father here." Issa, tr. fr. the Japanese.—LeOw
"**Were** you ever in Quebec." See Donkey riding
Were you on the mountain. Unknown, tr. fr. the Irish by Douglas Hyde.—CoBl
"**Werther** had a love for Charlotte." See Sorrows of Werther
West, Paul
"Of a sudden the great prima-donna."—BrLl
The West
Étude géographique. S. King.—BrA
The merry miner. Unknown.—HuS-3
Wild West. R. Boylan.—DuS
The winning of the TV West. J. T. Alexander.—BoH—BrA
West Virginia
Between the walls of the valley. E. Peck.—BrA
"The **west** was getting out of gold." See Looking for a sunset bird in winter
The **west** wind. Aileen Fisher.—FiC
"**West** wind to the bairn." Unknown.—MoB
"The **west** wind was a thief one day." See The west wind
Western magic. Mary Austin.—BrA
Western star, sel. Stephen Vincent Benét
"Americans are always moving on."—BrA
Westminster abbey
Birthday party. E. J. Coatsworth.—CoDh
Westminster bridge
Composed upon Westminster bridge, September 3, 1802. W. Wordsworth.—ArT-3—GrCt—PaH—WoP
Weston, Mildred
Central park tourney.—BrA—DuR—LaC
Cider song.—CoBn
Echo.—CoBn
Westward movement. See United States—History—Westward movement
Westwood, Thomas
The child and the sparrow.—ReBs
"A **wet** gray day—rain falling slowly, mist over the." See Morels
The **wet** litany. Rudyard Kipling.—GrS
"A **wet** sheet and a flowing sea." Allan Cunningham.—ArT-3—BlO—ClF—CoR
"**We've** been to the wars together." See To Lou Gehrig
"**We've** watched all about the upland fallows." See Lullaby
Wever, Robert
In youth is pleasure.—GrCt
"**Wha** is that at my bower-door." Robert Burns.—BuPr
"**Wha** kens on whatna Bethlehems." See The innumerable Christ
The **whale** ("At every stroke his brazen fins do take") See The progress of the soul
The **whale** ("Now I will fashion the tale of a fish") See Physiologus
The **whale** ("'Twas in the year of forty-nine") Unknown.—CoSs—GrCt
The **whale** ("What could hold me") Carmen Bernos de Gasztold, tr. fr. the French by Rumer Godden.—GaC
"**Whale** are blue, white." See Whales
Whale at twilight. Elizabeth Jane Coatsworth.—CoDh
Whale hunting. Sally Nashookpuk.—BaH
Whaler, James
Boy in a pond. See The runaway
The runaway, sel.
Boy in a pond.—ReO
Whalers. See Whales and whaling
Whales. Thea Faye Sakeagak.—BaH
Whales and whaling
Catching a whale. M. Elliott.—VrF
"Doth not a Tenarif, or higher hill." From Anatomy of the world: The first anniversary. J. Donne.—GrCt
Jack was every inch a sailor. Unknown.—DoW
July. N. Belting.—BeCm
"Luther Leavitt is a whale hunter." A. Brower.—BaH
"The ribs and terrors in the whale." H. Melville.—PlE
Square-toed princes. R. P. T. Coffin.—BrA
The whale ("At every stroke his brazen fins do take") From The progress of the soul. J. Donne.—GrCt
The whale ("Now I will fashion the tale of a fish") From Physiologus. Unknown.—ReO
The whale ("'Twas in the year of forty-nine") Unknown.—CoSs—GrCt
The whale ("What could hold me") C. B. de Gasztold.—GaC
Whale at twilight. E. J. Coatsworth.—CoDh
Whale hunting. S. Nashookpuk.—BaH
Whales. T. F. Sakeagak.—BaH
"**Whan** that Aprille with his shoures sote." See The Canterbury tales—The prologue
Wharf. Myra Cohn Livingston.—LiC
Wharves
Wharf. M. C. Livingston.—LiC
"**What** a fearful battle." See The chickens
"**What** a night. The wind howls, hisses, and but stops." See Snowstorm
"**What** a pretty kite." Issa, tr. fr. the Japanese by Harry Behn.—BeCs
"**What** a wonderful." Shiki, tr. fr. the Japanese by Harry Behn.—BeCs
"**What** a wonderful bird the frog are." See The frog
"**What** about caterpillars." See About caterpillars
What am I. Dorothy Aldis.—HuS-3—LaPh
"**What** are days for." See Days
"**What** are heavy? Sea-sand and sorrow." See Sea-sand and sorrow
"**What** are little boys made of." Mother Goose.—OpF—ReMg—WiMg
Boys and girls.—BrMg
Mother Goose rhymes, 10.—HoB

"**What** are little girls made of." See "What are little boys made of"
"**What** are the bells about? What do they say." See Birthday book
What are the most unusual things you find in garbage cans. James Schevill.—DuS
What are years. Marianne Moore.—PlE
"**What** are you carrying Pilgrims, Pilgrims." See The island—Atlantic Charter, A.D. 1620-1942
"**What** are you doing." See Somersaults & headstands
"**What** are you doing there, Robin a Bobbin." See Talents differ
What became of them. See "He was a rat, and she was a rat"
What bird so sings. John Lyly.—BlO
"**What** bird so sings, yet so does wail." See What bird so sings
"**What** bright bracelets you have. Do listen." See A girl speaks to her playmate
"**What** bring you, sailor, home from the sea." See Luck
"**What** can I give Him." See A Christmas carol—My gift
What can the matter be. See "Oh dear, what can the matter be"
"**What** could hold me." See The whale
"**What**, cry to be wash'd, and not love to be clean." See For a little girl that did not like to be washed
"**What** did Hiamovi, the red man, chief of the Cheyennes have." See The people, yes—All one people
"**What** did she see—oh, what did she see." See The cats have come to tea
What did you say. Eve Merriam.—MeI
"**What** do caterpillars do." See Caterpillars
What do we plant. Henry Abbey.—ArT-3
"**What** do we plant when we plant the tree." See What do we plant
"**What** do you see where you ride, kite." See The kite
"**What** do you sell, O ye merchants." See In the bazaars of Hyderabad
"**What** do you think." See What someone told me about Bobby Link
"**What** do you think a kite would do." See Someone asked me
"**What** do you think endures." See The greatest city
"**What** does it mean? Tired, angry, and ill at ease." See Beauty
"**What** does the bee do." Christina Georgina Rossetti.—ArT-3
"**What** does your tongue like the most." See A matter of taste
"**What** fairings will ye that I bring." See The singing leaves
"**What** happens to a dream deferred." See Lenox avenue mural—Dream deferred
"**What** happiness." Buson, tr. fr. the Japanese by R. H. Blyth.—LeMw
"**What** happiness you gave to me." See The yew-tree
"**What** has feet like plum blossoms." Unknown.—WyC
"**What** have you got to eat, poor man." See Poor man
"**What** have you looked at, moon." See To the moon
"**What** heart could have thought you." See To a snowflake
What her friend said. Varumulaiyaritti, tr. fr. the Tamil by A. K. Ramanujan.—AlPi
What hope is here. See In memoriam
"**What** hope is here for modern rhyme." See In memoriam—What hope is here
"**What** I know." See Night piece
What if. Myra Cohn Livingston.—LiC
"**What** if this world was full of happiness." Arlene Blackwell.—BaH
"**What** inn is this." Emily Dickinson.—DiPe
"**What** is a hoop." See Hoops
"**What** is a llano." See Aa couple of doublles
"**What** is Africa to me." See Heritage
"**What** is all this washing about." See Washing
"**What** is America." Joseph Francis Velez.—BaH
What is black. Mary O'Neill.—OnH
What is blue. Mary O'Neill.—OnH
What is brown. Mary O'Neill.—OnH
What is gold. Mary O'Neill.—OnH
What is gray. Mary O'Neill.—OnH
What is green. Mary O'Neill.—HoB—OnH
"**What** is it cries without a mouth." See Riddle
"**What** is it you're mumbling, old Father, my Dad." See By the Exeter river
What is love. A. P. Herbert.—CoBl (sel.)
"**What** is love, the poets question." See What is love
What is orange. Mary O'Neill.—OnH
What is pink. See "What is pink? a rose is pink"
What is pink ("Pink is the color of a rose") Mary O'Neill.—OnH
"**What** is pink? a rose is pink." Christina Georgina Rossetti.—ArT-3
What is pink.—BoGj—BrSg—HuS-3
What is purple. Mary O'Neill.—OnH
What is red. Mary O'Neill.—OnH
"**What** is the boy now, who lost his ball." See The ball poem
"**What** is the difference." See Color
"**What** is the matter with Mary Jane." See Rice pudding
"**What** is our innocence." See What are years
"**What** is this." Unknown, tr. fr. the Chippewa.—LeO
"**What** is this knowledge but the sky-stolen fire." See Nosce teipsum—Much knowledge, little reason
"**What** is this life if, full of care." See Leisure
"**What** is Tommy running for." See Tommy and Jimmy
What is white. Mary O'Neill.—OnH
What is yellow. Mary O'Neill.—OnH
"**What** is your favorite mystery." See Flying a ribbon

"**What** joy attends the fisher's life." See The fisher's life
"**What** kind of walk shall we take today." See On our way
"**What** lewd, naked and revolting shape is this." See Shopping for meat in winter
"**What** little throat." See The blackbird by Belfast lough
"**What** lovely names for girls there are." See Girls' names
"**What** makes the ducks in the pond, I wonder, go." See In the park
"**What** makes you look so black, so glum, so cross." See Eclogue
"**What** need you, being come to sense." See September 1913
What night would it be. John Ciardi.—LaPd—LaPh
"**What** of earls with whom you have supped." See The toad-eater
"**What** passing-bells for these who die as cattle." See Anthem for doomed youth
"**What** phantom is this that appears." See Helen of Tyre
"**What** ran under the rosebush." See Could it have been a shadow
What robin told. George Cooper.—ArT-3
What shall I give. Edward Thomas.—ThG
"**What** shall I give my daughter the younger." See What shall I give
"**What** shall we do for the striking seamen." Unknown.—HiL
"**What** shall we say it is to be forgiven." See Forgiveness
What she did in the morning, I wouldn't know, she was seated there in the midst of her resilient symptoms, always. Merrill Moore.—DuS
What she said. Milaipperun Kantan, tr. fr. the Tamil by A. K. Ramanujan.—AlPi
"**What** sight is this? . . . O'er dazzling snow." See The ghost-chase
What someone said when he was spanked on the day before his birthday. John Ciardi.—CiYk
What someone told me about Bobby Link. John Ciardi.—AgH—CiYk
"**What** sort of tether." See Lucretia Mott
"**What** splendid names for boys there are." See Boys' names
"**What** sweeter musick can we bring." See A Christmas caroll, sung to the king in the presence at White-hall
"**What** swords and spears, what daggers bright." See Frost
What the cock and hen say. See Cock and hen
What the girl said. Kapilar, tr. fr. the Tamil by A. K. Ramanujan.—AlPi
What the gray cat sings. Arthur Guiterman.—LiT—ReS
What the hyena said. Vachel Lindsay.—LiP
What the Lord High Chamberlain said. Virginia Woodward Cloud.—CoBb
What the lover said. Allur Nanmullaiyar, tr. fr. the Tamil by A. K. Ramanujan.—AlPi
What the tramp said. James Stephens.—StS
What then. William Butler Yeats.—YeR
"**What** thing am I." See Riddles
"**What** though the field be lost." See Paradise lost
"**What** time the rose of dawn is laid across the lips of night." See The angler's reveille
What to do. William Wise.—ArT-3
"**What** to do on a rainy day." See What to do
What Tomas said in a pub. James Stephens.—StS
"**What** way does the wind come? What way does he go." See Address to a child during a boisterous winter evening
"**What** were her thoughts, the woman, Bathsheba." See In the late afternoon
"**What,** what, what." See A threnody
"**What** will become." Barry Brown.—BaH
"**What** will go into the Christmas stocking." See Christmas stocking
"**What** will you do, God, when I die." Rainer Maria Rilke, tr. fr. the German by Babette Deutsch.—PlE
"**What** will you do when you grow up." See Elizabeth Blackwell
"**What** wond'rous life is this I lead." See The garden
"**What,** you are stepping westward." See Stepping westward
Whately, Richard
A serio-comic elegy.—BrSm
"**Whatever** he does, you have to do too." See Follow the leader
"**Whatever** place is poor and small." See The hut
"**What's** confidence." See Confidence
What's in the cupboard. Unknown.—GrCt
"**What's** in the cupboard, says Mr Hubbard." See What's in the cupboard
"**What's** in there." Mother Goose.—BrMg—MoB—ReOn
"**What's** New York." See Fiorello H. La Guardia
What's night to me. Sam Gilford.—LeM
"**What's** that." See The bat
"**What's** the good of breathing." See The frost pane
What's the news. See "What's the news of the day"
"**What's** the news of the day." Mother Goose.—OpF
What's the news.—BrMg
What's the railroad. Henry David Thoreau.—HiL
"**What's** the railroad to me." See What's the railroad
"**What's** your age." See Mother's party
"**What's** your name." See Pudden Tame
"**Whatsoever** things are true." See Philippians, Bible, New Testament
Wheat
High wheat country. E. L. Jacobs.—BrA
Wheatley, Phillis
His Excellency, General Washington.—HaK

On being brought from Africa to America.—HaK
To the Right Honorable William, Earl of Dartmouth.—HaK (sel.)
Wheel barrows
"Goes round the mud." Mother Goose.—BrMg
Old woman of Harrow. Unknown.—VrF
Wheelbarrow. E. Farjeon.—FaT
Wheelbarrow. Eleanor Farjeon.—FaT
Wheeler, Charles Enoch
Adjuration.—BoA
Wheelock, John Hall
Afternoon: Amagansett beach.—CoBn
Bonac.—PaH
Earth.—DuR
I sought you.—CoBl
I, too, I, too.—SmM
"Lift your arms to the stars."—CoBl
Prayer.—PlE
Return to New York.—PaH
Wheels. See also Bicycles and bicycling
Wheels. C. Lewis.—LeP
Wings and wheels. N. B. Turner.—ArT-3—HuS-3
Wheels. Claudia Lewis.—LeP
"**Wheels** over the mountains." See Wheels
"**Wheepy** whaupy." See Curlew
When. See The window
"**When** a cub, unaware being bare." Eve Merriam.—BrLl
"**When** a goose meets a moose." Zhenya Gay.—ArT-3
"**When** a jolly young fisher named Fisher." Unknown.—BrLl
"**When** a man hath no freedom to fight for at home." See Stanzas
"**When** a man's body is young." Unknown.—LeO
When a ring's around the moon. Mary Jane Carr.—ArT-3
"**When** a twister a-twisting will twist him a twist." See Twister twisting twine
"**When** all the ground with snow is white." See The snow-bird
"**When** all the other leaves are gone." See Oak leaves
"**When** all within is dark." See From Thee to Thee
"**When** at home I sit." See The little land
"**When** awful darkness and silence reign." See The dong with a luminous nose
"**When** bears are seen." See A moral alphabet—B stands for bear
"**When** boughs of spruces bend with snow." See Beneath the snowy trees
"**When** brother takes me walking." See The ordinary dog
"**When** Bunyan swung his whopping axe." See Folk tune
"**When** cats run home and light is come." See The owl
"**When** chapman billies leave the street." See Tam o' Shanter
"**When** Charles has done reading." See The rocking horse
"**When** children are good I have currants and cherries." See The gardener
"**When** children are naughty, and will not be dressed." See Dressed or undressed
"**When** Christ was born on Christmas day." See The stork
"**When** clouds appear like rocks and towers." Mother Goose.—ReOn
"**When** clouds appear, wise men put on their cloaks." See King Richard III—Wise song
"**When** cold December." Edith Sitwell.—McWs
"**When** coltsfoot withers and begins to wear." See Cuckoos
"**When** company came." See Peeking in
"**When** company is talking." See Talking
"**When** Daniel Boone goes by, at night." See Daniel Boone
When dawn comes to the city. Claude McKay.—BoH—LaC
When de saints go ma'chin' home. Sterling A. Brown.—BoA
"**When** descends on the Atlantic." See Seaweed
"**When** Enoch should have been at work." See The ne'er-do-well
"**When** Europe and romanticism." See Blackout
"**When** faces called flowers float out of the ground." E. E. Cummings.—CoBn
"**When** father is napping." See Peeking
"**When** father says." See So still
"**When** first my Jamie he came to the town." Unknown.—MoB
"**When** Frances goes to school, to write." See Look at your copy
"**When** from the brittle ice the fields." See Missel thrush
"**When** frost is shining on the trees." See At Mrs Appleby's
"**When** gentle April with his showers sweet." See The Canterbury tales—The prologue
"**When** George began to climb all unawares." See Encounters with a Doppelganger—A meeting
"**When** God at first made man." See The pulley
"**When** God had finished the stars and whirl of colored suns." See Ducks
"**When** good King Arthur ruled this land." Mother Goose.—OpF
Good King Arthur.—BrF
King Arthur.—BrMg
When grandmama was young. Elizabeth Jane Coatsworth.—CoSb
"**When** guests were present, dear little Mabel." See Our polite parents
"**When** Hitler was the devil." See The silent generation
"**When** human folk put out the light." See Kitten's night thoughts
"**When** I." See The rebel
"**When** I am a man and can do as I wish." See The conjuror
"**When** I am a man, then I shall be a hunter, O father." Unknown.—LeO
"**When** I am alone, and quite alone." See Hide and seek

"**When** I was a wee thing." Unknown.—MoB
"**When** I was as high as that." See A memory
"**When** I was born on Amman hill." See The collier
"**When** I was bound apprentice, in famous Lincolnshire." See The Lincolnshire poacher
"**When** I was but thirteen or so." See Romance
"**When** I was down beside the sea." See At the sea-side
"**When** I was just a little boy." See The ships of Yule
"**When** I was making myself a game." See Little rain
"**When** I was nine years old, in 1889." See John L. Sullivan, the strong boy of Boston
"**When** I was on Night Line." See Ego
"**When** I was once in Baltimore." See Sheep
"**When** I was one-and-twenty." See A Shropshire lad
"**When** I was one, I was in my skin." Unknown.—MoB
"**When** I was out one morning." See The shepherd
"**When** I was playing." See Playing
"**When** I was seven." See Growing up
"**When** I was sick and lay a-bed." See The land of counterpane
"**When** I was small, a woman died." Emily Dickinson.—DiPe
"**When** I was small and trees were high." See Tree-sleeping
"**When** I was very little." See The fish
"**When** I was young." See In the red
"**When** I was young." See The pit of bliss
"**When** I was young." Unknown, tr. fr. the Eskimo.—LeO
"**When** I was young and full o' pride." See Blow me eyes
"**When** I was young and in my prime." Unknown.—OpF
"**When** I was young and we were poor and I used to." See Modifications
"**When** I was young I used to go." Mother Goose.—OpF
"**When** I went out." See A spike of green
"**When** I went out." Akahito, tr. fr. the Japanese by Kennth Rexroth.—BaS—LeMw
"**When** I woke up this morning." See Spring
"**When** icicles hang by (or on) the wall." See Love's labour's lost
"**When** I'm going." See Going down the street
"**When** I'm in bed at night." See Night watchmen
"**When** I'm tucked into bed." See Storm at night
"**When** in disgrace with fortune and men's eyes." See Sonnets. William Shakespeare
When in Rome. Mari Evans.—BoA
When in the darkness. Alfred Tennyson.—TeP
"**When** in the darkness over me." See When in the darkness
"**When** Israel was in Egypt's land." See Go down, Moses
"**When** it is finally ours, this freedom, this liberty, this beautiful." See Frederick Douglass
"**When** it is the winter time." See Ice
"**When** it rained in Devon." See London rain
"**When** it rains." Aileen Fisher.—FiI
"**When** it rains on the sea." See All the fishes far below
"**When** it's just past April." See The flower-cart man
"**When** it's raining." See The chair house
"**When** Jacky drown'd our poor cat Tib." See Falsehood corrected.
"**When** Jacky's a good boy." Mother Goose.—OpF
Cakes and custard.—BrMg
Reward.—AgH
"**When** John Henry was a little boy." See John Henry
"**When** John Henry was about three days old." See John Henry
When Johnny comes marching home. Patrick Sarsfield Gilmore.—HiL
"**When** Johnny comes marching home again." See When Johnny comes marching home
"**When** Juan woke he found some good things ready." See Don Juan—Haidée
"**When** land is gone and money spent." Mother Goose.—ReMg
"**When** late I attempted your pity to move." See An expostulation
"**When** little heads weary have gone to their bed." See The plumpuppets
"**When** little Jane lifts up her head." See Hide-and-seek
"**When** lyart leaves bestrow the yird." See The jolly beggars
When Mahalia sings. Quandra Prettyman.—AdIa
"**When** making for the brook, the falconer doth espy." See Polyolbion—Hawking
"**When** Mazárvan the magician." See Vox populi
"**When** melancholy autumn comes to Wembley." See Harrow-on-the-hill
"**When** men were all asleep the snow came flying." See London snow
"**When** midnight comes a host of boys and men." See Badger
"**When** milkweed blows in the pasture." See Horse-chestnut time
"**When** Mrs Gilfillan." See Mrs Gilfillan
When monkeys eat bananas. David McCord.—McAd
"**When** monkeys eat bananas, these." See When monkeys eat bananas
"**When** Moses, musing in the desert, found." See The burning bush
"**When** mother says, No." See Consolation
"**When** mother takes me calling." See The extraordinary dog
"**When** my arms wrap you round I press." See He remembers forgotton beauty
"**When** my birthday was coming." See Little brother's secret
"**When** my brother Tommy." See Two in bed

"**When** the rain came which we had seen letting down its black hair at the windowed horizon." See At the windowed horizon
When the saints go marchin' in. Unknown.—PlE
When the sline comes to dine. Shelley Silverstein.—CoB
"**When** the stuffed prophets quarrel, when the sawdust comes out, I think of Roosevelt's genuine sins." See Roosevelt
"**When** the summer fields are mown." See Aftermath
"**When** the sun gets low, in winter." See Human things
"**When** the sun has slipped away." See The skunk
"**When** the tea is brought at five o'clock." See Milk for the cat
"**When** the turf is thy tower." See The grave
"**When** the voices of children are heard on the green and laughing." See Nurse's song
"**When** the voices of children are heard on the green and whisp'rings." See Nurse's song
"**When** the waters' countenance." See The wet litany
"**When** the white pinks begin to appear." Mother Goose.—OpF
"**When** the wind and the rain." Elizabeth Jane Coatsworth.—CoSb
"**When** the wind is in the east." See The wind
"**When** the words rustle no more." See Stillness
"**When** the world turns completely upside down." See Wild peaches
"**When** they heard the captain humming and beheld the dancing crew." See The post captain
"**When** they pull my clock tower down." See The clock tower
"**When** they said the time to hide was mine." See The rabbit
"**When** thou must home to shades of underground." See To shades of underground
"**When** three, he fished these lakes." See Fishermen
"**When** through the winding cobbled streets of time." See The noonday April sun
"**When** to the wood he came." See The history of Sam, the sportsman, and his gun, also, of his wife Joan
"**When** trees did show no leaves." See The ending of the year
"**When** trout swim down Great Ormond street." See Priapus and the pool
"**When** tunes jigged nimbler than the blood." See Song from a country fair
"**When** twilight comes to Prairie street." See The winning of the TV West
"**When** walking in a tiny rain." See Vern
"**When** we are in love, we love the grass." See Love poem
"**When** we behold." See Dahlias
"**When** we lived in a city." See Until we built a cabin
"**When** we locked up the house at night." See Locked out
"**When** we please to walk abroad." Izaak Walton.—MoS
"**When** we went out with grandmamma." Kate Greenaway.—GrT
"**When** we were little childer we had a quare wee house." See Grace for light
"**When** will the stream be aweary of flowing." See Nothing will die
"**When** wilt thou save the people." Ebenezer Elliott.—PlE
"**When** winds die down at dawn." See September
"**When** winter scourged the meadow and the hill." See Ice
"**When** wintry weather's all a-done." See The spring
"**When** Yankee soldiers reach the barricade." See Three poems about Mark Twain—Mark Twain and Joan of Arc
"**When** you and I." See When you and I grow up
When you and I grow up. Kate Greenaway.—GrT
When you are old. William Butler Yeats.—BoGj—CoBl—YeR
"**When** you are old and gray and full of sleep." See When you are old
"**When** you came, you were like red wine and honey." See A decade
"**When** You elect to call me, God, O call." See Prayer to go to Paradise with the donkeys
"**When** you have gone." Unknown, tr. fr. the Borneo.—LeO
When you walk. James Stephens.—LaPd—StS
"**When** you walk in a field." See When you walk
"**When** you watch for." See Feather or fur
When you're away. Samuel Hoffenstein.—CoBl
"**When** you're away, I'm restless, lonely." See When you're away
"**Whenas** in silks my Julia goes." See Upon Julia's clothes
"**Whence** comes the crooked wind." See La tour du sorcier
"**Whenever** I go down to the shore." See Some day
"**Whenever** I ride on the Texas plains." See Texas trains and trails
"**Whenever** I walk in a London street." See Lines and squares
"**Whenever** I walk to Suffern along the Erie track." See The house with nobody in it
"**Whenever** she looks down the aisle." Unknown.—BrLl
"**Whenever** the days are cool and clear." See The sandhill crane
"**Whenever** the moon and stars are set." See Windy nights
Where ("Houses, houses,—Oh, I know") Walter De La Mare.—DeBg
Where ("Monkeys in a forest") Walter De La Mare.—DeBg
"**Where** am I going." Leon Hargrove.—BaH
"**Where** are the daughters of Montezuma." Elizabeth Jane Coatsworth.—CoDh

"**Where** are the heroes of yesteryear." See Where, O where
"**Where** are the hound." See Finder, please return to Henry Thoreau
"**Where** are the old side-wheelers now." See The river boats
"**Where** are the songs of spring? Ay where are they." See To autumn
"**Where** are they hiding." See Chucklehead
"**Where** are they now, the softly blooming flowers." See Irises
"**Where** are we to go when this is done." See Sonnet
"**Where** are you going." See Holiday
"**Where** are you going." Issa, tr. fr. the Japanese.—LeOw
"**Where** are you going, my little kittens." See The little kittens
"**Where** are you going (to) my pretty maid." Mother Goose.—OpF—WiMg
The milk maid.—BrMg
"**Where** are you off to, two by two." See The lights
"**Where** can he be going." Issa, tr. fr. the Japanese by R. H. Blyth.—LeMw
"**Where** cart rins rowin to the sea." See The gallant weaver
"**Where** Covent-Garden's famous temple stands." See Trivia—The dangers of foot-ball
"**Where** did I come from mother, and why." See Christmas lullaby for a new-born child
"**Where** did Momotara go." See Momotara
"**Where** dips the rocky highland." See The stolen child
Where do rivers go. Unknown, ad. fr. the Japanese by Charlotte B. DeForest.—DePp
"**Where** do you go when." See Riding a fence
"**Where** does a river hurry so." See Where do rivers go
"**Where** does Cinderella sleep." See Parvenu
"**Where** does he wander." Chiyo, tr. fr. the Japanese by Harry Behn.—BeCs
"**Where** Europe and America build their arches." See The third continent
Where go the boats. Robert Louis Stevenson.—ArT-3—BoGj—HoB
"**Where** have these hands been." See Musician
"**Where** have you been." See Bonny Saint John
"**Where** have you been all the day." See The wee croodin doo
Where I went. See "I went up the high hill"
"**Where** is Anne." See Buttercup days
"**Where** is David? . . . Oh God's people." See In which Roosevelt is compared to Saul
"**Where** is Paris and Heleyne." Thomas of Hales.—GrCt
"**Where** is the grave of Sir Arthur O'Kellyn." See The knight's tomb
Where is the real non-resistant. Vachel Lindsay.—LiP
"**Where** is the star of Bethlehem." See Christmas 1959 et cetera
Where lies the land. Arthur Hugh Clough.—CoSs—GrCt
"**Where** lies the land to which the ship would go." See Where lies the land
Where, O where. Milton Bracker.—MoS
"**Where** on the wrinkled stream the willows lean." See The water ousel
"**Where** shall we our great professor inter." See A serio-comic elegy
Where the bee sucks. See The tempest
"**Where** the bee sucks, there suck I." See The tempest—Where the bee sucks
"**Where** the canyon spreads on either hand." See Hangman's tree
"**Where** the cities end, the." See Transcontinent
Where the hayfields were. Archibald MacLeish.—HaL
"**Where** the pools are bright and deep." See A boy's song
"**Where** the remote Bermudas ride." See Bermudas
"**Where** the world is grey and lone." See The ice king
"**Where** we walk to school each day." See Indian children
"**Where** were the greenhouses going." See Big wind
"**Where** were we." See Twenty-five
Where, when, which. Langston Hughes.—HaK
"**Wherever** fox or cat or crow." See Tracks in the snow
"**Wherever** I am, there's always Pooh." See Us two
Where's Mary. Ivy O. Eastwick.—ArT-3
"**Where's** the Queen of Sheba." See Gone
"**Whether** my bark went down at sea." Emily Dickinson.—DiPe
"**Whether** on Ida's shady brow." See To the Muses
Which hand. Kathleen Fraser.—FrS
"**Which** will you have, a ball or a cake." See Choosing
Whicher, George F.
Johan the monk. tr.—LiT
Juliana. tr.—CoBl
On the gift of a cloak. tr.—LiT
"**While** Fell was reposing himself on the hay." See On Fell
"**While** fishing in the blue lagoon." See The silver fish
"**While** I stay alone." Unknown.—BaS
"**While** it is alive, until death touches it." Emily Dickinson.—DiPe
"**While** moonlight, silvering all the walls." See The barn owl
"**While** my hair was still cut straight across my forehead." See The river-merchant's wife: A letter
"**While** sitting here looking toward the stars." Linda Curry.—BaH
"**While** stars are watching." See In a million years
"**While** the earth spins on." See Earth, moon, and sun

"The **white** moth to the closing bine." See The gipsy trail
The **white** owl. See Love in a valley
"**White** pebbles jut from the river-stream." See In the hills
White primit falls. Unknown.—GrCt
The **white** rabbit. E. V. Rieu.—SmM
White rose. Sacheverell Sitwell.—GrS
"**White** Rose is a quiet horse." See The four horses
White season. Frances M. Frost.—ArT-3—CoB
"**White** sheep, white sheep." See Clouds
"A **white** sheet on the tail-gate of a truck." See Elegy for a dead soldier
The **white** stag. Ezra Pound.—HaL
White Stone Bank. Wang Wei, tr. fr. the Chinese by Chang Yin-nan and Lewis C. Walmsley.—LeMw
"**White** Stone Bank river, shallow, clear." See White Stone Bank
"**White** violets I'll bring." See Flowers: For Heliodora
The **white** window. James Stephens.—ArT-3—HuS-3—StS
"**Whitie,** come fast." See Two puppies
Whitman, Walt
"Afoot and light-hearted, I take to the open road." See Song of the open road
After the sea ship.—CoSs
Animals. See Song of myself
Bivouac on a mountain side.—GrCt—LiT
Cavalry crossing a ford.—GrCt—WhA
The dismantled ship.—ClF—HoL
"A gigantic beauty of a stallion, fresh and responsive to my caresses." See Song of myself
Give me the splendid silent sun.—CoBn
The greatest city.—LaC
"I am afoot with my vision." See Song of myself
"I am he that walks with the tender and growing night." See Song of myself
"I believe a leaf of grass is no less than the journey-work of the stars." See Song of myself
"I celebrate myself." See Song of myself
I hear America singing.—ArT-3—BrA—HoB—HuS-3—WhA
"I hear America singing, the varied carols I hear."—LaPd
"I hear America singing, the varied carols I hear." See I hear America singing
"I think I could turn and live with animals." See Song of myself—Animals
Miracles. See Song of myself
O captain, my captain.—CoR—HiL—HuS-3
"On the beach at night."—GrCt
Out of the cradle endlessly rocking, sel.
Two guests from Alabama.—ReO
The ox-tamer.—CoB
The runner.—MoS
The same old law. See Song of myself
Song of myself, sels.
Animals.—CoB
"I think I could turn and live with animals."—LaPd
Song of myself.—LiT—SmM
"A gigantic beauty of a stallion, fresh and responsive to my caresses."—CoB—LaPd
"I am afoot with my vision."—CoB
"I am he that walks with the tender and growing night."—GrCt
"I believe a leaf of grass is no less than the journey-work of the stars."—ArT-3—LaPd
"I celebrate myself"
Song of myself.—WhA
Miracles.—HuS-3—LiT—SmM
The same old law.—ReO
Song of the open road.—WhA
"Afoot and light-hearted, I take to the open road."—ArT-3
Song of the redwood-tree.—PaH (sel.)
Two guests from Alabama. See Out of the cradle endlessly rocking
"When I heard the learn'd astronomer."—HoL
"The world below the brine."—CoBn
"You, whoever you are."—BrA
Whitman, Walt (about)
Song of myself, sels.
Animals.—CoB
"I think I could turn and live with animals."—LaPd
Song of myself.—LiT—SmM
"A gigantic beauty of a stallion, fresh and responsive to my caresses."—CoB—LaPd
"I am afoot with my vision."—CoB
"I am he that walks with the tender and growing night."—GrCt
"I believe a leaf of grass is no less than the journey-work of the stars."—ArT-3—LaPd
"I celebrate myself"
Song of myself.—WhA
Miracles.—HuS-3—LiT—SmM
The same old law.—ReO
Whittaker, Frederick
Custer's last charge.—HiL
Whittemore, Reed
Love song.—BrA
Summer concert.—BrA
Whittier, John Greenleaf
Barbara Frietchie.—HiL
The Bartholdi statue.—HiL
Brown of Ossawatomie.—HiL
The cable hymn.—HiL
The proclamation.—HiL
Skipper Ireson's ride.—CoSs—HiL
The snow. See Snow-bound
Snow-bound, sel.
The snow.—HuS-3
Whittington and his cat. Unknown.—VrF
"**Who** abdicated ambush." Emily Dickinson.—DiPe

"**Who** am I going to choose." Kathleen Fraser.—FrS
"**Who** am I that shine so bright." See A pretty thing
"**Who** are you, asked the cat of the bear." Elizabeth Jane Coatsworth.—ArT-3
"**Who** are you, Sea Lady." See Santorin
"**Who** are you that so strangely woke." See The princess of Scotland
"**Who** built Thebes of the seven gates." See Questions of a studious working man
"**Who** called? I said, and the words." See Echo
"**Who** calls? Who calls? Who." See For a mocking voice
"**Who** came in the quiet night." See The little fox
"**Who** can live in heart so glad." See The passionate shepherd—The merry country lad
"**Who** can surrender to Christ, dividing his best with the stranger." See Where is the real non-resistant
"**Who** ever had." See The wall of China
"**Who** fancied what a pretty sight." William Wordsworth.—WoP
"**Who** goes round my house at night." See Cruel Tom
"**Who** goes to dine must take his feast." Emily Dickinson.—DiPe
Who goes with Fergus. William Butler Yeats.—BoGj
"**Who** has not found the heaven—below." Emily Dickinson—DiPe
"**Who** has not heard of Whittington." See Whittington and his cat
Who has seen the wind. Bob Kaufman.—HaK
"**Who** has seen the wind." Christina Georgina Rossetti.—ArT-3—BlO—BoGj—HuS-3—LaPd
The wind.—HoB
"**Who** hath a book." Wilbur D. Nesbit.—ArT-3
"**Who** is king but Epiphanes." See Song of triumph
"**Who** is quick, quick, quick." See The swallow
Who is Silvia. See Two gentlemen of Verona
"**Who** is Silvia? What is she." See Two gentlemen of Verona—Who is Silvia
"**Who** is so proud." See A circus garland—The performing seal
"**Who** is that in the tall grasses singing." See Song for Naomi
"**Who** is the happy warrior? Who is he." See Character of the happy warrior
Who is the man of poise. See Bhagavad Gita
"**Who** is the man of poise, Krishna." See Bhagavad Gita—Who is the man of poise
"**Who** is't now we hear." See Alexander and Campaspe
"**Who** killed Cock Robin." Mother Goose.—OpF
The death and burial of Cock Robin.—BrMg—VrF
Who knows. Vachel Lindsay.—LiP
"**Who** knows if the moon's." E. E. Cummings.—HaL
"**Who** knows this or that." See Limits
"**Who** learned you to dance." Unknown.—MoB
Who likes the rain. Clara Doty Bates.—ArT-3—StF
"**Who** loves the rain." Frances Shaw.—ThA
"**Who** made the pie." Mother Goose.—OpF
The pie.—BrMg
"**Who** minds if the wind whistles and howls." See Windy morning
Who misses or who wins. William Makepeace Thackeray.—MoS
"**Who** misses or who wins the prize." See Who misses or who wins
"**Who** never lost, are unprepared." Emily Dickinson.—DiPe
"**Who** never wanted,—maddest joy." Emily Dickinson.—DiL—DiPe
"**Who**, or why, or which, or what." See The Akond of Swat
"**Who** pads through the wood." See The cat
Who pilots ships. Daniel Whitehead Hicky.—ThA
"**Who** pilots ships knows all a heart can know." See Who pilots ships
"**Who** plays with fire." See Primer of consequences
"**Who** said, Peacock pie." See The song of the mad prince
"**Who** saw the Forty-second." Unknown.—MoB
"**Who** saw the petals." See The secret song
"**Who** says that Soochow girls are fools." See A boatwoman
Who scans the meadow. Aileen Fisher.—FiI
"**Who** scans the meadow up and down." See Who scans the meadow
"**Who** sees the first marsh marigold." See A charm for spring flowers
"**Who** set that endless silence." See Death
Who stole the nest. Lydia Maria Child.—StF
"**Who** tells the little deer mouse." See Deer mouse
"**Who** was it that I lately heard." See Improper words
"**Who** was it that the thunder of fate." See Robert Gould Shaw
"**Who** will go drive with Fergus now." See Who goes with Fergus
"**Who** would not love." See The cat
"**Who** would true valour see." See The pilgrim's progress—The pilgrim
"**Whoever** discounts." See Oz.
"**Whoever** it was who brought the first wood and coal." See Banking coal
"**Whoever's** born on Christmas." See An Irish legend
"The **whole** world on a raft. A king is here." See Three poems about Mark Twain—The raft
Whoopee ti yi yo, git along little dogies. Unknown.—ArT-3
Git along, little dogies.—HuS-3
Whoops a daisy. Teddy Carr.—LeM
Who's here. Eve Merriam.—MeI
Who's in. Elizabeth Fleming.—BlO—ClF—ThA
"**Who's** me, a little black boy." See Me
"**Who's** that creature who's wearing a mask." See Hallowe'en
"**Who's** that dusty stranger? What's he doing here." See City sparrow

"**Who's** that knocking on the window." See Innocent's song
"**Who's** that tickling my back, said the wall." See The tickle rhyme
Who's who. W. H. Auden.—McWs
"**Whose** are this pond and house." Chang Liang-ch'en, tr. fr. the Chinese by Robert Kotewell and Norman L. Smith.—LeMw
"**Whose** cottage." Issa, tr. fr. the Japanese.—LeOw
"**Whose** is it then." Issa, tr. fr. the Japanese by R. H. Blyth.—IsF
"**Whose** little beast." See Donkey
"**Whose** little pigs are these, these, these." Mother Goose.—OpF
"**Whose** scarf could this be." Buson, tr. fr. the Japanese by Harry Behn.—BeCs
"**Whose** town did you leave." Richard Wright Hokku poems.—BoA
"**Whose** woods these are I think I know." See Stopping by woods on a snowy evening
"**Who've** ye got there?—Only a dying brother." See The brigade must not know, sir
"**Whsst,** and away, and over the green." See Nothing
"**Why.**" Onitsura, tr. fr. the Japanese by R. H. Blyth.—LeMw
Why ("Ever, ever") Walter De La Mare.—DeBg
Why ("I don't know why I'm so crazy") Myra Cohn Livingston.—LiC
Why ("Why do we hate") Joseph Francis Velez.—BaH
Why ("Why do you weep, Mother? Why do you weep") Walter De La Mare.—DeBg
Why ("Why take a little when you") Vanessa C. Howard.—BaH
"**Why** are you rabbits jumping so." See Why rabbits jump
Why art thou silent. William Wordsworth.—WoP
"**Why** are thou silent! Is thy love a plant." See Why art thou silent
"**Why,** as to that, said the engineer." See The ghost that Jim saw
"**Why?** Because all I haply can and do." See Why I am a liberal
"**Why** chidest thou the tardy spring." See May-day
Why did I write. See Epistle to Dr Arbuthnot
"**Why** did I write? what sin to me unknown." See Epistle to Dr Arbuthnot—Why did I write
"**Why** do bells for Christmas ring." See Song
"**Why** do I curse the jazz of this hotel." See The jazz of this hotel
"**Why** do the white man lie." Linda Curry.—BaH
"**Why** do we hate." See Why
"**Why** do you always stand there shivering." See The poplar
"**Why** do you cry." Unknown.—DoC
"**Why** do you weep, Mother? Why do you weep." See Why
"**Why** does a fire eat big sticks of wood." See A fire
"**Why** does my Anna toss her head." See The gaudy flower
"**Why** does the little dog stand by the door." See Night in early spring
"**Why** does the sea moan evermore." See By the sea
"**Why** does this seedy lady look." See The jilted funeral
"**Why** dost thou weep, my child." Unknown, tr. fr. the Belengi.—LeO
"**Why** fadest thou in death." See Song
"**Why** flyest thou away with fear." See To a fish of the brook
"**Why** for your spouse this pompous fuss." See On seeing a pompous funeral for a bad husband
"**Why,** here's a foolish little man." See The little coward
Why I am a liberal. Robert Browning.—BrP
Why I did not reign. Eve Merriam.—MeI
Why I voted the socialist ticket. Vachel Lindsay.—LiP
"**Why** is Mary standing there." See Sulking
Why isn't the world happy. Ramona Lewis.—BaH
"**Why** listen, even the water is sobbing for something." See The maid's thought
Why no one pets the lion at the zoo. John Ciardi.—DuR
"**Why** of the sheep do you not learn peace." See An answer to the parson
Why prejudice. Betty Chase.—BaH
Why rabbits jump. Unknown, ad. fr. the Japanese by Charlotte B. DeForest.—DePp
"**Why** should I care for the men of Thames." William Blake.—BlP—GrCt
"**Why** should my sleepy heart be taught." See The falcon
"**Why** should not old men be mad." William Butler Yeats.—YeR
"**Why** should we live when living is a pain." See What the tramp said
Why so pale and wan. See Aglaura
"**Why** so pale and wan, fond lover." See Aglaura—Why so pale and wan
"**Why** take a little when you." See Why
Why the owl wakes at night. Phyllis McGinley.—McWc
"**Why** the world is not happy makes me sad." See Why isn't the world happy
"**Why** was Cupid a boy." William Blake.—BlP
"**Why** were you born when the snow was falling." See A dirge
"**Why,** who makes much of a miracle." See Song of myself—Miracles
Wibbleton and Wobbleton. Mother Goose.—BrMg
Wickham, Anna
Silence.—CoBl
The tired man.—SmM
The **wicked** hawthorn tree. William Butler Yeats.—YeR
Widdemer, Margaret
The faithless flowers.—ThA

"I saw the wind today." P. Colum.—BoGj
Reminiscence II.—HaL
The wind.—CoR—LaPd
"I see the wind." K. Mizumura.—MiI
"I think that the root of the wind is water." E. Dickinson.—DiPe
"I went to the town." Unknown.—OpF
"In the evening glow." K. Mizumura.—MiI
"In the northwest wind." K. Mizumura.—MiI
In the treetops. A. Fisher.—FiI
"The least of breezes." Onitsura.—BeCs
"Like rain it sounded till it curved." E. Dickinson.—DiPe
"Little wind, blow on the hill-top." K. Greenaway.—ArT-3
Little wind.—BoGj—LaP
Lodged. R. Frost.—BrSg
"A lone gull." K. Mizumura.—MiI
March dreams. R. Henderson.—ThA
March wind. H. Behn.—BeG
"March winds and April showers." Mother Goose.—BrSg
Spring.—BrMg
"May wind is busy." K. Mizumura.—MiI
Mid-country blow. T. Roethke.—CoBn
Mr East's feast. Mother Goose.—AgH
"The moon's the north wind's cooky." V. Lindsay.—HoB—HuS-3—LaP—LaPd—ThA
"My children, my children." Unknown.—LeO
"My lady Wind, my lady Wind." Mother Goose.—OpF
The wind.—BrMg
Night wind in spring. E. J. Coatsworth.—CoDh
November day. E. Averitt.—DuR
Now close the windows. R. Frost.—HaL
"O wind, why do you never rest." C. G. Rossetti.—ArT-3
October wind. D. McCord.—McAd
Ode to the west wind. P. B. Shelley.—CoBn
"Of all the sounds despatched abroad." E. Dickinson.—DiPe
"Once again." K. Mizumura.—MiI
"Raging wind." K. Mizumura.—MiI
Riddle. E. J. Coatsworth.—CoSb
The secret. J. Stephens.—StS
Snowball wind. A. Fisher.—FiI
"Softly." Issa.—LeMw
The song of the wind bell. Ch'en Meng-chia. —LeMw
South wind. Tu Fu.—ArT-3—LeM
Spring wind. K. N. Agrawal.—AlPi
Stillness. M. Leaso.—LeM
A strong wind. A. Clarke.—CoBn
Sweet and low. From The princess. A. Tennyson.—BlO—HoB—HuS-3—TeP
A cradle song.—CoSs
Song.—SmM
"There came a wind like a bugle." E. Dickinson.—DiPe
The storm.—SmM
To a child dancing in the wind. W. B. Yeats. —YeR
To the thawing wind. R. Frost.—HaL
To the wind. From Rig Veda. Unknown.—AlPi
Trade winds. J. Masefield.—BoH—ClF
The trees and the wind. E. Farjeon.—FaA
The unknown color. C. Cullen.—BoH
"Waiting for the children." K. Mizumura.—MiI
"We must overcome the east wind." Unknown. —DoC
The west wind. A. Fisher.—FiC
"While the last wind of winter." K. Mizumura.—MiI
Who has seen the wind. B. Kaufman.—HaK
"Who has seen the wind." C. G. Rossetti.—ArT-3—BlO—BoGj—HuS-3—LaPd
The wind.—HoB
"Whose scarf could this be." Buson.—BeCs
The wind ("I saw you toss the kites on high") R. L. Stevenson.—ArT-3—HuS-3
The wind ("When the wind is in the east") Mother Goose.—BrMg
The wind ("The wind in a bad mood") K. Itta.—BaH
The wind ("Wind in the garden") D. McCord. —McE
Wind ("The wind is like the yeast in bread") R. Tanaka.—LeM
The wind ("The wind stood up, and gave a shout") J. Stephens.—CoBn—LiT—StS
The wind ("The wind—yes, I hear it—goes wandering by") W. De La Mare.—DeBg
The wind and the moon. G. MacDonald.—BoGj
The wind and the rain. W. W. Gibson.—ClF
A wind blows. E. J. Coatsworth.—CoDh
"The wind gives us." Issa.—LeOw
"The wind has such a rainy sound." C. G. Rossetti.—ArT-3
The sound of the wind.—BlO
The wind has wings. Unknown.—DoW
Wind in the trees. Unknown.—LeM
"Wind is a cat." E. R. Fuller.—ThA
Wind message. Unknown.—DePp
The wind of spring. M. C. Livingston.—LiC
"The wind was bringing me to school." J. Snyder.—LeM
"The wind was once a man." Unknown.—LeO
Wind, waves, and sails. M. La Rue.—CoSs
Wind weather. V. Brasier.—HuS-3
"Wind, wind." K. Mizumura.—MiI
Wind-wolves. W. D. Sargent.—ArT-3
A windy circus. L. Ray.—AlPi
Windy morning. H. Behn.—ArT-3
Windy nights. R. L. Stevenson.—ArT-3—BoGj —HoB—TuW
Windy tree. A. Fisher.—FiI
Windy wash day. D. Aldis.—ArT-3—LaP
Winter night. M. F. Butts.—ArT-3
"With hey, ho, the wind and the rain." From King Lear. W. Shakespeare.—ArT-3
Worms and the wind. C. Sandburg.—ReO
Wind. See "Arthur O'Bower has broken his band"
The **wind.** See "I saw the wind today"

The **wind**. See "My lady Wind, my lady Wind"
The **wind**. See "Who has seen the wind"
The **wind** ("I saw you toss the kites on high") Robert Louis Stevenson.—ArT-3—HuS-3
The **wind** ("When the wind is in the east") Mother Goose.—BrMg
The **wind** ("The wind in a bad mood") Kathy Itta.—BaH
The **wind** ("Wind in the garden") David McCord.—McE
Wind ("The wind is like the yeast in bread") Robert Tanaka.—LeM
The **wind** ("The wind stood up, and gave a shout") James Stephens.—CoBn—LiT—StS
The **wind** ("The wind—yes, I hear it—goes wandering by") Walter De La Mare.—DeBg
The **wind** and the moon. George MacDonald.—BoGj
The **wind** and the rain. Wilfrid Wilson Gibson.—ClF
"The **wind** and the wind and the wind blows high." See Skipping
"The **wind** became a green idea." See The March problem
"The **wind** begun (or began) to rock the grass." Emily Dickinson.—DiL—DiPe
A thunder-storm.—CoBn
"The **wind** billowing out the seat of my britches." See Child on top of a greenhouse
"**Wind**, bird, and tree." See The words
A **wind** blows. Elizabeth Jane Coatsworth.—CoDh
"The **wind** blows east, the wind blows west." See Hot cockles
"The **wind** blows high, the wind blows low." See Anne
"The **wind** blows out of the gates of the day." See The land of heart's desire
"The **wind** blows the rain into our faces." Charles Reznikoff.—LaC
"A **wind** came up out of the sea." See Daybreak
"**Wind** from the south, hook in the mouth." See How they bite
"The **wind** galing." See Wind in the trees
"The **wind** gives us." Issa, tr. fr. the Japanese.—LeOw
"The **wind** has some seeds." See Dandelions everywhere
"The **wind** has blown that searchlight out." See Autumn squall: Lake Erie
"The **wind** has picked me up." See The wind of spring
"The **wind** has such a rainy sound." Christina Georgina Rossetti.—ArT-3
The sound of the wind.—BlO
The **wind** has wings. Unknown, tr. fr. the Eskimo by Raymond De Coccola and Paul King.—DoW
"The **wind** in a bad mood." See The wind
"**Wind** in the garden." See The wind
Wind in the trees. Unknown.—LeM
The **wind** in the willows, sels. Kenneth Grahame
Ducks' ditty.—ArT-3—BoGj—CoB—LaP—LaPd—TuW
The song of Mr Toad.—BoGj
"**Wind** is a cat." Ethel Romig Fuller.—ThA
"The **wind** is blowing, blowing, blowing." See Wind message
"The **wind** is blowing, the ground is frozen." See A man is buried where the cold winds blow
"The **wind** is half the flower." See The flower
"**Wind** is in the cane. Come along." See Carma
"The **wind** is like the yeast in bread." See Wind
"The **wind** is sewing with needles of rain." See Two sewing
Wind message. Unknown, ad. fr. the Japanese by Charlotte B. DeForest.—DePp
The **wind** of spring. Myra Cohn Livingston.—LiC
"The **wind** of the marigold." See The field of the mice and the marigold
"**Wind** plays in the treetops." See In the treetops
"The **wind** stood up, and gave a shout." See The wind
"The **wind** was a torrent of darkness among the gusty trees." See The highwayman
"The **wind** was bringing me to school." James Snyder.—LeM
"The **wind** was once a man." Unknown, tr. fr. the Bushman.—LeO
"The **wind** was throwing snowballs." See Snowball wind
Wind, waves, and sails. M. La Rue.—CoSs
Wind weather. Virginia Brasier.—HuS-3
"**Wind** whines and whines the shingle." See On the beach at Fontana
"**Wind**, wind." Kazue Mizumura.—MiI
Wind-wolves. William D. Sargent.—ArT-3
"The **wind**—yes, I hear it—goes wandering by." See The wind
The **windhover.** Gerard Manley Hopkins.—PlE
The **windmill.** See "Blow wind, blow, and go mill, go"
The **windmill** addresses Don Quixote. Elizabeth Jane Coatsworth.—CoDh
Windmills. See Mills
The **window,** sels. Alfred Tennyson
When.—TeP
Winter.—TeP
"A **window-box** of pansies." See Window-boxes
Window-boxes. Eleanor Farjeon.—BrSg
"The **window** gives onto the white trees." See Schoolmaster
Windows
At the windowed horizon. E. J. Coatsworth.—CoDh
"Factory windows are always broken." V. Lindsay.—LaC—LiP
The frost pane. D. McCord.—HuS-3—McE
"Ginger, Ginger, broke the winder." Mother Goose.—OpF
Ginger.—BrMg
The magic window. E. Hammond.—StF
Under the window. K. Greenaway.—GrT
The white window. J. Stephens.—ArT-3—HuS-3—StS
"W's for windows." From All around the town. P. McGinley.—ArT-3

"The **wind's** an old woman in front of the rain." See Wind weather
"A **wind's** in the heart, a fire's in my heels." See A wanderer's song
"**Winds** of March, come sweeping through the long brown valley." See March dreams
"The **wind's** on the wold." See Inscription for an old bed
"The **winds** they did blow." See The squirrel
"**Winds** through the olive trees." See Long, long ago
Windsor, Kelvin
Wondering—LeM
A **windy** circus. Lila Ray.—AlPi
The **windy** city, sel. Carl Sandburg
Night.—LaC
Windy morning. Harry Behn.—ArT-3
Windy nights. Robert Louis Stevenson.—ArT-3—BoGj—HoB—TuW
Windy tree. Aileen Fisher.—FiI
Windy wash day. Dorothy Aldis.—ArT-3—LaP
Wine and cakes. See "Wine and cakes for gentlemen"
"**Wine** and cakes for gentlemen." Mother Goose. —ReMg
Wine and cakes.—BrMg—VrF
Wingfield, Sheila
Winter.—CoBl
Young Argonauts.—MoS
Wings
"If I had wings just like a bird." J. Stephens. —StS
Wings and wheels. N. B. Turner.—ArT-3—HuS-3
Wings and wheels. Nancy Byrd Turner.—ArT-3 —HuS-3
Winnebago Indians. See Indians of the Americas—Winnebago
The **winning** of the TV West. John T. Alexander.—BoH—BrA
Winsor, Frederick
"The hydrogen dog and the cobalt cat."—BrSm
Winter. See also December; January; March; Seasons; Snow
Address to a child during a boisterous winter evening. D. Wordsworth.—BlO
Address to a lark singing in winter. From Address to a lark. J. Clare.—ReBs
"All animals like me." R. Souster.—DoW
All winter. A. Fisher.—FiC
Alone. W. De La Mare.—GrCt
"Along the cold post road." Issa.—IsF
At last. W. De La Mare.—DeBg
At Mrs Appleby's. E. M. McWebb.—ArT-3—HuS-3
Birds at winter nightfall. T. Hardy.—ReBs
"Blow, blow, thou winter wind." From As you like it. W. Shakespeare.—GrCt
Heigh ho the holly.—ShS
Blue winter. R. Francis.—HoL
Brittle world. L. Sarett.—ThA
Candy house. E. J. Coatsworth.—CoSb
Caw. W. De La Mare.—DeBg
A child that has a cold. T. Dibdin.—GrCt
Cold blows the wind. J. Hamilton.—ClF (sel.)
"Cold winter now is in the wood." E. J. Coatsworth.—ArT-3—TuW
"Cruel winter wind." J. James.—BaH
The darkling thrush. T. Hardy.—CoR
Dog, midwinter. R. Souster.—CoB
End of winter. E. Merriam.—MeI
Flight. G. Johnston.—DoW
The frost pane. D. McCord.—HuS-3—McE
Frosted-window world. A. Fisher.—FiIo
Good hours. R. Frost.—GrS
The grass on the mountain. Unknown.—BoH—BrA
Haiku. D. Lippa.—LeM
Hard frost. A. Young.—CoBn
"Huddled starlings." K. Mizumura.—MiI
Human things. H. Nemerov.—CoBn
"I stand under the naked tree." L. McCall.—LeM
Ice ("When it is the winter time") D. Aldis.—ArT-3
Ice ("When winter scourged the meadow and the hill") C. G. D. Roberts.—CoBn—DoW
In the evening I walk by the river. Hsiu Ouyang.—LeMw
In winter. R. Wallace.—CoBn
Joe. D. McCord.—ArT-3—HoB—McE
The lady is cold. E. B. White.—PaH
Late winter. Laksmidhara.—AlPi
"Like a wave crest." Uda.—BaS
Looking for a sunset bird in winter. R. Frost. —ReBs
Lost. E. Recht.—LeM
Mad as the mist and snow. William Butler Yeats.—GrCt
A man is buried where the cold winds blow. D. G. Matumeak.—BaH
The morning star. E. Brontë.—GrCt
Nocturne. F. M. Frost.—CoBn
"The north wind doth blow." Mother Goose.—BlO—HuS-3—OpF—ReMg—SmM—WiMg
The north wind.—BrMg
O dear me. W. De La Mare.—ArT-3—SmM
Old Dan'l. L. A. G. Strong.—ClF—SmM
"On a winter day." C. Lewis.—LeP
Oregon winter. J. McGahey.—BrA—DuR
"Over the wintry." Soseki.—BeCs—LaPd
Pencil and paint. E. Farjeon.—LaPd
A robin. W. De La Mare.—GrCt—ReBs
"Shine out, fair sun, with all your heat." From The masque of the twelve months. Unknown.—GrCt
Shopping for meat in winter. O. Williams.—HoL
Signs of winter. J. Clare.—CoBn—HoL
Skate and sled. E. Farjeon.—FaA
"The sky is low, the clouds are mean." E. Dickinson.—DiPe
Beclouded.—CoBn
The sleepy day. H. Patel.—LeM
Snow. K. Orendurff.—LeM
The snow man. W. Stevens.—BoGj
"Snowflakes drift." K. Mizumura.—MiI
Song. W. J. Turner.—BoGj

Winter night ("A tree may be laughter in the spring") Collister Hutchison.—ArT-3
Winter ocean. John Updike.—CoSs
"The **winter** owl banked just in time to pass." See Questioning faces
Winter portrait. Robert Southey.—CoBn
Winter rain. Christina Georgina Rossetti.—CoBn
"**Winter** rose, and in one night fled away." See May day
Winter solstice. Sara Teasdale.—HoB
Winter song. Juan Ramón Jiménez, tr. fr. the Spanish by H. R. Hays.—LiT
Winter splendor. Elizabeth Jane Coatsworth.—CoDh
"**Winter** stalks." See Winter
Winter thaw. Elizabeth Jane Coatsworth.—CoDh
Winter the huntsman. Osbert Sitwell.—BlO—ClF
The **winter** trees ("Against the evening sky the trees are black") Clifford Dyment.—ClF
Winter trees ("I think that I shall never ski") Conrad Diekmann.—MoS
Winter troops. See Winter. Charles Cotton
"**Winter** uses all the blues there are." See Blue winter
Winter walk. Aileen Fisher.—FiIo
Winters, Yvor
April.—CoB—DuR
To be sung by a small boy who herds goats.—WeP
A **winter's** dream. Unknown, ad. fr. the Japanese by Charlotte B. DeForest.—DePp
The **winter's** tale, sels. William Shakespeare
"Daffodils."—ArT-3—BrSg—TuW
"Jog on, jog on, the foot-path way."—ArT-3
The merry heart.—ShS
The pedlar.—ShS
Some flowers o' the spring.—GrCt
"**Winter's** thunder." Mother Goose.—ReOn
Wintertime. Robert Louis Stevenson.—HuS-3
Wintry. David McCord.—McAd
Wintu Indians. See Indians of the Americas—Wintu
"**Wirgele-Wargele,** auf der bank." Mother Goose.—OpF
Wisdom, Paul
Night time.—LeM
Wisdom. See also Mind
Comparisons. From King Henry VI. W. Shakespeare.—ShS
Man of Thessaly. Mother Goose.—BrMg
There's wisdom in women. R. Brooke.—CoBl
"Three wise men of Gotham." Mother Goose.—OpF—WiMg
The wise men of Gotham.—BrMg
Wisdom ("I have known nights rain-washed and crystal-clear") F. Yerby.—BoA
Wisdom ("I stand most humbly") L. Hughes.—ArT-3
Wisdom cometh with the years. C. Cullen.—HaK
"A wise old owl lived in an oak." Mother Goose.—WiMg
The owl.—BrMg
Wise song. From King Richard III. W. Shakespeare.—ShS
Wit's pedlar. From Love's labour's lost. W. Shakespeare.—ShS
Wisdom ("I have known nights rain-washed and crystal-clear") Frank Yerby.—BoA
Wisdom ("I stand most humbly") Langston Hughes.—ArT-3
Wisdom cometh with the years. Countee Cullen.—HaK
Wise, William
Telegram.—ArT-3
What to do.—ArT-3
"The **wise** guys." See Kid stuff
Wise Johnny. Edwina Fallis.—ArT-3—BrSg
The **wise** men of Gotham. See "Three wise men of Gotham"
"The **wise** old apple tree in spring." See A pastoral
"A **wise** old owl lived in an oak." Mother Goose.—WiMg
The owl.—BrMg
"A **wise** old owl sat in an oak." See "A wise old owl lived in an oak"
Wise song. See King Richard III
The **wish** ("Each birthday wish") Ann Friday.—LaPh
A **wish** ("I want to climb the santol tree") Tomas Santos.—LeM
"**Wish,** and it's thine, the changeling piped." See Solitude
Wish at meal-time. John Farrar.—HoB
"A **wish** is quite a tiny thing." Annette Wynne.—ThA
"**Wish** upon a shooting star." See Shooting star
Wishes. See Wishes and wishing
Wishes ("I wish my eyes were big and blue") Edna Kingsley Wallace.—ThA
Wishes ("Oh, if you were a little boy") Kate Greenaway.—GrT—HoB
Wishes and wishing
Beach fire. F. M. Frost.—ArT-3
Being gypsy. B. Young.—ArT-3
The big Rock Candy mountains. Unknown.—GrCt
"The bird wishes it were a cloud." R. Tagore.—LeMf
The boy. R. M. Rilke.—LiT—SmM
A boy looking at big David. M. Swenson.—LiT
Circus hand. P. Dehn.—SmM
"Come, it is late in the day." Unknown.—DoC
Dialogue. E. J. Coatsworth.—CoDh
The donkey and the fluke. E. Merriam.—MeC
Fairy tale. A. Fisher.—FiIo
"Faith, I wish I were a leprechaun." M. Ritter.—ArT-3
The falling star. S. Teasdale.—ArT-3—HuS-3—LaPd—ThA
"The far-off mountains hide you from me." Unknown.—DoC
Five little chickens. Unknown.—LaPd
The grass on the mountains. Unknown.—BoH—BrA

Witches' song. From Macbeth. W. Shakespeare.—McWs
Song of the witches.—ShS
The witch's broomstick spell. Unknown.—GrCt
The witch's song. Mother Goose.—BrMg
A witch's spell. Unknown.—GrCt
Witches. See Witchcraft
The **witches.** See "Hey-how for Hallowe'en"
Witches ("A star-white sky") Linden.—LeM
Witches' charm. Ben Jonson.—BlO
The **witches'** ride. Karla Kuskin.—LaPd—LaPh
Witches' song. See Macbeth
The **witch's** broomstick spell. Unknown.—GrCt
The **witch's** song. Mother Goose.—BrMg
A **witch's** spell. Unknown.—GrCt
"**With** a bray, with a yap." See Ululation
"**With** a hop, and a skip, and a jump." W. O'Neill.—StF
"**With** a roof and its shadow it rotates." See The carousel
"**With** a scarf around his eyes." See Blindman's buff
"**With** a twitching nose." Richard Wright
Hokku poems.—BoA
"**With** Annie gone." See For Anne
"**With** black, wicked eyes, hairy thin legs and." See The spider
"**With** blackest moss the flower-plots." See Mariana
"**With** collars be they yoked, to prove the arm at length." See Polyolbion—Wrestlers
"**With** company coming." See Thanksgiving dinner
"**With** deep affection." See The bells of Shandon
"**With** feeble steps." Issa, tr. fr. the Japanese.—LeOw
With flowers. See "I've nothing else to bring, you know"
"**With** hairs, which for the wind to play with, hung." See On Lydia distracted
"**With** half a hundred sudden loops and coils." See The hurrying brook
"**With** hey, ho, the wind and the rain." See King Lear
With how sad steps, O moon. Philip Sidney.—GrCt
The languishing moon.—CoBn
"**With** how sad steps, O moon, thou climb'st the skies." See With how sad steps, O moon
"**With** innumerable little footsteps." See The centipede
"**With** its fog-shroud the." See Poems
"**With** leering looks, bull-fac'd, and freckl'd fair." See Jacob Tonson, his publisher
"**With** little here to do or see." See To the same flower
"**With** love among the haycocks." See A song
"**With** much ado you fail to tell." See A critic
"**With** myriad voices grass was filled." See John Deth
"**With** our sticks." See Tip-cat
"**With** roses muskybreathed." See Anacreontics
"**With** secrets in their eyes, the blue-winged hours." See A tree at dusk
"**With** shiny skin." See Wild horse
"**With** sprinkling eyes and wind-cherried noses." See Conversation about Christmas
"**With** sweetest milk and sugar first." See The nymph complaining for the death of her fawn
"**With** that voice." Issa, tr. fr. the Japanese by R. H. Blyth.—LeMw
"**With** the evening breeze." Buson, tr. fr. the Japanese by R. H. Blyth.—LeI
"**With** the eyes red." See The Cuban emigrant
With the roses. Juan Ramón Jiménez, tr. fr. thc Spanish. by H. R. Hays.—LiT
"**With** the spreading mists." Tsurayuki.—BaS
"**With** thee conversing I forget all time." See Paradise lost—Eve speaks to Adam
"**With** their lithe long strong legs." See Bullfrog
"**With** this round glass." See The magnifying glass
"**With** two 60's stuck on the scoreboard." See Foul shot
"**With** two white roses on her breasts." See A brown girl dead
"**With** voice unceasing." Fujiwara no Okikaze.—BaS
"**With** what smug elegance the small goat minces." See Nosegay for a young goat
"**With** wrinkled hide and great frayed ears." See A circus garland—The elephant
"**With** yellow pears." See Life half lived
Wither, George
"Shall I, wasting in despair."—CoBl
"**Within** a gloomy dimble she doth well." See The sad shepherd—Mother Maudlin the witch
"**Within** a thick and spreading hawthorn bush." See The thrush's nest
"**Within** a thicket's calm retreat." See The lion and the mouse
"**Within** my bed, the whole night thru." See Young love
"**Within** my house of patterned horn." See The tortoise in eternity
"**Within** one petal of this flower." Unknown.—BaS
"**Within** that porch, across the way." See The cat
Within the bush. See A rose-bud, by my early walk
"**Within** the bush her covert nest." See A rose-bud, by my early walk—Within the bush
"**Within** the neat cottage, beside the tall tree." See School
"**Within** the night, above the dark." See Swans at night
"**Within** the streams, Pousanias saith." See The last chance
"**Within** the town of Buffalo." See Niagara
"**Within** these dusky woods." See Keeper's wood
"**Within** this black hive to-night." See Beehive
"**Within** this grave do lie." Unknown.—BrSm
"**Within** your heart." See Hold fast your dreams

"**Without** a bridle or a saddle." Mother Goose.—OpF
Without benefit of declaration. Langston Hughes.—BoA
"**Without** contraries is no progression." See The marriage of heaven and hell
Without name. Paul Murray.—BoA
"**Withouten** you." See Little elegy
Wit's pedlar. See Love's labour's lost
Witt, Harold
"Dogs have as much right as people in Nevada."—DuS
The hawk.—DuS
Wives. See Married life
Wizards
The elf singing. W. Allingham.—HuS-3
Oz. D. McCord.—McAd
The song of seven. W. De La Mare.—DeBg
Wmffre the sweep. Rolfe Humphries.—PlE
"**Wmffre** the sweep was mad as a mink." See Wmffre the sweep
Wodehouse, E. A.
Afforestation.—MoS
"**Woefully** arrayed." Unknown.—GrCt
Wolcot, John
To a fish of the brook.—CoB
The **wolf.** Georgia Roberts Durston.—ArT-3
"The **wolf** also shall dwell with the lamb." See Isaiah
The **wolf** and the crane. Ennis Rees.—ArT-3
The **wolf** and the lioness. Ennis Rees.—ArT-3
"The **wolf** has come." Unknown.—WyC
"A **wolf** with a bone in his throat." See The wolf and the crane
"A **wolf,** with hunger fierce and bold." See The shepherd's dog and the wolf
Wolfe, Charles
The burial of Sir John Moore.—CoR
The burial of Sir John Moore after Corunna.—GrCt
The burial of Sir John Moore after Corunna. See The burial of Sir John Moore
Wolfe, Ffrida
Choosing shoes.—ArT-3—StF
Wolfe, Humbert
The blackbird.—ArT-3—BoGj—HuS-3
The boxer's face. tr.—MoS
The gray squirrel.—BoGj—CoB
The Greek anthology, sel.
"I saw no doctor, but, feeling queer inside." tr.—BrSm
Green candles.—SmM
"I saw no doctor, but, feeling queer inside." See The Greek anthology
On Dean Inge.—GrCt
The sluggard. tr.—MoS
Two sparrows.—SmM
The world's worst boxer. tr.—MoS
Wolfe, James (about)
Brave Wolfe. Unknown.—HiL
Wolfe, Thomas
Burning in the night.—BrA
Wollner, Paul
I love the world.—LeM
Wolves
The shepherd's dog and the wolf. J. Gay.—ReO
A story for a child. B. Taylor.—CoB
The Tantanoola tiger. M. Harris.—CaMb
Wind-wolves. W. D. Sargent.—ArT-3
The wolf. G. R. Durston.—ArT-3
The wolf and the crane. E. Rees.—ArT-3
The wolf and the lioness. E. Rees.—ArT-3
Woman
Flowers of darkness. F. M. Davis.—AdIa—BoA
"A woman is a branchy tree." J. Stephens.—StS
"A **woman** is a branchy tree." James Stephens.—StS
"A **woman** one wonderful morning." See Europa
"A **woman** who lived in Holland, of old." See Going too far
"**Woman,** your soul is misshapen." Unknown.—DoC
A **woman's** last word. Robert Browning.—BrP
Women. See also People—Portraits—Women
A boatwoman. Chao Yeh.—LeMw
Reflections outside a gymnasium. P. McGinley.—MoS
There's wisdom in women. R. Brooke.—CoBl
Women of Syracuse. E. J. Coatsworth.—CoDh
The women of Yueh. Li T'ai-po.—HoL
Women—Portraits. See People—Portraits—Women
Women of Syracuse. Elizabeth Jane Coatsworth.—CoDh
The **women** of Yueh. Li T'ai-po, tr. fr. the Chinese by Robert Payne.—HoL
Women's liberation
The old feminist. P. McGinley.—HiL
Wonder. Bernard Raymund.—CoB
Wonder wander. Lenore Kandel.—DuR
"The **wonder** was on me in Curraghmacall." See The two nests
"**Wonder** where they come from." See Clouds
"**Wonder** where this horseshoe went." See From a very little sphinx
"A **wonderful** bird is the pelican." Dixon Lanier Merritt.—BrLl
A **wonderful** man. Aileen Fisher.—FiIo
The **wonderful** weaver. George Cooper.—HoB
The **wonderful** world. William Brighty Rands.—ArT-3—HoB
Wondering. Kelvin Windsor.—LeM
Won't. Walter De La Mare.—DeBg
Wood, William
A deux.—CoBl
Wood
Fifty faggots. E. Thomas.—ThG
Getting wood. J. Tritt.—BaH
Iron. B. Brecht.—HoL
"The **wood** is full of rooks." See The farmer's gun
The **wood** of flowers. James Stephens.—LaPd—StS
"The **wood** shakes in the breeze." See The old tree
A **wood** song. Ralph Hodgson.—BoGj

The **wood-weasel.** Marianne Moore.—ReO
Woodchucks
Clover for breakfast. F. M. Frost.—HuS-3
Ground hog day. M. Pomeroy.—CoB
"How much wood would a wood-chuck chuck." Mother Goose.—ArT-3—HuS-3
The jolly woodchuck. M. Edey.—ArT-3—LaPd
"The **woodchuck's** very very fat." See The jolly woodchuck
Wooden hill. Mother Goose.—BrMg
The **woodlands.** William Barnes.—CoBn
The **woodman's** dog. William Cowper.—CoB
"The **woodpecker.**" Issa, tr. fr. the Japanese by R. H. Blyth.—LeOw
The **woodpecker** ("He walks still upright from the root") See Upon Appleton house—The hewel, or woodpecker
The **woodpecker** ("The woodpecker pecked out a little round hole") Elizabeth Madox Roberts.—ArT-3—HoB—HuS-3—LaP
"The **woodpecker** pecked out a little round hole." See The woodpecker
Woodpeckers
Flicker. D. McCord.—McAd
The hewel, or woodpecker. From Upon Appleton house. A. Marvell.—GrCt
The woodpecker.—ReBs
"His bill an auger is." E. Dickinson.—DiPe
"The rat-a-tat-tat." Issa.—IsF
"The woodpecker." Issa.—LeOw
The woodpecker. E. M. Roberts.—ArT-3—HoB—HuS-3—LaP
Woods, John
The unemployed blacksmith.—McWs
Woods. See Forests and forestry
"The **woods** were still and the snow was deep." See Christmas eve legend
Wool
All wool. A. F. Brown.—ArT-3
"Baa, baa, black sheep." Mother Goose.—ArT-3—BrMg—HuS-3—OpF—WiMg
Mother Goose rhymes, 21.—HoB
Woolf, Virginia
"Let us go, then, exploring."—CoBn
Woolly lambkins. Christina Georgina Rossetti.—HuS-3
A **word.** See "A word is dead"
"The **word** bites like a fish." See Words
"A **word** is dead." Emily Dickinson
A word.—ArT-3
Words
Aa couple of doublles. E. Merriam.—MeI
Baby Toodles. J. S. Newman.—CoBb
Be my non-valentine. E. Merriam.—MeI
"Butterfly, these words." Soseki.—BeCs
"Could any mortal lip divine." E. Dickinson.—DiPe
Double trouble. E. Merriam.—MeI
Gazinta. E. Merriam.—MeI
Gone forever. B. Mills.—DuR
Gossip. L. D. Robertson.—ThA
Having words. E. Merriam.—MeI
"He ate and drank the precious words." E. Dickinson.—DiPe
"I found the phrase to every thought." E. Dickinson.—DiPe
"A man of words and not of deeds." Mother Goose.—BlO—ReMg
A man of words.—ReOn
Mnemonic for spelunking. E. Merriam.—MeI
Nym and graph. E. Merriam.—MeI
Onomatopoeia. E. Merriam.—MeI
Onomatopoeia II. E. Merriam.—MeI
Ponjoo. W. De La Mare.—BrSm
Primer lesson. C. Sandburg.—HuS-3—TuW
The purist. O. Nash.—BoGj—BrSm
Skywriting. E. Merriam.—MeI
Song for my mother. A. H. Branch.—ArT-3
Space. C. Lewis.—LeP
Talk. D. H. Lawrence.—ClF
Their lonely betters. W. H. Auden.—BoGj—HaL
"There is a word." E. Dickinson.—DiPe
Tittle and jot, jot and tittle. E. Merriam.—MeI
"A word is dead." E. Dickinson
A word.—ArT-3
Words ("Out of us all") E. Thomas.—ThG
The words ("Wind, bird, and tree") D. Wagoner.—DuS
Words ("The word bites like a fish") S. Spender.—SmM
Words ("Out of us all") Edward Thomas.—ThG
The **words** ("Wind, bird, and tree") David Wagoner.—DuS
Words ("The word bites like a fish") Stephen Spender.—SmM
Words from an old Spanish carol. Ruth Sawyer.—LaPh
On Christmas morn.—LaPd
The **words** of Finn. Unknown.—GrCt
"The **words** of hymns abruptly plod." See Hymn
Wordsworth, C. W. V.
Song in praise of paella.—AgH
Wordsworth, Dorothy
Address to a child during a boisterous winter evening.—BlO
Wordsworth, William
After-thought.—WoP
Books. See The prelude
Character of the happy warrior.—WoP
Characteristics of a child three years old.—WoP
Childhood. See The prelude
Composed on a May morning, 1838.—WoP
Composed upon Westminster bridge, September 3, 1802.—ArT-3—GrCt—PaH—WoP
The daffodils.—BoGj—HoB—HuS-3—TuW
I wandered lonely.—CoR
"I wandered lonely as a cloud."—BlO—BoH—CoBn—SmM—WoP
Elegiac stanzas, suggested by a picture of Peele castle, in a storm, painted by Sir George Beaumont.—WoP
Fidelity.—ClF
Fishing. See The prelude
The fountain.—WoP
France. See The prelude
French revolution.—WoP

Boy with his hair cut short. M. Rukeyser.—CoR
Brass spittoons. L. Hughes.—BoA
The bricklayer. Unknown.—VrF
The chickens. Unknown.—StF
Five little chickens.—LaPd
Fatigue. P. Bacon.—LaC
I hear America singing. W. Whitman.—ArT-3—BrA—HoB—HuS-3—WhA
"I hear America singing, the varied carols I hear."—LaPd
"I meant to do my work to-day." R. Le Gallienne.—ArT-3—LaP—ThA
Living among the toilers. H. Percikow.—LaC
The man with the hoe. E. Markham.—BoH—PlE
The misery of mechanics. P. Booth.—DuS
On a tired housewife. Unknown.—SmM
Questions of a studious working man. B. Brecht.—SmM
"See-saw, Margery Daw (Jacky or Johnny shall have a new master)." Mother Goose.—OpF—WiMg
See-saw.—BrMg
Song for the lazy. Unknown.—DoC
Stevedore. L. M. Collins.—BoA
The stone-breaker. Nirala.—AlPi
There is power in a Union. Unknown.—HiL
"There was an old man who lived in a wood." Mother Goose.—HuS-3
"There's lots of ways of doing things." Unknown.—MoB
"Those who go forth before daylight. C. Sandburg.—HuS-3
Too old to work. J. Glazer.—HiL
"What shall we do for the striking seamen." Unknown.—HiL
"When I was young and in my prime." Unknown.—OpF
Work. H. Van Dyke.—ThA
Work without hope. S. T. Coleridge.—CoBn
Work. Henry Van Dyke.—ThA
Work songs
Blow, ye winds. Unknown.—CoSs
The Chinese bumboatman. Unknown.—CoSs
Come loose every sail to the breeze. Unknown.—CoSs
Dance the boatman. Unknown.—HiL
The fishes. Unknown.—CoSs
The gals o' Dublin town. Unknown.—CoSs
Haul away Joe. Unknown.—CoSs
A long time ago. Unknown.—CoSs
Lowlands. Unknown.—GrCt
Sea chanty. A. Burrows.—CoSs
The sea serpent chantey. V. Lindsay.—LiP
The whale. Unknown.—CoSs—GrCt
Work without hope. Samuel Taylor Coleridge.—CoBn
"**Working** is another way of praying." See Song of a Hebrew
World
"As for this world." Semimaru.—BaS
"At the time when the earth became hot." Unknown.—LeO
Auguries of innocence. W. Blake.—BlP—CoB (sel.)—SmM (sel.)
The beautiful. Unknown.—LeO
Blue. C. Lewis.—LeP
A crazy flight. M. C. Livingston.—LiC
Dead cow farm. R. Graves.—LiT
The earth ("Did you know, did you know") E. Farjeon.—FaT
Earth ("A planet doesn't explode of itself, said drily") J. H. Wheelock.—DuR
Earth and sky ("O potent earth, and heaven god-built") Euripides.—PlE
Earth and sky ("Oh sky, you look so drear") E. Farjeon.—BrSg
"The earth is not an old woman." D. Satyarthi.—AlPi
Earth, moon, and sun. C. Lewis.—LeP
Earth upon earth. Unknown.—GrCt
Earth's answer. W. Blake.—BlP
The end of the world. A. MacLeish.—McWs
Fire and ice. R. Frost.—HoL
Gloucester moors. W. V. Moody.—PaH
God's world. E. St V. Millay.—TuW
The good earth. K. Itta.—BaH
"A good world it is, indeed." Issa.—LeMw
Happy thought. R. L. Stevenson.—ArT-3—HuS-3
Heaven and earth. James I, King of England.—GrCt
"How and when and where and why." P. Gotlieb.—DoW
"I am he that walks with the tender and growing night." From Song of myself. W. Whitman.—GrCt
I dream a world. L. Hughes.—BoA—BoH
I love the world. P. Wollner.—LeM
I often wonder. Monk.—BaH
"I sit at my window this morning." R. Tagore.—LeMf
"If all the world were apple pie." Mother Goose.—ReMg
"If only the world." Minamoto no Sanetomo.—BaS
"If this little world to-night." O. Herford.—BrSm
Earth.—DuR
Introduction to the Songs of experience. W. Blake.—BlP
"It is the tears of the earth." R. Tagore.—LeMf
"It is there that our hearts are set." Unknown.—LeO
"The lilac is an ancient shrub." E. Dickinson.—DiPe
Listen to the unheard. C. Lewis.—LeP
Little children. T. N. Tsosie.—BaH
Looking through space. A. Fisher.—FiI
The lost world. R. Jarrell.—LiT (sel.)
The map. G. C. Oden.—BoA
"The mighty thoughts of an old world." T. L. Beddoes.—BoGj
Song.—GrS
A moment please. S. Allen.—AdIa—BoA—HaK
The motion of the earth. N. Nicholson.—LiT
My enemy. L. Curry.—BaH

World—*Continued*
Night thought of a tortoise suffering from insomnia on a lawn. E. V. Rieu.—CoB
"A piece of colored cloud shines on the stone well." Chien Hsu.—LeMw
"Ring around the world." A. Wynne.—ArT-3—HuS-3
The road to China. O. B. Miller.—StF
Song of the earth. E. J. Coatsworth.—CoDh
Song of the sky loom. Unknown.—LeO
Southbound on the freeway. M. Swenson.—BrA—DuR
"The spacious firmament on high." J. Addison.—PlE
Then as now. W. De La Mare.—DeBg—LiT
"This is a world full of Negroes and whites." D. Peterson.—BaH
"This is my letter to the world." E. Dickinson.—DiL—DiPe
To the terrestrial globe. W. S. Gilbert.—LiT
"To what shall I compare." Mansei.—BaS
The two deserts. C. Patmore.—CoBn
Two views of the planet earth. H. Behn.—BeG
Valentine for earth. F. M. Frost.—ArT-3—HoB
"The voice that beautifies the land." Unknown.—LeO
Wander-thirst. G. Gould.—ArT-3—ClF (sel.)—PaH
Warning to children. R. Graves.—BlO
A way of looking. C. Lewis.—LeP
A wee little worm. J. W. Riley.—LaPd
What Tomas said in a pub. J. Stephens.—StS
Why isn't the world happy. R. Lewis.—BaH
The wonderful world. W. B. Rands.—ArT-3—HoB
The world is too much with us. W. Wordsworth.—GrCt—WoP
"The world turns and the world changes." From The rock. T. S. Eliot.—ArT-3
"The world's coming to an end." J. Bryant.—BaH
The **world**, sel. Henry Vaughan
A vision.—HoL
"The **world** below the brine." Walt Whitman.—CoBn
"The **world** has held great heroes." See The wind in the willows—The song of Mr Toad
The **world** I see. Mari Evans.—HaK
The **world** is a mighty ogre. Fenton Johnson.—BoA
"The **world** is cold and gray and wet." See Young love
"The **world** is full of wonderful smells." Zhenya Gay.—ArT-3
"The **world** is lazy turning." See A crazy flight
"The **world** is not conclusion." Emily Dickinson.—PlE
"The **world** is so full of a number of things." See Happy thought
"The **world** is still deceived with ornament." See The merchant of Venice—Outward show
"The **world** is taking off her clothes." See Rondeau
The **world** is too much with us. William Wordsworth.—GrCt—WoP
"The **world** is too much with us; late and soon." See The world is too much with us
"The **world** is upsy-daisy." See General Post
"The **world** is very flat." See Night thought of a tortoise suffering from insomnia on a lawn
"The **world** of dew." Issa, tr. fr. the Japanese.—LeOw
"A **world** of short-lived dew." Issa, tr. fr. the Japanese.—LeOw
"The **world** they speak of." See Going away
A **world** to do. Theodore Weiss.—GrS
"The **world** turns and the world changes." See The rock
"The **world** turns softly." See Water
World war I, 1914-1918. See European war, 1914-1918
World war II, 1939-1945
Atlantic Charter, A. D. 1620-1942. From The island. F. B. Young.—ArT-3—BrA
The ballad of banners. J. Lehmann.—CaMb
Camptown. J. Ciardi.—HiL
Carentan O Carentan. L. Simpson.—CaMb
Children's crusade 1939. B. Brecht.—CaMb
Christmas eve under Hooker's statue. R. Lowell.—HiL
Christmas 1945. A. Hine.—HiL
Death of an aircraft. C. Causley.—CaMb
Dirge for the new sunrise. E. Sitwell.—PlE
Elegy for a dead soldier. K. Shapiro.—HiL
For the one who would take man's life in his hands. D. Schwartz.—HiL
In a bar near Shibuya Station, Tokyo. P. Engle.—BrA
Kilroy. P. Viereck.—HiL
The man in the dead machine. D. Hall.—DuS
Memorial to the great big beautiful self-sacrificing advertisers. F. Ebright.—HiL
Plato told him. E. E. Cummings.—BrA—HiL
Redeployment. H. Nemerov.—HiL
Sunday: New Guinea. K. Shapiro.—BrA
V-letter. K. Shapiro.—HiL
"The **world** was meant to be peaceful." Veronica Bryant.—BaH
The **world's** a sea. Francis Quarles.—GrCt
"The **world's** a sea; my flesh a ship that's mann'd." See The world's a sea
"The **world's** coming to an end." Juanita Bryant.—BaH
"The **world's** great age begins anew." See Hellas
The **world's** worst boxer. Lucilius, tr. fr. the Greek by Humbert Wolfe.—MoS
The **worm** ("As Sally sat upon the ground") Elizabeth Turner.—VrF
The **worm** ("Dickie found a broken spade") Elizabeth Madox Roberts.—BrSg—HoB
The **worm** ("Don't ask me how he managed") Raymond Souster.—DoW
The **worm** ("No, little worm, you need not slip") Ann Taylor.—BrSg
The **worm** ("When the earth is turned in spring") Ralph Bergengren.—BrSg

Worms. See also Caterpillars
"The aged dog." Issa.—IsF
The book-worms. R. Burns.—GrCt
"The Buddha." Issa.—IsF
The conqueror worm. From Ligeia. E. A. Poe. —PoP
"Fat father robin." D. McCord.—McE
"Getting colder." Issa.—LeOw
"Long man legless, came to the door staffless." Mother Goose.—OpF
"A measuring worm." Issa.—IsF
"Our little kinsmen after rain." E. Dickinson. —DiPe
The sick rose. W. Blake.—BlP—GrCt
A wee little worm. J. W. Riley.—LaPd
The worm ("As Sally sat upon the ground") E. Turner.—VrF
The worm ("Dickie found a broken spade") E. M. Roberts.—BrSg—HoB
The worm ("Don't ask me how he managed") R. Souster.—DoW
The worm ("No, little worm, you need not slip") A. Taylor.—BrSg
The worm ("When the earth is turned in spring") R. Bergengren.—BrSg
Worms and the wind. C. Sandburg.—ReO
Worms and the wind. Carl Sandburg.—ReO
"**Worms** would rather be worms." See Worms and the wind
Wotherspoon, Ralph
Our dumb friends.—CoB
The **would-be** merman. Vachel Lindsay.—LiP
"**Would** my house were on the cliff." Unknown. —BaS
"**Would** that the structure brave, the manifold music I build." See Abt Vogler
"**Would** that young Amenophis Fourth returned." See Litany of the heroes
"**Would** you have freedom from wage-slavery." See There is power in a Union
"**Would** you like to see a city given over." See The city of golf
"**Wouldn't** it be lovely if the rain came down." See Very lovely
"**Would'st** thou hear what man can say." See Epitaph on Elizabeth, L. H.
The **wraggle** taggle gypsies. See The raggle taggle gypsies
"**Wrapped** in a cloak." See Fog, the magician
The **wreck** of the Deutschland. Gerard Manley Hopkins.—LiT (sel.)
The **wreck** of the Hesperus. Henry Wadsworth Longfellow.—LoPl
The **wreckers'** prayer. Theodore Goodridge Roberts.—CoSs
Wrecks. See also Shipwrecks
It's here in the. R. Atkins.—BoA
"The **wren.**" Issa, tr. fr. the Japanese by R. H. Blyth.—IsF
Wren and dove. Unknown.—MoB
The **wren** hunt. Mother Goose.—BrMg
"The **wren** that rages when I sit." See No communication
Wrens
Cock Robin. Mother Goose.—ReOn
The cutty wren. Unknown.—ReOn
The dove says. Mother Goose.—BrMg
"Go now, my song." A. Young.—GrCt
The hunting of the wren. Unknown.—MoB
"It was on a merry time." Mother Goose.— OpF
Jenny Wren ("Her sight is short, she comes quite near") W. H. Davies.—CoB—ReBs
Jenny Wren ("Of all the birds that rove and sing") W. De La Mare.—ReBs
"Jenny Wren fell sick." Mother Goose.—ReOn —SmM
Mother Goose rhymes, 24.—HoB
Robin and Jenny.—BrMg
"Little Lady Wren." T. Robinson.—ArT-3
No communication. M. Van Doren.—ReBs
The robin and the wren. Unknown.—BlO
"The robin came to the wren's nest." Unknown.—MoB
"Robin, Robin Redbreast (cutty, cutty wran)." Unknown.—MoB
"The wren." Issa.—IsF—LeOw
Wren and dove. Unknown.—MoB
The wren hunt. Mother Goose.—BrMg
"Wrens and robins in the hedge." C. G. Rossetti.—ArT-3
Wrens of the lake. Unknown.—ReBs
"**Wrens** and robins in the hedge." Christina Georgina Rossetti.—ArT-3
Wrens of the lake. Unknown, tr. fr. the Irish by Robin Flower.—ReBs
"**Wrens** of the lake, I love them all." See Wrens of the lake
Wrestlers. See Polyolbion
Wrestling
Wrestlers. From Polyolbion. M. Drayton.—MoS
Wrestling. K. Fraser.—FrS
Wrestling. Kathleen Fraser.—FrS
Wright, Bruce McM.
The African affair.—BoA
Wright, David
Rousecastle.—CaMb—CoSs
Shanty.—CaD
Wright, James
A blessing.—DuS
By a lake in Minnesota.—BrA
Mutterings over the crib of a deaf child.—DuS
Wright, Judith
Egrets.—BoGj
Lyrebirds.—BoGj
Wright, Richard
Between the world and me.—AdIa—BoA
"The crow flew so fast"
Hokku poems.—BoA
"I am nobody"
Hokku poems.—BoA
"In the falling snow"
Hokku: "In the falling snow."—AdIa
Hokku poems.—BoA
"Keep straight down this block"
Hokku poems.—BoA

Wright, Richard—*Continued*
"Make up your mind snail"
Hokku poems.—BoA
"The spring lingers on"
Hokku poems.—BoA
"Whose town did you leave"
Hokku poems.—BoA
"With a twitching nose"
Hokku poems.—BoA
Wright, Richard (about)
To Richard Wright. C. K. Rivers.—AdIa—BoA
"A **wrinkled,** crabbed man they picture thee." See Winter portrait
"**Write** a limerick now. Say there was." David McCord.—BrLl
Writers and writing. See also Books and reading; Poets and poetry; also names of authors, as Lear, Edward (about)
After reading translations of ancient texts on stone and clay. C. Reznikoff.—GrS
A critic. W. S. Landor.—GrCt
The dream of all the Springfield writers. V. Lindsay.—LiP
The height of the ridiculous. O. W. Holmes.—HuS-3
"I am writer." J. Stephens.—StS
Skywriting. E. Merriam.—MeI
Sporus. From Epistle to Dr Arbuthnot. A. Pope.—GrCt
What then. W. B. Yeats.—YeR
Why did I write. From Epistle to Dr Arbuthnot. A. Pope.—GrCt
"**Writing,** I crushed an insect with my nail." See Interlude III
Written after swimming from Sestos to Abydos. George Gordon Byron.—ByP
Written in a year when many of my people died. See Alexander Campbell
Written in March. William Wordsworth.—ArT-3—BoGj—CoBn—TuW—WoP
March.—HoB
Written in very early youth. William Wordsworth.—WoP
"**W's** for windows." See All around the town
Wu-ti
The liberator.—ReBs
Wyatt, Sir Thomas
Of the mean and sure estate.—ReO (sel.)
Wylie, Elinor
An American in England.—PaH
"As I went down by Havre de Grace."—PaH
The bird.—McWs
The child on the curbstone.—LaC
The eagle and the mole.—ReO
The falcon.—HaL
Little elegy.—HaL
Madman's song.—HaL—ThA
Parting gift.—HaL
Peter and John.—CaMb
The puritan's ballad.—CoBl
Sea lullaby.—CoBn
The tortoise in eternity.—HoL—ReO
Velvet shoes.—ArT-3—BoGj—HuS-3—ThA
Wild peaches.—PaH
Wynken, Blynken, and Nod. Eugene Field.—HoB—HuS-3
"**Wynken,** Blynken, and Nod one night." See Wynken, Blynken, and Nod
Wynne, Annette
Columbus.—ArT-3
"Excuse us, animals in the zoo."—ArT-3
"Hearts were made to give away."—ArT-3
The house cat.—HuS-3
"I heard it in the valley."—ThA
"I keep three wishes ready."—ArT-3—HuS-3—LaPd—ThA
"I'm wishing the whole world Christmas."—ThA
Indian children.—ArT-3—HuS-3
Little folks in the grass.—ThA
"People buy a lot of things."—LaPd
"Ring around the world."—ArT-3—HuS-3
"A wish is quite a tiny thing."—ThA
Wyoming
Snow country. D. Etter.—BrA

X

[No entries under this letter.]

Y

The **yak** ("As a friend to the children commend me the yak") Hilaire Belloc.—BlO
The **yak** (For hours the princess would not play or sleep") Virna Sheard.—DoW
Yakamochi
"Clear is the bottom of the lake."—BaS
"Each season, more lovely."—BaS
"In the leafy treetops."—BaS
"Now it is spring."—BaS
"Turned towards the moon."—BaS
Yaks
Bird thou never wert. P. Bennett.—CoB
The yak ("As a friend to the children commend me the yak") H. Belloc.—BlO
The yak ("For hours the princess would not play or sleep") V. Sheard.—DoW
Yamabe no Akahito
"I wish I were close."—LiT
Yamanoue no Okura
"When I am in grief."—LeMw
Yang Wan-li
The temple bells of Yun Sui.—LeMw
Yankee Doodle. See "Yankee Doodle came (or went) to town"
"**Yankee** Doodle came (or went) to town." Mother Goose.—HuS-3—OpF
Yankee Doodle.—BrMg—GrCt
Yaqui Indians. See Indians of the Americas—Yaqui
Yardbird's skull. Owen Dodson.—AdIa—BoA
Yarmolinsky, Avrahm. See Deutsch, Babette and Yarmolinsky, Avrahm

Yarmon, Mary
Slave of the moon.—LeM
The **yarn** of the Loch Achray. John Masefield.—CoSs
The **yarn** of the Nancy Bell. William Schwenck Gilbert.—HoB—HuS-3
Yasuhide
Foam flowers.—LeMw
Yasui
"Wild ducks have eaten."—BeCs
Yayu
"When spring is gone, none."—BeCs
Yazzie, Harold Roy
"Want to be someone."—BaH
"**Ye** banks and braes and streams around." See Highland Mary
"**Ye** flowery banks o' bonie Doon." See The banks o' Doon
"**Ye** Hielands and ye Lawlands." See The bonny earl of Moray
"**Ye** rascals of ringers, ye merciless foes." See On bell-ringers
"**Ye** say they all have passed away." See Indian names
"**Ye** who pass by and would raise your hand." See To the wayfarer
"**Ye** young debaters over the doctrine." See The Spoon River anthology—The village atheist
"**Yeah** here am I." See Two jazz poems
Year. See also New year
"As one of us." Issa.—LeOw
The ending of the year. E. Farjeon.—FaA
"January brings the snow." Sara Coleridge.—ArT-3
The garden year.—HuS-3
Legacy. C. Morley.—DuR
The year's round. C. Patmore.—BrSg
"The **year** has made her will: she left to me." See Legacy
"The **year** is round around me now." See Green song
The **year's** at the spring. See Pippa passes
The **year's** round. Coventry Patmore.—BrSg
Yeats, William Butler
Adam's curse.—YeR
Anashuya and Vijaya.—LiT
Another song of a fool.—ReO
An appointment.—YeR
At Galway races.—MoS
The ballad of Father Gilligan.—McWs—PlE—YeR
Brown penny.—CoBl—YeR
The cap and bells.—GrCt—YeR
The cat and the moon.—BoGj—CoB—CoR—HaL—LiT—YeR
A coat.—YeR
"Come gather round me, Parnellites."—YeR
"Come gather round me, players all." See Three songs to the one burden
The death of Cuchulain.—GrCt
Down by the salley gardens.—CoBl
A faery song.—YeR
Fergus and the druid.—LiT
The fiddler of Dooney.—ArT-3—YeR
The fisherman.—MoS—YeR
For Anne Gregory.—McWs—YeR
The ghost of Roger Casement.—YeR
He remembers forgotten beauty.—YeR
He wishes for the cloths of heaven.—HoL—ThA—YeR
The host of the air.—LiT—YeR
The Indian upon God.—YeR
An Irish airman foresees his death.—BoGj—HoL—YeR
The lake isle of Innisfree.—ArT-3—CoR—PaH—ThA—YeR
The land of heart's desire.—PaH
Let all things pass away.—GrCt
The lover tells of the rose in his heart.—YeR
Mad as the mist and snow.—GrCt
Memory.—YeR
IX The four ages of man. See Supernatural songs
The old men admiring themselves in the water. BoGj—LiT—YeR
Politics.—YeR
A prayer for old age.—YeR
Red Hanrahan's song about Ireland.—YeR
The rose tree.—YeR
Running to paradise.—HaL—YeR
The scholars.—YeR
The second coming.—PlE
September 1913.—YeR
A song.—YeR
The song of the old mother.—HaL—YeR
The song of wandering Aengus.—ArT-3—BlO—BoGj—CoBl—GrS—HaL—HoL—McWs—SmM—ThA—YeR
The statesman's holiday.—YeR
The stolen child.—YeR
Supernatural songs, sel.
IX The four ages of man.—YeR
Three songs to the one burden, sel.
"Come gather round me, players all."—YeR
To a child dancing in the wind.—YeR
To a poet, who would have me praise certain bad poets, imitators of his and mine.—YeR
To a squirrel at Kyle-Na-No.—BlO—CoB—LaPd
To an isle in the water.—SmM—YeR
To be carved on a stone at Thoor Ballylee.—YeR
Two songs of a fool.—ReO
Two years later.—YeR
Under Ben Bulben.—YeR (sel.)
Under the moon.—PaH
Under the round tower.—GrS
The valley of the black pig.—GrCt
What then.—YeR
When you are old.—BoGj—CoBl—YeR
Who goes with Fergus.—BoGj
"Why should not old men be mad."—YeR
The wicked hawthorn tree.—YeR
The wild swans at Coole.—GrCt—PaH—YeR
Yeats, William Butler (about)
In memory of W. B. Yeats. W. H. Auden.—GrCt (sel.)

Yeats, William Butler (about)—*Continued*
To be carved on a stone at Thoor Ballylee. W. B. Yeats.—YeR
Under Ben Bulben. W. B. Yeats.—YeR (sel.)
Yekei Hoshi
"The cherry blossoms (of the)."—BaS
Yellow (Color)
Theme in yellow. C. Sandburg.—ArT-3—HuS-3
What is yellow. M. O'Neill.—OnH
"**Yellow-belly,** yellow-belly, come and take a swim." See Yes, by golly
The **yellow** bird. Unknown, tr. fr. the Chinese by Robert Payne.—ReBs
Yellow flutterings. John Keats.—CoB
Yellow fog. See The love song of J. Alfred Prufrock—"The yellow fog that rubs its back upon the window-panes"
"The **yellow** fog that rubs its back upon the window-panes." See The love song of J. Alfred Prufrock
"**Yellow** is the color of the sun." See What is yellow
"**Yellow** sun yellow." See The ballad of red fox
Yen Yun
The fall of the flowers.—LeMw
Yerby, Frank
Calm after storm.—BoA
The fishes and the poet's hands.—BoA
Weltschmerz.—BoA
Wisdom.—BoA
You are a part of me.—BoA
Yes, by golly. Unknown.—MoS
"**Yes,** crosswise the walk in the garden." See The rendezvous
"**Yes,** I remember Adlestrop." See Adlestrop
"**Yes,** it is sad of them." See Three bad children
"**Yes,** I've sev'ral kivers you can see." See Kivers
"**Yes,** Lord, I prick." See The hedgehog
"**Yes,** Nancy Hanks." See A reply to Nancy Hanks
"**Yes,** there's nothing cuter in all this world." See Pearls among swine
"**Yesterday.**" See Prediction
"**Yesterday** I skipped all day." See Tiptoe
Yesterday in Oxford street. Rose Fyleman.—ArT-3—LaPd
"**Yesterday** in Oxford street, oh, what d'you think, my dears." See Yesterday in Oxford street
"**Yesterday** you didn't like me." See Good and bad
"**Yet** ah, that spring should vanish with the rose." See The rubaiyát of Omar Khayyám
Yet do I marvel. Countee Cullen.—AdIa—BoA
Yet gentle will the griffin be. Vachel Lindsay.—HuS-3—LaPd—ThA
"**Yet** if his majesty, our soveraign lord." See The guest
"**Yet** once more, O ye laurels, and once more." See Lycidas
Yet the lean beast plays. Elizabeth Jane Coatsworth.—CoDh
Yevtushenko, Yevgeny
Lies.—DuS
On a bicycle.—LiT (sel.)
Schoolmaster.—LiT
Zima junction.—LiT (sel.)
The **yew-tree** ("Is there a cause why we should wake the dead") Vernon Watkins.—PlE
The **yew-tree** ("What happiness you gave to me") Unknown.—GrCt
Yew trees
The yew-tree ("Is there a cause why we should wake the dead") V. Watkins.—PlE
The yew-tree ("What happiness you gave to me") Unknown.—GrCt
Yogesvara
Characterization.—AlPi
"**Yokie** pokie." Unknown.—MoB
Yokomizo, Jill
"In my mountains."—BaH
"In the silent night."—BaH
Yokut Indians. See Indians of the Americas—Yokut
Yolp, yolp, yolp, yolp. Unknown.—ReO
"**Yonder** in the plum tree." Unknown.—BaS
"**Yonder** the long horizon lies, and there by night and day." See Wander-thirst
"**You.**" See Echo
You are a part of me. Frank Yerby.—BoA
"**You** are a part of me. I do not know." See You are a part of me
"**You** are disdainful and magnificent." See Sonnet to a Negro in Harlem
"**You** are French? Je suis." See Innuendo
"**You** are going out to tea to-day." See Manners
You are old, Father William. See Alice's adventures in wonderland—Father William
"**You** are old, Father William, the young man said." See Alice's adventures in wonderland—Father William
You are on U.S. 40 headed west. Vera White.—BrA
"**You** are the brave who do not break." See In time of crisis
"**You** brave heroic minds." See To the Virginian voyage
"**You** can dream of steamships sailing out of Naples." See Trains
"**You** can see me in the country." Unknown Riddles.—StF
"**You** can talk about yer sheep dorgs, said the man from Allan's creek." See Daley's dorg Wattie
"**You** cannot cage a field." See Lives
"**You** cannot put a fire out." Emily Dickinson.—DiPe
"**You** cannot rest behind the plate." See Villanelle
"**You** can't race me, said Johnny the hare." See The hare and the tortoise
"**You** can't see fairies unless you're good." See Fairies
"**You** common cry of curs, whose breath I hate." See Coriolanus—Coriolanus's farewell to his fellow-citizens as he goes into banishment
"**You** crash over the trees." See Storm

"**You** did late review my lays." See To Christopher North
You do it too. Margaret Langford.—StF
"**You** have been good to me, I give you this." See Idolatry
"**You** have slain your enemy." See Purification
"**You** hear the din and drone of birds." See Autumn flight
"**You** heard the screen door open." See May day
"**You** know the fellow." See A public nuisance
"**You** know the old woman." See The old woman
"**You** know the sitting on the train not-knowing feeling." See Flight
"**You** know, we French stormed Ratisbon." See Incident of the French camp
You know who. John Ciardi.—CiYk
"**You-know-who** knows all there is." See You know who
"**You** lifeless stones, at the immortal touch of the musical hands." See Music of stones
"**You** light the fire." Bashō, tr. fr. the Japanese by R. H. Blyth.—LeMw
"**You** looked at me with eyes grown bright with pain." See Parting after a quarrel
"**You** make a snowman." See Winter day
"**You** may call, you may call." See The bad kittens
"**You** may leave the clam on the ocean floor." See The clam
"**You** may never see rain, unless you see." See A dance for rain
"**You** may not believe it, for hardly could I." See The pumpkin
"**You** may talk about your groves." See Master Jack's song
"**You** might think I was in the way." See So run along and play
"**You** must wake and call me early, call me early, mother dear." See The May queen
"**You** need not pity Samson." See Samson
"**You** need not see what someone is doing." See Sext
"**You** nest in roof-tops where your scratching feet." See Chipmunks
"**You** never know with a doorbell." See Doorbells
"**You,** north must go." Unknown.—StF
"**You** pigeons on the temple roof." See Pigeon playmates
"**You** probably could put their names to them." See As when emotion too far exceeds its cause
"**You** raised your arms like wings." See You were shattered
"**You** really resemble." Unknown.—DoC
"**You** said that your people." See To Richard Wright
"**You** say, as I have often given tongue." See To a poet, who would have me praise certain bad poets, imitators of his and mine
"**You** say their pictures well painted be." William Blake.—BlP
"**You** see, merry Phillis, that dear little maid." See The tea party
"**You** see the ways the fisherman doth take." See Neither hook nor line
"**You** see this Christmas tree all silver gold." See Come Christmas
You shall be queen. Mother Goose.—BrMg
"**You** should never squeeze a weasel." See Don't ever seize a weasel by the tail
"**You** spotted snakes with double tongue." See A midsummer-night's dream
"**You** strange, astonished-looking, angle-faced." See The fish, the man, and the spirit—To a fish
"**You** sunburn'd sicklemen, of August weary." See The tempest—Holiday
"**You** think I am dead." See Talking in their sleep
"**You** want to integrate me into your anonymity." See Black Narcissus
You were shattered. Giuseppe Ungaretti, tr. fr. the Italian by Lowry Nelson, Jr.—LiT (sel.)
"**You** who cultivate fields." Unknown.—DoC
"**You** who have grown so intimate with stars." See To an aviator
"**You,** whoever you are." Walt Whitman.—BrA
"**You,** whose day it is, make it beautiful." See Song to bring fair weather
"**You** will go? Then go at once." See Then go at once
"**You** work in the factory all of your life." See Too old to work
"**You** would not recognize yourself if I should tell you." See Trinity: A dream sequence
"**You,** you are all unloving, loveless, you." See The sea
You'd say it was a funeral. James Reeves.—BrSm
"**You'd** say it was a funeral, a funeral." See You'd say it was a funeral
"**You'll** find, in French, that couplet's a little word for two." See Couplet countdown
"**You'll** find me in the laundromat—just me and shirts and stuff." See Laundromat
"**You'll** find whenever the new year comes." Unknown.—WyC
You'll love me yet. See Pippa passes
"**You'll** love me yet,—and I can tarry." See Pippa passes—You'll love me yet
"**You'll** mean what I say, tells prose." See Mona Lisa
"**You'll** wait a long, long time for anything much." See On looking up by chance at the constellations
Young, Andrew
At Amberley Wild Brooks.—ReO
The bee-orchis.—GrCt
The beech.—CoBn
The blind man.—ReBs
Christmas day.—CaD
Climbing in Glencoe.—MoS
Cuckoo.—GrCt
Cuckoos.—GrCt
Daisies.—BoGj
A dead bird. See A summer wish
The dead crab.—ReO
A dead mole.—CoB

Youth ("We have tomorrow") L. Hughes.—BoH—BrA—LiT
Youth ("We stood together") Unknown.—LeM
Youth ("We have tomorrow") Langston Hughes.—BoH—BrA—LiT
Youth ("We stood together") Unknown.—LeM
Youth and age. See also Birthdays; Childhood recollections; Old age; Youth
"Are not the joys of morning sweeter." W. Blake.—BlP
"The cherry tree blossomed. Black was my hair." Tomonori.—LeMw
The corner. W. De La Mare.—DeBg
Danny Murphy. J. Stephens.—CoR—StS
Father William. From Alice's adventures in wonderland. L. Carroll.—BoGj—LaP (sel.)—LaPd
You are old, Father William.—HoB
"You are old, Father William, the young man said."—ArT-3
The fountain. W. Wordsworth.—WoP
"Fresh spring, the herald of love's mighty king." E. Spenser.—GrCt
The frost. Tzu Yeh.—LeMw
George. D. Randall.—HaK
"How I yearn to be." Okura.—BaS
In the red. J. Stephens.—StS
Jack and the beanstalk. P. Goedicke.—DuS
John Anderson my jo. R. Burns.—BuH—BuPr
Mezzo cammin. H. W. Longfellow.—LoPl
Old age. From Thera-gatha and Theri-gatha. Unknown.—AlPi
The old beggar man. A. and J. Taylor.—VrF
The old knight. G. Peele.—GrCt
Old men and young men. J. Holmes.—McWs
Old woman of Croydon. Unknown.—VrF
Outdistanced. L. Rubin.—DuS
Piazza piece. J. C. Ransom.—GrS
Points of view. A. Lowell.—HaL
Rain. P. Williams.—LeM
The scholars. W. B. Yeats.—YeR
The skaters. J. Williams.—MoS
A song. W. B. Yeats.—YeR
The song of the old mother. W. B. Yeats.—HaL—YeR
Stanzas. G. G. Byron.—ByP
Stanzas written on the road between Florence and Pisa. G. G. Byron.—ByP
Those winter Sundays. R. E. Hayden.—AdIa—DuS
To a child dancing in the wind. W. B. Yeats.—YeR
To a young girl leaving the hill country. A. Bontemps.—HaK
To the virgins, to make much of time. R. Herrick.—GrCt
Two years later. W. B. Yeats.—YeR
"When I was young and in my prime." Unknown.—OpF
White primit falls. Unknown.—GrCt
"Why should not old men be mad." W. B. Yeats.—YeR
Wisdom cometh with the years. C. Cullen.—HaK
Youth. Unknown.—LeM
"**Youth** cocks his hat and rides up the street." See Points of view
"**Youth** of delight, come hither." See The voice of the ancient bard
The **youthful** gardener. Mary Elliott.—VrF
The **youthful** spring. Thomas Carew.—ClF
You've got to be taught. See South Pacific
"**You've** got to be taught to hate and fear." See South Pacific—You've got to be taught
Yuan Chieh
"Of gold and jewels I have not any need."—LeMw
Yuan Mei
Discovery.—LeMw
Only be willing to search for poetry. See "Only be willing to search for poetry, and there will be poetry"
"Only be willing to search for poetry, and there will be poetry."—LeMw
Only be willing to search for poetry.—LaPd
The **Yule** days. See The twelve days of Christmas
Yuma Indians. See Indians of the Americas—Yuma

Z

Zangwill, Israel
"The angels came a-mustering." tr.—PlE
Zaturenska, Marya
Water and shadow.—GrS
"A **zealous** lock-smith dyed of late." See On a puritanicall lock-smith
Zebra. Isak Dinesen.—BoGj
The **Zebra** Dun. Unknown.—HuS-3
Zebras
Zebra. I. Dinesen.—BoGj
The zebras. R. Campbell.—CoB
The **zebras.** Roy Campbell.—CoB
The **Zen** archer. James Kirkup.—PlE
Zenocrate
To entertain divine Zenocrate. From Tamburlaine the Great. C. Marlowe.—GrCt
Zeus
Europa. W. Plomer.—CaMb
Zima junction. Yevgeny Yevtushenko, tr. fr. the Russian by Robin Milner-Gulland and Peter Levi.—LiT (sel.)
The **zobo** bird. Frank A. Collymore.—BoGj
Zodiac, Signs of
The zodiac. E. Farjeon.—FaT
The **zodiac.** Eleanor Farjeon.—FaT
Zolotow, Charlotte
The little maple.—BrSg
"**The** zoo is a wonderful place." See Ballade of a zoo buff
Zoo manners. Eileen Mathias.—StF
"**Zooming** across the sky." See Up in the air

Zoos
Ape. From Creatures in the zoo. B. Deutsch.—DuS
At the zoo. A. A. Milne.—MiC
"At the zoo I remarked to an emu." Unknown.—BrLl
Ballade of a zoo buff. M. Bracker.—CoB
"A cheerful old bear at the zoo." Unknown.—BrLl
Come to think of it. J. Ciardi.—CiYk
"Excuse us, animals in the zoo." A. Wynne.—ArT-3
Exile. V. Sheard.—CoB
The good little girl. A. A. Milne.—CoBb
Inside the zoo. E. Merriam.—MeC
The monkeys. E. O. Thompson.—ArT-3
"One day I went out to the zoo." G. T. Johnson.—BrLl
Pete at the zoo. G. Brooks.—HaL—LaPd
Some brown sparrows. B. Fearing.—CoB—DuR
"The spangled pandemonium." P. Brown.—ArT-3
"There once was a barber of Kew." C. Monkhouse.—BrLl
Two from the zoo. E. Merriam.—ArT-3
Why no one pets the lion at the zoo. J. Ciardi.—DuR
Willy. Richard Moore.—DuS
Zoo manners. E. Mathias.—StF
Zummer stream. William Barnes.—CoBn
Zuñi Indians. See Indians of the Americas—Zuñi

DIRECTORY OF PUBLISHERS AND DISTRIBUTORS

ATHENEUM. Atheneum Publishers, 122 E 42 St, New York 10017
COWARD. Coward-McCann & Geoghegan, Inc, 200 Madison Av, New York 10016
CROWELL. Thomas Y. Crowell Company, 201 Park Av S, New York 10003
DELACORTE. Delacorte Press, 750 3d Av, New York 10017
DIAL. The Dial Press, Inc, 750 3d Av, New York 10017
DOUBLEDAY. Doubleday & Company, Inc, Garden City, New York 11530
DUTTON. E. P. Dutton & Company, Inc, 201 Park Av S, New York 10003
EVANS, M. M. Evans and Company, Inc, New York. Distributed by Lippincott
FOLLETT. Follett Publishing Company, 201 N Wells St, Chicago 60606
GARRARD. Garrard Publishing Company, 1607 N Market St, Champaign, Illinois 61820
HARCOURT. Harcourt, Brace & World, Inc, 757 3d Av, New York 10017
HILL & WANG. Hill & Wang, Inc, 72 5th Av, New York 10011
HOLT. Holt, Rinehart & Winston, Inc, 383 Madison Av, New York 10017
LIPPINCOTT. J. B. Lippincott Company, East Washington Square, Philadelphia 19105
LITTLE. Little, Brown and Company, 34 Beacon St, Boston 02106
LOTHROP. Lothrop, Lee & Shepard Company, Inc, 381 Park Av S, New York 10016
MACMILLAN. The Macmillan Company 866 3d Av, New York 10022
NORTON. W. W. Norton & Company, Inc, 55 5th Av, New York 10003
OXFORD. Oxford University Press, Inc, 200 Madison Av, New York 10016
PANTHEON BKS. Pantheon Books, Inc, 201 E 50th St, New York 10022
RANDOM. Random House, Inc, 201 E 50th St, New York 10022
REILLY. Reilly & Lee Books, 114 W Illinois St, Chicago 60610
SCOTT, FORESMAN. Scott, Foresman and Company, 1900 E Lake Av, Glenview, Illinois 60025
SCRIBNER. Charles Scribner's Sons, 597 5th Av, New York 10017
SIMON. Simon and Schuster, Inc, 630 5th Av, New York 10022
VANGUARD. Vanguard Press, Inc, 424 Madison Av, New York 10017
VIKING. The Viking Press, Inc, 625 Madison Av, New York 10022
WALCK. Henry Z. Walck, Inc, 19 Union Square West, New York 10003
WALKER. Walker & Company, 720 5th Av, New York 10019
WARNE. Frederick Warne & Company, Inc, 101 5th Av, New York 10003
WATTS. Franklin Watts, Inc, 575 Lexington Av, New York 10022
WORLD. The World Publishing Company, 110 E 59th St, New York 10022